The Leading Reference for Antique American Arms

FLAYDERMAN'S GUIDE TO ANTIQUE AMERICAN FIREARMS

...and their values

9th EDITION

Norm Flayderman

ABOUT THE COVER

Representing the newer end of the contents spectrum, the Colt Model 1911 pistol has become a sought-after collectible, and continues in use by military units, law enforcement personnel and private citizens.

The Model 1911 autoloading 45-caliber pistol was adopted in 1911, and Colt's first deliveries were made to Springfield Armory in early January 1912. Subsequently the Model 1911, with numerous modifications, has compiled an enviable service record with total production (to 1970) of over three million units, with most going to military contracts.

Author Norm Flayderman acquired the illustrated M-1911, frames and drawing from the Winchester Gun Museum in the mid-1970s when the museum contents were moved to the Buffalo Bill Museum in Cody, Wyoming. The Flayderman letter documenting the details of the acquisitions appears in the background, as does a letter from the Winchester Gun Museum, and is the sort of provenance that collectors value greatly. *(Courtesy Little John's Auction Service)*

Published by
Gun Digest® Books, an imprint of F+W Media, Inc.
Krause Publications • 700 East State Street • Iola, WI 54990-0001
715-445-2214 • 888-457-2873
www.krausebooks.com

To order books or other products call toll-free 1-800-258-0929
or visit us online at www.krausebooks.com, www.gundigeststore.com
or www.Shop.Collect.com

The views and opinions of the author expressed herein are not necessarily those of the publisher, and no responsibility for such views will be assumed.

All listings and prices have been checked for accuracy but the publisher cannot be responsible for any errors that may have occurred.

The opinions stated herein by the author as to the values of used firearms represent the views of the author and not necessarily those of the publisher. Obviously, the marketplace could yield different values for the subject firearms.

Library of Congress Control Number: 2006935760

ISBN 13: 978-0-89689-455-6
ISBN 10: 0-89689-455-X

Designed by Patsy Howell and Donna Mummery
Edited by Ken Ramage

Printed in the United States of America

Contents

ABOUT THE AUTHOR

Undoubtedly the world's best-known antique arms dealer and authority, Norm Flayderman's name has become synonymous with historic weapons of all types.

Having handled examples of most...if not all...known models and types of antique arms, Flayderman possesses a prodigious amount of information which he has shared freely with his fellow collectors. Scholarship in his chosen field is easily attested to by the "Acknowledgment" section of almost any antique arms book published within the past decades where his name will be carried, often as a major contributor, or as author of the "Foreword" or "Introduction."

Norm has received more honors and official recognition than any other professional dealer or collector in his field. An acknowledged arms historian, he acts in an advisory capacity to some of the most prestigious American museums and historical societies. He is Staff Arms Consultant by U.S. Army appointment to the famed Springfield Armory Museum, Arms Consultant by U.S. Marine Corps appointment to the Marine Corps Historical Center, Washington, D.C. and Quantico, Virginia, and Arms Consultant by Legislative Act and Governor's appointment to the State of Connecticut for their historic weapons collections. He most recently received appointment to the Board of Overseers of the U.S.S. Constitution Museum at the Navy Yard, Boston, Massachusetts. He has the unique distinction of being the only arms authority on the editorial/advisory staff of all three major national collector publications. Included among the most notable collections he has officially appraised or catalogued are the West Point Museum at the U.S. Military Academy, the famed Winchester Gun Museum at New Haven, Connecticut, and Cody, Wyoming, the Gettysburg National Museum, the venerable Colt Factory collection at Hartford, Connecticut, the renowned Kindig collection of Kentucky rifles and extensive arms and militaria collections at the Cowboy Hall of Fame, Oklahoma City and the Smithsonian Institution, Washington, D.C.

Widely known and respected in collecting circles in the United States and abroad, Norm's catalogs enjoyed the longest consecutive run of any ever issued in the antique arms field...over 120 editions in their 45-year span. The detailed descriptions in them, appearing with the earliest issues in the 1950s set new standards for the hobby. In his five decades of actively buying, selling and appraising American and European weapons he has handled a remarkably broad spectrum of antique and historic firearms, including some of the greatest rarities. It was his sincere interest in the entire range of them that was the stimulus to amass the immense storehouse of knowledge that is reflected in this book.

An impressive range of accomplishments for an exceptionally active career. Add to this a hitch in the U.S. Navy in WWII as an aerial photographer and later as an officer in the U.S. Air Force. More recently, in the 1980s, he served 4 years as Civilian Aide to the Secretary of the Army, in which capacity he often represented the U.S. Army and the Secretary on official business and functions. Graduation from Boston University and an earlier profession in photography all played important roles in his wide ranging career in antique arms.

Norm's interests are legion. His book, *Scrimshaw and Scrimshanders: Whales and Whalemen* (the indigenous folkart of the American whalemen and the history of whaling) is considered the definitive treatise on the subject. His most recent contribution to American arms lore, the massive sized, copiously illustrated *"The Bowie Knife; Unsheathing An American Legend"* met with resounding success when published in 2005. Honored with a foreword by a noted historian at the Smithsonian it received enthusiastic reviews by the press. Sorting out truth from myth, Norm produced the first reliable history of that iconic Bowie knife; from its origin to present-day. The Bowie's complex mix of history, hardware and tangle of deceptive folklore is at last placed in clear, accurate and logical perspective. He has authored two other books in the collecting field and numerous articles about antique weapons that have appeared in national publications. His multi-faceted career has often been a subject of feature articles appearing in national magazines and the popular press over the years. A little known facet of his interest is that in World War I aviation, a field in which he is also considered a competent authority.

The outdoors holds a special fascination for Norm. He is as much at ease behind the sights of a big bore double-rifle as he is in his professional career. He has stalked big game on safaris in many countries of Africa, where he bagged his share of record trophies; while Europe, Scandinavia, Canada and Iceland have often been on his hunting and fishing itinerary. Norm is among the handful of Americans to have hunted high in the Caucasus Mountains of southern Russia and the desolate Gobi Desert of Mongolia and Siberia. Hunting expeditions in the Himalayas of India, Poland and Turkey were followed by sporting treks in New Zealand, the Australian Outback and Tien Shan Mountains of the former Russian Republic of Kyrgyzstan, and more recently by a stirring adventure deep in the Amazon Jungle of Brazil.

Each day continues to hold something new and different for this busy fellow. He continues to take particular satisfaction in assuming the challenge and research of a subject that has been little studied, adding meaningfully to his chosen fields and American folklore. A student at heart, he has amassed extensive data for a number of ongoing research projects. As one of the most experienced historians in the field of American swords, he has labored on a planned guide, about the subject ever since his acquisition in 1955 of the most extensive collection of them ever assembled. Although long since disposed (through his catalogs), he had the foresight to photograph all of them individually; those illustrations were subsequently the basis for a significant addition to arms literature *"American Swords from the Philip Medicus Collection"* with the "Introduction" by Norm. Another pet project "waiting in the wings" is a graphic study of the Civil War years as witnessed through an unrivaled selection of military recruiting posters, printed proclamations, broadsides and handbills. The subject is one which the author is uniquely qualified to tackle and contribute to the lore of that momentous era. And there's more! Currently he is deeply engrossed in competing a study underway on another unique American primitive art form never previously studied, akin to the whaling sailor's art of "scrimshaw." The carvings produced by American soldiers of both North and South and the prisoners-of-war of both those armies during the Civil War were prolific. With the simplest of tools and the most common of materials they fashioned a wide range of fascinating items for themselves and the folks back home...tobacco pipes being their greatest output. Expectantly, that work and other favored "works in progress"...will find their way into print in the not too distant future.

Foreword

With thirty years in print and closing in on one million copies in circulation, this ninth edition of *Flayderman's Guide to Antique American Firearms* has dependably proven itself as the standard work and basic reference source in this challenging field of collecting considered by many its very bible. That remarkable achievement was recognized in short order, following issuance of the first edition three decades ago. Subsequent editions were received with similar enthusiastic, unstinting praise. This ninth revised and enlarged edition certainly maintains that impressive record of accomplishment. Perhaps the words of Mike Carrick, Staff Editor of the Questions and Answers columns of *The Gun Report* magazine, among the most influential publications dealing with historic firearms, said it best. Fielding a heavy volume of inquiries about antique arms on a daily basis, he wrote: "I have over 2,500 books on guns and edged weapons, but I have only [*Flayderman's Guide*] on my desk for constant daily use in answering my columns inquiries. Your *Guide* is the most useful book in my library." That same periodical commented in its earlier review of the second edition: "publication of *Flayderman's Guide* was revolutionary. It was the first to catalogue the whole field of collectible American firearms and divide it into logical groups, an instant success." And thus it has remained.

"…quite simply the best and most important study of antique American firearms ever written" said *Man at Arms Magazine*, the equally popular journal for antique arms collectors in their review of the sixth edition. In their commendation of Norm's 8th edition they noted: "Here at *Man at Arms* we get a pile of questions from readers [a large majority of which] could have been answered with a quick trip to *Flayderman's Guide*! Every edition is more comprehensive and accurate then the previous one," and that, too, is a tough one to beat!

Perhaps the ultimate testimony and confirmation of this *Guide* is to be found out in the real world or, to employ more fitting imagery, on the firing lines of the many gun shows held throughout the country where the book is in high evidence. Dog-eared, heavily worn and well-thumbed copies are to be spotted on (and under!) tables, kept readily accessible for instant reference. There are two-copy owners aplenty; retaining one on their library shelf the other for the road! By all counts that qualifies as the ultimate test by professionals and novices alike, who measure the book the toughest way by its accuracy and usefulness.

Flayderman's Guide is unique, the very first to embrace and catalog in a comprehensive encyclopedic manner the entire field of collectible antique American firearms. Over 4,000 of them are classified here, illustrated with over 1,800 detailed photographs. From its very inception it became the ultimate arms collectors and guntrader's reference, manual and handbook.

This expanded ninth edition brings to the field the latest up-to-date, essential technical and historical information in the treasury of arms lore; the veritable pillar of knowledge of this fascinating hobby. Many of these chapters have broken new ground for the collector. They provide experienced insights to assist the collector's understanding and appreciation of each of the many fields of firearms specialty.

Simultaneous with the very introduction of this indispensable manual, collectors and dealers of all stripes found new interest in the firearms cataloged, many not previously actively traded or avidly collected. With fresh, newly published data, much of it available at a mere glance only here, new collecting specialties were brought into the open. The book's impact was immediately felt in the marketplace and its long-term effects are much in evidence.

The catalog numbering system innovation Flayderman introduced with the second edition of this *Guide* was well-received by the collecting community. As expected, it immediately found its way into the general terminology and jargon of the collecting world, allowing hobbyists to talk in short-hand with unmistakable concurrence.

Both the general and the specialized arms press were generous in their approval from the very earliest publication of this Guide and the space they devoted to their reviews decidedly showed it! Critics were uniformly laudatory. These excerpts from a few widely known publications and by eminent authorities best summarize that commentary:

> *Field & Stream* magazine "…as a definitive work; you shudder at the amount of effort that must have been required to put it together."

> *Antiques & the Arts Weekly*: "*Flayderman's Guide* is the most authoritative price reference for American collectors that has ever been made available to collectors."

> *New York Times*: "A most valuable book for the person interested in truly old guns made in this country is Norm Flayderman's *Guide to Antique American Firearms*."

> *The American Rifleman*: "Coverage is thorough and material is arranged in a manner that permits easy access. The book is as valuable a general reference as any listed in its extensive bibliography."

> The *Guide* is the **only** book dealing with antique arms that was selected for the prestigious list compiled by the *American Rifleman* (the most widely circulated of all American firearms monthly periodicals) of the twelve most necessary and important books to be included in the gun expert's library! That was quite a recommendation!

> *Hobbies* magazine: "It soon became apparent to me just how much almost priceless data the volume contained for the collector who wanted a single volume reference work on virtually the entire range of antique American firearms."

> *The Daily News* Bangor Maine: "If knowledge is power in the collecting and dealing world *Flayderman's Guide* may be the ultimate weapon, at least to the gun fraternity."

> *Shooting Times*: "This book will not be bettered in its scope and field. If you are a collector, dealer or student of antique arms you will find yourself crippled without it."

Thomas E. Hall, curator, Winchester Gun Museum: "A splendid and brilliant work. After over 50 years of arms collecting and 29 years as curator of the Winchester Museum, I can say that it is a major contribution to arms literature."

Herb Glass, legendary American antique arms dealer: "If I had to settle for only one book in my arms library, [Flayderman's Guide] would be that choice."

Guns Magazine, by Elmer Keith, a renowned name in American firearms field: "The bible for the gun collector a must for all students of early American firearms!"

Stuart W. Pyhrr; curator of Arms and Armor; the Metropolitan Museum of Art, New York: "I also recommend your book to the public for its very practical discussion of condition and restoration as they affect the historical and monetary values of firearms."

And that brings me to the man and his credentials (as if the book is not enough!): One of the best-known antique arms dealers in the world, Flayderman has personally catalogued and described more firearms of all types than anyone else in gun collecting history. His own sales catalogs (issued from 1954 to 1998) were the most widely read and cited throughout the hobby. The 120 editions published over those years enjoyed the longest consecutive run of any ever issued and have become worthy collectors items in their own right! Collectors worldwide recognize him as a serious student in many specific fields and know him to freely share his knowledge.

In his years as a dealer Norm Flayderman has appraised and purchased some of the largest firearms collections in America. His expertise is often sought by well-known museums, historical societies and government agencies; his many formal appointments to their staffs being a fine measure of competence. There is more, but the point is obvious: Norm Flayderman is the right fellow to have produced this book. We are fortunate he has brought the same conscientious accuracy and insightful judgment to this Ninth Edition.

KEN RAMAGE, EDITOR
GUN DIGEST

Introduction

STAYING THE COURSE

This 9th edition marks the anniversary of 30 years in-print for this *Guide*! The continuous enthusiastic manner in which the preceding eight editions were accepted by my fellow collectors and dealers in this ever-fascinating hobby has been highly gratifying. The realization that all those many years sped by so swiftly cannot help but elicit a few personal remarks (with the reader's indulgence) for the excitement and pleasure afforded me by the provocative challenge of assembling, composing and editing these nine editions. Surveying the bustling, often changeable pace of the marketplace has proven a continual cause for attention. Along with that lively action, keeping an eye on the unceasing flow of newly published works, with its added bounty of freshly revealed data for this hobby, have managed to keep me on my toes and not allow for many dull moments. The mere quantity of that literature, embracing everything from major studies of firearms not previously examined to the minutiae of manufacturing details and variances (often the very essence of collecting), is amply affirmed by the bibliographies throughout this Guide.

The practice established with all prior editions of adding new information brought to my attention and reporting ever-changing collecting trends, has continued to make these *Guides* credible and useful tools for the collector. As originally anticipated when preparing the first edition of this *Guide* over three decades earlier (and since), it was inevitable there would be gaps in data or omissions for some models cataloged here, while numerous variants were certain to be lacking for many other entries. It was also recognized then, that with gradual maturing of the hobby, the future years held many changes in store for previously unrecognized American firearms to qualify as antique and gain admission to the ranks of the long-established, venerable arms collectibles. For many American firearms, that time decidedly arrived during the intervening years. They are noted by the inclusion of numerous previously overlooked and unstudied makes, models and variations. Chapter VIII (*Cartridge Handguns*) bears particularly valid witness to that observation. It is just such information that is proven worthy for addition to this 9th Edition and portends the future for other specialty fields of arms collecting.

An increasingly visible trend noticeable over the years, and one which may be reasonably accepted as an accurate barometer, has been the ever-increasing emphasis focused upon detail and manufacturing minutiae which continues to dominate numerous areas of collecting; especially the series of firearms made by major manufacturers such as Colt, Winchester, Remington, Smith & Wesson, etc. Recent decades have also seen greater, justly deserved, significance accorded to antique firearms directly associated with many historic eras and outstanding events of America's past as well as firearms identifiable to individuals that owned and carried them. Commensurate with that heightened appreciation has been a noteworthy advance in comparative values, not a few reflecting unprecedented gains based on great historical import.

IMPARTING NEW INFORMATION; INCURSIONS ON VIRGIN TERRITORIES

This updated 9th Edition is the largest and most extensive yet undertaken with over 1,200 revisions, modifications and an unprecedented wealth of significant new data and illustrations. Making use of every bit of available space in the 8th Edition for that profusion of fresh material, it was still necessary to increase the length of this work in excess of twenty percent. That detailed, practical information along with numerous entries never previously included are to be found throughout every chapter of this *Guide,* accompanied with a re-evaluation of over four thousand individual firearms. Once again, Chapter VIII *American Metallic Cartridge Handguns* continues among those sections reflecting an especially notable increase of information to include salient detail about handguns never previously catalogued and others that are finally placed in a proper perspective (such as the innocuous little revolvers known as "Saturday Night Specials" and the un-American named "British Bulldog" which has assumed a startling role in American arms collecting). Among other chapters noteworthy for the large numbers of new entries and additional factual data are those classifying the firearms of *Ethan Allen* (V-A); *Colt Firearms* (V-B); *Remington Firearms* (V-E); *Smith &Wesson* (V-G); *all the subsections* and categories of percussion handguns of Chapter VII; *American Military Longarms* (IX); and the numerous sections of Chapter XVIII *Miscellanea* (revealing reliable information on the once-questionable air rifle carried by Meriwether Lewis on the historic Lewis and Clark 1803 Exploring Expedition). Just about all bases have been covered.

As for those **"INCURSIONS ON VIRGIN TERRITORIES"** inferred in the caption above: I must admit to yielding to a personal fixation for challenging the subjects of *Dueling in America* and *Dueling Pistols* (Chapter VII-F). It appeared the time was right and long overdue to inject a note of skepticism and disbelief at the manner in which both subjects have been accepted *carte blanche* by collectors, historians and the public at large. Having examined the subject at reasonable depth for my recent study of the folklore, legend and myth of the Bowie knife (to refute a misconception that some American duels were actually fought with those knives), I became acutely aware that the entire subject was one fraught with misconceptions, distortions and outright fallacies. It was invariably treated in an utterly simplistic manner. Many of those same misrenderings of dueling practices were transposed directly to "Dueling Pistols." At first glance a simple, unassuming explanation was envisioned. However, with ever-increasing curiosity, as the topic was examined that doubtfulness heightened accordingly. Ostensibly there has been a general acceptance, across-the-board (lock, stock and barrel) of just about everything ever printed about those subjects for the past two centuries. It appears that no discernible voices were ever raised in disapproval or objection to even the most blatant distortions and delusions. I harbor the hope that my disputation and polemics might inject a note of rationality and logic into both subjects of "dueling" and "dueling pistols." Optimistically the gauntlet, thus thrown down, will not be found unmerited or irrelevant, but rather, will serve as a spark to motivate an enterprising historian, student or collector to accept that challenge to investigate the subjects at greater depth. They are deeply embedded in arms tradition as well as American folklore and deserve better treatment and judicious attention!

A persistently overlooked subject also due the attention of collectors is the relevance of early catalogs of firearms manufacturers and the merchants who sold those same guns. Others equally pertinent, are long outdated auction and other sales catalogs of notable American gun collections, many of which played historic, as well as informative roles in the story of antique American arms collecting. Quite a few of them continue to serve as important references to the present-day. Their significance has not been merely underrated, but entirely disregarded. A few are particularly worthy of veneration and are discussed in Chapter I (*Collecting Firearms*). Equally relevant have been the numerous periodicals devoted to antique firearms that have come and gone over the length of the 20th century. A résumé of their somewhat checkered past (also Chapter I) demonstrates the deserved critical recognition and proud status since achieved by this collecting field.

THE PULSE OF COLLECTING REMAINS STRONG, THE CLIMATE STIMULATING

It has been an exciting 6 years since the issuance of the last edition of this Guide. Much has happened in the antique arms world, generally mirroring the tenor of economic times in America. Reviewing my own comments in the previous 8 editions about the general health and climate of this arms collecting hobby affords the opportunity to get a handle on its stability and endurance, a reasonably accurate barometer to envision its development and anticipate its future. Cutting quickly to the bottom line: values, allure and demand for antique American firearms continues strong and robust just as they have since I first committed myself to print in this Guide over 30 years ago. A cursory reading of the "Introduction" of all those earlier editions amply confirms that conclusion. Collecting antique American firearms, and consequently the values of them, continues its unabated growth. That has proven quite the opposite trend of many other fields of collecting. Values have generally reflected a constant upward course throughout all the various ups-and-downs of the economic cycles of the stock market and the economy. With that track record, there is every reason to believe that this engrossing field of collecting will continue that same stable and healthy upward path, neither distracted by an influx of speculators, nor unbalanced by the excitement of awesome, record-shattering prices recently achieved for a few matchless, superlative rarities. The recent decade has witnessed increasing importance paid to minor manufacturing details and historical associations once thought insignificant. Quite often the respective arms are attended by a commensurate of value rise. Those changing patterns of collecting are often affected by the numbers of new collectors continually entering the field. Their outlook often differs from those old hands whose peripheral vision may have been blurred by years of concentration on a narrow field of specialty; possibly an instance of "not seeing the forest for the trees." Arms collecting does experience continual evolutionary change; most of it subtle, logical and enduring; occasionally profound and far-reaching. Those same possibilities continue to present themselves with the undertaking of each new research project in every area of this field. Nothing better exemplifies that comment than the recent entry on the collecting scene of the incongruously named "British Bull Dog" (see full story Chapter 8A-061). The disclosure of new factual material, often the minutiae, and for some the very essence of collecting, has been seen to open up new turf for the collector to explore, investigate and go gunning for (the analogy was inescapable).

If logically priced, antique firearms will continue to find a ready, if not eager market; just as they always have over the past half-century. I have written those identical words in all prior editions of this *Guide*. They continue to reflect my assessment of the present-day antique arms marketplace.

ARRIVING AT VALUES

The values reflected for the antique firearms cataloged in this 9th Edition have been carefully and rationally analyzed and determined on a piece-by-piece basis by my personally

conferring with many other dealers and collectors, each of whom are actively involved in this hobby and are cognizant of market conditions in their respective fields of specialty, including my own fifty years of actively buying, selling, trading and dealing in these very same estimable arms. There is no simple formula for arriving at values and value changes nor, would it be justifiable or accurate to simply assign a generalized, overall percentage of increase (or decrease) to all antique firearms or a particular specialized area or make of them. Each specialty of arms collecting is characterized by its own popularity and value trends. In some of those more narrowly focused fields of special interest, it often takes but a newly published research study, or merely a handful of active collectors to initiate an active search for those particular models to realize dramatic value changes. The broad range of values indicated for each of the listed firearms may be accepted as carefully considered, judicious, general guidelines that should be found of practical use in determining retail market values. To borrow phraseology in common usage by appraisers, these value guidelines would serve to ultimately determine "the full and fair market value as would have been paid for the [firearm] by a willing buyer to a willing seller in an open market, with both having knowledge of relevant facts." To expect that all collectors or traders would approach the estimation of values of antique firearms in the same manner or with the same practiced eye or with the same motives of buying and/or selling would be unrealistic. The highly subjective nature of placing dollar values on antiques of any type, firearms specifically, and the many motivations involved just do not make for unfailing exactness. It is commonly taken for granted that no two antique guns, in any condition less than new or like new, are rarely, if ever, identical; hence, should be evaluated on that individuality.

THE EXCITEMENT OF RECORD PRICES vs. CONVENTIONAL VALUE PATTERNS

Among the many exciting, newsworthy events that happened in the interim since the last edition have been the unprecedented, record-shattering prices, invariably realized at auction, for a wide variety of antique firearms. The startling numbers brought much favorable publicity and acclaim for this provocative field of collecting. Understandably, the media most often reports only those phenomenal prices for a handful of choice rarities, with little or no coverage given the more conventional arms, which comprise, by far, the major part of the collecting marketplace. It is essential for the collector, especially those newly introduced to the hobby, to recognize that such exceptional values (many running into the mid- and high-six figures) do not reflect across-the-board proportionate increases to all antique guns, and that those remarkable values seldom, if ever, reflect upon to weapons of the same make and model in lesser degrees of condition. The excitement created by so many record smashing American gun values was certainly provocative for the collecting community, and remains so to this day. It is of paramount importance to recognize that, almost without exception, such sensational values were established for antique firearms of equally outstanding rarity or condition or historical import. The values are certainly indicative of a new status achieved by the collecting of antique arms. They equally signify the continuing influx of an astute cadre of collectors with a deep understanding and appreciation for the ultimate, top-of-the-line for their respective fields of interest. However, the collector and dealer should not become blind-sided to the reality that those eye-opening, astounding prices were paid at public auction for equally eye-opening, astounding antique firearms. As for all other American arms, i.e. 99.9 percent of them, including the various ranges of grades of those listed and valued in this Guide, values will be seen reflecting more modest changes and increases. These remarks are certainly not intended to diminish the import of such values or the desirability, of the respective arms, but rather, to again call attention to the unique disparity of values for those ultimate specimens and caution the collector to keep in perspective the factors that affect and are responsible for establishing that other 99.9 percent of antique American firearms that are most apt to be encountered in the marketplace.

The values reflected by this 9th Edition confirm that prices have continued a just about an across-the-board rise, just as they had in every edition of this Guide over the past 30 years. Generally, firearms on the lower end of the condition scale reflect modest increases, while those in the upper levels of that same scale are shown to have disproportionately larger percentages of increased value owing to their greater demand in the marketplace.

THE DUAL RANGE OF CONDITIONS UTILIZED TO GRADE (AND VALUE) FIREARMS.

The dual grades of conditions shown for almost every listed firearm cataloged in this Guide represent the average range of condition in which that particular specimen *is most apt to be found offered for sale (or available for sale) in the collectors marketplace.* Merely using the same average condition grades for all guns of all types and periods would be as inaccurate, as it was unfair. All antique guns, regardless of their era of manufacture are not normally encountered in identical ranges of condition. That is especially evident with flintlock vs. percussion firearms vs. cartridge arms. In each instance the later manufactured weapon (especially those of post-Civil War through turn-of-century eras) is more likely to be found in a generally better range of condition. The dual ranges chosen for inclusion here have been based on my own experience in personally handling these exact types of firearms for over half a century, and in cooperation and concurrence with other professional dealers and collectors with long experience in various fields of specialization. Thus, a great majority of Civil War and earlier firearms are most often to be chanced upon in the dual range of *Good* and *Fine* while the majority of later manufacture arms (especially of the metallic cartridge era) will most often be seen listed in dual ranges of *Very Good* and *Excellent*. It is essential to recognize that those dual ranges are not hard and fast for all periods of manufacture. For instance: almost all Civil War carbines (Chapter VI-B) are listed in the lower ranges of Good to Fine, while a few specific models, such as the Smith carbine (9B-085); made during that same Civil War era, are most often found in better degrees of condition and hence are listed in the Guide under *Very Good* and *Excellent* as are Peabody carbines (9B-081). Other examples of differing ranges of conditions for various guns are especially evident in chapters discussing well-known gunmakers with extended production runs, such as Colt, Smith & Wesson, Remington, etc. Invariably their later cartridge models are encountered in finer average condition range than their earlier percussion models and are thus listed in this Guide.

Valuations for mint (or near mint) condition firearms have been purposefully avoided for almost all listings in this Guide. Essentially, they are not within the range of conditions chosen for inclusion in this Guide i.e. the category *most apt to be found for sale in the collectors marketplace.* Such optimum specimens are certain to be encountered; their frequency of availability in ever-diminishing numbers and vied for evermore furiously. With the search for such ultimate specimens in mint condition (or rare models in even lesser grades of Fine or Excellent) having reached imposing, often sensational price levels, they have sometimes been the subject of headlines and news stories in the firearms and general antiques press. Those lofty price plateaus have been primarily achieved at public auction (see further discussion Chapter I). There is little doubt that with the ever-rising popularity of almost all fields of collecting, especially of historical Americana and general antiques.and more particularly antique

American firearms, that such remarkable values for prime rarities are merited. However, it is essential that collectors (and dealers, too!) retain rationality and do not become distracted by such record-breaking values in the belief (or, more likely, hopes) that those same spectacular prices are transferable *pro rata* to identical model guns in lesser degrees of condition. Rarely, if ever does that occur. And, it is just at the juncture of irrepressible optimism that expectations overwhelm rational judgment to take precedence in buying or attempting to sell similar models in lesser grades of condition or quality; invariably to be met with disappointment. Those spectacular values established for equally spectacular lone specimens do not a market make. On occasion they cast a pall over segments of the marketplace in anticipation that new life has suddenly been breathed into a specialized area of collecting, all due to the record prices achieved and the publicity devoted to a single, or a mere handful, of rarities. Ultimately, the market settles back and resumes normalcy, sometimes to the disappointment of a few speculators, but to the relief of most others, dependent on who may be selling and who may be buying!

IMPACT OF THE COMPUTER AGE
The Internet, Websites, Dot.Coms and Email

Major changes have taken place since the issuance of the previous edition in the manner in which antique arms collecting in America is conducted and the impact of those changes continues to grow. They all came about in a relatively short time; their very first mention in these Guides was only in that last (8th) edition in 2001. Their significant effect has not merely altered the manner in which the commercial aspects of collecting are conducted, but encompasses the dissemination of information and communication between collectors, as well.

It's difficult not to sit up and take notice how the antiques market has adapted itself to the computer age and vice versa. Less than a decade ago it may have been thought incongruous, if not irreverent, to discuss such unlikely topics as time-honored, historical antiques and cutting-edge electronics in the same breath. How greatly have the tables turned! The computer and the Internet brought with them alternative collecting patterns, many of which have a direct effect on values.

It is reasonable to believe that others are destined for the future as the inexpensive means of world-wide communication continues its unceasing growth. Slowly and grudgingly, it even appears to be ensnaring the geriatric set, the old-timers and seasoned collectors who ultimately realized it was necessary to change gears to stay active in the game (myself included).

Among the more noticeable changes engendered by the computer is its use as a means for auction bidding, augmenting and very often supplanting the telephone. Allowing those same auction houses an instant world-wide audience via the Internet, combined with their issuance of exceptionally well-illustrated catalogs, also eliminated even the necessity to personally attend auctions for many potential bidders. Further evidence of change brought about by the computer has been the virtual disappearance of antique arms dealers' time-honored, printed mail-order catalogs. They are fast-vanishing from the scene, with but a handful of veterans still carrying the torch. On that score there's little doubt that the net's convenience as a means of buying, selling and trading antique arms has grown phenomenally, not merely by dealers, but allowing equal access for individual traders to the same enormous world-wide audience of arms collectors and potential arms collectors. My original observation in the 8th Edition, that the absence of many seasoned collectors [i.e. read: "old-timers"] from the electronic scene was influential in preventing it from reaching its full potential has distinctly given way to progress. It has become ever more apparent that traditional exchange of information via the postal system has yielded, with quickened pace, to email and the Internet. Inevitably, the future holds more useful distractions in store for these same remarkable systems.

The customary caveat and advice, offered to collectors since the early days of this hobby, to be aware of the small faction of fast buck artists, sharpers and con-men that sporadically operate on the periphery of this hobby at gun shows, and by mail order is equally applicable to the internet. The same sharks have rapidly adapted themselves to the computer age, often improving their questionable talents; enough, so to keep the collector on his toes! Firearms laws are also a matter of concern. Prior to free-wheeling and dealing electronically it is important that collectors be aware of laws and legal ramifications that may restrict the sale of various type firearms in state and interstate commerce.

IT ALL DEPENDS ON WHAT
THE MEANING OF "GOOD" IS! (Or What's In A Name?)

Semantics play an influential role in pricing; much more so than deserved. It's very likely a cause for misconception in arriving at values. Considerable belabored thought and discussion was devoted to the innocent, innocuous, rather humdrum phraseology "GOOD" as the term employed to portray condition of an antique firearm. The word is widely seen throughout this "GUIDE", valuing guns in one of the lowest condition ranges. Subject to varying interpretations, often at odds with one another, the term is universally used in firearms guides as well as those of other hobbies. More or less, a term of convenience, it usually indicates a grade of condition of the lower end of the scale. In its application to antique firearms, it may be both inept and misunderstood. All too often, collectors tend to make no correlation between the word itself and the actual condition it is supposed to describe.

Used in the context of describing antique guns, "GOOD" is merely a euphemism, i.e. a word or expression used in preference to a more direct word that sounds too harsh or disturbing; much like "between jobs" is substituted for "out-of-work"! "GOOD" is an artificiality, an over-nice word, agreeable to the ear to describe that, in antique gun collecting, is a condition that is really quite the opposite of that state! Unfortunately, it's often taken in its literal sense ("satisfactory in quality; excellent; genuine; sound; free from blemish; relatively fine quality; or at the meat market: a grade below 'choice; or 'prime'"; as per the dictionary)…when, what is talked about is really not "good" at all. So, please take note, "GOOD" as it is used in this "GUIDE" indicates antique American guns in the following condition:

> "Some minor replacement parts; metal smoothly rusted or lightly pitted in places, cleaned or reblued, principal lettering, numerals and design on metal legible; wood refinished, scratched, bruised, or minor cracks repaired; in good working order."

In other words, it's really rather low on the grading scale. Perhaps inappropriate and unsuited for the role, it is the term chosen for the only set of standards that were specifically adopted for antique guns that were established by the National Rifle Association many years ago; see full details and discussion in Chapter II. Thus, if the collector will bear in mind that the euphonious "GOOD" really indicates a fairly well worn specimen, he will be better able to gauge value.

INVESTORS, "INVESTMENT GRADE" GUNS
& RECORD PRICES

A steadying influence, likely the underlying reason, for continued health of this hobby (quite the opposite that occurred in many other collecting fields) is the fact that it has never been inundated by "investors" i.e. those who purchase only for the sake of financial gain with no appreciation for the arms themselves. Whether happenstance or not, most earning their livelihood from this hobby, with but few exceptions, never strenuously promoted only its profit potential, combining to make for stability in the American antique firearms market.

Hopefully it will never reach the point of self-aggrandizement, as have a few other collecting areas, where those dealing in the material consider themselves an "industry!".

Composed, mostly, of collectors, with but the smallest group of "investors," the antique arms market has been protected from the "boom or bust" wild swings of many other collecting fields. The fact that collectors did not desert the market in drastic economic swings has been a steadying influence, preventing any appreciable, price drop. "Investor" as it applies to gun collecting is not a derisive word but it does often imply that one has only a slight idea of the sphere in which they are operating. Those most successful in the long run are not "investors" attempting to forecast the market, but those who take the time to study the hobby to acquire an appreciation of it and buy items they will take pleasure from. It is this latter buyer who will invariably have the greatest gain when disposing of an item or collection. It is essential that the collector learn to discern misleading information disguised as "expert" opinion.

It has been noted that some other collecting markets have sustained well-reported diminishing buyers, prices and interest during various economic downturns. If and when they rebound, the euphemism currently in vogue by investors is "revitalize." The term has not found its way into this hobby.

CHANGING STANDARDS FOR CONDITION

Condition is, of course, a key factor in determining value. Chapter II discusses the subject at great length. There have been subtle changes over these past years, in the acceptance by collectors of antique arms in condition a grade or two below what was formerly accepted as the norm for various specialities. Although most apparent with Single Shot Rifles, the trend is equally observed with lever action rifles of all types and semi-automatic guns, among many others. In the 1950s through 1970s collectors of those types would only accept mint or near mint pieces with prices drastically falling off for anything below those grades. Commencing with the 1980s through to today, such arms are often prized in considerably lower grades. It was only in the late 1950s that gun collecting became mildly condition-conscious. The search for, and the acceptance of, the ultimate "factory new" or "mint" antique arms began to reach feverish pitch in the 1960s, 70s and early 80s. Although not reversing the trend (those ultimate condition pieces are still equally sought and vied for) there has been a noticeable lessening of goals, indicating the increasing shortage of such "factory new" antique arms. These altered collecting patterns are quite evident with today's collector and dealer, who may view the field from an entirely different perspective.

GUN SHOWS

There are literally dozens of gun shows throughout the U.S. on any given weekend. As far as antique and collector arms are concerned, there is a decided inverse ratio applicable: The more these shows proliferate, the less the quality and quantity of collectible arms are to be found on display. There are a few consistently fine, and usually exciting, shows throughout the year that have defined parameters for the type of antique and collectors arms allowed for display and sale. Established collector shows will be found a fine introduction to the hobby as long as the new collector tempers his enthusiasm with common sense! By far, the majority of gun shows are relegated to flea market status and the novice, especially, is cautioned that chances of finding the proverbial "sleeper" (i.e. falling into a sewer and coming up with a diamond) are greatly diminished. Very much in evidence at many of those shows are the same tired old guns offered by the same circuit riders at show after show, with the same tired, old, finger-smudged tags affixed.....with the same tired old prices! The tags themselves are the most obvious indication that the guns have been on the market, overpriced, for a long time.

GOALS & OBJECTIVES

The necessity for an accurate, up-to-date book encompassing all collectible American arms and their current market values was apparent; a one-volume source with simply stated, easily found specifications and corresponding prices. This book has been written to fill that want. It is intended to be of equal value and use to the advanced collector as well as to the neophyte; providing each with the basic material needed to assess values for a very wide range of American antique and collectors' firearms. The book is not intended as the very last word for collecting each specialized field and the reader is reminded of that throughout; especially where minute variances and nuances play an important role on specific models. The goal has been to arm the reader with all the facts necessary to quickly identify an arm and accurately evaluate it; or to at least determine that the piece is out-of-the-ordinary and possesses distinctive features requiring further research before hastily placing a value, possibly inaccurate, on it.

As the basic intent is to be both value and identification guide, considerable effort has been made to include as many known American made firearms as were manufactured on a production basis. Prototypes, experimental pieces or one-of-a-kind developmental or evolutionary models seldom seen are kept to a minimum. An equal effort has been made to assist the reader in determining prices for many types of American weapons which were individually hand crafted and are strictly one-of-a-kind. The Kentucky rifle is the most obvious example, but there are others as well, including Colonial weapons and many types of muzzle loading sporting rifles and fowling pieces. To attempt to include every American arm ever made would be quite inconceivable. It should therefore be obvious, but worthy of mentioning, that the mere fact a gun does not appear listed in this book, does not necessarily mean it is a priceless rarity. It does decidedly indicate, though, that the particular piece may have interesting potential and is well worth further research for identification.

Comment should be made on the incompleteness and inadequacies of certain other basic primers and guides for gun collecting. Some volumes played highly important roles in development of the hobby and were actually milestones in its evolution. In the light of present-day data and knowledge many of those books have been made obsolete, failing to keep pace with the great many collecting developments of the past five decades. Several major fields of American arms collecting were completely overlooked and in other instances the values reflected failed to keep step with actual market conditions. The lack of an up-to-date guide presented a major challenge. It was felt that such a work should be written in the light of personal knowledge and experience to offer the reader intimate glimpses into the field of collecting, insights not previously dealt with in any other books.

Another prime objective of this book is to make available a quick and easily-used reference to all those fields which have achieved primary and secondary importance in the past decades. Included are arms of specific makers that had never been previously treated as individual entities—but were insignificantly grouped among larger categories.

This work, based on research in published and unpublished sources and on practical day-to-day experience, seeks to correct earlier published inconsistencies and misinformation. Making available data about American arms, in an easily found manner, their significance may be better appreciated by a wider element of collectors and dealers alike; some of whom would not otherwise bother to dig out the facts for themselves. There is every reason to believe that by so doing a much wider interest will be generated in those collecting fields. It was found inappropriate to refer to some available published reference material where certain information had been unsubstantiated; in such cases material presented here about those particular arms includes only descriptions and values of the guns, which in all cases are based on first-hand practical experience.

Lastly, in presenting this work, it is intended to arm the reader with as many facts as possible about a particular field or specialty of collecting in order that he may have the opportunity to dig deeper for himself. To that end each chapter, or sub-group within a chapter, offers a bibliography of books available on that particular subject. It is a reasonable echo of the sentiments of everyone associated with arms collecting to state that an arms library, and knowledge of how to use it, is the collector's most important asset. If nothing more, the very awareness that such libraries do exist and that such titles are published should prompt further investigation.

LIMITATIONS

It would be quite impossible for a work of this wide scope to cover every conceivable variation and discuss every nuance of collecting; many of which significantly affect value. Neither can there be an infallible guide; no market in the world stands still and thus values cannot remain constant. By arming the reader with as many basic facts as space would allow, plus the details of the important published works in each field (so that all available tools to perform further research and investigation would be at his fingertips), the reader—with a bit of study, some forethought, some reading between the lines and, of course, a bit of luck- can assess the facts and the significant bits of minutiae which must be taken into account in arriving at values. The more unusual or special the weapon, the more thought, research and overall effort is required to arrive at an evaluation.

COVERAGE

For the most part the selection of American firearms in this work is those made prior to the turn of the century--1900. Some other semi-modern and modern pieces are included which, by general acceptance, are considered as "collectors" items. These latter pieces certainly could not be accurately called "antique" under the most severe definition of the word, but then again, that word as it is applicable to collecting is one that very often defies an exacting description. For the sake of the argumentation, a few definitions are presented from which the reader may make his own choice: From *Webster's New World Dictionary* "...ancient, old, of ancient times, out of date, antiquated, of or in the style of a former period, anything from ancient times, relic, made in a former period." A few substitute or synonymous words for "antique" from *Roget's International Thesaurus* are "...ancient, of yore, time honored, venerable, hoary, second hand, aged, archaic, of other times, out of date, old fashioned, oldfangled, obsolete etc." So, just where "antique" leaves off and a semi-modern piece begins is really a moot point. Some say it is with the muzzle-loading or percussion era, but that's not fair definition at all, for the early metallic cartridge arms cannot by any stretch of the imagination be considered "semi-modern." Choosing to avoid the pitfall of attempting to categorize "antique" American arms, attention is directed to listing and pricing all those generally considered as "collectible." The omission of certain modern arms no longer manufactured and which bring premium prices as collectors' items should not in any manner indicate that such pieces are not collectible. It merely reflects the feeling of the author that those guns are more often found in a "modern" collection and values more often seen in "modern" gun trading value guides and therefore beyond the scope of this volume.

ARRANGEMENT

Considerable thought was given to the arrangements of chapters and material within this book. Whenever and wherever possible, grouping has been alphabetical by the manufacturer's name, such as with the more well known, longer-active and prolific makers. For the most part their production has been itemized chronologically; in those few instances varying from this pattern the reasons are explained in the accompanying text.

All remaining arms are listed by major collecting type, e.g., American military handguns, American percussion pistols, American metallic cartridge pistols, etc. In some categories listings have been arbitrarily determined; as evidenced with primary and secondary martial handguns and longarms. A conscientious effort was made to list specimens under their most suitable categories; in some difficult cases the arbitrary choice was based on personal experience in dealing with those exact guns over many years.

Cross-indexing has been extensively used to assist the reader in quick identification or classification. The primary listing of a gun was determined by where it was felt the reader was most likely to first seek information; the cross-indexing allowed him to know that the gun might rightfully belong in another collecting group as well. This is especially true of items in the martial arms field which might be collected either for their military association or as the product of a specific manufacturer. The mere listing of an arm as a cross-indexed piece does not necessarily indicate or influence its importance in that particular collecting field.

Photographs of every major type or style of gun described are used; an important aid to identification. It was found both impossible as well as impractical to illustrate all pieces on an exact relative scale. Thus, not a few illustrations will be found disproportionate in size.

Guns are listed by their original factory terminology wherever possible and/or their traditional or collector designated "proper names." The sub-listings including alternative designations or popular "nicknames" (if any) preceded by the abbreviation "a.k.a." which merely means "...also known as..."

THE NUMBER SYSTEM AND HOW TO USE IT

The major innovation introduced in the Second Edition was a standardized numbering system for antique American guns. That was the first time such a reference mechanism was employed. It has since proven itself an asset to the hobby and continues to be employed in ever-widening usage, lending standardization afforded to but few other major collecting areas.

Numbers have been assigned to each gun and variation thereof listed in this book The system has been designed so that all firearms are simply and quickly located.

The first two digits (or single digit and alphabet letter) indicate the chapter and section in the book in which a particular weapon is found. The last three digits indicate the numerical order within that particular chapter in which the gun is listed, described and priced. Thus, Item 5B-025 indicates a gun found in Chapter V, section "B", Item 025 which is the Military Issue Colt Second Model Dragoon. Second example: 14-038 indicates a firearm listed in Chapter XIV, Item 038 which is a Peabody-Martini Creedmoor Mid-Range Rifle.

In instances where the collector has a gun not found listed in the book or a variant of one illustrated and described, simply use the reference "...similar to Number" and note the differences.

A TWO-EDGED SWORD

I am well aware that writing about, as well as establishing values for, an entire field of collecting may be likened to treading on thin ice. As has been the case with other books preceding this (in every field of collecting - guns included), the authors are damned for setting prices that are too low, being accused of doing so in order to buy such objects cheaply and hence make a killing for themselves; while on the opposite hand, they are damned for making the prices too high so they might sell their own items and hence, also make a killing! Writing price-guides is very much a two-edged sword. In either event, it is never possible to satisfy everybody and with the subjective nature of prices (especially antiques) and prices varying from section to section (as discussed later), it is quite possible—as a matter of fact it's assured—that not all parties are going to see eye-to-eye on values. All too often prices are based on grand expectations rather than first-hand knowledge. *With all candor, the reader is assured that I have no personal agenda to advance... or nest to feather...and, that a conscientious effort was made to reflect current retail value, in an open marketplace, for the listed antique arms in the various states of condition indicated.*

READER TAKE NOTE!

Quite likely the major misuse of a book such as this is the failure to read the "fine print." It has been the my experience, based on many years of observing human nature, that a great majority of those seeking an evaluation (and that includes advanced collectors, too) are guilty of seeing only what they want to see. They either don't (or won't) bother to read anything other than the listed price; which is very often the *highest* listed price without regard to condition. Jumping to such conclusions will likely result in disappointment. In order to utilize this book to the fullest, it is of the direct importance to read and digest the section discussing how various degrees of condition are arrived at and how those conditions radically affect price. Equally important is to know that desirable degrees of condition vary considerably with guns of different periods and makers. A discussion of condition has been purposely repeated throughout the book and it is strongly recommended that the reader often refers to that page in Chapter II giving details of standards for condition used for evaluations throughout this book.

COLLECTOR'S GIFT

Having set forth the motives and objectives for this book, and before leaving the reader to his own devices in buying, selling or trading, the author presents herewith a suggested format for an heraldic device the student may wish to use as a pattern for his personally devised crest or bookplate, signifying him a member of the arms collecting fraternity. The legend emblazoned within the riband stands as the most often heard, plaintive cry of the gun trader!

Norm Flayderman
Post Office Box 2446
Ft. Lauderdale, Florida 33303 U.S.A.

*I've got more than that in it!

Chapter I

Collecting Firearms

RECENT HISTORY AND PROGRESS OF ARMS COLLECTING

It is no exaggeration to say that the growth of the hobby of collecting antique firearms in the years following World War II has been phenomenal. Neither is it an exaggeration to claim for this field the right to be known as one of the fastest growing collecting pursuits since WWII. That era must decidedly be used as the turning point for all types of arms collecting, for it is only since then that these hobbies—especially in the field of American arms—have really taken off and risen to spectacular heights. Those decades since the war feature technological advances along with a tremendous rise in the general affluence of the American public. Plotting the mushrooming of technology and affluence on a graph alongside the increasing importance of antique weapons collecting and their concurrent immense increase in demand and value would undoubtedly show extremely close correlation. Earlier slowdowns in the pace of collecting have noticeably reversed themselves as this ninth edition goes to press. It continues to be brisk ... and in some areas, heated. Although the field is not broad enough nor considered sufficiently important by economists to have had any trend-studies made in the postwar decades, it can be said from first-hand knowledge that interest, demand and values in antique American arms have continued upward on a steady rise over the entire period. (Certain small segments of specialties within the field of American arms collecting have shown sudden spurts upwards in price, leveled off, and then even fallen slightly backward for a short period; those special areas, however, were extremely limited and in general had no influence on the overall antique American gun market.) This steady upward rise included every recessionary era in business and economic cycles. The economic setback of the early 1980s continued that rise to a lesser degree, evidencing a general leveling of prices, while the broad recession of the early 1990s had no adverse affect on antique American arms values which continued their upward trend. Such was definitely not the case in other areas of collecting; such fields as coins, stamps, art and silver are especially notable. This factor has gone unnoticed by antiques commentators and editorialists. The phenomenon is quite intriguing. The author lacks experience as an economist to interpret either the why or wherefore, but it is certainly worth noting and musing over.

Prior to World War II antique guns, especially American ones, were very much on the low end of the collecting world scale. A few of the early Colts, some of the scarcer American martial flintlock handguns, and fine Kentucky rifles were about the only arms which fetched anywhere near noteworthy values. Those values, though, in comparison to other collecting fields, were still on the bottom rung of the ladder; only rarely rising above a three figure status. Fine European arms and armor of the 18th century and earlier were then very much in demand, but the collecting fraternity for those types was also small in size. Collecting of American arms was very much a narrowly confined field that is easily evident by the limited number of short-lived publications devoted to the hobby, as well as few published research studies or books. Antique arms was hardly a field of any prominence when compared to such giants as the collecting of art, rare books, coins or stamps and other similar time-honored and popular hobbies and areas of investment. Since the War, the picture has changed drastically, but it is probably still very much a case of "not seeing the forest for all the trees." In living during the era and actually seeing the changes take place, it remains difficult to arrive at an overall perspective and visualize what the potential may actually be. Although certainly small by comparison to other collecting fields, the hard fact that not a few antique American arms have achieved price levels into the high six figure mark may very well be considered as a milestone and an indicator of what the future holds for what is still a very young collecting specialty. Proffered advice: condition will play an ever-increasing role in that future potential.

The foregoing remarks about price rises and new plateaus are not intended to indicate a feeling by the author that a stampede is about to take place (nor his hopes that it should!) in collecting American guns. Active, and thus close to this field in the postwar years, the author is hardly a disinterested reporter. He therefore very much wishes to emphasize his observations about the monetary aspects of this collecting hobby; for after all, value is very much what this book is all about.

Immediately following World War II, the collecting of antique arms gained ever-increasing popularity throughout the United States. Attributing this growth to any single specific reason would be in error, but a broad generality considered credible would relate the rising American economy and public affluence combined with the prominence given gun collecting by many writers. These two factors in combination allowed and inspired a relatively undiscovered or unexploited field to blossom. The same has happened in several other collecting pursuits and still takes place occasionally today. One wonders if anything remains "undiscovered."

With the mushrooming postwar awareness and interest in antique arms and the dramatic influx of new collectors, there simultaneously appeared a number of guides, handbooks and specialized studies. No doubt each book gave further impetus to the hobby. With the rapid spread of knowledge the collector was afforded the opportunity to pursue many avenues of collecting formerly denied him due to a lack of published information. Many of the new books spawned hosts of specialist collectors and students, quite frequently leading to further research studies published in book or periodical form. The effect, although not then obvious, is quite evident in retrospect.

The era of the 1950s ushered in a truly dramatic expansion in the hobby of gun collecting. During those years a few important periodicals devoted almost entirely to antique weapons entered the field, some surviving to the present day. Several other journals have since become available on the subject, and the array of publications now in print is quite impressive. The 1950s also saw the formation of new, as well as the expansion of existing, arms collecting clubs (many of them growing to giant size) throughout virtually every state in the Union. Although antique arms shows were well-known even before World War II, they were usually small private affairs far from achieving prominence in the press or in the arms world. In the 1950s various state clubs began attracting guests and exhibitors on a nationwide basis while at the same time expanding their exhibition facilities from small rooms to grand exhibition halls. In the early 50s it was quite possible to make a few important arms shows in a year; beginning in the 1960s and continuing to the present one could attend two or even three significant (sometimes enormous) shows almost every week of the year somewhere in the country!

Prices for antique arms began their sharp and steady upward trend in the 50s. From that point they never backslid. It is true that all values did not rise proportionately nor at the same time, but plotting on a graph would definitely show a continued and progressive rise on a rather steep incline (with but one narrow plateau) through the late 1990s reaching another slowdown after the turn of the century. A comparison of all preceding editions of this Guide, first available in 1977, confirms that trend. If the number of collectors were to be plotted on that same graph, the result would probably be an identically proportionate rise.

The great influx of new collectors and the increasing affluence of Americans, combined with a general inflationary trend in money and the decreasing supply of available antique arms, were chief factors in creating the steady overall price rise through the 1950s and 1960s. As earlier mentioned, the recessionary cycles in the economy rarely played a noticeable role in lessening either demand for guns or downward trends in their prices. Thus prices in most cases, if not continuing their rise, remained consistent or steady, then continued their upward trend the moment the economy resumed an even keel. In several instances highly specialized areas of arms collecting showed price rises out of proportion with the rest of the field. This was usually observed only in cases where a few collectors were attracted to a specialty and competed simultaneously for the very limited available specimens. A noteworthy example was Confederate handguns; always a rare commodity commanding prices commensurate with their importance. In the mid-1960s a number of new collectors caused a sudden increased demand, and prices quickly rose almost unaccountably 50 to 100 percent. The result was what might be termed somewhat of an hysteria in the market, particularly on the part of the neophyte collector. After a short period it was found that quite a few Confederate handguns were available with no takers, and a number of speculators trying to cash in on the demand found themselves holding the bag. The very fast and disproportionate price-rise had simply discouraged some of the new collectors who then gave up and went into other specialties; those who had speculated were loathe to take losses and thus for the next few years the Confederate handgun market merely stagnated.

Others were discouraged from entering the field due to the number of unsold and over-priced guns on the market. The passage of time and the general inflationary trend in the following years allowed the market to catch up with the prices of the Confederate handguns, and they once again took their rightful place of importance in the collecting field. Confederate handguns have not only continued to enjoy a healthy demand and solid sales, but now number among the arms showing the largest price increases. The Confederate handgun is but the most noteworthy example of disproportionate price increases; similar episodes have occurred in other highly specialized arms areas. Certain models and types of Winchesters have been caught up in this hysteria of sudden price rises only to find themselves being topped out. The passage of time, though, has found the market catching up with the prices. It does take some astuteness and common sense to recognize what is happening when very sudden and steep increases occur quite disproportionate to developments in the rest of the market.

Steady growth both in numbers of collectors and values of specimens, coupled with a vast amount of research studies and publications during the 1960s and continuing to the present contributed to the upward overall trend in the antique firearms field. It is interesting to note that the books currently available on antique guns and related subjects number in the many hundreds; yet there is still much room for improvement of many texts, and for new studies in relatively unexplored fields. A much larger number of titles have gone out of print and are difficult to locate.

In the early 1970s the greatest, often record-setting price increases were noted. Momentum remained high through the entire 70s and right on into the early 80s. True, there was a leveling off and a readjustment in the deep recession in the early 80s but prices (except in a few isolated instances) never slid backwards at any time and demand never slackened; over-priced mediocre merchandise merely stagnated much as it always had. Both demand and prices had increased almost on the same scale as the runaway inflationary trend common throughout most of the world in the late 70s. When inflation eased so too did the general price rise. The *demand* factor continued to reign supreme.

Reviewing the "Introductions" of the preceding eight editions of this Guide offers a credible means to get a handle on what has taken place in this hobby in the past 30 years; a practical and reasonably accurate barometer. The general trend certainly affects ever-increasing values and also recognizes the added emphasis focused upon detail and manufacturing minutiae which continue to dominate many areas of specialty collecting. Those same preceding years have seen greater significance, justly deserved, accorded to antique arms directly associated with specific eras and events in American history and the individuals that may have personally owned and carried them.

An interesting and influencing factor in changing the American antique arms market had been the entrance into the picture of the European buyer. Until the late 1960s, the European antique arms market, especially as it existed for the sale of American arms, played no role of any consequence. In fact, up to the 1960s Americans had been able to purchase large quantities of antique arms in Europe (both American made pieces as well as European arms) for import and sale throughout the United States. In the late 1960s this trend was completely reversed. Rising European affluence and a great influx of new collectors there caused rather meteoric rises in prices for arms in Europe, making it practically impossible for an American to purchase over there and import. European buyers (dealers and collectors) came to American shores to gather up great quantities of their own arms as well as American manufactured pieces to export for sale in their own countries. This situation was quite volatile and very much subject to the economy of the several countries involved as well as their currency restrictions (often subject to unpredictable fluctuations).

The European factor caused considerable change in the American market beginning in the early 1970s and was especially noticeable in affecting prices of American made guns of the Civil War and Indian War eras, mainly pieces in poor and mediocre condition. Quite a few Europeans have a great fascination with those periods of American history, and a heavy demand was created for weapons of those eras, partly influenced by a proliferation of television and movie Westerns. However, the European collector is generally not as discriminating a buyer condition-wise as is his American counterpart. Hence, the demand was much greater for lower quality pieces, and prices for those arms shot up disproportionately. Demand and sale of American arms oscillates in direct ratio to the fluctuations of the economies (and money restrictions imposed) of individual European countries. In the early 1980s the European buyer, once here in prodigious numbers, had, like the passenger pigeon and the buffalo ... or even the dodo bird ... become an almost extinct species! Although he no longer directly affected the American market, he left behind a very wide following of lovers forsaken who, like the mariner's wife, look forlornly to sea waiting for the ship to return! Those same "lovers scorned" continued their lonely vigil with many sitting on piles of mediocrity they had accumulated for the foreign market; one which had merely been a temporary aberration on the collecting scene! The hysteria those dealers created in their frenzy to accumulate hoards of ordinary merchandise for Europe, left a trail of carnage behind them in the many unknowing collectors and small-time dealers who thought their mediocre guns were suddenly turning into gold all over America ... never realizing that it was only the temporary, short-lived European market that kindled, and ultimately doused the demand!

The late 1980s and early 1990s saw a slow return of European and a few Scandinavian buyers to the American market searching for antique American arms as well as those of their respective countries. By the mid 90s even that sporadic trend slackened. Their impact has been much more modest than it was with the earlier wave. Restrictive gun laws in a few countries have caused some to limit the scope of their purchases here. While generally adding to the collectors' market, they have not generated the volatility attendant to their earlier entry.

Another interesting observation and reality of the antique arms business in America, and one for which no explanation is offered, is the changing pattern of the professional full-time antique arms dealer. In the 1940s and 1950s there were quite a few full-time dealers issuing catalogs on a regularly scheduled basis. The number of such dealers today has dwindled to the point that less than a handful regularly issue sales catalogs. Very possibly this number may dwindle to nil, since there are but the slightest signs of dealers coming into the field who intend to regularly catalog their merchandise. Likewise, there is an apparent decreasing number of full-time dealers who have retail establishments open to the public at regular hours and to which the collector may freely visit. The trend, with increasing frequency these past years, has shown a great influx of new and full-time dealers in the field, but their manner of conducting business is completely at contrast to the time-honored approach standard in almost every other collecting field. As a matter of fact, the *modus operandi* is peculiar to this antique arms business and offers an interesting insight into it. The general antique arms dealer of today—and most likely those of the future—normally conducts business along four parallel lines: he travels to the

better known and larger gun shows throughout the country; he advertises some of his best pieces in one or two of the better known and widely circulated antique arms publications; he has a small gun room or showroom associated with his home and will allow visits by appointment only; and, with ever-increasing frequency maintains a Web site on the Internet.

GUN AUCTIONS: THEIR IMPACT AND INFLUENCE

The many changes that have taken place over the years in the manner in which business transactions are conducted are likely best illustrated by the changeable roles and variable influence of gun auctions. That role has made a noticeable about-face since my last comments about their decreasing importance in the 8th Edition. Perhaps recounting their fluctuating history may place them in clear perspective for the collector and best indicate that variable influence and importance.

It was only with the 4th Edition of this Guide, in 1987, that first notice was even given to the significance of gun auctions. Until that decade, they made but minor inroads in the manner by which antique firearms were bought and sold in this country; their influence on arms values was negligible. Auction prices were invariably inconsistent over the past decades, subject to so many influences that their role as reliable price criteria was minimal at best.

The popular press, and even the gun press, occasionally reported a record auction price but usually failed to reflect what general, or average, prices were for that very same item when bought and sold in the usual course of the hobby. The American market had not been auction-oriented as far as antique guns were concerned, in direct contrast to the British market which had been, and is, very auction dominated. Proof was obvious by the very lack of gun auction houses in America or auction houses scheduling regular and frequent arms sales. The few firms game to try either held them at lengthy intervals or dropped them as unsuccessful. Within the past few years the foothold earlier established by a few reputable auction houses has increased dramatically. The author's prediction in earlier editions since 1987 that "... there is every likelihood that auctions will play an increasingly important role in the acquisition and disposition of antique arms ... may well portend the future" certainly was realized.

The following years of the 1980s through the mid-1990s witnessed the growth of a number of auction houses specializing in gun sales; at times becoming top-heavy. By the late 1990s I noted the growth of the auction market was in an "…unmistakable decline in both quality and quantity of arms attainable at auctions, i.e. those worthy of attracting attention and creating strong competitive bidding. Without such material, auctions are lackluster and so, too, are the prices realized." Further comment noted the downward trend, clearly visible in merely reviewing the numerous auction catalogs then being issued in which "…even the illustrations are frequently of endless quantities of monotonous, undiversified material. Auctions will continue to play an important role in arms collecting, very much governed by the class of merchandise they make available." The caption to that section of auction commentary said it all: "GUN AUCTIONS; THEIR DECREASING IMPORTANCE."

How the tables have turned! These last six years since that 8th Edition have witnessed a significant change in the influence of that auction market and the firms that participate in it. Certainly, the most obvious indicator has been the many record-breaking prices achieved by a wide variety of models and types of antique American firearms, their levels of quality and /or rarity.

The proliferation of superbly assembled and printed, color illustrated auction catalogs, the likes of which have never been previously seen in this field represent a credit to the auction houses that issue them and to the antique arms community in general (and they certainly place generations of gun catalogs that preceded them in their shadow). This great change of pace was ostensibly brought about by those few auction houses that had the foresight (and good fortune) to acquire from consignees significant outstanding specimens of antique arms and make them available on a reasonably steady basis. With proper promotion and marketing they frequently achieved startling values. Widely reported in both the general and the antiques press, those exceptional prices were ostensibly the stimulus for owners of similar material to take advantage of what was developing into a really hot market; there was no doubt that it truly was just that. In their aftermath, a veritable flood of great material, the very best of their respective types emerged on the auction scene and so it has remained. It is important that the collector bears in mind that those record values were achieved by what are considered to have been the very top, the *ne plus ultra*, of their particular category of firearm and that those very same prices seldom transpose to even slightly lesser rarity, quality or condition levels of identical models. There is little doubt that the notoriety of those auction values has been favorable for the hobby. They have certainly been responsible for a remarkable turnaround for a number of auction houses. In order that the neophyte collector as well as the veteran gun trader not be carried away by the excitement of those record-breaking values, it bears repeating that they have seldom had relevance or influenced values on antique arms of the same types if anything less than the very best or the most rare.

A few words about auctions are in order here for the collector ... and the dealer. Auctions will continue successful only if they do not revert to their former common practices of taking everyone's "cats and dogs" with protected prices, while allowing the very owners of those pieces to bid them up during the auction. These abuses were so flagrant that they colored the entire American gun auction market, with but a handful of notable exceptions. With reputations at stake, it has been observed that many houses have taken great precautions to keep their acts clean. When a legitimate collection has been offered at auction on a no-holds-barred basis, results have often been spectacular. Those results certainly attracted the attention of the collecting world and were equally noted by the auction houses themselves.

Many abuses as to which auctions have been, and still are, subject will continue to be the major stumbling block to their success. An uncomfortable feeling exists when auction houses either own all the material themselves or have given healthy loans or advances towards the material they are about to auction. By the very nature of these actions there is an obvious conflict of interest. For instance, if the collector seeks the auction house's advice, it is very difficult for the house to resist the temptation to push their own material instead of consignment items. The bidder enjoys greater peace of mind when the auction house has no vested interest.

A phenomenon peculiar to antique gun auctions that has been noticed by the author, is the lack of dealer "rings" or "pooling." The practice is illegal, but one that has been rampant for many years in the antique auction business in both America and abroad. The "ring" consists of a number of dealers who have conspired to rig the bidding, electing one member of their group to bid openly and purchase an item against the general public, thereby assuring that the item never brings a fair, or top, price. The owner or consignor is cheated from realizing full value for the item while the auction house is likewise cheated from realizing a higher commission. Following the auction the "ring" meets furtively and re-auctions the piece among themselves (the "knockout"), splitting the realized profit among themselves in

various proportions established beforehand. The author has never witnessed a dealer "ring" at work at an antique gun auction. Collectors and dealers have been found too independent and fiercely competitive ... which usually makes for a spirited auction! Of course, the possibility always exists for the exception to the rule. It is sincerely doubted that such tactics will make inroads in this particular field. The practice elsewhere has been quite vigorously prosecuted in recent years.

Auction galleries, in former years, were not the competitors to dealers that they have become today. Their increase in numbers has made acquisition of material by dealers considerably more difficult. A noticeable difference is the great emphasis by auction houses on "investment" and "profit" potential. Although dealers certainly are not immune to stressing that point, the more conservative will tend to downplay it. Auction galleries rarely have the time or expert personnel to advise or guide neophyte collectors as an experienced dealer might. For practical reasons many will not handle items below certain dollar values, which immediately eliminates segments of the collecting community.

In many instances the collector might find it practical and advantageous to use a reliable agent when buying at auction; either because his own expertise is weak or he is unable to personally view or attend the auction. Bidding agents usually charge a fee (10 percent seems about average) with such fees scaled downward if values reach five figures or more. It is a widely held opinion that the fee should be earned; to do so, the agent must be held responsible for more than merely bidding. While representing the collector, the agent should be answerable and held accountable for the authenticity of the item to be auctioned. Any doubts that he might have as to its originality should immediately be made known to the customer, at which time the responsibility then passes to the customer. When a bidder does not personally attend an auction, placing bids by mail or telephone with an auction house, without the use of a personal representative, it is possible that their bid may be used against them. Although telephone or mail bids should be used with the greatest of confidentiality, and it is assumed that a reputable house will do so, there have been enough unethical abuses of absentee bidding to create apprehension on the part of some bidders. Reputations of the auction house or the auction agent will certainly precede them. *Above all ... never bid on anything unless you have personally examined it ... or had a trusted representative examine it ... or have an ironclad money back guarantee from the auction house that it may be returned if found not as described.*

TRENDS IN COLLECTING

Undoubtedly the most significant trend in arms collecting is the constant search for weapons in pristine or close to "factory new" or "mint" condition. The most noticeable difference between the old-time American collections (those formed before 1950 and especially prior to World War II) and those of the postwar period is the overall condition of the latter group. In the earlier days, when guns were plentiful and quite inexpensive, very little concerted effort was made to seek only the finest or "ultimate" specimens. At the same time price differences for varying states of condition had a much smaller spread than in the current era. In articles dating from those earlier periods of collecting, condition is prominently mentioned as a desirable goal, but collectors then seldom sought the "ultimate" and quite often were satisfied with just reasonably clean specimens or those in a "fine" state and no more. The progression and advancement of the hobby, the spread of available knowledge and the great influx of new collectors have caused the search for perfection to become much more pronounced, to the point where among many this has achieved an almost fetish stage. Obviously the proportion of arms of any type in the "excellent" or "factory new" state is quite small in relation to overall quantities available; thus, the greatest price spreads will be found between average condition pieces and those in the top grades.

Another noticeable trend has been the increasing specialization to quite limited, confined fields. Much of this can be attributed to the wealth of data published in both book and periodical form, allowing the aficionados access to a guide for building their own collections. Without the availability of such material, it is extremely difficult to specialize in many areas, and the collector must have a bit of pioneering instinct to do so. The easy availability of arms literature and the steady stream of new research studies have in themselves spawned a host of sub-groups and sub-studies which in turn have identified other variations and types of arms that were heretofore unrecognized or completely overlooked. This is especially evident in some of the less expensive categories (the Damascus barrel breech-loading shotguns are an example); pieces which formerly were rarely collected or at best had severely limited followings. These types have generally achieved a much elevated status in recent years, with demand continuing to increase. A number of specialties have yet to be researched and documented, and remain as yet unexplored.

A dramatic change in collecting is the wholesale mobility of the collector himself due to the fantastic network of interstate highways built in the postwar years as well as the easy availability of air travel. Such advantages now taken for granted certainly serve to increase the collector's propensity to travel to all ends of the country in pursuing his hobby.

The increasing importance of antique arms well restored is a noteworthy development in the most recent years. The subject in general will be covered in Chapter III, but it is worthy of mention here as a decided trend in the collecting world. With the diminishing supply of fine specimens, combined with an increasing demand for those available, collectors have accepted restored arms on a wider basis than formerly. The subject is one sure to stir considerable debate and involves the matter of ethics; our purpose here is merely to report on what is occurring in the field rather than involve ourselves in dialectics.

Foremost among restorations is the reconstruction of flintlock arms; mainly in restoring to flintlock pieces that were earlier converted to percussion. At one time this practice was very much frowned upon, and even derided, by the majority of collectors. Feeling has mellowed considerably over the years and as long as there exists no intent to deceive the buyer into believing the specimen is in its original flintlock state, such restorations are not only acceptable, but are sometimes desirable. Of course, the work should be competently and accurately done. Certain other previously frowned upon restorations have become generally acceptable in recent years; these are usually on the earlier pieces of the muzzle-loading variety.

A very noticeable improvement in the postwar years has been clearly evident in the matter of arms descriptions. With the steady parade of value increases as well as the frequency with which specimens are advertised and sold through collector magazine mail order advertisements, the descriptive qualities of the advertisers have generally improved over earlier cataloging days. With no little sense of pride, the author feels that he has played an instrumental role in helping transform the general quality of the jargon of the collector and setting a pattern for the details necessary to provide a complete verbal description for mail order sales. In days when guns were inexpensive, a few words of description would often suffice for each item. With the great increase in values, every defect or fine point plays an important role in pricing; thus, to competently describe a gun, it should be reduced to a description of condition for each of the

various components. A quick sampling of dealer catalogs of earlier days and those that exist now will poignantly illustrate this trend.

THE ANTIQUE ARMS PRESS

Among the more interesting means to get a handle on collecting trends is to survey the history and background of the various periodicals devoted to antique arms that have come and gone over the years. I recently had the opportunity to do just that while preparing an article for the 50th anniversary of *The Gun Report*, the longest-running journal devoted exclusively to arms collecting and antique firearms. The retrospective proved to be a fascinating exercise. Should the aspiring scholar find the initiative to chart and graph all those many antique arms and their values over the decades, they would reflect not merely obvious value fluctuations (invariably substantial increases) but, more importantly, the changeable patterns of collecting that occurred.

Although all of the various journals and periodicals that preceded *The Gun Report* (and its contemporary *Man at Arms*) were short-lived, each in its own way was an important milestone in the collecting of antique firearms in America. The most probable cause of their individual failures was the lack of financial support by what was then but a small nucleus of dedicated antique arms collectors. In an article on this very same subject by the noted collector Henry M. Stewart in the November, 1974 issue of the *Monthly Bugle* (journal of the Pennsylvania Antique Gun Collectors Association), his research revealed that the earliest article in a national magazine dealing with antique gun collecting appeared in *Outing Magazine* in 1902 under the title "Collectors and Collections of Pistols." That was followed by a second article in 1903 in that same publication, "Pistols with Pedigrees." Likely the first American periodical solely devoted to the subject was the *Magazine of Antique Firearms*. Its first edition of 22 pages appeared in April, 1911 followed with consecutive issues monthly through August 1912. Published in Athens, Tennessee, its masthead declared it: "Official Organ of the American Society of Antique Weapon Collectors." Now approaching a century in age, those issues contained many excellent articles and illustrations and still make interesting reading.

With its introductory issue of March, 1923 *Stock and Steel*, billed as the "Official Organ of the Associated Firearm Collectors of America" was next in line for the American arms collecting world. This also short-lived monthly published in Marshalltown, Iowa ended with its fifth issue in July of that same year. It was the first of many equally transitory literary productions of F. Theodore Dexter whose name appears on the masthead. An intriguing fellow who deserves much recognition for the major role he played in the development of early arms collecting in America. "Dex," as he was more familiarly known, in 1923 earned his basic living in that small Iowa town playing piano in a movie house to accompany the silent films then in vogue. Eventually becoming a well-known, respected antique arms dealer, Dexter took pride over the years in advertising that he was a "commission dealer," i.e. preferring to handle fine antique weapons on a consignment basis rather than purchasing them outright. He maintained a high profile in the antique arms field for approximately three decades, the 1930s through 1960s. Operating primarily from Topeka, Kansas, he was the creative spirit behind many antique arms catalogs published under the guise of journals such as *Dexters Antique Weapon Trade Journal* in 1929, which featured a number of then prominent antique arms collections that Dexter sold on consignment for the owners. Subsequent sales catalogs, issued 1933-34 under the appearance of "journal" named *Arms Reference Club of America* (ARCA) were later changed to "*ARCA ARMS REVIEW.*" Other name changes followed erratically over ensuing years until October 1940; two later catalogs/journals in the early 1950s were equally short-lived. Although those publishing ventures may have had a rocky track record, they are not to be demeaned. They enjoyed a popular following and exerted considerable influence on the early American collecting market while equally credited with disseminating much valuable information. During the era Dexter issued those periodicals, he was also publishing a profusion of lists of illustrated antique firearms for sale.

November, 1939 witnessed the first issue of an antique arms journal that many consider to have pioneered the more scholarly articles of this hobby; the first to bear the name *The Gun Report*. Its large 8x12 format and four-column print made for a healthy measure of information. Each issue was accompanied by an inserted, smaller sized four-page monograph featuring a specific model of antique firearm. Published monthly in Akron, Ohio it lasted through April 1942. The very earliest conspicuous stirrings of the American arms collecting world are evidenced through the many advertisements, as well as the cross-section of articles contained in those issues. Of special note among those ads was that for the first edition of Charles E. Chapel's *The Gun Collectors Handbook of Values*, the notable, initial work to attempt to catalog all American antique firearms. A popular book, it enjoyed numerous editions through to the 1970s. The advertisements by many early antique arms dealers, who were soon to become the very backbone of the hobby, make equally interesting reading these many years later.

Next on the horizon, shortly following WWII and reflecting the initial rumblings of heightened interest in collecting antique arms was the noteworthy *Gun Collectors Letter* of October 10, 1946. Its first few issues were merely four-page brochures issued twice monthly. Quickly changing to monthly and growing in size, its name was shortened in December 1947 to merely *The Gun Collector*. Published in Madison, Wisconsin under the editorship of the knowledgeable collector and researcher G. Charter Harrison, Jr., it enjoyed a longer run than its predecessors. But, like them, it too was unable to find sufficient financial support to survive. Although growing in size and significance of contents, it soon changed to a bi-monthly, its issuance becoming increasingly sporadic until it was discontinued in 1953 with issue no. 48 to the dismay of American collectors. The gap left by that worthy publication did not go unnoticed by the collecting world, then experiencing its first substantial outward growing pains. The wealth of conscientiously researched articles, authored by some of the most well-known and creditable names in American arms collecting, brought home the awakened, critical need for such a publication. *The Gun Collector* continues to make absorbing and constructive reading; many of the articles in those issues are yet cited by collectors and authors of present day, or have proved to be the basis for numerous later scholarly studies.

With that checkered track record of defunct journals, collectors in the burgeoning hobby were at a loss for circulating newly completed studies on antique arms or even communicating easily and continuously among themselves. Except for a few sporadically appearing articles on historic firearms in the National Rifle Association's *American Rifleman* and occasional articles in *The Texas Gun Collector* (journal of the Texas Gun Collectors Association; inaugurated August, 1950 and devoted primarily to their organizational affairs) there was a distressing absence of a regularly issued trade journal. Talk of such need was widely prevalent, with the collecting world rife with rumors. Yet, no one leaped into the breach in the two year interim following departure of the *The Gun Collector*. The time could not have been more propitious for Kenneth Liggett, an enthusiastic arms collector and advertising manager of his local

Aledo, Illinois newspaper to step up to the plate. Acutely aware of the pressing need and recognizing the potential for such a journal, he established a newly renamed *Gun Report*, printing its first monthly issue June 1955, one and the same that celebrated its 50th anniversary of continuous printing in 2005. It continues to the present with well over 600 editions already to its credit and still going strong.

Two other creditable periodicals added substantially to the lore of American antique arms collecting in the years since inception of *The Gun Report*, offering that venerable publication but the slightest competition. *The American Arms Collector*, published by the Collectors Press in Towson, Maryland sustained a very short run of but eight issues between January, 1957 and October, 1958 while the *Arms Gazette*, published in Los Angeles, California enjoyed greater success in its seven-year run from 1973 to 1980. Both of those periodicals added significantly to this field of American arms collecting; many of their articles are regarded worthy of reference to present day.

Perhaps the growth of antique arms collecting as a hobby and the popularity of the guns themselves are best evidenced by the fact that it now supports two long-lived periodicals devoted entirely to the subject. With the establishment of *Man at Arms* by Andrew Mowbray in Rhode Island and the issuance in January, 1979 of the first edition of that monthly magazine, the collecting world has since been favored with two equally important, long-lived and widely read, regularly-issued authoritative journals.

Other privately published periodicals have also added significantly to the literature of arms collecting and continue to do so. Journals and bulletins such as those issued by the American Society of Arms Collectors, the Kentucky Rifle Association and the *Monthly Bugle* of the Pennsylvania Antique Gun Collectors Association as well as those by Colt and Remington arms collectors organizations (and other similar specialty societies) regularly contribute important articles regarding their various fields of concentration. Such publications however are limited in their circulation, usually restricted to their membership. The proliferation of such material further evidences the vastly increasing interest in the broad field of antique American firearms.

OLD GUN CATALOGS ARE NOT TO BE OVERLOOKED!

With the advent of the computer age, the proliferation of elegantly compiled, magnificently color-illustrated catalogs of antique firearms (issued almost exclusively by auction galleries) has been astounding! Quite a few are deserving of a permanent place on the arms student's shelf, particularly those that include noteworthy collections devoted to a specialized field such as the arms of an individual maker, or perhaps a specific category of firearm (e.g. military carbines, etc.), both of which often include scarce or rare variants seldom seen or mentioned in the usual published references. Such catalogs often serve as a valid source for factual data and manufacturing minutiae that are part and parcel of collecting. Although pre-computer age catalogs often fall short quality-wise when placed alongside those currently in vogue, many remain significant references, while others have achieved collectible status in their own right. Among more notable examples is that issued in 1973 of a conspicuously prominent American firearms collection, particularly renowned for its selection of Colt revolvers and longarms. The handsome 541-page, copiously illustrated (black and white), hard cover catalog *The William M. Locke Collection* (Biblio. Chap IV) serves not merely as a souvenir of the disposition of those many hundreds of superb firearms, but continues to serve as a source for research. Among other examples worthy of mention is the 1980 *Catalog of the Karl F. Moldenhauer Collection of Remington Arms* (Biblio. Chap V-E). The legendary catalogs issued by *Francis Bannerman Sons* of

New York City were unique. Early dealers in antique and government surplus firearms along with other weapons and equipment from the Civil War, Indian Wars, Spanish-American War and other eras, their business, founded in 1865 continued to the mid-twentieth century. The remarkable selection of material in their catalogs said to be "the greatest and best show of Military Goods, War Relics and Curios" was no idle boast; the quantity and broad range of arms and militaria available was unrivaled. Quite a few American arms collectors (including myself!) were introduced and inducted into collecting by those arresting, large, profusely photo and drawing-illustrated Bannerman catalogs, issued sporadically circa 1902-1960. Highly collectible in their own right, yet containing significant information on the background of many American arms, they are often mentioned in arms literature and continue to hold relevance for arms collecting to the present day. Bannermans played a major role in the development and history of antique arms collecting in America; its significance cannot be underrated and is deserving of long-awaited, intensive scholarly study.

THE BROOKS COLLECTION; PROGENITOR OF THE U.S. CARTRIDGE COMPANY COLLECTION

Vaguely remembered (if known at all) the 1899 catalog of the *A. E. Brooks's* [sic] *Collection of Antique Guns, Pistols, etc., Hartford, Connecticut* (Case, Lockwood & Brainard Co., Hartford Press) is said to be the first extensive illustrated listing of antique firearms assembled by an American collector. It classified and identified over 3,000 artifacts and relics, predominantly those of the Revolution, War of 1812, Civil War, Indian Wars and Spanish-American War. Almost 600 of those entries were antique firearms (mostly American) as emphasized by the subtitle: *Guns and Pistols from the Earliest Periods and a Complete Collection of all the Different Guns that were Used in Both Armies During the Civil War 1861 to 1865.* Privately published by the collector A. E. Brooks who stated in his "Prefatory" that he had been collecting, studying and researching the items for thirty years and that he solicited opinions of others "who may be interested in a collection of this character, with the view of correcting whatever errors may exist [and that the collection was] the most complete one in this country." On closing, he pointedly remarked "that the collection is now on exhibition at the [prestigious] Wadsworth Athenaeum [in] Hartford," apparently indicating the catalog was intended to accompany that display. Significant for the collector is Mr. Brooks' explicit statement that he had included with his catalog descriptions "the history of each piece so far as it is known to me. At the time of each purchase I invariably copied all the historic memoranda obtainable, or recorded the tradition as related by the former owner." Although such oral or other histories and provenances, unaccompanied by valid documentation, are subject to abuses and the occasional derisive comment about their reliability, it would be reasonable to assume that the preponderance of those ascribed histories in the Brooks captions (if not all) are genuine. Given the era the collection was assembled circa 1850s to 1890s, and the fact that many, if not most of such arms were acquired direct from the men that may have actually carried (or captured) them and their minimal monetary value, there ostensibly would have been little cause for owners who had disposed of their personal or family relics to fabricate spurious stories or, by Brooks likewise. At that time Civil War and Indian Wars weapons (including many of those captured from Indians), were merely secondhand items, some not yet considered obsolete. The mere fact that the sources of many of those arms and relics were still imbued with life would tend to preclude any inclination to fabricate specious origins and openly relate them in a catalog printed for local consumption.

THE BACKGROUND OF THE A. E. BROOKS COLLECTION

As so little has ever been written about the Brooks collection and its successor, the U.S. Cartridge Company, and as it has special significance for the American arms collector, a résumé of its background and a short chronicle of its history is relevant. The collection and A. E. Brooks, both received substantial recognition in the news media. Headlined: *"Valuable Collection of Firearms / Unique Specimens Owned by Mr. A. E. Brooks of Hartford,"* the *New York Times* article of May, 1894 offered interesting background on the formation of that vast assemblage of weaponry, including a portrait of the bearded A. E. Brooks, "who has spent his life [assembling the] collection which embraces not less than one thousand stands of arms, revolvers and pistols [and is] the most complete private collection in the country [of its kind]." The article continued at length with details of the gun collection "he began in 1859 and has done great and valuable work as a collector…the history of firearms will be materially benefited by his researches." The lengthy *Hartford Courant* article of February, 1897 is also worthy of special note. Captioned *"THE A. E. BROOKS MUSEUM TO BE DEPOSITED IN WADSWORTH ATHENAEUM'S SPLENDID COLLECTION OF FIREARMS AND AMMUNITION,"* it described much of that material then on display: "the collection [considered] largest of its class in the country and not excelled by any exhibit of its class in the country also [containing] cases of swords, bowie knives and daggers [etc.]." The *Courant* noted that the collection was being moved "from his place of business to the Wadsworth Athenaeum [as] Mr. Brooks is obliged to vacate the premises he now occupies at 387 Main Street [and] has offered to deposit the collection with the Athenaeum for exhibition and the trustees have accepted [and] will provide room for the 40 or more cases in which the collection has been numbered and cataloged by Mr. Brooks." The story mentioned the firearms and relics had been displayed at his "restaurant."

Further summarizing those articles along with some basic data from the U.S. Census returns of 1860, 1880 and 1910, finds that Abel E. Brooks was born 1834 in Massachusetts to parents who were hotel keepers. By 1854 Brooks relocated to Willimantic, Connecticut where he managed a restaurant for a few years, eventually erecting a larger building in 1860 named the "European House" (believed a restaurant, possibly a hotel) which he maintained until 1872 and relocation to Hartford. "Geers Hartford Directory" listed him as a "Saloon Keeper" or as a Liquor dealer or merchant and having two locations on Main Street, Hartford. Newspaper biographical sketches indicate that one of those was a restaurant in which the interior walls were decorated with thirty large cases of his antique firearms, while another eight cases of military relics were displayed in his den upstairs. Brooks collecting activities began in earnest in the mid-1850s and were relentlessly pursued to the late 1890s.

The initial change of ownership of the Brooks Collection was reported in the *Courant* of Jan. 24, 1902. It related that [his] "collection of war and other relics and curios" was to be transferred from the Wadsworth Athenaeum to Boston [for] exhibit at the show of the Massachusetts Sportsmens Association from mid-February to mid-March that year and "at the conclusion of [show] the guns, pistols and cannons will be taken by Paul Butler of Lowell, Mass., president of the U.S. Cartridge Company of that city. For many years this collection gave a distinction to Mr. Brooks's café on Main Street. After he went out of business most of the relics were deposited with the Athenaeum and there they have been ever since Mr. Butler, who has purchased the firearms, is a son of the late General Benjamin Butler. He is also president of the Massachusetts Sportsmens Association." Five years later, the *Courant* (May, 1907) reported that the Brooks collection of Indian relics had been sold at auction, the largest purchaser being the American Museum of Natural History. As for all the Civil War relics and other accessories, ordnance equipment and edged weapons, their whereabouts yet remains a mystery.

Following their acquisition and display of the gun collection (c. 1902) the U.S. Cartridge Company issued a 104-page photographically illustrated catalog, intended to accompany the exhibit at the Sportsmans' Show. (That first printing of the catalog is apparently quite rare.) The company later (c. 1910-20) revised and enlarged the catalog to 140 pages; copies of that undated edition are occasionally available on the collectors' market.

The widely known U.S. Cartridge Co., a major manufacturer of ammunition, was established in Lowell, Massachusetts in 1869 by the notable Civil War, Union Army General Benjamin F. Butler (later governor of Massachusetts, 1883). By 1870 he had secured complete control of the company, continuing to direct operations until his death in 1893, whereupon his son Paul Butler and other direct descendants assumed his controlling interest and management of the company. The Brooks collection, acquired in 1902, served to promote the company name. In 1904, following initial display at the Boston show, the company shipped it to Missouri for exhibit at the St. Louis Exposition. It was there that it was first viewed by the Smithsonian Institution's curator. Subsequent to the return of the firearms from St. Louis, the company entered negotiations with the museum to place the collection on loan. By 1906 it was sent, virtually in its entirety, to Washington, where it remained until 1931. The large file of correspondence generated in the ensuing years (on record in Smithsonian archives) chronicles the loan and eventual return of that collection. A majority of the stock of the U.S. Cartridge Co. was purchased in 1910 by the National Lead Company, however ownership of the gun collection remained in the estate of General Butler, reverting to his son Paul and other direct heirs in that year (National Lead Co. assumed 100 percent ownership of the company in 1919). In the years that followed, the Butler heirs carried on protracted correspondence with the Smithsonian, requesting return of the firearms collection; ultimately shipped back to them during August 1931. Whatever transpired during those years of their return to Massachusetts and storage in the decade that followed is unclear. By 1942 the collection was acquired by parties unknown and offered for sale through a small, paper-covered, unillustrated catalog issued by Robbins H. Ritter of East Hartford, Connecticut. It is apparent from that austere listing and accompanying single page price sheet that at least 565 antique firearms had been returned from the Smithsonian and had then been sold. The Ritter catalog commences with item no. 101 ending, in sequence, with no. 670, but omits a group of 53 pieces (item nos. 403-550 possibly sold prior to issuance of the catalog).

RELEVANCE OF THE BROOKS AND U.S. CARTRIDGE COMPANY CATALOGS FOR THE COLLECTOR

For today's collector, trader and dealer, both the Brooks and U.S. Cartridge Co. catalogs have a direct significance beyond their scarcity and value as collectibles. Seldom, if ever, mentioned is the unusual, corroborative historical information they include which is directly relevant to many guns described and illustrated in them. Certain antique arms (especially those of the Civil War) *directly identifiable* to the Brooks collection have sporadically appeared on the collectors market. Most that I have viewed had been totally unrecognized by collectors for the specific markings that identify them directly with entries in the Brooks (and by presumption the U.S. Cartridge) catalog and their consequent enhanced historical significance and market

value. It became evident after encountering specimens clearly traceable to the Brooks collection that he customarily marked each gun with his acquisition number, using small, individual die stamps of identical size which he applied in an unsystematic manner, usually to the stock (often the forearm) of his firearms. Most consisted of four numerals (although his Indian-owned and used longarms were struck with only single or double digits). Following verification of the authenticity of the stamped numbers, it becomes essential the Brooks catalog be utilized for identifying both provenance and historical background often associated with the weapon. Although each catalog entry is merely sequentially numbered, the Brooks acquisition number (to be matched with the firearm) is appended to each description. The numerous photographic plates illustrate showcases filled with guns, rather then individual specimens. Hence the photographs, although a valid means of cross-checking with the captions are not dependable for positive identification. At that juncture the U.S. Cartridge Co. catalog may be found particularly useful as those very same firearms are illustrated individually in larger size and detail. That latter catalog makes no mention of the Brooks collection and retains but few of the associated histories. With diligence and patience it is possible to match U.S. Cartridge Co. firearms to those of the Brooks catalog.

PRACTICAL ADVICE

Just one caveat for the collector contemplating acquisition of a weapon or other relic attributed to the Brooks collection! The watchword is "caution." Mr. Brooks die-stamp-on-the-wood identification system was amateurish and obviously subject to present-day forgery or other abuse (particularly so, as this is likely the initial discussion in modern arms literature of the history and significance of the collection). Hence, the uninitiated or overeager collector and trader should proceed with caution before tacit acceptance of die-stamped numbers matching those in the Brooks catalog. If confirmed genuine to the gun, that identification is certain to heighten its interest and desirability. Depending upon its published provenance and history of use, an increase in value, possibly substantial, may be warranted.

GENERAL VS. SPECIALIZED COLLECTIONS

Although there has been a decided trend towards specialization in collecting, there is no doubt that many collectors are still considered of the "general" category and many newcomers will undoubtedly follow these same "general" interests. Each field of collecting has its merits and undoubtedly satisfies the needs of the aficionado. Not a few extensive and fine "general" collections have been formed which have achieved wide notoriety. This type, though, does often tend to get out of hand, and is often associated with a "pack rat" syndrome— which may be likened to a squirrel storing nuts for the winter! Regrettably, a majority of these general arms groups are put together with no purpose at all in mind and tend more often than not to reflect just that attitude. At this point a word of caution is in order for those who might be embarking on a collecting career purely on an investment or speculative basis. The best advice would be to quit now while ahead! Many are the perils in store for purely investment-minded gun buyers. All too numerous have been the articles in recent years in leading financial journals as well as popular national publications about the remarkable price rises in antique guns and the often "big money" made, or which could have been made, on them. Such articles will surely continue to appear, but should they be the sole stimulus for a buyer entering the gun market, he may well be in for a very rude awakening.

It is certainly accurate to state that many collectors have turned handsome profits on their antique arms, especially by individuals who have been in collecting for some years; likewise a small handful of pure speculators have also made "killings" on a few very choice pieces. Rarely though do those above-mentioned financial journalists ever report the other side of the coin; many are the losers who entered collecting on a pure investment basis only to quickly find themselves much poorer for the experience. The articles rarely, if ever, are researched in depth, and in most instances rarely scratch beyond the surface. They either report the hysteria reached at a single auction as being indicative of the entire market, or concentrate on sensational prices acquired for a few pieces, or possibly note cataloged prices of a few pieces which do not accurately reflect actual sales! Experience and common sense should caution that it is impossible to wisely buy in the collecting field, whether antique guns, furniture, coins or art, unless the buyer is well armed with some knowledge of the field and the commodity and a good deal of patience. Few are those who have entered collecting on a purely speculative basis and have remained active very long. The very essence of collecting is the acquisition of knowledge ... and that takes time. A sincere interest in the items to be collected should be the key requisite for entering this field as a hobby; the ultimate return should be the enjoyment one has had from his collecting activities. Obviously money should be very well spent—just as an investment in anything of value should be carefully considered—and experience in the field of arms collecting has proved decidedly that prudent investments have brought very rich returns.

It is best to narrow a collection, especially a beginning one, to certain confined limits where a reasonable amount of management can be discerned by both the owner and the viewer. Taste and pocketbook will very likely determine the category. Examples of broad classifications which offer an array of possibilities might be to confine the collection only to muzzle-loading or breech-loading arms of specific eras or types (e.g., sporting weapons, military weapons, etc.). A fine and interesting area for broad specialization, and one which would cover the longest historical period, would be to show arms of all ignition types used in America and the many variations of each. Collections of these types offer intriguing as well as educational values. For the neophyte collector they offer the advantage of the broadest possible understanding of antique guns over a lengthy period, and at the same time present the opportunity to assemble a group of items having a wide general interest to others.

The last subject "wide general interest" is worth digressing for momentarily. It has been the author's feeling that one of the distinct inner satisfactions of collecting should be the ability to share and impart one's enthusiasm and interest to completely disinterested non-collectors and to see that spark of enthusiasm kindle itself within them. At the very least, the scope of the collection should be sufficient to arouse curiosity and elicit some feelings of interest on the part of the non-collector and visitor to the gun room. The more highly specialized and detailed a collection becomes, the less interesting it is to the public at large. As is often the case, especially with technically detailed collections (where the placement of a screw or a variant of a maker's mark may cause many hundreds of dollars difference in price), the owner finds it very difficult to talk enthusiastically to the casual non-collector gun room visitor. Although the collection may have great monetary value, it is of interest only to another dyed-in-the-wool collector. An arms group broader in scope and possibly associated with an historical era rather than concentrating on manufacturing variances will lend itself more easily to a display that is easily understood by the non-gun person. The majority of people visiting a collector's home or office, or wherever the pieces are displayed, are most likely not

fellow collectors. It is easier and generally more enjoyable, to give an interesting, or even exciting, tour through one's collection if it is of this broader scope. There is no intent here to disparage those highly specialized collections heavy in technical variations, for such pursuits are highly regarded and have made their own contributions to the antique arms field. It is obvious, though, that one loses his listening audience the more he becomes involved in detail and esoteric points. Thus, depending on one's needs and social mindedness, it is well worth remembering to what degree and with whom the collector would like to share his collecting activities.

Many are the avenues down which the collector may travel in pursuit of his hobby; the possibilities are just about limitless. Here are a few categories for starters: American military long guns or handguns; firearms of the Civil War or Indian War periods; firearms used by the frontiersmen covering the entire mid- and late 19th century; highly decorated American arms; arms of the same type used by famous Americans; firearms of specific American makers (either mass produced or hand crafted types); all guns made of one specific caliber (caliber 45-70 is a favorite in this field); firearms of unique mechanical designs; firearms designed for specific purposes (i.e., target rifles, fowling pieces for bird shooting, small bore hunting rifles, etc.) or guns bearing inscriptions tying them to specific events.

Quite a few arms of foreign manufacture played direct and important roles in various eras of American history. The two most notable were the Colonial, pre-Revolutionary years and the 1861-1865 Civil War years. The wide importation of those pieces (often under direct U.S. Government purchase or contract) and their wide acceptance and use during those periods have endeared them to the American gun collector. Such pieces are quite often found in well-rounded collections of American guns which encompass the respective eras. A few foreign pieces were so widely used and highly regarded that they are given equal status as an "American" collectors' item and are considered a necessary inclusion in certain American arms collections. The famed British "Brown Bess" of the American Colonial era, the French Model 1763 flintlock musket of Revolutionary America and the French made LeMat "grape shot" revolver of the Civil War period are certainly prime examples of these types. Other European pieces that are either direct infringements on American guns or made under license are noteworthy pieces for inclusion in American arms collections. European infringements of early Colts, Smith & Wessons, Winchesters and Henry rifles are prime examples of these types.

STARTING A COLLECTION

The reasons for collecting antique firearms are endless, but certain ones are basic. Although the investment angle must play a role, it should be but part and parcel of stronger motivations which tie the collecting activities to some personal preference that has captured the imagination and curiosity of the prospective collector. Appetites for gun collecting are often whetted by mechanical ingenuity, artistic features or historic associations. The possibilities and potential in collecting antique American arms are virtually unlimited; but these must be matched to both one's pocketbook and the amount of time one can devote to what can become a possessive mistress.

Probably the best approach to beginning a collection is to assemble a basic arms library and read those books thoroughly. But, alas, years of stressing this point and offering the same advice many times over has found it to be the least often accepted counsel. Whether time is too precious or gun money tends to burn a large hole in one's pocket, it seems the neophyte collector just cannot visualize that book hanging on two hooks on the wall! This note of sarcasm is well intended, if the collector-to-be can persevere and acquire a few recommended basic primers, he will find his money very well spent indeed. Larger city libraries are bound to have a good shelf of gun books as do many of the larger book stores; a few dealers specialize in arms books and issue catalogs, or, a visit to a gun show will usually find dealers with a wide variety of titles on hand. The Bibliography, Chapter IV, should be found helpful as a guide to basic works. Thoroughly digesting such primers will provide a good cursory knowledge of what gun collecting is all about. Recommended as a basic starter is the recently published *"331 Essential Tips and Tricks for the Gun Collector"* by S.C. Mowbray (2006). See Biblio. Chapter IV.

Armed with the basics, the next order of progression should be some astute travel—to a museum featuring a well-rounded or specialized collection (quite a few of these will be found throughout the country), to a gun collector's home, to a dealer specializing in antique arms, or to a nearby gun show; (none of these need be in any special order). New horizons will quickly be opened, especially at that visit to the first show where anywhere from a hundred to a thousand (or more!) tables may be seen displaying and offering for sale thousands of antique guns; a fascinating and unforgettable experience. Probably on display will be more guns than can be seen in most individual museums, plus a variety of accessories, parts and literature. The shows also offer an excellent forum for meeting with a very wide cross-section of collectors and dealers.

On the assumption the aspiring collector was able to attend that first gun show and not purchase anything (but some books), the next logical step should be to subscribe to a few of the regularly issued periodicals devoted to or featuring articles on collectors' arms. The importance of belonging to the National Rifle Association cannot be over-emphasized. Their highly respected and widely circulated publication *The American Rifleman* contains a great many informative articles for the gun collector, and the Association offers services to collectors who are members. Other periodicals devoted entirely to antique arms are of great value to the collector and should be subscribed to (see details in Bibliography). A host of other magazines covering modern weapons is readily available, and most of these carry some articles on antique and collectors' firearms. The importance of all these periodicals to the neophyte is not only their wealth of informative articles, but the profusion of advertisements of dealers and collectors nationwide who are offering their services or their lists or their items for sale. One of the best mediums of exchanges in the antique arms business is mail order. Advertisements and listings for all the regularly scheduled gun shows throughout the country will also be found in these publications.

Before money is laid down for that first gun, it would be wise to have selected a general area in which to confine one's collecting activities. Likely a choice was made by reading and by studying museum and private collections; at least some general guidelines should have been established, and the search for specimens can be confined to within a given category. A key asset for the neophyte is a mentor whose opinion is valued (and who is not trying to sell one of his own guns!); an outside impartial opinion as to the wisdom of the first choice will do much to start the collector on the right foot when making that first selection at a gun show or at a dealer's shop; it is also a great aid in building self-confidence. If on his own, then good common sense and judgment of human nature should take precedence when assessing circumstances surrounding the purchase of that first piece. Checking the reputation of a dealer or collector source is a worthy step, and remember that a guarantee, either verbal or written, is only as good as the party giving it.

The matter of *GUARANTEES* is worth dwelling on for a moment. Regardless of what one might be told about a gun, and even if said data is committed to writing, there are so many vagaries involved that unless the party making the guarantee is reputable, it will be found worthless. Proving an item is not what it is stated to be in a court of law is a highly involved process and a costly one as well. Courts and (most) lawyers know nothing about antique guns, so it is a matter of hiring witnesses (an expensive matter) and trying to educate judge and possibly jury as well! Unless a gun is worth many thousands of dollars, there is little likelihood that the aggrieved owner will ever get satisfaction if the seller does not choose to honor a complaint. In only the most flagrant violations does a collector have a chance to get together a consensus from the seller's peers and coerce him into making a disgruntled refund. This discussion is not intended to lessen the importance of acquiring a detailed bill of sale, which in some cases may deter the seller from passing off a spurious piece. A general observation in some five decades of dealing has shown that those highly detailed, multi-part bills are rarely asked for or offered, nor are they necessarily what they appear to be if the seller had larceny in his heart from the beginning! The entire subject has very broad legal and ethical implications not within the realm of discussion for this book, other than to bring them to the readers' attention and strongly stress the extreme importance of knowing the party from whom the purchase was made. It is very much a matter of a man's word being his bond. A source of satisfaction for the majority of those active in gun collecting is that such a statement stands not merely as a hackneyed cliche, but a standard of one's ethical code.

Undoubtedly the best rule-of-thumb on purchasing antique guns, and one that is heard repeatedly, is to limit one's buying as much as possible to quality and condition. Far better it is to have one good piece than a dozen "dogs." This is one of the most difficult points to get across to new collectors, especially when they are itching to buy that first piece! From studying human nature and collecting habits, it may be broadly stated that the new collector most often commits all the sins that he has been pointedly warned to avoid and that he ultimately comes to the realization that those were not such bad warnings after all. Those seeming bargains just are not bargains and are so damned hard to pass by! The mere fact that a gun bears a price tag and is being sold by a dealer or collector in his shop or at a show is not necessarily a measure of actual or accurate worth. That tag does not always indicate the actual price a seller is willing to accept. In some instances it may even be purposefully inflated, outlandishly so; a rather crafty device to tempt the prospective buyer to make an offer, after which the trap closes quickly on the unwary! The buyer must be prepared to analyze not only the weapon, but the person selling it, including their knowledge in that particular area, their method of doing business, their standing and reputation as a collector or dealer.

On auction buying: The final rule-of-thumb on bargains is worth remembering when it comes to attending an auction. Under no circumstances ever bid on any gun (or any other item for that matter) unless it has been very closely examined at the exhibition preceding the auction by yourself (preferably) or someone representing the collector and whose opinion is valued. This is a time-honored, unwritten rule equally applicable to neophyte as well as expert. The novice, with no idea of gun values, has no business bidding at an auction and is gently cautioned to possess his soul with patience and wait until he has some collecting experience under his belt before entering bidding competition. Common sense dictates that when one stands toe to toe and slugs it out price-wise—and that is what auctions are all about—he should at the very least know what he is doing.

SELLING ANTIQUE GUNS

There comes a time in every collector's life when he has to sell a gun or guns, or just try his hand at turning a profit. No matter how great the protestation, "... I never sell a gun ... I will never sell a gun ... I never sold a gun," everybody meets the situation face to face at one time or another. It is difficult to understand why a certain few collectors make a fetish of the claim that they never sold a piece, as if to do so were beneath one's dignity. You will meet these types often, but only rarely are their protestations credible. Some collectors are really more dealers than collectors; at least their buying, selling and trading activities run at a fever pitch, and they never seem to settle into any collecting pattern. A great majority of collector sales are due to a wide range of reasons, e.g., up-grading of specimens, disposing of items that no longer hold an interest, or a pressing and immediate need for cash. A number of for-sale methods are available depending on the time and effort one wishes to take. First to note is that the "book" or advertised or listed price for a specific piece is not always the one that can be realized for it. In some cases there may be no takers for the piece at any price. At this point the collector may acquire a quick education—and a most lasting impression—of one more detail of the fine art of gun trading!

Setting forth a listing in this book and neatly assigning a value to each piece tends very much to be misleading, especially to the neophyte or only casually interested owner of a gun or two. This is not unique to antique arms, but holds true for any collecting field. The mere fact that a gun is listed with a price in no way precludes that the owner must achieve that figure or even a predetermined percentage thereof. No central market place or bourse exists where all gun dealers and collectors conduct their transactions as on the stock or commodity exchanges; the arrangement is much looser with a great many variables; hit-or-miss is a more apt description. To avoid disappointment it is well to understand and be aware of the peculiarities and complexities involved in evaluating collectors' firearms.

Owning a rare gun with a healthy dollar value and realizing that value is at times analogous to "... being a horse of another color!" The collector should be aware that one gun is not as easily sold as another and that the demand factor greatly influences price and marketability. True, a great many very rare American guns are worth in the many hundreds or thousands of dollars; many will be seen listed in this work. Those pieces quite definitely fetch those prices when sold to a retail customer. The number of collectors for some of those particular type guns, however, may be extremely limited; as such, it is possible to occasionally experience not only sales resistance to a gun, but considerable lethargy as well. Possibly the only way that that particular piece might be sold would be to lower the price to a figure so attractive that it would be tantamount to forcing a sale. The same can hold true of a quite rare and valuable gun that is in great demand, but is in a very low grade of condition.

On the assumption that the collector has bought wisely and ably, he might well find that a dealer will pay him as high a price or more than any collector in the area. The dealer's own specialized clientele and access to a national market allows him to know exactly where to place that gun quickly, and in such instances he is usually willing to pay a premium price. The dealer normally pays cash on the spot for the item, whereas in many cases of private sales, the collector has to accept trade items in lieu of money. There is no general guide as to what gun dealers pay for their merchandise. To flatly state that they pay 50 percent of market value or to assign any fixed percentage would be absolutely erroneous. The only accurate statement is—a dealer expects to make a profit! With very fine conditioned pieces, numerous rare models and certain types for which he has a special demand (and for any number of other reasons), the

dealer is often in the position to pay the highest price for a piece and work on an extremely small profit margin to get it. This has been especially true in recent years. The dealer might even pay the so-called "book" value for a piece as he has been commissioned by a client to specifically acquire that model for a premium price. On the other hand, if that dealer has no demand or clientele for certain types of arms, then regardless of price, he might not want to invest money at all as it would represent completely dead merchandise for him. Many dealers are specialists themselves and handle only certain types for which they have an immediate following and will completely pass by pieces that are not of interest to them regardless of price. There are no generalizations that will apply to the subject of all arms dealers. A quite interesting observation is the fact that a tremendous amount of business is generated between dealers themselves, since most have their own followings and customers. If the dealer operates on a large scale and in mail order or makes all the major gun shows throughout the country, thus having access to a national market, it is obvious that he will have a wider range of interest and broader coverage of antique arms than the dealer who is conducting his business strictly on a local basis. In the latter case, the dealer will normally pay highest prices only for those pieces for which he has a walk-in local trade, whereas other items would be attractive to him only if they could be acquired well under "book" value allowing for wholesaling to other dealers. As a general statement, the larger the dealer and the broader his scope and sales coverage, the higher the prices he is willing to pay for merchandise.

If the collector does not realize the price he expected from a dealer or fellow collector, five other options are open to him for selling that arm at the greatest possible figure. Each requires time and effort on his part, but the results may prove worthwhile. The easiest method is to **take space at a regularly scheduled gun show** and display the arms to be sold as attractively as possible. A good opportunity is afforded to sell or trade there providing the price is realistic. Through actual show experience, where feverish trading often occurs, the collector will come across and very likely take for his own use much of the banter heard about the floor. Eavesdrop on any large gun show and chances are one will hear a chorus or two of the following elucidations during the course of the day, "... That's less than I paid for it! ... I don't care if I sell it or not! ... That's less than I got in it! ... I got more than that in it! ... If it doesn't move, you can bring it back!"

A second sales option available is the auction. This could prove both hazardous and expensive, and the collector should be well aware of the rules of the game. If the auction is "open" or "no reserve" (that is, one in which every item must be sold to the highest bidder) and it happens to be one of those bad days (influenced greatly by weather or economic conditions among other things), the gun could be sold for a pittance of its cost. Adding salt to the wound, the collector must pay the auctioneer's commission, normally from 10 to 30 percent. In some cases auction houses allow a reserve figure (i.e., a price under which an object will not be sold), a means of protecting against an under-value sale. But, with a reserve, a commission usually must still be paid to the auction house. The "reserve price" has its strong detractors as well as supporters. Two key factors to its successful use are the quality of the other material in the sale and the reputation of the auction house. On the latter subject, it's essential that the financial stability of auctioneers is verified and that they are bonded. Slow payments...and no payments...to consignors has been a cause for concern these past few years causing a few well known houses to enter bankruptcy proceedings. Other costs are likely to be incurred by the consignor, and these must be carefully weighed before entering into an agreement. Basic are such items as charges for insurance (know for certain who is insuring the items while in the possession of the auction house) and charges for cataloging, including extra reproduction fees for catalog illustrations.

Consignment is another method that can be utilized to realize a higher value from a collector's gun. Many dealers will accept certain select pieces from their clientele to sell on this basis. Consignment allows the dealer to add to his stock, permitting a broader selection of merchandise, without having to invest capital. Because of this, the dealer is willing to realize more for the collector than he would be willing to pay cash on the spot. The collector agrees to leave his gun with the dealer for sale at an agreed upon retail price. Details should be clearly understood, and the agreement made in writing. The collector further agrees to allow the dealer a flat percentage fee (normally about 20 percent) of the retail price if the item is sold. Should the item not be sold after a specified time, the collector has the right to take it back and to dispose of it at his own discretion. Normally, no charges are made to the collector if the piece is not sold, unless previously agreed upon. All these factors, especially the matter of the commission fee, should be definitely committed to writing at the time the consignment is made. A great many fine firearms are sold by this method. Advantages are obvious for both owner and seller. However, to utilize this method successfully one must choose wisely the dealer who is to handle the item. Most dealers are not interested in taking insignificant, low value items on consignment; e.g., pieces worth $100 or less; nor questionable objects requiring guarantees to their clientele while the consignee is relieved of all responsibility. Important in the choice of a consignment dealer is one that is not only reputable, but is financially reliable. In many instances the dealer sells his items on a time payment method (that is, the money comes in in dribs and drabs), or a trade may be necessary to realize the best transaction. In such instances it is important that the dealer pays the consignee the full agreed upon price the moment disposal is made, regardless of how he was paid for it or whether a trade was involved. Regrettably in many instances, consignment has proven an unpleasant experience for the collector as it was found that the dealer selling on a time payment method could not come up with all the money by the time the final payment came in. A trade situation also can prove to be a similar problem. It may be necessary where trading is involved that the consignee must sweat it out until each of the pieces taken in trade are themselves sold; sometimes an almost endless process. Thus, choose wisely and be sure to commit the agreement to writing.

The sales option requiring the greatest amount of time, but reaching the widest possible audience, **is advertising the gun** in one or more of the collecting periodicals. These are widely circulated throughout the United States and abroad, and present the collector with the very best chance of finding the ultimate specialized buyer most actively seeking that particular piece. Bear in mind that a considerable time lapse exists in mail order selling, from placing the advertisement to the date of publication and circulation; normally a minimum of two months. The collector must be prepared to service and answer all inquiries as well as to give full cash refund should the piece be returned by the buyer if not found up to specifications. Not a few well-known dealers active today started off by dabbling in part-time mail order. A cautionary note must be made with regard to buying and selling firearms of all types—especially through the mail: One must be familiar with the text of the Federal Firearms Act of 1968, which regulates interstate trade in firearms, and to be equally familiar with local and state firearms ordinances— decidedly a mixed bag! In the most general terms, guns made prior to December, 1898 are free of regulations under the Federal Act, but they do not conflict with or cancel any existing state or local laws in effect in one's area. The laws are readily available and their finer points can be checked with local gun clubs and organizations conversant with firearms regulations.

Trading as a final option. If all else fails, there's always gun swapping! Probably no other collecting hobby affords as many opportunities to trade as does antique firearms. This time-honored method is also a means of sharpening one's wits. With not a few collectors their major interest in the hobby is the action and satisfaction derived from the pure trading aspects. Depending on technique, it is very possible to amass quite an impressive collection with a minimum expenditure of cash and a little ingenuity and Yankee horse-trading. Likely superfluous would be a caution about trading values, but inasmuch as "... some never get the word" (to summarize an old story), only the reminder will be issued here that highly unrealistic prices are often encountered in the area where trading rather than sales is anticipated. The reason for this might possibly be the psychological advantage thought in allowing someone more for his gun in trade than could be attained for it in cash. The whole thing is based on both a not-too-cute or clever and often self-deceiving principle and brings to mind the classic story of the two $500 alley cats traded for the $1,000 mongrel dog!

GUN INSURANCE

Surrounded as we are with thieves, scoundrels, rogues, knaves, scalawags, prowlers and the light-fingered in this modern civilized era, the collector would do well to take safe-guards to protect his valuable guns. The hazard of fire is also ever-present. Not a few articles have been written on insurance; the subject is well covered in the James E. Serven book *The Collecting of Guns* and in several *American Rifleman* articles. In broadest terms, antique and collectors' firearms are not best covered under the most commonly used "Home Owners" policies. In most circumstances under that type coverage, a maximum fixed percentage (usually 10 percent) of the total value of the policy would apply to items such as firearms. Also, a limit or maximum dollar value would be set for any one piece, coverage generally applies only to guns actually on the premises and claims most often are paid on an actual cash or cost basis or even according to replacement cost less depreciation. Establishing some of these factors often entails considerable administrative as well as emotional problems after a loss has occurred. Special waivers and riders can cover some contingencies, but experience has shown that collectors rarely bother to adequately investigate their coverage for antique and collectors' guns under a Home Owner's policy. The result is very much a case of closing the barn door after the horse has gone.

One of the best and broadest types of coverage for antique and collectors' firearms is under policies known as "Fine Arts Floaters." Any good, knowledgeable insurance agent will be familiar with them. A number of attractive plans are even offered by some of the larger collecting organizations. The key feature of the Fine Arts policy is the fact that each and every gun in the collection is itemized and valued and kept on record with the insurance company and agent. These policies normally have provisions allowing for coverage even when the guns are on exhibit at a show and in transit. Should a loss occur, settlements are normally quicker and are generally for the amount on the scheduled list. It is, of course, quite necessary to continually up-date the schedule as prices change, or as items are bought or sold. Coverage under Fine Arts policies has not only been found to be broad in scope, but often features advantageous rates. They are well worth investigating.

APPRAISALS

Professional appraisals are often important in establishing values for antique and collectors' guns. Such evaluations are specified requirements for some insurance policies, for any estate and gift tax purposes, for tax plans of various types and damage and loss claims. They play an important role in determining originality of a collector's item, by supplying a professional opinion in writing.

The key to acceptability of the values or opinions stated in an appraisal by the party to whom they are submitted are the credentials and background of the appraiser. It is a simple matter to find anyone with the slightest knowledge of guns and have them write an evaluation, pulling figures out of the air so to speak; all that is needed is a typewriter and paper. However, the collector should well understand and remember that those evaluations are subject to review by quite a few official parties before acceptability and that one of the major features scrutinized is the credentials of the appraiser; his experience within the field of guns (not merely a general antiques appraiser) and his reputation are principal factors. Major appraisers associations are able to furnish lists of recognized experts whose specialty is firearms. A number of well-known dealers in the antique arms field are quite well qualified and handle evaluations as part of their normal business routine. Appraisal fees vary considerably and are dependent upon the qualifications and credentials of the appraiser, his expertise and professional affiliations, and, of course, his location. Fees are often based upon hourly and daily rates or on a flat rate based on quantity involved. The common practice of charging a percentage of the appraised value of the item or collection is looked upon unfavorably. It is no longer in use by most major auction houses and is actually forbidden in the bylaws of some major appraisers' associations.

RULES OF THE GAME—
THE COLLECTOR'S ETIQUETTE

A few basic rules should be strictly observed and adhered to when dealing with fellow collectors or handling firearms. These canons are based on plain, common sense, but it is surprising how many times they are broken unthinkingly. The briefest and simplest admonition and one which smacks of rural New England is "... keep your mouth shut and your hands in your pockets." Not only does this make sense, but since knowledge and experience are key elements of success in collecting, quite a bit can be learned by doing just that!

For starters, obey the most cardinal rule of them all—never point a gun, be it flintlock or otherwise, at anybody. Next most often heard and important rule of etiquette is never snap a hammer on any gun, modern or antique. Manners aside, snapping a hammer may do irreparable damage; metal striking metal can often break and replacement parts rarely exist. Sometimes the maxim, "He who breaks it, owns it" would be applicable, a speedy means of purchasing a piece that was neither desired nor affordable. If necessary to test the mechanical functioning of a gun and permission has been granted by the owner, then and only then is the hammer cocked. When the trigger is pulled, the hammer is let gently forward into its "off" or "fired" position, either by the thumb or by the other hand. This very same rule applies to the handling or mechanical functioning of any gun, antique or modern. Permission should first be obtained from the owner to even pick a piece up, and permission received before testing any mechanical function. Better still is to ask the owner to demonstrate the weapon himself.

When permission is granted for handling a firearm, it is important to do so properly. The hold should be on the wooden stock or grips; when this is not possible and the fingers must touch metal, the sides of the fingers (rather than the tips) should be used, at best they should be used gingerly. Fingers, and especially finger tips, leave a rust-causing residue; some

individuals do so greater than others, leaving a trail of carnage behind.

Don't be a cowboy with another's guns. Spinning cylinders is decidedly bad manners and potentially harmful; score marks may be caused on the cylinder periphery. Spinning guns Western style is as silly as it is hazardous. When the pistol drops, it may break both itself and the collector's toe, to boot. A few other senseless stunts which should be consistently avoided (and which indicate complete unfamiliarity and lack of etiquette) are the rapid and needless working of the breech of lever-action rifles TV Western style, the careless placement of a gun after viewing and handling (when longarms fall over they often tend to break the stock) and the shouldering and reshouldering of longarms as if they were to be fired or as if buying a new shotgun for field use. The latter, especially at a gun show, is tantamount to making a bloody nuisance of oneself and besides, an innocent bystander is likely to be poked in the head!

A subject on which to tread lightly and exercise restraint and common sense is money. If in a dealer's shop or at a show, a gun is marked with a price, the game is everybody's. If a gun is in a personal collection or "for exhibit only" the subject of values could be quite personal. To ask anyone, whether collector or dealer, how much they paid for it is completely out of order; that is nobody's business but their own. It is possible to ask how much they feel the piece is worth—even when it is not for sale— but only discretion and good judgment and, of course, the circumstances surrounding the question can suggest if the time is proper for such an inquiry. The essence of gun trading can be reduced to its very simplest denominator as that of engaging in friendly sociable relations while maintaining self-discipline and respect for another person's taste and property.

RESEARCH COME TO NAUGHT

A phenomenon all too common to this arms hobby is the disheartening frequency with which arms specialists, who have spent much of their collecting careers accumulating extensive research data, pass away before that valuable information is published or shared with fellow collectors. The commonness of such distressing instances appears inordinate in this arms field. I am aware of, and have personally collaborated with, numerous collectors over the years whose all-consuming interest and sole objective, fostered through years of study and handling antique firearms, was to commit that knowledge to writing and see it published. Their collecting experiences were broad in scope, often unique, having had access to innumerable antique arms no longer easily available; a firsthand knowledge through practical experiences seldom attainable. Yet, all too many of those lifetime projects were not carried through to a reasonable (and all too often, promised) conclusion; nor were those interminable accumulations of research documents passed along to others. All were merely forgotten, lost and irretrievable, much to the regret and sorrow of fellow collectors, many of who had been kept on tenterhooks in anticipation of seeing their collaborative efforts ultimately realized.

Aside from innate procrastination, it is suspected the source of inactivity rests with a simple piece of blank white paper! Assembling the vast treasury of notes, documents and raw material was relatively easy by comparison; both challenging and satisfying. Transposing that same material, in even the simplest format as a starting point, became for many a major roadblock. That appears to have particularly been the case for those who never previously faced the ultimate hurdle of the researcher, i.e. committing that knowledge to paper (or, the blank screen of a computer). It would be presumptuous (and ingenuous) to offer here suggestions to easily defeat that intimidating blank sheet of paper in order to get such a project underway. For a collector facing the prospect of such an obstacle, the mere knowledge that it exists and is easily overcome may offer especial incentive. You can take it from one who's been there; its worth giving it a shot!

LOADED GUNS: Safety Advice

Although instances are few and far between, the occasional loaded (part or full) antique firearm rears its ugly head. In the author's experience they are mostly found in single or double barrel muzzle-loading, percussion shotguns/fowling pieces; guns that, in their day, were kept easily accessible in readiness for an unwanted intruder. The need never presenting itself, the gun, at a later time, was moved and stored, its full charge forgotten ... but remaining to this day just as potentially dangerous. The same could (and did) happen with a few handguns and longarms of all types. In the interest of safety, all firearms, antique and modern, should be closely checked to ascertain they are empty. The very simple process requires only a wooden ram-rod or wooden measure at least as long as the gun's barrel. While pointing the muzzle away, slide the rod down the bore and mark the depth that it travelled. Remove the rod and place it alongside the barrel; if empty the lower tip of the rod should reach to the touch-hole (if flintlock) or the bolster and nipple (if perc.). If it comes up short it indicates there is an obstruction or a powder charge. Do not, under any circumstance, attempt to remove it by firing the gun ... extremely hazardous! If inexperienced, have a competent professional gunsmith look at the problem. It often turns out to be paper, cloth, stones, glass, etc. that were stuffed down the barrel by parties unknown. The potential hazard is sufficient to cause it to be handled on a "worst case" basis.

REGULATIONS, ORDINANCES & STATUTES

An awareness of rules, regulations and legislation pertaining to guns is requisite for the collector. He should familiarize himself with those of his local community and state as well as the Federal Gun Control Act (GCA) and National Firearms Act (NFA). Although the Federal Government and many states exempt "Antique firearms" from legislation and regulation, it should be understood that even the definition of "antique" is subject to different interpretation and definition. There is no simple, all-inclusive statement to absolve responsibility from legal ramifications of the myriad of gun laws. It's estimated there are over 10,000 of them on the books of towns, cities, counties, states and federally. Generally speaking...in the very broadest of terms...most firearms made in or before 1898 are considered "antique" and, with but few exceptions, are exempt from provisions of Federal firearms legislation. Quite a few states use that same cut-off date; others may use various dates or not address the subject of date at all. The Bureau of Alcohol, Tobacco and Firearms (BATF) of the U.S. Treasury Department is responsible for enforcement of Federal firearms laws. A copy of those laws and those of many states is available from BATF by request (Washington, D.C. 20226). A modest attempt was made to bring an awareness of a certain few, but not all, arms or devices found listed in this work that may fall under the provisions of the NFA or GCA. It is quite possible others are in those same categories. The reader is cautioned to verify the legal status of such arms if he is uncertain.

A Disclaimer About Serial Number Data: Included in various chapters throughout this work where serial number information may be utilized to indicate date of manufacture of various firearms, particularly for ascertaining status as "antiques" of pre-1898 manufacture: serial numbers and ranges are neither precise nor unerring and may be taken only as a general guide. The information is that which has been generally accepted by the collecting community and which has appeared in specialized works on the respective makers and/or manufacturers. Exact serial numbers (or serial number ranges) i.e. whether merely the date the manufacturer of the respective firearms cease production or the date the firearms were shipped from the factory of the respective gunmaker is often uncertain. In other instances serial ranges may have been broadly estimated by authors or researchers of the respective make or model.

COLLECTING ORGANIZATIONS AND ARMS MUSEUMS IN THE U.S.

Almost every state in the U.S. has an antique arms collecting club or association; many have more than one. At the last rough estimate, the count of such groups approximated 110. The best current listing with addresses of secretaries or presiding officers may be found in the annual edition of the *Gun Digest*, this most widely distributed work may be found in almost any sporting goods store or book store in America. Several collecting organizations place large advertisements in the two popular periodicals *Man at Arms* and *Gun Report* devoted entirely to antique weapons. Each magazine also publishes a calendar of scheduled gun shows. Collectors' organizations and shows run the gamut from loosely organized affairs to very professionally run exhibitions. Regardless of their size and quality, all offer the budding collector the opportunity to rub elbows with people of kindred spirits, and they certainly afford the opportunity to get acquainted with the entire hobby.

The United States is rich in museum collections of antique arms representing a fine cross-section of guns of all periods. These museum holdings range in size from small, highly specialized collections included with other exhibits in large public museums to extremely extensive, broad scope collections in museums devoted solely to weapons. One of the most detailed listings of collections available for public viewing is found in the highly recommended work *The Collecting of Guns*, edited by James E. Serven (*see Bibliography, Chapter IV*). Over 70 of these will be found, with notes on the nature of their arms group and details of their location and hours open to the public.

Chapter II

Values and Condition

Basic to the understanding of the monetary value of antique arms is the fact that stated figures are purely arbitrary, and there is no such thing as a fixed price. The discussion of gun values is highly subjective—as often are the values themselves. Social and emotional factors often affect an object's worth and in some cases to a very great degree. Rarely indeed will two experts look at a specimen and arrive at the exact same dollar value for it. With the more often encountered guns, those same two experts most likely would arrive at a price within 10 percent of each other; the disparity would rarely be more than 20 percent. A number of reasons account for the seeming lack of consistency in this hobby as opposed to the more clear cut, definable fields of coins, stamps or books. The primary factor is the size of the field itself; gun collecting does not have nearly the following of the latter three hobbies, nor does it have anywhere near the percentage of full-time large dealers issuing standard catalogs. The smaller known overall market and the looser interpretation of prices because of less published or otherwise maintained standards by professionals combine to make for a decidedly more eccentric market. Equally important is the fact that firearms do not neatly fill a definite grading category as do stamps, coins or books; this is made even more complex by the mechanical functions which weapons possess. Lastly, guns feature many more variables and irregularities than either stamps, coins or books; most important among these are historical associations, inscriptions, manufacturing variations, factory accessories, restorations and engravings.

In order not to discourage the reader at this point, it may be further quite emphatically and accurately stated that just about every weapon made does fall within distinct price guidelines and price categories. These figures are determined by what previous weapons of the same type have brought in the open market, by what closely similar weapons possessing a similar degree of demand and rarity have brought, or in the case of extremely rare, infrequently traded guns what they would bring based on experience and in the view of the influencing factors discussed within this section.

CORRECT IDENTIFICATION

Fundamental to establishing value is accurate identification of the gun. The mere similarity of a piece in contour and shape to one pictured herein or in another reference work, is hardly sufficient to conclude that the specimen is identical. Looks are deceiving when it comes to determining the fine points of gun identification and, consequently, value; jumping at conclusions is often dangerous and costly. As will be seen in the thousands of guns listed in this book and the many hundreds of photographs, there can often be great variances in price within a single model or type—which to the casual observer all look alike. A slight difference in markings, placement of screws or seemingly minor parts all play highly important roles in identification. The reader is urged to check all these minor technical points in the text accompanying each model after he has identified his piece from the illustration accompanying that text. To repeat again, the mere fact that a gun does not appear listed in this work (or is apparently unique) does not necessarily indicate it is either a priceless rarity or an unknown model. One should conclude that the specific piece certainly possesses an interesting potential and is well worth further research into its background and identification. Although this book does contain more descriptions, models and variant types than any other of its type ever published, gaps are inevitable.

AN INSIGHT TO 19TH CENTURY ARMS MAKING

Often overlooked, even though it has appeared in all preceding editions of this guide, is a particularly enlightening insight to the manner in which the American firearms business was conducted in the earlier nineteenth century through to the Civil War years. Such knowledge is readily gained from the study of Whitney firearms as discussed in the prefatory to the Whitney chapter (5-J) of this guide. A concise summary of seldom mentioned production, assembly and merchandising practices warrants the collector's understanding. It is logical to assume that what occurred with Whitney, applied equally to other gunmakers and has the likelihood to account for other previously unexplained model variations and anomalies. It becomes apparent from the section describing Whitney's five models known as "Good and Serviceable Arms" (Whitney's own terminology) that the art of gunmaking and merchandising was not the "exact science" that many authors and collectors might wish them to have been. Whitney's method of purchasing surplus parts and assembling guns for private sales other than to the U.S. government similarly accounts for similar arms that do not conform to strict government inspection standards. It is likely some of those marketing practices will account for occasional odd variants encountered. A gray area for certain, and the knowledge of which offers potential for abuse. Thus far, instances of the misuse of the information have not made any significant inroads in the arms collecting marketplace. However, knowledge of those nineteenth century practices of Whitney Arms Co. requires the attention of present-day collectors. More is read about them in Chap. 5-J.

THE WORD "VALUE"—A DESCRIPTION

Intrinsic value and monetary value are often inseparable to the collector. The highly subjective nature of the former and the general nature of this work precludes a discussion of it, and we shall confine ourselves purely to the latter.

According to *Webster's New World Dictionary* "value" is "...a fair or proper equivalent in money, commodities, etc., for something sold or exchanged; fair price. The worth of a thing in money or goods at a certain time; market price. The equivalent (of something) in money. Estimated or appraised worth or price; valuation." The *Roget's International Thesaurus* allows interchangeable use of value with "...worth, rate, par value, valuation, estimation, appraisement, money's worth, etc." Thus, it is obvious there are many interpretations as to what comprises value.

For the purpose of this particular work, it is important to be more specific in the use and definition of this key word. In order to do so, modification must be made to "fair market value," a more legalistic sounding term which has been quite strictly defined (by the Department of the U.S. Treasury in their publications concerning appraisals) as "...the price at which the property would change hands between a willing buyer and a willing seller, neither being under any compulsion to buy or sell and both having reasonable knowledge of the relevant facts."

Since there are no rigid fixed rules or formulas in arriving at the price of an antique or collector's firearm, it may be said that the "fair market value" of such arms is determined by considering all factors that reasonably bear on determining the price and which would be agreed upon between the willing buyer and the willing seller who were not under any pressure to act.

Having thus injected the word "price" into the discussion, it may be logically assumed that a current value in U.S. dollars has been assigned to all guns in this work. It may further be assumed that the dollar value shown here for the respective firearms are those prices known to have been realized or accurately estimated to be realized as "fair market value" when the piece changed hands between a willing buyer and a willing seller, neither of whom were under any pressure to act. In other words—based on the author's experience and very close acquaintance with the arms market and the highly regarded opinions of selected professional and non-professional authorities in the antique gun field, the prices reflected in this book are those which each gun would bring at retail on the nationwide collectors' market as it now exists.

FACTORS DETERMINING VALUE

Arriving at a price for an antique gun is often a most perplexing situation for the newcomer to collecting. An explanation and a bit of experience are necessary to understand how it is done, both in terms of complexities and the inequities. A classic example is a gun manufactured in very large quantities which brings five and ten times the price of a far rarer gun of which but a handful were made.

In broadest terms, the most important factors determining value are *Demand, Rarity and Condition*...in that order.

1. Demand

Demand is most clearly defined by reverting to our Webster's again where it is "...the desire for a commodity together with the ability to pay for it; the amount people are ready and able to buy at a certain price." That succinctly sums it up...the desire for a commodity.

Demand varies immensely in the collecting world for various type firearms; it can be inconstant, unsteady, fluctuating, spasmodic and erratic. Generally the reasons for varying degrees of demand can be logically explained. Often the astute collector, with an eye towards investment and potential future growth, has collected along lines in which demand has been very low and in time found himself with a collection that had appreciated immensely in value. This potential is not limited only to certain types or makes that are still relatively low in dollar value, but often exists in extremely expensive ones as well. The classic examples in the last decade have been in the very high-priced (seemingly so at the time) mint condition engraved Colts and Winchesters. In some cases these types rose in dollar value to astronomical heights, percentage-wise far outshining pieces way below them in dollar value. Of course, the classic analogy of tumbling into a sewer and emerging with a diamond is always hoped for and occasionally happens; known as finding a "sleeper" in the jargon of gun collecting. Many have made their sleepers happen with careful planning and foresight.

Some collector's guides and reference works assign degrees of "demand" on a numerical scale with the lowest number indicating little popularity or demand, increasing (apparently to a fever pitch!) as the numbers ascend the scale. This writer feels that such numerical scales not only hold little validity due to the rapid changes possible in gun collecting, but that they unfairly influence the collecting of a particular item and thus have been found quite impractical.

Demand varies geographically, and because of this, prices in many instances can be said to be regional. An excellent illustration of this point is American Colonial weapons. For the most part these are in low demand (if not unappreciated) in the mid- and far West; consequently Colonial weapons prices realized in those parts of the country are usually under those that can be realized in the East. Sales are also more difficult on a regional basis, with the best potential in the East, particularly where the arms were originally used. Further illustrative of our point are firearms used in the expansion of the American Western frontier, recognized as fine collectors' items and in demand throughout the United States. They are, though, in greater demand and achieve higher prices in those parts of the country where they actually were used—the West. Still another example is the identity of the maker or manufacturer. Colt and Winchester are in the highest degree of demand, while others whose products are equally fine and generally made in much smaller quantities are often found with considerably less devotees and consequently demand. The numbers of collectors actively seeking specimens by specific makers directly affects the demand and consequently the price for those pieces.

A fast diminishing eccentricity of the gun collecting market was the generalization that handguns were in greater demand and brought higher prices than longarms. No other reason can be offered for this other than differences in size. Possibly the basis in popular reasoning was that handguns were more practical to collect because of their smaller size and easier portability (and storability). It was thus an anomaly that many fine and rare long guns went begging for buyers while far more common handguns of similar period and type (often by the same maker) brought far greater values merely because of their size difference and the consequent archaic stigma. Along this same line, though, and an excellent example of the erraticism of the value market which contradicts the generality of handguns vs. longarms just stated, is the observation that demand and prices have always been higher for American longarms of the 18th century (especially the Revolutionary era and earlier) than for most handguns of the same era! Many of these disparities are in the process of being corrected, since as demand factors change, price follows suit.

Until quite recent times an unaccountable stigma has been attached to certain groups of collecting items, e.g., percussion or cartridge ignition systems, in effect making them noticeably less in demand than flintlock pieces; carbines were formerly much more desirable than muskets; rifles were assumed to be more important than shotguns; and percussion conversions were near the bottom of the strong demand items. In every instance no basis existed for this other than a very loose "traditional" sense of collecting practiced by a much smaller collecting world in an era when guns were available in quantity and within easy access of everyone's pocketbook. The complete reversal of the demand factor has upset most of the old cliches in collecting and shows every evidence of continuing to do so.

Overturning older practices and customs, the factor of demand continues to play the dominant role in current day pricing. One of the best case studies is the field of American flintlock martial handguns. Undoubtedly one of the "ultimate" areas for American gun collecting, these pieces have a number of attributes, among them historical association, rarity, a general handsome appearance, and a great variety of models, types and variations, allowing for a large collection. These guns have always been considered, even in the "old days," as among the ultimate of American collectors' items. They remain so to this day, but, in demand and price they have not shown nearly the interest nor increase evidenced by many equally and even less important types. Although demand for them has by no means diminished, a proportionate increase has not been noted in recent years. Likely this can be attributed to the fact that specimens have become so rare and hard to find that new gun collectors have not been attracted to this field nearly as often as to other specialties. Of course, martial flintlock handguns, like any other field, is subject to change, but the situation presents an interesting insight into the factor of demand.

The creation of demand has many facets. With Colts, Smith & Wessons, or Winchesters, their name and fame have preceded them. So much romance and lore surrounds many of the models of these makers. The great wealth of published material on them combined with the great quantities manufactured (consequently their greater availability) present a solid combination of attributes for collector demand. Other influencing factors are association with historical events, intriguing mechanical features, a wealth of published material about the arm (making it easy to collect and identify in all its variations), or a very reasonable or low price seemingly inconsistent with other pieces.

Reducing the entire subject to its very simplest terms: Without demand for a piece, regardless of rarity, it not only will bring a very low dollar value, but will be equally difficult to sell.

2. Rarity

The dictionary's definition will suffice for our purposes: "...the quality or condition of being rare (not frequently found; scarce; uncommon; unusual); specifically, uncommonest, scarcity, etc."

In gun collecting rarity may also be said to be the frequency with which a specimen is encountered. This is often, but not always, in direct relationship to the quantities in which that particular item was originally produced. In a great many cases this is simply determined; for instance, where studies in depth have been made on particular arms, and factory or government or other records have been scrutinized, the exact quantities produced of specific models have been determined. On such pieces it is quite simple to determine relative rarity of each of the various models and sub-types. With those weapons for which little or no research data exists, the degree of rarity is purely subjective and is based on either the experience of individuals

who have handled those same items for a long time (and are familiar with the frequency with which they appear on the market), or, in some cases, is highly speculative and based only on traditional (and sometimes erroneous) collectors' beliefs. The passage of time and the influx of a great many new collectors (hopefully including many diligent students and researchers) should continue the practice of continually publishing fresh data on American antique firearms. Such contributions will dispel and correct many earlier errors, allowing the present-day collector a much more accurate picture of the relative rarity of any individual piece.

Merely knowing the quantities in which a piece was manufactured is an insufficient basis for positively establishing relative rarity. Several models or variations were made in large quantities yet are still considered quite rare. Excellent examples are the various Smith & Wessons made and exported under contract for the Russian and Turkish governments with but a handful being retained in the United States—generally only a very few of the original huge quantities have filtered back into the collecting market. The Colt Berdan rifle is considerably scarcer than its quantity of production would indicate, as nearly the entire production was shipped to Czarist Russia, and surviving specimens are seldom seen. In other instances it may be found that the price of a single model gun is completely inconsistent as it changes from one degree of condition to the next. This occasionally occurs with a model manufactured in very large quantities and still readily found on the collectors' market, yet considered very scarce, if not rare, in a condition that only approximates "very good" or "fine" (NRA terms [*see below for the definitions of the NRA Condition Standards terms*]). Excellent examples are the Colt Dragoons, the martially marked Colt Single Action Army Revolvers, the martially marked Smith & Wesson single action "Americans" and "Schofields," as well as the Model 1859 and 1863 Sharps percussion cavalry carbines. All these were made in reasonably large quantities, widely issued and often heavily used with few, if any, left in the arsenal stores or in a drawer back home. Hence, surviving specimens almost invariably show very hard wear and use. In such instances the rarity factor as it affects price is very much oriented towards condition only and not quantity manufactured.

A curious and intriguing reality of rarity is the fact that a gun that was the most impractical and poorly made during its time and hence unpopular and manufactured in but small quantity may be found to be in this present day one of the rarest and sometimes most valuable of collector's items. At the same time the well made piece in its day, which enjoyed substantial popular sale, often stands in the shadow of the former on the hobbyist market. This fact is purely an often inconsistent observation and is not by any means a major determinant in price; the demand factor still weighs heavily.

It can thus be seen that although rarity is rather simply defined, extenuating circumstances exist which strongly affect that rarity as it relates to price and is not merely tied into numbers originally produced.

3. Condition

Although last in order as a factor influencing value, condition is the most often discussed and used word in relation to price. Even though more objective in nature than the demand or rarity factors, the subject, although easily defined ("...manner or state of being," Webster), has considerable margin for differences in opinion as to what that "state of being" actually is. Once a piece is less than "factory new" and the further that piece gets away from that condition, the greater the disparity of opinions about it. Basic human factors strongly affect opinion and often tend to color judgment; they cannot be discounted.

The seller of the gun has a natural propensity to lean towards over-estimation or over-description of condition—while the buyer is diametrically opposed and unless carried away with emotion or easily susceptible to sales pitches, would normally tend to underrate condition. It is at this juncture that good natured bantering, often playing a dominant role in transactions preceding the sale of any piece, evolves into a more heated and at times ill-humored debate!

There is good reason for the redundancy in our discussion of gun condition throughout this book; the subject cannot be treated lightly or without a certain amount of repetition in order to impress the reader with its importance. As earlier discussed, a decided trend noticeable in collecting has been the growing condition-consciousness of the market. This is not to say that the very lowest grades do not enjoy any popularity, for they decidedly do, but collectors have been justly educated by a wealth of literature on the subject to strive towards getting the finest conditioned specimens and are thus in a constant state of "up-grading." It will be found that with some models even small fluctuations in degrees of condition often increase values considerably. Each make and type of gun must be judged individually. A general rule-of-thumb is: The greater the demand for a gun, the greater the price change with degrees of condition. This is also very much the case with the rarity factor, but to a lesser degree. The admonishment which follows is directed solely towards those unfamiliar with antique guns and is of extreme importance: *Original finish that appears on a gun should be preserved at all costs.* Any cleaning should be executed with the greatest of care so as not to destroy any of that remaining finish. Many otherwise fine pieces have been considerably lessened in value because of promiscuous over-cleaning.

Prominent among the nuances of understanding condition is judging the amount of original finish; in the majority of cases this is bluing although others include casehardening, browning, nickel or silver plating, etc. Merely establishing or accurately estimating the percentage of finish remaining is not in itself quite sufficient. A feature that must also be taken into consideration is the condition of that original finish; whether dulled from age or in its factory bright condition, whether scratched or marred, etc. The identical percentage of original finish can fall into several degrees of condition. The knack for estimating finish is quite easily acquired, but it does necessitate actual first-hand experience in seeing and handling the guns themselves.

Another interesting observation on the eccentricities of the gun market with respect to "condition" is that the two most readily sold types of guns, and those which experience the least sales resistance when they are logically priced, are both the cheapest guns in the worst condition and the very finest guns in the ultimate degrees of condition. The defective pieces are attractive both for their extremely low price and the fact that they have a tremendous following of devotees who enjoy doing their own home gunsmithing (receiving either cash or therapeutic profit). In the case of the finest pieces they eventually reach the end of the line and never become available again. The best quality guns are vanishing from the active market and are the subject of heavy competition. The great bulk of antique guns available fall into the condition categories between these two extremes. The "in-between" are generally most readily available and are more often "churned" or turned-over by the many collectors in the constant process of upgrading.

STANDARDS FOR GRADING CONDITION

To understand values as shown throughout this book, it is essential to establish well-defined guidelines for various grades of condition. This subject has such wide latitude that a great diversion of opinions has always existed as to what should and what does constitute each degree of condition change as well as what words should be used to name these degrees. Likely the subject will never be resolved for the simple matter that firearms have so many variable factors that no one or two simple words can easily encompass their overall condition. As was stated earlier, once a piece is less than "factory new" and as near perfection as possible, opinions as to the exact condition of that piece will vary considerably.

In practice, i.e., mail-order sales, advertisements, catalogs, etc., simple one or two word descriptions of condition have not been found satisfactory. Up to the 1950s or so, those short one-worders would often be used in cataloging firearms. Although unsatisfactory, they were at least acceptable for the most part with no loud grumblings from collectors. This was especially true with the less expensive guns, many of which numbered under $50 in those days. As the field grew and the demand became greater (and consequently the prices), the need for more detailed descriptions, especially for mail-order sales, was quite apparent. It was one thing to sell a gun for $10 or $20—if the purchasing party found the piece below his expectations, he merely kept it, since to make the return wasn't worth the trouble. However, with prices ascending, buyers became much more discriminating, and it was worth their time to send those more valuable pieces back! Thus, in this day and age, there has evolved a very elaborate means for describing antique and collectors' firearms accurately for mail-order sales, and this has generally been the outgrowth of the system used in the author's own earlier catalogs. **No standard pattern is followed by all in the hobby,** and there is very little likelihood such will ever be the case. The general format developed to describe a firearm is a breakdown into various components, describing each separately. Thus, for an antique revolver, after the basic description including barrel length and any special mechanical features or markings, there should be individual details given for the percentage and condition of original finish remaining, the amount and location of rusting (almost every piece has some even to a minor degree); the condition of the metal, of the markings, and of the grips and the mechanical functioning of the piece. Any special defects (or attributes!) should also be noted. The buyer is thus less apt to be disappointed after seeing the piece, and the seller will minimize the amount of items returned to him with letters of disappointment.

The National Rifle Association through its committees on arms collecting has established a set of standards specifically for antique guns. Although all the words used in these standards or their definitions are not in everyday use by all collectors or dealers, these NRA guidelines are the closest to a code that the gun collecting field has. They are listed here with the permission of the NRA.

CONDITION STANDARDS FOR ANTIQUE FIREARMS

FACTORY NEW—all original parts; 100 percent original finish; in perfect condition in every respect, inside and out.

EXCELLENT—all original parts; over 80 percent original finish; sharp lettering, numerals and design on metal and wood; unmarred wood; fine bore.

FINE—all original parts; over 30 percent original finish; sharp lettering, numerals and design on metal and wood; minor marks in wood; good bore.

VERY GOOD—all original parts; none to 30 percent original finish; original metal surfaces smooth with all edges sharp; clear lettering, numerals and design on metal; wood slightly scratched or bruised; bore disregarded for collectors firearms.

GOOD—some minor replacement parts; metal smoothly rusted or lightly pitted in places, cleaned or reblued; principal lettering, numerals and design on metal legible; wood refinished, scratched, bruised or minor cracks repaired; in good working order.

(GOOD": Universally used, abused and misunderstood terminology. Be sure to read discussion relevant to it in "INTRODUCTION.")

FAIR—some major parts replaced; minor replacement parts may be required; metal rusted, may be lightly pitted all over, vigorously cleaned or reblued; rounded edges of metal and wood; principal lettering, numerals and design on metal partly obliterated; wood scratched, bruised, cracked or repaired where broken; in fair working order or can be easily repaired and placed in working order.

POOR—major and minor parts replaced; major replacement parts required and extensive restoration needed; metal deeply pitted; principal lettering, numerals and design obliterated, wood badly scratched, bruised, cracked or broken; mechanically inoperative; generally undesirable as a collectors firearm.

These NRA conditions have been used by the author as the guidelines for the value ranges in this work. In order to use this book correctly, the reader is urged to constantly consult these condition standards when assessing a gun before applying a value to it. They stand as the crux of the valuation matter.

FOR FIREARMS ON WHICH BLUE (or nickel) FINISH IS A MAJOR DETERMINANT OF VALUE:
the wide latitude given to "original finish" in the NRA "Standards" has been refined for this GUIDE:

"VERY GOOD" indicates a crisp piece with but traces of finish

"FINE" is a specimen with 30 percent finish

"EXCELLENT" indicates 80 percent finish

BLUE vs. NICKEL: On mass produced guns, invariably cartridge models, that list "blue or nickel" as standard, it is observed that blue frequently tends to bring a premium. That occurs more often on guns in the upper grades of condition and (on handguns) in the larger caliber models. Premiums are modest for "FINE", rising substantially for "EXC." and "FACTORY NEW/MINT." This axiom is a very broad generalization and not applicable across the board.

A few words from other collecting fields have been absorbed into gun collecting. Although the NRA standard term "factory new" is certainly the correct and most accurate description for a gun in that particular condition, it has been found in practice that the term most often used to denote "factory new" has been borrowed from the coin collecting field: "MINT." From time to time attempts have been made to discourage its use, but "mint" is an ingrained part of gun collecting terminology. Occasionally such terms as "unissued" or "unfired" are used synonymously for "factory new" or "mint."

CONDITION AND VALUE RANGES

Great consideration was given to the matter of range of values for use in this book. To maximize the readers' use thereof, it was felt appropriate to employ both a "high" range as well as a "low" one which would enable immediately learning the general overall price range that a particular gun carried; a range broad enough between the two prices to place specimens in intermediary grades. These two prices and the spread between them are sufficient to judge the relative increase from one degree to another, and with a little analytical thought the reader can reasonably assess guns both below and above the listed ranges. The matter of pricing "factory new" or "mint" guns or those close to that condition has been conscientiously avoided. Such prices are subject both to distinct differences in opinion as well as rapid fluctuations. As guns in those conditions are proportionately much fewer in number and

subject considerably to the whims and emotions of both buyer and seller, they are thus less logically valued than the more often encountered pieces.

A DUAL RANGE OF CONDITIONS (AND THEIR ACCOMPANYING VALUES) HAVE BEEN USED THROUGHOUT THIS GUIDE. Those dual ranges of condition reflected for almost every firearm cataloged throughout this guide, represent the average level of conditions in which each particular listed firearm *is most apt to be encountered (or offered for sale or available for sale) in the collectors' marketplace.* Cognizance of those dual ranges of condition and values is essential for making best practical use of this guide. Formerly included in this section of Chapter II of earlier editions of this guide, that vital information has been expanded and highlighted in the *"Introduction"* to this guide, ... which the reader is urged to attentively review.

OTHER FACTORS AFFECTING VALUE

There are other features of antique guns which play an important role in determining value. The prices listed in this book are for the standard style and grade manufactured piece of the maker or the "as issued" piece of government arsenals. Without producing an unwieldy, multi-volume price guide, it is physically impossible to identify and evaluate a host of variations, modifications, deviations and decorations that often can and do appear on a great many types of antique guns—each feature of which alters value. Every weapon must be judged on its individual merits, and this entails further research and effort on the part of the reader in order to determine just how good that particular gun might be and how to properly evaluate it in monetary terms. Some of these features are so often found in certain lines, e.g., Colts, Smith & Wessons, Winchesters, etc., that the subject has been individually covered in each of those respective sections. The matter is treated here as it affects antique American arms in general.

---

1. Cased Sets

Complete cased outfits are a desirable variant of many types of American firearms. They are most often seen in handguns although cased longarms occasionally appear. Styles of casings and accessories vary considerably; certain types, notably Colts and Smith & Wessons, are more often observed while in some other makes cased sets are practically unknown. The fact that an item is in its original case is an immediate enhancement of value. One cannot, however, arrive at a flat percentage price increase without having details of the case itself, its condition, its appearance and its accessories. For instance, a fine gun in its original and rare case is not greatly increased in value if the case is in poor condition. The mere rarity factor of a case is not sufficient to enhance value considerably because the poor condition of the case would detract from the gun when displayed. By the same token, that gun in that same case in fine condition would be worth a great deal more. The style and color of the lining is important as is the quality and condition of the lining and the compartments. Obviously, the cases that have been refitted internally (even though the box itself is original) are worth a great deal less than if untouched. The accessories included in the case each have an individual value and must be assessed both as to originality and correct type for that particular gun with their values considered in reaching a total for the outfit. Original paper labels of the maker or dealer that sold the gun also enhance value. Care should be exercised as such labels are often reproduced.

Cased sets are eagerly sought after and because of this have attracted not a few unscrupulous operators over the years who have manufactured for the over-eager, unsuspecting collector quite a few spurious specimens. The subject is covered in greater depth with some rules-of-thumb for spotting fake cases in the textual material accompanying the Colt section of this book, and the reader is referred there for more on the subject.

2. Matched Pairs

There exists no definite guide or even good rule-of-thumb for pricing antique arms found in matched pairs. There might be quite a few theories offered, but it is strictly a matter of catch-as-catch-can or what the market will bear! Of course, the primary determining factor is what make and model of gun is concerned. Some particular types (such as dueling pistols or large flintlock holster pistols) are often found in matched pairs and considered normal that way, while at the other extreme there are those pieces which are in very low demand and if found in pairs, the buyer is apt to say, "So what!" American percussion dueling pistols normally found as a pair would be so priced and when only a single such specimen is found it would have to be priced less than half of what the two would bring. Conversely, when a gun that is normally seen only as a single is found matched with another, the price would most likely be the value of each gun totalled plus an extra percentage for the rare situation of being found as a matched pair. The percentage is subject to wide fluctuations and no definite guidelines suggest how to determine a figure. A few observations, though, should be borne in mind:

(a) To be a matched pair, the guns must be truly that—matched, both in model, markings, finishes, grips and most important, condition. Serial numbers do not necessarily have to be in sequence or matched, but their closeness is a great asset.

(b) Merely finding two specimens of the same gun and keeping them together does not constitute a matched pair nor excite much collector interest. The pair should have features which demonstrate they have been kept together over the years. Of course, a double casing helps!

(c) Matching guns to one another more often prevails in Colts and Smith & Wessons or other pieces having exterior and easily visible serial numbers; if a gun necessitates stripping to locate the number, there is little reason to attempt finding a mate. A difference of 50 serial numbers has traditionally been considered the maximum spread acceptable in a matched pair, but that is by no means all-inclusive. There is no valid basis for this other than a general acceptance by a number of collectors. A larger serial number spread is accepted though, only when the pieces are otherwise virtually identical. In all cases this matching of pistols or revolvers into pairs will have little effect on some buyers, and that value must necessarily be enhanced is no foregone conclusion.

(d) A serial number sequence, i.e., one number following exactly after the other, is definitely considered a matched pair and in all cases increases the value of collectors' firearms. But, again, other factors must be weighed in determining value; the key will be condition. Not only must that match from gun to gun, but to be of any measurable value, condition should be rated fine or better.

3. Engraved Guns

Engraving or similar embellishments are found on guns of many American makers; some with a much greater degree of frequency than others. The major categories in engraved American arms are Colts, Smith & Wessons, Winchesters and Marlins. As a generality, it may be said that all antique arms which bear engraving or other fancy embellishments contemporary with the period of manufacture, other than as a standard feature, are considerably more valuable than the plain specimens. Some of these pieces were decorated at or for the factory, while others are known to have been engraved by the dealers or jewelers who sold them. On a great many specimens it is very difficult to determine where the engraving was done; it is important, though, for the modern day collector to determine when the engraving was done—then or now!

The demand for engraved antique American arms has always been strong, and hence, quite a few spurious specimens, many of which have been circulating for quite a few years, may be found on the market. The buyer is urged to carefully verify the authenticity of engraved or otherwise decorated guns before acquiring them.

No pat formula exists for evaluating fancy arms, but a few basic principles are predominant. Most important are the make and model of the gun and the desirability and demand for that model. Of equal importance is condition, for when prices start to rise, the buyer is interested not only in the exotica of decoration. The quality of the engraving or extra embellishments must also be taken into consideration. These can run from broad, simple scroll-like motifs on but a few parts to quite profuse, deep, finely detailed almost bas-relief motifs on all parts, at times including gold or silver inlay work. The latter types stand among the most exciting and eagerly sought after of all American collectors' firearms. Engraving and inlay work are not the sole features classifying a gun as fancy or embellished; fancy carving in the stock or grips or possibly even a special type of etching on the cylinder will also qualify the piece.

4. Grips, Stocks and Unusual Accessories

Gun stocks and pistol grips in most cases are of walnut and of standard issue. In the later metallic cartridge handguns gutta percha and hard rubber were in many cases substituted and are standard and so listed here. Fancy grips or stocks were a popular option from the factory or from dealers primarily from the mid-19th into the early 20th century. Many exotic materials were used, the most often elephant ivory (sometimes walrus), mother-of-pearl, black ebony, rosewood and fancy burled and Circassian grained woods. If in sound and complete (uncracked, broken or chipped) condition, a premium should be added to the normal value of the gun. Ivory and pearl are among the more desirable types and generally fetch higher prices than most woods. No clear or easy price formula exists, and normally the increase is anywhere from $20 to $75 at a maximum; although on a superb handgun of large size the value could be considerably more. It is, of course, very important to determine whether the grips are antique and an original fit, and it should be remembered that such grips have been made in modern times to enhance values for the unsuspecting. Thus, view them with care and caution.

Grips that bear fancy carving, either incised or relief, warrant an extra premium. In broadest terms, the fancier the carving and the finer quality and detailing of it, the higher the price. Such carving is more often seen on ivory than any other material, and depending on the size of the grips and the model on which they appear, prices for fine specimens certainly can be increased from a minimum of $75 to $100 and up; the better the condition and quality, the higher the value.

Exotic materials were also fitted to longarms, but less frequently than on handguns. The most often seen type of wood affecting value is the so-called select or Circassian grained walnut stocks. On the earlier handmade pieces one of the most desirable variations is the tiger-stripe curly maple. On production guns the select grain walnut stocks can often increase prices, but to what extent is very much dependent on the model of gun and, of course, condition. One of the most exotic stock types found on a few American longarms is rosewood. Depending on model and condition, the rosewood stock could increase a weapon's value considerably. A long-gun stock of elephant ivory is an extreme rarity, and any specimen judged to be original would be quite valuable.

A number of factory mounted special mechanical features or accessories add to the price of antique and collector firearms. Notable among these are varying styles of sights, especially on the fine single shot breech-loading target and lever action repeating rifles, e.g., Winchesters, Sharps, Remingtons and Marlin-Ballards. These types are also found with variances in levers, buttplates, palm rests and other options which were offered during their heyday; many are viewed as quite desirable by the modern day collector, thus commanding premium prices. Some government issue, U.S. military pieces are found with unusual arsenal accessories (usually sights), and these call for a price increase. Handgun accessories such as attachable shoulder stocks or interchangeable/spare cylinders will enhance value considerably. As with other non-standard features, the prospective buyer should proceed very cautiously in order to establish authenticity.

5. Presentation and Other Historically Associated Firearms

Guns bearing names, presentation inscriptions, or commemorative legends offer interesting potential for significant price increases. Those hand-engraved features appear in a variety of styles. Though most often seen on the backstraps of revolvers, they are also found on small inlaid grip plaques or carved on the stocks, either incised or relief. On most inscribed longarms the legends are engraved on plaques inset in the buttstock or (on lever actions or other breechloaders)

engraved on the receivers. The positioning or format of an inscription follows no set pattern, and the key to an evaluation is first to determine originality. Regrettably this area of arms collecting has been much abused by unscrupulous operators and spurious specimens are in circulation. Suggestions on how to spot a fake will be found in Chapter III of this book.

The challenge really begins after determining the authenticity of the inscription. If the gun is already accompanied by documents or has a known history and background, then much of the battle is over! What remains then is merely a matter of assessing value in proportion to the historical significance of the inscription. Should no known background of the names or legends appearing on the gun be available, then some detective work is in order. Establishing the history behind an inscription is quite important. In many cases, especially military presentations indicating names and regiments, backgrounds can be quite easily checked by searching military records through adjutant general departments which each state maintains or through the National Archives in Washington. All this can be accomplished through correspondence or by direct, on site, research.

In instances where inscriptions are present, but no identifying material is available and thus historical significance is unknown, then very little, if any, value can be added to the weapon. When revealing facts are known, values should increase in direct proportion to their significance. For example, a Colt Civil War revolver bearing the name of an officer and his regiment: Research documents that the officer was dismissed for cowardice in action and cashiered from the Army. This certainly is no illustrious history, but it is interesting and would likely increase the value of that gun 10 to 20 percent. Another piece of same type, same condition, similarly inscribed, but in which research proved the officer to have risen to command of the regiment and to have performed gallantly and heroically in battle, would add considerably to the piece and very possibly increase its value 50 to 100 percent, if not more. Although the most often observed type of inscription seems to be on Civil War era handguns, they are found on just about every type of firearm of every era. The price increase is in direct proportion to the historic relationship and importance that can be established for the gun. Establishing the significance of such guns usually requires considerable effort, and an equal effort may be involved in realizing the higher values for them. No two inscribed pieces are identical, and each must be weighed on its own merits and importance. One cannot simply and arbitrarily assign a price to such a piece; by the same token these items do offer an interesting and often exciting challenge to both buyer and seller.

6. Credibility of Documents

Certainly the greatest asset an inscribed gun can have is documentary evidence substantiating its originality. Regrettably collectors have often failed to realize the importance of such material, and when it was available, they overlooked acquiring it even if at no extra cost! The very best of such material is that which comes directly from the family whose ancestor originally owned the gun. Original letters, diaries, bills of sale or old news clippings have sometimes been kept intact and bear specific mention of the piece for identification. Such material is just about indisputable. In lieu of that, notarized affidavits from descendants of the original owner are quite important and do carry weight, especially where it can be reasonably accepted or perhaps proven that the particular gun has always remained in one family and been passed down generation to generation until final sale to the open market. It is important not to lose that chain of descent, and but a slight bit of effort is needed to draw up a brief statement as to background (how long the gun remained in the family, how it was passed down father to son, etc.), fully identifying it by description and serial number and any peculiar features. The seller must then notarize both the validity of the statement and his signature. Although the mere affidavit is in no way proof positive of the originality of the item (and the document is subject to abuses), it does add much to the strength of the background and credibility.

It is quite possible to considerably increase the value of an uninscribed (or otherwise historically unmarked) weapon that has historical association as long as substantiation can be made with documentary evidence. Value can be increased proportionately with the credibility of the documents; the closer they come to validating the piece "beyond the shadow of a doubt" the better the gun becomes. Excellent examples would be weapons known to have been used by Western badmen while performing nefarious deeds or by lawmen in their pursuit. Such pieces have always held a certain amount of morbid fascination (in the case of badmen) or romance of the West (in the case of the good guys). Of the literally thousands that the author has heard of over the years, but a handful ever turned out to be legitimate. Such items are worth a considerable amount of money, and their value is based chiefly on the strength of the accompanying documents. The buyer is cautioned to be extremely skeptical when buying such pieces merely accompanied by a dossier of documents which are actually completely peripheral. Quite often arms are offered for sale attributed to use by specific individuals and accompanied by tremendous amounts of data on those individuals. Although the data is found to be accurate as far as the individuals and historical events are concerned, on close scrutiny these materials fail to substantiate the originality of the gun itself and are rather "accessories after the fact!" In such cases the seller had hoped to overwhelm the unsuspecting buyer by the pure mass of documentary data, none of which substantiated the piece in any way. Thus, accompanying documents should always be carefully scrutinized and analyzed when they are instrumental in evaluating a piece.

The matter of inscribed historically associated guns and their values does not lend itself to simple formulas and offers one of the widest ranges of price variance in the gun market; they also offer the greatest challenges.

7. An Effective Tool For Historical Research

It has been surprising that the well-researched, multi-volume work "SERIAL NUMBERS OF U.S. MARTIAL ARMS" (Springfield Research Service) has not been better utilized by collectors. Augmented periodically, it offers a wealth of historical data, much of which may tend to increase values of certain firearms. The information is taken directly from U.S. Government archives, including those of the Springfield Armory, Office of the Chief of Ordnance, Adjutant General's Office, U.S. Marine Corps and U.S. Navy Bureau of Ordnance.

Listed by serial number sequence are many thousands of various handguns and longarms purchased by the U.S. from the Civil War to WWII. Data often includes place (or sometimes, unit) where issued. Guns range from Civil War Colt and Remington revolvers and cavalry carbines to WWII M1 rifles: Colt Single Actions, S&Ws, Springfield "Trap-door" longarms, Krags, M. 1917 rifles, Model 1911 autos and much more.

Of course, not every gun purchased by the U.S. is listed. And, it may be akin to looking for "a needle in a haystack." But, finding a gun among those listings could enhance its value appreciably. A WORD OF CAUTION: Locating a gun just one number apart from a listed piece doesn't count! It's considered a complete miss. The mere close proximity does not indicate that it was part of the same lot or issued to the same unit. Interesting, yes; premium value, no.

To make the best and most effective use of this "tool" for historical research, the collector would do well to contact the Springfield Research Service, P.O. Box 6322, Falls Church, Virginia 22040 or check their website: www.armscollectors.com/srs.htm. (An alternate, possibly upgraded, website: www.springfieldresearchservice.com) A vast amount of information from the archives and government records is available (for a modest fee) through them. Such data may add substantially to the historical significance (and often value) of some antique arms. The service offered also issues a quarterly "Newsletter" available upon subscription.

8. Unlisted or Unknown Variations

The mere fact that a model, sub-model or variation does not appear in this book should not be interpreted as proof the gun is a rarity. In no sense does the author wish to imply that every known variation or deviation from the manufacturer's "standard" gun has been located or cataloged! The reader is cautioned here, as he is throughout the book, not to jump to conclusions! The fact that a piece differs from standard might even suggest it is not entirely original. Much might have happened to an object that has been in existence 80 to 275 years since it left the factory or the maker's premises. Not a few interesting and fine quality alterations were made to guns over that period by very competent gunsmiths, often satisfying the owner's particular needs or whims. Both the quality of the workmanship of such alterations and the passage of time tend to give them the air of factory originality. At times the value of a gun may be enhanced due to the oddity factor. Most such alterations, however, when proven to be non-factory in origin normally do not increase the value of the gun and in many instances, actually detract from it.

When variations are found to be original, quite a number of factors must be weighed to assess the possible increase in value. Leading factors are the make and model of gun and demand for it on the collector market. The value of the variation may be said to increase in importance, and hence value, in direct proportion to the demand for the gun as a collector's piece. Thus, an unusual barrel length on a small caliber rimfire revolver of one of the lesser known makers may have merely a curiosity value for a few collectors and a price increase of 20 to 40 percent. That identical variation found on a similar period gun by one of the more eagerly sought after makers could very well increase value by 100 to 500 percent. Each situation must be analyzed carefully and weighed on its own merits.

Suspicions should be especially aroused at unique, not previously known or recorded, one-of-a-kind guns. Should more than one such ultra-rare piece turn up within a close time or geographic proximity then extreme caution and skepticism may be in order. When what is nontypical becomes typical should immediately be cause for concern.

It is in the area of variations that the counterfeiter and forger has had a veritable field day. As a matter of fact, he has the opportunity to hone his inventive abilities to a very fine edge. With the knowledge that variations do appear that have never previously been cataloged (one of the interesting aspects of gun collecting) quite a few intriguing variations have been made strictly to dupe the unwitting collector. Some of these were no doubt intended as good humored, pure practical jokes; an ingredient known from the days when guns had modest values. With the passage of years some of those early fakes or gags have acquired an age patina giving them a more credible appearance than the more recently made forgeries. The collector is forewarned of such specimens and should keep his wits about him when offered an unusual variant, coolly analyzing the piece and using good common sense as his basic guide.

9. Serial Numbers

An idiosyncrasy of gun collecting is the premium price often placed on arms with very low serial numbers; such prices being for the number alone and not for their indication of an early model or the fact that they indicate a low production. This number game plays a more important role with the large makers such as Colt, Smith & Wesson, and Winchester and is treated separately in the text within each of those sections. The serial number of the gun in no way affects its appearance, purpose or use and is merely a fascinating feature for some collectors on some guns. Before paying a premium price for numbers (one or two digits especially), the buyer is cautioned to learn a little about that gun's numbering system and whether or not the sequence was consecutive from "1" right through to the end of production, or whether serial numbers were in batch lots. Quite a few American guns are found with low serials since they were marked from "1" to "20" or possibly "1" to "100" and then numbering started all over again; look before you leap! Of equal importance is the fact that on many other types of American guns the serial number has yet to be found of any significance to collecting, and the best response on certain pieces to a very low digit serial is, "So what!" Although the numbers occasionally play a role in pricing, it is up to the reader to determine just how much by considering the other influencing factors.

10. Bores

Bores often play a significant role in establishing and affecting value. At times they are a primary factor, while with a great many other guns, bores play no influencing factor whatsoever. Generally, the importance of the bore condition may be weighed in direct proportion to the purpose of the weapon. For very fine percussion bench rest target rifles, long-range and mid-range single shot breech-loading target rifles, and items similar in nature, the bore was obviously an important feature when these arms were made and sold, and thus it is equally important to the collector today. On the opposite end of the scale are many guns (e.g., small pocket pistols) on which the bore is of no consequence whatsoever. Between these two poles lies a vast amount of pieces in which bores are of varying degrees of importance. Not a few collectors would immediately rule a piece out unless it has a fine bore; for others the bore is completely unimportant. The subject is also treated in those sections within this book devoted to guns where bore condition is a critical detail. Although the odds are heavily weighed against most collectors shooting an antique gun, part and parcel of the inspection process of a breechloader is to look down the bore; on muzzle loaders one goes out of his way to do so only with target rifles where this feature is absolutely important. A poor bore will very likely detract from both demand and price of a very fine quality piece, especially those designed for fine target shooting; a deteriorated bore or one ringed inside with a bulge evident on the outside of the barrel is a detriment to any gun and will detract both in price and demand. On handguns, bores are generally unimportant on the smaller caliber models, while on the larger sizes, especially pieces designed for target shooting, bores play a more dominant role.

Outstanding gold and silver mounted percussion sporting rifle in its original fitted case with accessories c.1850. Made by Daniel B. Wesson of Hartford, Conn. who, in 1854 with Horace Smith, founded one of America's most famous arms manufactories: Smith & Wesson. (*from N. Flayderman & Co. Catalog No. 104 of Oct., 1980*)

Chapter III

Restoration and Fakes
Where the Fine Line is Drawn

Spurious specimens and fraudulent practices are by no means of epidemic proportions; no more so than in any other field of collecting where valuable items are offered for sale. The collector is cautioned to be aware that in the antique arms field there have been, and continue to be, a certain number of unscrupulous individuals eager and willing to dupe the unwitting, the unsuspecting and the careless. Buyer ignorance and avarice are both dangerous where high values are concerned. Nefarious individuals have been active since the beginnings of the hobby, and new crops do come along. One of the earliest American periodicals devoted to this hobby, the *Magazine of Antique Firearms*, in its August, 1911 issue, discussed the widespread practice of making bogus antiques of all types, arms included, and looking "...upon the people of the U.S. as their best customers." True, such fakery was in all likelihood confined to European firearms, not becoming a cottage industry on U.S. shores until years later concurrent with the increased interest and value of American antique guns. If studies were made and graphs plotted, the lines reflecting the increase in values, the increase in collector numbers and the increase in forgers would merge. Fortunately it may be said that the good guys outnumber the bad guys by far, but forewarned is forearmed.

Gun clubs and organizations over the years have drawn codes of ethics and conduct applicable to both collectors and dealers. The most widely known is that of the National Rifle Association, reproduced in full at the end of this chapter. These codes generally identify practices relating to gun collecting that are considered unethical as well as general practices of unethical business behavior; the latter are for the most part relevant to any type of business transaction and not necessarily peculiar to arms collecting. These codes are both well intentioned and indisputable for their moral tenets. Although they function as guideposts and are observed (often in varying degrees) by most of the collecting world, a certain element exists who is either unaware of these codes—or would like to be. An honorable person would conduct himself according to the code while someone with larceny in his heart would ignore the rules whenever possible. A few comments should be made regarding codes in the light of reality; in other words, not what people should do, but what they in fact do! The reader should be aware that some recommended ethical practices are infrequently followed. Two especially flagrant examples are: (A) A marking under the stocks or elsewhere to indicate both date and nature of work performed when antique guns are either refinished or modern engraved; (B) Indication by a seller to a buyer that a piece has had "legitimate" restoration or completion of missing parts. In item A, it is rare to have a piece so marked, and the removal of such markings at some future date is a simple matter. In item B, a seller often advises a buyer that a piece has been restored, and to what extent; however, that story is usually watered down in the course of trades and sales down the line to the point where it is completely forgotten, overlooked or omitted in time. Thus, although the ethical practices of codes are worth following and often are, in the reality of gun trading certain rules are subject to abuse. Gradually or quickly as a piece changes hands, no one will remember exactly what happened, and it is very much up to the eyesight and judgment of the buyer to spot any inconsistencies on his own.

Following a code of ethics is a most worthy objective, but the buyer should always remember that he may be traveling in perilous waters. He should take nothing for granted, and rely on his own basic instincts, common sense and better judgment.

An absorbing book by a highly respected arms authority and one heartily recommended to all collectors interested in detecting fakes is *How Do You Know It's Old?* by Harold L. Peterson. Covering a wide range of interests, with a wealth of material on antique arms, it lays to rest many of the oft-quoted conundrums of collecting circles when trying to justify a questionable piece, e.g., "...it couldn't be a fake; nobody could spend all that time necessary to produce that and make any money," or "...I know this has to be old because of the circumstances under which I acquired it." The collector would do well to familiarize himself with the Peterson book, and may save considerable grief and money by absorbing a number of the finer points discussed.

Also worthy of the collector's attention, as it covers not only the foregoing subject but much of what follows here as well, is *331 + Essential Tips and Tricks; a How-To Guide for the Gun Collector* by S.C. Mowbray (see Biblio.)

What constitutes an ethical or "legitimate" restoration and differentiates it from an unethical or "illegitimate" one is quite debatable indeed. The subject begs for accurate definitions, yet constantly evades them. Not a few attempts have been made. Many of the definitions of "legitimate" restorations have apparent validity, but all seem to be the reflections of personal tastes of the interpreter. To further complicate matters, what is "legitimate" and what is not has had some change over the years. In current day practice certain restorations formerly thought "illegitimate" have acquired an air quite the opposite. An evolutionary process is at work as far as acceptability is concerned.

Bear in mind that almost anything man has made, another can reproduce or duplicate. Our intent here is not to philosophize about such practices nor suggest more codes condemning them, but rather to advise the reader what to expect by pointing out a few of the more obvious violations and how they might be detected.

The basic tenet which follows has proven itself valuable on countless occasions and is one which the author personally subscribes to and recommends: If in doubt, if a piece looks wrong or has something about it that you cannot put your finger on, if it just does not add up in your mind, the chances are the gun is wrong—pass it by. Very likely a few good pieces may be missed this way, but the law of averages will prove the practice a sound one. The mere fact that in looking at a gun one has an uneasy feeling is usually sufficient to indicate something is wrong. Whether or not one can put his finger on these vibrations is unimportant; the worst one can do at that point is try to rationalize something that is bad into being good, and here's where those old wives tales come into play like "...it's got to be good because of where it came from" or "...no one would take the time to make that kind of fake" or "...the price is so reasonable it couldn't be wrong." Emotions may cause an otherwise astute buyer to become carried away, making excuses to rationalize very obvious telltale clues such as color changes, patina, signs of pitting, etc. If time permits and other known examples are available for comparison, there is certainly a good basis for verifying the piece thoroughly. Often when confronted with the challenge of a possible fake, one's hopes of what one would like the gun to be takes precedence over good judgment. In other words, the buyer becomes his own worst enemy.

THE GREAT AMERICAN GUN SCAM

The story of the now infamous experimental Walker Colts may be found of interest, not merely as the author played a key role in their unmasking, but as an example of gullibility and poor judgement.

In 1931 a set of four unique, so-called experimental-transitional Colt Paterson-Walkers were featured in the catalog of a prominent arms dealer then offering a famous Colt collection. The revolvers, outrageous fakes fabricated by parties unknown, were subsequently sold for values equal then to what four fine Walkers would fetch on today's market. By 1937 they were the subject of a small book devoted solely to their fabricated and supposed rarity (*The Revolving Cylinder Colt Pistol Story 1839-1847* by J.H. Edgerly; see Biblio. Chap. V-B). They had become so well-accepted by the collecting world of the day that a respected arms historian illustrated and discussed them at length in his book *Whitney Firearms* (1946). In the 50s they reappeared on the cover of a well-known antique arms journal. The author acquired them when the owner's collection was dispersed in 1972, and in his catalog that same year exposed them as fakes; the entire page of that catalog later reproduced in the widely quoted *How Do You Know It's Old*. A few years following their sale as fakes and curiosities, the author was approached at an arms show by one of those characters that operates on the fringe of the collecting world. To his amusement he was given a tongue-lashing for ruining a swindle the fellow was about to close for those fakes, when his mark had somehow been shown the reprint of the exposé! The four revolvers had come full circle ...or almost.

The paths down which the expert restorer and forger have traveled are many. The subject is one which has been treated in print frequently over the years and is certainly worth a major study one day. Following are some points which the author has found to be the most pertinent in the matter of alterations. Some other factors involving restorations and fakes are beyond the realm of our coverage here, but are worth bearing in mind. These include such intriguing subjects as welding, brazing and barrel stretching (that is, restoring shortened barrels to their original length), altering guns from one model to another and reworking centerfire revolvers to rimfire models (as in a very few types of Colts and Smith & Wessons). The reader will often hear mention of using X-rays to detect certain types of fakes. This is an excellent method, but due to general inaccessibility and time limitations it is not utilized with any degree of frequency.

A note to bear in mind on polishing and refinishing: When confronted with a gun that has been heavily polished or has been entirely refinished, a danger signal should flash in one's mind. Both of these features, although not indicating the item has necessarily been tampered with, should call for a closer inspection. Polishing and refinishing can conceal a multitude of sins. By removing the normal patina and aging of the gun, the faker can obscure various areas that might have been worked over and such arms should be closely inspected.

A. REFINISHING

Refinishing antique guns is generally frowned upon; in quite a few instances it actually detracts from value, resulting in a less desirable and less valuable item (even though good money has been spent for the refinish). The practice of making a relatively worn gun, or one that has been heavily used, look like new is rather incongruous, and the effect on the gun is quite the same. Any antique item, especially a gun, used, and no longer new, should look its age and stand on its own merits. Refinishing is akin to taking an 80-year-old man and dressing him in the clothes of a teenager. Such a gun is, of course, simply detected and, for the most part, has the same value refinished as unrefinished. However, the restored status has changed the weapon's demand and desirability on the collectors' market. Where a very fine conditioned piece has been clearly refinished in an attempt to fool a collector, the question of intent may be raised. *Careful inspection* should be given original finishes in all cases to ascertain their originality.

Examine the gun in a good, strong light (daylight preferably); should the finish be suspect, a few other areas require close study with a magnifying glass: (1) Look for scratch marks or especially light rust pitting underneath the finish. If either is present, in all likelihood the gun has been refinished. Prior to putting on original factory finish most metal parts are polished clean and smooth and are free of any rust pitting or tiny pockmarks. In almost every instance scratches and pits are acquired after the gun has had its original factory finish. (2) Look very closely at all edges and markings. In order to realize a quality refinish, the metal must be cleaned and polished thoroughly. In so doing some sharpness will usually leave the edges (most noticeable on octagon barrels), and the markings are often lightened or even partially worn away. With markings once sharp and deep, the edges of the die struck impression are quite often rounded and smoothed over. (3) On revolvers standard with roll engraved scenes on the cylinder, a very careful inspection of this feature should be made for sharpness and clarity. Any wear, especially if uneven, beneath a blue finish would clearly indicate the piece was tampered with and very likely refinished.

B. MARKINGS AND NUMBERS

Markings are critical features in judging rarity and value of an antique gun and should be carefully scrutinized. Numbers are equally critical, but only on specific makes of guns—not all. Room for wrong-doing exists in each area, and it may be generally said that the alteration or "improvement" of markings is usually done with the intent to deceive and possibly even defraud. The matter becomes rather hazy though, once the gun leaves the original wrong-doer's hands and is traded down the line. Whether the original party who made and sold the piece told the next buyer what had been done is very much a moot point by the time the piece has been in general circulation and passed through a few hands. At that juncture the importance for the purposes of this book is not to comment on the gun's unethical manufacture, but how the unsuspecting purchaser may detect those incorrect marks or numbers which considerably detract from value and rarity. An inexpensive pocket magnifying glass is an indispensable aid and should be part of every collector's tool kit. Inspect all markings thoroughly; the more important they are for the gun, the closer they should be studied. Check for sharpness, depth and clarity. If the gun is heavily worn but the markings are sharp and clear, this obvious inconsistency indicates that some work has likely been performed. Markings should show the same even wear or rust pitting and corrosion found on the rest of the gun. Restamping or "freshening" the markings is not normally considered an asset or an improvement and most often will detract from the value. Worse still, any altering of markings to ones that never appeared on the gun is completely fraudulent.

Where remarking has been done with die stamps it will easily show up under a magnifying glass as inconsistent. In most cases where die stamps are used by forgers to re-mark or fraudulently mark a piece, they are single or individual dies, and the letters will appear quite uneven when magnified. The original manufacturers normally had stamps or rolls made on complete single dies which had a very even, regular appearance. It should be remembered, though, that the rarer and more valuable the piece, the more effort the expert forger will expend to fake it; thus, in some cases entire dies simulating those of the manufacturer have been made. Fortunately the use of these sophisticated dies is rare in comparison to the single stamp method. If the forger has freshened or re-marked the piece by hand engraving in a similar style to the original die stamp, this will quite easily show up under a magnifying glass; the consistency of the hand engraved markings are quite obviously different than those of the stamped markings. If well done, the hand engraved marks might fool the naked eye when not viewed closely, but are impossible to stand up under magnification.

Another investigatory avenue for the verification of authentic markings is any sign of age appearing within them, a detail seen best with magnification. If a gun has wear of any type, its markings should show the exact same percentage of wear and normal rust, pitting or corrosion, dents, scratch marks or mars of any form found on that same area of the gun proper.

The collecting world has been consistently warned about a few specific types of American arms which have been forged and regularly appear on the market. This book will call such pieces to the readers' attention wherever possible. A few of the most notorious types are worth discussion here. Most often seen and most often written about is the Model 1842 percussion U.S. martial pistol bearing "Palmetto Armory-Columbia, S.C." markings. Counterfeit dies were made by some unnamed forger to resemble the original markings for this model; the forger took the standard Model 1842 U.S. pistol with either Johnson or Aston markings; ground them off on both barrel and lock and then restamped these parts with the false Palmetto markings, afterwards aging the gun. Armed with foreknowledge and awareness, these arms are quite easy to spot. The dies do not match the original Palmetto markings exactly and, as is the case with most fakes, the faker cannot perfectly achieve the aged

patina on the metal. To detect this latter feature, though, does take some experience in distinguishing between false and genuine patinas.

A second gun known to have had its marks counterfeited is the Model 1842 boxlock U.S. Navy percussion pistol bearing "Deringer - Philadelphia" markings. Here too the faker has had dies similar to the original made. By taking the more often encountered Ames marked 1842 pistols, removing the lockplate markings, and restriking them with the Deringer die, he has made a more valuable (if undetected) piece. Again, the key features to study are the sharpness of the markings, their consistency with the pistol's overall condition and the patina of the metal. Of course, the very best method is to have a genuine specimen for comparison since spurious markings would not match the original when closely viewed.

A type of gun not infrequently seen with fake markings are the various sized Henry Deringer, Philadelphia, percussion pistols featuring agent/dealer barrel stampings. On these the lock and breech markings (of the maker) are usually genuine. Further discussion appears in the section pertaining to deringer pistols; the fake markings are normally detected in the same manner as on the foregoing Palmetto and Deringer types.

Serial numbers are critical with certain models and makes of guns while on others they bear very little importance. The most noteworthy make where serials play a prominent role is the Colt. Where serial numbers are required to match one another and are part of the valuation process, the stampings should be looked at very carefully. Numbers are subject to deceptive practices and alterations to improve value; a few fine points about them are worth noting. The subject has been discussed at length in the textual material accompanying the Colt section of this book, to which the reader is referred. This same discussion as it pertains to Colt is applicable to all other guns in which numbers are important.

C. ENGRAVING AND INSCRIPTIONS

In the areas of engraving and inscriptions the forgers have worked with considerable success for quite a few years. They have been especially prolific with fancy engraved guns while the inscribed presentation pieces have become more frequent only in recent years as historical specimens have acquired a greater degree of demand and significance. The presence of either fancy engraving or historic inscriptions (or both) adds considerably to the value of any gun, and hence, it is in both these areas that special care should be given in judging originality. It does take experience and practice to distinguish good from bad, and fortunately the majority of fakers leave telltale clues and are inept enough to allow for quick and easy spotting of their handiwork. As in any group of craftsmen (the word is used here loosely), there are degrees of talent; it is with the few clever, artistic workers that one must rely on the most expert eye to differentiate a bad piece.

A few basic details to check are: (1) The style of engraving. Some styles were not used in the period of manufacture while others are purely modern in form, shape and design and even appear incongruous on antique guns. The word style applies to both decorated and engraved guns as well as to the presentation or historical inscriptions on them. Several styles of lettering are purely modern in form and appearance and therefore could not be contemporary on antique guns. The study of known original specimens as well as considerable literature on the subject is helpful in determining background. (2) The wear and aging on either the engraving or the inscription should be consistent with the rest of the gun. Some engraved or inscribed specimens have been refinished, many of them in gold and silver plating. Remember, refinishes often cover a multitude of sins beneath, some of which can no longer be seen. When these refinishes appear on deluxe specimens, they should serve as a warning to inspect the gun closer.

D. RECONVERSIONS

The subject of reconversions often creates heated, emotional discussions. One such topic of debate is that of restoring flintlock guns that were converted (c. 1830s-1840s) to the percussion ignition system and have been returned to their original flintlock condition by gunsmiths in this modern era. The practice has its protagonists and its antagonists. Although reconversions are by no means thought unethical, it is strongly suggested and recommended that the fact of reconversion be made known by the seller. Ethical codes suggest an internal lock marking by the restorer to indicate such work. Only with considerable rarity has the author encountered a specific instance of such markings being made. As for disclosure to the buyer, that can be likened to the other repair and restoration work previously mentioned in which the whole matter becomes a moot point once the gun is in general circulation and has passed through three or four hands. By then whatever work was performed has either been accidentally or purposely forgotten, and the piece must stand on its own outward appearance. As with other restorative work—there are good workmen and bad workmen. A hack's handiwork is quite obvious; and the majority of the pieces encountered are amateurish. It is with the work of experts that the buyer must be especially careful; quite proper it is to say that all flintlocks should be inspected closely.

There is no firm formula for pricing a gun that has been converted from flintlock to percussion. On U.S. martial handguns or longarms percussion conversions can vary from 40 percent to 70 percent of the price of the piece for the same model in flintlock; it is dependent on the relative rarity and demand for each individual model. With other types of arms such as very fine Kentucky rifles or guns of exceptional quality or possessing unique features, the fact of a conversion may affect value to a much lesser degree; each piece must be evaluated on its own merits, importance and special attributes.

The price differential between an original flintlock and a restored flintlock is often considerable, no matter how fine the job of restoration. But a reasonable and accurate reflection of the general feeling of the collectors' market is that a fine restoration to a flintlock enhances both the appearance as well as the value of the gun. Collectors and dealers in general, though, are quite emphatic in stating that no matter how good the restoration to flintlock, that piece is never worth the same as the original flintlock specimen. Generally its value should be that of the percussion conversion plus whatever charges are involved in restoring it to flintlock, plus possibly a small premium or percentage above that if the work is of excellent quality. Thus, if a flintlock U.S. musket is worth $1,500 and that same piece as a percussion conversion is worth $400, the specimen that has been reconverted probably would be worth anywhere from $450 to $700 depending on the quality and cost of the restoration. When a restored piece is being offered and priced as an original flintlock, the questionable practices and intent of the seller arise. A few basic procedures helpful in **distinguishing reconversions** are: (1) Always remove the lock completely. (2) Closely examine the type of flashpan and method of attachment to the lock. That part presents the most difficulty to the restorer, and it is there where the most obvious telltale signs and defects will appear. The primary step would be to ascertain what type of flashpan was on the gun originally; with martial flintlocks a simple matter to check from several illustrated books and articles. The method of attaching the pan and its general appearance and fit are clues which suggest how long it has been on the gun. Remember that the flashpan is one part liable to much wear and to black powder

corrosion; the latter should be consistent and even on both the pan and the surrounding lock parts, all details quite evident when the lock is removed. Other telltale clues are the false aging or acid aging colors on the inside of the lock (if a new pan has been fitted), and possibly the absence of any pitting or rust corrosion on the inside of the lock, particularly when such signs are visible on the exterior of the pan itself. (3) Other lock parts should be closely inspected for aging consistent with the rest of the lock. However, such signs in themselves do not preclude that the piece is original as some of these parts could merely be replacements. (4) A key factor in establishing originality of a flintlock is the touchhole, an area where the restorers often fail miserably. Normally on converting to percussion, the flintlock touchhole was enlarged considerably in order to affix a large metal part (drum or bolster) to hold the percussion nipple. To restore this back to flintlock, the large aperture or hole left by the nipple and drum has to be closed and a new touchhole bored. Often one can easily detect signs of the larger hole having been bushed with telltale signs where the new metal has been fitted. In other cases clever welding and aging can conceal such clues. The best way to verify the touchhole is to remove the breech plug and tang from the barrel and examine the area from the inside. This, though, is quite difficult to accomplish and sometimes is not worth pursuing. Another method is the X-ray, a rarely used technique because of its inaccessibility as well as time and cost factors. The touchhole itself must be looked at closely, and if the gun shows considerable use and wear from firing and the touchhole is tiny with sharp edges, there is a decided inconsistency; normally the touchhole wears and enlarges with the greater use of the gun. (5) Verification of the fit of the lock should be carefully studied. Some reconversions have been cleverly made by merely installing a completely new and original flintlock to the gun. Besides checking the area of the touchhole as previously discussed, the entire aperture or mortise in the gun stock that holds the lock should be carefully scrutinized for new cuts or filled in areas.

All the foregoing are but the most obvious check points; no single detail is in itself conclusive evidence of restoration work. As an example, consider the matter of touchhole; on original flintlocks the touchhole was enlarged from very heavy wear and use to the point where rebushing was necessary during the period of its original use. Thus, it is necessary to take all factors into account when passing judgment on flintlocks.

E. BORES: RERIFLING AND SLEEVING

Bores are an important evaluating detail of some types of arms. When this feature plays such a role, it is important to watch for inconsistencies which would indicate alterations have been made. With many of the later single shot breech-loading target rifles or lever-action repeating rifles, calibers are often marked (but not always) on the barrel by the factory. A primary check would consist of verifying that the gun is in its original marked caliber and chambers a round for which it was originally intended. If not, there are clear indications that the bore was either shot out, rerifled and rechambered to something else close to the original caliber, or possibly changed at the whim of the original owner during its period of use. In either event, price is seriously affected in terms of the weapon's collectibility. The piece certainly continues to have value, but the figure is considerably less than if in the original "as made" caliber.

The most often encountered bore alteration is sleeving or relining. The original barrel is reamed or bored out, and a new liner is inserted and rifled to the desired size. Generally this sleeving or lining was done to suit the personal taste of the owner/shooter, whose concern was more with its functioning than its collector's appeal. However, relining merely to better the appearance and quality of an antique or collector's piece is not unknown. Only rarely is it possible to determine the reasons for reboring or relining on a gun, but usually this was to take the place of or cover up a barrel defect.

In many cases relining work is obvious and telltale signs indicate the nature of the work. Most noticeable are the marks seen at the muzzle or the breech of the barrel liner itself; the small seam visible between the two pieces of metal. Fine welding, though, can conceal this, and it is then a matter of verifying the rifling and the caliber. This may be difficult and is not always possible, but other signs may serve as tip-offs that something has happened. If one is familiar with the rifling of certain manufacturers, then looking down the bore is sufficient to give clues that the piece is suspect; liners rarely match original rifling. Kentucky rifles and other muzzleloaders are often found with smooth bores (as their rifling was shot out by use), and liners will sometimes be found. Besides the telltale clues of seam marks at the muzzle, a good tip-off is condition of the rifling, usually perfect and like new and thus inconsistent with the normal overall wear of the rest of a piece which likely had its bore shot out.

The more a gun's value is dependent on bore, the more detrimental to price will be a lining or sleeving job. Relined breech-loading arms of modern vintage would have their value lessened considerably whereas the more antique or muzzle-loading pieces (of course, depending on the type) are less affected. Two cases in muzzle-loading arms where sleeving or relining alters the price drastically downward are with heavy percussion bench rest slug rifles or fine target rifles. With both types rifling and bores are critical and specimens are actively sought because of the quality of their rifling and the makers' names that appear on them. Any alteration of bores affects price strongly.

F. AGING AND PATINA

One of the most often used words in antique collecting in general and guns in particular is "patina." The dictionary defines it as "...any thin coating or color change resulting from age, as on old wood; a fine crust or film on bronze or copper; is usually green or greenish blue and is formed by natural oxidation." For arms collecting purposes, patina is the color formed by natural aging on wood or metal. It is to collecting what aging is to whisky or wine. A collector's practiced eye quickly learns to discern genuine patina formed only by genuine aging vs. a false or faked patina caused by chemical or other agents. The knack for knowing patina is acquired through experience and involves quite a few subtleties; none of them difficult to master. It may be likened to a jeweler with the acquired talent of discerning various shades of coloration to seeking the ultimate blue-white in a diamond. With practice and exposure, the art can be skillfully mastered.

All woods and all metals age differently. As they age, they acquire color changes. In woods this is usually by absorption of paints, dyes, stains, grease, dirt in the hand that has rubbed it and any other number of materials, changing humidities and temperatures, light, air and smoke, etc. With metals, patina is usually caused by oxidation; in iron, aging brings rust causing a turn to brown; in brass or copper, the turn is to a very dark greenish color. There is no single exact shade or coloration of various patinas; just general tones and ones to which the practiced eye very much responds!

The subject of aging and patination is covered in quite a few books on antiques in general and in the Harold L. Peterson work *How Do You Know It's Old?* in particular; the reader is referred to those reference works. Our intention here is merely to advise of the importance of this feature and the fact that patinas are the source of highly important clues to both restorations and fakery.

Perfectly matching age patina is practically impossible; a few very expert workmen have come close (and those that might

have done so are obviously so good that no one as yet has been able to tell!). In the process of restoration it may be necessary to clean metal or wood in the area repaired to the point where patina is altered or destroyed; the patina must then be restored. Thus, if a piece under careful inspection shows variances in patination, this is usually a good sign that alterations were made and further investigation is in order. A standard agent for artificial aging on iron is acid. In varying strengths and formulas acids create patterns of pitting which are generally incorrect, differing decidedly from the normal age patterns still present on the gun.

Again the warning is repeated here that the buyer should be extremely wary of pieces that have been polished bright or refinished. What very likely happened is that repairs were made where it was impossible to match patina and thus, the restorer merely destroyed all existing patina giving the piece a new and consistent finish to conceal the work.

Patina in itself is a very desirable finish, particularly on iron when it has turned a nice, smooth, even brownish color. Although caused strictly by rusting and aging over the years, those shades of brown are often very rich, and they lend the piece a very mellow pleasing appearance. There are no maxims on acceptable patina, very much a matter of personal preference, but a general consensus is that when a piece has a fine patina, it should certainly be left intact and in no way marred or destroyed.

The creation of false patina is usually by means of a chemical. With iron the technique is most often some type of rusting or combination browning and rusting solution of which the formulas are numerous. Their purpose is to create in a few days or weeks an appearance equal to what would normally require years of honest use or aging. With woods, stains and varnishes are usually used to attempt the same thing. These processes are not necessarily detrimental to an antique gun, nor do they necessarily detract from value. They may be simply part of a very legitimate restoration or blending-over of a very minor and honest repair. Where they attempt to hide and conceal factors likely to significantly influence the value of that particular weapon, they are very much indicators to the buyer that he should proceed with caution.

G. REPRODUCTIONS

Quite a few faithfully copied, modern made reproductions of antique arms are on today's market. The great majority are of antique Colt revolvers, but others are based on Remingtons, Sharps, Smith and Gallager carbines, Civil War 1861 muskets, the French Model 1763 Charleville musket, the famed British flintlock Brown Bess musket and many individually crafted Kentucky rifles and pistols. More will come as muzzle-loading shooting, the fast growing hobby in the firearms field, continues to mushroom. All these reproduction guns have been made with the most honorable intentions for the vast black powder market, including those groups specializing in battlefield skirmishes and reenactments. As to be expected, the temptation was great for the untalented faker to try his hand with these reproductions, and thus a small number of spurious examples have found their way to the antique gun market and are sold as originals. They are found with the modern makers' markings removed and in a beat-up, battle-worn appearance with applied false patinas. Faked reproduction guns represent neither a threat to the collecting world nor to the forewarned collector, and in every case known to the author, the buyer exercised the most imprudent judgment in acquiring such a piece. As a majority of the reproductions are Colts, the subject is treated in greater detail in the text accompanying the Colt section of this book, to which the reader is referred.

BIBLIOGRAPHY

*Ackerman, R. O. *Care and Repair of Muzzle Loaders*. Albuquerque, New Mexico: Muzzle Loader's Library, 1966. A small 24 page monograph directed to the person who can accomplish the job with but basic hand tools.

*Ackley, P. O. *Home Gun Care and Repair*. Harrisburg, Pennsylvania: The Stackpole Company, 1969. A manual that has gone through numerous printings. Contains some good material on repairs and maintenance of collector guns.

*Angier, R. H. *Firearm Blueing and Browning*. Harrisburg, Pennsylvania: The Stackpole Company, 1936. Practical manual on the chemical and heat coloring of all barrel steels and other gun metals from earliest soft carbon to the latest "rustless."

Basic Gun Repair, Simple How-To Methods. Los Angeles: Petersen Publishing Company, 1973. Written for the beginner; shows some of the steps necessary in getting started. Some sections devoted to antique restoration.

Bish, T. L. *Home Gunsmithing Digest*, 3rd Edition. Northbrook, Illinois: DBI Books, Inc., 1984. Wide coverage from repairing, modifying, converting to maintaining and just "tinkering" with firearms.

*Brownell, R. *Gunsmith Kinks*. Montezuma, Iowa: F. Brownell & Son Publishers, 1969. Varied accumulation of shortcuts, techniques and comments by professional gunsmiths.

*Burch, M. *Gun Care and Repair*. New York: Winchester Press, 1978. Step-by-step "how-to" in words and photos on gunsmithing techniques.

*Carmichel, J. *Do It Yourself Gunsmithing*. New York: Harper & Row, 1977. 40 do-it-yourself installments by the respected shooting editor of *Outdoor Life*.

*Chapel, C. E. *Complete Guide To Gunsmithing: Gun Care and Repair*. Cranbury, New Jersey: A. S. Barnes & Co., Inc., 1962. Has gone through many printings. Wide coverage from the selection of tools to checkering and engraving.

The Gun Digest Book of Exploded Handgun Drawings. Northbrook, Illinois: DBI Books, Inc., 1992. Isometric views and parts lists of 488 modern and collector's handguns.

The Gun Digest Book of Exploded Long Gun Drawings. Northbrook, Illinois: DBI Books, Inc., 1993. Isometric views and parts lists of 488 modern and collector's rifles and shotguns.

Lister, R. *Antique Firearms - Their Care, Repair and Restoration*. New York: Crown Publishers, Inc., 1963. Describes and illustrates methods of stripping down, cleaning and reassembling the early firearms most commonly met with today; problems of rust, stubborn screws, damaged or missing parts, and general restorative work.

*Meek, J. B. *The Art of Engraving*. Montezuma, Iowa: F. Brownell and Son Publishers, 1973. Techniques of engraving and information on the subject in general to better judge the work of others.

*Mowbray, Stuart C. *331+ Essential Tips and Tricks; a How-To Guide for the Gun Collector*. Woonsocket, RI; Mowbray Publishing, 2006. Broad coverage of all components of collecting; special attention devoted to restorations and fakes.

*Newell, A. D. *Gunstock Finishing and Care*. Harrisburg, Pennsylvania: The Stackpole Company, 1949. Emphasis on modern firearms but some excellent material on antique and early gun stock finishes and refinishing techniques.

*Peterson, Harold L. *How Do You Know It's Old?* New York: Charles Scribner's Sons, 1975. A practical handbook of fakes for the antique collector and curator.

*Smith, L. W. *Home Gunsmithing the Colt Single Action Revolvers*. Philadelphia: Ray Riling Arms Book Company, 1971. Detailed information on the operation and servicing of this famed handgun.

*Stelle, J. P. & Harrison, W. B. *The Gunsmith's Manual*. New Jersey: Gun Room Press, 1972. An exact recreation of the original 1883 edition of this well known work. Much on making and repairing flintlock and percussion arms; the tools used for them.

Walker, R. T. *Black Powder Gunsmithing*. Northfield, Illinois: DBI Books, Inc., 1978. Wide coverage from replica building to the advanced, intricate art of restoration of antique muzzleloaders.

Walker, R. T. *Hobby Gunsmithing*. Northfield, Ill.: DBI Books, Inc. 1972. How to refinish repair, restore, restock, blue and accurize with simple tools.

Wood, J. B. *The Gun Digest Book of Gun Care Cleaning & Refinishing*: Book One—Handguns; Book Two—Long Guns. Northbrook, Illinois: DBI Books, Inc., 1984-85. Two-part series on how to care for, clean and refinish collector and modern firearms.

Wood, J. B. *Gunsmithing: The Tricks of the Trade*. Northbrook, Illinois: DBI Books, Inc., 1982. How to repair and replace broken gun parts.

*Wood, J. B. *The Gun Digest Book of Firearms Assembly/Disassembly*: Part 1: Automatic Pistols, Revised Edition; Part 2: Revolvers, Revised Edition; Part 3: Rimfire Rifles, Revised Edition; Part 4: Centerfire Rifles, Revised Edition; Part 5: Shotguns, Revised Edition; Part 6: Law Enforcement Weapons. Northbrook, Illinois: DBI Books, Inc., 1979-94. A six-part series of highly illustrated, step-by-step instructions for disassembling and reassembling all types of guns. Many collector guns are included.

(*) Preceding a title indicates the book is currently in print.

National Rifle Association
CODE OF ETHICS FOR GUN COLLECTORS AND DEALERS

'A listing of practices considered unethical and injurious to the best interests of the collecting fraternity.'

1. The manufacture or sale of a spurious copy of a valuable firearm. This shall include the production of full scale replicas of historic models and accessories, regardless of easily effaced modern markings, and it also shall include the rebuilding of any authentic weapon into a rarer and more valuable model. It shall not include the manufacture or sale of firearms or accessories which cannot be easily confused with the rare models of famous makers. Such items are: plastic or pottery products, miniatures, firearms of original design, or other examples of individual skill, plainly stamped with the maker's name and date, made up as examples of utility and craftsmanship and not representative of the designs or models of any old-time arms maker.

2. The alteration of any marking or serial number, or the assembling and artificially aging of unrelated parts for the purpose of creating a more valuable or unique firearm, with or without immediate intent to defraud. This shall not include the legitimate restoration or completion of missing parts with those of original type, provided that such completions or restorations are indicated to a prospective buyer.

3. The refinishing (bluing, browning, or plating) or engraving of any collectors weapons, unless the weapons may be clearly marked under the stocks or elsewhere to indicate the date and nature of the work, and provided the seller unequivocally shall describe such non-original treatment to a buyer.

4. The direct or indirect efforts of a seller to attach a spurious historical association to a firearm in an effort to inflate its fair value; efforts to "plant" a firearm under circumstances which are designed to inflate the fair value.

5. The employment of unfair or shady practices in buying, selling, or trading at the expense of young and inexperienced collectors or anyone else; the devious use of false appraisals, collusion and other sharp practices for personal gain.

6. The use of inaccurate, misleading, or falsified representations in direct sales or in selling by sales list, catalog, periodical advertisement and other media; the failure to make prompt refunds, adjustments or other proper restitution on all just claims which may arise from arms sales, direct or by mail.

Chapter IV

The Arms Library

The importance of a few basic titles to start the neophyte on the right foot has been discussed. As the collector progresses, he will soon find his greatest asset to be a good arms library, coupled with the knowledge of how to use it. Very likely this is one of the most underestimated and underutilized of all natural resources in collecting; whether in firearms or any other hobby. Research works are of key importance to the gun trader and the collector alike; especially so in this day and age with the strong competition prevalent. Utilizing the facts and minutiae gleaned from those reference works is very much analogous to separating the men from the boys on today's gun market. Just about everybody knows the basics, but the fine points—that's where some get lazy or lethargic, and that's where some of the biggest bargains, and even "sleepers" can still be found. Normally a collector's astuteness is in direct proportion to his reading list. Reading chapter and verse of most reference books is unnecessary, but one should at least be familiar with the general content and coverage of as many of the gun books as possible. Not all arms books are worthy of purchase. As a matter of fact, considerable misinformation and unsubstantiated facts are to be found between the covers of many titles, and hence, discretion must be used in their purchase. Following published reviews or seeking advice and opinions from knowledgeable fellow collectors is the best way of judging a book's value; the unworthy ones usually have acquired a reputation that precedes them.

In recent years the book market has been flooded with elegant examples of the publisher's art, exemplified by massive tomes illustrating exquisite arms from many leading museums and collections. Often derisively termed "coffee-table" editions, they are most often seen available during the height of the pre-Christmas selling frenzy when the gift-book market is at its peak and the book buyers sense of judgment and discretion is often at its lowest! These books are quite aptly named; first, they are so damned big they rarely fit on a library shelf, and thus the only place to put them is on a coffee table. Secondly, that position seems to be their chief redeeming value (as if some status

symbol) where they may be idly thumbed through to admire the handsome photography. It would be unfair to condemn them all, but the majority contain quite elementary texts and the guns illustrated are very often repeated book after book. The profusion of these volumes is becoming tiresome, and the collector (and his relatives too!) is warned to exercise judgment before laying out large sums for the coffee table titles. An observation of this aspect of the gun book market reveals that most are issued at very high prices and within a year are generally remaindered at prices substantially below the original retail. For the casual or even active gun trader such picture books do not offer much other than a few moments of idle musing.

Quite often gun books are themselves good investments. It is an interesting fact and one quite consistent over the years that many titles, especially those that are considered standard reference works or basic to various specialties, become more valuable the moment they go out of print. Quite a few arms books are published in limited quantities by small publishing firms or privately printed by the authors themselves.

In many instances once the first edition is out of print, there is little chance that the title will ever become available again. In such cases the price often can increase, two, three or four times over; based not on rare book status, but on the value of its information to the collector. Of course, in a great many instances the publisher does reprint the book if it has proved to be popular; but with present day publishing in a volatile state, one never knows if a book will ever come back once it is out of print. These remarks are not intended to spark any speculation in book buying (sometimes a hazardous game), but they do reflect the fact that arms books are worthy purchases from the financial standpoint as well as the literary.

A few dealers specialize in gun books and issue annual catalogs describing their complete stock. The annual edition of *Gun Digest* includes a detailed section covering most books currently in print on the subject of collecting as well as shooting, repairing, etc., antique and modern guns; also listed are various dealers handling these titles.

NOTE: _Separate bibliographies_
are included with each chapter of this work covering books
pertaining specifically to those respective sections.
The following listings include titles of broad introductory
nature and detailed studies of general interest.

BIBLIOGRAPHY

(*) Preceding a title indicates the book is currently in print.

Achtermeier, Wm. *Rhode Island Arms Makers & Gunsmiths 1643-1883*. Providence, Rhode Island: Man-at-Arms Publication, 1980. Covers makers from Colonial times to the demise of the Providence Tool Co., Rhode Island's largest maker in 1883.

*Adler, Dennis. *Metallic Cartridge Conversions. The History of the Guns and Modern Reproductions*. Iola, Wis. Krause Publications, 2003. Alterations, factory and otherwise, of percussion firearms (especially strong on Colts and Remingtons) from percussion to breech-loading cartridge.

*Adler, Dennis. *Blue Book of Airguns*. Minneapolis, Minn: Blue Book Pubs., 2001. Background of history and development; coverage essentially those of the post-1900 era (over 50 mfrs. and their products listed and valued).

Akehurst, R. *Antique Weapons For Pleasure And Investment*. New York: Arco Publishing Co., 1969. Advice on where and how to buy, points that affect values and hints on restoration.

Akehurst, R. *The World Of Guns*. London: Hamlyn Publishing Group, 1972. A broad general survey of all types of antique guns.

Amber, John T. (Compiler) *Ten Rare Gun Catalogs 1860-1899*. New York: Greenberg Pub., 1952. Exact reprints of ten famous American makers, including: "Winchester, 1875 & 1885 editions; Whitney Arms Co., 1878; S & W c. 1882; Wm. Wurfflein, Phila 1889; Parker Bros. c. 1899 and arms dealer G. W. Clafin & Co. 1886; J. H. Johnston, 1895."

Bailey, D. W., Hogg, I., Boothroyd, G. and Wilkinson, F. *Guns And Gun Collecting*. New York: Crown Publishing, 1972. Very fine color plates illustrating seven articles on various aspects of collecting.

*Baldwin, John. *Indian Guns, Spears and Shields of the American Frontier*. W. Olive, Mich. Early American Artistry Pub. Co., 2002.

Barnett, J.P. *The Life Saving Guns of David Lyle*. South Bend, Indiana: Town & Country Press, 1976.

Bennett, S. and Worthen, W.B. *Arkansas Made 1819-1870* Volume I. Fayetteville, Ark: University of Arkansas, 1990. Highly important, well-illustrated chapter on history of gunmaking and gunmakers in that state.

Bilby, Joseph G. *Civil War Firearms…Their Historical Background, Tactical Use and Modern Collecting and Shooting*. Conshohocken, Pa.: Combined Pub. Co., 1996. Merges technical data with details of their use on battlefield; a unit-by-unit study and how their performance and employment differed from popular conceptions.

Bingham, R.W. *Early Buffalo Gunsmiths*. Buffalo, N.Y.: Buffalo Historical Society, 1934. Monograph.

Blackmore, H. L. *Guns And Rifles Of The World*. New York: Viking Press, 1965. An excellent history of antique guns by an highly acclaimed author. Heavily illustrated with guns of all countries.

Blair, C. *European And American Arms c.1100-1850*. New York: Crown Publishers, Inc., 1962. Very broad scope and coverage by a noted authority.

Blair, C. *Pistols Of The World*. New York: Viking Press, 1968. An important treatise on the handgun; covers all types of all countries 16th to 20th centuries. Heavily illustrated.

Boddington, C. *America: The Men & Their Guns That Made Her Great*. Los Angeles, California: Peterson Publishing Co., 1981. Sixteen respected historians and firearms experts discuss how the development of weapons technology shaped American history in some famous as well as some little known incidents.

Boehret, P.C. *Arming The Troops 1775-1815: Arms Makers & Comments*. Easton, PA: Hobson Printing Co., 1967.

*Boorman, Dean K. *Guns of the Old West; an Illustrated History*. Guilford, Conn.: Lyons Press, 2002. An overview of the significant types of firearms used on the Western frontier beginning with Louisiana Purchase to c. 1890s.

Boothroyd, G. *The Handgun*. New York: Crown Publishers, Inc., 1970. A massive sized study of the evolution of handguns from matchlocks to automatics. Illustrating guns of all countries.

Bowman, H. W. *Famous Guns From The Smithsonian Collection*. New York: Arco Publishing Co., 1967. Informative text and illustrations on patent legislation, inventors, unique weapons and a wealth of historic detail, anecdotes, legends from this famous National collection.

Bowman, H. W. *Famous Guns From The Winchester Collection*. New York: Arco Publishing Co., 1958. One of America's most noted collections, the author has selected a group of outstanding specimens from flintlock to repeating rifles.

*Browning, J. and Gentry, Curt. *John M. Browning, American Gunmaker*. New York: Doubleday & Co., 1964; Browning Company, 1987. Biography of this famed inventor and his guns.

Buehr, W. *Firearms*. New York: Thomas Y. Crowell Co., 1967. Written for the novice; a quickly and easily read survey of history of guns, from handguns to cannon.

Butler, D. F. *United States Firearms-The First Century 1776-1875*. New York: Winchester Press, 1971. Account of design evolution of American small arms.

Byron, D. *Gunmarks*. New York: Crown Publishers, Inc., 1979. Tradenames, codemarks and proofs from 1870 to the present.

*Canfield, Bruce. *U.S. Infantry Weapons of the First World War*. Lincoln, R.I: Andrew Mowbray Publishers, 2000.

Carey, A. M. *American Firearms Makers*. New York: Thomas Y. Crowell Co., 1953. Listing of makers from Colonial period to end of 19th century with data on each. Widely used reference.

*Carman, W. Y. *A History of Firearms from Earliest Times to 1914*. Mineola, N.Y.: Dover Pub., Inc., 2004. Reprint of earlier 1955 work. Contains some useful references and entertaining anecdotes.

Chapel, C. E. *The Complete Book Of Gun Collecting*. New York: Coward-McCann, Inc., 1939, 1947, 1960. Answers a great many questions about collecting; especially useful to the new collector.

Chapel, C. E. *The Gun Collector's Handbook Of Values*. New York: Coward-McCann & Geoghegan, Inc., 1940, 1947 and numerous later revised editions. A pioneer work in the field of antique gun collecting. The first major attempt to codify, list and value a great many antique guns.

Chapel, C. E. *Guns Of The Old West*. New York: Coward-McCann, Inc., 1961. History and details of American firearms 18th and 19th centuries which opened the frontiers beyond the Alleghenies to the securing of territory to the West Coast.

Chinn, Col. George M. *The Machine Gun; History, Evolution & Development of Manual, Automatic & Airborn Repeating Weapons*. Washington, D.C.: Bureau of Ordnance, U.S. Navy, 1951. Vol. I of multi-volume set important for coverage of Gatling and other early U.S. types.

Cook, Grafton. *A.W. Spies: Importer, Outfitter & Fireman*. Niles, Mich.: Privately printed monograph, 1999. History of well known N.Y. arms dealer c. 1820's-1870's.

*Curtis, Chris C. *Systeme Lefaucheux: Continuing the Study of Pinfire Cartridge Arms* [and] *Their Role in the American Civil War*. Santa Ana, Calif.: Arms Lore Press, 2002.

*Demeritt, D. P., Jr. *Maine Made Guns And Their Makers*. Hallowell, Maine: Maine State Museum, 1973. Well researched and illustrated treatise on all types of arms produced in Maine. Revised, enlarged, 1997.

Dexter, F. Theodore. *Thirty-Five Years' Scrapbook of Antique Arms*. Topeka, Kansas: published by author, 1947. Two volumes. Includes many illus. and details of American and European guns including values as of 1947. Informative; interesting.

Dexter, F. Theodore. *Forty-Two Years' Scrapbook of Rare Ancient Firearms*. Los Angeles, Calif.: W. F. Lewis Publisher, 1954. Profuse photo illus. includes many rare American and European arms and their market values.

Deyrup, F. J. *Arms Makers Of The Connecticut Valley*. Northampton, Massachusetts: Smith College, 1948. Study of the economic development of the small arms industry 1798-1870.

*Dorsey, R. Stephen *Guns of the Western Indian War*. Eugene, Oregon: Collectors Library, 1995. Illus. & details of the many and various used by the "hostiles" and U.S. issued.

duMont, J. S. *Custer Battle Guns*. Ft. Collins, Colorado: The Old Army Press, 1974. Very important reference for all types of guns used by both sides in that historic encounter.

*Dunathan, A. T. *The American B.B. Gun*. South Brunswick, New Jersey: A. S. Barnes & Company, 1971. Basic guide to the field.

*Edwards, W. B. *Civil War Guns*. Harrisburg, Pennsylvania: The Stackpole Company, 1962. A classic and standard reference on the subject. The complete story of Federal and Confederate handguns and longarms and the many foreign imported types. Reprinted 1997, Thomas Pub., Gettysburg, PA.

Elman, R. *Fired In Anger*. New York: Doubleday & Co., Inc., 1968. The personal handguns of American heroes and villains from the gun used by Columbus through the guns of Indians, lawmen, bandits and assassins.

Farley, Captain J. P. *Army Revolvers and Gatling Guns*. Springfield, Massachusetts: National Armory, 1875. Reprint Circa 1960s. Official manual of Colt Single Action, S&W Schofield and the Gatling.

*Farrington, D. P. *Arming & Equipping the U.S. Cavalry 1865-1902*. Lincoln, Rhode Island: Mowbray Publishers, 2004. The firearms, edged weapons and accoutrements of the regular U.S. Cavalry from the Indian Wars to the Philippine Insurrection.

*Frey, Stephen. *Imported Military Firearms 1866-1899*. Pub. by author, Atlanta, Ga.; paper covers; plastic ring-bound. Lists and describes military arms of 17 foreign countries imported as "surplus" to sell on American market (through firms such as the famous Francis Bannerman of New York).

Ferree, G.B. *Ferree Family Gunsmiths*. F. Wayne, Ind.: privately printed, 1967. Noted family of Penna-Ky. riflesmiths.

Frith, J. and Andrews, R. *Antique Pistol Collecting*. London: The Holland Press, 1960. Evolution of handguns from hand cannon of 15th century to revolvers of mid-19th century.

*Frost, H. G. *Blades & Barrels*. El Paso, Texas: Walloon Press, 1972. Complete coverage of all combination firearms with knife or sword blades attached including many American specimens.

Fryer, D. J. *Antique Weapons A-Z*. London: G. Bell & Sons Ltd., 1969. General survey of collecting arms of all types from all parts of the world. Written as a guide for the novice.

*Garavaglia, L. A. and Worman, C. G. *Firearms of the American West 1803-1865*. Albuquerque, New Mexico: University of New Mexico Press, 1984. One of the most important works on subject. Wealth of detail. Reprinted 1997; U. of Colorado Press.

*Garavaglia, L. A. and Worman, C. G. *Firearms of the American West 1866-1894*. Albuquerque, New Mexico: University of New Mexico Press, 1985. Companion work of the above. Basic reference. Reprinted 1997; Univ. of Colorado Press.

Gardner, R. E. *Five Centuries of Gunsmiths, Swordsmiths And Armourers 1400-1900*. Columbus, Ohio: Walter F. Heer

Publisher, 1948. Important early listing of makers of all countries. Contains some material (such as cannon founders of America) which his later book *Small Arms Makers* does not have.

Gardner, R. E. *Small Arms Makers*. New York: Crown Publishers, Inc., 1963. A very important, often referred to, listing of American and European gun and sword makers with biographical detail.

*Gilkerson, William. *Boarders Away*. Lincoln, R.I.: Mowbray Publishers. Vol. I (1991). *Edged Weapons and Polearms*. Vol. II (1993). *Firearms of the Age of Fighting Sail 1626-1826*. Superb coverage. Most definitive on the subject with special attention to eras of American Revolution and War of 1812.

Gluckman, A. and Satterlee, L. D. *American Gun Makers*. Harrisburg, Pennsylvania: The Stackpole Co., 1953. A widely used, often referred to important listing of American gun makers 18th to 20th centuries with much data about them.

*Gooding, S. James. *Trade Guns of the Hudson's Bay Company, 1670-1970*. Alexandria Bay, N.Y.: (now the Museum Restoration Service) 2003. Definitive study of their various forms, manufacture and distribution; specialty weapons including pistols, fine guns, rifles and buccaneer guns also discussed.

*Gorman, Kit. *New Orleans Gunsmiths and Gun Dealers Until 1900*. Batchelor, Louisiana: P. Bazer Pub., 2006.

Greener, W. W. *The Gun And Its Development*. New York: Bonanza Books, 1967 Reprint. An exact reprint of the most important 9th Edition (1910) of an all time classic work, as important and useful today as when it was originally printed.

*Greener, W. W. *Modern Breech-Loaders: Sporting and Military*. Forest Grove, Oregon: Normount Technical Publications, 1971. Reprint of the 1871 classic; a leading treatise of breech-loaders of all types—shotguns, rifles and handguns.

*Groenewold, John. *Quackenbush Guns*. Mundelein, Illinois: pub. by author, 2000. Detailed study of famed maker responsible for earliest development of mass-produced airguns for short-range target and small game shooting; 1871-1943.

*Hamilton, T. M. *Colonial Frontier Guns*. Chadron, Nebraska: The Fur Press, 1981. Covers English, French, Dutch Frontier and trade guns; accounts of gunsmithing on frontier; studies of gun flints and shot sizes.

*Hamilton, T.M. *Firearms on the Frontier: Guns at Fort Michilimackinac 1715-1781*. Williamston, Mich.: monograph by Mackinac Island State Park Commission, 1976.

Hanson, Charles E., Jr. *The Northwest Gun*. Lincoln, Nebraska: Nebraska State Historical Society, 1955. Most significant treatise on Indian trade guns.

*Hanson, James A. *A History of the Fur Trade: When Skins Were Money*. Chadron, Nebraska: Museum of the Fur Trade, 2005. Includes information on Indian trade guns.

Hartzler, D. D. *Arms Makers of Maryland*. York, Pennsylvania: George Shumway Publisher, 1977. Excellent, detailed coverage of 18th and 19th century makers; military and sporting.

*Hartzler, D.D. & Whisker, J.B. *Gunsmiths of Maryland: Firelock Colonial Period Through Breech-Loading Patent Models; Featuring Longrifles*. Bedford, Pa.: Old Bedford Village Press, 1998.

Haynes, C. Vance *General Custer & His Sporting Rifles*. Tuscon, Arizona: Westernlore Press, 1996. History of his tow "trap door" Springfield sporters and Remington rolling block.

Hayward, J. F. *The Art Of The Gunmaker*. Volume I: 1500-1660; Volume II: 1660-1830. New York: St. Martin's Press, 1962, 1963. Important and often cited reference works. Detailed history European and American firearms; emphasis on techniques and styles of armament.

Heer, Eugene. *Der Neue Stockel*, Vols. I through III, Switzerland: Swiss Institute of Arms & Armor. Best and most often cited bibliography of makers. Over 2100 pages; 6500 maker's marks illustrated; 36,000 individual entries of gunmakers, gun stockers, decorators and designers from 1400 to WWI from 32 Nations. Many American makers included. Vol. III contains glossary and dictionary in English, French, German.

Held, R. *The Age Of Firearms*. Rev. Ed. Northfield, Ill.: DBI Books, Inc., 1970. A well-illustrated history of firearms from the invention of gunpowder to modern breechloaders.

Henderson, J. *Firearms Collecting For Amateurs*. London: Frederick Muller Ltd., 1966. A small, general overall survey of collecting with history of guns and advice on care, maintenance and display.

Hiller, Dennis E. *The Collectors' Guide to Air Rifles* (revised, enlarged Fourth Edition). Preston, U.K.: published by author, 1995.

Himmelwright, A.L.A. *Pistol and Revolver Shooting*. New York: Macmillan Company 1904, 1908, 1915, 1923, 1933. Important reference for American handgun target shoots and competitions 19th to early 20th century with the American (some European) handguns of famous makers used by the contestants.

Horn, W. R. *Gunsmiths And Gunmakers Of Vermont*. Burlington, Vermont: The Horn Company, 1976. A partial checklist from 18th century to 1900. Illustrations of arms and facsimiles of makers labels.

Hughes, J. B., Jr. *Mexican Military Arms; The Cartridge. 1866-1967*. Houston, Texas: Deep River Armory, 1968. Good details on American arms by various makers purchased and issued and Mexican military markings on them.

Hutslar, Donald A. *Ohio Gunsmiths & Allied Tradesmen*. Beverly, Ohio: Association of Ohio Longrifle Collectors. 5 Volumes, 1996-1998. Remarkable coverage.

*Irwin, John R. *Guns & Gunmaking Tools of Southern Appalachia*. Norris, Tennessee: Museum of Appalachia 1981. Locally known as the "squirrel" or "hog" rifle. These often highly accurate, graceful and serviceable arms were made in the mold of the traditional "Pennsylvania" rifle though simply embellished.

*Jenkins, Bill. *U.S. Military Match and Marksmanship Automatic Pistols*. Lincoln, R.I.: Mowbray Publishing, 2005.

Johnson, C. L. *A Checklist of 18th and 19th Century Illinois Gunsmiths*. York, Pennsylvania: George Shumway Publisher, 1974. Names, dates and locations of 630 Illinois makers. 2nd Edition 1982.

*Karcheski, W. J., Jr. *Selections from the Frazier Historical Arms Museum*. Louisville, Ky.: pub. by the museum, 2004. Illustrated survey of the fabulous, ever-enlarging collections of this newly formed, increasingly popular institution, rapidly becoming among most prominent in its field. Catalog; paper covers.

Kauffman, H. J. *Early American Gunsmiths 1650-1850*. Harrisburg, Pennsylvania: The Stackpole Co., 1952. Important listing of early American makers with illustrations of makers labels and guns.

*Katcher, Philip. *Sharpshooters of the American Civil War 1861-65*. Oxford, England: Osprey Publ., 2002. Close look at recruiting, training, deployment and the specialized military and civilian type rifles used.

Kennedy, David. *Guns of the Wild West; A Photographic Tour of the Guns that Shaped our Country's History*. Philadelphia, Pa.: Courage Books, 2005.

*Kirkland, K. *America's Premier Gunmakers—Browning*. New York: 1989.

Koller, L. *The Fireside Book Of Guns*. New York: The Ridge Press, 1959. History of firearms in America from the first explorers to modern sportsmen. Elegantly illustrated.

*Lewis, M.H. *The Gunsmiths of Manhattan 1625-1900: A Checklist of Tradesmen*. Alexandria Bay, N.Y.: Museum Restoration Service monograph, 1991.

Lewis, Jack. *Gun Digest Book of Single Action Revolvers*. Northfield, Illinois: DBI Books, 1982. Explores the history, folklore and fascination of the single action; written with the collector in mind.

Lindert, Albert W. *Gunmakers of Indiana*. Homewood, Illinois, 1968: Privately published by author.

Lindsay, Merrill. *The Lure of Antique Arms*. New York: David McKay Co., Inc., 1978. Excellent handbook for beginning American gun collectors.

*Macewicz J. P. *American Handgun Patents 1802-1924*. Bloomfield, Ontario, Canada: Museum Restoration Service, 1977. Often a key to identifying firearms. Lists over 1300 patents in chronological/numerical order; cross-indexed to the inventors.

Madaus, H. N. *The Warner Collector's Guide to American Longarms*. New York: Warner Books, 1981. Over 500 different shotguns muskets, rifles and carbines are described by maker, age, mountings and markings. Each arm assigned alphabet letter designation reflecting relative rarity and survival rate.

*Malloy, J. J., Thomas, D. S., White, T. A. *Percussion Ammunition Packets: Union, Confederate and European*. Gettysburg, Pa.: Thomas Publications, 2003. A remarkable study along with profuse illustrations of the various labeled packets of ammunition that accompanied American percussion handguns and rifles; also government-issued, labeled packages of paper-wrapped cartridges.

Marsh, R.E. & Flanagan, M.W. *Trap Guns for Pocket Gophers & Moles: A Collectors Manual*. Davis, Cal.: Privately printed, 1999.

*McAulay, John D. *Civil War Small Arms Of The U.S. Navy and Marine Corps*. Lincoln, R.I.: Andrew Mowbray Publishers, 1999.

McLean, D. B. (Editor). *The 1873 'Trapdoor' Springfield Rifle and Carbine & .45 Revolvers: Colt's M1873 & S & W Schofield*. Forest Grove, Ore.: Normount Armament Co., 1969. Paper cover pamphlet; illustrations and information from the original manuals. (Especially fine detail for the Springfield "Trapdoor.")

Moore, W. *Guns - The Development Of Firearms, Air Guns And Cartridges*. New York: Grosset & Dunlap, 1963. A general survey of antique guns told in pictures.

*Mowbray, Stuart C. *331+ Essential Tips and Tricks: A How-to Guide for the Gun Collector: A Practical Approach to Buying, Maintaining, Storage, Display, Photography and Much More*. Woonsocket, R.I: Mowbray Pub., 2006. Even includes specific instructions for detecting fakes and refinishing, alarms and insurance for the gun room and much more. Profusely illustrated.

Murry, Ellen N. *Code of Honor; Dueling in America*. Washington, Texas: Star of Republic Museum, 1984. Monograph, catalog of American duelling pistols.

National Rifle Association. *NRA Gun Collector's Guide*. Washington, D. C.: National Rifle Association, 1972. 75 of the best articles on gun collecting that appeared in the *American Rifleman* 1955 to 1970. A book of high value to the gun collector.

*Noe, D., Yantz, L.W., & Whisker, J.B. *Firearms From Europe: A History & Description Of Firearms Imported During The American Civil War By The United States And Confederate States*. Rochester, N.Y.: Rowe Publications, 1999.

*O'Meara, Robert H. *The Guns of the Gunfighters: Lawmen, Outlaws & Hollywood Cowboys*. Iola, Wis.: Krause Pub., 2003. Guns are illustrated with contemporary photographs and brief biographies of the men that carried them.

*O'Neal, Bill. *Encyclopedia of Western Gunfighters*. Norman, Okla.: University of Oklahoma Press, 1979 (hard cover; later editions paper cover). Details on 255 gunmen, their aliases, occupations; brief biographies and accounts of verified gunfights (chronologically).

Parsons, John E. and DuMont, John S. *Firearms in the Custer Battle*. Harrisburg, Penna.: Stackpole Company, 1953. A significant reference to the subject.

Paul, V.A. *Missouri Gunsmiths To 1900*. Washington, Missouri: Obscure Place Pub. Co., 2000.

Peterson, H. L. *Encyclopedia Of Firearms*. New York: E. P. Dutton & Co., Inc. 1964. A wealth of information on a variety of topics from 14th century hand cannon to 20th century Lewis gun.

Peterson, H. L. and Elman, R. *The Great Guns*. New York: Grosset & Dunlop, Inc. and The Ridge Press, 1971. Well prepared, elegantly illustrated history from hand cannon to modern Colts and Winchesters.

Peterson, H. L. *Pageant Of The Gun*. New York: Doubleday & Co., Inc., 1967. An informative history of firearms conveying the excitement and drama of ten centuries of arms development. 55 greatly varied stories covering such subjects as whaling guns, fowlers, duellers, target shooting, etc.

Peterson, H. L. *The Treasury Of The Gun*. New York: Ridge Press/Golden Press, 1962. Magnificently illustrated story of six centuries of gun development. American and European guns associated with historic events.

Phillips, H. & Tyler, T. *Vermont's Gunsmiths & Gunmakers to 1900*. Dorset, Vermont: Two Damn Yankees Pub., 2000. Includes inventors, patentees of firearms and accountrements, manufactories and armories.

Phillips, Roger F. and Klancher, Donald J. Bloomfield, Ontario, Canada: Museum Restoration Service, 1982. Numerous weapons were American.

*Pitman, General John. *The Pitman Notes on U.S. Martial Small Arms and Ammunition 1776-1933*. Vol. I *Breech-Loading Carbines of U.S. Civil War*. Armory Publications: Tacoma, Washington 1987. Vol. II *Revolvers and Automatic Pistols* Thomas Publications: Gettysburg, Pa. 1990. Vol. III *U.S. Breechloading Rifles and Carbines, Cal. 45*. Thomas Publications 1991. Vol. IV *U.S. Magazine Rifles and Carbines Caliber .30*. Vol. V *Miscellaneous Notes Caliber .58, 50, 30; Confederate and Foreign*. Significant research material from previously unpublished manuscripts; exceptional drawings by U.S. Army Ordnance officer with 40 year career.

Pollard, H. B. C. *A History Of Firearms*. Boston and New York: Houghton Mifflin Co., 1926. A significant early work for collectors; small arms of all types and countries from 14th to 19th century.

*Pritchard, Russ A., Jr. *Civil War Weapons and Equipment*. Guilford, Conn.: Lyons Press, 2003. Broad, generalized survey; profusely illustrated.

*Rattenbury, Richard. *Packing Iron; Gunleather of the Frontier West*. Milward, N.Y.: Zon Int'l Pub. Co., 1993. For the military and Western collector a superbly illus., yet serious, detailed study.

Riling, R. *Guns And Shooting, A Selected Chronological Bibliography*. New York: Greenberg: Publisher, 1951. Listing of 3,000 American and foreign books on guns and shooting 16th through 20th century. Valuable reference for arms collector.

*Rosa, J. G. *Guns of the American West*. London, England: Arms & Armour Press, 1985. General survey for the popular market.

*Rosa, Joseph *Age of the Gunfighter; Men & Weapons on the Frontier, 1840-1900*. N.Y. City: Smithmark Publications, 1993. Fascinating reading & illus.; overall general survey of gun types.

Rosa, J. G. & May, R. *The Pleasure Of Guns*. London: Octopus Books, 1974. Very general survey of antique arms with numerous color illustrations.

Rosebush, W. E. *American Firearms and the Changing Frontier*. Spokane, Washington: Eastern Washington State Historical Society, 1962. Use of specific types of firearms in American frontier expansion from the Black Hawk War through conquest of California.

Rosebush, W. E. *Frontier Steel, The Men And Their Weapons*. Appleton, Wisconsin: C. C. Nelson Publishing Co., 1958. Covers the period from the Black Hawk War through the Mexican War and the Conquest of California.

*Russell, C. P. *Firearms, Traps And Tools Of The Mountain Men*. New York: Alfred A. Knopf, 1967, and reprinted by the University of New Mexico Press, Albuquerque, New Mexico, 1977. A guide to the equipment of the trappers and fur traders who opened the West from the 1820s to the 1840s.

Russell, C. P. *Guns On The Early Frontiers*. Berkeley and Los Angeles: University of California Press, 1957, Reprint 1980, University of Nebraska. A history of firearms from Colonial times through the years of the Western fur trade.

Rywell, M. *Gun Collectors' Guide*. Harriman, Tennessee: Pioneer Press, 1955, 1961, 1965. General introduction to the hobby answering many questions often asked by the neophyte. Subtitled "Old Guns for Profit."

Satterlee, L. D. (Compiler). *Ten Old Gun Catalogs*. Chicago: Gun Digest Association, Inc., 1962. Exact reprint of the original catalogs of American makers and dealers: Merrill, 1864; Peabody, 1865, 1866; Henry, 1865; Spencer, 1866; National, 1865; Folsom, 1869; Great Western, 1871; James Brown, 1876; Homer Fisher, 1880; Remington, 1877.

Satterlee, L.D. *Catalog of Firearms for the Collector*. Detroit: Private Published, 1927, 2nd Edition, 1939. Among earliest, pioneer attempts to codify antique firearms; emphasis on American.

Satterlee, L. D. *Fourteen Old Gun Catalogs for the Collector*. Chicago, Ill.: Gun Digest Association, 1962. (Reprint of limited 1940 ed.) Includes Maynard catalog, 1885; Ballard & Marlin catalog 1888; Stevens catalog 1888; Stevens-Pope, 1902; Colt catalog 1896; plus eight Sharps catalogs 1859 to 1880. Important basic tool for the collector, student.

Sawyer, C. W. *Firearms In American History 1600 To 1800*. Boston: Privately published by the author, 1910. The first important reference on Colonial American arms. Still considered a classic.

Sawyer, C. W. *Firearms In American History - Volume Two - The Revolver*. Boston: The Arms Company, 1911. One of the primary works on American revolving handguns and longarms.

Sawyer, C. W. *Our Rifles*. Boston: The Cornhill Company, 1920. One of the very first and important reference works on American longarms of all periods. For many years a basic reference source.

Schroeder, J. J., Jr. (Editor). *Gun Collector's Digest*. Northbrook, Illinois: DBI Books, Inc., Vol. I, 1974, Vol. II, 1977, 3rd Edition, 1981, 4th Edition, 1985, 5th Edition, 1989. Compilations of illustrated articles on a great many phases of gun collecting.

*Schwing, N. *Standard Catalog of Firearms*. Iola, Wisc: Krause Publications, 11th Edition, 2001. Identification & values modern European & American plus many antique American arms. Principles and fairness demand it be listed; vanity ... and ego ... insist it's not comparable to *FLAYDERMAN'S GUIDE*!!

*Sellers, Frank M. *American Gunsmiths*. Highland Park, New Jersey: The Gun Room Press, 1983. Basic reference. Over 19,000 listings: gunmakers, patentees, gunsmiths.

Serven, J. E. (Editor). *The Collecting Of Guns*. Harrisburg, Pennsylvania: The Stackpole Company, 1964. Recommended for novice and expert alike. 33 chapter tour of the gun collecting world with chapters on individual collecting fields. Almost exclusively devoted to American arms.

Serven, J. E. *Conquering The Frontiers*. La Habra, California: Foundation Press, 1974. Stories of American Pioneers and the guns which helped them establish a new life.

Serven, J. E. *Two Hundred Years Of American Firearms*. Northfield, Illinois: DBI Books, Inc., 1975. A history of American made guns and their influence on the nation's growth.

*Shaffer, Rutledge and Dorsey. *Gun Tools; Their History and Identification*. Eugene, Oregon: Collectors Library Pub., 1992. First lengthy, detailed listing all known U.S. issue and factory made tools to accompany firearms. Vol. II, 1997, Dorsey & Shaffer.

Sharpe, P. B. *The Rifle In America*. New York: William Morrow & Company, 1938: Funk and Wagnalls Company, 1947 and subsequent editions. A milestone in arms books. A classic with a wealth of data on most American makes; especially strong on cartridge models by Winchester, Stevens, Ballard, Marlin, Mossberg, Savage, etc.

*Shelton, L. P. *California Gunsmiths 1846-1900*. Fair Oaks, California: Far West Publishers, 1977. Five hundred California makers listed.

*Sherayko, Peter. *Tombstone: The Guns and Gear*. Shadow Hills, Cal.: Caravan West Productions, 2005. Firearms, saddlery, clothing used in Tombstone during its heyday.

Shields, J. W., Jr. *From Flintlock To M1*. New York: Coward-McCann, 1954. History of American longarms; almost entirely devoted towards military models.

*Smith, Graham. *Warman's Civil War Weapons*. Iola, Wisc.: Krause Pub., 2005. Over 300 color illus. of five categories of handguns, carbines, rifles, muskets (plus swords and edged weapons) with specifications for each (not a price guide); alphabetically arranged.

*Smith, Gene P. and Curtis, Chris C. *The Pinfire System*. San Francisco, Cal.: Bushman-Brashaw Pub. Co., 1983. Includes information of American interest especially those pinfires purchased and used during the Civil War.

Smith, W. H. B. *Gas, Air & Spring Guns of the World*. Harrisburg, Pennsylvania: Telegraph Press, 1957. Basic reference.

*Springfield Research Service. *Serial Numbers of U.S. Martial Arms*. Vol. I (1983). Vol. II (1986). Vol. III (1990). Vol. IV (1995) and quarterly newsletters. Silver Spring, Maryland: Springfield Research Service. Vast wealth of information on government purchased arms from Civil War through 20th century.

Steindler, R. A. *The Firearms Dictionary*. Harrisburg, Pennsylvania: Stackpole Books, 1970. Defines, explains, illustrates phrases, terms, nomenclature and terminology of firearms, ammunition, accessories and gun repair techniques.

Steinwedel, L. W. *The Gun Collector's Fact Book*. New York: Arco Publishing Company, 1975. A general guide; where and how to buy antique arms; what affects value; hints on restoration.

Suydam, Charles R. *Bulls-Eyes and Sharpshooters*. American Society of Arms Collectors: Reprint as a monograph from their bulletin No. 62 (1990). Covers the little known, accurate, noiseless, small, indoor target pistols.

*Swinney, H. J. *The New York State Firearms Trade*. Maynardsville, Tenn.: T. Rowe Pub., 2006. A remarkable five-volume set with thousands of illus. A unique undertaking alphabetical listing (with details) of all gunsmiths, gunmakers, agents, manufacturers, importers, patentees of NY State; Volume V devoted entirely to New York City. A treasure house of valuable information; there is nothing quite its equal in scope.

Swinney, H. T. *New York State Gunmakers*. Cooperstown, New York: Freeman's Journal Press, 1951. Checklist of New York gunsmiths and manufacturers. Some biographical detail.

*Taffin, John. *Single Action Sixguns*. Iola, Wisc.: F & W Publications, 2006. From percussion revolvers to modern-day manufacturers.

Taylerson, A. W. F. *The Revolver*. New York: Crown Publishers (Volume I: "1818-1865;" Pub. 1968; Vol. II "1865-1888;" Pub. 1966; Vol. III "1889-1914;" Pub. 1971.) A classic work on all types of revolvers; much on American-made models.

Taylerson, A. W. F. *Revolving Arms*. New York: Walker & Company, 1967. History of mechanically-rotated revolving cylinder firearms in England, on the continent and in the United States from their inception to present day.

Tunis, E. *Weapons - A Pictorial History*. Cleveland & New York: World Publishing Company, 1954. A broad overall survey of weapons of all types from Roman times to World War II.

Trefethen, J. B. (Compiler) and Serven, J. E. (Editor). *Americans And Their Guns*. Harrisburg, Pennsylvania: Stackpole Books. The history of the National Rifle Association.

U. S. Cartridge Company's Collection of Firearms. Old Greenwich, Connecticut: We, Inc., circa, 1970s. Reprint of the original catalog circa 1920s of one of the most famed early collections of antique firearms; many specimens of which appear on the market in this era.

United States Martial Collectors Arms. San Jose, California: Military Arms Research Service, 1977. Highly informative, lengthy list of 850 U.S. inspectors and their marks, serial numbers and production quantities for approximately 70 U.S. pistols, rifles and commemorative firearms, etc., circa 1800s to present day.

VanRensselaer, S. *American Firearms*. Watkins Glen, New York: Century House, 1947. An important and widely used listing of American gunsmiths and arms manufacturers and patentees with descriptions of their arms.

*Walter, John. *The Greenhill Dictionary of Guns and Gunmakers*. London, England: Greenhill Books, 2001 (also Stackpole Books, Penna.). From Colt's first patent to present day, 1836-2001. Military small arms, sporting arms, airguns; designers, mfrs, inventors, trademarks, etc.

West, B. *Savage and Stevens Arms & History*. Azusa, Cal.: published by author, 1971.

West, B. *Browning Arms & History*. Azusa, Cal.: Published by author, 1972.

*Whisker, J.B., Bryan, G., Russo, L., McKnight, R. *Gunsmiths of the Carolinas 1660-1870*. Bedford, Pa.: Old Bedford Village Press, 1994.

Whisker, James B. *Arms Makers of Colonial America*. Selinsgrove, Pa.: Susquhanna University Press, 1992.

Whisker, James B. *The Gunsmith's Trade*. Lewiston, N.Y.: E. Mellon Press 1992. Sociological study.

Whisker, James B. *Arms Makers of Philadelphia*. Privately published circa 1990. Monograph; Paper covers.

Whisker, James B. *Arms Makers of Pennsylvania*. Selinsgrove, Pa: Susquehanna Univ. Press, 1990. Detailed listing of makers to 1900 with emphasis on Kentucky rifles.

Whisker, James B. *Gunsmiths of Virginia*. Bedford, Pa: Old Bedford Village Press, 1993.

Wilkinson, F. *Antique Firearms*. New York: Doubleday & Company, Inc., 1969, and reprinted by the Presidio Press, San Rafael, California, 1978. Traces the history of firearms from 14th century to modern repeating rifles.

*Wilson, R.L. *The Peacemakers; Arms and Adventure in the American West*. New York, N.Y. Random House, 1992. Most lavishly illustrated, fascinating work yet devoted to the subject. Highly recommended.

Wilson, R. L. (Editor). *Antique Arms Annual*. Waco, Texas: Antique Arms Annual Corporation, 1971. One of the most ambitious undertakings in antique arms publishing. Important articles by noted arms authorities. Lavish illustrations of exceptional American arms.

Wilson, R. L. *L. D. Nimschke Firearms Engraver*. Teaneck, New Jersey: John J. Malloy Publisher, 1965 (reprint 1993). The personal records and patterns of one of the most noted of all early American gun engravers who worked for over one hundred different makers including Allen, Colt, Winchester, Remington, Sharps, Smith & Wesson, Ballard and many others.

*Wilson, R. L. *Steel Canvas; The Art of American Arms*. N.Y. City: Random House, 1995. Lavishly produced, important study of the very finest of American arms; all types; all eras.

*Wilson, R. L. *Ruger & His Guns; History of the Man, the Company & the Firearms*. N.Y. City: Simon Schuster, 1996.

Wilson, R. L. *Price Guide to Gun Collecting*. New York: Ballentine Publishing Group. First edition 1998.

*Wilson, R. L. *Silk and Steel: Women at Arms*. New York: Random House Pub., 2003. A unique work and reference with profuse illus of European and American women (most 19th to early 20th centuries), from all walks of life, as exhibition, professional and sporting fields of shooting…and their guns; includes those courageous ladies in the military and at war; lady gunmakers, engravers, collectors and those of Wild West show fame.

Winant, Lewis. *Firearms Curiosa*. New York: Greenburg Publisher, 1955 (with many subsequent reprints). Classic guide to all the strange, freakish and combination type weapons including many of American origin.

Winant, L. *Early Percussion Firearms*. New York: William Morrow & Company, 1959. A history of early percussion firearms ignition from Forsyth to Winchester 44-40. An often cited work.

*Winter, Frederick R. *U.S. Naval Handguns 1808-1911*. Lincoln, R.I.: Mowbray Publishers 1990.

*Wolff, Eldon G. *Air Guns*. Milwaukee, Wisconsin: Milwaukee Public Museum, 1958. The most important treatise on the subject; 15th to 19th centuries.

*Worman, Charles G. *Gunsmoke and Saddle Leather: Firearms in the 19th Century American West*. Albuquerque, N.M.: Univ. of N.M. Press, 2005. Massive in size and information by noted arms authority and researcher. Chapters dedicated to many different phases of Western history and development including others for Winchesters, Colts, Sharps and more.

Worman, Charles G. "Firearms in American History. A Guide for Writers, Curators and General Readers." Yardley, Pa.: Westholm Pub., 2007. Development and use of them from the 16th through end of 19th century. Highly recommended.

The William M. Locke Collection. East Point, Georgia: The Antique Armory, Inc., 1973. A highly important, copiously illustrated catalog of one of the most important and famous American arms collections.

-----*Guns at the Little Bighorn*. Lincoln, R.I.: Mowbray, Inc., 1988. A monograph with reprint of six articles from *Man-At-Arms*.

-----*The Rifle 1885-1888*. Reprint by Broadfoot Publishing Company, Wilmington N.C. 1990 in two volumes of the complete four year run of the first magazine (published monthly) devoted to shooting sports in U.S. Wealth of detailed text, illus, ads on all makes American arms.

-----*Shooting and Fishing 1886-1906*. Reprint in three volumes plus index, 1991 by Broadfoot Publishing Company, Wilmington, N.C. of the thirty volumes of monthly magazines that succeeded "The Rifle." Significant references.

*-----*Cody Firearms Museum Official Guide* Cody, Wyoming: Buffalo Bill Historical Center, 1991. Also distributed by Mowbray Publishers, Lincoln, R.I.

-----*Gun Report Index June 1955 to May, 1990*. Aledo, Illinois: Gun Report, 1996. Index to 35 years of articles on antique arms.

*-----*Guns of the Gunfighters*. Los Angeles: Petersen Publishing Co., 1975. From Wild Bill Hickok to Bonnie & Clyde. Paper covers.

-----*Henry of Boulton; A Pennsylvania Gunmaking Family & Its Firearms*. Nazareth, Pa.: Jacobsburg Historical Society, 1988. Famous makers; good for military & Indian trade gun research. Paper covers; monograph.

-----*Indian Trade Guns*. Union City, Tenn.: Pioneer Press, 1982. Compilation of various historical society archeological research papers and other information that supplements Hansen's *N.W. Gun*.

*-----*Man At Arms 15 Year Index 1979-1993*. Lincoln, R.I.: A. Mowbray Publishers, 1993.

-----*Digest of Advertising For Firearms & Ammunition 1873-1940*. 2 Vols. Canton, Conn.: Armsco Press, 1998.

-----*Longarms In America*. Vol. I & II. American Society Of Arms Collectors. Compilation by G.E. Weatherly of 98 articles from the A.S.A.C. *Bulletins*. 1998.

*-----*Civil War Arms Makers And Their Contracts*. Lincoln, R.I.: A Mowbray Pub., 1998. Facsimile reprint of original 1862 Ordnance Dept. reports. Edited by S. Mowbray & J. Heroux. Important basic research source; wealth or original data.

*-----*Civil War Arms Purchases And Deliveries*. Lincoln, R.I.: A. Mowbray Pub. 2000. Edited by S. Mowbray. Significant basic research source; vast amount of data.

-----*John M. Browning Armory*. Ogden, Utah: Browning Arms Co., 1960 pamphlet with history of the famous firm.

-----*A History of Browning Guns from 1831*. St. Louis, Mo.: Browning Arms Co., 1942, pamphlet; soft cover; 60 pages.

-----*U.S. Military Arms; Dates of Manufacture from 1795*. Brownsboro, Texas: Art and Reference House Pub., 1989. Small pocket guide with soft covers categorically listing handguns and longarms by U.S. arsenals and commercial manufacturers.

PERIODICALS

Armax ... Journal of the Cody Firearms Museum
   Published semi-annually by the Museum c/o Buffalo Bill Historical Center, P.O. Box 1000, Cody, Wyoming, 82414.

American Rifleman
   Published monthly by The National Rifle Association of America, 1600 Rhode Island Avenue, N.W., Washington, D.C. 20036

The two most widely read often cited journals almost exclusively devoted to antique arms:

The Gun Report

   Published monthly by World-Wide Gun Report, Inc., P.O. Box 111, Aledo, Illinois 61231. Vol. I, No. 1, June, 1955 to present.

Man-At-Arms

   Published bi-monthly by Man-At-Arms Magazine, 54 East School St., Woonsocket, Rhode Island 02895. Vol. I, No. 1, Jan. 1979 to present.

Other periodicals that have played a role in the history of antique arms collecting:

Arms Gazette

Wallace Beinfeld, Editor. Los Angeles, Cal.: W. Beinfeld Publishing. Vol. I, No. 1 Sept. 1973 to Vol. VIII, 1980.

The American Arms Collector

Hugh Benet, Editor. Towson, Maryland. Collectors' Press, Inc. Vol. I, No. 1 Jan., 1957 to Vol. II, No. 4 Oct. 1958.

Gun Collectors Letter

(changed in 1947 to *The Gun Collector*). Charter Harrison, Editor and publisher, Madison, Wisconsin. Issue No. 1 Oct., 1946 to Issue No. 48 in 1953. Influential series.

The Gun Report

F.W. Funk & R.E. Patterson, Editors. Akron, Ohio: Gun Report, Inc., Pub. Vol. I, No. 1 Nov., 1939 to Vol. III, No. 6 April, 1942.

Magazine Of Antique Firearms

G.E. Brown, Editor. Athens, Tenn.: J.N. Clements, Publisher. Vol. I, No. 1 April, 1911 to Vol. IV, No.2 Aug., 1912.

Stock And Steel

F. Theodore Dexter, Editor. Marshalltown, Iowa: Associated Firearm Collectors of America Pub. Vol. I March 23, 1923 to Vol. I, No. 5 July, 1923. The first of a long list of arms publications by this noted commission dealer. All that followed were sales oriented.

Texas Gun Collector

Published by the Texas Gun Collectors Association, Houston, Texas. Various editors over their long run from August, 1950 to present day.

(Top) Left Side: Inscribed "***Shooting The Tiger With The Single Shooter***" depicts four hunters: one being eaten by a tiger; two others running frightened pursued by tigers; another in background taking aim with a "single shooter."

(Bottom) Right Side: Inscribed "***Winchester Repeating Rifle***" depicts well dressed gentlemen hunter with binoculars while Chinese servant stands by holding his Winchester rifle and two dead tigers to one side. Signed in four places by the famous Winchester engraver C. F. Ulrich.

(N. Flayderman & Co. Catalog No. 100. Oct., 1976.)

Chapter V-A

Ethan Allen
(Allen & Thurber, Allen & Wheelock, E. Allen & Co.)

An honored name in American gunmaking history and one significant in the field of arms collecting is that of Ethan Allen of Massachusetts. A prolific manufacturer of firearms of many types over a lengthy period, his arms were widely purchased and well respected for their quality and sturdiness. The Allen pepperbox was the major competitor to the Colt revolver until well into the 1850s, and like the Colt, it came to symbolize a standard type of arm of its era in the developing American saga. Ethan Allen was one of the first U.S. producers of handguns for commercial sale made on the interchangeable parts principle; he was also among the first private gunmakers to operate on a comparatively large scale.

Allen marked guns have always enjoyed a strong demand and sale on the collector's market. The wide variety of types available and their usually moderate and low price range in relation to some other more expensive makes readily accounts for their broad following. It is even possible to say there is a relative inequity about this price disparity and that Allens are deserving of a more elevated position in the hierarchy of collecting. Much of this may be attributed to the lack of definitive information on the maker, his successive companies, and the products themselves. Allen arms possess all the characteristics necessary to attract a wide following of devotees: Manufacture in reasonably large quantities; a number of basic models; a great many variations; manufacture over a long time period; and excellent historical associations with America's adventurous Western Frontier period. That price disparity and concurrent inequity are now nearing an end.

Although there are, and long have been, a few highly advanced students and collectors, the field has generally lacked for the heated competition found in some other American firearms specialties such as Colts, Remingtons, and martial arms. Much of the fault may be attributed to the lack of a concise, basic guide to the subject which would allow the average collector or trader to be reasonably aware of the extent of Allen material, and to distinguish a rarity from a common specimen.

Until recent years, little had been written about the subject. A pioneer work, *The Story Of Allen & Wheelock Firearms,* was published in 1965 in limited edition. Covering but one facet of Allen arms, it pointed out the wide range of material available and served as the first partial cataloging of the field. The subsequent publication, in 1973, of *Ethan Allen, Gunmaker,* reviewing the broad scope and importance of Allen weapons, lent considerable impetus to this field of collecting. Although the latter work primarily is a biography of Ethan Allen, it covers his entire line of arms in a manner that greatly assists the collector seeking a basic sequential guide—including essential points for identification of various models and sub-models. With the publication, in 2006, of *Ethan Allen and Allen & Wheelock; Their Guns and Their Legacy*, collectors are liberally provided with a remarkably broad spectrum of manufacturing and marking variations of these popular arms. There is every reason to believe that the wealth of detail, textually as well as photographically, will have an impact on the collecting of not only Allens, but pepperboxes and American percussion handguns in general. The collectors' marketplace will eventually sort out from that wealth of material the variations and minutiae that will ultimately affect value increases for specific models.

This chapter fills the much-needed guide for simplified identification of all Allen arms, placing them in perspective chronologically and value-wise for the collector. The pepperbox section was especially prepared with that in mind. For the first time, collectors have at their fingertips an easily used reference for these significant American firearms. The chapter is generally arranged by type of gun (i.e. single-shot pistols, multishots, pepperboxes, revolvers and long arms) with each group in a general chronological order. Many of these Allens were made simultaneously and thus several models overlap chronologically. An earnest effort was made to describe and illustrate as many well-known and major variations of each model as have been generally recognized and which are known to materially affect values...perhaps markedly! Not every known variation of Allen arms is listed; a number of the less important types as well as a few extremely rare, if not unique, variants are known and are possible to encounter. The above-mentioned, newly published 2006 Allen book is a most worthy reference and includes such anomalies. With the advent of that wealth of new data about these important gunmakers, such previously unrecognized or relatively unappreciated variations and variants are likely to reflect increasing popularity. Values indicated here merely reflect their current market price and not what conceivably "might be" or "should be" based on their rarity. As information disseminates widely and identification becomes easier, there is every possibility that, with time, values on many of these previously unexamined or unidentified types could be directly affected. Following the progress of this unique group of American firearms in the ensuing years will prove worthwhile.

As with other American firearms of the era, Allens may be found with several extra features that can and do influence value considerably. The most often encountered extra is fancy grips. Ivory is the most likely to be observed, but other exotic materials were also employed, e.g., pearl or rosewood. On occasion the collector may find heavy all-metal German silver, or in a few instances pewter (these latter two are known generally with scroll and floral engraving on them). Fancy grips add to the desirability and value of arms on which they appear. The reader is referred to Chapter II for information on pricing such extra features. Relief carved grips may be seen on Allens and are in great demand, adding considerably to a specimen gun's value.

Elaborately engraved pieces will at times be observed on various models of Allens and are quite rare. Many Allen handguns were cased, and these most often are in the pepperbox and small caliber revolver types. Desirability and values are also increased considerably with such items; the subject is covered in Chapter II to which the reader is again referred.

On not a few Allens, particularly the earlier types, **agents' names** may be found marked in addition to or instead of the usual Allen markings. This is an important feature and does affect value, in some cases significantly. The reader is referred to the section treating Allen pepperboxes within this chapter for further discussion of agents' markings and how to assess proportionate price increases for them.

A few basic facts concerning Ethan Allen and his companies will prove useful to the reader and collector. The first dispels a myth, while the others are of assistance in placing Allen arms in their proper chronological order and general periods of manufacture and sales.

Contrary to an unfounded, but popular belief, Ethan Allen, the arms inventor and manufacturer (1806-1871) bore no relationship to the American Revolutionary hero of the same name. As far as can be ascertained, the sameness of the inventor's and the war hero's names is merely coincidence (Charles Allen of Hopkins & Allen likewise). The popularity of the surname Allen has also been the cause of some confusion as quite a few other American gunmakers—many of them New Englanders, and some achieving notoriety of their own—bore this same surname. Hence, a certain vagueness arises among the uninitiated when Allen arms are discussed.

In 1831 Ethan Allen embarked on his manufacturing career with the production of cutlery in the small Massachusetts hamlet of Milford. It was there that he received his foundation and experience in metal working and commercial manufacturing. The products believed made at that factory were shoemakers' tools, knives, and various other devices for cutting. In that same year he moved to North Grafton, Massachusetts, a nearby village where he continued manufacturing the same line of items and where it is thought Allen had his first exposure to the arms trade with the fabrication of a cane gun patented by Dr. Roger Lambert of Upton, Massachusetts. Evidently with that experience under his belt, and his personal assessment of the market as ready for his gun making ability, Allen embarked on his firearms career with the first production of his underhammer "Pocket Rifle," in late 1836.

In 1837 Allen was granted his first patent providing for double action operation of a percussion pistol, leading to the manufacture of his "Tube Hammer" pocket pistol and ultimately to the development of his famed pepperbox. In that same year he formed a partnership with Charles Thurber, his brother-in-law. Their manufacturing operations continued at Grafton, Massachusetts until 1842 when, in order to expand their operation and likely make use of better power facilities and broader labor market, relocation was made to the thriving manufacturing center of Norwich, Connecticut, where the firm remained until 1847.

It is not positively known why the location was changed to Worcester, Massachusetts in 1847. It is surmised that better plant facilities and lower prices, and easier means of transportation, were more attractive there. Business continued as Allen & Thurber until 1854, when Thomas P. Wheelock, another brother-in-law of Ethan Allen who had been with the firm since its inception in Grafton, was taken in as a full partner; the name then changed to ALLEN, THURBER & COMPANY. It thus remained until 1856 when, with the retirement of Charles Thurber, the trade name was altered to ALLEN & WHEELOCK. This latter identification remained on the firm's products from 1856 through 1865.

Thomas Wheelock died in 1864 at age 51. The following year Ethan Allen reorganized and renamed the company "E. ALLEN & CO.," which by then included two of Allen's sons-in-law, Sullivan Forehand and Henry Wadsworth. The company operated under that E. Allen & Co. name until Ethan Allen's death in 1871 when it once again underwent a name change to FOREHAND & WADSWORTH (see Chapter VIII-A). With the death of Henry Wadsworth in 1890 it was reorganized and renamed FOREHAND ARMS COMPANY. Despite Sullivan Forehand's death in 1898, it operated under his name until 1902 at which time the company name and remaining inventory on hand was purchased by the HOPKINS & ALLEN MANUFACTURING CO. (no relation of Ethan Allen) of Norwich, Connecticut. Principals of the firm, Samuel and Charles Allen, are said to have been employees of the Ethan Allen firm at an earlier date.

In addition to his many patents for firearms, Ethan Allen was well-recognized as the inventor of special equipment (patented in 1860) for the manufacture of cartridges...machinery that was to remain in popular use by himself and others for many years. Allen & Wheelock also manufactured quite a few sizes and calibers of rimfire and lipfire ammunition. Boxes bearing the A&W label are eagerly sought after by gun and ammunition collectors alike!

A name that often appears linked with the Allen firm and has a more direct association than the usual agent's marking which may be found on some Allen firearms is that of William H. Onion, a nephew of Ethan Allen. Onion established himself in business in New York City in the early 1850s and it is fairly evident from labels on cased guns, as well as advertisements in periodicals of the era, that William Onion was both in business with and financially backed by his uncle and by Thomas Wheelock and Charles Thurber. For a short period he even operated under the name ONION & WHEELOCK. This close association to the factory and its owners makes cased outfits with the Onion & Wheelock labels or markings quite desirable.

Listed below is the chronological order of the Allen firms with the various names they operated under, locations and dates of each: A quick method of identifying the era and relative scarcity of most Allen marked weapons.

E. ALLEN Grafton, Massachusetts 1831-1837
ALLEN & THURBER Grafton, Massachusetts 1837-1842
ALLEN & THURBER Norwich, Connecticut 1842-1847
ALLEN & THURBER Worcester, Massachusetts 1847-1854
ALLEN THURBER & CO. Worcester, Massachusetts 1854-1856
ALLEN & WHEELOCK Worcester, Massachusetts 1856-1865
E. ALLEN & COMPANY Worcester, Massachusetts 1865-1871

BIBLIOGRAPHY

(NOTE: Material on Allens, especially pepperboxes, may be found in several other books covering American firearms appearing in complete bibliographic listings elsewhere in this book, notably Chapter IV and Chapter VII Pepperboxes. These are: *American British and Continental Pepperbox Firearms* by Jack Dunlap, *Pepperbox Firearms* by Lewis Winant, *The Collecting of Guns*, Edited by James E. Serven, and Sellers & Smith, *American Percussion Revolvers*.)

*Henry, Paul. *Ethan Allen and Allen & Wheelock; Their Guns and Their Legacy.* Woonsocket, Rhode Island: Mowbray Pub. Co., 2006. A "must have" for the study and collecting of these makers; a remarkable wealth of detail in text and color illustrations.

*Mouillesseaux, Harold R. *Ethan Allen, Gunmaker: His Partners, Patents And Firearms.* Ottawa, Canada: Museum Restoration Service, 1973. A major guide to the subject with a great wealth of biographical material on Ethan Allen and his partners as well as details on their products.

*Thomas, H. H. *The Story of Allen & Wheelock Firearms.* Cincinnati: Krehbiel Company, 1965. (Distributed by Rutgers Book, N.J.) The first work devoted solely to Allen arms, a pioneer in its field with numerous photo illustrations.

(*) Preceding a title indicates the book is currently in print.

Lambert Patent Percussion Cane Gun   *See Chapter VII-C, Lambert (E. Allen's first gun making venture).*

Ethan Allen First Model Pocket Rifle

First Model Pocket Rifle made by Ethan Allen, Grafton, Massachusetts. Underhammer Single Shot Pistol. Made c. mid-1830s through c. 1842; total quantity a few thousand.

31 caliber standard, but also made in 32, 34, and 44, with varying frame sizes; box like frame shape standard. Rifled barrels of from 5-1/8" to 9", part octagon, part round. Made without ramrod; mountings of iron. Saw handle grips of walnut (sometimes rosewood), usually with silver oval inlays. Scroll engraving standard on frames of later production.

Batch numbers only under barrel or top of strap. Standard marking on frame: E. ALLEN/GRAFTON/MASS. and POCKET RIFLE/CAST STEEL/WARRANTED. Dealer or agent markings sometimes present, e.g., A. W. SPIES MISSISSIPPI POCKET RIFLE, and will add premium to the values. Frequent advertisements in the St. Louis "Missouri Republican" by Allen dealers Mead & Adriance of that city (see 7E-021) often mentioned this model. The Jan. 27, 1838 issue offered it as "...the celebrated Mississippi

Rifle Pistol." An earlier edition, Jan. 11, 1837 advised they had three dozen on hand that were "...highly recommended by all who have used them as excellent for sportsmen or for defense." MEADE & ADRIANCE agent markings as well as those of WOLF & GILLESPIE are also occasionally encountered on this early Allen and add premium to the value shown.

5A-001

| 5A-001 | Values—Good **$550** | Fine **$1,275** |

Ethan Allen Second Model Pocket Rifle

5A-002

Second Model Pocket Rifle, Underhammer Single Shot Pistol. Made c. late 1830s into the 1840s. Limited production estimated

at a few hundred. Features basically as on the First Model, but having a rounded frame contour and bag type grip. This is the first firearm to bear the Allen & Thurber name; usually seen marked CAST STEEL/WARRANTED/POCKET RIFLE ALLEN & THURBER/WORCESTER, MASS Earlier and scarcer markings with address GRAFTON, MASS. (worth premium to value). Varying lengths part round/part octagon barrels (4"to 6" usual). Usual backstrap on "Worcester" marked, narrow type 1/4" width; most early "Grafton" marked specimens with wider (1/2") backstraps. Agent or dealer markings not observed on this model.

| 5A-002 | Values—Good **$500** | Fine **$1,150** |

Allen & Thurber Tube Hammer D.A. Pistol

Tube Hammer Single Shot Pistol, by Allen & Thurber, Grafton, Massachusetts. Made late 1830s to early 1840s. Total production estimated at a few hundred.

Small caliber pocket pistol of double action type, with a spurless hammer resembling a curved tube. Short part round, part octagon barrel. Iron with walnut grips, each having a small oval inlay and wide 15/32" gripstrap.

Serial numbered. ALLEN'S PATENT on frame and P.M./E.A. 1837 on barrel, and sometimes with GRAFTON, MASS. address.

5A-003

A scarce early Allen with the basic pepperbox grip and frame profile and double action mechanism, this is the pistol pictured in the Allen patent of November 1837. It was also the basis of the 1837 patented action used on pepperboxes (low tension screw type):

5A-003   Values—Good **$750**   Fine **$1,850**

Allen & Thurber D.A. Bar Hammer Pistol

Single Shot D.A. Bar Hammer Percussion Pistol made by Allen & Thurber, Grafton, Norwich and Worcester. Norwich marked specimens quite rare with only a few known and worth a premium. Made c. 1830s to period of the Civil War; total quantity of several thousand estimated.

28 to 36 calibers. Barrel lengths vary from about 2" to 10"; barrels are of the screw-off type, allowing for breech-loading; half round/half octagon. Very long barrel lengths usually bring higher values. Short barrel types known as muff pistols.

Walnut grips. Blued finish.

Marked with batch numbers. Numerous variations may be found within this group; frames either plain or with simple, broad scroll engraving.

Earliest type with handle set at sharp angle to frame and ALLEN & THURBER/GRAFTON MASS.in two lines on side of the hammer; oval inlay on each grip; has the 1837 patent type action. Backstrap width 7/32". Earliest specimens with 15/32" (wider) backstraps worth premium. Estimated production approximately 200:

5A-004   Values—Good **$500**   Fine **$950**

As above, angle of handle not quite as sharp, and bearing ALLEN'S PATENT/CAST STEELon barrel; with or without oval grip inlays; has the 1845 patent type action. Production estimated at less than 200 and less often encountered than first type:

5A-005   Values—Good **$500**   Fine **$950**

Last type, with arched shape to handle and longer frame; varied later type markings of the Worcester period; not necessarily including maker's name; 1845 patent type action; majority of production of this style. Found with all three type Worcester markings:

5A-006   Values—Good **$200**   Fine **$575**

5A-004

5A-005

Allen & Thurber Sidehammer Target Pistol

Single Shot Sidehammer Target Pistol made by Allen & Thurber. An improved type over previous single shot Allen pistols. Made c. late 1840s into the 1850s. Total production estimated at a few hundred.

Calibers 34, 41, and 45. Barrels part round, part octagon, and vary in length from about 6" to 10".

Barrel markings ALLEN & THURBER, WORCESTERor ALLEN THURBER & CO, the latter quite scarce and will bring premium value.

Wooden ramrod beneath the barrel. Rear sight mounted near breech of barrel and extending back behind hammer (where engages adjustment screw). Trigger guard with or without spur (earlier type lacks spur and has single grip screw). Very early models had full octagon barrels, are quite scarce and will command premium values. Usually the very long barrel lengths will bring small premium prices as well as specimens with more elaborate sights than the usually encountered open type described above:

5A-007   Values—Good **$400**   Fine **$1,250**

Large Frame Type. About identical profile to that pictured for 5A-007 with noticeably larger frame and longer handle; the grips fastened by two screws. Trigger guard with long outside finger spur also standard. Barrel lengths of 10 and 12 inches.

5A-007.2   Values—Good **$550**   Fine **$1,500**

5A-007

Allen & Thurber Center Hammer Pistol

Single Shot Center Hammer (Boxlock) Percussion Pistol made by Allen & Thurber, Allen Thurber & Co. and Allen & Wheelock, with the so-called Shotgun-Type hammer. Made c. late 1840s to period of the Civil War; total quantity of a few thousand.

32, 36, and 44 calibers (the latter rare). Barrel lengths from about 3 to 12 inches; half round/half octagon. Single action mechanism, the hammer offset slightly to the right to allow for sighting.

Walnut grips. Blued finish.

5A-008

Serial (batch) numbered. Barrel marking: ALLEN AND THURBER, ALLEN THURBER & CO, or ALLEN & WHEELOCK

An advantage of this pistol was the quite simple action, large caliber, and generally long barrel length. Numerous variations exist in this type. The very long barrels usually bring higher values:

5A-008 Values—Good **$175** Fine **$500**

Allen & Thurber Double Barrel Single Trigger

Double Barrel Single Trigger Pistol made by Allen & Thurber, Allen Thurber & Co., Allen & Wheelock. Made c. 1850s; total quantity estimated from 500 to 1,000.

34 and 36 caliber. Double (side-by-side) barrels, in length from 3" to 6" (longer length worth premium). Double hammers with single trigger.

Walnut grips. Blued finish. Ramrods sometimes present.

Serial (batch) numbered. Flute between barrels may be marked ALLEN & THURBER, ALLEN THURBER & CO or ALLEN & WHEELOCK Unmarked specimens may be encountered.

An attempt to produce a pocket pistol of increased (two shot) firepower, the mechanism has the unique feature of a single trigger which releases both hammers individually (on two separate pulls) when both are cocked simultaneously. Earliest models have tension screws on inside gripstrap; these screws discontinued on later production.

Identical pistols marked BRUCE & DAVIS and SPALDING & FISHER are believed to be of Allen & Thurber manufacture (most likely made by them on order and marked with trade names). No documentary evidence has been found to substantiate this:

5A-009 Values—Good **$400** Fine **$900**

5A-009

Allen Thurber & Co. Target Pistol

5A-010

Target Pistol with Attachable Stock made by Allen Thurber & Co. Made c. early 1850s in limited quantity.

31 and 36 caliber. Barrel lengths of about 11" to 16" octagonal; or part octagon/part round (often on A&W-marked specimens). Wooden ramrod beneath barrel. German silver and iron mountings. Deluxe engraving on major parts, excepting barrel.

Serial numbered. Marked on barrel ALLEN THURBER & Co./WORCESTER/CAST STEEL Specimens known marked also ALLEN & THURBER and ALLEN & WHEELOCK Values same.

These sophisticated arms featured a high standard of craftsmanship, special sights (including peep, and tube and ball), false muzzles and bullet starters, and set triggers. They were apparently standard cased with a full array of accessories.

Considered as scarce and a prized specimen for an Allen collection, or for the collector of New England arms.

The attachable stock has fancy patchbox on right side and oval escutcheon plate inlaid on left side.

Values are for complete gun with false muzzle and attachable stock. Cased outfits, as often encountered, are valued considerably higher, with both the condition of the case and the inclusion of accessories affecting such increased values. The absence of the false muzzle detracts considerably from the value and desirability of most specimens (if they show provisions for one originally) as does the absence of the stock:

5A-010 Values—Good **$2,750** Fine **$8,500**

Pistol only, without attachable stock:
5A-010.5 Values—Good **$900** Fine **$3,000**

Allen & Wheelock Center Hammer Pistol

Center Hammer Straight Line Percussion Pistol made by Allen & Wheelock, a.k.a. "In-Line" or "Straight Away" (as nipple is 'in line with the barrel and bore). Made c. 1858 to 1865; total quantity about 500.

31 to 38 caliber. Single shot. Barrel lengths from 3" to 6"; variations in barrels are encountered with some full octagon or full round; others part round, part octagon. The long barrel length will usually bring a slightly higher value. Iron frame standard; brass frame known but very rare.

Walnut grips.

Serial (batch) numbered. Barrel marking: ALLEN & WHEELOCK..usual markings most often seen on octagon barrels; round barrels seldom encountered with markings. This deringer type arm was one of the simplest of all Allen firearms. The frame was one piece, and the mechanism was an uncomplicated single action; the barrels were occasionally surplus revolver barrels from other Allen models on which production had ceased. A variant of the handle shape is also encountered with a more evenly arched profile versus earlier "quick drop" profile:

5A-011

5A-011   Values—Good **$250**   Fine **$600**

ALLEN PEPPERBOXES

Among the most popular and best selling handguns of their day, the Allen pepperboxes were the first American double action revolving arms. The long period of their manufacture from the 1830s to the early 1860s attests to their wide popularity and commercial success. For a decade or more after the introduction of Sam Colt's revolver, the Allen pepperbox enjoyed far wider sales and notoriety as a handgun; contemporary accounts usually attest to that fact. The Allen pepperbox found wide acceptance among a general cross section of the American public as a reliable and inexpensive weapon of defense. Quite a few of them were sold to emigrants heading west and not a few found their way to California with the 49ers, turning up in the gold regions of that fast burgeoning area. They were also highly popular, primarily in larger dragoon sizes, with military men in both federal and state militia service, and are known to have seen campaign use in the Seminole Wars of Florida, and in the Mexican and Civil Wars. A number of specimens appear in fine collections with inscriptions on them directly associating them to military usage and ownership.

More types and variations occur within the Allen pepperboxes than any other Allen product, and very likely any other model of gun by any other American manufacturer. It is estimated that about 50 basic types were made from their first introduction in the 1830s to final production in the 1860s. Of these there exist numerous sub-types and a great many variations have been identified.

Allen pepperboxes have always enjoyed a wide following in the dual collecting categories of Allen arms and American pepperboxes. Their attractiveness is based on a close association with many important eras of American history, the popularity of their maker's name, and the several variations in which they can be found, acquired and accumulated. Very likely the major problem experienced in collecting them has been the lack of a definitive, systematically categorized check-list of all models, sub-models and variants. Allen pepperboxes have thus far had not a little literature written about them, yet they have managed to elude a simplified, reasonably complete detailed listing and itemization (the very first, and meager, attempt appearing in the April, 1911 issue of the short-lived *Magazine Of Antique Firearms*) which the average collector or merely mildly interested gun trader finds so essential for reference. In attempting to break through that barrier, the author has established the first simplified guidelines for identification and evaluation of these highly important American arms. It is essential for the reader to understand that in pioneering new territory, especially in a field such as the Allen pepperboxes (which were manufactured in so many styles and variations), the simplified listings in this chapter represent the most often encountered, basic styles plus some of the better known variations and rarities. In order to grasp, and consequently properly evaluate, the importance of pieces not falling within any of these listings (specimens of which the reader may encounter), it is essential that he perform further research on his own.

It is indicative of the difficulty of systematically categorizing Allen pepperboxes that all prior works on the subject have thus far avoided a confrontation with the problem. These guns just have not lent themselves to the neat systematized presentations that such arms as Colts and Smith & Wessons have. This certainly does not lessen their importance nor their value; it merely presents the collector with more of a challenge and further allows the serious student a chance to accumulate knowledge and shed some very important light on the field. The reader is also referred to Chapter VII-B (American Percussion Pepperboxes) for further information about these arms.

Fundamental to the identification and evaluation of Allen pepperboxes are a few observations concerning their manufacture at three different locations, their two basic styles (i.e., 1837 and 1845 patents), the few features commonly found in most types (enumerated below) and the fact that *CONTRADICTIONS OFTEN OCCUR.*

For the sake of systematization, Allen pepperboxes are divided into three basic groups: (1) Those made at Grafton, Massachusetts, c. mid-1830s to 1842; (2) those made at Norwich, Connecticut, c. 1842 to 1847; (3) those made at Worcester, Massachusetts, c. 1847 to 1865.

The two basic subdivisions of Allen pepperboxes made at the latter two locations are those of the 1837 patent type and of the 1845 patent type. These are key identifying features, especially in the Norwich made pepperboxes, and are easily recognized and verified by the collector.

The 1837 patent type has a one-piece straight (more or less) mainspring which fits into a small clip at the base of the inside strap (underneath the grips). The screw which adjusts the tension on that spring (and which can be observed by the eye on the outside of the gun) appears on the inside (or front) gripstrap very close to the bottom or butt of the handle.

The 1845 patent type has a large "U" shaped mainspring and the tension adjusting screw (which is easily observed on the outside of the gun) appears approximately in the center of the inner (or front) gripstrap of the handle.

A few other features more or less common to all Allens of all three types are factory standard walnut grips; early ones often have long narrow oval German silver inlays (known in collectors' terminology as "spangles"). A variety of other types of grips are found on Allen pepperboxes and are discussed in the prefatory text of this section. The usual finish on standard pepperboxes was blued barrels and frames with casehardened hammers, although other finishes are seen with varying degrees of frequency. These too will alter values upward depending on their originality and type.

Indicative of manufacturing economy introduced by Allen is his utilization of the integral nipple with barrels. Only on the early Grafton-made models are removable nipples seen; all other Allen pepperboxes have nipples milled integrally with barrels.

A feature standard with most Allens (it will be so noted where normally not encountered) is hand-engraved designs on the frame and nipple shields. Types and styles vary and are described in the following listings; it should be noted that rarely will specimens be found identical on any type as they were all hand engraved and for the most part quickly, but well executed. For the expert, engraving style, although repetitive and varying slightly, is sufficient to place a piece within a certain time and place of manufacture. Highly embellished, custom engraved specimens are sometimes seen having designs covering sections of the barrel as well as much finer quality workmanship on the frame; such pieces—when proven original—command premium values and must be judged individually on their own merits.

Serial numbers on Allens are not a good method of judging either period of manufacture or variation. They are manufacturing batch numbers and hence, will be noted with but very few digits and in a low series.

Barrel lengths of the various models and types fall within general patterns which are detailed in the following descriptions. It has been observed that varying lengths, as long as they fall within known patterns, do not normally affect values nor demand. Of course, should bona fide unique or extra long lengths occur as is always possible, such a piece would merit a considerable premium.

Another major feature in understanding the general sequence of production of early Allen pepperboxes as well as evaluating them is the shape, and especially the angle at which the grip or handle is set to the frame. This is a nuance which is not easily categorized in a listing such as the present one, and tends very much to cloud the issue for our purposes. The collector, however, should be very much aware of this and it is certainly well worth his effort to review the subject, quite well discussed in *Ethan Allen, Gunmaker*. The matter of grip angle is decidedly introduced in our listings, but variants do occur within them which require further attention on the reader's part. Mention is made of major handle variations when important for basic identification. Five major angles have been categorized by Allen collectors: (A) The "quick drop" grip in which the handle is set at a very sharp, almost right angle to the frame, as found on the earliest Grafton and Norwich specimens. This is the first style and the most easily observable. (B) The so-called "slow drop" grip in which the handle is still at a sharp angle to the frame, but slightly more curved than the early type. (C) Full "dog leg" grip and (D) semi "dog leg" grip, both of which have the early long handles normally with oval

"spangles" or escutcheons, but are not set at nearly the sharp angular positions of the early, first two types. (E) The most commonly encountered evenly arched "late rounded" grip as found on most of the Worcester manufactured pieces.

Among the other details to which the serious collector should pay heed are the use of grip pins, "spangles" (the long oval narrow German silver grip inlays), numerous marking variations and the sizes and shapes of marking dies.

The pitman (or connecting rod) and ratchet features are often mentioned and referred to in Allen pepperbox literature. These features first appear in the Grafton series and were continued throughout all other Allen pepperboxes. They consisted of an inner series of cam teeth on the base of the barrel unit and a square pin below the cylinder pin extending from the breech. When hammer is at full cock the square pin extended from the breech and locked the cylinder for the moment of firing.

A feature found on several late Grafton and Norwich pepperboxes is a slotted hammer for sighting (at the rear of the hammer a rectangular slot which is used to sight through). It is estimated that less than one-third of the late Graftons and approximately one-third of all Norwich production were made with this feature. The incidence of their survival seems to be less than formerly indicated and does call for a small premium to their value. Front sights were not usual and the presence of them will also add a premium to value.

DEALER, DISTRIBUTOR OR AGENT MARKINGS

The presence of dealers' or agents' markings on Allen pepperboxes is an important feature affecting value. Such markings may be considered scarce and often appear on a variety of types of Allens and can increase their prices from a minimum of 20 percent to possibly 100 percent or more, depending on the marking and the model of pepperbox. Certain agents' markings are more likely to be seen than others, e.g., **J. G. Bolen**, or **A. W. Spies & Company**, while others are considered quite scarce, e.g., **Young, Smith & Company**, **Lane & Read**, **Tryon**, and **Hyde & Goodrich**; still others may be considered rare, such as **J. Eaton, Meade & Adriance, Canfield Bros., S. Sutherland, Wolfe & Gillespie, P. Evans** and no doubt some that have yet to be recorded! In most cases where agents' names appear, some of the other standard markings (such as the Norwich or Worcester address) or even the Allen company name will be omitted and normally only the ALLEN'S PATENT markings will appear on the hammer. The reader should bear in mind, as previously stated, that contradictions often occur.

Grafton Production Pepperboxes

Grafton-made pepperboxes were not only Allen's first production, but are among the scarcest for the collector and may generally be regarded as the most valuable. It is within this group that collectors have singled out the earliest, and one of the smallest of Allen's pocket sizes to apply the quaint name "The Dainty

5A-012

Grafton." Two other sizes of Grafton-made pieces are found and are usually referred to as the "standard" and the "dragoon." These early Allens are easily distinguished by both their "Grafton, Mass." address markings and the very sharp angle at which the grip is set to the frame; the so-called "quick drop." They usually are also seen with the very tiny die-stamp markings (the so-called No. 1 die—1-1/2 millimeters in letter height), considerably smaller than on the later Norwich and Worcester production arms. A nuance worth investigating for the advanced collector is the absence and later introduction of the internal pitman and ratchet mechanism which is a distinguishing feature of variations within the Grafton line.

"DAINTY" OR SMALL POCKET SIZE. The first pepperbox manufactured by Allen. Six-shot. 28 caliber. Removable, numbered nipples. Barrel lengths vary; normally of approximately 2-3/4" to 3". Most specimens with engraved frame bearing simple, leaf-like designs with some specimens plain, unengraved. Often marked ALLEN'S PATENT on left sideplate in very tiny block letters, and on left side of hammer ALLEN & THURBER/GRAFTON, MASS. also in tiny No. 1 die size. Made without nipple shield:

5A-012   Values—Good **$2,000**   Fine **$6,000**
STANDARD OR MEDIUM SIZE. Barrel lengths vary, approximately 3" to 5". Six-shot. 31 caliber.

Early Type. Removable, numbered nipples; fluted barrel ribs; wide backstrap (over 1/2" width). Frame either plain or with very simple broad leaf hand-engraved designs; left side of frame often found (but not always) with tiny ALLEN'S PATENT markings. Hammer marked ALLEN & THURBER/GRAFTON, MASS. in tiny letters:

5A-013   Values—Good **$1,100**   Fine **$3,250**

5A-014

Second Type. Distinguished by first use of integral nipples; wide backstrap (over 1/2" width), hammer markings identical to above, but not found with sideplate markings; usually bears simple engraved frame designs; fluted barrel ribs. There are known specimens with full hexagonal shaped barrels which are considered very rare and will command premium values:

5A-014   Values—Good **$1,100**   Fine **$3,000**

Third or Late Type. Similar to above. Its most easily identifiable feature is the narrow backstrap (about 5/16" width). It is on this model that Allen first used a nipple shield, although not all specimens are found with this feature. Top of hammer marked in tiny letters ALLEN'S PATENT. Side of

hammer marked ALLEN & THURBER/GRAFTON, MASS. Full hexagonal barrels also known on this type but are considered quite rare and will bring premium values:

5A-015   Values—Good **$875**   Fine **$2,750**
DRAGOON SIZE. Large frame. Six-shot. 36 caliber. Barrel lengths approximately 5-1/2" to 6". All variations have wide backstrap. All made without nipple shield and all have fluted barrel ribs.

Early First Type. Plain, unengraved frame; unmarked sideplate; removable numbered nipples; fluted barrel ribs; side of hammer marked ALLEN & THURBER/GRAFTON, MASS. in tiny letters (No. 1 die) and on top of hammer, ALLEN'S PATENT.

5A-016   Values—Good **$1,750**   Fine **$4,000**

Second Type. Simple engraved frame designs; removable numbered nipples; same markings as above. Internal change showing use of the pitman and ratchet:

5A-017   Values—Good **$1,500**   Fine **$3,750**

5A-018

Third Type. Similar to above. Quickly distinguished by its integral/fixed nipples. Also shows use of the pitman and ratchet:

5A-018   Values—Good **$1,400**   Fine **$3,500**

Fourth or Last Type. Similar to above. Quickly identified by its hand engraved nipple shield:

5A-018.5   Values—Good **$1,400**   Fine **$3,500**

Norwich Production Pepperboxes

Similar in style to the earlier Grafton pepperboxes, particularly in the sharp angle where the handle joins the frame and the use of long, narrow, oval shaped German silver inlays (spangles) on grips. The earliest Norwich specimens have the so-called "quick drop" grip with this angular juncture becoming less severe in later Norwich production running the gamut to the so-called "slow drop" and full and semi "dog leg" grips. Such nuances are often very important and are felt by some advanced collectors to be classified as a distinct category of the Norwich line, but this is felt beyond the scope of categorization of this work.

All Norwich pepperboxes are six-shot. The earliest Norwich pepperboxes have the so-called No. 1 die (tiny 1-1/2 millimeter letter height) markings on the top of hammer and matching ALLEN & THURBER/NORWICH C-T on side of the hammer. It is quite firmly believed that these pieces were made at Grafton and assembled at Norwich. The first Norwich manufactured pieces have the larger so-called No. 2 die (2-1/2 millimeter letter height) markings on top side of hammer and PATENTED CAST STEEL on barrel group (while the early ones were either unmarked or bore only CAST STEEL).

Almost all Norwich specimens bear the simple hand engraved scroll/floral designs on the frame. Marking variations are numerous and are not always uniform for both barrels and hammer. A most important factor in categorizing the Norwich

production is the use of the 1837 patent (with the tension screw for mainspring on lower handle near butt) and the more commonly encountered 1845 or later type patent which is quickly identified by the tension screw for mainspring located about in the center of the inner gripstrap. The collector should be aware that many of the 1845 or "later" types will be observed which bear the older 1837 patent markings. This merely indicates use of the marking die from earlier production which had not yet been discontinued, or even the use of stock or bin parts in the assembly of the guns; an interesting feature, but one which does not normally increase nor affect the value of a specimen. Normal markings ALLEN & THURBER/NORWICH, C-T on hammer (except where agent's marks appear) with patent dates or CAST STEEL on barrels.

There was no small or pocket size frame made in this Norwich group. A few of the hammerless models with short barrel lengths are occasionally seen referred to as "pocket size" or "model" Norwich production, but they actually do not constitute a distinct size variation. Their frame size is the same as "standard" and their short barrels merely give them the appearance of being smaller.

STANDARD OR MEDIUM SIZE. ALLEN & THURBER/NORWICH C-T **marked pepperboxes. Early Style With 1837 Patent Actions;** usually marked with 1837 patent date. Barrel lengths from approximately 3" to 5" are usual. Engraving of scroll/floral designs on frame. Where nipple shields are used, they have the rolled type (as opposed to the hand engraved) scroll designs.

5A-019

Bar hammer style; fluted barrel ribs; made without nipple shield:
5A-019   Values—Good **$425**   Fine **$1,150**

Identical to above, but with nipple shield:
5A-020   Values—Good **$450**   Fine **$1,250**

5A-021

Bar hammer type with flat barrel ribs; made without nipple shield:
5A-021   Values—Good **$400**   Fine **$1,100**

Identical to above with nipple shield:
5A-022   Values—Good **$375**   Fine **$1,000**

5A-023

Hammerless (concealed hammer) type with conventional trigger and trigger guard; flat barrel ribs; without nipple shield (none has been encountered with shield and such would be considered very rare):
5A-023   Values—Good **$950**   Fine **$3,000**

5A-024

Hammerless type as above, but with distinctive ring trigger; made without shield; flat barrel ribs:
5A-024   Values—Good **$725**   Fine **$2,000**

Identical to above, but with shield:
5A-025   Values—Good **$800**   Fine **$2,200**

5A-026

Bar hammer type with ring trigger; fluted barrel ribs; made without nipple shield (rare):
5A-026   Values—Good **$550**   Fine **$1,400**

Identical to above, but with conventional trigger guard:
5A-026.5 Values—Good **$550**   Fine **$1,400**

5A-027

Identical to above, but made with nipple shield having the roll type scroll engraving; rare:
5A-027   Values—Good **$550**   Fine **$1,400**

STANDARD OR "MEDIUM" SIZE WITH 1845 TYPE PATENT. (Hammerless types have not been observed in this style and would be considered quite rare.)

5A-028

Bar hammer; nipple shield and flat barrel ribs:
5A-028   Values—Good **$350**   Fine **$1,200**

Ring trigger model with bar hammer and nipple shield; flat barrel ribs:
5A-029   Values—Good **$550**   Fine **$1,250**

5A-029

Ring trigger as above without nipple shield; these are found with very small No. 1 type die markings ALLEN'S PATENT on top of hammer; only known case where apparently Allen reverted to the use of a discontinued die:
5A-030   Values—Good **$625**   Fine **$1,400**

DRAGOON SIZE NORWICH PEPPERBOXES, 1837 PATENT ACTIONS. Large frame; barrel lengths usually 6".

5A-036

Bar hammer with conventional trigger and trigger guard; fluted barrel ribs; made without nipple shield:
5A-031   Values—Good **$875**   Fine **$2,500**

Identical to above, but with nipple shield:
5A-032   Values—Good **$875**   Fine **$2,500**

Identical to above, but flat barrel ribs and made without nipple shield:
5A-033   Values—Good **$750**   Fine **$2,250**

Ring trigger model. Made without nipple shield; fluted barrel ribs:
5A-034   Values—Good **$750**   Fine **$2,250**

DRAGOON SIZE NORWICH PEPPERBOXES, 1845 TYPE ACTIONS

Bar hammer with conventional trigger and trigger guard; flat barrel ribs; with nipple shield:
5A-036   Values—Good **$750**   Fine **$2,250**

Ring trigger model with flat barrel ribs; made without nipple shield:
5A-037   Values—Good **$875**   Fine **$2,500**

5A-035

5A-038

Ring trigger model made without nipple shield and flat barrel ribs:
5A-035   Values—Good **$875**   Fine **$2,500**

Ring trigger model with nipple shield (rare):
5A-038   Values—Good **$950**   Fine **$2,600**

Worcester Production Pepperboxes

There is no doubt that after the move from Norwich to Worcester, the company continued either the production or at least the assembly of parts shipped from their Norwich facilities. Documentary evidence does not exist as to which models were first made or introduced by the Worcester factory, but it has been quite thoroughly agreed upon by most Allen students that many models were simultaneously produced. The earliest style of Worcester marked pepperboxes decidedly show characteristics of Norwich types and they may be aptly called "transitional." These are distinguished by their "dog leg" handles with noticeable angular juncture to the frame, quite distinctly setting them off from the overall Worcester-made pepperbox. The Worcester product generally conforms to a style of an evenly rounded frame (versus the flatter frames of Norwich and earlier production), with the handles having a gentle or evenly arched shape as they meet the frame. This latter, standard type is not usually found with the oval inlays or "spangles." The true transitional "Worcester" marked model is likely that with the conventional trigger and hammer, 5" barrel, flat wide ribs with rolled scroll design on nipple shield, dog leg handle and spangles on grips. The next later transitional type has the rose and vine engraved shield.

The most conventional Worcester pepperboxes are those with the shorter appearing handle of the so-called "bag" shape. Nipple shields are standard on Worcester pepperboxes (except where noted below) and bear a very simple hand engraved scroll motif on most pieces with the later models having no design there at all. Hand engraved motifs are easily distinguishable from the earlier Norwich roll embellished nipple shields. Transitional and very early Worcester pieces will be observed with the Norwich style roll engraving and may be considered

quite scarce. Frames of all Worcester pepperboxes are quite standard with the broad hand engraved scroll/floral designs. Worcester made pepperboxes are all of the 1845 patent type. Except for the one single action model (so noted below), all conventional Worcester production was double action with bar type hammer. Concealed hammer types are known and specimens identified as original are considered rare.

SMALL OR "POCKET SIZE" WORCESTER PEPPERBOX. Calibers 25, 28, 31, and 34 (in four-shot only). Found in four-, five- and six-shot styles. Five-shot variety most commonly encountered in this size. Four-shot a distinctly different model as noted below. Marking of all three types of the Worcester era, 1847 to 1865 (see preface). Majority of these small sizes have fluted barrels. Barrel lengths 2-1/2" to 4".

5A-039

Fluted barrels with engraved nipple shield separately affixed; most often seen with hand engraving on shields:
5A-039   Values—Good **$325**   Fine **$750**

5A-040

Fluted barrels with nipple shield made integral with frame:
5A-040 Values—Good **$325** Fine **$750**

5A-041

Fluted barrels without nipple shield; no provision for same and usually plain, unengraved frame. ALLEN & WHEELOCK marked only and one of the very last styles made at Worcester:
5A-041 Values—Good **$325** Fine **$750**

Similar to above frame without nipple shield, but having the rebated barrels of 5A.040. A transitional type. Numbers must match to be original:
5A-041.5 Values—Good **$350** Fine **$850**

5A-042

Four-shot pepperbox 34 caliber. Found only with ALLEN & WHEELOCK markings. Fluted barrels. A distinctly different style than all other Allens in the method of attaching barrels to frame; an integral extension at rear of barrels affixes to frame rather than the standard use of a center support bored through the barrel units to the muzzle. Variance noted in locking devices. Simple engraved design standard on frames; all are made without recoil shield. Single indentation at rear of barrels between nipples for hammer safety rest:
5A-042 Values—Good **$450** Fine **$1,400**

STANDARD OR MEDIUM SIZE. This is the most often encountered size and very likely the group with the widest variations of types and markings. Caliber usually 31 or 32. Five- or six-shot; ribbed and fluted barrels usually varying 3" to 5". Conventional triggers only (ring triggers have not been observed in Worcester production). Markings are of all three Worcester styles. Simple broad scroll/floral engraved frames are standard. The most often seen styles and some of the very scarce variations are:

> **Early transitional type** with handle of "dog leg" style as carry over from Norwich production; oval inlay in grips; flat narrow barrel ribs. ALLEN & THURBER, WORCESTER markings only and the rolled type engraving of Norwich style on nipple shield. Very scarce:
> **5A-043** Values—Good **$375** Fine **$1,250**

5A-043

5A-044

Similar to above with Norwich style handle, but hand engraved nipple shield and wide flat barrel ribs:
5A-044 Values—Good **$375** Fine **$1,150**

5A-045

Bag shaped, evenly curved standard Worcester style handle with rounded frame; wide flat barrel ribs; engraved nipple shield. One of the most often seen styles:
5A-045 Values—Good **$375** Fine **$1,100**

Identical to above with fluted barrels:
5A-045.5 Values—Good **$375** Fine **$1,100**

5A-046

Single action, shotgun type hammer with wide flat barrel ribs; engraved nipple shield; bag shaped handle. Normally seen with sideplate fastening on right side. A rare variation is known (and will bring considerable premium) with sideplate on left side; another very rare variation recorded is fitted with fluted barrels. Specimens proven original worth considerable premium:
5A-046 Values—Good **$700** Fine **$2,250**

Hammerless type with conventional trigger and nipple shield. In this case nipple shield is merely a narrow short projection at the top of the frame rather than completely encircling frame:
5A-047 Values—Good **$950** Fine **$3,000**

5A-048

Bag shaped handle. Frame size noticeably larger and is midway between the "Standard" and "Dragoon" (recent collector terminology names it the "Baby Dragoon"). Worcester production. 6 shot. Engraved nipple shield; flat barrel ribs:

5A-048   Values—Good **$450**   Fine **$1,200**

DRAGOON SIZE. Easily identified by its massive proportions. 36 caliber. Six-shot. Approximately 6" barrels (varying slightly). Conventional bar type hammer and trigger; broad scroll/floral engraving standard on frames. A few rare variations are known to appear in this style such as the bar hammer with short cocking spur which allows for single action operation; such pieces demand substantial premiums. These large "Dragoons" are termed by collectors "49'ers" as so many of them are known to have been carried by those heading west in the earlier years of the Gold Rush.

5A-049

Early transitional style with "dog leg" handle having features of Norwich production; oval grip inlay; wide flat barrel ribs; hand engraved nipple shield; trigger guard

without spur as seen on later types. Usually marked only ALLEN & THURBER, WORCESTER.

5A-049   Values—Good **$875**   Fine **$2,750**

5A-050

Standard Worcester production with bag shaped, evenly arched handle; spur projecting from rear of trigger guard; engraved nipple shield; wide barrel ribs; marked ALLEN & THURBER or ALLEN & WHEELOCK ALLEN, THURBER & CO. markings are known, but rare and will bring premium value):

5A-050   Values—Good **$950**   Fine **$3,000**

5A-051

As above, but with fluted barrels; spur projecting from rear of trigger guard; markings usually ALLEN & THURBER ALLEN & WHEELOCK markings are known, but considered rare and will bring a premium value while ALLEN, THURBER & CO. are believed to exist, but none has yet been recorded and would certainly bring premium also:

5A-051   Values—Good **$950**   Fine **$3,000**

Allen & Wheelock Large Frame Pocket Rev.

Bar Hammer Double Action Pocket Model Percussion Revolver, Large Frame Type, made by Allen & Wheelock, a.k.a. "Transitional Pepperbox-Revolver." C. 1857 into early 1860s; quantity estimated as high as 1500; however, actual production more likely near 500. Specimens seldom seen; very scarce.

34 caliber (various listed as 32 caliber). Five-shot round cylinder, bearing roll engraved forest scene decoration, including deer and dogs. 3" to 5" octagonal barrels, without sights.

Walnut grips of bag shape. Blued finish; casehardened cylinder, hammer and trigger.

Serial (batch) numbered. Markings noted below under values.

The first revolver made by Allen, the design shows obvious influences of his pepperbox production, particularly in the bar hammer, double action, and overall appearance of frame and grips. Numerous variations of lesser importance may be found on this model including several different styles of hammer rests on rear of cylinders.

Early model, having cylinder pin of threaded type, with slot for screwdriver; screws into the frame (beneath the barrel); about 400 estimated made, however, survival rate apparently low and this considered hardest to find by collectors. Marked ALLEN & WHEELOCK (frame) and PATENTED APRIL 16, 1845 (hammer):

5A-052   Values—Good **$450**   Fine **$1,200**

5A-052

Transition type; as above, but with sliding type cylinder pin secured by screw through bottom of the frame; frame length forward of the cylinder, 11/16"; estimates of quantity made range from 50 on up:

5A-053   Values—Good **$325**   Fine **$1,100**

Medium frame type; (a.k.a. "Late Production" type in earlier editions of this "guide"). Has identical profile and caliber of that illustrated; also five shots. Slightly smaller cylinder (1-1/2" long vs. the larger 1-5/8") and a smaller, lighter frame. Barrel marking usually: ALLEN & WHEELOCK WORCESTER, MASS./ALLEN'S PATENT APRIL 16, 1845. Hammer marking as on previous models, although placement may vary:

5A-054   Values—Good **$300**   Fine **$1,000**

Allen & Wheelock Small Frame Pocket Rev.

Bar Hammer Double Action Pocket Model Percussion Revolver, Small Frame Type, a.k.a. "Transition Pepperbox-Revolver." Made by Allen & Wheelock c. 1858 into early 1860s; total quantity about 1,000.

5A-055

About identical profile to above "Large Frame" and "Medium Frame" but noticeably smaller; hammer is evenly rounded vs. the double "bends" in profile of the Large Frame type."

30 caliber (variously listed as 31 cal.). 5-shot round cylinder 1-1/4" long bearing roll engraved forest scene, including deer and ducks. 2" to 3-1/2" octagonal barrels, without sights.

Walnut grips of bag shape. Blued finish.

Serial (batch) numbered. Barrel marking: ALLEN & WHEELOCK, MASS./ALLEN'S PATENT APRIL 16, 1845 Specimens encountered with patent date marking on hammer.

All the small frame size pistols were fitted with the late cylinder pin, of sliding type, secured by a screw through bottom of the frame. Variations of hammer shape and forward section of trigger bow (at point where it joins frame) also noted:

5A-055   Values—Good **$400**   Fine **$1,250**

Allen & Wheelock Sidehammer Pocket and Belt Revolvers

Sidehammer Pocket and Belt Model Revolvers by Allen & Wheelock. Made c. 1858-1861; total quantity as noted below under values.

28 caliber Pocket Model, small frame, octagon barrel lengths 2" to 5". 32 caliber (seen variously listed as 31 and 34 cal.). Belt Model with larger or medium size frame, octagon barrels from 3" to 6" with longer 7-1/2" barrels known and considered rare, worth premium. Cylinders all five-shot and roll engraved with forest scene and varying total of deer. Cylinder pins enter frame from rear, screw into position.

Walnut grips. Blued finish; casehardened cylinder, hammer and trigger guard.

5A-057

Serial (batch) numbered. Barrel markings as indicated below.

As noted under the Navy Model revolvers, a number of variants will be encountered in the Allen & Wheelock Sidehammers. Due to the limited numbers produced, complete classifications have yet to be made and published. Quite a few minor variations noted.

Early production type; lateral friction style catch on left side of sideplate/trigger guard, to secure trigger guard/loading lever into position for firing (see illustration of side hammer early production Navy for this feature). Barrel marking: ALLEN & WHEELOCK and ALLEN'S PATENT JAN. 13, 1857. Various estimates have been made for production of these two calibers, but no documentary evidence has been found to support production figures. For collecting purposes both may be said to be rare and very probably less than 100 of each were produced:

5A-056   Values—Good **$550**   Fine **$1,500**

Standard model; catch for trigger guard of spring loaded type and mounted on rear of guard. Variations appear in shape of cylinder pins, and two or three screw sideplates. Barrel marking: ALLEN & WHEELOCK WORCESTER, MASS./ALLEN'S PATENTS JAN. 13, 1857, SEPT. 7, 1858. 28 and 31 caliber specimens (estimated approximately 750 to 1000 of each made):

5A-057   Values—Good **$375**   Fine **$1,150**

Allen & Wheelock Sidehammer Navy Revolver

Sidehammer Navy Model Percussion Revolver by Allen & Wheelock. Made c. 1858-1861; total quantity as noted below under values.

36 caliber. Large frame size. 6-shot round cylinder with roll engraved forest scene including rabbit, deer and doe motif. Octagonal barrel, 5-1/2" to 8" with the latter the most often encountered. However, that longer 8" bbl. will usually bring a premium of 10 to 15 percent.

Walnut grips. Blued finish; the cylinder, hammer and trigger guard casehardened.

Serial (batch) numbered. Barrel markings as noted below.

Some confusion exists in studying the Allen & Wheelock Sidehammer revolvers, due to the number of variants encountered and the relatively small quantities produced. The Navy Model is the most readily identifiable, and is one of the most sought after types. Although no government contracts were given for this model, it is considered by collectors as a martial type.

5A-058
Early Production

5A-059
Standard Production

Early production type; lateral friction style catch on left side of sideplate/trigger guard, to secure trigger guard/loading lever into position for firing. Barrel marking: ALLEN & WHEELOCKand ALLEN'S PATENT JAN. 13, 1857. About 100 made:

5A-058   Values—Good **$1,250**   Fine **$4,000**

Standard model; catch for trigger guard of spring loaded type and mounted on rear of guard. Barrel marking: ALLEN & WHEELOCK WORCESTER, MASS./ALLEN'S PATENTS JAN. 13, 1857, SEPT. 7, 1858. About 750 made:

5A-059   Values—Good **$1,150**   Fine **$3,500**

Allen & Wheelock Center Hammer Army

5A-060

Army Model Center Hammer Percussion Revolver by Allen & Wheelock. Made c. 1861-1862; total quantity usually estimated about 700. However, from the frequency with which this piece appears, it would seem that considerably more were made, hence there is strong likelihood numbers were merely assembly numbers.

44 caliber. 6-shot round cylinder rebated at nipple end. 7-1/2" half round, half octagon barrel.

Walnut grips. Blued finish, with casehardened hammer and trigger guard.

Serial (batch) numbered. Barrel markings: ALLEN & WHEELOCK. WORCESTER, MASS. U.S./ALLEN'S PT'S. JAN. 13, 1857. DEC 15, 1857, SEPT. 7, 1858.

An improvement over the Sidehammer revolvers, the main features of the Army Model are the centrally located hammer and the cylinder pin entering from the front. Variations are known in the method of attaching nipples to cylinder with slight changes in shape of nipple wells. Records show that 536 Allen revolvers were bought by the U. S. government in 1861; they do not, however, indicate which model. It has been generally assumed that these were all the 44 caliber Army type. Martially marked specimens are very rare and will command premium values if fully validated. It is known that a very small group of them (believed to be in this large 44-caliber "Army" size were issued to the 2nd and 3rd regiments of Michigan cavalry during the Civil War:

5A-060   Values—Good **$1,000**   Fine **$4,000**

Allen & Wheelock Center Hammer Navy

5A-061

Navy Model Center Hammer Percussion Revolver by Allen & Wheelock. Made c. 1861-1862; total quantity estimated 500 as with the Army Model, it is assumed the "serial" numbers more likely

represent assembly numbers, hence quantity manufactured is very possibly larger than 500.

36 caliber. 6-shot round cylinder rebated at nipple end. 7-1/2" octagon barrel; also made in 5", 6", and 8" lengths. The 7-1/2" and 8" lengths are worth a 10 to 20 percent premium.

Walnut grips. Blued finish, with casehardened hammer and trigger guard.

Serial (batch) numbered. Barrel marking: ALLEN & WHEELOCK WORCESTER, MASS. U.S./ALLEN'S PT'S. JAN. 13, DEC. 15, 1857, SEPT. 7, 1858.

The center hammer model evolved from the Sidehammer series, and is believed to have been made after the Allen & Wheelock lipfire Army and Navy production. No government contracts were given for this model, but it is considered a martial piece by collectors:

5A-061   Values—Good **$750**   Fine **$3,000**

Allen & Wheelock "Providence Police"

Providence Police (so-called) **Model Center Hammer Percussion Revolver by Allen & Wheelock.** Made c. late 1850s—early 1860s; total quantity about 700.

36 caliber. 5-shot round cylinder with rebated section at nipple end. Octagonal barrel standard at 3" or 4" length (5" barrels scarce and worth premium).

Walnut grips. Blued finish.

Serial (batch) numbered. Although these arms are all unmarked, they are decidedly the product of Allen & Wheelock and are so considered. Such features as the cylinder pin and gas deflector encircling the pin and the typical A&W styling can be observed in the frame, hammer, and cylinder configuration.

Collectors know this large caliber spur trigger revolver by the "Providence Police" name, as presumably specimens were made for use by the Providence, Rhode Island, police department,

5A-062

although no conclusive evidence exists to verify this fact. Variations have been noted in the single or two screw fastening of the sideplate:

5A-062   Values—Good **$375**   Fine **$1,250**

Allen & Wheelock Center Hammer Lipfire Army

Army Model Center Hammer Lipfire Revolver, a.k.a."2nd Model Lipfire," by Allen & Wheelock. Made c. early 1860s; total quantity about 250.

44 lipfire. 6-shot round cylinder with notches for cartridge lips at rear wall. 7-1/2" half round, half octagon barrel.

Walnut grips. Two shapes to the grips/butts are known which constitute distinct variations. The most commonly encountered (as illustrated) known as the "narrow" grip is evenly tapered in contour; a rarely found shape known as the "flared" or "bell" type has the contour of grip widening noticeably at butt. Blued finish, with casehardened hammer and trigger guard.

Serial (batch) numbered. Barrel marking: ALLEN & WHEELOCK, WORCESTER, MASS. U.S./ALLEN'S PAT'S SEP. 7, NOV. 9, 1858.

Quite similar to the Army Model Center Hammer percussion revolver, the lipfire was contemporary, and likely would have continued except for a successful patent infringement against Allen & Wheelock by Smith & Wesson. Collectors sometimes erroneously confuse the lipfire Army as a conversion from percussion. It was actually manufactured prior to the percussion model. Although no government contracts were given for this model it is considered by collectors as a martial piece.

5A-063

First Model. Loading gate hinged at top.

Narrow grip:
5A-063   Values—Good **$1,100**   Fine **$3,750**

Flared grip:
5A-064   Values—Good **$1,400**   Fine **$5,000**

Second Model. Loading gate hinged at bottom.

Flared grip:
5A-065   Values—Good **$950**   Fine **$3,500**

Narrow grip:
5A-066   Values—Good **$875**   Fine **$3,000**

Allen & Wheelock Center Hammer Lipfire Navy

Navy Model Center Hammer Lipfire Revolver, a.k.a."3rd Model Lipfire," by Allen & Wheelock. Made c. early 1860s; total quantity about 500.

36 lipfire. 6-shot round cylinder with notches for cartridge lips at rear wall. 8" octagonal barrel; also made in 4", 5", and 6" lengths (7-1/2" reported).

Walnut grips. Blued finish, with casehardened hammer and trigger guard.

Serial (batch) numbered. Barrel marking: ALLEN & WHEELOCK WORCESTER, MASS. U.S./ALLEN'S PATENTS SEPT. 7, NOV. 9, 1858

As with the Army Model Lipfire revolver, the Navy type was discontinued due to infringement pressure from Smith & Wesson. Collectors should not confuse the lipfires with conversions; in fact it appears that the lipfires predated Allen & Wheelock's production of the percussion Center Hammer Army and Navy Revolvers. Although no government contracts were given for this model, it is considered by collectors as a martial piece. Variations as found in the Army Model have not been encountered on this model:

5A-067   Values—Good **$750**   Fine **$2,250**

5A-067

Allen & Wheelock Sidehammer Lipfire Pocket

Pocket Model Sidehammer Lipfire Revolver, (former term 1st Model Lipfire disused), **by Allen & Wheelock.** Made c. early 1860s; total quantity estimated at several hundred.

32 lipfire. 6-shot round cylinder with notches for cartridge lips at rear wall. Barrel lengths of 4", 5", and 6"; octagonal. Cylinder pin entering frame from front section of the barrel lug. Loading gate on frame is locked by long ratchet type (rack and pinion) loading lever unit affixed to left side of barrel just ahead of the cylinder. Variations have been noted in the plate on left side of breech of barrel covering the rack and pinion; early models have noticeable angular shape to right side and will bring a premium value; later, commonly encountered specimens, are evenly rectangular.

Serial numbered. Barrel marking: ALLEN & WHEELOCK WORCESTER, MASS. U.S./ALLEN'S PATENTS SEPT. 7, NOV. 9, 1858, JULY 3, 1860. Specimens also known and worth premium bearing ETHAN ALLEN & CO.markings.

This rather unusual design featured the spur trigger combined with the sidehammer associated with percussion Allen & Wheelocks, and the cylinder, barrel lug, and cylinder pin arrangement associated with the Center Hammer percussion and lipfire models. This model was made in lipfire only, and is not to be confused with conversions:

5A-068   Values—Good **$450**   Fine **$1,750**

5A-068

Allen & Wheelock Center Hammer Lipfire Pocket Revolver

Pocket Model Center Hammer Lipfire Revolver, a.k.a.,"4th Model Lipfire," by Allen & Wheelock. Made c. 1861-1863. Total quantity estimated less than 200.

25 caliber lipfire. 7-shot round cylinder with notches for cartridge lips at rear. Octagon 3" barrel. Easily distinguished by

5A-069

its solid frame, spur trigger contours and the small circular sideplate on left frame with the retaining screw off-center. Although one known specimen bears Allen & Wheelock markings (very rare), this model is normal and correct with the complete absence of makers markings:

5A-069   Values—Good **$375**   Fine **$1,150**

COMMENTARY ABOUT A&W LIPFIRE REVOLVERS: Quite a few were converted after manufacture to accept rimfire (and in some instances, centerfire) cartridges. Alterations possible by A&W, but never proven; generally assumed such conversions were accomplished by parties unknown. Details about the various methods of conversion are best read in *Ethan Allen and A&W: Their Guns* by P. Henry (q.v.). Decidedly collectible,; their values usually lessened by 25 percent, often greater.

Allen 32 Sidehammer Rimfire Revolver

32 Sidehammer Rimfire Revolver by Allen & Wheelock and Ethan Allen & Co. Made c. 1859-1862; total quantity estimated over 1,000.

32 rimfire (with 6-shot cylinder). Barrel lengths from 2-7/8" to 5"; all barrels octagonal. Iron frame standard. A few specimens with brass frames are known and may be considered rare. It is believed they are to be found only on the Third Model.

Walnut grips. Blued finish.

Serial (batch) numbered. Barrel marking: ALLEN & WHEELOCK WORCESTER, MASS. U.S./ALLEN'S PATENTS SEPT. 7, NOV. 9, 1858 On the frame of most specimens made after this date: JULY 3, 1860. Cylinder scene of dogs chasing rabbit (often very lightly rolled) is observed on some, but not all specimens; usually encountered on earlier production only.

As with the 22 caliber Sidehammer series, the styling is typical of most Allen & Wheelock revolvers, and the cylinder pin usually enters from forward of the barrel lug. A number of variations will be found (classified into at least eight distinct types), but three basic variants are significant in terms of pricing. Some lesser details will affect price slightly. First and second models have the so-called "quick drop" shape to handle (see illustration) while the handle of third model noticeably arches more evenly, resembling the handle of the Smith & Wesson Model 2 Army. First and second models also have mortised front sights while most third models are often fitted with blade type sights.

First Model; identified by obtuse angle, rounded contoured profile at rear of topstrap (where hammer enters frame). Cylinder pins of button head type, secured by screw entering front of frame. Abrupt drop grip profile. Does not include the JULY 3, 1860 date stamping:

5A-070   Values—Good **$275**   Fine **$950**

Second model; front of topstrap (over the cylinder) is bevelled (i.e. curved) gradually to meet barrel; rear of strap at right angle to hammer at its point of entry. JULY 3, 1860 date marking usually present on frame:

5A-071   Values—Good **$250**   Fine **$850**

**5A-070
First Model**

**5A-071
Second Model**

**5A-072
Third Model**

Third model; front of topstrap machined down (narrower) and has concave slope to where it meets barrel. JULY 3, 1860 frame marking usually present. Later specimens have ETHAN ALLEN & CO. barrel markings, with 1858 and 1861 patent dates:

Long 1-1/8" cylinder type (as shown):
5A-072   Values—Good **$225**   Fine **$675**

Short 1" cylinder type:
5A-072.5   Values—Good **$200**   Fine **$625**

Allen 22 Sidehammer Rimfire Revolver

22 Sidehammer Rimfire Revolver made by Allen & Wheelock, Ethan Allen & Co. Made c. 1858-1865; total quantity estimated over 1,500.

22 rimfire; 7-shot cylinder. Barrel lengths from 2-1/4" to 4". All barrels octagonal. Iron frame; a few specimens with brass

frames and others with part octagon/part round barrels are known and may be considered quite rare.

Walnut grips. Blued finish.

Serial (batch) numbered. Barrel marking: ALLEN & WHEELOCK WORCESTER, MASS. U.S./ALLEN'S PATENTS SEPT. 7, NOV. 9, 1858

On the frame (on most specimens made after date): JULY 3, 1860. Cylinders on issues one through six are engraved with five circular panels depicting mounted rider, standing Indian (seal of Massachusetts), ship and other military trophy designs.

These distinctive sidehammer pistols feature the typical styling of most Allen & Wheelock revolvers, and the cylinder pin usually enters forward of the barrel lug. Quite a few variations will be found in these models, and eight distinct types are known. The most important of these are listed below. Many lesser variants will affect price slightly.

Quite a few of these side-hammer 22s are encountered in original factory wooden cases (usually with a panel inside bored to accept numerous rounds of rimfire cartridges...and value will at least double, often much more). There is also a very rare type of case made of Gutta-percha (usually black a.k.a. "hard rubber") fitted especially for this model. The outer cover is designed with high relief scroll work.

5A-073

Early model; cylinder pin of long, narrow, round shape entering from rear; hammer strikes to right of center; grip frame has comparatively sharp drop. Grooved topstrap for sighting. *Scarce:*
5A-073   Values—Good **$275**   Fine **$900**

5A-074

Second issue; with short button tip cylinder pin entering from front of frame with large retaining screw under forward section of frame, and hammer strikes at center; grooved topstrap for sighting; very scarce:
5A-074   Values—Good **$300**   Fine **$950**
Third issue; rear entry cylinder pin with short projecting button tip; V-notch rear sight; beveled type frame; considered the scarcest type:
5A-075   Values—Good **$375**   Fine **$1,000**

5A-076

Minor details identify the **Fourth, Fifth, Sixth, and Seventh issues,** values of which are about equal. Watch for front entry cylinder pin, V-notch rear sight at back section of topstrap, quick drop and later more gradually curving grip profile, and (Seventh Issue) name change in markings to Ethan Allen & Co:
5A-076   Values—Good **$150**   Fine **$500**

5A-077

Eighth issue; has bird's head shape grips, small sideplate, and the Ethan Allen & Co. or E. Allen & Co. markings. It later was made under the Forehand and Wadsworth name:
5A-077   Values—Good **$175**   Fine **$450**

Allen & Wheelock 32 Center Hammer S/S

32 Center Hammer Single Shot Pistol by Allen & Wheelock. Made c. early 1860s; total quantity between 500 and 1,000.

32 rimfire caliber. Full octagonal or part octagonal/part round barrel, usually of 4" or 5" length; pivots to the right for loading and found both with and without automatic ejection.

Walnut grips. Blued or nickel plated finish.

Serial (batch) numbered. Barrel marking: ALLEN & WHEELOCK/WORCESTER, MASS.

An unusual deringer type pistol, the frame and hammer profiles show the Allen & Wheelock styling. The top of the recoil shield has a projecting lip which covers the breech of the barrel and fits at forward edge into a grooved recess near breech of barrel. Two distinct overhang or projecting lip sizes are noted: (a) the short lip which terminates at point where barrel is grooved; (b) the long lip which extends 1/4" beyond the barrel groove.

Part octagon/part round barrels (found with or without ejector):

Long overlap or lip:
5A-078   Values—Good **$225**   Fine **$550**

5A-079

5A-081

Short overlap or lip:
5A-079   Values—Good **$250**   Fine **$600**

Made without lip:
5A-080   Values—Good **$175**   Fine **$500**

Octagon barrels (found with or without ejector);

Long overlap:
5A-081   Values—Good **$225**   Fine **$650**

Short overlap:
5A-082   Values—Good **$250**   Fine **$700**

Made without overlap (Note: hammer profile should be identical to that shown for others of this model):
5A-083   Values—Good **$275**   Fine **$675**

5A-083

Allen 22 Center Hammer Single Shot

22 Center Hammer Single Shot Pistol. Made by Allen & Wheelock and E. Allen & Co., c. early 1860s. Total quantity limited.

22 rimfire caliber. Except for rare variation as noted below barrels are part round/part octagon varying from 2" to 5-1/2"; pivots to right for loading; with or without automatic ejection. Finish, serial markings as on 32 caliber size, but frames are smaller and with scooped out, flat sides. Known markings include ALLEN & WHEELOCK, E. ALLEN & CO.

5A-084

5A-085

5A-086

Square butt style; iron frame only:
5A-084   Values—Good **$175**   Fine **$550**

Bird's head butt style; iron frame (brass scarce; will bring premium):
5A-085   Values—Good **$150**   Fine **$450**

Early variation; full octagon barrel and rounded iron frame as seen on the 32 caliber style; observed with and without crowned muzzle; rare:
5A-086   Values—Good **$325**   Fine **$950**

E. Allen & Co. Vest Pocket Deringer

5A-087

22 Vest Pocket Single Shot Deringer by E. Allen & Co. c. 1869-1871. Total quantity estimated several thousand.

22 rimfire, breech loaded. Brass frame. 2" octagon/round barrel. Pivots to right for loading; made without extractor.

Serial (batch) numbered.

Walnut grips. Blued or plated barrel with brass frames bright. Barrel marking E. ALLEN & CO. MAKERS.

One of smallest American made deringer type pistols; overall measures just 4":
5A-087   Values—Good **$275**   Fine **$750**

E. Allen & Co. 32 Deringer

5A-088

32 Deringer Pistol by E. Allen & Co. Made c.1865 to 1871. Total quantity very limited; believed less than the 41 Deringer.

32 rimfire breechloader. Part round/part octagon barrels with lengths known 2", 3-1/2" and 4" (barrel thicknesses vary also; both thin and thick walled); 6" barrel rare, worth premium. Pivots to the right for loading; automatic extraction.

Walnut grips; iron frame; bird's head butt. Blued or plated finish. Brass frame rare; worth premium.

Serial numbered. Barrel markings: E. ALLEN & CO WORCESTER MASS./ALLEN'S PAT MCH.7. 1865.Large frame and handle size about same as the 41 Deringer but contours unique to this model. Very scarce:
5A-088   Values—Good **$250**   Fine **$650**

E. Allen & Co. 41 Deringer

41 Deringer Pistol by E. Allen & Co. Made c. 1865-1871; total quantity very limited; estimated at under 2,000.

41 rimfire breechloader. Barrel part round, part octagon or full octagon, usually of 2-1/2" to 2-7/8" length. Pivots to the right for loading and automatic extraction.

Walnut grips. Blued or plated finish.

Serial numbered. Barrel marking: E. ALLEN & CO./WORCESTER MASS. and ALLEN'S PAT. MCH 7 1865.

First model; as above, with part round, part octagon barrel:
5A-089   Values—Good **$675**   Fine **$2,250**
Second model; as above, but with octagon barrel; less often seen:
5A-090   Values—Good **$750**   Fine **$2.500**

5A-089
First Model

Allen & Wheelock Single Shot Center Hammer Muzzle-Loading Rifle

5A-091

Single Shot Muzzle-Loading Center Hammer Percussion Rifle by Allen & Wheelock (a.k.a. "No. 10 Inside Cock"). Made c. 1850s. Quantity unknown; very limited.

Made in various calibers and barrel lengths. Also made as a smoothbore shotgun.

Iron mountings; lock casehardened, the barrel browned. Wooden ramrod beneath barrel.

Walnut buttstock with crescent shaped buttplate; no forestock. Stock usual; earlier production had narrow iron forend.

Serial numbered. Barrel marking: ALLEN & WHEELOCK

A distinctive feature is the center hung hammer slightly offset to the right to allow for sighting, and the long integral iron frame extending full length of the wrist. *Rare*:

5A-091   Values—Good **$450**   Fine **$1,500**

Allen Single Shot Sidehammer Muzzleloader

5A-092

Single Shot Muzzle-Loading Sidehammer Percussion Rifle by Allen & Wheelock, Allen & Thurber, Allen Thurber & Co. Made c. 1840s into early 1860s. Total quantity estimated at a few hundred.

Various calibers; octagonal barrels, varying in length and weight, but generally around 28" to 32".

Iron mountings; lock area generally casehardened; the barrel browned.

Walnut buttstock, patchbox sometimes present. Buttplate usually crescent style, although shotgun type encountered. Iron or German silver forend. Wooden ramrod beneath barrel.

Serial numbered.

Markings known indicating manufacture by Allen & Wheelock, Allen & Thurber, and Allen Thurber & Co. Note that barrels were made available to the trade, and these will sometimes be observed retaining Allen markings, the balance of the weapon being by an individual gunsmith. A distinctive Allen feature is the metal frame extending back to form the straight grip. In arriving at an evaluation, consideration must be given not only to condition, but to quality of workmanship, sights, engraving (if present), patchbox. Values shown are for plain, unembellished specimens. This model may be encountered in a great many variations and varying degrees of decoration (i.e., engraving) with special sights or buttplates, false muzzle, patchbox, etc., all of which will affect value upwards, with considerable increases for elaborate, fine condition specimens:

5A-092   Values—Good **$600**   Fine **$2,750**

Allen Combination Rifle-Shotgun

Combination Rifle-Shotgun, with Side-by-Side or Over-Under Barrels by Allen & Thurber, and Allen Thurber & Co., Allen & Wheelock and E. Allen & Co. Percussion muzzle-loader. Made c. 1840s into the late 1860s; total quantity limited.

Caliber/gauge combinations known include what may be the standard, 38 caliber and 12 gauge. Barrel lengths about 28" to 34".

Iron mountings.

5A-094

Walnut buttstock and forend, patchbox may be present. Wooden ramrod beneath barrel.

Serial numbered. Barrel rib markings of the four types as indicated above.

These arms are very scarce and very little information is known or recorded about them. Values shown are for plain specimens. As with the preceding single shot percussion rifle, any embellishments or accessories will alter price upwards: Side-by-Side:

5A-093   Values—Good **$875**   Fine **$3,500**
Over/Under:
5A-094   Values—Good **$1,100**   Fine **$4,000**

Allen & Wheelock Sidehammer Breechloader

5A-095

Breech-Loading Sidehammer Percussion Rifle by Allen & Wheelock. Made c. 1855-1860; total quantity less than 500.

36 to 50 caliber. Barrel lengths vary; part round, part octagon. The breech mechanism often known as the "FAUCET" or "TAP" breech, due to the lever opening device's resemblance to a water faucet. Takedown feature apparently standard on all models. Takedown bolt on underside of frame.

Iron mountings; lock casehardened, the barrel browned.

Walnut stocks, with earlier specimens sometimes having patchbox.

Serial numbered. Barrel marking: ALLEN & WHEELOCK/ALLEN'S PATENT JULY 3, 1855 Also marked AT & CO. inside the lockplate.

This quite distinctive rifle is further evidence of the tremendous versatility of Allen. The unusual breechloader is encountered in many different variations of style and quality, all of which will affect value upwards and add premiums; a number of fine engraved specimens have also been encountered. At least one of these "tap actions" is known as a military model carbine with a number of distinctive features not seen on others. It is assumed made for military trials of the post-Civil War era; documentary evidence has yet to surface:

5A-095   Values—Good **$750**   Fine **$3,500**

Allen Thurber & Co. Other Rifles and Shotguns

Other Allen Thurber & Co. Rifles and Shotguns.

An Allen Thurber & Co. advertisement of c. 1854-1856 notes the company was manufacturing (among other products) "Double Rifles, Double Rifle and Shot, Single and Double Shot Guns." The collector may expect therefore to locate some specimens within those categories not covered in the present volume. Specimens of percussion single barrel and side by side double barrel shotguns are illustrated in the Mouillesseaux and

Henry books, but at present very little data is available. An approximate value guide can be gained by consideration of figures given for more common types, bearing in mind that usually single barrel percussion shotguns were a mass market item, and thus generally of comparatively low value.

As with other Allen rifles and shotguns, these types may be found in various qualities, grades of workmanship and extra embellishments, all of which will affect values upwards

5A-096

5A-097

depending on their importance to the gun. Values reflected below are for plainest grades.

Side lock double barrel 12 gauge percussion shotgun: 26" damascus barrels. Broad scroll engraving on locks and hammers. Each lock marked E. ALLEN & CO. MAKERS One-piece walnut stock with checkered wrist. Also made in 16 gauge and worth small premium:

5A-096   Values—Good **$400**   Fine **$1,250**

Iron frame, sidehammer double barrel 10 gauge and 12 gauge percussion shotgun: Rounded iron frame with protruding square take down bolt (requires wrench) on underside. 30" and 32" damascus barrels. Marked on center rib of barrels ALLEN & WHEELOCK/WORCESTER or ALLEN & THURBER/WORCESTER Two-piece walnut stock and forend:

5A-097   Values—Good **$350**   Fine **$1,000**

Allen Thurber & Co. Whaling Gun

5A-097.3

Large, heavy percussion, muzzle-loading whaling gun for shoulder firing whale harpoon or an explosive whale bomb lance (the latter most often used.) c. 1854-1856. Quantity unknown; extremely rare.

Known recorded specimens with 1-1/8" bore; thick wall 22" part octagon/round barrel (outside diameter at muzzle 2"); iron frame with side hammer; 38" overall; weight 24 pounds. Walnut stock; iron buttplate. No provision made for ramrod. Marked on barrel ALLEN THURBER & CO / WORCESTER and NO. 2 / CAST STEEL.

Further research may reveal an intriguing story. The most widely made and used of this style bomb lance guns were those of C. C. Brand of Norwich, Conn., whose whaling guns are unmarked (q.v.). His best known has an heavy, iron, skeleton stock cast integral with the frame; the earliest attributed to him has a walnut stock and closely similar (with but minor variation) to ALLEN'S WHALING GUN (etc.) WITH IMPROVEMENTS BY C.C. BRAND. The use of that name may be mere coincidence as it refers to Oliver Allen of Norwich, Conn. inventor of a bomb lance in 1846, believed to have first designed the gun.

C.C. Brand guns were sold in three sizes, the "No. 1" with 7/8" bore; "No. 2" 1-1/8" bore; "No. 3" 1-1/4" bore; weights varying accordingly. Thus far only the No.2 size has been recorded for the ALLEN THURBER & CO. marked gun:

5A-097.3   Values—Good **$4,500**   Fine **$7,500**

Allen Thurber & Co. Punt or Market Hunter's Gun

5A-097.5

Massive size, percussion, muzzle-loading half stock fowling piece made by Allen Thurber & Co. c.1854-1856. Quantity unknown but would have been extremely limited. Very rare.

Known, recorded specimen 4 gauge; 35" part octagon/round barrel. Unique, massive 7-1/4" lockplate (illus. shows standard lock next to gun for comparison); weight 18 lbs. Marked on both the barrel and lock ALLEN THURBER & CO / WORCESTER

5A-097.5   Values—Good **$1,750**   Fine **$4,000**

Allen Drop Breech Rimfire Rifle

Drop Breech Single-Shot Rimfire Rifle (a.k.a. "Falling Block Rifle") by Allen & Wheelock, Ethan Allen & Co. Made c. 1860-1870s; total quantity estimated at 1,500 - 2,000.

Variety of rimfire calibers 22 through 44 (a number of these viewed with later conversions to centerfire). Both the smallest and largest calibers scarcer and usually bring premium values. Varying length barrels (usually part octagon/part round) 23 to 28 inches average; others known. Iron frame standard (brass frames extremely rare and worth substantial premium). Two frame sizes; largest calibers (usually 42 and 44 RF on larger frame). Sides of frames observed with flat or rounded configurations. Some specimens of both size frames were fitted

with a simple take-down feature whereby barrel could be easily separated from frame and removed (by a small pin easily knocked out on frame; larger frames on later production with a tapered square-headed screw). Trigger guard acts as lever to open breech and eject cartridge; hammer cocked manually. Rear sight lever mounted on left side of frame with lever to manually elevate or lower; graduated numeral markings to pre-set. Sights on late manufacture replace with leaf type.

Iron mountings; blued barrel; case hardened frame, hammer and trigger guard.

Walnut buttstock and forend observed with many variations; some fitted with sling swivels and metal forend caps.

5A-098

Serial numbered. Barrel marking: ALLEN & WHEELOCK/ALLEN'S PAT. SEPT. 18, 1860 or E. ALLEN & CO./WORCESTER MASS/ALLEN'S PATENT. SEPT. 18, 1860

The hammer profile and trigger guard operation show the distinct styling of certain Allen & Wheelock arms. Short barreled, large caliber specimens with sling swivels are often considered by collectors as a secondary martial type carbine, and bring a slightly higher value as do takedown models. Quite a few of this type are found with the FOREHAND & WADSWORTH markings; prices will be approximately the same as Allen marked specimens. This well-known Allen rifle is encountered in many different qualities and grades including engraved specimens, fancy wood and checkering; varying buttplates, etc. Values adjusted upwards depending on the embellishments and quality of engraving. Much information and illustrations of variations and qualities of the "Drop Breech" rifle in the P. Henry work; see Biblio.):

5A-098 Values—Good **$325** Fine **$1,200**
Rifle with special "Allen Patent 1860" (marked) rotary disk tang peep sight:
5A-098.5 Values—Good **$475** Fine **$1,400**

Allen & Wheelock Lipfire Revolving Rifle

5A-099

Lipfire Revolving Rifle by Allen & Wheelock. Made c. 1861-1863; total estimated less than 100.

44 lipfire. 6-shot round cylinder with cuts to allow projection of lip at breech for firing. Barrel length approximately 26" to 28", round with octagon breech section.

Iron mountings; blued, with casehardened frame, hammer, and trigger guard. Walnut buttstock and forend; note crescent shaped buttplate. Trigger guard operates the ejector rod for cartridges.

Serial numbered. The few specimens known do not bear marker's markings.

Based on the Army Model Center Hammer Lipfire revolver, Allen & Wheelock was attempting to add still another variation of firearm to their diverse line. The result for today's collector was one of the scarcest of revolving rifles:
5A-099 Values—Good **$5,500** Fine **$20,000**

Allen & Wheelock Percussion Revolving Rifle

5A-100

Percussion Revolving Rifle by Allen & Wheelock. Made c. 1861-1863. Estimated less than 20.

44 caliber percussion. 6-shot. 26" and 28" round barrels known, but lengths can vary. Rammer operated by moving forward the trigger guard. Variations noted in few known specimens and all are considered as experimental pieces.

On the few specimens known no maker's markings appear. Very rare:
5A-100 Values—Good **$8,000** Fine **$22,500**

Allen "Hinge-Breech" Double Shotgun

5A-101

Breech-Loading Double Barrel "Hinge-Breech" Shotgun by Ethan Allen & Co. Made c. 1865-1871; quantity estimated at several hundred or more.

10, or 12 gauge; barrel lengths about 28" (an 8 gauge reported and would be rare). These unusual arms, covered by Allen patents of 1865 and 1868, had the novel feature of a trapdoor breech fitted with a locking lever/handle.

Serial numbered. Breech trapdoor marked ETHAN ALLEN & CO./WORCESTER, MASS. On barrels: FINE LAMINATED STEEL.

Walnut stocks, checkered.

Produced in three grades, the pricing provided herein is based on the standard, lowest production type, which will be rather plain, and lacking the fancy features of deluxe engraving and checkering as found on the best grade pieces. An unusual accessory, and extreme rarity if proven original, is a steel chamber insert or short (auxiliary) rifled barrel for use in this piece allowing for the use of rifle cartridges:

5A-101   Values—Good **$450**   Fine **$1,500**

Chapter V-B

Colt Firearms

I n the world of antique arms collecting, there is no name more illustrious than that of Colt. In the hearts of many it is synonymous with the American revolver. From their beginnings in 1837, the guns of this maker have a proud and distinct association with virtually every event in American history in war and peace where weapons were used and carried. The quality of the product which led to its ultimate great and lasting success, joined with the fact that many models were manufactured in large quantities, are two major reasons in making Colt collecting vie for top honors as one of the most actively pursued specialties in the arms field. More simply stated, the commercial success of Colt, their longevity and the high production quantities, have afforded more collectors an opportunity to acquire specimens of a broad range of models. Not a few rare American handguns will bring less than half the price of a common Colt merely because the demand has yet to be created for them, nor may they offer either the collecting possibilities or historical associations that the often far commoner Colt does. The collector may well ponder this simply stated fact; it affords interesting possibilities for the future-looking collector on a long range basis.

The lure of Colt collecting is a strong one, pointed out by both the sheer numbers of collectors and the quantity of published works on the subject. Competition for specimens is spirited and very minute variations of seemingly minor points can often cause very great price fluctuations within a single type. Undoubtedly the broadest spread of values can be found within Colt collecting with prices for the commonest specimens starting around $100 and a few extreme rarities and ultra fancy historic specimens achieving prices in the high six figures! By far, the majority of Colts are valued in the three to lower four-figure price range.

Of no small significance in this field is the amount of published data available to the serious collector. Writers have been more prolific about Colts than any other antique weapon. There are a number of extremely fine reference works easily available to verify all major points on every model as well as a vast wealth of related minutiae. The two necessary classics in the Colt field are *The Book of Colt Firearms* (Sutherland and Wilson) and *Colt Firearms From 1836* (Serven). The field is so vast that the collector often specializes within it, e.g., by collecting only percussion Colts or cartridge models; he may even limit himself further by pursuing only Model 1849 Pocket revolvers or Model 1851 Navies, or Single Actions. In each of these three fields a very large and interesting collection is possible. Each also has a number of well documented and researched reference works available dwelling at great length on the most finite of details. Surprisingly, with all the known facts about Colts, published

and otherwise, there is always new and fresh information appearing on the subject. Here is an endless source for the researcher; veritably a bottomless mine allowing for extensive and varied investigation.

As previously mentioned, some often innocuous appearing variations and differences can cause great fluctuations in values. In no other specialty are these nuances more evident than with Colts; it is well worth understanding and learning these subtle distinctions as they could make quite a difference in values.

Generally speaking "condition" is the key word in Colt collecting and Colt prices. Seemingly minor differences in condition often cause considerable variance in price. The earlier the gun and the rarer the model, the more this price difference becomes apparent with changes in condition. The percentage of original finish remaining on the gun is extremely important. The condition of that finish—that is, whether it is bright and untouched looking or has been dulled and worn—is equally important. Like acquiring a taste for fine wine, a well-turned ankle or good horse flesh, the talent for judging finish is an acquired one and likely mastered with considerable more ease!

This Colt section lists in chronological order of manufacture every Colt model made from the first Paterson, New Jersey, product to the early double action revolvers and automatics at the turn of the century. The cut-off point was arbitrarily chosen for the models generally considered by the collecting field as the "antique" types. It can be accurately stated that all Colts have a collectibility; most certainly those in which production has ceased. As quite a few such arms fall in the area considered "modern," they were not felt suitable for inclusion in this work. An attempt has been made to include every so-called standard or major variation of each model manufactured; however, the reader should take note that the mere fact that a variation he might encounter does not appear within this listing does not necessarily mean that said item is great or rare. It should, though, immediately indicate that further research on that piece is worthwhile—the specimen may very well be worth considerably in excess of the standard type found listed.

Rare Colt variations do show up (most, but not all have been listed in the known reference works) and they can be encountered on almost any model in a wide array of features. Those most obvious are odd barrel lengths or calibers, unusual non-standard markings and possibly even basic changes in contour, most especially in the grip area. At this point a further caution must be stated—do not jump to conclusions! The fact that a piece differs from standard does not necessarily mean that it is original! In the 75 to 160 years that the gun might have been in existence, much could have happened after having left the factory; some changes strictly to satisfy the whims of those who used it. Many interesting alterations were made by competent gunsmiths during the period of use; these have acquired an air of originality through the years. When such alterations prove to be non-factory in origin, they generally do not enhance the value of the gun and might very well detract from it. The possibility is ever present too that some latter-day mechanic with larceny in his soul has "improved" the piece merely to catch the unsuspecting collector. When encountering unusual variations, your own common sense and better judgment will have to take precedence.

Variations are quite difficult to evaluate, especially when they are one-of-a-kind. Such features as unique or extra long or extra short original barrel lengths, or major contour changes might be considered important variations and may very well alter the value anywhere from double to five times normal value or possibly more. Such factors as general condition of the gun, its model and period, must all be taken into account and analyzed in pricing these variations. A very minor, uninteresting variation might only slightly (if at all) affect the price of a very late 19th century cartridge Colt revolver, whereas the same variation encountered on an early single action Colt or percussion revolver could very well double the price. Each must be taken on its own merits and a little detective work must be performed to establish precedence of other similar specimens or pieces of similar importance that have been sold in the past. There is considerable room for enhancing values on such a piece, but it requires effort on the part of the reader to find out just how much!

The most basic check point to be made on an antique Colt is the serial number. On all the percussion revolvers—and on a great many of the later cartridge types—all the major component parts should bear matching serial numbers. On most percussion specimens this check is very simply made by quickly scanning the piece to verify if numbers are all matching. If they do not, this doesn't make the gun any less of a collector's item, but that fact does make it less valuable. An antique Colt Model 1860 revolver used in the Civil War and now with mismatching numbers on some parts (for instance, the barrel number does not match that of the rest of the gun), is still a genuine Civil War military used revolver that very likely was reassembled in the field during the heat of combat (for the parts were interchangeable) with no thought given to the collector's value 140 years hence! The gun is just as romantic as one with matched numbers and may even have some known history attached to it, but from the collector's point of view and the dollars to be placed on it, it just cannot bring what the matched number revolver does. Depending on the condition and quality of it, price can fall anywhere from 10 percent to 50 percent of the matched number specimen.

A further word about numbers. On minor parts such as the barrel wedge, if unnumbered or mismatched, the price is rarely affected. There are some purists who will not want that gun with the mismatched wedge number in their collection and it might be slightly more difficult to sell, but its value is the same whether the number matches or not. A mismatched number on a loading lever will most definitely detract from the value, but if the condition matches the gun, the mismatched number will probably affect it only 10 percent or less. A mismatched number on any other major piece is serious as far as value is concerned. It will be found that sometimes collectors blink their eyes at a mismatched number—almost as if it did not exist. This is true only on a superlative specimen that might be mint or about mint condition. If that mismatched number appears on a major part, yet the part matches in condition, it will be found that the mint or near mint gun will still fetch just about (though not quite as much) as the matched number specimen. This seems to occur only on pieces in superlative condition, but again, there is a definite sales resistance to them on the part of many collectors. The only other major numbering error that does seem to occasionally occur and which has a valid background, is a transposed digit. Colts were all hand-numbered with individual die stamps for each digit and human errors did occur. For instance a Colt Model 1851 Navy with all matching numbers 5432 has a serial number on the cylinder stamped 5423. It may be taken for granted (especially if the condition of the cylinder matches that of the rest of the gun) that this was merely a defect caused by a workman transposing the two last digits when he hand-stamped the dies. It has been the author's experience that such single transposed numbers might embitter a few purists who would turn up their noses at such a piece, but the majority of collectors would gladly accept the gun and pay exactly the same for it as other matched number pieces. A further tip on inspecting numbers—and worth mention in passing: that is, a piece with a mismatched number which somewhere along the line has been "improved" by matching the number again. The mismatched number had been ground off and then the piece was die stamped with new numbers matching the existing numbers. In almost every example encountered, it is near impossible to match dies perfectly to the existing numbers on the gun. If suspicious, examine the numbers with a magnifying glass. In almost every instance the dies used to stamp the suspicious numbers will not match identically with those of the Colt factory dies; chances are the gun part was spuriously altered.

Original blue finish, as previously mentioned, is a key factor in determining the value of a Colt. To easily outline a simple formula on how to tell original blue finish from reblued is somewhat like trying to describe the color red! For a starter it would be best to compare a known fine original blued Colt with a reblued one. Your eyes should immediately pick up just that right color tone which is Colt's and no one else's. It doesn't take long to acquire the knack of it; just a little care and patience. Original Colt finishes are quite distinctive—especially on antique pieces—and rarely, if ever, have they been accurately duplicated by present-day methods. There are, of course, other dead giveaways to tell if the gun has been refinished. Such material has been covered in the introductory chapters to this book and the reader is referred to them.

A Colt that is sometimes observed and easy to spot as refinished is the piece that has apparently much "original" finish including bluing on the cylinder, yet no cylinder engraved scene remains. A classic excuse is "… It must have been one that left the factory without engraving." Well that just isn't the case and it didn't happen, so watch out for those types. Another matter of interest and a point worth bearing in mind is the feature of cylinder engraving on antique Colts. When these scenes do appear on many models, the design was rolled into the steel of the cylinder under very heavy pressure, making an indentation in the surface. Hence, it takes quite an amount of wear to obliterate these designs. When a piece appears that apparently has considerable original finish on most of the gun and yet the cylinder design is worn smooth and cannot be seen, it is also a good time to look it over very closely; chances are there has been some type of alteration to the gun. It is just plain common sense that the blue finish—which is merely a super thin surface-applied coloration—would wear much more quickly than the deep die impressed designs on the metal itself. There is, of course, considerably more to Colt collecting than these few pointers; they are, though, a good start for the uninitiated gun trader!

A little further discussion of finish; blue versus nickel. On Colts, especially with the later cartridge revolvers and automatics, the choice condition specimens (those mint or near mint), will fetch about equal prices for blue or nickel when that finish is normally found and is standard to the piece. When finish shows wear and declines, there then exists a decided value difference. A gun with 70 percent blue finish is considered quite fine and is usually quite appealing to the eye; that very same gun with only 70 percent nickel finish remaining very often has a blemished or spotted appearance and might very well show considerable hard wear as well. From the point of view of original preservation, nickel was by far the sturdier, harder wearing finish; from the point of view of esthetics to the collector, nickel doesn't quite stack up to the blued guns after it shows some wear. Thus, as a general rule-of-thumb, for guns that are not mint or near mint, blued finish specimens are in somewhat higher demand and more eagerly sought after as they generally have a better appearance. Also, that same blued gun will normally fetch more in price than the same model with an identical percentage of nickel remaining. This principle is certainly not hard and fast, many exceptions exist depending on the individual specimen.

Bore conditions on Colts are often important in establishing or affecting values. This is especially true with later cartridge types of large size and caliber and a number of the cartridge rifles and shotguns. Generally bores do not play an important role in pricing the percussion revolvers, although a very poor or deteriorated bore with a major defect very likely will detract from the price. On the big single and double action cartridge revolvers and especially those in target grades as well as the lever action and pump action rifles, bore is quite important to consider when arriving at value and it should at least match in grade the exterior condition of that piece. In many other instances bore will not affect the value one way or the other, but it most decidedly will influence the desirability for that particular piece on the collector's market. A number of collectors might immediately rule a piece out unless the bore is fine; likewise there are others who just do not care.

Fancy original factory engraved specimens will be found in every model of Colt. All engraved Colts are desirable and all are considerably more valuable than plain specimens. After that generality, it becomes a new ball game for the collector or dealer trying to evaluate a piece in monetary terms. Considerable care and study should be given before determining same. Fortunately the subject is treated in a number of works and is covered at great depth in the classic *The Book of Colt Engraving* by R. L. Wilson.

From Colt's beginnings at Paterson, New Jersey, and continuing through to present day, the Colt factories have employed engravers to work full-time for them decorating arms for special presentation or gift purposes or at the request and order of their customers. Earliest pieces are usually decorated very sparsely with floral and scroll motifs. As the years progressed, designs became more elaborate and lavish. Factory engravers are often unknown; most master engravers are known by name and style. Engraved specimens are usually priced by the model on which these designs and motifs appear. Some are very often encountered like the Model 1849 Pocket revolver and the small 22 caliber "Open Top" spur trigger revolver. Style of engraving and quality are factors influencing value; some patterns are very commonly found while others are rare; extremely deep engraving in which the designs appear to be in high relief is a very rare style as are panels on various parts of the gun in which patriotic motifs or portraits or unusual scenes appear. Original gold or silver inlays are great rarities, seen only on the most elaborate Colt arms. Condition plays a highly important role on engraved guns also. Engraving on the very early pieces, that is, the Paterson series, the Dragoons, Baby Dragoon and Wells Fargo models, are among the least encountered, and hence, some of the more valuable. It is on these fancy engraved specimens of all types that competition and bidding is the keenest. At the very least, and the lowest quality and condition, the presence of engraving will at a minimum double the price. From that point on, it is up to the reader to do some leg work. To be noted and *well remembered*: In the engraved

Colt line some of the most flagrant violations in the ethics of arms collecting are found. Demand has always been so strong and the market so wide for engraved Colts that spurious specimens have been circulating for quite some time, many of them almost beginning to acquire the patina of age! Forewarned is forearmed.

Grips are an important facet of Colt collecting. Usual factory installed grips were walnut; specimens herein are priced for their standard factory installed types. The factory on many occasions, especially on fancy engraved pieces, used more exotic materials such as ivory, pearl or burled and circassian grained wood; a few very rare specimens were even custom stocked with wood from the famed Connecticut Charter Oak tree (some are so marked). Assuming that grips are in good condition, (that is, not broken, chipped, cracked or badly worn) original factory plain, uncarved ivory or pearl grips on smaller specimens are worth a minimum of $75 extra and at a minimum $100 to $175 extra on the large models. On rare models or extremely early models, fancy grips would be worth considerably more. Seemingly minor features such as original checkering on ivory grips—if established as factory work—would bring an added premium. Factory grips bearing high relief carving (usually encountered with patriotic, military or eagle motifs) would immediately place them in the scarce, often rare, category and at least $400 should be added—providing they are in sound condition. Price could be increased considerably depending on elaborateness and quality of carving. Again, a word of caution is offered: Grips should be inspected very closely to determine originality. As prices are high and demand great, these too have brought forth a whole host of spurious specimens.

Early ivory grips are usually one piece; later types appear as one piece but have a wood block in center joining them. Almost all pearl grips are two piece. First use of the gilt medallion with rampant horse trademark, deeply inset in grip, was 1911; after 1920 the medallion was flush with surface.

Cased outfits are often encountered in Colt collecting. It was a common occurrence during the day of their manufacture to sell complete sets. Standard casings normally consisted of: A walnut box with velvet lining over the compartmented type interior; the revolver itself; a number of accessories including a two-cavity bullet mold, a powder flask (often marked "Colt's Patent," but not always), a combination screwdriver-nipple wrench, possibly a packet of cartridges and a small canister of percussion caps. Cased sets are most often encountered in the percussion series and are quite scarce in later cartridge models. Most often seen is the Model 1849 Pocket revolver, followed by the Model 1851 Navy. From that point on the scarcity increases noticeably. The earliest revolvers of the Paterson series and those in the Dragoon series are very rare. Generally, the commonest type case, that is, for the 1849 Pocket model, may be worth by itself $1,000 to $2,000, while in the 1851 Navy size, it would be worth, in very fine condition, approximately $3,000 (empty) on the current collector's market. Occasionally a rare form of case is encountered such as a double size or even a triple size, considered great rarities. Another highly desirable type is the so-called "French Style", usually made of an elaborately grained, exotic wood, often brass edged and having a lining of plush materials which is recessed in contour shape specially fitted for the specific gun; accessories are usually extra fancy also. Such cases are highly sought after and, depending on their condition, can add considerably to the gun. The collector is cautioned to carefully inspect any Colt case encountered. This has been an especially lucrative area for the unscrupulous for the past 50 years. There are but few general rules-of-thumb for spotting a fake case and no definitive guides. It takes a little experience and know-how; but a few of the most basic features are mentioned here. For starters, turn the case over and see what the underside looks like. If there is no wear on it at all (or only the slightest) or it has been heavily refinished, then be wary. A genuine case always shows considerable wear on the underside and the wood itself is unfinished and will have acquired a nice patina that only age can give it. Following that, take a good look at the compartmenting and the overall fit. Genuine cases were well made by competent workmen; this is where many fakers fall down. Another feature worth checking is the condition of the material and the point where aging occurs. Normally a gun sitting in a case for a century will have caused certain indentations, grease marks and stains and there will be a certain amount of fading. None of these features will offer proof positive as to the originality of the case, but they are good starting points. Printed paper labels, usually "DIRECTIONS FOR LOADING" are often found intact, affixed to the inner lid of a Colt casing. They add interest and desirability to the outfit and possibly a small premium to value. Such labels have been copied, falsely aged and added to outfits to make them more attractive. They are most often encountered on mediocre conditioned outfits or an antique box relined to resemble an authentic Colt case. They should be closely examined.

Quite a few antique copies and infringements were made of Colt revolvers during the height of their popularity and fame. A few were even made in Europe under license from Col. Colt—most notably the Model 1851 Navy. A number of unauthorized copies of varying degrees of quality were made in Belgium, France, Turkey, Austria, Spain and probably Mexico. Some copies were made as late as the turn of the century or in the early 20th century. All are bona fide antique collector's items and all are certainly considered suitable for inclusion in a Colt collection. Prices vary considerably with style, quality of workmanship, period of manufacture and, of course, condition. Most often encountered are copies of the Model 1851 Navy. Fine conditioned specimens of good workmanship bring comparable prices to the Hartford made Navies, possibly just slightly less. Those of lesser qualities (and there are many) usually bring less than 50 percent of Hartford made pieces. Dragoons were also copied, but not quite as faithfully as the Navies and usually undersized; they are valued considerably less. A few specimens exist of Paterson copies and are considered quite rare if a faithful facsimile. A number of less accurate copies were made only generally following the Colt pattern are considered peripheral to a Colt collection. In the later cartridge era, quite a few copies and spurious infringements were made. Generally speaking they bring considerably less (often but a fraction) than the price of the Colt after which they were fashioned. Quite a few interesting examples of single action infringements exist and represent interesting curiosa in a collection. Price-wise and quality-wise, they are far removed from the Colt made Single Action. Of course, the Confederate copies of Colts are a field to themselves and have been treated as such in their own chapter in this work.

In the last decades, with the popularity of reenactments of Civil War battles and revival of black powder muzzle loading shooting, a wide range of modern made, faithful, recreations of Colt revolvers have been produced and are readily available on the market. A small number of spurious repros, that is, those that have been fake-aged to resemble antiques, have filtered into the antique arms market. There should be no cause for alarm. The collector duped by one has no one to blame but himself. Although some repros have been quite cleverly aged, they rarely, if ever, have been found expert enough to fool even the novice who is armed with but the slightest degree of knowledge and common sense. It is hoped that this statement will not be construed as a challenge to the prospective faker! In every instance encountered or investigated it has been found that anyone selling these fakes knows exactly what they are and that usually the buyer has failed to exercise good judgment. There

are many points about these reproductions that make them quite readily identifiable as such and as yet it has not been found that they are any threat to antique gun collecting. The buyer would do well to steer a wide path around anyone known handling this type of arm and passing them off as genuine antiques. The most often encountered disclaimer by one peddling such weapons, when asked as to its originality, is "…I don't know, that's the way I got it!"

Except for a limited amount of percussion revolvers made at Paterson, New Jersey (1836-42) and their short lived London, England factory (1852-57), all Colt revolvers, regardless of markings on the barrel, were made in the Hartford, Connecticut factories. Although the great bulk of Colt percussion revolvers bear the barrel markings "Address Sam'l Colt - New York City," Colt merely maintained a large sales office there. The barrel markings were applied to take advantage of the name of that famed city since Colt felt that address lent his products more prestige than a Hartford address. The early Colts which bear Hartford markings, most notably those in the Model 1849 Pocket revolver series, had that address applied in order to distinguish them from regular Hartford production; such pieces were actually made from parts shipped back from the closed Colt London factory. Of the *London* marked pieces, basically only the Model 1849 and Model 1851 Navy were made there in quantity. Almost all others, even though bearing *"London"* markings of some type, were most likely made in the Hartford plant. The *"London"* markings were applied in Hartford with the pieces being specifically earmarked for sale abroad and to capture the English market. The complete story of these *"London"* guns and markings can be found discussed at great length in Colt reference works. Many interesting variations appear in them and some are extremely rare.

Low serial numbers are an enticing feature on all Colts. They in no way affect the appearance nor the operation of the piece nor represent a variance of any type; merely an eccentricity of Colt collecting. Anything with three digits or lower is most desirable in a Colt serial number and a premium may be added for it. If a two-digit number is present, the premium would be higher and if a single digit serial number, the premium may possibly double the price. There is no fixed rule and in most instances it is a case of "what the market will bear." One will find that in some cases the number doesn't impress everybody, and with a premium too high, even a top-notch collector would pass it by.

Colt collectors and researchers will be pleased to learn that factory records of serial numbers for some earlier percussion revolvers and the great majority of cartridge models remain in existence and have been maintained to the present. For percussion models the following are available in the specific serial ranges indicated: **Model 1851 Navy Revolver**: serials 98,000 to 132,000; **Model 1861 Navy Revolver**: Serial No. 1 through 12,000; **Model 1860 Army Revolver**: Serial No. 1 through 140,000. Some "**Pocket Model 1849 Revolver**" serials are available (best to inquire first by phone or letter); numbers also available for the **Model 1871-72 Open Top** revolver and all of the **Single Action Armies** through serial number range 343,000 (plus the single-action 44 rimfire. Also, most other cartridge handguns. Limited records are available for the **Colt Lightning Rifles** and most of the double-barrel **1878 and 1883** shotguns as well as other long arms. To acquire a detailed schedule of the varied information available and research fees applicable write to: COLT ARCHIVE PROPERTIES LLC., P.O. Box 1868, Hartford, Conn. 06144-1868 (telephone: 860-236-6311). Recently the archive offered a "premium telephone service" for the Colt Single-Action Revolvers and an "expedited phone service" for all other models.

New collectors will be pleased to learn there is an organization (founded in 1980) that has devoted itself specifically to Colt firearms. In addition to scheduled meetings, members receive a quarterly magazine which includes informative articles about many facets of Colt collecting. For further details, contact: COLT COLLECTORS ASSOCIATION, P.O. BOX 2241, LOS GATOS, CALIFORNIA 95031...or their website: www.coltcollectorsassoc.com.

To acquire a general perspective and time sequence for all Colt models that are listed in this section, a very brief history of the Colt company is useful. The subject has been so widely and well covered in numerous works and at such great length and depth that to attempt a history would do it injustice. A chronological review of Colt company history appears in the appendix of *The Book of Colt Firearms*.

Samuel Colt (1814-1862) inventor of the revolver bearing his name, secured his first patent in February, 1836. A stock company known as the "Patent Arms Manufacturing Company" was formed in 1836 to manufacture these revolvers at Paterson, New Jersey. The company went into bankruptcy in 1842 with considerable litigation ensuing between Colt and the other investors in the immediately following years. During the years 1843 to 1846, Samuel Colt produced no further pistols. In 1847, with the assistance of a U. S. Government contract, he manufactured the famed "Walker Colt" at the factory of Eli Whitney in Whitneyville, Connecticut, and in the following year, 1848, he reestablished himself with his own factory at Hartford, Connecticut, where Colt firearms have been made ever since.

The reader is urged to review the introductory material to this book, giving the exact definition of the NRA Standards which comprise the terms good, very good, fine and excellent.

BIBLIOGRAPHY

*Bady, D. B. *Colt Automatic Pistols*. Los Angeles: Borden Publishing Company, 1955, 1956, 1971 (Revised and enlarged 1973). An important and standard reference for Colt automatics.

Barnard, Henry. *Armsmear*. Hartford: Mrs. Samuel Colt, 1868. With reprint by Beinfeld Publishing Co., North Hollywood, 1978. Biography of Sam Colt by his wife. Considered a rarity amongst Colt collector items.

*Boorman, Dean K. The History of Colt Firearms. London, England: Salamander Books, 2001. Wide coverage; introductory text designed to appeal to a broad audience. Profuse color and b&w illustrations.

*Breslin, J. D., Pirie, W. Q., Price, D. E. Variations of Colt's New Model Police and Pocket Breech-Loading Pistols. Lincoln, Rhode Island: Andrew Mowbray Inc. Publishers, 2002. A type-by-type guide to Colt factory, small-frame conversions from percussion to cartridge of the Model 1862 "Police" and "Pocket Navy" revolvers...many of which were actually made as cartridge pistols. A significant reference.

Brown, David M. *The 36 Calibers of the Colt Single Action Army*. Albuquerque, New Mexico: David M. Brown Publisher, 1965. Mostly a catalog of one-man's collection with emphasis on variations, chambering and markings. Some of the material does not stand up under the light of critical examination.

*Brunner, John W. The Colt Pocket Hammerless Automatic Pistols. Williamstown, N.J.: Phillips Publications, 1998.

*Campbell, Robert. Model 1911 Automatic Pistol. Accokeek, M.D.: Stoeger Publishing, 2005.

*Clawson, C.W. *Colt .45 Service Pistols; Models Of 1911 And 1911A1*. Ann Arbor, Michigan: Privately published by author 1991.

*Cochran, K. *Colt Cavalry, Artillery and Militia Revolvers*. Rapid City, South Dakota: Cochran Publishing Co., 1987. Much detail on all models and minutiae.

*Cochran, K. *Colt Peacemaker British Model*. Rapid City, South Dakota: 1984.

*Cochran, K. *Colt Peacemaker Ready Reference Handbook*. Rapid City, South Dakota: 1985.

*Cochran, K. A. *Colt Peacemakers Encyclopedia*. Rapid City, South Dakota: Privately published, 1986. Voluminous entries and illustrations. Volume II published 1991, Rapid City, South Dakota: Cochran Publishing Co.

Cochran, K. A. *Peacemaker: Evolution and Variations*. Rapid City, South Dakota: Colt Collector Press, 1975. Coverage from the Model 1851 Navy through the birth of the Peacemaker listing many of the known variations.

Colt, Mrs. Samuel. *"A Memorial of Caldwell Hart Colt."* Hartford, Conn.: Privately printed, 1894. Memoir about only child of Samuel Colt that reached adulthood.

Edgerly, James H. *"The Revolving Cylinder Colt Pistol Story 1839-1847."* Topeka, Kansas: Privately printed, 1937. Monograph. Written to support validity of four allegedly rare transitional Colt Walkers exposed as fakes 35 years later.

Edwards, W. B. *The Story of Colt's Revolver*. Harrisburg: Stackpole Company, 1953. An excellent, highly detailed biography of Sam Colt with considerable important data on the development and manufacture of the guns also.

Fluck, John J. *Colt-Root Model 1853*. Topeka, Kansas: F.T. Dexter, Publisher, 1950. Significant first study of the Root (24-page monograph).

*Garton, George. *Colt's S.A.A. Post War Models*. N. Hollywood, California: Beinfield Publishing Co., 1979. Revised edition: Highland Park, N.J.: Gun Room Press, 1987. Wealth of data. Important reference.

*Goddard, W. H. D. *The Government Models; Development of the Colt Model of 1911*. Lincoln, R.I.: Mowbray Publishing Co., 1988. Great wealth of detail; fine illustrations.

*Grant, E. S. *The Colt Legacy*. Providence, R. I.: Mowbray Publishing Co. 1982. The story of the Colt Armory at Hartford, 1855-1980. Company history with considerable information on firearms, also.

Grant, Ellsworth S. *The Colt Armory; A History of Colt's Manufacturing Co*. Lincoln, R. I. Mowbray Publishing, 2005. Revised, re-titled and considerably enlarged reprint of 1980 Edition. A classic work.

*Greeley IV, Horace *The Colt U.S. General Officer's Pistol* Lincoln, Rhode Island: Mowbray Publishers, 1989. Definitive account of these unique autos with extensive tables of serials and dates of issue.

Grennell, D. *The Gun Digest Book of the .45*. Northbrook, Illinois: DBI Books, Inc., 1989.

*Hamilton, John G. *Colt's History & Heroes*. Aledo, Illinois: World Wide Gun Report, Inc. 1963. Discusses Colt's popularity due to role in America's history; defines historical, presentation, inscribed pistols and those associated with history by some form of written evidence; how to authenticate the historical pistol.

Hacker, L. *Colt Single Action Army Revolver*. Little Rock Arkansas: Privately published, 1982. Pocket guide of serial numbers reprinted 1989 by Pioneer Press, Union City, Tenn.

Haven, C. T. and Belden, F. A. *A History of the Colt Revolver*. New York: William Morrow and Company, 1940 (numerous reprints circa 1960s-70). One of the earliest Colt books; necessary for complete Colt book shelf, but mostly superseded by later works.

Hemphill, J.R. *Colts From Texas And The Old West*. Actworth, Georgia. Star Printers, 1990. A browsing book. Mostly fuzzy, poorly lighted photos, slight text.

Hosley, William *Colt: The Making of an American Legend*. Amherst, Mass: University of Mass., 1991. Fine Colt family and factory history.

*Houze, Herbert G. *Colt Presentations From the Factory Ledgers 1856-1869*. Lincoln, Rhode Island: Andrew Mowbray Inc. - Publishers, 2003. A primary source and reference documenting hundreds of Colt presentations and gifts of firearms.

*Houze, Herbert G. *Samuel Colt Arms, Art, and Invention*. New Haven, Conn.: Yale University Press in association with Wadsworth Athenaeum Museum, Hartford, Conn., 2006; printed as a catalog to accompany the most important collection of Colt revolvers (including the personal collection of Samuel Colt) ever assembled. This sumptuous work adds significantly to Colt lore. An important reference.

Houze, Herbert G. *Colt Rifles and Muskets 1847 to 1870*. Iola, Wisc: Krause Publications, 1996.

*Hughs, James B. *The Gatling Gun Notebook; A Collection of Data and Illustrations*. Lincoln, R.I.: A. Mowbray Publishers, 2000.

*Jenkins, Bill. *U.S. Military Match and Marksmanship Automatic Pistols*. Lincoln, R.I.: Mowbray Publishing, 2005. Primarily concentrates on the Colt M1911 and other Colts with inclusion of S&Ws, High Standards, etc.

*Jordan, R.M. and Watt, D.M. *Colt's Pocket '49. Its Evolution Including Baby Dragoon & Wells Fargo...*(mfd. at Hartford & London). Loma Mar, Cal.: Privately pub. by author D.M. Watt. 2000. An highly significant study that will likely become the the basic text for the model. Issued simultaneously with a pocket-size "Summary."

Keogh, G. *Samuel Colt's New Model Pocket Pistols*. Ogden: Privately published by the author, 1964. Detailed study of the Root Model 1855 side hammer revolvers. Classic and standard reference to the subject.

Kopec, J.A. and Fenn, H.S. *Colt Cavalry & Artillery Revolvers: A Continuing Study*. Newport Beach, Cal.: Graphic Publishing, 1994.

*Kopec, J., Graham, R. and Moore, C. K. *A Study of the Colt Single Action Army Revolver*. LaPuente, California: Privately published by the author, 1976. Standard reference; massive size with wealth of associated material. Reprinted 2006.

*Kopec, John A. *Colt Cavalry And Artillery Revolvers*. Whitmore, California: Kopec Publications, 1994. Continuing, detailed study of Colt single actions by noted authority.

Kuhnhausen, J. *The Colt Double Action Revolvers; A Shop Manual*. Vols. I & II. Idaho: VSP Publishers, 1988. Parts lists and detailed breakdown drawings.

*Longfield, G.M. and Basnett, D.T. *Observations on Colt's Second Contract Nov. 2, 1847*. Alexandria Bay, N.Y.: Museum Restoration Service, 1998. Monograph (see 5B-024).

Lord, D. M. *Colt Bibliography*. Privately published by the author, 1966. Lists hundreds of articles appearing in most well known arms periodicals and books on Colt firearms.

Maxwell, S. L. *Colt-Burgess Magazine Rifle*. Dallas, Texas: Taylor Publishing Company, 1985. Highly detailed coverage.

McDowell, R. Bruce *"A Study of Colt Conversions & Other Percussion Revolvers."* Iola, Wisc: Krause Publications, 1997. Significant treatise and major reference.

Mills, F. P. *Colt Double Rifles*. Greenfield: Privately published by the author, 1953. Important reference and study of these rare Colt longarms.

Mitchell, J. L. *Colt—the Man, the Arms, the Company*. Harrisburg: Stackpole Company, 1959. Reference source for much original material; exact facsimiles of original letters and documents relating to Sam Colt and the factory up to 1865.

Moore, C. K. *Colt Revolvers and the U.S. Navy 1865-1889*. Bryn Mawr, Pennsylvania: Dorrance & Co., Inc., 1987.

*Moore, C. Kenneth *Colt Single Action Army Revolvers And The London Agency*. Lincoln, Rhode Island: Mowbray Publishers, 1990. Detailed study of relationship between Hartford and their British agency.

*Moore, C. Kenneth *Colt Single Action Army Revolver Study; New Discoveries*. Lincoln, R.I.; Mowbray Publishing, 2003. A follow-up to his earlier and classic work (co-authored with Kopec); updated with much new material from original archives; important serial number data.

*Moore, C. Kenneth. *Colt Single Action Army Revolvers; U.S. Alterations*. Lincoln, R.I.: Mowbray Publishers. Comprehensive study of the so-called "Artillery Model."

*Murphy, Bob *Colt New Service Revolvers*. Aledo, Illinois: Gun Report, 1993. Monograph.

Ogle, John *Colt Memorabilia Price Guide*. Iola, Wisc.: Krause Publications, 1998.

*O'Meara, R.H. *Colt's Single Action Army Revolver*. Iola, Wisc.: Krause Publications, 1999. Introductory source for black powder shooters and about Single Action Legend, romance and rivals.

Parsons, J. E. *New Light on Old Colts*. New York: Privately published by the author, 1955. Detailed study from the Colt Civil War shipping ledgers; much original source information.

Parsons, J. E. *The Peacemaker and Its Rivals*. New York: William Morrow and Company, 1950. An all-time classic on the Colt Single Action Army, its evolution, antecedents, rivals, popularity, variations and data on its volume, serial numbers and sales.

*Parsons, J. E. *Samuel Colt's Own Record*. Hartford: Connecticut Historical Society, 1949. Important reference on the design and production of the Walker Colt from the original records of transactions with Walker and Eli Whitney in 1847.

Parsons, John E. *"Catalog of Loan Exhibition of Percussion Colt Revolvers & Conversions 1836-1873."* N.Y. City: Metropolitan Museum of Art, 1942. Milestone in Colt collecting; first major exhibit by an important museum.

Phillips, P. R. & Wilson, R. L. *Paterson Colt Pistol Variations*. Dallas, Texas: Jackson Arms, 1979. Highly detailed, profusely illustrated definitive reference for Paterson longarms and handguns. A work of major significance.

*Phillips, W. G. & Vervloet, J. P. *U.S. Single Action Cartridge Handgun Holsters 1870-1910*. Bloomfield, Ontario: Museum Restoration Service, 1987. Detailed, well illustrated monograph.

*Potocki, John *The Colt Model 1905 Automatic Pistol*. Lincoln, R.I.: A. Mowbray Publishers, 1998.

Rapley, Robin J. *Colt Percussion Accoutrements 1834-1873*. Privately published by author: Newport Beach, California, 1994. Extensive, detailed, pioneer work. Profusely illustrated. Soft covers.

*Rapley, Robin J. *The History and Identification of Colt Accoutrements 1834-1911: Paterson to Automatic.* Christchurch, New Zealand: Published by author, 2006. Entirely new, much updated, greatly enlarged work. Classic coverage of this highly significant subject. Hard covers.

Renwick, William G. *The Folding Trigger Paterson Colt.* Privately published by author, 1934. First significant treatise on the model. Monograph.

Rhea, D. & V. *How the Colt Navy .36 Was Fired.* Wood River, Illinois, 1985.

Roes, K.T., (Editor) *Colt and its Collectors.* Wordsworth Publisher, 2003. Catalog of Colt collectors association exhibit; Colt, The Legacy of a Legend. At the Buffalo Bill Historical Center, Cody, Wyoming.

Rohan, J. *"Yankee Arms Maker."* N.Y. City: Harper & Bro., 1935. Biography of Samuel Colt with some facts askew.

Rosa, J. G. *Col. Colt London.* London: Arms and Armour Press, 1976. Detailed reference on Colt's London factory and the arms produced there and bearing those markings.

*Rosa, Joseph G. *Colt Revolvers And The Tower Of London.* London, England: Royal Armory, 1988. General study of Colts with some specific data on English models and usage. Soft covers.

Rywell, Martin *"Trial of Samuel Colt."* Harriman, Tenn: Pioneer Press, 1955. The landmark case Colt won over Mass. Arms Co. for patent infringement. Actual court transcript. A major source of information on the manufacture of revolving arms of the period.

Serven, J. E. *Colt Firearms From 1836.* Santa Ana: The Foundation Press; numerous updated editions since the original in 1954. One of the most important, often referred to and widely respected Colt references. Reprinted 1992.

Sheldon, D. *A Collector's Guide to Colt .38 Auto-Model 1900.* Willernie, Minnesota, 1987.

Shumaker, P. L. *Colt's Variations of the Old Model Pocket Pistol,* 1848-1872. Beverly Hills: Fadco Publishing Company, 1957 (revised edition 1966). Classic reference; highly detailed study of the Baby Dragoon and Model 1849 Pocket revolvers in all their variations.

*Silva, Lee A. *The Wyatt Earp—Colt "Buntline Special" Controversy.* Newport Beach, Cal.: Graphic Publications, 1995.

Sutherland, R. Q. and Wilson, R. L. *The Book of Colt Firearms.* Kansas City: Privately published by R. Q. Sutherland, 1971; reprinted 1993 by Blue Book Publishing Co. One of the most important reference works ever published on the subject. Massive in size and scope; exquisitely illustrated.

*Swayze, N. L. *'51 Colt Navies.* Yazoo City: Privately published by the author, 1967. Classic reference on the Colt Model 1851 and its many variations. Reprinted by the Gun Room Press, Highland Park, New Jersey, 1991.

Sweeney, Fred *A Guide To The Proper Accoutrements For Hartford Produced Percussion Colt Revolvers.* Privately published by author, 1993. Spiral bound.

Tivey, T. *Colt Rifle 1884-1902.* New South Wales: Clouston & Hall, 1984. Covers the Colt Burgess and Lightning models.

Ulrich, Arthur L. *"A Century of Achievement."* Hartford, Conn: Colt F.A. Co., 1936. Among first Colt histories. Paper covers.

Virgines, George E. *The Saga of the Colt Six Shooter* New York City: Frederick Fell, Inc. 1969.

Wahl, P. & Toppel, D. *"The Gatling Gun."* N.Y. City: ARCO Publishing, 1965. The most important reference to the subject. Highly regarded.

Whittington, Robert D., III. *The Colt Whitneyville-Walker Pistol.* Hooks, Texas: Brownlee Books, 1984. A study of the pistol and the men associated with its development, manufacture and use.

*Whittington, Robert D. III. *The Walker's Walker Controversy Solved.* Hooks, Tex. Privately published, 2003. Monograph and follow-up to author's earlier work (q.v.) about uncertainty of serial numbers of famous Colt Walker Model given by Colt to Capt. Walker.

*Wilkerson, Don *The Post-War Colt Single Action Revolver 1955-1975.* Dallas, Texas: Taylor Publishing Co. 1978; second edition 1980. Detailed coverage of famed single action in its most recent series and variations since WWII.

Wilkerson, Don *The Post-War Colt Single Action Revolver 1976-1986.* Dallas, Texas: Privately published by author, 1986.

*Wilkerson, Don *Colts Single Action Army Revolver; Pre-War/Post-War Model.* Minneapolis, Minnesota. Privately published by author 1991.

Wilkerson, Don *Colt Double-Action Revolver Model of 1878.* Marceline, Missouri: Walsworth Publishing Co., 1998. Exceptionally detailed coverage of the many variations and illustrations of the well known Colt "Double Action Frontier."

*Wilkerson, Don *Colt Scouts Peacemakers In New Frontiers In .22 Caliber* Kansas City, Missouri: Cherokee Publications, 1993.

Wilson, R. L. *The Colt Heritage: The Official History of Colt Firearms—1836 to the Present.* New York: Simon and Schuster, 1979. The "official" history as authorized by the Colt Firearms Division. The Colt story from its beginning through 1978 with elaborate serial number tables as an appendix; exceptional illustrations.

*Wilson, R. L. *Colt—An American Legend.* New York: Abbeville Press, 1985. Basically same as *The Colt Heritage* (see above) with added material on serial numbers.

Wilson, R. L. & Hable, R. E. *Colt Pistols 1836 … 1976.* Dallas, Texas: Jackson Arms Company, 1976. A unique presentation of one of the finest Colt collections assembled; exceptional color illustrations; authoritative text.

Wilson, R. L. *The Book of Colt Engraving.* Los Angeles: Beinfeld Publication Inc., 1974, revised and expanded edition 1982. A very detailed and thorough study of Colt engraving from earliest period to modern times; exquisitely illustrated.

*Wilson, R. L. *The Colt Engraving Book, c. 1832-1921, Volume I.* Greatly enlarged edition of Wilson's earlier *Book of Colt Engraving* (q.v.). *Volume II "c. 1919-2000."* New York: Bannerman's Publishers, 2001 (both volumes). Sumptuous editions; exceptional illustrations.

Wilson, R. L. *Colt Commemorative Firearms.* Wichita: Colt Engraving Vol. I Kidwell, 1969. Detailed guide and reference on modern made Colt commemorative firearms.

*Wilson, R. L. *The Paterson Colt Book: The Early Evolution of Samuel Colt's Repeating Arms.* Palo Alto, California: Strutz-LeVett Publishing Co., 2001. Extensive coverage of all earliest Colts revolving arms with detail and exceptional color illustrations.

*Wilson, R. L. *Colt's Dates of Manufacture 1836-1978.* Hamilton, Ohio: 1985. Serial numbers all models by year.

Wilson, R. L. *The Arms Collection of Colonel Colt.* Bullville, New York: H. Glass, 1964. Story of Samuel Colt's personal and unique arms collection.

Wilson, R. L. *The Rampant Colt.* Spencer, Indiana: T. Haas, 1969. Study of all Colt trade marks and their use including material on a variety of other Colt memorabilia.

Wilson, R. L. *Samuel Colt Presents*. Hartford: Wadsworth Atheneum, 1961. Finely detailed and illustrated catalog of the famed exhibition of some of the most important and historic Colts ever assembled. An important reference work.

Wilson, R. L. *Fine Colts: The Dr. Joseph A. Murphy Collection*. Doylestown, PA: Republic Publishing Co., 1999. Lavishly color illustrated work about noted American Collection.

Wooten, Ben H. *A Study of Colt's New Model Army Pistol 1860*. Privately published, circa 1950's. Monograph.

_____*Colt's From The Wm. E. Locke Collection*. Lincoln, R.I.: Mowbray Publishing, 1996. Many important Colts from very famous collection; often referred to.

*_____*A Century of Achievement 1836-1936: Colt*. Boulder, Colorado: Paladin Press. 2006 reprint of famous 1937 edition of Colt's catalog issued to commemorate their century in business. Review of their history and principal firearms made over that period plus their 1937 catalog.

_____*The Russian Colts*. Los Angeles, Cal.: Beinfeld Publications 1976. Catalog of loan exhibition by Russia's Hermitage Museum, St. Petersburg to N.Y. Met. Museum of famous Colts presented by Sam'l Colt to Russian Czars.

(*) Preceding a title indicates the book is currently in print.

Patersons in Perspective

A significant research project culminating in the publication of *Paterson Colt Pistol Variations* (*see Bibliography*) brought to light important data that has revised considerably information about Patersons in previously published works. Models are now accurately placed in their correct sequence with correct nomenclature (actually used by Samuel Colt) along with updated and corrected information on calibers, quantities and variants; all of which are shown in a clearer perspective.

Colt Pocket Model Paterson Revolver No.1

5B-001

5B-002

Pocket Model Paterson Revolver (No. 1). Made c.1837-38; total of about 500 manufactured.

28 caliber. 5-shot cylinders. Barrel lengths from 1-3/4" to 4-3/4"; octagonal in shape, without attached loading levers. Cylinder length 1-1/16".

Grips of varnished walnut. Blued finish on all metal parts.

The smallest size of Paterson handgun, the "Baby Paterson" had its own serial number range, from 1 through about 500. Standard barrel marking was: - Patent Arms M'g Co. Paterson N·J.-Colt's Pt.-. Serial number stampings generally are not visible until taking the gun apart (on some a number can be noted on the bevel at bottom of the grip). So-called Centaur scene with the word COLT and the company's four-horse-head trademark was roll engraved on the cylinder.

The Pocket Model was the first handgun made at the Colt Paterson factory. So diminutive in size that short barreled specimens seem like miniatures, the Baby Paterson is the smallest Colt percussion revolver made.

Basic variations are:

Standard Model, without attached loading lever, rear of cylinder rounded or square back:

5B-001   Values—Good **$17,500**   Fine **$50,000**

Ehlers Model (also known as Fourth Model Ehlers) named after John Ehlers, a major stockholder and later officer of the Patent

Arms Manufacturing Company who took over after it went into bankruptcy. These revolvers were semi-finished at the time of the litigation; when Ehlers assumed ownership of the firm, he completed manufacture, assembled and merchandised them.

This constitutes a distinct, separate model, with attached loading lever; capping channel on recoil shield; cylinder 31/32" length with rounded rear; barrel marking lacks the M'g Co. merely having a space where these marks had been removed from the roll die. Total of about 500 made (including the "Fifth Model Ehlers" of the Belt Model No. 2). Made c.1840-43. *Rare:*

5B-002   Values—Good **$20,000**   Fine **$55,000**

Colt Belt Model Paterson Revolver No. 2

Belt Model Paterson Revolver (No. 2). Made c.1837-40; totaling approximately 850 (including the No. 3 Belt Model).

5B-003

5B-004

31 caliber. 5-shot cylinders. Barrel lengths from 2-1/2" to 5-1/2"; octagonal; without attached loading levers.

Varnished walnut grips. Blued finish on all metal parts.

A straight gripped version of the Belt Paterson, the No. 2 Model shared its serial range, from 1 through about 850 with the No. 3 Belt Model. Barrels were marked: Patent Arms M'g Co Paterson N-J. Colt's Pt. Usually it is necessary to disassemble the pistol before discovering serial number stampings (on some the number is visible on the bevel at bottom of the grip). Cylinder scene: the roll engraved Centaur motif, including COLT within the four-horse-head trademark.

A quick means of identifying the No. 2 Belt pistol from the Baby Paterson is by comparison of weights. A 4" barrel Baby weighs only 11 ounces, while the No. 2 pistol of the same barrel length weighs 20 ounces. All No. 2 Belt pistols have the straight type grip.

Standard Model, without attached loading lever; rear of cylinder either rounded or square back:

5B-003   Values—Good **$18,500**   Fine **$47,500**

Ehlers Model (also known as Fifth Model Ehlers), a distinct, separate model, with attached loading lever; capping channel on

recoil shield; cylinder 1-1/16" length with rounded rear; barrel markings lack the M'g Co having a space where these had been removed from the roll die. Total about 500 made (including the 4th Model Ehlers of the Pocket Model No. 1). Made c.1840-43. *Rare:*

5B-004   Values—Good **$18,500**   Fine **$50,000**

Colt Belt Model Paterson Revolver No. 3

Belt Model Paterson Revolver (No. 3). Manufactured from about 1837 to 1840; total run of approximately 850 (including the No. 2 Belt Model).

31 caliber; 5-shot cylinders. Barrel lengths from 3-1/2" to 5-1/2"; octagonal in shape, with or without attached loading levers.

Grips of varnished walnut. Blued finish on all metal parts; a few pistols had casehardened hammers.

This medium size series of Paterson pistols shared the serial number range with the No. 2 Belt Model, beginning with 1 and running to about 850. Barrels were marked: Patent Arms M'g Co. Paterson N-J Colt's Pt. Serial numbers generally not visible until taking the gun apart (though on some will be observed on the butt area of the grip). The Centaur scene, with the word COLT and the four-horse-head trademark was the roll engraved cylinder scene.

The Belt Model series was the only group of Paterson revolvers produced having two types of grips—the straight and the flared styles. Attached loading levers are scarce in the Belt production, and the round shouldered cylinders are more often seen than the straight or square back type.

5B-005

5B-006

The major variations are:

Standard pistol, with flared grip; without attached loading lever:

5B-005   Values—Good **$30,000**   Fine **$70,000**

Standard pistol; flared grip *with attached loading lever* and capping cutout on the recoil shield. Very rare:

5B-006   Values—Good **$32,500**   Fine **$75,000**

Colt Holster Model Paterson Revolver No. 5

5B-007

5B-008

Holster Model Paterson Revolver (No. 5) (also known as the "Texas Paterson"). Manufactured c. 1838-40; in a total of about 1,000.

36 caliber. 5-shot cylinders. Barrel lengths from 4" to 12"; standard at 7-1/2" and 9". All are octagonal in shape, with or without attached loading levers.

Grips of varnished walnut. Metal parts blued, with casehardened hammer and frame.

The largest size in the Paterson handgun production, the "Texas" Model had its own serial range, numbered from 1 up through about 1000. Barrels were marked: Patent Arms M'g. Co. Paterson N·J.-Colt's Pt. Serial numbers generally cannot be observed without taking the pistol apart; but at the least are often found on the bottom of the grip. Cylinder roll scene was the stagecoach holdup, including the word COLT.

The Texas Paterson has had the greatest appeal to the collector, due to its large size, the relatively heavy caliber, and the association of the type with the Texas Ranger Jack Hays and verified use by military and civilians on the frontier. Many of the specimens of this model known today show rather hard use, and thus a Texas Paterson in outstanding condition is one of the great prizes of Colt collecting. A verified martially marked specimen is a great rarity and worth a considerable premium.

Major variations are:

Standard model, without attached loading lever, and with rounded or square shoulders to the cylinder:

5B-007   Values—Good **$50,000**   Fine **$110,000**

Standard model, with attached loading lever, capping cutout on the recoil shield, and rounded shoulders to the cylinder:

5B-008   Values—Good **$55,000**   Fine **$120,000**

Colt First Model Ring Lever Rifle

First Model Ring Lever Rifle. Manufactured c. 1837-38; total production about 200. Pulling the ring lever cocked the hammer and turned the cylinder for each shot.

34, 36, 38, 40, and 44 calibers. 8-shot cylinders standard (10-shot rare and worth premium). Barrel lengths standard at 32"; octagonal in shape, with or without attached loading levers.

5B-009

Varnished walnut stocks, having cheek piece usually inlaid with the Colt four-horse-head trademark. Metal parts blued, with browned barrel.

First of Colt's longarm production, the No. 1 or First Model rifle was marked in its own serial range, from 1 on up through about 200. Barrels were marked on the top: Colt's Patent Patent Arms Man'g. Co., Paterson, N. Jersey. Serial numbers appear on various parts, most of them visible only when the rifle has been disassembled. The cylinder roll scene depicts horsemen and a centaur coursing a deer; the word COLT is also present.

Ironically Colt's initial factory production of firearms was in rifles—the No. 1 Ring Lever—and not in handguns, which came a few months later. Thus, the First Model Rifle is of extreme importance to the advanced Colt collector. Limited in production to but 200, these arms are *rare*. The First Model is

quickly differentiated from the Second Model by the presence of the topstrap extended over the cylinder of the former.

The two basic variations are:

Standard model, without attached loading lever, without capping channel in the recoil shield, and with square-backed cylinder configuration:

5B-009   Values—Good **$18,500**   Fine **$50,000**

Improved model. Factory fitted loading lever attached and the addition of a spring held detent underneath trigger guard to permit the cylinder to be revolved while loading (instead of removing cylinder for loading), locking the ring lever to permit this. The addition of a capping groove on the recoil shield and the rounding of the back of the cylinder were also factory improvements and came before the permanent loading lever. Thus these improvements were performed while the rifles were still in inventory and serial numbers are not an accurate guide as these improvements are found as low as serial number 16:

5B-010   Values—Good **$19,000**   Fine **$55,000**

Colt Second Model Ring Lever Rifle

5B-011

Second Model Ring Lever Rifle. Manufactured c. 1838-41; the total produced approximately 500. The ring device served to cock the hammer and revolve the cylinder for each shot.

44 caliber. 8-shot cylinder standard (10-shot rare and worth premium). Standard barrel lengths of 28" and 32"; octagonal in shape, with or without attached loading levers.

Varnished walnut stocks, with cheekpiece (but *not* inlaid with the Colt trademark as standard in the First Model Rifle). Metal parts blued, with browned barrel.

Second Model Rifles were serial numbered in their own range, from 1 on up through about 500. Barrels were marked: Patent Arms M'g. Co. Paterson, NJ.-Colt's Pt. Serial numbers on various parts, usually visible only when the rifle has been disassembled. The cylinder roll scene is of horsemen and a

centaur coursing a deer; the word COLT is present, as is a small house (the latter not present on the First Model cylinder roll).

Though not as rare as the First Model Ring Lever Rifle, the Second Model is still a difficult arm to locate, and as with its predecessor, is seldom found in good condition. The quick means of telling one model from the other is the lack of a topstrap extension over the cylinder on the Second Model.

There are two basic variations:

Standard model, without attached loading lever, with capping channel in the recoil shield, and having the squareback or rounded type cylinder:

5B-011   Values—Good **$12,500**   Fine **$35,000**

Improved model with attached loading lever, capping channel in recoil shield, rounded shoulders of cylinder and other features as mentioned in the "Improved Model" of 1st Model Ring Lever rifle:

5B-012   Values—Good **$14,000**   Fine **$37,500**

Colt Model 1839 Carbine

Model 1839 Carbine. Made c. 1838-41; total quantity approximately 950. Features an exposed hammer, and does not have a ring lever cocking device.

525 smoothbore caliber. 6-shot cylinder. Standard barrel length of 24", but other lengths (notably 28" and 32") also known; round shape excepting bevels present at the breech; with or without attached loading levers.

Varnished walnut stocks. Metal parts blued, the barrel browned.

Manufactured in its own serial number range, beginning with 1 and continuing through about 950. Barrels were marked: Patent Arms M'g. Co.Paterson, N.J.-Colt's Pt. Serial numbers on various parts, generally visible only when the gun has been disassembled. The cylinder roll scene is one of the most elaborate in the Paterson production, featuring scrolls, Colt markings, and panels of a naval battle, land battle, and a hunter and trophy lion.

The Model 1839 Carbine proved to be the most practical and popular of all Colt arms from the Paterson period. It was so

5B-013

5B-014.5

highly regarded by Samuel Colt that he seriously considered re-introduction of the model when developing his revived business in Hartford. A quick identification of the model is the cylinder length of 2-1/2" and the exposed hammer.

Basic variations are:

Standard model, with attached loading lever on the barrel lug and round backed cylinder:

5B-013 Values—Good **$12,500** Fine **$27,500**

Earliest production (rare) without attached loading lever, square-backed cylinder, and a capping groove cut near the top of the right recoil shield:

5B-014 Values—Good **$15,000** Fine **$40,000**

Standard First/early type without attached loading lever and round backed cylinder. Every indication is that this is the model purchased by the "Republic Texas, 1839":

5B-014.5 Values—Good **$14,000** Fine **$32,500**

Government purchase Carbines with WAT inspector mark on the left side of the stocks; fitted with attached loading levers. 360 pieces purchased by U.S. Government (in four orders). Extreme care should be exercised in the acquisition of this piece:

5B-015 Values—Good **$25,000** Fine **$90,000**

Long cylinder variant. 3-1/4" cylinder with proportionately longer frame to accommodate. Estimated quantity made 25 to accept the larger musket size charge. Approximately half of these burst on firing. *Extremely rare:*

5B-016 Values—Good **$15,000** Fine **$40,000**

Colt Model 1839 Shotgun

5B-017

Model 1839 Shotgun. Manufactured c. 1839-41; in a total run of about 225. The mechanism is the same as on the Model 1839 Carbine, with an exposed hammer.

16 gauge. 6-shot cylinder. Standard barrel lengths of 24" and 32"; round shape (without bevels at the breech) and made without attached loading levers.

Varnished walnut stocks. Metal parts blued; the barrel browned in a Damascus decor.

Produced in an individual serial range, numbered from 1 on up through about 225. On right side of the barrel lug: Patent Arms M'g. Co. Paterson, N.J.-Colt's Pt. Serial markings on various parts, but most of these visible when gun has been taken

apart. Dramatic and sizable cylinder roll scene, of scrolls, Colt markings, and three panels depicting the American eagle, a deer-hunting sequence, and an Indian with bird hunters.

The quite limited total production proves the Model 1839 Shotgun to have been of little popularity in its day. The type did have some potential as a repeating military musket, but the failure of the Paterson enterprise early in the 1840s cut short such possibilities for success. The Model 1839 Shotgun is one of the greater rarities in Colt's longarm production, and specimens seldom appear on the market. For quick identification measure the cylinder length—3-1/2" (as compared to the 2-1/2" of the Model 1839 Carbine):

5B-017 Values—Good **$8,500** Fine **$27,500**

Colt Walker Model Revolver

Walker Model Revolver. Manufactured in 1847, with a total production of approximately 1,100.

44 caliber. 6-shot cylinder. 9" part round, part octagonal barrel. A massive 4 lbs. 9 oz. in weight.

One piece walnut grips. Casehardened frame, hammer, and lever; balance blued; excepting plain brass trigger guard, and the cylinder "in the white".

Serial numbering in five companies, A, B, C, D, and E, beginning with the number 1 in each grouping. The five company series combined totaled 1,000 revolvers.

Barrel marked: ADDRESS SAM⸱ COLT NEW-YORK CITY. On the right side of the lug: US/1847. Cylinder roll engraved with a Texas Ranger and Indian fight scene; but this is frequently missing on surviving specimens due to years of service and neglect. Government inspector markings were applied to the grips and various metal parts, but these too are often worn or rusted off.

The Walker is the greatest prize of any Colt collection. Slightly more than 10 percent of the original total manufactured have survived to appear in modern day collections and museums. A great many reproductions and fakes have been made, and a number of badly mutilated specimens have been heavily restored.

The buyer should exercise extreme caution in acquiring a Walker.

Standard Walker, A, B, C, D, E Company serial ranges:

5B-018   Values—Fair **$42,500**
            Very Good (no finish) **$125,000**

The special group of an additional 100 Walkers in the so-called "Civilian Range"; these had no U.S. inspector markings, bore numbers from 1001 through about 1100, and were otherwise like the military Walker pistols. Valuewise this is a "gray" area. This model is scarcer and will bring a premium to advanced Colt collectors, while others prefer martially marked specimens and

5B-018

pay more for them. This group of 100 tends to be found in better average condition:

5B-019   Values—Fair **$37,500**
            Very Good (no finish) **$110,000**

Colt Whitneyville Hartford Dragoon Revolver

Whitneyville Hartford Dragoon Revolver (also known as the "Transition Walker"). Made late in 1847, in a total quantity of about 240.

44 caliber. 6-shot cylinder. 7-1/2" part round, part octagonal barrel.

One piece walnut grips. Casehardened frame, hammer, and lever; the balance blued. Gripstraps have been noted in varying finishes; trigger guards of brass and backstraps either steel or brass.

Serial numbered from about 1100 through 1340, picking up from where the Civilian Series Walker pistols left off.

Barrel marked: - ADDRESS SAM^L COLT NEW YORK-CITY -; some variation noted, including a few barrels unmarked. Variations also appear in the COLTS/PATENT mark on left side (and sometimes right) of the frame. Cylinder bearing the roll engraved scene of a Texas Ranger and Indian fight. However, as the cylinder is slightly shorter/narrower than that used on the Walker revolver a very narrow section of that cylinder scene is lacking.

Actually of greater rarity than the Walker Model, the Whitneyville Hartford Dragoons are sometimes called the "Transition Walker," since some of the production parts were left over from the predecessor model. The two major frame variations in the Whitneyville Hartford are: 1. Cutout at the rear of the frame, into which fits a curved portion of the grips, and 2. Straight-back frame. The trigger guard on both variants slants back into the grips, rather than being in a vertical juncture as would be standard on later Dragoon pistols. Among other distinctive details to note are the very slender, or "Slim Jim," appearance of the grips, and the short trigger and cylinder stop screws of early frames (thus not passing completely through).

One of the great Colt rarities, the Whitneyville Hartford Dragoon has been an attractive challenge to fakers; *caveat emptor*!

Cut-out Frame Type:

5B-020   Values—Fair **$20,000**
            Very Good (without finish) **$65,000**

Straight Back Frame Type:

5B-021   Values—Good **$11,000**   Fine **$37,500**

5B-020
Cut-out Frame Type

5B-021
Straightback Frame Type

Colt First Model Dragoon Revolver

First Model Dragoon Revolver. Manufactured 1848 - c. 1850; total of about 7,000.

44 caliber. 6-shot cylinder. 7-1/2" part round, part octagonal barrel.

Grips of one piece walnut. Casehardened frame, hammer, and lever; the balance blued. Gripstraps standard of brass, silver plated for civilian sales, and left unfinished for the military.

Serial numbered from about 1341 through about 8000, continuing the sequence from the Whitneyville Hartford Dragoon.

Barrel marked: ADDRESS SAM^L COLT, NEW-YORK CITY -. COLT'S/PATENT on the left side of the frame; often accompanied by U.S. (on government purchased and issued specimens) centered beneath. Texas Ranger and Indian fight scene roll

engraved on the cylinders. Cylinders also bear roll-engraved panel marking in large letters **COLT'S PATENT** accompanied by second panel **MODEL U.S.M.R.** ("U.S. Mounted Rifles"). A

5B-022

scarcer variant is marked **U.S. DRAGOONS** in place of the U.S.M.R. marks, and will add premium to value.

Identifying features of the First Model are: Continuation of the square backed trigger guard, the cylinder stop slots oval, and the juncture of grips, gripstraps, and frame forming a straight vertical line. Early series pistols have some notable carryovers from the Whitneyville-Hartford Dragoon, while later specimens show improvements of evolution leading into the Second Model pistols. A few late First Models were cut to accept detachable

shoulder stocks (all three types; see 5B-030/031/032/033); work and adaptation performed after guns were mfd.; very rare. **Military issue** First Model with government inspector markings on the grips and various metal parts:

5B-022	Values—Good **$5,000**		Fine **$35,000**

Civilian First Model; varnished walnut grips and standard finish (U.S. often present on frame):

5B-023	Values—Good **$5,000**		Fine **$30,000**

U.S. Walker Replacement Dragoon

U.S. Walker Replacement Dragoon. Also known as the "pre-1st Model Dragoon" and the "Fluck" Dragoon (after the late John J. Fluck whose detailed research in 1956 first identified the gun as a distinct model). Manufactured in 1848.

44 caliber. 6-shot cylinder; 7-1/2" part round/part octagon Colt Walker barrels that were re-worked by Colt factory to this shorter length.

Closely resembling the First Model Colt Dragoon. Just 300 of these were made by Colt for the U.S. government to replace Colt Walkers that had burst or otherwise failed while in U.S. service. These revolvers were actually accepted by the U.S. as part of the 1,000 piece contract for Walkers. They utilize many original Walker and Walker-reworked parts by Colt.

Serial number range approximately 2216 to approximately 2515; the numbers of the tiny Walker type.

Finish: blued barrel with casehardened frame and loading lever; cylinder usually left bright. Cylinder has rolled engraved scene of Texas ranger and Indian fight and an identifying feature of this model is the pressure ridge (characteristic of rolled scenes on Walker cylinders) at the rear of the cylinder near the locking notches.

The longer backstrap similar to the Walker makes for an unusual grip profile with the butt angling downward toward the rear. The trigger guard is from the Walker model, Colt factory re-worked. Markings COLT'S/PATENT/U.S. are positioned towards the center of the left side of the frame. Specimens of this model show an uneven quality in workmanship and other features such as double stamped barrel markings and metal flaws. Inspector markings are: WAT (in oval cartouche) on right grip and JH (in oval) on left side; inspector mark P appears on various metal parts.

Second only to the Whitneyville-Hartford in the limited quantity produced, this Walker replacement revolver is one of

5B-024

the ultra-desirable variations in Colt's Dragoon series and among the first of Colt's revolvers produced at Hartford for U.S. military issue:

5B-024	Values—Good **$12,500**	
	Fine (little or no finish) **$37,500**	

More recently, tentatively renamed "Colt's Second Contract Dragoon" (not to be confused with "Second Model Dragoon.") A 1998 detailed study "Observations on Colt's Second Contract, Nov. 2, 1847" (see Bibliography this chapter) adds complication and controversy to this rare model. The authors have theoretically identified 1000 (rather than 300) of this enigmatic Colt, contracted in 1847 and delivered in four shipments, each with their own variations, in 1848. The four types appear in serial ranges 2001 through 3000. As the survey is conjectural and was based on examination of "...well over a dozen" specimens, which may be too small a number to draw definitive conclusions, and is yet to be tested in the market place. its acceptance and impact is untried. It certainly is worthy of taking into consideration. Articles published in the January and May 2004 issues of the *Gun Report* also take exception to the "Fluck" theory.

Colt Second Model Dragoon Revolver

Second Model Dragoon Revolver. In production c. 1850-51; total made about 2,700.

44 caliber. 6-shot cylinder. 7-1/2" part round, part octagonal barrel.

Grips of one piece walnut. Casehardened frame, hammer, and lever; the remainder blued. Gripstraps standard of brass,

5B-025

plated in silver for civilian sales, and left unfinished for the military.

Serial range from about 8000 through about 10700, the sequence continuing from the First Model Dragoon.

Barrel markings are two slight variations of: ADDRESS SAM COLT NEW-YORK CITY. COLT'S/PATENT on the left side of the frame, with government issue revolvers having U.S. centered beneath. The Texas Ranger and Indian fight scene was roll engraved on the cylinders. U.S.M.R. cylinder markings most often encountered; U.S. DRAGOONS scarce and bring an added premium.

Identification of the Second Model is quickly made by looking for the distinct combination of square-back trigger guard and rectangular cylinder stop slots. Subtle changes were appearing in the mainspring type, the hammer (adding a roller bearing), and the trigger guard width as seen from the front. Both vertical and horizontal loading lever latches were in evidence. As with the First Model Dragoon a few were later fitted (about a year after their manufacture) for all three variants of the attachable shoulder stock (see 5B-030 to 033). (Authentic specimens worth premium values).

The Second Model is of greater scarcity than either the First or the Third Dragoon pistols, and among its most desirable variations are the NEW HAMPSHIRE and MS (Massachusetts) marked militia issues. Only a few of these are known to collectors, and only a few hundred were originally made; they normally appear in the serials within about 10000 to the lower 11000 range.

Military issue Second Model with government inspector markings on the grips and various metal parts:

5B-025   Values—Good **$4,500**   Fine **$30,000**

Civilian Second Model; varnished walnut grips and standard finish:

5B-026   Values—Good **$4,250**   Fine **$27,500**

NEW HAMPSHIRE or MS militia issue Second Model:

5B-027   Values—Good **$5,250**   Fine **$35,000**

Colt Third Model Dragoon Revolver

Third Model Dragoon Revolver. Manufactured from c. 1851 to c. 1861; in a total of about 10,500.

44 caliber. 6-shot cylinder. 7-1/2" part round, part octagonal barrel.

Grips of one piece walnut. Casehardened frame, hammer, and lever; the remainder blued. Gripstraps standard of brass, plated in silver for civilian sales, and left unfinished for the military.

Serial numbering began about 10200 (overlapping with some of the Second Model) and continued to about 19600.

Barrel markings are two slight variants of: ADDRESS SAM COLT NEW-YORK CITY. As standard with predecessor models, COLT'S/PATENT was stamped on the left side of the frame, with government issue revolvers having U.S. centered beneath. The Texas Ranger and Indian fight scene was roll engraved on the cylinders. U.S.M.R. cylinder markings most often encountered; U.S. DRAGOONS scarce and bring an added premium.

Spotting a Third Model is relatively easy—simply look for the combination of rectangular cylinder stop slots and rounded trigger guard, the two basic features. Several variations have been noted in this type. Most important are:

Shoulder Stocked Pistols: An estimated 1,200 to 1,500 Third Models were cut for attachment of shoulder stocks. The stocks were in three basic types—the First pattern attached to the revolver via two prongs which engaged two slots in the backstrap; the Second type attached by one prong engaging a slot in the backstrap, and a hook which clamped onto the butt; the Third, and most commonly encountered pattern, had extensions on its yoke which fit into cutouts on each side of the revolver's recoil shield, and had a hook which clamped onto the butt. All three stock designs were made plain (standard) or with canteen inserts. Backstrap slots serve basically to identify Third Model Dragoons cut for the First and Second type shoulder stocks; pistols cut for the Third type are standard with four-screw frames, notched recoil shields, a groove in the heel of the backstrap, folding leaf sights dovetailed onto the barrel (through the roll die marking), blued steel backstrap, and half moon shaped front sight.

Both First and Second pattern of stocks are found in the serial range of 13,000 to 16,000. Both are very rare. (First Pattern a bit more so). Third Pattern stock is the type standard on all four percussion Colt revolvers adapted for stocks (the Dragoon, 1860

5B-028

Army; Model 1851 Navy and 1861 Navy). Usually found in serial range 16,000 to 17,000 and range 18,000 to 19,000.

A quite scarce variation of martially marked Third Models is that found with the hand engraved marking on the barrel lug: C.L. DRAGOONS These pistols are militia issues, and are similar to the NEW HAMPSHIRE and MS guns found in the Second Model production.

The Third Model is the least scarce of all Colt Dragoons, and is the most representative type of Dragoon production. The collector looking for a specimen of the Colt "four pounder" should start with the Third Model.

Standard Third Model Dragoon revolver:

5B-028   Values—Good **$4,000**   Fine **$25,000**

Martially marked (U.S., and government inspector stampings) Third Models:

5B-029   Values—Good **$4,250**   Fine **$30,000**

Shoulder-stocked revolvers. Those fitted for shoulder stocks usually found with iron backstraps, although a few retained original brass backstraps. Dragoons fitted for third type (most commonly encountered) attachable stock have four-screw frames.

First and Second types, Pistol:
5B-030   Values—Good **$4,750**   Fine **$30,000**

First and Second types, Stock:
5B-031   Values—Good **$5,500**   Fine **$10,000**

Third type, Pistol:
5B-032   Values—Good **$4,000**   Fine **$27,500**

5B-030

Third type, Stock:
5B-033   Values—Good **$3,750**   Fine **$8,500**
(Note: If stock has canteen insert feature worth 25 percent to 50 percent premium.)
C.L. Dragoon variation: a survey of known specimens found almost all with 8" barrels. A single specimen of the M-1851 Navy also known with identical markings. Formerly believed to denote "CONNECTICUT LIGHT DRAGOONS," more recent evidence indicates the markings designate the *CROCHERON*

LIGHT DRAGOONS an Alabama militia unit later mustered into Confederate service as Capt. Halloway's Company of Alabama cavalry:
5B-034   Values—Good **$12,000**   Fine **$60,000**

8" barrel variation; generally high serial numbers (18000 and above), very limited production; scarce (iron backstrap very rare; worth premium of 25 percent):
5B-035   Values—Good **$6,250**   Fine **$37,500**

Colt Hartford English Dragoon Revolver

Hartford English Dragoon Revolver. Parts made in Hartford, and the final assembly and finish done at Colt's London factory, c. 1853-57; approximately 700 total production.

Basically this Dragoon is a variation of the Third Model (see illustration of standard third Model). The first detail to note for identification is the exclusive serial range from 1 through about 700. British proof stampings are on the breech end of the cylinder and on the left side of the barrel lug (crown over a V and a crown over GP monogram). Grips were most always varnished walnut, and finishing for the metal parts of the revolver was in the fine quality English style blue and color hardening; gripstraps were of brass and silver plated.

Barrel markings were usually one of two variations of ADDRESS SAMᴸ COLT NEW-YORK CITY, but a few pistols bear the

hand engraved inscription: COLᴺ COLT. LONDON Frame markings COLTS/PATENT usually hand-engraved on all models; the Texas Ranger and Indian cylinder roll scene was standard.

Some surprising variations are recorded in this model, because Colt's was cleaning up their parts stock of leftovers from earlier production. Thus, a few pistols were made with square-back trigger guards, some had frames cut for shoulder stocks, V-type mainsprings, and so forth. At least 20 percent of the Hartford English Dragoon production was engraved, in London, and in British style scrolls. About 200 revolvers (many of them engraved) were returned to Hartford in 1861, for use in the Civil War.
Standard Hartford English Dragoon revolver:
5B-036   Values—Good **$3,750**   Fine **$20,000**

Colt Model 1848 Baby Dragoon Revolver

Model 1848 Baby Dragoon Revolver. Manufactured from 1847 through 1850; total of approximately 15,000.

31 caliber. 5-shot cylinder on all variations. Barrel lengths of 3", 4", 5", and 6"; all are octagon, with or without attached loading levers (rare with lever).

Grips of one piece varnished walnut. Casehardened frame, hammer, and lever; remainder blued. The gripstraps of silver plated brass.

The first pocket model to be made at Colt's Hartford factory, the Baby Dragoon was a diminutive version of the early 44 caliber Dragoon revolvers; the square-back trigger guard is a distinguishing feature. The serial range began with 1, and continued through about 15500. Two types of barrel markings were used, each reading: ADDRESS SAMᴸ COLT/NEW-YORK CITY, but one having bracket finials at each end. COLTS/PATENT was marked on the left side of the frame. The cylinder scene for early revolvers is a portion of the Texas Ranger and Indian fight roll as standard on the 44 caliber Dragoons. Later guns (after range of about 10500 to 11000) are standard with the famous stagecoach holdup design.

Major variations: Most Baby Dragoons do not have attached loading levers; the latter feature began to appear in the serial range of about 11600. Pistols without the lever do not have loading cutouts on the right side of the barrel lug; those with levers factory installed will have the cutout. Cylinder types are another basis for determining variants in this model: These are classified by combinations of the roll engraved scene and the shapes of the cylinder stop slots (round and then oval on early guns; rectangular on the late production). Still another detail is in the length of the frame; late production pistols are slightly longer, and this is visible by noting the increased distance between the front of the cylinder and the back of the barrel lug.

As the first pocket Colt revolver made since the collapse of the Paterson enterprise, the Baby Dragoon is an attractive piece to collectors. Such pioneer features as the square-back trigger

guard, low serial numbers, oval stop slots, Ranger and Indian cylinder scene, and lack of loading lever are all of particular appeal. With a limited production total, the model offers quite a contrast in scarcity to the successor model, the 1849 Pocket Revolver. Because of their value, and as serial ranges often overlap with the more common "Pocket Models", this has been an area subject to deception. Deceitfully altered trigger guards (from rounded to squareback) and plugged/welded barrel lugs (where plunger of loading lever was fitted) are sometimes encountered.

Considerable detail on the Baby Dragoon was published in P.L. Shumaker's *Colt's Variations of the Old Model Pocket Pistol* and Jordan & Watts *Colt's Pocket '49; Its Evolution* (see Biblio). Basic breakdown of variations is as follows:
Pistols with the Texas Ranger and Indian fight cylinder scene, in varying barrel lengths; and without attached rammer levers; serial range through about 11600 (some overlap with stagecoach scene cylinders):
5B-037   Values—Good **$2,500**   Fine **$11,500**
Pistols as above, with left hand barrel stamping, no capping groove on right side of recoil shield. Serial range 1 to 150:
5B-038   Values—Good **$3,250**   Fine **$17,000**

5B-037

Pistols as above, but with the stagecoach holdup cylinder scene; and oval stop slots. Serial range about 10400-12100 (note overlap with other variations):

5B-039   Values—Good **$2,500**   Fine **$14,000**

Pistols as above, with stagecoach holdup cylinder, scene and rectangular cylinder stop slots. Serial range approximately 11000 to 12450 (note overlap with other variations):

5B-040   Values—Good **$1,750**   Fine **$11,000**

Pistols with the stagecoach cylinder scene, and with attached rammer levers; rectangular cylinder stops; serial range approximately 11600 to 15500:

5B-041   Values—Good **$2,750**   Fine **$15,000**

5B-041

Colt Model 1849 Pocket Revolver

Model 1849 Pocket Revolver. Production began in 1850, and continued through 1873; total of the Hartford made series was about 340,000 (by December 1865, the year the Civil War ended, serial number range had reached approximately 280,000). The London Model 1849 totaled about 11,000 and is covered separately below.

31 caliber. 5- and 6-shot cylinders. Barrel lengths of 3", 4", 5", and 6"; octagonal in shape, with or without attached loading levers (majority had levers).

Grips of one piece varnished walnut. Casehardened frame, hammer, and lever; remainder blued. The gripstraps of silver plated brass; a few of steel, blued or silver plated. Oval trigger guards standard, in two sizes.

Successor to the Baby Dragoon, the Model 1849 Pocket was very much a diminutive version of the Model 1851 Navy. The 1849's serial numbering continued that of its predecessor (with some overlap), beginning at about 12000 and continuing through about 340000. Three basic barrel markings were employed (on U.S. made specimens); and their progression is one means of classification for the Model 1849. Their serial ranges are: ADDRESS SAM COLT/NEW-YORK CITY (14400 through c. 187000; two variations in marking known); ADDRESS SAM COLT/HARTFORD CT (164000 to about 206000); and ADDRESS COL. SAM COLT NEW-YORK U.S. AMERICA, known as the "one line New York" (187000 to about 340000). Rarely encountered is: ADDRESS.COL: COLT./LONDON found in high serial ranges. As to be expected, some overlapping of marking does appear from one serial range to another. Standard throughout production was the COLTS/PATENT stamping on the left side of the frame. Also standard was the stagecoach holdup roll design on the cylinder. The London made pistols are in a category by themselves.

More Model 1849 Pocket pistols were produced than any other Colt percussion firearm. With 23 years of steady production this model underwent a great many changes, hence numerous variations are encountered. Some are highly significant for the collector (and most are so noted here) while others are interesting or curious but will rarely or significantly alter basic values. A fairly complete collection of the Model 1849 would require at least 200 revolvers. Recommended sources for

5B-043

all variations are Shumaker's *Colt's Variations of the Old Model Pocket Pistol* and the very recent, highly detailed Jordan & Watts *Colt's Pocket '49.* Among those details considered are markings, types of trigger guards, loading cutouts, loading lever latches, sights, hammers, finishes, engraving, etc. An alleged variant that rears its ugly head occasionally is the so-called M. 1849 with "dragoon type barrel" (part round/octagon). A few are known as far back as the 1930s; some thought to have been altered in jest to tease a fellow collector (in an era when the gun had but slight value). In the interim such pieces have even acquired some genuine aging. Regardless of fact that specimens appear in the Belden & Haven book and the famous collection exhibited at the Metropolitan Museum of Art, 1942 Catalog, the consensus of expert opinion is that no such variant was made. (The author exposed that 1942 fake in his own 1981 catalog.)

Standard model, in 4", 5", or 6" barrel (the latter often tend to bring a premium), with attached loading lever, and small brass trigger guard:

5B-042   Values—Good **$550**   Fine **$1,250**

Same as above, with large brass trigger guard:

5B-043   Values—Good **$475**   Fine **$1,150**

Standard model, in 4", 5", or 6" barrel, with attached loading lever, and with steel gripstraps:

5B-044   Values—Good **$575**   Fine **$2,000**

Same as above with ADDRESS-SAM'L COLT/HARTFORD CT. Large brass trigger guards and five-shot cylinders most commonly encountered (six-shot cylinders worth premium). Specimens with large iron trigger guards rare and worth premium:

5B-045   Values—Good **$600**   Fine **$1,750**

Crowned Muzzle Variation of Model 1849. One-line New York address; found within serial range 331, 600 to 322,993. Muzzles of the octagon barrels have been neatly rounded (i.e. "crowned") in attempt to protect the bore at that critical point while equally protecting the holster from the usual sharp edges of the muzzle as the gun is inserted or withdrawn. All those thus far recorded had 5-shot cylinders and 4" barrels.

5B-045.2   Values—Good **$750**   Fine **$2,250**

Martially marked Model 1849; 50 purchased by U.S. Navy 1861. Few authentic specimens observed in 203000-204000 serial range with two line Hartford address, large brass trigger guard. Markings vary slightly; include anchor at top of barrel near breech, inspector marks P/GG on outside wall of cylinder, block letters USN at top of brass backstrap and U.D.C. (Union Defense Committee) on underside of butt:

5B-045.5   Values—Good **$6,000**   Fine **$20,000**

Same as above with two line LONDON barrel marking, but without British proofs and serial number in the high Hartford production range (above 143,000). Rare:

5B-046   Values—Good **$575**   Fine **$2,500**

So-called "Wells Fargo" model; made without loading lever; 3" octagon barrel with breech extension and long frame (both as standard on all M. 1849's); small rounded trigger guard. Quantity approx. 4,000. Specimens appear mixed in with serial range 15,000 to 164,000. Origin of terminology obscure; no known affiliation with Wells Fargo so exercise caution should such markings be seen (spurious examples known).

A few variants of this scarce model are worth premiums: (A) early production with short frame and short barrel extension as on "Baby Dragoon". (B) 4" barrel; serial range 14-15,000. Very rare. (C) large brass trigger guard; quantity approx. 1,250. (D) small steel guard in serial range 147,000; quantity approx. 75. (E) large steel guard; quantity approx. 175:

5B-047   Values—Good **$1,000**   Fine **$6,500**

London-made pistols, identified by their own serial range (1 through 11,000) are basically the same as Colt's contemporary Hartford production (1853-57). Quality of the London pistols was superior to that of Hartford. Usual markings ADDRESS COL: COLT./LONDON

Early London made; Serial numbers under 1000. Most with brass gripstraps and small rounded trigger guard. Variations

5B-047

noted. Earliest specimens (serial range, 1 - 265 with one line hand engraved markings COL. COLT. LONDONor SAM COLT. LONDON rare and worth premium:

5B-048   Values—Good **$525**   Fine **$1,400**

Later London-made; steel gripstraps and large oval trigger guard. Three variations noted among this group:

5B-049   Values—Good **$500**   Fine **$1,250**

Colt Model 1851 Navy Revolver

Model 1851 Navy Revolver. Brought out in 1850 and manufactured through 1873; 215,348 of this model were made in Hartford. By December 1865, the year the Civil War ended, serial numbers of the Model 1851 had reached approximately 185,000. Colt's London factory turned out about 42,000 of the Model 1851, and these are detailed separately below.

36 caliber. 6-shot cylinder. 7-1/2" barrel; octagonal, with attached loading lever.

Grips of one piece varnished walnut. Casehardened frame, hammer, and lever; remainder blued. The gripstraps of silver plated brass; a few of steel, finished in blue.

Serial numbers began at 1 and the highest number recorded was 215348. Three basic barrel markings (American production) were used; their sequence is a means of classification for the model. The markings and their approximate serial ranges are: - ADDRESS SAM⋅ COLT NEW-YORK CITY - (1 - 74000); - ADDRESS SAM⋅ COLT. HARTFORD CT. - (74000 - 101000); - ADDRESS COL. SAM⋅ COLT NEW-YORK U.S. AMERICA - (101000 - 215348). Throughout production the left side of the frame was marked: COLTS/PATENT. Also standard was the roll engraved cylinder scene, depicting a battle between the Texas Navy and that of Mexico.

The Model 1851 was Colt's prime medium caliber handgun in the percussion period of manufacture in Hartford. As one of the most popular of American antique arms, the Navy has come to be recognized as a collecting specialty of its own. The number of variations is considerable, all detailed in the standard reference work '51 Colt Navies, by Nathan L. Swayze. Basic to classification of variants are trigger guard types, markings, contours of certain parts, materials of gripstraps, and attachable shoulder stocks. Caution advised for so-called "Dragoon variant" with part round/octagon barrel. As with M. 1849 (see

details), consensus of expert opinion believes variant never made by Colt and likely all specimens spurious.

First Model Square-back Trigger Guard; In serial range 1 - 1250 (however, a more recent study published in *Gun Report,* August 2006, indicates that serial range is more likely 1 - 800); recognizable by the square-back trigger guard, and screw under the wedge:

5B-050   Values—Good **$5,000**   Fine **$32,500**

Second Model Square-back Trigger Guard; Serial range 1250 - 4200; square-back trigger guard and the wedge screw above the wedge. A few are found in serial ranges up to 4500, and it is in those ranges especially where caution is advised as bogus specimens turn up; the usual round trigger guard is spuriously altered to square-back shape. Usually the workmanship is obvious; a few require very careful scrutiny.

5B-051   Values—Good **$3,250**   Fine **$22,500**

Third Model; Serial range 4200 - 85000 (a few in ranges as low as 3600); featuring the small rounded brass trigger guard:

5B-052   Values—Good **$900**   Fine **$4,500**

Fourth Model; Serial range 85000 - 215348; having the large rounded brass trigger guard:

5B-053   Values—Good **$900**   Fine **$4,000**

(Note: Some overlap exists between the various serial ranges.)

IMPORTANT VARIATIONS from the above are:

Iron gripstraps; most often seen having large trigger guard:

5B-054   Values—Good **$950**   Fine **$4,500**

Barrels marked - ADDRESS COL. COLT LONDON -(U.S. made; high serial ranges):

5B-055   Values—Good **$900**   Fine **$4,000**

Martially marked Navies, with U.S. on the left side of the frame (beneath COLTS/PATENT), government inspector marks **on the** grips and on various metal parts. A highly detailed study

5B-050

5B-053

5B-058

"Marking Variations of U.S.N. Inspectors on Colt 1851 and M. 1861 (percussion & conversion) Revolvers" in May, 2000 "Gun Report" may play a role in adding premium values to some U.S.N. revolvers.

Brass Straps:
5B-056   Values—Good **$1,650**   Fine **$11,500**

Iron Straps:
5B-057   Values—Good **$1,850**   Fine **$14,000**

Cut for shoulder stock attachment. The same three basic types of stock attachments were made as in the Third Model Dragoon (*q.v.* for description). Rarest are the **First** and **Second type attachments:**

First type stocks most often observed in serial range 56,000; **Second type** in serial range 69,000; **Third type** in various ranges from 67,000 to 192,000 (see "*Book of Colt Firearms*" for specific numbers). Stocks with the canteen insert may be encountered in all three types. The large majority of stocks were sold to the civilian market (silver plated, brass mountings and varnish finished wood stocks standard); military models very rare (oil finished, walnut stocks standard).

Pistol:
5B-058   Values—Good **$2,000**   Fine **$11,500**

Stock:
5B-059   Values—Good **$4,000**   Fine **$9,500**

Third type attachment, in which the pistol features a four screw frame, cutouts on the recoil shield, and (sometimes) lanyard swivels on the trigger guard strap:

Pistol:
5B-060   Values—Good **$1,900**   Fine **$11,000**

Stock:
5B-061   Values—Good **$3,750**   Fine **$8,500**

(Note: The presence of the canteen insert in the shoulder stock adds 25 percent to 50 percent of the stock's value.)

THE LONDON MODEL 1851 NAVY revolver is quite similar to its contemporary made at Colt's Hartford factory; however, the London pistols have their own serial range (1 through 42000), they feature large trigger guards, and blued or (uncommon) silver plated steel gripstraps. Standard barrel marking: ADDRESS. COL: COLT.LONDON, British proofmarks present on the breech end of the cylinder and on left side of the barrel lug. Manufacturing dates were 1853 through 1857. The two standard models are:

First Model; Serial numbers in the range 1 to approximately 2000, brass gripstraps (some trigger guards square-back [rare and worth a considerable premium], but small round was standard), several parts of Hartford make:
5B-062   Values—Good **$950**   Fine **$4,250**

Second Model; Serial range from approximately 2000 to end of production, all parts London made, steel gripstraps with the trigger guard of large rounded size (small iron trigger guard rare; worth premium):
5B-063   Values—Good **$900**   Fine **$3,850**

British, Canadian, Australian, Austrian and other martially-marked New York and London-marked 1851s. There are quite a few variations of British War Department markings (**W.D.** accompanied by motif of arrow; known as the "Broad Arrow") to indicate government ownership; Canadian marks (**U.C.** for Upper Canada and **L.C.** for Lower Canada); Australian police and military ownership marks; Austrian government **KM** ("Kriegs Marine" Imperial Navy markings, usually with a serial number and most often seen marked on the top of the brass backstrap) and other obscure foreign military-marked Navies. Such identifiable, authentic markings usually increase values a minimum of 25 percent to those; possibly as high as 100 percent or more depending on their rarity, historic associations. Information on such markings is found in the J. Rosa work *Colonel Colt London* and N. Swayze's *'51 Colt Navies* (see Biblio.)
5B-063.5

Colt Model 1855 Sidehammer Pocket Revolver and "Charter Oak" Grips

Model 1855 Sidehammer Pocket Revolver. Most commonly known among collectors as the "Root Model" after Elisha K. Root, the noted Colt designer (although Samuel Colt himself actually was the inventor of this model). Entered into production in 1855, and discontinued c. 1870. Made in two distinct serial sequences, with the total quantity approximately 40,000. The model was Colt's only percussion handgun built on the solid frame principle, in contrast to the firm's standard design of barrel and cylinder which are readily removable from the frame. Other features permitting the quick identification of Model 1855 pistols are the hammer mounted on the right side of the frame, the spur trigger, the cylinder pin's entry into the frame from the rear, and the "wraparound grip" secured to the backstrap (no trigger guard strap is present).

Serial numbering is in two sequences, based on caliber. The first production, in 28 caliber, is numbered 1 through about 30,000. (Made through to 1861).The second production, in 31 caliber, is numbered separately from 1 through 14,000 range (by the end of the Civil War in 1865 they reached approximately to

10000 range). Most pistols with octagonal barrels were chambered for 28 caliber, and had only 3-1/2" barrel lengths. All pistols with round barrels are 31 caliber, and have either 3-1/2" or 4-1/2" barrel lengths. Standard finish throughout production was casehardened hammer and loading lever; the balance blued.

Standard grips are one piece, varnished walnut (unique in all of the Colt handgun line). A few of these Root models were fitted with special oak wood grips made from Connecticut's most famous and historic ancient tree, under which its original royal charter had been signed centuries earlier. In 1865 the tree was toppled by a violent storm and ultimately its remains were acquired by Samuel Colt. Aside from having some personal furniture (including a carved cradle) made from that wood, Colt fitted a small group of these Root models with grips also made from it, popularly named "CHARTER OAK." A number of those handguns were handsomely engraved and also inscribed with a presentation from Colt personally, mentioning that very fact "...Charter Oak Stock" on some of them. A few plain Root models were also fitted with those Charter Oak grips. Values for authentic specimens may be increased upwards considerably depending on historic inscription, engraving and condition.

A thorough classification of the seven basic variations of the Sidehammer series has been made by S. Gerald Keogh, in the monograph *Samuel Colt's New Model Pocket Pistols*. The breakdown is by details of barrel length, shape, and marking, cylinder shape and roll engraving, means of securing the cylinder pin, cylinder pin type, caliber, loading levers, and so forth. Rather complicated, only basics are noted here:

Models 1 and 1A; 3-7/16" octagon barrel, full octagon loading lever, Hartford barrel address without pointing hand motif, 28 caliber, Cabin and Indian cylinder scene, serial range 1 - 384. Minor difference: capping groove cutout on right recoil shield of Model 1 is 1/2" (serial range 1-175); groove is 5/8" on Model 1A (same as on all other models):

5B-064   Values—Good **$950**   Fine **$6,500**

Model 2; 3-1/2" octagon barrel, Hartford barrel address with pointing hand motif, 28 caliber, Cabin and Indian cylinder scene, serial range 476 - 25000:

5B-065   Values—Good **$425**   Fine **$1,250**

Model 3; 3-1/2" octagon barrel, Hartford address, pointing hand motif, used until approximately serial 26000, 28 caliber, full fluted cylinder, serial number range 25001 to 30000:

5B-066   Values—Good **$425**   Fine **$1,250**

Model 3A; 3-1/2" octagon barrel, Hartford address, 31 caliber, full fluted cylinder, serial number range 1 to 1350:

5B-067   Values—Good **$475**   Fine **$1,450**

Model 4; 3-1/2" octagon barrel, Hartford barrel address without pointing hand motif, 31 caliber, full fluted cylinder. Serial range 1351 - 2400:

5B-068   Values—Good **$475**   Fine **$1,450**

Model 5; 3-1/2" round barrel, COL. COLT NEW-YORK, etc. barrel address, 31 caliber, full fluted cylinder, serial range 2401 - 8000:

5B-069   Values—Good **$385**   Fine **$1,100**

Model 5A; Same as Model 5, except the barrel length of 4-1/2"; serial range also the same:

5B-070   Values—Good **$600**   Fine **$1,850**

Models 6 and 6A; 3-1/2" and 4-1/2" round barrels, COL. COLT NEW-YORK, etc. barrel address, 31 caliber, stagecoach holdup cylinder roll scene, Model 6 has 3-1/2" barrel, 6A has 4-1/2" and worth premium. Serial range 8001 - 11074:

5B-071   Values—Good **$425**   Fine **$1,100**

Models 7 and 7A; 3-1/2" and 4-1/2" round barrels, COL. COLT NEW-YORK, etc. barrel address, 31 caliber, stagecoach holdup cylinder roll scene, screw-in cylinder retains the cylinder pin. Model 7 has 3-1/2" barrel, 7A has 4-1/2" and worth premium. Serial range 11075 - 14000:

5B-072   Values—Good **$625**   Fine **$2,250**

5B-065

5B-069

Colt Model 1855 "First Model" Sporting Rifle

Model 1855 "First Model" Sporting Rifle. Manufactured c. 1856-59; total run of about 1,000.

36 caliber. A very limited number in 40 caliber. 6-shot cylinder. Barrel lengths standard in a variety of lengths, 15" and 18" in carbine size, and 21", 24", 27" and 30" in the rifle size; round in shape, semi-octagonal at the breech.

Varnished or oil finished walnut stocks. Metal parts blued, with casehardened hammer and lever.

The first of Colt's production of revolving longarms in Hartford, and one of the few sidehammer longarm groups to be individually serial numbered; the range from 1 up through 1000. The standard barrel marking: COLT'S PT./1856 and ADDRESS COL. COLT/HARTFORD CT. U.S.A.Cylinder roll scene of a hunter firing at five deer, found only on the First Model Sporting Rifle.

Quick identification of this model can be made by the oiler device attached to the left side of the barrel lug, the lack of a forestock, the unique cylinder roll scene, and the spur type trigger guard. NOTE: the serial numbers on oiler device and its fasteners seldom match that of the rifle.

Major variations are:

Early production; with hand engraved marking in old English letters on the barrel (Address S. Colt Hartford Ct. U.S.A.), low serial numbers:

5B-073   Values—Good **$3,500**   Fine **$12,500**

Standard production model, as described above; rifle length barrels:

5B-074   Values—Good **$3,250**   Fine **$10,500**

Standard production model, but with carbine length barrels:

5B-075   Values—Good **$3,250**   Fine **$10,500**

5B-073

5B-074

Colt Model 1855 Half Stock Sporting Rifle

5B-076

Model 1855 Half Stock Sporting Rifle. Made c. 1857-64; estimated production of 1,000 to 1,500.

Calibers 36 and 44 with 6-shot cylinder; large caliber 56, 5-shot. (A few made in 40 and 50 calibers; 6-shot cylinders.) Barrels standard in 24", 27", and 30" lengths; round with semi-octagonal breech.

Varnished or oil stained walnut stocks. Metal parts blued, the hammer and lever casehardened.

Serial numbering in the Half Stock Sporting Rifle group is rather complicated, since these were in ranges by calibers, and military rifles and carbines of the same calibers thus were included, as was the Full Stock Sporting Rifle. Standard topstrap

marking: COLT'S PT./1856 and ADDRESS COL. COLT/HARTFORD CT. U.S.A. Cylinders were fluted, and thus roll engraved scenes not present.

For identification purposes, look for the half stock forend, and the rifled barrel (to avoid confusion with the smoothbore Model 1855 Shotgun). Some quite attractive variations have been observed in the Half Stock Sporting group, in special sights, frames, trigger guards, adjustable set triggers, and so forth. Some outstanding engraved and presentation pieces have come from this model. Values about the same for either large scroll type trigger guard or small conventional type:

5B-076   Values—Good **$3,500**   Fine **$10,000**

Colt Model 1855 Full Stock Sporting Rifle

Model 1855 Full Stock Sporting Rifle. (Not illus.) Manufactured c. 1856-64; the total limited to a few hundred specimens. Virtually identical to Full Stock Military Rifle but without sling swivels and has crescent shaped buttplate.

36, 40, 44, 50, and 56 calibers (calibers 40 & 50 very scarce and will bring a premium). 5-shot cylinder (56 caliber) and 6 shots for all other calibers. Barrel lengths of 21", 24", 27", 30" and 31-5/16"; round with semi-octagonal breech.

Again serial numbering in the series is complicated, since these were in ranges by calibers, and thus military rifles and carbines of the same calibers were included, as was the Half Stock Sporting Rifle. Standard topstrap marking: COLT'S

PT./1856 and ADDRESS COL. COLT/HARTFORD CT. U.S.A. Cylinders standard fluted, and without roll engraved scenes.

Identifiable by the full stock forend, the lack of bayonet fixture on the muzzle end, and the general use of sporting style sights. It is possible to confuse this model with some of the full stock military revolving rifles and rifled muskets. In the event of uncertainty, the reader should carefully study the detailed material presented in *The Book of Colt Firearms*. Considerable variation of details will be observed, generally in sights, trigger guards, frames, barrel lengths, and calibers. As noted in the Half Stock Sporting group, some important engraved and presentation arms have come from this model:

5B-077   Values—Good **$3,500**   Fine **$11,000**

Colt 1855 Military Rifle and Rifled Musket

Model 1855 Military Rifle and Rifled Musket. Made c. 1856-64; estimated total production of 9,310.

44 and 56 calibers. 5-shot cylinder (56 caliber) and 6 shots for the 44. 64 caliber very rare; worth premium.

Barrel lengths of 21", 24", 27", 31", 31-3/16", 31-5/16", 37-5/16" and 37-1/2"; round in shape with semi-octagonal breech.

Oil stained walnut stocks. Metal parts blued; hammer and lever casehardened.

As with most of the Model 1855 Sidehammer longarms, the serial number is complex, due to the factory practice of numbering by calibers; thus Full and Half Stock rifles and the various Carbines of identical calibers are all together. Standard topstrap marking for 44 caliber arms: COLT'S PT./1856 and ADDRESS COL. COLT/HARTFORD CT. U.S.A.Standard for the 56

caliber: COL. COLT HARTFORD CT. U.S.A.Cylinders were fluted, and without roll engraved scenes.

A combination of details enables quick identification of the Military Rifle and Rifled Musket: Full stock forend, aperture for bayonet attachment (either a proper bayonet lug, or front sight machined to accept socket), military sights, and U.S. markings (the latter present on government issued arms). Some confusion is possible between the Military Rifle and the Full Stock Sporting Rifle; when in doubt consult the detailed data in *The Book of Colt Firearms*. A notable degree of variation exists in these arms, in sights, trigger guards, frames, barrel lengths, calibers, markings, finishes, and bayonets. Specimens in caliber 64 are very rare; they are found with barrel lengths of 31-1/4" in smoothbore and rifled. Serial numbers fall below 100. They both accepted the

5B-078

socket-type bayonets. There is no 50 caliber model believed made in this military rifle. Reportings of this 50 caliber are believed to have been confused with the full stock sporting rifle which resembles it.

Major variations are:

Standard type for angular bayonet, U.S. markings:
5B-078   Values—Good **$5,500**   Fine **$22,500**

Same as above, without U.S. markings:
5B-079   Values—Good **$3,500**   Fine **$10,000**

Standard type for saber bayonet, U.S. markings:
5B-080   Values—Good **$5,500**   Fine **$22,500**

Same as above, without U.S. markings:
5B-081   Values—Good **$3,250**   Fine **$10,000**

Colt Model 1855 Revolving Carbine

Model 1855 Revolving Carbine. Made c. 1856-64; estimated total production 4,435.

36, 44 and 56 calibers. 5-shot cylinder (56 caliber), and 6 shots for the 36 and 44. Barrel lengths of 15", 18", and 21". A 24" variation, the "Artillery Model," also manufactured. All barrels round in shape with semi-octagonal breech.

Varnished or oil stained walnut stocks (former for civilian sales, latter for military). Metal parts blued; the hammer and lever casehardened.

In common with most of the Model 1855 Sidehammer longarm production, the serial numbering is complex. The factory practice was to number by calibers; thus, Carbines, Full and Half Stock Sporting Rifles, and Military Rifles and Rifled Muskets—of the same caliber—are all numbered together. The company address markings can be confusing. The majority of 36 and 44 caliber Carbines have the topstrap legend: COLT'S PT./1856 ADDRESS COL. COLT/HARTFORD CT. U.S.A. The 56 caliber Carbines customarily marked on the topstrap: COL. COLT HARTFORD CT. U.S.A. Cylinders were fluted, and without roll engraved scenes.

Quick identification of most carbines is from the lack of a forend (the only exception noted below), presence of lanyard rings or swivels (on frames and/or stocks), sights usually military type, and the generally short barrel length. The one variation having a forend is the "Artillery Model," quite rare, and fitted with the saber type bayonet; these were 56 caliber, with 24" barrel, and had two barrel bands on the forend. Very rare are Carbines in 40 and 50 calibers.

Major variations are:

Standard Carbine in 56 caliber, with military quality finish, no forend stock, and 15", 18" and 21" barrels:
5B-082   Values—Good **$3,250**   Fine **$10,000**

Standard Carbine in 44 caliber, with military quality finish, no forend, and 18" and 21" barrels:
5B-083   Values—Good **$3,250**   Fine **$9,500**

Standard Carbine in 36 caliber, with military quality finish, no forend, and 18" and 21" barrels:
5B-084   Values—Good **$3,250**   Fine **$9,500**

Artillery Model Carbine, 56 caliber, with 24" barrel and forend, and bayonet lug on muzzle:
5B-085   Values—Good **$3,500**   Fine **$16,500**

"British Carbine," 56 caliber, serial range 10000 - 12000. Barrel lengths from 21" to about 30"; usually with British proofmarks and brass trigger guards and buttplates:
5B-086   Values—Good **$3,250**   Fine **$9,500**

5B-082

5B-085

Colt Model 1855 Revolving Shotgun

Model 1855 Revolving Shotgun. Made c. 1860-63; total of about 1,100.

10 and 20 gauges (75 and 60 calibers respectively). 5-shot cylinders. Standard barrel lengths of 27", 30", 33", and 36" also known, primarily in the 10 gauge production. All barrels round, with semi-octagonal breech.

Varnished walnut stocks. Metal parts blued, with casehardened hammer and lever. Some barrels were finished brown; and some stocks oil stained.

Serial numbered as a separate group from other Model 1855 production, the shotgun range began with 1 and continued through 1100. 10 gauge specimens bore the standard topstrap marking: COL. COLT HARTFORD CT. U.S.A. 20 gauge guns standard marked on the topstrap: COLT'S PT./1856 and ADDRESS COL. COLT/HARTFORD CT. U.S.A. Cylinders fluted, and thus were not roll engraved.

Shotguns are quickly identified by their smoothbore, the usually present trigger guard marking of 60 or 75 cal. (though

5B-088

not found on the scroll guard arms), the serial numbering under 1100, the shotgun style buttplates, and the lack of rear sights. *Ultra-rare* are specimens of either gauge having full stock forends.

Major variations are:

10 gauge Shotgun, with small oval trigger guard, large frame size, and buttstock without checkering:

5B-087   Values—Good **$3,000**   Fine **$6,000**

10 gauge Shotgun, with large scroll type trigger guard, large frame size, and checkered buttstock:

5B-088   Values—Good **$3,000**   Fine **$6,000**

20 gauge Shotgun, with small oval trigger guard, small frame size, and buttstock without checkering:

5B-089   Values—Good **$3,000**   Fine **$6,000**

20 gauge Shotgun, with large scroll type trigger guard, small frame size, and checkered buttstock:

5B-090   Values—Good **$3,000**   Fine **$7,500**

Colt Model 1860 Army Revolver

5B-091

5B-092

Model 1860 Army Revolver. In production from 1860 through c. 1873; total of about 200,500 made. Serial numbers reached about 156,000 by December, 1865 and the end of the Civil War.

44 caliber. 6-shot rebated cylinder. 7-1/2" (early production only) and 8" barrels; round, with the creeping style loading lever.

Grips of one piece walnut. Casehardened frame, hammer, and lever; remainder blued. The gripstraps standard as follows: Brass trigger guard, blued steel backstrap.

Serial numbers began at 1 and continued through about 200500. The two basic barrel markings were: -ADDRESS COL. SAM^L COLT NEW-YORK U.S. AMERICA- and -ADDRESS SAM^L COLT HARTFORD CT.- (early production only). Standard on the left side of the frame was the stamping: COLTS/PATENT. On the left shoulder of trigger guard strap: 44 Cal. Cylinder roll scene of the battle between the Texas Navy and that of Mexico (Same as applied to the 1851 and 1861 Navy Models).

Successor to the Third Model Dragoon, the Model 1860 Army ranks third in total number produced of the various models of percussion Colt handguns. It was the major revolver in use by U.S. troops during the Civil War, and 127,156 of the Model 1860 Army were acquired by the Union government for that conflict. Key variations and their values are as follows:

Fluted Cylinder Army; Cylinders had full flutes, and thus lacked roll engraved scenes. Barrel lengths were 7-1/2" and 8", their markings either the New York or the Hartford addresses. A very few of earliest production fitted with the shorter M. 1851 Navy size grip; very rare variant. Frames usually of the four screw type, with the recoil shield cut for attachment of shoulder stock. Appear in the serial range 3 to about 8000; the total production estimated at 4000:

5B-091   Values—Good **$2,500**   Fine **$11,000**

Standard Round Cylinder Army; The cylinder roll engraved with the Naval Engagement scene. 8" barrel length, most marked with the New York address, but some early specimens are Hartford-marked. Army (large) size grip; blued steel backstraps, brass trigger guards. Frames of the four screw type until about serial range 50000, at which point the fourth screw (for engaging shoulder stock yoke) was dropped. Most of the production sold to the U.S. government, and marked with inspector stampings on the grips and various metal parts:

5B-092   Values—Good **$950**   Fine **$7,500**

Civilian Model Round Cylinder Army; The same as the Standard Round Cylinder pistol, except for the three-screw frame and the lack of cuts for shoulder stock attachment. New York barrel address standard. The finish on Civilian Army revolvers was generally superior to the usual military contract pieces:

5B-093   Values—Good **$900**   Fine **$7,000**

The number of variations in the 1860 Army is not at all as extensive as in the Model 1849 Pocket or the Model 1851 Navy. The Army's period of manufacture was shorter, and by the time of its introduction, the Colt revolver had reached a pinnacle of evolution employing the percussion ignition system.

OTHER VARIATIONS of the Model 1860, sought by collectors:

Attachable shoulder stocks were made in the Second and Third patterns (as detailed in the material on the Third Model Dragoon, *q.v.*).

The Third type stock is the most often encountered of the military issue "Armys;" large quantity was purchased by government contract early in Civil War. Brass yokes and buttplates usually unfinished on military issue stocks while many sold to civilian market most often silver-plated.

Stock for the fluted cylinder Army, Second type (attaches to back of handle and butt); very rare:

5B-094   Values—Good **$4,250**   Fine **$10,000**

5B-095

Stock for the fluted or round cylinder Army, Third type (yoke type; standard style):

5B-095   Values—Good **$3,500**   Fine **$8,500**

(Note: A 25 percent to 50 percent premium is placed on stocks having the canteen insert. Whether for fluted or round cylinder model determined by serial range.)

"LONDON"-marked Model 1860 Army. All of these were made at the Hartford plant, but bear the barrel marking ADDRESS COL. COLT LONDON. Backstraps and trigger guards are blued steel. Specimens viewed in serial ranges 158,000, 167,000 and 168,000 very scarce:

5B-096   Values—Good **$2,000**   Fine **$10,000**

Colt Model 1861 Navy Revolver

Model 1861 Navy Revolver. Manufactured 1861 through c. 1873; total of 38,843 produced. (Serial numbers approached 28,000 range by December 1865, the year the Civil War ended.)

36 caliber. 6-shot cylinder. 7-1/2" barrel; round, with the creeping style loading lever.

Grips of one piece varnished walnut. Casehardened frame, hammer, and lever; remainder blued. Brass gripstraps, plated in silver.

Serial numbering began at 1 and continued through 38843. The single standard barrel marking was: - ADDRESS COL. SAM. COLT NEW-YORK U.S. AMERICA. -. COLTS/PATENT was stamped on the left side of the frame. 36 CAL on the left shoulder of the trigger guard strap. The cylinder roll scene (often very light on this model) depicted the battle between the Texas Navy and that of Mexico.

A streamlined version of the Model 1851 Navy, the 1861 is one of the most attractive of all Colt percussion handguns. However, limited in production quantities and in years of manufacture, the number of variations is few. The key types:

5B-097
Fluted Cylinder Model

Fluted Cylinder Navy; Only about 100 of these were made, in serial range from 1 to approximately 100. Cylinders are fluted, and bear no roll engraved motif. However, the fluted cylinders were marked **PAT. SEPT 10TH 1850** within one of the flutes.

5B-097   Values—Good **$6,500**   Fine **$40,000**

Standard production model, with the features as described above:

5B-098   Values—Good **$950**   Fine **$8,000**

Shoulder Stock Navy; Found only in the serial ranges 11000 and 14000, about 100 were produced. Only the Third type stock was made for the Model 1861 (see Third Model Dragoon for description of the type). Frames of the four screw design, with the recoil shield cut for engaging the stock yoke. Serial number on stock (to match gun) appears on bottom tang of yoke with letter "S" usually marked below each serial. It is also possible to find a stock fitted with the canteen variant; extremely rare:

Stock:
5B-099   Values—Good **$4,250**   Fine **$10,000**

Pistol:
5B-100   Values—Good **$3,750**   Fine **$16,000**

5B-101
Standard Model

U.S. Martial marked; Several hundred were sold to both the Army and Navy during the Civil War. Many of these bear no inspector markings; when inspector marks are present they mostly appear on the grips and in single letters on various metal parts. Occasionally U.S.N. found on the brass butt of naval contract pieces. Although U.S. markings beneath COLTS PATENT on frame are reported, such marks are very rare and worth premium. Beware of spurious U.S. frame marks. See 5B-056 Martial Colt 1851 for reference to detailed study of U.S.N. markings.

5B-101   Values—Good **$2,750**   Fine **$17,500**

London-marked specimen fitted with iron gripstraps; -ADDRESS COL. COLT LONDON-on barrel. These were all manufactured in Colt's Hartford plant for their London office. Rare:

5B-102   Values—Good **$2,000**   Fine **$12,000**

Revised Understanding, Assumptions And Conclusions About The Colt Model 1862 "Police" And Model 1862 "Pocket Navy" Revolvers

Extensive, comparative analytical studies on both these percussion revolvers and their conversions to cartridge models of same (see 5B-127 through 5B-132), most notably those published in the American Society of Arms Collectors (Bulletin No. 85 April, 2002); *Man at Arms* magazine (issue no. 3, 2003); and *"The Rampant Colt"* bulletin of the Colt Collector's Association (Summer 2004) culminated in completion of a major study *Variations of Colt's New Model Police and Pocket Breechloaders* by Breslin, Pirie and Price (see Biblio). Similar to the two ground-breaking works on the Colt Pocket Model of 1849, their survey distinguished numerous variations o these 36-caliber models that have not been previously catalogued, as well as clarifying and distinguishing others that are now recognized in a new light. These two models, always popular among collectors, have been contentious as far as terminology was concerned. The

authors stated their case well. As the results of their study are so newly imparted and yet to be fully absorbed by the collecting world … or in the marketplace … it is found impracticable to re-classify the long-familiar, usual listings (as in this "guide"). The impact of those findings is yet to be determined. Awareness of the new data may possibly affect the popularity (hence values) of some of those variations, perhaps elevating their status … and consequently "demand" in the marketplace. Some of the conclusions the authors reached may yet be confirmed "beyond shadow of doubt" (as the authors have stated) and they remain assumptions, based mostly on statistical survey of a significant sampling of the guns. Among those important assumptions is their conclusion that these two models were made individually, each in their own serial number range and not, as previously believed, having shared the same serial range.

Colt Model 1862 Police Revolver

Model 1862 Police Revolver. Made from 1861 through c. 1873. Recent studies concluded that this model did not share its serial numbering with the so-called "1862 Pocket Navy" (below) and was numbered in its own range from 1 through approximately 48,000 range. (By December 1865, the year the Civil War ended, the serial number range had reached approximately the 32,000 range.)

36 caliber. 5-shot rebated and half fluted cylinder. 3-1/2" (rare), 4-1/2", 5-1/2", and 6-1/2" barrels; round, with the creeping style loading lever.

Grips of one piece walnut. Casehardened frame, hammer, and lever; remainder blued. The gripstraps of silver plated brass.

Serial numbers began at 1 and continued (with the Model 1862 Pocket Navy) through approximately 47000. The standard barrel marking was: ADDRESS COL. SAM- COLT NEW-YORK U.S. AMERICA. On the left side of the frame: COLTS/PATENT. Stamped within one of the cylinder flutes: PAT SEPT. 10th 1850.

The Model 1862 Police is considered by many collectors as the ultimate in streamlined design by Colt's factory in the percussion period. Due to slow sales and the demand for metallic cartridge arms, several thousand of the late production of the Model 1862 Police and the Pocket Navy were converted from percussion to cartridge use. The result has been to add to the desirability of these arms in their original cap and ball configuration.

5B-104

Variations of the Model 1862 Police follow:

Early specimens with the barrel marking: ADDRESS SAM- COLT/HARTFORD CT Silver plated iron gripstraps:

5B-103   Values—Good **$800**   Fine **$3,000**

Same as above, with silver plated brass gripstraps:

5B-104   Values—Good **$750**   Fine **$2,500**

Standard version of the Model 1862 Police, in 4-1/2", 5-1/2", or 6-1/2" barrel lengths. NEW YORK barrel address:

5B-105   Values—Good **$600**   Fine **$2,000**

As above, but wit h steel gripstraps, and L beneath serial numbers on bottom of gun; for sales to England. Usually found with British proofmarks:

5B-106   Values—Good **$650**   Fine **$2,250**

As above, but with ADDRESS COL. COLT/LONDONbarrel marking. Generally high serial ranges, and *rare*:

5B-107   Values—Good **$1,100**   Fine **$4,750**

Colt Pocket Model of Navy Caliber Revolver

Pocket Model of Navy Caliber Revolver; in earlier days of collecting, erroneously called the "Model of 1853" and in more recent times named the "Model 1862 Pocket Navy" revolver. Now more correctly termed the "Pocket Model of Navy Caliber" or merely "Pocket Navy." Recent studies concluded that it was numbered in its own serial range, and not, as formerly believed, having shared the number series with the Model 1862 Police (above). Exact years of production undetermined; estimated sometime between 1863 and 1865 extending to approximately 1872. Under 22,000 manufactured (of which a large percentage were either shipped as factory conversions to cartridge or made originally as cartridge models). Serial numbers of all "New York"-marked specimens fall in that serial range (under 22,000); a small group of "LONDON"-marked specimens (see 5B-110) recorded in the serial range 37,000!) The "Pocket Model of Navy Caliber" has always been among the scarcer of the Colt percussion revolvers. Its basic variations are as follows:

36 caliber. 5-shot round, rebated cylinder. 4-1/2", 5-1/2", and 6-1/2" barrels, octagonal, with the Model 1851 Navy style hinged loading lever.

Grips of one piece walnut. Casehardened frame, hammer, and lever; remainder blued. The gripstraps of silver plated brass.

Serial numbering began at 1 and continued (with the Model 1862 Police) through approximately 47000. It is not known for certain whether the number 1 was marked on the Model 1862 Police, or the Pocket Navy—or perhaps both. Some duplication

is considered likely to have occurred. The standard barrel marking was: ADDRESS COL. SAM- COLT NEW-YORK U.S. AMERICA. On the left side of the frame: COLTS/PATENT. The cylinder roll scene was the stagecoach holdup.

5B-108

Standard version, in 4-1/2", 5-1/2", or 6-1/2" barrel lengths:

5B-108   Values—Good **$625**   Fine **$2,250**

New York barrel address, with blued steel grip straps and L markings with most serial numbers (for English market):

5B-109   Values—Good **$700**   Fine **$2,750**

ADDRESS COL. COLT/LONDONbarrel marking, with British proofmarks and blued steel grip straps. (These were made at the Hartford factory for sale in their London office. Very limited production. Serial numbers recorded in the 17,000, 34,000, 37,000 and 39,000 serial ranges). Rare and seldom encountered.

5B-110   Values—Good **$950**   Fine **$4,500**

Thuer Conversion Colt Revolvers

Thuer Conversion Revolvers. Manufactured c. 1869-72; in a total production of about 5,000. The Thuer was Colt's first production of revolving firearms chambered for metallic cartridges. Production was in several models, as pointed out in the valuations listed below.

31, 36, and 44 calibers; all in the specially designed tapered Thuer cartridge. The design of these arms also allowed for changing of cylinders, in order to employ the cap and ball system. All cylinders were six-shot. Barrel lengths varied according to model.

Grips and finishes were standard according to the various models. This was also true with serial numbers, which generally appear in the higher ranges. Barrel, frame, and serial number markings were likewise conventional. However, distinctive to all Thuer conversions is the marking on the conversion ring (positioned at the breech end of the cylinder): PAT.SEP./15.1868; an *E*, in script, was marked on the ring at the eject position.

Besides the markings, the Thuer rings are easily identifiable by the presence of a turning knob, the rebounding firing pin, the ejection mechanism, and the fact that, with removal of the cylinder, the ring itself is removed as a separate unit. The ring fits over an extension left on the breech end of the cylinder where metal was machined off. Barrel lugs of the following models were machined on the right side to allow for front loading of the cylinders with the Thuer cartridge: Model 1849 Pocket, 1851 Navy, 1860 Army, 1861 Navy, 1862 Police, 1862 Pocket Navy. (Note: Though failing to prove a practical product, the Thuer's status as the first metallic cartridge revolving Colt firearm places specimens in a prized category for the Colt collector. Limited production has made the type quite desirable but has also attracted a certain amount of faking. Collectors should be extremely wary when acquiring this model.)

Major models are as follows:

Model 1849 Pocket revolver, various barrel lengths:
5B-111   Values—Very Good **$4,750**   Exc. **$12,500**
Model 1851 Navy:
5B-112   Values—Very Good **$5,000**   Exc. **$14,000**
Model 1860 Army:
5B-113   Values—Very Good **$5,500**   Exc. **$16,500**

5B-112
1851 Navy Conversion

5B-113
1860 Army Conversion

Model 1861 Navy:
5B-114   Values—Very Good **$5,500**   Exc. **$16,500**
Model 1862 Police:
5B-115   Values—Very Good **$4,500**   Exc. **$11,500**
Model 1862 Pocket Navy:
5B-116   Values—Very Good **$4,500**   Exc. **$11,500**
(Note: Also known, but extremely rare, are Thuer conversions in the Dragoon, Model 1855 Sidehammer revolver, and the Model 1855 Sidehammer rifle. These demand a premium.)

Richards Conversion, Colt 1860 Army Revolver

Richards Conversion, Model 1860 Army Revolver. Made c. 1871-78; total production of about 9,000.

44 Colt centerfire. 6-shot rebated cylinder. 8" barrel; round, with ejector rod attached, loading lever removed and the barrel lug plugged.

Grips and finish standard for the Model 1860 Army; breechplate casehardened.

Serial numbering in two ranges: One group which began at 1 and ran to approximately 8700 (including the Richards-Mason model), and another which was within the Model 1860 Army serial sequence from about 167000 - 200614. Barrel marking: - ADDRESS COL. SAM· COLT NEW-YORK U.S. AMERICA -. On the left shoulder of trigger guard strap: 44 CAL. Cylinder roll depicts the naval engagement scene.

Quick identification of the Richards can be made by noting the following details: Conversion breechplate having a firing pin, integral rear sight, and a rim which projects slightly over the breech end of the cylinder, the Model 1860 barrel lug contour retained, and the ejector rod extending out of the tube significantly (in direction of the cylinder). The Richards proved a much more practical conversion than the Thuer, and is a popular early metallic cartridge revolver with collectors.

12-Slot Cylinder Variation: The first group (quantity unknown) of Richards Conversions were fitted with cylinders bearing 12 notches for the cylinder stop (versus the usual six notches). Earliest of these were Army cylinders which had the notches added at the time of conversion while other cylinders were newly-made for the existing percussion 1860 revolvers. The details were published initially in the May, 2002 issue of *Gun Report* magazine (by R.B. McDowell). An unknown quantity (likely small) of newly manufactured 12-notch cylinders were never utilized; some subsequently found their way to the

collectors' market years later "on the loose." Hence, caution should be exercised on acquisition of the early 12-notch Richards Conversion, in order to ascertain it was originally assembled that way! Note: an occasional 12-stop cylinder has been encountered on the "transition" (a.k.a. "Second Model" Richards as well as the 1860 Richards-Mason Conversion (5B-120); such oddities have been determined to be not factory original variations.)

5B-117

Major variations are:
Standard model (a.k.a. "First Model"):
5B-117   Values—Good **$1,000**   Fine **$4,500**
U.S. marked specimens, the U.S. on left side of the barrel lug, serial numbers mixed, (with a *second set* of conversion numbers next to original numbers), government inspector marks present:
5B-118   Values—Good **$3,000**   Fine **$14,000**
Transition model (a.k.a. "Type II" or "Second Model") between the Richards and Richards-Mason; has barrel and ejector type of the former, and conversion plate and hammer of the latter, 1871 and 1872 patent dates marked on left side of the frame:
5B-119   Values—Good **$1,600**   Fine **$5,750**

Richards-Mason Conversion, Colt 1860 Army

Richards-Mason Conversion, Model 1860 Army Revolver. Major production period c. 1877-78; total of about 2,100.

44 Colt centerfire. 6-shot rebated cylinder. 7-1/2" and 8" barrels; round and of special production having a smaller lug area than the Richards Model; ejector rod attached.

Grips and finish standard for the Model 1860 Army; breechplate casehardened. Nickel plating not unusual.

Serial numbered within the range of the Richards Model, the Richards-Mason running from 5800 to about 7900. Barrel marking either -ADDRESS COL. SAM⸱ COLT NEW-YORK U.S. AMERICA -, or COLT'S PT. F.A. MFG. Cᵒ HARTFORD, CT. U.S.A. On the left side of the frame are 1871 and 1872 patent dates. 44 CAL on the left shoulder of the trigger guard strap. Cylinder roll depicts the naval engagement scene.

5B-120

Identifying characteristics allowing for quick identification of this model are: Breechplate without integral rear sight, cut away at top to allow for the hammer to strike the cartridge, no projecting front rim on the conversion plate (as on the Richards Model), and the special barrel made for the R-M group:

5B-120   Values—Good **$1,275**   Fine **$5,500**

Conversion of the Colt Model 1851 Navy

Conversion of the Model 1851 Navy. Made primarily in the mid 1870s; total production of about 3,800.

38 rimfire and 38 centerfire. 6-shot cylinders. 7-1/2" barrels; octagonal, with ejector rod attached, and the loading lever removed and barrel lug plugged.

Grips and finish standard for the Model 1851 Navy. Nickel plating not unusual.

Serial numbering in two ranges: The major group (special series for metallic cartridge) which began at 1 and ran to about 3800, and another which was within the percussion series of about 41000 to 91000 (the latter all naval alterations, and noted separately in the valuations below). Barrel marking: ADDRESS

5B-121

COL. SAM⸱ COLT NEW-YORK U.S. AMERICA- or -ADDRESS SAMᴸ COLT HARTFORD CT.-. Left side of the frame marked either COLTS/PATENT or with 1871 and 1872 patent dates. The cylinder roll is of the naval engagement scene.

The major variations and their values are:

Standard model, produced from previously unfinished and unassembled parts (all pieces from the 1 - 3800 serial range); the method of alteration was the same as in the Richards-Mason Model 1860 Army:

5B-121   Values—Good **$800**   Fine **$3,750**

U.S. Navy Conversions, were made from Model 1851 pistols returned to the factory (the serial group 41000 - 91000 as noted above). Navy inspector markings present (note USN on buttstrap), 1871 and 1872 patent dates stamped over COLTS/PATENT on the frame, blued and casehardened finish; iron gripstraps standard. See 5B-056 Martial Colt 1851 for reference to detailed study of U.S. Navy markings.

5B-122   Values—Good **$1,750**   Fine **$6,000**

Civilian pistols sent to Colt's factory for conversion, and thus appearing from various serial ranges from the percussion production:

5B-123   Values—Good **$800**   Fine **$3,500**

Conversion of the Colt Model 1861 Navy

Conversion of the Model 1861 Navy. Made primarily in the mid 1870s; total production of about 2,200.

38 rimfire and 38 centerfire. 6-shot cylinders. 7-1/2" barrels; round, with attached ejector rod, and the loading lever removed and barrel lug plugged.

Grips and finish standard for the Model 1861 Navy. Nickel plating not unusual.

Serial numbering in two ranges: Group beginning at around 100 and running up through about 3300, and another within the percussion series and generally of four digits (the latter all naval alterations, and noted separately below). Standard barrel marking: -ADDRESS COL. SAM⸱ COLT NEW-YORK U.S. AMERICA -. The left side of frame marked either COLTS/PATENT or with 1871 and 1872 patent dates. Cylinder roll scene of the naval engagement.

The major variations and their values are:

Standard model, made from previously unfinished and unassembled parts (all pieces from the c. 100 - 3300 serial range); the method of alteration the same as the Richards-Mason Model 1860 Army:

5B-124   Values—Good **$850**   Fine **$3,750**

5B-124

U.S. Navy Conversions, made from Model 1861 pistols returned to the factory (serial group mainly of four digit numbers). Standard Navy inspector markings, including USN on buttstrap; iron gripstraps standard. 1871 and 1872 patent dates stamped over COLTS/PATENT on the frame, blued and casehardened finish. See 5B-056 Martial Colt 1851 for reference to detailed study of U.S. Navy markings.

5B-125   Values—Good **$1,400**   Fine **$6,500**

Civilian pistols sent to Colt's factory for conversion, and thus appearing from various serial ranges from the percussion production:

5B-126   Values—Good **$750**   Fine **$3,250**

Conversions to Cartridge of the Colt Model 1862 "Police" and "Pocket Model Navy" Small Frame Revolvers

The major conversion groups made by the Colt factory of percussion revolvers to breech-loading cartridge models were with the Model 1862 "Police" revolver and the "Pocket Model of Navy Caliber." Numerous styles and variations are recorded. Approximately 32,000 were altered or produced as original cartridge pistols, utilizing parts of those small frame "Police" and "Pocket Navy" models. In some instances reworked parts from the Model 1849 Pocket Revolver ("Old Model Pocket"; 5B-042) were utilized. Estimated that about 13,000 were factory conversions from percussion models and approximately 20,000 were newly made as cartridge models. When frames and parts from the Pocket Model of 1849 were utilized they are usually observed in the serial range 273,000 to 328,500.

Collecting and categorizing these "Small Frame Conversions" has long been a source of confusion for collectors. Very little reliable data have been available. Increased collector interest and well researched studies have placed these models and their many variations in a more accurate perspective. (Additional significant information directly pertaining to these conversions is included with the commentary immediately preceding the Percussion Model 1862 Police Revolver 5B-103 et al.)

Colt 4-1/2" Octagon Barrel Revolver

4-1/2" Octagon Barrel Revolver. Made c. 1873-75; total quantity estimated 2,000 (all believed from converted percussion revolvers).

38 rimfire. 5-shot cylinder. The octagonal barrel without ejector, the loading lever cutout plugged.

Serial numbering as noted in preface material; in percussion and metallic cartridge ranges. Barrel marking: -ADDRESS COL. SAM^L COLT NEW-YORK U.S. AMERICA-. Left side of the frame marked either COLTS/PATENT *or* with 1871 and 1872 patent dates. Cylinder roll scene depicts the stagecoach holdup.

Key identifying features are the 4-1/2" octagonal barrel without ejector, and the cylinder with stagecoach holdup scene:

5B-127

5B-127	Values—Very Good **$650**	Exc. **$3,000**

Colt Round Barrel Pocket Navy with Ejector

Round Barrel Pocket Navy with Ejector. Made c. 1873-75; total quantity about 2,000.

38 rimfire and 38 centerfire. 5-shot cylinder. Distinctive round barrel and lug contour with attached ejector rod; plugged loading lever area. 4-1/2", 5-1/2", and 6-1/2" barrel lengths.

Serial numbering as noted in preface material; in percussion and metallic cartridge ranges. Barrel marking: COLT'S PT.F.A.MFG.C^O/ HARTFORD CT.U.S.A. On the left side of the frame were stamped 1871 and 1872 patent dates. Cylinder roll scene depicts the stagecoach holdup.

Distinct identifying features are the round barrel and special barrel lug, presence of ejector rod, loading gate on the conversion breech plate, and the roll engraved cylinder:

5B-128

5B-128	Values—Very Good **$850**	Exc. **$3,400**

Colt 1862 Police & Pocket Navy, with Ejector

Model 1862 Police and Pocket Navy, with Ejector. Made c. 1873-75; total quantity about 6,500.

38 rimfire and 38 centerfire. 5-shot cylinder. Round barrels altered from the standard Model 1862 Police percussion type; plugged in the loading lug area, but still retaining much of the original profile. 4-1/2", 5-1/2", and 6-1/2" barrel lengths.

Serial numbering as noted in preface material; in percussion and metallic cartridge ranges. Barrel marking:-ADDRESS COL. SAM^L COLT NEW-YORK U.S. AMERICA-. On the left side of the frame COLTS/PATENT *or* either of two forms of 1871 and 1872 patent dates. Cylinder roll scene depicts the stagecoach holdup, but not present on half-fluted cylinders.

Quick identification possible by the distinct barrel lug contour, presence of the ejector rod, and the presence of the left-over percussion loading cutout in the lower section of the barrel lug.

5B-130

Conversion having rebated, roll engraved cylinder:
5B-129   Values—Very Good **$825**   Exc. **$3,000**
Conversion having rebated, half-fluted cylinder:
5B-130   Values—Very Good **$950**   Exc. **$3,750**

Colt Round (Ctg.) Barrel Model, with Ejector ("Solid Barrel Type")

Round (Cartridge) Barrel Model, with Ejector. (Not illus.) Made c. 1873-75; total quantity about 6,500.

38 rimfire and 38 centerfire. 5-shot cylinder. The distinct round barrel design was made specifically for this model, and was not altered from the percussion. 4-1/2", 5-1/2" and 6-1/2" barrel lengths.

Serial numbering as noted in preface material; in percussion and metallic cartridge ranges. Barrel marking: COLT'S PT.F.A.

MFG.C°/ HARTFORD CT.U.S.A. On the left side of the frame were stamped 1871 and 1872 patent dates. Cylinder roll scene of the stagecoach holdup.

Can be identified quickly by the barrel lug contour (can be confused only with the Round Barrel Pocket Navy with Ejector), presence of the ejector rod, and the lack of any plug in the barrel lug:

5B-131   Values—Very Good **$750**   Exc. **$3,000**

Colt 3-1/2" Round (Ctg.) Barrel, w/o Ejector ("Solid Barrel Type")

3-1/2" Round (Cartridge) Barrel Model, without Ejector (a.k.a. "Solid Barrel Type"). Made c. 1873-80; total quantity about 10,000 (of which approx. 6,500 were converted from Pocket Model 1849 revolver parts; the additional estimated 3,500 made as original cartridge guns).

38 rimfire and 38 centerfire. 5-shot cylinder. The 3-1/2" round barrel without ejector was manufactured specifically for this model, and was not altered from the percussion.

Serial numbering as noted in preface material; in percussion and metallic cartridge ranges. Barrel marking: COLT'S PT.F.A.MFG.C°/HARTFORD CT. U.S.A. On the left side of the frame were stamped 1871 and 1872 patent dates. Cylinder roll scene of the stagecoach holdup.

Instantly identifiable by the stubby 3-1/2" round barrel without ejector rod; loading gates seldom present. Of all models

5B-132

of the 1862 Police/Pocket Navy conversions, the 3-1/2" Round Barrel type is the most common. Specimens were shipped as late as the 1880s:

5B-132   Values—Very Good **$600**   Exc. **$2,450**

Colt Model 1871-72 Open Top Revolver

Model 1871-72 Open Top Revolver. Manufactured c. 1872-73; in a total quantity of about 7,000.

44 rimfire. 6-shot cylinder. 7-1/2" barrel; made specifically for this model, and not to be confused with the Richards-Mason conversion.

Varnished walnut grips. Metal parts blued, the hammer casehardened; some brass gripstraps made, and these were finished in silver plating.

Serial numbered in its own range, the Open Top series began with 1 and ran through about 7000. Barrel Marking: -ADDRESS COL. SAM⊦ COLT NEW-YORK U.S.AMERICA-. On the left side of the frame of about the first 1000 pistols was stamped COLTS/PATENT; the balance of production was marked with 1871 and 1872 patent dates. 44 CAL on the left shoulder of the trigger guard strap. Cylinder scene is the naval engagement.

The model is quickly identifiable by the lack of a conversion breechplate, the straight cylinder (not rebated), and the Richards-Mason type barrels but having an integral rear sight. As the direct predecessor to the Single Action Army, the Open Top 44 is highly prized by collectors. Its limited production and the hard use many experienced has made the model one of the more difficult of major Colt revolver types to obtain.

Major variations are:

Standard model, 7-1/2" barrel, New-York barrel address marking, Army size grips:
5B-133   Values—Good **$2,500**   Fine **$9,500**
Same as above, but with Navy size grips:
5B-134   Values—Good **$3,000**   Fine **$11,000**
Late production, with COLT'S PT.F.A.MFG.C°.HARTFORD, CT. U.S.A. barrel address marking:
5B-135   Values—Good **$2,750**   Fine **$10,000**
Any of the above models having 8" barrel, or COLTS/PATENT frame marking bring an added premium.

5B-134

Colt Single Action Army Revolver

Single Action Army Revolver. A legendary American gun. Contracted and issued in large quantities by the U.S. Army during the Indian Wars; widely carried in the "golden days of the old west" by the most illustrious of lawmen and most notorious of outlaws. A.k.a. "Peacemaker", "Frontier Six-Shooter", "Equalizer", "Hog-leg", "Thumb-buster" and more recently "First Generation" for pre-World War II production 1873-1940 (included here); popularly known as merely the

"Single Action" among collectors. "Second Generation" (1956-1978) and "Third Generation" (1978-present) types are easily recognized by large letters "SA" after serials or letter-number combinations on commemoratives and custom guns. (Post-WWII types not covered.) Total quantity, including Flattop Target model and Bisley Model (both numbered in same range) 357,859 of which 310,386 were this standard model. (Those under No. 182,000 (approx.) made prior to Dec. 31, 1898.)

Most popular calibers for collectors are 45 (150,683 made); 44-40 (64,489 made). Other popular calibers: 41 (16,402 made); 38-40 (38,240); 32-20 (29,812 made).

Other scarce and rare calibers with respective quantities follow. Values and premiums are usually in direct relation to quantity produced: (except where noted all are centerfire) 22 RF (107); 32 RF (1); 32 Colt (192); 32 S&W (32); 32-44 (2); 38 Colt (1,011); 38 Colt (up to 1914 1,011); 38 Colt (after 1922 1,365); 38 S&W (9); 38 Colt Special (820); 38 S&W Special (25); 38-44 (2); 357 Magnum (525); 380 Eley (1), 44 Smoothbore (15), 44 RF (1,863); 44 German (59); 44 Russian (154); 44 S&W (24); 44 S&W Special (506); 45 Smoothbore (4); 45 Auto (44); 450 Boxer (729); 450 Eley (2,697); 455 Eley (1,150); 476 Eley (161).

Barrel lengths were standard in 4-3/4", 5-1/2", and 7-1/2". Lengths listed in the Colt serial ledgers run from 2-1/2" on up to 16". Ejector rod standard, mounted on the right side of the barrel.

Long barreled Colts with attachable, skeleton-type Colt made shoulder stocks are commonly called "Buntline Specials" after the legendary Dime Novel author Ned Buntline. He allegedly had five made for presentation to Dodge City lawmen, a story debunked by critical arms and Western students. Some special order Single Actions with varying long length barrels were made and attachable shoulder stocks could be separately purchased from Colt for them (or any Single Action). All are considered rare. Though these types have acquired the nickname of "Buntline Special," the so-called "true" Buntline is a special flat top single action in the serial range of 28800 through 28830, with folding leaf rear sight and barrel length varying from 10" to 16". Considered an extreme rarity. All of those long barreled models with stocks fetch values far in excess of those shown here but each must be valued on its own individual merit and unique features.

Grip types vary, beginning with walnut (either oil stained or varnished), and changing to eagle and shield pattern hard rubber at the serial range about 75000. At the range about 165000 these were succeeded by rampant colt hard rubber without the eagle and shield design. A variety of special grips were available, particularly in ivory and pearl, sometimes carved; quantities, however, were relatively limited.

Finish was standard blued, the frame and hammer casehardened. Nickel plating was fairly common. Silver, gold, and other finishes could be ordered, but are scarce.

Serial numbering began with 1 and continued through 357859. The only exception to the sequence was the special 44 Rimfire Model, which is considered individually below. Barrel address markings went through two standard types:
+COLT'S PT. F.A. MFG. Co. HARTFORD, CT. U.S.A.+ (serial range 1 to approximately 24000). Slanted, italic markings.
COLT'S PT. F.A. MFG. Co. HARTFORD, CT. U.S.A.(serial range 24000 to end of production; in single line on barrels of 5-1/2" and longer).

Patent date markings were on the left sides of the frames. The sequence was as follows: Two line marking of 1871 and 1872 dates (beginning of production through about 34000). Three line marking of 1871, 1872, and 1875 dates (34000—about 135000). Two line marking of 1871, 1872, and 1875 dates (135000 to end of production). A rampant colt trademark was stamped next to the patent dates, beginning at about the 130000 range, and continued in slightly varying formats through the end of manufacture.

The stamping of serial numbers on cylinders ceased about 120000; no serial appeared on that part thereafter. Around 144000 Colt introduced the transverse, spring-loaded catch for the cylinder pin (located on the front of the frame just below barrel) to replace the cylinder pin retaining screw. Generally believed to be the demarcation of the use of black powder loads

for smokeless, high pressure loads, it should be specifically noted that such is not the case! By 180000 (October, 1898) Colt warned against the use of smokeless powder and continued to do so until early 1900 (approx. 192000) when they first stated their smokeless guarantee.

Most caliber markings appeared on the left side of the barrel; excepting the early production (up through about the 130000 serial range), where marks were usually on the trigger guard area.

The variety of other marks classified is extensive, and includes government inspector and proof stampings, Colt factory inspector stamps, serial numbering, various inscriptions (e.g., W.F. & Co.), etc., etc.

Caution: Since 1981 there have appeared on the market a number of extremely clever, well-made, completely spurious Colt single-action FAKES of the martially marked 45 caliber model and the 44/40 caliber with the etched barrel panel. Other fake single action rarities will undoubtedly show up, too. Close scrutiny is mandatory when acquiring these types; bills-of-sale from the seller with guarantees of authenticity should be obtained.

Classification of these famous Colt single actions, and the identification of their myriad of variants is so extensive that there are currently 15 books specifically dealing with the subject. Quite a few of those works are of major significance to understanding them (*see Bibliography this chapter*).

5B-136

BASIC VARIATIONS AND THEIR VALUES:
Early production revolvers, 45 caliber, 7-1/2" barrel, with so-called "pinched frame" (constriction in the topstrap to form the rear sight), and slanted barrel address (serial range about 1 to 100):
5B-136   Values—Good **$27,500**   Fine **$110,000**
Early Martially Marked Model, 7-1/2" barrel with slanted address markings (most of the first 24,000 pistols produced), in 45 caliber, with U.S. markings and inspector stampings:
5B-137   Values—Good **$5,000**   Fine **$40,000**
Standard models above the serial range 24000 to end of production; common calibers, e.g., 45, 44-40, 38-40, 32-20, etc. Longer barrel lengths and largest calibers in greater demand and tend to bring higher values. Those made for smokeless powder (after c. 1898) to end of production tend to bring lesser values than indicated:
5B-138   Values—Good **$1,500** Fine **$5,000** Exc. **$10,000**
Rare calibers: Depending on the quantity produced of each specific caliber (and, of course, condition) prices of this model can increase from 50 percent to 500 percent.
Civilian arms with the early slanted barrel address, 45 caliber, 7-1/2" barrels (no U.S. government markings):
5B-139   Values—Good **$2,500**   Fine **$9,500**
U.S. martially marked revolvers with conventional barrel address, 7-1/2", 45 caliber, government inspector markings:
5B-140   Values—Good **$3,750**   Fine **$11,500**
Springfield Armory and Colt factory refinished U.S. martially marked revolvers with 5-1/2" barrels; so called ARTILLERY

MODEL. Three variations: TYPE I all mixed serial numbers; TYPE II barrel number mismatched, other numbers match, worth small premium; TYPE III all matching numbers, very scarce, worth premium:

5B-141   Values—Good **$1,750**   Fine **$6,000**
Made for British Market with Pall Mall London address markings:
5B-142   Values—Good **$1,400**   Fine **$5,000**
44 rimfire series, individual serial range of from 1 to about 1800, 44 Henry caliber, made c. 1875-80, majority with 7-1/2" barrels:
5B-143   Values—Good **$4,750**   Fine **$35,000**
22 rimfire series, 7-1/2" barrel. Total 107 made (flat-top model not included); 90 of these utilized frames and some parts of the 44 r.f. series (*q.v.*) with serial numbers in the 44 r.f. special range

5B-145

1 - 1800; others fall mostly in serial range 135000. 22 CAL marked on side of trigger guard:
5B-143.2   Values—Good **$4,500**   Fine **$27,500**
44-40 revolvers with etched COLT FRONTIER SIX SHOOTER barrel marking (left side); within serial range about 21000 to about 130000:
5B-144   Values—Good **$2,000**   Fine **$10,500**
Sheriff's or Storekeeper's Model. Made without ejector rod or ejector housing. Right forward side of frame made without provision for the ejector housing. 4" barrel most commonly encountered with majority of other barrel lengths from 2-1/2" to 4-3/4" and a small group with 7-1/2". Various calibers:
5B-145   Values—Good **$5,000**   Fine **$30,000**
Wells Fargo & Company revolvers, bearing the W.F. & Co. markings on the butt, and documented by Colt factory ledgers, 45 caliber, usually 5-1/2" barrels:
5B-146   Values—Very Good **$5,000**   Exc. **$12,500**
Long fluted cylinder model, made in the serial range 330001 - 331480, to use up double action cylinders:
5B-147   Values—Very Good **$2,500**   Exc. **$7,500**
(Note: Among the important details affecting collector valuations are calibers, barrel lengths, special markings, variations in sights, frames, ejector rods, hammers, cylinder pin locking devices and grips. The number of variants catalogued by collectors is very extensive. Fortunately the Colt factory ledgers are nearly complete for this model. The collector should perform careful and thorough research on rare and/or high value pieces prior to acquisition.)

Colt Flattop Target Model Single Action Army

Flattop Target Model Single Action Army. Made c. 1888 to about 1896; a few in later years; total quantity approximately 925.

Values shown are for following calibers and quantities known made of each: 22 RF (107); 38 Colt (122); 41 (91); 45 (100); 450 Boxer (89); 450 Eley (84).

Premiums usually added to rarer calibers: 32 Colt (24); 32 S&W (30); 32-44 (9); 32-20 (30); 38 S&W (39); 38 Colt Special (7); 38-44 (11); 380 Eley (3); 38-40 (19); 44 Russian (51); 44 S&W (51); 44 S&W Special (51); 44-40 (21); 455 Eley (37); 476 Eley (2).

7-1/2" barrel standard. Variants known, most prominent being the mis-named "Buntline Specials."

Grips of checkered hard rubber; checkered walnut also available. Metal parts blued, with casehardened hammers.

Serial number markings within the range of about 127000 - 162000, with a few in higher ranges; numbered in the sequence

5B-148

of the Single Action Army. Barrel marking: COLT'S PT. F.A.MFG.C° HARTFORD, CT.U.S.A. Frame markings of 2-line 1871, 1872, and 1875 patent dates and the rampant colt were standard. Caliber markings on left side of the barrel for most of the production.

A highly prized variation of the Single Action Army, the identifying details are the flattop frame with rear sight dovetailed into position, the removable sight insert in the front sight post, and the lack of a groove in the topstrap. Colt serial ledgers indicate that a wide range of variation exists in the Flattop Single Action series, notably in sights, calibers, and—to a lesser extent—in barrel lengths.

Standard model, blued finish, 7-1/2" barrel:
5B-148   Values—Very Good **$4,250**   Exc. **$11,500**
Model for British market. Barrel has regular COLT/HARTFORD one line markings with addition of DEPOT 14, PALL MALL LONDON:
5B-148.5   Values—Very Good **$3,750**   Exc. **$10,500**
Rare calibers and variations: As with the standard single action, there are many calibers considered either scarce or rare. Prices can increase 50 percent to 500 percent depending on relative rarity and quantities produced of other calibers. Reference works should be consulted for verifying such facts. Variations in barrel lengths other than 7-1/2", unusual finishes, grips or London barrel markings will demand a premium value on this model.

Colt Bisley Model Single Action Army Revolver

Bisley Model Single Action Army Revolver. Made c. 1894-1915; the total production approximately 44,350 (not including an additional 976 in the Flattop Target model).

Values shown are for most often encountered calibers and respective quantities: 32-20 (13,291); 38-40 (12,163); 41(3,159); 44-40 (6,803); 45 (8,005).

Premiums usually added to rarer calibers: 32 Colt (160); 32 S&W (18); 32-44 (14); 38 Colt (412); 38 S&W (10); 38 S&W Special (2); 38-44 (6); 44 Smoothbore (1); 44 Russian (90); 44 S&W (29); 45 Smoothbore (2); 450 Eley (5); 455 Eley (180).

Standard barrel lengths 4-3/4", 5-1/2", 7-1/2"; also known with 3", 3-1/2", 4" lengths not fitted with ejector housing; rare; worth premium. Various custom lengths known; very rare.

Grips of checkered hard rubber with rampant colt decor. Metal parts blued, with casehardened frame and hammer.

Serial numbered within the range of 156300 - 331916, in the sequence of the Single Action Army. Barrel marking: COLT'S PT.F.A.MFG.C⁰. HARTFORD,CT.U.S.A. Frame markings of 2-line 1871, 1872, and 1875 patent dates and the rampant colt were standard. Caliber markings on left side of the barrel, accompanied by: (BISLEY MODEL). The Bisley is one of the few Colt revolvers to be stamped with its model designation.

Easy identification of the Bisley is made by its name marked on the barrel. Other points of identification include: the hunch-backed backstrap and grip profile, the low profile wide spur hammer, and large trigger guard bow. Source of the name was the shooting ground in England at which Great Britain's national target matches have been held since the nineteenth century. Despite its target design, the Bisley proved a popular firearm for other purposes, and occasionally specimens can be seen in faded photographs from the American frontier. Sales were good in England, but most Bisleys were bought by American customers. Black powder models are scarce. In lesser condition grades they

5B-149

tend to bring 10 percent to 20 percent premium while in "EXC" and better they may bring up to 50 percent premium.

Standard model, blued and casehardened finish:

5B-149   Values—Good **$850**   Fine **$2,500**

Model for British market. Barrel has regular COLT/HARTFORD one line markings with addition of DEPOT 14, PALL MALL LONDON:

5B-149.5   Values—Good **$950**   Fine **$2,500**

Rare calibers and variations: As with the single action model, many calibers are considered either scarce or rare. Prices can increase 50 percent to 500 percent depending on relative rarity and quantities produced of other calibers. Colt references should be consulted to verify such facts. Variations in barrel lengths other than the three basic sizes, or unusual finishes, grips, London markings will demand a premium value.

Colt Bisley Model Flattop Target Revolver

Bisley Model Flattop Target Revolver. Made c. 1894 to 1913; total produced about 976.

Values shown for the following calibers and respective quantities: 32-20 (131); 38 Colt (96); 38-40 (98); 44-40 (78); 45 (97); 455 Eley (196).

Premiums usually added for rarer calibers: 32 Colt (44); 32 S&W (17); 32-44 (17); 38 S&W (5); 38-44 (47); 41 (24); 44 German (62); 44 S&W (64).

Standard barrel length 7-1/2"; custom lengths known; very rare.

Grips of checkered hard rubber; with checkered walnut also available. Metal parts blued, with casehardened hammers.

Serial numbered within the range 156300 - 325000; within the sequence of the Single Action Army. Barrel marking: COLT'S PT.F.A.MFG.C⁰. HARTFORD,CT.U.S.A. Frame markings of 2-line 1871, 1872, and 1875 patent dates and the rampant colt were standard. Caliber markings on left side of the barrel, accompanied by: (BISLEY MODEL).

In addition to the features standard to the Bisley model, the Target Model features the flattop frame with rear sight dovetailed into position, the removable sight insert in the front

5B-150

sight post, and the lack of a groove in the topstrap. A fair degree of variation has been noted in the Bisley Flattop group, reflecting the particular interests of target shooters.

Standard model, blued finish, 7-1/2" barrel:

5B-150   Values—Very Good **$3,750**   Exc. **$10,000**

Model for British market. Barrel has regular COLT/HARTFORD markings with addition of DEPOT 14, PALL MALL LONDON:

5B-150.5   Values—Very Good **$3,750**   Exc. **$8,500**

Rare calibers and variations: See note regarding same on the standard Bisley single action. Identical price increase will apply in the matter of rare calibers, odd barrel lengths other than the standard 7-1/2", finishes, grips or London markings.

Colt House and Cloverleaf Model Revolvers

House Model Revolver. Manufactured c. 1871-76; total quantity of 9,952. Serial numbering began with 1 and continued through the highest number. More popularly known among collectors as the "Jim Fisk model" due to its infamous use by a blackmailer to murder the notorious financier-playboy Jim Fisk in January, 1872 in New York City. The sordid affair over a woman received much attention of the news media of the era.

41 rimfire caliber (short or long ctg.). Basic types categorized as follows:

4-shot cylinder model, known as the Cloverleaf (due to the four-leaf clover appearance of the cylinder from front or rear), was made

in 1-1/2" and 3" barrel lengths. Most of the production (totaling 7,500 pieces) were of the 4-shot type, and the majority of these had 3" barrels; these were marked: COLT'S HOUSE PISTOL/HARTFORD CT. U.S.A. The left side of 1-1/2" barrels bore: COLT.

5-shot cylinder model (with straight, non-fluted cylinder), known as the House Pistol, was made only in a 2-5/8" barrel length. Total production was about 2,150, with serial numbers above the 6100 range. Distinctive marking is in the topstrap groove: PAT. SEPT. 19. 1871.

Grips of both 4- and 5-shot pistols were varnished walnut or rosewood. Standard finish of frames nickel plated or plain, the

5B-152

5B-153

balance of major parts nickel plated or blued. Brass frames on all models.

Major variations are:

Cloverleaf Model, with 1-1/2" round barrel; 4-shot cylinder; ejector rod is contained within the cylinder center pin and is removable for use, without necessity to remove cylinder (octagon barrel rare; worth 25 percent to 50 percent more):

5B-151   Values—Good **$825**   Fine **$2,750**

Cloverleaf Model, with 3" round barrel; 4-shot cylinder.

5B-152   Values—Good **$450**   Fine **$1,250**

House Model, standard 2-5/8" barrel, 5-shot cylinder. The cylinder pin was in combination with the ejector, necessitating removal of the cylinder in order to eject ctgs.

5B-153   Values—Good **$400**   Fine **$1,100**

Colt First Model Deringer

First Model Deringer (actual Colt terminology). Made c. 1870-90; total production about 6,500.

41 rimfire caliber. Single shot. 2-1/2" barrel, pivoting down and to the left for loading.

5B-154

All steel construction, without wooden grips. Barrel standard either blued, or nickel or silver plated; the frames nickel or silver plated. A few with solid silver frames/handles are known (made on special order). Extremely rare and worth considerable premium.

Serial numbered in its own range, beginning with 1 and continuing through approximately 6500. Barrel marking: COLT'S PT.F.A.MFG.C°/ HARTFORD CT. U.S.A./№ 1. 41 CAL may be found beneath barrel release button, on right side of the frame. Scroll engraving standard, and this was one of the very few Colt arms issued with that feature on the complete production. (a plain, *unengraved* specimen considered a rarity!)

The model was based on the design of the National No. 1 Deringer, and was the first single shot pistol made by the Colt company. The National Arms Company (original mfrs. of this pistol) was purchased in its entirety by Colt in 1870.

5B-154   Values—Good **$625**   Fine **$2,750**

Colt Second Model Deringer

Second Model Deringer (actual Colt terminology). Made c. 1870-90; in total quantity of about 9,000.

41 rimfire caliber. Single shot. 2-1/2" barrel, pivoting down and to the left for loading. Approximately 200 reportedly made in caliber 41 centerfire (very rare: worth premium if authenticated).

Checkered and varnished walnut grips. Barrel standard either blued, or nickel or silver plated; the frames nickel or silver plated. A few with solid silver frames (made on special order) are known. Extremely rare and valuable.

Serial numbered in its own range, beginning with 1 and continuing through approximately 9000. Barrel marking: COLT'S PT.F.A.MFG.C°/HARTFORD CT. U.S.A./№ 2. 41 CAL may be found beneath barrel release button, on right side of the frame. Scroll engraving standard, and the No. 2 was among the very few Colt arms issued with that feature on the complete production.

Quickly identifiable by the № 2 marking on top of the barrel, and from the presence of grips. Design source for this model was the National No. 2 Deringer (*q.v.*).

Major variations are:

Standard model, the frame of iron, varnished and checkered walnut grips:

5B-155   Values—Good **$550**   Fine **$2,000**

5B-155

Early model, (first 200) frame of iron, varnished and checkered walnut grips, the barrel marking: ADDRESS COL. COLT/HARTFORD CT. U.S.A:

5B-156   Values—Good **$1,000**   Fine **$3,250**

Brass frame model. A few with brass frames and the First Type barrel markings are known (rare and worth premium); they appear in the serial 1500 range. More often encountered are brass frames in the serial range 2500 with the second type marks:

5B-156.5   Values—Good **$900**   Fine **$3,250**

41 Centerfire Model. Likely less than 200 were chambered for centerfire; most being sold through Colt's London agency. Standard iron frame type with special C.F. hammer and round recoil plate:

5B-157   Values—Good **$1,250**   Fine **$3,750**

Colt Third Model Deringer

Third Model Deringer (collector terminology; also known as the "Thuer"). Made c. 1870 - 1912; the production total approximately 48,000. Yearly production quantities and serial ranges unknown.

41 rimfire caliber. Single shot. 2-1/2" barrel, pivoting to the right for loading.

Varnished walnut grips. Blued barrels, the bronze frames nickel or silver plated. Plating not uncommon on the barrels as well.

Serial numbered in its own range, beginning with 1 and continuing through approximately 48,000. Barrel marking: **- COLT -** in italics for most of the production, but in tiny block letters for the first 200 pistols. 41 CAL usually stamped on left side of the frame. Unlike the No. 1 and No. 2 Deringer pistols, engraving was not standard on the Third Model series.

Identifiable by their 41 caliber and the barrel pivoting sideways. Intermittently since 1959 the Colt factory has manufactured 22 caliber versions of the Third Model, but a 41 caliber pistol has not been re-introduced. The Third or Thuer Deringer outsold by nearly three times its No. 1 and No. 2 companions.

(Note: A premium added if the rampant colt and C marking present on the frame, or for Colt London Agency markings, or chambered for 41 centerfire.)

First type, earliest production: Quickly distinguished by the relief bolster (raised area) through which the barrel screw is fitted on the forward, underside of the frame. Barrel markings - COLT - (in tiny block letters). Short, high hammer spur. Serial number range approx. 1 to 200:

5B-158   Values—Good **$1,450**   Fine **$6,500**

First type, later production: As above with the raised bolster on forward section of frame, high hammer spur but with **- COLT -** in large italic letter markings on the barrel (the same as found on the standard last model). Serial approx. 200 to 2,000:

5B-159   Values—Good **$725**   Fine **$2,600**

5B-158
First Type

5B-160
Standard Model with sloping hammer

Standard Model: Distinguished by the absence of the raised bolster on forward frame. Earlier production has the short high hammer; later production with a sloping hammer and a more moderate curve to the handle. (On medium and lower conditioned specimens, values usually the same for either type. In top grades of condition the short, high hammer spur style brings a small premium.) Markings **- COLT -** (in large italic letters on barrel). Varnished walnut grips, plated frame and blued or plated barrel:

5B-160   Values—Good **$275**   Fine **$650**

Colt Open Top Pocket Model Revolver

Open Top Pocket Model Revolver. Made c. 1871-77; total production of about 114,200.

22 Short or Long rimfire caliber. 7-shot cylinder. 2-3/8" and 2-7/8" barrel lengths.

Grips of varnished walnut. Blued or nickel plated cylinders and barrels: the brass frames nickel plated. Silver plating (on frame) not uncommon.

Serial numbered in its own range, beginning with 1 and continuing through to end of production. Barrel markings in four distinct variations of: COLT'S PT. F.A. MFG. Cº/HARTFORD CT. U.S.A. Stamped on left side of frame: 22 CAL.

A distinct type due to the open top frame, the barrel and cylinder easily removed by releasing the pivoting latch, the spur trigger, and the 7-shot non-fluted cylinder with the stop slots near the muzzle end. The Open Top 22 had an excellent sales record, but success was cut short due to the flood of the market by cheap pistols known to collectors as "suicide specials."

A rare variation (worth premium value) known on very early, low numbered specimens, has circular, tapered firing pin which enters frame through a circular hole (*vs.* usual thin flat plate firing pin which fits through matching narrow slot at top of frame).

Major variations are:

Early production having 2-3/8" or 2-7/8" (worth premium) barrel with ejector; high spur hammer most often encountered:

5B-161   Values—Very Good **$550**   Exc. **$1,500**

5B-161

5B-162

Standard model, 2-3/8" barrel length without ejector rod; with high spur hammer:

5B-162   Values—Very Good **$200**   Exc. **$500**

As above, with sloping spur hammer (above 22000 serial range):

5B-163   Values—Very Good **$200**   Exc. **$500**

Colt "New Line" Series Of Cartridge Revolvers

This line of five solid-frame, spur-trigger revolvers, ranging in caliber and size from 22 to 41, was newly introduced in 1873. Initially they met with much success, yet production for most calibers ceased by the late 1870s. Only the 32-caliber model continued until 1884. Tremendous proliferation of very inexpensive competitive types of near-identical appearance, by both American and European manufacturers, eventually caused Colt, unwilling to sacrifice their quality of materials and workmanship, to drop the line.

Alternate Names (i.e. Nicknames) For "New Line" Revolvers

B. Kittredge & Company of Cincinnati, Ohio, noted firearms dealers and among Colt's major outlets in the Midwest, introduced an innovative marketing twist by coining newly-conceived names (especially for their advertising) for each of these handguns: "The LITTLE COLT" (22 caliber); "THE PONY COLT" (30 caliber); "THE LADIES COLT" (32 caliber); "THE PET COLT" (38 caliber) and "THE BIG COLT" (41 caliber). Such markings were actually applied to some of those various models. Engraved on the right side of barrels, the markings, reportedly in script fashion, were hand-engraved, apparently at the Colt factory (disputation contends Kittredge applied those markings). Quantities unknown; judging by frequency of appearance, extremely limited. Collectors cautioned to be wary of marked specimens. It appears more spurious examples known than genuine ones! Authenticated specimens very rare and worthy of considerable premium.

Colt New Line 22 Revolver

New Line 22 Revolver. In production c. 1873-77; total made approximately 55,343.

22 rimfire caliber. 7-shot cylinder. 2-1/4" barrel length.

Grips of varnished rosewood. Nickel plated finish, or nickel plated frame with the balance blued.

Serial numbering in a distinct range, beginning with 1 and continuing to the end of production. Two standard barrel markings, variants of: COLT'S PT. F.A. MFG. CO./HARTFORD, CT. U.S.A. (additional line barrel marks DEPOT 14 PALL MALL LONDON very scarce and worth premium). Left side of barrel etched: COLT NEW 22 (earliest production does not have this etched panel; very scarce); and 22 CAL stamped on left side of the frame. 1874 patent date marking present on pistols after 16000 serial range.

This was the only 22 caliber pistol manufactured in Colt's New Line group, and as with the Open Top 22, manufacture was cut short by the overwhelming competition of cheap "suicide special" handguns. The New Line 22 type is quickly distinguished by the solid frame construction, 7-shot fluted cylinder, and the flat-sided barrel.

Major variations are:

First Model, in the serial range 1 - 16000; basically identified by the short cylinder flutes, the cylinder stop slots on outside, and the lack of patent date markings:

5B-164   Values—Very Good **$200**   Exc. **$550**

**5B-164
Short Cylinder Flute**

**5B-165
Long Cylinder Flute**

Second Model, in the serial range 16000 - 55343; has long cylinder flutes, the locking slots on cylinder back, and patent date stamping on the barrel:

5B-165   Values—Very Good **$175**   Exc. **$450**

Colt New Line 30 Caliber Revolver

New Line 30 Caliber Revolver. (Not illus.) Same as 32 Caliber with long flutes. Made c. 1874-76; total quantity of about 11,000.

30 rimfire caliber. 5-shot cylinder. Barrel lengths of 1-3/4" and 2-1/4"; round.

Grips of varnished rosewood. Full nickel plated finish, or blued with casehardened frame.

Serial numbering was in an individual range, beginning with 1 and continuing to end of production. Two barrel markings standard, variants of: COLT'S PT.F.A. MFG. Cº/HARTFORD, CT. U.S.A. Left side of barrel etched: COLT NEW 30. Marking 30 CAL. sometimes present on the frame or butt.

Still another victim of the stiff competition from "suicide specials," the 30 caliber New Line remained in production only three years, and is one of the more desirable of types in the series. The 30 is an unusual chambering for a Colt firearm, and this was the *only* product made by the company in that caliber.

Major variations are:

Standard model, in 2-1/4" barrel length; long fluted cylinder:

5B-166   Values—Very Good **$225**   Exc. **$600**

Same as above, but with 1-3/4" barrel:

5B-167   Values—Very Good **$300**   Exc. **$875**

Colt New Line 32 Caliber Revolver

New Line 32 Caliber Revolver. Made c. 1873-84; in a total quantity of about 22,000.

32 rimfire and 32 centerfire calibers. 5-shot cylinder. Barrel lengths of 2-1/4" and 4".

Varnished rosewood grips. Nickel plated finish, or blued with casehardened frame.

Serial numbering began with 1, and continued to the end of production. However, 38 and 41 caliber New Line, New House and New Police revolvers are believed to have been included. Two barrel markings standard, variants of: COLTS PT.F.A.MFG. CO./HARTFORD, CT. U.S.A. Left side of barrel etched: COLT NEW 32 (except on approximately the first 3,000 made and the very last made in 1884). On the left side of the frame: 32 CAL; if C also present, the letter indicates "centerfire."

The 32 outnumbered all other pistols in the New Line group, excepting the 22 caliber model. This was Colt's first production model handgun chambered for 32 caliber metallic cartridge ammunition.

Major variations are:

First Model, in the serial range 1 - 10000; features short cylinder flutes, the cylinder stop slots on the outside, no patent date markings, 2-1/4" barrel:

5B-168   Values—Very Good **$185**   Exc. **$550**

Second Model, in the serial range 10000 - 22000; having long cylinder flutes, the locking slots on cylinder back, 1874 patent date stamping on the barrel, 2-1/4" barrel:

5B-168

5B-169

5B-169   Values—Very Good **$185**   Exc. **$550**
Either of the above, in 4" barrel length:
5B-170   Values—Very Good **$425**   Exc. **$1,275**

Colt New Line 38 Caliber Revolver

5B-171

New Line 38 Caliber Revolver. Manufactured c. 1874-80; the total quantity about 5,500.

38 rimfire and 38 centerfire calibers. 5-shot cylinder. Barrel lengths of 2-1/4" and 4".

Grips of varnished rosewood. Nickel plated finish, or blued with casehardened frame.

Serial numbering was in the same range as the New Line 41 caliber revolvers; the series began with 1, and continued through

about 12516. Some numbering believed shared with the 32 New Line serials. Two barrel markings standard, variants of: COLTS PT. F. A. MFG. CO./HARTFORD, CT. U.S.A. Left side of the barrel etched: COLT NEW 38 (except on the earliest, low numbered specimens). On the left side of the frame: 38 CAL.; if C also present, the letter indicates "centerfire."

The 38 New Line is an attractive model to collectors because of the relatively large caliber, and the limited production.

Major variations are:

First Model, in the serial range 1 - 3200; having short cylinder flutes, the cylinder stop slots on the outside, and no patent date markings; 2-1/4" barrel:

5B-171   Values—Very Good **$275**   Exc. **$600**

Second Model, in serial range 3200 - 12516; with long cylinder flutes, the locking slots on cylinder back, 1874 patent date stamping on the barrel; 2-1/4" barrel:

5B-172   Values—Very Good **$225**   Exc. **$550**
Either of the above, in 4" barrel length:
5B-173   Values—Very Good **$500**   Exc. **$1,400**

Colt New Line 41 Caliber Revolver

New Line 41 Caliber Revolver. Made c. 1874-79; total quantity about 7,000.

41 rimfire and 41 centerfire calibers. 5-shot cylinder. Barrel lengths of 2-1/4" and 4".

Grips of varnished rosewood. Nickel plated finish, or blued with casehardened frame.

Serial numbering in the same range as the New Line 38 caliber revolvers; the series began with 1, and continued through about 10700. Some numbering believed shared with the 32 New Line serials. Two barrel markings standard, variants of: COLTS PT. F. A. MFG. CO./HARTFORD, CT. U.S.A. Left side of the barrel etched: COLT NEW 41 (except on the very earliest, low numbered specimens). On the left side of the frame: 41 CAL; if C also present, the letter indicates "centerfire."

The 41 caliber chambering and rather business-like appearance has inspired a special enthusiasm for this model from collectors. The production is fairly limited, and as with

5B-174

most of the New Line models, variation is split into the First and Second types:

First Model, in the serial range 1 - 3200; with short cylinder flutes, the cylinder stop slots on the outside, and no patent date markings; 2-1/4" barrel:

5B-174   Values—Very Good **$300**   Exc. **$900**

Second Model, in serial range 3200 - 10700; having long cylinder flutes, the locking slots on cylinder back, 1874 patent date stamping on the barrel; 2-1/4" barrel:

5B-175   Values—Very Good **$300**   Exc. **$900**
Either of the above, in 4" barrel length:
5B-176   Values—Very Good **$675**   Exc. **$1,850**

Colt New House Model Revolver

New House Model Revolver. Manufactured c. 1880-86; the total quantity about 4,000. Found in serial range 10300 to 25700.

38 and 41 centerfire calibers; rare in 32 c.f., few made (worth premium). 5-shot cylinder. 2-1/4" barrel.

5B-177

Grips of varnished rosewood or walnut, or of checkered hard rubber with COLT oval embossed. Nickel plated finish, or blued with casehardened frame.

Serial numbering shared with various other models of New Line and New Police pistols, in 32, 38, and 41 calibers. Barrel marking: COLT'S PT. F.A. MFG. C⁰./HARTFORD, CT. U.S.A. (additional DEPOT 14, PALL MALL LONDON barrel markings scarce, worth premium.) Left side of barrel usually etched (late production stamped) with caliber designations, e.g., COLT HOUSE 38, COLT NEW 38, or NEW HOUSE 38. Caliber designations may be found on left side of the frame. Some barrels have 1874 patent date marking.

Distinctive details identifying the model include the square profile of the butt (in contrast to the bird's head grip of most New Lines), the 2-1/4" barrel without ejector rod, and the thin loading gate on the right recoil shield. All cylinders were of the long fluted type, with the stop slots at the back:

5B-177   Values—Very Good **$350**   Exc. **$950**

Colt New Police "Cop and Thug" Revolver

New Police "Cop and Thug" Model Revolver. Made c. 1882-86; total quantity not more than 4,000. Found in serial range 14450 to 21500 continuing to end.

38 centerfire caliber. 32 and 41 CF calibers quite rare. 5-shot cylinder. Barrel lengths of 2-1/4", 4-1/2", 5" and 6" (all but the shortest fitted with ejector rod).

Grips of hard rubber embossed with the Cop and Thug motif and COLT oval. Nickel plated finish, or blued with casehardened frame.

Serial numbering shared with various other models of New Line and New House pistols, in 32, 38, and 41 calibers. Barrel marking: COLT'S PT. F.A. MFG. C⁰./HARTFORD, CT. U.S.A. (additional DEPOT 14, PALL MALL LONDON markings scarce; usually found with rosewood grips). Etched or stamped on left side of barrel with caliber designations, e.g., COLT NEW 38 or NEW POLICE 38. Caliber designations may be found on the left side of the frame, and some barrels have 1874 patent date markings.

The New Police is the only New Line model having the ejector rod as a standard feature. The Cop and Thug grips (found on a majority of the production) also serve to identify the type. The low relief scene depicts a "cop" arresting a "thug," and is located between the stock screw and butt on each grip panel. **Prices given are for specimens having this type grip** (and must be in reasonably good condition—if chipping or very worn, demand and price fall accordingly); with plain grips deduct

5B-178
with close-up
of grips

approx. 15 to 25 percent from values. All cylinders were of the long fluted type, and the stop slots were at the back.

Major variations are:

Standard model, 38 caliber, with ejector rod on barrel:
5B-178   Values—Very Good **$850**   Exc. **$3,000**
Same as above, except with 2-1/4" barrel and without ejector:
5B-179   Values—Very Good **$575**   Exc. **$2,000**
Standard model, with ejector rod on barrel, but chambered for 41 centerfire caliber. Caliber 32CF more rare and worth premium:
5B-180   Values—Very Good **$1,000**   Exc. **$3,250**

Colt Model 1877 "Lightning" D.A. Revolver

Model 1877 "Lightning" Double Action Revolver. Made 1877 - 1909; total production 166,849. Under serial number 111,500 (approx.) made prior to Dec. 31, 1898.

Standard calibers were 38 Colt (the "Lightning") and 41 Colt (the "Thunderer"). Approx. 200 were chambered for 32 Colt caliber (found in serial range 66,000 through 121,000) extremely rare; worth substantial premium. Other calibers known on special order fetch strong premiums if authenticated. In

common usage both calibers are called: "Lightning." 6-shot cylinder. Barrel lengths vary from 1-1/2" to 10". Standard lengths were 2-1/2" to 3-1/2" without ejector, and 4-1/2" to 6" with (no barrels were made shorter than 4-1/2" with ejector).

Majority of production had checkered hard rubber grips with oval rampant colt embossed motif; earlier revolvers had checkered one piece rosewood. Finished in blue, with casehardened frame; second in quantity was nickel plating.

Serial numbering began with 1 and continued through 166849. Barrel address marking: COLT'S PT.F.A.MFG.C°/HARTFORD. CT. U.S.A. Three line patent date marking (1871, 1874, and 1875) on left side of the frame, usually accompanied by rampant colt stamp. Caliber designation on either the trigger guard or on left side of the barrel.

The Lightning was Colt's first production of a double action revolver. Its sales record was impressive, but the mechanism was rather intricate and specimens are often found malfunctioning. The similarity of barrel and frame to the Single Action Army is part of the Lightning Model's appeal to collectors; as is the distinctive bird's head grip profile. Increasingly, arms enthusiasts are devoting attention to this somewhat neglected but quite interesting Colt handgun. A relatively broad range of variations exist in the Lightnings, particularly in barrel lengths, markings, finishes, grips, and in sundry other details. "Billy the Kid" (William Bonney) carried the Lightning the night he was shot by Pat Garrett; John Wesley Hardin was known to have carried a "Thunderer." Major types are as follows:

Standard model, without ejector, in barrel lengths between 2-1/2" and 3-1/2":

5B-181   Values—Very Good **$400**   Exc. **$1,450**

Same as above, but in remaining barrel lengths (some ultra-rare, e.g., 1-1/2" or 6", and bring a premium price):

5B-182   Values—Very Good **$400**   Exc. **$1,450**

Standard model, with ejector, in barrel lengths between 4-1/2" and 6":

5B-183   Values—Very Good **$425**   Exc. **$1,600**

Made for British market, with or without ejector. Usual COLT/HARTFORD barrel marks with addition DEPOT 14, PALL MALL LONDON and British proofmarks:

5B-184   Values—Very Good **$425**   Exc. **$1,600**

Made for The American Express Co. marked on backstrap AM. EX. CO. Quantity approx. 1,200, all of which are documented on Colt's factory ledgers:

5B-185   Values—Very Good **$1,000**   Exc. **$2,500**

(Note: A premium placed on checkered rosewood grips, on pistols chambered for the *rare* 32 Colt caliber, and on long barrel lengths [7" to 10"].)

5B-181

5B-183

Colt Model 1878 "Frontier" D.A. Revolver

Model 1878 "Frontier" Double Action Revolver. Made 1878 - 1905; the total production 51,210. Under serial number 41,000 (approx.) made prior to Dec. 31, 1898.

Standard calibers were 32-20, 38-40, 41 Colt, 44-40, and 45; also made but scarce (or rare) were 22 rimfire, 38 Colt, 44 Russian, 44 German Government, 44 S&W, and 450, 455, and 476 Eley. 6-shot cylinder. Barrel lengths standard of 4-3/4", 5-1/2", and 7-1/2" with ejector, and 3", 3-1/2" and 4" without ejector. However, lengths are know from as short as 2-1/2" and as long as 12".

Major share of the series had checkered hard rubber grips with oval rampant colt embossed motif; earlier revolvers had checkered and varnished walnut of two piece type. Blued finish standard; second in quantity was nickel plating. Serial numbering began with 1 and ran through to the highest number, 51210. Barrel address marking (in one or two lines):

5B-187
Standard Model

COLT'S PT.F.A.MFG. C°. HARTFORD CT. U.S.A. No patent date stampings. Designations of caliber were on either the trigger guard or on the left side of the barrel.

The Frontier Double Action is one of the largest frame revolvers made by Colt's. It is easily identified by the frame and grip profile (note solid construction, with the trigger guard removable), the thin loading gate, the two piece grips, and the cylinder which (like the Lightning Model 1877) does not swing out for loading. One reason for the popularity of the Model 1877 is the chambering for large calibers, and the similarities it has to the Single Action Army. Increasingly, collectors are finding the Model 1878 Frontier an attractive area in the Colt field.

Major variations are:

Standard model, without ejector, in barrel lengths of 3", 3-1/2", and 4", and in the five most common calibers; in collector terminology the "Sheriff's Model":

5B-186   Values—Very Good **$600**   Exc. **$2,250**

Standard model, with ejector, in barrel lengths of 4-3/4", 5-1/2", and 7-1/2". The Mexican government purchased 500 of these with 7 1/2-inch barrels in 45 caliber in 1890 through a dealer in Mexico City. Checkered hard rubber grips and marked on left frame with an oval, die-struck motif of a sunburst-like design and liberty cap in its center accompanied by smaller letters **"R"** and **"M"** respectively on either side of the sunburst. Very scarce; worth premium value.

5B-187   Values—Very Good **$625**   Exc. **$2,250**

Made for British market, with or without ejector. Usual COLT/HARTFORD barrel marks with addition DEPOT 14, PALL MALL LONDON and British proofmarks:

5B-188   Values—Very Good **$500**   Exc. **$1,650**

Model 1902 "Alaskan" or "Philippine Constabulary Model" revolver, sold on contract to the U.S. Ordnance; extra-large trigger and trigger guard, U.S. inspector stampings, 6" barrel, 45 caliber, lanyard swivel on butt, and blued finish; total made about 4,600, in serial range 43,401 - 48,097 (a few reported in higher ranges).

Although commonly known among collectors as the "ALASKAN MODEL" and less commonly as the "PHILIPPINE CONSTABULARY MODEL," it has been established that the only correct nomenclature is that with "PHILIPPINE" title. Also confirmed that the oversized trigger guard which distinguishes this variant will not allow for its use in cold weather (i.e. Alaska) while wearing gloves (as formerly believed) but rather, it allows for an elongated trigger in order to offer better leverage for double-action firing, necessitated by the stronger hammer spring added by special request of the U.S. Army c. 1901. (The misnomer clarified in *Colt's Double Action Revolver Model 1878* by Wilkerson (1998) and article by D. Chamberlain in *Gun Report* (Feb. 2002). Noted that a few observed with **"W.C. Co."** markings on left frame, identified as those of the "Western

5B-189
Model 1902

Costume Co." an early Hollywood theatrical/motion picture prop house and likely purchased as government surplus for use in early hollywood Westerns.

5B-189   Values—Very Good **$900**   Exc. **$3,000**
(Note: A premium placed on barrel lengths other than the standard ones noted above.)

Colt Model 1889 Navy Double Action Revolver

Model 1889 Navy Double Action Revolver. In production 1889-94; the total made approximately 31,000.

38 Colt and 41 Colt calibers. 6-shot cylinder. Standard barrel lengths of 3", 4-1/2" and 6".

Checkered hard rubber grips with oval rampant colt embossed motif. Blued finish; nickel plating not uncommon. Serial numbered in its own series, beginning with 1 and up through approximately 31000. Barrel marking of Colt company name, Hartford address, and 1884 and 1888 patent dates. Caliber designations appear on the left side of the barrel.

5B-190

The Model 1889 is quite important to collectors because it was the first swingout cylinder double action in the Colt line. Certain features allow for quick identification, among them: The 1884 and 1888 patent dates in the barrel marking and the long fluted cylinder having the locking slots at the back. The cylinders revolve counter-clockwise. The serial numbers are often confused with assembly numbers: The former are found stamped on the *butt*, while the latter are in the cylinder area, and elsewhere.

Major variations are:
Standard model, in 4-1/2" and 6" barrel lengths, blued or nickel plated, with checkered hard rubber grips:
5B-190   Values—Very Good **$375**   Exc. **$950**
Same as above, but in 3" barrel length:
5B-191   Values—Very Good **$450**   Exc. **$1,150**
U.S. Navy contract. Total 5,000 serial range 1 to 5000. Blue finish; 6" barrel, plain walnut grips. 38 caliber. Butt marked U.S.N., serial number, inspector initials, date 1889. Between 1896 and 1900 total of 4,637 returned to Colt for Conversion to Model 1895 cylinder locking system and refinishing. Values shown for altered revolvers; original unaltered specimens (total 363) rare; worth considerable premium:
5B-192   Values—Very Good **$850**   Exc. **$2,250**

Colt New Army and Navy Revolver

New Army and Navy Revolver, Models of 1892, 1894, 1895, 1896, 1901, and 1903. Made from 1892 through c. 1907; total of approximately 291,000. Under serial number 115,000 (approx.) made prior to Dec. 31, 1898.

38 Colt and 41 Colt calibers; 38 S&W made in lesser quantity. 6-shot cylinder. Standard barrel lengths of 3" (scarce and will bring premium), 4-1/2" and 6".

Checkered hard rubber grips with oval rampant colt embossed motif; plain walnut standard on contract purchases of the government. (Note: Army rubber grips often included a date stamping within the COLT oval motif.) Blued finish; nickel plating not uncommon.

Serial numbering in their own series, though overlapping in higher numbers with the successor model, the Army Special; New Army and Navy range from 1 through about 291000. Barrel marking of Colt company name, Hartford address, and 1884 and 1888 patent dates; 1895, and then 1901 were added to

later models. Designations of caliber marked on left side of the barrel.

The Models of 1892 to 1903 represent developments and improvements in Colt's double action Army and Navy size revolvers. Differences from one model to the next are generally minor, and sometimes can be detected only by examining interior parts. All models have the short cylinder flutes and the two sets of stop slots on the outside of the cylinder; the cylinders revolve counter-clockwise. As with the Model 1889 Navy, the serial numbers are often confused with assembly numbers: The serials appear on the *butt*, while assembly numbers (two or three digits only) are in the cylinder area. (Note: Special markings occasionally found and some, especially Wells Fargo & Co., when verified, command premium prices.)

Basic variations are:
Standard Models, 1892, 1894, 1895, 1896, 1901 and 1903, civilian sales:

5B-193   Values—Very Good **$185**   Exc. **$475**
Same as above, but military orders:

    Navy variations, 38 caliber, 6" barrel, plain walnut grips, Butt marked "U.S.N."/anchor/38D.A./P/inspector initials/date. Inspector initials on wood grips. Lanyard swivel standard.
5B-194   Values—Very Good **$350**   Exc. **$1,100**

    Army variations, 38 caliber, 6" barrel, plain walnut grips, Butt marked "U.S. Army/Model/1892" with serial number and inspector initials. Wood grips also with inspector marks.
5B-195   Values—Very Good **$300**   Exc. **$1,000**

    Total 8,000 manufactured under 2 contracts 1892-93. At least 7490 known altered at Springfield for mechanical defects. Values shown for modified guns; those in unaltered state worth premuim. Identified basically by 1888 as last patent

5B-193

date on barrel, inspector mark "DM" left grip and "RAC" right grip, left frame, cylinder and barrel; no screw visible under cylinder latch.

Colt Model 1905 Marine Corps D.A. Revolver

Model 1905 Marine Corps Double Action Revolver. Manufactured 1905-09; in a total of 926. Basically a variation from the New Army and Navy Revolver series, late production.

    38 Colt and 38 S&W Special calibers. 6-shot cylinder. 6" barrel.

    Varnished and checkered walnut grips. Blued finish.

    Serial numbering in an individual range, beginning at 10001 and continuing through 10926. Marine Corps issue revolvers were butt marked with USMC stampings, and with numbers (beginning with 1) running in sequence with the Colt production serial (thus gun number 10001 bore USMC number 1). Barrel address of Colt's in Hartford, with 1884, 1888, and 1895 patent dates. Caliber designations on the left side of the barrel.

    The Marine Corps Model is one of the ultra-desirable handguns in Colt's double action revolver production. With a total made of only 926, and most of these experiencing service use, the surviving arms are few. The Marine Corps association also adds to the model's status and importance. For quick identification: Distinctive grips, serial range, and grip frame type. Cylinders revolve counter-clockwise.

    Basic variants are:
Standard model, with USMC butt markings, bore serials 10001 - 10800; found in more worn condition than civilian types:
5B-196   Values—Very Good **$1,000**   Exc. **$3,500**
Standard model, civilian sales only; bore serials 10801 - 10926:
5B-197   Values—Very Good **$750**   Exc. **$2,500**

5B-196

Colt New Service Double Action Revolver

New Service Double Action Revolver. Made from 1898 through 1944; in a total run of about 356,000 (including Shooting Master and other variations).

    Variety of calibers from 38 Colt to 476 Eley. 6-shot cylinder. Barrel lengths from 2" to 7-1/2", with most common in 4-1/2", 5-1/2" and 7-1/2".

    Until c. 1928 checkered hard rubber with COLT oval were standard grips, after 1928 these were discontinued in favor of checkered walnut having Colt medallion inset. Blued finish standard; nickel plating not uncommon.

    Serial numbering in an individual range, beginning at 1 and continuing through approximately 356000. Barrel markings of Colt company name, Hartford address, and patent dates of 1884

5B-198

and 1900, *or* 1884, 1900 and 1905, *or* 1884, 1905 and 1926. Left side of barrel marked with model designation (e.g., NEW SERVICE) and caliber; the military model stamped: COLT D.A. 45.

    The New Service was Colt's largest framed double action swingout cylinder revolver. It also boasts one of the longest production runs of any D.A. Colt—some 46 years. A number of variations are known in the series, and the basic types are as follows:
Old Model revolver; serial numbers from 1 to about 12000; hard rubber COLT oval grips, NEW SERVICE model marking on sideplate:
5B-198   Values—Very Good **$400**   Exc. **$1,000**
Old Model New Service Target; serials about 6000 - 15000; checkered walnut grips, 7-1/2" barrel, flattop frame, NEW SERVICE model sideplate marking:
5B-199   Values—Very Good **$650**   Exc. **$1,750**
Improved Model revolver; serials about 21000 - 32500; hard rubber COLT oval grips, has Colt positive lock mechanism (various internal and external improvements):
5B-200   Values—Very Good **$375**   Exc. **$900**
Improved Model New Service Target; features of the Improved Model standard revolver; but still including flattop frame, checkered walnut grips (with Colt medallion inlays), and 7-1/2" barrel:
5B-201   Values—Very Good **$675**   Exc. **$1,750**

Model 1909 US Army and US Navy; within serials 30000 - 50000; walnut grips, 45 Colt caliber, 5-1/2" barrel:

> **Army** revolver bears U.S. ARMY MODEL 1909 butt markings:
> **5B-202**   Values—Very Good **$400**   Exc. **$1,100**

> **Navy** with U.S.N. butt markings. Quantity 1,000:
> **5B-203**   Values—Very Good **$575**   Exc. **$1,750**

Model 1909 U.S. Marine Corps; virtually the same as above, but with varnished and checkered walnut grips (gripframe of smaller profile), USMC butt markings. Quantity 1,400:
5B-204   Values—Very Good **$1,250**   Exc. **$4,000**

Model 1917 U.S. Army; within serials 150000 - 301000; walnut grips, 45 Colt and 45 ACP calibers, 5-1/2" barrel. Improved version of the Model 1909 revolver. U.S. ARMY MODEL 1917 butt markings. Quantity 154,000:

5B-205   Values—Very Good **$260**   Exc. **$500**

Civilian Model 1917; scarce variation limited to about 1,000 revolvers, and made up by Colt's from leftover parts of the Model 1917 U.S. Army production; serials in 335000 and 336000 range; 45 ACP caliber and barrel so marked; lack U.S. ARMY butt markings:

5B-206   Values—Very Good **$325**   Exc. **$800**

Late Model New Service; began approximately in the 325000 serials, and continued through end of production; checkered walnut grips with Colt medallion inlays, various improved production features:

5B-207   Values—Very Good **$325**   Exc. **$650**

Shooting Master revolver; within serials of about 333000 - 350000; checkered walnut grips with Colt medallion inlays, various calibers from 38 S&W Special to 45 Colt (larger calibers bring premium values), 6" barrel standard. Caliber designation and COLT SHOOTING MASTER on left side of barrel; target sights, and *flattop frame*:

5B-208   Values—Very Good **$525**   Exc. **$1,100**

(Note: A number of variances from standard types exist in the sizable production of New Service revolvers. Some of the unusual and odd variations will command an added value; a majority of very minor variations will not. A thorough and detailed study may be found in the Wilson-Sutherland book.)

Colt Camp Perry S.A., Single Shot Target Pistol

Camp Perry Single Action, Single Shot Target Pistol. Made from 1926 to 1941 (less than 100, believed experimentals, made in 1920; all with serials under 100). Total quantity 2,525; among smallest production of all Colt cartridge handguns. 22 Long Rifle caliber. One shot chamber, mounted on crane, and pivoting down and to the left for loading (as on conventional Colt double-action revolver). 8" and 10" barrels.

Checkered walnut grips with rampant Colt medallion inset. Blued finish.

Serial numbered in individual range, from 1. Barrel marking (top): COLT'S PT. F.A. MFG. CO./HARTFORD CT. U.S.A. On left side of chamber: CAMP PERRY MODEL; and on the barrel, the caliber marking.

A unique model of Colt double action handgun, the Camp Perry was named after the site of U.S. pistol, revolver, and rifle competition in Ohio. The type is distinguished by its single shot construction, the unusual barrel lengths, and the quite limited production (which was made on the frame of the Double Action revolver; without recoil shield).

5B-209

Standard model; with 10" barrel length:
5B-209   Values—Very Good **$500**   Exc. **$1,250**
Variation, having 8" barrel (standard after 1934, serial range about 2150):
5B-210   Values—Very Good **$500**   Exc. **$1,250**

Colt New Pocket Double Action Revolver

New Pocket Double Action Revolver. Manufactured 1893 - 1905; total run of about 30,000. Under serial number 11,900 (approx.) made prior to Dec. 31, 1898.

32 Colt and 32 S&W calibers. 6-shot cylinder. Barrel lengths from 2-1/2" to 6".

5B-211

Checkered hard rubber grips with COLT oval motif. Finishes either blued or nickel plated.

Serial numbering in an individual range, beginning with 1 and continuing through approximately 30000; serials then continued by the Pocket Positive Model. Barrel marking of Colt company name, Hartford address, and 1884 and 1888 patent dates. COLT'S NEW POCKET stamping on left side of frame.

The New Pocket began a long line of pocket size double action swingout cylinder revolvers made by Colt's. Model identification can quickly be made by the serial number range, and the New Pocket frame stamping.

Basic variations are:
Standard model, but early production, without 1884 and 1888 patent barrel markings:
5B-211   Values—Very Good **$125**   Exc. **$375**
Standard model, with 1884 and 1888 markings, and in 2-1/2", 3-1/2", and 6" barrel lengths:
5B-212   Values—Very Good **$100**   Exc. **$300**
(Note: Premium placed on 5" barrel specimens.)

Colt New Police 32 Double Action Revolver

New Police 32 Double Action Revolver. Made c. 1896-1907; total produced about 49,500. Under 4,600 (approx.) made prior to Dec. 31, 1898.

32 Colt, 32 Colt New Police, and 32 S&W calibers. 6-shot cylinder. Barrel lengths of 2-1/2", 4", and 6".

Checkered hard rubber grips with COLT oval motif. Finished either in blue or nickel plating.

Serial numbering in an individual range, from 1 on up through approximately 49500 (and including the New Police Target Model): numbers then continued by the Police Positive 32 Model. Barrel marking of Colt company name, Hartford address, and 1884 and 1888 patent dates. COLT'S NEW POLICE stamped on left side of the frame.

The New Police 32 was the second pocket size double action swingout cylinder revolver brought out by Colt's factory. It was given a substantial boost by Theodore Roosevelt and the New York City Police Department, purchasers of better than 4,500 specimens, all with the backstrap marking: NEW YORK POLICE. The New Police 32 is quickly identified by the serial range, 1884 and 1888 patent markings, and the frame marking: NEW POLICE.

Basic variations are:

5B-213

Standard model, blue or nickel finish:
5B-213 Values—Very Good **$90** Exc. **$275**
New Police Target model; 6" barrel, flattop target frames and target sights, otherwise basically same as standard model; total production about 5,000:
5B-214 Values—Very Good **$250** Exc. **$650**
(Note: Premium placed on New York Police contract revolvers, and other specially roll marked revolvers.)

Colt Model 1900 Automatic Pistol

Model 1900 Automatic Pistol. Manufactured 1900-03; total run of about 3,500.

38 rimless smokeless caliber. Magazine held 7 shots. Barrel length 6".

Walnut, checkered walnut, or hard rubber grips. Blued finish; the hammer and combination sight/safety casehardened.

Serial numbered from 1 on up through about 3500; numbers then continued by the Model 1902 Sporting Pistol. Left side of the slide marked BROWNING'S PATENT, with 1897 patent date, and the Colt company name and Hartford address. Caliber designation and AUTOMATIC COLT on right side of the slide.

An extremely significant pistol to the collector, the Model 1900 was Colt's *first* production in the category of automatic handguns. In its own way this is the "Paterson" of Colt autos, and several of its features are quite primitive when compared to

5B-215

later developments. Long slide without slide stop, pointed hammer spur, rear sight doubling as a safety (later replaced by sight mounted in dovetailed fashion), rather straight grip.

Major variations are:

Standard model, with rear sight also serving as hammer safety:
5B-215 Values—Very Good **$1,450** Exc. **$6,000**
As above, but hammer safety rear sight altered to conventional rear sight:
5B-216 Values—Very Good **$800** Exc. **$2,000**
Pistols with slide serrations on front area of slide (above serial range of about 2000):
5B-217 Values—Very Good **$1,250** Exc. **$5,500**
U.S. Navy model, marked USN and number on left side of the frame, with the Colt serial number on right side of frame:
5B-218 Values—Very Good **$2,750** Exc. **$6,500**
U.S. Army model, two contracts (as below) intermingled in the commercial series production. Each contract marked on left trigger bow U.S.

Although quantities purchased of this Army model somewhat higher than Navy model, they appear with less frequency, and in more worn states of condition, hence values usually higher:

First contract, total quantity 75; in serial range under 200. Plain, smooth walnut grips with inspector's cartouche on left grip dated 1900 over initials JTT:
5B-219 Values—Very Good **$7,000** Exc. **$19,500**

Second contract, total quantity 200. Serial range 1501 to 1700. Checkered walnut grips. Inspector's initials RAC marked on left side of trigger bow:
5B-219.5 Values—Very Good **$5,000** Exc. **$17,500**

Colt Model 1902 Sporting Automatic Pistol

Model 1902 Sporting Automatic Pistol. Made 1903-08; in a total quantity of about 7,500.

38 rimless smokeless caliber. Magazine capacity 7 shots. Barrel of 6" length.

Hard rubber, checkered grips with COLT and rampant colt motifs. Blued finish, the hammer casehardened.

Serial numbers continued the series begun by the Model 1900 Automatic, beginning at the range about 3500, and continuing through approximately 10999; some pistols in the range 30000 - 30190. Slide markings of four basic types; the first identical to that on the Model 1900; the second with the patent date part of marking in three lines (including 1897 and 1902); the third with patent date marking in two lines and including 1897 and 1902; and the fourth the 1897 and 1902 dates and PATENTED in two

5B-220

lines but without reference to Browning. Caliber designation and AUTOMATIC COLT on right side of slide.

The second model of Colt Automatic Pistol, identification can be confusing, but basic details to note are: 1897 and 1902 patent date slide markings, rear sight dovetailed onto breech area of slide, rounded butt shape, rounded hammer spur, long slide, and lack of a slide lock device (on left side of frame). Comparison should be made with the Model 1902 Military, and differences are noted in the text on that model.

Basic variations of the Model 1902 Sporting are:
Standard model, the serrations on the front section of slide; below serial range of about 9500:
5B-220   Values—Very Good **$500**   Exc. **$2,250**
Standard model, the serrations on the rear section of the slide; made in serial range about 9500:
5B-221   Values—Very Good **$450**   Exc. **$2,000**

Colt Model 1902 Military Automatic Pistol

Model 1902 Military Automatic Pistol. Manufactured c. 1902-29; in a total of approximately 18,000.

38 rimless smokeless caliber. Magazine capacity 8 shots. Barrel length 6".

Hard rubber, checkered grips with COLT and rampant colt motifs. Blued finish, the hammer casehardened.

Quite unusual serial numbering, which began at 15001, and went *backward* to 11000; then began at 30200, continuing to 47266. Numbers were shared with the Model 1903 Pocket (Hammer type) Automatic within the years 1918-29. Three types of slide markings on the left side, as follows: First type, has patent part of marking in three lines (with 1897 and 1902 dates); second type, with patent date marking in two lines and including 1897 and 1902, and BROWNING reference; the third type, has 1897 and 1902 dates and PATENTED in two lines (but without reference to Browning). Caliber designation, AUTOMATIC COLT, and MODEL 1902 on right side of slide.

With several similarities to the Model 1902 Sporting Pistol, the Model 1902 Military can be distinguished by the following details: Slide lock device on left side of frame, MODEL 1902 markings on slide, magazine capacity of 8 cartridges, square butt profile, and presence of lanyard swivel on left side of the butt. The Model 1902 Military is the most often encountered of the "long slide" early Colt automatic pistols, and boasts a comparatively lengthy production run.

Basic variations are:
Early production model, having slide serrations at the front section:
5B-222   Values—Very Good **$500**   Exc. **$2,250**
Standard production, with the slide serrations at the rear section; hammers either rounded or of the spur type:
5B-223   Values—Very Good **$450**   Exc. **$1,750**
Special group of U.S. Army marked pistols; within the serial range 15001 - 15200; have inspector stampings and slide serrations at the front:
5B-224   Values—Very Good **$3,750**   Exc. **$12,500**

5B-222

5B-223

Colt Model 1903 Pocket Automatic Pistol

Model 1903 Pocket Automatic Pistol. Made c. 1903-29; the total quantity approximately 26,000.

38 rimless smokeless caliber. Magazine capacity 7 shots. Length of barrel 4-1/2".

Hard rubber, checkered grips with COLT and rampant colt motifs. Blued finish, the hammer casehardened.

The serial numbering in sequence from 16001 through 47226; from 30200 to end of production the numbers shared with the

1902 Military Model Pistol. Same three types of slide markings as on the Model 1902 Military Pistol (*q.v.*). Caliber designation and AUTOMATIC COLT on right side of slide.

The Model 1903 Pocket Automatic is generally identical to the Model 1902 Sporting, with the notable exception of the shorter slide. This was Colt's first pocket size automatic, and features a long production record for a comparatively primitive model of automatic type.

5B-225

Basic variations are:

Early production model, with the rounded hammer (serials to about 22000). Blue finish on these did not hold up well, consequently they are difficult to find in finer grades of condition:

5B-225   Values—Very Good **$250**   Exc. **$1,000**

Standard model, having the spur type hammer (serials after about 22000):

5B-226   Values—Very Good **$225**   Exc. **$875**

Colt Model 1903 Hammerless 32 Pocket Auto

Model 1903 Hammerless 32 Pocket Automatic Pistol a.k.a. "Model M." Manufactured c. 1903-46; total quantity over 572,000.

32 ACP Caliber. Magazine capacity 8 shots. Barrel lengths 4" and later 3-3/4".

Three types of hard rubber grips with COLT and rampant colt embossed motifs used through 1924; balance of production checkered walnut with Colt medallion inlays. Blued finish standard; a large number nickel plated with pearl/medallion grips.

Serial numbered from 1 through 572215 including a small group marked U.S. PROPERTY. A variety of slide markings have been catalogued, to be expected from such a large total manufacture. Patent dates (earliest production 1897 only; later 1903 added) and Colt company name and Hartford address standard on left side; right side marked AUTOMATIC COLT which changed to COLT AUTOMATIC c. 1915; second line CALIBRE 32 RIMLESS SMOKELESS.

Few models of any Colt handgun outnumber the diminutive 1903 Hammerless 32 in total quantity produced. The first concealed hammer automatic in the firm's line, it offers the collector a number of variations, particularly in markings and grip styles.

Major variations are:

1st Type: 4" barrel with barrel bushing; serial range from 1 to 71999:

5B-227   Values—Very Good **$200**   Exc. **$550**

5B-227

2nd Type: 3-3/4" barrel with barrel bushing; serial range 72000 to 105050:

5B-228   Values—Very Good **$175**   Exc. **$425**

3rd Type: 3-3/4" barrel without barrel bushing; serial range 105051 to 468096:

5B-229   Values—Very Good **$165**   Exc. **$350**

4th Type (Commercial): 3-3/4" barrel with added magazine safety; serial range 468097 to 554000:

5B-229.5   Values—Very Good **$165**   Exc. **$350**

4th Type (Military): 3-3/4" barrel with added magazine safety. Right frame marked U.S. PROPERTY. Blue (worth premium) or Parkerized finish. Serial range 554001 to 572214:

5B-230   Values—Very Good **$750**   Exc. **$1,750**

Colt Model 1905 45 Automatic Pistol

Model 1905 45 Automatic Pistol. Manufactured 1905-11; in a total run of approximately 6,100. Plus special military contract in separate serial group (201 made).

45 rimless smokeless caliber. Magazine capacity 7 shots. Barrel length 5". Snub hammer changed to spur type after serial range 3600.

Grips of checkered and varnished walnut. Blued finish; the hammer casehardened.

Serial numbered from 1 on up. Two basic types of markings on left side of the slide; the first having 1897 and 1902 patent dates, with Colt company name and Hartford address, the second also having 1905 date, with Colt name and Hartford address. On the right side of all slides: AUTOMATIC COLT/CALIBRE 45 RIMLESS SMOKELESS.

The Model 1905 was Colt's first automatic chambered for 45 caliber ammunition; the cartridge was a forerunner of the 45 ACP. Readily identifiable features are the nearly vertical grip angle, the 45 rimless smokeless caliber, and the rectangular slide

5B-231

shape (lacking the escalloped lower section standard on the Model 1911 45 Automatics).

Major variations are:

Early model, having 1897 and 1902 patent dates in the slide marking (serial range below about 700):

5B-231   Values—Very Good **$1,250**   Exc. **$4,000**

Standard model, with 1897, 1902, and 1905 patent dates on the slide (serial range above about 700):

5B-232   Values—Very Good **$775**   Exc. **$3,250**

Shoulder stocked pistols; the stocks of metal and leather, doubling as holsters; pistols have grooved frames to accept stock attachment, and are within specific serial number ranges. Classified "Curio & Relic" and subject to the provisions of Gun Control Act. Complete with stock:

5B-233   Values—Very Good **$6,500**   Exc. **$17,500**

Special military variation, numbered within individual serial range of 1 - 201, and known to collectors as the 1907 contract pistol; has K.M. inspector stamping, lanyard loop on frame, and external indicator to show if chamber loaded; spur hammer and grip safety:

5B-234   Values—Very Good **$7,000**   Exc. **$20,000**

5B-232

Colt Model 1908 Hammerless 25 Caliber Auto

Model 1908 Hammerless 25 Caliber Automatic Pistol. Factory designation "Model N" denoted frame size. Made c. 1908-41; the total quantity 409,061. The smallest auto in the Colt line.

25 ACP caliber. Magazine capacity 6 shots. Barrel length 2".

Hard rubber, checkered grips with COLT and rampant colt embossed motifs were standard until serial range of about 335000; thereafter checkered walnut with Colt medallion inlays were used. Blued finish standard; fair number in nickel plating.

Individually serial numbered from 1 through 409061. Three basic markings were used on the left side of the slide, earliest type including 1896, 1897, and 1903 patent dates, Colt company and Hartford address marking; the second type adding a 1910 date; and the third type adding a 1917 date. On the right side of the slide, standard throughout manufacture: COLT AUTOMATIC/CALIBRE 25.

Basic variants are:

Early production model, with 1896, 1897 and 1903 dates on the left side slide marking; through serial range of about 20000; rubber grips:

5B-235   Values—Very Good **$250**   Exc. **$500**

Standard model, with dates as above, plus either 1910 or 1910 *and* 1917; former type with rubber grips; latter with rubber or checkered walnut:

5B-236   Values—Very Good **$250**   Exc. **$500**

U.S. Property marked; No known formal government contracts or Colt records showing direct sale. However, definite proof of

5B-235

U.S. ownership and marking. Almost all likely for clandestine WW II O.S.S. use (after war, the Central Intelligence Agency). Most acquired in small lot purchases by U.S. Ordnance Dept. direct from dealers/jobbers; some even second hand and by gift.

Usual markings U.S. (or "United States") PROPERTY; some with Ordnance cross-cannon/flaming bomb/circle insignia. Die size and placement of marks vary depending on arsenal or facility where applied. None observed with proofs or inspector markings; most with Parkerized finish. (Most definitive study MAN-at-ARMS, Feb., 1995.) Caution should be exercised as spurious examples known:

5B-237   Values—Very Good **$950**   Exc. **$2,750**

Colt Model "M" Hammerless 380 Pocket Auto

5B-238

Model "M" Hammerless 380 Pocket Automatic Pistol; a.k.a. "Model 1908 Hammerless" and "Model 1903 Hammerless." Manufactured from 1908-1945; total quantity over 138,000.

380 ACP caliber. Magazine capacity 7 shots. Barrel length 3-3/4" only.

Three types of hard rubber grips with COLT and rampant colt embossed motifs used up to 1924; balance of production checkered walnut with Colt medallion inlays. Blued finish standard; large quantity also made with nickel plated finish.

Serial numbered in individual series from 1 through 138009. Left side of slide marked with two patent dates (1897 and 1903) with Colt company name and Hartford address. Right side marked AUTOMATIC COLT (after 1915 changed to COLT AUTOMATIC) with second line reading CALIBRE 380 HAMMERLESS.

The actual factory designation for both the 380 and 32 hammerless was merely "Model M." The use of issue dates as model names is apparently a later collector designation.

Basic variations are:

1st Type: 3-3/4" barrel with barrel bushing; serial range from 1 to 6251:

5B-238   Values—Very Good **$400**   Exc. **$700**

2nd Type: 3-3/4" barrel without barrel bushing; serial range 6252 to 92893:

5B-238.3   Values—Very Good **$275**   Exc. **$450**

3rd Type (Commercial): 3-3/4" barrel with added magazine safety: serial range 92894 to 133649:

5B-238.8   Values—Very Good **$275**   Exc. **$425**

3rd Type (Military): 3-3/4" barrel with added magazine safety; right side of frame marked U.S. PROPERTY. Blued finish; serial range 133650 to 138009. Some in this group may have an "M" preceding the serial number:

5B-239   Values—Very Good **$950**   Exc. **$2,500**

Colt Model 1909 45 Automatic Pistol

Model 1909 45 Automatic Pistol. Manufactured 1910; quantity made approximately 23.

45 rimless, smokeless caliber. Magazine capacity 7 shots. Barrel length 5". High polished blued finish; casehardened hammer, grip safety and mainspring housing. Checkered walnut grips. Serial numbered 0 to 23 on left frame.

Markings: Patent dates 1897, 1902, 1905 with Colt name and Hartford address on left side of slide; AUTOMATIC COLT CALIBRE 45 RIMLESS SMOKELESS on right slide.

The Model 1909 manufactured as a trial pistol for the U.S. military; never slated for commercial sale. It marks the advent of single-link decoupling of the barrel/slide. Extremely rare.

Few recorded sales. Values variable; likely in mid five figures for specimens in top condition grades.
5B-239.5

5B-239.5

Colt Model 1910 45 Automatic Pistol

Model 1910 Automatic Pistol. Manufactured 1910; quantity approximately 10.

Caliber, magazine capacity, barrel length, checkered grips, and finish all similar to above (hammer bright blue). Serial numbered 1 through 10 on left frame.

Slide markings same as Model 1909.

The Model 1910 exhibits first appearance of the slanted grip profile of its ultimate successor, the famous Model 1911 series. It also has development features directly attributed to John Browning. Extremely rare.

Few recorded sales. Values variable; likely in mid five figures for specimens in top condition grades.
5B-239.6

5B-239.6

Colt Model 1911 Special Army 45 Automatic Pistol

Model 1911 Special Army 45 Automatic Pistol. (Not illus.) Manufactured 1911; total quantity 12. About identical in appearance/profile to Model 1911 Civilian/Military series following.

Caliber, magazine capacity, barrel length, checkered grips, finish (blued hammer) similar to Model 1910 above. Serial numbered 1 through 12 on left frame.

Slide markings, patent dates identical to above with Colt rampant colt trademark at left rear of slide. Has thumb safety.

This pistol was the final victor in the Colt-Savage trials and direct predecessor of the Model 1911. Extremely rare.

Few recorded sales. Values variable; likely in mid five figures for specimens in top condition grades.
5B-239.7

Colt Model 1911 Automatic, Civilian Series

Model 1911 Automatic Pistol, Civilian Series. (Not illus., identical to Military Model.) Introduced in 1911 and still in production; total production of original serial range (through 1970) of C336169. Serial number prefix C denotes the Civilian Model.

45 ACP caliber. Magazine capacity of 7 shots. Barrel length 5".

Serial numbering began with C1 and continued through end of production of prefix C arms, in 1970; successor model not evaluated. Slide markings are quite varied, and best analyzed by reference to pages 432 and 433 of *The Book of Colt Firearms.* Basically, on right side of slide appears the caliber and COLT AUTOMATIC marking; on the left side patent dates (after c. 1938

dates no longer used in slide markings), and the Colt company name and Hartford address. GOVERNMENT MODEL on pistols post c. 1946.

Other than the world famous 45 Automatic profile, the quickest means of determining if a pistol is from the Model 1911 Civilian group is from the C serial number prefix. Because of the significant number of variants in both the Civilian and Military Model 1911 (and M1911A1) production, many collectors specialize only in the "Colt 45 Auto." Its unique service record, hard-hitting ballistics, and world wide recognition contribute to the strong appeal of these arms in the collector market.

Major variations of the Civilian series are:

Early production model, having 1897, 1902, 1905, and 1911 patent dates in the slide markings (through serial range about C-4500):

5B-240 Values—Very Good **$550** Exc. **$1,750**

Standard model pistols, within the serial range approximately C-4500 to C-130000; Model 1911 type with straight mainspring housing:

5B-241 Values—Very Good **$550** Exc. **$1,750**

455 caliber British Contract pistol; bear serial numbers of own series (began with W10001, and continued through to over W21000). CALIBRE 455 on right side of slide; made in 1915 and 1916:

5B-242 Values—Very Good **$700** Exc. **$1,850**

Scarce Russian order pistols with ANGLO ZAKAZIVAT (in Russian characters) marking; totaled about 14,500 arms in 45 ACP; within the serial numbers about C-50000 to C-85000:

5B-243 Values—Very Good **$2,500** Exc. **$6,000**

Model 1911A1 pistols; began at the range of about C-130000; and are quickly identified by the arched mainspring housing:

5B-244 Values—Very Good **$550** Exc. **$1,250**

Colt Model 1911 Automatic, Military Series

Model 1911 Automatic Pistol, Military Series. Manufactured 1912-57; in a total production of about 2,695,000. These pistols do not have the C serial prefix, as found in the Civilian arms.

45 ACP caliber. Magazine capacity of 7 shots. Barrel length 5".

Serial numbers classified into three basic groups, the major of which was the Colt factory and other contractors' series in the range 1 - 2693613, the Remington-UMC production of 1 - 21676, and the government arsenal pistols (have X prefixes). Slide markings are somewhat involved, but subdivide into the following: On left side, first type with 1897, 1902, 1905 and 1911 patent dates, and Colt company name and Hartford address; the second type adding 1913 patent date, and continuing the Colt name and Hartford address; and the third type was a reorganization of the patent date markings and Colt-Hartford data of the second variation. Standard on right side of slides was MODEL OF 1911, followed by either U.S. ARMY or U.S. NAVY or U.S.M.C. (very rare markings). Note UNITED STATES PROPERTY standard frame marking.

Inspector markings: Pointed out under the variation categories detailed below.

No model of Colt handgun even approaches the total manufacturing run of the Model 1911 and M1911A1 Automatic pistols. Though the Single Action Army is every bit as famous, its total of 357,859 is paltry in comparison to the over 2,695,212 Military series pistols and over 336,000 Civilian arms. However, the purpose of the military series was decidedly for wartime use, and such service greatly reduced the proportion of arms surviving to the present in respectable condition. It is sometimes quite difficult to obtain fine conditioned specimens, despite the great numbers produced in most variations.

The major variants are as follows:

Model 1911 pistol made by Colt's factory during World War I period, serial range from 1 to about 629500; JMG, WGP and GHS inspector markings; straight mainspring housing; blued finish. Serial numbers below 10000 add a premium:

5B-245 Values—Very Good **$650** Exc. **$1,800**

5B-245

With U.S.N. markings:

5B-246 Values—Very Good **$1,200** Exc. **$3,000**

Model 1911A1 pistol, by Colt's factory; beginning in 1924; serial range 700001 - end of production (2380013); RS inspector markings; arched mainspring housing; Parkerized finish standard:

5B-247 Values—Very Good **$650** Exc. **$1,400**

Same as above, with blued finish:

5B-247.5 Values—Very Good **$750** Exc. **$1,600**

North American Arms Company series; quite a desirable variation, production was limited to about 100; bear company slide markings, with the serials on slide (WWI period):

5B-248 Values—Very Good **$8,500** Exc. **$25,000**

Springfield Armory Model 1911 pistol; within serial range of 72751 - 133186; total of 25,767 produced; bear Colt and Springfield Armory markings, eagle motif and Ordnance Department flaming bomb on frame and slide. (Note: Approximately 100 made prior to World War I for sale through the Director of Civilian Marksmanship and bear N.R.A. markings on the frame near the serial number. Value approximately twice that shown here. Be wary of spurious specimens.):

5B-249 Values—Very Good **$1,750** Exc. **$5,000**

Remington-UMC Model 1911 pistol; serial range 1 - 21676; having Colt and Remington-UMC slide markings, and E or B inspector stamps:

5B-250 Values—Very Good **$600** Exc. **$1,750**

Singer Manufacturing Company Model 1911A1 pistol; serial range S800001 - S800500; S. MFG. CO/ELIZABETH N.J. slide markings; blued finish (not Parkerized); only 500 made; JKC inspector markings:

5B-251 Values—Very Good **$5,000** Exc. **$17,500**

Union Switch & Signal Company Model 1911A1 pistol; serial range 1041405 - 1096404; slides include marking: U.S. & S. CO./SWISSVALE.PA. U.S.A.; about 40,000 made; RCD, HA, and R inspector markings:

5B-252 Values—Very Good **$950** Exc. **$2,250**

Remington Rand, Inc. Model 1911A1 pistol; serial ranges are several, the lowest number is 916405, and the highest 2619013; about 900,000 total made; REMINGTON RAND INC. slide marking; FJA, G, and HS inspector markings:

5B-253 Values—Very Good **$800** Exc. **$1,500**

Ithaca Gun Company, Inc. Model 1911A1 pistol; serial ranges are several, the lowest number 856405, and the highest 2693613; about 400,000 total made; ITHACA GUN CO. slide marking; FJA, G, and HS inspector markings:

5B-254 Values—Very Good **$800** Exc. **$1,500**

(Note: For further information, detailed serial number breakdown, markings, and other data, the author recommends *Colt Automatic Pistols* by Donald B. Bady, and Wilson-Sutherland, *The Book of Colt Firearms*. The amount of detail for the advanced collector is extensive.)

Colt Model 1861 Special Musket

5B-255

Model 1861 Special Musket. Manufactured 1861-65. Production usually estimated at 75,000. Recent information from government records indicates that the total was 100,000 and that many of them supplied for state contracts; this will explain the numerous specimens encountered with N.J. (New Jersey) markings on both barrel and stock.

58 caliber. Single shot muzzleloader made on government contract for use in the Civil War. 40" barrel standard; three barrel bands.

Oil-stained walnut stock. Metal parts for most of the production were finished "in the white," but bluing was standard on nipples, rear sights, and various screws. Barrels fastened to forend by three oval, split-ring iron barrel bands, tightened into place by clamping screws at the bottom of each band. Late production models fitted with solid iron bands retained in place by long narrow springs inletted in the stock as on the standard M1861 contract musket.

No serial numbers were used in the standard production of the Model 1861 Musket. On the lockplate is stamped:

U.S./COLT'S PT F.A. MFG CO./HARTFORD CT.The date of manufacture appears behind the hammer, e.g., 1861. An American eagle was marked on the bolster, and government inspector stamps are on several parts.

An unknown quantity, (likely sizeable) of Colt M1861 Muskets were sold on the civilian market during the Civil War. Some of them had failed to pass the more stringent government inspections yet were definitely serviceable. Classified by Colt as "Second Class U.S. Rifle Muskets" all are identified by their lack of the distinctive eagle marking on the bolster and the usual U.S. government inspector markings. Colt had agreements with the eminent New York City military outfitters and arms dealers Schuyler, Hartley & Graham who sold 2,500 of those muskets to the state of Connecticut in July, 1863. Values approximately the same as for the government-marked specimens

5B-255   Values—Very Good **$1,500**   Exc. **$3,750**

(Note: Further details on the 58 caliber "Special Musket" appear in Chapter IX, U.S. Military Longarms.)

Colt Berdan Single Shot Rifle

5B-256

Colt Berdan Single Shot Rifle. Breechloader with "trapdoor" breech system; made in rifle (standard model) and carbine types. Manufactured from 1866 to about 1870. Total of all types exceeded 30,000.

42 centerfire cartridge. Single shot. Rifle barrels measured 32-1/2", and the carbines 18-1/4".

Serial numbering of the Russian contract rifles (which represented nearly all of the Colt Berdan production) ran from 1 on up; and followed the barrel marking Colt's Fire Arms Factory Hartford America No. (in Russian Cyrillic letters). Arms for American sales bore Colt's name and the Hartford address in English on the barrel.

Ironically the Berdan was the Colt company's first metallic cartridge firearm. Patent for the weapon's breech system had been taken out by Hiram Berdan, known for his legendary Civil War "Sharpshooters" Regiment. The Colt Berdan rifle and carbine represent a pioneer American product in the rapidly growing field of breechloading metallic cartridge military firearms. These weapons are difficult to obtain due to the fact that nearly all of the production was shipped to Russia, and few have returned.

Basic variants are:

Standard model, Russian-order rifles, with Cyrillic barrel markings and serial numbers (numbers also marked on bottom of barrel); total quantity of about 30,000:

5B-256   Values—Very Good **$600**   Exc. **$1,250**

Carbines with Cyrillic barrel markings; made in hopes of quantity orders by the Russians; total of not more than 25 made; half stocked:

5B-257   Values—Very Good **$3,000**   Exc. **$6,000**

Carbines with Colt, Hartford barrel markings; in attempt to win orders from U.S. government; approximately 25 or less made; half stocked:

5B-258   Values—Very Good **$5,000**   Exc. **$10,000**

Standard model military rifle, with Colt barrel markings in English; serial numbers not always present; total quantity in 42 caliber of not more than 100:

5B-259   Values—Very Good **$2,500**   Exc. **$5,000**

(Note: A quite rare 45-70 variation of the American version Colt Berdan rifle was also produced, as were variations of the Berdan made up as target rifles [also bearing American markings]. These arms demand a premium.)

Colt Laidley Military Rifle

Colt Laidley Military Rifle. Single shot breechloader with rolling block, split breech, type action (but unlike the Remington

5B-259.5

or Whitney). Made c. 1867. Total produced 50 of which 25 were in 45 centerfire caliber and 25 in 50 centerfire.

Barrel length 36". Full walnut stock, 2 band fastened. Serial numbered 1 through 50 under barrel. Only marking on the lower numbered specimens F.R.B. under barrel or on front of frame (Franklin R. Bull, Chief Arms Inspector of Springfield Armory sent to Colt's to help in manufacture of the rifle).

Designed by Col. T.T.S. Laidley, U.S. Army, but not adopted for U.S. service. At Laidley's request, Colt made these 50 rifles (on plans obtained from Springfield Armory) for submission to Russian ordnance officers. Laidley design was also the basis for the Whitney-Laidley rifle (*q.v.*):

5B-259.5   Values—Very Good **$2,250**   Exc. **$3,500**

Colt-Franklin Military Rifle

5B-260

Colt-Franklin Military Rifle. Bolt action breechloader, having a gravity-feed box magazine. Made in 1887-88; the total produced about 50.

45-70 caliber. Magazine capacity 9 shots. Barrel length of 32-1/2".

Serial numbering from 1 on up. Some specimens marked with U.S. government inspector stamps, VP and eagle head, A, U,

and US. Colt company name and Hartford address barrel markings not always present.

One of the great rarities in Colt's production, the Franklin was patented by a vice president of the firm, General William B. Franklin. The hope was for quantity sales to the United States government. The weapon had some basic failings, not the least of which was the quite primitive magazine, and the rifles made appear to have been for experimental and test purposes:

5B-260   Values—Very Good **$4,500**   Exc. **$8,500**

Colt Model 1878 Double Barrel Shotgun

5B-261

Model 1878 Double Barrel Shotgun, Exposed Hammers. Made from 1878-89; in a total quantity of 22,690.

Gauges: 10 and 12. Side by side barrels; sidelocks. Barrel lengths standard at 28", 30" and 32"; other lengths available on order. All barrels manufactured in Belgium and sent "in the white" to Colt's where they were assembled and finished in a great variety of "Damascus" patterns (see discussion of same, Chapter XVII) many reaching complex and aesthetic heights and far greater than the mere four styles/grades (TWIST...FINE TWIST...LAMINATED...DAMASCUS) advertised for them. Occasionally found with extra set of matched numbered barrels; worth premium of 50 percent or more. Double triggers.

Oil stained or varnished checkered walnut stocks (uncheckered on very plainest grade); pistol grip standard; straight stocks scarcer and usually bring premium. Metal parts

finished as follows: Locks, breech, and forend mounts casehardened; barrels blued or browned, and feature damascus patterns.

Serial numbering from 1 on up; marked in various positions, but most quickly located on the trigger guard tang. Barrel rib marked: COLT'S PT. F. A. MFG. CO. HARTFORD CT. U.S.A.Gauge markings on bottom of breech area of barrels. Colt's Pt. F. A. Mfg. Co. marked on lockplates.

Colt's first double barrel shotgun proved to be a success until competition from less expensive foreign products became excessive. Enthusiasts regard the Colt Model 1878 as one of the finest quality shotguns made in American history. Not a few of these arms continue in use today—though their firing with modern loads (even weak ones) is *not* recommended.

Major variations are:

Plainest grade, merely line engraving bordering edges of locks, or with just the slightest simple scroll engraving; uncheckered, or very plain checkered stock; broad, coarse "Damascus" patterns on barrel finish:

5B-261   Values—Very Good **$425**   Exc. **$1,150**

Medium Grade, with more profuse scroll, or simple scene engraving, checkering of better quality as are the patterns of the "Damascus" finishes of the barrels:

5B-261.5   Values—Very Good **$625**   Exc. **$1,750**

Finest Grade, profusely engraved, often with detailed game scenes; very delicate and ornate patterns in the "Damascus" barrel finish; elaborate checkering and stock work:

5B-262   Values—Very Good **$1,100**   Exc. **$5,500**

(Note: Colt factory ledgers are complete on the Model 1878 shotgun, and provide an exhaustive amount of detail.)

Colt Model 1883 Double Barrel Shotgun

5B-263

Model 1883 Double Barrel Shotgun, Hammerless.
Manufactured from 1883-95; total quantity about 7,366.

Gauges: 10 and 12 (8 ga. known; very rare). Side by side barrels; boxlock action. Barrel lengths standard at 28", 30", and 32"; variations made on special order-lengths as short as 18" and long as 36" recorded. As with the Model 1878 shotgun, all barrels were imported from Belgium and assembled and finished at the Colt factory (see details above). Occasionally found with extra set of matched numbers barrel and worth premium of 50 percent or more. Double triggers.

Oil stained or varnished checkered walnut stocks; pistol grip standard; straight stocks scarcer and usually bring premium. Metal parts finished as follows: Frames and forend mounts casehardened; barrels blued or browned, and feature Damascus patterns of varying grades and qualities.

Serial numbered from 1, with the range 3057 to 4056 left out to suggest a higher production than actually made. Highest recorded number 8366. The serial is quickly located on the trigger guard tang. Barrel rib usually marked: COLT'S PT. F. A. MFG. CO. HARTFORD, CT. U.S.A.Marking of gauge on bottom of breech of barrels. Each side of frame may be marked: COLT. Usually engraved on bottom of frame is the inscription: PATENTED AUG. 22. SEP. 19. 1882.

Among finest quality firearms made in Colt's long history, the Hammerless Model 1883 ranks among the best grade doubles produced in the entire American arms trade. The limited number completed and the great pains devoted to handling specific orders from often fussy shooters means that a considerable degree of quality and variety is evident in the Model 1883 series. A review of Colt factory serial ledgers shows the exhaustive attention devoted to this pride of the Colt line.

Major variations are:

Standard model, with light engraving, and average checkering; in either 10 or 12 gauge:

5B-263   Values—Very Good **$600**   Exc. **$1,500**

Finer, Fancier Damascus patterns on barrels; scroll engraved designs on frame:

5B-263.5   Values—Very Good **$750**   Exc. **$2,250**

Fanciest grade in which greatest variations in quality observed. Elaborate engraving, often with game scenes; delicate Damascus barrel patterns. Values shown for average specimens, exceptional examples worth premiums:

5B-264   Values—Very Good **$1,000**   Exc. **$4,750**

(Note: Colt factory ledgers are complete on the Model 1883 shotgun, and supply exhaustive details.)

Colt Double Barrel Rifle

5B-265

Double Barrel Rifle. Made c. 1879-85; total quantity of about 35. One of the great rarities of Colt collecting.

Calibers are variations of the 45-70. Side by side barrels; sidelocks. Standard barrel length at 28". Double triggers.

Oil stained or varnished checkered walnut stocks. Metal parts finished as follows: Locks, breech, and forend mounts casehardened; barrels blued or browned; balance of metal parts usually blued.

Serial numbering from 1 on up; marked in various locations, but immediately located on trigger guard tang. Two numbers from the Model 1878 Shotgun group were 293 and 397. On the barrel rib: COLT'S PT. F. A. MFG. CO. HARTFORD CT. U.S.A.On lockplates: COLT'S PT. F. A. MFG. CO.

One of the ultra-rarities in Colts, the Double Rifle has a unique appeal to the collector because it was the brainchild of Caldwell Hart Colt, the playboy son of Samuel Colt. Caldwell was an avid gun enthusiast, and maintained a collection at the family home, Armsmear. The major share of Double Rifle production is believed to have been for Caldwell and his friends. This model is not to be confused with the Model 1878 Hammer Shotgun, a few specimens of which have been altered spuriously into double rifles. The Colt Double Rifle is a prize for the advanced collector:

5B-265   Values—Very Good **$10,000**   Exc. **$27,500**

Colt-Burgess Lever Action Rifle

5B-266

Colt-Burgess Lever Action Rifle. Made 1883-85; the total production 6,403.

44-40 caliber. 15-shot magazine and 25-1/2" barrel (rifle), and 12-shot magazine—20" barrel (carbine).

Oil stained walnut stocks. Metal parts blued (barrel and magazine tube occasionally browned); casehardened frames rare, worth premium; the hammer and lever casehardened.

Serial numbering from 1 on up to 6403. Colt company name and Hartford address marking on top of the barrel, accompanied by patent dates from 1873 to 1882. On bottom of the lever: +BURGESS'S PATENTS+.

The only lever action firearm made in any quantity in Colt's history, the Burgess was part of the company's attempt to offer shooters a broad range of hand and long guns. According to tradition, and generally considered to be a factual story, the Winchester factory responded to the Colt-Burgess with a showing of revolving handguns that just might go into production—if Colt continued manufacture of their new lever

action! After what must have been considerable expense of tooling up, Colt's suddenly discontinued the Burgess, and today specimens are justifiably prized by collectors. Only a few have survived in fine condition, and the total production run was quite limited. Breakdown was 2,593 carbines and 3,810 rifles.

Major variations are:

Standard model rifle, 25-1/2" barrel, full magazine, blued and casehardened finish (some barrels browned); octagonal barrel; 2,556 made of which 35 had part octagonal, part round barrels; very rare, worth premium:

5B-266 Values—Good **$950** Fine **$4,750**

Same as above, but with round barrel (1,219 made):

5B-267 Values—Good **$1,000** Fine **$4,750**

Standard model carbine, 20" barrel, full magazine, blued and casehardened finish (1621 made):

5B-268 Values—Good **$1,500** Fine **$5,250**

Baby Carbine, with lightened frame and barrel; identified in Colt factory ledgers (972 made):

5B-269 Values—Good **$1,750** Fine **$6,000**

Colt Lightning Slide Action, Small Frame

5B-270

Lightning Model Slide Action Rifle, Small Frame. Produced 1887-1904; the total quantity 89,912. Under serial number 35,300 (approx.) made prior to Dec. 31, 1898.

22 caliber short and long rimfire. 24" barrel the standard length. Factory records indicate special order lengths 9-1/2 inches to 24 inches were also made (and should be verified before acquiring).

Oil-stained walnut stocks; either plain or checkered. Metal parts blued; hammer casehardened.

Serial numbered from 1 on up to 89912. On the barrel the Colt company name and Hartford address marking, with patent dates from 1883 to 1887. Caliber marking on the barrel at breech.

In the Small Frame, 22 caliber slide action rifle, Colt's made a Lightning Model designed for small game shooting and "plinking," the first gun of its kind in the factory's history. Like the Medium Frame Lightning, the 22 was so well constructed that at this writing some specimens are still in service. Competitors' 22s increasingly made sales difficult, and in the early 20th century the Small Frame Lightning was finally discontinued. Despite the considerable total number produced, the basic variation of the 22 Lightning is:

Standard model; 24" barrel, either round or octagonal; half magazine; straight buttstock:

5B-270 Values—Very Good **$325** Exc. **$1,000**

Colt Lightning Slide Action, Medium Frame

Lightning Model Slide Action Rifle, Medium Frame. Made 1884-1902; in a total quantity of 89,777. Under serial number 84,000 (approx.) made prior to Dec. 31, 1898.

32-20, 38-40, and 44-40 calibers (A few in each caliber made in smooth bore; rare; worth premium). 15-shot (rifle with 26" barrel), or 12-shot (carbine, with 20" barrel) magazines. Rifles available in various lengths.

Oil stained walnut stocks; forends usually checkered. Metal parts blued; the hammer casehardened.

Serial numbered from 1 on up to 89777. Colt company name and Hartford address marking on top of barrel, with 1883 patent

dates *or* with 1883, 1885, 1886, and 1887 patent dates. Caliber markings located on breech end of the barrels.

The Medium Frame was the first type Lightning Slide Action brought out by Colt's factory. It shared chamberings with the Single Action Army and the Double Action Model 1878 Frontier revolvers, in the 32-20, 38-40, and 44-40, and thus could serve as a companion arm. In league with such arms as the Model 1878 and 1883 double barrel shotguns, Colt's was obviously attempting to capture much more of the gun market than solely handguns. Production of the Medium Frame was rather substantial, but still only minor in comparison with Winchester's

5B-271

lever action competitor arms. Of all the Lightning rifles, the Medium Frame series offers the greatest degree of variation; they are also appealing to collectors because of the revolver calibers.

Major variants are:

Standard model rifle, 26" barrel, either round or octagonal, first type barrel marking (patent dates 1883 only); without sliding breech cover:
5B-271   Values—Very Good **$500**   Exc. **$2,000**
Standard model rifle, same as above, but with more common patent barrel marking (1883, 1885, 1886, and 1887); with sliding breech cover:
5B-272   Values—Very Good **$475**   Exc. **$1,500**
Military rifles or carbines; with sling swivels, bayonet lugs, shortened magazine tubes, and carbine type buttplates; 44-40

caliber; various barrel lengths:
5B-273   Values—Very Good **$1,400**   Exc. **$5,500**
Carbine of standard type, with 20" barrel; adjustable military type sights; round barrel, and carbine buttplate:
5B-274   Values—Very Good **$875**   Exc. **$3,750**
Baby Carbine; same as above but of slimmer construction in barrel area; weight of 5-1/4 lbs., rather than the standard carbine's weight of 6-1/4 lbs.:
5B-275   Values—Very Good **$1,450**   Exc. **$4,750**
San Francisco Police Rifles; 44-40 caliber; blued finish, with SFP 1 to SFP 401 number markings on lower tang:
5B-276   Values—Very Good **$1,000**   Exc. **$3,750**
(Note: Presence of deluxe features, such as pistol grip stocks, command added premium.)

Colt Lightning Demonstrator

Colt Lightning Cutaway Demonstrator. Factory skeletonized with various shape apertures all parts to view internal mechanism. At least 50 known made 1885-1890 and sent to various Colt dealers for sales promotion purposes (likely others also). Large majority Medium Frame size (other types worth premium). Barrels shortened near breech; stocks by rear tang. If serial number indicates post-1898 manufacture it falls under provisions of GCA and is treated as any modern gun: (also note: a few spurious specimens are known).

5B-276.5

5B-276.5   Values—Fine **$2,500**   Exc. **$4,500**

Colt Lightning Slide Action, Large Frame

5B-277

Lightning Model Slide Action Rifle, Large Frame. Made 1887-94; the total produced 6,496.

Calibers from 38-56 to 50-95 Express (worth premium). Standard rifle barrel length of 28", and carbine of 22". Rifles available in various lengths.

Oil stained walnut stocks; the forends checkered. Metal parts blued; the hammer casehardened.

Serial numbered from 1 on up to 6496. Colt company name and Hartford address marking on top of barrel, with patent dates of 1883, 1885, 1886, and 1887. The caliber markings on left side of the breech end of the barrel.

By far the scarcest of Lightning Colt rifles is the Large Frame group. These rather mammoth slide actions were chambered for big game cartridges, but from a practical standpoint were no competition for the lever action equivalents made in large quantities by Marlin and Winchester. The short production run and limited number of Large Frame (usually called "Express Model") Lightnings classifies them rather closely in value with

the Lever Action Colt-Burgess rifles. However, there are a fair number of variations in the former, particularly due to varying barrel lengths, calibers, and combinations of stocks, sights, and finishes.

The basic variants are:
Standard model rifle, with octagonal 28" barrel, full magazine:
5B-277   Values—Very Good **$950**   Exc. **$3,750**
Same as above, but with round barrel:
5B-278   Values—Very Good **$950**   Exc. **$3,750**
Carbine of standard type, with round barrel, 22" length, full magazine, and any caliber; military style sights, carbine buttplate; 9 lbs. total weight:
5B-279   Values—Very Good **$2,750**   Exc. **$8,000**
Baby Carbine, with round barrel, 22" length but of lighter and more slender construction; weight of 8 lbs.:
5B-280   Values—Very Good **$3,750**   Exc. **$12,500**
(Note: Presence of deluxe features, such as pistol grip stocks, command added premium.)

The author with Models 1874 and 1877 ("Bulldog") Gatling guns on cover of his 1959 catalog.

Colt Gatling Gun

Colt Gatling Gun. The first practical machinegun. Invented by Dr. Richard J. Gatling, Indianapolis, Indiana 1861; patented as an "Improvement in Revolving Battery Guns" Nov., 1862. Among most fascinating and largest of antique Colt firearms actively collected.

Resembling a massive pepperbox, the gun lent its name to a common noun once popular (now out of vogue) to describe a repeating handgun … the "gat." They saw service in numerous historic engagements throughout the world from the 1860's to slightly after the turn of the century. The outcome of the skirmish at Little Big Horn is debated to this day; had Custer not chosen to leave his three Gatling batteries at Fort Lincoln when he set out to campaign, could the tide of the battle have turned?

Gatling's invention covered a hand cranked repeating firearm with multi-barrels arranged around a central shaft and individual strikers (later, bolts with firing pins) for each charge (or chamber). The 1862 patent and his development models were hopper-fed, 6 barrel, percussion .58 caliber, using reloadable, individual, auxiliary steel chambers; each fitted with a nipple for the percussion cap. A second model of 1862 was chambered for 58 caliber rimfire metallic cartridges, eliminating the auxiliary chambers. Although given Army trials, the gun was not adopted. Gatling did succeed in interesting Union General Benjamin Butler who purchased 12 guns with personal funds late 1863. Made by the Cincinnati Type Foundry Works, the guns saw service at the siege of Petersburg, June, 1864. The U.S. Navy reported favorably on the gun and also purchased a few during the war; there are no known photographs or records of their use.

Gatling had eight of his guns in 1" caliber made in 1865 by the Cooper Firearms Company of Philadelphia (q.v.). Given extensive trials the gun was officially adopted in 1866 and the fledgling Gatling Gun Company given its first important U.S. order for 100 guns (50 in caliber .50CF; 50 in caliber 1"); most were ten barrel types, a few six barrel. The arrangement for Colt to make the guns was the beginning of the long association with the **Gatling Gun Company.** Although retaining its name it was ultimately absorbed by Colt.

Gatlings were made in many varieties, from the early Models 1865-66, the Model 1874 (in 45-70 caliber and considered among collectors as "classic"), M. 1879, M1881 and others in the 80's; M1893 in 30-40 Krag caliber; M. 1895 chambered for 6mm USN; M1903 cal 30-03 and later altered for cal .30-06; declared "obsolete" by U.S. Ordnance in 1911. They were available in numerous configurations and various mountings from large two-wheel field carriages, tripods, naval deck cones and police wagons to unique camel saddles for desert warfare. Among the most revealing documents is a factory price list c. 1880's describing the host of calibers, numbers of barrels and varying lengths and cartridge feed devices, etc. Calibers shown were from .42, .43, .45, .50, .55, .65, .75 to 1". Collectors are partial to the U.S. issue 45-70 types of the Indian Wars, however all are rare and highly desireable. Most Gatlings have open/exposed barrels, a lesser group is entirely encased in brass. Among those the Model 1877 "Bulldog" with five 18" barrels, weighing 90 pounds, usually on tripod mount, highly desirable, especially for its size. The very rare, diminutive "Police Model 1893" is a great prize with its six short 12" barrels cal 45-70 weighing about 74 pounds.

Colt and Gatling markings on earlier models are usually on a large, heavy, round cast brass plate affixed to the rear brass housing GATLING'S/BATTERY/GUN (patent dates)/MADE BY COLT'S/PT. FIRE ARMS MFG. CO./HARTFORD, CONN. U.S.A.with various dates. (**Collectors take note:** that plate was quite accurately reproduced a few years ago as a novelty item, some of which have found their devious way into the collectors' market.) On later models markings were elaborately hand engraved on that same area. Model dates, caliber and serial number are most often seen.

Best references are *The Gatling Gun* (Wahl & Toppel), *The Book of Colt Firearms* (Wilson/Sutherland) and *The Machine Gun* (Col. Chinn, Vol I).

Gatling Values: The subject obviously demands further study by an owner wishing to sell a Gatling or the collector seeking to acquire one. The myriad of variables allow for but the broadest of generalizations. As with any collectible firearm, condition and completeness are important. It has been the author's observation that any Gatling in near complete condition, lacking a mount of any type, rusted and pitted (but NOT a dug relic!) and in restorable working order is valued in the $20,000 range. Average going prices for various models in complete mechanical order (some minor replaced parts, showing wear, lightly pitted, etc.) with their original yoke and on an authentic, desirable type mount have been $40,000 to $70,000. From that point it's another ball game where aesthetics, condition and rarity play significant roles and prices hovering between the high five figures and low 6 figures are not unknown.
5B-281

Samuel Colt personal presentation book-cased outfit. Long considered among the most rare type of Colt casing. Engraved Colt Model 1862 revolver with accessories. Both the pistol and the gold-embossed, red leather-covered case bear inscriptions from Sam Colt to Mrs. John B. Floyd, wife of the then recently resigned Secretary of War and soon-to-be Confederate General, John B. Floyd of Virginia. (*N. Flayderman & Co., c. 1970*)

Chapter V-C

Manhattan Firearms Company

The collecting of Manhattan firearms is an excellent—if not classic—case of having a published work on a previously unexploited field open new vistas for the collector and consequently precipitate an immediate alteration of values. The pioneer work *Manhattan Firearms* by Waldo E. Nutter, published in 1958, was important from dual viewpoints. As one of the first in-depth studies about a then-obscure arms subject, it received wide circulation from a major publishing firm in a field where almost all prior books had covered the more traditional subjects of collecting, i.e., Colts, Smith & Wessons, U.S. martial arms, etc. As such, the Nutter book represented the beginnings of the thirst for wider knowledge in all aspects of antique American arms. *Manhattan Firearms* also made available to the average collector a neatly categorized and itemized pattern for collecting guns that could be simply understood and followed by the average arms enthusiast, including the dealer and gun trader.

Prior to the book's publication, Manhattan arms enjoyed but a limited following and rather insignificant values for the great majority of specimens. There being no guidelines to follow, and the average collector having no idea what constituted a rarity as distinguished from a common specimen of Manhattan, these arms suffered a general lethargy in their collectible status. Immediately upon release of the Nutter book, there was a noticeable change in values and demand for Manhattan firearms and they have enjoyed a far greater and ever-increasing popularity in the collecting world; unquestionably their status had been elevated considerably. Published data had created both a demand and market for a specialized collecting area.

The several models and variations of Manhattan firearms offer the collector an excellent opportunity to assemble an impressive arms group, and not a few collections of significant proportions have been formed in recent years. But as with other fields, small nuances often play important roles in value. The collector, when encountering pieces that are unlisted herein, is urged to research the variances himself in order to assess the importance of them before hastily evaluating a specimen.

A basic check to be made on Manhattan 36 caliber Navy type revolvers is the verification that all serial numbers on major component parts are matched. On this model, as with Colts, serial numbers appear externally on all major parts. As similarly applicable to Colts, a mismatched number does not make a gun less of a collector's item, but it does make it less valuable. Very minor pieces such as a barrel wedge should not affect value at all; a mismatched number on a loading lever will detract from the value, but if the condition matches the gun it will do so only slightly, probably ten percent or less. Information concerning this subject appears in the Colt chapter and is worth reading for the Manhattan collector also.

The U.S. Ordnance is known to have purchased one small order for 36 Manhattan revolvers (caliber unknown) in late 1861, very possibly at the request of an individual regiment commander, there being no recorded contract. As there is every likelihood that such guns were not martially marked, extreme caution should be exercised should such a specimen be offered. Those guns in 36 caliber and considered "Navy" size are classified by collectors as a secondary martial handgun. A number of such pieces were privately purchased and carried by officers and men of both the Army and Navy during the Civil War. A few presentation and inscribed specimens have been observed in well known collections. Such inscribed or marked pieces, when authentic, are considered quite scarce in this field and their values are enhanced considerably.

Fancy, highly embellished Manhattans are occasionally encountered. The engraving on the 36 caliber Navy size is often identical to the style found on Colts of the period and a few exceptionally elaborate or very ornate specimens are known. All models of Manhattans may be found with grips other than the standard walnut, with ivory being the most often encountered. Fancy grips, if original to the gun and if in sound and complete condition, add a premium to the normal value of the gun. The reader is referred to Chapter II for further information on this subject.

Cased outfits are quite rare in the Manhattan line and very few are known. The collector should be wary of jumping to conclusions by the mere presence of a Manhattan in an original antique case with accessories. A number of cases used by other American makers will fit various models of Manhattans. But our statement regarding rarity of such cases should not lend stimulus to the opportunist to place Manhattans in other makers' cases to increase their value disproportionately. It has been found in the author's experience that a cased Manhattan, even though far rarer than a cased Colt, would not be increased to any greater degree in value than any other cased gun unless some special feature, e.g., a label or other unique identifying Manhattan device, were found in the case to prove that it was distinctly Manhattan! The presence of a "Manhattan Firearms Company" marked bullet mold in a case is also not in itself sufficient to identify the case as being Manhattan-made. Such bullet molds, although scarce, are quite often observed on the collectors' market and were evidently sold with the gun, but not necessarily with the case.

These arms, despite the impressive name and address marking of MANHATTAN and NEW YORK CITY, were never manufactured in that city or for that matter in that state. A thumbnail sketch of the company's history should prove of interest for the collector and help understand the sequence of their evolution and manufacture.

The expiration of Samuel Colt's master patents for the revolver in 1857 signaled the opening of the flood gate for competitive firearms. Among the most significant of these new products were those of Manhattan Firearms Manufacturing Company. Many of their guns hold special interest because of their close similarity to the Colt (e.g., the 31 caliber Pocket Model and the 36 caliber Belt or "Navy" Model). Unlike Colt, Manhattan's output came to be accepted primarily by the civilian market, and sales to the military were limited to private purchases by individual officers or enlisted men.

The company was founded, mainly by a group of New Jersey businessmen, and incorporated in New York City in 1856. Their first manufacturing facilities were in Norwich, Connecticut, where the single shot percussion pistols and pepperboxes were made, and possibly the earliest manufacture of some of their 31 caliber percussion revolvers. Thomas Bacon, later to found his own well know firm in Norwich, was superintendent of manufacturing at Norwich and evidently also acted as private contractor for some of the parts supplied to Manhattan.

Manhattan's first firearms were classified for later historians in a legal case tried before the New London County, Connecticut, Supreme Court of Errors, in 1859, entitled MANHATTAN FIREARMS MANUFACTURING

COMPANY VS. THOMAS K. BACON. The text of this intriguing document, published in the Nutter book, *Manhattan Firearms*, offers interesting details of the arms then being manufactured by Manhattan as well as insights to the company's early business history.

In 1859 manufacturing facilities were moved to Newark, New Jersey, where they remained for the duration of the company's existence. Manhattan's corporate history lasted somewhat less than 20 years. In that time, the company made over 150,000 handguns varying from single shot percussion pistols to pepperboxes to pocket and Navy size percussion revolvers, to metallic cartridge revolvers. Some of their production was issued bearing trade names other than their own such as HERO or the LONDON PISTOL COMPANY.

Successor to the Manhattan firm in 1868 was the American Standard Tool Company, also of Newark, New Jersey. American Standard lasted five years, forced out of business in 1873 during the great fina¬ncial panic of that year. Its product line was far more restricted in the arms field than its prolific predecessor.

BIBLIOGRAPHY

Nutter, Waldo E. *Manhattan Firearms*. Harrisburg, Pennsylvania: Stackpole Company, 1958. Pioneer work on the subject and the basic guide in its field.
(*) Preceding a title indicates the book is currently in print.

Manhattan Bar Hammer Single Shot Pistols

Bar Hammer Double Action Single Shot Pistols. Made c. 1856-late 1850s; total quantity estimated about 1,500. Production in Norwich, Connecticut.

31, 34, and 36 calibers. Barrel lengths from about 2"-4"; and of half round, half octagonal shape.

Two piece walnut grips of bag shape. Blued finish.

Serial numbers in lots, possibly based on barrel lengths, and in sequences from 1. Standard marking, on left side of the hammer: MANHATTAN F.A. MFG. CO./NEW YORK Frame engraving standard. The Bar Hammer Single Shots are of

5C-001

importance to the collector for their scarcity, and their position as the earliest of Manhattan company products:

5C-001   Values—Good **$225**   Fine **$550**

Manhattan Shotgun Style Hammer S.S. Pistols

Shotgun Style Hammer Single Action Single Shot Pistols. Made c. 1856-late 1850s; total quantity estimated about 500. Production in Norwich, Connecticut.

36 caliber. Barrel lengths about 5"-6"; half round and half octagonal in shape.

Two piece walnut grips of bag shape. Blued finish.

Serial numbers do not indicate quantities manufactured but were rather batch or manufacturing numbers—hence almost all found will have low numbers. Standard marking: MANHATTAN F.A. MFG. CO. NEW YORK

Decorative engraving on the frame was standard.

Identified by the centrally pivoting shotgun style hammer, the relatively large overall size, and the presence of front and rear sights. This model is one of the scarcest of Manhattan firearms:

5C-002

5C-002   Values—Good **$250**   Fine **$600**

Manhattan Pepperbox Pistols

Pepperbox Pistols. Made c. 1856 to late 1850s; total quantity of various types estimated at from 2,500 to 3,000. Production in Norwich, Connecticut.

28 caliber (often described as 31). Barrel lengths usually of 3", 4", and 5"; number of shots varies, as indicated below. All models were double action.

Two piece walnut grips of bag shape. Blued and casehardened finishes.

Serial numbering believed to be based on the number of shots, and the barrel lengths, and appear in various series. Standard marking, first found on the barrels, and later on left side of the hammer: MANHATTAN F.A. MFG. CO./NEW YORK Not all specimens bore this legend; later specimens dropped the address. CAST STEEL on barrel. Standard with frame engraving. **Three-Shot;** 3" barrel group; hand turned; very scarce:

5C-003   Values—Good **$450**   Fine **$1,250**
Five-Shot; 3", 4" or 5" barrel group; turned automatically when trigger pulled, a standard feature of all models excepting the Three-Shot:
5C-004   Values—Good **$325**   Fine **$975**
Six-Shot; 3" or 4" barrel:
5C-005   Values—Good **$325**   Fine **$975**
Six-Shot; 5" barrel; the scarcest of all Manhattan pepperbox pistols:
5C-006   Values—Good **$450**   Fine **$1,250**

5C-004

5C-005

Double Action Pepperbox

An unusual and unique variant of an American pepperbox as well as rare Manhattan. The single specimen viewed had a serial number that would indicate about 40 or 50 were made. 6 shot; 31 caliber. large oversize trigger bow to accommodate the double action trigger. Most unusual features are the nipples which are set in straight line with the 4" barrels (much like Blunt & Syms pepperboxes; q.v.). Hammer almost flush fitted at top of bold scroll engraved frame operates with a rolling motion.

Marked on barrel rib MANHATTAN F.A. MF'G CO. PATENT APPLIED FOR:
5C-006.5   Values—Good **$1,750**   Fine **$4,500**

5C-006.5

Manhattan Pocket Model Revolvers

Pocket Model Revolvers. Made c. 1858-1862. Total quantity of the two series about 4,800. Produced in Newark, New Jersey.

31 caliber. 5- or 6-shot cylinders, with roll engraved stagecoach holdup scene. Barrel lengths of 4", 5", or 6"; octagonal in shape; value premium placed on 5" and 6" lengths.

Two piece walnut grips. Blued finish, with casehardened hammer and loading lever.

Serial numbered from 1 on up, beginning with the First Series, and continuing to completion in the Second. Scroll engraving standard on the frame.

These Pocket Model revolvers offered some features which were patented and original with Manhattan, but basically they counted on their similarity to the Colt Model 1849 Pocket revolver for sales appeal. It was however rather unusual to find a mass produced repeating handgun on which hand engraving was a standard feature. Specimens known with transitional features of both series and worth premium.

Series I Pocket Model; 5-shot cylinder, with 10 cylinder stop slots. Small size trigger guard and grips. Patent date not present on frame, and the barrel marked: MANHATTAN FIRE ARMS/MANUFG. CO.NEW-YORK. Serial range from 1 to about 1000. Three examples of an unusual variant of this Series I have been identified with 5-shot, plain, unengraved cylinders having only five stop slots; all with serials under 500 (including an engraved and presentation-inscribed model). Rare and worth premiums.
5C-007   Values—Good **$375**   Fine **$1,000**

5C-007

5C-008

Series II Pocket Model; 6-shot cylinder, with 12 cylinder stop slots. Large size trigger guard and grips. Marked on frame: DECEMBER 27, 1859, and on barrel in one line: MANHATTAN FIRE ARMS MF'G.CO.NEW YORK Frames and gripstraps usually plated. Serial range from about 1000 to about 4800:
5C-008   Values—Good **$350**   Fine **$950**

Manhattan/London Pistol Company Variation

London Pistol Company variation, made by Manhattan. Percussion revolver made during the period of the Series I and early Series II Pocket Model Manhattans (*q.v.*), and differing from those arms as follows: Barrel marking LONDON PISTOL COMPANY, frame stamping (beneath cylinder) PATENTED DEC. 27, 1859, and various defects evident (e.g., casting pits, imperfections in engraving, irregular grip frame shape, and cylinder bolt screw extending through frame's right side). These LONDON PISTOL COmarked revolvers were Manhattan's means of utilizing and marketing second quality, sub-standard arms without impairment to their name. The result for the present-day collector is a variation more valuable, and far scarcer, than the finer quality production!

Total quantity estimated at a few hundred; serial numbers intermingled with Series I and early Series II. Variations are often seen on these "London" models exhibiting transitional and mixed features of both the Series I and II.

5 shot Series I type. Most often encountered. Serial numbers generally under 1000 with a few reported in the low teens:

5C-009   Values—Good **$425**   Fine **$1,200**

6 shot Series II type. Very Scarce. Serial numbers reported under 2000 range:

5C-009.5   Values—Good **$500**   Fine **$1,400**

Manhattan 36 Caliber Model Revolvers

36 Caliber Model Revolvers, a.k.a. "Navy Type". Made c. 1859-68; total quantity estimated about 78,000. Produced in Newark, N.J.

36 caliber. 5- and 6-shot round cylinders roll engraved in five decorative oval panels with military and naval scenes. 4", 5", and 6-1/2" octagonal barrels.

One piece varnished walnut grips. Blued finish, with casehardened frames, hammers, and levers, and silver plated brass gripstraps.

Serial numbered from 1 on up. Barrel markings and variations as noted below.

Manhattan's 36 caliber revolver series bears a close resemblance to the Colt Model 1851 Navy, and also to the Model 1849 Pocket. Close comparison of the Manhattan 36 to the Colt competition reveals that the former product featured its own advantages, and that fact is surely a major reason for the weapon's considerable sales success. (Note: 6-1/2" barrels worth approx 25 percent premium.)

5C-010

Series I 36 Caliber Model; serial range from 1-4200; 5-shot; barrel marking MANHATTAN FIRE ARMS MFG. CO. NEW YORK Note: The "1859" patent date does *not* appear on the cylinder. Premium placed on the first 1,000 revolvers, identified by the trapezoidal shaped cylinder stop slots (found below serial range 800), and thicker grips (below serial range 1000):

5C-010   Values—Good **$450**   Fine **$1,250**

Elaborately engraved Manhattan 36-caliber "NAVY" revolver with handsome relief-carved ivory grips. (*N. Flayderman & Co.*, c. 1995)

As above, but with 6" barrel (about 500 made, serial range below 1000):

5C-011   Values—Good **$675**   Fine **$1,500**

Series II: serial range about 4200-14500; barrel marking as above; 5-shot cylinder includes 1859 patent date marking:

5C-012   Values—Good **$450**   Fine **$1,250**

Series III; serial range about 14500-45200; barrel marking in one line: MANHATTAN FIRE ARMS CO, NEWARK N.J. 5-shot cylinder includes 1859 patent date. First appearance of the spring plate mounted on face of recoil shield is seen on an estimated few thousand early Series III under serial 21000 (worth premium) then discontinued and found later as standard on the series IV below:

5C-013   Values—Good **$450**   Fine **$1,250**

Series IV; serial range about 45200-69200; barrel marking in two lines: MANHATTAN FIRE ARMS CO. NEWARK N.J./PATENTED MARCH 8, 1864. 1859 patent date on 5-shot cylinder. Spring plate mounted on face of recoil shield, to prevent charge spreading from fired chamber:

5C-014   Values—Good **$425**   Fine **$1,250**

5C-015

Series V; distinguished by its 6-shot cylinder. Serial range from 1 to 9000, in its own series. Barrel address and cylinder date marking as noted above for Series IV variation. Tapered type loading lever on all barrel lengths except 4". Spring plates (worth premium) may or may not be present. Production of Series V arms estimated from June 1867-December 1868:

5C-015   Values—Good **$475**   Fine **$1,500**

Manhattan 22 Caliber Pocket Revolvers

22 Caliber Pocket Revolvers. Made c. 1860-61 (1st Model) and c. 1861-62 and 1868-1873 (2nd Model). A close copy in many respects of Smith & Wesson First Model 1st Issue and 2nd Issue type 22 revolvers. Total quantity made about 17,000; in Newark, New Jersey.

22 rimfire caliber. 3" octagonal, ribbed barrel.

Two piece varnished walnut or rosewood grips. Blued finish, with silver plated frame.

Serial numbered from 1 on up, in separate series for the First and Second Models. Two types of barrel marking, as noted under variations discussed below. Scroll engraving standard on side flats of the barrels.

Until production was halted by law suit, the Manhattan 22 caliber revolvers were not only well made, but they sold rapidly The company apparently had no fear of possible legal action from Rollin White or S&W, as apparent from open marketing, and the standard marking of company name and address appear on most of the pistols produced.

First Model, First Variation; rounded brass frame having circular iron frame plate, 7-shot cylinder, stop on frame topstrap, and the stop slots at breech end of cylinder; 6-groove rifling and barrel; usually not signed (when marked appears as on second variation noted below). Barrel latch overlapping side of frame bottomstrap and lower barrel lug. Approximately 1,600+ made:

5C-016   Values—Good **$275**   Fine **$675**

First Model, Second Variation; as above, but with circular brass frame plate, 3-groove rifling, marking on barrel (in an arc motif): MANHATTAN FIRE ARMS/MANUFG./CO/N.Y. Serial range about 1600+ to about 4800:

5C-017   Values—Good **$225**   Fine **$550**

First Model, Third Variation; as above, but having hammer spur curving gracefully to the rear and somewhat downward. Serial range about 4800 into the 7000s:

5C-018   Values—Good **$225**   Fine **$550**

First Model, Fourth Variation; as above, but the barrel latch no longer overlaps forward section of frame bottomstrap. Serial range from the 7000s to about 9000+:

5C-019   Values—Good **$225**   Fine **$550**

Second Model; flat brass frame fitted with large oval sideplate, chambered for 22 long cartridge (and thus having longer cylinder; measuring 15/16"), 7 shots, stop on frame bottomstrap, and the stop slots at front section of cylinder, roll engraved cylinder (Indian and settler motif), barrel marking on the top rib: MANHATTAN FIRE ARMS MF'G. CO NEW YORK and 1859 patent date on bottom. Total production about 8,000:

5C-020   Values—Good **$200**   Fine **$475**

Variant; believed made by Manhattan; plain, unengraved and unmarked revolver with serial number under 400. Its rarity not completely established, but a decided variation:

5C-021   Values—Good **$150**   Fine **$350**

American Standard Tool Co. revolver; substantially identical to the Manhattan marked type but with barrel marking: AMERICAN STANDARD TOOL CO. NEWARK, N.J. Approximately 40,000 manufactured. The standard model was plain and undecorated. Engraved specimens however are quite commonly encountered and they do bring premium values over the standard model:

5C-022   Values—Good **$175**   Fine **$400**

5C-016

5C-020

Manhattan/American Standard Hero S.S. Pistol

Manhattan Fire Arms Company and American Standard Tool Co., Newark, N.J. Hero Single Shot Pistol. Made c. 1868-73 (possibly earlier); total quantity about 30,000.

34 caliber. Round, screw off, smoothbore barrels in various lengths with 2" and 3" most commonly encountered.

Two piece varnished walnut grips, of bag shape. Blued with brass frame left bright, and casehardened hammer.

Manhattan product made without serial numbers, but numbers present on the American Standard pistols. Markings noted below.

Known as the "poor man's deringer" the Hero pistol was believed to be Manhattan's last percussion firearm and thought to be brought out in their last year of existence (1868). Recent evidence tends to show that date might have been earlier. The Bacon Mfg. Company (*see Chapter VIII-A for history*) apparently made a similar, if not identical, pistol that appeared in an advertisement by them c. 1861. Numerous unmarked Hero pistols may possibly be the product of Bacon or even Iver Johnson; values for completely unmarked specimens usually slightly less.

The American Standard Tool Co., successor of Manhattan, was set up to manufacture firearms and to make tools. It lasted only from 1868 to 1873. Pistols occasionally encountered marked only HERO without company markings are valued the same as the more common American Standard type (see also "Uncle Sam" 7C-038.5).

Hero pistol by Manhattan Fire Arms Co.; without serial numbers and with HERO/M.F.A. CO. marking; total made about 5,000:

5C-023   Values—Good **$250**   Fine **$500**

Hero pistol by American Standard Tool; bearing serial numbers, and marked A.S.T.Co/HERO. Barrels also made in 2-1/2" length. Total made about 25,000:

5C-024   Values—Good **$225**   Fine **$450**

5C-023

Chapter V-D

Marlin
(including Ballard and Marlin-Ballard)

A source of irritation and complaint for many collectors over the years has been that the arms and history of this significant American inventor and manufacturer have suffered from a lack of definitive information and a basic collecting guidebook. Surprisingly, as one of the major American gun makers, with well over a century of continuous operations and having produced a substantial quantity of longarms and handguns (in a host of variations) there were but few attempts, most of them aborted, to perform the research necessary to give collecting impetus to this field. That need was finally well met with the publication (1989) of the encyclopedic *Marlin Firearms* by William Brophy. Marlins have generally been collected on a piecemeal basis (*i.e.*, handguns included in deringer or revolver collections, Ballards in single shot rifle groups, and lever action in hit-or-miss groups) rather than as complete assemblages reflecting the entire sequence. Although the "last word" on the subject will be found in the Brophy book, it is with considerable satisfaction that the author lays claim to this chapter as among the "first words" about Marlins in their entirety.

Although a prolific group of arms of very high quality, the Marlin is still very much in the "affordable" category price-wise, offering the collector, researcher and student a relatively broad potential.

A great wealth of information (but by no means near-complete) has been available for many years on the popular Marlin-Ballard single shot rifles. Marlin pistols have been relegated almost to obscurity information-wise, while their lever action rifles, a major product of the company, are long overdue for justly deserved recognition as an important segment of the American repeating arms field. One reason for the relatively obscure position of Marlins has been their inclusion in a few published works that have long since gone out of print or the rather incomplete and incoherent coverage in works that have received very limited circulation, or at best, were nothing more than a repetition of catalog descriptions and continuance of "old wives" tales having no basis in fact.

The author has departed from the more or less standard style of firearm descriptions with the Marlin lever action rifles. This was due to their prominence as well as the lack of definitive and statistical data, and since so much new information has been unearthed quite essential in assessing both rarity and value. The reader will therefore find herein the most complete material published to date on the subject of variations of calibers, barrel lengths and quantities for many of the lever action models; all data gleaned directly from the original factory records. As previously mentioned, this does not represent the "last word" on the subject, but is certainly a substantive starting point for anyone interested in Marlins. It is hoped that this section will prove a valuable reference for those collecting or trading in the field.

Marlin handguns also offered a considerable challenge to list and describe and it is with a sense of satisfaction that they are to be found herein completely and accurately categorized and evaluated for the first time, with a great deal of fresh information as to quantities made and identification of variations and markings.

Ballard rifles—often a field of study and collecting by themselves—are placed in a clearer perspective for the *very first time ever* and are discussed at great length in the prefatory text to that section.

Marlin values tended to fluctuate considerably with changes in condition. For the most part they did not reflect the more moderate price gradations that similar guns of their contemporaries maintain (e.g., Colt, Winchester and Smith & Wesson). This was especially noticeable with handguns and lever action rifles, while the Ballards more or less reflect trends similar to other American single shots. Those price fluctuations were likely caused by the fact that no definitive guide had been available to the collecting world and hence, with the condition-conscious market that evolved in past decades (where almost any gun of any maker in superb condition became highly desirable), only those specimens in the highest condition grades had been actively sought by collectors-at-large rather than Marlin specialists. With changing collecting patterns and the publication of definitive data about Marlins, that trend has reversed itself.

The original factory finishes of Marlin rifles are noteworthy. The brilliant casehardening colors standard on the receivers of their single shot and repeating rifles as well as the high quality of blued finishes on barrels have been a major reason for their great popularity (especially in the finer degrees of condition) and their attractiveness to the collector. A generalization and rule-of-thumb for collecting Marlin firearms would place the earlier and scarcer models as desirable in all grades of condition, whereas the most salient feature affecting demand and evaluation of the later, more common and widely produced types is condition.

Bore conditions are often a major factor in evaluating the Marlin-Ballard series, as most were made for fine, accurate target shooting. Bores do not play a dominant role in evaluating the early pre-Marlin-Ballards. The reader is referred to Chapter XIV and the sections dealing with Winchester single shot rifles and the Sharps New Model 1874 (in Chapter V) where the subject of bores is discussed in some detail.

Quite a few Marlins of all types were factory engraved. As with all other American arms, such fancy embellishments are in strong demand and usually prices for them are greatly in excess of those for standard, plain specimens. This subject has also been discussed throughout the book, notably in Chapter II and the introductory text to many of the American arms makers. Marlin lever action rifles were available with varying degrees of factory engraving. Ornate specimens are highly desirable and may be rated on a par with similarly decorated Winchesters. Often the same engravers worked for both makers. Factory engraving was available on custom order on almost all models of Ballards, while on some of the fancier, higher grades engraving was standard, and is so indicated in the descriptions and prices in this section. Handguns may also be found with varying degrees of decoration, but to a much lesser degree than longarms. Although quite scarce, values on most engraved Marlin handguns increase more moderately than those of their contemporaries (i.e., Colt or Smith & Wesson, etc.). The most commonly encountered simple scroll/floral engraved motifs normally increase values from 50 percent to 100 percent. Finely cut, elaborate specimens are seldom seen and must be evaluated individually, based on their quality and rarity.

Cased Marlin handguns are seldom encountered; however, the lesser frequency of their appearance on the collectors' market is not sufficient to increase their values disproportionately. The most usual form of casing is a walnut box with simple compartmented lining similar in style to that used by Smith & Wesson (and very probably many of those cased Marlins are in fact in Smith & Wesson boxes which on some models are interchangeable). Values may be increased based on style, completeness and condition of the box.

Where grips are other than standard (ivory and pearl were available from the factory at extra cost), values may be increased proportionately providing their condition is complete and sound. The reader is referred to Chapter II for a detailed discussion of the subject. Ivory or pearl grips will normally increase values of Marlin handguns approximately $50 to $100.

Factory records of serial numbers exist for most Marlin lever actions from serial No. 4000 (c. 1883) to No. 355,000 (c. 1906). No records are available for any Marlin handguns, Ballard rifles, shotguns or 22 rifles (except lever actions) made prior to 1948. Those Marlin records are now maintained by the Cody Firearms Museum at the Buffalo Bill Historical Center, 720 Sheridan Ave., Cody, Wyoming 82414. For the modest fee of $55 ($30 to members of the Cody Firearms Museum) per rifle the collector is afforded the opportunity to acquire original manufacturing data. Information usually found includes model number, caliber, barrel length, date of manufacture and any special order or custom features. Shipping information and names of purchasers are rarely available.

Serial Numbers Marlin Lever Action Repeaters: Various models did not have individual blocks of numbers assigned. It is believed models were randomly numbered in sequence as they were shipped rather than as they were manufactured. Thus, a M. 1897 numbered 1501,001 entered June 1, 1897 may be recorded in just one day prior to a M. 1894 No. 150, 002. Reportedly, those under serial No. 175,500 may possibly be those made prior to Dec. 31, 1898; further verification is called for.

This section, and certainly any "well-rounded" Marlin collection, includes some of the predecessor Ballard arms made at Worcester and Newburyport, Massachusetts. The development of the Ballard system and the succession of companies that manufactured the arm are of direct importance and relevance to the collector of Marlins.

A brief, but general history of the Marlin Firearms Company is helpful in establishing for its products a clear historical perspective. The founder, John Mahlon Marlin (1836-1901), a former employee of the Colt Firearms Company at Hartford, launched his own business in New Haven c. 1863. The first weapon made is generally considered to be small a single shot 22 caliber deringer type pistol. Early production was confined to single shot handguns, with revolver manufacture starting after 1870. With the expiration of the Rollin White patents (owned by Smith & Wesson), Marlin (as did many other American makers) entered into revolver production. His first types were quite similar to those produced by Smith & Wesson and Colt (in their New Line series).

In 1873, the Brown Manufacturing Company of Newburyport, Massachusetts, then making the Ballard's patent rifle, was sold under mortgage foreclosure proceedings. Patent rights to the Ballard, plus a group of arms and parts in various stages of production, were acquired by Charles Daly of the large New York arms dealers Schoverling & Daly. Daly arranged with John Marlin to continue manufacture of the Ballard rifles, with Schoverling and Daly handling sales and distribution exclusively in the early years. Evidently, Daly himself bought into the Marlin firm at that time, eventually becoming its president and later selling his interest back to John Marlin in 1893. Business progressed sufficiently to the point where reorganization proved necessary and, in 1881, the Marlin Firearms Company was formed. Manufacturing continued heavily in the Ballard single shot rifle line while simultaneously their first lever action repeater (the Model 1881, named for the year of incorporation) was developed and marketed. By the late 1880s the era of the single shot waned and Marlin discontinued the Ballard (around 1890 or 1891), devoting all their efforts to the rising popularity of lever action rifles, later adding a line of pump action shotguns. On John Marlin's death in 1901 the operation was continued by his two sons, and other specialties were added to their line. Most notable of these was the Ideal Cartridge Reloading Manufacturing Company in 1910 (later sold to Lyman in 1925) with a diversified array of bullet molds, reloading tools and accessories.

Early in the period of the First World War, the firm was sold to a New York syndicate (1915) and renamed the Marlin-Rockwell Corporation. All the company's wartime energies were devoted to the manufacture of machine guns. The cessation of hostilities saw no revival in the manufacture of sporting arms, with management showing little interest in the field and merely maintaining a repair department to service pre-war Marlin sporting arms and maintain good will for the company name.

By 1921 a new organization—the Marlin Firearms Corporation—was formed, but manufacturing operations never got rolling. By 1923 the firm went into receivership, ultimately reaching the auction block. Purchase in its entirety was made by Frank Kenna in that year, revitalization began, and once again Marlin entered the field of sporting firearms, manufacture continuing (with exception of the war years 1942 to 1945) to the present day as the Marlin Firearms Company. The company has remained within the Kenna family to present and devotes most of its energies to sporting firearms.

BIBLIOGRAPHY

(Note: Important sources for information are factory catalogs issued beginning with the early 1880s. Other material about Marlins and Ballards may be found in bibliographic listings elsewhere in this book, notably Chapters IV, V and XIV. These are: *The Rifle In America* by Philip Sharpe, the three volumes on single shot rifles by James Grant, *100 Years Of Shooters And Gun Makers Of Single Shot Rifles* by Kelver, *U.S. Military Small Arms 1816-1865* by Reilly, and many reprints of original Marlin catalogs.)

*Brophy, William S., Lt. Col., U.S.A.R., Ret., *Marlin Firearms; A History of the Guns and the Company That Made Them*. Harrisburg, Pennsylvania: Stackpole Books, 1989. The major work in this field; massive in size and scope; likely to remain unequaled in importance.

*Dutcher, John T. *Ballard, The Great American Single Shot Rifle*. Denver, Colo.: Privately printer for the author, 2002. Considerably updates information on the significant American rifle. All known models; details of the Ballards used during Civil War and Western expansion; target and customized types.

Ellis, Richard S. *"The Midas Marlins."* Rock Island, Illinois: Privately published. Monograph, catalog of exceptional engraved rifles.

*Layman, George J. *"Guide To The Ballard Breechloader."* Union City, Tenn: Pioneer Press, 1997. In-depth study each model and their ctgs.

Wolff, Eldon G., *Ballard Rifles In The Henry J. Nunnemacher Collection*. Milwaukee, Wisconsin: Public Museum of the City of Milwaukee, 1945; Second Edition 1961. Highly detailed study of Ballards and Marlin-Ballards with a wealth of data on accessories. Substantial non-analyzed statistical data taken from many specimens.

(*) Preceding a title indicates the book is currently in print.

Marlin Handguns

"XL Derringer"

"XL Derringer" marked Single Shot 41 Rimfire Deringer. Often attributed to Marlin, recent evidence indicates manufacture by Hopkins & Allen. *See Chapter VIII-A for listing.*

Marlin First Model Deringer

First Model Deringer Single Shot Pistol, a.k.a. "Baby 22" or (incorrectly) as the "Model 1863." Made c. 1863 to 1867. Total quantity estimated as high as 4,000, but specimens do not appear as commonly as that number would seem to indicate. 22 caliber rimfire. 2-1/16" part round/part octagon barrel swings sideways for loading.

Brass frame with front section (area beneath barrel) fluted on sides. Frames often plated; barrels standard blued. Rosewood grips.

Top of barrel marked: J. M. MARLIN / NEW HAVEN, CT. Serial numbers mixed with other models.

These scarce pistols represent the first production of handguns by John Marlin. Features to note in addition to the above are the absence of sights and an extractor. Not a few unmarked deringers may be seen which are very similar to this model, but not having the small protruding plunger on the underside of the frame immediately to the rear of the pivot screw. They have not been established nor are considered as Marlin manufacture and are priced merely as inexpensive, unmarked single shot deringers:

5D-001   Values—Good **$325**   Fine **$800**

5D-001

Marlin O.K. Model Deringer

O. K. Model Deringer Single Shot Pistol. Made c. 1863 to 1870. Total quantity estimated at 6,000.

Calibers 22 and 30 rimfire; cal. 32 rare, worth premium. Part round/part octagon barrels vary from 2-1/8" (22 caliber) to 3-1/8" (32 caliber).

Brass frame with flat sides; barrel swings sideways to load; rosewood grips. Frames plated; barrels standard blued, but often plated also. Walnut or rosewood grips. A few known with square butt; very rare; worth premium.

Serial numbers mixed with other models. Right side of barrel marked: J. M. MARLIN/NEW HAVEN. CT. Top of barrel marked: O.K. Values approximately 15 percent less when unmarked or marked O.K. only.

In common with the "First Model" deringer, there was no extractor:

5D-002   Values—Good **$275**   Fine **$750**

5D-002

Marlin Square Butt O.K. Deringer   *See item 8A-104*

Marlin Victor Model Deringer

Victor Model Deringer Single Shot Pistol. (Not illus.) Made c. 1870-1881. Total quantity estimated about 2,000. Identical in contours to the "O.K." but larger in size.

Caliber 38 rimfire. 2-11/16" barrel, part octagon/part round; swings sideways for loading. Rosewood grips.

Flat sided brass frame. Finish either blued barrel with plain frame or full plated.

Serial numbers mixed with other models. Marking on right side of barrel: J. M. MARLIN/NEW HAVEN. CT./PAT. APRIL. 5. 1870. Top of barrel: VICTOR.

This model featured an extractor and the larger 38 caliber cartridge:

5D-003   Values—Good **$375**   Fine **$1,400**

Marlin Never Miss Deringer

Nevermiss Single Shot Deringer. Made c. 1870-1881. Total quantity estimated about 5,000.

Calibers 22, 32, and 41 rimfire. 2-1/2" round barrel swings sideways for loading.

Brass frames with fluted sides (on forward sections under barrels) similar to the First Model. All three sizes fitted with extractors. Finish either blued barrel with plated frame or full plated. Rosewood grips.

Serial numbered. Marked on right side of barrel: J. M. MARLIN/NEW HAVEN. CT./PAT. APRIL. 5. 1870. Top of barrel marked: NEVER MISS.

22 Caliber Size. Estimated quantity 900:
5D-004   Values—Good **$375**   Fine **$1,400**

5D-004

32 Caliber Size. Estimated quantity 2,600:
5D-005   Values—Good **$275**   Fine **$950**
41 Caliber Size. Estimated quantity under 1,000:
5D-006   Values—Good **$950**   Fine **$2,500**

Marlin Stonewall Deringer

Marlin "Stonewall" Single Shot Deringer. Made c. 1870s. Total quantity estimated 200. Rare.

Caliber 41 rimfire. Similar in style to the Nevermiss (above) with slightly smaller brass frame size and slightly varying contour shape.

Marked STONEWALL on top of barrel with J.M. MARLIN / NEW HAVEN, CONN. PAT. APRIL 5, 1870 on side:
5D-006.5   Values—Good **$2,000**   Fine **$4,500**

Marlin Percussion Burglar Alarm

Percussion Burglar Alarm invented by George W. Bigelow of New Haven, Conn. and patented April 10, 1860; manufactured by J.M. Marlin. An unusual and rare Marlin associated item: (1) the only percussion ignition by Marlin; (2) possibly the very first Marlin, although manufacture estimated as late as 1865. Quantity made unknown; rare.

All iron. 3" overall. Marked on side of hammer PAT. APR 10, 1860. The device would detonate the percussion cap after the window or door jamb, in which it was inserted, was opened by an intruder.

Specimen known in original pasteboard box, fully and boldly labelled BIGELOW'S PATENT BURGLAR ALARM MANUFACTURED

5D-006.7

BY J.M. MARLIN & CO, NEW HAVEN, CONN.(only known use of term "& CO." with Marlin name.)
Percussion Alarm Device:
5D-006.7   Values—Very Good **$325**   Exc **$600**
Alarm Device with Labelled Box:
5D-006.8   Values—Very Good **$1,250**   Exc **$2,500**

Marlin O.K. Pocket Revolver

O.K. Pocket Revolver. (Not illus.) Made c. 1870 to 1875. Total quantity estimated about 2,000. Identical in contour to the "Little Joker" with variant shape to center pin and bar latch for same in front of frame.

Caliber 22 rimfire short. 2-1/4" round barrel. Straight, unfluted cylinder; seven shots. Brass frame with circular removable sideplate having concentric grooving or flutes on left side. Nickel plated throughout or nickel frame with blued cylinder and barrel. Rosewood grips; bird's head butt. Serial numbered.

Marked on top of barrel: O.K. and J. M. MARLIN, NEW HAVEN. CONN. U.S.A.

The removable cylinder pin also acted as extractor rod:
5D-007   Values—Very Good **$225**   Exc **$650**

Marlin Little Joker Pocket Revolver

Little Joker Pocket Revolver. Made c. 1871-1873. Total quantity estimated at 1,100.

Caliber 22 rimfire short. 2-1/4" round barrel with flat sides. Straight, unfluted cylinder; seven shots. Brass, spur trigger, solid frame with circular removable sideplate having concentric grooving or flutes on left side. Nickel plated throughout; rosewood grips; bird's head butt. Serial numbered.

Marked on top of barrel: LITTLE JOKER. Marked on left side of bbl: J. M. MARLIN. NEW HAVEN, CONN. U.S.A.

Broad scroll and floral engraving as well as pearl or ivory grips were apparently all standard features, and values reflect same. A few known specimens are plain, unengraved. They are apparently quite scarce that way and should be worth a premium:

5D-008   Values—Very Good **$350**   Exc. **$950**

5D-008

Marlin XXX Standard 1872 Pocket Revolver

XXX Standard 1872 Pocket Revolver. Made c. 1872 to 1887. Total quantity estimated about 26,000.

Caliber 30 rimfire. Two basic types of tip-up barrels: First Style 3-1/8" octagonal ribbed barrel; Later Style 3" round ribbed barrel. 2" barrel very scarce; worth premium. Three cylinder styles as noted below; all five-shot.

Brass frame with spur trigger and bird's head butt. Rosewood grips with hard rubber having raised monogram M.F.A. Co. on a star motif used in late production. Standard finish, nickel plated throughout; silvered frame with blued barrel scarce.

All barrels marked on top: XXX STANDARD 1872 with other markings noted below. Serial numbered. The XXX identification was reference to the 30 caliber with a companion model known as the XX Standard chambered for 22 caliber.

Note: shorter barrel lengths were made on custom order and worth premium if original; longer barrel lengths on these models not known.

Octagon Barrel Type; 30 rimfire short. Made 1872-73. Estimated quantity 500. Flat sides at breech or lug of barrel; non-fluted, straight cylinder. Also marked on left side of barrel: J. M. MARLIN - NEW HAVEN. CT.:

5D-009   Values—Very Good **$300**   Exc. **$900**

Round Ribbed Barrel, Non-Fluted Cylinder Type; a.k.a. "Transition type". 30 rimfire short. Made 1873. Estimated quantity 500. Breech of barrel and lug deeply grooved. Cylinder non-fluted, straight style. Left side of barrel marked: J. M. MARLIN. NEW-HAVEN. CT. U.S.A. PAT. JULY 1. 1873:

5D-010   Values—Very Good **$350**   Exc. **$950**

Round Ribbed Barrel, Short-Fluted Cylinder Type; 30 rimfire short. Made 1873-76. Estimated quantity 10,000. Barrel as on

5D-009
Octagon Barrel Type

5D-012
Round Barrel Long-Fluted Cylinder Type

above, but cylinder with half length flutes and stop slots near breech end; barrel marking as above:

5D-011   Values—Very Good **$175**   Exc. **$600**

Round Ribbed Barrel, Long-Fluted Cylinder Type; 30 rimfire long caliber. Made 1873-76. Estimated quantity 15,000. Barrel as above. Cylinder has longer flutes than above type and frame is 3/16" longer. Barrel markings as above:

5D-012   Values—Very Good **$175**   Exc. **$550**

Marlin XX Standard 1873 Pocket Revolver

XX Standard 1873 Pocket Revolver. Made c. 1873 to 1887. Total quantity estimated about 10,000.

Caliber 22 long rimfire. Two basic styles of tip-up barrels. Earliest 3-1/8" octagonal ribbed design; later style 3" round ribbed. 2" barrel very scarce; worth premium. Seven-shot round cylinders both fluted and unfluted.

Brass frames; spur triggers; bird's head butt. Rosewood grips with hard rubber having relief monogram M.F.A. Co. used on later production. Standard finish nickel plated throughout.

All barrels marked on top: XX STANDARD 1873 with other markings as noted below. Serial numbered.

The XX identification referred to the 22 caliber.

Octagon Barrel, Non-Fluted Cylinder Type; made 1873; estimated quantity 500; flat sides at breech/lug of barrel. Left side marked: J. M. MARLIN-NEW HAVEN. CT.:

5D-013   Values—Very Good **$375**   Exc. **$1,400**

Round Ribbed Barrel, Non-Fluted Cylinder Type; made 1874; estimated quantity 500; breech of barrel/lug deeply grooved.

Left side of barrel marked: J. M. MARLIN NEW-HAVEN. CT. U.S.A. PAT. JULY. 1. 1873. A.k.a. "Transition type":

5D-014   Values—Very Good **$375**   Exc. **$1,400**

Round Ribbed Barrel, Fluted Cylinder Type; made 1875-87; estimated quantity 9,000; same as above, with the cylinder fluted:

5D-015   Values—Very Good **$175**   Exc. **$575**

5D-015

Marlin No. 32 Standard 1875 Pocket Revolver

No. 32 Standard 1875 Pocket Revolver. Made c. 1875 to 1887. Total quantity estimated about 19,500.

Caliber 32 rimfire. 3" round tip-up barrel. Round, fluted five-shot cylinder made in two lengths for either short or long cartridges.

Brass frame, spur trigger, bird's head butt. Rosewood grips on earlier pieces with hard rubber having raised monogram M.F.A. Co. used on later production. Standard finish nickel plated throughout or nickel plated with blued barrel and cylinder.

All barrels marked on top: NO. 32 STANDARD 1875 with other markings as noted below. Serial numbered.

This series was similar to the XXX Standard 1872 with differences in the front section of frame and cylinder.

First Type. Barrel marked on left side: J. M. MARLIN. NEW HAVEN, CT. U.S.A. PAT. JULY 1. 1873. Caliber 32 short rimfire. Made 1875. Estimated quantity 1,500:

5D-017

5D-016   Values—Very Good **$175**   Exc. **$550**
Second Type. Barrel marked as above. Caliber 32 short or long with corresponding cylinder lengths. Made 1876-87. Estimated quantity 18,000:
5D-017   Values—Very Good **$175**   Exc. **$550**

Marlin 38 Standard 1878 Pocket Revolver

5D-018

38 Standard 1878 Pocket Revolver. Made c. 1876 to 1887. Total quantity estimated about 12,000.

Caliber 38 centerfire. 3-1/4" round ribbed tip-up barrel. Five-shot fluted cylinder.

Steel frame with spur trigger and flat butt and removable sideplate. Standard finish full nickel plated throughout. Hard rubber grips with relief initials in panel at top J.M.M. on early production and M.F.A. monogram on later types (c. 1881).

Barrel markings on left side: J. M. MARLIN. NEW HAVEN. CT. U.S.A. PAT. JULY. 1. 1873. Barrel marked on top: 38 STANDARD 1878. Serial numbered:
5D-018   Values—Very Good **$250**   Exc. **$750**

Marlin Model 1887 Double Action Revolver

Model 1887 Double Action Revolver. Made c. 1887 to 1899. Total quantity estimated about 15,000.

Calibers 32 and 38 centerfire. Both basically identical in contour; the 38 has shorter cylinder flutes (illustrated). 3-1/4" round ribbed top break barrel. Fluted five-shot cylinder for 38 caliber and six-shot for 32.

Steel frame; spur trigger with flat butt. Nickel plated finish most often encountered with blued trigger guard and other minor parts, although full blued finish also not unusual. Hard rubber grips.

Standard markings on top of barrel: MARLIN FIREARMS CO. NEW HAVEN CONN. U.S.A./PATENTED AUG. 9. 1887. On very early pieces patent dates do not appear and the markings PAT. APPLIED FOR are on left side of barrel; such pieces will bring a premium value.

5D-019

The Model 1887 was the last revolver made by Marlin, and was their first and only double action handgun:
5D-019   Values—Very Good **$200**   Exc. **$550**

Marlin Lever Action Rifles

Marlin Model 1881 Lever Action Rifle

Model 1881 Lever Action Rifle. Made c. 1881 to 1892. Total quantity estimated slightly over 20,000. (Surviving records start with Serial No. 4001.)

Calibers 32-40, 38-55, 40-60, 45-70 (worth premium), and 45-85. Tubular magazine beneath barrel (eight-shot with 24" barrel and in 45-70 and 40-60 calibers). Top ejection. Octagon barrels

standard; round barrels scarce and will bring premium value. Buckhorn rear and blade type front sights.

Blued finish with casehardened hammer, lever and buttplate. Varnished walnut stocks.

Markings: **First Style,** found on early 1881s: J. M. MARLIN NEW HAVEN, CONN. U.S.A. PAT'D. FEB. 7 '65. JAN. 7 '73, SEP. 14

5D-020

'75. NOV. 19 & 26 '78. JUNE 3 '79. DEC. 9 '79. NOV. 9 '80(all on one line). **Second Style:** Identical to First Style, but on two lines. **Third Style:** Identical to First Style, on two lines with addition at end of words REISSUE NOV. 9, 1880.

Caliber marking on top of barrel at breech.

The first lever action Marlin rifle. The key patents in production and design were by the prolific Andrew Burgess, but John Marlin and others also contributed patent details. It was Marlin who put all the features together into the finished—and highly regarded—firearm. Capable of handling large calibers like the 45-70, the Model 1881 was years ahead of the Model 1886 Winchester, and proved a very popular rifle. A number of optional extras were available, such as set triggers, and will increase values depending on their importance. A feature such as an extra heavy barrel is quite rare and will increase value substantially.

Values shown are for the most commonly encountered barrel lengths and calibers. Prices may be increased according to relative rarity. The following production totals are shown in factory records:

Caliber 32 = 1,785; 38 = 3,563; 40 = 6,261; 45 = 4,769.

Barrel lengths: 20", just four made; 21-1/2", just one made; 22", just two; 24" = 2,788; 26" = 277; 28" = 12,482; 30" = 780; 32" = 42; 34" just three. A total of 13 were also manufactured as original smoothbore shotguns.

Early Model 1881. One-line J. M. MARLIN markings. Serial numbers below 600. 28" or 30" barrels. Calibers 45-70 and 40-60. Made c. 1881 only. Front of receiver has a 3/4" rebate; removable trigger plate:

5D-020 Values—Very Good **$1,400** Exc. **$3,750**

Standard Model 1881. Second and Third Style markings. Made c. 1882 to 1892. Serial numbers range from about 600 to 51233 (include also later models). Made in various calibers. Barrels usually 24", 28" or 30"; other lengths made as noted above from 1889. Does not have the rebate at front of receiver or removable type trigger plate:

5D-021 Values—Very Good **$1,000** Exc. **$3,000**

Light Weight Rifle. Made c. 1884 to 1892. Frame is 3/16" thinner than standard models. Made in calibers 32-40 and 38-55 as standard. Width of lever 7/16" (standard model 1/2"). Lighter barrel weight and smaller diameter than standard (3/4" at muzzle). 24" and 28" barrels standard with 26" very scarce:

5D-022 Values—Very Good **$1,000** Exc. **$3,000**

Marlin Model 1888 Lever Action Rifle

5D-023

Model 1888 Lever Action Rifle. Made c. 1888 to 1889. Total quantity estimated 4,814.

Calibers 32-20, 38-40, and 44-40. Tubular magazine beneath barrel (holds 13 rounds with 24" barrel). Octagonal barrels most often encountered. Round barrels available on special order; part octagon/part round barrels, pistol grip stocks also quite scarce and will bring premium. See below.

Top ejection. Buckhorn rear and blade type front sights.

Blued finish with casehardened hammer, lever and buttplate. Plain walnut stocks.

Serial numbered in range 19559 to 27854. Barrel marking: MARLIN FIREARMS CO. NEW HAVEN, CT. U.S.A./PATENTED OCT. 11, 1887. Caliber marking on top of barrel at breech.

Marlin's second lever action rifle, the Model 1888 featured a short throw mechanism suitable for the shorter length pistol cartridges for which it was chambered. The well known inventor Lewis Hepburn was instrumental in the design of this model. Overall weight was light 6-1/2 to 7 lbs.

Values indicated for calibers and barrel lengths in most common production. Prices may be increased according to relative rarity. The following production totals are shown in factory records:

Calibers 32-30 = 1,298; 38-40 = 1,776; 44-40 = 1,727.

Barrel lengths: 16", just one made; 20" = 25; 22", just one; 24" = 4,312; 26" = 264; 28" = 198; 30", just one; 44", just one.

Octagon barrels = 4,548 made; round barrels = 266; part octagon/part round, just 23 made:

5D-023 Values—Very Good **$950** Exc. **$3,000**

Marlin Model 1889 Lever Action Rifle

Model 1889 Lever Action Rifle. Made c. 1889 to 1899. Total of about 55,072.

Calibers 25-20 (very rare); 32-20; 38-40; and 44-40 (worth premium). Tubular magazine beneath barrel (holds 13 rounds with 24" barrel). Octagon or round barrels standard; available in lengths from 24" to 32" (at 2" intervals). Also made in 20" carbine. Buckhorn rear and blade type front sights.

Blued finish with casehardened hammer, lever and buttplate. Plain walnut stocks.

Serial numbered in the range 25000 to 100000; having numbering range overlaps with other models. Barrel marking: MARLIN FIRE-ARMS CO., NEW-HAVEN, CT. U.S.A./PATENTED OCT. 11. 1887. APRIL. 2. 1889. Caliber marking on top of barrel at breech. Top of frame marked: MARLIN SAFETY.

5D-024

This was Marlin's first lever action having the solid top frame and side ejection; basically the Model 1888 redesigned. It may be quickly identified by its lever latch. The Model 1889 was the true forerunner of modern lever action Marlins, all of which featured the side ejection—Lewis Hepburn was instrumental in its development. A number of optional features were available such as special sights, deluxe stocks, various magazine lengths and barrel shapes, etc. which will add premiums in value depending on their relative importance and rarity.

Values indicated are for calibers and barrel lengths in most common production. Prices may be increased according to their relative rarity. The following production totals are shown in factory records:

Calibers: 25-20, just 34 made; 32-20 = 15,441; 38-40 = 18,635; 44-40 = 20,934.

Standard Rifle. 24" barrel standard. Total 46,285 manufactured. Barrel lengths from production records: 15", just 40 made of which 10 were octagon and 30 round; 20" = 676; 22", just 10 made; 24" = 39,363; 26" = 3,729; 28" = 2,268; 30" = 165; 32" = 99; 40", just three made:
5D-024   Values—Very Good **$500**   Exc. **$1,400**
Carbine. Saddle ring affixed to left side of receiver; special carbine style buttplate. Total made 8,685. 20" standard with 8,354. Other lengths rare and will bring premium (327 made with 15" barrel and four with 24" barrel):
5D-025   Values—Very Good **$900**   Exc. **$1,750**
Musket. 30" barrel with full stock, forend and magazine. Total production just 68 of which 62 were in caliber 44-40 and just 3 in caliber 38-40 with calibers of the three remaining specimens unknown. Very rare:
5D-026   Values—Very Good **$3,500**   Exc. **$6,500**

Marlin Model 1891 Lever Action Rifle

Model 1891 Lever Action Rifle. Made c. 1891 to 1897. Total quantity 18,642, includes all variations.

Calibers 22 rimfire and 32 rimfire/centerfire. Tubular magazine made in three lengths (half type, three-quarter length and full). 24" octagon barrels most often encountered. Buckhorn rear and blade type front sights.

Blued finish with casehardened hammer, lever and buttplate; flat shotgun style buttplate also seen. Plain walnut stock. (Shown in illustration with pistol-grip stock, a feature which is worth a premium.)

Serial numbered in range 37492 to 118000 (overlaps with other models).

Barrel markings, **First Variation:** MARLIN FIRE-ARMS CO. NEW-HAVEN, CT. U.S.A./PAT'D NOV. 19. 1878. APRIL 2. 1889. AUG. 12. 1890. Top of frame marked: MARLIN SAFETY.

Barrel markings, **Second Variation:** Identical to above, but patent date of MARCH 1, 1892 added.

Marlin's first lever action chambered for 22 cartridges, the Model 1891 was also the first repeating rifle made to accept 22 Short, Long and Long Rifle cartridges on an interchangeable basis. The new gun helped round out the company's offering in lever actions by adding the small caliber to the medium and large caliber arms already in production. The Model 1891 has a separate trigger and sear with a safety system which requires the

lever to be closed to fire the gun. This feature was dropped on all subsequent caliber 22 lever action rifles.

Values are for the most commonly encountered 24" barrel lengths. Prices may be increased according to relative rarity of other lengths. The following production totals are shown in factory records:

Barrel lengths: 20", just two made; 21", just one made; 22", just one made; 24" = 18,086; 25", just one made; 26" = 283; 27", just one made; 28" = 259; 30", just four; 32", just one; 40", just one made.

Barrel styles: Octagon most common. There were 3,435 also made with round barrels and just 233 made with part octagon/part round barrels. Engraved and deluxe styles extremely scarce in this model.

First Variation. Caliber 22 rimfire only. *Side loading*, made with short magazine only. Approximately 5,000 manufactured:
5D-027   Values—Very Good **$750**   Exc. **$2,000**
Second Variation. Calibers 22 rimfire (worth premium) and 32 rimfire and centerfire. (Not illus.) Identical to Model 1892. The latter caliber more often encountered. *Tube loading* with full length magazine underneath the 24" barrel. Tang markings MODEL/1891 are found on specimens after serial range 112000 (approx.). Round barrels are scarcer and worth premium:
5D-028   Values—Very Good **$300**   Exc. **$875**

5D-027

Marlin Model 1892 Lever Action Rifle

5D-029

Model 1892 Lever Action Rifle. Made c. 1895 to 1916. Total estimated quantity approximately 45,000.

This rifle is the same as the Model 1891 Second Variation, tube loading, described above with the following exceptions: Upper tang marked MODEL 1892 (later changed to MODEL '92); receiver blued, improved ejector, wider firing pin and improved safety feature. Has one-piece sear and trigger.

Calibers 22 rimfire (scarce) and 32 rimfire and/or centerfire. Barrel lengths 24", 26", and 28" round, octagon or part octagon/part round; half and full magazines.

Serial numbered in range of 90000 to 412000 (overlaps with other models). Some have "A", "C", or "D" prefix for new number series c. 1912 to 1915.

Crescent style rifle buttplates with heel (or tang) were used until 1906, after which the "S" curved buttplate (made without a tang or heel) was used.

Numerous extra or special features were available (including a casehardened receiver) which will add to values depending on the nature of the special feature and condition of the gun. Not made in take-down. (See the improved version of this model—the Model 1897 which was made as a take-down only.)

22 caliber:

5D-029   Values—Very Good **$350**   Exc. **$1,000**

32 caliber:

5D-030   Values—Very Good **$250**   Exc. **$825**

Marlin Model 1893 Lever Action Rifle

Model 1893 Lever Action Rifle. Made c. 1893 to 1935. Total quantity estimated from 850,000 to 1,000,000.

Calibers 25-36; 30-30; 32 Special; 32-40; 38-55. Full length tubular magazines standard. Octagon or round barrels in lengths from 24" to 32" (at 2" intervals). 20" carbine also made. Buckhorn rear and blade type front sights.

Finish: Casehardened receiver, hammer, lever and buttplate; blued barrel and magazine tube. Varnished walnut stocks.

Serial numbered generally in the range 81393 to 355504 (through 1906), but a few appear in higher series and also observed in individual series with letter prefixes; overlaps various other models.

Barrel markings: MARLIN FIRE-ARMS CO. NEW-HAVEN, CT. U.S.A./PATENTED. OCT. 11. 1887. APRIL 2. 1889. AUG. 1. 1893. After 1919 marking of THE MARLIN FIREARMS CORPORATION/NEW HAVEN, CONN. U.S.A.-PATENTED.Caliber marking on top of barrel at breech. Rifles made after 1904 have marking on left side of barrel SPECIAL SMOKELESS STEEL. Marked on upper tang MODEL 1893 (and in later production MODEL '93).

The Model 1893 was Marlin's first lever action rifle chambered for the new smokeless powder cartridges. Numerous special order features were available such as sights,

take-down, barrel shapes, stocks, etc. and such features will add premiums to value depending on the nature of them and the condition of the gun. The Models 1936 and 36 follow this design and are about identical to it.

Standard Rifle; as above. Early production in calibers 38-55 and 32-40. Upper tang lacks MODEL 1893 markings on early guns:

5D-031   Values—Very Good **$350**   Exc. **$1,200**

Later Production Rifle; Circa 1895 to 1916. BLACK POWDERor SPECIAL SMOKELESS STEEL marked barrels for all calibers:

5D-032   Values—Very Good **$325**   Exc. **$1,100**

Special Lightweight Rifle; take-down type. 18" or 20" part round/part octagon barrel. Forend 1" shorter than standard. Short magazine. Straight stock with shotgun style buttplate:

5D-033   Values—Very Good **$425**   Exc. **$1,275**

Carbine; 20" round barrel, full magazine, carbine style buttplate; saddle ring on left side of frame. 61 were made with 15" barrel and one with special 15-1/2" barrel; these will bring considerable premiums. These shorter lengths fall under the provisions of the Gun Control Act and therefore before acquiring a specimen, the legality should be verified. Carbine type folding leaf rear sights:

5D-034   Values—Very Good **$450**   Exc. **$1,400**

5D-033
Standard Rifle with Take-Down Feature

5D-034
Carbine

**5D-035
Musket**

Musket; 30" round barrel; full stocked forend fastened by two barrel bands; cleaning rod fitted beneath barrel; carbine style buttplate. Fitted for socket type bayonet. Late production in 30-30 caliber only having a 24" round barrel and fitted for a knife type bayonet. Values for the most widely made calibers; others will bring an added premium. Only 31 are known made: 25-36 caliber just one made; 30-30 caliber just five made; 32-40 = 22; 38-55 just two made; one other recorded made, but caliber unknown:

5D-035   Values—Very Good **$3,250**   Exc. **$5,750**

Marlin Model 1894 Lever Action Rifle

Model 1894 Lever Action Rifle. Made c. 1894 to 1935. Total quantity approximately 250,000.

Calibers 25-20, 32-20, 38-40, and 44-40. Full length tubular magazine. Octagon or round barrels in lengths from 24" to 32" (at 2" intervals). 20" carbine also made. Buckhorn type rear and blade front sights.

Finish: Casehardened receiver, hammer, lever, buttplate and frame (hammers blued after 1900); blued barrel and magazine. Varnished walnut stocks.

Serial numbered in the range 107678 to 355245 (through 1906); overlaps with various other models. Barrel marking: See below. Caliber marking at top of barrel near breech.

The short action of the Model 1894 was possible due to the relatively short length of the cartridges it was chambered for. Overall design was close to that of the Model 1893. As with most Marlin lever actions, a variety of special order features were available. Their presence will usually add extra values depending on the nature of the special feature and the overall condition of the rifle. These include take-down features and rifle barrels of 22" and shorter.

Early Type Rifle. Barrel marking: MARLIN FIRE-ARMS CO., NEW. HAVEN, CT. U.S.A./PATENTED OCT. 11, 1887. APRIL 2. 1889. Top of frame marked MARLIN SAFETY. No model markings appear on tang. Made in calibers 38-40 and 44-40 only:

5D-036   Values—Very Good **$350**   Exc. **$1,000**

Standard Rifle. Barrel marked as above with additional patent date AUG. 1, 1893. The markings on the top of the frame were omitted. Tang markings MODEL 1894 or, in later production, MODEL '94 There is an overlap in the use of both markings—with the full date generally being earlier. Crescent style rifle buttplates used until 1906, after which changed to the "S" style (made without heel or tang). Made in all four calibers:

5D-037   Values—Very Good **$300**   Exc. **$950**

Carbine. 20" round barrel with full magazine and carbine style buttplate; saddle ring on left side of receiver. 935 were made with 15" barrels, 29 with 14" barrels and just three with 12" barrels. All of these latter will bring considerable additional premium values, however, these short lengths fall under the provisions of the Gun Control Act and the status of their legality should be verified before acquiring one:

5D-038   Values—Very Good **$450**   Exc. **$1,250**

Baby Carbine. As above with six-shot half magazine. Weighs just 5-1/2 lbs. Made in calibers 38-40 and 44-40:

5D-039   Values—Very Good **$750**   Exc. **$1,850**

Musket. 30" round barrel with full forend fastened by two barrel bands. Made for either angular or knife type bayonets. Ramrod fitted below barrel. Carbine style buttplate and sights. Total made 152 c. 1894 to 1906. 97 in caliber 38/40 and 55 in caliber 44/40. Over half of quantity made was purchased by the Bureau County, Illinois, prison and were marked (at the prison) BUREAU COUNTY on the receiver. Values indicated are for such marked specimens. Those without the County markings will bring a premium:

5D-040   Values—Very Good **$2,250**   Exc. **$4,000**

**5D-036
Rifle**

**5D-038
Carbine**

**5D-039
Musket**

Marlin Model 1895 Lever Action Rifle

**5D-042
Lightweight Rifle**

Model 1895 Lever Action Rifle. Made c. 1895 to 1917. Total quantity approximately 18,000.

Calibers 33 W.C.F., 38-56, 40-65, 40-70, 40-82, 45-70 (worth 20 percent premium), and 45-90. Full length tubular magazine standard. Octagon or round barrels in lengths from 26" to 32" (at 2" intervals). 20" also made and scarce. Buckhorn type rear and blade front sights.

Finish: Casehardened receiver, hammer, lever; blued barrel and magazine. Varnished walnut stocks.

Serial numbered in the range 131135 to 338279 (through 1906); overlaps with various other models. Barrel marking: MARLIN FIRE-ARMS CO., NEW HAVEN, CT. U.S.A./PATENTED. OCT. 11. 1887. APRIL 2. 1889. AUG. 1. 1893. Caliber markings at top of barrel near breech. Top of frame marked (before c. 1903) MARLIN SAFETY. Upper tang marked: MODEL 1895. Barrels after c. 1896 marked: SPECIAL SMOKELESS STEEL.

The Model 1895 was Marlin's large hunting caliber rifle and was considered a companion type in the company's line to the Models 1893 and 1894. Overall design and patents were the same for all three, and the result was an impressive offering to the shooting public. As a collector's item, the Model 1895 is considered quite scarce and desirable. A variety of special order features were available for it and their presence will add extra values depending on the nature of them and condition of the gun. Included was the take-down feature, unusual barrel lengths (e.g., 20" or 32"), pistol-grip buttstock, etc.

Standard Rifles. Made through c. 1912 in all calibers above except 33 W.C.F.:

5D-041   Values—Very Good **$750**   Exc. **$3,000**

Lightweight Rifles. Made in 45-70 and 33 W.C.F. (introduced c. 1912) only, c. 1912 to 1917. Weight about 7 lbs. with 22" barrel and half magazine which was not previously available:

   Cal. 33 W.C.F.:
   5D-042   Values—Very Good **$625**   Exc. **$1,500**

   Cal. 45-70:
   5D-043   Values—Very Good **$875**   Exc. **$2,750**

Carbine: 22" round barrel and full magazine; saddle ring affixed to left side of receiver; carbine style buttplate and sights. Just five were recorded made with a special short 15" barrel (c. 1906) which will bring considerable premium value, however, the status of their legality must be verified (see similar carbines Model 1893 and Model 1894 with short barrels):

5D-044   Values—Very Good **$1,500**   Exc. **$6,500**

Marlin Model 1897 Lever Action Rifle

Model 1897 Lever Action Rifle. Made c. 1897 to 1917. Total quantity estimated approximately 125,000.

Caliber 22 rimfire. Round, octagon or part octagon/part round barrels 24", 26", or 28". Full or half magazines. Take-down type action standard. Buckhorn rear and blade type front sights.

Finish: Casehardened receiver, hammer and lever; blued barrel and magazine. Varnished walnut stocks.

Serial numbered in the range 150021 to 354487 (through 1906) with other serials having letter "A" prefix; overlaps with various other models. Barrel marking: MARLIN FIRE-ARMS CO., NEW-HAVEN, CT. U.S.A./PAT. APR. 2. 1889. AUG. 12. 1890. MAR. 1. 1892. Top of frame marked: MARLIN SAFETY. Inside of receiver marked: PAT. JUNE 8, 1897. Upper tang marked: MODEL 1897 or, on later production, MARLIN MODEL '97.

Available only as a take-down, the 1897 was an improved version of the Model 1892. In 1922 it was redesignated the Model 39 with production continuing to present. Many options were available, and when present, these will usually add premium to the value depending on their nature and the overall condition of the rifle.

Standard Rifle. Top of receiver rounded:

5D-045   Values—Very Good **$300**   Exc. **$1,000**

"Bicycle Rifle." Usual barrel length of 16" with full magazine. Could be ordered with barrels up to 28", but magazines on all lengths were 16". Rare:

5D-046   Values—Very Good **$875**   Exc. **$3,000**

Late Production Rifle. With flat top receiver:

5D-047   Values—Very Good **$250**   Exc. **$950**

5D-045

See also Savage Model 1895 Rifle, Chapter XIII (13-021).

Marlin Shotguns

Marlin Pump/Slide Shotguns

Marlin's line of slide or pump, bolt and lever action shotguns is substantial. These are categorized by the model identifications: Model 1898, 16, 17, 19, 19-S, 19-G, 19-N, 21, 24, 26, 28, 30, 31, 42, 43, 44, 49, 53, 60, 63, and 410. Serial numbering was shared by all the pump action guns beginning with the Model 1898, so there is considerable overlapping. The hammerless models are numbered in their own series while the Model 60 and the Model 410 each had individual series. Approximately 1916 a new series of numbers commenced using the prefix "A."

From a collector standpoint, the types considered in the present volume are the pump actions through the Model 30 and the lever action Model 410.

Information presented here is not in the same detail as for the lever action rifles, but will enable identification and evaluation for all types. An indication of the quantity produced may be had from the factory statistics that approximately 150,000 slide action shotguns were made in the years 1898 to 1912.

In general the shotgun grades differed as follows: "A" Grade—plain gun without checkering or engraving and barrel usually marked Special Rolled Steel Barrel. "B" Grade—plain gun with checkered, nicely figured grain walnut stock; matted barrel marked Special Smokeless Steel Barrel . "C" Grade—special selected fancy walnut wood checkered stock; matted barrel marked as in "B" and with simple scroll and game scene engraving on receiver. "D" Grade—imported circassian walnut selected grain checkered stock; matted barrel with marking as in "B" above; elaborate engraved scroll and game scene panels on receiver; gold plated screws and trigger. It is quite possible to encounter variations in any of these features.

Marlin Model 1898 Slide Action Shotgun

Model 1898 Slide Action Shotgun. (Not illus.) Made c. 1898 to 1905. 12 gauge. Total quantity estimated at 55,000.

The first commercially available Marlin shotgun; featured a visible hammer, take-down construction and the frame appears much like the firm's larger caliber lever action rifles.

Available in 26" to 32" (interchangeable) barrels; standard with full choke. Five-shot tubular magazine.

Top of barrel marked: MARLIN FIREARMS CO., NEW HAVEN CT., U.S.A. with second line bearing patent dates 1894 and 1896. No model marks present. Serial numbered.

Finish blued with casehardened hammer. Varnished walnut pistol-grip stock. Made in various grades; standard type as described above.

Barrel serial numbers do not agree with receiver numbers. The suffix to barrel number indicates the choke (i.e., C = cylinder; F = full choke, etc.).

Standard Model 1898:
5D-048	Values—Very Good **$150**	Exc. **$450**

Brush or Riot Gun: With 26" barrel and cylinder bore:
5D-049	Values—Very Good **$200**	Exc. **$600**

Marlin Model 16 Slide Action Shotgun

Model 16 Slide Action Shotgun. (Not illus.) Made c. 1904 to 1911. 16 gauge. Total quantity estimated approximately 5,000.

Virtually identical to the Model 1898 except for the 16 gauge chambering, 26" and 28" barrels, and the marking 16 GA on breech of barrel and MARLIN MODEL 16 on upper tang.

Barrel marking of company name and patent dates include added years 1889, 1900, and 1904.

Made in various grades. Value given for standard type.

Early production of this model has 1898 patent dates and does not have the model designation on the tang. It is considered quite scarce and will bring a premium:
5D-050	Values—Very Good **$125**	Exc. **$400**

Marlin Model 17 Slide Action Shotgun

Model 17 Slide Action Shotgun. (Not illus.) Solid frame; visible hammer. Made c. 1906 to 1908. 12 gauge. Total quantity estimated at 5,000.

Upper tang marked: MARLIN MODEL NO. 17. Barrel lengths as below. All with cylinder bores. Barrel markings as on Model 16 with same patent dates. Varnished walnut straight stocks (no pistol grip).

Standard Model; 30" or 32" barrel:
5D-051	Values—Very Good **$125**	Exc. **$400**

Brush Gun; 26" barrel:
5D-052	Values—Very Good **$125**	Exc. **$450**

Riot Gun; 20" barrel:
5D-053	Values—Very Good **$200**	Exc. **$500**

Marlin Model 19 Slide Action Shotgun

Models 19, 19-S, 19-G, and 19-N Slide Action Shotguns. (Not illus.) All take-down style with visible hammer. Made c. 1906-1907. 12 gauge. Total quantity estimated about 25,000.

Upper tang marked: MODEL 19.

Barrel lengths from 26" to 32". Some variation in barrel markings, but basically the same as on the Models 16 and 17. Varnished walnut pistol grip stock. The Model 19 was the standard. Model 19-S included two extra screws for locking forend. Model 19-G had a rib cut, and a cut in the frame with special lug to prevent locking bolt disconnecting from action slide during quick or rough use. The 19-N had both of the 19-S and 19-G details and a new type forend and tubular magazine.

The Model 19 was the successor to the Model 1898. Production was four grades, with just basic differences shown in the below listings.

Grade A. Plain:

| 5D-054 | Values—Very Good **$150** | Exc. **$400** |

Grade B. Pistol grip fancy grained stock:

| 5D-055 | Values—Very Good **$225** | Exc. **$500** |

Grade C. Fancier wood than Grade B above with engraved receiver:

| 5D-056 | Values—Very Good **$450** | Exc. **$1,400** |

Grade D. Deluxe wood and finish; fancier and more profuse engraving and often with gold plated screws and trigger:

| 5D-057 | Values—Very Good **$600** | Exc. **$2,250** |

Marlin Model 21 Slide Action Shotgun

Model 21 Slide Action Shotgun. (Not illus.) Take-down; visible hammer. Made c. 1906-1909. 12 gauge. Total quantity estimated at 7,000.

Upper tang marked: MARLIN MODEL NO. 21. Barrel lengths from 26" to 32". Barrel markings as on the Model 19. Varnished walnut straight grip stock.

The Model 21 was known as the Trap Model due to the straight stock. It was available in four grades with the basic differences noted below.

Grade A. Plain:

| 5D-058 | Values—Very Good **$150** | Exc. **$400** |

Grade B. Checkered grip and forearm:

| 5D-059 | Values—Very Good **$225** | Exc. **$500** |

Grade C. Fancy grained wood with checkered grip and forearm, with engraved receiver:

| 5D-060 | Values—Very Good **$450** | Exc. **$1,400** |

Grade D. Extra fancy checkered grip and forend with more profuse engraved receiver and often gold plated screws and trigger:

| 5D-061 | Values—Very Good **$600** | Exc. **$2,250** |

Marlin Model 24 Slide Action Shotgun

Model 24 Slide Action Shotgun. (Not illus.) Take-down; visible hammer. Made c. 1908-1915. 12 gauge. Total quantity estimated at 16,000.

Upper tang marked: MODEL NO. 24. Barrel lengths from 26" to 32". Barrel markings as on the Models 19 and 21 except for added patent dates of 1908 and 1909. Varnished walnut, pistol grip stock.

A distinguishing feature of the Model 24 is a pinch-type magazine tip and a metal support at each end of the forend wood. It was available in four grades with basic differences noted below.

Grade A. Plain:

| 5D-062 | Values—Very Good **$150** | Exc. **$400** |

Grade B. Checkered pistol grip stock and forend:

| 5D-063 | Values—Very Good **$150** | Exc. **$500** |

Grade C. Fancy grained checkered pistol grip stock and forend with engraved designs on receiver:

| 5D-064 | Values—Very Good **$450** | Exc. **$1,400** |

Grade D. Extra fancy checkered pistol grip stock and forend. Profuse engraved receiver and often gold plated screws and trigger:

| 5D-065 | Values—Very Good **$600** | Exc. **$2,250** |

Marlin Model 26 Slide Action Shotgun

Model 26 Slide Action Shotgun. (Not illus.) Solid frame; visible hammer. Made c. 1909-1915. 12 gauge. Total quantity estimated at 12,000.

Upper tang marked: MARLIN MODEL NO. 26. Barrel lengths 30" and 32". Barrel marking the same as the Model 24. Varnished walnut straight grip stock. The Model 26 replaced the Model 17 and was produced only in solid frame.

Standard Grade:

| 5D-066 | Values—Very Good **$125** | Exc. **$450** |

Brush Gun: With 26" barrel and cylinder bore:

| 5D-067 | Values—Very Good **$150** | Exc. **$500** |

Riot Gun: 20" barrel and cylinder bore:

| 5D-068 | Values—Very Good **$225** | Exc. **$550** |

Marlin Model 28 Slide Action Shotgun

Model 28 Slide Action Shotgun. (Not illus.) Take-down; hammerless. Made c. 1913-1915. 12 gauge. Total quantity estimated at 6,000.

Does not have model markings. Standard barrel lengths 30" and 32"; full choke.

Left side of barrel marked: MARLIN FIREARMS CO., NEW HAVEN, CONN. U.S.A. and 1896, 1904, 1906, 1908, and 1909 patent dates. Varnished walnut pistol grip stock.

This was the first Marlin slide action shotgun commercially available having the hammerless design. Available in four grades and trap types with basic differences noted below.

Grade A. Plain:

| 5D-069 | Values—Very Good **$125** | Exc. **$400** |

Grade B. Checkered stock and forend:

| 5D-070 | Values—Very Good **$225** | Exc. **$500** |

Grade C. Fancy grained wood with checkered stock and forend; engraved receiver:
5D-071   Values—Very Good **$450**   Exc. **$1,400**
Grade D. Extra fancy checkered wood; profuse engraved receiver and often with gold plated screws and trigger:
5D-072   Values—Very Good **$600**   Exc. **$2,250**

Grade T. Matted top rib on barrel; fancy grained checkered stock with high comb:
5D-073   Values—Very Good **$400**   Exc. **$1,250**
Grade TS. Matted top rib; plain checkered stock; plain grade:
5D-074   Values—Very Good **$250**   Exc. **$875**

Marlin Model 30 Slide Action Shotgun

Model 30 Slide Action Shotgun. (Not illus.) Take-down; visible hammer. Made c. 1911 to 1915. Total quantity estimated at 3,000. 16 or 20 gauge. Matted barrels; standard lengths of 26" and 28"; full choke. Lowest Grade (A) barrels marked Special Rolled Steel Barrel, while others marked Special Smokeless Steel Barrel with damascus also available on Grade D.

Upper tang marked: MODEL 30 or MODEL 30-20.

Left side of barrel marked: MARLIN FIREARMS CORP., NEW HAVEN, CT. U.S.A. with 1908 and 1909 patent dates. Varnished walnut pistol grip stock.

Available in four styles with basic differences noted below.
Grade A. Plain; available 16 gauge only:
5D-075   Values—Very Good **$150**   Exc. **$400**
Grade B. Checkered pistol grip stock:
5D-076   Values—Very Good **$225**   Exc. **$500**
Grade C. Fancy grained checkered stock with engraved receiver:
5D-077   Values—Very Good **$500**   Exc. **$1,500**
Grade D. Extra fancy checkered stock with profuse engraved receiver and often gold plated screws and trigger:
5D-078   Values—Very Good **$600**   Exc. **$2,250**

Marlin Lever Action Shotgun

Marlin Model 410 Lever Action Shotgun

5D-079

Model 410 Lever Action Shotgun. Made c. 1929 to 1932. Estimated quantity approximately 6,500.

410 gauge (2-1/2" shell). Five-shot tubular half magazine beneath barrel. 22" or 26" round barrel.

Finish blued with casehardened lever and hammer. Varnished walnut pistol grip stock. Hard rubber shotgun style buttplate.

Serial numbered from 1 on up (with and without "U" prefix). Marked on upper tang: MARLIN/410. Embossed on buttplate: MARLIN.

Utilizing the basic Model 1893 rifle receiver, the Model 410 used a 2-1/2" shot shell. The demise of this model was brought about by the introduction of the longer shot shell which could not be accommodated. The Model 410 was also primarily used as a give-away gun c. 1930 with the purchase of four shares of Marlin Preferred Stock:
5D-079   Values—Very Good **$600**   Exc. **$1,750**

Ballard Rifles And Carbines And Their Makers

Numbered among the most famous of American single shot breech-loading rifles, with much arms literature devoted to it, the Ballard rifle, until the 6th edition of this guide, eluded an accurate chronicle of its development. The first five editions of this book specifically mentioned that anomaly. Leaning heavily on the research and unpublished manuscript of Howard Michael Madaus, former curator at the Milwaukee Public Museum and the famous Cody Firearms Museum at Cody, Wyoming, the following is the *first* comprehensive account of the sequence of makers and events that ultimately led to the long and distinguished line of great American single shots, the Marlin-Ballard. This is by no means the entire story, nor is it intended to be. There certainly is much yet to learn about the subject. It should, however, place the development of these early Ballards in much clearer perspective and rectify many misconceptions previously held. Significant detail about all Ballards is further catalogued and interpreted in *Ballard, The Great American Single Shot Rifle* by Dutcher (see Bibliography).

Invented by Charles H. Ballard of Worcester, Mass. and granted patent number 33631 on November 5, 1861, the rifle had

a short and somewhat checkered career 1862 to 1873 until becoming the mainstay of the Marlin line.

The firm of Joseph Merwin and Edward P. Bray of New York City, were primarily sales agents for various gun manufacturers. As is noted on many Ballards, they were sole "agents" for them and played important roles in the various companies formed to make the guns. Merwin and Bray also held the patent for the dual ignition system (use of a percussion nipple on the breech block) in order that the arm could be fired either rimfire or percussion cap. That innovation was introduced in 1864.

The Ballard was manufactured by five different firms as outlined below. It is estimated that approximately 24,000 was the total production by all five makers of which approximately 50 percent went to fill Civil War military orders, the state of Kentucky being the largest contractor.

1) Ball and Williams of Worcester, Mass. 1862 to 1865. The largest makers of the five with great majority of their production for military use.

2) Dwight, Chapin & Company of Bridgeport, Conn. 1863 to 1864. As Ball and Williams were running their factory at full capacity, agents Merwin and Bray brought this firm into the picture to capture a lucrative government contract. Very limited production with very few pieces accepted by government inspector; contract was forfeited and company filed for bankruptcy. Balance of contract taken over by Ball and Williams.

3) R. Ball & Company, Worcester, Mass. 1865 to 1866.
Company renamed after Williams retired in July of 1865. Ball was incapacitated shortly after, with the company continuing in business under management of his son-in-law. With the war over, diminishing sales and lack of government orders, severe manufacturing cutbacks were made. After 1-1/2 years of struggling and limited production the company was sold with all its machinery to E.P. Bray (Merwin and Bray partnership had been dissolved in November of 1866) and the Merrimack Arms and Manufacturing Company and moved in its entirety to Newburyport, Mass.

4) Merrimack Arms and Manufacturing Company, Newburyport, Mass. 1867 to 1869.
Production continued to be rather limited, the firm taken over by the Brown Manufacturing Company.

5) Brown Manufacturing Company, Newburyport, Mass. 1869 to 1873.
They continued the Ballard line in the same facilities until economic conditions and depression in the United States saw sales diminish, forcing them into bankruptcy. Company was sold at public auction under mortgage foreclosure proceedings. The Ballard patent rights and evidently some of the rifles in various stages of production, along with miscellaneous parts, were purchased by Schoverling and Daly, arms dealers of New York City, who arranged with John M. Marlin of New Haven to continue manufacturing.

Marlin utilized some parts from the Brown operation on his earliest production (q.v.) and distribution was handled by Schoverling and Daly. The result of the combination of Marlin's mechanical and manufacturing expertise combined with the salesmanship of the latter two partners was a highly developed series of single shot rifles, revered by collectors as among the finest ever produced.

Operations continued under the John M. Marlin name until 1881 when the business was incorporated as the Marlin Firearms Company under which all subsequent Ballard rifles were made until their discontinuance c. 1891. The exact year production ceased is unknown; generally the date is thought to be somewhere subsequent to the issuance of the 1888 catalog in which these Ballards were last listed. Their phasing out was basically in deference to the rising popularity of the repeating rifle, to which the Marlin Firearms Company devoted their major attentions.

A major distinction easily seen on Ballards, and one which quickly dates their era and manufacture is the presence of tangs on the frame (i.e. extensions on rear of frame, top and bottom, which seat into the stock for fastening to the gun). Prior to 1867 all Ballards had outside, visible tangs. Post 1867, with the take-over by Merrimack Arms and Manufacturing Co., and subsequently Brown Manufacturing Co., all Ballards had internal tangs extending through the hollow in the stock, fastened by a bolt from the underside of the butt. A second, readily recognizable feature in all Ballards (except 100 of the very first production) is the external extractor, in the shape of a short rounded post or lever, manually actuated, on the underside of the forearm.

Some confusion exists as to the calibers in which all Marlin-Ballards were made. Those most commonly mentioned and encountered are listed in the following descriptions, but the reader should note that others may be observed. Marlin-Ballards were listed in catalogs in more or less standard calibers, but the factory would provide on custom order almost any chambering for a client; hence, it is possible to encounter a wide range of calibers and values should be assessed on either the rarity or desirability of special sizes. Pre-Marlin-Ballard rifles were all made in rimfire calibers. A tremendous amount of manufacturing variations may be encountered, especially in Marlin-Ballards. These are most noticeable in hammer profiles, breechblocks and other significant components. A highly detailed study of these appears in the Eldon Wolff monograph of specimens in the Nunnemacher Collection of the Milwaukee Public Museum (see Bibliography).

Often reported, but never seen, are rifles allegedly bearing Ballard Arms Company, Fall River, Massachusetts, markings. No known specimen has ever been viewed by the author and competent authorities believe the reportings of such specimens are erroneous and based on earlier, unverified sources.

Ballards were popular both for hunting and target; in that latter capacity many achieved great notoriety. In the Marlin era, they were widely recognized for outstanding workmanship and testimonials to their accuracy and finishes were many—and well deserved. Surviving specimens of the fancier long range models or of any Ballards in very fine grades of condition are among the most eagerly sought after of the single shot target line today. It is also significant to note that Ballard rifles were among the earliest of metallic cartridge guns marketed successfully in the United States.

Ballard Rifles and Carbines by Ball and Williams

Ballard Rifles and Carbines by Ball and Williams, Worcester, Mass. 1862-1865. First and largest makers. Total quantity all models approximately 15,600. Majority of production to fill Civil War military orders. Serial range 1 to 15600 approximately.

Usual markings: BALL & WILLIAMS/WORCESTER MASS and BALLARD'S PATENT/NOV.5.1861 and MERWIN & BRAY.AGTS/NEW YORK. Marking usually appear on breech end of barrel up to serial 9000; on sides of frame after that period. One piece breech blocks up to serial 9700; two piece "split" breech blocks after that period.

Finish: Blue barrels and frames; casehardened frames reported but not viewed; would be worth premium if original. Walnut stocks. Frame shape all models (except for 46 caliber military rifle) is octagon/faceted.

Earliest manufacture. Recognized by its inside extractor; only pre-Marlin Ballard with this feature. Circa 1862. Estimated less than 100 made; serial numbers 1-100 approximately. (Not illustrated).

All believed caliber 38 rimfire. Full octagon barrel 24" to 28":
5D-080   Values—Good **$1,100**   Fine **$4,000**
Sporting Rifle. Estimated quantity made 5,000. Calibers 38, 44 & 46 rimfire (32 rf. worth premium). Octagon or part octagon/part

**5D-081
Sporting Rifle**

5D-082
44 Cal. Carbine

5D-084
Military Rifle

round barrel is 24", 26" or 28". (30" bbl. is round, in 46 rf. only and in 15000 serial range.):

5D-081   Values—Good **$550**   Fine **$2,000**

Carbine. From all indications it appears that the entire production (until the end of the Civil War, April, 1865) of approximately 6,600 carbines went to fill military contracts. The state of Kentucky, having found the Ballard carbine favorably reported for use by Kentucky Cavalry, after purchasing 3,000 pieces, contracted for 1,000 more in November of 1863 (these appear in serial 6,000 range) acquiring another 600 on the open market from rejects of U.S. government purchase. Ballards saw much service with many Kentucky cavalry outfits such as the 3rd, 6th, 8th, 11th, 12th, 13th and 45th Mounted Infantry in a great many campaigns, including Atlanta, pursuing Morgan and numerous guerrilla skirmishes. 2nd Iowa, also with distinguished record, known armed with some. The state of New York purchased 500 carbines approximately September, 1863. Carbines do not have specific markings to identify them as Kentucky or New York purchases.

Caliber 44 rimfire (dual ignition system very rare) 22-1/8" part round/part octagon barrel. Sling swivels affixed to barrel band and underside of butt (frame mounted sling rings not used):

5D-082   Values—Good **$850**   Fine **$2,500**

U.S. Contract Carbines. Caliber 44 rimfire. 22" part octagon/part round barrel. Sling swivels on barrel band and underside of butt (frame mounted sling rings not used).

Ball & Williams received a U.S. government contract in January 1864 for 5,000 carbines. They delivered 1,000 of them by March 16, 1864 and another 500 August 1, 1864, forfeiting the balance of the contract due to receiving higher prices from their Kentucky contracts. These U.S. contract pieces are identified by either the large inspector marks **MM** in script in an oval cartouche on the left side of the stock (serial ranges 6600-6800) and later block initials MM stamped on all major metal parts and the comb of the butt stock (serial range 9800-10500). 1,200 of these U.S. purchased Ballards were sent to Vermont to arm that state's militia following the raid on St. Albans, Vermont by a band of Confederate prisoners who had escaped to Canada. Another 600 carbines made for the government contract were rejected, sold on the "open" market and purchased by the state of Kentucky for their Cavalry September 1864:

5D-083   Values—Good **$2,750**   Fine **$4,750**

Military Rifles. Two types of Infantry rifles were made. The total of 4,000 pieces was entirely contracted by the state of Kentucky. Both types were marked KENTUCKY (as specified below). Earlier studies of the Ballard rifle, and the first five editions of this book, concluded that the KENTUCKY markings did not indicate state ownership, but rather a "promotional" term indicating rifles of this type were merely of "state of Kentucky pattern". With the known contracts by the state and known production by Ball & Williams, it is now established quite conclusively that those KENTUCKY markings do specifically indicate state ownership and issuance.

Military Rifle Caliber 44 Rimfire. 1,000 contracted by and delivered to the state of Kentucky by April 5, 1864. 30" barrel. Short carbine type forestock with single barrel band. KENTUCKY marked on the round barrel. Octagon shape frame. Serial range between 7100 and 8500:

5D-084   Values—Good **$850**   Fine **$2,500**

Military Rifle Caliber 46 Rimfire. 3,000 contracted by and delivered to state of Kentucky between July 1864 and March 1865. Serial ranges between 9400 and 13100. 30" round barrel. Marked KENTUCKY on top of the rounded frame. Full forend fastened by three barrel bands.
Note: Contract originally specified 56 caliber rimfire but was changed to 46 rimfire:

5D-084.5 Values—Good **$775**   Fine **$2,250**

Dual Ignition System (a.k.a. "alternate ignition"). Combination rimfire and percussion. Swivel striker on hammer for either the standard rimfire cartridge or the percussion nipple mounted on the breechblock. Hammer marked: PATENTED JANUARY 5, 1864. Almost exclusively seen on sporting models. System patented by Merwin & Bray first appears on Ballards in 14000 serial range in mid-1865. Small premium value often asked. Refer to "Sporting Rifle" No. 5D-081:

5D-085

Brass Frame Models. Encountered only on sporting models. Under 50 estimated made. Specimens occur in serial ranges approximately 180 to 200; 310 to 320; 1490 to 1500. Frames with silver finish. Breech blocks and levers also brass:

5D-086   Values—Good **$1,400**   Fine **$3,250**

Dwight, Chapin & Company and Ball & Williams Ballards

Dwight, Chapin & Company Bridgeport, Connecticut production 1863-1864 with contract completion by Ball & Williams of Worcester, Mass. 1864.

In October 1862, N.Y. City firearms dealers Merwin and Bray (see Chapter 8-A) were successful in acquiring a U.S.

Government contract for 1,000 each of larger caliber 56-56 Ballard rifles, carbines. (In reality 52RF; see discussion IX-B, Spencer rifles.) As the Ball & Williams facilities were operating at full capacity, M&B contracted with the Connecticut firm of Dwight, Chapin & Co. to manufacture the guns (Dwight was a

5D-086.2
56-56 Cal. Carbine

former superintendent of Springfield Armory). Dwight, Chapin was unable to meet delivery specifications of the contract, causing their business failure. Their total delivery was but 115 carbines by September 1863.

At the bankruptcy proceedings M&B acquired the completed carbines and unassembled parts for rifles and carbines and had Ball & Williams complete assembly and production of them.

(Note of interest: At the Dwight, Chapin bankruptcy sale the factory and machinery were acquired by Oliver Winchester who utilized both to manufacture the famous Model 1866 Winchester rifle and carbine. Chapin was kept on with the Winchester Company as Secretary).

Dwight, Chapin markings are on the 115 carbines delivered on U.S. contract; it is possible that they may occur on some later completed carbines acquired by Ball & Williams, but more likely such markings were removed by B&W.

Total quantity of approximately 1,800 pieces are chambered for the 56-56 Spencer cartridge (earlier reported 54 caliber is incorrect). All have the large rounded frame; all are in their own serial range of 1 to approximately 1800. All utilize the two-piece "split breech" block. A few of these large frames were possibly utilized to make Sporters. Quantity unknown.

Dwight, Chapin & Company Carbines. 22" round barrels. Serial numbers approximately 1 to 115.

Marked on left frame: DWIGHT, CHAPIN & CO/BRIDGEPORT, CONN. Over MERWIN & BRAY/AGT'S N.Y./Serial Number. Right frame marked BALLARD'S PATENT/NOV.5,1861.

U.S. Government inspector markings D (of E.M. Dustin) appears on most parts including block, hammer, barrel, buttplate, lever with EMD at comb of buttstock near buttplate:

5D-086.2   Values—Good **$3,500**   Fine **$10,000**

Ball & Williams Assembled Carbines. Identical to above. Neither Dwight, Chapin & Co. or Ball & Williams markings were used. Only the Ballard patent and Merwin & Bray marks (as above) appear.

Approximately 1,000 were manufactured/assembled. All were purchased by the state of Kentucky by April 1864:

5D-086.3   Values—Good **$950**   Fine **$2,500**

Ball & Williams Assembled Rifles. 30" barrel; full walnut forend fastened by three barrel bands.

Approximately 835 rifles are estimated to have been completed. It is recorded that 35 were sold to Colonel James Montgomery's 2nd South Carolina Colored Infantry (35th U.S.C.T.) and 600 were sold to the state of Kentucky (April 1864) and issued to the 4th Kentucky Mounted Infantry. No specific regimental identifying markings are known for either:

5D-086.4   Values—Good **$1,400**   Fine **$2,750**

R. Ball & Company Ballard Rifles and Carbines

R. Ball and Company, Worcester, Massachusetts, 1865-1866. Based on serial number ranges it is estimated that 2200 Ballards were manufactured; most were sporting rifles. Serial numbers continued in sequence from the Ball & Williams in approximate 16000 to 18000 range. Almost all fitted with the dual ignition (cartridge/percussion) system. Markings: BALLARD'S PATENT/NOV.5.1861 and MERWIN & BRAY AGTS/NEW YORK (neither BALL & WILLIAMS or BALL & CO. marks were used).

Carbine: 44 rimfire. Round frame; 22" round barrel. Quantity estimated 200+. It is known that New York state purchased 100 carbines March, 1866 for issue to prison guards; no specific

marking known:

5D-086.5   Values—Good **$1,250**   Fine **$2,750**

Sporting Rifle: 32, 38, 44, 46 rimfire. Octagon, part octagon/part round barrels 24", 26", 28", 30". Octagon frame shape:

5D-086.6   Values—Good **$850**   Fine **$2,500**

Military Rifle: 46 rimfire. 30" barrel; round frame. Full forend fastened with three barrel bands:

5D-086.7   Values—Good **$1,500**   Fine **$3,250**

Shotgun: 20 gauge. 30" round barrel; round frame with sight groove at top. Very few made:

5D-086.8   Values—Good **$500**   Fine **$950**

Merrimack Arms & Manufacturing Co. Ballard Rifles & Carbines

Merrimack Arms & Manufacturing Co., Newburyport, Mass. 1867-1869. Total production estimated 2,200; almost all sporting rifles.

All markings on left frame in four lines: MERRIMACK ARMS & MFG. CO. / NEWBURYPORT, MASS. / BALLARD'S PATENT / NOV. 5, 1861. Most, probably all, rifles made by Merrimack had the dual percussion/cartridge system. Serial range approximately 18000 to 20300.

Sporting Rifles: 32, 38, 44 and 46 rimfire. (22 and 50 rf. rare and worth premiums). Octagon and part round/part octagon barrels 24", 26", 28", 30". Octagon shaped frame. Single set trigger rare and worth premium:

5D-087   Values—Good **$850**   Fine **$2,500**

Carbine: 44 rimfire 22" round barrel; round frame. Estimated quantity under 200, of which 70 were sold to New York state for prison guard use and issued to Sing-Sing Prison December, 1869:

5D-088   Values—Good **$1,400**   Fine **$3,250**

Military Rifle: Few reported in 46 rimfire; 30" barrel, round frame. Rare. This model also known in .50 rf.; believed submitted for U.S. Government trials; very rare, worth premium over value shown:

5D-089   Values—Good **$1,400**   Fine **$3,250**

Shotgun: 20 gauge rimfire (a unique reloadable copper shell); 30" round barrel; round frame with sight groove at top. Quantity estimated less than 50:

5D-090   Values—Good **$500**   Fine **$950**

Brown Manufacturing Company Ballard Rifles

Brown Manufacturing Company, Newburyport, Mass. 1869 to 1873. total quantity made estimated at 1,700.

Markings on left frame BROWN MFG. CO. NEWBURYPORT MASS and BALLARD'S PATENT/NOV.5,1861. Serial numbers continued in sequence from Merrimack guns to approximately 22000.

Although company literature listed carbines and shotguns, it is believed none were made.

Sporting Rifles: Identical to those made by Merrimack Arms Co. (see above). Calibers 22 and 50 rimfire also rare and worth premiums. Single set trigger feature and takedown models also known and worth premiums. Difficult to estimate quantities made, but minimum of 500 and likely more:

5D-090.5   Values—Good **$850**   Fine **$2,500**

Military Rifle: It has been estimated that as many as 1000 military rifles were made, (possibly in anticipation of an European contract that likely did not materialize) and subsequent to the closure of the factory many were purchased by

5D-090-8
Frame Extractor Variant

the well known Boston, Mass. arms and sporting goods firm of Williams Read & Sons who sporterized them for civilian sales.

46 rimfire. 30" barrel; full forend; 3 barrel bands. Round frame. About identical to those made by Ball & Williams (#5D-084.5) but with tangless frame and omission of KENTUCKY markings:

5D-090.6   Values—Good **$750**   Fine **$2,250**

Grip (Frame) Extractor Sporting Rifle: Distinguished by the small, checkered, sliding catch at each side of the frame. Manually grasped and pulled rearward to extract spent cartridge. Found only on early production Brown rifles. Estimated quantity less than 50:

5D-090.8   Values—Good **$1,150**   Fine **$3,000**

FREUND CONVERSIONS OF BALLARD RIFLES

Conversions by the famous Freund Brothers of Cheyenne, Wyoming Territory of early Ballard rifles. Although their conversions of Sharps Model 1874 and Borchardt Model 1878 rifles are more widely known (see Chapter V-F Sharps), that famous Western firm of gun dealers and gunsmiths widely advertised in their 1879 (and likely other) catalog their conversions of Ballard rifles to accept their "Freund's Improved Breech Mechanism" (as per illustration here). They claimed the factory-supplied breech had "...a very serious defect" in forcing the cartridge into the barrel and lacking strength. Their "New Improved Breech" not only overcame those defects but allowed

the use of larger caliber ammunition with heavy charges. Ballard rifles encountered with that authentic Freund breech and bearing their usual markings on the barrel "FREUND BROS." or "FREUND & BRO." usually justifies premiums of at least 100 percent which will rise accordingly with top-conditioned specimens. Collectors should bear in mind that Freund Brothers were large dealers in firearms as well and very likely sold Ballard rifles along with many other makes without such breech conversions and which will also bear those same Freund markings. If authentic, premium values are well-justified (at notably less than rifles fitted with the "Freund breech").

9

BALLARD RIFLE,
WITH FREUNDS' IMPROVED BREECH MECHANISM.

The above cut represents a Ballard rifle with our new improved breech action. The shooting qualities of the barrel and the general finish of the Ballard rifle are inferior to none; but, unfortunately, it has, in our opinion, a very serious defect in its breech movement, possessing no facilities for forcing the cartridge to its proper position in the barrel, and lacking the strength in the resisting parts so essential to a reliable service gun. By inserting our

10

new improved breech movement, we have overcome both these defects. Our breech movement forms a direct resistance at a right angle to the line of recoil, against heavy charges. Without our movement, the Ballard gun cannot offer the necessary resistance to heavy charges of powder. For this reason, they have not as yet made a 40 calibre gun to shoot 90 grains of powder; the strain is so great. Consequently, they have made cartridges to suit the gun. But, to meet the demands of the public the gun must be made to suit the cartridges in market. By applying our movement to the Ballard gun, this is accomplished, and any cartridges in the market may be used with perfect safety. We make this movement either with single or double extractors, as ordered, and when applied to the Ballard rifle, it becomes equal to any in the market. The Ballard rifle possesses an advantage over the Sharps in use, in the fact of its having a cleaning-rod attached; to attach it to the Sharps rifle would entail additional expense. This gun is splendidly sighted for hunting or target practice, and has double triggers. By the insertion of our new movement, we make a direct resistance in the rear, and there is neither spring nor strain, and there is less recoil.

In conclusion, we say that we guarantee every rifle which we alter to our new breech movement, and if any rifle fails to conform in every respect to our representations, we will take it back and pay all charges of transportation, besides refunding the purchase money. We make the insertion of our new breech movement a specialty, but are prepared to do any work, whether new or repairs, in the gun-making line.

In sending orders, be particular to describe fully the size, length, and weight of barrel, the calibre, single or double trigger, specify whether the pistol grip is desired, and whether plain, open or peep sight is preferred, that no error may occur.

Orders may be addressed to F. A. Dammann, who has our agency, or to us.
                                                    FREUND BROS.,
                                              CHEYENNE, Wy. Ter.

Marlin-Ballard Rifles

Made by John M. Marlin at New Haven c. 1875 to 1881 and the Marlin Firearms Company, New Haven c. 1881 to 1891. Total quantity produced is estimated at approximately 40,000.

It's relevant to note that James Grant, the most prolific and often referred to author of books about single shot rifles, in his first, and still most important work "Single Shot Rifles", has not only devoted the first and lengthiest chapter to the Marlin-Ballard, but states in the opening sentence of the first page "… It is fitting that the most famous and beloved of all old single shots should have the place of honor (in this book)."

The arms of both firms are basically identical as are the model names and numbers, with but few exceptions as noted. The basic changes are the markings: J. M. MARLIN NEW HAVEN. CONN. U.S.A./BALLARD'S PATENT. NOV. 5, 1861 appears on those made prior to 1881; and MARLIN FIREARMS CO. NEW HAVEN CT. U.S.A./PATENTED FEB. 9. 1875./BALLARD'S PATENT NOV. 5. 1861 is on those made subsequent to 1881. The 1875 patent date covered John Marlin's reversible firing pin for dual usage of either rimfire or centerfire cartridges and is marked on guns provided with that feature. As production advanced through the years and most rimfire cartridges were generally discontinued, so too was the reversible firing pin, becoming generally obsolescent. Thus, those rifles made without the reversible pin will not bear the 1875 patent date.

All Marlin Ballards have the octagon or faceted top of the forward section of the frame/receiver and those of the Marlin Firearms Company (post-1881) have the fluted or grooved sides. Casehardening was the standard finish of all frames. Most barrels were either octagonal or part octagonal/part round with blued finishes standard.

Among other features distinguishing the Marlin-Ballards from all other Ballards are the inside tang and inside extractors. The serial number range for this inside extractor type is approximately 500 to 17000 for the J. M. Marlin marked rifles, and from 17000 to approximately 40000 for the Marlin Firearms Company marked rifles.

Almost all the following described rifles may be seen with either J. M. Marlin or Marlin Firearms Company markings (except where noted) and prices generally are the same for either marking. In some instances advanced or highly specialized collectors may wish to pay premiums for the earlier J. M. Marlin specimens, but such nuances will only be evident by a careful survey of the field and the potential market.

Engraved specimens in various grades were standard on some models and are so noted in the following descriptions, with values reflecting same. When engraving was not a standard feature, it was usually available at an extra price. When such decoration is found, premiums are added to the value. The subject of deluxe arms and relative values has been discussed at considerable length in the section concerning Winchesters.

The models described and listed herein are in their basic configurations as usually listed by Marlin in their catalogs. A tremendous variety of sights, stocks, levers, set triggers, special buttplates, barrel lengths and weights were available for extra charges. When such features are not standard and are seen on specimens available on the collectors' market, they usually will add value premiums. The amounts of such premiums are very much dependent on the nature of the options and the condition of the subject rifle. The longest barrel lengths (unless standard) and the heaviest barrel weights are scarce and quite desirable; such features will usually add at least 25 percent to values.

Studying original (or reprint) Marlin catalogs sheds much light on the collecting of these Ballards. Many options that were available on models when first introduced were dropped in later years. In a few instances, nomenclature itself varies from catalog to catalog for the same gun contributing to the difficulty of their positive identification. The Ballard No. 6 is a classic example while the No. 7 was listed in a few varieties that tend to be very confusing.

Barrel weights often vary for the same gun and are so indicated in original catalogs. The customer evidently had his choice between regular and medium weight barrels which were not considered as an "extra" at the time, nor did they require a premium in the basic cost. Many rifles are listed in two weights in Marlin catalogs, clearly indicating different barrel sizes.

Some Marlins were listed in catalogs as standard with barrel lengths of 32" or more. Unless these are long range rifles where such extreme lengths are standard, the general rule-of-thumb for the collector in making an evaluation would be to place a premium for most with 32" or longer barrel lengths.

Although Marlin catalogs and literature often state that frames are "extra heavy" and subsequent arms collecting literature has chosen this catalog phraseology to indicate there are two different sized frames (or options available), such was decidedly not the case, at least as far as a custom option was concerned or a special weight for larger calibers. Frames varied somewhat in contours and there was a basic frame for a straight grip model *vs.* a slightly curved frame for pistol grip stocked rifles. The majority of frames were made with 1-1/4" thickness while another group of 1-9/32" thickness was used on certain of the Schuetzen models. These frames apparently were merely manufacturing variants; the slightly thicker one was not intended to be known as the "extra heavy" or stronger type. The words "extra heavy" used consistently throughout some of the catalogs (and as subsequently repeated by modern authors), were merely used to originally indicate that *all* Marlin-Ballards had frames that were heavy enough, if not more so, to hold the loads for which they were designed. The use of such terminology then was no different than it is in today's advertising, whether it be cough syrup, toothpaste, gasoline or gun frames! Those larger 1-9/32" frames apparently were used only on the Model No. 6, 6-1/2, and 10, and in later versions only made by the Marlin Firearms Company. They seem only to be *manufacturing variances* and apparently have nothing to do with the strength of the frame or the loads they are designed to take.

Listings of calibers attributed to the various models herein are not all inclusive. Considerable confusion exists as to what calibers were available for each model and undoubtedly the practice of custom-chambering many on customer request would make such a complete listing impossible. Calibers described here are the usual ones either listed in catalogs or which have been otherwise recorded. There is every likelihood that others will be seen, and premiums to values, if any, must be judged on the desirability or rarity of that particular caliber and, of course, its originality (i.e., not a reboring and rechambering of the gun in present day).

Model names, numbers or designations do not appear on the rifles themselves. A few other odd variants and models were issued by Marlin that are not included here and might possibly be encountered on the collectors' market. Some were introduced and offered in catalogs for but a year or two at most and made only in the smallest quantities. Such nuances and esoteric features may be found in works such as the James Grant *Single Shot Rifle* series.

The Ballard rifle was one of the most famed and respected names in shooting history during the latter 19th century. These same guns continue to be in great demand today. It is important for the collector to realize that many Ballards have been rebarreled over the years as well as rebored and rechambered. Such factors affect prices drastically, hence, it is of the utmost importance that they be inspected quite closely for originality. During the era of their use some were rebarreled by the custom makers Harry Pope, George Schoyen, Axel Peterson and others of note. In such instances premiums may be added to values depending, of course, on the model on which alteration was performed and the condition. It is very much a matter of name, fame and reputation of the riflesmith as to whether values are to be added or subtracted!

External Extractor Ballard Hunter's Rifle

External Extractor Ballard Hunter's Rifle. Made by John M. Marlin, New Haven, Connecticut; c. 1875 to 1876. Total quantity estimated at less than 300.

44 caliber rimfire and centerfire. 24" to 28" round barrels. Breechblock utilized the John Marlin innovation of reversible firing pin allowing for use of both rim and centerfire cartridges.

Distinguishing feature is the external extractor lever as used on earlier Newburyport production.

Finish: Casehardened receiver with blued barrel. Two-piece walnut stock.

Left side of frame marked: J. M. MARLIN. NEW HAVEN. CONN. U.S.A./BALLARD'S PATENT. NOV. 5. 1861. Serial numbered in range 1 to 500.

5D-091

Very similar in appearance to sporting style rifles made by Brown Manufacturing Company (and Ball and Williams) and obviously using many earlier fabricated parts acquired by Marlin after acquisition of the remnants of the Brown Manufacturing Company:

5D-091   Values—Good **$900**   Fine **$2,250**

Note: Prices include original sights where indicated. If sights are missing deduct 20 to 30 percent of price.

Ballard No. 1 Hunter's Rifle

Ballard No. 1 Hunter's Rifle. (Not illus.) Made by J. M. Marlin, c. 1876 to 1880. Believed found only with the J. M. Marlin markings and made prior to change-over to Marlin Firearms Company.

Caliber 44 rim or centerfire. 26", 28", and 30" round barrels. Reversible firing pin and internal extractor. Serial numbered in the 300 to 500 range. Scarce:

5D-092   Values—Very Good **$1,000**   Exc. **$3,250**

Ballard No. 1-1/2 Hunter's Rifle

Ballard No. 1-1/2 Hunter's Rifle. Made c. 1879 to 1883.

Usual caliber 45/70, but also made 40/63 and 40/65. 30" and 32" round barrels. Differing from the No. 1 mainly in

chambering for centerfire calibers:

5D-093   Values—Very Good **$1,500**   Exc. **$3,750**

5D-093

Ballard No. 1-3/4 "Far West" Hunter's Rifle

Ballard No. 1-3/4 "Far West" Hunter's Rifle. (Not illus.) Made c. 1880 or 1881. Believed made only by J. M. Marlin and so marked.

A variant of the Ballard No. 1-1/2, differing only in having a double set trigger and ring style lever:

5D-094   Values—Very Good **$2,000**   Exc. **$4,500**

Ballard No. 2 Sporting Rifle

5D-095

Ballard No. 2 Sporting Rifle. Made c. 1876 to 1891.
32 and 38 rim or centerfire and 44 centerfire calibers. 26", 28", and 30" octagon barrels. Reversible firing pin. Rocky Mountain type open sights. Centerfire brings 10 to 20 percent higher values:

5D-095   Values—Very Good **$700**   Exc. **$2,000**

Ballard No. 3 Gallery Rifle

Ballard No. 3 Gallery Rifle. (Not illus.) Made c. 1876 to 1891.
Caliber 22 short or long rimfire. 24", 26", 28", and 30" octagon barrels.

Basically identical to the Model No. 2 Sporting Rifle except chambered for this small caliber. Rocky Mountain type sights:

5D-096   Values—Very Good **$750**   Exc. **$2,000**

Ballard No. 3F Fine Gallery Rifle

5D-097

Ballard No. 3F Fine Gallery Rifle. Made c. late 1880s. A variant of the No. 3, featuring pistol grip stock with pronged off-hand style nickeled buttplate and a full loop lever.
26" octagon barrel. Oil finished stock. Scarce:

5D-097   Values—Very Good **$1,100**   Exc. **$3,500**

Ballard No. 3-1/2 Target Rifle

Ballard No. 3-1/2 Target Rifle. (Not illus.) Made c. 1880 to 1882.
A variation of the No. 4 Perfection Rifle, differing as follows: 30" octagon barrel; checkered stock with shotgun type butt; tang

peep sight and globe front sight. Chambered for 40/65 cartridge:

5D-098   Values—Very Good **$1,750**   Exc. **$4,500**

Ballard No. 4 Perfection Rifle

Ballard No. 4 Perfection Rifle. (Not illus.) Made c. 1876 to 1891. Chambered for a variety of calibers from 32/40 to 50/70; all centerfire. The larger express calibers worth premium.

26" to 34" barrels (the longer lengths bring premiums). Rocky Mountain sights standard:

5D-099   Values—Very Good **$1,750**   Exc. **$4,500**

Ballard No. 4-1/2 Mid Range Rifle

Ballard No. 4-1/2 Mid Range Rifle. (Not illus.) Made c. 1878 to 1882.
A variant of the No. 4 Perfection with the following differences: Fancy, checkered pistol grip stock; shotgun butt; single trigger; 30" part round/part octagon barrel. Chambered

for calibers 38/40, 40/65, and 40/70. Vernier tang peep sight and globe front sight. Plain grade:

5D-100   Values—Very Good **$2,250**   Exc. **$5,000**
5D-100.5   Engraved Grade:
                Values—Very Good **$4,500**   Exc. **$8,000**

Ballard No. 4-1/2 A-1 Mid Range Target Rifle

5D-101

Ballard No. 4-1/2 A-1 Mid Range Target Rifle. Made c. 1878 to 1880.

A variant of the No. 4-1/2 Mid Range with following differences: Engraved scroll designs on both sides of the frame including inscription on left BALLARD A-1 and on right side MID RANGE. Sold with a choice of shotgun or rifle type stock; horn forend tip and the best grade of Vernier tang rear sight and windgauge spirit level front sight. Also came equipped with an extra mount at heel of buttplate for rear position. Apparently listed only in calibers 38/50 and 40/65, but probably available in other calibers on order:

5D-101 Values—Very Good **$4,250** Exc. **$8,000**

Ballard No. 5 Pacific Rifle

5D-102

Ballard No. 5 Pacific Rifle. Made c. 1876 to 1891.

Listed in a great variety of calibers from 38/50 to 50/70 (including such popular ones as 45/70, 44/40, 44/100, etc.). Catalogs specifically noted that Marlin would not make the gun on custom order in any caliber smaller than 38/55. 30" and 32" medium to heavy weight octagon barrels. Rocky Mountain sights. Rifle buttplate.

The distinctive feature of the gun is the presence of a ramrod mounted under the barrel and double set triggers. Ring shaped lever also standard:

5D-102 Values—Very Good **$2,000** Exc. **$5,000**

Ballard No. 5-1/2 Montana Rifle

Ballard No. 5-1/2 Montana Rifle. (Not illus.) Believe made only by the Marlin Firearms Company. First introduced c. 1882. Made to approximately 1884.

A variant of the No. 5 Pacific Rifle with the following differences: Made in caliber 45 Sharps (2-7/8") only and with extra heavy weight barrel including ramrod mounted underneath; rifle or shotgun style butt with checkered steel buttplate:

5D-103 Values—Very Good **$6,500** Exc. **$12,500**

Ballard No. 6 Schuetzen Off-Hand Rifle

Ballard No. 6 Schuetzen Off-Hand Rifle. (Not illus.) Made only by J. M. Marlin c. 1876 to 1880.

40/65, 44/75, and 38/50 centerfire calibers. 30" and 32" octagon barrels. Vernier tang peep and spirit level front sights.

Schuetzen style, high combed select grain walnut stock with cheek piece; nickeled finish; Swiss type buttplate. Loop and spur type lever; double triggers. Plain, not engraved (as differentiated from the Marlin Firearms No. 6):

5D-104 Values—Very Good **$3,000** Exc. **$7,500**

Ballard No. 6 Schuetzen Rifle

5D-105

Ballard No. 6 Schuetzen Rifle made only by Marlin Firearms Company. Circa 1881 to 1891.

32/40 and 38/55 centerfire calibers. 32" part round/part octagon barrel. Vernier rear peep and spirit level front sights. Loop and spur type lever; double set triggers.

Schuetzen style high combed stock with cheek piece, checkered at wrist; Swiss type buttplate with nickel finish; horn forend tip.

Fancy scroll, floral and animal scene engraving standard on frame:

5D-105 Values—Very Good **$4,250** Exc. **$8,500**

Ballard No. 6-1/2 Off-Hand Mid Range Rifle

Ballard No. 6-1/2 Off-Hand Mid Range Rifle. (Not illus.) Made c. 1880 to 1882.

40/65 Everlasting caliber only. 28" and 30" part round/part octagon barrels.

Schuetzen style select grain stock with a higher comb than the No. 6; cheek piece; heavy type Schuetzen buttplate with nickeled finish. Plain, non-engraved frame:

5D-106 Values—Very Good **$2,500** Exc. **$5,250**

Ballard No. 6-1/2 Rigby Off-Hand Mid Range

Ballard No. 6-1/2 Rigby Off-Hand Mid Range Rifle. (Not illus.) Made c. 1880 to 1882.

38/50 and 40/65 centerfire calibers. 26" and 28" round Rigby type barrels (a distinctive feature of the Rigby barrel is the relief raised ribs at the extreme breech end of barrel where they join frame). Mid-range Vernier rear peep and globe type front sights.

Fancy grain checkered pistol grip stock with cheek piece and nickel plated Swiss type buttplate; forend tip and pistol grip caps of horn. Single trigger and ring type lever.

Fancy hand engraved scroll work and animal motif scenes standard on both sides of frame. Those with a gold inlaid arrow design on the upper Rigby flat are worth a premium when found on any variation of Rigby barrel:

5D-107   Values—Very Good **$4,000**   Exc. **$9,000**

Ballard No. 6-1/2 Off-Hand Rifle

Ballard No. 6-1/2 Off-Hand Rifle. The successor to both other No. 6-1/2s. (Not illus., similar to 5D-105 except with pistol grip stock and single trigger.) Made by Marlin Firearms Company only, c. 1883 to 1891.

38/55 and 32/40 centerfire calibers. 28" and 30" Rigby type round barrels. Vernier rear peep and spirit level front sight.

Loop lever. Single trigger. Select grain Schuetzen type stock with cheek piece; checkered pistol grip; short pronged off-hand style buttplate with nickeled finish. Horn forend tip and pistol grip cap. Scroll engraving standard on both sides of frame and very slight at breech end of barrel:

5D-108   Values—Very Good **$4,000**   Exc. **$9,000**

Ballard No. 7 Long Range Rifle

Ballard No. 7 Long Range Rifle. (Not illus.) Made c. 1883 to 1890 by Marlin Firearms Company only.

Details generally as below. Essentially the same as the A-1,

but plain and not engraved. Plain walnut stock with plain adjustable rear and globe front sights or Vernier sights.

5D-109   Values—Very Good **$4,250**   Exc. **$8,500**

Ballard No. 7 "Creedmoor A-1" Long Range

5D-110

Ballard No. 7 "Creedmoor A-1" Long Range Rifle. Made c. 1876-1886.

44/100 and 45/100 usual calibers, but chambered for others. 34" part round/part octagon barrel. Long range (1,300 yard) Vernier tang peep sight with an extra mounting base at heel of buttplate for alternate location; spirit level windgauge front sight.

Select grain checkered pistol grip Creedmoor type (high heel) butt with shotgun style buttplate; horn forend tip.

Hand engraved scroll work designs on action standard with large fancy letters on left side BALLARD A-1, and on right side LONG RANGE

5D-110   Values—Very Good **$5,000**   Exc. **$10,000**

Ballard No. 7 A-1 Long Range Rifle

Ballard No. 7 A-1 Long Range Rifle. (Not illus.) Made c. 1879 to 1883.

A variant of the No. 7 "Creedmoor A-1" having fancier, higher grade stocks and improved grade of sights. A key feature on this one is apparently the straight checkered stock and

forearm (instead of the usual pistol grip). Specifications otherwise generally the same. Engraving on frame standard with the fancy BALLARD A-1 on left side of frame and LONG RANGE on right side:

5D-111   Values—Very Good **$5,000**   Exc. **$10,000**

Ballard No. 7 A-1 "Extra" Long Range Rifle

Ballard No. 7 A-1 "Extra" Long Range Rifle. (Not illus.) Made c. 1879 to 1883.

Another variation of the A-1 in their highest grade. The distinctive feature is the 34" Rigby type round barrel (with raised ribs near breech where it joins frame).

This was available in their fanciest deluxe grades. Engraving usually very profuse fancy scroll and animal motifs. Forend tip,

pistol grip cap and buttplate of horn. Long range and windgauge sights. Creedmoor style checkered pistol grip stock.

These were more or less individually made to the customer's specifications and considerable variation is encountered on them. Only small quantity was believed manufactured. Rare:

5D-112   Values—Very Good **$5,500**   Exc. **$12,000**

Ballard No. 8 Union Hill Rifle

Ballard No. 8 Union Hill Rifle. (Not illus.) Made by Marlin Firearms Company 1884 to 1890.

38/55 and 32/40 calibers. 28" and 30" part round/part octagon barrels. Adjustable type mid-range tang peep sight with globe type front sight. Full loop lever; double set triggers.

Checkered pistol grip stock; short pronged off-hand type buttplate nickeled finish. Plain, non-engraved frame. Essentially a lower grade No. 6-1/2 Off-Hand and one of the most popular rifles in the Marlin-Ballard line:

5D-113   Values—Very Good **$2,250**   Exc. **$4,500**

Ballard No. 9 Union Hill Rifle

Ballard No. 9 Union Hill Rifle. (Not illus.) Made by Marlin Firearms Company, c. 1884 to 1891.

A variant of the No. 8 Union Hill, differing in having a single

trigger (with same style lever). Vernier mid-range rear peep and windgauge front sights:

5D-114   Values—Very Good **$2,000**   Exc. **$4,000**

Ballard No. 10 Schuetzen "Junior" Rifle

Ballard No. 10 Schuetzen "Junior" Rifle. (Not illus.) Made by Marlin Firearms Company, c. 1885 to 1891.

A variant of the Union Hill, differing in its overall heavier weight (approximately 12 lbs.), 32" part round/part octagon barrel and a lighter short pronged off-hand style buttplate. Mid-

range Vernier rear peep sight and adjustable windgauge front sight. Pistol grip checkered stock. Made in calibers 32/40 and 38/55. Highly popular model in the series:

5D-115   Values—Very Good **$2,250**   Exc. **$5,000**

Chapter V-E

Remington Firearms

This chapter represents the most complete, coherent listing of all Remington arms made to c. 1900, both long guns and handguns, with significant comprehensive specifications and technical data about the types or models themselves and their numerous variations. Although not the definitive story of Remington arms, this chapter in its eight prior editions has grown to become a prime reference for this famous maker.

One of the major American manufacturers and a significant field of antique arms collecting, there has been, until now, a surprising shortage of detailed, published data defining the specifications, peculiarities and variations of the numerous Remington models that the world of collecting tirelessly seeks.

The importance of Remington in the collecting field as well as its historical associations over a very lengthy era of American history (the longest life of any U.S. arms maker) are on a par with other major areas of collecting that have been considered in the forefront of interest, demand and values, i.e., Colt, Smith & Wesson, Winchester. Until recent years, the lack of an easily usable, dependable reference work was not merely an anomaly for this popular area of collecting, but an annoying obstruction.

For almost a half-century the major guide to the arms of this prominent maker was *Remington Handguns* by Charles Karr. Published in 1947, it subsequently enjoyed numerous reprintings (without essential change), remaining until the mid-1990s the most often quoted for Remington handguns. It yet remains a milestone in Remington and American arms lore. But, as the author himself wrote in his foreword: "...This little volume represents one more foundation stone in the edifice which is the story of the handgun in America...let us hope that it represents but the first of major contributions." And so it has remained for fifty years! Although a few other works contributed to Remington lore in the following decades, it was not until 1997 with the remarkable exhibition *"The Guns of Remington"* (with hundreds of their arms) sponsored by the Remington Society and the Cody Firearms Museum...and publication of the voluminous hardcover catalog of that show (H. Madaus, Editor)...followed by R. Marcot's *Remington, America's Oldest Gunmaker* in 1998 that literature and basic references about these makers and their arms began to offer the collector, the long-overdue wealth of necessary detail the field deserved. Other significant references have since followed, including the encyclopedic *History of Remington Firearms* (R. Marcot) in 2005. The growing library of Remington literature has benefited not only the individual collector but has also been influential in heightening interest in the specialized field of collecting Remington arms.

These last few years have seen great interest in Remington arms and Remington research. Spearheaded and sponsored by the Remington Society of America, a number of detailed studies have been undertaken and published that have been of immense assistance to the collecting world. The Remington Society maintains a website at www.remingtonsociety.com and also issues an informative, scholarly quarterly "Journal."

In compiling this chapter the author has drawn on the expertise of well-respected Remington collectors, the Remington Arms Museum and his own half century experience in handling the guns of this maker. Members of the Remington Society of America have been most generous in their cooperation in making this chapter the most up-to-date, important reference that it has become. In 1997 the Society sponsored an exhibition of 850 Remington firearms at the Cody Firearms Museum. The enormity of such an undertaking is unlikely to ever be duplicated. The catalog of the exhibition (*qv*) is already a collector's item.

A few guns, such as the Rolling Block Action rifles and pistols and Hepburn rifles were made in seemingly endless variations; both worthy of volumes devoted solely to each and offering potential for exhaustive research. Exact quantities made are now known for some models and are reflected in revised figures. They may be at variance with earlier published figures.

Conspicuous by its absence is the so-called Remington-Elliot Skeleton Stock Rifle (the Vest-Pocket Deringer with the very long barrel and attachable or folding stock). There is a complete dearth of information about this gun which has always been a subject of controversy among collectors. The possibility exists that it was a Remington product—while, on the other side of the fence, there is every reason to believe that the company never had anything to do with its manufacture. All specimens observed utilized the 41 caliber deringer action and breech; the barrel having been cut off with the breech bored out and a new barrel sweated into the existing action. With no accurate records verifying their factory originality, and with the variations that have been seen on them (many showing a lack of consistency), the author felt the reader would be best served by mentioning them here, rather than including them as a known Remington-made gun. Many that have been viewed have every indication of being genuine, antique "of the period" pieces and as such are considered both rare and desirable collectors' items. Nevertheless, the collector should be extremely wary of this particular type of arm as it was, and is, highly susceptible to forgery and not a few spurious specimens appear on the market. In other words—who made them, and when—is still unknown! If they prove to be original Remington, so much the better.

The field of Remington handgun conversions (i.e., from percussion to cartridge) is also fertile for research. Quite a few variations in conversions, especially in the larger 36 and 44 caliber handguns, have never been completely listed and undoubtedly will reflect price variances (for the scarcer types) when more definitive data is known about them. Of course, with statistical studies hoped for in the future, several scarcities might appear. At present rarity for some can only be approximated, based on the experience of advanced collectors and dealers who have handled specimens over the years. Statistics are not always the best guide to rarity. As shown throughout other fields of arms collecting, they are merely good indicators. *Bear in mind that contradictions exist and appear with a reasonable frequency.* That's when the cupidity of the seller and the gullibility of the buyer must be separated! When such contradictions and variances appear, they are in many cases logically explained; it does take some thought and investigation and, of course, careful consideration by a practiced eye along with logical and practical reasoning to determine if the arm has been spuriously altered or is an authentic factory variation.

The field of Remington single shot rolling block pistols is certainly a good example of the latter point. Remington produced many parts in anticipation of contracts which never materialized; thus, variations of target pistols (using those parts) are numerous. This particular field is often difficult because of the possibility of contemporary and modern gunsmith alterations of the Military Model 1871 Pistol. Variations have been noticed in the No. 7 rifle (mostly in extractors) which seem to indicate the factory salvage of available parts on hand during their era of production.

For ease in use, this chapter was arranged into two basic sections: The **HANDGUNS** section is basically in the chronological order which they were produced. A few changes were made in the interest of ease and use of the book, such as placing the Rider Single Shot Pistol at the commencement of the deringer section and keeping all single shot rolling block pistols in one group rather than splitting them.

The **LONGARMS** section is basically in chronological order, but again, a few exceptions were made in the interest of ease of reference by the reader. Most notable is the inclusion of all the rolling block arms as one unit even though a few later models (such as the Hepburn) are out of numerical sequence. Shotguns, for the most part, were kept together out of chronological order as a distinct separate section.

For the Remington specialist, a major asset is the collecting of original (or reprint) Remington catalogs. A great deal of information may be gleaned from them, especially in the seemingly endless variations, notably in the single shot rifle line. For the researcher these catalogs are key tools.

THE CASE OF THE WANDERING APOSTROPHE! With a sense of mild amusement the author brings to the attention of Remington buffs a curious error apparently committed in most studies in which markings on Remington arms have been reported (and brought to light in the 9th Edition of this work). It is observed on many early Remingtons that the actual placement of the apostrophe mark after the word "REMINGTON" has been inaccurately reported...indicating that either the researcher/writer had misread that marking...or the error was made by the typesetter or proofreader. Investigation reveals that the apostrophe mark (used to denote ownership) on various models was applied inconsistently by the factory itself, sometimes viewed as **REMINGTONS'** or **REMINGTON'S.** Those same misreadings and oversights have invariably been carried through in similar manner by later researchers (sometimes compounding the error!), until reporting it here. Admittedly, the oversight is of minor consequence, one that may have but faint chance of causing distress. However, as markings play an integral role in the literature and collecting of firearms, that error was eligible to be recognized.

Having thus fired this opening gun at the "wandering" apostrophe, every effort has been made to correct the placement of that mark in the descriptions in this chapter. Possibly not all bases are yet covered! Based on past experience I have every reason to believe that collectors and readers will bring such oversights to the author's attention.

The reader is urged to review the introductory material to this book regarding nuances of collecting—many of which affect values in Remington arms. The prefatory material in the chapters concerning Colt and Smith & Wesson arms contain considerable discussions of matters directly and equally applicable to Remingtons. At the risk of redundancy and in order not to try the patience of the reader, a few salient points are touched upon here.

As with all antique and collectors' arms—and especially with the more popular widely manufactured models, Remington included— *condition* is the key word, strongly affecting demand as well as value.

Rare variations do appear in the Remington line, and as easily attested by the foregoing text, there are many yet to be listed or widely known. Such variations could be encountered on almost any model; the most obvious being odd barrel lengths, unusual non-standard markings and possibly even basic changes in contour. The reader is reminded not to jump to conclusions, but to investigate such features very closely, especially if contemplating paying a premium price for them! Many alterations could have been, and were, made by competent gunsmiths during the actual period of use of the gun and have thus acquired a genuine aging and appearance of "originality" throughout the years. Even though interesting, when such variations prove to be non-factory in origin, they generally do not enhance the value of the gun, and very likely will detract from it.

The subject of blue finish *vs* nickel finish (especially as found on a number of the later cartridge models) is quite thoroughly discussed in the Colt and Smith & Wesson chapters. That material should be reviewed as it applies equally to Remingtons. To encapsulate—in just about new or mint condition a gun with blued or nickel finish will bring about the same price. In worn condition (for example, 50 percent blue *vs.* 50 percent nickel finish remaining) the blued gun will fetch a considerably higher value and will be found in stronger demand.

Original engraved specimens are encountered in Remingtons, but with much less frequency than Colts or Smith & Wessons. As a matter of fact, engraved Remingtons are quite rare (the only exception to this example is the Magazine Deringer Model). Engraving, particularly in the percussion handguns, is usually quite simple in form and a great deal less elaborate than the engraved Colt. Occasionally on a fancy Remington percussion handgun a full cylinder scene may be observed; usually acid etched *vs* the rolled design found on Colts. The subject of increased values for deluxe specimens has been discussed thoroughly in the introductory chapters of this book as well as the Colt chapter. Engraved specimens may also be found in the Remington longarms line, primarily on fancy rolling blocks, but rarely on a Remington Hepburn. In all of these, the engraving is usually much more profuse than on the early handguns and of quite fine quality. All may be considered very scarce or rare.

Cased outfits in Remingtons are also rare. They are encountered with a much less degree of frequency than in the Colt line. Value-wise, however, prices are increased relatively proportionate to the manner in which cased Colts are increased, although an exceptionally fine conditioned or complete specimen, the percentage of increase may be higher than a comparative Colt.

The use of exotic grip materials (other than the standard specified factory supplied types) will add to the value of a gun.

Ivory is the most often encountered type of special grips; other materials are occasionally seen. Pearl is quite often used on the later, small size metallic cartridge revolvers. Values increase in direct proportion to the type of gun on which they appear and the quality and condition of the grips themselves are always key factors. This subject has also been quite well covered throughout the book. (See "Rem. Smoot Revolvers" regarding Celluloid grips.)

As with Colts, there have been within recent years a wide range of modern made, faithful recreations of Remington arms. For the most part these are reproductions of the "New Model" Army and Navy type revolvers and Remington Model 1863 "Zouave" 58 caliber percussion rifles. The reader is referred to the discussion of similar Colt replicas in the text accompanying that section; the same "caveats" will apply. In essence, though, there is no cause for alarm on these reproductions—and the few spurious specimens that have turned up (fake aged to resemble antiques) have not in any way affected the market nor are they considered any major threat.

The matter of bores *vs* price is another subject covered in other segments of this book, notably in the Winchester, Colt and Single Shot Rifle chapters, and is often important in establishing values as well as affecting demand. Generally, bores do not play a major role with most Remington handguns except for the single shot target models. This is not to say that bores are unimportant, though, and the reader is referred to a general discussion of this subject in the preface to the Winchester chapter as well as the discussion of the Model 1874 Sharps sporting rifles.

In order to place the arms in clearer perspective, the collector will find it useful to have a general knowledge of the history of the Remington Arms Company and its founders. The Remington name is first associated with American arms circa 1816 when Eliphalet Remington II is said to have started making barrels at his father's forge near the modern village of Ilion, N.Y. to supply the busy gun trade in the central New York area. Their barrel making manufacture considerably expanded in 1828, with their move to what is now Ilion, N.Y. where they located along the Erie Canal, by which they shipped their products. Evidence has yet to surface to substantiate any early gun making activities by the Remingtons other than the manufacture of barrel and possible rifle mountings. (*For more complete details of this facet see 5E-068.*)

The first verifiable instance of Remington manufacture of entire guns dates to 1848 with their purchase of gun making machinery from the Ames Company of Chicopee, Mass., taking over their uncompleted contract for Jenks breechloading percussion carbines for the U.S. Navy. (*see 9B-063*) At about that same time Remington took over a defaulted contract (from John Griffith of Cincinnati) for 5000 of the U.S. Model 1841 Percussion "Mississippi" rifles, (*see 9A-285*) their first opportunity to expand on a large, mass production basis. Other contracts for the Model 1841 followed soon after in the early 1850's.

Eliphalet Remington had taken his son Philo into the business with him in 1844, the firm's name changing at that time to "E. REMINGTON & SON." By 1852 two more sons, Samuel and Eliphalet Jr. entered the business, the firm's name again changed to "E. REMINGTON & SONS" reflecting the new partnership.

Improvements and modifications were frequently made and introduced to Remington manufacturing techniques. Both the founder and his successors were essentially arms makers and manufacturers, not inventors or innovators. They sought and acquired inventions from others. This likely contributed to much of their success, as witnessed by their long history.

Their first handgun production commenced in 1857 with the introduction of the Remington-Beals Pocket revolvers. The outbreak of the Civil War caused the firm to devote almost all its energy to military production of longarms and handguns, although an 1862 advertisement of theirs offered "… cast steel, stubs twisted and refined iron rifle barrels; brass, German silver and iron gun mountings; gun locks, gun materials, telescopes for rifles, rifling machines, gun stocks, barrels ribbed, patent breeched and cone-seated; rifle barrels patent muzzled, ball starters, molds … and … engraving done in best style."

Their 1870 catalog, as well as later issues, still offered cast steel, iron and twisted barrels of varying types and weights as well as matched barrels for double rifles and shotguns in varying grades and brass, iron and German silver gun mountings.

Eliphalet (II), the founder, died in 1861 and management was taken over by his eldest son, Philo. By 1865 the company was reorganized from a partnership to a corporation, but retained the same name E. Remington & Sons.

In the post-Civil War years, as will be attested to by the following listings of their products, the company entered the field with a large variety of successful competing arms. They prospered substantially in the lucrative foreign market, garnering several large orders for their famous rolling block line.

Samuel Remington died in 1882; his share of the business was sold to Philo who assumed full management of the company. But, by 1886 neither Philo nor Eliphalet III were able to rescue the company from grave financial reverses and the firm went into receivership. It was reorganized as the Remington Arms Company. Control passed from the family to the famed New York military and sporting goods firm of Hartley and Graham in 1888, the same partners that were the founders (in 1867) of the Union Metallic Cartridge Company of Bridgeport, Connecticut.

Operating under the same firm name of the Remington Arms Company from 1888 to 1912), Remington was merged by Hartley and Graham with their own Union Metallic Cartridge Company and the name changed to Remington-U.M.C., under which it operated until 1934-35 when again it was reorganized, the name reverted to Remington Arms Company, Inc. That name has continued in use to the present day. Controlling interest in the firm since 1933 was by the Dupont Corporation, who in 1993 sold that interest to Clayton, Dubilier, Rice, an investment group.

BIBLIOGRAPHY

(Note: An important source for information is original factory catalogs issued sporadically over the years; a highly significant recent find was the extensive illustrated 1870 Remington catalog containing a wealth of detail. Other information about Remington arms may be found in works appearing in bibliographic listings elsewhere in this work. They are: *The Collecting Of Guns*, edited by Serven; *Single Shot Rifles* and *More Single Shot Rifles* by James J. Grant; *The Rifle In America* by Phil Sharpe; *American Percussion Revolvers* by Frank Sellers and Samuel E. Smith; *United States Military Small Arms 1816-1865* by Robert M. Reilly; *Catalog Of The William M. Locke Collection*; *Identifying Old U.S. Muskets, Rifles And Carbines* by Colonel Gluckman; and *Civil War Guns* by William B. Edwards.)

Ball, Robert W. *Remington Firearms: The Golden Age of Collecting*. Iola, Wisc: Krause Publications, 1995.

Hatch, Alden. *Remington Arms In American History*. New York: Rinehart and Company, Inc., 1956. Basically the historic development of the Remington Arms Company with some data on various models produced.

Hatfield, R. E., *Remington's Vest Pocket Pistol...and the Saw-handle-Grip Pocket Pistol*. Private Pub. 1997. Small Monograph. Heavy on statistics based on assumed individual serial ranges for each caliber.

*Hatfield, Robert E. *Remington's Vest Pocket Pistols*. Lincoln, Rhode Island: Andrew Mowbray Publishers, 2002. An in-depth study, in great detail, of the four uniquely named "Vest Pocket Pistols."

*Janzen, J.L. *Bayonets of the Remington Cartridge Period*. Broken Arrow, Oklahoma: Cedar Ridge Publications, 1994.

Karr, Charles Lee, Jr. and Karr, Caroll Robbins. *Remington Handguns.* Harrisburg, Pennsylvania: Stackpole Company, 1947; Second Edition 1951. Many subsequent reprintings. Basic guide in use.

Kirkland, K.D. *America's Premier Gunmakers: Remington.* New York, N.Y.: Exeter Books, 1988. Part of a series of various makers. Cursory coverage.

Landskron, J. *Remington Rolling Block Pistols.* Buena Park, Calif: Rolling Block Press, 1981. Important data about numerous models and variations of this widely produced, famous handgun.

Larson, E.D. *Remington Tips.* Union City, Tennessee: Pioneer Press, 1975. Monograph. 3rd revised edition 1996 published by author; Ayer, Mass. (earlier Arizona: Wolfe Pub. 1992). Revised 3rd Edition, 1996; Pub. by author, Ayer, Mass. Important data about this famous firearm.

*Layman, George. *The Military Remington Rolling Block Rifle.* 3rd revised edition 1996 published by author; Ayer, Mass. (earlier Arizona: Wolfe Pub. 1992). Revised 3rd Edition, 1996; Pub. by author, Ayer, Mass. Important data about this famous firearm.

Lyles, G.R. and Moldenhauer, K. *Remington Double Derringer Alias Remington Over and Under.* Hagerstown, Maryland: Privately published monograph, 1982.

*Madaus, H.M., Compiler. *The Guns Of Remington* Dayton, Ky: Biplane Pub. 1997. Sponsored by Remington Society & Cody Firearms Museum; massive history of Remington with 850 superb color illus. of their guns 1816 to present as exhibited in the most important Remington exhibition ever assembled.

*Marcot, Roy M. *Remington, America's Oldest Gunmaker.* Peoria, Ill.: Primedia Publications, 1998. Remington Co. authorized history; a work of major significance.

*Marcot, Roy. *The History of Remington Firearms.* Guilford, Conn: The Lyons Press, 2005. Clearly and succinctly one of most significant and encyclopedic works reporting the story of the company as well as its products. All models listed in chronological order.

*Myszkowski, Eugene. *The Remington Lee Rifle.* Latham, N.Y.: Excalibur Publications, 1994. Detailed coverage.

*Myszkowski, Eugene. *Remington Autoloading & Pump-Action Rifles: A History of the Centerfire Models 760, 740, 7400 & 7600.* Tucson, Ariz: Excalibur Publications, 2002.

*Parker, Harry J. *A Study of Remington's Smoot Patent & Number Four Revolvers.* Santa Ana, Calif: Arms Lore Press, 2003. A detailed study of these spur trigger pocket handguns often termed (incorrectly) "New Line Revolvers" in arms literature.

Peterson, Harold L. *The Remington Historical Treasury Of American Guns.* New York: The Ridge Press, 1966. A history of Remington from earliest times to present interwoven with the development of their various arms.

*Phillips, Roger. *Remington Large-bore Conversion Revolvers.* Regina, Sask., Canada: 2005. A coherent analysis of the various methods used to produce viable cartridge revolvers of Remington design from experimental and trial types to production models.

*Schif, Charles. *Reminton's First Revolvers: The Rem-Beals .31 Caliber Revolvers.* Woonsocket, R.I.: Mowbray Pub., 2007. Important guide to these earliest and smallest Rem. period handguns.

*Schreier, K. F. Jr. *Remington Rolling-Block Firearms.* Union City, Tennessee: Pioneer Press, 1977. A general survey of these famed Remingtons. Not highly definitive but a good introduction to the subject.

*Semmer, Charles G. *Remington Double Shotguns.* Private published by author, 1996. Thorough coverage with very detailed illustrations.

The Karl F. Moldenhauer Collection of Remington Arms. Hyannis, Mass.: Richard Bourne Auction Co., 1980. Hard bound, auction catalog of largest, most well-known collection of Remingtons. Fine source book for information not available elsewhere: great variety of models, types, and sub-types. Prices realized at auction included.

*Ware, D.L. *Remington Army and Navy Revolvers 1861-1888.* Albuquerque, N.M.: University of N.M. Press, 2007. A fresh perspective on these important series of large caliber handguns.

Williford, D.F., Jr. *Molds For Remington Percussion Revolvers And Revolving Rifles.* Fairmont, West Virginia: Privately published, 1991. Monograph, spiral bound.

(*) Preceding a title indicates the book is currently in print.

REMINGTON HANDGUNS

Remington-Beals 1st Model Pocket Revolver

First Model Beals Pocket Revolver. Made c. 1857-1858. Total quantity estimated between 4,500 and 5,000.

Percussion 31 caliber. Five-shot round cylinder. 3" octagon barrel.

Grips of gutta percha with smooth finish. Blued overall finish with casehardened hammer and german silver trigger guard. Few specimens with iron trigger guards scarce; worth premium in value (Earliest trigger guards brass, silver plated. Worth small premium).

Serial numbered in batches located underside of barrel, top inside of trigger guard, left side of buttstrap and bottom of grip. Barrel marking: F. BEAL'S PATENT, JUNE 24, '56 & MAY 26, '57on all variations except the earliest (as shown below). Topstrap over the cylinder markings as shown below. Cone front sights usual. Some early ones dovetailed blade type german silver.

A major distinguishing feature is the outside mounted pawl on the left frame which serves to rotate the cylinder. On all variations except the last (see below) it is a short, curved arm (as illus.).

The Beals was Remington's first revolver. Its introduction coincided with the expiration of Samuel Colt's master patent in 1857.

The terminology adopted to identify these variations is that assigned by the pioneer study published October, 1960 in *GUN REPORT*:

Issue 1. Markings appear on the topstrap only in 4 lines F. BEALS' PATENT/JUNE 24, 1856/REMINGTONS/ILION N.Y. Barrel unmarked. Wide cylinder locking notches between nipples also act as hammer rests:

5E-001   Values—Good **$500**   Fine **$1,200**

5E-001

Issue 2 and Issue 3. Topstrap markings REMINGTONS'/ILION, N.Y. Very narrow locking notches (do not act as hammer rest) between nipples:

5E-001.4   Values—Good **$325**   Fine **$875**

Issue 4. Topstrap markings MANUFACTURED by/REMINGTONS'/ILION N.Y. No locking notches; the nipple

wells serve as notches:

5E-001.6   Values—Good **$325**   Fine **$875**

Issue 5. Topstrap markings and nipple wells as locking notches identical to Issue 4. The frame mounted pawl is round, identical to that on the Beals 2nd Model below:

5E-001.8   Values—Good **$450**   Fine **$1,000**

Remington-Beals Prototype "Army" Revolver

Prototype Beals "Army" Percussion Revolver. Made c 1856; quantity unknown, likely under 10.

Percussion 44 caliber. 8-inch octagon barrel. 6-shot round cylinder. Single action. 2-piece walnut grips. No provision for loading lever.

Very little known or recorded of this huge revolver. Immediately identifiable by its near-identical profile to the First Model "Pocket Revolver" as above. Two specimens are thus far identified bearing serial numbers under 10. Markings on top of frame **F. BEALS PATENT JUNE 24TH, 1856.** As with the First Model Pocket Revolver this huge handgun (measuring 12 inches overall) has wide cylinder locking notches between nipples which also act as hammer rests.

Illustrated and described here as an example of the type of antique firearm that always has the possibility of showing up at

5E-001.9

the least expected moment and...possibly place! An extreme rarity with others possibly waiting to be discovered! Value estimated mid-five figure range.
5E-001.9

Remington-Beals 2nd Model Pocket Revolver

5E-002

Second Model Beals Pocket Revolver. Made c. 1858-1859. Quantity likely under 1,000.

Percussion 31 caliber. Five-shot round cylinder. 3" octagon barrel.

An improved version of the First Model, it differed as follows: Squared butt; checkered hard rubber or walnut grips; spur type trigger; outside disc pawl on left side of frame. Barrel markings: BEALS PATENT 1856 & 57, MANUFACTURED BY REMINGTONS' ILION, N.Y. Serial numbers on bottom of barrel and left gripstrap (beneath grips) from 1 to approximately 1000: cylinders either plain or acid etched with floral designs (worth premium).
5E-002   Values—Good **$2,250**   Fine **$8,500**

Remington-Beals 3rd Model Pocket Revolver

Third Model Beals Pocket Revolver. Made c. 1859-1860. Total quantity about 1,000.

Percussion; 31 caliber. Five-shot round cylinder, 4" octagon barrel, spur type trigger.

Grips of checkered hard rubber (variant shown in illus.) having squared butt profile. Blued overall finish.

Serial numbered in batches; located under barrel and left side of butt frame. Barrel marking: BEALS PAT. 1856, 57, 58 and MANUFACTURED BY REMINGTONS', ILION, N.Y.

Larger than its predecessors, it is the only Beals pocket revolver fitted with a rammer type loading lever. The lever must be lowered before the center pin (type also used on large frame

5E-003

Beals Army and Navy revolvers) can be removed. Cylinder length is 1-5/8" as compared to 1-1/8" on Second Model:
5E-003   Values—Good **$800**   Fine **$3,250**

Remington-Rider Pocket Revolver

Rider Pocket Model Revolver. Made c. 1860 to 1873 in percussion with altered specimens made for 32RF metallic cartridge after 1873. Estimated quantity approximately 2,000 total both types.

Percussion, 31 caliber. Five-shot mushroom shaped cylinder. 3" octagon barrel. Large, oval shaped German silver trigger guard.

Checkered hard rubber grips. Standard finishes either blued with silver-plated frame if percussion model, blued with nickel-

plated frame (or full nickel) if conversion model. Values same for all types.

Serial numbers under barrel, under grip and inside trigger bow. Barrel marking: MANUFACTURED BY REMINGTONS', ILION, N.Y., RIDERS PT. AUG, 17, 1858 MAY 3, 1859.

This distinctive double action revolver was designed by Joseph Rider of Newark, Ohio. Remington's contracted with Rider for the manufacture of the Pocket Model, and he became a

5E-004

5E-005

valued employee of the company, moving to Ilion. One of the first double action revolvers made in quantity in the United States, in its factory conversion to metallic cartridge form it was probably the first American double action cartridge revolver. A few variations have been noted—early specimens have dovetailed cone type front sight while later production had the pin type front sight.

Percussion Model:

5E-004	Values—Good **$300**	Fine **$950**

Factory Conversion to Metallic Cartridge: Factory installed newly made cylinder with removable cover at rear in place of percussion cylinder; slight modification of hammer to allow interchangeable use of percussion or cartridge cylinders. Those leaving factory as original cartridge are serial numbered on frame ahead of trigger. Later production without capping groove. 3" barrel standard; 2-1/2" and 2" scarce, worth premium (2" marked only "REMINGTON'S/ILION, N.Y."):

5E-005	Values—Very Good **$275**	Exc. **$700**

Remington-Beals Army Model Revolver

5E-006

Beals Army Model Revolver. Made c. 1861-1862. Quantity made estimated 1,900. 50 percent to 80 percent to U.S. Army. It is known that almost the same quantity was also purchased on the open market; such revolvers will not bear government inspector marks.

Percussion; 44 caliber. Six-shot round cylinder. 8" octagon barrel with barrel threads concealed by frame. Cylinders do not have safety notches.

Walnut grips. Blued finish with casehardened hammer and blued loading lever. German silver cone sight; high spur hammer.

Serial numbered from 1 on up; located under barrel, on side of grip frame and inside trigger guard tab. Barrel marking: BEALS PATENT SEPT. 14, 1858/MANUFACTURED BY REMINGTONS' ILION, N.Y.

The small caliber Beals pocket types were quickly followed by Remington's first large frame, large caliber Navy and, later, Army revolvers. From these early 44 and 36 caliber handguns evolved improved models, produced in greater quantities, and soon giving rival makers—particularly Colts—stiff competition.

Standard Beals Army:

5E-006	Values—Good **$1,150**	Fine **$3,750**

Martially marked Beals Army: Usually observed in serial number range above 725 (lowest number thus far recorded) (previously 859). Recent information from archives reveals 750 passed U.S. inspection. Such marked specimens are quite rare, however. Due to known pressure to get the guns delivered and production problems at factory it's possible many not marked; equally possible they suffered high attrition rate:

5E-007	Values—Good **$1,400**	Fine **$7,500**

Remington-Beals Navy Model Revolver

Beals Navy Model Revolver. Made c. 1861-1862. Total quantity estimated at 14,500. Substantially identical in appearance to the Beals Army, but slightly smaller.

Percussion; 36 caliber. Six-shot round cylinder without safety notches. 7-1/2" octagon barrel; barrel threads concealed by frame.

Walnut grips. Blued finish with casehardened high spur hammer; cone sight.

Serial numbered from 1 on up and overlapping numbers in the Model 1861 Navy range. Barrel marking: BEALS PATENT SEPT. 14, 1858/MANUFACTURED BY REMINGTONS' ILION, N.Y.

Early production: Has small integral rod extension (about 1-1/2") forward of the single wing cylinder pin and fitting into a slot in the rammer lever in order that the cylinder pin could not be withdrawn. Very limited production, estimated 200 and all fall in serial range under #200:

5E-008	Values—Good **$950**	Fine **$4,000**

Standard Beals Navy; double wing cylinder pin:

5E-009	Values—Good **$750**	Fine **$2,250**

5E-008

Martially marked: Approximately 400 to 500 made were sold to the U.S. Army and bear martial markings. Specimens quite scarce: most in serial range 13,000 to 15,000:

5E-010	Values—Good **$900**	Fine **$3,000**

U.S. Navy Marked: An unknown quantity, likely under 1,000, were acquired by the Navy early in the Civil War directly from Remington and possibly some on the open commercial market. They have no identifying martial markings. In 1866 the Navy took inventory of its small arms; those still serviceable were marked with a small, deep-struck anchor on the barrel near the frame (some still aboard vessels and smaller stations were overlooked and not so-marked.) Such specimens are rare; buyers are advised to exercise extreme caution as spurious anchor markings are known:

5E-010.4 Values—Good **$1,400** Fine **$4,000**

U.S. Navy Conversion To 38 Centerfire: In 1875 the Navy returned to the factory 1,000 various models Remington 36 percussion revolvers for conversion to 38CF; the "IMPROVED DESIGN" with ejector rod and loading gate. Included were a small, unknown quantity of Beals (see above item 5E-010.4) Some, not all, had anchor marking. It is assumed that all Beals Navies thusly converted were part of that contract as Remington's only known conversion of this model was for this contract; none commercially:

5E-010.6 Values—Good **$850** Fine **$3,000**

Remington 1861 Army Revolver

Model 1861 Army Revolver, a.k.a. "Old Model Army." Made c. 1862. Total quantity estimated 6,000.

Percussion; 44 caliber. Six-shot round cylinder. 8" octagon barrel. Early manufacture used the Beals type frame with *concealed barrel threads at breech*; about mid-production the exposed barrel thread frame (as illustrated) introduced. German silver cone sight.

Walnut grips. Blued finish with casehardened high spur hammer. Serial numbering commenced at the end of Beals Army production, continuing to approximately #15000. Barrel marking: PATENTED DEC. 17, 1861/MANUFACTURED BY REMINGTONS', ILION, N.Y.

Quick identification made by noting the channel cut along top of loading lever to allow removal of the cylinder pin without lowering the lever. This feature was actually found not acceptable for military service and many were returned to the factory to have the rammer channel blocked by a filister screw, making it necessary to drop/open the loading lever to remove the cylinder pin. General shape of Remington percussion revolvers was introduced by the 1861 Army and prevailed to the end of percussion revolver production. On late manufactured specimens safety notches were introduced at the rear of the cylinder and loading lever changed to New Model type.

Apparently almost all production went to fill U.S. government orders and therefore almost all specimens will bear military markings (inspector stamps on left grip usually). Civilian, or non-military marked weapons, although scarcer, will not bring premium values. Most show heavy wear. Better condition specimens scarce.

Martially marked standard percussion model:

5E-011

5E-011 Values—Good **$750** Fine **$2,500**

Factory Conversion To Metallic Cartridge: Few, if any, believed converted by Remington. All thus far observed have been non-factory. Specimens, if proven factory work:

5E-012 Values—Good **$850** Fine **$2,500**

Remington 1861 Navy Revolver

Model 1861 Navy Revolver, a.k.a. "Old Model Navy." (Not illus.) Made c. 1862. Total quantity estimated at 7,000. Substantially identical to Model 1861 Army, but slightly smaller.

Percussion; 36 caliber. Six-shot round cylinder. 7-3/8" octagon barrel. Early manufacture used the Beals type frame with concealed barrel threads at breech; about mid-production exposed barrel threads introduced. In late production cylinder safety notches also introduced. Cone sight.

Walnut grips. Blued finish with casehardened high spur hammer.

Serial numbered from end of Beals Navy production. Barrel marking: PATENTED DEC. 17, 1861/MANUFACTURED BY REMINGTONS' ILION, N.Y.

As on the Model 1861 Army, there is a channel cut along the top of the loading lever which acts as a major feature of identification. It appears that almost all production of this model, too, went to fill U.S. government orders and hence, almost all will be found with military markings. Those without same, which would be considered quite scarce, will not necessarily bring a premium value.

Martially marked standard percussion model:

5E-013 Values—Good **$750** Fine **$2,250**

U.S. Navy purchased; As with the Beals Navy #5E-010.4, likely under 1,000 purchased direct from Remington, etc. Other circumstances, details, markings identical for U.S.N. Beals (q.v.):

5E-013.5 Values—Good **$950** Fine **$3,250**

Factory conversion to metallic cartridge: None believed converted by Remington for the civilian/commercial market. See 5E-014.6 below and 5E-010.6 for same circumstances:
5E-014

Factory conversion with Army markings None believed to have been altered:
5E-014.5

U.S. Navy conversion to .38 centerfire: Circumstances identical to those of the Beals U.S.N conversions 5E-010.6 (q.v.). Small quantity of M. 1861 Navies returned to Remington as part of the 1,000 piece conversion contract, 1875:

5E-014.6 Values—Good **$700** Fine **$2,000**

Remington New Model Army Revolver

New Model Army Revolver. Made c. 1863-1875. Total quantity estimated approximately 122,000.

Percussion; 44 caliber. Six-shot round cylinder. 8" octagon barrel; threads visible at breech end. Safety notches on cylinder shoulders between nipples.

Walnut grips. Blued finish; casehardened low spur hammer. Screw-in type steel front sight on most; early production had mortised cone sight of the 1861 model. Grip frame reduced 3/16".

Serial numbers continue from Model 1861 Army and commence approximately in the 15000 range, cylinders usually

5E-015
Standard Model

unnumbered. Barrel marking: PATENTED SEPT. 14, 1858/E. REMINGTON & SONS, ILION, NEW YORK, U.S.A./NEW MODEL

One of the major handguns of the Civil War, the New Model Army was the stiffest competitor to Colt's Model 1860 Army. The New Model Army was also the last of Remington's 44 caliber percussion revolvers. The famous showman William F. "Buffalo Bill" Cody carried a "New Model Army" c. 1866-mid 1870's for buffalo hunting and the Indian Wars and claimed "It never failed me."

Standard model; with government inspector stamping on left grip (initials within cartouche) and sub-inspector initials on various other parts. Total about 106,000:
5E-015   Values—Good **$700**   Fine **$2,500**
Civilian specimens; lacking government inspector markings: quantity approximately 15,000:
5E-016   Values—Good **$700**   Fine **$2,000**
State of New Jersey purchases; marked N.J. on barrel. Acquired by the state for Civil War issue. 1,000 purchased under contract and most are found in quite fine states of condition:
5E-017   Values—Good **$700**   Fine **$2,000**
Transitional model. Three varieties of transitional types between the Model 1861 and New Model have been observed, almost all appearing within the 10000 to 22000 serial range: Old

Model style markings without "New Model." Other earlier features also noted as carry-over from Model 1861:
5E-018   Values—Good **$700**   Fine **$2,250**
Factory conversion to accept metallic cartridges. Both 5-shot and 6-shot. Calibers 46 rimfire or 44 rimfire and centerfire, and 45 centerfire. Made both with and without ejector rods; Rollin White markings on cylinder: PATENTED APR 3'd 1855 worth premium. Many non-factory, private gunsmith conversions are encountered on this *New Model* and unless some documented history of use and/or circumstances of conversion, their values are considerably less than factory types:
5E-019   Values—Good **$650**   Fine **$1,750**

5E-019
Conversion with Ejector

5E-019
Conversion without Ejector

Remington New Model Navy Revolver

New Model Navy Revolver. (Not illus.) Made c. 1863-1878. Total quantity approximately 28,000. Substantially identical to New Model Army, but smaller.

Percussion; 36 caliber. Six-shot round cylinder. 7-3/8" octagon barrel; threads visible at breech end. Safety notches on cylinder shoulders between nipples.

Walnut grips. Blued finish; casehardened low spur hammer.

Serial numbers from about 23000 continuing from the Model 1861 Navy. Barrel marking: PATENTED SEPT. 14, 1858/E. REMINGTON & SONS, ILION, NEW YORK U.S.A./NEW MODEL As with the Army Model, this New Model Navy proved to be a stiff competitor to its Colt counterpart.

Standard model, non-military marked:
5E-020   Values—Good **$800**   Fine **$2,250**
Martially marked model; Contrary to earlier descriptions, as far as can be determined there were NO "New Model" Navies purchased by the Army. The U.S. Navy purchased 4300, none of which are known to have government markings (small individual letter markings on various parts are internal factory

applied). In 1866 the Navy took inventory of its smallarms; those still serviceable were then marked with a small anchor on the barrel near the frame (some still aboard vessels and at small stations were overlooked and not marked). Caution is recommended before acquiring specimens with the anchor marking as spurious examples known:
5E-021   Values—Good **$900**   Fine **$3,000**
Factory conversion to breech-loading metallic cartridge. Calibers 38 centerfire or rimfire. Made c. 1873 to 1888. Many of these were not conversions, but actually left the factory as cartridge revolvers:
5E-022   Values—Good **$600**   Fine **$1,600**
U.S. Navy conversion to 38 centerfire: In 1875 the Navy gave Remington a contract to convert 1,000 36 caliber of their percussion revolvers to 38CF "IMPROVED DESIGN" with ejector rod and loading gate. The large majority of the 1000 pieces the Navy returned were "New Models". (see 5E-010.6 & 5E-014.6 also). Values for anchor marked specimens:
5E-022.5   Values—Good **$850**   Fine **$1,900**

Remington New Model S/A Belt Revolver

New Model (Single Action) Belt Revolver. Made c. 1865-1873 in percussion; made in cartridge subsequent to 1873. Total quantity estimated from 2,500 to 3,000.

Percussion; 36 caliber. Six-shot round cylinder. 6-1/2" octagon barrel; threads visible at breech end. Safety notches on cylinder shoulders between nipples.

Walnut grips. Blued finish; casehardened hammer. Some

specimens nickel plated throughout or with nickel plated frame and balance blued. Values about the same.

Serial numbered with the Remington-Rider New Model Double Action revolver. Barrel marking: PATENTED SEPT. 14, 1858/E. REMINGTON & SONS, ILION, NEW YORK U.S.A./NEW MODEL

A smaller version of the New Model Navy, quick means of identification are the screws which enter the frame from the right side, and the short barrel length.

Standard model as described above:

Some early specimens were made on the double action style frame, identification made by placement of mainspring and will bring premium:

5E-023   Values—Good **$475**   Fine **$1,400**

Factory conversion to breech-loading to accept metallic cartridges; 38 caliber.

5E-024   Values—Good **$450**   Fine **$1,250**

5E-023

Remington-Rider D/A New Model Belt Revolver

Double Action New Model Belt Revolver. Made c. 1863-1873 in percussion with subsequent production as metallic cartridge. Total quantity estimated at 3,000 to 5,000.

Percussion; 36 caliber. Six-shot round cylinder. 6-1/2" octagon barrel; threads visible at breech end. Safety notches on cylinder shoulders between nipples.

Walnut grips. Blued finish; casehardened hammer. Some specimens overall nickel plated or with nickeled frame and balance blued. Values about the same all types. (Silver finished worth premium)

Serial numbered, probably along with the New Model Single Action Belt revolver. Usual barrel marking: MANUFACTURED BY REMINGTONS', ILION, N.Y./RIDER'S PT. AUG. 17, 1858, MAY 3, 1859. Later specimens and most conversions marked PATENTED SEPT. 14, 1858/E. REMINGTON & SONS, ILION, NEW YORK, U.S.A./NEW MODEL

One of easiest of Remingtons to identify with its distinctive double action mechanism. Screws enter on right side of frame.

Standard model as described above:

5E-025   Values—Good **$650**   Fine **$2,250**

Fluted cylinder models earliest production c1863-65.; identical to above, but with a distinctive full fluted cylinder found on 3-digit or lower numbered specimens. Estimated at few hundred produced:

5E-026   Values—Good **$850**   Fine **$3,000**

Factory conversion to breech-loading metallic cartridge; 38 caliber with special factory installed two-piece cylinder. Variations in sights have been noted. As with other conversions loading levers have been left intact:

5E-027   Values—Good **$600**   Fine **$1,500**

5E-025
Standard Model

5E-026
Fluted Cylinder Model

5E-027
Factory Conversion

Remington New Model Police Revolver

New Model Police Revolver. Made c. 1865-1873 in percussion with subsequent production as factory alterations to cartridge. Total quantity estimated at 18,000.

Percussion; 36 caliber. Five-shot round cylinder with safety notches on cylinder shoulder. Octagon barrels in varying lengths 3-1/2", 4-1/2", 5-1/2", and 6-1/2". (6-1/2" length brings small premium.)

Walnut grips. Blued finish. Casehardened hammer. Other finishes overall nickel plated or nickel plated frame with balance blued. Values about same for all types (silver finished worth premium).

Serial numbered from 1 on up. Barrel marking: PATENTED SEPT. 14, 1858 MARCH 17, 1863/E. REMINGTON & SONS, ILION, NEW YORK U.S.A./NEW MODEL

5E-028
Standard Model

5E-029
Factory Conversion

Designed to compete with the Colt Model 1862 Police and Pocket Navy revolvers, this arm was a scaled down version of the Remington Navy and Belt Models. Frame screws enter from right side.

Standard model in original, unaltered percussion as described; scarce:

5E-028   Values—Good **$475**   Fine **$1,200**

Note: Altered/converted models (as below) with percussion cylinders only worth 20 percent less.

Factory conversion to metallic cartridge; All believed made for 38 Rimfire only. Special two piece factory cylinder and frame alteration to accept it. Majority of this model made as alterations and original cartridge. Offered by factory with spare, interchangeable perc./ctg. cylinders; worth premium if present:

5E-029   Values—Good **$375**   Fine **$1,000**

Remington New Model Pocket Revolver

New Model Pocket Revolver. Made c. 1865-1873 in percussion; subsequent production as metallic cartridge conversions. Total quantity estimated at 25,000. Majority made as conversion or as original cartridge.

Percussion; 31 caliber. Five-shot round cylinder; safety notches on cylinder shoulders. Octagon barrels of 3", 3-1/2", 4", 4-1/2", the latter two being quite scarce and bring premium values.

Walnut grips. Blued finish; casehardened hammer. Varying finishes including overall nickeled or nickeled frame and balance blued with prices about the same for all types (silver finish worth premium).

Serial numbered from 1 on up. Barrel marking: PATENTED SEPT. 14, 1858 MARCH 17, 1863/E. REMINGTON & SONS, ILION, NEW YORK U.S.A./NEW MODEL(1858 date only same value).

Quickly identified by its distinctive spur trigger and very small frame size.

First Type; earliest production; percussion. As described above, but all brass frame and brass sheath/spur trigger. (A very small undetermined quantity, starting with serial No. 1, have iron spur triggers; worth premium):

5E-030   Values—Good **$875**   Fine **$2,750**

Second Type; in original/unaltered percussion. Identical to above, but iron frame with brass sheath/spur trigger:

5E-031   Values—Good **$400**   Fine **$1,200**

Third Type; in original/unaltered percussion. Identical, but all iron throughout including sheath/spur trigger:

5E-032   Values—Good **$350**   Fine **$850**

Note: Altered 2nd and 3rd types with percussion cylinder worth 20 percent less.

Factory conversion to metallic cartridge: 32 Rimfire only. Special factory two piece cylinder. Offered (optional) with interchangeable percussion cylinder; worth premium if present:

5E-033   Values—Good **$265**   Fine **$475**

5E-031
Second Type

5E-033
Factory Conversion

Remington-Rider Single Shot Deringer

Rider Single Shot Deringer, a.k.a. "Parlor Pistol." Made c. 1860-1863. Total quantity estimated at 200.

5E-034

Percussion; 17 caliber. All brass 3" barrel integral with the all brass frame. Two-piece breech (the basis for the patent).

Brass grips also integral with frame and barrel. Finish standard as silver plated throughout.

Not serial numbered. Barrel marking: RIDER'S PT./SEPT 13, 1859.

Smallest of all Remington pistols, very little data is known about this model. The sole propellant force was the percussion cap. Buyer is urged to be extremely wary of spurious specimens:

5E-034   Values—Very Good **$3,750**   Exc. **$8,000**

Remington Zig-Zag Deringer

Zig-Zag Deringer, a.k.a. "Zig-Zag Pepperbox." (Original 1862 factory advertising termed it "Elliot's Pocket Revolver.") Made c. 1861-1862. Total less than 1,000.

22 rimfire short caliber. Six-shot barrel cluster with zig-zag grooves at breech end, a key part of the revolving mechanism. 3-3/16" barrel group. Ring type trigger; double action system with concealed hammer. Loads through port in frame at breech. Hard rubber grips. Blue or silver finish or combination of both. Screws enter frame from left side on some specimens, right side

5E-035

on others, there apparently being no continuity on this feature. Variations also observed on mainspring set screws.

Serial numbered on left grip frame under grips. Markings: ELLIOT'S PATENT/AUG. 17, 1858/MAY 29, 1860., and MANUFACTURED BY REMINGTON'S, ILION, N.Y.

Remington's first handgun designed for metallic cartridge ammunition. Patented by William H. Elliot, who became one of the company's more prolific inventors:

5E-035 Values—Good **$1,250** Fine **$3,750**

Remington-Elliot Deringer 22RF

Elliot Deringer 22RF, a.k.a. "Pepperbox." (Termed by Remington as their "New Repeating Pistol [Elliot's Pat.] No. 1"). Made c. 1863-1870's. Total quantity combined for this 22 caliber (estimated 30 percent of total) with the larger 32 caliber model about 25,000.

22 rimfire caliber. Five-shot stationary barrel cluster with revolving firing pin; barrels fluted and 3" overall. Ring type trigger. Barrel group tilts forward for loading and extraction.

Hard rubber, rosewood or walnut grips. Blued or silver finish or full nickel plated or nickeled frame with balance blued. Blue finish usually brings premium.

Serial numbered bottom of barrel and inside frame. Barrel markings MANUFACTURED BY E. REMINGTON & SONS, ILION, N.Y./ELLIOT'S PATENTS/MAY 29, 1860-OCT. 1, 1861.

5E-036

An improved version of the Zig-Zag Deringer, this new pistol was made in the greatest quantity of any Remington ring trigger pistol:

5E-036 Values—Good **$385** Fine **$1,000**

Remington-Elliot Deringer 32RF

Elliot Deringer 32RF, a.k.a. "Pepperbox." (Termed by Remington as their "New Repeating Pistol [Elliot's Pat.] No.2.") Made c. 1863-1888. Total quantity of this (estimated 70 percent of total) and the 22 caliber type about 25,000.

32 caliber rimfire. Four-shot stationary barrel cluster. Barrels 3-3/8" in length and ribbed. The gun otherwise has all features and details similar to that described above for the 22 caliber model:

5E-037 Values—Good **$350** Fine **$875**

5E-037

5E-037

5E-038

Remington Vest Pocket Pistol

Vest Pocket Pistol, a.k.a. "Saw Handle Deringer." (Termed by Remington as their "No. 1" size.) Made c. 1865-1888. Total quantity estimated approximately 17,000 to 20,000.

22 rimfire caliber. Single shot with hammer doubling as breechblock. 3-1/4" round barrel with octagon breech made integral with frame.

Walnut grips. Overall blued, silver or nickel plated finish or combination of two.

Serial numbered underside of barrel and grip frame. Barrel marking: REMINGTON'S ILION, N.Y. PATENT OCT. 1, 1861 with early production completely unmarked.

5E-038

This unusual and quite distinctive small deringer type pistol was another invention of William H. Elliot:

5E-038   Values—Good **$275**   Fine **$800**

Remington Vest Pocket Pistol

Vest Pocket Pistol, a.k.a. "Saw Handle Deringer." Made c. 1865-1888. Total quantity estimated at 15,000 or less. Calibers 30, 32, and 41 rimfire (38 rimfire often listed, but improbable such caliber ever made; most likely due to misgauging the 41 caliber model). Barrel lengths as noted below. Split breech type action.

Rosewood or walnut grips. Blued, silver or nickeled finish overall or combination of two.

Serial numbered. Barrel marking: REMINGTON'S. ILION, N.Y./PATD. OCT. 1, 1861. NOV. 15, 1864. (These two dates referring to both the Elliot and Rider Patents.)
Standard model in 41 caliber rimfire. 4" part octagon/part round barrel; termed by factory their "No. 3" size. Quantity estimated 14,000:
5E-039   Values—Good **$425**   Fine **$1,250**
32 rimfire caliber; Quantity estimated 300-500. Long thought to be custom ordered this caliber appears in their 1870 catalog as a standard gun known as their "No. 2" size. 3-1/2" part

5E-039

octagon/part round barrel; iron frame standard; brass frame on early models rare and will bring premium value. 30 rimfire caliber rare. Quantity estimated 500. Will bring premium:
5E-040   Values—Good **$450**   Fine **$1,250**
Note: According to 1997 Hatfield study quantities for .30 and .32 cals larger than indicated here. Based on assumptions that each caliber numbered in separate series, data may be erroneous. Empirical evidence in the marketplace would appear to negate the findings of the survey.

Remington-Elliot Single Shot Deringer

5E-041

Elliot Single Shot Deringer. (Factory termed it "Vest Pocket Deringer Pistol [Elliot's Patent]".) Made c. 1867-1888. Total

quantity estimated approximately 10,000 (likely less).

41 rimfire caliber. 2-1/2" round barrel screwed into frame. An ingenious mechanism consisting of trigger, combination hammer-breechblock and mainspring.

Walnut grips. Blued, silver or nickel plated finish or combination of two. Values about the same.

Serial numbered under barrel. Barrel marking: REMINGTONS, ILION, N.Y. ELLIOT PAT. AUG. 27, 1867.

Another creation of William H. Elliot's, this unusual, diminutive pistol is one of the most practical of American deringers:

5E-041   Values—Good **$675**   Fine **$1,500**

Remington Double Deringer

Double Deringer, a.k.a. "Model 95 Double Deringer," a.k.a. "Over-Under Deringer." Made c. 1866-1935. Total quantity estimated at over 150,000.

41 rimfire short. 3" round, superposed barrels; tips upward for loading and extraction, locked by a pivoting key on right side of frame. Firing pin automatically switched from barrel to barrel.

Walnut, rosewood or checkered hard rubber grips. Blued or nickeled finish or combination thereof. Serial numbering varied; some in sequence, but most in batches. Orderly sequences difficult to access. Barrel markings as below.

Another design of William H. Elliot, the Double Deringer is probably the best known of all American deringer type pistols.

The fact that it remained on the market for 69 years is evidence of its exceptional merit, practicality and popularity.

Major types as shown below are divided by marking differences. All types except for the earliest production of Type I have manual extractor between barrels.

CAUTION: Inspect specimens closely. A cracked or broken barrel hinge is a common fault and will decrease value up to 50 percent.
Type I, Early Production, a.k.a. Model No. 1. Made without extractor. Barrel markings in center ribs between barrels on each side: E. REMINGTON & SONS, ILION, N.Y. on one side; ELLIOT'S PATENT DEC. 12, 1865 on opposite side. Made c. 1866. Quantity estimated at under 2000.

Note: Less than 100 of the initial production of this Type I, Early production had rare variant markings with words MANUFACTURED BY preceding the usual E. REMINGTON & SONS marks. Serials under 100. Very rare and worth premium:

5E-042   Values—Good **$750**   Fine **$2,500**

Type I, Transitional, a.k.a. Model No. 1, First Variant. Markings same as above in center ribs between barrels. Made c. 1867-1868; with extractor. Quantity estimated only 100:

5E-043   Values—Good **$850**   Fine **$2,750**

Type I, Late Production, a.k.a. Model No. 2. Markings identical to above, but are in two lines along the top of the upper barrel. Has extractor. Made c. 1868. Estimated quantity 14,000:

5E-044   Values—Good **$325**   Fine **$850**

Type II, a.k.a. Model No. 3. Marked REMINGTON ARMS CO., ILION, N.Y. in one line along top of upper barrel. Made c. 1888-1911. Estimated quantity 80,000:

5E-045   Values—Good **$275**   Fine **$775**

Type III, a.k.a. Model No. 4. Marked REMINGTON ARMS - U.M.C. CO., ILION, N.Y. in one line along top of upper barrel. Made c. 1912-1935. Estimated quantity 55,000:

5E-042

5E-046   Values—Good **$275**   Fine **$775**

Type III, Late Production, a.k.a. Model No. 4, Third Variation. Although estimated production c. 1935, more likely WWI era because of serial range. Marked as above. Simple fluting between barrels (instead of the distinctive rib). Hammer grooved instead of knurled. Matte type gray-blue finish. Quantity estimated at 500:

5E-046.5   Values—Very Good **$850**   Exc. **$2,000**

Remington-Rider Magazine Pistol

Rider Magazine Pistol. Made c. 1871 to 1888. Total quantity estimated approximately 15,000 (likely less). They were not serial-numbered.

32 rimfire extra-short. Five-shot magazine located below the 3" octagon barrel. Breechblock/cartridge carrier device positioned adjacent to hammer; magazine loads from muzzle end.

Walnut grips standard, although often encountered with rosewood, pearl or ivory. All parts nickel plated most often encountered. Also seen with casehardened frame and blued barrel, but quite scarce and will bring premium. Barrel marking: E. REMINGTON & SONS, ILION, N.Y./RIDERS PAT. AUG. 15, 1871.

This Joseph Rider invention is one of the most unusual of nineteenth century pocket pistols and one of the first metallic cartridge weapons using a tubular magazine. One of the few instances in American arms where engraved specimens are more commonly encountered than plain, unembellished ones. The latter, though scarcer, do not bring higher prices:

5E-047   Values—Very Good **$800**   Exc. **$2,500**

5E-047

Remington-Smoot Revolvers (and Celluloid Grips)

The **Remington-Smoot Breech-Loading Metallic Cartridge Revolver.** Although classified and termed throughout most modern literature on the subject of Remington arms as the New Line Revolvers (Numbers 1, 2, 3, and 4), it appears that they have suffered an injustice. No such terms were applied by Remington who named them in their sales literature as both **Remington No. 1 Revolver** or **Smoot's Patent-New Model**. It is felt that factory nomenclature on these should be used and reintroduced to the language of collecting. Blue finish specimens in all models are scarce and worth premium.

These Remington-Smoot Models No. 1 through No. 4 Revolvers are occasionally found with **ivory-like grips made of celluloid.** An obvious oddity and one that piqued the curiosity of a few advanced collectors. The origins, and the material itself, remained unexamined (merely termed, as an expedient, "ivory" or taken for granted as ivory) until publication in the June, 1990 *Bulletin* of the Remington Society in an article by Dr. H. H. Parker (and his later *Study of Remington's Smoot...Revolvers*). It was then proven conclusively that the material was indeed, celluloid. Many of those grips (but not all) are fitted on the underside with a cast metal backing plate, thought to strengthen and provide stability for the grips. No Remington catalogs of the era ever mentioned the use of celluloid, furthering the enigma. Neither was there any distinction made when "ivory grips" were offered as options for prospective buyers. One might be tempted to ridicule celluloid as just a cheap imitation of ivory, or disparage Remington for deviousness for its use. However, there may be more to the story than first meets the eye. Cursory research of "celluloid" credits its invention as the first successful plastic material that introduced the beginnings of a major world industry. Invented in 1868 by an Albany, New York printer J.W. Hyatt, celluloid was patented in 1870; first commercial use evidently for dental plates. Production continued in 1871 by the "Celluloid Manufacturing Company" of Albany ("Celluloid" registered as a trade name with the U.S. Patent office, 1873). The wide uses for the material spawned vigorous growth in the expanding plastics industry; between 1872 and 1880 sixteen companies were licensed for the production of various products and novelties made from material (Remington not among them). Although conjecture infers that Remington manufactured the ivory-appearing grips, there is reason to believe it was not the case. However, Remington was certainly among the first to recognize the potential of that material for grips. With both inventor and earliest manufacture of "Celluloid" in close proximity to the Remington Factory (and concurrent with Remington's use of it) there is, ostensibly, more to the story than first meets the eye. It has the makings of an interesting sidelight to the history of these **SMOOT REVOLVERS**...worth of the efforts of an enterprising researcher.

Remington-Smoot New Model No. 1 Revolver

No. 1 Revolver—New Model (Smoot's Patent); probably most easily termed Remington-Smoot New Model No. 1, a.k.a. erroneously "New Line Revolver No. 1." Made c. 1875-1877. Estimated quantity 3,000.

30 rimfire short. Five-shot cylinder 13/16" overall. 2-13/16" octagon barrel integral with frame.

Walnut or checkered hard rubber grips. Blued (scarce) or full nickel plated finish.

Serial numbered. Barrel marking: E. REMINGTON & SONS, ILION, N.Y./ PAT. W. S. SMOOT OCT. 21, 1873.

A competitor to the Colt line of metallic cartridge pocket revolvers, the Remington-Smoot featured an unusual design in which the frame, barrel and ejector housing were all of one piece. The rod ejector was another special design. It differs from the "New Model No. 2" noticeably stepped-down about one inch below the ball tip.

5E-049

Early production; revolving recoil shield. Made 1875. Estimated quantity 650. *Very scarce:*
5E-048   Values—Very Good **$550**   Exc. **$1,500**
Standard model; total made 2300. Recoil shield solid, affixed rigidly to frame:
5E-049   Values—Very Good **$200**   Exc. **$550**

Remington-Smoot New Model No. 2 Revolver

No. 2 Revolver—New Model (Smoot's Patent); probably most easily termed Remington-Smoot New Model No. 2, a.k.a. erroneously "New Line Revolver No. 2." (Not illus.; about identical in contours to New Model No. 1.) Made c. 1877-1885. Total of approximately 3,000.

32 rimfire short and 30 rimfire short. Five-shot cylinder 7/8" long. 2-3/4" octagon barrel forged integral with frame.

Checkered hard rubber grips. Blued (scarce) or full nickel plated finish.

Serial numbered 1 to approximately 2000. Barrel marking identical to New Model No. 1. Believed made only with solid recoil shield.

A unique and confusing feature is the two calibers in which this Model No. 2 is found, the 30 rimfire being made simultaneously with the Model No. 1 in the same caliber.

Extensive research and survey of this Model No. 2 reveals that approximately one-third of production (about 600 pieces) were in 30 r.f. while the balance of 1,400 were 32 r.f. Some difficulty will be encountered in distinguishing each variant as they are identical in size and contour. Best and basic method is by an accurate caliber gauge and actually fitting a case in the respective chamber. Other differences are in a stepped-down ejector rod on the Model No. 2 versus a non-stepped rod in the Model No. 2. When viewed from the front, there is a thicker wall on the cylinder of the 30 r.f. Serial numbers seem to fall in the lower ranges on the 30 caliber model also.

32 caliber type:
5E-050   Values—Very Good **$225**   Exc. **$550**
30 caliber type:
5E-050.5   Values—Very Good **$250**   Exc. **$600**

Remington-Smoot New Model No. 3 Revolver

No. 3 Revolver—New Model (Smoot's Patent); probably most easily termed Remington-Smoot New Model No. 3, a.k.a. erroneously "New Line Revolver No. 3." Made c. 1878-1888. The total estimated of about 25,000 includes both grip styles.

38 rimfire short (also made 38 centerfire which will bring premium value). Five-shot cylinder 1-13/16" long. 3-3/4" octagon barrel screwed into frame.

Checkered hard rubber grips. Blued (scarce) or full nickel plated finish. Most, but not all, serial numbered. Barrel marking identical to Model No. 1 and No. 2.
Note: There is an obvious inconsistency in values versus quantities manufactured of this "Model 3." Regardless of fact that earliest production is estimated highest, the incidence of their appearance on collectors' market continue to make them scarcer style and most valuable. Production figures based on

"Guns of Remington" (*q.v.*), possibly arrived at from a statistical sampling of the Model 3 in "Arms Gazette" Dec., 1974. It drew many of its conclusions from serial number data. The fact that 25 percent of specimens studied were unnumbered and the Remington numbering system was erratic may have led to incorrect conclusions.

Saw-handle style; ribbed type octagon barrel. Estimated quantity 6,000 of this last production type:
5E-051   Values—Very Good **$250**   Exc. **$575**
Bird's head grip style; octagon barrel made with rib, quantity estimated at 6,500:
5E-052   Values—Very Good **$250**   Exc. **$650**
Earliest production 1878; birds's head butt; barrel made without rib, quantity estimated 12,500.:
5E-052.5   Values—Very Good **$400**   Exc. **$800**

5E-051

5E-052

Remington New Model No. 4 Revolver

No. 4 Revolver—New Model; probably most easily termed Remington New Model No. 4, a.k.a. erroneously as the "New Line Revolver No. 4." Total quantity estimated at approximately 23,000. C. 1877-88.

Caliber 38 rimfire or centerfire short; 41 (estimated 20 percent of production) rimfire or centerfire short. Five-shot cylinder 1-1/16" long. 2-1/2" round barrel screwed into frame and made without ejector rod, checkered hard rubber grips. Blued or full nickel plated finish. Most, but not all, serial numbered. Barrel marking: E. REMINGTON & SONS, ILION, N.Y.:

5E-053   Values—Very Good **$200**   Exc. **$400**

5E-053

Remington Iroquois Pocket Revolver

Iroquois Pocket Revolver. Made c. 1878-1888. Total quantity estimated approximately 10,000:

22 rimfire. Seven-shot plain or fluted cylinder (scarce). 2-1/4" round barrel screwed into frame and made without ejector rod.

Checkered hard rubber grips. Blued or nickel plated finish.

Not serial numbered. May be encountered marked on top of barrel only IROQUOIS or marked on side of barrel only REMINGTON, ILION, N.Y. When both markings present a slight premium to value is added. Often encountered completely unmarked and correct that way; value 20 percent less.

This well constructed pocket arm was a major competitor to the Colt New Line 22 in outside appearance and was a scaled down version of the Remington New Model No. 4.

Plain, straight cylinder type:
5E-054   Values—Very Good **$325**   Exc. **$650**
Fluted cylinder type:
5E-054.5   Values—Very Good **$375**   Exc. **$750**

5E-054

5E-054.5

Remington Model 1875 Single Action Army

Model 1875 Single Action Army Revolver. (a.k.a. "IMPROVED ARMY OR FRONTIER ARMY") Made c. 1875-1889. Total quantity estimated approximately 25,000 to 30,000.

Calibers: 44 Remington CF (not marked on gun) approx. the first 16,000 guns; 44-40 (marked just "44" on front flat of frame or bottom of grip) and .45 (marked same and scarcer; worth 20 percent premium) balance of production; both marked on grip, later on frame, last on trigger bow. 45 cylinder slightly longer to prevent accidental insertion in 44 frame.

Six-shot fluted cylinder. 7-1/2" round barrel standard with few made in original 5-3/4" length considered quite rare and

5E-055

Close-up of Mexican Gov't markings on Model 1875 Single Action Army

worth premium; extreme caution should be exercised in acquisition as many in this length are spurious. Distinctive feature of the 1875 is the web-like contour on the underside of the ejector housing.

Walnut grips. Blued finish with casehardened hammer and loading gate; or nickel plated finish. Lanyard ring at butt. Standard early; optional later.

Earlier production numbered in sequence 1 to approx. 14,000. Numbered in batches (mostly up to 3 digits) after that, accounting for many low numbered pieces seen. Barrel marking: E. REMINGTON & SONS, ILION, N.Y. U.S.A.

An attempt to compete with the Colt Single Action Army, the Remington lacked the advantage of Colt's early start in government sales. Considerable mystery still surrounds this model. Although much speculation of sale to U.S. military, no known contracts. 639 nickel plated M. 1875's were purchased by U.S. Interior Dept. 1883 for use of Indian Police on western reservations; no known data of specific government markings. Records yet to surface of the known contract c. 1875 for 10,000 M. 1875's for Egyptian government. Currently believed only very small quantity made or delivered; Egypt at the time remiss in large sums owed Remington for rolling block rifles. Fact that almost every known specimen has turned up in U.S. (less than handful in Europe; three in Egypt) supports that contention. Markings generally accepted as Egyptian contract (worth approx. 20 percent premium) are a stamped cartouche on grip with "FR" or "JWR" (markings identical to U.S. inspector type) and "R" with star motif on side of barrel and frame.

Approximately 1,000 purchased by Mexican Gov't. c. 1880s. Marked RdeM usually on barrel, cylinder and frame; also distinctive Mexican liberty cap and sunburst in sunken hallmark. Rare; worth premium:

5E-055 Values—Good **$900** Fine **$3,250**

Remington Model 1888 (Transition) Single Action Army

Model 1888 Transition Single Action Army. (a.k.a. New Model Pocket Army). Made circa 1888-1889. Total quantity of less than 1,000. (Not illus; identical to Model 1890 Single Action shown below.)

Long an enigma for collectors, the factory originality of this big single action was questioned, and at times, quite passionately disputed. Although advanced Remington collectors acknowledged the originality of specimens, there was such a dearth of substantiating, documentary evidence that the gun was relegated to an undecided, often dubious, status. Its demand, and consequently value, as a collector's item suffered accordingly.

With the surfacing of an obscure 1889 catalog of the famous New York arms and sporting dealers Hartley and Graham, where it is well illustrated and called the *New Model Pocket Army*, the mystery has apparently been solved. It is significant to understand that Hartley and Graham assumed control of Remington Arms Company in 1888. Very likely these single actions were made for them specifically, using many parts on hand at the factory. The catalog illustrates the 1888 alongside the standard Model 1875.

Caliber 44-40. Although catalog advertises barrel as 5-1/2", many measure 5-3/4". Ejector housing identical to the Model 1890 (without the web). Barrel address is that of the Model 1875 E. REMINGTON & SONS, ILION, N.Y.U.S.A. Most specimens have lanyard ring at butt. Many, but not all are marked 44 or 44W on left grip; some with caliber markings on left frame or at rear of the trigger guard, further indicating Hartley & Graham's new management use of leftover parts. Finish blue or nickel.

It is not yet established if the serial numbers are in sequence or in batch numbers, but all recorded serials are under 1000. Assembly numbers are found under barrel, top of ejector and often on front of frame, a feature not usually seen on other .44 caliber Model 1875s.

Note: Exercise caution on acquisition of this Model 1888. Not a few Model 1875s, usually well-worn and with barrels shortened during time of use, have been spuriously altered to resemble Model 1890s. With the knowledge of this authentic 1888 transitional piece, there exists a more fertile field to snare the unsuspecting:

5E-055.5 Values—Good **$950** Fine **$3,750**

Remington Model 1890 Single Action Army

Model 1890 Single Action Army Revolver. Made c. 1891-1896. Total quantity approximately 2,020. Recent research reveals the quantities manufactured and shipped in the following years: 1891 (125); 1892 (844); 1893 (538); 1894 (467); 1895 (none); 1896 (just one).
44-40 centerfire only. Six-shot cylinder. 5-1/2" or 7-1/2" round barrel lacking the web (of the Model 1875) beneath the ejector rod housing.
Checkered hard rubber grips with monogram RA in panel at top. Blued or full nickel plated finish.
Serial numbered from 1 on up. Barrel marking: REMINGTON ARMS CO., ILION, N.Y.
This quite scarce successor to the Model 1875 Army, and competitor to the Colt Single Action Army, is one of the most sought after of Remington handguns. The buyer should exercise

5E-056

extreme caution in the acquisition of this model as not a few Model 1875s have been reworked to resemble it:
5E-056 Values—Good **$1,400** Fine **$5,500**

Remington Model 1891 Double-Action Revolver

Model 1890 (so-called) Double-Action Revolver. A curious handgun variously reported as the "Model 1891 Tip-up Mexican" (in *Remington Handguns* by Karr, 1956) and the "Remington M1891 Revolver" (in *Mexican Military Arms; 1866-1967* by Hughes, 1968; both works using partial or rough drawing illustrations only). To this day no known example has been viewed or recorded. Apparent that Remington designed such a revolver (the illustration here from Remington archives) but no other records verify its actual manufacture. Reportedly made with top-break barrel (of unknown length), five-shot cylinder; grips of black, hard rubber...and allegedly supplied under Mexican government contract for a total of 2,000 pieces that was completed by (or before) 1895 and bearing "REMINGTON ARMS CO., ILION, N.Y." barrel marks along with so" some indication" of Mexican government ownership. No prototype, experimental or production specimen has yet materialized. Believed never evolved beyond the drawings and possibly some rumored "component parts." It is, of course, possible that Remington did negotiate a contract and designed such a handgun for Mexico. Should such a specimen turn up: caveat emptor!

5E-056.5

5E-056.5

Remington 1865 Navy Rolling Block Pistol

Model 1865 Navy Rolling Block Pistol. Made c. 1866-1870. Total produced originally estimated at approximately 1,000; since revised to approximately 6,500 (*see Model 1867*).

50 rimfire. Single shot. 8-1/2" round barrel. Distinctive spur type trigger.

Walnut grips and forend. Blued barrel with casehardened frame, breechblock, trigger, trigger sheath and hammer.

Serial numbered under barrel ahead of forend. Frame marking: REMINGTONS, ILION N.Y. U.S.A. PAT. MAY 3 NOV. 15TH, 1864, APRIL 17TH, 1866.

The first of the Remington Rolling Block Pistols, readily identifiable by its spur trigger. Generally recognized as one of strongest actions ever made, the "Rolling Block" name comes from the pivoting action of the breechblock and hammer which acting together form a secure closure to the barrel on firing.

Martially marked model; in addition to above, bears inspector markings on right side of frame P and FCW, inspector's initials

5E-057

on left side of grip and naval anchor on top of barrel near breech:
5E-057   Values—Good **$1,100**   Fine **$3,750**
Civilian model; identical to above, lacking inspector markings described above:
5E-058   Values—Good **$850**   Fine **$2,500**
Centerfire model; quite often these are encountered with breechblocks adapted for centerfire only. It is possible a number were issued that way while others were altered by merely interchanging later centerfire breechblocks:
5E-059   Values—Good **$650**   Fine **$1,600**

Remington 1867 Navy Rolling Block Pistol

Model 1867 Navy Rolling Block Pistol. Made c. early 1870s. Total quantity unknown. Most recent theories believe this model never manufactured, but rather are all converted Model 1865s (hence, accounting for the shortage of that model).

50 caliber centerfire. Single shot. 7" round barrel.

Walnut grips and forend. Blued finish with casehardened frame, breechblock, trigger, trigger guard sheath and hammer.

Serial numbered under barrel ahead of forend; assembly numbers under grips. Frame marking: REMINGTONS ILION N.Y. U.S.A./PAT. MAY 3 NOV. 15TH, 1864 APRIL 17TH, 1866.

Modified from the Model 1865, it appears that all of these Model 1867s were government contracted for and will bear martial markings of **P** and **FCW** on right side of frame, and inspector's initials in script on left side of grips. Most, but not all, will have additional markings of an anchor and **I./W.D.W.** or **I/H.E.** on barrel near breech. It is possible that some without martial markings may be encountered; if so, they would be considerably scarcer, but they would not fetch higher values.

5E-060

(Note: this action with its naval markings used for a cadet rifle—*see 5E-084.5*.)
Naval marked 1867 as described above:
5E-060   Values—Good **$750**   Fine **$2,000**
1867 transitional type; identical to above, but civilian and not martially marked although many bear British proof marks. 8-1/2" barrel. Major distinguishing feature is the grip screw which enters through the rear frame strap passing through the grip and threaded into the backstrap itself (as opposed to the normal grip fastening with two wood screws):
5E-061   Values—Good **$600**   Fine **$1,250**

Remington 1871 Army Rolling Block Pistol

Model 1871 Army Rolling Block Pistol. Made c. 1872-1888. Total quantity approximately 6,000 plus.

50 centerfire. Single shot. 8" round barrel.

Walnut grips and forend. Blued finish with casehardened frame and trigger guard; hammer and breechblock finished bright.

Serial numbered. Frame marking: REMINGTONS ILION, N.Y. U.S.A./PAT. MAY 3 NOV. 15TH, 1864 APRIL 17TH, 1866 P20S.

Most of these were sold to the U.S. government and bear martial markings (approximately 5,000) which include government inspector initials on barrel and grips (usually

5E-062

C.R.S.), although civilian models are scarcer (estimated 900 made), they normally bring the same price.

Quite a few Model 1871 Armies (as well as the Model 1891 and 1901 Target Pistols) were altered and converted by gunsmiths right up to present day, to other calibers and with various barrels for shooting and target purposes. The collector should be wary not to confuse such later refinements with special work available from the factory.

The distinctive profile of the Model 1871 evolved from improving its Navy predecessors; most noticeable is the hump at the rear of the frame:

5E-062   Values—Good **$525**   Fine **$1,750**

Remington 1891 Target Rolling Block Pistol

Model 1891 Target Rolling Block Pistol. Made c. 1892-1898. Total quantity shown on factory records at 116, however larger quantities are possible.

22 long and short rimfire; 25 Stevens; 32 S&W rimfire and centerfire. Single shot. 10" half octagon/half round barrel (made also in 8" and 12" lengths which will bring an extra premium).

Walnut grips and forend. Blued finish with casehardened frame and trigger guard; hammer bright. Although serial numbered, numbering system indecipherable. Barrel marked: REMINGTON ARMS CO. ILION, N.Y. Left frame marked: REMINGTONS ILION, N.Y. U.S.A./PAT. MAY 3 NOV. 15TH, 1864 APRIL 17TH, 1866 P S (these latter two marks indicating a military receiver).

One of the most difficult of all Remington handguns to obtain; buyer should be extremely cautious that it is not merely a later gunsmith's alteration. It should further be realized these were over-runs of the Model 1871 Army contract receivers. Rear sights were standard as modified buckhorn type while front sight was blade type:

5E-063   Values—Very Good **$900**   Exc. **$2,500**

5E-063

Remington 1901 Target Rolling Block Pistol

Model 1901 Target Rolling Block Pistol. Made c. 1901-1909. Total of 735 made, as indicated by factory records.

5E-064

22 short and long rifle rimfire; 25-10 rimfire; 44 S&W centerfire. Single shot. 10" half octagon/half round barrel.

Original profusely checkered forend and grips. Blued finish barrel and frame as well as other parts.

Barrel and frame markings same as Model 1891 (with omission of inspector markings P and S). Major identifying features: The thumb lever (or ear) on breechblock offset horizontally in order to stay out of line of sight; adjustable rear sight mortised into top of frame; front sight ivory bead type on wide blade mortised into barrel.

This scarce pistol was the last of Remington's Rolling Block handgun production, bringing to a close over 44 years production.

5E-064   Values—Very Good **$900**   Exc. **$2,500**

Remington Mark III Signal Pistol

Mark III Signal Pistol. Made c. 1915-1918. Total quantity approximately 24,500. 10 gauge chambered for a special shot type shell charged with special powder only intended to direct a flare into the air. Single shot. 9" round iron barrel; tips downward to load. Brass frame with spur type trigger.

Walnut grips. Dull black finish on barrel; brass left bright.

Serial numbered. Barrel marking: THE REMINGTON ARMS - UNION METALLIC CARTRIDGE CO., INC. MARK III, REMINGTON BRIDGEPORT WORKS BRIDGEPORT, CONNECTICUT U.S.A.This arm classified as "Curio and Relic" under Federal Firearms Regulations by the Bureau of A,T and F:

5E-065   Values—Very Good **$225**   Exc. **$400**

5E-065

Remington 1911 & 1911A1 45 Caliber Auto   *See Colt Firearms, Chapter V.*

Remington Model 51 Automatic Pistol

Model 51 Automatic Pistol. 3-1/2" round barrel. Grip and manual safeties; magazine safety. Checkered hard rubber grips with Remington/UMC markings in panel. Blue-black finish.

Markings under serial number 63000: THE REMINGTON ARMS - UNION METALLIC CARTRIDGE CO. INC./REMINGTON ILION WKS. N.Y.U.S.A. PEDERSEN'S PATENTS PENDING. Markings over number 63000: REMINGTON ARMS CO. INC. ILION WKS N.Y. U.S.A./PEDERSEN PATENT (with 1920-21 patent dates).

Note: a small anchor marking often seen on many of these is an internal factory inspector's mark and does not indicate any U.S. Navy contract or purchase.

Caliber 380: 7 shots. Made c.1918-1934. Quantity approximately 54,500. Serial numbered 1 to 60800. Rear of slide has nine grooves under serial number 40000; above that number 15 grooves and Remington trademark added to frame, caliber stamped on barrel:

5E-066

5E-066	Values—Very Good **$275**	Exc. **$550**

Caliber 32: 8 shots. Made c.1921-1934. Quantity approximately 10,200. Serial numbered from 60801 to 70280 and 90501 to 92627:

5E-067	Values—Very Good **$300**	Exc. **$675**

REMINGTON LONGARMS

See Chapter IX, American Military Longarms, for the following Remington made arms:

Model 1841 Percussion Contract "Mississippi" Rifle

Model 1861 Percussion Contract Rifle-Musket

Remington Conversion With Maynard Tape Primer of U.S. Model 1816 Musket

Jenks U.S. Navy Percussion Breech-Loading Carbine With Maynard Tape Primer

Merrill, Latrobe and Thomas Percussion Breech-Loading Carbine

Model 1870 Rolling Block Navy Rifle by Springfield Armory

Model 1871 Rolling Block Army Rifle by Springfield Armory

Experimental Model 1870 Carbine and Army Rifle by Springfield Armory

A New Perspective On Remington Flintlock And Percussion Sporting Rifles

In very recent years considerable attention has been paid to solving the puzzle of what a "true" Remington flintlock or percussion sporting rifle looked like. The first five editions of this work discussed the subject in the broadest possible terms due to the almost complete lack of definitive data. Although no closer now to describing these elusive rifles...should they have ever existed...the passage of time and extensive research have revised attitudes about them; attitudes that are quite contrary to traditional belief and legends that are often repeated as fact.

Current judgment by "Remington" scholars is that Eliphalet II, the first Remington name associated with the arms trade, made barrels only for approximately the first 30 years, never turning out a complete gun during that period.

The issue would appear put to rest by the well documented article of H.J. Swinney (*Gun Report*, April, 1987). Nowhere among the many early references quoted is there the slightest mention of gun-making by Remington in those early years. There are, however, among those references to official government documents and various published works numerous citations indicating their barrel making activities, including the following excerpts:

> From Gordon's *Gazetteer Of The State Of New York*, published in 1836: *...Remington's manufactory of rifle barrels is in the town providing a return of $15,000 (profit) per annum.*

> From J. Leander Bishop's *A History Of American Manufacturers From 1608 To 1861*, published in Philadelphia, 1861, under the listing Remington, this quote: *...for many years (after 1828) the business was limited to the fabrication of barrels.* There is every indication that

Bishop made that statement from information he obtained from Eliphalet Sr. the founder; from the horse's mouth, so to speak. Bishop went on to state that complete guns were not made until the military orders (Jenks carbine for the Navy and the Model 1841 rifle) were received.

Tradition has it, that while working at his father's forge near Ilion, New York (German Flats) Eliphalet produced his first entire rifle, somewhere between the years 1816 and 1828. Fact seems to indicate that he turned out barrels only, and not too many at that. The forge was producing farm tools and implements to meet local needs, the addition of gun barrels apparently was the logical expansion of their output to a fertile area, that of supplying the many gunsmiths working in the central New York area. There certainly was no mass production of such barrels, much less guns. Of the handful of flintlocks that have surfaced attributed to Remington, none have been judged a "true" example of his work, other than possibly the barrel; and that, too, is questionable. It continues to be a matter for contention if such early (1816-1828) barrels were even marked, or how, and in what form those markings were applied.

The forge relocated to Ilion in 1828; in that same year Eliphalet Senior died. His prior barrel making venture having been successful, Eliphalet II installed machinery for barrel making in that new forge. Judging by the number of REMINGTON marked barrels appearing on percussion halfstock rifles of other makers, as well as reviewing census records of Remington output, their product was well received. Although a majority of such marked barrels are found on guns of New York state makers, all northeastern states are liberally represented, and to a lesser extent, makers of most other states and territories, as far west as California.

It has yet to be determined in exactly what eras those barrels were made; they are best judged by the known makers whose names most often appear on the rifles. Remington markings may give a clue: large block letters REMINGTON in a curved arch are believed earlier than the more often observed (and assumed last style) block letters in a straight line. Seldom seen is "REMINGTON STUBS TWISTED". The only determination for the lesser seen P. & S. REMINGTON mark is that it was used, presumably, after 1840. REMINGTON markings are most commonly viewed on the underside of barrels, occasionally on the side, seldom on top; further attesting to the generally accepted belief that only barrels were made in those first three decades.

Percussion sporting rifle locks marked REMINGTON are thought to have been imported already stamped with their name, a not uncommon practice. It has not been established if the factory made other gun accessories and mountings for the trade, or at what dates. The REMINGTON marking is occasionally found on the inside of a patchbox door. 1858 is the earliest date yet noted for advertisements for such mountings.

The great disparity in rifles which bear REMINGTON markings on barrels or locks appears to be further evidence that entire rifles were not factory products. It is rare that any two such pieces are even closely identical, leading to the logical assumption that if the company were in the gunmaking business, their products would closely follow a general pattern or design. The handful of elegantly embellished, elaborately

marked Remington rifles that are known do not discount the possibility that Remingtons were gunsmiths and makers. Rather, it is felt such rifles represent family presentation pieces, made for them by gunsmiths close to their factory operation, the Remingtons having formed relationships with some of the finest makers of their era.

Thus, the complete lack of documentary or other substantiating evidence strongly suggests that Remington's first venture into the manufacture of complete firearms was not until their contract for the Jenks breech-loading carbine for the U.S. Navy c. 1840s. The reader is referred to Chapter XII *Percussion Sporting and Target Rifles* for advice on valuing rifles with REMINGTON markings, which, in almost all instances, will be used in combination with the name of the gun maker who merely bought his barrel blank, and possibly lock, from Remington. In such cases a slight premium is occasionally added to the rifle's value. Frequently percussion rifles are encountered with REMINGTON markings only, with the absence of any other identification. In view of all the foregoing, it is the considered opinion of the author and most Remington students, that such pieces, although falling in a "gray" or questionable area, were made by other parties. Such rifles are primarily valued for their quality and condition, with a premium at times added for the Remington name. Should a percussion sporting rifle (or flintlock!) be proven of unquestioned factory manufacture, its value must be determined on an individual basis.
5E-068

Remington Revolving Percussion Rifle

5E-069

Revolving Percussion Rifle. Made c. 1866-1879. Total quantity estimated at less than 1,000.

Caliber 36 and 44. Six-shot round cylinder with safety notches at shoulder. 24" and 28" barrels apparently standard; 26" barrels advertised but not usually encountered. Full octagon barrels usual; half octagon/half round barrels scarce.

Walnut buttstock with crescent buttplate (two types, flat and pointed seen), scroll type trigger guard with spur below trigger bow. Blued finish with casehardened or blued hammer, frame and loading lever. Brass or iron trigger guard.

Serial numbered from 1 on up and all those noted to date have been below 1000. Barrel marking: PATENTED SEPT. 14, 1858/E. REMINGTON & SONS, ILION, NEW YORK, U.S.A./NEW MODEL

Although using frame design of the **New Model** revolver series, it is larger and cylinder is 3/16" longer than the New Model

Army. It also has a special extra long length loading lever which is an important feature in identifying authentic specimens.

Two types of rear sights are encountered, either a folding leaf type or open buckhorn style; front sights are blade type. Mountings on stock are either iron or brass with the latter most often seen.

36 caliber percussion model as described above; most often encountered type:
5E-069   Values—Good **$1,500**   Fine **$5,500**
44 caliber percussion as above; very scarce:
5E-070   Values—Good **$2,000**   Fine **$6,500**
Factory conversion to breech-loading metallic cartridge; special installed cylinder .38 or .44 rimfire. 46 caliber rimfire known, worth considerable premium if original. *Very rare:*
5E-071   Values—Good **$1,500**   Fine **$4,000**

Remington Rifle Cane

Rifle Cane, a.k.a. "Cane Gun." 1858 patent of J.F. Thomas, master mechanic at Remington. Made c. 1858-1866 in percussion; quantity estimated under 500. Made c. 1866-1888 in breech-loading metallic cartridge; estimated quantity 1,800. A primary comparative study "Remington Rifle Canes" by E.L. Burka in the American Society of Arms Collectors "Bulletin" (April, 2002) estimated total production of these as high as 4,500 basing that quantity on serial numbers observed on various models (he

concluded each type serial numbered in its own range). Based on that larger quantity, surviving specimens would clearly indicate that the rifle cane suffered a high rate of attrition.

Single shot; concealed mechanism in the screw-off upper section and handle. Outer covering of cane shaft and handle of gutta percha. Loaded and cocked by pulling back on handle; concealed button type trigger. Narrow German silver band below handle. Barrel lengths vary. Overall approximately 33–36-1/2".

5E-072

5E-072.1

5E-074.5

5E-074

The Remington Rifle Cane.

JUST THE THING FOR TAXIDERMISTS.

No. 1 Cane weighs 16 oz.   No. 2, 24 oz.

Protection against Dogs and Highwaymen.

Remington markings vary and have been viewed stamped on the gutta percha and occasionally on the iron tip of shaft; markings not in evidence on some specimens. Serial numbered. Variant style handles (other than those listed below) are known.

Remington advertised these as "Just the thing for taxidermists [and]...protection against dogs and highway men."

Has considerable interest as an oddity and scarce Remington. The company's first longarm made for metallic cartridges. These rifle-canes declassified by the A.T. and F. Bureau from former classification as "curios or relics" and are no longer considered NFA weapons, but rather "antiques" and therefore not subject to the Gun Control Act regulations.

PERCUSSION MODELS: 31 CALIBER ONLY (and CONVERSIONS TO 32 RIMFIRE presumed completed by Remington Factory). Although 44 caliber and .410 bore reported by earlier studies, recent investigation indicates error caused by inaccurate measurements. Estimated 500 percussion (including conversions) produced." Both types usually marked J.F. THOMAS PATENT/FEB'Y 9, 1858/ILION, N.Y. Four distinct handle shapes advertised as "standard" but others known.

Standard handles; either (1) "L" or right-angle shape, (2) arched, curved shape, (3) bulbous or golf-club shaped:
5E-072   Values—Very Good **$4,250**   Exc. **$7,500**

Ball and claw shape handle (standard style):
5E-072.1 Values—Very Good **$4,500**   Exc. **$8,000**

CARTRIDGE MODELS: Calibers 22RF and 32RF. Two types gutta percha handles standard, with ivory handles (and likely others) on special extra order. Two variant breech actions. More recently estimated that approximately 2,000 of each caliber were manufactured. Usually marked: REMINGTON & SONS/ILION, N.Y./PATENT FEB'Y 9, 1858 (later production substituting **"PAT EXTEND FEB 9, 1872."** for the 1858 Pat. date).

Plain curved handles 32RF (add premium for 22RF):
5E-073   Values—Very Good **$3,500**   Exc. **$5,500**

Large dog head handle with detailed designs along back; 32RF:
5E-074   Values—Very Good **$4,500**   Exc. **$8,500**

Small dog head handle; smooth design; 22RF:
5E-074.5 Values—Very Good **$4,500**   Exc. **$8,500**

Ivory and other variant handles (if original c. 1858-1888):
5E-075   Values—Very Good **$2,500**   Exc. **$4,750**

Remington 1863 Percussion Contract Rifle

Remington Model 1863 Percussion Contract Rifle, a.k.a. "Zouave Rifle." Made c. 1862-1865. Total quantity 12,501.

58 caliber; single shot muzzleloader. 33" round barrel (with either 3-groove or 7-groove rifling) fastened by two barrel bands.

5E-076

Large lug at right side of barrel near muzzle for attaching saber type bayonet.

Brass mountings. Blued barrel, casehardened lock with all brass parts finished bright. Tulip head steel ramrod. Walnut stock. Brass patchbox at right side of butt.

Lock markings: Ahead of hammer American eagle over small U.S.; in two lines under bolster REMINGTON'S/ILION, N.Y.; at rear horizontally dated 1863; breech of barrel marked with date and V/P (eaglehead) proof with inspector initials and STEEL. Tang of buttplate marked U.S.

One of the best made and designed military arms of the Civil War era. The origin of the name "Zouave" for this rifle has yet to be revealed. In official documents and the U.S. contract it was termed "Harpers Ferry Pattern." The great majority of them found in higher grades of condition suggest they were not issued; their usage remains a mystery:

5E-076   Values—Very Good **$2,750**   Exc. **$4,500**

Remington Barrels for U.S. Navy "Plymouth" Pattern Rifles. *See 9A-312.5.*

Remington Single Barrel Muzzle-Loading Percussion Shotgun

Remington Single Barrel Muzzle-Loading Percussion Shotgun. Made c. 1866 through 1870s. Illustrated and described in their 1873, 1877 and 1878 factory catalogs. Quantity unknown, but their 1873 catalog mentioned "… having made and sold 10,000 within the past few years we feel warranted in resuming their manufacture."

20 gauge. 35" round barrel; muzzle crowned. Narrow, flat iron frame with center hung hammer (deep "V" notched sighting slot on hammer head); completely unmarked except for possible P proof and inspector initials on underside of barrel (may not be consistent on all specimens). Walnut stock and short forend with iron tip; iron trigger guard and butt plate. Extremely simple construction:

5E-076.5

5E-076.5   Values—Good **$225**   Fine **$550**

Remington Double Barrel Percussion Shotgun

Remington Muzzle-Loading Percussion Double Barrel Shotgun. A little known or reported facet of Remington's history was their sale of imported English percussion single and double barrel shotguns. They advertised in Ilion (and likely other N.Y.) newspapers in 1855 through 1856 having for sale "....single and double fowling guns, imported by themselves" (other ads "....inspected by themselves.") Identified single barrel specimens are not yet known. IMPORTED BY E. REMINGTON & SONS, ILION, N.Y. is marked on the center rib of double barrel style. Although dimensions, quality, bore size likely varies, specimen viewed was English (not marked by maker), plain grade, bar type locks, Damascus barrels, Birmingham proof marks; straight walnut stock; iron mountings. Authentic marked specimens rare:

5E-076.7   Values—Good **$850**   Fine **$2,250**

Remington-Beals Single Shot Rifle

5E-077

Remington-Beals Single Shot Rifle. Made c. 1866-1870. Quantity unknown; estimated at less than 800.

32 and 38 long rimfire. Standard barrel lengths of 24", 26", 28"; part round/part octagon. Sporting style folding leaf rear sight.

Blued finish; iron mountings. Walnut stock with straight grip; made without forend. Serial numbered.

Barrel marked: BEALS PATENT JUNE 28, 1864. JAN. 30, 1866/E. REMINGTON & SONS, ILION, NEW YORK. Frames were brass on majority of production; iron occasionally seen, quite scarce and will bring a premium value.

The action of this unusual arm is of lever type, which, when lowered moves the barrel forward for loading and extraction:

5E-077   Values—Good **$325**   Fine **$950**

The Remington Rolling Block Action

Among the most notable and widely manufactured of all antique American arms is the sturdily built, easily operated Remington Rolling Block action. Made in so many models and variations over such a long period that many of them were disregarded by the marketplace, a mere handful creating a spark of collector interest. More recent years have favored these eminent arms with detailed, in-depth studies (see Biblio.) that have systematically categorized each and every model, substantially enhancing (and enriching) their collector as well as historical interest.

The basic principle for the so-called rolling block breech was patented by Leonard M. Geiger in 1863. The action was improved by Remington's own genius, Joseph Rider, and first produced as the "Split Breech" carbines (q.v.). Rider continued to develop the mechanism until finally perfected in 1866 with further improvements patented in April, 1866, August, 1867, and November, 1871.

The rolling block was an interlocking system of hammer and breech determined to be one of the strongest actions of its era and capable of handling any ammunition then produced. Popularity was due not only from its tremendous strength, but the simplicity of action: (a) Hammer cocked; (b) breechblock very simply rolled backward and downward by pressure of thumb on the projecting ear-like lever on the side of the block; simultaneously the spent cartridge was extracted; (c) by merely rolling breechblock into place, gun was ready to fire (in its final refinement the hammer was also locked at the full cock position).

The rolling blocks are divided into two basic styles for collector purposes: (1) Military, (2) Sporting. Each group, especially the latter, has its own sub-categories.

Production was over a remarkably long period, 1867 to 1934 (in one form or another) with over a million of the military models and carbines made. Important detail and production charts of these models is available in "The Military Remington

Rolling Block Rifle" by G. Layman; 3rd Edition (q.v.).

The rolling block was produced in four basic action sizes or types which, in many cases, are also model number designations. The largest of these actions was the No. 1, first introduced in 1868, and the smallest was the No. 4, introduced in 1890:

No. 1 Action: 1-1/4" wide. Largest of the rolling blocks; chambering from small bores to the largest and heaviest calibers.

No. 1-1/2 Action: About identical in profile and dimensions to the No. 1 above but narrower in width and lighter in weight. Not chambered for the heavier calibers.

No. 2 Action: 1-1/8" wide. Chambering generally for the less potent cartridges of medium sizes with several for pistol size cartridges. Easily distinguished by the arched or curved contour at rear sides of action where it joins stock.

No. 3 Action: Not a rolling block type. This was the Remington-Hepburn, falling block breechloader.

No. 4 Action: Made in rimfire calibers 22, 25/10 Stevens and 32. A lightweight rolling block action quite short size; the forward section of the receiver (especially the receiver ring into which the barrel is screwed) is noticeably narrower than either of its predecessors (the Models No. 1 or No. 2).

No. 5 Action: Large action similar to the No. 1 size, but designed for "Smokeless High Powered Cartridges" and first introduced in 1898. Has the extraction device for rimless cartridge cases. The last of the large frame rolling blocks.

Remington Single Shot Breech-Loading Carbine

5E-078
Type I

5E-079
Type II

Single Shot Breech-Loading Carbine, a.k.a. "Split Breech Remington." All types were made under sub-contract from Remington by the Savage Revolving Arms Co. of Middletown, Conn. Made c. 1865-1866. Total quantity indicated below.

46 and 50 rimfire. The predecessor of the famed "Rolling Block" design. 20" round barrel fastened by single barrel band. There is considerable difference in the size of the actions of each type. The 50 caliber is much larger and heavier throughout the action, barrel and the stock.

Iron mountings. Walnut buttstock and forend. Blued finish with casehardened action; some specimens found entirely nickel plated (post 1870).

Serial numbered. Tang of breech marked: REMINGTON'S ILION, N.Y./PAT. DEC. 23, 1863 MAY 3 & NOV. 16, 1864.

Remington's earliest production longarms chambered for metallic cartridge ammunition. Of historic interest as they appear to be the last type arm supplied to the Union government

on contract prior to the end of the Civil War. Prices below are for martially marked specimens. Examples not so marked will bring slightly less.

Type I. 46 rimfire. U.S. contract March, 1864 for 1,000; amended Dec., 1864 for total 5,000. First delivery 1250 in Feb., 1865; then 1,500 Mar., 1865; final by Apr. 30, 1865. Civil War issue, if any, unknown. 3,600 of these were repurchased by Remington from the U.S. in 1870 and promptly resold to France for use in the Franco-Prussian War. Small size action; very curved trigger; long breech; short hammer; short forend. Sling ring affixed to left side of frame. Inspector's initials left side of stock:
5E-078   Values—Good **$950**   Fine **$3,500**
Type II. 50 rimfire. U.S. contract Oct., 1864 for 15,000. First delivery 1,000 not until Sept., 1865; final delivery by May, 1866. U.S. resold almost entire lot back to Remington in 1870 who then promptly sold to France for use in Franco-Prussian War. Specimens very scarce. Short breech; long hammer; long 9-3/4"

forend; rifle type buttplate; sling ring and bar on left side of frame and some specimens fitted with sling swivels on both buttstock and barrel band:

5E-079 Values—Good **$1,000** Fine **$3,750**

Type III. Civilian/Sporting Models. After completion of both military contracts, all remaining parts, dies and machinery were returned by Savage to Remington where carbines (both frame sizes) were assembled in various calibers and configurations. Stocks of fancy and select grain are occasionally seen. Quantity was likely under 1,000. These models were advertised in the catalog of 1866:

5E-079.5 Values—Good **$575** Fine **$1,500**

Remington Rolling Block Conversions Of Civil War Muskets

Remington Rolling Block Conversions of Civil War Model 1861/1863 Percussion Muzzle-Loading Rifled Muskets.

Exacting details on these arms are elusive, at best. It is known that they definitely were made in 58 caliber centerfire and 50-70 caliber centerfire, and specimens have been observed in 58 caliber rimfire and 43 Spanish centerfire.

Some 50-70 caliber specimens have quite positively been attributed to Springfield Armory manufacture utilizing Remington supplied actions. It is not known where the 58 caliber models were sold, but very probably to state militias and possibly the Federal government. It will have to await more diligent research to unearth facts concerning these latter types. They are quite scarce, however, and considered as both U.S. martial longarms and early Remingtons. It is also an observation that invariably these conversions, when encountered, are in very heavily used condition and finer grades will bring premiums especially if inspectors' marks are very clear. Features common to all are the rear sight of short single leaf Model 1864 U.S. type; oil finished walnut stocks with iron mountings.

Markings on tang: REMINGTON'S ILION, N.Y. U.S.A./PAT. MAY 3^D. NOV. 15TH 1864, APRIL 17TH 1866.

Springfield Armory conversion. Circa 1868; total quantity 504 in 1868. Caliber 50-70. 39-3/8" Civil War musket barrel with a new liner brazed in. Civil War musket stock used to make the two-piece stock. Three-band fastened forend 34-3/16" long; 13-3/16" buttstock with inspector stamps E.S.A. and S.W.P. in individual cartouches. Model 1863 musket type ramrod 38-5/16" long screws into stud in front of rolling block action. Very rare; few known specimens as almost the entire lot was altered by Springfield Armory in 1869 by shortening to 36" barrel, 2 band fastened with 3 digit serial on top of barrel:

5E-080 Values—Good **$1,150** Fine **$3,000**

Shortened Springfield Armory conversion. Identical to above with barrel shortened to 36"; forend shortened accordingly and two-band fastened; the third band spring slot filled in with wood. Model 1868 type ramrod and ramrod stop. It is obvious that these arms are shortened from the 39-3/8" style described above. A very scarce longarm with very few known:

5E-081 Values—Good **$1,000** Fine **$2,500**

58 caliber centerfire conversions. Made by Remington and many other arms dealers, including Hartley & Graham of New York. Quantities unknown; but encountered with much greater frequency than either of the Springfield Armory conversions. Encountered in both 36" barrel (full stock two-band fastened) and 39" barrel (full stock three-band fastened). Altered Civil War musket stocks. Specimens normally observed without inspector markings and if same are observed on wood, they would be worth premium. Values indicated are for the 36"; 39" specimens would be worth at least value indicated here with premium value possible:

5E-082 Values—Good **$375** Fine **$700**

Remington U.S. Navy Model 1867 Rolling Block Carbine

U.S. Navy Model 1867 Rolling Block Carbine; c. 1868-1869. Quantity made 5095 (the overrun of 95 carbines were sold commercially). Earlier editions of this work reported the carbines to have been "assembled at Springfield Armory with actions made by Remington." Recent revised information indicates they were made and assembled entirely at the Remington factory. Over 50 percent of those manufactured were later altered to other caliber carbines *and rifles*. This model very scarce in original configuration and caliber. Two hundred of the carbines altered to 45-70 caliber were purchased by the state of South Carolina and marked "SC" on their upper tangs.

50-45 centerfire. 23-1/4" barrel with short forend fastened by single barrel band. Short single leaf rear sight. Barrel blued with casehardened frame. Iron mountings. Walnut stock oil finished. Sling swivels on barrel band and underside of butt. (Caution suggested if ring bar and ring also present. Believed recently added to "improve" value) Markings on tang behind hammer: REMINGTON'S, ILION, N.Y. U.S.A./PAT. MAY 3^D. NOV. 15TH 1864, APRIL 17TH 1866. Inspector markings on right frame P/FCW/(anchor). Inspector initials in cartouche at wrist of stock also:

5E-083 Values—Good **$850** Fine **$2,500**

5E-083

Remington Model 1867 Navy Cadet Rolling Block Rifle

Model 1867 Navy Cadet Rolling Block Rifle. Made by Springfield Armory c. 1868 utilizing Remington actions only; the same action as the 1868-9 Navy Carbine. Quantity made 498.

Caliber 50-45 centerfire cadet cartridge. 32-1/2" round barrel; typical Springfield Armory three-groove rifling. Barrels have a brazed-in liner, the same as on the Model 1866 Trap-Door Rifles.

5E-084

Actions identical to the Navy Carbine described above bearing anchor marking on left side of frame and P/F.C.W. on right side of frame. Casehardened action with bright barrels and hardware. Rear sight identical to that used on Model 1864 Civil War musket. Overall length 47-3/8". Made without provision for sling swivels.

Markings on tang identical to that described above for Navy carbine and heel of buttplate marked U.S.

This Cadet Rifle has much in common with the Model 1867 Springfield trap-door cadet rifle; takes the same bayonet and has the same front sight, upper and lower barrel bands, nose cap, buttplate and ramrod identical except for length. Very scarce:

5E-084   Values—Good **$875**   Fine **$2,500**

Remington Cadet Rifle With Model 1867 Pistol Action

Cadet Rifle With Model 1867 Pistol Action. (a.k.a. "Pistol Framed Cadet Rifle." Not illus.) Another Remington enigma solved by careful study of old gun catalogs and the detailed story of these "Cadets" by E. Hull in the Feb., 2005 *Gun Report*. Clearly described in the 1903-1904 catalog of Hartley & Co. (who then owned the Remington Arms Company) as "...made from obsolete material by the Remington Arms Company especially for us". Advertised by Hartley as their "REMINGTON CADET RIFLE NO. 205". Intended for sale to the many military schools and cadet

corps quasi-military boys organizations popular during that turn-of-the-century era. The 5,000 Cadet Rifles that the Hartley & Co. 1904 catalog reported having sold is believed merely exaggerated sales talk; reliable estimates place figure at approximately 1,000. Caliber .50 Remington Pistol CF. 28" blued or browned barrel; full walnut stock fastened by two barrel bands. Action is that of the Model 1867 U.S. Navy Rolling Block Pistol (*see 5E-060*) with the Navy inspector markings P/FCW still in evidence:

5E-084.5   Values—Good **$225**   Fine **$350**

Remington New York State Contract Rolling Block Rifles and Carbines

New York State Contract Rolling Block Rifles and Carbines. (Not illus.) Made for New York State National Guard c. 1872. Total quantity estimated at 15,000. Three-line Remington markings and patent dates on tang. Finish blued with casehardened action. Iron mountings with sling swivels on rifle and ring bar and sling ring on left frame for carbine. Walnut stocks oil finished. A few features distinguish the model: extremely high, curved hammer spur; thumb lever for breech block protrudes outward instead of up; safety locking action which automatically returns hammer to half cock when breech is closed.

Caliber 50-70 c.f. Rifle has 36" barrel fastened by three barrel bands to forend; carbine has short forend fastened by single barrel band. 22" barrel. Inspector marks on left side of stock at wrist with cartouche in "banner" or serpentine-like shape and inspector initials H.B.H. inside; others seen with US. N.Y. markings on right butt with two inspector markings on left wrist. On many the top of comb of stock has regimental letter and number markings:

Full stock rifle:

5E-085   Values—Good **$475**   Fine **$950**

Saddle ring carbine; 22" barrel:

5E-086   Values—Good **$550**   Fine **$1,100**

U.S. Springfield Rifles with Remington Rolling Block Actions   *See Chapter IX-A.*

Remington Rolling Block Military Rifles and Carbines

Rolling Block Military Rifles and Carbines. Large No. 1 size action. Made c. 1867-1888. Quantities totaling over 1,000,000. Made for both domestic and foreign sales. In some cases only actions were supplied for foreign contracts with the guns themselves being assembled abroad and in other cases, entire guns were made abroad under license from Remington. The majority, however, appear to be of Remington manufacture. The factory practice of utilizing surplus parts from military and other contracts and selling to the commercial market accounts for many other variations and anomalies. The author has yet to discover any great collecting nuances on these rolling blocks; their value and demand would be basically according to their condition and caliber. Odd or unusual markings, especially if in English and decipherable, might enhance values also. Should a complete study and statistical survey be performed on them,

there is every possibility that values could be enhanced. Under present market conditions, however, they are still one of the most commonly encountered of all antique arms. In the 1960s they were imported from abroad (purchased as surplus from foreign governments) in tremendous quantities in all types, sizes and grades of condition with the lesser quality pieces actually being sold by the pound as sales promotions! Many of them were primarily of value (and many still are) for their rugged actions for conversions to modern sporters.

Values indicated herewith are median prices for specimens in the more obsolete, less desirable calibers—which are the most often encountered. More popular and desirable calibers, if proven original, will add a premium to the value.

Bores are usually of importance only on the more desirable calibers and will definitely influence their price. For the rest, the

5E-087

bores are a matter of personal preference and except for the very highest grades of condition, have not been found greatly influential in values.

Barrel lengths vary considerably on rifles from approximately 30" to 39" with forends either two-band or three-band fastened. Carbines vary in length from 19" approximately to 22" with short forend, single-band fastened. The most desirable are the carbines having ring bars and saddle rings affixed to left side of frame. The buyer should inspect carbines very carefully for many rifles were shortened in modern times both to make them more desirable and to fetch the higher values.

Remington markings appear in two or three lines on tang behind hammer. Caliber markings not normally encountered. A whole host of foreign markings may be encountered including English, Chinese, Arabic, Turkish, Spanish and many others.

The gun was officially adopted by Denmark as their official arm in 1867; by Norway and Sweden in 1868; by Spain in 1869; by Egypt in 1870 and Argentina in 1879.

Both the rifle and carbine were purchased by the Mexican Government and are usually encountered with deep struck markings "R de MEXICO" (or merely "RM") on top of breech, accompanied with markings near breech of barrel of a deep sunken, round sunburst-like motif with liberty cap in center over large letters "RM" below. Mexican-marked specimens usually bring premium values over those shown.

Full stock military rifle:

5E-087   Values—Good **$250**   Fine **$475**

Saddle ring carbine:

5E-088   Values—Good **$350**   Fine **$650**

Note: Prices shown here for all Remington target rifles include sights where specified. If sights missing, deduct 20 to 30 percent from price (see note in Chapter XIV also).

Remington No. 1 Rolling Block Sporting Rifles

No. 1 Rolling Block Sporting Rifles Various Types. Overall period all types c. 1868-1888; details of dates, where known are given with individual listings below.

As with the Winchester single shots, the Sharps Model 1874 and the Marlin-Ballard single shots—these Rolling Block Sporters were offered with a great variety of features, calibers, barrel lengths, weights, finishes, stocks, buttplates and sights; all of this resulting in a field of wide opportunities for the collector who wishes to specialize. A very general breakdown of major types follows herewith and it must be noted that a great many variations exist and may be encountered. No complete comprehensive guide exists detailing each type and all its variations and calibers and possible combinations, nor is data available as to quantities manufactured, and hence they are merely estimated when possible. Considerable information about them may be found in the James Grant, *Single Shot Rifles* series of books.

Many special features will increase values and they should be carefully noted. The following listings detail the arms as they were more-or-less offered in their standard, least embellished, basic model type, and are valued accordingly. Extra accessories when not listed as standard will enhance values and may include: Double set triggers; single set trigger; a wide range of sights including Vernier types and front sights with spirit levels; varying quality of stocks and various styles of buttplates.

Standard finishes on all were: Blued barrel with casehardened action. Remington markings with Ilion, New York address and varying patent dates are found on tang behind hammer. Barrels usually marked E. REMINGTON & SONS, ILION, N.Y.

Bore conditions are quite important in evaluating these sporters. At very least, its condition should be rated as good as the outside condition, if not better. Bore condition may be relegated to secondary importance only in the case of exceptionally unusual features such as a very heavy barrel weight, rare markings (such as a western gun maker or gun dealer's name) or other feature that might give it an association with an historical event or personage.

As will be noted from the following listings, there are a great many calibers that these arms were chambered for and these listings do not reflect them all. Values are for the more commonly encountered types. Premiums may be added to the piece for such calibers as 45-70 and other highly popular shooters' calibers as well as those in the largest 50 caliber sizes.

Sporting Rifle No. 1. Possibly as many as 12,000 manufactured. Calibers include 40-50, 40-70, 44-77, 45-70, 50-45, 50-70 and other centerfires with some rimfire calibers also encountered including 44 and 46. 28" and 30" octagonal barrels standard; round barrels are encountered, scarcer, and in finest grades will bring premium. Folding leaf type rear sight; dovetailed blade front sight. Great many options available each of which will add

5E-089
Sporting Rifle No. 1

5E-090
Long Range Creedmoor

5E-091
Mid-Range Target

to value. With heavy octagon barrel in 50-70 will bring premium 50 to 100 percent in centerfire calibers:

5E-089　　Values—Very Good **$1,100**　　Exc. **$3,250**
As above in 22 or 32 rimfire:

5E-089.2　　Values—Very Good **$800**　　Exc. **$2,250**
Long Range "Creedmoor" Rifle. Made c. 1873-1890. Quantity estimated as few hundred. Calibers 44-90, 44-100, 44-105 centerfire standard; others evidently available on custom order. 34" part octagon/part round barrel standard. Long range Vernier sight mounted on tang with globe front sight. Plain grain checkered pistol grip buttstock with checkered forend having iron cap standard on most (could be had in plain uncheckered stock too). Fancy grains of wood will bring premiums as will special sights, buttplates, spirit levels, etc. One of the finest Remington arms produced:

5E-090　　Values—Very Good **$3,750**　　Exc. **$7,500**
Mid-Range Target Rifle: Circa 1875-1890. Calibers 40-70, 44-77, 45-70, 50-70. Part octagon/part round barrels 28" and 30". Advertised in five basic stock styles from straight sporting to pistol grip Creedmoor with great variety of sights. Values here for a checkered pistol grip stock with a Vernier tang peep sight and globe front sight (plainer specimens should bring proportionately less):

5E-091　　Values—Very Good **$2,000**　　Exc. **$4,750**
Short Range Rifle: Made c. 1875-1890. Several thousand produced. Centerfire calibers 38 extra long; 40-50; 44 S&W; 44 extra long. Rimfire calibers 38 extra long; 44 extra long and 46. 26" and 30" full octagonal or round barrels. Variety of sights.

Values here for combination peep and open rear sight and Beach front sight. Values also reflect checkered pistol grip stick, although available with others in centerfire calibers:

5E-092　　Values—Very Good **$1,400**　　Exc. **$3,500**
As Above in rimfire calibers:

5E-092.2　　Values—Very Good **$1,150**　　Exc. **$2,500**
Black Hills Rifle: Made c. 1877-1882. Caliber 45-60 centerfire. 28" round barrel. Plain open sights. Plain, straight stock. Advertised by the company as "...designed for hunters and sportsmen generally, when requiring a well made, reliable gun at a moderate price. Using a cheap, but strictly first class ammunition":

5E-093　　Values—Very Good **$2,000**　　Exc. **$4,000**
Shotgun: Made c. 1870-1890s. Quantity several thousands. 30" and 32" laminated (Damascus) or plain barrels.

　　Model "No. 1": 16 gauge; chambered for interchangeable use of 16 Brass or 20 ga. paper shells. Shotgun buttplate:
　　5E-094　　Values—Very Good **$300**　　Exc. **$750**

　　Model "No. 2": (described in their 1893 catalog) 20 gauge; still chambered for same 16 Brass or 20 ga. paper shells. Made mostly with military rifle parts and barrels. Military buttplate:
　　5E-094.5　　Values—Very Good **$300**　　Exc. **$750**
Light Baby Carbine: Made c. 1885-1910. Estimated quantity a few thousand. Earliest production chambered for calibers 44 rimfire and 44 centerfire with both 18-inch or 20-inch barrels (scarce and worth premium). Majority of production (later mfr.) in caliber 44-40 with 20-inch very lightweight round barrels only. Available in blue or nickel finish (blue scarcer). Carbine type forend fastened with single barrel band. Weight just 5-3/4 lbs. Ring bar and saddle ring on left frame. Scarce:

5E-095　　Values—Very Good **$1,100**　　Exc. **$2,750**

5E-094
Shotgun

5E-095
Light Baby Carbine

Remington Model 1-1/2 Sporting Rifle

5E-096

Model 1-1/2 Sporting Rifle. Manufactured c. 1888-1897. Estimated several thousand manufactured. Standard No. 1 frame, but otherwise a lightweight version (narrower frame width) of the No. 1 sporting rifle. Rimfire calibers 22; 25 Stevens; 25 long; 32; 38 long and extra long. Centerfire calibers 32-20; 38-40; 44-40. Medium weight octagon barrel from 24" to 28". Straight, plain walnut stock with blade type front sight:

5E-096 Values—Very Good **$600** Exc. **$1,400**

Remington Model 2 Sporting Rifle

Model 2 Sporting Rifle. Made c. 1873-approximately 1910. Quantity estimated a few thousand. Made in a great variety of rimfire calibers from 22 to 38 as well as centerfire from 22 to 38-40, 44-40. 24" and 26" octagon barrel standard. Sporting type rear sight with notched elevator adjustment device and bead front sight standard. Blued finish with casehardened frame. Iron mountings. Walnut stock of the so-called "perch-belly" type having a slight rounded curve to under-section of butt. Remington markings on earlier specimens appear on tang; were later moved to left side of frame. Available with considerable amount of special order features, many of which (such as Vernier and windgauge sights, pistol-grip checkered stocks, etc.) will increase values. Set triggers not available on this model.

5E-097

Easily distinguished by its smaller size action than the No. 1 and the distinctive curved configuration to the rear sides of the frame where it joins stock. Centerfire calibers values (rimfire valued approx. 20 percent less):

5E-097 Values—Very Good **$500** Exc. **$1,200**

Remington New Model No. 4 Rolling Block

5E-098

New Model No. 4 Rolling Block Rifle. Made c. 1890-1933. Quantity made estimated at over 50,000.

Chambered for rimfire calibers 22, short, long and long rifle; 25 Stevens; 32 short and long. 22-1/2" octagonal barrels standard for most of production (24" also in 32 caliber) with round barrels available in latter years towards end of production. V-notch rear and bead front sights standard. Finish blued with casehardened frame. Iron mountings. Various markings encountered of company name, address and patent dates. Take-down model available after turn of the century and can bring slight premium in the finer grades of condition. Remington's lightest and smallest rolling block:

5E-098 Values—Very Good **$175** Exc. **$475**

Remington Model No. 4 S "Military Model" Rolling Block Sporting Rifle

5E-099

Model No. 4 S "Military Model" Rolling Block Sporting Rifle, and "Boy Scout Rifle." Made c. 1913-1923. Approximate quantity made estimated from 10,000 to 25,000. Caliber 22 rimfire short and long. 28" round barrel with musket type forend fastened by single barrel band. Stud for knife type bayonet rarely encountered; affixed at underside of barrel (the bayonet and its scabbard very rare and specimens are seldom seen). Earliest production bears frame markings AMERICAN BOY SCOUT, standard frame markings MILITARY MODEL.

Made on the New Model No. 4 action.

The exact background of the name Boy Scout for this rifle is obscure, but it seems that this was never the officially adopted arm of the group known today as the Boy Scouts of America. The subject is discussed at considerable length in James Grant's *Boys' Single Shot Rifles*. Very likely private military academies for young boys were among the buyers:

5E-099   Values—Very Good **$750**   Exc. **$1,750**

American Boy Scout marked (without bayonet). Made 1913 only. Rare:

5E-099.5 Values—Very Good **$1,750**   Exc. **$3,500**

Remington No. 5 Rolling Block Rifles and Carbine

5E-100
Sporting & Target Model

5E-101
Military Rifle

No. 5 Rolling Block Rifles and Carbine. Made c. 1897-1905. Three basic styles as described below. Total quantity estimated at 100,000. Plus French Military contract of 100,291. Action of identical large size as the No. 1, but made to chamber smokeless cartridges.

Calibers and barrel lengths as noted below. Finish blued with casehardened frame and buttplate. Stocks as below. Patent markings on tang with Remington name and address as well as caliber along top of barrel.

In effect, the last of the major size rolling blocks, its greatest weakness being the lack of a magazine to allow competition with the many new repeaters, particularly the Mauser, then available.

The Model 1897 rifle and carbine were both purchased by the Mexican government. Specimens will be found with the added markings "REPUBLICA MEXICANA" over the outline design of a Mexican eagle with a snake in its beak. Will usually fetch premium values.

Sporting and target rifle. Made c. 1898-1905. Calibers 30-30; 303 British; 7mm; 30-40 Krag; 32-40 H.P.; 32 U.S. and 38-55. 28" and 30" barrels standard (the latter on 30 U.S.). Plain, straight stock and half type forend with short curl at tip. Open type rear sights. Only advertised extras were set triggers and will bring premium:

5E-100   Values—Very Good **$1,750**   Exc. **$5,000**

Model 1897 military rifle. Made c. 1897-1917. Caliber 7mm and 8mm Lebel and 30 U.S. (the latter bringing slight premium). Full musket type forend fastened by two barrel bands with stud for knife type bayonet at tip of forend; wooden hand guard along top of barrel between receiver and lower band; sling swivels. Majority made for export (and so advertised) to South and Central America. Also available in a later variation, often referred to as the Model 1902, with automatic ejection, otherwise identical:

5E-101   Values—Very Good **$400**   Exc. **$950**

Carbine. About identical to the military rifle in same calibers, but with 20" barrel and short carbine forend (and wooden barrel cover) fastened by single band; ring bar and ring on left side of frame. Majority of production for export:

5E-102   Values—Very Good **$425**   Exc. **$1,100**

Remington No. 6 Falling Block Rifle

5E-103

No. 6 Falling Block Rifle. Made c. 1902-1933. Exact quantities unknown, but over 250,000 or more.

Rimfire calibers, 22 short, long, long rifle (will bring small premium) and 32 short and long; also available in smoothbore for shot cartridges.

20" round barrel. Very light weight piece intended solely for the young boys' market. All actions are take-down type with knurled knob for barrel release on underside of frame. Action a very modified thinned-down version of the rolling block with small projecting knob on block to operate breech. Made in

number of variations over its long production run. Finishes standard in blue throughout; the earliest type will have casehardened frames and will bring slight premium in the finer grades of condition:

5E-103   Values—Very Good **$175**   Exc. **$475**

Remington No. 7 Rifle, Rolling Block Action

5E-104

No. 7 Rifle, Rolling Block Action. Made c. 1903-1906. Less than 500 were made.

Rimfire calibers 22 short and long rifle and 25-10 Stevens. 24", 26", and 28" part octagon/part round barrels. Made on the Model 1871 pistol action.

Blued barrel with casehardened action and trigger guard. Marked REMINGTON ARMS CO. ILION, N.Y. U.S.A. on barrel and

standard two-line Remington and patent date markings and P and S identical to Model 1871 pistol on left side of frame. Very distinctively shaped full checkered pistol-grip stock and checkered forend; hard rubber buttplate with Remington monogram in shield design. Lyman type, folding, tang peep sight mounted on uniquely designed bracket behind hammer. One of the most unusual Remington arms as well as last rolling block introduced:

5E-104   Values—Very Good **$2,500**   Exc. **$7,500**

Ingersoll Life-Line Gun

Ingersoll Life-Line Gun. An unusual special order variant of the rolling block. Patented 1885 by Simon Ingersoll of Stamford, Conn. Made for the "Ingersoll Life-Line Company" utilizing No. 1 action (of the N.Y. State contract type) with special fitted, short, thick .44 barrel and very heavy nickel plated all brass stock marked at wrist "Remington Arms Co. Ilion, N.Y." and the Ingersoll patent dates "Dec. 8, 1885/Sept. 7, 1886." Ingersoll advertised the gun "Every Sea Side resort should have the Life-Line Gun ready for instant use to save life in case of fire or drowning [they] are indispensable for steamers, pleasure yachts and ships...it can also be used for throwing a harpoon in the seal and whale fisheries." Factory records indicate at least 25 were made for Hill & Stover, N.Y. who owned the Ingersoll Co. in 1888; one in 1895; 28 in 1899. It's possible others were made, but from their appearance on the collectors' market, they would be considered rare. Other similar appearing line throwers with rolling block actions and all metal stocks are known, but not believed to be fabricated by the Remington factory.

5E-104.5   Values—Very Good **$1,150**   Exc. **$2,500**

Reading Remington Barrels

Although it's not possible to check factory records to verify the original accessories or equipment that Remington Rolling Block and Remington-Hepburn Sporting and Target Rifles were originally shipped with, there are certain markings that appear on the underside of their barrels of great assistance to the collector. The forend needs only to be removed to view them. The following commonly encountered markings (in large size, block letters) indicate the rifle left the factory with these extra features:

D.T. = Double (set) Triggers
S.T. = Set Trigger (i.e. single set trigger).
P.G. = Pistol Grip

SIGHTS = Usually indicates extra target sights other than standard.

E.S. = Extra Sights. This tends to be confusing; it has been found to occasionally imply that a gun has both its normal sights (as called for in catalog) as well as an extra sight or sights … or, in some cases, merely has a set of sights that are other than standard.

The No. 3 Remington-Hepburn Rifle

Designed by Lewis L. Hepburn, Superintendent of Remington's mechanical department, and also a member of the

American Creedmoor International Shooting Team, this distinctive falling block action rifle was patented in 1879 and first introduced in 1880. Remington listed numerous variations in their catalogs until approximately 1907. The side mounted lever on the frame operates the breech, which drops downward; a very strong, simply worked and constructed action.

Certain features are common throughout all Hepburns, such as finishes: quite handsome casehardened action with the barrel blued. Checkered pistol grip buttstocks are common to all Hepburns except for the full stock "Creedmoor Military" model and the under-lever so-called "Walker" type. On lower grades the forends are plain without checkering but these could be specially ordered checkered. Finer grades had matching checkering standard. Forend tips vary: Hardened metal on the early production hunting rifles was later changed to hard rubber or horn, inset along the underside of the tip. Fancy match grades usually carried casehardened or nickel plated tips or on special order, full horn or rubber to match the pistol grip caps. Various styles of double set triggers were available. Caliber markings are usually stamped on the underside of barrel just ahead of the forend. Barrels are marked E. REMINGTON & SONS, ILION, N.Y. or REMINGTON ARMS CO. Marked on the right side of the action HEPBURN'S PAT. OCT. 7th, 1879.

Hepburns are often difficult to simply categorize. It appears that factory nomenclature for some of the models changed over the years and names did not always remain consistent. As standard models and variations were dropped, others were introduced. Hence an intensive study is required to fully clarify the subject. Almost all important and basic models are included here. The reader should also note that certain information accompanying the description of the Remington rolling block rifles (*q.v.*) is applicable to these Hepburns also. Prices and descriptions as they appear below are for the standard grade of each model. Custom features will add varying premiums. Considerable further information may be found in the James Grant book *Single Shot Rifles*.

Condition is very important both internally and externally on Remington-Hepburns and very much affects not only the demand factor, but values; although to a slightly lesser degree on the extremely rare models or variants.

Remington-Hepburn No. 3 Sporting and Target Model

5E-105

Remington-Hepburn No. 3 Sporting and Target Model. Made c. 1883-1907. Quantities unknown, estimated at 8,000 to 10,000.

Listed in a tremendous variety of calibers from 22 Winchester centerfire to 50-90 Sharps straight. Barrel lengths 26", 28", and 30". Available either round or octagon; part round/part octagon. Sporting, open type rear sights standard with elevator adjustment; blade type front sight. Special weight heavier barrels and more popular caliber sizes (especially those for various 45s and 50s) will bring premiums. Buttstock made without cheekrest:

5E-105   Values—Very Good **$1,250**   Exc. **$4,500**

Remington-Hepburn No. 3 Match Rifle

5E-106

Remington-Hepburn No. 3 Match Rifle. Made c. 1883-1907. Quantity unknown, estimated at less than 1,000.

Chief distinguishing feature is the larger buttstock with high comb and the nickel plated pronged Schuetzen type or "Swiss" buttplate. Made for fine target shooting in short and mid-range matches.

Calibers 25-20 Stevens; 25-21 Stevens; 25-20; 25-25; 32-40; 38-40; 38-50; 40-65.

Made in two distinct grades: "A Quality" and "B Quality." Major distinguishing features between the two: The "A Quality" had plain grained walnut stock with cheekrest and uncheckered forend; Beach combination front and tang peep sight. The "B Quality" had fancy select grained stock, large cheekrest, matching checkering on forend, Vernier tang peep sight and windgauge front sight with spirit level. Double set triggers were an extra feature and will bring slight premium:

"A" Quality No. 3 Match:
5E-106   Values—Very Good **$2,000**   Exc. **$5,000**
"B" Quality No. 3 Match:
5E-107   Values—Very Good **$2,750**   Exc. **$6,000**

Remington-Hepburn No. 3 Long Range Creedmoor

5E-108

Remington-Hepburn No. 3 Long Range Creedmoor. Made c. 1880-1907. Quantities unknown, believed but a few hundred.

Calibers 44 (2.6"), 44-100, 44-90 straight. 32" or 34" octagon/round barrel with tall long range Vernier rear peep and windgauge spirit level front sight. Shotgun butt with hard rubber buttplate. A second base for the rear Vernier peep sight is mounted at heel of stock. Deluxe wood grains and checkering on forend were extra features and premium should be added:

5E-108   Values—Very Good **$3,500**   Exc. **$8,000**

Remington-Hepburn No. 3 Mid-Range Creedmoor Rifle

Remington-Hepburn No. 3 Mid-Range Creedmoor Rifle. (Not illus.) Very similar to the Long-Range Model, but shorter 28" barrel with the short Vernier tang peep sight and windgauge front sight with spirit level. Calibers 40-65 and 40-65 straight:

5E-109   Values—Very Good **$2,250**   Exc. **$5,500**

Remington-Hepburn No. 3 High-Power Rifle

Remington-Hepburn No. 3 High-Power Rifle. (Not illus.) Believed introduced around 1900 and made to c. 1907. Quantities unknown; believed limited. Made for the smokeless cartridges; calibers 30-30; 30 Government; 32 Special; 32-40 H.P.; 38-55 H.P.; 38-72. 26", 28", and 30" round barrels standard. Open type hunting sights. Other features available such as double set triggers, fancier grain wood and checkered forend will add premium:

5E-110   Values—Very Good **$1,750**   Exc. **$4,000**

Remington-Hepburn No. 3 Long Range Military Rifle

5E-111

5E-112

Remington-Hepburn No. 3 Long Range Military Rifle. Made c. 1880s; quantities unknown; extremely limited. Chambered for 44-75-520 Remington straight cartridge. Round 34" barrel.

Full musket type forend fastened by two barrel bands. Plain, uncheckered, straight stock with standard military type barrel sights (Vernier sights add premium). This model is designed specifically for competition in the Creedmoor contests:

5E-111   Values—Very Good **$2,500**   Exc. **$5,000**

Fancy grade. Identical to above with checkered pistol grip stock and very fancy, almost full checkered forend. Vernier type long-range tang peep sight and windgauge spirit:

5E-112   Values—Very Good **$4,250**   Exc. **$8,000**

Remington-Hepburn No. 3 Schuetzen Match

Remington-Hepburn No. 3 Schuetzen Match Rifle, a.k.a. "Under-lever Hepburn," a.k.a. "The Walker-Hepburn." Unique feature is the under-lever which operates breech with no provision for side lever. Under-lever in the shape of an exceptionally fancy large scrolled trigger guard. Two styles (see below) medium-heavy weight 30" or 32" part octagon/part round barrel (weight 11 to 13 lbs.). Very fancy large Schuetzen type checkered butt and forend with high cheekrest; massive

5E-114

Swiss type pronged buttplate; double set triggers; wind gauge Vernier tang peep and hooded front sight; palm rest.

Buyer must be very cautious on this model. Very few specimens known and there are many spurious pieces as well as alterations that look like the Walker, but are not original factory.

The very ultimate for rarity in both the Remington line and the American single shot rifle line.

Breech-loading; with Remington Walker barrel:

5E-113   Values—Very Good **$12,500**   Exc. **$27,500**

Muzzle-loading; with Remington Walker barrel fitted with a removable false muzzle (the Walker name usually appears underneath) and accompanied by brass bullet starter. Other loading accessories were supplied and if intact are worth extra premium:

5E-114   Values—Very Good **$17,500**   Exc. **$40,000**

Remington Single Shot Bolt Action Rifle

Remington Single Shot Bolt Action Rifle. Made c. 1868-69. Total quantity less than 50 (numbers as high as 45 recorded on five known specimens to date).

Caliber 43 Egyptian c.f. (45-70 reported, but not viewed). Barrel length 31-1/2". Full walnut stock fastened by two barrel bands. Iron mounts and cleaning rod.

Receiver markings REMINGTON'S/ILION N.Y. U.S.A./PATENT 1868 with Birmingham, England script cipher proofmarks **VPB** with crown on both receiver and breech of barrel. Underside of barrel marked A & T (Adams and Tait, Birmingham, England, gun barrel makers). One specimen reported (not viewed) REMINGTON AND SONS/ILION N.Y./PATENT 1869.

5E-114.5

Made by Remington (under U.S. patent #86,690 issued Feb. 9, 1869 to Samuel Remington) with some barrels added in England:

5E-114.5   Values—Very Good **$2,000**   Exc. **$3,750**

Remington-Keene Magazine Bolt Action Rifle

Remington-Keene Magazine Bolt Action Rifle. Made c. 1880-1883. Total quantity estimated at 5,000.

45-70 caliber most widely made and most popular and in demand. Also made in 40 caliber and 43 caliber. 24-1/2" round barrel standard on sporting rifles. Also available part octagon/part round barrel and will bring premium.

Standard finish blued throughout; casehardened hammer. Iron mountings. Walnut straight stock standard with pistol grip optional and worth premium as are select grain woods.

Marked on left side of breech E. REMINGTON & SONS, ILION, N.Y./PATENT FEB. 24. MARCH 17. 1874 JAN. 18. SEPT. 26, 1876. MAR. 20. JUL. 31. 77.

Remington's first production bolt action firearm, the Keene had an outside, visible hammer; with bolt closed, hammer was manually cocked. Mechanism included a magazine cut-off allowing for use as a single shot if desired. Various models as listed below:

Hunter's or sporting rifle; as described above:

5E-115   Values—Very Good **$875**   Exc. **$2,000**

Frontier model; made for the U.S. Department of the Interior for arming Indian Police 1880-1881. 24" barrel with carbine style barrel band at muzzle; sling swivels; carbine buttplate without flanged top and marked U.S.I.D. with serial number on left side of frame and also government inspectors' marks on frame and stock. Quantity estimated 620 to 800. (More recent research appears to indicate quantity mfd. likely under 500.)

5E-116   Values—Good **$2,750**   Fine **$6,000**

Carbine model; 22" barrel with full stock running almost to muzzle fastened by two barrel bands and iron forend tip; sling swivels on upper band and underside of butt. Magazine carries seven cartridges. Short folding leaf military type rear sight and military buttplate. *Very scarce:*

5E-117   Values—Very Good **$1,400**   Exc. **$3,250**

5E-115

5E-118

Army rifle; 32-1/2" barrel, full stock running almost to muzzle fastened by two barrel bands with narrow iron forend cap. Sling swivels upper band and underside of butt.

The rifle is very scarce. The U.S. Army evidently only used a few examples in the 1881 trials and made no further purchases. A martially marked specimen would be worth a substantial value over that shown here:

5E-118   Values—Very Good **$2,000**   Exc. **$4,000**

Navy rifle; identical to above, just slightly shorter 29-1/4" barrel. The U.S. Navy purchased 250 of these in 1880 which are believed to have been issued to the Marine Corps for field tests. Barrels marked at breech U.S./anchor/P/WWK:

5E-119   Values—Very Good **$2,750**   Exc. **$5,000**

Remington-Lee Magazine, Bolt Action Rifles

Remington-Lee Magazine, Bolt Action Rifles. Made c. 1880 to 1907. Total quantity in excess of 100,000 with majority for export.

Standard finish blued. Majority of production was military muskets with full stocks fastened by two barrel bands; carbines with short stock single band fastened; sporting rifles fastened by screw from underside of forend. Detachable box magazines under stock just ahead of trigger guard and are a major feature for quick identification.

In 1880, the U.S. Navy contracted with James Paris Lee of Bridgeport, Connecticut for 300 full stock 45-70 caliber rifles of the type invented (and patented 1879) by Lee. The Lee Arms Company was formed to produce the guns and let a contract to Sharps Rifle Company to actually manufacture them. Sharps discontinued all operations in 1881 and the Lee parts and tools were turned over to Remington Arms Company who completed the guns for the Navy contract. Remington was also licensed to produce the Lee Rifles for foreign sales and made some slight modifications to the action. As a result of various contracts with both foreign governments, the U.S. Army and Navy, further modifications were made resulting in several variations for which "Model" designations and/or classifications have been applied by collectors. Such terminology was not always recognized by either Remington or the Lee Arms Company, who retained patent and sales control throughout the manufacturing life of the guns. Serial numbers, with the exception of the Model 1879, are in the same series. All models were made in three basic variations: Military Rifle, Military Carbine and Sporting Rifle of which the Military Rifle is by far the most common.

Model 1879: Made by Sharps. Flat sided magazine. Total quantity made approximately 300 with most of them military model. But one carbine made and a very few sporting rifles (rare, will bring considerable premium). Military model has 28" barrel, full stock, two-band fastened; caliber 45-70. Barrel marked: SHARPS RIFLE CO. BRIDGEPORT, CONN. and in a rectangular cartouche OLD RELIABLE. *Rare:*

5E-120   Values—Good **$2,500**   Fine **$5,000**

Model 1879: By Remington. Right side of magazine flat; left side with raised rib for cut-off device. Marked on receiver: LEE ARMS CO. BRIDGEPORT, CONN. U.S.A. and PATENTED NOV. 4, 1879.

U.S. Navy Model; 29-1/4" round barrel; full stock two-band fastened. U.S. Navy inspector marks, proof and naval anchor near breech of barrel. Caliber 45-70. Approximately 1,300 made:

5E-121   Values—Good **$675**   Fine **$2,000**

Military Rifle; identical to above without U.S. military markings. Majority made for export. Caliber 45-70 or 43-77 (43 Spanish). This latter caliber brings about 25 percent less than the 45-70s valued here. Some found with Chinese barrel markings. Approximate quantity made 1,000:

5E-122   Values—Good **$425**   Fine **$1,000**

Sporting Rifle; caliber 45-70 or 45-90. 28" or 30" part round/part octagon barrel. Pistol grip sporting type half stock. Approximately 400 to 500 made. Rare:

5E-123   Values—Good **$625**   Fine **$1,400**

Models 1882 and 1885: Magazine has two grooves down each side to guide the cartridge lifter. Only differences in these models is in the extractor and cocking knob on bolt, both of which are larger on the Model 1885. The Model 1882 marked: LEE ARMS CO. BRIDGEPORT, CONN., U.S.A. and PATENTED NOV. 4, 1879; or E. REMINGTON & SONS, ILION, N.Y. U.S.A. SOLE MANUFACTURERS & AGENTS The Model 1885 may be found with either of the above two described markings or REMINGTON ARMS CO./ILION, N.Y. U.S.A. and LEE PATENT NOV. 4. 1879.

Model 1882 U.S. Army Contract; 32" round barrel; full stock two-band fastened. Caliber 45-70. Marked U.S. at breech with inspector initials and also inspector markings on right side of stock. Quantity made estimated at 770:

5E-124   Values—Good **$675**   Fine **$1,750**

Model 1885 U.S. Navy Contract; as above with inspector marking on left side of stock and on receiver ring naval inspector's initials and anchor. Quantity made estimated at 1,500:

5E-125   Values—Good **$675**   Fine **$1,750**

Military Models Not Under U.S. Contract; made for various foreign governments and civilian sales. Calibers 45-70, 43 Spanish, 45 Gardner, 42 Russian. A great many of these were made for foreign export and are found with foreign markings. Approximately 10,000 of the Model 1882 manufactured and

5E-124
M1882

5E-131
M1889 Sporting Rifle

60,000 of the Model 1885. Prices tend to be generally the same for both. Values indicated are for the most popular 45-70. Although some of the other calibers are considerably scarcer, they generally tend to bring about 25 percent less. 32" barrel:

5E-126   Values—Good **$425**   Fine **$875**

Model 1882/1885 Carbines; 24" round barrel. *Very scarce:*

5E-127   Values—Good **$675**   Fine **$1,750**

Model 1882/1885 Sporting Rifles; calibers 45-70 and 45-90. 26" and 30" octagon barrels; sporting style half stock. Estimated quantity made 200. *Very scarce:*

5E-128   Values—Good **$650**   Fine **$1,750**

Model 1899: Three grooves on each side of magazine. Made mostly for smokeless powder cartridges. Considerable changes in the extractor to adapt for rimless cartridges. Calibers as below. Markings: REMINGTON ARMS CO./ILION, N.Y. PATENTED AUG. 26th 1884. SEP'T 9th 1884. MARCH 17th 1885. JAN. 18th 1887. Made c. 1899 to 1907.

Full Stock Military Rifle; calibers 6mm USN; 30-40; 303 British; 7mm; 7.65mm. Similar to the Model 1882/1885 with noticeably different contour to tip of forend which is designed to accept a knife type bayonet. Also easily distinguished by the wooden

barrel cover from lower band to receiver; slightly different contour to bolt and cocking piece. 29" barrel. The 30-40 caliber will bring a 10 percent to 20 percent premium:

5E-129   Values—Very Good **$500**   Exc. **$950**

Military Carbine; counterpart to the above rifle, chambered for the same cartridges; 20" barrel; three-quarter carbine style stock fastened with single barrel band and also having distinctive barrel cover extending from band to receiver. The 30-40 caliber will bring approximately a 10 percent to 20 percent premium:

5E-130   Values—Very Good **$650**   Exc. **$1,500**

Sporting Rifle; calibers as above and also 30-30; 303; 32 Special; 32-40; 35 Special; 38-55; 38-72; 405; 45-70; and 45-90. 26" or 28" octagonal barrels or 24", 26", and 28" round barrels. Walnut half stock with grasping grooves along sides of forend and standard with checkered pistol grip. Open type front and rear sporting sights. Very fancy, select grained wood or custom sights available and will bring varying premiums. The more popular calibers will also bring premiums from 10 percent to 25 percent. Total quantity manufactured estimated at 7,000:

5E-131   Values—Very Good **$450**   Exc. **$950**

Remington Berthier Bolt Action Rifle

5E-132

Remington Berthier French Army Model 1907/15 Bolt Action Rifle. (Named incorrectly the "Remington Lebel Bolt Action Rifle" in earlier editions). Utilizes a Mannlicher three-round clip. Made under contract for the French government circa 1915. Exact quantities made and/or delivered unknown; estimated a few thousand to as high as 50,000. Remington references mention the U.S. purchased a quantity of these in WWI that were issued to the

American 369th and 372nd Negro Infantry regiments of the A.E.F. that served with French forces in Europe during that war.

8mm Lebel caliber. 31-1/2" barrel. Full stock. Blued finish.

Marked on right side of barrel at breech RAC 1907-15. Marked on left side of action in script REMINGTON/M'LE 1907-15:

5E-132   Values—Very Good **$275**   Exc. **$500**

Remington Mosin-Nagant Bolt Action Rifle

5E-133

Remington Mosin-Nagant Bolt Action military rifle made under contract for the Russian government circa 1916-1918. Exact quantity unknown but over 650,000. Original contract for one million terminated by Russian Revolution of 1918.

7.62mm caliber; 32" barrel. Full stock. Blued finish.

Marked on top of barrel at breech in arch design REMINGTON/ARMORY/ (DATE). Marked on top of breech with the crest of Czar Nicholas II:

5E-133   Values—Very Good **$250**   Exc. **$425**

Remington-Enfield Bolt Action Rifle *See U.S. Model 1917 Magazine Rifle, Chapter IX-A.*

Remington-Whitmore Model 1874, Model 1876, Model 1878 Double Barrel Hammer Shotguns and Rifles

5E-134

Remington-Whitmore "Lifter Action" Model 1874, Model 1876, Model 1878 Double Barrel Hammer Shotguns and Rifles. Made c.1874 to 1882 (Model 1876 only to mid-1880s). Total quantity estimated at few thousand.

10 and 12 Gauge Models 1874, 1876. 10 Gauge only Model 1878. 28" and 30" steel barrels with blued finish standard; Damascus barrels available as option (collector values same). Case hardened locks and breech. Walnut pistol grip or straight stock.

Barrel rib marked E. REMINGTON & SONS, ILION, N.Y. Model 1874 only marked at top of breech on latch A.E. WHITMORE'S PATENT AUG.8.1871. The Model 1878 (made 1878 to mid-1880s) was "streamlined" and made without the flashplates on lower breech frame; renamed the "New Model Heavy Shotgun".

One of the very first mass produced, reasonably priced, double barrel shotguns made in the U.S. Pulling upward on breech lever at top of frame opened barrels. Few options

1874   1876/78

available; fancy, select grain and checkered stocks, or engraved action and locks are worth premium values.

Standard hammer double shotgun:
5E-134   Values—Very Good **$450**   Exc. **$1,200**
Combination rifle/shotgun. *Very scarce:*
5E-135   Values—Very Good **$1,400**   Exc. **$4,500**
Double rifle: Identical to that described above, but original rifle barrels. Very rare, few made. Extreme caution should be exercised when acquiring specimens to insure that they are not lined shotgun barrels:
5E-136   Values—Very Good **$3,750**   Exc. **$10,000**

Remington Model 1882 & Model 1883 Double Barrel Hammer Shotguns

5E-137

Model 1882 and Model 1883 Double Barrel Hammer Shotguns. Made c. 1882-1889. Total quantity estimated at approximately 5,000.

10 and 12 gauge. 28" and 30" steel or damascus barrels.

Walnut straight or half pistol grip stock; blued finish with damascus barrels having twist finish; casehardened locks and action; hard rubber or steel buttplate. Barrels marked E. REMINGTON & SONS, ILION, N.Y. No lock markings.

The Model 1883 is basically the same as the Model 1882 with lower, curved hammer spur (see chart below) and improved sighting. Very scarce; worth 20 percent premium.

Conventional top lever action. Available in select grain woods, finer checkering and engraving all which will increase value proportionately; at least six varying grades advertised originally:
5E-137   Values—Very Good **$450**   Exc. **$1,100**

Remington Model 1885, Model 1887, Model 1889 Double Barrel Hammer Shotguns

5E-138
Model 1889

Model 1885, Model 1887, Model 1889 Double Barrel Hammer Shotguns. Made c. 1885-1909. Total quantities unknown, estimated over 30,000.

10, 12, 16 gauge; barrel lengths 28" to 32"; available in steel or damascus barrels. Details about the same as for previous shotguns. Available in great many grades and varying degrees of embellishments all of which will increase value proportionately. Prices here for standard, plain grades. All these represent improvements over the Model 1882, all of them being very similar in appearance to it with but slight contour changes and hammer shape.

Models 1885 and 1887 marked on barrel rib E. REMINGTON & SONS, ILION, N.Y., U.S.A. Model 1889 marked REMINGTON ARMS

| 1882 | 1883 | 1885/87 | 1889 |

CO. on both locks and barrel rib:

5E-138   Values—Very Good **$450**   Exc. **$1,100**

NOTE: Between 1882 and 1889 Remington manufactured inserts to convert shotguns into rifles. Rifle sights were included with the accessory. Where such inserts are present with Remington shotguns values increase 50 to 100 percent.

Remington Hammerless Shotguns Model 1894 and Model 1900

5E-139
Model 1894

5E-139.5
Model 1900

Hammerless Shotguns Model 1894 and Model 1900. Made c. 1894-1910. Total produced unknown, but several thousands.

10, 12, and 16 gauge (Model 1900 in 12 and 16 only). Barrel lengths from 26" to 32" of steel or damascus twist. Value below for plain grades; available with many options and many grades, all of which will increase prices proportionately.

Both models bear the Remington Arms Co. logo on sides of the receivers and often on the barrel ribs as well:

Model 1894: Total Quantity 14,000:
5E-139   Values—Very Good **$450**   Exc. **$1,400**
Model 1900: Total quantity 95,000:
5E-139.5   Values—Very Good **$425**   Exc. **$1,100**

Remington Single Barrel Model 1893 & Model No. 9 Shotguns

Remington Single Barrel Model 1893 and Model No. 9 Shotguns. Outside hammer, side cocking Model 1893 (a.k.a. No. 3) shotgun made 1893-1903 and Model No. 9 made 1902-1910. Total quantity of both estimated 50,000.

10, 12, 16, 20, 24 and 28 gauge. Blued barrel in various lengths 28" to 34". Case-hardened frames. Hard rubber buttplates with Remington logo.

About identical, the Model 1893 has a button release on

forend and standard ejector. Model No. 9 with screw released forend and auto ejector. Plain, pistol grip walnut stock. Markings REMINGTON ARMS CO. ILION, N.Y. U.S.A.; encountered with and without patent dates.

Shotguns 10, 12, 16 and 20 Gauge:
5E-140   Values—Very Good **$150**   Exc. **$400**
Gauges 24 and 28; very scarce:
5E-141   Values—Very Good **$225**   Exc. **$500**

5E-140

Chapter V-F

Sharps Firearms

Among the illustrious names in American firearms history is that of Christian Sharps, originator of a line of extremely practical, sturdy, long-lived and often quite handsome military and sporting rifles and handguns. Sharps arms are associated with several major historical events which shaped American destiny in the 19th century. The substantial quantities in which many of his models were made is testimony to their widespread popularity with both the military and the public during their period of manufacture and use. Undoubtedly the most widely used and popular cavalry weapon of the Civil War was the Sharps carbine. Certainly, one of the guns that most quickly comes to mind in considering the opening and expansion of the West following the Civil War, is the Sharps "Buffalo" rifle. The gun was so closely associated in Western lore (and especially that concerning the meat hunters of the Old West) that its name was often used synonymously by writers of the period to indicate any big game rifle. Although no such terminology was ever applied by the Sharps Company, in actuality a great many models of Sharps are called by present day collectors and authors "Buffalo Rifles."

Sharps models are chronologically arranged in this chapter, with all major variations and sub-models listed and identified. Most Sharps specimens are simply recognized; it is with the Model 1874 rifle that much confusion exists in correctly classifying various types. The reader is cautioned to be especially careful before quickly categorizing a Model 1874 and special note of that is made under that respective listing.

Considerable misinformation as well as large gaps in information characterize much of what has appeared in print about Sharps firearms. A great deal remains to be written on the subject. Much of the material appearing in this chapter is fresh data not previously published. It is hoped this presentation will help rectify and clarify as well as simplify the field of Sharps collecting. A substantial amount of data, particularly quantities manufactured, was gleaned directly from original Sharps manufacturing records which are still in existence.

Sharps longarm prices are very much determined, as are other American antique arms, by condition. Demand is usually quite strong for all Sharps in just about all conditions, largely due to the great historical associations of these arms. It seems that almost all Sharps percussion military models of the Civil War era were issued and saw considerable service; they are seldom found with any amount of finish remaining, thus the very fine conditioned specimens do tend to bring noteworthy premiums. This equally applies to those general types known as the "Buffalo Rifles," the heavy duty, serviceable, plain weapons that made their way west in the 1870s and the 1880s, and were the working gun of that part of America. Fine conditioned specimens are quite difficult to find and for the most part, those working guns show wear and use. But, with all the lore surrounding them, they are still very much in demand.

It is with the fine and fancy grades of Model 1874, 1877 and Borchardt sporting and target rifles that slight variances in grades of condition and bores play an important and influencing role in values. The more the gun is designed for use as an accurate competition sporting or target rifle, the more these features are important to value; slight fluctuations affect demand and value considerably. Such features as the absence of a Vernier tang sight on a Creedmoor (where it is standard and part of the original issue with the gun) are a detriment to value, whereas the absence of a sight on one of the more commonly encountered "working" models (also a type that might easily be located) would be of only minor significance.

Occasionally gunsmith's or agent's names are found marked on Sharps rifles, indicating that they merely handled and sold the piece as dealers. Such markings add a premium to value, the figure fluctuating with the notoriety of the name. Those same markings may also indicate that a special modification, peculiar to the individual gunsmith, was performed on the rifle (F.W. Freund of Cheyenne, Wyoming was especially noted and is highly desirable). Such custom, marked alterations are worth increased premiums.

Engraved and lavishly decorated Sharps are known in almost all models and are quite eagerly sought after. Designs run from simple scroll and floral work to fancy engraved panels depicting hunting and western scenes. Decoration of deluxe arms was executed by a number of famous as well as unnamed engravers of the era. The mere presence of original engraving enhances Sharps value considerably. As with other fine American arms, in order to achieve high demand and high value, it is important to have equally fine grades of condition. Sharps four-barrel pepperboxes are more often engraved than other type Sharps arms and often encountered with grips other than factory standard, usually of ivory and occasionally bearing relief carving.

A brief biography of the founder and a review of the companies that manufactured his arms will prove helpful to understand his sequence of firearms: Christian Sharps (1811-1874) worked for the famed New England inventor John Hall at the Harpers Ferry Arsenal, where he learned the principles of arms manufacturing. Sharps' own first breechloader was patented in 1848. In 1850 he moved to Mill Creek, Pennsylvania (near Philadelphia), and contracted with the old, well established arms manufacturing firm of A. S. Nippes at Mill Creek where the first two models of Sharps sporting rifles were made. Finding it difficult to finance further arms projects in the Philadelphia area, Christian Sharps went to New England where an arrangement was made with the well known firm of Robbins and Lawrence to manufacture the new breechloader at their factory in Windsor, Vermont (c. 1851). The corporation to manage and sell the arms was formed and headquartered in Hartford, Connecticut as the Sharps Rifle Manufacturing Company. Christian Sharps served as technical advisor to the company, receiving a royalty on guns manufactured. Arms production continued in Vermont until approximately 1855 at which time manufacturing changed to Hartford, continuing under the name of Sharps Rifle Manufacturing Company until 1874. The firm was then reorganized as the Sharps Rifle Company, remaining in Hartford through 1876. Hartford operations ceased in 1876 and the plant was moved to Bridgeport where it continued under the same name, Sharps Rifle Company, until 1881.

To collectors' good fortune many of the original Sharps Company ledger books are intact and privately owned. Records are near complete for almost all cartridge models; lacking for many of the percussion guns. The owner of those records passed away (since the 8th edition of this work). We understand information is still to be furnished about Sharps serial numbers and recommend checking the website www.antiqueguns.com/places.htm ("Researching your Guns") for up-to-date information. Christian Sharps' relations with the Sharps Rifle Manufacturing Company were rocky at best. In 1853 he severed all connections with Hartford, with no evidence that he was ever further associated with it. He returned to Philadelphia and in 1854 formed C. Sharps & Company where he commenced manufacturing with a breech-loading percussion single shot pistol and pistol-rifle; in 1859 with four-shot pepperboxes. In 1862 he entered partnership with William Hankins forming a new company known simply as Sharps and Hankins. Production continued under that name with four-barrel pepperboxes and single shot breech-loading rifles and carbines (with sliding barrel actions); almost the entire production was devoted to military work. The partnership was dissolved in 1866 and Christian Sharps reverted to the C. Sharps & Company name. He resumed manufacture of four-barrel pepperboxes. The firm ceased existence with Christian Sharps' death in 1874.

BIBLIOGRAPHY

(NOTE: A considerable amount of material on Sharps may be found in several other books covering American firearms; a few of the more important titles worth checking are: *The Rifle in America,* by Philip Sharp; *Single Shot Rifles* and *More Single Shot Rifles* by James J. Grant; *U. S. Military Small Arms 1816-1865* by Robert M. Reilly; *U. S. Muskets, Rifles and Carbines* by Arcadi Gluckman; and *The Collecting of Guns* edited by James E. Serven and all of the McAulay carbine and rifle books see Chap. IX.)

*Balentine, F.J.P., *Freund & Brothers Pioneer Gunmakers To The West.* Newport Beach, Cal. Graphics Publishers, 1997. Impressive, extensive, well illustrated.

*Coates, E.J. & McAulay, J.D. *"Civil War Sharps Carbines & Rifles.* Gettysburg, Pa: Thomas Publications, 1996. Significant reference; much on units using Sharps and even quite a bit on serial numbers and individuals to whom issued.

Hopkins, Richard E. *Military Sharps Rifles and Carbines,* Volume I. San Jose, California: Book Shelf Press, 1967. Pioneer work on the subject; considerable data and detail of value; more recent information on the subject has disproven some points discussed.

Kelver, Gerald O. *"Frank & George Freund & The Sharps Rifle;* Pioneer Gunmakers of Wyoming Territory & Colorado." Ft. Lupton, Colo.; private published monograph, 1986.

*Marcot, Roy M. *Civil War Chief of Sharpshooters Hiram Berdan, Military Commander and Firearms Inventor.* Irvine, California: Northwood Heritage Press, 1989. Profusely illustrated biography; important data on Sharps military rifles.

*Rywell, Martin. *Sharps Rifle, The Gun That Shaped American Destiny.* Union City, Tennessee: Pioneer Press, 1957. Short explanatory text with brief history of Sharps and his companies; mostly exact reprint of original period testimonials, brochures and catalog sections from Sharps Rifle catalogs along with exact reprints of patent drawings and applications.

Satterlee, L. D. (Compiler). *Fourteen Old Gun Catalogs for the Collector.* Originally published very limited edition 1940 with widely circulated reprint Gun Digest Association, Chicago, Illinois, 1962. Very valuable basic tool and guide for the collector. Exact reprints of eight original Sharps catalogs 1859 to 1880 plus reprints of other American makers catalogs of the same era.

*Sellers, Frank. *Sharps Firearms.* Denver, Colorado: Sellers Publication, 1982; 8th printing, Alstead N.H. The most important reference work ever published on the subject. Definitive, comprehensive coverage of all models and variations with historical background, performance data, information about cartridges and Sharps loading tools.

Sellers, Frank M. & Bailey III, Dewitt. *Sharps Firearms, Volume III, Part III, Model 1874 Rifles.* Denver, Colorado: Privately published, Frank M. Sellers. Highly authoritative definitive guide to the Model 1874 rifle and all its many varieties. Great wealth of data and much exact information from original company records. Widely cited and used.

Smith, Winston O. *The Sharps Rifle, Its History, Development and Operation.* New York: William Morrow & Co., 1943. The pioneer work on the Sharps rifle. Good basic information, but the important detail material especially on variations has been found lacking in the light of more recently unearthed information.

Sword, Wiley. *Sharpshooter: Hiram Berdan, His Famous Sharpshooters and Their Sharps Rifles.* Lincoln, R.I.: Mowbray Publishing Co., 1988. History of famed Civil War outfit.

(*) Preceding a title indicates the book is currently in print.

Sharps Model 1849 Rifle

Model 1849 Rifle (a.k.a. 1st Model Sharps). Made by A. S. Nippes, Mill Creek, Penna., for Christian Sharps. Made c. 1850. Total quantity likely less than 100.

5F-001

5F-001
Close-up action of Sharps Model 1849

36 and 44 caliber percussion breechloader with circular disk type automatic capping device on right side of the breech. Standard barrel length, 30".

Brass or iron patchbox, buttplate, and forend cap; a wooden cleaning rod mounted beneath the barrel.

Walnut stocks: note the slow curve profile to bottom contour of the buttstock.

Serial numbered from 1 on up. Specimens usually marked: A.S. NIPPES/MILL CREEK PA.

This quite rare first model in the Sharps series is highly prized by collectors and only a few examples are known. The most distinct identifying feature is the priming mechanism, covered by an upward-pivoting circular brass lid. Minor variations are evidenced on all specimens:

5F-001   Values—Good **$8,000**   Fine **$17,500**

Sharps Model 1850 Rifle

Model 1850 Rifle (a.k.a. 2nd Model Sharps). Made by A. S. Nippes for Christian Sharps; Butterfield & Nippes, Philadelphia (Kensington), Pennsylvania, distributors. Manufactured c. 1850; total quantity approximately 150.

36 and 44 caliber percussion (other calibers known) breechloader with Maynard tape primer mounted on the lock on right side of breech. Standard barrel length 30".

Iron patchbox and buttplate; brass forend cap. Wooden cleaning rod mounted on underside of barrel.

Walnut stocks quite similar to the First Model Sharps: note the slow curve profile to bottom contour of the buttstock.

Serial numbered from 1 on up. Specimens usually marked: on breech SHARPS PATENT/1848; on primer cover

MAYNARD/PATENT/1845; on barrel MANUFACTURED/BY/A.S. NIPPES/ MILL CREEK, PA.

One of the rarest of all Sharps firearms, the Second Model can be quickly identified by the similarity to the First Model, and the Maynard priming mechanism on the breech. Both Models also feature the long, curved back-action lockplate. The Second Sharps Rifle is important historically as the earliest sporting type longarm equipped with the Maynard tape primer. Also known in carbine length with 22" part octagon, part round barrel; caliber 52. Approximately 6 made. Rare; worth premium:

5F-002   Values—Good **$6,500**   Fine **$15,000**

5F-002

*5F-002
Close-up action of
Sharps Model 1850*

Sharps Model 1851 Carbine

5F-003

Model 1851 "Box Lock" Carbine. Made by Robbins & Lawrence, Windsor, Vermont, for Sharps Rifle Manufacturing Co., Hartford, Connecticut, c. 1852-55. Total quantity 1,857.

52 caliber percussion breechloader, using Maynard tape primer contained beneath a hinged trapdoor on front of lock which opens downward for loading. Easily distinguished by the hammer which is mounted *inside* the lock. 21-5/8" barrel.

Brass buttplate and barrel band, secured by a screw into stock, or by front end of sling ring bar.

Walnut stocks; brass patchbox on most except martial marked (Army & Navy) models and sporting model.

U.S. and inspector markings on the barrel of government purchased pieces; serial number and C.SHARPS/PATENT/1848 on the tang; EDWARD MAYNARD/PATENTEE/1845 on primer door; ROBBINS/&/LAWRENCE on barrel.

An important collector's piece; the first Sharps made as a military arm.

Martially marked carbine for U.S. Army: Order for 200 in 1854 changed to 150 guns; all delivered to 1st and 2nd U.S. Dragoons

in Texas and New Mexico. Serials 100 to 250. In 1855 another 25. Barrel marked "U.S. / S.P.K." and "U.S." / 1852" on heel of buttplate:

5F-003   Values—Good **$7,000**   Fine **$17,500**

Martially marked carbine for U.S. Navy; 60 to N.Y. Navy Yard 1853 for use in North Pacific Exploring Expedition. Forty recorded being aboard U.S.S. Vincennes; 10 aboard U.S.S. John Kennedy, 1853. Marked on heel of buttplate "USN" with tiny five point star between each letter. Serial numbers in 300 range:

5F-003.2   Values—Good **$7,500**   Fine **$20,000**

Standard carbine without military markings:

5F-003.5   Values—Good **$4,000**   Fine **$10,000**

Sporting rifle; as above with varying barrel lengths (longer) both round and octagon; the forend screw fastened without barrel band. Calibers 36, 44, and 52. Approximately 400 produced:

5F-004   Values—Good **$4,000**   Fine **$10,000**

(Note: Less than a handful [believe just 4] were produced as shotguns; one of most recognizable features, the lack of rifle type rear sights and bead type front sights. Very rare.)

Sharps Model 1852 Carbine

5F-005
Carbine

Model 1852 "Slanting Breech" Carbine. Made by Robbins & Lawrence, Windsor, Vermont, for Sharps Rifle Manufacturing Co., Hartford, Connecticut, c. 1853 to 1855. Total quantity approximately 5,000.

52 caliber percussion breechloader with Sharps patent pellet primer mounted in the lockplate. 21-1/2" barrel.

Brass buttplate, patchbox and barrel band. Blued finish with casehardened frame, breechblock, lock, lever and trigger plate. Variations seen in saddle ring bar and ring mounting.

Walnut stocks with patchbox in butt.

Serial numbered within the range of approximately 2050 to 7500. Barrels usually marked: SHARPS RIFLE/MANUFG. CO./HARTFORD, CONN.and may also bear U.S. and inspector stampings; on the tang: SHARPS/PATENT/1848 and the serial number; on the lockplate: C.SHARPS'/PATENT/1852. Occasionally this model is found with British proof marks indicating purchase by the British government and although a scarce feature, it does not normally command higher value.

This was the earliest Sharps having the distinctive relief contoured "slanting breech" on the frame. A key feature pinpointing the Model 1852 is the retaining spring on right rear section of the forend, serving to secure the lever hinge pin. Also standard was the sling ring slide bar extending from left side of the breech to the barrel band.

Standard model:
5F-005 Values—Good **$2,500** Fine **$6,000**
Martially marked carbine for U.S. Army: total 225 c. 1854 with most to U.S. 2nd Dragoons, Indian fighting in West. Markings as on M.1851:
5F-006 Values—Good **$3,750** Fine **$8,000**
Martially marked carbine for U.S. Navy: 150 delivered 1856. Some specifically intended to arm ship leaving for duty for "…a station infested with pirates and (Sharps carbine) might be called on". Markings as on M.1851; patch box final may also have inspector initials and date:
5F-006.2 Values—Good **$5,500** Fine **$12,500**
Sporting Rifles; as above with varying barrel lengths (round or octagon). Approximately 600 made. Calibers 36, 44 and 52:
5F-007 Values—Good **$3,000** Fine **$5,500**
Military Rifles; as above with 27" barrel and stud for saber bayonet; carbine type forend. Approximately 60 made:
5F-008 Values—Good **$6,000** Fine **$17,500**
Shotguns; as above, smoothbore and with shotgun bead type front sight and no provision for rear rifle sight. Approximately 73 made:
5F-009 Values—Good **$1,750** Fine **$4,000**

Sharps Model 1853 Carbine

5F-010
Carbine

Model 1853 Slanting Breech Carbine (a.k.a. The John Brown Model). Made by Robbins & Lawrence, Windsor, Vermont, for Sharps Rifle Manufacturing Co., Hartford, Connecticut until October 1856 and made by the Sharps Rifle Manufacturing Co. in Connecticut thereafter. Years of manufacture 1854 through 1857. Total quantity carbines approximately 10,500. 52 caliber; Sharps pellet primer system mounted in lock. 21-1/2" barrel.

Finish and mountings as on Model 1852, including brass patchbox; later production changed to iron. Walnut stocks.

Serial numbered within the range of about 9000 to 19000. Barrel markings SHARPS RIFLE/MANUFG. CO./HARTFORD, CONN.: tang markings: C. SHARPS/PATENT/1848 and serial number; lockplate markings: SHARPS/PATENT/1852 (early ones have an apostrophe in word SHARP'S; late ones omit it.)

To quickly distinguish this model from the Model 1852, note the small spring retained stud mounted in right side of frame to retain the lever hinge pin. In actuality, according to Sharps Manufacturing Co. itself, the Model 1852 and 1853 were the same model; the former being totally made in Windsor, Vermont, and the latter at Hartford, Connecticut. Four types of sling rings and ring bars are noted on the M1853; Sporting model carbines often seen without provision for sling rings. Numerous other minor variations are encountered.

Standard model:
5F-010 Values—Good **$2,000** Fine **$5,500**

"John Brown Sharps" and "Beecher's Bibles"

The Model 1853 carbine is known to collectors as the "John Brown Sharps" for its association with that firebrand abolitionist in the mid-1850's. It is occasionally referred to in some "Bleeding Kansas" and arms literature as "Beecher's Bibles" after the noted

5F-012
Shotgun

5F-013
Military Rifle

minister Henry Ward Beecher, who was quoted in the *N.Y. TRIBUNE,* Feb., 1856, as stating there was more moral power in one Sharps carbine than 100 bibles. The carbine story is best told in *SHARPS FIREARMS (q.v.)* and *PLOWS & BIBLES: RIFLES & REVOLVERS: GUNS OF KANSAS TERRITORY*, (D. Watts, Kansas Historical Society, Vol. 21, No. 1; Spring, 1998). There is some dissension about quantities intended for John Brown's use. There is evidence that both pro-slavery and anti-slavery factions owned Sharps carbines. Although it was but one of many diverse types of firearms used, "…nothing else could match the Sharps as a symbol of the free-state cause…it became a badge of the free-stater (and) the mere possession of (one) could mark a man as an enemy of the territorial government and its supporters." (Watts, "PLOWS & BIBLES"). Members of various Abolitionist "Emigrant Aid Societies" in the East raised funds to purchase at least 900 Model 1859 carbines for the struggle. (Serial numbers of 400 are found in "SHARPS FIREARMS.") Not all of them reached Kansas, nor is there conclusive evidence that John Brown received them in Kansas. Many reached no further than supporters in Tabor, Iowa. Many (or all) of that lot, subsequently sent back east, have been directly associated with his raid on the U.S. Arsenal at Harpers Ferry, Virginia in 1859. Recorded serial numbers for the 400 carbines are almost all in the range 10,000 to 18,000 (none 11,000). Values shown for specimens with positive identification by serial or with otherwise documented identification. Near misses, interesting, but values same as standard model:

5F-010.2   Values—Good **$5,500**   Fine **$12,500**

Martially marked U.S. military carbine. Identical to above with U.S. inspector markings. Estimated quantity 250:

5F-010.5   Values—Good **$4,500**   Fine **$9,500**

Sporting Rifle; as above; made 1854 to 1859 in calibers 36, 44 and 52; varying barrel lengths 24" to 34" with 27" the standard; octagon barrels most commonly encountered with 2,240 manufactured; round barrels 600 manufactured; and part octagon/round rare with only 110 manufactured. Brass furniture on early production; iron standard on later ones. Varied finishes offered with white, blue or brown barrels; casehardened action and furniture (if iron); plain or plated brass furniture; oil or varnish finish stocks. More fancy grade 1853 Sporting rifles were made than any other model; with 30 major variations listed in factory records not counting barrel lengths and finish:

5F-011   Values—Good **$1,500**   Fine **$4,500**

Shotgun; as above; made 1854 to 1856. Serial number range 8300 to 17300. Total quantity approximately 320. Made in 24, 26, 28, 32 and 90 bore; with majority in 26 bore (approximately 58 caliber). Distinguishable by lack of rear sight, bead front sight; often a groove on top of frame for sighting:

5F-012   Values—Good **$1,400**   Fine **$3,500**

Military Rifle; identical in contour to carbine with carbine type short forend and longer 27" barrel with stud for saber type bayonet. Approximately 204 made; serial number range 15000 to 17000:

5F-013   Values—Good **$4,750**   Fine **$17,500**

Sharps Model 1855 U.S. Carbine

Model 1855 U. S. Carbine. Sharps Rifle Manufacturing Co., Hartford, Connecticut. Made c. 1856-57. Quantity under 800.

52 caliber percussion breechloader; with Maynard tape primer beneath hinged trapdoor opening downward for loading. 21-3/4" barrel.

Brass buttplate, patchbox, and barrel band. Blued finish, with casehardened frame, breechblock, lock, lever, trigger plate, and lever latch. Walnut stocks. Note the sling ring mount of short length mounted on left side of the buttstock and breech.

Serial numbered within the range about 17000 to 22000. Barrel markings: SHARPS RIFLE/MANUFG. CO./HARTFORD CONN. On tang: SHARPS/PATENT 1848. On primer cover: EDWARD MAYNARD/PATENTEE 1845

Another scarcity in the Sharps field, the Model 1855 U.S. was the last of the slanting breech carbines, and was in production when the Robbins & Lawrence and Sharps firms suffered significant losses. The former actually failed, and Sharps Rifle Manufacturing Co. took over Robbins & Lawrence operations.

5F-014
Carbine

5F-015
Model 1855 Navy Rifle

Standard model:
5F-014   Values—Good **$4,750**   Fine **$17,500**
Martial Marked U.S. Army Carbine: Quantity 600; most issued to 1st Dragoons in California and 2nd Dragoons in Texas. Barrel marked "U.S. / JH":
5F-014.2   Values—Good **$7,500**   Fine **$20,000**
Martial Marked U.S. Navy Carbine: Quantity 100 c. 1857. Caliber 577. Barrel 18". Marked on heel of buttplate "USN" with a tiny five point star between each letter. Finial of patchbox marked with inspector "SCR" over "1857". It is recorded that 100 of those carbines were issued to U.S. naval vessels subsequently sent on the Paraguay expedition of 1858-1859.
5F-014.4   Values—Good **$8,500**   Fine **$25,000**

Model 1855 U.S. Navy Rifle; as above but with 27" barrel; 54 cal. forend of carbine type but slightly longer in length; stud for saber type bayonet on underside near muzzle. Total made approximately 263; c. 1856. Serial numbered within range about 20000 to 21000. Markings as above and usually naval anchor at breech of barrel denoting U.S.N. purchase. 200 were received by the U.S. Navy in 1857. The frigates USS Wabash and USS Merrimack each received 35; smaller quantities to USS Mississippi and USS Minnesota.
5F-015   Values—Good **$5,500**   Fine **$16,500**
Model 1855 Sporting Rifle; 28" octagon barrel. Extremely rare; only 12 listed as being made:
5F-016   Values—Good **$4,750**   Fine **$14,000**

Sharps Model 1855 British Carbine

5F-017

Model 1855 British Carbine. Sharps Rifle Manufacturing Co., Hartford, Connecticut. Made c. 1855-57; total quantity about 6,000. About identical to the U.S. Model 1855.

577 caliber percussion breechloader, having Maynard tape primer beneath hinged trapdoor opening downward for loading. 19" or 21" barrel; with approximately 3,000 of each length produced.

Brass buttplate and patchbox; the barrel band of wide configuration, and of iron. Blued finish, with casehardened frame, breechlock, lock, barrel band, lever, trigger plate, and lever latch. Walnut stocks. Sling ring of type as found on the Model 1855 U.S. Carbine, of short length, and mounted on left side of frame and on wrist of buttstock.

Serial numbered within the range about 19000 to 29000. Barrel and tang markings include British proofs; otherwise basically the same as on the Model 1855 U.S. Carbine.

Despite the significant manufacturing total, the Model 1855 British Carbine is a difficult item to obtain, since issue and use were primarily in foreign lands, under aegis of the British Empire. However, a few specimens are known to have returned to America for service in the Civil War. Unusual markings may be observed on foreign issue pieces, such as regimental identifications, or later-stamped police registration numbers:
5F-017   Values—Good **$4,000**   Fine **$8,000**

Sharps New Model 1859, 1863 and 1865 Carbines and Rifles

New Model 1859, 1863 and 1865 Carbines and Rifles. Sharps Rifle Manufacturing Co., Hartford, Connecticut, c. 1859 to 1866; total quantity all types approximately 115,000.

52 caliber all models percussion breechloader, so-called *straight breech* models; Sharps pellet priming system integral with lockplate. Variations as noted below in value section.

Markings included model designation on top of barrel near breech, i.e., NEW MODEL 1859, NEW MODEL 1863 or NEW MODEL 1865; also on the barrel SHARPS RIFLE/MANUFG. CO./HARTFORD, CONN.; on the left side of the receiver C. SHARPS PAT./SEPT. 12TH 1848; on the lock (near center) C. SHARPS' PAT./OCT. 5TH 1852, and (upper front section) R. S. LAWRENCE PAT./APRIL 12TH 1859. Other Lawrence markings and patent date appear on the rear sight and H. CONANT PATENT/APRIL 1, 1856 appears on rear of breechblock.

Stocks all were walnut, oil finished with inspector markings on left side at wrist. Finish generally blue barrel with casehardening on receiver, breechblock, lock, lever and trigger plate. Carbines have sling ring bars (finished white) affixed to left side of receiver extending to the middle of the wrist. Furniture all models is iron except where noted on first few New Model 1859 carbines.

Considerable confusion and misinformation has appeared about these three models leading to misunderstanding about them. It is hoped that the description and simplification here will correct most of what has preceded.

These straight breech models were a definite improvement over the earlier slant breech types and are the most common of the Sharps rifles and carbines, accounting for approximately 65

**5F-018
Carbine**

**5F-023
Military Rifle**

percent of total Sharps production. While these pieces are usually designated as three distinct models and actually bear such markings (New Model 1859, New Model 1863, New Model 1865), in actuality they are all one model. The difference in designation being merely a difference in barrel markings, a cleanout screw in the breechblock and minor sight change. Minor improvements were made throughout production and New Model 1859 markings will be found on barrels of guns which have the so-called New Model 1863 improvements; variations found within the models themselves are more important to the collector than barrel markings, consequently all straight breech models for ease in understanding should be considered together.

Percussion straight breech models were numbered consecutively from approximately 30000 to approximately 150000. At serial number 100000, a new marking was introduced, the use of the prefix C (the Roman numeral designation for the number one hundred). This prefix C designates the serial number 100000 (and definitely does not indicate, as has been erroneously reported, the word "carbine"); in other words, serial number C1 would indicate the serial number 100001. Considerable overlap exists in serial numbers between all three "New Models," but general ranges are: New Model 1859 in the range of approximately 30000 to 75000; New Model 1863 in the range from approximately 75000 to 140000; New Model 1865 in the range from approximately 140000 to 145000. Well over 100,000 Sharps rifles and carbines of these models were purchased and used by the U.S. Army and Navy during the Civil War (with the exception of the very early New Model 1859). Major types are:

CARBINES: All with 22" barrels.

New Model 1859 Carbine; early type. All brass furniture with brass patchbox. Approximate quantity made 3,000. State of Georgia bought 1600 from Sharps; another 400 on commercial market, 1860; known issued to Georgia cavalry and infantry units:
5F-018   Values—Good **$2,500**   Fine **$7,000**

New Model 1859 Carbine; iron furniture with patchbox. Approximate quantity manufactured 30,000. Early 1861 the Navy purchased small lot (quantity and source unknown) not fitted with saddle ring and ring bar; serials in 40,000 to 44,000 range. Worth premium if authentic:
5F-019   Values—Good **$1,750**   Fine **$3,750**

New Model 1863 Carbine; iron furniture with patchbox. Approximately 20,000 manufactured:
5F-020   Values—Good **$1,750**   Fine **$3,750**

New Model 1863 Carbine; iron furniture made without patchbox. Approximately 40,000 manufactured:
5F-021   Values—Good **$1,750**   Fine **$3,750**

New Model 1865 Carbine; iron furniture made without patchbox. Approximately 5,000 made:
5F-022   Values—Good **$1,750**   Fine **$4,500**

MILITARY RIFLES: All rifles (except where noted in one instance) have 30" round barrels with full forends fastened with three barrel bands; all have iron patchboxes.

New Model 1859 Rifle; lug for saber type bayonet near muzzle. Approximately: 1,500 for Army contract; 2,800 for Navy contract:
5F-023   Values—Good **$2,250**   Fine **$5,000**

Same as above adapted for socket bayonet. Estimated quantity 1000 (and likely larger) for U.S. Army contract:
5F-023.5 Values—Good **$2,250**   Fine **$5,000**

New Model 1859 Rifle issued to Col. Hiram Berdan's 1st and 2nd Regiments of U.S. Sharpshooters. 2000 purchased/issued c.1862. Authenticated examples in serial range 54,374 to 57,567 (Marcot), but possible that specimens may occur in range as low as 36,000 (Sellers). Found fitted for both type bayonets; most with double set triggers. Depending on authentication and features, values at very minimum 50 percent over those shown above:
5F-023.7

New Model 1859 Rifle; with extra long 36" barrel having bayonet lug near muzzle. This has a correspondingly longer forend. Approximately 600 manufactured. Usually found with blued receivers serial range 36-37,000:
5F-024   Values—Good **$3,000**   Fine **$5,000**

New Model 1863 Rifle; adapted for socket type bayonet; approximately 6,150 manufactured in serial range C30,000 to C40,000:
5F-025   Values—Good **$2,000**   Fine **$3,750**

Same as above; with lug for saber type bayonet. Approximately 1,000 made:
5F-025.5 Values—Good **$2,000**   Fine **$3,750**

New Model 1865 Rifle; made without bayonet lug; approximately 1,000 manufactured:
5F-026   Values—Good **$1,750**   Fine **$3,500**

(Note: Some specimens of military rifles were fitted with double set triggers and when found will command a small added premium value.)

**5F-027
Sporting Rifle**

5F-028
Coffee Mill Carbine

SPORTING RIFLES: One of the rare items produced during the Civil War era were octagon barrel sporting rifles; made in both the New Model 1859 and 1863 types. These were made using rejected actions that the government would not accept. Few were produced and most were fitted with fancy walnut stocks, double set triggers; octagonal barrels fitted on most. Estimated production about 100:

5F-027   Values—Good **$2,750**   Fine **$7,500**

COFFEE-MILL SHARPS: A very famous and rare variation of Sharps carbines is the so-called "Coffee-Mill" model. Built into the buttstock is a unique grinding device (with a removable handle) and various slots for same. Overlooked data, recently brought to the author's attention, revises that reported in the earlier seven editions. Correspondence and orders of the War Dept. and Ordnance Office of January, 1865 (as reprinted in the Journal of the Company of Military Historians, 1979, Vol. 31 No. 4) indicate the different purpose of the device. It was invented by Lieut. Col. Walter King, 4th Missouri Cavalry (an outfit that had its share of chasing the notorious guerrilla leader Quantrill). Intended by King as an integral part of "Cavalry Raiding Equipments," he was permitted to "…adapt his invention at his own expense to a sufficient number of arms now in use to arm a squadron (of approx.) one hundred and that it be submitted to trial in the field." When and where trial took place is unknown. According to the Ordnance Board that met in Washington Jan. 6, 1865, to examine the "…small mill ingeniously arranged in the stock of a carbine with which corn or wheat is ground into meal suitable for cooking purposes…" the "Raiding Equipment" was found impractical and unsuitable for adoption; Col. King was highly commended. The device has been observed usually on M. 1859 and M. 1863 carbines and also known on a M. 1853. Extreme caution should be exercised in purchasing any specimen of this rare variant; not a few spurious examples have been made over the past half century… and longer.

A two-part article "Col. King's Carbine Milling Device" by A.F. Lustyik (Nov. & Dec. 2005 *Gun Report*) added significantly to the lore of this unique device and plausibly concluded that the quantity actually adapted for the "grinder" was considerably less than the 100 authorized.

5F-028   Values—Good **$17,500**   Fine **$45,000**

Metallic Cartridge Conversions of New Models 1859, 1863 & 1865

Conversions to Metallic Cartridge of New Model 1859, 1863 and 1865 Carbines and Rifles. (Not illus.; identical in contour to the percussion models.) Following the Civil War, the U.S. Government in 1867 decided to convert many of their percussion military arms to metallic cartridge breechloaders. The Sharps was one of those selected for conversion and contracts were given to Sharps Rifle Manufacturing Co. to alter rifles and carbines of their manufacture. A total of 31,098 carbines and 1,086 rifles (of all three styles, i.e., New Model 1859, 1863 and 1865) were converted. In addition to the normal inspector markings found on Sharps percussion arms, an extra inspection stamp (initials DFC in a ribbon cartouche) was marked in the center of the left side of the buttstock. Conversion carbines are of two major types: (A) Original six-groove bores. (B) Relined bores with three-groove rifling. Conversions were refinished by the factory; when condition of the original stock required that it be replaced, a buttstock with no patchbox was used in all cases, regardless of the original model designation. Conversions bearing the "New Model 1865" markings will command a premium value.

Variations are:

CARBINES:

Conversion to 52-70 rimfire carbines. Total production unknown, but extremely limited:

5F-029   Values—Good **$2,000**   Fine **$4,000**

So-called 52-70 conversion with spring loaded firing pin. (a.k.a. M. 1867). Quantity 1900. Most are M. 1863 type. Although using original barrels with 6 groove .52 bores (a few lined examples) the carbines were intended to chamber the standard 50-70CF round:

5F-030   Values—Good **$1,500**   Fine **$3,500**

Identical above with usual cam type firing pin. (a.k.a. M. 1868). Original 6 groove bore; chambered the 50-70 round:

5F-030.5   Values—Good **$1,500**   Fine **$3,000**

Conversion to 50-70CF with 3 groove lined barrel. Cam type firing pin (also M. 1868). Quantity approx. 27,000. (Note: Government allowed all bores under .5225 to be unlined; all over that size to be lined to .50. Both to utilize same round):

5F-031   Values—Good **$1,500**   Fine **$3,500**

RIFLES:

Conversion of rifles to 50-70 centerfire. All with the three-groove lined barrels. Total 1,086 estimated made:

5F-032   Values—Good **$1,750**   Fine **$4,000**

Sharps New Model 1866 Military Rifle

New Model 1866 Rifle. Sharps Rifle Manufacturing Company, Hartford, Conn. Made c. 1866. Quantity unknown; extremely limited.

Caliber 50 rimfire. Barrel length 30 inches. Standard finish blued barrel and casehardened action; iron mountings. Lawrence patent rear sight. Usual SHARP'S MANUFG. CO barrel markings. R. S. LAWRENCE markings on lockplate, with additional lock markings NEW MODEL 1866 Specimens easily recognizable as the action and frame is tilted at a slight angle backwards (instead of vertical) and the lever that actuates the dropping breech has altered shape to allow for the use of a cam to operate breech block. An extreme rarity, examples of authentic specimens have yet to appear in the collectors' marketplace.

5F-032.5

Sharps New Model 1869 Carbine and Rifle

5F-033
Carbine

New Model 1869 Carbine and Rifle. Sharps Rifle Manufacturing Co., Hartford, Connecticut. Made c. 1869-1871. Total quantity less than 1,000.

44-77, 50-70 (2" case) and 60 calibers (possibly others). Barrel lengths 26", 28" and 30" on sporting rifles and 30" on military model.

Standard finish: blued barrel, barrel bands, lever latch and patchbox (if present); casehardened frame, buttplate, trigger plate and lever.

Walnut stock; oil finished for military arms and varnish finish for sporting styles. Pewter tip on forend of sporting type.

Standard markings on the barrel SHARPS RIFLE/MANUFG. CO./HARTFORD CONN on the frame C. SHARPS' PATENT/SEPT 12TH 1848.

The Model 1869 action is easily distinguished by the lockplate which is not adapted or fitted for the percussion pellet primer parts. Although similar to the later 1874 Model lockplate, it is much thicker (3/8") while the 1874 is but 3/16" thick.

Major Variations are:

CARBINE; Caliber 50-70 centerfire; 22", 24" or 26" round barrel; saddle ring bar as on the Model 1859/1863. Approximately 500 made:
5F-033   Values—Good **$2,500**   Fine **$4,500**

MILITARY RIFLE; Caliber 50-70 centerfire; 30" round barrel; full forend fastened with three barrel bands. Very scarce. Approximately 100 made:
5F-034   Values—Good **$2,750**   Fine **$6,000**

SPORTING RIFLE; The 26" barrel 44 caliber is most commonly encountered followed by the 50 caliber with short round barrel; these latter are distinguished from military carbine by lack of barrel band on forend and the presence of a pewter forend tip. The markings NEW MODEL 1869 usually are present on top of barrel or on the lockplate. Approximately 50 made:
5F-035   Values—Good **$3,250**   Fine **$7,500**

Springfield Altered Sharps Model 1870s

5F-036

Model 1870 Springfield Altered Sharps Rifle and Carbine. Springfield Armory and Sharps Rifle Manufacturing Co. Made c. 1870, in total quantity of about 1,300.
50-70 centerfire breechloader. 35-1/2" barrel.

Walnut stocks; frame, breechblock, lock, lever, trigger plate, and lever catch were casehardened; the barrel, barrel bands, buttplate, sling swivels, and ramrod were left in the white. The full forend is fastened with two barrel bands (instead of three as on other Sharps military rifles) and it has iron ramrod. Serial numbered on the upper tang of breech and on left side of the barrel. Frame marking: C. SHARPS PAT./SEPT. 12TH 1848. On the buttplate: US.

This rather scarce variation of the Sharps was not merely an adaptation utilizing existing Civil War parts. According to Ordnance Reports the Springfield Armory newly fabricated parts necessary to complete these rifles. The two basic models on Sharps actions are:

First Type; action a conversion from percussion straight breech type includes lockplate marking: R. S. LAWRENCE PAT./APRIL 12TH 1859 and C. SHARPS' PAT./OCT. 5TH 1852. Approximately 700 made:
5F-036   Values—Good **$1,650**   Fine **$4,500**
Second Type; using the early Model 1874 style action and lockplate shows no provisions for pellet primer system. The serial range from 1 to 300 and separate from the First Type:
5F-037   Values—Good **$2,500**   Fine **$6,500**
Springfield Armory Trial Carbine; Made c. 1871. Total quantity 308. Caliber 50-70. 22" barrel with forend noticeably longer than usual Sharps type. Utilizes a percussion Sharps action converted to centerfire. All other parts are Springfield Armory manufacture with musket type buttplate; Model 1870 Springfield "trap-door" carbine rear sight (the long leaf overlaps the base considerably) graduated to 700 yards:
5F-038   Values—Good **$5,000**   Fine **$9,500**

BUFFALO RIFLES

"Sharps Rifle" was often synonymous with "Buffalo Rifle" in Western lore; near-generic in its use to describe the large caliber, heavy barrel, very plain grade, breech-loading rifles in regular use

by professional buffalo hunters during the height of the era c. 1867-1882. Although other makers (notably Remington) were used, the Sharps was, by far, the most widely favored … and reported. To minimize the sound of the gunshot and prevent the herd from stampeding, shooting was done from a stand at long range, often using cross-sticks or other form of rest. Heavy barrels made for steadier aim and allowed for faster shooting, their larger size expanding more slowly as they heated in rapid shooting.

Hunters often used two rifles to lessen heating (which decreased accuracy). In earlier years calibers from 40-90 to large .50 were in favor; by 1876 the .45 (2-7/8") became popular as did the heavier barrels, with rifles weighing in between 13-1/2 lbs. and 16-1/2 lbs. usually and invariably fitted with double set triggers.

Sharps Model 1874 Rifle

Model 1874 Rifle. Manufactured by the Sharps Rifle Manufacturing Co., Hartford, Connecticut, and the Sharps Rifle Co., Bridgeport, Connecticut, c. 1871-1881 (although the gun actually started production 1871, the name "Model 1874" was not applied to the rifle until a few years later). Various quantities as listed below.

The Model 1874 offers a great variety of features, calibers, barrel lengths, weights, finishes, stocks, buttplates and sights. The result is a field of very wide opportunities for collectors offering them a specialty of only the Model 1874 if they so choose. A general breakdown of major types follows herewith, but it must be noted that many, many variations exist. The very best and most accurate reference for this model may be found in *Sharps Firearms* (Sellers) and *Sharps Firearms/Model 1874 Rifles,* (Sellers and Bailey).

Extra care should be taken before quickly categorizing a Model 1874. The "Sporting Rifle" style which was made in the largest quantity of any 1874 (6,500 manufactured) was ordered from the factory in a multitude of variations, many of which closely approximate the features of the rarer "Creedmoor, Mid-Range, Long-Range" styles; thus, it is quite possible to misidentify an 1874 and consequently incorrectly evaluate it. Many of the fancy "Sporting Rifles" have double set triggers which could not be used on "Creedmoor" rifles as the rules of the range at that time were quite rigid as to weight, sights and single trigger. If all such criteria is not met, the gun cannot be a "Creedmoor." To add to the possibility of misidentification it should be further noted that the mere fact that a gun might meet the Creedmoor criteria is not in itself conclusive evidence that the gun is a "Creedmoor" or other special target grade model. When in doubt the reader should consult references on the subject and fellow collectors knowledgeable in the Sharps line. Excellent quality, substantially priced, reproductions of the M. 1874 Sharps have been made in recent years; available in many variations and calibers. The author has yet to encounter one that is spuriously altered to resemble an antique. However, that possibility is worthy of bearing in mind.

Many special features add to values and should be noted carefully. Such accessories as double set triggers; various single triggers; checkered triggers and a whole range of tang sights including Vernier types and front sights with spirit levels, as well as varying quality degrees of stocks all affect and, depending on the model, add to values (if the item is standard for that particular model, then it includes the accessory; if it is not standard and purely extra, then the value should be increased).

Standard finishes were: blued barrel, bands, lever latch; casehardened frame, buttplate, trigger plate and lever.

Walnut stocks with oil finish for military arms and varnish finish for civilian and sporting arms.

Serial numbering featured the C prefix up to C54800 after which the "C" prefix was dropped and the number was marked in full. Three basic styles of barrel markings are encountered: (1) SHARPS RIFLE MANUFG. CO. HARTFORD, CONN This marking appears in three variations: (A) Three-line marking up to 1873; (B) A two-line marking up to 1874; (C) A one-line marking c. 1874. (2) SHARPS RIFLE CO HARTFORD, CONN.C.1874 to 1876. (3) SHARPS RIFLE CO BRIDGEPORT, CONN.1876 and later. The famous Sharps trademark OLD RELIABLE was added to barrel markings in 1876 and is normally found only on Bridgeport marked pieces; its presence on a Hartford marked gun indicates the use of left over parts after the dissolution of the company which were assembled at a later date and sold. They are still fine collectors' items. Caliber markings also appear on the top of the barrel near breech. Hartford barrels are easily distinguished from those made at the Bridgeport factory as they have a relief round collar at the base of the barrel where it fits into frame; Bridgeport barrels do not have this feature.

CAUTION. Sharps "Creedmoor", "Long Range" and "Mid-Range" Models: If lacking their Vernier/target sights (usual to those models) values shown lessened approx. 20 to 30 percent.

The most easily distinguished feature of the Model 1874 is the thin lockplate (just 3/16" thick) and which is made specially for cartridge model rifles with no provisions for the percussion pellet priming device. HARTFORD address usually worth about 15 percent premium. SPORTING MODELS (only) in 50 cal. and rifles with authentic markings of a Western gunmaker, agent or dealer may bring premiums of 50 percent to 100 percent. Basic models are:

Sporting Rifle; single or double triggers; open sights; calibers 40, 44, 45 and 50; barrels either full octagon or half octagon/half round from 22" to 36" in length; barrel weights from 7-1/2 pounds to 25 pounds. Premium values should be added to the heavier barrels; a rule of thumb being the larger and heavier, the more the premium. Approximately 6,500 made of this sporting rifle:

5F-039   Values—Good **$3,500**   Fine **$9,000**

Military Rifle; calibers 50-70 and 45-70 standard, but others available. 30" barrel with full forend fastened by three barrel bands. Serial number range above C50000. Approximately 1,769 made. Variations occur within this and will be found both with and without patchbox:

5F-040   Values—Good **$2,500**   Fine **$5,500**

Military Carbine; caliber 50-70 centerfire standard, but others available. Virtually identical to the Model 1859/1863 and distinguished by its very thin lockplate. Approximately 456 made:

5F-041   Values—Good **$2,500**   Fine **$6,000**

5F-042
Hunter's Rifle

**5F-045
Mid-Range**

Hunter's Rifle; single trigger, open sights. Calibers 40, 44, 45 and 50. Round barrels 26", 28" and 30" in length. Approximately 592 made:

5F-042	Values—Good **$3,000**	Fine **$7,000**

Creedmoor Rifle #1; made for target competition; 10-pound weight, single trigger, 44-90 caliber, but other calibers known; 32" octagon barrel; the pistol grip and forend checkered; the rear sight having a Vernier scale for firing up to 1300 yards; elaborate interchangeable front sight of globe and split bar type complete with windgauge. 134 made:

5F-043 Values—Very Good **$7,500** Exc. **$22,500**

Creedmoor Rifle #2; a less deluxe target rifle than above; less than 10 pounds in weight, with single trigger, 44-90 caliber, 32" octagon barrel. Straight style buttstock; Vernier peep rear sight, globe and split bar front sight having windgauge; only 12 made:

5F-044 Values—Very Good **$7,000** Exc. **$20,000**

Creedmoor Rifle #3; less than 10 pounds weight, having single trigger, 44-90 caliber, 30" octagon barrel. Butt of broad flat type; rear sights of peep and open type allowing elevation up to 1000 yards; globe front sight. 3 made:

5F-045 Values—Very Good **$5,500** Exc. **$17,500**

Mid Range Rifle #1; approximately 9 pounds in weight; single trigger, 40-70 caliber standard, other calibers available. 30" octagon or half round/half octagon barrel; the pistol grip and forend checkered. Rear sight of peep type having Vernier scale with graduations up to 600 yards; front sight of windgauge and spirit level type; 102 made:

5F-046 Values—Very Good **$5,750** Exc. **$17,500**

Mid Range Rifle #2; as above, but with straight stock checkered; 71 made:

5F-047 Values—Very Good **$5,000** Exc. **$12,500**

Mid Range #3; approximately 9 pounds in weight; single trigger, 40 caliber, 30" octagon or half round/half octagon barrel; stocks as on #2 except not checkered. Rear sight of peep type, the front a globe. 4 made:

5F-048 Values—Very Good **$5,000** Exc. **$11,000**

Long Range Rifle #1; less than 10 pounds in weight; single trigger, 44-90 caliber standard 1875-1876 and 45-100 thereafter, 34" barrel; pistol grip and forend checkered, with escutcheon plate of silver. Rear sight of peep type having Vernier scale with graduations up to 1300 yards; front sight an interchangeable globe and split bar having windgauge and spirit level. Approximately 87 made:

5F-049 Values—Very Good **$6,500** Exc. **$20,000**

Long Range Rifle #2; as above but lacking escutcheon plate and of a less deluxe finish. Approximately 258 made:

5F-050 Values—Very Good **$5,500** Exc. **$17,500**

Long Range Rifle #3; like the #2 model, but of plain finish; straight, checkered stock. Approximately 75 made:

5F-051 Values—Very Good **$5,000** Exc. **$15,000**

Long Range Rifle #4; as above but with plain, uncheckered stock and sporting tang sight and globe front sight. Approximately 9 made:

5F-052 Values—Very Good **$5,000** Exc. **$14,000**

Business Rifle; brought out in 1876, this economy variation was of 10-1/2 pounds weight, with double trigger, 26", 28" and 30" round barrel, in calibers 40-70 or 45-75, and with V-notch type adjustable rear sight. Approximately 1,604 made:

5F-053 Values—Good **$3,500** Fine **$5,750**

Schuetzen (or German pattern) Rifle; 30" octagon barrel, caliber 40-50. Checkered pistol grip stock and forend with large pronged Schuetzen type buttplate; double set triggers; tang sight. All with Bridgeport address. Approximately 69 made almost all of which were purchased by members of a New York shooting club:

5F-054 Values—Very Good **$6,500** Exc. **$15,000**

The So-Called "A" Series Sporting Rifles; made from left over parts c. 1879-1882; great variety of features. Easily distinguishable by the letter "A" marked inside an octagonal panel on the receiver; serial number range from 200001 to 200700. Majority made from altered percussion actions. Made in 40 and 45 caliber. Variety of barrel styles, lengths and weights. Estimated total manufactured at 700 with a great majority going to well known Denver, Colorado, dealers Carlos Gove and J. P. Lower and may be found with their name also marked on barrel (worth a premium in value):

5F-055 Values—Good **$3,500** Fine **$7,000**

**5F-051
Long Range Rifle #3**

The So-Called Meacham Conversion; although not a Model 1874 Sharps, this gun is often confused with it. Made from altered Civil War percussion carbine actions with serial numbers in the range under C50000 and ground down percussion lockplates with usually unmarked barrels having English type rifling and a special non-Sharps style forearm. Altered, assembled and sold by the firm of E. C. Meacham of St. Louis, Missouri, c. 1880s. A similar type conversion was made in the Sharps factory from 1879 to 1881 for several of the large wholesale houses. Those made by Sharps have regular Sharps barrel markings while the "Meachams" have unmarked barrels or rather coarse and irregular duplications of the Sharps marking:

5F-056 Values—Good **$2,750** Fine **$5,500**

Note: Prices include sights as specified. If sights lacking deduct approximately 20-30 percent from price.

Sharps Model 1877 Rifle

5F-057

Model 1877 Rifle (a.k.a. "The English Model"). Made by Sharps Rifle Co., Bridgeport, Connecticut, c. 1877-1878. Total quantity approximately 100.

Caliber 45 (either 2.6" or 2.4" case). Barrel lengths 34" and 36".

Standard finish was blued barrel and buttplate; casehardened frame, lockplate, hammer, lever and trigger plate.

Checkered walnut stock and forend varnish finished.

Barrel marking SHARPS RIFLE CO. BRIDGEPORT, CONN. OLD RELIABLE. Left side of frame SHARPS RIFLE CO./PAT. APR. 6, 1869 and C. SHARPS PAT./SEPT. 12TH 1848.

The Model 1877 was made to supply the Creedmoor or target shooters with a long range rifle specifically adapted to Creedmoor rules; i.e., weighing 10 pounds or less with single trigger and metallic sights. These pieces were designed for extremely long range shooting, the idea being to get most of the weight in the barrel; therefore Sharps designed an action that was extremely light allowing almost a pound more of weight to be put into the barrel of the gun. This piece is quickly distinguishable by the uniquely shaped narrow back-action lock quite different from all other vertical breech Sharps:

5F-057 Values—Very Good **$8,500** Exc. **$27,500**

FREUND MODIFIED SHARPS RIFLES and "WYOMING SADDLE GUN"

Brothers Frank and George Freund, German gunsmiths, immigrated to the United States in 1857; Frank later serving with the Union Army during the Civil War. By 1867 they had found their way west, practicing their profession in various towns newly spawned by the Union-Pacific Railroad as it built its way through the territory. Relocating to Denver in 1871 they operated as Freund & Brother until 1875, selling out to the well known dealer and gunsmith J.P. Lower. Immediately re-establishing themselves that same year in Cheyenne, Wyoming Territory they operated as Freund Bros. and Freund & Bro. (both these markings used on their rifles). The firm split up in 1880, George going to Colorado where he remained until his death in 1911, Frank remaining in Cheyenne until 1886, closing shop and returning to Jersey City, New Jersey; passing away in 1910. Both brothers patented many gun improvements, Frank being the most prolific.

Their markings on Sharps (or other make American rifles) normally denote their having merely handled/sold the gun as dealers and agents for the Sharps Rifle Company and will command a premium in value, as is discussed in the preface to this chapter. Freund markings have always seemed to possess a bit more lure for the collector for the fact that so many famous Americans and Westerners are known to have purchased rifles from them, including Generals Phil Sheridan, George Cook and Theodore Roosevelt. Often, Sharps (and other American) rifles are found with FREUND PATENT markings on uniquely designed front and rear sights sold by the Freunds. Such accessories and markings are deserving of increased premiums to the rifle's value.

Of major significance to the collector, and a feature that commands the highest premiums added to "Freund" marked Sharps rifles is the addition of Freund patented modifications (to breech-block, extractors, firing pin, etc.) that may be found

5F-057.5

on various models and grades of rifles; a very few as late as Frank's move to Jersey City in the 1880s. The ultimate Freund-Sharps rifles of the Models 1874 and 1877 are those elaborately engraved, bearing very large FREUND/CHEYENNE markings and in bold lettering FAMOUS AMERICAN FRONTIER or BOSS GUN, the maker's not too subtle name for his handiwork! Approximately 300 of the top-of-the-line rifles were produced. Values of these titled, and highly desirable pieces range in the low to mid-five figures.

A unique Freund carbine, built entirely by Freund on design of his own modified Sharps action, was known and advertised by him as the "Wyoming Saddle Gun". Estimated that approximately 30 were made. Calibers and barrel lengths vary. Example illustrated here .40 caliber; 18" barrel, 35" overall. Light scroll engraving around edges. Hand engraved, large markings on lock and action FREUND'S PATENT/WYOMING ARMORY, CHEYENNE, WYOMING. Breech block marked

FREUND'S PAT. 1876, 1877. Freund markings elsewhere; two-piece cleaning rod in butt:

5F-057.5   Values—Very Good **$35,000**   Exc. **$65,000**

A Note About Valuing "Freund" Marked Rifles. Although the great majority of conversions were made at Cheyenne, Wyoming a few were made after they moved to Jersey City, in 1886. All such arms usually bear barrel markings "FREUND BROS." or "FREUND & BRO." The mere marking of their names does not indicate that the particular rifle is a conversion however! As noted, the Freunds were large dealers in firearms of all types and many guns that were merely sold by them will also bear those same markings. *There is no doubt that the mere name alone will add a premium value to the gun so marked. However only if it has the actual Freund conversion to the breech will that premium be substantial usually a minimum of 50 percent often over 100 percent of normal value, determined ultimately by condition.* **5F-057.8**

SHARPS HAMMERLESS RIFLE MODEL OF 1878, with Freunds' Breech Block (top view), showing the cartridge projecting. Price for altering to this system, $25.00.

The following is from the Deadwood Times, the leading paper of the Black Hills, and our readers will see from this what is thought of the Freunds inventions, etc., in "the Land of Gold:"

A SHARPS RIFLE (top view), With Freunds' Improved Breech Mechanism Adjusted.

This style of breech-block having resistance of axial light on each side with Freunds' new firing-pin, half-cocking slide and cover, see engraving, page 14.

For adjusting the improvement, $35.00. Work first-class in all respects.

5F-057.8

Sharps-Borchardt Model 1878 Rifle

Model 1878 Sharps-Borchardt Rifle. Made by Sharps Rifle Co., Bridgeport, Connecticut, c. 1878-1881; total quantity approximately 8,700.

Calibers, barrel lengths and shapes, and stock styles varied considerably, according to the type variation. A general breakdown of types appears below, but many variations exist in barrel lengths, weights, sights, stocks, etc. Note single trigger with sliding safety lock device.

Standard finishes as follows: Blued or casehardened frame, lever, and trigger; blued barrel, buttplate and barrel bands (if present).

Walnut stocks, oil finished on military arms, and varnished for civilian.

Serial numbering on bottom of barrel and frame; sometimes on left side of frame. All variations within common serial sequence.

Standard markings: On barrel, OLD RELIABLE/SHARPS RIFLE CO. BRIDGEPORT CONN./U.S.A.; on left side of frame: BORCHARDT PATENT/ SHARPS RIFLE CO. BRIDGEPORT CONN./U.S.A.

With its distinctive hammerless action and flat-sided frame, the Sharps-Borchardt arms are quite modern in appearance. Developed by Hugo Borchardt who became more famous in later years for his automatic pistol as well as the basic design for the Luger pistol.

Carbine; 45-70 caliber, 24" barrel; saddle ring mounted on left side of the frame; one barrel band. Military style sights. Limited production; and the last model of Sharps carbine; approximately 384 made:

5F-058   Values—Good **$2,000**   Fine **$4,500**

Military Rifle; 45-70 caliber, 32-1/8" barrel; full forend fastened by two barrel bands; ramrod beneath barrel. Military type sights. Approximately 6,900 produced; a number sold in foreign countries:

5F-059   Values—Very Good **$1,750**   Exc. **$3,750**

Mid-Range Rifle; approximately 9 pounds in weight; 40 caliber, 30" barrel. Pistol grip buttstock and forend checkered; rear sight a Vernier peep with graduations to 600 yards, and an open

5F-058
Carbine

5F-060
Mid-Range Rifle

5F-062
Hunter's Rifle

5F-064
Sporting Rifle

hunting type on barrel. Hard rubber paneled action with walnut panels extra. Also made in deluxe grades of varying degrees of extras and fancy finishes and engravings; these will command premium prices accordingly. Approximately 215 made. Caution: If lacking the Vernier target sights, value approximately 20 percent less:

5F-060   Values—Very Good **$5,000**   Exc. **$8,500**
Long Range Rifle; slightly less than 10 pounds weight; 45 caliber, chambered for 2-4/10" case length; varying barrel lengths. The pistol grip buttstock and forend checkered; rear sight a new style Vernier with graduations to 1,200 yards, the front sight of windgauge and spirit level type and having interchangeable aperture and pin-head discs. Hard rubber panel in each side of action standard with walnut panels extra. Also available in varying deluxe grades, which command premium prices accordingly. Approximately 230 made. Caution: If lacking the Vernier target sights, value approximately 20 percent less:

5F-061   Values—Very Good **$6,500**   Exc. **$17,500**
Hunter's Rifle; about 8-1/2 pounds weight; 40 caliber, 26" barrel. Plain stocks without checkering or pistol grip. Chambered for 1-7/8" case length. Approximately 62 made:

5F-062   Values—Good **$2,000**   Fine **$4,500**
Business Rifle; 10 pounds weight; 40 caliber, chambered for 2-1/2" case length; 28" octagon or round barrel. Plain stocks without checkering or pistol grip. Approximately 89 made:

5F-063   Values—Good **$2,250**   Fine **$5,000**
Sporting Rifle; weights vary from 9 to 12 pounds; 45 caliber with 2-1/10" case length; 30" barrel of round or octagonal shape. Plain stocks. Approximately 610 made:

5F-064   Values—Very Good **$2,750**   Exc. **$6,000**
Officer's Rifle; 9 pounds weight; 45 caliber, with 2-1/10" case; 32" barrel. The stocks of medium fancy grade, and the finish of extra quality. On each side of the frame an inlaid hard rubber panel. Approximately 48 made:

5F-065   Values—Very Good **$4,500**   Exc. **$8,500**
Express Rifle; 9-1/2 pounds weight; 45 caliber, with 2-7/8" case; 26" octagonal barrel. Fancy grade of stocks, with checkered pistol grip and forend; buttplate of hard rubber; fitted with sling staples. Rear sight of two leaved type having platinum lines; the front sight long beaded; upper surface of the barrel mat finished. Available with double triggers. Approximately 31 made:

5F-066   Values—Very Good **$6,500**   Exc. **$15,000**
Short Range Rifle; 9-3/4 pounds weight; 40 caliber, with 1-7/8" case; 26" round barrel. Plain stocks, but the pistol grip and forend checkered; buttplate of hard rubber. Rear sight of short vernier type and sights include windgauge. Approximately 153 made:

5F-067   Values—Very Good **$3,750**   Exc. **$7,500**

Sharps Double Barrel Shotgun

Double Barrel Breech Loading Shotgun; c. 1878-79. (not illus.) Sharps announced in their 1878 catalog they were tooled up to manufacture fine quality shotguns. Although they half-heartedly attempted to acquire tools and machinery from George H. Fox (founder American Arms Co.) of Boston, they chose instead to have 10 and 12 gauge doubles made for them in England. Quantity unknown; extremely limited with

Webley being largest supplier, sending about 150 by 1879. Side lever (just one top lever); plain side locks marked **"SHARPS RIFLE CO."**; rebounding hammers; Damascus barrels marked on center rib **"OLD RELIABLE"** in panel and **"SHARPS RIFLE CO. BRIDGEPORT, CONN."** Very plain grade pistol grip stock.

5F-067.5   Values—Very Good **$3,250**   Exc. **$5,500**

Lee Bolt Action Rifle made by Sharps   *See Remington-Lee, Chapter V.*

C. SHARPS & CO.
SHARPS & HANKINS
PHILADELPHIA 1854-1874

Sharps Breech-Loading Single Shot Pistol

Breech-Loading Single Shot Percussion Pistol. Made by C. Sharps & Co., Philadelphia, c. 1854 to 1857. Approximately 850 total pieces produced of two major types.

Action is the dropping block, lever activated type based on Sharps' 1848 patent; the action being just about a miniature edition of the carbine and rifle type. Calibers, lengths and markings as indicated below. Iron mountings; no forend under barrel; walnut grips; percussion pellet priming device made integral with frame. Finish blued barrels with casehardened action, breech, lever and hammer or blued barrels and frames.

One of the major reasons Sharps left the Hartford firm was their refusal to manufacture these dropping block single shot pistols as they felt there would be no market for them. The very limited number made by Sharps in Philadelphia seems to prove their correct judgment. Two major types were produced:
First Type; caliber 31 to 34; 5" round barrel. Marked in oval panel on left frame SHARPS PATENT/ARMS MF^ed FAIRMOUNT/PHILA.

5F-068

PA. Total produced approximately 500. Serial numbered from 1 to 500 approximately. Varnished walnut grips:
5F-068   Values—Good **$2,000**   Fine **$4,500**
Second Type; slightly larger overall. 36 caliber. 6-1/2" round barrel. Marked on right frame C. SHARPS & CO./PHILA. PA.or C. SHARPS & CO'S/RIFLE WORKS/PHILA. PA.and on left side of frame C. SHARPS/PATENT/1848. Approximately 350 produced. Serial numbered 470 to 950 approximately:
5F-069   Values—Good **$2,000**   Fine **$5,000**

Sharps Pistol Rifle

Pistol Rifle. Made by C. Sharps & Co., Philadelphia, in the mid and late 1850s; production limited.

31 and 38 caliber percussion breechloader, using the falling block action, opening downward on movement of trigger guard/lever. Barrel lengths vary but standard at approximately 28". Initially manufactured using the Breech-Loading Pistol action, most specimens were made having a special Pistol Rifle action.

Early specimens with German silver buttplate, forend cap, and escutcheon plates for forend which was secured by a wedge. Standard production featured iron mountings.

Serial numbered. Markings as noted below.

Relatively little is known of these scarce and unusual weapons. Specimens are difficult to locate and are highly prized by collectors.
First type; utilizing pistol action; includes ramrod mounted beneath the barrel and German silver mountings. Left side of

frame marked C. SHARP'S PATENT 1848-52. Approximately 50 made:
5F-070   Values—Good **$2,750**   Fine **$6,000**

5F-071

Standard model; having special Pistol Rifle action; lacks ramrod; iron mountings. Left side of frame marked: C. SHARPS & CO. PHILADA. PA. Approximately 600 made:
5F-071   Values—Good **$2,750**   Fine **$6,000**

Sharps Percussion Revolver

Percussion Revolver. Made by C. Sharps & Co., Philadelphia, c. 1857-58 in a total quantity of about 2,000.

25 caliber; 6-shot round cylinder. 3" octagonal ribbed barrel, of tip-up type.

Two piece walnut grips. Blued finish.

Serial numbered from 1 on up. Barrel marking: C. SHARPS & CO., PHILA. PA.

Bearing a close resemblance to the early 22 caliber Smith & Wesson revolvers, several minor variations have been discerned in this desirable Sharps product. The pistol is important as an early specimen of Sharps handgun production:

5F-072

5F-072   Values—Good **$1,000**   Fine **$3,000**
(Note: A few specimens will be encountered bearing the agent's marking WM BRYCE & CO.,in place of standard Sharps marks. These will command a slightly higher value.)

Sharps and Sharps & Hankins Breech-Loading 4-Shot Pepperbox Pistols

Breech-Loading 4-Shot Pepperbox Pistols. By C. Sharps & Company and Sharps & Hankins, Philadelphia. Made c. 1859 to 1874. Quantities made in the many thousands.

The pepperboxes of both these makers are treated here under a single heading as it is felt this is the proper way to treat them (and they have been thusly listed in other well known works on the subject) in the order of their introduction and manufacture. See historical note regarding Sharps partnership with Hankins preceding this section.

Calibers 22, 30 and 32 short and long rimfire; barrel lengths vary from 2-1/2" for 22 caliber to 3-1/2" for the Sharps & Hankins Model 3. The 4-barrel cluster slides forward for loading. All specimens have rotating firing pins mounted either in frame or on hammer. Varying finishes, but standard with a blued barrel and silver plated frame for the brass frame models, and casehardened finish on iron frame models. Grips standard, either walnut or gutta-percha. The following are the four major models with most often encountered and well known variations of each. Other variants are known and depending on the nature of it, values may be increased accordingly.

Model 1; caliber 22 rimfire; generally brass frames except where noted. Marking C. SHARPS & CO. PHILADA, PA.on left side and C. SHARPS PATENT 1859 on right side, either on the barrel or the frame. Straight line marking on barrel or frame is early and scarce; circular marking around the hammer screw most often encountered. Wood grips standard on all except Model 1A. Major variants:

Model 1A

Model 1A; most often encountered; straight standing breech and straight grip to frame juncture; gutta-percha grips. Barrel release on underside at front of frame. Serial numbered 1 to 60000 and 1 to 5000 (when number 60000 was reached numbering commenced again with number "1"; thus later features may be found with low serial numbers); over 60,000 manufactured:

5F-073   Values—Good **$300**   Fine **$575**

Model 1B

Model 1B; fluted standing breech and rounded grip to frame juncture; barrel release on left side of frame. Serial numbered 1 to 3200. Approximately 3,200 manufactured:
5F-074   Values—Good **$325**   Fine **$625**

Model 1C; fluted standing breech; round grip to frame juncture; barrel release underside front of frame. Serial numbered 1 to 26000. 26,000 manufactured:
5F-075   Values—Good **$300**   Fine **$575**

Model 1D; identical to 1C above except iron frame. Serial numbered 22000 to 23000. Approximately 1,100 manufactured; rare:
5F-076   Values—Good **$600**   Fine **$1,500**

Model 1E; distinguished by its rounded standing breech (which looks identical to the breech on the Model 4 type or the Sharps and Hankins type) and rounded grip to frame juncture. Barrel release on underside, forward part of frame. Specimens encountered in 2100 serial range. Only 50 estimated manufactured; rare:
5F-077   Values—Good **$950**   Fine **$3,500**

Model 2; caliber 30 rimfire with medium size brass frame. Markings same as Model 1. Variations are:

Model 2A; straight standing breech and straight grip to frame juncture. Serial numbered 1 to 30000 and 1 to 5000. Checkered gutta-percha grips. 26,500 manufactured:
5F-078   Values—Good **$275**   Fine **$600**

Model 2B; straight standing breech and rounded grip to frame juncture. Wooden grips standard. Serial numbered 1 to 4000. Approximately 3,700 manufactured:
5F-079   Values—Good **$300**   Fine **$675**

Model 2C; fluted standing breech and round grip to frame juncture, wooden grips standard; serial numbered 3700 to 8000. Approximately 5,000 manufactured:
5F-080   Values—Good **$300**   Fine **$675**

Model 2D; fluted standing breech and straight grip to frame juncture, checkered gutta percha grips standard; serial numbered 1 to 1200. Approximately 1,200 manufactured:
5F-081   Values—Good **$425**   Fine **$1,200**

Model 2E; straight standing breech and straight frame to grip juncture; floral gutta percha grips standard. Note frame size of this model smaller than all other Model 2 types. Serial numbered 1 to 1000. Approximately 1,000 manufactured:
5F-082   Values—Good **$625**   Fine **$1,600**

Model 2F; identical to Model 2E above with longer 3-1/2" barrels. Quantity estimated manufactured 25:
5F-082.5 Values—Good **$1,750**   Fine **$4,000**

Model 3
(Sharps & Hankins)

Model 3; Sharps & Hankins Models. Caliber 32 short rimfire. Marked ADDRESS SHARPS & HANKINS, PHILADELPHIA, PENN. on top of the barrel and SHARPS PATENT/JAN. 25, 1859 on right side of frame. Smooth gutta-percha, checkered gutta-percha or wood grips standard on all models. Four major types. Serial numbers run from 1 to 15000 and the models are scattered throughout these number ranges with generally "A" models being the earliest and "C" models latest:

Model 3A; circular sideplate on left frame by hammer screw. Button barrel release on left frame just ahead of hammer screw. Approximately 2,500 manufactured:
5F-083   Values—Good **$300**   Fine **$875**

Model 3B; made without the circular sideplate; barrel release identical to above. Approximately 2,000 manufactured:
5F-084   Values—Good **$300**   Fine **$900**

Model 3C; made without sideplate; barrel release moved forward slightly with various internal differences. Generally found with a shell extractor mounted vertically between the barrel grooves at breech. Approximately 9,000 manufactured:

5F-085   Values—Good **$300**   Fine **$900**

Model 3D; very similar in appearance to above, but the barrel release (although still a button) is plunger type instead of pivoting bar. Distinguished by the absence of the frame screw on forward section of frame. Approximately 2,500

Model 4

manufactured:

5F-086   Values—Good **$300**   Fine **$900**

Model 4; The bird's head grip/butt model marked C. SHARPS PATENT JAN. 25, 1859 on right frame. Caliber 32 long rimfire. Variations are:

Model 4A (a.k.a. "Bulldog"); 2-1/2" barrel retained by screw in front underside of frame. Serial number range 1 to 3,690. Approximately 2,000 manufactured:

5F-087   Values—Good **$375**   Fine **$1,100**

Model 4B; 2-1/2" barrel retained by pivoting barrel catch mounted at front of frame. Serial numbered 1000 to 11000. Approximately 9,000 manufactured:

5F-088   Values—Good **$350**   Fine **$1,000**

Model 4C; 3" barrel retained by pivoting barrel latch at front of frame. Serial numbered from 11000 to 15000. Approximately 4,000 manufactured:

5F-089   Values—Good **$350**   Fine **$1,100**

Model 4D; 3-1/2" barrel with variations in retaining methods; not serial numbered. Approximately 25 estimated made. Buyer should exercise caution as spurious specimens are seen fitted with longer barrels from the Sharps & Hankins pepperbox (*q.v.*):

5F-090   Values—Good **$1,500**   Fine **$4,000**

Boxed and Cased Sharps Model 1 and Model 2 Pepperboxes

Closed case Sharps Model 1A

Although it's conceivable to find all models of Sharps pepperboxes cased in wooden boxes with compartment-type linings it is apparent that only Model 1 and 2 types were more commonly boxed at the factory and are more often encountered on the collector's market. The paperboard type box with full label on the inner lid "DIRECTIONS FOR USE OF SHARPS PATENT REPEATER" is the most often observed style, usually found with plain unengraved models. Subject to condition of the pepperbox (as well as the paperboard box) minimum premium of 50 percent (often 100 percent and more) is justifiable. The second type of casing is very rare and seldom encountered; made of black gutta percha with hinged lid; high relief decorated with floral and scroll motifs; the dark velvet lining on inner lid fancy scroll embossed. This style case usually observed with fancier, engraved specimens. At a minimum 100 percent premiums are merited, and often increased depending on quality of engraving.

European-Manufactured Sharps Four-Barrel Pepperboxes

Only two foreign manufacturers were licensed by Sharps to make copies of their four-barrel pepperbox. In early 1860 the firm of Tipping & Lawden of Birmingham, England produced three variations of a pepperbox, whose profiles closely resemble the Sharps "Model One" type. Each of them bore the markings "TIPPING AND LAWDEN/SHARPS PATENT" on the left frame around the hammer screw. Approximately 6,000 are estimated manufactured circa 1860s-1870s and are classified as three "Models": **Model 1:** caliber 22 rimfire; total made 2,000...**Model 2:** calibers 7mm, 8mm, 30 rimfire, 32 rimfire. Total made 4,000...**Model 3:** 9mm, .340. total made 250 larger frame; rare and worth premium. (Quite a few were engraved in varying degrees of profuseness.) Generally valued on the American market approximately the same as American-made counterparts; the scarcer calibers and larger sizes fetching premiums. Tipping & Lawdens are occasionally encountered bearing other name markings (*in addition* to their own) merely denoting various retail outlets that sold the pistols, or possibly a sub-contractor employed to finish them.

The only other European manufacturer *licensed by Sharps* to manufacture copies of their four-barrel pepperboxes was L. GHAYE of Liege, Belgium, circa 1861. He manufactured almost identical copies of the Sharps Model 1A and 2A. Quantities are unknown but believed very limited. Specimens bear markings **C. SHARPS PATENT 1859** in a circle around the left frame hammer screw along with Liege, Belgium (**LGE** in circle) proof marks. Values approximately same as American-made Sharps (a scarce variant by Ghaye, noticeably different than American models is fitted with a large under-lever to open barrels and a small swivel lever on side of breech for extractor (and will fetch premium values). Best source for information on these and other European types is F. Sellers *Sharps Firearms*.

Collectors should be aware that there were quite a few other antique infringements of the Sharps pepperbox, all of them fine collector's items of varying degrees of value...*and also in more recent decades there have been modern-made copies of these Sharps pepperboxes manufactured in Japan, Italy and elsewhere.* When considering such unknown types, exercise caution.

Sharps & Hankins Model 1862 Carbine

Model 1862 Carbine. Sharps & Hankins, Philadelphia, made c. 1862-65; total quantity of about 8,000.

52 rimfire breechloader, the barrel sliding forward on opening of the combination trigger guard/lever. Barrel breech enters into recoil shield of frame 1/8".

Brass buttplate; all other mountings of steel; casehardened action. First model with firing pin on hammer (scarce, worth premium); 2nd model floating type firing pin mounted on recoil shield. Oil hole in the extractor well. Sling swivel on bottom of buttstock, but sling ring on left side of frame is scarce.

Walnut stocks. Blued finish, with casehardened frame, upper and lower tangs, lever, and hammer casehardened.

Serial numbered from 300 on up (mixed with Model 1861 rifle numbers). Frame on right side marked: SHARPS/&/HANKINS/PHILADA; marked on left side: SHARPS/PATENT/1859.

Several distinct variations were produced in the Model 1862 series, as follows:

Navy type; 24" barrel, with leather covering as protection against rusting. Official records indicate total Navy purchases of 6,686. Leather secured by two screws at breech of barrel, and a band of steel at muzzle. Believed to have seen extensive service aboard various vessels which may account for many seen with damaged leather:

5F-091   Values—Good **$1,100**   Fine **$3,000**

Navy type with leather covering badly deteriorated or lacking:

5F-092   Values—Good **$400**   Fine **$500**

Army type; 24" blued barrel; lacks screws and screw holes for retaining leather covering of the Navy type. Encountered with or without the saddle ring fixture on left frame. Estimated quantity made 500 with approximately 200 ordered by U.S. Army 1865:

5F-093   Values—Good **$1,100**   Fine **$4,000**

(Note: A few of the Army type were made experimentally in other calibers; authenticated specimens rare; worth premium values.)

Short Cavalry type; 19" blued barrel; saddle ring mounted on left side of frame. Sometimes called the 11th New York Volunteer Cavalry Model, since that unit is known to have used this type; often observed having tinned finish; limited production of approximately 1,000; and sometimes found with Navy inspector markings P/HKH on left frame:

5F-094   Values—Good **$1,250**   Fine **$4,500**

5F-091
Navy Model

5F-094
Short Cavalry Model

Close-up of action
Sharps & Hankins
5F-091 through 5F-095

5F-095

Sharps & Hankins Model 1861 Navy Rifle

Model 1861 Navy Rifle. Sharps & Hankins, Philadelphia, made c. 1861-62; total quantity about 700. U.S. Navy purchased 600 under contract 1862 and another 100 on the commercial market. Used mostly to arm Marine guards aboard ship; some known on gunboats on the Mississippi.

52 caliber rimfire breechloader, the barrel sliding forward on opening of the combination trigger guard/lever. 32-3/4" barrel.

Steel mountings except for brass buttplate; made without a ramrod; bayonet lug on bottom of muzzle end of barrel for saber bayonet found on most, but not all specimens. Firing pin mounted on face of hammer.

Walnut stocks; full forend fastened with three barrel bands. Blued barrel and barrel bands; the frame, lower tang, hammer, lever, forend cap and upper tang casehardened. Specimen known with full leather covered barrel as on carbine. Very rare; worth premium.

Serial numbered from 1 to about 700 (mixed with Model 1862 carbine numbers). Frame on right side marked: SHARPS/&/ HANKINS/PHILADA.; marked on left side: SHARPS/ PATENT/1859:

5F-095   Values—Good **$1,400**   Fine **$4,500**

Montana Territory-marked Sharps buffalo rifle. Standard Civil War Model 1863 Sharps carbine altered/remade c. 1870s by known Western gunsmith. Market "A.B. CHARPIE/HELENA, MT." on the 24-inch octagon barrel. Caliber 50; weight 12 pounds. Shown here with two rare ammo belts with original brass buckles of famous Colorado firearms dealers "C. GOVE & SONS" and "JOHN P. LOWER/SPORTSMEN [sic] DEPOT"-both of Denver. Bowie knife also marked by Lower, Denver. (*N. Flayderman & Co. Catalog No. 116, 1992*)

Chapter V-G

Smith & Wesson

The product of one of the most prolific of American makers, Smith & Wesson arms have always enjoyed great popularity in the collecting field. From the viewpoint of the many models produced (and the variations of each), total quantities of various models, and the general affordability of most to the average collector, S&Ws have attracted quite an impressive following. The background and early history of the company and the men for whom it was named is well worth reading and is easily found in the S&W reference works. The collector is often puzzled as to why the early lever action repeating Volcanic type S&W pistols are not usually found in a S&W book or chapter, but more often in one pertaining to Winchester arms; the following brief background of the firm should clarify the matter.

Horace Smith and Daniel Wesson, both of Massachusetts and each with an extensive background in the arms manufacturing industry, went in partnership in 1852 for the manufacture of a lever action, repeating magazine handgun that was an evolutionary development from the earlier Hunt & Jennings patents. Smith and Wesson manufactured these handguns (known to collectors as the Iron Frame Volcanics) in their factory at Norwich, Connecticut. Total production of the Volcanics was about 1,000 pieces. In mid-1855 Smith and Wesson sold their shares of ownership in the company to the newly organized Volcanic Repeating Arms Company. Smith remained with the new company as plant manager for a short period while Wesson stayed on as plant superintendent; manufacturing facilities moved to New Haven, Connecticut. Both Smith and Wesson shortly thereafter left the employ of this new Volcanic Repeating Arms Company, and each eventually returned to Springfield, Massachusetts, severing all ties with the earlier companies. The Iron Frame Volcanics were changed to brass frame types under the new management in New Haven; the company entering bankruptcy in 1857. Taken over by Oliver Winchester and renamed the "New Haven Arms Company," it was changed to the Winchester Arms Company in 1866.

Horace Smith and Daniel Wesson formed a second partnership in 1856 for the development and manufacture of a revolver chambered for a self-contained metallic cartridge. This gun was to revolutionize the firearms industry and was the first of a long line of revolvers to carry the famed S&W name.

Volcanic type S&Ws are cross-indexed in this section as their action and mechanical features were the predecessors of the Winchester and are to be found with that group of arms. A well rounded S&W collection most certainly will include these Iron Frame S&W Volcanics.

A troublesome feature, but basic to an understanding of S&Ws, is mastery of the terminology. There is no doubt, and

there seems to be general agreement, that it is at times quite tedious and confusing—while in other instances it can be downright perplexing! The redundancy of the word "Model" is most disagreeable. For instance, "Model No. 1, 1st Model" or better yet, "Model 3 Russian 3rd Model"—that's one you could almost read the same frontwards as well as backwards! Don't let it get the best of you; it only hurts on first glance and once you really get into S&Ws, everything falls into place quite nicely. To use another cliche—don't fight 'em, join 'em when it comes to nomenclature. A disconcerting situation for many years has been the liberal misuse and alteration of the actual factory names and nomenclature by collectors and writers (especially in the early days of collecting). Thus today we have a hodgepodge of names that have been applied for many years to many of these models which has often led to a confusion in cataloging specimens by both collector and dealer alike. Exemplifying the confusion that often existed with the collecting of S&Ws before their accurate and identifiable differentiation by later writers is this statement in the classic and pioneer work *The Gun Collector's Handbook of Values* to be found under the listing of the 1st Model Russian revolver: "… This whole business of Russian markings is confused. The factory records are confused, and the author of this book is confused. The situation offers a golden opportunity for some fool to obtain a Doctor of Philosophy degree, or some arms dealer to get out a paperbound pamphlet and charge too much for it." I think the reader will find that the problem has since resolved itself. Although still requiring some study, the material is all there waiting for him.

The standard reference work most commonly considered throughout the collecting world, and certainly a book deserving of the laurels passed its way, is the Jinks and Neal, *Smith & Wesson 1857 to 1945, A Handbook For Collectors*. This major work, first published in 1966 and since revised and updated, is recognized as a basic guide in this field for all models. The authors have classified the weapons by the original factory terminology which is the accepted form and in use throughout this chapter on S&Ws. The factory identified their basic models by frame sizes (e.g., Model 1, Model 2, Model 3, etc.) and from each of these varied sizes, several types developed or were produced; hence, the modification of almost every one of the models which created the tongue-twister names. "Standard Catalog of S&W" by Supica and Nahas, 1996 (q.v.) has also gained a deserved place as a major guide to this field.

Many S&Ws are better known in the collecting world by their nicknames, and these are also given following the official designation. For instance, you will rarely see the "Model No. 3, 1st Model" ever called that; it will invariably be termed the "1st Model American." Included with each listing therefore are all the popular nicknames and other designations by which each revolver is "also known as" (a.k.a.).

For ease in use and identification, this S&W section has been generally arranged by calibers, in ascending order, from the smallest, 22, to the largest, 455; each of the various models within those calibers is arranged chronologically in order of manufacture, from earliest to latest. In a few instances where basic models were made in various calibers (e.g., the "New Model No. 3"), the gun will be listed under that caliber most often encountered with the variants of calibers and styles found in sub-listings for that particular gun.

It is quite true that there are a number of apparently very uninteresting variants found lurking in the S&W field and listed as individual models. This is especially evident in the numerous Hand Ejector models of 32, 38 and 44 calibers—all made in the late 19th and early 20th centuries. Some of the variants can only be identified by disassembling the piece. Unless you are a dyed-in-the-wool, highly advanced specialist in S&Ws or an avid fancier of manufacturing technicalities, many of these pieces might not hold a fascination for you. There are so many other fine, interesting and historically associated S&Ws in this field that the collector has ample room to amass an impressive collection prior to involving himself with the minutia of internal variances.

There are a number of features peculiar to S&Ws that the collector will do well to arm himself with. Of major importance is the difference between nickel finishes and blue finishes.

In the top-most grades of condition—that is, mint or near mint—blue or nickel finished guns will fetch about equal prices. When finishes show wear and grades of condition descend, there is a decided difference in the price of blued or nickeled guns. Hence, a gun with 70 percent blue finish and smooth even wear is considered quite fine and most likely will be quite appealing to the eye; that very same gun with only 70 percent nickel finish remaining very likely will not look nearly as good and in some cases could even show very heavy wear. Although percentages are the same, the blued gun will normally fetch more in price and will normally be in greater demand. This by no means should be taken to indicate a hard and fast principle; it is merely a rule-of-thumb and a general observation.

Bore conditions on S&Ws are often important in determining value. Generally, on the early, small caliber models bores are unimportant. As the guns progress upward in size and caliber as well as date of manufacture, bores tend to become more important in establishing values. This is especially so with the fine target models and the big single actions, especially those in target grades. In many instances it will be found (depending on whether one is either buying or selling a gun) that the bores might not affect the actual values of the piece, but might make it more difficult to sell by lessening the demand for it. A very poor bore or one that has ringed the barrel inside causing an outward bulge will most definitely affect the price downward.

In many instances price differences exist between different issues of the same model, and these are seemingly inconsistent with the quantity differences (i.e., numbers manufactured) of those issues. This is accounted for by the collectors' demand and interest in the model itself for the importance of the variance. Often variances within a specific model that are found in mediocre condition will all be priced similarly; whereas in the upper grades of condition, they may be found to vary extensively in price. This again may be accounted for by the interest and demand on the collector's market for that particular model.

Often a perplexing anomaly to the uninitiated is the case of closely similar models in which the commoner specimen brings more money than the scarcer piece. This is very simply attributed to the fact that the commoner piece has greater collector interest and demand. It is certainly possible that as time progresses, the situation could well change and it is in just such situations as this that the future-conscious collector/investor might wish to consider closely. A good example is the 32 caliber Safety 1st Model revolver of which approximately 91,500 were made. The type, merely by virtue of its being the "1st Model," brings a higher price than the 2nd Model of this same revolver of which approximately 78,500 were made.

Of further interest to the S&W collector is that in the small caliber revolvers, especially 32 and 38 caliber double action types, the longer 6" barrels, even though standard and likely made in the same quantities as the shorter barrel lengths, will normally bring a slightly higher premium merely because of their longer length and generally more eye appealing appearance.

Bear in mind that the serial number ranges listed throughout this section are rarely exact and changes irregularly occurred on the exact serial number given. These are offered as an approximate termination point for one change to another. Quite definitely an overlap exists in almost all serial number ranges from one variance to another. Guns in each model were not always assembled in exact numerical order and hence, in the transitional period (somewhere near the termination serial number range for the model) a later gun could be found with the serial number still in the range of the earlier model. Therefore, it is necessary to check all the fine points and features of the gun and not rely solely on serial numbers.

Occasionally a five-pointed, small star marking will be found on the butt of a S&W. At one time this marking was thought to indicate only a factory refinished gun. Indeed, the stamp has been found on many factory refinished pieces. The marking indicates considerably more than that, however, and will also be found on S&Ws that still have their original, untampered factory finish. The star indicates the gun has been returned to S&W for a repair of some type and was processed through their repair department. The work could have been anywhere from a minor internal adjustment, or replacement part, to a major overhaul.

The stamping Made for Smith & Wesson is occasionally encountered on the revolvers of other makers; most notably those of Moore, Bacon and Pond. That legend was applied by those manufacturers after having lost a patent infringement suit to S&W in 1862. The marking is of decided interest to the S&W collector and pieces so stamped are often a part of a well rounded S&W arms group. Presence of Made for Smith & Wesson adds 20 to 40 percent premium to the value of those guns by other makers.

The marking Made for Smith & Wesson is also encountered on the small 22 caliber revolvers by Rollin White Arms Company and the Lowell Arms Company. Those guns were actually made under contract to S&W and thus should not be considered as infringements. The S&W marking on either Rollin White or Lowell Arms revolvers decidedly make them of interest in a S&W collection, enhancing their values some 20 to 40 percent. Approximately 4,300 Rollin White revolvers bore the S&W marking, as did over 7,500 of the Lowell Arms Company guns.

INFRINGEMENTS AND COPIES OF S&WS are occasionally encountered. Some of those are quite intriguing and well made; most notably of the Model 1, 2nd Issue, and the Model 2 Army. Most of these are of British or Belgian manufacture and often bear interesting markings, some identical to the Springfield-made S&Ws. Very noteworthy copies of the "New Model Russian" (Model 3 Russian, 3rd Model) revolver were made both in Germany and by the Russian government at their arsenal in Tula with total production in excess of 150,000. Those are important enough to be included in this section and will be found described and listed with that model. No accurate or complete study has ever been made in the area of infringements and copies, but a well rounded S&W collection should contain a few specimens of the more interesting and good quality types. Although their values are not the subject of this work, it is worth mentioning that in fine condition they have brought prices closely comparable to the American specimens from which they were fashioned; demand, however, is not as great. Many of the later Spanish, and possibly even Mexican made, copies of the double action S&Ws of all types are encountered. These are in very low demand, with prices moderate, not even closely approximating the genuine S&Ws.

The models and their variants listed in this section are those considered standard factory production pieces and will be most often observed by the collector and student. One's eye should always be on the lookout for the unlisted variants which do occasionally appear and which are most certainly choice collector's items and enthusiastically sought after. They can be found in almost all models and they can cover a broad array of features. The most obvious details are custom, extra-long or extra-short barrel lengths (in the latter the collector must be extremely cautious to determine authentic specimens from those that are merely cut down) to complete changes in contour and handle shapes. A word of caution—don't jump at conclusions; what the eye sees and the heart feels may not always be what the gun actually is! Alterations and mutilations were not infrequently made during the period of use by itinerant gunsmiths at the whims of owners. Some of these gunsmiths were extremely fine workmen and with the passage of time, the arm may have acquired a patina of age suggesting factory originality. When, on close scrutiny, the variance turns out not to be factory and merely an alteration (albeit an interesting one) this does not often enhance its value and usually will detract from it. It again bears mention that odd and unusual variations have been made in modern times on antique S&Ws to deceive the unsuspecting collector. When encountering such a piece, and unfamiliar with it, the collector is urged to consult with known authorities.

Original variants are often difficult to price and may be one-of-a-kind pieces. However, they are not priceless! If the variant is an uninteresting or extremely minor one, it will normally affect the value but slightly. If, however, the variant is an extra long custom barrel length or some unique, extremely intriguing feature (special caliber, etc.), it might very well make the piece anywhere from double to five times normal value.

Grips often affect S&W prices. The use of plain ivory or pearl grips on S&Ws, if in fine, unbroken condition, will certainly add to the value of any gun. Occasionally unusual hard rubber variant types are found on S&Ws and are also worth watching out for. In the small caliber models, ivory or pearl handles can increase the value anywhere from $35 to $125 depending on condition and the style of grip. On the very large caliber models, especially the single actions, values could be increased anywhere from $85 to $300. In many of the later S&Ws it is important to differentiate between original grips and privately purchased ones. Most of those that are factory original manufactured after 1890 will bear a small inset gilt medallion embossed with the S&W monogram.

Occasionally observed on ivory grips and but rarely on pearl are high relief carved designs; usually of military or eagle or patriotic motifs. Such carving will greatly enhance the value of any gun and the grips at a minimum should be worth at least $150 more; especially so if found on the big single action models. Condition is a very important factor in evaluating such grips and badly worn ones would not be considered in these higher dollar values.

A significant number of S&Ws will be found bearing fancy engraved designs. It is important to distinguish original factory engraving, original period engraving and modern applied engraving. This can only be done through experience and verification by persons knowledgeable in the S&W line. No attempt will be made to treat the subject here. Presence of original engraving on any S&W will greatly enhance its value.

The value will be in direct proportion to the degree to which the engraving is applied. Of extreme importance is condition of the gun itself. An original engraved specimen will, at a minimum, at least be doubled in price. With that as a stepping stone, further research must be done to verify the type and quality of the engraving in order to determine market value of the gun. Some S&Ws are not uncommonly found engraved while other models are extremely rare. Condition continues to be a highly important factor affecting both value and desirability.

Several variations of original factory and dealer casings are encountered with S&Ws. Depending on condition, they also will do much to enhance the value of the guns they contain. Casings are usually of walnut with wool baize covered compartments, accommodating the gun, a few spare accessories, and a packet of ammunition. Values are determined by the models for which the cases are fitted. Cases for small caliber models (through to 38) are most often observed, while the large casings, especially for the big single actions, are rarely seen. 1st Model, 1st Issue 22s are occasionally found in a hard gutta-percha case with the relief design of the pistol itself on the outer lid. (See two types of those gutta percha cases for S&W Model No. 1 "First Issue" and "Second Issue" revolvers along with descriptions on the following page.) Walnut cases normally range in value from $225 to $600 for the smaller types with double that and more for some of the rare large sizes.

ORIGINAL FACTORY LABELED BOXES. Plain, unengraved Smith & Wessons (beginning with earliest models) were usually sold packaged in labeled, factory pasteboard boxes. Most did not survive due to the ravages of time, their obvious weaknesses and the fact that many were never needed once the gun was removed from the box. A generous cross-section of the types and labels are illustrated here. For the collector such labeled boxes are extremely desirable and will enhance values of the matching revolvers. On the earliest models those boxes may increase premiums 100 percent, often more, dependant on condition and rarity. Condition of box and the label are important. Some boxes for earliest models include fine illustrations of the actual gun on labels on the cover, adding a desirable extra feature. The condition of the revolver within the box is a key element; in most instances such handguns will be found in exc. + (or better) condition.

Low serial numbers usually enhance value. Although in no way affecting the manufacture or the appearance or the purpose of the gun, the quest for such numbers and increased values of same are an established idiosyncrasy of the collecting world! Broad generalization would place three digits or lower to be a most desirable feature on any S&W with a slight premium for same; if two digits, the premium should be higher and if just a single digit, the premium could conceivably double the price— but not necessarily. There is no fixed rule.

Smith and Wesson factory records are intact for almost all models. The company offers the service of identifying those pieces for which factory records exist for a $30.00 fee. Write to Office of the Historian, S&W, P.O. Box 2208, Springfield, Mass. 01101. Such data usually includes only the exact material that actually appears on their records.

The reader is reminded to take note that the dual range of conditions and their accompanying prices are especially evident throughout this S&W section. The subject and the reason for this is quite thoroughly treated in Chapter II of this book and it should be referred to and reviewed in order that its use may be understood.

The reader is further urged to review the introductory material to this book, especially the section of Chapter II where the exact definition of the NRA standards which comprise the terms used to describe condition here.

BIBLIOGRAPHY

*Boorman, Dean K. *The History of Smith & Wesson Firearms* Guilford, Conn.: Lyons Press 2002. Issued simultaneously with the 150th anniversary of S&W. Coverage includes S&Ws up to present; investing in them; shooting them.

*Chicoine, David R. *Smith & Wesson Sixguns of the Old West* Lincoln, R.I.: Andrew Mowbray Publishers, 2004. Fine guide to the early large frame S&Ws; the revolvers that made S&W's reputation on the frontier, battlefield and shooting range.

*Jinks, R. G. and Neal, R. J. *Smith and Wesson 1857-1945*. New York: Barnes and Company, 1966; Revised Edition 1975. Reprint 1996; R&R Books, Livonia, N.Y. A most authoritative and complete work on the subject; considered a standard reference for S&W collectors.

Jinks, R. G. *History of Smith & Wesson*. Los Angeles, California: Beinfeld Publishing Co, 1978. Details the evolution and development of Smith & Wesson handguns (including the Volcanics) 1852–1977. Highly authoritative and a companion volume to the author's earlier work.

Jinks, Roy G. *Artistry in Arms, The Guns of S&W*. Springfield, Mass: S&W, 1991. Superbly illus., finely designed catalog of special exhibition of rare and elegantly engraved antique S&Ws.

Lyons, A. *Smith and Wesson Collectible Pocket Pricing Guide*. Grover City, California: 1988.

McHenry, R. C. and Roper, W. F. *Smith and Wesson Handguns*. Huntington, West Virginia: Standard Publications, Inc., 1945. The first guide to S&W collecting and history with information of value but generally superseded by the Jinks and Neal work.

Parson, J. E. *Smith and Wesson Revolvers—The Pioneer Single Action Models*. New York: William Morrow and Company, 1957. A superb detailed study of early production, combining a wealth of data on both the company and their products.

*Pate, Charles W. *Smith & Wesson American Model in U.S. and Foreign Service* Woonsocket, R.I.: Andrew Mowbray Pub., 2006. In-depth study on these famous early single actions; includes important serial number information also.

*Supica, J. & Nahas, R. *Standard Catalog Of Smith & Wesson*. Iola, Wis.: Krause Publications, 1996. Lots of new S&W information; necessary companion for the Jinks & Neal work. Updated 3rd Edition, 2006.

(*) Preceding a title indicates the book is currently in print

S&W Iron Frame Volcanic   *See Winchester Firearms, Chapter V, and prefatory text to this chapter.*

Smith & Wesson 22 Caliber Models

S&W Model No. 1 First Issue Revolver

Model No. 1 First Issue Revolver. Manufactured 1857-60; total run of about 11,671.

22 short rimfire caliber. 7-shot non-fluted cylinder. Barrel length of 3-3/16"; barrels are octagonal.

Rosewood grips, the butt shape square. Brass frame silver plated, the barrel and cylinder blued.

Serial numbered in individual range, starting with 1 and continuing through 11671, serials then continued by the succeeding model. Barrel marking features company name and address; and on the cylinder, 1855 patent date (later specimens also included 1858 date marking).

The Model No. 1 First Issue was Smith & Wesson's first metallic cartridge firearm, beginning a long line of weaponry still very much in the forefront of the industry at this writing. This was a tip-up revolver, on which the barrel pivoted upwards, hinged to the forward end of the topstrap. Distinguishing features include the rounded contour of the sides of the frame and the circular sideplate.

*Model No. 1
First Issue*

**Left: Bayonet type barrel catch of first and second types.
Right: Spring-loaded side projection barrel catch
on all other Model No. 1 series.**

Second style case

Earliest style case

Model 1
First Issue

First Type. Distinguished by presence of a recoil plate revolving with the cylinder. Bayonet type barrel catch, projecting from frame bottomstrap and a small key fitted to left side of recoil shield which acts as retainer for revolving recoil plate. Serial range from 1 to low 200s:

5G-001   Values—Good **$6,500**   Fine **$15,000**

Second Type. Serial range of about early 200s to about 1130; varies mainly in having altered form of attachment of the recoil plate to frame with exterior key not present. Bayonet style barrel latch:

5G-002   Values—Good **$3,000**   Fine **$7,000**

Third Type. Serial range of about 1130s to approximately 3000+; improved method of fastening of the barrel with a catch (used on rest of Model 1 series, all issues) that had side projections and was spring loaded:

5G-003   Values—Good **$1,250**   Fine **$3,000**

Fourth Type. Serial range of about 3000+ to 4200+; recoil plate area altered and its diameter significantly reduced:

5G-004   Values—Good **$900**   Fine **$2,250**

Fifth Type. Serial range about 4200+ to 5500+; rifling change from three grooves to five:

5G-005   Values—Good **$900**   Fine **$2,250**

Sixth Type. Serial range approximately 5500+ to about 11671. Rotating recoil device eliminated and instead a ratchet was made an integral part of cylinder; other modifications also made:

5G-006   Values—Good **$900**   Fine **$2,000**

There are two rare type, original factory issued, black **gutta percha**, hinged lid cases for early S&W Model 1 Revolvers; both First and Second Issue types (the only models believed so equipped). *Earliest style* had a high relief design of that same First Issue molded into its cover along with relief lettering: "MANUFACTURED ONLY BY SMITH & WESSON/SPRINGFIELD MASSACHUSETTS" with decorative relief scroll and floral designs at each corner. The edges of the border of the lid were a series of miniature relief designs of that same revolver. The *second style case* (believed scarcer) similar in size and styling with relief floral designs each corner; center motif a relief panoply of six flags and shield, stack of cannon balls in center. Second style does not bear S&W markings. Interiors identical both styles, includes a gutta percha compartment to hold 22 cal. cartridges; and embossed velvet lining inside lid. Both cases were made by Littlefield Parsons & Company for S&W. The second style of cases believed to have also been used for the later production "First Issue revolvers," but most have been observed with the "Second Issue" revolvers. Condition is, of course, important when assessing premium values. Very minor chips or nicks are not significant as a rule; values for cases (without revolvers enclosed) are known to have fetched from $950 to $3,500 in fine condition.

S&W Model No. 1 Second Issue Revolver

Model No. 1 Second Issue Revolver. Made 1860-1868; total production about 117,000.

22 short rimfire caliber. 7-shot non-fluted cylinder. 3-3/16" octagonal barrel.

Rosewood grips, the butt shape square. Blued barrel and cylinder, with silver plated brass frame, or full plating in nickel or silver.

The serial numbering continuing from the Model No. 1 First Issue, beginning at about 11672 and continuing through to about 128000. Company name and address on the barrel; on the cylinder 1855 and 1859 patent dates were marked, and at serial range about 20000 an 1860 date was included.

Readily distinguishable from the Model No. 1 First Issue by the flat sides of the frame and irregular shaped sideplate, but the Second Issue is otherwise quite close in appearance to its predecessor. A scarce variation on early production has a "square cut" side plate rather than the standard evenly curved type; worth premium. (See also discussion "Infringements and Copies" in prefatory text to this chapter.)

5G-007

Standard model; early type with 1855 and 1859 patent date cylinder markings:

5G-007   Values—Good **$325**   Fine **$650**

Standard model, with 1855, 1859, and 1860 date markings:

5G-008   Values—Good **$275**   Fine **$575**

Approximately 4,402 revolvers (having the three patent dates) marked 2D QUAL'TY on barrel lug; these had slight defects and were sold at discount:

5G-009   Values—Good **$1,200**   Fine **$2,500**

S&W Model No. 1 Third Issue Revolver

Model No. 1 Third Issue Revolver. Made 1868-1881; total production approximately 131,163.

22 short rimfire caliber. 7-shot fluted cylinder. 2-11/16" and 3-3/16" round ribbed barrels.

Rosewood grips, the butt of bird's head shape. Blued barrel and cylinder, with nickel plated frame, or full blue or nickel plating.

Serial numbered in their own range, beginning with 1 and continuing through end of production, 131163. Company name and address on the barrel, along with 1855, 1859, and 1860 patent dates.

Basically an improved type from the Model No. 1 First and Second Issue revolvers, featuring the fluted cylinder, round barrel, and bird's head type grip. As on the previous models, extraction of cartridges is accomplished by removing the cylinder, and using the rammer pin to poke out the empties. Seven guns were marked 2D QUAL'TY. Rare; worth premium.

5G-010

Standard model, of 3-3/16" barrel length; the barrel markings on the top rib:
5G-010   Values—Very Good **$225**   Exc. **$475**
Standard model, of 2-11/16" barrel length; the markings on the side of the barrel:
5G-011   Values—Very Good **$700**   Exc. **$1,500**

S&W First Model Single Shot Pistol

First Model Single Shot Pistol (a.k.a. Single Shot Model 1891). Manufactured 1893-1905; total production approximately 1,251.

22 long rifle, 32 S&W, and 38 S&W calibers. Single shot; 6", 8", and 10" barrels (markings "H.M. POPE" on top rib of barrel, indicating custom work by that noted riflesmith, worth premium).

Checkered hard rubber grips, extension type with square butt. Blue or nickel plated finish.

Serial numbering was in the same range as the 38 Single Action Third Model Revolver, from 1 to 28107. Company name and address on the barrel, with 1875, 1877, and 1880 patent dates.

5G-012

An unusual and scarce target pistol, the First Model Single Shot has the profile of a revolver, retains the revolver recoil shield and is topbreak action. Its frame was that of the 38 Single Action Third Model. A popular target pistol of its day, some specimens saw match use by the United States Olympic Team. A rare variation commanding a substantial premium price is the combination set: The 38 Single Action Third Model frame, cylinder, and barrel, with 22, 32, or 38 caliber single shot barrels; generally cased together with accessory items, including standard and target grips. Spuriously assembled sets are known. Important to check for matching numbers on all major components.

Standard model, chambered for the 22 long rifle cartridge; 862 made:
5G-012   Values—Very Good **$600**   Exc. **$1,000**
Standard model, chambering in 32 S&W caliber; 229 made:
5G-013   Values—Very Good **$1,150**   Exc. **$2,000**
Standard model, chambering for 38 S&W; 160 made:
5G-014   Values—Very Good **$1,200**   Exc. **$2,250**

(Note: 1,947 single shot barrels were sold separately, made in the three production calibers; they were not completed into guns at the factory. A complete serial number listing of the 1,251 First Model Single Shot Pistols made by Smith & Wesson is given in the Jinks and Neal book.)

S&W Second Model Single Shot Pistol

Second Model Single Shot Pistol. Made 1905-1909; total produced 4,617.

22 long rifle caliber. Single shot; 10" barrel standard; single action.

Checkered hard rubber grips, extension type with square butt. Blue or nickel plated finish.

Serial numbered in their own range, from 1 on up through 4617. Company name and address on the barrel, but not including patent dates. A distinguishing feature is the frame, which has been altered from revolver by removal of the recoil shield and will not accommodate a revolver cylinder, as did the First Model Single Shot.

Standard model, with 10" barrel not marked with patent dates:
5G-015   Values—Very Good **$600**   Exc. **$1,200**
Standard model, but fitted with a First Model Single Shot Pistol barrel (which thus includes 1875, 1877, and 1890 patent date

5G-015

markings); 22 caliber. 10" barrel standard. 8" barrel worth 30 percent premium; 6" length 50 percent premium.
5G-016   Values—Very Good **$600**   Exc. **$1,200**

S&W Third Model Single Shot Pistol

Third Model Single Shot Pistol (a.k.a. Single Shot Perfected; Olympic Model Single Shot). Manufactured 1909-1923; total production 6,949.

22 long rifle caliber. Single shot; 10" barrel standard.

Checkered walnut grips, extension type with square butt. Blued finish. Serial range 4618 to 11641.

In this instance the frame is an altered version of that in use on the 38 Double Action Perfected Model, and was machined so a revolver cylinder could not be used. An interesting feature is that the Third Model Single Shot could be fired double action, as well as single action, and thus its trigger is located at the center

5G-017

area of the trigger guard.

5G-017   Values—Very Good **$550**   Exc. **$1,000**

S&W Straight Line Single Shot Pistol

Straight Line Single Shot Pistol. Made 1925-36; total quantity 1,870.

22 long rifle. 10" barrel. Sights mounted on breech and muzzle of barrel.

Walnut grips with S&W monogram inlays. Blued finish.

Serial numbered in individual range from 1 on up. Company name marking, and patent date stampings of 1901, 1908, 1909, and 1923.

Having the appearance of an automatic pistol, the Straight Line's barrel pivots left for loading and extraction. The hammer pulls straight back, rather than pivoting as on conventional handguns. Minor variations for this model are detailed in the Jinks and Neal book.

5G-018

Pistol without case or accessories:
5G-018   Values—Very Good **$750**   Exc. **$1,200**

Cased set of pistol and accessory items:
5G-019   Values—Very Good **$1,100**   Exc. **$2,000**

S&W First Model Ladysmith Revolver

5G-020

First Model Ladysmith Revolver (a.k.a. Model M Hand Ejector 1st Model). Made 1902-1906; total production 4,575.

22 long caliber. 7-shot fluted cylinder. 2-1/4", 3" and 3-1/2" barrel lengths.

Checkered hard rubber grips, rounded butt. Blued or nickel plated finish.

Serial numbered in an individual range, beginning with 1 up to 4575. Company name and address barrel marking, and patent dates of 1899, 1900, and 1901.

The Ladysmith revolvers are quite popular with collectors, in part due to their diminutive size, and because of use by women as a personal defense weapon. Daniel B. Wesson himself was the designer, and the Ladysmith was S&W's first 22 revolver since the Model No. 1 Third Issue had been discontinued in 1881. The First Model Ladysmith can be quickly identified by noting the checkered cylinder release button on the left side of the frame:

5G-020   Values—Very Good **$750**   Exc. **$1,750**

S&W Second Model Ladysmith Revolver

Second Model Ladysmith Revolver. Manufactured 1906-1910; total produced approximately 9,400.

22 long caliber. 7-shot fluted cylinder. 3" and 3-1/2" barrel lengths.

Checkered hard rubber grips, rounded butt. Blued or nickel plated finish.

Serial numbering continued from that of the First Model Ladysmith, and is in the range 4576 to 13950. Barrel marking includes the company name and address, and the patent dates 1899, 1900, and 1901.

The Second Model's major difference from the First Model Ladysmith is in the system of locking the cylinder into position. The thumb release on the left side of the frame was discontinued,

5G-021

and in its place a locking device was added to the bottom of the barrel. The design was such that the cylinder pin was locked at both ends:

5G-021   Values—Very Good **$650**   Exc. **$1,500**

S&W Third Model Ladysmith Revolver

Third Model Ladysmith Revolver. Made 1910-1921; total production approximately 12,200.

22 long caliber. 7-shot fluted cylinder. 2-1/2", 3", 3-1/2", and 6" barrel lengths.

Plain walnut grips with S&W medallion inlays; square butt profile. Blued or nickel plated finish.

5G-022

Serial numbering picked up where the Second Model Ladysmith had left off, and is in the range 13951 to 26154. Barrel marking includes the company name and address, and patent dates of 1896, 1901, 1906, and 1909.

The Third Model is quickly distinguished by the smooth walnut grips and the square butt profile. The cylinder locking system continued that as used on the Second Model Ladysmith. (Note: Use of pearl or ivory grips commands a premium, and these special order features are seen occasionally.)

Standard model, in 2-1/2" (worth premium), 3" or 3-1/2" lengths:

5G-022   Values—Very Good **$575**   Exc. **$1,250**

As above, but with 6" barrel and standard sights (scarcer than below):

5G-023   Values—Very Good **$1,750**   Exc. **$3,500**

The 6" barrel model, with target sights:

5G-024   Values—Very Good **$1,600**   Exc. **$3,000**

S&W 22/32 Hand Ejector Revolver

22/32 Hand Ejector Revolver (a.k.a. 22/32 Bekeart Model). Made c. 1911-53; total production approximately 1,000 (the "true" Bekeart Model); several hundred thousand were made of the standard 22/32 Hand Ejector revolvers.

22 long rifle. 6-shot fluted cylinder. 6" barrel length.

Checkered walnut grips of extension type, with square butt; and inlaid S&W medallions. Blued finish.

Serial numbering began with 1. Barrel marking includes the company name and address, caliber designation, and the patent dates 1906, 1909, and 1914.

The impetus for this model came from the San Francisco arms dealer Phil B. Bekeart, who urged S&W to make a target 22 revolver having a heavyweight frame. To back up his confidence in such a gun, he ordered 1,000 himself. These 1,000, in the serial range of 1 to about 3000, are the true Bekeart Model (see below).

True Bekeart Model, within the serial range 1-3000, but total production of 1,000 specimens. Features as noted above, but

5G-025

included a separate serial stamping on grip bottom, special sights (in many respects the revolver was the same as the 32 Hand Ejector Model of 1903 Second Change):

5G-025   Values—Very Good **$625**   Exc. **$1,250**

Balance of production (any specimens not the true Bekeart Model):

5G-026   Values—Very Good **$350**   Exc. **$750**

Smith & Wesson 32 Caliber Models

S&W Model No. 1-1/2 First Issue Revolver

Model No. 1-1/2 First Issue Revolver (a.k.a. Old Model 1-1/2). Made from 1865-1868; the total production approximately 26,300.

32 rimfire caliber. 5-shot non-fluted cylinder. 3-1/2" octagon barrel standard; 4" barrel scarce, worth premium.

Rosewood grips, with square shaped butt profile. Blued or nickel plated finish.

5G-027

Serial numbered from 1 up to about 26300; serials then continued by the succeeding model. Company name and address barrel marking, with 1855 and 1859 patent dates (later specimens also included 1865 marking).

The Model No. 1-1/2 First Issue was S&W's initial production of a 32 caliber revolver. This series was a beefed up version of their Model No. 1 22 rimfire revolver, offering the more substantial performance of a 32 caliber round. The barrel pivots from the front of the topstrap, and ejection was done by removing the cylinder and pushing each cartridge out with the rammer pin. An unusual historical note is that most parts for the 1-1/2 First Issue were manufactured by a Middletown, Connecticut, firm, King & Smith, and S&W did the final fitting and assembly. Six were marked 2D QUAL'TY. Rare, worth premium.

Standard model, with 1855 and 1859 patent date marking:

5G-027   Values—Very Good **$350**   Exc. **$750**

As above, but also including the 1865 marking, which was added in the serial range of about 15304 to 15653:

5G-028   Values—Very Good **$350**   Exc. **$750**

S&W Model No. 1-1/2 Second Issue Revolver

Model No. 1-1/2 Second Issue Revolver (a.k.a. New Model 1-1/2). Manufactured 1868 1875; in a total run of about 100,700.

32 rimfire long caliber. 5-shot fluted cylinder. 2-1/2" and 3-1/2" round barrels.

Rosewood grips, with bird's head butt profile. Blued or nickel plated finish.

Serial numbering continued the range begun by the Model 1-1/2 First Issue Revolver, from about 26301 to 127100. Company name and address marking, with 1855, 1859, and 1865 patent dates, were on the top of the barrel.

An improved version of the First Issue revolver, the Second Issue has a more streamlined appearance. Internally it features the cylinder stop in the topstrap, rather than in the bottomstrap as on the First Issue. 41 were marked 2D QUAL'TY. Rare, worth premium.

Standard model, 3-1/2" barrel:
5G-029   Values—Very Good **$250**   Exc. **$500**
As above, but 2-1/2" barrel; markings on side of barrel:
5G-030   Values—Very Good **$575**   Exc. **$1,250**

5G-029
Standard Model

5G-031
Transition Model

Transition model, made by fitting First Issue cylinders and barrels to Second Issue frames; within the serial range of about 27200-28800; estimated between 650 and 1,500 produced:
5G-031   Values—Very Good **$1,750**   Exc. **$3,750**

S&W Model No. 1-1/2 Single Action Revolver

Model No. 1-1/2 Single Action Revolver (a.k.a. 32 Single Action). Made 1878-1892; total production of 97,574.

32 S&W caliber. 5-shot fluted cylinder. 3", 3-1/2", 6", 8", and 10" round barrels.

Grips of plain wood or checkered hard rubber; both types with bird's head butt profile. Blued or nickel plated finish.

Serial numbering in an individual range, from 1 on up to 97574. Barrel marked with company name and address, and with 1865, 1869, 1871, 1875, and 1877 patent dates.

5G-033

A key detail in the design of the Model No. 1-1/2 Single Action is its topbreak action. The barrel pivots on the bottom framestrap, and latching on the topstrap just forward of the hammer. Another important characteristic is the rebounding hammer, so made for safety when carrying a fully loaded revolver. As the barrel is opened downward, all cartridges are automatically extracted. This was S&W's first 32 caliber revolver with automatic ejection and made in the break-open style.

The major variance in this model is the strain screw (for adjusting tension on mainspring) located in the forestrap of the grip and which is found on most specimens after approximately serial range 6500. Early specimens (serial range 1 to 1300) lack the patent dates of April 20, 1875 and December 18, 1877, and for the advanced collector are worth a slight premium.

Early production without strain screw. (Serial range approximately 1 to 6500). Barrel lengths 3" to 6":
5G-032   Values—Very Good **$225**   Exc. **$475**
Later production with strain screw:
5G-033   Values—Very Good **$185**   Exc. **$375**
Long barrel lengths. 8" and 10" with strain screw:
5G-034   Values—Very Good **$1,000**   Exc. **$2,750**

S&W Model No. 2 Old Model Revolver

Model No. 2 Old Model Revolver (a.k.a. Model No. 2 Army). Manufactured 1861-1874; total production 77,155.

32 rimfire long caliber. 6-shot non-fluted cylinder. 5" and 6" octagonal barrels usual; 4" rare. A few 8" and 10" extreme rarities.

Rosewood grips with square butt profile. Blued or nickel plated finish and scarce "half plate" finish (*i.e.* silver plated frame with blued cylinder and barrel); in better states of condition will bring premium.

Serial numbering an individual range, from 1 to 77155. Barrel marking was company name and address; and 1855, 1859, 1860 patent dates stamped on cylinder.

Similar in outward appearance to the Model No. 1-1/2 First Issue, the Model No. 2 Old Model can be readily identified by the differing patent date marking, the presence of the cylinder stop on the topstrap, and the 6-shot cylinder. Another significant difference is barrel lengths. The Model No. 2 was a popular personal sidearm with many officers and enlisted men during

5G-035

the Civil War. General George Armstrong Custer is known to have owned a pair of these. Specimens with serial under 35731 (produced by May 1, 1865) will bring small premium because of possible Civil War usage. The notorious western gunslinger "Wild Bill" Hickok, while marshal of Deadwood was carrying a Model 2 "Army" (as well as aces and eights) the night he was shot in August 1874. Rare markings 2D QUALITY were applied to 35 "Armies" with slight defects and are worth premium values. Interesting and rare variations are found in this model. An unique collection, formed solely with the Model 2 "Army" was

sold at auction Feb., 2001 by Butterfield's, San Francisco. Their catalog which also includes much data from factory records is a valuable reference for these "Armies." (See also discussion "Infringements and Copies" in prefatory text to this chapter.)
Standard model, early production having two pins in the topstrap (holding cylinder stop); serial range 1 to about 3000. 5" or 6" barrel:
5G-035   Values—Very Good **$1,000**   Exc. **$2,500**
B. KITTREDGE & Co./CINCINNATI, O. marked on side of barrel. 2600 were purchased by that well-known arms dealer in 1862, of which 730 were sold by them, under contract, to the state of

Kentucky and delivered by Sept. 1862 and subsequently issued to the 7th Kentucky Cavalry. Values below are for KITTREDGE marked specimens. Those under No. 7715 with possible 7th Ky. Cavalry use are worth premium:
5G-035.5   Values—Very Good **$1,500**   Exc. **$3,500**
Standard model, balance of production, and having three pins holding the cylinder stop in the topstrap. 5" or 6" barrel:
5G-036   Values—Very Good **$750**   Exc. **$2,000**
Same as above, but 4" barrel. This variation quite rare, but watch for forgeries or alterations. Made c. 1866-67. Three-pin type only:
5G-037   Values—Very Good **$2,250**   Exc. **$5,000**

S&W 32 Double Action First Model Revolver

32 Double Action First Model Revolver. Made in 1880, in a total quantity of 30.

32 S&W caliber. 5- shot fluted cylinder. 3" round barrel.

Hard rubber grips, plain black. Blued or nickel plated finish.

Serial numbering in an individual range, from 1 to 30. Company name and address barrel marking, with patent dates of 1865, 1869, 1871, 1877, 1879, and 1880. Two variations exist in date stampings on this model revolver.

One of the rarest of all S&W revolvers, the 32 Double Action First Model—from the standpoint of rarity alone—is out of the reach of most collectors. One of its most striking structural details also accounts in part for the rarity of the model; the sideplate is straight sided, later found to be a cause for weakness in the frame.

5G-038

The plain black hard rubber grips are also a specific feature to note. This was S&W's first 32 caliber double action topbreak revolver; ejection was automatic on pivoting down the barrel:
5G-038   Values—Very Good **$4,500**   Exc. **$10,000**

S&W 32 Double Action Second Model

5G-039

32 Double Action Second Model Revolver. Manufactured 1880-1882; total production 22,142.

32 S&W caliber. 5-shot fluted cylinder. 3" round barrel.

Hard rubber grips, with checkered or floral patterns and S&W monogram stampings (note: shown in illus. with pearl grips). Blued or nickel plated finish.

Serial numbering continued that begun by the 32 Double Action First Model, and continued through to 22172. Company name and address barrel marking, with patent dates of 1865, 1869, 1871, 1879, and 1880.

The major difference between this model and its *rare* predecessor is the somewhat oval (or irregular) contour adopted of the sideplate. A secondary variant is noted in the embellished grips, as contrasted to the plain stocks of the First Model:
5G-039   Values—Very Good **$225**   Exc. **$350**

S&W 32 Double Action Third Model Revolver

32 Double Action Third Model Revolver. Produced 1882-1883; in a total run of 21,232.

32 S&W caliber. 5-shot fluted cylinder. 3", 3-1/2", and 6" barrels.

Hard rubber grips, with checkered pattern and S&W monogram. Blued or nickel plated finish.

Serial numbering continued from the 32 Double Action Second Model, from 22173 to 43405. Company name and address barrel marking, with patent dates of 1865, 1869, 1871, 1880, and 1882.

Quite similar to its Second Model predecessor, the 32 Double Action Third Model did vary considerably internally. Changes were most obviously reflected in the cylinder periphery, no longer including a long "free groove" as previously, and now with one set of stop notches instead of two; and the flutes

became longer. The trigger guard continued to have the slight reverse curve (almost a squareback) rear profile:
5G-040   Values—Very Good **$200**   Exc. **$325**

5G-040

S&W 32 Double Action Fourth Model Revolver

32 Double Action Fourth Model Revolver. Made from 1883-1909; total production about 239,600. (Serial numbers under 209,300 (approx.) made prior to Dec. 31, 1898.)

32 S&W caliber. 5-shot fluted cylinder. 3", 3-1/2", 6", 8", and 10" barrels; these latter two quite scarce and will bring premium values.

Hard rubber grips, with checkered pattern and S&W monogram. Blued or nickel plated finish.

Serial numbers continued from the 32 Double Action Third Model, and ran from 43406 to about 282999. Company name and address barrel marking, with patent dates of 1865, 1869, 1871, 1880, and 1882 *or* (late production) 1880, 1882, and 1889.

Improvements from the previous model were in the trigger, trigger guard (note oval shape, having dropped the reverse curved back profile), and internally in the cylinder stop and sear. Note that the transition between the Fourth and Fifth Model of

5G-041

the 32 Double Action covers some 10,000 serial numbers (in the range 278677-288529):

5G-041   Values—Very Good **$200**   Exc. **$325**

S&W 32 Double Action Fifth Model Revolver

32 Double Action Fifth Model Revolver. (Not illustrated; substantially identical to the Fourth Model.) Manufactured 1909-1919; total produced about 44,641.

32 S&W caliber. 5-shot fluted cylinder. 3", 3-1/2", and 6" barrels.

Hard rubber grips, with checkered pattern and S&W monogram. Blued or nickel plated finish.

Serial numbering from about 283000-327641; continuing the range from the Fourth Model revolvers (the transition between

the two models covers some 10,000 serials, in the range 278677-288529). Company name and address barrel marking, with patent dates of 1880, 1882, and 1889.

A major detail identifying the Fifth Model is the front sight integral with the barrel, rather than an insert pinned into position as on previous models of the 32 Double Action. The Fifth Model was the ultimate evolution of the 32 caliber break open double action begun by the First Model, in 1880:

5G-042   Values—Very Good **$200**   Exc. **$325**

S&W 32 Safety First Model D.A. Revolver

32 Safety First Model D.A. Revolver (a.k.a. 32 Safety Hammerless New Departure and Lemon Squeezer). Made 1888-1902; total produced 91,417.

32 S&W caliber. 5-shot fluted cylinder. 2", 3", and 3-1/2" round barrels.

Checkered hard rubber grips with S&W monogram impression. Blued or nickel plated finish.

Serial numbered from 1 to 91417, the range then continued by the succeeding model. Company name and address barrel marking, with patent dates of 1877, 1880, 1883, and 1885.

Known to many as the "Safety Hammerless" (among other nicknames), the 32 Safety First Model was unusual in three major respects: The hammer was concealed, and thus the revolver could only be fired double action, and a safety bar set onto the backstrap had to be simultaneously squeezed to allow for firing. The origin of one nickname, "Lemon Squeezer" is obvious. Size was small, so the 32 Safety First Model D.A. was truly a pocket hideaway revolver. Made on the break open

5G-043

principle, a significant detail of the First Model is the location of the knurled barrel release at the back center of the topstrap, rather than on the sides as on later models.

Standard model, 3" or 3-1/2" barrel:

5G-043   Values—Very Good **$250**   Exc. **$450**

2" barrel revolvers, with markings on side of barrel:

5G-044   Values—Very Good **$425**   Exc. **$750**

S&W 32 Safety Second Model D.A. Revolver

32 Safety Second Model D.A. Revolver. Made 1902-1909; total of about 78,500.

32 S&W caliber. 5-shot fluted cylinder. 2", 3", 3-1/2", and 6" barrels.

Checkered hard rubber grips with S&W monogram. Blued or nickel plated.

Serial numbered from 91418 to about 170000 (overlap with the Third Model in the range 163082-175772). Company name and address barrel marking, with patent dates of 1877, 1880, 1883, and 1885.

5G-045

Two major details distinguish the Second Model from its predecessor: The adoption of the T-shaped barrel catch with two knurled buttons (one each side of topstrap), and the necessary changes in the topstrap to accommodate the T-catch. The revolver continued to be a pocket hideaway type, except for the addition of a 6" barrel to the line.

Standard model, in 3", 3-1/2" and 6" (worth premium) lengths:
5G-045 Values—Very Good **$200** Exc. **$400**
As above, but in 2" barrel, known as the "Bicycle Revolver"; the barrel markings rolled on the side (rather than on top), and the patent marking with less dates:
5G-046 Values—Very Good **$425** Exc. **$750**

S&W 32 Safety Third Model D.A. Revolver

32 Safety Third Model D.A. Revolver. (Not illus.; similar to 32 Safety Second Model D.A.) Manufactured 1909-37; total quantity approximately 73,000.

32 S&W caliber. 5-shot fluted cylinder. 2", 3", and 3-1/2" barrels. Checkered hard rubber grips with S&W monogram. Blued or nickel plated finish.

Serial numbering from about 170000-242981.

Changes slight from the predecessor model, and are most noticeable in the barrel marking on 3" and 3-1/2" barrels, which read only: S & W SPGFD MASS, and on 2" barrels S & W only (on side). Slight sight fastening changes also noted. All such differences are detailed in the Jinks and Neal book.
Standard model:
5G-047 Values—Very Good **$185** Exc. **$400**
2" barrel model:
5G-048 Values—Very Good **$425** Exc. **$750**

S&W 32 Hand Ejector First Model D.A.

32 Hand Ejector First Model D.A. Revolver (a.k.a. Model I Hand Ejector or Model 1896 Hand Ejector). Made 1896-1903; total quantity of 19,712.

32 S&W long caliber. 6-shot fluted cylinder. 3-1/4", 4-1/4", and 6" barrels.

Checkered hard rubber grips with S&W monogram; of either round butt or square butt, extension target type. Blued or nickel plated finish.

Serial numbered from 1-19712, in individual range. Company name and address marking on the cylinder, with patent dates 1884, 1889, 1894, and 1895. Placement for these markings was on the chambers, between the flutes.

The 32 Hand Ejector First Model D.A. was S&W's maiden entry into the production of swingout cylinder revolvers. Locking into position was by spring tension on the cylinder pin; by pulling forward on the pin, the cylinder could be swung out

5G-049

for loading and extraction. Another unusual feature was the positioning of the cylinder stop in the topstrap. Still another was the location of the rear sight about central in the topstrap above the forward end of the cylinder. Variation with short hammer spur in serial range 5500 to 6000 scarce; worth premium:
5G-049 Values—Very Good **$325** Exc. **$650**

S&W 32 Hand Ejector Model of 1903

32 Hand Ejector Model of 1903 (a.k.a. Model I Hand Ejector Model of 1903). Made 1903-04; total quantity of 19,425.

5G-050

32 S&W long caliber. 6-shot fluted cylinder. 3-1/4", 4-1/4", and 6" barrels.

Grips and finishes same as 32 Hand Ejector First Model.

Serial numbered from 1-19425, in individual range. Company name and address marking on the barrel, with patent dates 1889, 1894, 1895, 1896, 1898, 1901, and 1902.

Design of the Model of 1903 was in marked contrast to that of the 32 Hand Ejector First Model. Main differences were in the location of the cylinder stop in the bottomstrap of frame, locking of cylinder pin at each end, and releasing of cylinder by pushing forward the thumb piece on left side of the frame. Barrel made without rib, and bore company and patent markings; no patent markings appear on the cylinder:
5G-050 Values—Very Good **$225** Exc. **$350**

S&W 32 Hand Ejector Model of 1903, 1st Change

32 Hand Ejector Model of 1903, First Change (a.k.a. Model I Hand Ejector Model of 1903 First Change). (Not illus.; similar to previous model.) Made 1904-06; total quantity of 31,700.

Caliber, cylinder, and barrel lengths same as 32 Hand Ejector Model of 1903.

Grips as on Model of 1903, but some also made in walnut.

Serial numbered from 19426-51126. Company name and address marking on the barrel, with patent dates 1889, 1894, 1895, 1896, 1898, 1901, 1902, and 1903.

Changes from the preceding model were minor, primarily as follows: Longer stop notches on cylinder and longer stop cut in frame, internal changes to trigger and rebound catch, and removal of shoulder on extractor rod and reduced extractor rod bushing hole:

5G-051 Values—Very Good **$200** Exc. **$350**

S&W 32 Hand Ejector Model of 1903, 2nd Change

32 Hand Ejector Model of 1903, Second Change (a.k.a. Model I Hand Ejector Model of 1903 Second Change). (Not illus.; similar to previous models.) Made 1906-09; total quantity of 44,373.

Caliber, cylinder, and barrel lengths same as preceding variations.

Grips as on preceding variation.

Serial numbered from 51127-95500. Company name and address marking on the barrel, with patent dates of early production same as 32 Hand Ejector Model of 1903 First Change; later production dropped the dates 1895, 1898, and Dec. 17, 1901.

Differs from the First Change primarily internally, thus the most useful means of identification is by serial number range:

5G-052   Values—Very Good **$200**   Exc. **$350**

S&W 32 Hand Ejector Model of 1903, 3rd Change

32 Hand Ejector Model of 1903, Third Change (a.k.a. Model I Hand Ejector Model of 1903 Third Change). (Not illus.; similar to previous models.) Made 1909-10; total quantity of 624.

Caliber, cylinder, and barrel lengths same as preceding variations.

Grips as on preceding variation.

Serial numbered in the range 95501-96125. Company name and address marking on the barrel, without patent date markings. February 6, '06 marked on side of rebound slide. Differs from the Second Change primarily internally; identification is thus best made by serial number range:

5G-053   Values—Very Good **$225**   Exc. **$400**

S&W 32 Hand Ejector Model of 1903, 4th Change

32 Hand Ejector Model of 1903, Fourth Change (a.k.a. Model I Hand Ejector Model of 1903 Fourth Change). (Not illus.; similar to previous models.) Made in 1910; total quantity of 6,374.

Caliber, cylinder, and barrel lengths same as preceding variations.

Grips as on preceding variation.

Serial numbered in the range 96126-102500. Company names and address marking on the barrel, without patent date markings. February 6, '06 on side of rebound slide.

Differs from the Third Change internally; identification is thus best made by serial number range:

5G-054   Values—Very Good **$200**   Exc. **$350**

S&W 32 Hand Ejector Model of 1903, 5th Change

32 Hand Ejector Model of 1903, Fifth Change (a.k.a. Model I Hand Ejector Model of 1903 Fifth Change). (Not illus.; similar to previous models.) Made 1910-17; total quantity of about 160,499.

Caliber, cylinder, and barrel lengths same as preceding variations.

Grips as on preceding variation.

Serial numbered in the range 102501 to about 263000.

Company name and address marking on the barrel, with patent dates 1894, 1895, 1896, 1901, 1906, and 1909. Patent date on rebound slide no longer present.

Differs from the Fourth Change primarily internally; identification can be done via serial number range, and patent date markings on barrel:

5G-055   Values—Very Good **$200**   Exc. **$350**

S&W 32 Hand Ejector Third Model

32 Hand Ejector Third Model (a.k.a. Model I Hand Ejector Third Model). (Not illus.; similar to previous models.) Made 1911-42; total quantity of about 271,531.

Caliber, cylinder, and barrel lengths same as preceding variations of Model of 1903.

Grips of checkered hard rubber, impressed with S&W monogram, and of round butt type.

Serial numbered in the range about 263001-534532. Company

name and address marking on the barrel, with patent dates 1901, 1906, 1909, and 1914 (early production). Later production with patent dates 1906, 1909, and 1914.

Differs from the 32 Hand Ejector Model of 1903 Fifth Change primarily internally; identification can be done via serial number range, patent date barrel markings, and the standard hard rubber stocks and service style front and rear sights:

5G-056   Values—Very Good **$200**   Exc. **$300**

S&W 32-20 Hand Ejector First Model D.A.

32-20 Hand Ejector First Model D.A. Revolver. Made 1899-1902; total quantity 5,311 (however, specimens seldom turn up).

32-20 Winchester caliber. 6-shot fluted cylinder. 4", 5", 6", and 6-1/2" barrel lengths.

Checkered hard rubber or walnut grips; the rubber including S&W monogram impression; rounded butt profile. Blued or nickel plated finish; hammer and trigger casehardened.

Serial numbered from 1 to 5311, in individual range; later continued by successor models. Company name and address marking on the barrel, with patent dates 1884, 1889, 1895, 1896, and 1898.

5G-057

One of the earliest of S&W swingout cylinder revolvers, the 32-20 Hand Ejector First Model has a rather modern appearance, including the cylinder release thumb piece on the left side of the frame. However, the forward end of the cylinder pin is not secured, lacking the lug which is a characteristic of subsequent revolvers:

5G-057   Values—Very Good **$425**   Exc. **$675**

Note: If original S&W factory TARGET SIGHTS present on any of these 32-20 models, premium values of three to five times values shown.

S&W 32-20 Hand Ejector Second Model 1902

32-20 Hand Ejector Second Model 1902. (Not illus.; similar to the following model.) Made 1902-05; total quantity 4,499.

32-20 caliber. 6-shot fluted cylinder. 4", 5", and 6-1/2" barrels.

Grips same as 32-20 Hand Ejector First Model. Blued or nickel plated finish.

Serial numbered from 5312-9811. Company name and address marking on the barrel, with patent dates 1889, 1895, 1896, 1898, and 1901.

Quite close in appearance to the First Model, except primarily in the presence of a lug on bottom of the barrel for locking of front end of cylinder pin. Identification can also be made from the serial number range:

5G-058   Values—Very Good **$350**   Exc. **$550**

S&W 32-20 Hand Ejector Model 1902, 1st Change

32-20 Hand Ejector Model 1902, First Change. Made 1903-05; total quantity of 8,313.

Same caliber, cylinder, and barrel lengths as Second Model 1902.

Grips same as Second Model 1902, with addition of checkered walnut having a square butt profile. Blued or nickel plated finish.

Serial numbered from 9812-18125. Company name and address marking on the barrel, without patent date markings.

Quite similar in appearance to the Second Model 1902, excepting in the larger barrel diameter and the larger frame where barrel screws into position. Identification can also be

5G-059

made using the serial number range:

5G-059   Values—Very Good **$275**   Exc. **$475**

S&W 32-20 Hand Ejector Model 1905

32-20 Hand Ejector Model 1905. (Not illus.; similar to previous model.) Made 1905-06; total quantity of 4,300.

Same caliber, cylinder, and barrel lengths as previous model.

Grips same as previous model. Blued or nickel plated finish.

Serial numbered from 18126-22426. Company name and address marking on the barrel, with patent dates 1889, 1894, 1895, 1896, 1898, and 1901.

Quite similar in appearance to the Model 1902, First Change, excepting primarily in the cylinder stop cut and slot, and in the shape of the trigger. Identification also aided by reference to the serial number range:

5G-060   Values—Very Good **$275**   Exc. **$475**

S&W 32-20 1905 Hand Ejector, 1st Change

32-20 Hand Ejector Model of 1905, First Change. (Not illus.; similar to previous model.) Made c. 1906-07; total quantity of about 11,073.

32-20 caliber. 6-shot fluted cylinder. 4", 5", 6", and 6-1/2" barrel lengths.

Grips same as previous model; made with both round and square butts. Blued or nickel plated finish.

Serial numbered from 22427 to about 33500. Company name and address marking on the barrel, with patent dates 1889, 1894, 1895, 1896, 1898, 1901, and 1906.

Quite similar in appearance to the Model 1905, excepting in various internal details, identification is aided by reference to the serial number range, and the presence of specific patent date markings on barrel:

5G-061   Values—Very Good **$275**   Exc. **$475**

S&W 32-20 1905 Hand Ejector, 2nd Change

32-20 Hand Ejector Model of 1905, Second Change. (Not illus.; similar to previous models.) Made c. 1906-07 to 1909; total quantity of about 11,699.

Same caliber, cylinder, and barrel lengths as previous model.

Grips same as previous model, including with round and square butts. Blued or nickel plated finish.

Serial numbered from about 33501-45200. Company name and address marking on the barrel, with patent dates 1894, 1895, 1896, 1901, and 1906. Rebound slide bore patent marking February 6, '06.

Quite similar in appearance to the Model 1905, First Change, excepting in various internal details. Identification is aided by consulting the serial number range, and noting the presence of specific patent date markings on the barrel, and on the rebound slide:

5G-062   Values—Very Good **$275**   Exc. **$475**

S&W 32-20 1905 Hand Ejector, 3rd Change

32-20 Hand Ejector Model of 1905, Third Change. (Not illus.; similar to previous models.) Made 1909-15; total quantity 20,499.

32-20 caliber. 6-shot fluted cylinder. 4" and 6" barrels.

Grips same as previous model; including with round or square butts. Blued or nickel plated finish.

Serial numbered from about 45201-65700. Company name and address marking on the barrel, with patent dates 1894, 1895, 1896, 1901, and 1906. 1909 date added on late production.

Basically the same as the Model of 1905, Second Change, identification can be made by referencing the serial number range, and by noting the absence of the February 6, '06 patent marking (formerly on rebound slide):

5G-063   Values—Very Good **$275**   Exc. **$475**

S&W 32-20 1905 Hand Ejector, 4th Change

32-20 Hand Ejector Model 1905, Fourth Change. (Not illus.; similar to previous models.) Made 1915-40; total quantity 78,983.

32-20 caliber. 6-shot fluted cylinder. 4", 5", and 6" barrels.

Grips same as previous model; including with round and square butts. Blued or nickel plated finish.

Serial numbered from 65701-144684. Company name and address marking on the barrel, with patent dates 1901, 1906, 1909, and 1914. Late production specimens bear last three dates only.

Quite similar in appearance to the Model of 1905, Third Change, excepting in certain sight details, and in various internal parts. For identification, consult serial number sequence and patent date markings:

5G-064   Values—Very Good **$240**   Exc. **$450**

S&W Model 320 Revolving Rifle

5G-065

Model 320 Revolving Rifle (a.k.a. S&W Revolving Rifle). Made 1879-1887; total run of 977.

320 S&W rifle caliber. 6-shot fluted cylinder. 16", 18", and 20" round barrels.

Checkered hard rubber (mottled red color) grips with S&W monogram impression; rounded butt profile. The forend also of checkered hard rubber and of the same mottled coloration. Attachable shoulder stock of select walnut, with a checkered hard rubber (black) buttplate, bearing the S&W monogram impression. Blue finish usual; nickel scarce; worth premium.

Serial numbered from 1 to 977, in individual range. Company name and address marking on the barrel, with patent date markings of 1865, 1869, 1871, 1875, and 1877.

This scarce and unusual revolving rifle might be termed the Smith & Wesson "Buntline Special," in the combination of a long barreled revolver with an attachable shoulder stock. The Model 320 was constructed using the frame, cylinder, and basic action of the New Model No. 3 Revolver. Some minor differences were made in the hammer and trigger, and the barrel was made of two pieces. Standard were leather carrying cases, with accessories.

The Model 320 is one of the major prizes in a S&W collection, and to find a complete cased set is a challenging task (worth $2,000 to $3,000 premium).

The stock numbers (found inside) are assembly numbers only and thus do not match those of the revolver. Values noted below are for revolver complete with stock. If stock is missing values about 40 percent less.

Revolver with stock. 16" barrel (239 made) or 20" barrel (224 made):

5G-065   Values—Very Good **$7,000**   Exc. **$15,000**

As above. 18" barrel (514 made):

5G-066   Values—Very Good **$6,000**   Exc. **$14,000**

Smith & Wesson Automatic Pistols

S&W 35 Automatic Pistol

35 Automatic Pistol (a.k.a. Model of 1913). Made 1913-21; total quantity 8,350.

35 S&W Automatic caliber. 7-shot magazine. 3-1/2" barrel.

Grips of plain walnut with S&W monogram inlays. Blued or nickel plated finish.

Serial numbered from 1 on up. Company name markings, and patent dates of 1910, 1911, and 1912.

The only S&W made to fire the unusual 35 S&W Automatic cartridge, the Model of 1913 had a rather short life due to the relatively high cost of the ammunition, the occasional use of 32 ACP cartridges (cheaper, but caused not infrequent

5G-067

malfunctions), and the expense of manufacture of the pistol itself. Basic design of the Model of 1913 had been purchased by S&W in Europe. Basic features are detailed in Jinks and Neal,

including identification of the eight variations of manufacture. Specific serial ranges are listed for each type:

5G-067   Values—Very Good **$275**   Exc. **$600**

S&W 32 Automatic Pistol

32 Automatic Pistol. Made 1924-36; total quantity 957.

32 ACP caliber. 7-shot magazine. 3-1/2" barrel.

Grips of plain walnut with S&W monogram inlays. Blued finish.

Serial number range from 1 on up. Company name marking on the left side of the barrel assembly. Patent date markings of 1910, 1911, 1916, and 1921.

The 32 Automatic was brought out as an improved version of the 35 Automatic, with several distinct changes: Barrel fixed to frame (could not be pivoted up to clean), disconnect included for magazine, rear safety device discontinued, reduced recoil spring employed, and certain other features. The 32 Automatic is a S&W collector's prize, due particularly to the quite limited production total of but 957:

5G-068

5G-068   Values—Very Good **$1,250**   Exc. **$2,250**

Smith & Wesson 38 Caliber Models

S&W 38 Single Action First Model Revolver

38 Single Action First Model Revolver (a.k.a. "Baby Russian" and Model No. 2 First Issue). Manufactured 1876-1877; total quantity of 25,548.

38 S&W caliber. 5-shot fluted cylinder. 3-1/4" and 4" round barrels.

Checkered hard rubber grips with S&W monogram impression were standard on nickel plated revolvers; wood grips used on the blued specimens. Revolvers standard in blued or nickel plated finish (blue will bring premium).

Serial numbering in individual range from 1 to 25548. Company name and address marking on the barrel, with patent date markings of 1865, 1869, 1871, and 1875.

The pocket size, the topbreak action, and the spur trigger are all identifying features of the "Baby Russian." A few slight variations appear such as an unusual safety device on frame (discontinued after approximately first 100 were made); and

frame plates on the first 10 percent (approximately) of production were retained by one screw, all later pieces by two screws. Such variations will command a premium value:

5G-069   Values—Very Good **$350**   Exc. **$750**

5G-069

S&W 38 Single Action Second Model Revolver

5G-070

38 Single Action Second Model Revolver (a.k.a. Model 2 Second Issue). Made 1877-1891; total run of 108,255.

38 S&W caliber. 5-shot fluted cylinder. 3-1/4", 4", 5", 6", 8", and 10" round barrels.

Checkered hard rubber grips with S&W monogram impression were standard on nickel plated revolvers; wood

grips generally found on blued specimens. Standard finish in blue or nickel plating (blue will bring premium).

Serial numbered in individual range from 1 to 108255. Company name and address marking on the barrel, with patent date markings of 1865, 1869, 1871, and 1875.

Basically a continuation of the 38 Single Action First Model revolver, the Second Model has a shorter extractor housing under the barrel due to improvements in the ejection mechanism. The housing difference provides a quick visual means of identifying the Second Model.

Standard model, in 3-1/4", and 5" barrel lengths (4" bbl. worth 10 percent premium; 6" bbl. approx. 100 percent premium):

5G-070   Values—Very Good **$250**   Exc. **$475**

As above, but in 8" and 10" lengths:

5G-071   Values—Very Good **$1,500**   Exc. **$4,500**

S&W 38 Single Action Third Model Revolver

38 Single Action Third Model Revolver (a.k.a. Model 1891 Single Action and Model No. 2 Third Model). Produced 1891-1911; total quantity of about 26,850.

38 S&W caliber. 5-shot fluted cylinder. 3-1/4", 4", 5", and 6" barrel lengths.

Checkered hard rubber grips with S&W monogram

5G-072

impression. Blued or nickel plated finish.

Serial numbered from 1 to 28107; also including in the number series the Single Shot First Model and the 38 Single

Action Mexican Model, both of which are covered under separate headings. Company name and address marking on the barrel, with patent dates of 1875, 1877, and 1880.

Visually this S&W is quite similar in contour to the New Model No. 3, but *much smaller*. A major feature in contrast to the First and Second Model predecessor revolvers is the presence of a trigger guard. The Third Model also has a rebounding hammer, and MODEL OF 1891 was included in the barrel rib marking. An unusual advantage of the Third Model was its availability as a "combination gun," able to accept an exchange single shot barrel in 22, 32, or 38 caliber. When found with the combination variations (having matching numbers) a premium in value should be added:

5G-072　　Values—Very Good **$750**　　Exc. **$2,000**

S&W 38 Single Action Mexican Model

38 Single Action Mexican Model. Manufactured 1891-1911; total produced about 2,000.

38 S&W caliber. 5-shot fluted cylinder. 3-1/4", 4", 5", and 6" barrels (5" and 6" bbls. 10 percent to 20 percent premiums).

Checkered hard rubber S&W monogram grips or walnut. Blued or nickel plated finish.

Serial number range was included within that of the 38 Single Action Third Model Revolver, from 1 to 28107. Company name and address marking on the barrel, with patent dates of 1875, 1877, and 1880.

The Mexican Model's salient details are the flat sided hammer, the spur trigger, and the lack of a half-cock notch on the hammer. The trigger assembly was a separate part fitted to the frame and not made integral with it. Otherwise the type is basically a 38 Single Action Third Model revolver. As the name implies, sales for the Mexican Model were targeted primarily to the export market. Collectors should note that "spur trigger

5G-073

kits" were available, which enabled making a 38 Single Action Third Model into a Mexican Model, and thus extreme care must be exercised in purchasing this model. One obvious giveaway of kit use is the flanged contour of the 38 Single Action Third Model's hammer sides. Exchange single shot barrels in 22, 32, or 38 caliber were also available for the Mexican Model revolvers:

5G-073　　Values—Very Good **$2,000**　　Exc. **$4,750**

S&W 38 Double Action First Model Revolver

38 Double Action First Model Revolver (a.k.a. 38 D.A. First Issue). Made in 1880; total quantity of about 4,000.

38 S&W caliber. 5-shot fluted cylinder. 3-1/4" and 4" round barrels.

Checkered hard rubber grips with S&W monogram impression; rounded butt profile. Blued or nickel plated finish.

Serial numbering from 1 to about 4000, and continued by the successor model production. Company name and address marking on the barrel, with patent dates of 1865, 1869, 1871, and 1875.

The first S&W revolver of the double action mechanism in 38 caliber, the Model is closely related to the 32 Double Action First Model. Distinctive design details are in the series of grooves encircling the cylinder, and the two sets of stop notches. Like its 32 caliber counterpart, the sideplate has a squared appearance, rather

5G-074

than the oval shape of later production. Barrel release catch (just forward of the hammer) is of the T type. And the trigger guard profile has a reverse curve ("squareback") contour at its rear:

5G-074　　Values—Very Good **$550**　　Exc. **$1,200**

S&W 38 Double Action Second Model Revolver

38 Double Action Second Model Revolver (a.k.a. 38 D.A. Second Issue). (Not illus.; similar in appearance to First Model.) Produced 1880-1884; in a total run of about 115,000.

38 S&W caliber. 5-shot fluted cylinder. 3-1/4", 4", 5", and 6" barrels.

Checkered hard rubber grips (black or mottled red color) with S&W monogram impression; rounded butt. Blued or nickel plated finish.

Serial numbers continued that from the First Model, and are within the range of approximately 4001 - 119000. Company name and address marking on the barrel, with patent dates of 1865, 1869, 1871, and 1875 (early production), and 1865, 1869, 1871, 1879, and 1880 (late production).

The Second Model was a continuation of the First Model, with the improved contour of the sideplate (now rounded instead of the previous squared appearance). The change was done to increase frame strength:

5G-075　　Values—Very Good **$275**　　Exc. **$450**

S&W 38 Double Action Third Model Revolver

38 Double Action Third Model Revolver. Made 1884-1895; total quantity of about 203,700.

38 S&W caliber. 5-shot fluted cylinder. 3-1/4", 4", 5", 6", 8", and 10" barrels.

Checkered black hard rubber grips with S&W monogram impression; round butt. Blued or nickel plated finish.

The serial numbering continued from the Second Model, running from about 119001 - 322700. Company name and address marking on the barrel, with patent dates of 1865, 1869, 1871, 1880, and 1882.

Changes from the Second Model were most obvious in the cylinder and trigger areas. Cylinder flutes became longer, the long grooves were dropped, as was one set of the stop notches. Due to internal improvements the pronged back to the trigger became a solid arched piece partially sheathed within the back section of the trigger guard. The American Express Company purchased over 1,000 of this and the 4th Model (below) in varying quantities 1892-1905. Marked AM. EX. Co. with serial

5G-076

number (under 4 digits) on backstrap; worth 25 percent to 50 percent premium. Exercise caution.

Standard model, barrel lengths from 3-1/4" to 6":
5G-076   Values—Very Good **$275**   Exc. **$375**
As above, but in 8" and 10" lengths:
5G-077   Values—Very Good **$1,250**   Exc. **$3,000**

S&W 38 Double Action Fourth Model Revolver

38 Double Action Fourth Model Revolver. (Not illus.; similar to 38 D.A. Third Model.) Manufactured 1895-1909; total run of about 216,300 (serial numbers under 382,000 (approx.) made prior to Dec. 31, 1898).

38 S&W caliber. 5-shot fluted cylinder. 3-1/4", 4", 5", and 6" barrels.

Checkered black hard rubber grips with S&W monogram impression; also available were target type checkered hard rubber of the extension type with square butt. Blued or nickel plated finish.

Serial numbers carried on from the Third Model, from about 322701 - 539000. Company name and address marking on the barrel, with patent dates of 1880, 1882, and 1889.

The Fourth Model was an improvement over the Third in its reduced trigger pull and by a new sear, and subsequent changes internally to the hammer. The Second, Third, and Fourth Model 38 Double Action revolvers represent three of the largest production runs of S&W firearms in the 19th and early 20th centuries:
5G-078   Values—Very Good **$225**   Exc. **$350**

S&W 38 Double Action Fifth Model Revolver

38 Double Action Fifth Model Revolver. (Not illus.; similar to 38 D.A. Third and Fourth Models.) Made 1909-1911; production run of about 15,000 (however, specimens available on the collectors' market always scarce).

38 S&W caliber. 5-shot fluted cylinder. 3-1/4", 4", 5", and 6" barrels.

Checkered hard rubber grips with S&W monogram impression; also available were target type checkered hard rubber or walnut stocks of the extension type with square butt.

Serial numbering continued from the Fourth Model, and are from about 539001 - 554077. Company name and address marking on the barrel, without patent date stampings.

The Fifth Model differs from the Fourth in the lack of patent markings on the barrel, and in the use of an integral sight blade on barrels having standard (not target) front sights. An internal change was in the barrel catch cam:
5G-079   Values—Very Good **$450**   Exc. **$750**

S&W 38 Double Action Perfected Model

5G-080

38 Double Action Perfected Model. Manufactured 1909-20; total production of 59,400.

38 S&W caliber. 5-shot fluted cylinder. 3-1/4", 4", 5", and 6" barrels.

Checkered hard rubber grips with S&W monogram

impression; also available with target type checkered hard rubber or walnut stocks of the extension type with square butt.

Serial numbered in individual range from 1 on up. Company name and address marking on the barrel, with patent dates 1896, 1901, 1906, and (on late specimens) 1909.

This is an important specimen for the collector, as it was the last S&W break open revolver made, and their ultimate achievement of the type in overall design. Distinctive details include the barrel/cylinder release catch on the topstrap and the thumb release catch on the left side of the frame (both having to be operated simultaneously to open the barrel), the trigger guard integral with the frame, and the lockplate on the right side of the frame. Rare variant with left frame not cut for, nor provided with the thumb release. Specimens generally found in 52,000 range; worth premium:
5G-080   Values—Very Good **$250**   Exc. **$550**

S&W 38 Safety First Model D.A. Revolver

38 Safety First Model D.A. Revolver (a.k.a. "New Departure 38 Safety First Model"). Made in 1887, in a total quantity of about 5,125.

38 S&W caliber. 5-shot fluted cylinder. 3-1/4", 4", 5", and 6" round barrels (the 6" length quite rare).

Checkered hard rubber grips with S&W monogram impression. Blued or nickel plated finish.

Serial numbers ran from 1 to 5250, with some overlap with the successor model. Company name and address barrel marking, with patent dates of 1869, 1877, 1880, 1883, and 1885 (first production); later specimens with patent dates of 1877, 1880, 1883, and 1885.

Like its 32 caliber "Safety Hammerless" counterpart, this model featured a concealed hammer, a safety bar in the backstrap, and a topbreak action. Firing could only be done in double action. This was a more potent version of the 32, and both models share the "Lemon Squeezer" and "Safety Hammerless"

5G-081

nicknames. A distinguishing detail on the 38 First Model is the so-called "Z-bar" barrel latch in the topstrap, which when pushed sideways allowed for tipping down the barrel and cylinder for loading and extraction.

Standard model, 3-1/4", 4", and 5" barrels:
5G-081   Values—Very Good **$450**   Exc. $**900**
As above, but with 6" barrel:
5G-082   Values—Very Good **$875**   Exc. **$1,750**

S&W 38 Safety Second Model D.A. Revolver

38 Safety Second Model D.A. Revolver. Manufactured 1887-1890; total of about 37,350.

38 S&W caliber. 5-shot fluted cylinder. 3-1/4", 4", and 5" barrels (6" barrel worth 40 percent premium).

Checkered hard rubber grips with S&W monogram impression. Blued or nickel plated finish.

Serial numbering continued from the 38 Safety First Model (with some overlap) and are in the range approximately 5001 - 42483. Company name and address barrel marking, with patent dates of 1877, 1880, 1883, and 1885 (first production); later revolvers with 1880, 1883, 1885, 1887, 1888, 1889, and 1890 dates.

The major distinguishing feature of the Second Model is the barrel catch, which is a small knurled thumb piece at the top of the frame just behind the topstrap:

5G-083

5G-083   Values—Very Good **$300**   Exc. **$725**
U.S. Martially marked model. 100 of these were purchased by U.S. government 1890 in serial range 41333 to 41470. Blued finish; 6" barrel; U.S. marked on left side of barrel lug:
5G-083.5   Values—Very Good **$3,750**   Exc. **$7,500**

S&W 38 Safety Third Model D.A. Revolver

38 Safety Third Model D.A. Revolver. Made 1890-1898; total run of about 73,500.

38 S&W caliber. 5-shot fluted cylinder. 3-1/4", 4", 5", and 6"

5G-084

barrels (6" bbl. valued at 40 percent premium).

Checkered hard rubber grips with S&W monogram impression. Blued or nickel plated finish.

Serial numbering continued from the 38 Safety Second Model, from 42484 - 116002. Company name and address barrel marking, with patent dates of 1880, 1883, 1885, 1887, 1888, 1889, and 1890.

Major evolutionary differences between the Second and Third Model revolvers are: Barrel release catch fitted into and protruded from the rear section of the topstrap, and is pushed downward to function; frame contour in that area altered accordingly; the trigger contour was changed at top front and a pin was added to the trigger guard. Other changes primarily internal in nature were also made:
5G-084   Values—Very Good **$250**   Exc. **$475**

S&W 38 Safety Fourth Model D.A. Revolver

38 Safety Fourth Model D.A. Revolver. Manufactured 1898-1907; total quantity of about 104,000 (serials under 119,000 (approx.) likely made prior to Dec. 31, 1898).

38 S&W caliber. 5-shot fluted cylinder. 3-1/4", 4", and 5" barrels (6" bbl. valued at 25 percent premium).

Checkered hard rubber grips with S&W monogram impression. Blued or nickel plated finish.

Serial numbering continued from the 38 Safety Third Model, from 116003 to about 220000 (overlap with the Fifth Model in the

5G-085

range about 216500 - 222310). Company name and address marking on the barrel, with patent dates of 1880, 1883, 1885, 1887, 1888, 1889, and 1890 (early production); later revolvers with 1883, 1885, and 1889 dates.

Improvements found in the Fourth Model include adoption

of the T-type barrel catch with two knurled side knobs on the topstrap, and adding the barrel marking (left side): 38 S&W CTG. To insert the T-catch, changes were also necessary in the topstrap and frame:

5G-085   Values—Very Good **$225**   Exc. **$425**

S&W 38 Safety Fifth Model D.A. Revolver

38 Safety Fifth Model D.A. Revolver. (Not illus.; similar to 38 Safety Fourth Model D.A.) Produced 1907-1940; total made about 41,500.

38 S&W caliber. 5-shot fluted cylinder. 2", 3-1/4", 4", 5", and 6" barrels (6" bbl. valued at 25 percent premium).

Checkered hard rubber grips with S&W monogram impression, or checkered walnut. Blued or nickel plated finish.

Serial numbers continued from the 38 Safety Fourth Model, from about 220000 - 261493 (overlap with the Fourth Model in the range about 216500 - 222310). Company name and address

marking on the barrel, without patent date stampings; SMITH & WESSON and 38 S&W CTG. were marked on the left and right side of barrel respectively.

The Fifth Model is distinguished by the front sight blade being integral with the barrel, lack of patent dates in the barrel marking, addition of S&W and caliber marking on barrel sides, and minor changes in the barrel catch area.

3-1/4", 4", 5", and 6" barrel specimens:
5G-086   Values—Very Good **$225**   Exc. **$450**
2" barrel version:
5G-087   Values—Very Good **$550**   Exc. **$1,250**

S&W 38 Hand Ejector, M&P 1st Model

38 Hand Ejector, Military & Police First Model Revolver (a.k.a. Model 1899 Army-Navy Revolver). Made 1899-1902; total run of 20,975.

38 Long Colt and 38 S&W Special calibers. 6-shot fluted cylinder. 4", 5", 6", and 6-1/2" barrels.

Checkered hard rubber grips with S&W monogram impression, or checkered walnut. On the latter an impressed circular panel was in the upper section of each stock; these were plain for civilian sales, and marked with inspector initials for Army issue. Blued or nickel plated finish.

Serial numbered from 1 to 20975; continued by the successor model. Company name and address marking on the barrel, with patent dates 1884, 1889, 1895, 1896, and 1898.

The 38 Hand Ejector M & P First Model is one of the earliest of S&W swingout cylinder revolvers. Locking of the cylinder into position was by a thumb catch on the left side of the frame; no latch was present on the bottom of the barrel, to engage the front end of the cylinder pin.

Standard model, civilian series (the bulk of production):
5G-088   Values—Very Good **$425**   Exc. **$800**

5G-088

U.S. Navy Model, delivered year 1900, in a total quantity of 1,000, and in the S&W serial range 5001 to 6000. 6" barrels, finished in blue, with checkered walnut grips; 38 Long Colt caliber. The butt bears markings U.S.N., an anchor, inspector initials, and special Navy serial range (1 to 1000):
5G-089   Values—Very Good **$950**   Exc. **$2,000**

U.S. Army Model, delivered in 1901, total quantity of 1,000. 6" barrels, finish blued, grips checkered walnut with inspector initials K.S.M. in panel on right grip and J.T.T. 1901 on left grip. 38 long Colt caliber. Marked on butt: U.S. ARMY / MODEL 1899. S&W factory serial range 13001 - 14000:
5G-090   Values—Very Good **$1,100**   Exc. **$2,250**

S&W 38 Hand Ejector, M&P 2nd Model

38 Hand Ejector, Military & Police Second Model Revolver (a.k.a. Model 38 Hand Ejector Military & Police Model 1902). Made 1902-03; total of 12,827.

38 S&W Special and (special Navy order) 38 Long Colt calibers. 6-shot fluted cylinder. 4", 5", 6", and 6-1/2" barrels.

Checkered hard rubber grips with S&W monogram impression, or checkered walnut. On the latter an open circle device was in the upper section of each stock. Blued or nickel plated finish.

Serial numbered from 20976 - 33803. Company name and address barrel marking, with patent dates 1889, 1894, 1895, 1896, 1898, and 1901.

Improvements in the Second Model from its predecessor include the locking lug or latch on bottom of the barrel, increased extractor rod diameter, and minor internal changes.

Standard model, civilian series (bulk of production), chambered only for 38 S&W Special:
5G-091   Values—Very Good **$275**   Exc. **$750**

5G-091

U.S. Navy Model, delivered c. 1902. In the S&W serial range 25001 - 26000, and bearing on the butt: U.S.N./[anchor motif] /38.D.A./[arrow through a lying-down S]/No/[serial designation of Navy, from 1001-2000]J.A.B. 38 Long Colt U.S. service caliber, 6" barrel:
5G-092   Values—Very Good **$800**   Exc. **$2,000**

S&W 38 Hand Ejector, M&P 1902, 1st Change

38 Hand Ejector, Military & Police Model 1902 Revolver, First Change. (Not illus.; similar to previous model.) Made 1903-05; total quantity 28,645.

38 S&W Special caliber. 6-shot fluted cylinder. 4", 5", and 6-1/2" barrels.

Checkered hard rubber grips with S&W monogram impression, or checkered walnut; both of round butt type. After 58000 serial range checkered walnut square butt grips also available. Blued or nickel plated finish.

Serial numbered from 33804 - 62449. Company name and address barrel marking.

This model S&W is identical to the 32/20 Hand Ejector Model 1902 First Change, excepting chambering. Changes from the 38 Hand Ejector Military & Police Second Model were in an enlarged diameter to the barrel thread, and a corresponding increase in the diameter of the barrel hole in frame. Changes were also made in the yoke and the yoke cut in the frame (again due to the enlarged barrel).

Standard model, as above, with round butt type grips of either walnut or hard rubber:

5G-093   Values—Very Good **$250**   Exc. **$575**

Standard model, but with square butt to frame and square butt checkered walnut grips (appear after 58000 serial range only):

5G-094   Values—Very Good **$275**   Exc. **$650**

S&W 38 Hand Ejector M&P, Model 1905

38 Hand Ejector Military & Police, Model 1905. (Not illus.; similar to previous model.) Made 1905-06; total quantity 10,800.

Caliber, cylinder, finishes, barrel lengths, and grips same as Model 1902, First Change. Available with both round or square butts.

Serial numbered from 62450 - 73250. Company name and address barrel marking, with the patent dates 1889, 1894, 1895, 1898, and 1901.

An improved version of the Model 1902, First Change, with the major differences in the cylinder stop cut and the corresponding frame stop slot. Minor internal changes also made. A convenient means of identification is via the serial number range, and patent date markings on barrel:

5G-095   Values—Very Good **$250**   Exc. **$500**

S&W 38 Hand Ejector M&P 1905, 1st Change

38 Hand Ejector Military & Police Model 1905, First Change. (Not illus.; similar to previous model.) Made 1906-c. 1908; total quantity unknown due to overlap with the Model 1905, Second Change (total of both models was 73,648).

38 S&W Special caliber. 6-shot fluted cylinder. 4", 5", 6", and 6-1/2" barrels.

Grips same as Model 1905 predecessor; available with both round or square butts. Blued or nickel plated finish.

Serial number range began at 73251, but last number of production as yet undetermined. Company name and address barrel marking, with the patent dates (first production) 1889, 1894, 1895, 1896, 1898, 1901, and 1906. Late production barrels bear patent dates 1894, 1895, 1896, 1901, and 1906.

Changes which brought about this model were relatively minor, and were internal:

5G-096   Values—Very Good **$250**   Exc. **$500**

S&W 38 Hand Ejector M&P 1905, 2nd Change

38 Hand Ejector Military & Police Model 1905, Second Change. (Not illus.; similar to previous model.) Made c. 1908-09; total quantity unknown due to overlap with the Model 1905, First Change (total of both models was 73,648).

Caliber, cylinder, barrel lengths, finishes, and grips same as Model 1905, First Change; available in both round or square butt.

Serial number range beginning presently unknown, but the last number of production was 146899. Company name and address barrel marking, with the patent dates 1894, 1895, 1896, 1901, and 1906.

Changes from the previous model were relatively minor, although one key feature to note is the presence of the patent date February 6, '06 on the rebound slide:

5G-097   Values—Very Good **$250**   Exc. **$500**

S&W 38 Hand Ejector M&P 1905, 3rd Change

38 Hand Ejector Military & Police Model 1905, Third Change. (Not illus.; similar to previous model.) Made c. 1909-15. Total quantity 94,803.

38 S&W Special caliber. 6-shot fluted cylinder. 4" and 6" barrel lengths.

Grips and finishes same as preceding model; available in both round or square butts.

Serial numbered from 146900 - 241703. Company name and address barrel marking, with patent dates 1894, 1895, 1896, 1901, 1906 and (on late production) 1909.

Minor internal changes were made, as well as the knob in the extractor rod becoming a solid fixture instead of screwed into position. The patent date marking on the rebound slide was discontinued. Double action throw differs in this model as compared to predecessor variations:

5G-098   Values—Very Good **$250**   Exc. **$475**

S&W 38 Hand Ejector M&P 1905, 4th Change

38 Hand Ejector Military & Police Model 1905, Fourth Change. (Not illus.; similar to previous model.) Made 1915-42; total production approximately 458,296.

38 S&W Special caliber. 6-shot fluted cylinder. 2", 4", 5", and 6" barrels; 2" barrel scarce and will bring a premium.

Grips and finishes same as preceding model; available in both round or square butts.

Serial numbered from 241704 to about 700000. Company name and address barrel marking, with patent dates 1901, 1906, 1909, and 1914 (late production marked with only the last three dates).

Changes in this model were primarily internal, and details are provided in Jinks and Neal. A useful aid for identification is to consult the serial number range, and the patent date barrel markings:

5G-099   Values—Very Good **$225**   Exc. **$450**

Smith & Wesson 44 Caliber Models

S&W Model No. 3 First Model Single Action

Model No. 3 First Model Single Action Revolver (most commonly known as First Model American). Manufactured 1870-1872; total of about 8,000.

44 S&W American and (rare) 44 rimfire Henry calibers. 6-shot fluted cylinder. 8" round barrel; and few reduced to 6" length.

Walnut grips; squared butt profile. Blued or nickel plated finish.

Serial numbering in an individual range, from 1 to about 8000; continued by succeeding model. Barrel marking of company name and address, with patent dates of 1860, 1865, and 1869.

In the First Model American the S&W company produced their first topbreak revolver. It preceded the Colt Single Action by over three years, and historically has a fine association with the American West. "Buffalo Bill" Cody purchased an "American" in 1874 and was known to have carried it before his days as a showman. Wyatt Earp allegedly carried one at the "shootout at the O.K. Corral" and some were known carried at the Little Big Horn in 1876. Part of the design was for automatic extraction as the barrel pivoted full forward. The new six-shooter was also S&W's initial heavy caliber revolver to enter into production. Collectors have noted a number of variations, several of them due to the company's utilization of parts which had become out-of-date from changes in the later Model 3 Russian First Model contract revolvers. Major variants in the First Model American are as follows:

5G-100

Standard model, 44 S&W American cartridge; approximately first 1,500 revolvers had a small vent hole drilled into the extractor housing (visible when looking at barrel assembly from bottom):
5G-100   Values—Good **$1,800**   Fine **$4,500**
As above, 44 S&W American caliber; lack hole in bottom of extractor housing (bulk of production run):
5G-101   Values—Good **$1,250**   Fine **$3,750**
Transition Model American revolvers; 44 S&W American caliber; beginning in the serial range about 6466 - 6744 continuing to 8000; can be recognized quickly by shorter cylinder (1.423", rather than 1.450" of earlier specimens), and interlocking type hammer-barrel catch design (notch in hammer). Subdivisions have been made by collectors within this model:
5G-102   Values—Good **$1,600**   Fine **$4,250**
Special group of Transition Model revolvers, in the serial range 3500 - 3900; believed to have come from the early production of Old Model Russian S.A. Revolvers:
5G-103   Values—Good **$1,600**   Fine **$4,250**
Rare group of about 100 First Model American revolvers chambered for the 44 rimfire Henry caliber; serial numbers dispersed throughout the entire series of the model:
5G-104   Values—Good **$2,750**   Fine **$7,000**
U.S. Army order of 1,000 revolvers; U.S. marked (top of barrel), and with OWA inspector stamp on left grip. A and P letter stampings also present; serial number range 125 - 2199. Premium for nickel plated specimens (200 made); blued finish was standard. Serial numbers of government inspected pieces can be verified in Jinks and Neal, Parsons and Supica books:
5G-105   Values—Good **$5,500**   Fine **$12,500**
Nashville Police Contract. Distinguished by its 6" barrel and large, slightly slanted markings almost full length of backstrap "Nashville Police No.---" (numeral 1 to 32). Rare variant; 32 made on special order for that city, 1871. The few known specimens in 3400-3500 range; blued; walnut grips. Should be verified with factory letter.
5G-105.5   Values Approx. 50 percent or more than "U.S" type (5G-105).

S&W Model No. 3 Second Model Single Action

Model No. 3 Second Model Single Action Revolver (most commonly known as Second Model American). Made 1872-1874; total produced about 20,735.

44 S&W American and 44 rimfire Henry calibers. 6-shot fluted cylinder. 8" round barrel standard; but also known in (rare) 5-1/2", 6", 6-1/2", and 7", which will command a premium price; be wary of altered specimens.

Walnut grips with squared butt profile (hard rubber also known, and are scarce). Blued or nickel plated finish.

Serial numbers continued from the First Model American production, from about 8000 to 32800 (includes Model 3 Russian First Model commercial revolvers). Barrel marking of company name and address, with patent dates of 1860, 1865, and 1869.

The Second Model American is quickly identified from the First Model by the larger diameter trigger pin, and the projection or "bump" on each side of the bottom of the frame (just above the trigger) to accommodate that increase. Another difference appears in the front sight, the German silver blade having been replaced by a steel one. This Second Model has the notch in top of hammer. Later changes were made near the end of

production. These very minor variations can affect values slightly for the advanced collector.
Standard model, 8" barrel length, 44 S&W American caliber:
5G-106   Values—Good **$1,400**   Fine **$3,500**
As above, but in 44 rimfire Henry. A total of 3,014 were made; 2,157 of which did not have the notched hammer:
5G-107   Values—Good **$2,500**   Fine **$6,000**

5G-106

S&W Model 3 Russian First Model

Model 3 Russian First Model Single Action Revolver (most commonly known as Old Old Model Russian). (Not illus.) Manufactured 1871-1874; a total of about 5,165 (commercial and rejected contract arms) and 20,014 Russian contract specimens.

44 S&W Russian caliber. 6-shot fluted cylinder. Commercial production in 6", 7", and 8" barrels; Russian contract revolvers in 8" length.

Walnut grips with squared butt profile. Blued or nickel plated finish.

(Note: No illustration shown, since the basic contour about identical to the First and Second Model American.)

Serial numbering of the commercial production was in the serial range of the American Model, from about 6000 to 32800. Serials of the contract arms were in the range of 1-approximately 20000. Contract pieces either have Russian Cyrillic markings, or (where ground off and rerolled) S&W company name and address, and patent dates, and RUSSIAN MODEL as standard on the commercial Old Old Model Russian. The standard barrel marking on the latter is the company name and address, 1860, 1865, and 1869 patent dates, and RUSSIAN MODEL

Basically a variation of the Second Model American revolver, the Old Old Model Russian differs in its chambering and (on approximately the first 3,000 production) the smaller diameter of the trigger pin (and subsequent lack of the projection on each side of frame bottom). The balance of this model did have the larger trigger pin and the accompanying frame projection to accommodate it. Most of the 5,165 First Model Commercials bear barrel markings in English, and include the legend: RUSSIAN MODEL A few are marked in Cyrillic, as noted below. Contract revolvers delivered to the Czar's government were marked in Cyrillic, which translated to: "Smith & Wesson arms factory. Springfield, America."

Standard commercial model; barrel markings in English, including words RUSSIAN MODEL (the notorious western outlaw John Wesley Hardin carried this model and in 1874 did in a Texas lawman with it, narrowly escaping a lynch mob). Total made about 4,665; 8" barrel version. Premium added for 6" or 7" lengths:

5G-108 Values—Good **$1,400** Fine **$3,500**

Contract revolvers, delivered to the Russian government; serial range from 1 - 20000. 44 S&W Russian caliber. Cyrillic barrel roll, and a Russian double headed eagle stamped near the breech end, underneath which are inspector initials. Butt swivels were standard. Rarely encountered due to shipment of almost all to Russia:

5G-109 Values—Good **$3,000** Fine **$7,500**

Rejected Russian contract revolvers, generally with markings in English (same as commercial production), but sometimes with Cyrillic barrel roll (latter commanding added premium). Serial numberings in both instances were from the Russian contract series; about 500 produced:

5G-110 Values—Good **$1,750** Fine **$4,500**

Note About Serial Numbers: on S&W 1st Model Americans (5G-100) through New Model Russians (5G-117) serial number is found on butt only with assembly numbers on all other parts (usually on cylinder, barrel and latch, and under the grip on butt). With very few exceptions, the assembly numbers match each other but do not match the serial number. This rule will generally hold true excluding those made for Russian and Japanese contracts.

S&W Model 3 Russian Second Model

Model 3 Russian Second Model Single Action Revolver (most commonly known as Old Model Russian). Manufactured 1873-78; in a total quantity of about 85,200 (see value listings below for basic breakdown by types).

44 S&W Russian and 44 rimfire Henry calibers. 6-shot fluted cylinder. 7" barrel length.

Walnut grips of rounded butt profile. Blued or nickel plated finish.

Serial numbering was rather complex, and is important in establishing variants and their authenticity. Here is a model of S&W which requires careful study by collectors to fully understand the rather wide range of variations. Reference works should be consulted for minute, yet important points. Serial number groupings, markings, and other details are encountered which affect values; the basic variants only are listed here. This model is easily recognized by its spurred trigger guard, the 7" barrel, and the rounded butt contour with humpbacked gripstrap.

5G-111

Standard commercial model; 44 S&W Russian caliber. Company name and address barrel roll with -AUG. 13, 69. RUSSIAN MODEL termination. Total production 6,200:

5G-111 Values—Good **$875** Fine **$2,500**

Standard model, 44 rimfire; approximate production 500:

5G-112 Values—Good **$2,500** Fine **$6,000**

Russian contract model; 44 S&W Russian caliber. Total made estimated at 70,000, but are rarely encountered due to the shipment of most specimens to Russia. Cyrillic barrel marking with double eagle near end:

5G-113 Values—Good **$1,750** Fine **$4,750**

Special Turkish Model series; 44 rimfire Henry caliber; first lot of 1,000 in this caliber made on special order with special rimfire frames and numbered 1 - 1000. Rare:

5G-114 Values—Good **$2,250** Fine **$5,500**

Second lot of approximately 2,000 pieces made from altered centerfire frames and numbered in commercial series. Extreme caution must be taken in identifying authentic specimens:

5G-115 Values—Good **$2,000** Fine **$5,000**

Japanese government variation; within the serial range 1 - 9000. Generally found with Japanese naval markings (anchor with two wavy lines on the butt and/or proof mark on barrel), and these are in addition to the usual English markings. 44 S&W Russian caliber. Barrel roll ends in -JAN. 19, 75 REISSUE JULY 25, 1871 (so-called "re-issue" stamping). 5,000 produced:

5G-116 Values—Good **$1,750** Fine **$4,500**

S&W Model 3 Russian Third Model

Model 3 Russian Third Model Single Action Revolver (most commonly known as New Model Russian). Made 1874-78; total run of about 60,638.

44 S&W Russian and (smaller quantity) 44 rimfire Henry calibers. 6-shot fluted cylinder. 6-1/2" barrel length.

Walnut grips of rounded butt profile. Blued or nickel plated finish.

Serial numbering rather complex, and is usually instrumental in establishing authenticity of numerous variants. Reference books on the subject should be carefully studied in verifying specimens. Famous Western lawman (dispatched "Billy the Kid") Pat Garrett believed to have carried the model.

Differences between the New Model Russian and its predecessor are primarily in the shorter extractor housing on the barrel, and its integral front sight (contrasting to the pinned front sight of the Old Model). Barrels were standard in 6-1/2" length. **Commercial production;** English markings; 44 S&W Russian caliber. Barrel address terminated in: AUG. 24,69. RUSSIAN MODEL. Total of about 13,500:

5G-117

5G-117   Values—Good **$875**   Fine **$2,250**
Commercial production; English markings; 44 rimfire caliber:
5G-118   Values—Good **$2,000**   Fine **$4,500**
Russian contract revolvers; totalled 41,138, and were serial numbered separately for each contract, beginning with 1. 44 S&W Russian caliber. Cyrillic barrel address; with the double eagle near the breech end, beneath which either KO or HK inspector initials were usually stamped. Rarely encountered since most were shipped to Russia:
5G-119   Values—Good **$2,000**   Fine **$4,500**
Copies by Ludwig Loewe Co.; Berlin, Germany, made for the Russian government under contract. Identical to the above but with different Cyrillic barrel marking. Bears HK inspector stamping:
5G-120   Values—Good **$1,400**   Fine **$3,500**
Copies by Ludwig Loewe; for commercial sale with barrel markings in English:
5G-121   Values—Good **$1,150**   Fine **$3,000**
Copies by the Russian government arsenal, Tula; identical to the S&W product, except for the different Cyrillic barrel markings, which also included a date:
5G-122   Values—Good **$1,400**   Fine **$3,750**
Turkish Model; 44 rimfire Henry caliber. Bear W inspector mark on butt. 5,000 made, using centerfire frames altered to accept the rimfire hammer:
5G-123   Values—Good **$2,000**   Fine **$4,250**
(Note: Extreme caution recommended in acquiring a specimen of this variation.)
Japanese Model; marked on the butt with an anchor and two wavy lines. 1,000 produced for the Japanese government:
5G-124   Values—Good **$1,750**   Fine **$3,750**

S&W New Model No. 3 Single Action Revolver

New Model No. 3 Single Action Revolver. Although factory records indicate manufacture/shipping 1878-1912, most recent reference (Supica/Nahas book; q.v. from information received direct from S&W) states "…all frames were mfd. by 1898 making the gun an antique." (This is verified except for the 38-40 No. 5G-133.) Total quantity 35,796.

44 S&W Russian was the standard caliber; made in limited quantities were 32 S&W, 32-44 S&W, 320 S&W Revolving Rifle, 38 S&W, 38-40, 38-44 S&W, 41 S&W, 44 rimfire Henry, 44 S&W American, 44 S&W Russian, 44-40, 45 S&W Schofield, 450 Revolver, 45 Webley, 455 Mark I, and 455 Mark II. 6-shot fluted cylinder. 3-1/2", 4", 5", 6", 6-1/2", 7", 7-1/2", and 8" barrels.

Checkered hard rubber (with S&W monogram impression) or walnut grips (after c. 1907 S&W monogram inlays standard in walnut grips). Blued or nickel plated finish.

Serial numbered in individual range from 1 to 35796. The standard barrel marking was the company name and address, with the patent dates 1865, 1869, 1871, 1875, and 1877; in the serial range 29625 - 31008 date markings were discontinued from use.

Quite a bit of variation exists in the New Model No. 3 series, and from the standpoint of design, performance, and historical interest, these revolvers are considered among the most sought after of S&W firearms. Among features standard to all variations were the break open mechanism with the barrel pivoting on the lower framestrap, automatic ejection as the barrel opened fully, and the rebounding type hammer (the latter in use nearly always). 1-7/16" cylinder length was standard, but 1-9/16" sometimes encountered above serial 30000. A collector could pursue solely variations of the New Model No. 3 Single Action as his specialty, much as many Colt enthusiasts concentrate only on the Single Action Army revolver. Reportedly the model used

5G-125

by Bob Ford to send Jesse James to his maker. Annie Oakley known to have ordered three of them.

Major variations are:
Standard model; 44 S&W Russian caliber; 6-1/2" barrel most often encountered. Specimens in other lengths command higher values; the farther away from the 6-1/2" norm usually the greater the premium. Blued or nickel plated; patent dates included on the barrel address marking:
5G-125   Values—Very Good **$950**   Exc. **$2,750**
As above; but without patent date barrel marking (only a few thousand made):
5G-126   Values—Very Good **$950**   Exc. **$2,750**
(Note: Premium placed on revolvers chambered for calibers other than 44 S&W Russian. The added value varies with both the rarity and desirability of the caliber.)
State of Maryland Model; only 280 made, all plated in nickel, 44 S&W Russian caliber, 6-1/2" barrel, walnut grips. Serial numbers 7126 - 7405. Butts marked U.S.; HN and DAL stampings also present on other parts; and the date 1878 above DAL appears on the left grip. Purchased from S&W and inspected by the U.S. government at the specific request of the Governor and Adj. Gen'l of Maryland to the U.S. Army's Chief of Ordnance in 1878.

These 280 revolvers were supplied "…to the extent of the funds then due {Maryland} under the provisions of the Militia Act."
5G-127   Values—Very Good **$4,500**   Exc. **$10,000**
Japanese Navy Model; within serial ranges 5426 - 5701 (first order), and 9001 - 9600 (second order). Later purchases, in higher serial ranges, were made by the Japanese government through the S&W importer serving Japan. This latter group may total as many as 1,500+. Major identifying markings are an anchor on the framestrap, with or without two wavy lines:
5G-128   Values—Very Good **$1,600**   Exc. **$3,250**
Japanese Artillery Model, with serials in the 25000 range, and Japanese character markings on the left side of the extractor housing. Blued finish, and 7" barrels. Butt swivels and an added serial range (also on butt) are also characteristic of this pistol:
5G-129   Values—Very Good **$1,850**   Exc. **$4,000**
Australian Model, serial numbered in the early 12000 and early 13000 range, total of 250 (7" barrel, with attachable shoulder stocks) and 30 (6-1/2" barrel, without shoulder stocks). All revolvers were nickel plated and in 44 S&W Russian caliber. Broad arrow mark of the Australian Colonial Police is on revolver butt and on lower tang of the shoulder stock. The 2 screws that fasten yoke to wrist of stock enter from right side, an anomaly on Australian contract.

For gun only:
5G-130   Values—Very Good **$1,500**   Exc. **$3,500**
For stock only:
5G-131   Values—Very Good **$1,250**   Exc. **$2,250**

Argentine Model, total of 2,000 sold to the Argentine government by New York dealers Hartley and Graham. Bear factory markings in front of trigger guard. EJERCITO/ARGENTINO. Serial number range between 50 to 3400:
5G-132   Values—Good **$1,750**   Fine **$3,500**
U.S. Revenue Cutter Service Issue; the predecessor of the U.S. Coast Guard. "Shelf" purchases 1890, from stock in batches: some from factory, others from dealers. Varying length barrels 5", 6", 6-1/2"; nickel and blued. No known distinctive markings. Serials in ranges 17,000 to 27,800. At least 140 recorded in Supica/Nahas and most in Jinks/Neal (q.v.). Value to be determined after further study published; estimated as high as the State of Maryland model:
5G-132.5
(Note: About 40 percent of New Model No. 3 production was exported, not only to Japan [the major foreign client], Argentina, and Australia, but to England, Spain, and other European countries, to Cuba, and parts of Asia. Certain proof or other foreign stampings will add only slightly to the value of an otherwise standard revolver.
New Model No. 3 chambered for 38-40 Winchester caliber. Made 1900-1907, in total quantity of only 74. 4" and 6-1/2" barrels. Serial numbered in individual range from 1 to 74. Company name and address barrel marking, with patent dates 1865, 1869, 1871, 1875, and 1877. Note 1-9/16" long cylinder and subsequent long topstrap:
5G-133   Values—Very Good **$5,000**   Exc. **$12,500**

S&W New Model No. 3 Target Single Action

New Model No. 3 Target Single Action Revolver. (Not illus.; similar to New Model No. 3.) Manufactured 1887-1910; total produced 4,333.

32-44 S&W target and 38-44 S&W target calibers. 6-shot fluted cylinder. 6-1/2" round barrel.

Checkered hard rubber or walnut grips; the rubber including S&W monogram impression; rounded butt profile. Blued or nickel plated finish.

Serial numbering from 1 to 4333, in individual range. Company name and address marking on the barrel, with patent dates of 1865, 1869, 1871, 1875, and 1877 (dates discontinued about midway through production).

S&W made this desirable revolver identical to the New Model No. 3 series in special chambering for the 32-44 and 38-44 target rounds. An accessory available, and rather scarce today,

was an attachable shoulder stock.

(Note: Caliber markings were added on the barrel [left side] in the serial range of about 3567 - 3832; revolvers so marked command a slight premium.)
32-44 caliber standard model; with 1-7/16" cylinder; 2,621 produced:
5G-134   Values—Very Good **$900**   Exc. **$2,500**
Same as above, but with 1-9/16" cylinder; 299 made:
5G-135   Values—Very Good **$1,000**   Exc. **$2,850**
38-44 caliber standard model; having 1-7/16" cylinder; 1,023 produced:
5G-136   Values—Very Good **$1,000**   Exc. **$2,850**
Same as above, but with 1-9/16" cylinder; 390 made:
5G-137   Values—Very Good **$1,100**   Exc. **$2,850**

S&W New Model No. 3 Turkish Model

New Model No. 3 Turkish Model Single Action Revolver. (Not illus.; similar to New Model No. 3.) Made 1879-1883; total quantity 5,461.

44 rimfire caliber. 6-shot fluted cylinder. 6-1/2" barrel length. Checkered walnut grips. Blued finish.

Serial numbering was in an individual range, from 1 to 5461. Company name and address barrel marking, with patent dates of 1865, 1869, 1871, 1875, and 1877. Additional markings were P (cylinder and frame bottomstrap), U (on barrel) and AFC (upper circle of left grip).

Basically this was the New Model No. 3 revolver, but chambered for 44 rimfire cartridges. Special inspector and proof

stampings are another feature, as is the individual serial range. Butt swivels were standard. This is a difficult model to locate in fine condition, due to the hard use specimens experienced in Turkish service.
Standard model; features as noted above; total of 5,281 made (281 on a later order):
5G-138   Values—Good **$1,750**   Fine **$4,000**
Contract overruns of 58, (sold by S&W to dealers Wexel & DeGress) and 121 (sold by S&W to dealers Shoverling, Daly, and Gales); these have the same markings as above, serial numbers may be found for all of these in the Jinks and Neal book:
5G-139   Values—Very Good **$2,250**   Exc. **$5,000**

S&W New Model No. 3 Frontier Single Action

New Model No. 3 Frontier Single Action Revolver. (Not illus.; similar to New Model No. 3.) Made 1885-1908; total quantity of 2,072.

44-40 Winchester caliber, with a significant quantity converted to 44 S&W Russian. 6-shot fluted cylinder. 4", 5", and 6-1/2" barrel lengths.

Checkered hard rubber grips with S&W monogram impression, or checkered walnut. Blued or nickel plated finish.

Serial numbers ran in an individual range, from 1 to 2072. Company name and barrel address marking, with 1865, 1869, 1871, 1875, and 1877 patent dates.

Besides the 44-40 caliber and individual serial numbering, the New Model No. 3 Frontier was distinguishable from the standard New Model No. 3 by the 1-9/16" long cylinder. Even those specimens converted to 44 S&W Russian had the long cylinder. Extractor type was the hook, rather than the rack and gear design. Competition with the Colt Single Action Army was the main inspiration for the New Model No. 3 Frontier, but it fell short of that goal. For this reason a fair amount of the production was converted to the 44 S&W Russian caliber.

Standard model; 44-40 caliber, sold commercially in the United States:

5G-140   Values—Very Good **$1,750**   Exc. **$4,000**

Japanese purchase revolvers, converted to 44 S&W Russian and shipped in 1895 and 1896. Serial numbers are listed in the Jinks and Neal book. Total of 786:

5G-141   Values—Very Good **$1,250**   Exc. **$2,750**

Shoulder Stocks For S&W Large Single-Action Revolvers

Detachable shoulder stocks (a.k.a. "Extension stock" or "Attachable stock") were made in limited quantities for various models of their large singe-action revolvers. Most were supplied and fitted to the guns at the factory; apparently none were serial-numbered to match the gun (see exception 5G-131 Australian Model) and shipped with the gun from the factory. Stocks could be purchased individually at later date, requiring the owner to have to adapt revolver for it. (If the serial number is visible on the butt of revolver when stock is affixed on the gun, it is likely factory-adapted.) Illustrated is the general style and configuration of walnut stock on all 4 types.

Generally a 10 percent to 30 percent premium may be added to those guns which can be authenticated as factory-adapted for stock. That premium should correspond to the rarity of the revolver.

Caution: Copies of these stocks were made in Spain (some apparently in the late 1800s or very early 1900s) contemporary with Spanish copies of the S&W revolvers. Although collectible, they are valued considerably less than those of S&W manufacture.

Only the revolving rifle stock 5G-141.7 is valued for blued finish. The other three types are valued for nickel yokes (blued finish worth 20-30 percent premium).

5G-141.5 Stock for Model No. 3 First Model single action Nos. 5G-100/101/102/103/104 and **Model 3 Russian First Model** Nos. 5G-108 and 5G-110. Iron buttplate. A total of 604 manufactured.

5G-141.5   Values—Very Good **$2,000**   Exc. **$3,000**

5G-141.6 Made to adapt to Model 3 Russian Second Model Nos. 5G-111/112/114/115…and **Model 3 Russian Third Model** Nos. 5G-117/118/123/124. Iron buttplate. Total of 941 manufactured by S&W.

5G-141.6   Values—Very Good **$2,500**   Exc. **$3,500**

5G-141.7 For Model 320 Revolving rifle 5G-065/066. Of the total 977 produced the great majority had long upper tang (on the wrist of stock). A small quantity with variant short tang will likely bring premium. Hard rubber buttplate with "S&W" monogram in a circular panel. Blued finish standard on the yoke.

5G-141.7   Values—Very Good **$3,000**   Exc. **$4,000**

5G-141.8 For New Model No. 3 Single Action. Nos. 5G-125 through 5G-141 (almost never found fitted to 5G-127/129/132/132.5/133/139). Hard rubber buttplate with "S&W" monogram in circular panel. Total of 1000 produced including those for the Australian Model (5G-130/131 which were marked with the "Broad Arrow" and Contract Number).

5G-141.8   Values—Very Good **$1,000**   Exc. **$2,000**

5G-141.5

5G-141.6

5G-141.7

5G-141.8

S&W 44 Double Action First Model Revolver

44 Double Action First Model Revolver (a.k.a. New Model Navy or D.A. Frontier). First produced 1881; listed in company catalogs to early 20th century and shipped up to 1913. Latest reference (Supica/Nahas book; q.v. from information received direct from S&W) states "…all frames manufactured prior to 1899 (thus) an antique." Quantity 53,590.

44 S&W Russian (standard), with a limited quantity in 38-40 and 44-40 Winchester. 6-shot fluted cylinder. 4", 5", 6", and 6-1/2" barrel lengths. 2 only with verified 8" barrel.

Checkered hard rubber (with S&W monogram impression) or walnut grips (after c. 1900 S&W monogram inlays may be present). Blued or nickel plated finish.

Serial numbered in an individual range from 1 to 54668. Company name and address barrel marking, with patent dates of 1865, 1869, 1871, 1879, and 1880.

Quite similar in shape to the 32 and 38 caliber Double Action First Model revolvers, (but much larger) the 44 D.A. First Model is distinguished by the cylinder having two sets of stop notches and the long "free grooves" between the central set, the 44 S&W Russian chambering, and the use on most specimens of 1-7/16" long cylinders. Belle Starr "The Bandit Queen of Indian Territory" carried this big double action. Texas gunfighter John Wesley Hardin was holding a nickel finished one as he fell dead to the floor of El Paso's Acme Saloon, August 19, 1895.

Standard model, 44 S&W Russian caliber; varying barrel lengths between 4" and 6-1/2"; 1-7/16" cylinder:
5G-142   Values—Very Good **$750**   Exc. **$1,850**

5G-142

As above, but with 1-9/16" cylinder (late production and scarce):
5G-143   Values—Very Good **$850**   Exc. **$2,000**
As above, 38-40 caliber, 1-9/16" long cylinder, with 4", 5", and 6-1/2" barrel lengths. Serial numbering in individual range, from 1 to 276. Caliber designation marked on left side of the barrel. A rare variation:
5G-144   Values—Very Good **$3,500**   Exc. **$6,000**
As above, 44-40 caliber (a.k.a. Double Action Frontier), 1-9/16" long cylinder, with 4", 5", 6", and 6-1/2" barrel lengths. Total production 15,340; serial numbered in an individual range, beginning with 1. After c. 1900 the patent date markings on barrel were dropped from use. 44 WINCHESTER CTG. standard marking on left side of the barrel:
5G-145   Values—Very Good **$875**   Exc. **$2,250**

S&W Model 44 D.A. Wesson Favorite

Model 44 Double Action Wesson Favorite. Manufactured 1882-1883, in a total quantity of about 1,000.

44 S&W Russian caliber. 6-shot fluted cylinder. 5" barrel length.

Checkered hard rubber or walnut grips; the former with S&W monogram impression. Blued or nickel plated finish; the latter much the most common.

Serial numbering was within the range of the 44 Double Action First Model revolvers; specifically between the numbers about 8900 - 10100. Company name and address marking was on the cylinder periphery, and included the patent dates 1865, 1869, 1871, 1879, and 1880.

The Wesson Favorite is closely similar to the Model 44 Double Action First Model, except as follows: Various cuts were made to reduce weight (e.g., note grooves on sides of frame between trigger guard and cylinder), cylinder diameter was smaller in the front (flute) section, barrel diameter was smaller, a special sight groove was cut along most of the barrel top, and

5G-146

company markings and patent dates were on the cylinder instead of the barrel rib.
Standard model; finished in nickel plating:
5G-146   Values—Very Good **$3,750**   Exc. **$10,000**
Standard model, but finished blue:
5G-147   Values—Very Good **$5,000**   Exc. **$12,000**

S&W 44 Hand Ejector First Model Revolver

44 Hand Ejector First Model Revolver (a.k.a. 44 Triple Lock or 44 Hand Ejector New Century). Made 1908-15; total quantity of about 15,375.

44 S&W Special (standard caliber), and 44 S&W Russian, 44-40, 45 Colt, 45 S&W Special, 450 Eley, and 455 Mark II calibers. 6-shot fluted cylinder. 4", 5", 6-1/2", and 7-1/2" barrel lengths.

Checkered walnut grips, square butt, without S&W monogram on early models; inset gold monogram on later models. Blued or nickel plated finish.

Serial numbered from 1 to 15375; an additional 5,000 were manufactured in a separate serial number series from 1 to 5000 in the 455 MKII caliber. These guns are classified as the 455 MKII

First Model, resulting in serial number duplication. Company name and address barrel marking, with patent dates 1894, 1895, 1896, 1901, and 1906.

Due primarily to the serial number overlap pointed out above, there is some confusion in studying this model of S&W revolver. Jinks and Neal provide full details and the basic variations are noted below. (Note: The nickname "Triple Lock" comes from the use of the standard dual locking devices for the cylinder, and the added security of a lock on the yoke front engaging the extractor rod casing.) Specimens with original factory fitted target sights worth approximately 50 percent premium.

Standard model, chambered for 44 S&W Special, or 450 Eley:
5G-148   Values—Very Good **$1,250**   Exc. **$2,000**

Standard model, but chambered for 44 S&W Russian, 45 S&W Special:
5G-149   Values—Very Good **$2,500**   Exc. **$15,000**
As above, chambered for 44-40 or 45 Colt:
5G-149.2   Values—Very Good **$2,500**   Exc. **$5,000**

Conversion model; made by S&W from standard production, altering the chambering to 455 Mark II caliber (done as an order from the British government during WWI). Serial numbers listed in Jinks and Neal. Total 666 British order, and 142 for commercial sale:
5G-150   Values—Very Good **$700**   Exc. **$1,400**

Special model (a.k.a. 455 Hand Ejector First Model), chambered for 455 Mark II cartridge; and serial numbered 1 to 5000. Note

5G-148

that some of these arms were converted to 45 Colt caliber. Identification is aided by presence of proof-marks (British or Canadian) on frame:
5G-151   Values—Very Good **$625**   Exc. **$1,250**

S&W 44 Hand Ejector Second Model Revolver

44 Hand Ejector Second Model Revolver. Made 1915-37; total quantity approximately 34,624.

44 S&W Special (standard), 38-40, 44-40, and 45 Colt calibers. 6-shot fluted cylinder. 4", 5", 6", and 6-1/2" barrel lengths.

Checkered walnut grips, square butt, with or without S&W monogram inlays. Blued or nickel plated finish.

5G-152

Serial numbered from 15376 to about 50000. Company name and address barrel marking, with patent dates (early production) 1901 and 1906, (middle production) 1901, 1906, and 1909, and (late production) 1906, 1909, and 1914.

Several internal changes appear in the Second Model revolver, as well as discontinuance of the third locking device and the heavy barrel lug. Cylinder size (and consequently the frame cut for cylinder) were made somewhat larger. Serial sequence is a useful assist in identification of second Model revolvers. Special factory target sights occasionally encountered on this model. A rare feature worth an approximate premium of $100 over values shown.
Standard model, chambered for 44 S&W Special:
5G-152   Values—Very Good **$500**   Exc. **$1,000**

As above, but chambered for 44-40 or 45 Colt:
5G-153   Values—Very Good **$1,000**   Exc. **$2,000**
(Note: 38-40 is an extreme rarity, and, though advertised by the company, specimens have yet to be found; would command a premium value.)

S&W 44 Hand Ejector Third Model Revolver

44 Hand Ejector Third Model Revolver (a.k.a. Model 1926 Hand Ejector Third Model). (Not illus.; similar to previous model.) Made 1926-50; total produced prior to WWII approximately 33,054.

44 S&W Special (standard), 44-40, and 45 Colt calibers (these latter two very rare—even more so than First and Second Model and worth considerable premium). 6-shot fluted cylinder. 4", 5", and 6-1/2" barrel.

Grips and finishes same as on Second Model.

Serial numbered from 28358 to 61412 (prior to WWII), and continued following the war to 1950. Company name and address barrel markings, with patent dates 1906, 1909, and 1914. Hammer and trigger above serial range 33561 bear marking:

Reg. U.S. Pt. Off. Post WWII specimens include S prefix with the serial number.

A basic detail for identifying this model is the heavy barrel lug construction (as used on the 44 Hand Ejector First Model or "Triple Lock" revolver), but lacking the third locking device. Other changes were internal. Special factory target sights occasionally encountered on this model. A rare feature worth an approximate premium of $100 over values shown.

Standard model; 44 S&W Special caliber:
5G-154   Values—Very Good **$1,000**   Exc. **$2,000**

As above, chambered for the 44-40 or 45 Colt:
5G-154.2   Values—Very Good **$2,000**   Exc. **$4,500**

Smith & Wesson 45 Caliber Models

S&W First Model Schofield Single Action

First Model Schofield Single Action Revolver. Manufactured 1875; total of 3,035 made.

45 S&W caliber. 6-shot fluted cylinder. 7" barrel length.

Walnut grips, with square butt profile. Blued finish standard; nickel plating scarce.

Serial numbered from 1 to 3035. Company name and address marking on the ejector housing, including patent dates of 1865,

5G-155

1869, 1871, and 1873 (latter date missing on some early production specimens).

The U.S. Ordnance Department ordered almost the entire production of this model. Distinctive features were in the barrel catch (attached to the frame, rather than to the topstrap), the gracefully shaped frame, and the shorter ejector housing on the barrel. A round recoil plate was inserted in the frame, through which the hammer struck the cartridges. Many were issued to the U.S. 4th Cavalry, seeing service in the Geronimo Campaign and the black troopers of the 9th and 10th U.S. Cavalry, the

intrepid "Buffalo Soldiers" of the Indian Wars. The James brothers, Jesse and Frank, Cole Younger of Younger Brothers, James Gang and Quantrill Raiders notoriety and U.S. Marshall Bill Tilghman also reported carrying the Schofield. "Lonesome Charley" Reynolds, Chief Scout for Custer is also known to have carried a Schofield.

Standard model; military issue, with inspector markings on various parts, and U.S. at butt. 3,000 made:
5G-155   Values—Very Good **$4,000**   Exc. **$10,000**

Commercially sold specimens; totaling about 35; without U.S. or inspector markings. *Rare:*
5G-156   Values—Very Good **$5,500**   Exc. **$12,500**

Wells Fargo & Company variations; two distinct styles of markings (with inventory number) on right side of ejector housing of the barrel: (1) Vertical die stamped block letters W.F.&Co's Ex. (2) Slanted italic letters without the s in Co's. Inventory number matches serial number of gun. Barrels shortened to 5". Sold as government surplus to Schuyler, Hartley & Graham, N.Y. dealers, who in turn sold them to Wells Fargo. A desirable and colorful variation:
5G-157   Values—Good **$3,500**   Fine **$6,000**

S&W Second Model Schofield Single Action

Second Model Schofield Single Action Revolver. Made 1876-1877; total produced 5,934.

45 S&W caliber. 6-shot fluted cylinder. 7" barrels.

Walnut grips, with square butt profile. Blued finish standard; nickel plating scarce.

Serial numbering continued the range begun by the First Model Schofield; and ran from 3036 to approximately 8969. Company name and address marking on the ejector housing, including patent dates of 1865, 1869, 1871, and 1873.

This was an improved version of the First Model Schofield, and differed from its predecessor as follows: Recoil plate no longer used in the frame, the barrel catch having an oval, scooped center section (when viewed from top) and knurled, and the somewhat flatter trigger shape.
Standard model; military issue, with inspector markings on various parts and U.S. on butt. Total contract 5,285:
5G-158   Values—Very Good **$4,000**   Exc. **$9,000**

Commercially sold specimens; totaling about 650:
5G-159   Values—Very Good **$3,500**   Exc. **$8,500**

Wells Fargo & Company variation; identical to that described in the First Model Schofield:
5G-160   Values—Good **$3,500**   Fine **$6,000**

5G-158

S&W 455 Mark II Hand Ejector First Model

455 Mark II Hand Ejector First Model Revolver (a.k.a. Model 455 Caliber Mark II Hand Ejector First Model). (Not illus.; similar to 44 Hand Ejector First Model.) Made 1914-15; total

quantity 5,000. See 44 Hand Ejector First Model Revolver for details:
5G-161   Values—Very Good **$350**   Exc. **$675**

S&W 455 Mark II Hand Ejector Second Model

455 Mark II Hand Ejector Second Model (a.k.a. Model 455 Caliber Mark II Hand Ejector Second Model). (Not illus.; similar to 44 Hand Ejector Second Model, without the lug.) Made 1915-17; total quantity 69,754.

455 Mark II caliber. 6-shot fluted cylinder. 6-1/2" barrel.

Checkered walnut grips, square butt, with S&W monogram inlays. Blued or nickel plated finish.

Serial numbered from 5001 to 74755. Company name and address barrel marking, with patent dates 1901 and 1906.

Key differences are in the absence of the third locking device, the absence of the large encasing section of the barrel lug, and a slightly larger cylinder and corresponding increased size of the

cut in frame for the cylinder. Serial range data is an aid to the identification of this model.

Standard English model:
5G-162   Values—Very Good **$425**   Exc. **$700**

Canadian government purchase (totalling 14,500 specimens), with proof stampings on frame:
5G-163   Values—Very Good **$450**   Exc. **$750**

Conversions of government model specimens to 45 Colt caliber (British or Canadian proof marks present on frame):
5G-164   Values—Very Good **$425**   Exc. **$700**

Wesson Fire Arms Co. Double Barrel Shotgun

Double Barrel Breech-Loading Shotgun. By Wesson Fire Arms Company of Springfield, Mass., c. 1868-70. Total quantity about 219.

12 gauge. Side by side barrels (it is possible that other types of shotguns were manufactured by the firm, but if so, specimens have yet to surface).

Standard barrel length 30", double triggers, straight type buttstock with skeleton steel buttplate and checkered butt.

This quite rare specimen of D.B. Wesson inventiveness, although a product of the Wesson Fire Arms Company, is well within the realm of Smith & Wesson collector's items. Patents were held by D.B. Wesson, John Stokes, and by Wesson and John H. Blaze. Chief officer of the company was D.B. Wesson President, and Horace Smith, C.E. Buckland, and J.W. Storrs were directors. Quality of production was excellent, with not a few guns finely engraved by the Gustave Young shop. It is believed many of these were fabricated in the S&W factory and then finished nearby. The intertwined monograms of D. Smith and D.B. Wesson appear on underside of barrels of marked specimens.

5G-165

Standard model, the barrel marked WESSON FIRE ARMS Co SPRINGFIELD MASS. Serial numbered on the trigger guard strap:
5G-165   Values—Very Good **$2,750**   Exc. **$5,000**

Specimens as above, but without serial number or barrel address marking:
5G-166   Values—Very Good **$1,850**   Exc. **$3,750**
(Note: Premium placed on specimens based on degree of engraving and deluxe stockwork.)

Smith & Wesson experimental single-action "American" revolver. Caliber 44 rimfire. Unique split cylinder ejector system. Accompanied with the matching barrel and split cylinder of an experimental S&W Model 1, Third Issue 22 rimfire revolver marked "MODEL 1868."
(N. Flayderman & Co. Catalog No. 42 of October 1959)

Chapter V-H

Stevens Arms Company

No name is better known to the older crowd of collectors and shooters (the over-seventy set) than that of Stevens. Not a few arms enthusiasts were weaned (shooting-wise) on one form or another of Stevens' famed line of boy's rifles.

Very likely the most prolific maker (and certainly one of the best) of arms for young boys, the firm is justly recognized and equally known for its superb "Ideal" series of single shot target and sporting rifles. Stevens' extensive and varied line of single shot pocket and target handguns made over its 78-year history has also come to be respected in collecting circles.

A favorite of shooters and collectors and the subject of a sizable bibliography, quite a bit of information and lore are available concerning the Stevens longarms. Handguns, regrettably, have suffered most over the years from a lack of definitive data and thus only the most easily recognized models or those in the finest condition tended to achieve any significant values on the collectors' market. With the publication of *Stevens Pistols And Pocket Rifles* (*see bibliography*), the collecting world was provided with an accurate, detailed and reliable guide to the entire series of handguns and thus afforded the opportunity to easily identify—and consequently evaluate—each type as to importance and relative rarity. A great asset for the collector and student in this line is the array of company catalogs issued over a long period of time, revealing a great wealth of data covering standard models and their many variations.

A reasonable generalization for collecting in this field would hold that the earlier and scarcer models are highly desirable in any condition, whereas with the later, more widely produced and commonly seen types, a basic key to demand and evaluations are the better degrees of condition. This is particularly true with guns specifically made for fine, accurate target shooting, in which bore condition is a major factor. The subject is discussed at length in the sections dealing with the Winchester Single Shot and the Sharps New Model 1874 rifles, to which the reader is referred.

Fancy embellishments, (e.g., engraving) were standard on some of the Ideal model rifles. Such decoration is reasonably common in less elaborate grades (i.e., simple broad floral and scroll motifs) while available as extra options in varying degrees of elaborateness on almost the entire Ideal series. On handguns, however, engraving may be considered rare and few specimens are encountered.

Cased Stevens handguns are also considered rare and specimens are seldom seen. Some of the so-called "bicycle" or "pocket rifles" were cased in a walnut box with simple compartmented lining and if in reasonably sound, complete and

original condition should increase values at least 50 percent or more. The very elaborate cases with fancy plush, recessed and contour shaped linings are practically unknown in the Stevens line (a few exquisite specimens have been recorded—but are few and far between).

Stevens handgun grips invariably are the standard walnut "as issued." The substitution of ivory or other exotic materials is infrequent, but values do not necessarily increase in direct proportion to their rarity—but rather more in line with those of other American handguns. Ivory grips are likely to be seen more often on the Off-Hand Target No. 35 model than any other of the series.

The collector, trader and dealer should familiarize himself with the Gun Control Act of 1968 (as administered by the Bureau of Alcohol, Tobacco and Firearms of the U.S. Treasury Department) when it comes to buying or dealing in the Stevens so-called "bicycle rifles" or, more aptly and correctly known "pocket rifles." When found without shoulder stocks, they are merely treated as a normal handgun, however, accompanied by their detachable skeleton stock (or if in shotgun bores) they fall into entirely different classifications. Many of these were originally quite restricted as to the ease in which they could be freely bought, sold or traded. With the clarification of their original date of manufacture, some have since been reclassified from the most restrictive categories and currently considered as "curios and relics" (more or less meaning they must be handled as modern firearms, but may be reasonably and legally sold and purchased by those having proper licenses). Others have been completely declassified and removed from the "curio and relic" category and are considered as strictly "antiques" and hence, not subject to any of the provisions of the Gun Control Act. The author has made mention of the more recent classifications as they existed at the time of publication, however, the collector is urged to verify the status of a particular model to ascertain its most current classification. It should be further noted that not only do classifications occasionally change, but often a specific model made in various calibers may be found in dual classifications, one for each of the respective calibers.

Stevens "Pocket Rifles" were sold with matching serial numbers on their detachable shoulder stocks and the pistols to which they were fitted. The prices indicated in this section for complete "Pocket Rifles" with detachable shoulder stocks are for matching numbered specimens. Prices should be revised downward approximately 20 percent when shoulder stock numbers are mismatched to the gun.

The history of the Stevens Arms Company, as well as the background of the man for whom it was named are interesting ones. Familiarity affords the collector a greater insight into the guns and places sequence of manufacture (and variations) in sharper focus. It may also serve to heighten interest in a number of the models.

The founder of this long lived firm, Joshua Stevens (born Chester, Massachusetts, 1814), had an impressive association with many of the famed New England gun makers before attempting an independent manufacturing career.

Stevens was primarily a tool maker with secondary talents as a businessman. As an innovator or inventor, his role was not one of major significance. The patents he did acquire were, for the most part, merely improvements on arms already in production. As a matter of fact, almost his entire line of pistols and rifles was based on the identical tip-up design utilizing his major patent of September 6, 1864, a pistol action design, with the barrel tipping upward from the rear when released by a catch on the frame.

Stevens' earliest training was as an apprentice tool maker in 1834, with his first gun-making experience acquired in 1838 as an employee of C. B. Allen, Springfield, Massachusetts, then engaged in the manufacture of the Elgin Cutlass Pistol and Cochran Turret Guns. Stevens is known to have worked for Eli Whitney in 1847 and to have played a role in the manufacture of the famed Whitney-Walker Colts then being made under sub-contract. When Samuel Colt took over the manufacture of his revolvers after the Walker and moved the machinery to his own Hartford plant, Stevens went along to that factory. After leaving over a difference of opinion in pistol design, (Stevens was working on one he thought better!), he entered partnership with Edwin Wesson and William H. Miller in the late 1840s, manufacturing percussion revolvers in Hartford, based on the Leavitt patent of 1837. Very few specimens are known of this arm and the quantity produced is believed to have been extremely small.

By 1850, Stevens was in the employ of the Massachusetts Arms Company in Chicopee Falls, devoting his talents to superintendence of production. During that time he was issued patents for improvements on percussion revolvers then being made by the company. On September 6, 1864, Stevens took out his most important patent—that for the tip-up action on a single shot pistol. After a lengthy career as a tool and gun maker for others, Joshua Stevens entered an independent manufacturing and business venture on his own.

The company grew very slowly and remained quite small at its quarters in a remodeled grist-mill in Chicopee Falls. By 1870 there were still less than 60 employees working and this number dropped to even less in the hard-times of the 1870s. Although the complete succession of handguns may be seen in the following descriptions, it should be noted that guns were not then the sole product of the company, since machine tools and associated items were under simultaneous production.

It was not until 1880 that some expansion was carried out. Up until that time the company was known as J. STEVENS AND CO.; the "AND CO." consisting of W. B. Fay and James Taylor, two businessmen who had formed a partnership with Stevens and had given financial backing.

The firm was incorporated in 1886 as the J. STEVENS ARMS & TOOL CO. with the old partnership dissolved. Financial interest, however, was basically in the hands of the original three partners. Growth was maintained at a rather slow pace and by 1895, the company still employed less than 50 people. As in earlier years, the tool business continued to account for a major amount of production.

In 1896, I. H. Page, one of the incorporators of the company, and also an employee (bookkeeper) as far back as 1886, assumed complete control, becoming President by buying out the shares held by Stevens and James Taylor. Stevens continued an active career with other non-gun or manufacturing businesses in the Chicopee Falls area and lived to the ripe old age of 92, passing away in 1907.

The Stevens Arms and Tool Company, under the aegis of I. H. Page, grew quickly after 1896, adding considerably in manufacturing space and employees, until by 1901 it had 900 workers. By 1902 company advertising boasted that "… it was the largest producer of sporting firearms in the world." By 1915 and the outbreak of World War I, Stevens was a leader in the American arms business as a maker of target and small game hunting guns.

Interesting to note is that Stevens, for all its fame and importance as a gun manufacturer, never made a military arm of any type. During World War I the plant was turned over to the New England Westinghouse Company, under whose direction it continued until the cessation of hostilities. In 1916, reorganization was carried out under the new name J. STEVENS ARMS COMPANY.

Purchased in its entirety by the Savage Arms Company in 1920, the operations of the two concerns were merged, with Stevens operated as a subsidiary. When Savage moved from Utica, New York, to Westfield, Massachusetts, in 1960, the old Stevens factory in Chicopee was abandoned. For all practical purposes the company then ceased to exist but with its name remaining on a few products of Savage as the last vestiges of its fame.

As an aid to identification and manufacturing dates, the following markings are found on Stevens Arms[†]:

1864 to 1886: J. STEVENS & CO. CHICOPEE FALLS, MASS. PAT. SEPT. 6, 1864 (all in one line) or J. STEVENS & CO. CHICOPEE/FALLS, MASS. PAT. SEPT. 6, 1864 (in two lines).

1886 to 1916: J. STEVENS A & T CO./CHICOPEE FALLS, MASS. USA PAT. SEPT. 6, 1864 (in two lines) or J. STEVENS A & T CO./CHICOPEE FALLS, MASS. USA (in two lines).

1916 to 1942: J. STEVENS ARMS CO./CHICOPEE FALLS, MASS. USA (in two lines).

[†]Note: The above markings revise and update those stated in the classic work *Stevens Pistols And Pocket Rifles* which in two instances (1886-1916 and 1916-1942) reflect typographical errors.

BIBLIOGRAPHY

(Note: Information about Stevens Arms may be found in several books covering the broad field of American firearms. These volumes appear in complete bibliographic listings elsewhere in this work, notably Chapters II and XIV. They include: *The Rifle In America* by Phil Sharpe, The 5 works on single shot rifles by James Grant, *The Breech-Loading Single Shot Match Rifle* by Major Roberts and Ken Waters, *One Hundred Years Of Shooters And Gun Makers Of Single Shot Rifles* by Kelver, *The Story Of Pope's Barrels* by Ray Smith, and *14 Old Gun Catalogs* compiled by L. D. Satterlee and many reprints of factory catalogs) and *Savage & Stevens Arms* by B. West.

Cope, Kenneth L. *Stevens Pistols And Pocket Rifles*. Ottawa, Ontario, Canada: Museum Restoration Service, 1971. The basic, pioneer, and definitive guide to the subject.

*Kimmel, Jay. *Savage & Stevens Arms Collector's History*. Portland, Oregon: Corey-Stevens Pub. Co., 1990. Reprints of important articles and original catalogs plus textual material by author; much valuable information.

----J. Stevens Arms & Tool Co., *A Short Illustrated History*. Canton, Conn.: Armsco Press. c.1995.

(*) Preceding a title indicates the book is currently in print.

Handguns
Pocket Pistols

Stevens Vest Pocket Pistol

Vest Pocket Pistol. Made c. 1864 to 1876. Quantity made originally estimated about 500; serial number study seems to indicate total quantity may be as high as 1,200.

Caliber 30 rimfire most often encountered; caliber 22 rimfire rare. 2-7/8" part octagon/part round tip-up barrel.

Finish: Nickel plated iron frame with blued barrel or overall blued. Fish-tail shaped handle with rosewood grips. Extractor found on later produced pieces.

Earliest production marked only VEST POCKET PISTOL, while later made pieces (above Serial No. 120 approximately) also bear markings on top of barrel: J. Stevens & Co./Chicopee Falls, Mass. in two lines, some entirely unmarked. Patent date does not appear. Serial numbered.

Also nicknamed the "Kickup Model," this diminutive deringer shared with the Old Model Pocket Pistol the distinction

5H-001

of launching the Joshua Stevens line of guns.

30 rimfire. Estimated quantity 1000:
5H-001   Values—Good **$950**   Fine **$2,750**
22 rimfire. Estimated quantity 200:
5H-001.5   Values—Good **$1,400**   Fine **$3,750**

Stevens Old Model Pocket Pistol

5H-002

Old Model Pocket Pistol (a.k.a. 1st and 2nd Types/Models). Made c. 1864 to 1886. Total quantity estimated about 15,000.

Calibers 22 and 30 short rimfire. 3-1/2" part round/part octagon tip-up barrel.

Brass frame (rare with iron frame; worth premium) with the removable semi-circular sideplate (very late models did not have that circular inspection plate on left frame). Finish: Frame nickel or silver plated; barrel blued or nickel plated. Rosewood grips; flat butt. Only minor differences distinguish the two models: front of frame on second model wider to provide more strength for hammer pivot screw; and head of barrel release stud had a slotted and flared top. Values apparently same for both types.

Barrel markings: J. Stevens & Co. Chicopee/Falls, Mass. Pat. Sep 6 1864 Serial numbered.

This small handgun shares with the Vest Pocket Model the distinction of starting the Stevens Company line. The general style of it set the standard for the majority of Stevens pistol production well into the 20th century:

5H-002   Values—Very Good **$125**   Exc. **$400**

Stevens Gem Pocket Pistol

Gem Pocket Pistol. Made c. 1872 to 1890. Total production estimated about 4,000.

Calibers 22 and 30 short rimfire. 3" part octagon/part round barrel swings sideways to load.

Brass frame with nickel plated finish; barrel blued or nickel plated. Walnut or rosewood grips; bird's head butt.

Marked only: GEM on barrel and does not bear Stevens Company name or address. Serial numbered.

A distinctive Stevens deringer type pistol and their only handgun made without the tip-up barrel feature:

5H-003

5H-003   Values—Very Good **$400**   Exc. **$1,250**

Stevens 41 Caliber Deringer Pistol

5H-004

41 Deringer Pistol. Made c. 1875. Total quantity estimated under 100.

Caliber 41 rimfire. 4" part round/part octagon tip-up barrel.

Brass frame with semi-circular sideplate either nickel or silver plated finish; barrel blued. Walnut grips; bird's head butt.

Few specimens known observed with two-line STEVENS markings on top flat or left flat of barrel; others unmarked.

A rare type with but a handful located:
5H-004   Values—Good **$2,250**   Fine **$5,000**

Stevens 22 Caliber Deringer Pistol

22 Deringer Pistol. Made c. 1875. Total estimated under 25. Very rare.

22 rimfire. 4" part round/part octagon barrel. Iron frame with semi-circular sideplate; nickel finish; barrel blued. Walnut grips. Barrel markings: J. STEVENS & CO CHICOPEE/FALLS, MASS. PAT. SEPT.6. 1864.

Very ungainly, awkward appearance. Has the small frame of the "Old Model Pocket" with an extended front end and the very large bird's head handle of the 41 Deringer. Caution advised; be certain barrel and frame matched and not merely composite:

5H-004.5

5H-004.5   Values—Good **$1,250**   Fine **$3,000**

Stevens Single Shot Pistol

Single Shot Pistol (a.k.a. 3rd Type/Model). (Not illus.) Made c. 1886 to 1896. Total quantity estimated about 25,000.

Calibers 22 and 30 short rimfire. 3-1/2" part round/part octagon tip-up barrel. Basically identical in contours to the Old Model Pocket Pistol.

Brass frame made both with and without the semi-circular sideplate; firing pin and rear sight on hammer; nickel or silver plated finish; barrel blued or nickeled. Walnut grips; flat butt.

Barrel markings: J. STEVENS A & T CO. Either with or without patent date.

Basically the Old Model Pocket Pistol under a new name. The barrel marking differentiates it from its predecessor:

5H-005   Values—Very Good **$125**   Exc. **$300**

Stevens No. 41 and Tip-Up 41 Pocket Pistols

No. 41 and Tip-Up No. 41 Pocket Pistols. Recent research has shown all these small Stevens pocket pistols/deringers, starting with the Old Model Pocket #5H-002, to be one continuous series circa 1864 to 1916, consisting of 5 basic types. The following two are now identified, in collector assigned terminology, as the 4th and 5th types, or models.

There has been, and continues to be, confusion over the nomenclature of these two models. Stevens, in their advertising and catalogs named them "No. 41" and "Tip-Up No. 41" or "No. 41 Tip-Up;" these latter two used interchangeably. They are two distinct "models" and the differences are readily apparent.

Both pistols have iron frames with firing pin mounted in the recoil shield. Both are made without sideplates. Part round/part octagon barrels 3-1/2" will vary just slightly. Mushroom type barrel release buttons. Finish: nickel; nickel and blue; full blue.

Barrel markings on both J. STEVENS A & T CO./CHICOPEE FALLS, MASS. USA without patent dates. Style of markings only, differ, as below:

"No. 41" Pocket Pistol/Deringer (a.k.a. 4th Model). c. 1898-1902. Estimated quantity 28,000.

Small frame size (same as 5H-002 and 5H-005). Note that the breech of the barrel is flush with top of recoil shield as on those earlier models. Markings in block letters.

5H-006

5H-006.7

22 rimfire:
5H-006   Values—Very Good **$125**   Exc. **$350**

30 caliber rimfire; made in early production of this model; scarce:
5H-006.5 Values—Very Good **$150**   Exc. **$375**

"Tip-Up No. 41" (a.k.a. "No. 41 Tip-Up" and/or 5th Model). c. 1903-1916. Estimated quantity 80,000. Made in 22 rimfire only.

Easily recognized by its larger, thicker frame, thick walled barrel and thicker grips. Most noticeable is the top of the recoil shield which is grooved for sight and rises much above the breech of the barrel. Markings are in block letters or slanted script letters:

5H-006.7 Values—Very Good **$100**   Exc. **$275**

Target and Sporting Pistols

Stevens Six Inch Pocket Rifle

The Six Inch Pocket Rifle. Made c. 1869 to 1886. Total quantity estimated about 1,000.

5H-007

Caliber 22 short or long rimfire. 6" part octagon/part round tip-up barrel. Firing pin on hammer.

Brass frame with semi-circular sideplate finished either in nickel or silver plating; barrel blued. Walnut or rosewood grips; flat butt.

Barrel markings are all two line style: J. STEVENS & CO. CHICOPEE/FALLS, MASS. PAT. SEPT. 6, 1864. Serial numbered.

Advertised by Stevens as the "Old Model Pocket Rifle, Six Inch Barrel ..." this was their earliest model of target pistol. It was not intended for use with a detachable shoulder stock: (Note value 20 percent to 30 percent less if sights missing):
5H-007   Values—Good **$275**   Fine **$650**

Stevens-Lord No. 36 Pistol

Lord No. 36. Made c. 1880 to 1911. Total quantity estimated about 3,500.

Rimfire calibers 22 short and long rifle, 22 W.R.F., and 25 Stevens. Centerfire calibers 32 Short Colt, 38 Long Colt and 44 Russian. 10" or 12" part round/part octagon tip-up barrel. Firing pin in frame with bushing.

Brass or iron frames with nickel plated finish; barrel blued. Checkered walnut grips with very wide, weighted and flared butt cap.

All of those made prior to 1886 have the one-line markings: J. STEVENS & CO. CHICOPEE FALLS MASS. PAT. SEPT. 6, 1864 These markings appear on guns up to approximately serial range of 600 and hence, are scarcer than the later markings and should bring a slight premium. Guns made after 1886 bear either version of the

5H-008

two-line J. STEVENS A & T CO. marking (*q.v.*). Serial numbered.

Origin of the name for this pistol was Frank Lord, a prominent competitive pistol shooter of the period. Of all Stevens target pistols, the Lord Model boast the greatest popularity and the most years of availability. Those in the large centerfire calibers quite scarce and will bring a premium:

5H-008   Values—Very Good **$550**   Exc. **$1,250**

Stevens-Conlin, First Issue Pistol

Conlin, First Issue. Made c. 1880 to 1884. Total produced estimated about 500.

Calibers 22 or 32 short or long rimfire. 10" or 12" part

5H-009

round/part octagon tip-up barrel. Firing pin in frame with bushing.

Brass spur trigger frame with semi-circular sideplate; nickel plated finish. Barrel blued. Walnut checkered grips with wide, weighted and flared butt cap. Very late production of this model may have an added oval trigger guard with finger spur extension. This feature, if original, is quite scarce and will add a premium to the value of the piece.

Barrel markings are all two-line: J. STEVENS & CO. CHICOPEE/FALLS, MASS. PAT. SEPT. 6, 1864. Serial numbered.

The inspiration for the naming of this model was James S. Conlin who owned and operated a very popular and famous shooting gallery on Broadway in New York City:

5H-009   Values—Very Good **$750**   Exc. **$1,750**

Stevens-Conlin No. 38, Second Issue Pistol

Conlin No. 38, Second Issue. Made c. 1884 to 1903. Total produced estimated about 6,000. (However, frequency seen much less than Gould model and valued about same.)

Rimfire calibers 22 short and long rifle, 22 W.R.F., 25 Stevens and 32 long. Centerfire caliber 32 Short Colt. 10" or 12" part round/part octagon tip-up barrel. Firing pin in frame with bushing. Rear sight screw adjustable for windage and elevation.

Iron or brass frame made without sideplate. Finish: Nickel plated frame with blued barrel. Checkered walnut grips with wide, weighted and flared iron butt cap.

Earlier production has two-line markings J. STEVENS & CO. CHICOPEE/FALLS, MASS. PAT. SEPT. 6, 1864 (scarcer), while the

5H-010

majority are seen with either style of the two-line J. STEVENS A & T CO. markings. Serial numbered:

5H-010   Values—Very Good **$550**   Exc. **$1,450**

Stevens-Gould No. 37 Pistol

Gould No. 37. (Not illus.) Made c. 1889 to 1903. Total quantity estimated about 1,000 (but likely larger).

About identical to the Conlin No. 38, Second Issue, without the finger spur on trigger guard.

Same calibers, sights, breech type and barrel lengths and shapes as Conlin No. 38, Second Issue.

Iron frame nickel plated; barrel blued. Checkered walnut

grips with wide, weighted and flared iron butt cap. Firing pin in frame with bushing.

Marked with either style of the two-line J. STEVENS A & T CO. name and address (*q.v.*).

Gould was named for the prominent late 19th century arms expert and writer, A. C. Gould:

5H-011   Values—Very Good **$450**   Exc. **$1,000**

Stevens Offhand Target No. 35 Pistol

Offhand Target No. 35. Made c. 1907 to 1916. Total quantity estimated about 35,000. About identical in contour to the Gould No. 37.

Rimfire calibers 22 short and long rifle, 22 Stevens-Pope, 22 W.R.F. and 25 Stevens. 6", 8", or 10" part round/part octagon tip-up barrels. Firing pin in frame without bushing.

5H-012

Iron frame finished either blue or nickel plated; barrel blued. Plain uncheckered walnut grips with wide, weighted and flared butt cap. Rear open sight adjustable only for elevation.

Barrel markings are all two-line J. STEVENS A & T CO. without patent date. Serial numbers all above 25000 range.

Should not be confused with the Gould No. 37 which will bear serial numbers under the 25000 range. Another differentiating feature from the No. 37, is the absence of a firing pin bushing:

5H-012   Values—Very Good **$150**   Exc. **$450**

Stevens Offhand No. 35 Pistol

Offhand No. 35. (Not illus.) Made c. 1923 to 1942. Total quantity manufactured recorded at 43,357. Identical to the Offhand Target No. 35, and on specimens made after 1929, the trigger guard is more primitive appearing, being stamped of sheet metal rather than cast.

Caliber 22 long rifle or 410 gauge. 6", 8", 10", 12-1/4" part round/part octagon barrels.

Iron frames either nickel plated, casehardened or blued; barrels blued.

Barrel markings: J. STEVENS ARMS CO./CHICOPEE FALLS, MASS. USA.

Stevens last manufactured pistol. Specimens in 410 shotgun gauge (or any other shot cartridge) are subject to the provisions (and restrictions) of the National Firearms Act:

5H-013   Values—Very Good **$150**   Exc. **$375**

Stevens Auto Shot No. 35 Pistol

Auto Shot No. 35. (Not illus.) Made c. 1929 to 1934. Total quantity estimated about 2,000.

410 gauge 2" shotgun shell. 8" or 12-1/4" part octagon/part round barrel; smoothbore. Firing pin in frame without bushing.

Iron frame. Overall blue finish. Either plain walnut or checkered (scarce) grips; wide, weighted flared butt cap.

Markings: J. STEVENS ARMS CO./CHICOPEE FALLS, MASS. USA. Serial numbered.

Basically this is the "Offhand No. 35" merely renamed and in shotgun gauge with a rather primitive appearing stamped trigger guard instead of the earlier cast type. The original manufacture of these was halted with the passage of the National Firearms Act in 1934 which restricted the use of shot cartridges in handguns. This handgun is subject to the provisions (and restrictions) of the National Firearms Act and collectors should not attempt to acquire or dispose of specimens unless complying fully with those provisions:

5H-014   Values—Very Good **$400**   Exc. **$1,250**

Stevens Diamond No. 43, First Issue Pistol

Diamond No. 43, First Issue. Made c. 1886 to 1896. Total quantity estimated at about 25,000.

Calibers 22 short and long rifle rimfire. 6" or 10" part round/part octagon tip-up barrels. Firing pin in frame with bushing (early variant with firing pin on hammer worth premium).

Brass frame with semi-circular sideplate standard in almost all production except the last 5,000 (and these are worth a slight premium). Nickel plated frame with blued barrel. Plain walnut grips with flat butt.

5H-015

Marked with either version of the J. STEVENS A & T CO. two-line style with those bearing the patent dates most often seen. Serial numbered:

5H-015   Values—Very Good **$150**   Exc. **$450**

Stevens Diamond No. 43, Second Issue Pistol

Diamond No. 43, Second Issue. (Not illus.) Made c. 1896 to 1916. Total quantity estimated about 70,000.

Identical in contour to the First Issue.

Caliber 22 short and long rifle and 22 Stevens-Pope. Same breech style, barrel lengths and shapes as First Issue. Firing pin in frame without bushing.

Iron frame (without sideplate) either nickel plated or blued;

barrel blued. Walnut grips; flat butt.

Markings are all two-line J. STEVENS A & T CO. style without the patent date. Serial numbering commences at approximately 26000 and shares same serial range with the Reliable Pocket Rifles, Second Issue. Further identifying feature distinguishing this from the First Issue is the lack of a firing pin bushing. Quite often found with British proofs which will not affect values:

5H-016   Values—Very Good **$150**   Exc. **$375**

Stevens Target No. 10 Pistol

Target No. 10. Made c. 1919 to 1933. Total quantity produced 7,131.

Caliber 22 long rifle rimfire. 8" round tip-up barrel; firing pin in frame.

Steel frame. Full blue finish. Checkered hard rubber grips. Markings in two-lines on left side of frame: J. STEVENS ARMS

5H-017

CO./CHICOPEE FALLS, MASS. USA. Serial numbered.

Although appearing outwardly to be a semi-automatic pistol, the No. 10 was made only as a single shot. A manual cocking stud extended at rear of frame. Deluxe models were available with blued barrel, browned frame, nickeled finished trigger and barrel release, and checkered aluminum grips. Premiums may be added to value for such specimens:

5H-017   Values—Very Good **$150**   Exc. **$375**

Pocket Rifles

Light Frame Types (Frames 5/8" Width)

Stevens Old Model Pocket Rifle

5H-018

Old Model Pocket Rifle. Made c. 1869 to 1886. Total quantity estimated about 4,000.

Caliber 22 short or long rimfire. 8" or 10" part octagon/part round barrel. Spring actuated extractor. Firing pin on hammer.

Brass frame with semi-circular sideplate. Either nickel or silver finished; barrel blued. Shoulder stock black japanned or nickeled. Grips either walnut or rosewood.

Barrel markings all two-line: J. STEVENS & CO. CHICOPEE/FALLS, MASS. PAT. SEPT. 6, 1864.

Stevens made this model by adapting the Old Model Pocket Pistol and adding a longer barrel to it, improving the sights and fitting the butt with a mount to engage the attachable stock. Serial numbering in the range of the Old Model Pocket Pistol. Reclassified from a "curio and relic" under Federal Firearms regulations to its proper status as an antique and hence, not subject to Gun Control Act provisions:

Complete With Detachable Shoulder Stock:
5H-018   Values—Very Good **$550**   Exc. **$1,500**
Pistol Only Without Stock:
5H-019   Values—Very Good **$250**   Exc. **$600**

Stevens Reliable Pocket Rifle, First Issue

Reliable Pocket Rifle, First Issue. (Not illus.) Made c. 1886 to 1896. Total quantity estimated about 4,000.

Calibers 22 short, long and long rifle rimfire. Contours identical to the Old Model.

A continuation of the Old Model Pocket Rifle under a new model designation. Basic variance being the extractor now linkage actuated. Grips of either walnut or rosewood.

Detachable stock as above.

Markings are all the J. STEVENS A & T CO. with patent date.

Reclassified from a "curio and relic" under Federal Firearms Regulations to its proper status as an antique and hence, not subject to Gun Control Act provisions:

Complete With Detachable Shoulder Stock:
5H-020   Values—Very Good **$550**   Exc. **$1,500**
Pistol Only Without Stock:
5H-021   Values—Very Good **$225**   Exc. **$550**

Stevens Reliable Pocket Rifle No. 42, Second Issue

5H-022

Reliable Pocket Rifle No. 42, Second Issue. Made c. 1896 to 1916. Total quantity estimated about 8,000. About identical to Old Model with altered profile to detachable stock only.

Caliber 22 long rifle and Stevens-Pope rimfire. 10" part octagon/part round barrel.

An altered version of the First Issue, differing mainly in caliber and use of iron for the frame material. Firing pin mounted in frame without bushing. Grip lengthened by approximately 1/2" and the skeleton type shoulder stock has a slightly altered shape and is wider at butt end with larger opening.

Markings: J. STEVENS A & T CO. Almost all appear to be without the use of patent date. Serial numbered in common with the Diamond No. 43, Second Issue (range 26000 to 100000) and with Reliable Pocket Rifle No. 42, Second Issue.

This model is classified under the Gun Control Act as a "curio and relic." No exact production/serial number information is available for this model. However, any of them which can be documented as being produced prior to 1899 would be considered as "antiques" and hence not subject to G.C.A. provisions:

Complete With Detachable Shoulder Stock:
5H-022   Values—Very Good **$550**   Exc. **$1,500**
Pistol Only Without Stock:
5H-023   Values—Very Good **$225**   Exc. **$550**

Medium Frame Types (Frames 1" Width)

Stevens New Model Pocket Rifle, First Issue

5H-024

New Model Pocket Rifle, First Issue. Made c. 1872 to 1875. Total quantity estimated about 8,000.

Caliber 22 and 32 short or long rimfire (30 rf. rare, worth premium). Barrel lengths 10", 12", 15", or 18", and either part octagon/part round or full octagon. Firing pin on hammer.

Brass frame with semi-circular sideplate finished either in nickel or silver plate; barrel blued. Walnut or rosewood grips. Detachable shoulder stock nickel finished.

Barrel marking: J. STEVENS & CO. CHICOPEE/FALLS, MASS. with patent date.

Stock fitted into dovetail at butt with upper section secured by knurled screw directly into backstrap of handle. Longest barrel lengths will bring slight premiums. This model has been declassified under the Federal Gun Control Act from "curio and relic" to an antique, and as such, not subject to the Gun Control Act provisions.

Complete With Detachable Shoulder Stock:
5H-024   Values—Very Good **$475**   Exc. **$1,250**
Pistol Only Without Stock:
5H-025   Values—Very Good **$225**   Exc. **$550**

Stevens New Model Pocket Rifle, Second Issue

New Model Pocket Rifle, Second Issue. (Not illus.) Made c. 1875 to 1896. Total quantity estimated about 15,000. About identical to First Issue.

Basically the same as its predecessor, the major difference in the firing pin mounting in the frame with a bushing (rather than on the hammer itself). Late specimens eliminated the sideplate also.

Calibers 22 short, long, long rifle rimfire, 22 W.R.F., 25 Stevens and 32 long rimfire or centerfire. Frame nickel plated with barrel blued; detachable stock nickeled finish.

Barrel marking: J. STEVENS & CO. CHICOPEE/FALLS, MASS.or J. STEVENS A&T CO.with either marking accompanied by patent date.

As with the above First Issue, this has been reclassified under the Gun Control Act as an antique, and therefore no longer subject to Gun Control provisions:

Complete With Detachable Shoulder Stock:
5H-026   Values—Very Good **$475**   Exc. **$1,250**
Pistol Only Without Stock:
5H-027   Values—Very Good **$225**   Exc. **$550**

Stevens Vernier New Model Pocket Rifle

Vernier New Model Pocket Rifle. (Not illus.) Made c. 1884 to 1896. Total quantity estimated about 1,500.

Basically identical to the New Model Pocket Rifle, Second Issue, but with the addition of a Vernier tang peep sight on the backstrap and an open sight at breech end of barrel located further up the barrel than the Second Issue. Made in same calibers as above except 25 Stevens.

Barrel marking: J. STEVENS & CO. CHICOPEE/FALLS, MASS.or J. STEVENS A&T CO.with either marking accompanied by patent date. The sights are very important; if lacking, value lowered 30 to 40 percent.

This has been reclassified under the Gun Control Act as an antique, and therefore no longer subject to Gun Control Act provisions:

Complete With Detachable Shoulder Stock:
5H-028   Values—Very Good **$650**   Exc. **$1,750**
Pistol Only Without Stock:
5H-029   Values—Very Good **$400**   Exc. **$875**

Stevens New Model Pocket Shotgun

New Model Pocket Shotgun. (Not illus.) Made c. 1876 to 1917. Total quantity estimated about 3,000.

Calibers 38 or 44 Stevens Everlasting, 38-40 or 44-40 shot and 410 gauge. 10", 12", 15", or 18" part octagon/part round barrels. Substantially same as preceding pocket rifles.

Brass frame with semi-circular sideplate, nickeled finish; barrel blued. Detachable shoulder stock nickeled finish. Rosewood or walnut grips

About identical to New Model Pocket Rifle, Second Issue (with same markings), except for its smoothbore shotgun type barrel. Often known as the "Taxidermist Model" for its preference by some hunters for obtaining skins with minimum damage. Most calibers of this model are classified under Gun Control Act as "curio and relic;" caliber 44 Everlasting is considered an "antique" and not subject to G.C.A. (likely 38 Everlasting, too, but not verified), while those in 410 gauge are subject to provisions and restrictions of the N.F.A. No exact production/serial number information is available for this model. However, any of them (except 410) which can be documented as being produced prior to 1899 would be considered as "antiques" and hence not subject to G.C.A. provisions:

Complete With Detachable Shoulder Stock:
5H-030   Values—Very Good **$600**   Exc. **$1,500**
Pistol Only Without Stock:
5H-031   Values—Very Good **$325**   Exc. **$700**

Stevens New Model Pocket Rifle No. 40

5H-032

New Model Pocket Rifle No. 40. Made c. 1896 to 1916. Total quantity estimated about 15,000.

Calibers 22 long rifle, 22 W.R.F., 22 Stevens-Pope, 25 Stevens rimfire and 32 long rimfire or centerfire. 10", 12", 15", and 18" octagon or part octagon/part round barrels. Firing pin in frame without bushing.

Iron frame finished either blued or nickel plated; barrels blued. Detachable shoulder stock nickel plated. Walnut grips.

Barrel markings all J. STEVENS A & T CO. without the patent date.

A modification of the New Model Pocket Rifle, this No. 40 has a longer grip, modified rear sight and trigger with trigger guard. Classified under the Gun Control Act as a "curio and relic," no exact production/serial number information is available for this model. However, calibers 25 Stevens rimfire and 32 Long rimfire and any of them which can be documented as being produced prior to 1899 would be considered as "antique" and hence not subject to G.C.A. provisions:
Complete With Detachable Shoulder Stock:
5H-032   Values—Very Good **$400**   Exc. **$1,250**
Pistol Only Without Stock:
5H-033   Values—Very Good **$200**   Exc. **$550**

Stevens New Model Pocket Shotgun No. 39

New Model Pocket Shotgun No. 39. (Not illus.) Made c. 1896 to 1905. Total quantity estimated about 1,000.

A shotgun version of the No. 40 above, differing only in its smoothbore barrel and chambered for 38 or 44 Stevens Everlasting, 38-40, 44-40 shot or 410 gauge. Shotgun type sights.

Barrel markings all J. STEVENS A & T CO. without patent date.

Classification for this model under the Gun Control Act is identical to that described above for the "New Model Pocket Shotgun." Only the caliber 410 subject to the provisions of the National Firearms Act:
Complete With Detachable Shoulder Stock:
5H-034   Values—Very Good **$575**   Exc. **$1,400**
Pistol Only Without Stock:
5H-034.5   Values—Very Good **$325**   Exc. **$700**

Stevens Vernier New Model Pocket Rifle No. 40-1/2

Vernier New Model Pocket Rifle No. 40-1/2. (Not illus.) Made c. 1896 to 1915. Total quantity estimated about 2,500. Virtually identical to the New Model Pocket Rifle No. 40, but with addition of a Vernier peep sight on the backstrap and an open sight at breech end of the part octagon/part round barrel. Like the No. 40, it also has full oval trigger guard with conventional trigger. The sights are very important; if lacking, value lowered 30 to 40 percent.

Classified under the Gun Control Act as a "curio and relic." No exact production/serial number information is available for this model. However, any of them which can be documented as being produced prior to 1899 would be considered as "antiques" and hence not subject to G.C.A. provisions:
Complete With Detachable Shoulder Stock:
5H-035   Values—Very Good **$700**   Exc. **$1,500**
Pistol Only Without Stock:
5H-036   Values—Very Good **$400**   Exc. **$900**

Heavy Frame Types (Frames 1-1/4" Width)

Stevens Hunter's Pet Pocket Rifle No. 34

5H-037

Hunter's Pet Pocket Rifle No. 34. Made c. 1872 to 1900. Total quantity estimated at about 4,000.

Made in a great variety of calibers from 22 short rimfire to 44-40 centerfire. 18", 20", 22", and 24" part octagon/part round barrels. Largest calibers and longest barrels will command premium value. Iron frame nickel plated; barrel blued.

Detachable shoulder stock nickel finished. Walnut grips. A very small quantity of these were made with brass frames and such specimens will command 50 percent to 100 percent premiums in values. Firing pin in frame with bushing.

Earlier specimens bear the first type J. STEVENS & CO., etc. one-line markings, whereas later manufactured bear both types of the two-line J. STEVENS A & T CO. markings. Prices are the same for all types.

A very popular short rifle of the period, the factory is known to have made some specimens fitted with matching 20 gauge shotgun barrels and others were known to have been sold with interchangeable barrels of varying calibers. Classified under the

Gun Control Act as a "curio and relic." As with other "pocket rifles" of this type, any which can be documented as being produced prior to 1899 would be considered as "antiques" and hence not subject to G.C.A. provisions:

Complete With Detachable Shoulder Stock:
5H-037   Values—Very Good **$650**   Exc. **$1,650**
Pistol Only Without Stock:
5H-038   Values—Very Good **$275**   Exc. **$750**

Stevens Vernier Hunter's Pet Pocket Rifle No. 34-1/2

Vernier Hunter's Pet Pocket Rifle No. 34-1/2. (Not illus.) Made c. 1884 to 1900. Total quantity estimated about 1,200.

About identical to the above with the addition of a Vernier tang peep sight fitted on the backstrap and special front and rear sights for barrel (the rear sight positioned considerably further forward than on the No. 34). Serial number of the Vernier peep sight matches that of the gun.

Markings identical to above except very few are found with the earliest J. STEVENS & CO., etc. type. The sights are very

important; if lacking, value lowered 30 to 40 percent.

Classified under the Gun Control Act as a "curio and relic." Its status would be identical to that described above for the "Pocket rifle No. 34."

Complete With Detachable Shoulder Stock:
5H-039   Values—Very Good **$750**   Exc. **$1,850**
Pistol Only Without Stock:
5H-040   Values—Very Good **$425**   Exc. **$875**

Longarms

Stevens Tip-Up Rifles

Without Forend

With Forend

This series was first introduced in the 1870s and manufactured in several variations until the line was discontinued c. 1895. Officially termed by Stevens in their catalogs as rifles No. 1 through No. 15, each was correspondingly named, e.g., "Open Sight Rifle"; "Combined Sight Rifle"; "Expert Rifle"; "Premier Rifle"; "Ladies' Rifle"; "Crack Shot Rifle," etc. There exists in certain arms literature and among non-advanced collectors some confusion as to the exact nomenclature on these. For instance, the 1888 catalog assigns rifles No. 15 and No. 16 the official names of "Crack Shot Rifles," yet subsequent catalogs assign these same numbers to two different boys' rifles (q.v.).

Until a detailed statistical survey is made on the Tip-Up rifles and until simplified identification may be made for each numbered model of the series, it may be generally stated that most specimens (with exceptions noted in the following descriptions) are sought primarily on the basis of their condition, with minor differentiating points not playing key roles in either collecting or evaluating them.

The best means of identifying each model is through original or reprint Stevens catalogs. Of course, considerable information may be gleaned from the various James Grant books on single shot rifles.

Stylistically the Tip-Ups are all about identical with a distinctive nickel plated iron frame (often termed "step-down" type). Frames might vary slightly in contour, with just three sizes noted: the rifle size, shotgun size and a lighter weight type made for the so-called LADIES' MODELS. Either full octagon or part octagon/part round barrels will be found, with standard lengths on most models of 24", 26", 28", and 30"; the Ladies' rifle only was standard in 24" and 26". Variances also are noted in the shape of

the trigger guard with either a flat trigger guard tang or the so-called "pistol grip shape" of the lower tang.

Model numbers are frequently, but not always, found on these tip-ups. They can be seen (without removing the trigger guard) on the lower tang of the stock, just under the lower "loop" that is formed as an extension of the trigger bow. When numbers are not present, distinctions between the less expensive models (Nos. 1 through 6 as well as Nos. 15 and 16) which were not equipped with wooden forends and the Model Nos. 7 through 14 which were equipped with a matching wooden forend. Other major features which will increase value are the use of select grains of wood for the stock, Swiss type nickel plated buttplates and large tang and Vernier peep sights. Of course, full length Stevens telescopic sights if present will also add premiums. When originally offered through the Stevens catalogs, the only options were in barrel lengths and calibers. Other features such as fancy grained stocks and sights served to distinguish one model from another, and hence, were factory standard with those models.

Calibers often are an identifying feature for the tip-up series and the reader is again referred to original catalogs as well as the Grant single shot rifle books for detailed specifications. Calibers varied from 22 rimfire to 44 centerfire.

Finish is quite standard throughout all the series, with nickel plated actions, trigger guards and buttplates, and blued barrels. Generally condition, both exterior and bores, serves as the most important factor in creating demand and establishing values.

Brass frames are encountered on very early model rifle size Tip-Ups. Highest serial recorded 1291. Cursory research indicates first 500-600 likely all in brass with brass intermixed with iron frames to about serial 1300. Although scarce, only slight premiums likely:

Tip-Up Rifles Without Forends. Plain grain walnut stocks; open sights; octagon or part octagon/part round barrels (Nos. 1 through 6, 15 and 16):
5H-041   Values—Very Good **$300**   Exc. **$650**

Tip-Up Rifles With Matching Walnut Forend. Octagon/round barrels; Swiss type buttplates; large folding tang peep sights and open barrel sights; plain grain walnut stocks (fancy grain wood brings premium), Nos. 7 through 10:

5H-042 Values—Very Good **$550** Exc. **$1,400**

Ladies' Models Tip-Up Rifles. A distinctive style easily distinguished from the others in the series by its slightly smaller lighter weight frame; shorter buttstock and forend with the latter having a wide metal joint on its lower end (where it meets the frame) that is not seen on any other tip-up number; has pistol grip shaped trigger guard tang; calibers 22 rimfire and 25 rimfire only. 24" and 26" light weight octagon/round barrel. Made in four distinct models:

No. 11. Plain wood; open sights:
5H-043 Values—Very Good **$650** Exc. **$1,150**

No. 12. Fancy grained wood; open sights:
5H-044 Values—Very Good **$850** Exc. **$1,750**

No. 13. Beach type front, open rear and Vernier tang sights; plain walnut stock:
5H-045 Values—Very Good **$1,000** Exc. **$2,250**

No. 14. As above, but with extra fancy grained stock and forend:
5H-046 Values—Very Good **$1,250** Exc. **$2,750**

Tip-Up Shotgun. 10, 12, 14, 16, and 20 gauge; 30" and 32" barrels of either twist or plain finish; frames finished nickeled or browned; made with matching forend. These could be purchased with interchangeable (matched number) barrels and forend, and if accompanying the shotgun, will increase value of the piece 15 percent to 25 percent, depending on quality and condition:

5H-047 Values—Very Good **$200** Exc. **$400**

Stevens Ideal Single Shot Rifles

Study and identification of this series is often confusing to the neophyte and the advanced trader—or for that matter, just about anyone who is not a Stevens specialist! Sorting out a few basic facts will help to understand this famous group of guns and place them more clearly in perspective.

In 1893 Stevens introduced the first of their famous series of single shot rifles known as the IDEAL model; a falling block type lever action made over the years in a great many calibers, variations and styles. First made as the Model 44, these numerals indicated both a model number and name, while the action used on that type was utilized for other Stevens single shot rifles through to the Model No. 54.

In 1904 Stevens introduced a similar appearing, newer, stronger action, the No. 44-1/2, newly designed for smokeless powder. The older 44 action was discontinued on all heavier caliber rifles and made only in lighter calibers 22 rimfire, 25 Stevens rimfire, 32 long rimfire, 25-20 centerfire and 32-20 centerfire (and even these latter centerfire calibers were eventually discontinued).

The 44-1/2 was both a rifle model number as well as an action only, incorporated and used on the other Stevens models up to the No. 54 and the No. 56; supplanting this newer type action on the very same model that had formerly utilized the 44 style action.

Thus, many numbers of the Ideal series of Stevens will be found with two distinct action types. On models which may be found with either type action, the one with the 44-1/2 will normally bring higher values. On mint or near mint/factory new specimens, the price disparity is small—possibly 10 percent, but as condition falls off, the disparity becomes greater—averaging 15 percent to 30 percent. On lesser conditioned pieces, especially those in larger calibers or which might have value for their action to rebuild as a modern shooter, the stronger 44-1/2 action is certainly in heavier demand and will bring a higher value. Thus, it is very much a matter of to whom and for what purpose the gun is sold.

The 44-1/2 action, although resembling the earlier falling block 44 action is quite different from it and was termed by Stevens as a "sliding bolt" type with the breechblock sliding vertically in the receiver. Upon closing, the breech starts forward and upward simultaneously (a "rocking" motion) and after seating the cartridge in the chamber, it slides vertically upward into place.

Model numbers are usually found marked on the front face of the action (forend must be removed to see). On very late production rifles these numbers are often seen on the lower tang, behind the trigger. Standard models, numbers 44, 44-1/2, 044-1/2, will be so marked. If rifle is a higher or custom grade, numerals 45 through 54 will often be seen (but no indication to differentiate the 44 or 44-1/2 action used). These higher

numerals usually create confusion as the rifle they are marked on does not resemble the Stevens catalog description of that particular model number. Such rifles were special orders and merely variations.

The basic differences in identifying the old 44 from the 44-1/2 action are: (a) The 44 has a hump-like side profile (or silhouette) to the frame from the point just behind the hammer to extreme rear where it joins the stock. The 44-1/2 has a very even downward curve in that same area. (b) The 44 action has a screw in the center of the left side of the receiver slightly ahead and below the breechblock, whereas the 44-1/2 has no screw at that point. (c) On the 44 action the screw head for the lever hinge pin is visible on the left side of the receiver, whereas on the 44-1/2 only the blank, smooth end of the hinge pin is seen on the left side of the receiver.

Both the 44 and the 44-1/2 are take-down types allowing for interchangeable barrels. Manufacture continued through 1916 on most and to the 1930s on a few of the more popular styles. As the models developed and newer ones were introduced, a very wide range of options became available, allowing for a tremendous amount of variation; so many that the collector can concentrate exclusively on Ideals and find it difficult to exhaust the possible combinations. Model numbers may often be confusing as the first types with 44 frame were originally introduced as the Nos. 107, 108, 109, 110. After the company reorganized in 1896, model numbers were changed to the more familiar Nos. 44 through 55. Old Stevens catalogs are of extreme significance to the collector, containing a great wealth of important data; quite a bit will be found at variance with information shown in some of the more popular present-day reference works.

Models are described here in their basic styles as listed by Stevens catalogs. Other options (such as telescope or other special sights, stocks, levers, set triggers, special buttplates, barrel lengths or weights) if not standard will usually add a premium to the value—the amount of the premium very much depending on the nature of the option and the condition of the rifle on which it appears. Barrels were made up to 34" in length and in five weights. The longest lengths and the heaviest weights are quite scarce and will add 25 percent and often more to values. It is interesting to note when reading Stevens catalogs that many options offered when models were first introduced, were subsequently dropped and not available in later years. Basic features were sometimes changed as the model remained in the line.

Finishes of the Ideals are generally blued barrels with casehardened receivers. Engraved specimens (in various grades) were standard on some models and are so noted in the following descriptions and are reflected in their values. Where engraving is not a standard feature of the rifle, in many cases it was available at an extra price; such engraving when found will certainly add premiums to the value. The subject has been well discussed in other sections of this book.

Stevens-Pope Barrels

In 1901 Stevens succeeded in luring one of America's most famed riflesmiths, Harry M. Pope, of Hartford, to work for them. From this venture the famed "Stevens-Pope" specialty line grew. The union was short-lived, however, due to personality clashes between the old master and company officials. Originally contracted for a five year period, Pope severed his union with the company c. 1903 and went his own way. The story is quite a famous one in American arms as well as in Stevens factory history, and is well recorded in just about every book on the subject of Stevens or American single shot rifles. As a matter of fact, an entire book is devoted to Harry Pope's specialties (*The Story Of Pope's Barrels*). For purposes of identification and evaluation here, suffice to say that c. 1901 to 1903 a special line of barrels were custom made under Harry Pope's supervision at the Stevens factory. These barrels are mentioned and listed in the various Stevens catalogs of the period as "extras" and could be custom ordered in many styles, weights, lengths and calibers. During that short period of Harry Pope's employ at Stevens the company actually issued an extensive, well-illustrated *Stevens-Pope Catalog of Rifle Barrels and Specialties*, highly descriptive of Pope accessories and the rifles. The basic identifying feature is the name STEVENS-POPE marked on the top of the barrel in addition to the standard factory markings. Rifles came in two basic styles: (a) The usual breech-loading type and (b) muzzle-loading type, i.e., a regular barrel, but with a detachable false muzzle and bullet starter.

No simplified formula exists for pricing these arms. The collector must do some research into the nuances of Pope's work, the style of his rifling, as well as the arm on which it appears in order to arrive at an accurate value. A general rule-of-thumb would have it that on standard breech-loading Stevens

with "Stevens-Pope" marked barrels, values may be increased 25 percent to 50 percent, and with muzzle-loading barrels values may be increased 50 percent to 100 percent or possibly even more. A key factor is not merely the name Stevens-Pope, but the condition of the gun. If the rifling is in poor condition, then the gun is not much more than a curiosity for the major price factor is the state of the bore. It is also very important to establish that the bore is the original Pope as cut at the factory and not one later recut or enlarged by some other riflesmith. If the latter, the value is reduced considerably! A last feature to note is that the muzzle-loading type was originally accompanied by a false muzzle. Said muzzle must be intact with the gun! If lost and missing, it is like finding an automobile without an engine—detracting considerably from an increased premium.

One small nuance on Stevens-Pope barrels is the fact that those bearing Serial No. 1 through 1200 are considered more valuable than specimens with higher numbers. Pope was quite disgruntled with his arrangement at the factory and never stayed out his full contract. It is known that barrels numbered up to Serial No. 1200 were made directly under his supervision, and hence, seem to be in somewhat stronger demand. They will bring a premium price over barrels bearing later serial numbers which were made under the same system with the same tools and machinery, but not under Pope's personal supervision. The factory continued the "Stevens-Pope" system for a few years afterwards. Almost all of the barrels made under Pope's personal supervision were fitted with the 44 type action. The 44-1/2 was not introduced until 1904 subsequent to Pope's severing association with the factory, although the Stevens-Pope operation did continue without his supervision in the latter years.

Note also that Stevens offered a service of re-rifling other makers' barrels (if sent in individually by customers) to Stevens-Pope bores. As specifically advertised in their catalog "… We recut rifles of other makes or smaller calibers to larger sizes with the same outfit and guarantee as for a new barrel, etc." Hence, the collector may occasionally encounter an apparent anomaly of a Winchester, Remington or other rifle bearing additional "Stevens-Pope" markings; accounted for in light of the foregoing. Also to note are the barrels with Stevens-Pope rifling made for the standard U.S. Model 1898 Springfield Krag action. They are discussed in the American Military Longarms section, Chapter IX (*q.v.*).

STEVENS BARRELS ON OTHER MAKE ACTIONS

Stevens catalogs also noted "New barrels (not necessarily those of H.M. Pope) 24 to 34 inches…octagon or half octagon…will be fitted to center-fire Ballard, Sharps hammerless (Borchardt), Remington, Winchester single shot actions using old fore-ends (an extra charge for new fore-ends)…and to Maynard actions, but owing to extra work require extra charge." A wide range of calibers were offered from .22 to 40-70.

Note: Prices include sights as specified. If sights lacking deduct approximately 20-30 percent from price.

Stevens "Removable Sideplate" Ideal Rifle

Removable Sideplate Ideal Rifle. Made c. 1893 to mid-1894. Quantity estimated (together with the removable sideplate "Favorite") about 2,000. Calibers 22 rimfire through 38 centerfire. Part octagon/part round barrels varying in length.

Stevens' first underlever single shot. Based on the Ottis W. Horr patent, August 11, 1885. Actually listed in company advertising flyer of November, 1893, as the "STEVENS IDEAL." The predecessor of that famous model and closely resembling it; sides of receiver more exposed with angular openings and a

5H-047.5

removable plate on right side of receiver. Has quick take-down system with variations noted for both slip shanks and threaded shanks. Variations in four-screw and five-screw frames also:

5H-047.5   Values—Very Good **$1,500**   Exc. **$4,000**

Stevens Ideal Rifle No. 44

5H-048

Ideal Rifle No. 44. Made c. 1894 to 1933. Total quantity estimated at about 100,000.

Calibers 22, 25, and 32 rimfire and 25-20, 32-20, 32-40, 38-40, 38-55, and 44-40 centerfire. Also made on special order in 22 short rimfire, 22-7-45 W.R.F., 22-15-60, and special Stevens calibers of 25-21, 25-25, 28-30-120, 32-20, and 32 Ideal. After 1904 available only in 22, 25 Stevens and 32 long rimfire calibers and 25-20 and 32-20 centerfire calibers. Eventually the latter two were discontinued also.

Standard barrels were of No. 2 weight and part octagon/part round; 24" for rimfire and 26" for centerfire. Rocky Mountain front sight and open sporting rear sights.

Standard finish: Casehardened frame with blued barrel. Oil finished walnut stocks; nickel plated rifle style buttplate in center fire calibers:

5H-048   Values—Very Good **$450**   Exc. **$1,100**
As above in rimfire calibers:
5H-048.2   Values—Very Good **$350**   Exc. **$900**

Stevens Ideal Rifle No. 44-1/2

5H-049

Ideal Rifle No. 44-1/2. Made c. 1903 to 1916.

Same calibers as No. 44 and also on special order in 30-30 and 30-40 U.S. (quite scarce and will bring premium).

Barrel lengths, types and sights as on No. 44. Many options available including barrel lengths up to 34" and Stevens-Pope barrels; shotgun or Swiss butt, etc. in center fire calibers:

5H-049   Values—Very Good **$750**   Exc. **$1,850**
As above in rimfire calibers:
5H-049.2   Values—Very Good **$625**   Exc. **$1,400**

Stevens Ideal English Model Rifle No. 044-1/2

5H-050

Ideal English Model Rifle No. 044-1/2. Made c. 1903 to 1916.

Calibers 22, 25 and 32 rimfire and 25-20 and 32-20 centerfire. On special order calibers 22 short and 22-7-45 W.R.F. and 22-15-60, 25-21, 25-25 and 28-30-120 Stevens centerfire and others. 24" part round/part octagon barrel (for rimfire calibers) and 26" for centerfire calibers. Barrels very tapered. Rocky Mountain front sight and V type sporting rear sight.

Finish blued with casehardened frame. Oil finished walnut stock; shotgun style hard rubber buttplate.

The Model 044-1/2 differed mainly in its shotgun butt, weight and very tapered barrel. Numerous options were available including full octagon barrel, loop lever, Swiss buttplate, various barrel lengths. Some of the options available in early years were later dropped in center fire calibers:

5H-050   Values—Very Good **$850**   Exc. **$2,000**
As above in rimfire calibers:
5H-050.2   Values—Very Good **$650**   Exc. **$1,400**

Stevens Ideal "Range Model" Rifle No. 45

Ideal "Range Model" Rifle No. 45. Made c. 1896 to 1916. Similar to above with wide range of calibers from 22 short rimfire to 44-40.

Basic differences are the Beach combination front and open rear barrel sights with Vernier tang sight and Swiss buttplate.

Part octagon/part round No. 2 barrel standard with 26" for rimfire cartridges and 28" for centerfire. Numerous options available:

5H-051

44 Action in center fire calibers:
5H-051   Values—Very Good **$850**   Exc. **$1,750**
As above in rimfire calibers:
5H-051.2   Values—Very Good **$750**   Exc. **$1,400**
44-1/2 Action in center fire calibers:
5H-051.5   Values—Very Good **$1,000**   Exc. **$2,250**

As above in rimfire calibers:
5H-051.7   Values—Very Good **$850**   Exc. **$1,750**

Stevens Ideal "Range" Model Rifle No. 46

Ideal "Range" Model Rifle No. 46. (Not illus.) First made c. 1896.

Identical to the No. 45 except fancy grained stock. The model number was dropped shortly after its introduction and the fancy grained stock was merely included as an extra with the No. 45.
5H-052

Stevens Ideal "Modern Range" Rifle No. 47

5H-053

Ideal "Modern Range" Rifle No. 47. Made c. 1896 to 1916.

Available in a wide range of calibers from 22 rimfire to 44-40 centerfire. Barrels standard as part octagon/part round; 26" length for rimfire and 28" for centerfire.

Basically same as the Ideal Range No. 45 with addition of the following: Pistol grip buttstock; Swiss style buttplate; full loop style lever (of a design similar to those found on lever action repeating rifles of the era); Beach type front and open rear barrel sights with Vernier tang peep sight. Numerous options were also available:

44 Action in center fire calibers:
5H-053   Values—Very Good **$1,250**   Exc. **$2,250**
As above in rimfire calibers:
5H-053.2   Values—Very Good **$875**   Exc. **$1,750**
44-1/2 Action in center fire calibers:
5H-053.5   Values—Very Good **$1,400**   Exc. **$2,750**
As above in rimfire calibers:
5H-053.7   Values—Very Good **$1,100**   Exc. **$2,250**

Stevens Ideal "Modern Range" Rifle No. 48

Ideal "Modern Range" Rifle No. 48. (Not illus.) Made c. 1896 to 1916.

Identical to the No. 47, but with deluxe, fancy grained checkered pistol grip stock and forend. Like the No. 46, this model was later discontinued after its introduction and merely included as an extra with the No. 47.
5H-054

Stevens Ideal "Walnut Hill" Rifle No. 49

5H-055

Ideal "Walnut Hill" Rifle No. 49. Made c. 1896 to 1930s.

Considerable range of calibers from 22 rimfire short to 44-40. 28" and 30" part round/part octagonal barrels standard either No. 2 or No. 3 weight. Globe interchangeable front sight and Vernier tang peep (with a number of other options available).

Standard finish blued barrel with casehardened frame. Varnished and checkered, pistol grip plain walnut stock with high comb and cheek-piece. Swiss type buttplate; full loop lever. Globe interchangeable windgauge front sight and tall Vernier tang peep (barrel not mortised for rear sight). Engraving in a variety of patterns was standard on the receivers. Numerous extra options were available including many Schuetzen styles in levers, buttplates, palm rests, etc.

The Walnut Hill series is highly regarded by Stevens collectors and aficionados of the single shot rifle. It has a high rating for accuracy and the model remained in production into the second quarter of the 20th century:
44 Action:
5H-055   Values—Very Good **$1,750**   Exc. **$4,500**
44-1/2 Action:
5H-055.5   Values—Very Good **$2,500**   Exc. **$6,500**

Stevens Ideal "Walnut Hill" Rifle No. 50

Ideal "Walnut Hill" Rifle No. 50. (Not illus.) Identical to the Model 49, but with fancy grained stock. This model number was used until 1916 when discontinued and the fancy stock was merely included as an "extra" with the No. 49. In 1927 the model number was revived and used until 1932:

5H-056   Values—Very Good **$1,750**   Exc. **$4,500**

Stevens Ideal "Schuetzen Rifle" No. 51

5H-057

Ideal "Schuetzen Rifle" No. 51. Made c. 1896 to 1916. Basically the Walnut Hill No. 49, but with following extras as standard: Double set triggers, extra fancy Swiss type checkered stock of select grain and with cheekpiece—made in straight stock without pistol grip; large heavy Schuetzen style buttplate and short loop lever with two-piece wood panel insert. Globe interchangeable front and Vernier tang rear peep sights; barrel not mortised for rear sight. A number of "extras" were available including palm rest, bullet starter and false muzzle, special sights and variations in barrel lengths and weights. Scroll engraved designs on the receivers were standard. This model usually encountered in the No. 4 barrel weight:

44 Action:
5H-057   Values—Very Good **$2,750**   Exc. **$5,750**
44-1/2 Action:
5H-057.5   Values—Very Good **$3,500**   Exc. **$8,000**

Stevens Ideal "Schuetzen Junior" Rifle No. 52

Ideal "Schuetzen Junior" Rifle No. 52. (Not illus.) Made c. 1897 to 1916.

Quite similar to the No. 51, but having the following features: Either the full loop type or three-finger spur lever; engraving of better quality and fancier on receiver; fancy grained checkered pistol-grip stock and heavy Schuetzen style buttplate. Usually found with a No. 3 or No. 4 weight barrel. Numerous special extra options were available:

44 Action:
5H-058   Values—Very Good **$2,750**   Exc. **$6,000**
44-1/2 Action:
5H-058.5   Values—Very Good **$3,500**   Exc. **$8,000**

Stevens Ideal "Schuetzen Special" Rifle No. 54

5H-059

Ideal "Schuetzen Special" Rifle No. 54. Made c. 1897 to 1916 (No No. 53 appears to have been made or issued in the Ideal line).

Quite similar to the Schuetzen Junior No. 52, but differing in the following details: Massive Swiss style long curved prong buttplate; special finger lever; straight type checkered stock with a walnut two-piece panel in the finger lever to form a better grip; double set triggers; standard barrel length of 30" and 32"; palm rest sometimes advertised as standard in various catalogs. Large array of extra options were also available. Stevens highest grade; fine quality and profuse engraving was standard on it:

44 Action:
5H-059   Values—Very Good **$4,000**   Exc. **$9,000**
44-1/2 Action:
5H-059.5   Values—Very Good **$5,500**   Exc. **$12,000**

Stevens Ideal "Ladies' Model" Rifle No. 55

Ideal "Ladies' Model" Rifle No. 55. (Not illus. Identical in appearance to No. 56.) Made c. 1897 to 1916.

Calibers 22 short and long rimfire, 22-7-45 W.R.F., 25 Stevens rimfire and 32 long rimfire. 24" part octagon/part round barrel standard (with longest length available on special order 26"). Beach combination front sight, open type rear and Vernier tang peep sight.

Blued finish; casehardened frame. Believed made on the "FAVORITE" action (see 5H-065). Checkered pistol grip buttstock and forend with the plain (No. 1) "S" curved lever; Swiss style buttplate standard (and preferred), but was available as standard with shotgun style hard rubber buttplate.

A light weight nicely made single shot, especially geared to the ladies' and boys' market and proved one of the most popular of the Stevens rifles. Made on the "Favorite" frame. Differs from "Ladies' Model 21" (5H-068) as barrel is threaded into frame and secured with screws:

5H-060   Values—Very Good **$1,250**   Exc. **$3,000**

Stevens Ideal "Ladies Model" Rifle No. 56

5H-061

Ideal "Ladies Model" Rifle No. 56. Made c. 1906 to 1916. About identical to the No. 55, but also available on special order in centerfire calibers 22-15-60, 25-20 Stevens, 25-21, 25-25, 28-30-120 and 32-20. 24" octagon/round barrel standard for rimfire and 26" for centerfire.

Fancier grained checkered walnut stocks; tapered barrel. Made only on the 44-1/2 action:

5H-061   Values—Very Good **$2,250**   Exc. **$4,500**

Stevens Ideal "Semi-Military Rifle" No. 404

5H-062

Ideal "Semi-Military Rifle" No. 404. Made c. 1910 to 1916.

Caliber 22 rimfire only. 28" round barrel. Globe type front sight (with interchangeable discs) and Lyman No. 42 receiver sight with cup disc.

Blued barrel with casehardened frame. Walnut straight stock with semi-beavertail forend 12" in length and checkered; forend fastened with screw on underside (does not use barrel band) and sling swivel fitted to underside of barrel just ahead of forend. Shotgun style hard rubber buttplate Plain (No. 1) "S" shaped lever:

5H-062   Values—Very Good **$750**   Exc. **$1,250**

Stevens Ideal "Armory Model" Rifle No. 414

Ideal "Armory Model" Rifle No. 414. (Not illus.) Made c. 1912 to 1932.

Caliber 22 short or long rifle rimfire. 26" round barrel on the 44 type action. Rocky Mountain front sight, Lyman receiver rear sight (made specifically for this gun); tang tapped also for sights.

Blued barrel with casehardened frame; walnut straight stock with semi-beaver tail style forend fastened by single barrel band. Sling swivel on barrel band and underside of butt; shotgun hard rubber buttplate. Plain (No. 1) "S" shaped lever. Styling of this model was that of a military musket:

5H-063   Values—Very Good **$450**   Exc. **$900**

Boys' Rifles

Stevens was one of America's most prolific makers of small caliber rifles for young boys. Many of their varied line of such arms have achieved considerable collector status over the years and are listed here in chronological order by year first made. The exclusion of their extensive series of bolt-action types does not indicate their lack of collectibility, but merely an arbitrary cut-off point chosen by the author. It has been his experience that these following described rifles have always been quite popular as "antique" collectors' arms and have met with an ever-increasing demand and interest in recent years.

Stevens "Favorite" Rifles

Stevens "Favorite" Rifles. Made c. 1893 to 1939. Quantity estimated made (of all styles) approximately 1,000,000.

5H-064
First Model Favorite

Caliber 22 (in BB, CB, short, long and long rifle), 25, and 32 rimfire as standard; also made in 22-7-45 (22 W.R.F.). 22" part round/part octagon barrel; plain open sights.

Blued barrel with casehardened frame. Oil finished walnut stocks; shotgun style hard rubber buttplate.

The Favorite series was one of the most popular and best selling of all Stevens rifles. It offered dual advantages of take-down and interchangeable barrels. For changing to another caliber barrel, it was necessary to change breechblocks; a quickly done process.

A great many marking variations may be encountered; all will include the Stevens "A & T" name and many (but not all) include the model name FAVORITE.

5H-065
Standard Model Favorite

5H-068
Favorite Ladies' Model

Favorites, like the Tip-Up series, were made in numerous model types (No. 17, 18, 19, 21, 27, etc.). Over their long years of production many manufacturing variations occurred. It may be generally stated that collector interest and value-wise they are sought primarily on the basis of their condition, and minor differentiating features which often distinguish one model from another have not played important roles in either seeking them or evaluating them, except for a few of the most advanced specialists! Basic differences in models (such as the 17, 18, and 19) are merely sights.

A few of the more important types are listed here. Those that are found with features such as Vernier or other tang sights may have values increased proportionally:

First Model Favorite. Made 1893 to 1894. Rare. Noticeably different from later production with a removable plate on right side of receiver. Calibers 22 and 25 rimfire only. Quantity manufactured estimated at less than 1,000 and possibly but a few hundred:
5H-064   Values—Very Good **$750**   Exc. **$1,750**
Standard Model "Favorite" No. 17. The basic type. Plain open sights:

5H-065   Values—Very Good **$250**   Exc. **$600**
Favorite Shotgun No. 20. Chambered for caliber 22 or 32 rimfire shot cartridges with smoothbore barrel. Open type front sight and made without rear sight:
5H-066   Values—Very Good **$200**   Exc. **$500**
Favorite Bicycle Rifle No. 21. Shorter 20" barrel. Rocky Mountain front and Stevens leaf rear sights were standard, although various sight options were available including Verniers. Premiums may be added if accompanied by the original leather edged canvas carrying case in sound condition. Made c. 1898 to 1903:
5H-067   Values—Very Good **$250**   Exc. **$600**
Favorite Ladies' Model No. 21. The discontinued number of the Bicycle Rifle was given to this model. Made c. 1910 to 1916. 24" barrel standard, but 26" available. Fancy grained checkered pistol-grip stock and forend; Swiss buttplate; Beach type front and open rear sight with Vernier tang sights:
5H-068   Values—Very Good **$1,250**   Exc. **$3,000**

Stevens "Sure Shot" Rifle No. 23

5H-069

Stevens "Sure Shot" Rifle No. 23. Made c. 1894 to c 1897 or 1898. Caliber 22 rimfire. 20" round barrel swings sideways to right

to load with barrel release button on left frame.
Made without forend. The system is very similar to that on many of the early deringer single shot pistols including that of the Stevens "Gem." Very scarce:
5H-069   Values—Very Good **$1,150**   Exc. **$2,250**

Stevens "Crack Shot" Rifle No. 16

5H-070

Stevens "Crack Shot" Rifle No. 16. Made c. 1900 to 1913.
Calibers 22 and 32 rimfire. 20" round barrel. Plain open sights.
Finish blued barrel with casehardened frame. Two-piece oil finished walnut stocks, hard rubber buttplate.
Marked CRACK SHOT on the barrel along with usual Stevens markings.
This was another economy model Stevens which featured take-down construction. The action was of a rolling block type

operated by a thumb lever on the right side. It was the second model with this same designation and name; the earlier had been assigned to one of the Tip-Up series that had been discontinued in the 1890s:
5H-070   Values—Very Good **$150**   Exc. **$550**

Stevens "Crack Shot" Rifle No. 16-1/2

Stevens "Crack Shot" Rifle No. 16-1/2. (Not illus.) Made c. 1900 to 1913.

Identical to the No. 16, but chambered and bored for 32 rimfire shot cartridges:

5H-071   Values—Very Good **$150**   Exc. **$550**

Stevens "Maynard Junior" Rifle No. 15

5H-072

Stevens "Maynard Junior" Rifle No. 15. Made c. 1902 to 1912.
Caliber 22 rimfire. 18" part round/part octagon barrel.
Overall blued finish. Stock roughly cut by bandsaw from thin walnut board; edges rounded; a few later production better finished. Case hardened frame and varnished wood specimens known; worth premium.
Usual Stevens markings and also STEVENS-MAYNARD, JR.

This was an economy model in the Stevens line and its mechanism was taken from the Maynard rifle of the Civil War era:

5H-072   Values—Very Good **$250**   Exc. **$600**

Stevens "Maynard Junior" Rifle No. 15-1/2

Stevens "Maynard Junior" Rifle No. 15-1/2. (Not illus.) Made c. 1902 to 1912.

Identical to the No. 15, but smooth-bore and chambered for 22 rimfire shot cartridge:

5H-073   Values—Very Good **$250**   Exc. **$600**

Stevens "Little Krag" Rifle No. 65

5H-074

Stevens "Little Krag" Rifle No. 65. Made c. 1903 to 1910.
Caliber 22 rimfire. Single shot bolt action. 20" round barrel.
One-piece stock with short forend fastened to barrel by large screw with swivel top on underside of forend.
Usual Stevens barrel markings and also LITTLE KRAG. Blued finish. Scarce:

5H-074   Values—Very Good **$350**   Exc. **$700**

Stevens "Little Scout" Rifle No. 14

5H-075

Stevens "Little Scout" Rifle No. 14. Made c. 1906 to 1910.
Caliber 22 rimfire. 18" barrel. The one-piece stock quickly distinguishes it from the following Model 14-1/2. Take-down screw on underside of forend. Usual company name markings on barrel as well as LITTLE SCOUT:

5H-075   Values—Very Good **$125**   Exc. **$400**

Stevens "Little Scout" Rifle No. 14-1/2

5H-076

Stevens "Little Scout" Rifle No. 14-1/2. Made c. 1911 to 1941.

Caliber 22 rimfire. 20" barrel. Rolling block type action very similar to the No. 14, but sturdier frame and made with two-piece stock (which distinguishes it from the No. 14) with entire receiver and frame exposed (casehardened). Barrel marked with usual company name and address and LITTLE SCOUT:

5H-076 Values—Very Good **$125** Exc. **$400**

Stevens "Marksman" Rifle No. 12

Stevens "Marksman" Rifle No. 12. (Not illus.) Made c. 1911 to 1930.

Calibers 22, 25, and 32 rimfire. 22" tip-up barrel operated with "S" type under-lever. Blued barrel and frame.

Usual company name and address markings and MARKSMAN.

Action very similar to the Maynard Junior No. 15:

5H-077 Values—Very Good **$175** Exc. **$500**

Stevens "Crack Shot" No. 26 Rifle

Stevens "Crack Shot" No. 26 Rifle. (Not illus.) Made c. 1912 to 1939.

Calibers 22 and 32 rimfire. 18" barrel standard, but also available in 20" round barrel. Action very similar to the Little Scout No. 14. Two-piece stock. Blued overall or blued barrel and casehardened frame. Standard company name and address on barrel and left frame marked CRACK SHOT 26:

5H-078 Values—Very Good **$125** Exc. **$400**

Stevens "Crack Shot" No. 26-1/2 Rifle

Stevens "Crack Shot" No. 26-1/2 Rifle. (Not illus.) Identical to the above, but chambered and bored for 22 and 32 rimfire shot cartridges with smoothbore barrel.) Made c. 1912 to 1939:

5H-079 Values—Very Good **$125** Exc. **$400**

Stevens "Featherweight" Rifle No. 101

Stevens "Featherweight" Rifle No. 101. (Not illus.) Made c. 1914 to 1916.

Caliber 44 XL, 44 W.C.F. shot and 44 Game-Getter (all were interchangeable). This small piece was in fact a "44 Gauge" shotgun. Also offered in No. 3 Eley or 9mm calibers for export.

Identical in appearance to the Marksman No. 12 described above with a 26" round shotgun barrel and shotgun sights. Scarce. Estimated quantity made approximately 5,000:

5H-080 Values—Very Good **$225** Exc. **$500**

Stevens "Junior" Rifle No. 11

Stevens "Junior" Rifle No. 11. (Not illus.) Made c. 1924 to 1931.

Caliber 22 rimfire. 20" barrel. Stamped frame with rolling block type action and thumb lever on right.

Slab type stock made without buttplate. Blued finish.

Usual company markings and also STEVENS JUNIOR on barrel. The company's last effort in making an inexpensive, light weight rifle for young boys:

5H-081 Values—Very Good **$125** Exc. **$350**

Other Stevens of Interest

Stevens "Visible Loading" Pump Rifle

5H-082

"Visible Loading" Repeating Pump Action Rifle No. 70. Made c. 1907 to early 1930s. Includes in series also the Nos. 70-1/2, 71, 71-1/2, 72, 72-1/2.

Caliber 22 rimfire. 20" round barrel with three-quarter length magazine tube. Finish blued barrel with casehardened frame.

The model number differences indicate sight combinations only. The standard No. 70 had open sights. Vernier and other sights will bring small premiums in the finer conditioned specimens:

5H-082 Values—Very Good **$150** Exc. **$500**

Stevens "Gallery" No. 80 Pump Rifle

5H-083

Repeating "Gallery" No. 80 Pump Rifle. Made c. 1906 to 1910.
Caliber 22 rimfire. 24" round barrel with three-quarter length magazine tube. Open sights. Blued overall finish. Steel cap on the very short forend:

5H-083	Values—Very Good **$150**	Exc. **$350**

Stevens "High Power" Lever Action Rifle

5H-084

"High Power" Repeating Lever Action Rifle No. 425. Made c. 1910 to 1917. Estimated quantity made 26,000.

All calibers were for Remington centerfire cartridges 25, 30, 32 and 35 (Rem. CF). 22" round barrel with two-thirds length magazine tube; side ejection; full loop lever. Full blued finish. Walnut stocks:

5H-084   Values—Very Good **$550**   Exc. **$1,250**

No. 430. Identical to above, but with fancy grained checkered stock and forend:

5H-085   Values—Very Good **$800**   Exc. **$1,500**

No. 435. Identical, but with extra fancy checkered stock and forend; matted top of receiver with engraved designs edging border of receiver on both sides and on lever:

5H-086   Values—Very Good **$1,250**   Exc. **$3,000**

No. 440. Identical, but with fancy checkered stock and full engraved scenes and panels on receiver (with bear design, etc.); engraved forend tip and lever:

5H-087   Values—Very Good **$2,250**   Exc. **$5,000**

Stevens Three Trigger Shotgun

Three Trigger, Outside Hammer Double Barrel Shotgun. (Not illus.) Made 1876 to 1884. Estimated quantity few thousand.

10 and 12 gauge. 30" and 32" Damascus barrels; action and hammers case hardened. Was advertised as available with one rifle and one shot barrel in calibers 38 and 44; very scarce and worth premium of at least 50 percent.

An unusual appearance with double trigger guards and three triggers. Front guard and single trigger are to release latch to open barrels:

5H-088   Values—Good **$450**   Fine **$900**

Prices and descriptions of Stevens handguns as shown in an Iver Johnson catalog c.1890s.

Chapter V-I

Frank Wesson
(including Wesson & Harrington and Harrington & Richardson)

Indicative of the relative infancy of several categories of the American arms collecting field as well as the fact that many areas are still wide open for research and exploitation are these series of arms by Frank Wesson and associated firms. It is hardly likely that any other family name has had greater impact, nor been more widely involved, in 19th century American gun making. Frank Wesson's older brothers carved independent gun making careers, each achieving fame and success in their respective fields. Daniel B. Wesson was noted as the co-founder of the estimable firm of Smith & Wesson (*q.v.*) while Edwin Wesson was widely noted for his superb quality muzzle-loading, handcrafted percussion sporting and target rifles, considered to be some of the finest of the era.

Surprisingly little published material appears in modern day gun literature concerning Frank Wesson and his arms, and much of that is either erroneous or at best repeats generalities of early day authors, often not based on fact. Yet—his arms are relatively easily found and common on the collectors' market, testifying to their wide manufacture, popularity and public acceptance over a reasonably long period.

As with other sections of this book listing and describing various series of arms by American makers in which the author disclaims being the "last word" on the subject, he does take considerable pride in claiming this to be the "first word" in the Frank Wesson field! As will be seen from the following descriptions, the handguns and rifles of Frank Wesson offer a wide potential for the collector to amass a reasonably extensive collection encompassing an interesting cross-section of 19th century arms from single shot target pistols, deringers, revolvers, and pocket rifles to sporting rifles, while price-wise most are very much in the still easily "affordable" categories.

Although not reported here in detail as very little is known about them, it is also quite possible to locate double barrel shotguns and double rifles as well as shotgun-rifle combinations (and even barrel inserts to convert shotgun to rifle) that were also turned out in small quantities by Wesson.

Price fluctuations on the collectors' market for most of these arms have been extremely slight, based mainly on the lack of guidelines and knowledge about the guns themselves. Major types and styles (i.e., two-trigger rifles, pocket rifles and deringers) have been easily recognized, but the recognition has been accompanied by an almost complete lack of information and data on the numerous and distinct variations available. Thus, values indicated herein are based on the current collectors' market which has generally operated without prior knowledge of quantitative, chronological or manufacturing differences which normally affect values. It is quite conceivable that this first, basic listing of each of the production models and their major variations will affect values and more closely align them with price differences of variations of other well known American arms manufacturers. The author wishes neither to speculate nor recommend the reader pursue the purchase of any specific type, but certainly notes the value fluctuations observed in many collecting fields upon the publication of detailed data, in which values are based strictly upon manufacturing variances and other subtle distinctions.

A sufficient amount of new material included with the breakdowns of the various Wesson models should place all of his arms—especially the "pocket rifles" and the two-trigger series—in much clearer perspective for the collector. As will be seen in the two-trigger rifles, a definite chronological order exists—one which encompasses quite a few easily recognized major differentiating features. Other factors to note are the inclusion of interchangeable, matched numbered barrels which may occasionally accompany a specimen. When so equipped and numbers are matching, values may be increased proportionally. Sets are known, with a total of three, four and even more barrels of varying calibers and bores. Note also that a few two-trigger Wessons are known bearing very fine quality, profuse engraved motifs that were obviously executed by some of the noted engravers of the era. There do not appear to be any standardized patterns, but the engraving invariably is of the highest degree with motifs of fancy scroll and floral designs, sometimes with exceptional paneled depictions of game scenes. Arms so embellished must be priced individually on their own merits using the guidelines established in Chapter II.

Engraving is rarely seen on the Frank Wesson pocket rifles and only a few specimens are known. This generally holds true for other Wesson handguns as well as Wesson & Harrington and Harrington & Richardson revolvers. Engraving (when present) is normally of the broad scroll and floral type and decidedly not of the profuse, ornate degree sometimes seen on the two-trigger rifles. Values, of course, may be increased for any engraved specimen with percentages very much dependent on quality and elaborateness of the designs, and particularly on condition.

Most of the nomenclature used to describe the various models in the following section are modern day terms of convenience coined by Wesson collectors. The same holds true for the Wesson & Harringtons and Harrington & Richardsons. Insufficient promotional and advertising literature has survived to know what the manufacturer originally called all of his models. In some cases the maker never even bothered to name a new product thus leaving it for the first writer on the subject to coin his own in latter day! For instance, on the Model 1870 Pocket Rifles, Wesson used only the term "New Model" in his promotional literature but it has not yet been determined if this applied to the roll-over mechanism, merely the half-cock variation or to the frame mounted firing pin. Thus the author has avoided its use, leaving the matter for resolution by a more astute writer!

Frank Wesson "pocket rifles" as they were called by the maker are also popularly known to collectors as "bicycle rifles" and occasionally as "buggy rifles." These were originally manufactured and sold with matched serial number, attachable shoulder stocks. The values shown in the following descriptions are for complete "pocket rifles" with their *matched number* stocks or for the pistol without same. Prices should be revised downward approximately 15 percent to 20 percent when the shoulder stock is mismatched to the gun.

The "pocket rifles" with their attached stocks were originally classified under the National Firearms Act as "collectors' items" and "curios or relics." In more recent rulings in effect at the time of publication of this book, they have been declassified and hence, are no longer considered covered under the provision of that Federal act, therefore being identified as "antiques." Hence, they are not subject to the Gun Control Act provisions. The declassification by the Treasury Department did not specifically itemize and name the Wesson series (as were the Stevens), but merely mentioned the "Frank Wesson Bicycle Rifle with Accompanying Shoulder Stock." It is assumed that this covers all Frank Wesson bicycle rifles (and that individual nomenclatures were not known or realized as they were on Stevens) and thus assumed that all Wesson bicycle rifles are within that one declassification. The collector or trader is certainly urged to verify this interpretation.

Walnut or rosewood grips were invariably standard on all Wesson handguns and are so indicated. Ivory is occasionally encountered on the Frank Wesson deringers and Wesson & Harrington revolvers and tends to increase values (providing the ivory is excellent in condition) about 10 percent to 20 percent, depending on the model and the gun's overall condition. Ivory (or other exotic material) grips are rare on the pocket rifles, but this specific detail would not necessarily increase values more than normally except for the most advanced collectors. On H&R handguns ivory or pearl might occasionally be substituted for the standard wooden or hard rubber grips and would be worth a premium of approximately 10 percent.

Although the Frank Wesson name is not associated with any currently produced firearm, it is inextricably associated with the history and background of Harrington & Richardson, a noted name in American gun making in continuous operation since 1875. Thus, the Wesson guns (those individually manufactured by him as well as by the partnership of Frank Wesson and Gilbert Harrington and those subsequently by Gilbert Harrington and William Richardson) may be said to form an unbroken chain of American arms making from 1859 to 1985. All are treated in this one section in hopes of spelling out the influence and importance of Frank Wesson in the arms history of the United States and showing the role that Wesson rightfully deserves in the collectors' world. A brief history of all three firms will place the man, the companies and their respective guns in sharper focus.

Frank Wesson (1828-1899) learned his trade as a gun maker under the tutorship of his elder brother Edwin in Northboro, Massachusetts, and Hartford, Connecticut. A great deal remains to be known about his earlier formative years. It is thought that after Edwin's death in 1848, Frank emigrated (probably the lure of the gold rush) to California where he was engaged in gun making; returning in the late 1850s to Worcester where he established himself in business under his own name c. 1859.

In October of 1859, Frank Wesson and Nathan Harrington (the uncle of Gilbert Harrington) were granted a patent for the arrangement of a breech locking bolt, breech elevating spring and wedge shaped recess to accommodate the rim of a cartridge—all of which features were those incorporated on Wesson's earliest two-trigger rifles and tip-up pistols. In 1871 Wesson entered into partnership with his nephew, Gilbert H. Harrington, for the production and sale of small spur trigger pocket revolvers made under the patent protection issued to Harrington in that same year. Wesson meanwhile likely continued to manufacture single shot pistols and rifles under his own name, whereas the revolver manufacture, although produced in the same factory owned by Wesson, was a separate venture marketed under the "Wesson & Harrington" name.

The partnership was short-lived and was dissolved late in 1874 or early 1875. Wesson returned to his individual business, continuing with the manufacture of his two-trigger rifles, pocket rifles and deringers until 1888. Harrington, in 1875, formed another partnership with a former Wesson employee, William A. Richardson. Evidently, no ill-will existed between Harrington and his uncle as the new H&R firm moved into an adjacent building to the Wesson factory where it commenced the manufacture of revolvers based on the former Wesson & Harrington designs. The new firm continued to grow in size, changing to ever-larger locations and facilities within Worcester. By 1888 it had incorporated as the Harrington & Richardson Arms Company, Inc. and by the time both founders had deceased (1897), it was producing 200,000 revolvers annually. After 102 years in Worcester, the firm moved in 1973 to Gardner, Massachusetts. H&R continued to function under that name until recent times.

BIBLIOGRAPHY

(Note: There are no books devoted solely to the arms of these makers. Some material about them may be found in the following works which are noted in other bibliographic listings in this book: *The Breech-Loading Single Shot Match Rifle* by Major Roberts and Ken Waters; *The Muzzle Loading Cap Lock Rifle* by Ned H. Roberts; *Single Shot Rifles* and *More Single Shot Rifles* by James J. Grant; *100 Years Of Shooters And Gun Makers Of Single Shot Rifles* by Gerald O. Kelver and *The Rifle In America* by Phil Sharpe; *Handguns Americana* by DeWitt Sell; *Collector's Guide to American Cartridge Handguns* by DeWitt Sell; *Collector's Handbook of U.S. Cartridge Revolvers 1856-1899* by W. B. Fors; *Suicide Specials* by Donald Webster.)

Larson, E.M. *Variations Of The Smooth Bore H&R Handy-Gun.* Takoma Park, Maryland: Privately Published, 1993. Small, pocket sized, highly definitive, well researched story of all models of this unique handgun.

----*A Short Illustrated History of the Harrington & Richardson Arms Co.*, Canton, Conn.: Armsco Press, c.1996.

Two-Trigger Frank Wesson Rifles

Made at Worcester, Massachusetts c. 1859 to 1888. Serial numbering and sequences have yet to be determined. It is likely that each of the five types below were numbered in their own series and therefore total quantities have been estimated in excess of 35,000.

A great variety of two-trigger Wessons are seen on the collectors' market. It remains for a diligent researcher to neatly categorize these arms which were made over a lengthy period of time and were quite obviously highly popular and well used in their era.

A tip-up type action with the forward trigger acting as release for the barrel. The initial October 25, 1858 patent was for a breech-locking bolt, the breech elevating spring and wedge shaped recess in the standing breech to accommodate the rim of a metallic cartridge. Finishes on all early types and military carbines were blued overall; later sporting types had nickeled frames (casehardened frames occasionally seen) with blued barrels.

Calibers on all models were standard at 22, 32, 38, and 44, with all earlier types made through 1870s rimfire only; later varieties as noted in combination rim and centerfires. The 22 caliber models in all types are scarcer and will bring premium values.

Unless otherwise noted, all barrels on all types are octagon averaging 24" to 28". Lengths will vary with no appreciable price differences except for excessive measurements of 32" or longer which will bring premiums.

Marking variations have been noted, but have not been completely categorized and apparently have no effect on values. The most commonly seen are found on the barrel: F. WESSON/ WORCESTER, MASS. accompanied by F. WESSON/PATENTED OCT. 25, 1859 (on earliest type) or F. WESSON'S PATENT/OCT. 25, 1859 and NOV. 11, 1862 (on all other types). The latter patent date refers to the flat, slotted link affixed to the side of the frame and the breech of the barrel, limiting the travel of the barrel in its tip-up action when the breech is opened.

Considerable lesser variations including slight contour changes are seen on Wessons and apparently do not affect values unless of a major nature. Values shown are for standard, plain grade specimens. Variances such as select wood, checkering, fancy sights, and engraving will add premiums to the value as noted in the preface.

First Type; rounded iron frame and forend all forged integral. Made c. 1859 to 1863 or 1864. Estimated quantity approximately 2,000. Not fitted with extractor. Slotted link to limit travel of breech when opened on *right side* of frame and barrel. Breech of barrel relieved (recessed) at each side allowing for removal of spent cartridges by fingers (often necessitating use of a ramrod). Most of production believed made in 24" carbine length and in 44 rimfire caliber (22 rimfire known and worth premium); possibly also made in 32 and 38 rimfire, but premium values for these are doubtful. The stock of the so-called sporting models has a

peculiar flattening along the underside of butt with crescent shaped buttplate; carbine stock flattened along top of comb, fitted with military style buttplate and equipped with sling swivels (no carbines noted are equipped with sling rings). German silver blade type front sight with fixed rear sight for sporting rifle and three-position folding leaf sight on military carbine:

Sporter:

5I-001	Values—Good **$350**	Fine **$800**

Brass frame sporting Model. Very little known about these; observed in sporting types only:

5I-002	Values—Good **$750**	Fine **$1,500**

Military Carbine. 24" barrel with sling swivels. Caliber 44 rimfire: Total quantity approx. 4,500:

5I-003	Values—Good **$600**	Fine **$1,100**

Kittredge & Co. Marked Military Carbine. Well known Ohio sporting goods and arms dealers and agents for many American gun makers of the era, including Frank Wesson. Kittredge very often added their own markings to guns. They are also known to have supplied 760 Wesson carbines to Indiana; 1366 to Kentucky and many to Kansas and Missouri for state units. Values shown here are for carbines with the additional markings B. KITTREDGE & CO./CINCINNATI, O. If state militia markings also appear and can be completely authenticated, values may be increased at least 100 percent. Although 151 were reported in earlier editions having been purchased by the U.S. shortly after the Battle of Gettysburg, it has been found that they were merely purchased under Federal authority for the state of Ohio and thus, not sent for U.S. Ordnance inspection. Wesson carbines bearing "U.S." markings (of any type) or state military markings should be viewed with great caution. The author is not aware that any were so marked:

5I-004	Values—Good **$1,250**	Fine **$2,250**

5I-005

Second Type; similar to above; made c. 1863 or 1864 to 1875 or 1876. Estimated quantity 5,000. The slotted link moved to the left side of the barrel and frame with a manually operated ejector (long, narrow bar with round knob handle) on right side of barrel breech. All rimfire calibers as noted above. Apparently made in sporting models only, including carbine lengths:

5I-005	Values—Good **$350**	Fine **$800**

Third Type; made c. 1872 to 1888. Estimated quantity made 7,500. The most notable, and easily distinguished, feature is the adjustable hammer striker for use with either rimfire or centerfire cartridges. Rounded iron frame as above. Majority are made with a two-position striker on hammer which may be used to fire (in the conventional manner) the rimfire cartridges through a slot in the recoil shield of the frame; striker may be retracted in the flat hammer face used to strike a floating firing

5I-001

pin in the frame for centerfire cartridges. Later production (believed scarcer, but value premiums would be paid only by most advanced Wesson collectors) have an adjustable striker on the hammer to selectively fire either of the two floating firing pins (rimfire and centerfire). **Double barrel** (side-by-side) rifle/shotguns are known (rare: worth substantial premium). Specimens 14 gauge by 44 centerfire with 24-inch round barrels recorded; fitted with double hammers and extra large trigger bow to accommodate three triggers.

5I-006   Values—Good **$350**   Fine **$800**

Fourth Type; made c. 1872 to 1888. Estimated quantities 7,500. A noticeably larger and heavier rounded iron frame. Made in sporting models only. Invariably found with the double floating firing pins in frame as described above. Officially named in Frank Wesson advertising literature as the "**No. 2 Mid-Range Sporting and Gallery Rifle.**" Made in all four calibers, rimfire and centerfire. Checkered pistol grip stock standard with folding tang peep sight. 28" and 30" part round/part octagon barrel. Globe front and open type rear sights. Very scarce:

5I-007   Values—Very Good **$850**   Exc. **$2,250**

Fifth Type; large, heavy weight, flat framed sporter. Officially termed in Wesson literature "**New Model**." Made c. 1876 to 1888. Estimated quantity approximately 15,000. Invariably

5I-008

found (and so advertised by Wesson) to accommodate centerfire and rimfire cartridges with double firing pins, but variations known with centerfire pin only. Plain, straight, uncheckered stock standard (pistol grips worth premium); folding tang sight. Other distinct variations have been noted in this type and specimens may be observed with or without removable sideplate on frame as well as rounded or flat sided forends (the latter feature felt to be the very last of production and worth a premium to specialists in the Wesson field):

5I-008   Values—Very Good **$700**   Exc. **$1,750**

Under-Lever, Falling Block Wessons

The exact dates of manufacture not known; believed from the early or mid-1870s through the 1880s. All of these very well made rifles display exceptionally fine quality workmanship. A great many variants have been noted on all three types. Quantities as listed below.

Frank Wesson was obviously one of the first cartridge "wildcatters." Calibers listed below for the various basic styles are those as described in a Wesson brochure of 1876 about them. Actual data, however, on many known specimens proves production to have run the gamut in caliber sizes from popular ones to Wesson wildcats, and about the only way to get proof positive of the caliber of one of these rifles is to take a chamber cast. The key to values on these rare pieces are not calibers, but rather model and condition.

Markings vary considerably and are relatively unimportant for values. The standard markings listed below are those that have been recorded for most specimens. Variances such as the shape of pistol-grip and stock contours and other features are also quite widely noted.

Nomenclature as listed below for each of the three models is exactly as termed by Wesson in his advertising promotional literature. Considerable data about these three types (statistical and comparative) may be found in the James Grant book *More Single Shot Rifles*.

No. 1 Long Range Rifle. Side hammer type; back action lock; firing pin in breechblock. Very closely resembles rifles made by the noted Edinburgh, Scotland, maker, Alexander Henry. Quantity made estimated at less than 50 and very probably less than 25. Rare. 34" or longer full octagon or part octagon/part round barrel. Overall weight about 10 lbs. Fancy grained checkered pistol grip stock and forend; shotgun butt. Two-position (tang and heel of butt) long range Vernier rear peep sight; spirit level, windgauge front sight. Advertised in calibers 44-100 and 45-100 with many variations known. Usual markings F. WESSON MFR. WORCESTER, MASS./LONG RANGE RIFLE CREEDMOOR.(with or without No. 1 at end of second line):

5I-009   Values—Very Good **$6,000**   Exc. **$17,500**

5I-009
No. 1 Long Range

5I-010
No. 2 Long & Mid-Range

5I-011
No. 1 Mid-Range & Sporting

No. 2 Long and Mid-Range and Hunting Rifle. Side hammer type; firing pin in bolster on right side of receiver; rounded iron frame. Quantity made estimated at less than 100 and very likely under 75. 28" to 34" full octagon barrel (32" and 34" lengths will bring premium). Fancy grained, checkered straight stock and forend; shotgun butt. Two-position (tang and butt) Vernier rear peep sight; spirit level, windgauge front sight. Usual barrel markings (varies considerably): F. WESSON, MAKER/WORCESTER, MASS. The 32" and 34" barrel lengths usually have additional markings: LONG RANGE RIFLE CREEDMOOR under the Wesson name. Calibers were not advertised on Wesson literature, but recorded specimens vary from 35 to 45:

5I-010   Values—Very Good **$4,000**   Exc. **$9,500**

No. 1 Mid-Range and Sporting Rifle. Centrally mounted hammer. Estimated quantity made less than 25. Although the rarest of the three types, it will usually bring about the same as the No. 2 Long Range except for the most advanced of Wesson or single shot specialists who might pay premiums comparable to the No. 1 Long Range. Part round/part octagon barrels vary in length from 28" to 34". Fancy grained checkered pistol grip stock and forend; shotgun butt. One or two-position Vernier rear peep sight; spirit level, windgauge front sight. Advertised calibers were 38-100, 40-100, and 45-100, but recorded specimens vary considerably:

5I-011   Values—Very Good **$6,500**   Exc. **$15,000**

Frank Wesson Handguns

Frank Wesson Manual Extractor Pistol

5I-012.2
Large Frame

5I-012
Small Frame

Small Frame Single Shot Manual Extractor Pistol. Made circa 1856-1857. Total made estimated approximately 200.

Caliber 22 rimfire, full octagon barrel approximately 4". Very slender, brass frame and handle with square butt; spur trigger. Barrel releases (tips up to load) by depressing button latch under forend. Major distinguishing feature is the manually operated, relief, knurled extractor on breech of barrel (a specimen is known identical but without this extractor feature).

Maker's markings not present. Believed serial numbered in its own range beginning with "1" on up:

5I-012   Values—Good **$450**   Fine **$1,000**

Large Frame Manual Extractor Target Pistol. About identical to above but almost twice the size. Caliber 22 rimfire; 6-1/2" octagon barrel; rear barrel sight adjustable for elevation. Manufactured circa 1856-1857. Quantity estimated at less than 50.

5I-012.2   Values—Good **$650**   Fine **$1,450**

Frank Wesson & Nathan Harrington Pistol

Small Frame Single Shot Pistol. Made 1859. Quantity estimated about 100.

Caliber 22 rimfire. Brass frame. Distinguished by its all-round two-step barrel. Looks like a cross between 5I-012 and 5I-013. Spur trigger; square butt. Two line WESSON & HARRINGTON barrel markings.

Made during the short lived (about 6 months) partnership with *Nathan* Harrington, the uncle of Gilbert Harrington (of Wesson & Harrington/Harrington & Richardson):

5I-012.5   Values—Good **$550**   Fine **$1,250**

5I-012.5

Frank Wesson Small Frame Single Shot Pistols

Small Frame Single Shot Pistols. Made c. 1859 through early 1880s. Total made approximately 15,000.

Caliber 22 short rimfire. 3-1/2" part octagon/part round

barrels standard, but lengths will vary from 2-7/8" to 6".

Chief distinguishing feature is the brass frame. Spur trigger; square butt; rosewood or walnut grips.

5I-013
First Type

5I-014
Second Type

Serial numbered; see below. Barrel markings: first type F. WESSON/PATENTED OCT. 25, 1859. Second type FRANK WESSON WORCESTER MASS/PAT'D OCT. 25, 1859 & NOV. 11, 1862

Barrels tip up at breech to load by pulling rearward on the long projecting lever on underside of frame. Designed primarily for plinking and gallery use.

First Type, a.k.a. Model 1859. Distinguished by the round sided frame and large irregular sideplate. Serial numbered in its own range from 1 through approximately 2500:

5I-013   Values—Good **$200**   Fine **$550**

Second Type, a.k.a. Model 1862. Distinguished by the flat sided frame and interrupted circular sideplate. Serial numbered in its own range 1 through approximately 12000:

5I-014   Values—Good **$175**   Fine **$475**

Frank Wesson Medium Frame S.S. Pistols

Medium Frame Single Shot Pistols. Made c. 1859 through early 1870s. Total made approximately 2,000.

Calibers 30 short or long, 32 short rimfires. 4" part round/part octagonal barrels standard, but length variations from approximately 3" to 6".

Iron frames standard (occasionally encountered in brass frame and will bring premium); spur trigger; square butt; rosewood or walnut grips. Identical action to the small frame model with barrels tipping up to load and long projecting lever latch beneath frame.

Barrel markings of first and second types identical to above.
First Type, a.k.a. Model 1859. Distinguished by narrow frame at barrel hinge and short trigger. Serial numbered in its own range approximately 1 through 1000. Variant known with full octagon barrel and low 2 digit serial; rare; worth premium:

5I-015   Values—Good **$200**   Fine **$650**

Second Type, a.k.a. Model 1862. Distinguished by wider frame at barrel hinge and longer trigger. Serial numbered in its own range 1 through approximately 1000:

5I-016   Values—Good **$200**   Fine **$650**

5I-015
First Type

5I-016
Second Type

Frank Wesson Small Frame Tip-Up Pocket Rifle

Tip-Up Pocket Rifle Model 1862, Small Frame. Made c. 1865 to 1875. Total made unknown, estimated at less than 100 and numbered within the serial range of the Second Type Small Frame Single Shot Pistol.

5I-018

Calibers 22 rimfire. Single shot. 6" part round/part octagon barrel (slightly varying lengths have been noted).

Brass frame standard, spur trigger; square butt; rosewood grips; no extractor.

Standard barrel markings: FRANK WESSON WORCESTER, MASS/PAT'D OCT. 25, 1859 & NOV. 11, 1862

Fitted with detachable, skeleton type shoulder stock (rare) which fits into special narrow butt cap with mortised slot. Adjustable peep sights.

Pistol with Stock (usually not numbered):
5I-017   Values—Good **$875**   Fine **$2,250**
Pistol Only (lacking stock):
5I-018   Values—Good **$450**   Fine **$1,250**

Frank Wesson Med. Frame Tip-Up Pocket Rifle

5I-019

Tip-Up Pocket Rifle Model 1862, Medium Frame. Made c. 1862 to 1870. Total quantity estimated at under 500.

Calibers 22, 30, and 32 rimfire. The latter is the most commonly encountered; only very advanced collectors might wish to pay slight premium for 22 or 30 calibers. 10" to 12" part round/part octagon barrels standard, but lengths will vary slightly.

Iron frame; spur trigger; square butt; rosewood grips; brass butt cap.

Barrel markings identical to above. Serial numbered in their own range beginning with 1 on up.

Fitted with detachable skeleton type shoulder stock and special wide mortised butt cap (into which stock fits). Also fitted with extractor for spent cartridges and adjustable peep sights.

Pistol with Matched Number Stock:
5I-019   Values—Good **$575**   Fine **$1,250**

Pistol Only (lacking stock):
5I-020   Values—Good **$250**   Fine **$650**

Frank Wesson Small Frame Superposed Pistol

Two-Shot Superposed Pistol, Small Frame, a.k.a. "Vest Pocket" or "Watch-Fob" Deringer. Made c. 1868 to 1880. Total quantity estimated less than 3,000.

Caliber 22 short rimfire. 2" and 2-1/2" octagonal superposed barrels with knurled area between them. Overall length 4" to 4-1/2".

Brass frame; spur trigger; bird's head butt; rosewood grips. Serial numbered from 1 on up.

Two styles of hammers are noted on this very tiny pistol; a straight spurred hammer (usually called the "Vest Pocket" model) and a round ring type hammer with circular piercing in it (usually known as the "Watch-Fob" model). Although the straight type is less often encountered, the ring hammer has been found more interesting in style to collectors and therefore both types bring about the same value.

A highly desirable feature occasionally found on this model is a sliding dirk in the center section between the two barrels, and when encountered a premium of 25 percent or more may be added to the value.

5I-021

First Type. Markings placed vertically on the barrel; FRANK WESSON/WORCESTER, MASS/PAT DEC 15, 1868 Muzzles of barrels crowned:
5I-021   Values—Good **$750**   Fine **$2,250**

Second Type. Markings placed horizontally in one line along barrel: FRANK WESSON WORCESTER MASS Pt DEC 15/68 Muzzles squared:
5I-022   Values—Good **$725**   Fine **$2,000**

Frank Wesson Med. Frame Superposed Pistol

Two-Shot Superposed Pistol, Medium Frame. Made c. 1868 to 1880. Total quantity estimated at 3,000.

Caliber 32 short rimfire. Superposed octagonal 2-1/2" barrels with knurled area between them. 3-1/2" barrels rare.

Brass frame; spur trigger; bird's head butt; rosewood grips.

Serial numbered, but numbering range not fully understood. Believed to be from 1 to 2000 and commencing again with No. 1. Earlier production with half-fluted barrels as shown; later with full flutes.

5I-023

Often referred to as "over and under" deringers; barrels are manually revolved. Occasionally encountered with a sliding double edged dirk in the center section between the two barrels (only on 3-1/2" model) and quite desirable. Approximately 50 percent premium or more.

Although variously reported in .38 cal., none other than prototype believed made.

First Type. Distinguished by flattened grips, a sharper drop to the angle at which the handle is joined to the frame; short barrel flutes. Markings positioned vertically on the barrel: FRANK WESSON/WORCESTER. MASS./PT. APPLIED FOR
5I-023   Values—Good **$375**   Fine **$1,250**

Second Type. Distinguished by wider grips, less angular drop to the handle and short barrel flutes. Markings positioned vertically on the barrel: FRANK WESSON/WORCESTER MASS/PAT DEC 15, 1868:
5I-024   Values—Good **$375**   Fine **$1,250**

Third Type. Distinguished by the full fluted barrels and horizontally positioned one line markings: FRANK WESSON WORCESTER MASS Pt. DEC 15/68
5I-025   Values—Good **$375**   Fine **$1,250**

Frank Wesson Large Frame Superposed Pistol

Two-Shot Superposed Pistol, Large Frame. Manufactured c. 1868 to 1880. Total made estimated at 2,000.

Caliber 41 short rimfire. 3" octagonal barrels, full fluted, with sliding double edged dirk in center section standard on all specimens.

Brass frame, spur trigger, bird's head butt, rosewood grips.

As with the smaller sizes, these "over and under" deringers also have manually revolved barrels with small locking latch on underside of frame.

First Type. 3 line markings identical 5I-24 above, vertically at breech of barrel:

5I-026   Values—Good **$950**   Fine **$2,650**

Second Type. 3 line markings identical above; barrel flutes extended almost to breech partially through markings; PT. July 20, 1869 on side of barrel, horizontal:

5I-026.5   Values—Good **$950**   Fine **$2,650**

Third Type. 1 line marking, horizontal on side of barrel; FRANK WESSON WORCHESTER, MASS. PAT. DEC. 15, 1868, JULY 20, 1869. Long barrel flutes as above:

5I-027   Values—Good **$950**   Fine **$2,650**

5I-026

Frank Wesson 1870 Small Frame Pocket Rifle

5I-028
First Type

Model 1870 Pocket Rifle, Small Frame, a.k.a. "Sportsman's Jewel." Made c. 1870-1890. Total quantity roughly estimated at 3,000.

Caliber 22 rimfire, single shot. Barrels 10", 12", 15", 18", and 20", and either full octagon or part octagon/part round. Longest lengths often worth premium.

Spur trigger; square butt; rosewood grips.

Believe serial numbered in two ranges from 1 to 2200 and then commencing again with No. 1.

Fitted with skeleton type detachable shoulder stock and easily distinguished by its different breech action, the barrel turns or rotates on its axis to the right to load (vs. tip-up of earlier action).

First Type. Brass frame. Part round/part octagonal barrel and internal half cock. Barrel marking: FRANK WESSON WORCESTER, MASS./PATENT APPLIED FOR

Pistol With Matched Number Stock:

5I-028   Values—Very Good **$475**   Exc. **$1,200**

Pistol Only (lacking stock):

5I-029   Values—Very Good **$200**   Exc. **$550**

Second Type. Brass frame. Full octagonal barrel with internal half cock. Barrel marking: FRANK WESSON WORCESTER, MASS./PATENTED MAY 31, 1870.

Pistol With Matched Number Stock:

5I-030   Values—Very Good **$475**   Exc. **$1,200**

Pistol Only (lacking stock):

5I-031   Values—Very Good **$200**   Exc. **$550**

Third Type. Iron frame. Distinguished by the external push-button half cock mounted on the left side of frame. Full octagon barrel. Markings identical to second type.

Pistol With Matched Number Stock:

5I-032   Values—Very Good **$475**   Exc. **$1,200**

Pistol Only (lacking stock):

5I-033   Values—Very Good **$200**   Exc. **$550**

Frank Wesson 1870 Med. Frame Pocket Rifle

Model 1870 Pocket Rifle, Medium Frame, a.k.a. "Sportsman's Jewel." Made c. 1870-1893. Total made roughly estimated at 5,000.

Calibers 22 and 32 rimfire, single shot. Full octagonal barrels in varying lengths 10" to 22" (longest lengths often bring premiums).

Spur trigger; square butt; rosewood grips.

Barrel markings all types: FRANK WESSON WORCESTER, MASS/PATENTED MAY 31, 1870. Believe serial numbered in three ranges with numbering pattern indecipherable. Although there

is a discernible difference in overall size, the width at the breech (varying from 22/32" to 25/32") is the most positive way of identifying this from the smaller frame model (averaging 18/32" width at breech).

With detachable shoulder stock and the same rollover breech action as the above.

First Type. Brass frame. Distinguished by an internal half cock.

Pistol With Matched Number Stock:

5I-034   Values—Very Good **$550**   Exc. **$1,250**

Pistol Only (lacking stock):

5I-035   Values—Very Good **$250**   Exc. **$575**

5I-036
Second Type

Second Type. Iron frame. Distinguished by an external push-button type half cock.

Pistol With Matched Number Stock:
5I-036   Values—Very Good **$550**   Exc. **$1,250**

Pistol Only (lacking stock):
5I-037   Values—Very Good **$225**   Exc. **$500**

Third Type. Iron frame. Distinguished by an external push-button half cock and the addition of a third screw to the left side of the frame for locking against the main barrel supporting screw. Frame size on this type usually runs the full 25/32" thickness.

Pistol With Matched Number Stock:
5I-038   Values—Very Good **$550**   Exc. **$1,250**

Pistol Only (lacking stock):
5I-039   Values—Very Good **$225**   Exc. **$500**

Frank Wesson Model 1870 Pocket Shotgun

Model 1870 Pocket Shotgun. (Not illus.) Made c. 1870 to 1875. Total estimated at less than 100, possibly less than even 50.

Calibers 38 and 44 centerfire shot cartridges. Single shot. Barrels usually 15" part round/part octagon, but may vary.

Iron frame; spur trigger; square butt; rosewood grips.

Serial numbered in their own range from 1 on up. Barrel markings FRANK WESSON WORCESTER, MASS./PAT'D OCT. 25, 1859 & NOV. 11, 1862 (an unexplained anomaly as the weapon employs the 1870 patent design).

Made with skeleton type detachable shoulder stock and having most of the characteristics of the Medium Frame 1870 Pocket Rifle above with the exception of the octagon/round barrel and patent markings. Surprisingly, and regardless of its antiquity, this particular model has not been removed (as of 1997) from the provisions and restrictions of the N.F.A. and collectors should not acquire or dispose of specimens unless complying. Values shown below are those that would be applicable if, and when, reclassified and "antique."

Pistol With Matched Number Stock:
5I-040   Values—Very Good **$750**   Exc. **$1,750**

Pistol Only (lacking stock):
5I-041   Values—Very Good **$350**   Exc. **$750**

Frank Wesson 1870 Large Frame Pocket Rifle

5I-042
First Type

Model 1870 Pocket Rifle, Large Frame. Made c. 1870-1880. Total made estimated at less than 100, possibly less than 50.

Calibers 22, 32, 38 and 44 rimfire; single shot. Barrels full octagon in varying lengths from 15" to 24".

Brass or iron frames for both types; spur trigger; square butt; rosewood grips.

Barrel markings: FRANK WESSON WORCESTER, MASS/PATENTED MAY 31, 1870.

Serial numbered in its own range from 1 on up.

Has the same roll-over type action as lighter weight models. Quickly discernible from them by its very long frame length and wide 26/32" breech.

Made with detachable skeleton type shoulder stock which fits into mortise on the wide butt cap.

First Type. Automatic extractor which lifts the cartridge out of the breech when barrel is rolled to the open position.

Pistol With Matched Number Stock:
5I-042   Values—Very Good **$1,250**   Exc. **$3,250**

Pistol Only (lacking stock):
5I-043   Values—Very Good **$650**   Exc. **$1,500**

Second Type. Has the standard Wesson extractor which slides in a dovetail on the right side of barrel.

Pistol With Matched Number Stock:
5I-044   Values—Very Good **$1,100**   Exc. **$3,000**

Pistol Only (lacking stock):
5I-045   Values—Very Good **$650**   Exc. **$1,500**

Frank Wesson and Gilbert Harrington Handguns

Wesson & Harrington No. 1, 22 Cal. Revolver

Model No. 1, 22 Caliber Revolver. Made c. 1871 to 1873. Total quantity estimated at 2,500, but specimens quite scarce.

Caliber 22 short rimfire; seven-shot fluted cylinder. 3-3/16" octagonal barrel.

Brass frame; spur trigger; bird's head butt. Frame silver plated with barrel and cylinder blued or full nickel. Rosewood grips.

Barrel markings WESSON & HARRINGTON, WORCESTER, MASS. PAT. FEB. 7. JUNE 13 '71.

5I-046

Serial numbered in its own range from 1 on up.

Distinguishing features are the contoured ejector rod which slopes upward into the cylinder pin (affixed to underside of barrel by a screw); frame which is fitted to the curve of the cylinder necessitating removal of a small wedge of bottomstrap in order to remove cylinder:

5I-046   Values—Very Good **$250**   Exc. **$650**

Wesson & Harrington No. 2, 22 Cal. Revolver

Model No. 2, 22 Caliber Revolver. (Not illus.) Made c. 1874 to 1879. Total quantity estimated at 15,000.

Caliber 22 rimfire short. Seven-shot fluted cylinder. 11/16" or 3-3/16" octagonal barrels.

Iron frame; spur trigger; bird's head butt. Available either full nickel or full blued finish; rosewood grips.

Barrel markings same as Model No. 1.

Serial numbering ranges not fully known, either in its own series or continuation of the Model 1 range.

Similar to the Model 1, but displaying improvements. Most easily distinguished are the push-type cylinder pin with spring button release, frame no longer contoured to the cylinder curve, and lacks the removable frame wedge in bottomstrap.

Transition Type. Retains the brass frame of the Model No. 1 and oval cylinder pin release button. Otherwise displays features of Model No. 2. Quantity made estimated at 500:

5I-047   Values—Very Good **$225**   Exc. **$600**

First Type. Short cylinder pin and ejector rod; frame notched on right side at point where barrel is fitted to it; three-groove rifling:

5I-048   Values—Very Good **$150**   Exc. **$475**

Second Type. Long cylinder pin and ejector rod; unnotched frame; five-groove rifling. Late production may have Harrington & Richardson markings:

5I-049   Values—Very Good **$150**   Exc. **$475**

Wesson & Harrington No. 3, 32 Cal. Revolver

Model No. 3, 32 Caliber Revolver. Made c. 1874 to 1879. Total quantity estimated at 15,000.

Caliber 32 rimfire short. Five-shot fluted cylinder. 11/16" octagon barrel.

Iron frame; spur trigger; bird's head butt. Full blue or full nickel finish; rosewood grips.

Barrel markings same as Model No. 1.

Believed serial numbered in its own range from 1 on up.

About identical in contour to Model 2 above, but larger size.

First Type. Short cylinder pin and ejector rod; frame notched at junction where barrel enters it; three-groove rifling:

5I-050   Values—Very Good **$150**   Exc. **$450**

Second Type. Long cylinder pin and ejector rod; unnotched frame; five-groove rifling; lever type cylinder pin release on left

5I-051

side of frame. Scarce:

5I-051   Values—Very Good **$350**   Exc. **$750**

Third Type. Distinguished by use of the spring loaded button type cylinder pin release, otherwise same as Second Type:

5I-052   Values—Very Good **$150**   Exc. **$450**

Wesson & Harrington No. 4, 38 Cal. Revolver

Model No. 4, 38 Caliber Revolver. (Not illus.) Made c. 1875 to 1877. Total quantity estimated at 500. Calibers 38 rimfire or 41 rimfire; the latter scarcer and worth premium.

Five-shot fluted cylinder. 3-1/2" octagon barrel.

Iron frame; spur trigger; bird's head butt. Available either full nickel or full blue finish; rosewood grips.

Barrel markings same as Model No. 1. Serial numbered in its own range from 1 on up.

About identical in contours to Models 2 and 3 above and easily distinguished by its large size and caliber:

5I-053   Values—Very Good **$275**   Exc. **$650**

Wesson & Harrington No. 5 Revolver

Model No. 5 Non-Ejecting Revolver. Made c. 1875 to 1876. Total estimated at 4,000.

5I-054

Calibers 32 rimfire (seven-shot), 38 and 41 rimfire (both five-shot). 2-15/32" octagonal barrel.

Iron frame; spur trigger; bird's head butt. Available either full nickel or full blue finish. Rosewood grips.

Barrel markings WESSON & HARRINGTON. WORCESTER MASS and often the additional markings PAT. MAY 23, 1876. The larger caliber model is marked on topstrap 41 CALIBER. Serial range uncertain, possibly a continuation from Model 4.

Built on the frame of the Model No. 4, but with shorter barrel, without ejector rod and a short cylinder pin.

32 or 38 caliber:

5I-054   Values—Very Good **$150**   Exc. **$425**

41 caliber:

5I-055   Values—Very Good **$300**   Exc. **$750**

NOTE: Wesson & Harrington Models Nos. 2, 3, 4, 5 are occasionally seen with H&R markings which were used at the very end of production of those respective models. Very scarce and worth premium.

Harrington and Richardson

H&R Model No. 1 Revolver

Model No. 1 Revolver. Made c. 1877 to 1878. Quantity estimated at 3,000. Calibers 32 (seven-shot) and 38 (five-shot) rimfires. 3" octagon barrel.

Iron frame; spur trigger; bird's head butt. Checkered hard rubber grips. Full nickel finish only.

Barrel markings HARRINGTON & RICHARDSON WORCESTER, MASS/PAT MAY 23, 1876. Believe serial numbered in range continuing the Wesson & Harrington Model No. 5.

Very similar to the Wesson & Harrington Model No. 5, with noted variances being topstrap not raised at breech and has full length sighting groove:

5I-056

5I-056   Values—Very Good **$125**   Exc. **$300**

H&R Saw-Handled Frame Spur Trigger Revolvers

Saw-Handled Frame Spur Trigger Revolvers. Made c. 1878 to 1883. Quantities listed below.

Features common to all models: Fluted cylinders; octagonal barrels; iron frame; spur trigger; flat butt. Nickel finishes.

Earlier production all types distinguished by the H&R

5I-057

emblem on the checkered hard rubber grips. Later production bears American shield design (often referred to in company literature as "New Design of 1878"). Values same for both types.

Barrel markings same as Model No. 1.

Model 1-1/2 Revolver. Quantity estimated at 10,000. Caliber 32 rimfire. Five-shot. 2-1/2" barrel:
5I-057   Values—Very Good **$85**   Exc. **$250**

Model 2-1/2 Revolver. Quantity estimated at 5,000. Caliber 32 rimfire with seven-shot cylinder. 3-1/4" barrel:
5I-058   Values—Very Good **$100**   Exc. **$300**

Model 3-1/2 Revolver. Quantity made estimated at 2,500. Caliber 38 rimfire; five-shot; 3-1/2" barrel:
5I-059   Values—Very Good **$125**   Exc. **$325**

Model 4-1/2 Revolver. Quantity made estimated at 1,000. Caliber 41 rimfire; five-shot; 2-1/2" barrel:
5I-060   Values—Very Good **$225**   Exc. **$625**

H&R Model 1880 Double Action Revolver

Model 1880 Double Action Revolver. Made c. 1880 to 1883. Quantity estimated at 4,000.

Calibers 32 (six-shot) and 38 (five-shot) S&W centerfire. Fluted cylinders. 3" round barrels. Solid frame; saw-handle style. Fancy hard rubber grips with sunburst and scroll design. Full nickeled finish.

Barrel markings HARRINGTON & RICHARDSON, WORCESTER, MASS with 1880 patent date. Serial numbered from 1 on up.

H&R's first double action revolver, based on Peter Holter Patent of January 20, 1880:

5I-061

5I-061   Values—Very Good **$175**   Exc. **$450**

H&R The American Double Action Revolver

The American Double Action Revolver. (Not illus.) Made c. 1883 to 1940. Total estimated at 850,000.

Calibers 32 centerfire (six-shot), 38 and 44 centerfire (five-shot; worth 100 percent plus premium). Fluted cylinders. Round barrel on early production (worth premium); later

octagonal barrels. 2-1/2" standard, but 4-1/2" and 6" optional. This same model made in either 32 or 38 rimfire, known as the "H&R BULLDOG" revolver and so marked.

Solid frame with modified saw-handle. Full nickel finish with blue on later production. Fancy hard rubber grips with scroll design.

Marked on topstrap: THE AMERICAN DOUBLE ACTION. Later production bearing company name on barrel.

Variant of this was made with a safety hammer patented 1887 and marked SAFETY HAMMER DOUBLE ACTION:

5I-062   Values—Very Good **$70**   Exc. **$165**

H&R Young America Double Action Revolver

The Young America Double Action Revolver. (Not illus.) Made c. 1884 to 1941. Total estimated at 1,500,000.

Calibers 22 rimfire (seven-shot) and 32 S&W centerfire (five-shot). Round barrel on earliest (worth premium) with later production all octagonal. 2" standard with 4-1/2" and 6" optional. Also made in 32 rimfire and known as the "YOUNG AMERICA BULLDOG" (and so marked).

Solid frame with modified saw-handle. Full nickel finish standard, but later production in blue also.

Standard markings: YOUNG AMERICA DOUBLE ACTION on topstrap with later production bearing company name also.

The Safety Hammer version, patented in 1887, marked: YOUNG AMERICA SAFETY HAMMER. A special variant of the Safety Hammer type with 1-1/8" round barrel issued and marked VEST POCKET (worth 25 percent premium):

5I-063   Values—Very Good **$70**   Exc. **$150**

H&R Shell Extracting Revolver

H&R Shell Extracting Revolver (as originally named in advertising literature) a.k.a. "Hand Ejector". (Not illus.) Made c. 1886 to 1888. Quantity estimated at 6,000.

Calibers 32 centerfire and 32 H&R long centerfire (six-shots) and 38 S&W centerfire (five-shots). 3-1/4" round ribbed barrel.

H&R's first top-break revolver, based on the American Double Action Model frame. Full nickel finish. Hard rubber grips with scroll design.

Early barrel markings: HARRINGTON & RICHARDSON,

WORCESTER, MASS. U.S.A. Later production marked: HARRINGTON & RICHARDSON ARMS COMPANY/WORCESTER, MASS. U.S.A. PAT'D OCT 4th 1887. Serial numbered in its own range.

Center pin protrudes under barrel and is used to manually eject cartridges. Earliest production has two guide pins for the star shaped ejector while later production has push-button on barrel latch to hold cylinder catch open. Values apparently the same for both types:

5I-064   Values—Very Good **$175**   Exc. **$450**

H&R Automatic Ejection D/A Revolvers

Automatic Ejection Double Action Revolvers. Dates and quantities as listed below.

Calibers 32 centerfire and 32 H&R long centerfire (six-shots) and 38 S&W centerfire (five-shots). 3-1/4" round ribbed barrels standard for both types.

Top break action, full nickel finish both types. Markings as below:

Model 1. Made c. 1887 to 1889. Quantity estimated at 5,000. Fancy hard rubber grips with scroll work design. Barrel markings same as Shell Extracting Revolver with later production having 1887 patent date:

5I-065   Values—Very Good **$100**   Exc. **$350**

Model 2. Made c. 1889 to 1940. Total quantity estimated at 1,300,000. Also available in 2-1/2", 4", 5", and 6" barrels. Checkered hard rubber grips with H&R target design. Later production also available in blue. Markings vary throughout, but always bear company name on barrel rib and often one or more patent dates. Most indicate model name on left side and caliber on right side of barrels. Similar to Model 1 with redesigned frame having flattened bottomstrap, more squared curves to backstrap and smaller, more graceful hammer. Numerous internal changes over its period of production. Also

5I-067
Automatic Bayonet Revolver

made with a patented safety style hammer known as the "Police Automatic":

5I-066   Values—Very Good **$60**   Exc. **$185**

Automatic Eject Revolver With Knife Attachment. Officially named by H&R **"Automatic Bayonet Revolver."** Made only in 38 c.f. according to their 1902 advertising. Made c. 1901 to 1917. Estimated quantity 2,000. 4" round ribbed barrel with 2-1/4" double edge folding knife mounted on underside at muzzle. Checkered hard rubber grips with H&R target design. Available blue or nickel. Serial numbered in range of Model 2 above. Considered a distinct "arms curiosa" by collectors:

5I-067   Values—Very Good **$575**   Exc. **$1,450**

H&R Smooth Bore Handy-Gun

5I-067.5

H&R Handy Gun. c. 1920s to 1934. Estimated quantity 54,000. Earlier reported that serial numbers were included with the M.1915 shotgun; more recent research seems to indicate numbered in their own series 1 to 54,000 (approx.).

410 gauge and 28 gauge smooth bore; 22 rimfire, 32-20 (likely few other c.f. also) with rifled barrels. Three models and numerous variations based on finish, markings, top lever, etc.

Usual markings HARRINGTON & RICHARDSON, WORCESTER, MASS. U.S.A. and HANDY-GUN. Markings such as

ESSEX GUN WORKS and HIBBARD are occasionally seen and merely represent "private labels" made by H&R for others.

Smooth bore and shot shell types subject to restrictions of National Firearms Act and cannot be freely traded unless complying:

Values only if NFA registered:
Chambered for 28 Gauge:
5I-067.5   Values—Fine **$575**   Exc. **$1,200**
Chambered for 410 Gauge:
5I-067.7   Values—Fine **$500**   Exc. **$900**

H&R Self-Loading (Semi-Automatic) Pistols

H&R Self-Loading (Semi-Automatic) Pistols. Dates and quantities as listed below.

Standard finish both types blue, but also available in nickel. Checkered hard rubber grips with H&R monogram in center panel. Each size serial numbered in its own range from 1 on up.

Markings on left side of slide H&R SELF-LOADING with caliber. Right side of slide marked in three lines with company name, address, and patent dates AUG. 20, 1907, APR. 13, NOV. 9, 1909.

Semi-automatics designed by Webley & Scott of England who licensed H&R to manufacture and market them in the United States.

Caliber 25 (6.35mm): Made c. 1912 to 1916. Quantity 16,630. Six-shot magazine capacity. 2" barrel:
5I-068   Values—Very Good **$175**   Exc. **$475**

Caliber 32 (7.65mm): Made c. 1916 to 1924. Total 34,500. Eight-shot magazine capacity. 3-1/2" barrel:
5I-069   Values—Very Good **$175**   Exc. **$425**

5I-068

5I-069

H&R Hammerless Double Barrel Shotgun

H&R's Hammerless (Anson & Deeley) Double Barrel Shotgun. Made c. 1882 to 1885. Quantity unknown; estimated between 3,000 and 4,000.

12 gauge with 28" or 30" Damascus barrels; 10 gauge with 30" or 32" Damascus barrels.

Checkered, select grain stock; casehardened engraved frame. Serial numbered in its own series from 1 on up.

Believed to be the first American made hammerless double shotgun. Designed by Anson & Deeley of Birmingham, England who licensed H&R to market them in the U.S.

Available in four grades from "A" (their highest) to "D".

Anson & Deeley markings on lockplates with Harrington & Richardson markings on barrel rib and buttplate.

"D" GRADE. Plainest style; slight border engraving:
5I-070   Values—Very Good **$350**   Exc. **$950**

"C" GRADE. Better wood and better Damascus finish to barrels; slight engraving:
5I-071   Values—Very Good **$400**   Exc. **$1,150**

"B" GRADE. High quality engraving, fancier select grained wood and a Damascus finish to barrels:
5I-072   Values—Very Good **$700**   Exc. **$2,500**

5I-070

"A" GRADE. Extra select grained wood, fine Damascus finish to barrels, finest quality profuse fancy engraving; small gold inlay plate for owner's initials on buttstock:
5I-073   Values—Very Good **$1,250**   Exc. **$4,000**

Chapter V-J

Whitney Arms Company

Eli Whitney and the companies that bore his name are as familiar to collectors as Colt, Smith & Wesson and Winchester. There is no disputing Whitney's stature among American arms manufacturers and inventors.

No other American gun maker produced such a broad range of arms over as many historic and important eras as did Whitney. The name appeared on weapons of many models and styles from the earliest American flintlocks to lever action repeating rifles and included a host of handguns from percussion to breech-loading metallic cartridge types. Surprisingly, with this prodigious issue and the glamour and romance of the Whitney name, their products for the most part remained very much overshadowed, both in demand and price, by many of their peers. This may be attributed to a lack of definitive information about Whitney arms as well as the almost complete lack of guidelines for pursuing the field.

Whitney-marked arms of all types have enjoyed a brisk sales over the years, but have certainly never reached their potential based on importance. A few Whitneys have been in great demand, such as the contract Model 1798 contract muskets (possessing a great historical connotation) while others of far greater rarity have literally gone begging for buyers as they were completely unrecognized in rarity and importance. This is especially evident with some of the early contract flintlocks and many of the breech-loading metallic cartridge single shot and lever action rifles.

Fuller's work *Whitney Firearms*, published in 1946, stands as the major effort in advancement of knowledge of this field and presents much data of value for the collector today. However, it does have several gaps of information; some pieces shown attributed to Whitney have since been identified as of either dubious originality or the product of other companies. The author is not to be faulted, for his contribution to arms collecting lore and Whitney history has been immense. The book was written in an era in which the quest for arms information had just awakened, and was based on the meager information then available. A significant amount of Whitney data and correspondence has been found in the intervening years, but very little has been published on the subject since the Fuller book. Much of the information in the present chapter is based on that data and on the practical experience of advanced Whitney collectors and the author in owning, collecting and dealing in the arms themselves. While it is hoped that this section will contribute to the interest and knowledge of this significant American maker and his guns, this author is well aware of the gaps and inconsistencies that exist and which remain to be explained. No implication is made that this chapter represents a definitive study of Whitney arms. Rather, the author hopes that subsequent studies will treat the subject in depth. Some models should be more appropriately named, *e.g.*, the so-called "pre-Model 1812" flintlock muskets, which were more likely fashioned after evolutionary changes of the Model 1795 Springfield, with development parallel to that as described for 1808 contract arms (*q.v.*). It thus remains for future historians to resolve the pattern of development of some Whitney arms. This guide has confined itself to their recognition and identification, with nomenclature occasionally dictated by expediency.

The unearthing of original Whitney correspondence and the deeper research into archival material have aided in logically explaining certain weapons that were an enigma to the collector (for instance, the Massachusetts Sea Fencible musket) and in solving the mystery surrounding others (e.g., revealing Whitney as the manufacturer of the MANTON marked Civil War musket formerly thought to have been of British manufacture). Much of this new data is based on original documents, letters, diaries and company correspondence of the Whitneys housed at Yale University Library; material never tapped previously. Eventually the entire Whitney story should be told, amplifying much of the information shown here. The subject is unquestionably a worthy one.

Intriguing insights to the arms business as it existed in the first half of the nineteenth century and through the Civil War years may be gleaned from the study of Whitney firearms. What occurred with Whitney very likely applied to other manufacturers as well, and hence, may account for previously unexplained model variations. Primary among these insights are Whitney's machinations in the manufacture and sale of military longarms in the 1850s and early Civil War years. It is quickly apparent from the section describing the firm's five models known as "Good and Serviceable Arms" (Whitney's own terms) as well as some of their odd type Civil War 58 caliber muskets (termed by Whitney "good and serviceable arms not requiring gauge inspection") that the art of gun making and selling (as well as that of collecting) is not the exact science that writers and collectors would wish them to be. Quite a deal of intrigue and "behind closed door" dealings existed in the buying, selling, manufacturing and assembly of guns in America!

Having seen Whitney's method of purchasing surplus parts and assembling guns for private sale to other than U. S. government agencies, it certainly follows suit and may be assumed that other manufacturers engaged in similar activities—accounting for a number of other weapons on the American collectors' market which do not conform to strict governmental inspection standards. It remains for future researchers to bring these facts out. Also obvious is that during the era of manufacture of flintlock muskets Whitney not only sold guns that were not passable by government inspection, but also sold guns from other assembled contracts (left-over parts). This must have been standard practice of the day and will very well account for some of the odd-balls found in collecting arms by other makers. It is in this rather gray area that both the manufacturer of yesterday perpetuated abuses for the sake of sale and that the collector of today must exercise the most careful judgment to distinguish between the genuine antique that did not conform originally and that which may be a spurious modern composite. In this area gullibility most often prevails!

Further apparent after reading this Whitney chapter is that pure numbers/quantities manufactured are not in themselves the major influencing factor in collectors' values. Excellent examples are in the Phoenix, Laidley and Remington type rolling blocks as well as various lever action Whitneys. All of these were made in reasonably large, if not impressive, quantities; yet specimens of most types do not occur with the frequency seemingly indicated by the quantities produced. In great measure this is attributable to the very large quantities and contracts made and sold by Whitney to foreign countries, particularly to South and Central America (as noted in the original Whitney correspondence of the Yale Archives). In other cases the mystery yet remains as to where the arms went. The Phoenix is a prime example. Apparently made in reasonably large quantities (in relation to other American arms and collectors' rarities) they do not turn up with a frequency even approximating the numbers in which they were known to have been made and sold. When specimens are found, they most often are in very well used condition. This fact has been observed by the author over the years and equally noted by others in the field. The prices reflected in the present section are those considered retail values on a national basis for the market as it exists currently and not speculatively based on what they "should bring" according to their presumed rarity.

A further insight to nineteenth century arms manufacturing may be gleaned from the various alterations performed by Whitney for the famed New York firm of Hartley and Graham (formerly Schuyler, Hartley and Graham). The groups of sporterized trap-door Springfield 45-70s and altered Allin muskets to cadet muskets and carbines proved that such work was decidedly done by well known firms such as Whitney and lend credence to the fact that other contemporary manufacturers undoubtedly performed the same type of alterations. Their specimens remain yet to be discovered and identified for the collector.

A phase of Whitney manufacturing most significant to the collector and one that certainly should not be understated or passed over lightly was their first handgun manufacturing experience—the production under contract for Samuel Colt of the famed Colt Walker revolver, more aptly termed the Whitneyville-Walker. The story is told in detail in just about every book on Colt firearms and it is mentioned but briefly here.

A few years after the closing of his Paterson, New Jersey, factory, Samuel Colt received a contract from the U.S. government to build a large 44 caliber percussion holster pistol for use by mounted troops in the Mexican War. Without manufacturing facilities of his own and possessing a large order for 1,000 revolvers, he sought out the most logical facilities to sub-contract the work for him—those of Eli Whitney. Colt assigned his entire contract to Whitney and received an agreement to share in the profit as well as retaining ownership for special tools or machines purchased or made for the manufacturing of the Walkers. The entire contract for 1,000 pieces was made by Whitney for the government, plus 100 more for civilian sales—totaling 1,100 in all. All subsequent revolvers were made by Colt at his own factory, which was quickly established in Hartford. The entire group of Whitneyville-

Walkers was manufactured in 1847. It is a moot point as to which type of collection the Whitneyville-Walker is more deserving to be included. They are generally considered as Colts and about all information on them is normally encountered in books concerning that subject. The Walkers certainly are equally deserving of a place of importance and honor in a well rounded, complete Whitney collection.

The reader should be aware that four so-called "Collins/Improved" model Whitney-Walkers illustrated and discussed in the 1946 *Whitney Firearms* book have since been exposed as bogus. A more complete story about them is told in Chapter III, sub-heading: *The Great American Gun Scam.*

The author has not personally viewed or encountered all of the various calibers listed for the breech-loading single shot and lever action rifles. Many of the calibers might be extremely rare. Insufficient research has been done in this field to accumulate statistical data on the subject. The calibers listed are taken from original Whitney correspondence, sales literature, and catalogs of the period. It is conceivable that in some cases calibers mentioned as being available were never made, or at best were one of a kind. At this date there is no way of determining this.

Experimental, prototype, or trial pieces are known in Whitney firearms. Those that most readily come to mind are the large 36 caliber hooded cylinder percussion revolver and an interesting brass frame single shot percussion breech-loading rifle of the 1850s with a large breech rotating lever on the right side of the action. Such items are of distinct rarity and demand. Their values are usually commensurate with the importance of the arm itself (i.e., whether longarm or handgun, military or sporting, and of course, condition). As with the products of other large American arms makers, variations and other unusual features will occasionally be encountered, e.g., odd barrel lengths, nonstandard markings, and sometimes even contour changes. Some may be of original Whitney factory work while others are not. The subject is discussed in both the preface of this book and in the introductory text to the Colt chapter; the reader is referred to those respective sections.

Factory installed or applied extra features such as engraving or fancy grips can and do influence values significantly. Considering the large numbers of handguns made by Whitney, surprisingly few are found with these extras. Engraving on percussion handguns is rarely seen, although some specimens are known. Embellishments are most often encountered on the small rimfire spur trigger metallic cartridge revolvers. The use of ivory or other exotic materials for grips is also rather sparse in the Whitney percussion line, although the frequency with which these features may be observed is certainly much greater than that of engraving. Ivory grips are frequently encountered on the small metallic cartridge revolvers. These additional features increase the desirability and value of the arms on which they appear. The reader is referred to Chapter II for information in pricing such extras.

It is possible to encounter engraved Whitney longarms of the metallic cartridge era and such items are classified as very rare. These pieces would be considered highly desirable and in great demand; values would be very much dependent on both quality of the engraving and condition of the arm on which they appeared.

Conversions of Whitney revolvers from percussion to breech-loading metallic cartridge types are occasionally encountered. The majority of these are rim or centerfire types, although a few lipfires have also been seen. Most conversions are on the 36 caliber Civil War Navy type revolvers; some smaller pocket models are also known. There is no written record that such alterations were made at the Whitney factory, these were generally believed the products of individual gunsmiths. More recent research seeks to prove that a small group of the 36-caliber

"Navy" revolvers, all with identical, highly professional alterations held strong possibilities of being converted by Whitney...or, if not. perhaps (on a long shot) at a U.S. government arsenal. Stay tuned for future developments!

Of paramount importance to the collecting of Whitney arms is some knowledge of the founder, Eli Whitney, Sr., his son, and the companies that they created and managed. Their story is an important and often exciting one in American arms manufacturing history and holds not a little fascination for the collector, historian and researcher. It is covered here in brief to assist the reader in understanding the broad scope of these guns.

Eli Whitney, Sr. (1765-1825) achieved fame at an early age with his invention of the cotton gin in 1793—but one year after his graduation from Yale College. His inventive and mechanical genius completed the design and working model for this major scientific advance in a mere ten days! Results from use were immediate and it is not an overstatement that probably no other development in the history of invention had such tremendous and sudden economic impact as Whitney's invention of the cotton gin.

Through an unfortunate chain of circumstances which prevented immediate and proper patenting of his invention, and due to a loose-jointed partnership arrangement, Whitney's invention was widely copied and infringed upon. Although, after a number of years he ultimately realized legal recognition of his claim, Whitney had lost the immediate advantages of financial gain from the cotton gin and earned but little monetarily from it.

However, Whitney's mechanical and inventive genius had widely come to be acknowledged and recognized. After his disillusionment and lack of financial return from the cotton gin episode, he turned to other pursuits, deciding upon the manufacture of firearms.

Based on his reputation and character, Whitney was able to obtain in 1798 a large contract for 10,000 "stand of arms" from the U. S. government. Even though he had no previous gun making or manufacturing experience, financial backers were readily available to establish him in business. His proposal as submitted contained a unique aim "… to make the same parts of different guns, as the locks for example, as much like each other as the successive impressions of a copper-plate engraving." Although never achieving interchangeability of parts on the early Model 1798 flintlock muskets, this proposal was possibly the first inference in America of a system of parts interchangeability—a major step in American industrial development. Popular accounts often give credit for interchangeability to the Model 1798; this was not actually the case. Whitney devised tools and machines for making separate parts and by so doing added significantly to the advancement of the art of manufacturing. He accomplished his original goal by proving that workmen with little or no experience could operate machinery and with it turn out in quantity a great multitude of gun parts with marked precision. By so doing he succeeded in reducing quite complex processes to a series of rather simple operations; all of this done through the use of jigs and other labor saving devices. The very first true interchangeability of parts was not achieved until the manufacture of the Model 1819 Hall breech-loading flintlock rifle.

Presiding over his New Haven factories, Whitney continued producing guns for various government contracts until his death in 1825. No known civilian type arms bearing his name have come to light from that era; nor is it known that he made anything other than military longarms during his lifetime.

From the inception of his manufacturing activities, Eli Whitney called his facilities a "private armory." He believed the government needed a firm such as his to support the requirements for muskets in the U.S. The company was referred to as the "Whitneyville Armory" during his lifetime and until 1863 when the company was incorporated as the "Whitney Arms Company." Subsequent to that year all reference to the operation in official correspondence bore that heading.

Prior to his death Whitney entered into contract with his two nephews, Philos and Eli Whitney Blake, to manage the operation of his gun factory as his son, Eli Whitney, Jr., was still a minor. The Blakes ran the armory until 1834 at which time the interim trustees of the estate, Henry Edwards and James Goodrich, continued operations of the factory through 1842. In that year Eli Whitney, Jr. came of age and took over the reins of management.

Continuing with the manufacture of contract flintlock muskets for the U. S. government, Eli Whitney, Jr. moved into large quantity contracts of the Model 1841 percussion rifle. His early diary entries indicate he experienced extreme money problems and the Model 1841 production created most of these. Even though contract quantities of the Model 1841 were large and production continued until 1855, it proved to be an unprofitable undertaking. In subsequent ventures, aside from his handgun manufacturing, Eli Whitney, Jr. was concerned primarily with making guns from U.S. government auction parts, and in using imported parts as well as residual parts purchased at auction from the Robbins and Lawrence Armory in Windsor, Vermont. His correspondence and diaries of the era indicate that he was something less than a good businessman and was often preoccupied with calculating profits before he made or sold his products. They further show his search for bargains and maneuvering to buy at the "lowest possible price." While his father had been the mechanical and investing genius, the younger Whitney, despite patents of his own, did not possess the same ingenuity or business acumen. Considerable material, including gun barrels, was purchased on the European market while condemned parts from U.S. armories came from the American surplus market. With the foreclosure, after bankruptcy, of the Robbins and Lawrence Armory in 1857, Whitney purchased large quantities of Enfield stocks and gun parts and, evidently, some gun making machinery and/or machine tools. As late as 1862 he was still attempting to sell surplus materiel from the Windsor, Vermont, armory and large lots of Enfield rifle stocks. The company concerned itself in the mid-1850s with the building of serviceable arms that resembled the standard government issue weapons, and achieved nearly the same selling price—but did not have to undergo the rigid inspection and other formalities of sale to the U.S. government.

With the Whitneyville-Plymouth rifle and 1863 contracts for the Civil War 58 caliber musket, Whitney moved back into the area of devoting his efforts almost entirely towards State and Federal government production. After the cessation of Civil War hostilities, he sought and acquired patents for breechloaders, entering into competition of Federal trials for adoption of such arms. Failing to attract government contracts for any of his patents, he readily engaged and continued in the manufacture of breech-loading single shot firearms and lever action arms of various types. Much of this production was sold abroad. It is in the post-Civil War era through the 1870s that he very much expanded the company's offerings to the sporting market along with the military. His single shot and repeating rifles were competitive with Winchester, but they were never a very serious threat and did not achieve the popularity of those more firmly entrenched arms.

With advancement of age and the diminishing sales of his products, Eli Whitney, Jr. began search for a buyer for the company as early as 1883. His son Eli Whitney, III apparently played no active role with the firm. Severe business reverses by 1888 proved too late to save the Whitney Arms Company and a sale was negotiated with Winchester Repeating Arms Company which acquired the properties, assets and equipment of Whitney in 1888.

The Whitney factory was immediately closed and the property operated under lease by Winchester until 1903 at which time it was sold to the New Haven Water Company. Winchester moved machinery and tools to its main plant in New Haven following their purchase and the entire Whitney firearms line was withdrawn from the market. Winchester did not manufacture rifles utilizing Whitney actions which had been in current production at the time of their acquisition. So ended some 90 years of manufacture in the firearms field under the famous name of Whitney.

An interesting collection of Whitney and other New England makers' arms and artifacts (regrettably no factory records) are at the Eli Whitney Museum in Whitneyville, New Haven, Conn. on the site of the original Whitney Armory.

BIBLIOGRAPHY

(Note: Material about Whitney may be found in other books on American firearms. A few of the more important titles [to be found listed in bibliographies elsewhere in this book] are: *The Rifle In America* by Sharpe; *American Percussion Revolvers* by Sellers and Smith; *Civil War Guns* by Edwards; *U.S. Military Small Arms 1816-1865* by Reilly; *Identifying Old U.S. Muskets, Rifles and Carbines* by Gluckman; *Single Shot Rifles* by Grant; *More Single Shot Rifles* by Grant; *Lever Action Magazine Rifles* by Maxwell; *The Colt Whitneyville-Walker Pistol* by Whittington and American Military Shoulder Arms Vol. II* by Moller. *Ten Rare Gun Catalogs 1860-1899* by Amber which contains a reprint of the 1878 Whitney catalog.)

Cooper, C. & Lindsay, M. *Eli Whitney & The Whitney Armory*. Whitneyville, Conn.: Eli Whitney Museum 1980. Whitney's pioneer manufacturing work; identification of Whitney muskets; list of New Haven makers; chapter on Simeon North.

Fuller, Claud E. *The Whitney Firearms*. Huntington, West Virginia: Standard Publications, Inc., 1946. First and only book entirely devoted to Whitney arms. A wealth of important biographical and technical information based on limited material available at time of publication. Note considerable gaps and a lack of definitive information on technical detail of the guns and their variations.

Hall, K.L. & Cooper, C. *Windows On The Works: Industry On The Eli Whitney Site 1798-1979*. Hamden, Conn., Whitney Museum, 1984

Thrower, Charles W. *Whitney Firearms*. Unpublished manuscript in possession of the author; Wellesley, Massachusetts.

(*) Preceding a title indicates the book is currently in print.

LONGARMS

Whitney 1798 U.S. Contract Musket

5J-005
Whitney 1798 U.S. Contract Musket (Style III)

5J-001
Style close up

5J-005
Style III

U.S. Contract of 1798 Flintlock Musket (Basic U.S. Model 1795 or Charleville Pattern). Manufactured Circa 1801-1809. Total quantity delivered 10,000. Made in three distinct types.

69 caliber single shot muzzleloader; 43-3/4" round barrel fastened by three barrel bands; small stud for socket bayonet at top of barrel 1-1/4" from muzzle.

Iron mountings with trigger guard having pointed finial towards muzzle and rounded lower end. All metal parts finished bright. Steel ramrod with button tip.

Black walnut stock with comb; oil finished; inspector markings on left side opposite lock.

Barrel marked with inspector marking of James Carrington (C.P. overlay) or Robert Orr (which appears in a sunken cartouche as two concentric circles) and an oval indicating government proof.

Lock marked U. STATES in arch design positioned vertically at rear and NEW HAVEN under eagle motif ahead of hammer. The lower rear end of frizzen spring terminates in a distinct double pointed or spear shape.

This first Contract for 10,000 guns represented one-quarter of the Model 1795 guns contracted for by the Government, and attested to the faith and confidence placed in Eli Whitney. Without prior exposure to arms manufacturing he worked, invented, designed and with time established the finest private Armory of the period.

His guns, while not totally dimensionally interchangeable as some had hoped, did approach interchangeability with special jigs and fixtures.

STYLE I. Distinguished by the flat lockplate with pointed, teat-like projection at rear; flat hammer; *faceted, integral* iron flashpan;

a curl to the lower forward projection of the frizzen. Inspector markings on stock of Noble Orr (N.O.) and D. Wadsworth (W.) Only 1,000 of this first style produced and considered quite rare, especially so as most believed shortened and later condemned:

5J-001   Values—Good **$6,000**   Fine **$22,500**

Same; Converted to Percussion:

5J-002   Values—Good **$1,500**   Fine **$3,000**

STYLE II. Very similar to first style with pointed teat-like projection at rear of lock, but with rounded brass flashpan mounted at an inclined angle. Inspector markings of Robert Orr only on stock, a fancy U.S. in an oval with ORR framed in lower portion. Only 1,000 manufactured:

5J-003   Values—Good **$1,650**   Fine **$4,250**

Same; Converted to Percussion:

5J-004   Values—Good **$600**   Fine **$1,000**

STYLE III. Easily distinguished by the evenly rounded rear of the lock, terminating without the pointed teat-like projection. The hammer is rounded; same brass flashpan as Style II and the lower forward projection of the frizzen is flat, quantity approx. 8,000. All bear the inspection marks of Robert Orr except the last 500 bearing those of Charles William (V over CW):

5J-005   Values—Good **$1,500**   Fine **$3,500**

Same; Converted to Percussion:

5J-006   Values—Good **$500**   Fine **$850**

Whitney 1798 Conn. Contract Musket

Connecticut Militia Contract 1798 type Flintlock Musket (Basic U.S. Model 1795). (Not illus.) Manufactured c. 1804-1810. Total quantity delivered 112.

Musket will duplicate Style III of the U.S. Contract; except the lock will not have U. STATES on it. The inspection was by the State of Connecticut whose seal is a shield containing three bunches of grapes stamped in wood opposite lock. CONNECTICUT is usually stamped on the sideplate and the gun will carry a rack number from #1 to 112.

Connecticut contracted for 112 muskets starting in 1804 to replace the old Brown Bess then being used by the First Company of the Governor's Foot Guard:

5J-007   Values—Good **$1,600**   Fine **$3,750**

Same; converted to percussion:

5J-008   Values—Good **$600**   Fine **$950**

Whitney N.Y. Contract Pre-1812 Musket

New York Militia Contracts pre-Model 1812 Flintlock Musket (basic configuration of the Whitney Model 1812 and predecessor to it). (Not illus.; see U.S. Model 1812 Contract.) Manufactured c. 1808-1812. Total quantity delivered 4,000.

The State of New York as a part of their contract to Whitney in 1808 instructed him to modify the 1798 musket as follows: (A) Make the barrel heavier by 4 to 8 ounces from the center to the breech. (B) Heavier limbs on the lock. (C) Two to four more threads on the breech plug. (D) Thicker grip on the stock. (E) Seasoned wood. From these changes evolved the basic features carried through the State Contracts to his obtaining the Model 1812 Government Contract in 1812.

69 caliber single shot muzzleloader; 42" round barrel fastened by three barrel bands; small stud for socket bayonet at top of barrel 1-1/4" from muzzle; 6-5/8" lockplate.

Iron mountings with trigger guard having pointed finial towards muzzle and rounded other end. All metal parts finished bright. Steel ramrod with button tip or trumpet tip.

Black walnut stock without comb, oil finished with inspector markings on left side opposite lock. State inspectors were John McLean (wavy edged circle around V/BY/I.M.) or a Mr. Peck (whose mark is not known).

Barrel will have the usual P in an oval indicating proof and stamped S.N.Y. (State of New York).

Lock marked with eagle motif over N. HAVEN or only N. HAVEN in a scroll; rounded hammer; rounded brass flashpan mounted at an inclined angle; double pointed spear shape tip on

5J-009
Early Production

5J-009
Late Production

the frizzen spring:

5J-009   Values—Good **$1,600**   Fine **$3,000**

Same as above; Converted to Percussion:

5J-010   Values—Good **$500**   Fine **$800**

Whitney Conn. Contract Pre-1812 Musket

Connecticut Militia Contracts pre-Model 1812 Flintlock Musket (basic configuration of the Whitney Model 1812 and predecessor to it). Manufactured c. 1810-1812. Total quantity delivered 1,400.

69 caliber single shot muzzleloader, 42" round barrel fastened by three barrel bands; small stud for socket bayonet at top of barrel 1-1/4" from barrel.

Iron mountings with trigger guard having pointed finial towards muzzle and rounded lower end. All metal parts finished bright. Steel ramrod with button or trumpet head.

Black walnut combless stock, oil finished with State inspector's mark, the State shield with three bunches of grapes on the left side opposite the lock; a large S.C. (State of Connecticut) is sometimes stamped or burned into the top of the stock.

Barrel with P in oval proof and usually also stamped S.C.

Earlier locks will resemble the contract 1798 Style III Contract without U. STATES and the remainder will have only N. HAVEN in a scroll. Rounded hammer; rounded brass flashpan mounted at an inclined angle; double pointed spear shaped tip on frizzen spring:

5J-011   Values—Good **$1,600**   Fine **$3,000**
Same as above; converted to percussion·
5J-012   Values—Good **$500**   Fine **$800**

Whitney U.S. Contract 1812 Musket

U.S. Contract of 1812 Flintlock Musket. Manufactured from 1812-1824. Total quantity manufactured 18,000.

69 caliber single shot muzzleloader; 42" round barrel fastened by three barrel bands; small stud for socket bayonet at top of barrel 1-1/4" from muzzle.

Iron mountings with trigger guard having pointed finial towards muzzle and rounded lower end. All metal parts finished bright. Steel ramrod with button head.

Black walnut stock without comb, oil finished with inspector markings on left side opposite lock. Inspected by D. Wadsworth, S. Fuller, J. Newbury, L. Sage, A. Hubbard with their initial stamps. J. Newbury inspected most of this contract.

The only barrel mark usually seen is the P in oval proof.

Lock marked only N. HAVEN in a scroll. Rounded hammer, rounded brass pan on inclined angle. The lock will fall into one of three categories and the measurement of the small of the stock (or wrist) will vary.

Whitney convinced the government in 1812 to contract for the somewhat special musket that he had been building for State Contracts. This musket incorporated advancements in design that were not found in the arms then being made for by the government under the 1808 contracts. Whitney's Model 1812 musket ultimately became the basis for the U.S. Model 1816 musket. The Model 1812 like its forerunner, the Contract of 1798, were made in lots of ten and did not have dimensionally interchangeable parts.

STYLE I. The earliest has a lock 6-5/8" long by 1/8" thick; double pointed frizzen spear shaped tip of spring, and the frizzen screw 1-11/16" in from the end of the lock. Circumference of wrist of buttstock 5-1/4" to 5-3/8"; estimated production 5,000:

5J-013   Values—Good **$1,250**   Fine **$2,750**

As above; converted to percussion:
5J-014   Values—Good **$500**   Fine **$750**

STYLE II. Intermediate design will have a lock 6-1/2" long by either 1/8" or 3/16" thick; frizzen spring of either one or two points, and the frizzen screw 1-11/16" in from the end of the lock. Thicker wrist circumference 5-5/8" to 5-7/8". Estimated production 2,000:

5J-015   Values—Good **$1,250**   Fine **$2,750**

As above; converted to percussion:
5J-016   Values—Good **$500**   Fine **$750**

STYLE III. The later lock is 6-1/2" long by 3/16" thick, single point on frizzen spring and the frizzen screw 1-7/8" in from the end of the lock. Wrist circumference as in Style II. Estimated production 11,000:

5J-017   Values—Good **$1,250**   Fine **$2,750**

As above; converted to percussion:
5J-018   Values—Good **$500**   Fine **$750**

NEW YORK STATE PURCHASE. The first 1,000 muskets manufactured on this contract, because of a conflict between the government and Whitney, were not U.S. inspected nor accepted and quickly purchased by the State of New York under Governor D. Tompkins. They were, however, inspected by James Carrington under Whitney's direction and bear his C superimposed over P at breech of barrel which also is stamped SNY and P proof in sunken oval. They otherwise duplicate Style I of the 1812 contract:

5J-019   Values—Good **$1,250**   Fine **$2,750**

As above; converted to percussion:
5J-020   Values—Good **$500**   Fine **$750**

5J-017
Style III

Whitney Mass. Contract 1812 Musket

5J-023
Type II

5J-021
Type I

Massachusetts Militia Contract Model 1812 Flintlock Musket. Manufactured c. 1815.

Massachusetts (including Maine) in 1815 contracted for over 1,455 arms (of various makers) to issue to the State Militia Forces. Reimbursement from the Federal Government for these contracts was not made until many years later after a long and often bitter suit by the State. As Massachusetts had not been a very willing participant in the War of 1812, the Federal Government was not easily convinced to pay for its arms bills.

TYPE I. (a.k.a. "Sea Fencible Musket.") Typical Model 1812 Whitney flintlock (Style III), but has the buttstock thinned down considerably and is fitted with a uniquely shaped, thick brass buttplate with a rounded projection on its heel. The barrel stamped M.S. (State of Massachusetts); a rack number (usually two digits) on buttplate; five digit number stamped at top of barrel between the straps of upper barrel band (reason unknown; numbers all seem to appear in the 10,000, 11,000, or 12,000 series). Lock marked N. HAVEN in scroll.

Although this has been previously identified as a "Sea Fencible Musket" and/or a "Navy Contract" musket, it seems that such attributions are not the case. However, no further, or better, designation has been assigned, leaving the reason for the uniquely shaped buttplate an enigma. Quantity likely less than 100:

5J-021	Values—Good **$1,600**		Fine **$3,750**

As above; converted to percussion:

5J-022	Values—Good **$800**		Fine **$1,250**

TYPE II. A Style II or III Model 1812 flintlock musket; stock has a comb and usual iron buttplate; stamped in the wood with a V over S.F. all in a diamond over M.S. The barrel has the usual P in an oval M.S. and the five digit number. Lock marked N.HAVEN in scroll. While the exact number of muskets sold to Massachusetts is unknown, it is felt based on other contracts they number less than 300:

5J-023	Values—Good **$1,400**		Fine **$2,750**

As above; converted to percussion:

5J-024	Values—Good **$500**		Fine **$750**

Whitney 1822 U.S. Contract Musket

5J-025

U.S. Contract of 1822 Flintlock Musket (Basic U.S. Model 1816 with 1822 improvement). Manufactured under two contracts from 1822 until 1841. Made with three distinct lock plate markings.

69 caliber single shot muzzleloader, 42" round barrel fastened by three bands with band springs; stud for socket bayonet at top of barrel 1-1/4" from muzzle.

Iron mountings; trigger guard has rounded ends and sling swivel is part of the trigger guard. Steel ramrod with button head. U.S. stamped on heel of buttplate.

Black walnut stock, oil finished, with inspector markings on left side opposite lock.

FIRST CONTRACT. Quantity 15,000; bears lock markings U.S. over P & E.W. BLAKE to right of hammer and NEW HAVEN over date (from 1826 to 1830) at rear. The barrel was originally browned on this contract; inspectors were John Newbury (JN), Asabel Hubbard (AH), Luther Sage (L.S.), James Carrington (JC), Joseph Weatherhead (J.W.), Justin Murphy (JM), Elisha Tobey (ET), Jacob Perkin (J.P.), George Flegel (G.F.), James Bell (JB). P in circle proof, inspectors initials and U.S. stamped at breech. The tang usually bears the same date as the lock.

Whitney was to start delivery in 1824, but due to his illness and death in January, 1825, the Government extended the first delivery until January, 1826. Philos and Eli Whitney Blake were nephews of Eli Whitney, Sr. They had entered into contract with their uncle to run the factory prior to his death and took over all manufacturing operations subsequent to his passing. The Blakes left the armory in 1834. Interim trustees were appointed until Eli Whitney, Jr. came of age and assumed control of operations:

5J-025	Values—Good **$1,250**		Fine **$2,500**

Same as above; converted to percussion:

5J-026	Values—Good **$450**		Fine **$700**

SECOND CONTRACT. Signed in 1830 and extended through 1841; quantity 24,000. The locks from 1830 to either 1837 or 1838 will have a branch and crossed arrows, U.S. and E. WHITNEY in the center and at rear N. HAVEN and date from 1830 or 1838. Locks dated from 1837 until 1841 are identical, but omit arrow and branch motif. The tang usually bears the same date as the lock. Inspectors were R. Chandler (RC), C. W. Hartwell (CWH), A. D. King (ADK), Thomas Warner (TW), Luther Sage (LS), Asa Hubbard (AH), N. W. Patch (NWP), Justin Murphy (JM), D. LeGro (DLG), E. A. May (EAM), H. Tracy (HT), W. North (WN), O. W. Ainsworth (OWA), J. N. Sollace (JNS), J. Stillman (JS), W. A. Thornton (WAT):

5J-027	Values—Good **$1,250**		Fine **$2,500**

As above; converted to percussion:

5J-028	Values—Good **$450**		Fine **$700**

Whitney So. Carolina Contract 1816 Musket

South Carolina Militia Contract Model 1816 (1822 Improvement) Flintlock Musket. (Not. illus.) Manufactured c. 1837. Total quantity delivered 800 to 1,000. Identical to the second U. S. Contract of 1822. Lock markings E.WHITNEY in center (without the arrow and branch motif) and N. HAVEN over date 1837 or 1838 at rear.

Does not bear inspector marking by the U. S. government, but does have the usual P in oval barrel proof. Definitive information on this contract not available; they are also believed marked SO. CAROLINA on breech of barrel or stamped in stock:

5J-029	Values—Good **$2,500**		Fine **$5,000**

As above; converted to percussion:

5J-030	Values—Good **$2,250**		Fine **$3,500**

Whitney Composite 1816 Musket

Composite or Class II muskets from Residual Model 1816 Contract Parts. (Not. illus.) Made by Whitney of parts not up to full Federal Standards (Class I), but yet not rejected by them. Manufactured c. 1842. Total quantity sold 1,000.

This group of muskets were offered to the U.S. Navy in 1842 and it is unknown who actually purchased them. Probability is they were ultimately sold to a state for militia use. They do not carry the usual U.S. inspection marks although they do bear the P in oval

proved barrel and possibly a state marking; worth small premium:

| 5J-031 | Values—Good **$1,250** | Fine **$2,000** |

As above; converted to percussion:

| 5J-032 | Values—Good **$450** | Fine **$700** |

Whitney 1816 Mass. Percussion Conversion

Massachusetts Militia (Sea Fencible or Coast Artillery) Contract, Model 1816 converted to Percussion with brass buttplate.

Converted c. 1851. Total number of conversions estimated at less than 300.

Whitneys, Springfields and Waters Model 1816 converted to percussion with a considerably thinned buttstock and fitted with a heavy brass buttplate about identical to the Type I Massachusetts Militia Contract Model 1812. The plate has a rack number and M.S. stamped on the barrel. A five digit number may be found on the barrel between the straps of the upper barrel band.

While the actual source of the conversion is unknown, it is listed under Whitney as the majority of the conversions seem to be of that manufacture. Apparently all are found as conversions

only. The reason for the unique brass buttplate (a few iron are known) has yet to be determined. Earlier identification as a "Sea Fencible" or "Navy Contract" musket is apparently incorrect. (*See also 5J-021 this chapter*):

| 5J-033 | Values—Good **$800** | Fine **$1,250** |

5J-033

Whitney 1841 U.S. Percussion Rifle

5J-034

Whitney 1841 U.S. Percussion Rifle. Made 1843 to 1855; total production 26,500 under four contracts (*see also Chapter IX-A "U.S. Model 1841"*).

54 caliber; 33" round barrel fastened by two barrel bands; not adapted for bayonet. Browned finish.

Brass mountings and patchbox. U.S. marked on buttplate. Blued trigger, bandsprings, and screwheads; casehardened lock. Steel ramrod with brass tip. (Altered later to iron tips to accept pointed Minie bullet). Walnut stock, oil finished; inspector marks left side opposite lock. Inset brass blade frontsight; seven groove rifling. Marked V/P/U.S. with various inspector initials

and (after 1848) STEEL at breech. Tang dated same as lock. "V" notch open type rear sight.

Lock marked E. WHITNEY over U.S. ahead of hammer; N. HAVEN with date (1843 through 1855) vertically at rear. (Although reported in prior editions as only 100 made in 1855, records indicate that quantity much larger; 1855 date appears on this and long range model below).

These were young Whitney's first contracts after assuming leadership of the company. Although he supplied large quantities of well-made rifles, the contract price was never adequate to cover the tooling and set-up costs. In later life he wrote that he had spent thirteen of his best years with the Model 1841 and really never made a profit:

| 5J-034 | Values—Good **$1,250** | Fine **$4,250** |

South Carolina Contract and Other Whitney Model 1841 Rifles

South Carolina Contract and Other Whitney Model 1841 Rifles. (Not illus.) Although most details lacking, it is known that some U.S. contract M1841s failed government inspection and such guns were sold to the more lucrative market supported by state militias and to meet the urgent needs of emigrants and adventurers opening the Western frontier and heading for the California gold fields. Details of markings on those latter types not known but likely will be standard Whitney M1841s lacking

inspector markings. Although quite possible other state markings will be recorded there are two known contracts (November and December, 1849) for total 274 pieces to South Carolina. Lock marked E.WHITNEY over SC with N.Haven/1849 at rear. Blade type front sight affixed to upper strap of top barrel band; bayonet lug on underside near muzzle for socket type bayonet. Very rare:

| 5J-034.5 | Values—Good **$3,000** | Fine **$6,000** |

Model 1841 U.S. Whitney Adapted For Long Range

Model 1841 U.S. Whitney Adapted for Long Range. (Not illus.) Made 1855. Quantity 600. Identical #5J-034 with altered steel tip ramrod to accept the Minie pointed bullet. Bayonet stud with projecting, 1" narrow guide rail for saber type bayonet. Front of

stock shortened slightly with new, shorter, double strap barrel band. Long range rear sight with 2-1/2" base. Lock and tang with "1855" date:

| 5J-035 | Values—Good **$1,500** | Fine **$4,250** |

Whitney "Good and Serviceable Arms"

Good and Serviceable Arms. The following Whitney longarms (through number VJ-047.5) were made by Whitney from the mid-1850s through the Civil War years. Together with surplus parts from his Model 1841 contracts, Whitney purchased quantities of condemned parts from the Springfield and Harper's Ferry Armories, parts from the Robbins and Lawrence factory at Windsor, Vermont when their arms contracts were forfeited, and quantities of European and American parts when they could be inexpensively acquired and assembled the following models. They were sold to states and private militia companies as "good and serviceable arms not to be subject to government inspection with gauges." He had just completed the Model 1841 contracts and found it a profitless venture, thus, the assembly of inexpensive parts into non-gauge controlled production gave him a saleable product at a fair price, yet with a substantial profit. His manufacturing emphasis was with such arms until he went into full production of the U.S. Navy Plymouth rifle and U.S. contract .58 caliber muskets in 1863 "...I expect to be more particular in my government work than in my state work, as the State inspection is not with gauges. The inspector only examines the finished gun, which we agree to furnish good and serviceable."

Earlier editions of this work first brought to light these "Good and Serviceable Arms," identifying, describing and illustrating all of them. In the lengthy interim between that pioneering study of the First Edition, the arms have been researched in greater depth, and placed in more proper chronological order and with greater detail. The author has leaned heavily upon the study by Howard Michael Madaus "Percussion Martial Longarms of Eli Whitney, Jr." published in *Armax; Journal of the Winchester Arms & Museum* (Volume II Number 1) to make the story of these interesting arms current. In order not to disturb this Guide's identification numbers, the original order has been retained (except where noted); the correct chronological order, varying but slightly, is found in the Madaus article.

See also NEW HAMPSHIRE *marked* M.1842 *style musket made by Whitney* 9B-035.

(A) M1841 "Good and Serviceable" Rifles. With no government contracts and a general business slowdown between 1855 and 1861 Whitney made every effort to utilize surplus parts from his M1841 contracts. As late as 1864, New York military outfitters Schuyler, Hartley and Graham advertised in their well-known catalog the "Mississippi Rifle," although no maker's name was given. There is every reason to believe that they were (or, at least, many of them were) those made by Whitney. Recorded variations are:

Type I: OHIO marked. About standard to U.S. contract of 1855 but with earlier "V" notch open rear sight; no stock inspection marks; stud for saber type bayonet (found with or without the narrow one inch rail guide); short double strap top barrel band. Standard lock markings found both with or without US. Large OHIO markings branded on left side of stock to rear of sideplate. Although "Ohio markings" are found on regular U.S. contract M1841s, the state also purchased separately 420 "Mississippis" direct from Whitney, using Schuyler, Hartley and Graham as their agent. Values are for OHIO marked rifles; without OHIO markings values are 25 percent less than shown.

There is strong evidence that Georgia and Mississippi both purchased quantities of these M1841s in 1860-61 before the outbreak of hostilities, direct from Whitney and through agents D.C. Hodgkins of Macon, Georgia:
5J-035.2 Values—Good **$1,500** Fine **$4,500**

Type II: Similar to above, but no patchbox. Circa 1856-57. Bayonet stud with 1" guide rail. Locks found both with and

without US. Usually without US on buttplate. Sights vary; most thought to be Sharps Model 1853 carbine type:
5J-035.3 Values—Good **$1,250** Fine **$3,000**

Type III: Similar to above. Circa late 1850s. Quantity unknown. With Iron patchbox. Brass bow on iron trigger strap. Stud for socket type bayonet. Early, wide type double strap barrel band. No US on lockplate; has US on butt:
5J-035.4 Values—Good **$1,500** Fine **$3,250**

Type IV: Circa late 1850s. No patchbox. Brass bow on iron trigger strap. No US on lock or butt. No provision for bayonet. Early type Model 1841 open sights:
5J-035.5 Values—Good **$1,250** Fine **$3,000**

5J-036

(B) Model 1855 (Maynard Tape Primer) Rifle-Musket Style: Circa 1861. Quantity 350 estimated. 58 caliber. 40" bright finish barrel fastened by three barrel bands. Iron mountings of M1855 style with Enfield type pewter forend cap, band springs and "wing" style brass lockscrew ferrules. Barrels rifled with seven grooves (unique to Whitney on these types). Locks were condemned or defective, but complete, M.1855 Maynard Tape Primed style, usually, but not always, dated 1858 (their original date of U.S. Armory manufacture) but marked E.WHITNEY/N.HAVEN forward of hammer. Only variations noted are sights: Type I used long 2-5/16" base with folding leaf and slide: Type II shorter 1-5/16" base with single "L" shaped leaf with pierced aperture.

This model known to have been issued to the 8th Connecticut Volunteer Infantry:
5J-036 Values—Good **$1,500** Fine **$3,500**
(C) Model 1855 (Maynard Primer) Rifle Style: (In the first five editions of this Guide was number 5J-040). Made circa 1860-61. Estimated total 100 (approximately 50 of each type).

Whitney acquired a number of U.S. Model 1855 rifle barrels (33") dated 1858 and 1859 from surplus or condemned material sold by the Harper's Ferry Arsenal. The barrels were already three groove rifled (58 caliber) with front sights and bayonet lugs (without the guide rail) of arsenal type.

A key identification feature is the M1855 lockplate (acquired as surplus or condemned from U.S. arsenal) which was never milled for the Maynard primer and the "high hump" ground down to generally fit the contour of the stock (similar to that found on the Confederate Richmond Armory Type III longarms. *See Chapter X*). Lock marked E.WHITNEY ahead of hammer. Brass M1841 barrel bands with narrow double strap top band. Slight variances distinguish the two types: Earlier has sight base 2-7/8" from breech with M1855 lockscrew ferrules; later type sight base 5-5/8" from breech with Enfield style "winged" ferrules. The three-digit number usually seen on bayonet stud not a serial; likely intended to match fitting of bayonet. Whitney numbering

5J-036.5

**5J-038
Enfield Type Rifle—Musket**

on tang of iron buttplate on earlier production; near muzzle of barrel on later made. Brass trigger strap with iron trigger bow:
5J-036.5   Values—Good **$1,500**   Fine **$2,750**

5J-037 Richmond Type Humpback Lock Rifle-Musket
(Editions 1 through 5) Reclassified 5J-047.5 (*q.v.*).

(D) Whitney-Enfield Style Muskets and Rifles: All the transactions and machinations that transpired with the machinery, tools, jigs and surplus parts left over from the defunct Vermont factory of Robbins & Lawrence are yet to be told. After entering bankruptcy proceedings caused by failure to complete their contract with the British government for percussion Enfield rifle-muskets (for Crimean War use) their plant was sold to Lamson & Goodnow of Vermont, the machinery last being recorded located at Hartford, Connecticut under the control of the Sharps Rifle Company by 1860. It is known that Whitney acquired at bargain prices 5,000 sets of the solid type, iron, barrel bands for the Enfield rifle and quantities of stock blanks, at the liquidation auction in Vermont. It is also known that as late as 1863 Whitney was trying to sell thousands of surplus Enfield stock blanks as well as surplus Enfield rifling machines. He likely acquired other lesser manufacturing items at the liquidation, contributing to the reason that he chose to manufacture longarms on the general pattern of the British Enfield. The Whitney-Enfields are only generally similar, at best, to the British pattern, clear indicating Whitney's use of parts other than the Robbins & Lawrence-British Enfields. Two distinct types were made:
(1) Rifle-Musket: Made c. 1859-1862. Quantity estimated 3,500. Caliber 58. Seven groove rifling. 40" barrel (instead of 39" British length), bolster and clean-out screw similar to Model 1855 U.S. Takes socket bayonet. Full stock fastened by three iron Enfield solid type barrel bands; pewter forend cap of Enfield design cast direct to stock; Enfield type "winged" brass lockscrew escutcheons; iron buttplate of Enfield style; two piece trigger guard (brass bow/iron strap) instead of one piece brass Enfield type. Long base rear sight.
    Distinctive flat, flush fitted lockplate vastly different than Enfield style; narrow upward projection between bolster and stock; marked only E.WHITNEY near center. Awkwardly shaped hammer.

Records indicate that the state of Maryland purchased 2,000 of these in 1860 following the John Brown Raid, all of which delivered in 1861 and issued to Maryland Volunteer Militia. 370 of those pieces were seized by Southern sympathizers from a warehouse in the city during the Baltimore riots on the night of April 19, 1861 and undoubtedly saw later Confederate service.
    The state of Georgia contracted with Whitney for 1,700 of these in November 1860 and it is believed at least 1,225 were delivered by February 1861. Another 75 were purchased in late 1860 by the "Enterprise Guards" of Clark County, Mississippi (eventually Company B, 14th Mississippi Infantry). Obviously, many others were likely sold to Northern Militia through various agents and dealers. No specific markings are known indicating their Northern or Southern regimental usage. Such markings if authentic would increase values 50-100 percent from those shown below. The collector is urged to use extreme caution if such markings are present:
5J-038   Values—Good **$1,150**   Fine **$2,750**
(2) Enfield Type Rifle: Made c. 1859-1862. Same Enfield style configuration as above but with shorter 33" barrel fastened by two barrel bands. Same mountings (very small quantity only encountered with brass Enfield type trigger guard).

> **Type I:** Large oval, iron patchbox on right butt (brass known; very rare); no bayonet stud; M1841 rifle sights with brass blade front inset in barrel; open type, V-notch rear. Estimated quantity under 150:
> **5J-039**   Values—Good **$2,000**   Fine **$3,750**

> **Type II:** Oval, iron patchbox with lug for saber type bayonet; slightly shortened forestock to accept bayonet; iron blade front sight; long range rear sight with tall, ladder leaf. Quantity estimated 300. It is now reasonably certain that it is this Type III that was rejected by the State of Mississippi who ordered 1500 rifles in 1860 thinking they were purchasing the "true" Model 1841 rifles. Although only 60 have formerly been believed delivered to the state, the correct quantity is 160, the initial delivery (and the one most often mentioned) of 60, with 100 more delivered before the contract was terminated:
> **5J-039.2** Values—Good **$2,000**   Fine **$3,750**

> **Type III:** Similar to above, with stud for saber-bayonet but made without patchbox. Basic difference between this and Type IV is rear sight; this fitted with long 2-5/16" base and long range ladder/leaf. Quantity estimated at least 200; it is established that at least some companies of the 10th Rhode Island Infantry were armed with the Type III:
> **5J-039.4** Values—Good **$1,500**   Fine **$2,750**

**5J-039.2
Enfield Type Rifle**

Type IV: Similar above; without patchbox; has Whitney made short base rear sight similar to U.S. style, but without the stepped sides, short "L" shaped leaf with small aperture. At least 336 of this type and possibly as many as 500 were purchased by the U.S. directly from Schuyler, Hartley & Graham of N.Y. in 1861. Total quantity estimated 600:
5J-039.6 Values—Good **$1,500**   Fine **$2,750**

5J-040. Model 1841 "Mississippi" Style Rifle. (Editions 1 through 5) Reclassified 5J-036.5 (*q.v.*).

Whitney 1861 Navy Percussion Rifle

5J-041

Model 1861 U.S. Navy Percussion Rifle (a.k.a. Plymouth Rifle). Manufactured under the contract of July, 1861, with delivery of 10,000 guns completed in 1864.

69 caliber, single shot muzzleloader, 34" round bright finished barrel fastened with two bands.

Iron mountings throughout, U.S. stamped on buttplate, steel ramrod with large cylindrically shaped tip pierced with small hole.

Black walnut stock, oil finished with inspectors marks in the wood on side opposite lock. Typical inspection initials will be JHG or FCW. The trigger guard has a spur finger grip behind the guard bow and the rear sling is mounted on the stock near the buttplate.

Barrel has three groove rifling, small iron blade front sight, markings are V,P over eagle, date of 1863, 1864 on top flat. Inspector marks FCW or W (both Frank C. Warner) or JHG (John H. Griffiths). Unique long range leaf type rear sight graduated to 1,000 yards. Large bayonet lug on right side of muzzle.

1st Style lockplate marking of large eagle-shield-flag motif ahead of hammer; beneath bolster: U.S./WHITNEY-VILLE: at rear of hammer, dated 1863, vertically.

2nd Style lockplate marking of small eagle-shield motif over U.S. ahead of hammer; WHITNEY-VILLE under bolster. Date 1863 or 1864 at rear of lock, stamped vertically. Values similar.

Whitney undoubtedly assembled guns from the residual parts of this contract and rifles resembling the contract guns with minor modifications, such as trigger guards without a finger spur are occasionally encountered. Permission was granted by the Navy to utilize the M1861 Rifle-Musket lock. The numbers stamped on barrel tangs are not serials. They were applied by Whitney in order to match up the saber bayonets provided by Collins & Co. which required individual hand fitting.

Inspiration for design of this arm was the French military "Carabine a Tige" percussion rifle. The Plymouth was produced under recommendation of Captain John A. Dahlgren, one of the U.S. Navy's most well known ordnance officers. The nickname "Plymouth" was derived from the U.S.S. Plymouth aboard which the gun was originally developed c. 1856-1858 while the vessel's primary mission was the testing of new naval ordnance and under command of Captain Dahlgren. (*See 9A-312.5 Chapter IX-A, pattern rifle for Whitney "Plymouth" rifle made by Washington Navy Yard*):
5J-041   Values—Good **$1,500**   Fine **$4,000**

Whitney U.S. Contract 1861 Rifle-Musket

U.S. Government Contract—Model 1861 Rifle-Musket. (Not illus.) Manufactured under contract of October 17, 1863, and completed delivery of 15,000 guns. *See Chapter IX, "American Military Longarms," Model 1861 Rifle-Musket.*

58 caliber, single shot muzzleloader, 40" round bright barrel fastened with three bands.

Iron mountings throughout, U.S. stamped on buttplate, steel ramrod with swell and tulip tip.

Black walnut stock, oil finished with inspectors marks in the wood on the opposite side from the lock. Typical inspection initials JHG, FCW and HW.

Barrel has three-groove rifling, standard Model 1861 front and rear sights, V-P over eaglehead proof and date 1863 or 1864 with inspectors initials of JHG, FCW, W or HW.

Lock has small eagle over U.S. in the center; WHITNEYVILLE on forward lock and date 1863 or 1864 at rear.

This contract was made to conform to strict government gauge control. Whitney had an earlier contract for 40,000 guns signed December 24, 1861, which he did not press ahead on, but rather spent all his energies on tooling-up and producing the state contracts and the Plymouth rifle contract. He had, however, secured gauges and produced parts for that first contract of 1861 and thus when he signed the second contract of October, 1863, voiding the first, he was able to ship guns to the government a few days later:
5J-042   Values—Good **$900**   Fine **$3,000**

Whitney Connecticut Contract M1861 Muskets

Whitney Connecticut Contract M1861 Muskets. (Not illus.) Contract 1861 for 6,000 arms completed; contract 1862 for 8,000 arms completed. Total 14,000 delivered by April 1863. Conforms very closely to Standard U.S. Model 1861 Percussion .58 caliber rifle-musket (*q.v.*) with following differences:

1) Pewter forend cap

2) No "US" on butt

3) Seven groove rifling with three groove only at end of production

4) Whitney made rear sight dovetailed into barrel, 1-5/16" base; single "L" shaped leaf with pierced aperture

5) Steel ramrod with straight shank and brass tip. These gave trouble; in 1863 Whitney shipped state sufficient straight shank, tulip head ramrods to replace the earlier brass rods.

Inspector markings not usually found on stocks; barrel inspectors JHS and H on much of production with later manufacture G.W.Q. Barrels accept the British Enfield bayonet which Whitney admitted importing from England while most later production made to accept the U.S. socket bayonet.

In 1861 Whitney chose to concentrate his efforts on pursuing the more profitable state contracts, not accepting a U.S. government order until 1863. He called these "...nearly of Springfield pattern" advising that he was less particular in his state contracts. As he advised the state prior to his second contract, his guns were sold as "...good, safe and serviceable arms, and all parts will interchange as well as those previously made (First Contract), but they are not to be subject to a minute inspection of government gauges."

It is definitely known that the 22nd and 27th Connecticut Volunteer Infantry were issued these M1861 muskets. There are strong indications that the following Connecticut regiments were also issued them: 13th, 14th, 15th, 16th, 18th, 20th and 21st:

Early production: Lock markings E.WHITNEY over N.HAVEN ahead of hammer; undated at rear. These are scarcer and usually encountered in quite worn condition:

5J-043   Values—Good **$850**   Fine **$2,750**

Later production: Circa 1862-63. Lock marked with large eagle and panoply of flags over large lettering WHITNEYVILLE ahead of hammer. Undated:

5J-044   Values—Good **$850**   Fine **$2,750**

Whitney "Manton" Marked 1861 Rifle-Musket

Whitney "Manton" Marked 1861 Rifle-Musket. (Not illus.) Made circa 1862-63. Quantity unknown; very limited; likely well under 2,000.

Except for the lock markings the gun is about identical to the Connecticut Model 1861 Contracts above. Barrel inspector markings G.W.Q. and also with proofs V and P on most specimens.

Lock marked ahead of hammer in fancy large Old English Gothic style letters MANTON with date 1862 at rear (lock likely produced in that year; believed arms not assembled until 1863 which was earliest date when Whitney rifled the bores with three grooves).

Specimens rare; reported that barrels can vary 39" or 40" and some may be of European import, thought to have been purchased from Colt who had earlier contracted in England for rifle-musket barrels that were subsequently found slightly undersized. It is believed that the "Manton" markings were applied as quality of these arms was not up to Whitney standards, having been made with inferior and surplus parts from his Second Connecticut Contract. It is conjectured that he used the name "Manton," that of an old, established British gun making firm, noted for quality, to give these second-class arms a patina of quality. Long an enigma for collectors, the puzzle of the background of this musket was solved when correspondence in Whitney's own hand revealed that he made them to be sold as "near Springfields." He even denied that they were his until considerable interest was shown in them, at which time he quoted manufacturing and delivery figures...admitting to lock markings.

The New York agents Fitch and Waldo purchased 1,074 of these "Mantons" from Whitney in 1863 which were ultimately sold to New York State for the re-activated militia as a consequence of the New York City Draft Riots. Surviving specimens are quite rare:

5J-045   Values—Good **$2,000**   Fine **$4,000**

Whitney Flush Lock M1861 Type Rifle-Musket

Flush Lock Plate Model 1861 Type Rifle-Musket (a.k.a. "Direct Vent Rifle-Musket"). (Not illus.) Made c. 1863. Estimated quantity under 100.

Configuration about identical to above Connecticut Contract M1861 muskets. 58 caliber; barrel accepts the M1861 socket type bayonet. Whitney style unstepped, single leaf rear sight with aperture. Three groove rifling. Inspector marks G.W.Q. at breech and V over P with six pointed star. Forend cap on most of pewter; other of iron. Flat bolster, flush with the lockplate and made without clean-out screw.

Completely flat, non beveled lockplate fitted flush with stock. Marked with large eagle and panoply of flags over WHITNEYVILLE in large letters with 1863 date at rear.

Another of Whitney's "Good and Serviceable Arms Not Requiring Gauge Inspection" and sold through various arms agents for state militia regiments.

Long musket: 40" barrel fastened by three bands:

5J-046   Values—Good **$1,100**   Fine **$2,750**

Short variation: 30" barrel fastened by two bands. So called "Artillery Model" by collectors. Definitive information not available as to their Civil War manufacture...or post-War alterations for Cadet or school usage by military goods dealers. See Chapter IX where "Artillery Models" discussed at length in section about Civil War 58 caliber muskets. Value if 30" is original length would be same as musket:

5J-047

5J-047.5

Whitney "Humpback" Lockplate M1861 Type Rifle-Musket

"Humpback" Lockplate M1861 Type Rifle-Musket (in first 5 editions of this Guide was 5J-037). Made c. 1863. Quantity estimated 200.

58 caliber. 39" barrels. General conformation of the M1861 Connecticut Contract Rifle Musket. Distinctive feature the "High-humpback" lockplate unmilled for the Maynard Tape Primer; likely the remainder of locks that Whitney had earlier purchased and used for his Model 1855 Type rifle (5J-036.5). Although identically resembling those used on the Confederate Richmond muskets, there is no Confederate association to these lockplates.

Lock markings in center E.WHITNEY/N.HAVEN with very weak second line, indicating c.1862 when die was discarded and changed to a newer style markings. Three groove rifling also would clearly indicate manufacture c. 1863.

A very scarce piece on which variations are found: Mostly, but not all, pewter forend caps; most buttplates of iron;

lockscrew escutcheons of both brass winged Enfield style and round, iron M.1861 style. Very scarce. Elements of the 21st Connecticut Infantry were known to have been armed with this. Very scarce:

5J-047.5   Values—Good **$1,100**   Fine **$3,000**

Whitney Percussion Shotguns

Percussion Shotguns—Double and Single Barrel, Muzzle-Loading. Manufactured 1866-1869. Quantity unknown, but probably few thousand each. Records indicate that 997 double and 355 single barrels made in year 1867 alone. Patent No. 59110 of October 23, 1866, covered the percussion design.

Gauges: The single shot is a reamed out surplus 58 caliber rifled barrel; about 60 caliber (20 gauge). Factory advertising offered double barrel models in "… 10 to 18 bore as per gun gauge" and barrels for these doubles were specifically manufactured for them; lengths advertised from 28" to 36" but it appears that 30" was standard; barrels were blued.

Barrel markings: WHITNEY ARMS CO., WHITNEYVILLE, CONN. HOMOGENEOUS WROUGHT STEEL Serial numbers from 1 on up.

Varnished walnut stock with rather crude checkering at the wrist. Frames on both the single and double types have a 1" circular removable plate allowing access to the inner mechanism. Brass tipped wooden ramrod.

These shotguns are quite scarce. Although reasonable quantities believed manufactured, survival rates quite small with the single barrels less often encountered:

5J-048   Values—Good **$400**   Fine **$850**

5J-048
Single Barrel

5J-048
Double Barrel

Whitney Swing-Breech Carbine

5J-049

Whitney Swing-Breech Carbine. Made c. 1866. Total produced less than 50.

46 rimfire, single shot carbine made to Whitney's Patent 44,991 of November 8, 1864. The barrel is 22" long, round and blued throughout. A button on the right side of the frame releases the breechblock, it is swung sidewise for inserting the

cartridge. A metal lug under forearm manually operates the shell extractor. May have double set triggers. A very rare carbine and only a few known to exist:

5J-049   Values—Good **$1,750**   Fine **$2,750**

Whitney-Cochran Carbine

Whitney-Cochran Carbine. Made c. 1866-1867. Total produced estimated at less than 50.

44 rimfire, single shot carbine made by Whitney Arms under license from J. W. Cochran; principally utilizing his Patent 47088 of April 4, 1865. 28" round barrel most often encountered; blued finish. Walnut varnished stock and forearm; saddle ring on left side of frame. Opening of the trigger guard-lever, raises the breechblock; loading is from underside. Single leaf rear sight and wedge type front sight. Barrel markings WHITNEY ARMS CO. - WHITNEYVILLE, CONN. and the breechblock J. W. COCHRAN N.Y. PAT'D/APR 4, 1865 & FEB'Y/20, 1866 Cartridge manually ejected by means of lever on the side of the tang. Primarily made

5J-050

for the 1867 U.S. Government Carbine Trials. The gun was not accepted:

5J-050   Values—Good **$1,250**   Fine **$2,500**

Whitney "Excelsior" Single Shot Top Loaders

5J-051

Whitney "Excelsior" Single Shot Top Loading Rifle or Carbine. Made c. 1866-1870. Total produced less than 200.

38, 44, and 50 rimfire, single shot rifle. Various length octagon and round barrels, standard length 28"; blued finish. Resembles the Cochran and Peabody designs, and probably an outgrowth of Whitney's Cochran work. When on safety—a ring latch (affixed to front of block) disengages the block, allowing it to pivot downwards exposing the barrel. Loading from the top; hand ejector lever under the barrel on the forearm on early types.

Later style has a thumb actuated lever on the right side (variations encountered). Center mounted hammer; adaptable for either rimfire or centerfire cartridges. Marked WHITNEY ARMS CO. - WHITNEYVILLE CONN on barrel. Serial numbered on underside of frame and barrel. V-notch rear sight and folding pin front sight. The carbine has the saddle ring on the left side of the frame:

5J-051   Values—Good **$950**   Fine **$2,250**

Whitney-Howard Lever Action Single Shot

5J-052

Whitney-Howard Lever Action, Hammerless, Single Shot Breechloader, a.k.a. the Howard THUNDERBOLT. Made c. 1866-1870. Total production estimated less than 2,000.

Caliber 44 rimfire usual; other calibers known and worth slight premium value. Shotgun 20 gauge or 58 caliber centerfire. Barrel lengths and types as indicated below.

Black walnut stock varnish finished. Blued finish to frame and barrel.

Invented and patented by Charles and Sebre Howard 1862-1866, with early production evidently built under contract by Whitney for the Howards, and later production by Whitney for sale to the general public with their own line of guns. Trial tested but rejected for military purchase by the State of New York and the U.S. Army in their carbine trials of 1867.

Markings normally encountered on the barrel with unmarked specimens known. Four distinct marking variations have been observed, all four types bearing both the Howard and Whitney names. Markings either bear legend MANUF'D FOR HOWARD BROTHERSor merely HOWARD'S PATENTSfollowed by dates and also WHITNEY ARMS CO. WHITNEYVILLE, CONN.

The locking mechanism was the weak point, blowing open on occasion. Whitney correspondence in 1882 mentions that he had long since returned all parts for these guns to the Howard Brothers in Detroit, Michigan, having ceased manufacturing the gun and that parts were available from the Howards. This very likely accounts for some of the unusual variations such as English marked specimens that are occasionally encountered as

the Howards may have assembled and sold such pieces themselves. One of these "Thunderbolts" is known and recorded as a handgun (an extreme rarity).

An early variant form is known which has ejector port on right side and slight contour change in breech/receiver area. This type will bring a premium value approximately 20 percent to 50 percent above standard styles.

Rifle; caliber 44 rimfire; barrel lengths 22" to 28" with 24" length apparently standard; single leaf folding rear sight standard; blade front sight; stocks often seen with checkering at wrist. Specimens known with double set triggers and other special features which if proven original will fetch a premium value. A military rifle-musket with 29" barrel and unique fitted bayonet is known and considered very rare (At least two muskets are known and worth substantial premium values...and if accompanied by the bayonet, an additional premium):

5J-052   Values—Good **$350**   Fine **$750**

Carbine; similar to above with barrels varying 18-1/2" to 19". Estimated less than 200 manufactured. Normally not encountered with saddle ring and this device if present will add a premium to the value:

5J-053   Values—Good **$425**   Fine **$875**

Shotgun; as above; 20 gauge smoothbore (approximately 58 caliber) centerfire. Barrels 30" to 40" with 36" apparently standard length. Estimated less than 200 manufactured:

5J-054   Values—Good **$250**   Fine **$425**

Whitney Phoenix Breechloader

Whitney Phoenix Breechloader. Made c. 1867-1881. Total produced all types estimated at 25,000. Various styles and calibers as shown below.

An easily identified model with unique, very narrow breechblock hinged on right side of receiver and lifting upward to load. Serial numbered. Three variations of extraction systems observed.

The Phoenix is somewhat of a mystery. Although the estimated production figures (taken from original correspondence) tend to indicate quite extensive quantities were made, the gun is not as often encountered as the figures imply. An especially noticeable feature with this model is the well used, if not worn, condition in which they are usually found; fine conditioned specimens are quite scarce.

5J-055
Sporting Rifle

5J-058
Shotgun

5J-059
Military Rile

The Phoenix production gun is based on the patent issued to Whitney in 1874; its exact origin is unknown although it resembles James Warner's 1864 Patent breechloader. They have been observed as breech-loading conversions in 58 caliber of the U. S. Model 1861 musket (considered a rarity) with a massive Phoenix type breechblock and bearing Whitney Arms Company barrel markings. Such pieces were possibly made for the trials of 1867.

All production Phoenix longarms bear only the marking PHOENIX, PATENT MAY 24, 74 with the caliber normally stamped at breech. The Whitney name does not appear. Barrels finished blued; receivers either blued or casehardened.

Rifle; sporting and target grades. Total production estimated less than 2,000, centerfire 38, 40, 44, 45, 50; rimfire 32, 38, 44. 26" to 30" round or octagon barrel; leaf type rear sight and blade front sight. Black walnut, varnished stock and forend. Values given are for the plain specimens in common calibers. This model may be encountered in numerous variations: special target sights, pistol grip and deluxe stocks or longer barrel lengths, all of which affect value upwards as do the scarcer and largest calibers:

5J-055   Values—Good **$650**   Fine **$1,500**

Schuetzen Rifle; total production very limited, centerfire 38, 40, 44 with 30" or 32" octagon, round or half round blued barrels. Large Schuetzen type, fancy grained polished walnut stock, checkered grip and forearm. Nickel plated Swiss type buttplate, Vernier and windgauge sight with spirit level, horn forend tip, variations include double set trigger, odd calibers. Rare:

5J-056   Values—Good **$1,100**   Fine **$2,750**

Gallery Rifle; Total production very limited, 22 caliber rimfire, octagon or half octagon blued barrel 24" in length. Rare:

5J-057   Values—Good **$400**   Fine **$1,250**

Shotgun; Total production less than 5,000 (estimated). 10, 12, 14, 16, 22 gauge, blued steel barrels 26", 28", 30" 32" in length with shorter lengths known. Occasionally encountered unmarked. Many of the earlier barrels were 58 caliber musket barrels worked over:

5J-058   Values—Good **$250**   Fine **$500**

Military Rifle or Musket; total production estimated at 15,000. Great majority made under contract for Central and South American countries; small quantities sold to State Militias. Calibers 433, 45, 50 centerfire. 35" barrel blued; walnut stock with 3-band fasteners; full forends. An American martially marked specimen with markings on barrel VP over eagle .45 caliber - 70 Gr. would be considered quite rare and command a substantial premium. Rarely encountered in any variation:

5J-059   Values—Good **$950**   Fine **$2,500**

Carbine (Civilian); total production estimated less than 500. 44 caliber centerfire, 24" round barrel with blued or brown finish; casehardened frame; military style buttplate, single barrel band, screw fastened; military sights and saddle ring on left side of frame:

5J-060   Values—Good **$875**   Fine **$2,250**

Carbine (Military); total production less than 1,000. 433, 45, 50 caliber centerfire, 20-1/2" round barrel; casehardened frame, iron buttplate, single barrel band screw fastened, military sights and saddle ring left side of frame. These were made mostly under contract for Central and South America and thus very rare:

5J-061   Values—Good **$875**   Fine **$2,250**

Whitney-Laidley Style I Rolling Block

Whitney-"Laidley" Style I Rolling Block Action, a.k.a. Split Breech Whitney. Made c. 1871-1881. Total production all types estimated at 40,000 to 50,000. Various styles and calibers shown below. Identifying features are the flat frame sides and four major breech parts.

In 1870 Whitney purchased the manufacturing rights to the 1866 Patent on a rolling block type action issued to T.S.S. Laidley and C. A. Emery and proceeded to obtain a series of patents in his name to improve the action and compete with Remington. Style I covers the series of improvements on the basic four-piece (hammer, locking cam, thumb-piece plate, breechblock) design. While the Whitney was a good design, Remington's was simpler and because of an earlier start enjoyed greater acceptance.

Whitney entered this gun in the New York State Trial of 1871 as well as Government Trials and did not win a U.S. contract. As with the Phoenix line, the estimated production figures, taken from original correspondence, indicate rather extensive quantities manufactured and may have been embellished by Whitney to help sales. The gun is not encountered with the frequency which the production figures imply and is rather scarce and in some models quite rare. Rifles chambered for centerfire usually bring 10 to 30 percent more than rimfire.

Sporting and Target Rifle; total production estimated at 5,000. 38, 40, 44, 45, 50 centerfire and 32, 38, 44 rimfire calibers with chambering for special calibers on order. Guns standard with blued barrel and casehardened receiver and hammer. Standard

5J-062
Deluxe Sporter

5J-062
Deluxe Sporter

5J-065
Military Rile

barrel lengths 24" to 30" available round, octagon or half octagon. Markings typical WHITNEYVILLE ARMORY CO. PATENTED OCT 17 '65, RE-IS'D JUNE 25, '72, DEC 26 '65-RE-IS'D OCT 1, '67, MAY 15 '66, JULY 16 '72on tang. Caliber marked near breech of barrel. Values given are for the plain specimens in common calibers. This model may be encountered in numerous variations: special target sights, pistol grip and deluxe stocks (with Swiss buttplate) or longer barrel lengths, all of which affect value upwards as do the scarcer and largest calibers:

5J-062   Rimfire Calibers:
             Values—Very Good **$650**   Exc. **$1,750**
5J-062.5   Centerfire Calibers:
             Values—Very Good **$950**   Exc. **$2,750**

Creedmoor Rifle No.1; total production less than 100. 44 caliber with 32" or 34" octagon, half octagon or round barrel; pistol grip, polished stock; checkered grip and forearm; Vernier and windgauge sights with spirit level. The top flat of the receiver is engraved WHITNEY CREEDMOOR Blued barrel and casehardened frame. Rare:
5J-063   Values—Very Good **$3,500**   Exc. **$7,000**

Creedmoor Rifle No.2; 40 caliber with 30" or 32" barrels, otherwise same as above. Rare:
5J-064   Values—Very Good **$2,250**   Fine **$4,500**

Military Rifle or Musket; total production estimated at 30,000. These guns were mainly made for South and Central American contracts with few specimens found in U.S. collections and those usually in heavily worn condition. 433, 45, 50 caliber centerfire standard; 44 caliber very rare. The 433 and 45 calibers have 35" barrels and the 50 caliber has a 32-1/2" barrel. Full stocked forend fastened by three barrel bands, the top band marked PAT NOV 8, 1874. Tang markings as shown above. Black walnut stock, oiled finished. Specimens were purchased by the Mexican government (cal. 11mm Spanish) will be encountered (worth premium value) with markings on top of barrel in deep stamped

oval panel with sunburst-like motif and a liberty cap in center and large letters "RM" below the panel:
5J-065   Values—Good **$750**   Fine **$1,750**

Gallery Rifle; Production estimated less than 500. 22 caliber rimfire long or short, 24" octagon or half octagon standard and longer lengths an extra. Typical marking and variations the same as shown under Rifle-Sporting and Target. Barrel blued and receiver section casehardened. Values are for plain specimens; extra features increasing value:
5J-066   Values—Very Good **$450**   Exc. **$1,200**

Carbine (Military); total made estimated at less than 5,000 with most of production shipped to Central and South America. 433, 45, 50 caliber centerfire, 20-1/2" round blued barrel and casehardened frame and hammer; black walnut stock; military sights; saddle ring and bar on left side of receiver; tang markings as above. Specimens purchased by the Mexican government (cal. 11mm Spanish) will be encountered (worth premium value) with markings on top of barrel in deep stamped oval panel with sunburst-like motif and a liberty cap in center and large letters "RM" below the panel:
5J-067   Values—Good **$750**   Fine **$1,400**

Montreal Police marked (on barrel) military carbine. Cal. 43. Contract 1875 by Montreal, Canada for 60 with socket bayonets; for prisoner escort use. Serial range 6700-7500; heel of buttplate with police numbers 1-60:
5J-067.5   Values—Good **$850**   Fine **$1,850**

Carbine (Civilian); total production less than 1,000 46 rimfire with 19-1/2" round barrel; 44 rimfire or centerfire with 18-1/2" round barrel (scarcer). Finish; blued barrel with casehardened frame and hammer termed by Whitney "The plain Military Finish." Available also full nickel plated. Tang markings as above:
5J-068   Values—Good **$750**   Fine **$1,400**

Whitney-Remington Style II Rolling Block

Whitney-"Remington"—Style II Rolling Block. Made c. 1881-1888. Total production all types estimated 50,000. Upon the expiration of Remington's Patent on the basic rolling block action, Whitney essentially copied the action and called it his "New Improved System;" in his correspondence he referred to it as his "Remington Type." Easily distinguished from the Style I, the action having only two major parts (hammer, breechblock) and the frame is rounded. Upper tang is usually marked WHITNEY ARMS COMPANY, NEW HAVEN CT USAand caliber

marking at breech of barrel. Serial numbered. Rifles chambered for centerfire usually bring 10 to 30 percent more than rimfire.
No.1 Sporting and Target Rifle; total estimated production 3,000. 38-40, 40-60, 44-40, 45-60, and 50-95 caliber centerfire, 38, 44 caliber rimfire. Round, octagon and part octagon barrels in varying lengths 26" to 30". Walnut varnished stock and following variations: Values given are for plain specimens in common calibers. This model may be encountered in numerous variations—special target sights, pistol grip and deluxe stocks or

5J-069
Sporting & Target Rifle

5J-069

5J-071
Military Rifle

5J-072
Carbine

longer barrel lengths, all of which affect value upwards as do the scarcer and largest calibers; (rimfire approx. 20 percent less):

5J-069   Values—Very Good **$875**   Exc. **$2,250**

No.2 Sporting Rifle; a lighter weight version of the #1 size with slightly smaller and noticeably lighter frame for the smaller calibers in which the gun was made. 22 short, long, 32 short, long, 38 long and 44-40 centerfire calibers. Values for plain specimens, special features such as sights, deluxe stocks will affect value upwards:

5J-070   Values—Very Good **$550**   Exc. **$1,400**

Military Rifle or Musket; total production estimated 39,000. 433, 45 calibers centerfire with 35" barrel and 50 caliber with 32-1/2" barrel. As with Style I, documentation shows most of production went to Central and South America and surviving specimens in U.S. very scarce, if not rare. Tang markings the same as Style I or WHITNEY ARMS CO., NEW HAVEN, CT. U.S.A.

otherwise similar to Style I:

5J-071   Values—Good **$650**   Fine **$1,750**

Carbine (Military); total production estimated 5,000. All features similar to Style I with the later style action. Most of production to Central and South America:

5J-072   Values—Good **$650**   Fine **$1,750**

Carbine (Civilian); total production estimated 2,000. Same details as the Style I with later style action. Occasionally found marked LITTLE WONDER #2 on top of barrel:

5J-073   Values—Good **$650**   Fine **$1,600**

Shotguns; total production estimated less than 1,000. Made from both Style I and Style II frames. Usually 20 gauge, but also found in 12, 14, 16 gauge. Found with markings of both Style I or Style II guns or unmarked. Barrel length is 26" to 30" with lengths of 20" to 23" also common:

5J-074   Values—Very Good **$275**   Fine **$500**

Whitney-Burgess-Morse Lever Action Repeater

Whitney-Burgess-Morse Lever Action Repeater. Made c. 1878-1882. Total production estimated at less than 3,000. Caliber standard in 45-70, but others known as mentioned below. Magazine tube mounted under barrel. Walnut stocks. Blued finish on barrels and frames. Serial numbered.

Early or 1st Type models 1878-79 were top loaded, fitted with serpentine or "S" shaped lever. These are considered very rare and will bring a considerable premium over the values indicated for usual encountered 2nd Type. 2nd Type were side loading, the design changed in early 1879, retaining the same "S" shaped lever.

Barrel markings in two lines G. W. MORSE PATENTED OCT. 28th 1856, and caliber markings at breech 45 CAL 70 GR. CF. Markings on tang behind hammer A. BURGESS PATENTED JAN 7th 1873, PATENTED OCT 19th 1873in three lines.

Variations most often observed include thickness of magazine tubes and tube bands; placement of screw fastening forend tip; found both with and without trap door in buttplate for cleaning rod.

Serial numbers marked inside on bottom floor plate on early specimens and on lower tang of trigger plate on later production.

5J-075
Sporting Rifle

Whitney entered into a license agreement with Andrew Burgess early in 1878 to build the magazine-lever action gun covered under G. W. Morse Patent of 1856 and A. Burgess' Patents Jan. 7, 1873 and Oct. 19, 1875; Burgess believed to have been paid a royalty on guns made. Correspondence indicates the first lot of 1,000 guns was finished around January, 1879, and before that year was out, he had to recall all of them and rework the magazine loading system as the cartridge often got under the carrier and also the point of one shell would explode the one above it while being moved from the magazine to the receiver chamber.

Whitney termed the gun "The Burgess Repeating Rifle." It did not gain public acceptance; its basic design was intended to seek military contracts, making it too heavy for a sporting rifle.
Sporting Rifle; production estimated 1,500. 28" octagon or round barrel, 9 shots, completely blued with casehardened hammer. Varnished black walnut stock and forend. Buckhorn rear and German silver blade front sights. Value shown for standard specimen. The gun is known with various combinations of sights, double set triggers; such features will increase values accordingly:
5J-075 Values—Very Good **$1,250** Exc. **$3,500**

Military Rifle or Musket; production estimated at 1,000. 33" round barrel, full forend fastened by two bands with sling swivel on upper band; military sights; oil finished walnut stock. 11 shots; fitted for either an angular or saber bayonet. Also chambered for caliber 433 Spanish and 42 Russian:
5J-076 Values—Very Good **$1,750** Exc. **$4,000**

Carbine; total production estimated at 500. 22" round barrel; carbine ring affixed to left frame; 7 shots; oiled finished walnut stock with full length forend extending nearly to muzzle and fastened with single barrel band:
5J-077 Values—Very Good **$2,500** Exc. **$4,750**

Whitney-Kennedy Lever Action Repeater

5J-079
Sporter with S-Lever

5J-081
Carbine with S-Lever

5J-081
Carbine with Standard Lever

Whitney-Kennedy Lever Action Repeater, a.k.a. Whitney Kennedy-Tiesing. Made c. 1879-1886. Total production estimated at 15,000.

Made in two distinct frame sizes; see details below.

Magazine tube mounted under barrel. Walnut stock. Blued finish to frame and barrel with casehardened lever and chamber; casehardened frame occasionally encountered and in finer grades of condition worth premium values, as are original nickel finished pieces in top condition grades only.

Two-line barrel markings vary WHITNEY ARMS CO, NEW HAVEN, CONN. U.S.A. or WHITNEYVILLE ARMORY, CT. USA or WHITNEY KENNEDY MF'D BY WHITNEY ARMS CO NEW HAVEN, CONN, U.S.A. Occasionally just the single word KENNEDY appears after the Whitney name, divorced from the rest of the markings; with few specimens known marked only KENNEDY. Caliber markings stamped at breech.

Tang markings appear in variation also, but usually show the Burgess Patents of Jan. 7, 1873, and April 1, 1879, as well as the Kennedy Patent of May 13, 1879, and the Kennedy-Tiesing Patent of Aug. 12, 1879.

Serial numbers apparently 1 to approximately 5000 after which letter prefix series were used, alphabetically in sequence A-T with each letter having number series 1 through 1000.

Major variation is the use of the serpentine or "S" shaped lever of the earlier Burgess Model in production through mid-1883 (less often encountered and worth a small premium to value) at which time lever was changed to the full loop type. Other lesser variations also noted. Trap door in buttplate; cleaning rod standard on all models except the 32-20 caliber of later type.

The Whitney-Kennedy was an outgrowth of and improvement to the Burgess and underwent several minor design changes during its years of production.

SPORTING RIFLE:
Small or light frame; weight 9 lbs; forearm length 9-1/16"; loading aperture on frame 1-1/4". Caliber 44-40, 38-40 and in later production 32-20. 24" round, octagon or part octagon barrels; full or half magazines; Buckhorn rear and German silver blade type front sights standard. Values shown are for plain, standard specimen. A wide variety of original accessories and factory extras are encountered on these including many types of sights, engraving, nickel finished; fancy and deluxe grades of stocks, double set triggers and extra long barrel lengths—each feature of which must be evaluated on its own merit and importance as with other similar makes with values adjusted upwards accordingly:
5J-078 Values—Very Good **$950** Exc. **$2,500**

Large or heavy frame; weight 9-1/2 lbs; forearm length 10-1/4"; loading aperture on frame 1-1/2". Used with heavier and Express calibers 40-60, 45-60, 45-75, 50-90 (quite rare and brings a premium); 26" and 28" barrels. Other features as above. Value shown for standard types with special features as listed above increasing values:

5J-079 Values—Very Good **$1,150** Exc. **$2,750**

Military Rifle or Musket; production estimated at 1,000. Made in large frame size only. Majority of muskets were made for contracts shipped to Central and South America and thus all specimens on collectors' market are rare. Full wooden forend fastened by two bands; sling swivel on upper band and buttstock; oiled finished walnut stock; military style sights. 32-1/4" round barrel, 11- or 16-shot magazine in 40-60, 44-40, 45-60 calibers. Fitted for either angular or saber bayonet:

5J-080 Values—Very Good **$1,750** Exc. **$3,500**

Carbine; production estimated 1,000. Small frame calibers 44-40 and 38-40 with 20" round barrel and 12-shot magazine; large frame calibers 40-60 and 45-60 with 22" round barrel and 9-shot magazine. Carbine style forend with single barrel band; single leaf rear sight. Most of production apparently sent to South and Central America:

5J-081 Values—Very Good **$1,750** Exc. **$3,500**

Whitney-Scharf Lever Action Repeater

5J-082
Sporting Rifle

5J-083
Military Rifle or Musket

Whitney-Scharf Lever Action Repeater a.k.a. Model 1886. Made c. 1886-1888. Total production estimated at less than 2,000.

Calibers 32-20, 38-40, and 44-40. Barrel lengths as noted below. Blued finish with casehardened lever and hammer. Walnut stocks; half and full magazines. Solid buttplate without trap door for cleaning rod.

Barrel markings WHITNEY ARMS COMPANY, WHITNEYVILLE, CONN. with caliber marked at breech. Tang marked WHITNEY ARMS COMPANY, PAT'D DEC 21, 1886in two lines. Serial numbered.

The Kennedy was not gaining in popularity, expensive to make and Whitney needed a better lever action gun. The William C. Scharf Patent of December 21, 1886, was assigned to E. Whitney and production commenced. It was a fine gun, but too late to save the Whitney Arms Company. They were forced to sell out to Winchester in 1888. Actually as early as 1883 Whitney was making overtures to potential purchasers indicating he wished to retire.

Sporting Rifle. Barrel lengths 24", 26", 28" in round, octagon or part octagon. Values shown for standard specimen with open sights. Same variations as found in Whitney-Kennedy may be seen on this and same value changes will apply. Surviving specimens are seldom encountered:

5J-082 Values—Very Good **$925** Exc. **$2,500**

Military Rifle or Musket. Production estimated at less than 50. Calibers 44-40 and 45-60. 32-1/2" round barrel; full wooden forend fastened by two barrel bands; sling swivel on upper band and buttstock; military style sights; fitted for either socket or saber type bayonet. Very rare:

5J-083 Values—Very Good **$3,000** Exc. **$5,500**

Carbine. Production estimated at less than 50. Calibers 38-40 and 44-40. Swivel ring on left frame. Barrel length 20" with full magazine. Typical carbine type half length forend retained by single barrel band. Single leaf folding rear barrel sight; very rare:

5J-084 Values—Very Good **$3,500** Exc. **$6,000**

Whitney Double Barrel Shotguns

5J-085

Double Barrel, Breech-Loading Centerfire Shotguns. Made 1870-1874. Estimated less than 2,500 manufactured.

10, 12, and 16 gauges; damascus steel barrels; standard length 28" to 32" with shorter lengths known. Blued overall finish or browned damascus striped barrels. Stock and forearm varnished black walnut and usually checkered at wrist. Serial numbered under buttplate, forend, bottom tang and under barrel. Normally found with engraving on receivers.

Early barrels marked (using up percussion barrels) WHITNEY ARMS CO, WHITNEYVILLE, CONN. HOMOGENEOUS WROUGHT STEEL, E. WHITNEYS, PATENT OCTOBER 23, 1866 and later WHITNEY ARMS CO, WHITNEYVILLE, CONN, E. WHITNEYS PATENT OCTOBER 23, 1866, JULY 27, 1869.

Distinctive appearance with two trigger guards in series; forward trigger releases the barrels:

5J-085   Values—Good **$285**   Fine **$750**

HANDGUNS

Whitney Hooded Cylinder Pocket Revolver

Hooded Cylinder Percussion Pocket Model Revolver; manually revolved cylinder. Made c. 1850-53; total quantity about 200.

28 caliber. 6-shot round (hooded) cylinder with etched decoration. Octagonal barrel varying in length from 3" to 6". Button on top, rear of frame releases cylinder to revolve.

Two piece walnut grips of bag shape. Blued finish; brass frame and cylinder hood silver plated.

Serial numbered from 1 on up. E. WHITNEY N. HAVEN CT (on barrel), and PATENT and APPLIED FOR on opposite sides of the cylinder hood.

The first production revolver by Whitney after his contract manufacture of the Walker Colt (1847), the Hooded Cylinder Model was made with some apprehension because of Samuel Colt's litigation against the Massachusetts Arms Co. Some changes were made in the Hooded Cylinder pistols as a result

5J-086

of Colt's victory in the suit. Cylinders before that decision had the nipples recessed in individual deep apertures; post trial specimens featured grooves between each nipple aperture; the last production, and scarcest, had rebated cylinders exposing the nipples:

5J-086   Values—Good **$1,500**   Fine **$3,500**

Whitney Prototype Hooded Cylinder Revolver

5J-086.2

Hooded Cylinder Percussion Belt Size Revolver; likely the prototype for the preceding pocket model. Made circa 1850. (Quantity unknown, very limited. Rare.

36 caliber with round 4-1/2" to 6" barrels; five-shot only. Brass frame; bag shape walnut grips. Blued finish to steel; silver finish to the brass usual. Specimens known are all unmarked (possibly due to the patent situation). Note: Model made without trigger guard; distinct difference to contour of the hooded cylinder; nipples sunk in wells in the side of the plain cylinder.

5J-086.2   Values—Good **$4,000**   Fine **$9,500**

Whitney Two Trigger Pocket Revolver

Two Trigger Percussion Pocket Model Revolver. Made c. 1852-1854; total quantity about 650.

32 caliber. 5-shot with round cylinder having etched decoration. Octagonal barrel varying in length from 3" to 6".

Two piece walnut grips with squared butt profile. Blued finish; brass frame; square back trigger guard.

Serial numbered from 1 on up. Markings as noted below.

The novel feature of this revolver was the forward trigger's use as a release and lock for the *manually* turned cylinder. Whitney was still being cautious and attempting to avoid any patent litigation problems with Samuel Colt.

Standard model; the frame of brass; trigger guard iron. Marked: E. WHITNEY N. HAVEN CT (on barrel), and PATENT APPLIED FOR (on frame). About 600 produced:

5J-087   Values—Good **$500**   Fine **$1,600**

5J-087

Iron Frame model; the trigger guard of brass. Made without markings, except for serial number. About 50 made:

5J-088   Values—Good **$700**   Fine **$2,000**

Whitney Ring Trigger Pocket Revolver

Ring Trigger Percussion Pocket Model Revolver. Made c. 1854-1855 under Whitney Patent No. 11,447 of August 1, 1854 (it evaded all of Colt's patent claims). Total quantity estimated less than 50. Rare.

31 caliber. Six shots; 4-inch octagonal barrel. Blued finish: walnut grips. All specimens observed have fancy etched designs on the cylinder and almost all are unmarked.

Although somewhat similar in appearance to the Whitney-Beals Pocket Revolver (see following) it should not be confused with that model. Most noticeable is the absence of the large shield (i.e. "hood") attached to left side of frame covering part of cylinder. To fire, hammer is manually cocked; when trigger is activated it revolves cylinder and releases hammer, allowing it

5J-089

to fall and fire the chamber. Timing mechanism not always proper, causing malfunction.

5J-089   Values—Good **$3,500**   Fine **$7,500**

Whitney-Beals' Patent Pocket Revolver

Beals' Patent Ring Trigger Percussion Pocket Revolver, a.k.a. "Walking Beam Pocket Revolver." Made c. 1854-late 1860s. Total production about 3,200.

Calibers, cylinders, frames and barrels as shown below. All cylinders bore etched decoration.

Two piece walnut grips with squared butt profile. Blued finish; large shield attached on the left side almost covering the entire side of the cylinder.

Serial numbered in more than one range. Markings as noted below.

5J-091

The Walking Beam model takes its name from part of the mechanism's similarity to the walking beam steam engine of the day. The basic design was patented by Fordyce Beals, later to assign some important patents to the firm of E. Remington & Sons. Variations are known in grip and frame shape, cylinder pin, latch and ring size.

First Model; brass frame, 6-shot 31 caliber cylinders; 2" to 6" octagonal barrels. On cylinder shield: F. BEALS/NEW HAVEN, CT. or BEAL'S PATENT. About 50 made:

5J-090   Values—Good **$1,200**   Fine **$3,250**

Standard 31 caliber model; iron frame, 7 shots; 2" to 6" octagonal barrels. Marked ADDRESS E. WHITNEY/WHITNEYVILLE, CT. and BEALS PATENT/SEPT. 1854 or F. BEALS/PATENT/SEPT. 1854 or the patent date JUNE 24, 1856. About 2,300 made:

5J-091   Values—Good **$475**   Fine **$1,400**

Standard 28 caliber model; iron frame; 6-shot; 2" to 6" octagonal barrels. Marked ADDRESS E. WHITNEY/WHITNEYVILLE, CT. and F. BEALS/PATENT/SEPT. 1854. About 850 made; 7-shot specimens rare, worth premium:

5J-092   Values—Good **$550**   Fine **$1,750**

Whitney Copy of Colt 1851 Navy

Whitney Copy of Colt Model 1851 Percussion Navy Revolver. (Not illus.) Made c. 1857-1858. Estimated quantity 300 to 400. About identical in configuration to the Colt Model 1851 (*q.v.*).

36 caliber. 6-shot; round cylinder. 7-1/2" unmarked octagon barrel. Major distinguishing features from Colt are the two-piece walnut grip fastened with screw and cylinder bearing the Whitney (1st Type) design cylinder scene of eagle, shield, lion motifs. Blued finish.

Extremely little known about these arms other than their existence and some slight mention of them in Whitney and

government correspondence. It is possible that Whitney utilized original Colt parts purchased as surplus and reworked in the manner that he did with longarms during that same era; making "good and serviceable" guns from parts. It is equally possible that he fabricated the entire gun. A theory exists based on notes in Whitney correspondence that a majority of these Colt type revolvers were sold through a Texas agent to Mexico in the 1850s after their rejection by the Chief of Ordnance in 1858:

5J-093   Values—Good **$1,750**   Fine **$4,500**

Whitney Navy & Eagle Co. Revolvers

Navy Model Percussion Revolver and Eagle Co. marked Revolvers. Made c. late 1850s-early 1860s. Total quantity about 33,000.

36 caliber. 6-shot round cylinder with two types roll engraved decoration as on Pocket Models. The roll engraved scene is usually applied lightly and difficult to view clearly or easily. Octagonal barrel, standard length 7-1/2", but from 4"-8" known, and rare; such variant barrel lengths commanding premium prices. Iron frame.

Two piece walnut grips. Blued finish, with casehardened loading lever.

Serial numbered from 1 on up for each of the two basic models. Barrel marking: E. WHITNEY/N. HAVEN. Other markings as noted below. Note: Presence of government inspector stampings add a premium of at least 25 percent, often greater.

The Whitney Navy is among the first practical solid frame revolvers, and was an early competitor to the Colt following expiration of the latter's master patents in 1857. The gun was quite popular in the Civil War and much of its production saw service in that conflict; over half of the standard Second Model was purchased by the Army and Navy, and by various states. Any authenticated U.S. government or state marks will add

Details of U.S. Naval
markings on barrel
and cylinder

premium values (as mentioned above). Usual naval contract marks are "U.S." and anchor stamped on top of barrel near frame and on cylinder (as illustrated here) valued at 40 percent or greater premium. The Navy purchased approximately 4,300 Whitney "Navies." *Civil War Small Arms of the U.S. Navy and Marine Corps* by McAulay (see Chap. IV) lists many U.S. vessels and Navy Yards which received quantities (and serial rangers for some).

FIRST MODEL. The usual Whitney markings are omitted on most of the 1st Model Navies. The markings EAGLE CO. appear on most specimens above serial number 500 to approximately the 1200 number range. The reason for the use of this trade name has not been documented. His use of this device is known on other guns, most notably the MANTON marked 58 Civil War musket (*q.v.*) and small cartridge model revolvers.

5J-094
First Model, 1st Type

1st Type; frame of comparatively light construction with very noticeably thin topstrap over cylinder; no loading lever assembly. Lacks barrel markings. Iron trigger guard. Eagle, shield and lion cylinder scene. Square juncture of grips with frame. About 100 made:
5J-094   Values—Good **$1,450**   Fine **$4,000**

2nd Type; (not illustrated); as above, but with attached loading lever, ball type lever catch. About 200 made:
5J-095   Values—Good **$950**   Fine **$3,250**

3rd Type; (not illustrated); as above, but has three screw frame (above models had four screw frames) and three piece center linked loading lever. Serial range about 300-800:
5J-096   Values—Good **$800**   Fine **$2,750**

(NOTE: Above serial range about 500, most specimens have barrel marking: EAGLE CO.)

4th Type; serial range about 800-1500. Distinguished by the rounded juncture of grips with frame. Safety notch for hammer now found on back of cylinder. Usually barrel marked EAGLE CO., but may bear E. WHITNEY/N. HAVEN roll:
5J-097   Values—Good **$800**   Fine **$2,750**

SECOND MODEL

5J-097
First Model, 4th Type

1st Type; (not illustrated); frame of heavier, stronger construction; brass trigger guard. Cylinder pin secured by wingnut on forward section of the frame, right side, just one safety notch at rear of cylinder. Barrel marking now standard: E. WHITNEY/N. HAVEN. Cylinder scene of the eagle, shield and lion; ball type latch at end of loading lever. Serial range began with 1; about 1,200 made:
5J-098   Values—Good **$750**   Fine **$2,250**

2nd Type; (not illustrated); cylinder machined with six safety notches at back; serial range about 1200-13000:
5J-099   Values—Good **$675**   Fine **$2,000**

3rd Type; ball type loading lever latch changed to the Colt or "wedge" type; serial range 13000-15000:
5J-100   Values—Good **$675**   Fine **$2,000**

4th Type; (not illustrated); cylinder roll scene of eagle, lion, naval engagement, and shield bearing rib and marked WHITNEYVILLE. Serial range 15000-25000:
5J-101   Values—Good **$675**   Fine **$2,000**

5J-100
Second Model, 3rd Type

5th Type; (not illustrated); as above, but with large trigger guard; serial range 25000-29000:
5J-102   Values—Good **$675**   Fine **$2,000**

6th Type; (not illustrated); as above, but the rifling changed from 7 grooves to 5; serial range 29000 to 34000:
5J-103   Values—Good **$675**   Fine **$2,000**

Whitney Pocket Model Percussion Revolver

Pocket Model Percussion Revolver. Made c. late 1850s-early 1860s. Total quantity about 32,500.

31 caliber. 5-shot round cylinder, roll engraved with eagle, shield, and lion motif and on later production similar motifs

with the addition of naval engagement and shield with WHITNEYVILLE in riband. Octagonal barrels of lengths from 3" to 6". Iron frame.

Two piece walnut grips. Blued finish, with casehardened loading lever.

Serial numbered from 1 on up, for each of the two basic models. Other markings as indicated below.

Variations and evolution of the Pocket Model is closely associated with that of the Navy Model. In design the Pocket Model was a considerable advance over earlier attempts and allowed for the automatic revolution of the cylinder on cocking of the hammer. Expiration of Colt's master patents in 1857 allowed the significant improvements.

FIRST MODEL

1st Type; (not illus.) frame of comparatively light construction; especially noticeable in the thin topstrap over the cylinder; Made without loading lever; has small curved lever at front of center pin as on 5J-087. Square juncture of grip to frame. Most unmarked (except serial number). Premium for those with topstrap stamping: ADDRESS E. WHITNEY/WHITNEYVILLE, CT. Serial range about 1-250. About identical in contour to 1st Model, 1st Type Whitney Navy, but in smaller size:

5J-104   Values—Good **$850**   Fine **$2,000**

2nd Type; (not illus.); as above, but with attached loading lever. Serial range about 250-500:

5J-105   Values—Good **$575**   Fine **$1,500**

3rd Type; (not illus.); as above, but has three screw frame (predecessors had four screw frames). Serial range about 500-1100:

5J-106   Values—Good **$450**   Fine **$1,100**

4th Type; (not illus.); as above, but with safety notch added to cylinder. Serial range about 1100-1500:

5J-107   Values—Good **$450**   Fine **$1,100**

5J-109

5th Type; as above, but with round juncture of grip to frame. Serial range about 1500-end of production for First Model:

5J-108   Values—Good **$450**   Fine **$1,100**

SECOND MODEL

1st Type; frame of heavier, stronger construction noticeably thicker topstrap. Cylinder pin secured by wingnut on forward section of right side of frame. Round juncture of grip to frame. Barrel marking standard: E. WHITNEY/N. HAVEN. Cylinder roll scene of eagle, shield and lion motif. Ball type latch on loading lever. Serial range began with 1; about 8,000 of this style produced:

5J-109   Values—Good **$375**   Fine **$875**

2nd Type; (not illus.); as above, but the cylinder scene of the eagle, shield, lion and naval engagement with legend: WHITNEYVILLE in riband across shield. Serial range about 8000-12000:

5J-110   Values—Good **$375**   Fine **$875**

3rd Type; (not illus.); as above, but loading lever latch changed from ball type to the Colt or "wedge" type. Serial range about 12000-late in production:

5J-111   Values—Good **$375**   Fine **$875**

4th Type; (not illus.); as above, but rifling changed from 7 grooves to 5. About 1,000+ produced:

5J-112   Values—Good **$400**   Fine **$1,100**

Whitney "New Model" Pocket Revolver

"New Model" Percussion Pocket Revolver a.k.a. Root Type Pocket Model. Made c. 1860-1867; total quantity estimated less than 2,000.

28 caliber. 6-shot cylinder, roll engraved with eagle, shield, and lion motif. 3-1/2" octagonal barrel. Iron frame.

Two piece walnut grips. Blued finish.

Serial numbered from 1 on up. Barrel marking: E. WHITNEY/N. HAVEN.

This gun was pictured in an 1860 Whitney gun advertisement. It was introduced to compete with the Model 1855 Colt Root and has obviously been closely patterned after it.

5J-113

The most noticeable difference is the centrally mounted hammer. Whitney referred to this gun as his "New Model":

5J-113   Values—Good **$400**   Fine **$1,250**

Whitney Rimfire Breechloading Revolvers

Rimfire, Breech-Loading Revolvers. Made c. 1871-1879. Total quantity approximately 30,000.

Calibers 22, 32 and 38 rimfire. Brass, solid frame construction in three sizes according to caliber; spur or "sheath" type trigger; bird's head butt. Variety of finishes; all nickel or nickeled frame with blued cylinder and barrel are most usually encountered.

Grips either rosewood or hard rubber as factory standard with ivory or pearl often encountered and worth a premium in value.

Octagonal barrels with lengths as shown; other lengths known and worth premium if original. Usual barrel markings WHITNEYVILLE ARMORY all types followed by CT. USA or USA or WHITNEYVILLE CONN: specimens found both with and without

PAT MAY 23, 1871. The very short 1-1/2" barrels are marked just WHITNEYVILLE.

Cylinders on all three types both round and fluted styles.

The button release for the cylinder pin is rectangular on earlier specimens, round on later production. Serial numbered.

Original Whitney records/correspondence indicates they produced all three types with trade names as shown below. These guns are identical to their regular models with the absence of any Whitney markings and the substitution of the trade name. Other sheath trigger American revolvers bear almost identical trade names to some of these, but only those that are identical to Whitney manufacture in configuration are considered their product.

The sizes (i.e., No. 1, No. 1-1/2) as given below are the terms used by Whitney in their sales literature to describe these guns. There yet exists among collectors some confusion about the nomenclature used by Whitney to identify these various models and quantities made of individual models. It has been established by factory literature and subsequent research that the revolver was also made in caliber 30 (see 5J-115.8).

SIZE/MODEL NO. 1

22 rimfire, 7 shots, 3-1/4" octagon barrel (round barrels scarce; worth 25 percent premium). Total production estimated 3,500. Major variations:

Straight, unfluted cylinder, brass frame. Earliest style. Marked WHITNEYVILLE or UNION, N.Y.:
5J-114   Values—Very Good **$175**   Exc. **$500**

Narrow cylinder, short flutes, brass frame. Marked WHITNEYVILLE or EAGLE CO.:
5J-115   Values—Very Good **$125**   Exc. **$400**

Wide Cylinder, long flutes, brass frame. Marked WHITNEYVILLE or EAGLE CO. Many latch variants seen:
5J-115.3 Values—Very Good **$135**   Exc. **$425**

MONITOR marked. Iron frame, straight cylinder, round barrel. Specimens reportedly marked DEFENDER also, but not viewed:
5J-115.7 Values—Very Good **$125**   Exc. **$375**

SIZE/MODEL NO. 1 30 CALIBER VARIANT

30 rimfire Variant (recently brought to light). Whitney actually advertised the gun in this caliber and specimens are known and recorded. Although Whitney's description listed it as a "No. 2" model (with other discrepancies recorded in those factory listings) the 30 RF examples have been observed in the same size as "Wide Cylinder" (as 5J-115.3 above) with a 5-shot, short flute cylinder. Examples known marked WHITNEYVILLE or EAGLE ARMS CO. Rare.
5J-115.8

SIZE/MODEL NO. 1-1/2

32 rimfire, 5 shots, 3-1/2" octagon barrel. Two cylinder lengths known; cylinder catch variations, also:

WHITNEYVILLE marked; production estimated at 15,000:
5J-116   Values—Very Good **$125**   Exc. **$350**

EAGLE CO. (tradename) marked; estimated production 1,000:
5J-117   Values—Very Good **$125**   Exc. **$350**

SIZE/MODEL NO. 2

32 rimfire, 6 shots, 5" octagon barrel. Iron or brass frame (iron scarcer, worth premium):

WHITNEYVILLE marked; production estimated at 2,000:
5J-118   Values—Very Good **$125**   Exc. **$375**

EAGLE CO. (tradename) marked; estimated production 1,000:
5J-119   Values—Very Good **$125**   Exc. **$375**

SIZE/MODEL NO. 2-1/2

38 rimfire, 5 shots, barrel lengths 1-1/2" (worth 25 percent premium) and 3". Iron or brass frame (iron scarcer, worth premium). Numerous cylinder catch variations noted:

WHITNEYVILLE marked; production estimated at 5,000:
5J-120   Values—Very Good **$125**   Exc. **$400**

EAGLE CO. (tradename) marked; production estimated at 1,000:
5J-121   Values—Very Good **$125**   Exc. **$375**

5J-114
Size / Model No. 1 Early Style

5J-115
Size / Model No. 1

5J-115.3
Size / Model No. 1 Wide Cylinder

5J-115.7
Size / Model No. 1 Monitor Marked

5J-116
Size / Model No. 1-1/2

5J-120
Size / Model No. 2-1/2

Chapter V-K

Winchester Firearms
(and Their Predecessor Arms)

Synonymous with the development and expansion of the American West is the name of this famed American gun. The romance and lore surrounding the name certainly has much to do with the collector interest in the guns of this illustrious maker. Of course, not all Winchesters were instrumental in "winning the West." A great many have been associated with important personages in all parts of the world including Presidents and crowned heads, while many others have gained considerable prestige by their trusted dependability and use on celebrated expeditions, safaris, and hunts throughout the world, to just plain putting meat on the table—for over a century.

What helps make them so attractive from the collector's point of view are the many models and variations of each which exist as well as the large quantities in which most were manufactured; certainly a testimony to their popularity as well. The mere fact that there were many made and hence a reasonably large amount are still in existence, affords the average collector the opportunity to rather readily acquire specimens.

It may be accurately said that all Winchesters have collector appeal. Some models still in production today have variations in their earlier production that have already achieved a collectible status. A cut-off point for what is generally considered in the "antique" Winchester collecting field was arbitrarily established for this section, terminating with models introduced or commencing production approximately at the turn of the century. However, a few successor models of the 20th century which substantially bore the same characteristics and appearance of earlier pieces have been included.

This Winchester section is arranged by style of action: lever action, single shots, bolt and pump action rifles and all shotguns. A general attempt has been made to follow a chronological order within each grouping, although where not strictly adhered to the reasons will be obvious. Many Winchesters were simultaneously manufactured and the more popular ones enjoyed very long sales runs well into the 20th century.

Surprisingly, with all the published works that have appeared on the subject of Winchester, there is still room for more research to come. A number of fine books are available to the collector for use as standard guides in pursuing the hobby and there are endless avenues in which one can specialize. The broadness of the Winchester field is such that numerous segments worthy of special studies remain in relatively unexplored areas, while others have room for improvement and updating.

Paramount to the collecting of Winchesters and their evaluation is condition. Small fluctuations in the percentage of original finish still remaining can often increase value considerably. This is especially true with earlier models. Although the percentage of blue (and case hardening if it appears) is the usual guideline for placing a gun in a specific category of condition, it must be taken into consideration what condition that blue finish is actually in. For instance, is it still bright and in its original issued state—or has it dulled considerably from age? Thus, pure percentages as a guideline can tend to be misleading without amplification. The prices reflected herein for the two most often encountered grades of condition will be found an accurate guide. It must be remembered that there are many nuances in the pricing of Winchesters and that often seemingly minor factors will play a role in affecting values. Such information can only be gleaned from a further study of the subject.

A great many Winchesters were made available to the public—and are so listed in their catalogs—in wide varieties of styles, finishes, barrel lengths, barrel weights and a whole host of optional accessories, e.g., single and double set triggers and sights of many styles. Some of these features have considerable importance and many will enhance the value of the gun on which they appear; often times a very rare accessory or feature can affect the price considerably. The variations that can and do occur are veritably endless; they comprise one of the intriguing aspects of collecting Winchesters. Certainly arbitrary is the listing of the variants of each model in this section. It is felt that every major variant of each model as well as variants that are generally accepted as "standard" are included herein. The collector is cautioned to watch for variants and sub-variants and a multitude of accessories that will affect values. The several reference works on Winchester should be consulted for verification of these features as well as establishing their relative scarcity.

Bore condition is an influencing factor in Winchester values. Although chances are that very few intend to shoot an antique Winchester being considered, it is a part of the examination process to look down the bore and see if it sparkles—or doesn't. In the case of a very fine quality and conditioned specimen, there is no doubt that a mediocre or poor bore will detract from its demand and its value. This is especially so on those High Wall and Low Wall Winchester single shots where bore is a major determining point in arriving at value. About the only Winchester in which a bore is relatively unimportant (except in the finest and highest priced specimens) is the brass frame Model 1866. A great amount of these show heavy use and bores are normally just as bad. Of course, a ringed bore causing even the slightest bulge evident on the outside of the barrel is a detriment to any firearm and will definitely detract from its value and desirability—price should be revised downwards accordingly.

Very likely one of the most sought after variations and one which affects value considerably is the deluxe feature to be found on many of the models. This usually entails having extra fancy grained wood (in various grades too) with checkered pistol grip or straight stock and matching forend. Such features greatly enhance the value, and it is very much dependent on which model the deluxe feature appears as to what the value increase might be. In other words, on some they are quite often encountered, while on others they may be considered rare. Verification of such features is found in many of the easily available Winchester reference works.

Original factory engraved Winchesters are a completely new ball game. No attempt to price such specimens has been made; it would be completely unfair to both the buyer and seller or owner of such pieces. This is a highly specialized field in which quite a few factors must be taken into account in order to arrive at value. Fortunately there is a wealth of printed material available to study and digest, chief of which is the highly respected definitive *The Book of Winchester Engraving* by R. L. Wilson. Suffice it to say that the factory did custom engraving on all models in various degrees and qualities as well as price ranges. Following these "standard" grades they performed extra fancy custom work that was done either by their own engravers or custom contract engravers. Depending on the model, the style and class of engraving, and the condition of the specimen, prices can start at the very least from double the amount of a plain specimen and progress to six figures. Obviously these latter prices are few and far between and represent the ultimate in the engraver's art as well as the finest for condition. As the reader can see, there is a broad range into which engraved specimens can fall. Extreme caution should be exercised in the acquisition of engraved specimens. Many Winchesters were engraved years after they left the factory at the whim of the owner and having thus achieved age and antiquity, they give the appearance of being factory original. Although their value is undoubtedly enhanced over a plain specimen, they decidedly do not possess the desirability, demand or value of an original factory engraved piece. There are also not a few spurious engraved Winchesters to be found on the market engraved by unscrupulous purveyors to capture the pocketbook of the unwary.

A very low serial number on a Winchester is an enticing feature. No fixed rules or even good rules-of-thumb exist on how to add values for low numbers; it is just a collector eccentricity. Generally speaking, three digits or lower will add a premium to the value of an antique Winchester. Two digits or a single digit number could possibly increase the price 25 to 50 percent or more.

Original factory warehouse records of serial numbers exist for many (but not all) antique Winchesters Model 1866 through Model 1907. Those records are now at the Cody Firearms Museum which offers a service for collectors to identify rifles for which records are still on file. A modest fee of $55.00 per gun ($30.00 to members of the Firearms Museum) is charged. Address letters to: Cody Firearms Museum, c/o Buffalo Bill Historical Center, 720 Sheridan Ave., Cody, Wyoming 82414. Museum letters include data that appears in ledger books kept by the Winchester warehouse, entered when the gun was received from the factory. Usually logged-in was date received, model, caliber, barrel length, custom work (i.e. engraving, special markings, etc.) special sights and date shipped from the warehouse, along with numbers of any special work orders. Where a gun was standard, i.e. barrel lengths or calibers were the only one that particular model was then made, such information was often overlooked. The buyers' names or destinations for the guns on leaving the warehouse were rarely included.

This section, and consequently a well rounded or "complete" Winchester collection, contains the predecessor arms that led to the ultimate design and manufacture of the first Winchester. The dual paths of development of both the mechanical systems of the weapons and the financial affairs of the companies that manufactured these predecessors are inextricably tied to each other. With each of these evolutionary pieces, the textual material includes some of the historical background of the particular piece and its association with the true "Winchester."

A brief background on the evolution of the company name "Winchester" is helpful in understanding the subject. It all began with the Hunt's Patent repeating rifle c. 1848, subsequently improved upon by Lewis Jennings, c. 1849 to 1852, and manufactured in the shops of Robbins & Lawrence in Windsor, Vermont; the shop foreman was B. Tyler Henry (of later Henry rifle fame). Production ceased in 1852 with the investors suffering heavy losses. After a lapse of two years, Horace Smith and Daniel Wesson, c. 1854, took up where the Jennings left off; in their plant at Norwich, Connecticut, their lever action repeating magazine pistol (the Iron Frame Volcanic) was manufactured with B. Tyler Henry prominently employed in its production, c. 1854 to 1855. In that latter year the company was re-incorporated as the "Volcanic Repeating Arms Company;" Oliver F. Winchester entered the picture as a stock holder. The new Volcanic Repeating Arms Company acquired the entire rights of patents and assets from Smith & Wesson; Smith stepped out of the picture and Wesson shortly thereafter. In February, 1856, production of the brass frame Volcanic pistol was changed to the New Haven plant; by August the company had experienced great financial problems and became insolvent in 1857 with the entire assets sold to Oliver Winchester. In April of that year, the company reorganized as the New Haven Arms Company and continued to manufacture the brass frame Volcanic pistol and rifle. B. Tyler Henry, as shop superintendent, in successful experiments redesigned in large rifle size the Volcanic action to use large caliber rimfire metallic cartridges—also developed by himself. The famed Henry lever action repeating rifles were manufactured from 1860 through 1866. Oliver Winchester served as chief executive officer of the New Haven Arms Company and continued as such when the name was changed in 1866 to the "Winchester Repeating Arms Company."

The reader is urged to review the introductory material to this book (especially Chapter II) giving the exact definition of the NRA standards which comprise the terms used to describe conditions for each of the following guns.

BIBLIOGRAPHY

*Adler, Dennis. *Winchester Shotguns*. Edison, N.J.: Chartwell (Book Sales Inc.) 2006. A detailed overview of the Winchester shotgun line from their earliest English imports to the present day. Well-illustrated.

*Boorman, Dean K. *The History of Winchester Firearms*. England: Salamander Books, 2001. A well-illustrated concise account of this famous company from their beginnings to present day.

Butler, D. F. *Winchester '73 and '76, The First Repeating Centerfire Rifles*. New York: The Winchester Press, 1970. Devoted exclusively to these two models with a great deal of fine detail about them.

*Cambell, John. *The Winchester Single Shot*. Vol. I. Lincoln, R.I: Andrew Mowbray Publishers, 1995. Definitive details on the "High Wall" and "Low Wall" and accessories. Vol. II, 1998.

*Canfield, Bruce N. *Winchester in the Service*. Lincoln, R.I.: Mowbray Publishers, 1991. All models purchased under U.S. Government contract from the Hotchkiss in 1877 to the M1 carbine of WWII.

Fadala, S. *Winchester's 30-30 Model 94*. Harrisburg, Pennsylvania: The Stackpole Company, 1986.

*Giles, R. T. and Shuey, D. L. *One Hundred Years of Winchester Cartridge Boxes, 1856-1956*. Atglen, Pa: Schiffer Pub, Ltd. Guide and identification for matching Winchester boxed cartridges to the guns chambered for them.

*Houze, Herbert G. *Winchester Repeating Arms Co.; Its History And Development 1865-1981*. Iola, Wisc: Krause Publications, 1994.

*Houze, Herbert G. *Winchester Bolt Action Military & Sporting Rifles 1877 to 1937*. Lincoln R.I.: Mowbray Publishing, 1998.

*Houze, Herbert G. *The Winchester Model 1876 'Centennial' Rifle; Its True Origins and Subsequent Production*. Lincoln, Rhode Island: Mowbray Inc., Pub., 2001. Corrects several misconceptions about origin and evolution of this famous lever-action rifle. Important reference.

Johnson, Burton, Pugsley, Hall et al. *Winchester Repeating Arms Co. Firearms Reference Collection*. Salt Lake City, Utah: Lynhame Sayce Co. 1991.

*Kowalski, David D. (Editor) *Standard Catalog of Winchester* Iola, Wisconsin: Krause Publications, 2000. Comprehensive Price Guide for vast cross-section of Winchester products with 2,500 illustrations. Contributions by well-known collectors and students.

Lee, R. M. and Wilson, R. L. *The Art of the Gun (Vol. IV) Winchester Firearms Masterpieces*. Sparks, Nevada: Yellowstone Press. 2002. Numerous rare examples from well-known Robert Lee collection accompanied by brief text.

*McDowell, R. B. *Evolution of the Winchester*. Tacoma, Washington: Armory Publications, 1985. Great wealth of detail and data on the Hunt, Jennings, Smith-Jennings, S&W, Volcanic. Henry and very early Winchesters.

Madis, G. *Experimental Winchesters*. Brownsboro, Texas: Art and Reference House (n.d.). Series of drawings of rifles c. 1870 to WWI.

*Madis, G. *The Winchester Book*. Lancaster, Texas: Privately published by the author; First Edition 1961; Revised and Enlarged 1969, 1971 and 1977. A very extensive, detailed study of all Winchester collector firearms; profusely illustrated and considered a standard reference work.

*Madis, G. *The Winchester Handbook*. Tyler, Texas: Art & Reference House (n.d.). Smaller, concise version of *The Winchester Book*. Covers all models from 1849; details variations.

*Madis, G. *Winchester Dates of Manufacture*. Tyler, Texas: Art & Reference House, 1981 and 1984. Includes year of manufacture and total guns made from date of introduction to date discontinued; serial ranges for each year. 80 models from 1849 to 1984.

*Madl, John T. *Identifying Your Model 1886 Winchester*. Sault Ste. Marie, Mich: Lake Superior State University (2005). Systematically examines the popular lever action; its history and construction. Monograph; spiral bound.

*Muerrle, P. *Winchester; The Way It Really Was*. Madison, Conn: Private printed by author, 1996. Personal recollections of factory c. 1918 to c. 1960's.

Parsons, J. E. *The First Winchester*. New York: William Morrow and Company, 1955 (enlarged slightly 1960). Devoted primarily to the Henry rifle and the Model 1866 Winchester with considerable data on the Models 1873 and 1876 also. Classic work; highly regarded.

*Pirkle, A. *Winchester Lever Action Repeating Firearms-Vol. I Models-1866, 1873, 1876*. Tustin, Cal.: North Cape Pub., 1994.

*Pirkle, A. *Winchester Lever Action Repeating Firearms-Vol. II Models of 1886 & 1892*. 1996.

*Pirkle, A. *Winchester Lever Action Repeating Firearms-Vol. III Models of 1894- & 1895*. 1999.

Renneberg, Robert C. *The Winchester Model 94; The First 100 Years*. Iola, Wisconsin: Krause Publications, 1991. Much detail and minutiae of this famous rifle.

Rule, Roger C. *A Catalog of 20th Century Winchester Repeating Arms*. Northridge, Cal.: Alliance Books, 1984. Complete Winchester catalog coverage for all Winchester products.

Rule, R. C. *The Rifleman's Rifle; Winchester's Model 70, 1936-1963*. Northridge, California: Alliance Books, Inc., 1982. Great detail; fine illustrations on this popular, very collectible bolt action sporting rifle.

Schwing, Ned. *Winchester Slide Action Rifles*. Vol. I *Models 1890 and 1906*; Vol. II *Models 61 and 62*. Iola, Wisconsin: Krause Publications, 1992 and 1993 respectively.

Stadt, R. W. *Winchester Shotguns and Shotshells*. Tacoma, Washington: Armory Publications, 1984. Fine detail, profuse illustrations from double barrel hammer types, lever and pump styles to Model 59 auto.

*Sword, Wiley *The Historic Henry Rifle: Oliver Winchester's Famous Civil War Repeater*. Lincoln, Rhode Island, Mowbray Pub., 2002. Important addition to Winchester (and Civil War military arms) literature. Significant original source information. Much on Civil War usage by various regiments; serial number data.

*Webster, Tom *Winchester Rarities*. Iola, Wisconsin: Krause Publications, 2001. Catalog of the diverse advertising materials of Winchester prior to 1935; much rare and uncommon Winchester memorabilia. Color illustrated.

Stone, George W. *The Winchester 1873 Handbook*. Arvada, Colorado: Frontier Press, 1973. Wealth of minutia about this one model.

Trolard, T. *Winchester Commemoratives*. Plano, Texas: Commemorative Investments Press, 1985. Fine color illustrations; profuse detail each rifle.

*Watrous, G. R., Rikhoff, J. C. and Hall, T. H. *The History of Winchester Firearms 1866-1975*. New York: Winchester Press, 4th Revised and Updated Edition 1975. The only factory authorized and published guide to all Winchester firearms from the earliest through the most currently produced. Wealth of important data. A standard reference; widely used and cited.

*Webster, Tom *Winchester Rarities*. Iola, Wisconsin: Krause Publications, 2001. Catalog of the diverse advertising materials of Winchester prior to 1935; much rare and uncommon Winchester memorabilia. Color illustrated.

Williamson, H. F. *Winchester—The Gun That Won the West*. Washington: Combat Forces Press, 1952; with many subsequent reprintings. Primarily a business history of the company; contains a great deal of intriguing and important firearms history also.

Wilson, R. L. *Winchester: The Golden Age of American Gunmaking and the Winchester 1 of 1000*. Cody, Wyoming: Buffalo Bill Historical Center, 1983. Superb color plates.

Wilson, R. L. *The Book of Winchester Engraving*. Los Angeles: Beinfeld Publishing, Inc., 1975. Highly detailed, very thorough study of Winchester engraving from earliest period to modern times; superbly illustrated.

*Wilson, R. L. *Winchester Engraving*. Palm Springs, California: Beinfeld Publishing Company, Inc., 1990. Revised and considerably enlarged edition of the above classic work.

*Wilson, R.L. *Winchester in American Legend*. New York, N.Y.: Random house, 1991. History of the company from its beginnings to present; all models; exceptional color illustrations.

___Winchester Factory Catalogs. A major source of information is many thick, detailed, illustrated catalogs issued over the long span of the company's life. Original issues are considered collector's items, and are often quite available; most have been reproduced at one time or another and readily available at modest prices.

(*) Preceding a title indicates a book is currently in print.

Hunt Repeating Rifle

5K-001

The Hunt Repeating Rifle. The first "Winchester" made is the hardest of all models to obtain. Invented by Walter Hunt, who also designed the cartridge (known as the "Rocket Ball"), the gun had the unusual designation of "Volition Repeater." The cartridge was a hollow bullet containing the powder inside, backed by a pierced disk which permitted ignition via a separate priming device. Hunt's pioneer rifle is so rare that only one specimen is known, and that is in the Winchester Museum collection. No sales are on record in modern times, and thus no estimate of value is presented here. Manufacture was c. 1847-48, but not in any quantity. The illustrated Hunt Rifle indicates the unique appearance of this ultimate in Winchester rarities: (Note: The Winchester story began in 1849, with the Hunt, and proceeded through a variety of other types before the Winchester Repeating Arms Company was chartered in 1866. Although Oliver F. Winchester did not enter into the picture until about 1855, the historic and mechanical background of the firm is properly traced through the Hunt, the Jennings, Smith & Wesson, Volcanic, and the New Haven Arms Company.) **5K-001**

Jennings Rifle

5K-002
Jennings Repeating Rifle

5K-002.5
Jennings Breechloading Rifle

The Jennings Rifle. Successor to the Hunt Repeating Rifle. Made by Robbins and Lawrence at their factory in Windsor, Vermont. Although their contract called for 5,000 repeating rifles, it is believed that less than 1,000 in all variations were manufactured with the repeaters likely not produced in quantities greater than for testing or evaluation purposes. The firm's foreman, B. Tyler Henry, would later play a major role in the development of the rifle and ammunition for the Volcanic, New Haven, and Winchester arms companies. The Jennings is important in Winchester evolution because it served to bring together the talents of Henry, Horace Smith, and Daniel Wesson. Their efforts led ultimately to quite historic developments in lever action repeating firearms.

The Jennings and Smith-Jennings Rifles have only recently been properly classified by the detailed study appearing in *Evolution of the Winchester* (R.B. McDowell).

Markings vary; all (except the First Model) are usually marked 0MROBBINS AND LAWRENCE - MAKERS - WINDSOR, VT. and PATENT 1849. They are occasionally seen marked in an oval panel on the frame PATENT 1849/C.P. DIXON AGENT/NEW YORK...or a combination of both markings. Serial numbers were in a minimum of four groups, all starting with 1.

All Jennings Rifles and Smith-Jennings Rifles (except those converted to muzzle-loading percussion) were made to utilize the Hunt "Rocket Ball" cartridge with a pill primer; all are 54 caliber. **Jennings Repeating Rifle;** made c. 1848-49.

Ring-lever-trigger operates mechanism within long oval trigger guard; automatic pill primer. Unmarked. Tubular magazine loaded from front. Very rare; quantity manufactured unknown, but likely only a few produced for testing and evaluation purposes. No known sales in recent times: **5K-002**

Jennings Breechloading Rifle. Made c. 1850-51. Single shot. Factory converted or made from Jennings repeater parts. "Rocket Ball" cartridge loaded through right side of frame; ring trigger operates breech and the automatic pill primer device. Magazine tube made smaller in diameter and used for carrying cleaning rod. The Rocket Ball cartridge having insufficient power made the rifle impractical for hunting or military purposes likely leading to its lack of success and small quantity produced. As many of these were later altered by local gunsmiths to muzzle-loading, they are quite scarce. Erroneously classified in earlier editions of this Guide as "First Model" (5K-002):

5K-002.5   Values—Good **$1,500**   Fine **$3,500**

Jennings Factory Muzzle-Loading Rifle. Made c. 1852 only. New smaller frame using remaining parts from unsuccessful breechloading models. Ring trigger cut and altered to spur trigger; trigger guard re-formed with an indented bow. Breech of barrel plugged, striker pin on hammer ground flush, percussion nipple fitted on top of frame. Listed in previous editions of this Guide as number 5K-004:

5K-003   Values—Good **$950**   Fine **$1,750**

Non-Factory Converted Jennings to Muzzle-Loading Rifle. (Not illus.) Made c. 1850s. Encountered usually on the Second Model Jennings (above). Quality of workmanship varies greatly; unlikely any two of these are identical. Barrels plugged in usual

5K-003
Jennings Factory
Muzzle-Loading Rifle

manner with trigger guards, triggers, hammers altered, modified or replaced:

5K-003.5   Values—Good **$500**   Fine **$900**

Smith-Jennings Rifle

5K-004
Jennings Repeating Rifle

5K-004.5
Jennings Breechloading Rifle

5K-004.6
Third Model Smith-Jennings

The Smith-Jennings Rifle. Horace Smith, an experienced gunsmith (and soon after of Smith & Wesson fame) was engaged to improve the Jennings Rifle c. 1851. He was issued a patent August, 1851 for an improved action and Robbins and Lawrence commenced manufacture of the repeater. All took the "Rocket Ball" cartridge and were pill primed. *All three models are repeating rifles*; all caliber 54. Markings are the same as on the Jennings (see above) retaining the *1849* patent date.

In earlier editions of the Guide, this rifle was termed "Second Model Smith-Jennings" number 5K-003. It is now more correctly listed as follows:

First Model Smith-Jennings; made 1851. Quantity approximately 500. Ring type lever-trigger without trigger guard. Front loading tubular cartridge magazine under barrel. Automatic pill magazine for priming the "Rocket Ball" ammunition. Flat sided (usually engraved) frame with evenly rounded forward undersection. Most often encountered of the three models:

5K-004   Values—Good **$3,500**   Fine **$7,000**

Second Model Smith-Jennings; made c. 1851-52. Quantity less than 400. Very similar to First Model with improved pill priming system and cartridge carrier position spring. Frame has pronounced bulge on undersection resulting in nickname "pregnant frame Jennings":

5K-004.5   Values—Good **$4,000**   Fine **$8,500**

Third Model Smith-Jennings; made 1852. Quantity less than 200. Long slender frame with escalloped (hollowed-out or fluted) lower sides of frame. Pill priming system further improved; side loading port changed from a simple swinging plate to one which slid open/closed within two channels:

5K-004.6   Values—Good **$4,500**   Fine **$9,500**

S&W Lever Action Repeating Pistols

Smith & Wesson Lever Action Repeating Pistols. The next Winchester predecessor arms made after the Jennings were the Smith & Wesson repeaters. These were based on a Horace Smith and Daniel B. Wesson patent of 1854, and are historically intriguing due to the fact that the S&W firm today is famous for its success with revolvers.

The S&W Lever Action pistols were made in Norwich, Connecticut, c. 1854-55. The estimated total production was only about 1,700. Featuring the lever action mechanism, they have integral, front loading magazines located beneath the barrel. The self-contained cartridge was a special type, the hollowed out conical bullet containing the powder, and backed by the primer.

An important pioneer arm to both Smith & Wesson and Winchester collectors, the quite limited production total makes these pistols highly prized and difficult to obtain.

5K-005
.31 caliber "No. 1 Pistol"

5K-006
.41 caliber "No. 2 Pistol"

The basic models are:

31 Caliber No. 1 Pistol; 4" barrel, bag shaped varnished wooden grip, all steel construction with engraved frame. The lever with a round finger hole. Blued finish with browned barrels. Serial number usually found beneath the grips. Standard marking on barrel flats: SMITH & WESSON, NORWICH, CT.and PATENTED FEBRUARY 14, 1854 and CAST STEEL. Quantity made approximately 1,200:

5K-005   Values—Good **$3,250**   Fine **$12,500**

41 Caliber No. 2 Pistol; 8" barrel, flat bottomed varnished wooden grip, all steel construction with engraved frame. Note spur on bottom of the round finger hole of the lever. Blued finish with browned barrels. Serial number usually beneath grips. Generally marked on barrel top flat: SMITH & WESSON NORWICH, CT./CAST-STEEL PATENT. Also made with 6" bbl. and worth premium. Quantity made under 500:

5K-006   Values—Good **$5,500**   Fine **$15,000**

NOTE: Calibers for S&W and Volcanic Arms have been variously listed as 30 and 38 cal.
Correct sizes are 31 cal. and 41 cal. as shown.

Volcanic Lever Action Pistols and Carbines

5K-011

5K-007

5K-008

Volcanic Lever Action Repeating Pistols and Carbines, by the Volcanic Repeating Arms Company. In July of 1855, the Smith & Wesson name was changed to the Volcanic Repeating Arms Company, opening still another chapter in Winchester history. Business was carried on under the Volcanic name from 1855 to 1857, at which time it was reorganized as the New Haven Arms Company. Oliver F. Winchester, a successful manufacturer of clothing, became an increasingly active investor in the lever action arms, having first purchased stock in the Volcanic firm c. 1855. Smith and Wesson both dropped out of the enterprise c. 1855-56.

The breakdown of Volcanic arms is presented in the following model listings. All guns were of the same caliber, 41, and fired the patented, specially designed cartridges (though improved) of the Smith & Wesson type; magazines of integral structure, located beneath the barrel. The Volcanics began with serial 1, and have been observed marked in excess of the number 3000. Standard markings of all models, on the barrels: THE VOLCANIC/REPEATING ARMS CO./PATENT NEW HAVEN CONN/FEB 14, 1854. Marking variations are noted in these. Finish: Unfinished brass frames; the barrels blued. (Note: Engraved specimens, cut in a large, open scroll pattern, are often encountered. These arms command an added premium.)
Lever Action Navy Pistol; 6" barrel, 41 caliber, brass frame, flat-bottomed varnished walnut grip, rounded finger hole in the lever. VOLCANIC barrel markings as noted above. Quantity estimated 1,200:

5K-007   Values—Good **$3,500**   Fine **$8,000**

Lever Action Navy Pistol; same as above but with 8" barrel. Quantity estimated 1,500:

5K-008   Values—Good **$3,500**   Fine **$8,000**
(Note: Pistols as above fitted with shoulder stocks demand a premium.)
Lever Action Navy Pistol; as above but with 16" barrel, and attachable shoulder stock. Quantity estimated 300. Rare.

Pistol:
5K-009   Values—Good **$5,000**   Fine **$16,000**

Pistol with Stock:
5K-010   Values—Good **$8,500**   Fine **$22,500**
Lever Action Carbine; 41 caliber, barrel length of 16-1/2" utilizing left-over barrels from Navy Pistol. Long and straight, varnished walnut, buttstocks, with crescent type brass buttplate. VOLCANIC markings as noted above:

16-1/2" barrel:
5K-011   Values—Good **$7,000**   Fine **$17,500**

21" barrel made only by New Haven Arms Co. (*q.v.*):
5K-012

25" barrel made only by New Haven Arms Co. (*q.v.*):
5K-013

Volcanic Lever Action Pistols and Carbines by New Haven Arms Co.

Volcanic Lever Action Repeating Pistols and Carbines, by the New Haven Arms Company. Due to increasing financial pressures, the Volcanic firm was reorganized into the New Haven Arms Company, in April of 1857. However, Volcanic remained as the trade name for the lever action pistols and carbines. A key means of telling the "Volcanic Volcanics" from the "New Haven Arms Company Volcanics" is the omission of VOLCANIC marks and change to PATENT FEB. 14, 1854/NEW HAVEN,CONN. Marking variations are also noted in these.

5K-014

5K-015

The New Haven Arms Company's Volcanic production lasted from 1857 to 1860, and the breakdown of models is presented below. The cartridge type, magazine, and other basic features remained as on the "Volcanic Volcanics." Total manufactured of the New Haven Volcanics is estimated at about 3,300; serial numbering began with 1. Finish: Unfinished brass frames; the barrels blued. (Note: Engraved specimens, cut in a large, open scroll pattern, are often encountered. These arms command an added premium.)

Lever Action No. 1 Pocket Pistol; 3-1/2" and 6" (Target type) barrels (scarce and will bring a premium), 31 caliber, small size brass frame, flat-bottomed varnished walnut grip, round finger hole in the lever. VOLCANIC barrel markings as on Volcanic Arms Company pistols, but including 1854 patent date and New Haven address:

3-1/2" barrel. Quantity estimated 850:
5K-014　　Values—Good **$2,750**　　　Fine **$5,000**

6" barrel. Quantity estimated 225:
5K-015　　Values—Good **$3,250**　　　Fine **$6,750**

Lever Action No. 2 Navy Pistol; 8" barrel, 41 caliber large size brass frame, flat-bottomed varnished walnut grip, round finger hole in lever. VOLCANIC barrel markings as above, including 1854 patent date and New Haven address. Quantity estimated 1,000:
5K-016　　Values—Good **$3,750**　　　Fine **$8,000**

No. 2 Navy Pistol identical above with 6" barrel. Quantity estimated 300:
5K-016.5　Values—Good **$4,250**　　　Fine **$9,500**

Lever Action Navy Pistol; large frame model as above, but with 16" barrel, and attachable shoulder stock. Quantity unknown; extremely limited; very rare. Great caution should be exercised in acquiring this variant:

Pistol:
5K-017　　Values—Good **$5,000**　　　Fine **$15,000**

Pistol with Stock:
5K-018　　Values—Good **$7,500**　　　Fine **$22,500**

Lever Action Carbine; 41 caliber, barrel lengths of 16-1/2", 21", and 25". Large brass frame. Long and straight, varnished walnut, buttstocks with crescent type brass buttplate. Barrel markings as above, including 1854 patent date and New Haven address. Quantity estimated 1,000 for all three lengths:

16-1/2" barrel:
5K-019　　Values—Good **$7,000**　　　Fine **$17,500**

21" barrel:
5K-020　　Values—Good **$8,000**　　　Fine **$24,000**

25" Barrel:
5K-021　　Values—Good **$9,000**　　　Fine **$27,500**

5K-019

5K-020

5K-021

See also Walch Revolver 7A-117

Henry Rifle

Henry Rifle. Made 1860-66; total quantity approximately 14,000. (overlap with model 1866).

44 rimfire caliber. Tubular magazine integral with the barrel, and located beneath it. 15 shots. 24" barrel length standard.

Oil stained walnut stocks. Blued finish; brass frames usually left plain.

Serial numbers overlap the Model 1866. Highest Henry range is about 14000. Major serial number location on the top of breech

end of barrel; marked: HENRY'S PATENT. OCT. 16. 1860/ MANUFACT'D BY THE NEW HAVEN ARMS. CO. NEW HAVEN. CT.

The Henry Rifle was developed from the Volcanic, and was built around the new 44 rimfire cartridge. Both the new rifle and the cartridge were designed by B. Tyler Henry. A basic feature of the 44 rimfire was the use of a metallic casing, rather than the undependable self-contained powder, ball and primer bullet of the Volcanic. Loading continued to be from the muzzle end of

5K-022
Iron Frame Henry

5K-023
Early Brass Frame Henry

the magazine. A distinctive identifying feature of the Henry is the lack of a forend, and the absence of a loading gate on either side of the frame. Made in relatively limited quantities, and a revolutionary weapon in Civil War service, the Henry is one of the major collector's items in the entire Winchester field. The model is difficult to obtain in fine condition and commands premium prices in all its variations. Quite a few company-size Union outfits, especially those from Kentucky, Illinois, Indiana and Missouri purchased at their own expense, and carried, Henry rifles. Much significant information on the development and history of this important rifle, its production, sale and usage by the military during the Civil War is found in *The Historic Henry Rifle* by W. Sword (q.v.).

Iron Frame Model. The most desirable Henry variation, featuring the frame of iron, rather than the standard brass. Rounded type iron buttplate at its heel; no lever latch; sporting style adjustable leaf rear sights. Quantity estimated 275. Serial number range 1 to 400:

5K-022 Values—Good **$30,000** Fine **$100,000**

Early Brass Frame Model. As above, but the frame and buttplate of brass. With or without lever latch. Serial numbers overlap iron frames. Total made about 1,500:

5K-023 Values—Good **$11,500** Fine **$35,000**

Late Brass Frame Model. As above, but the heel of the **brass** buttplate (**adopted approx. serial range no. 4,000**) has a pointed profile. Lever latch standard. Serial range primarily above about 2500 (overlap with early M1866 brass frame rifles):

5K-024 Values—Good **$10,000** Fine **$30,000**

U.S. Government Purchased and Issued Henry Rifles. Total quantity 1,731 acquired between 1862 and 1865. Most in serial range 3000 to 4200. Known issued to 1st Maine and 1st District of Columbia Cavalry Regiments, (more than 200 were captured Sept. 1864 from the 1st D.C. Regiment and issued to the 7th, 11th and 35th Virginia (Confederate) Cavalry); small quantity trial issues to other units. Believed brass frames only. Inspector

markings C.G.C. at breech of barrel and stock. Extremely important information about government purchases and serial number ranges of same will be found in *The Historic Henry Rifle* (by W. Sword, q.v.) some of which may add significantly to historic significance and premium values.

5K-025 Values—Good **$20,000** Fine **$70,000**

Cleaning or wiping rods issued with all Henry rifles. Earliest types were jointed, four-piece hickory wood rods with small iron fittings for assembly. The four sections were stowed in the butt stock through a hinged brass door in buttplate. Later rods were four pieces of steel with brass tip stowed in butt in same manner. However, the aperture and the loading port was narrower in diameter, hence the earlier wooden rod will not fit into that later style! Reported that some earlier wooden rods may bear "CGC" inspector markings to accompany government contract rifles.

5K-025.5

Briggs Patent Henry Rifle. Although the King's Patent (May 22, 1866) hinged loading gate adapted to a Henry rifle became the device used to facilitate loading cartridges from the receiver in the M.1866, other methods were experimented with. Best known and most practical is the Briggs Patent of Oct. 16, 1866 which allowed for loading the magazine tube immediately in front of the receiver. Made only experimently, there are a handful of known examples that have come on the market. One method, made without a forearm, had the entire magazine tube slide forward; the other (illus. here) is fitted with a uniquely designed brass forend which slides forward to expose the bottom end of the magazine for ease in loading. Few recorded sales; values minimum in low five figures; upward considerably dependant on condition.

5K-025.5

Winchester Model 1866 Rifle

Model 1866 Rifle. Manufactured c. 1866-98; total produced approximately 170,101.

44 rimfire caliber. Tubular magazine located beneath the barrel. Distinctive brass frame.

Oil stained walnut stocks. Metal parts finished as follows: Lever and hammer casehardened; barrel browned or blued, magazine tube blued, the brass furniture left a natural finish.

Serial numbering overlaps that of the Henry Rifle, and began at about 12476. Until about the 20000 serial range the number was marked beneath the buttstock on the left side of the upper tang. Thereafter the number could be found on the lower tang and was visible without removing the buttstock.

These arms are not marked "Model 1866," and are easily distinguished by their brass frames with loading gates, and the

presence of forestocks. Winchester Museum serial records are only partially complete on the 1866 production. Popularly known on the frontier as the "Yellow Boy", the Indian also called it "many shots" along with "heap firing" guns. The '66 is the repeating rifle most deserving of the name "The Gun That Won The West."

Rifles: Standard with 24" barrel, octagonal through about the serial range 100000, at which time round barrels became common. Brass frame, buttplate, and forend cap (steel cap became standard after serial range 135000). The buttplate of the crescent type.

Carbines: Standard with 20" round barrel and two barrel bands. Brass frame and buttplate, the latter of the distinctive curved profile. Saddle ring mounted on the left side of the frame.

Muskets: Standard with 27" round barrel, 24" magazine, and

5K-028
M. 1866 Rifle

5K-029
M. 1866 Carbine

5K-032
M. 1866 Musket

17" forend. Three barrel bands present, and the buttplate of carbine style.

Major variations are:

First Model 1866 (a.k.a. "Flatside"), tang serial number concealed by the buttstock, "Henry drop" in profile of frame at the hammer area, frame does not flare out to meet forend, upper tang has two screws, flat loading gate cover, Henry and King's patent barrel marking, serial range 12476 to about 15500 (with some overlap with Henry Rifle).

Rifle version of the First Model (not fitted with forend cap):
5K-026   Values—Good **$14,000**   Fine **$45,000**

Carbine version of the First Model:
5K-027   Values—Good **$7,000**   Fine **$22,500**

Musket version of the First Model: (None produced)

Second Model 1866, concealed "inside" serial marking on the tang (early production through about 19000 serial range), flared frame to meet the forend, the "Henry drop" frame profile has turned to a graceful curved shape in the hammer area, Henry and King's patent barrel marking for most of production, serial range about 15500 to 23000+.

Mexican military purchase: Late in 1866 President Benito Juarez purchased 1,000 Model 1866 rifles (most likely 5K-028; possibly 5K-030; not to be confused with muskets or carbines). They were soon delivered to Monterrey in the State of Nuevo Leon. Only marking thus far recorded is a small circular stamp at top of receiver with a crudely outlined eagle, wings downward and letters "N.L." (Nuevo Leon) on left of circle; an issue or serial number above circle. Whether that marking indicated solely a Nuevo Leon state issue or was marked on all

the contract is unknown. Authenticated specimens worthy of premium values.

Rifle:
5K-028   Values—Good **$4,500**   Fine **$12,500**

Carbine:
5K-029   Values—Good **$4,000**   Fine **$11,500**

Musket: None known to be produced.

Third Model 1866, serial marked in block numerals behind the trigger (and thus visible without removing stock), flared frame to meet forend, and the curved frame profile in hammer area not as pronounced as the First and Second Models; Winchester, New Haven and King's Patent barrel marking, serial range about 23169 (lowest recorded number to date) to 149000.

Rifle:
5K-030   Values—Good **$4,000**   Fine **$11,000**

Carbine:
5K-031   Values—Good **$3,750**   Fine **$9,500**

Musket:
5K-032   Values—Good **$2,500**   Fine **$6,500**

Fourth Model 1866, the serial number marked in script on the lower tang near lever latch, flared frame to meet forend, the curved frame profile in hammer area even less pronounced than the Third Model, barrel marking same as the Third Model, serial range about 149000 to 170101. Late production iron mountings.

Rifle:
5K-033   Values—Good **$3,250**   Fine **$9,000**

Carbine:
5K-034   Values—Good **$2,750**   Fine **$8,500**

Musket:
5K-035   Values—Good **$2,500**   Fine **$6,500**

(Note: A premium placed on round barrels on rifles, as these are less frequently encountered than octagon.)

Winchester Model 1873 Rifle

Model 1873 Rifle. Made c. 1873-1919; total produced approximately 720,610 (figure includes 19,552 made in 22 rimfire).

32-20, 38-40, and 44-40 calibers. Tubular magazine located beneath barrel. The frames of iron with sideplates, and noticeably different from the Model 1866 predecessor.

Oil stained or (less common) varnished walnut stocks. Blued finish, with hammers, levers and buttplates casehardened; frames also not uncommon casehardened.

Serial numbering in individual series from 1 on up; located

on the lower tang. MODEL 1873 and Winchester markings appear on the upper tang; caliber markings usually are present on bottom of the brass elevator block (see bottom of frame) and on the barrel at breech. Winchester name and address marking on the barrel, with King's Improvement patent dates.

To the good fortune of collectors, Winchester Museum factory records are virtually complete for the Model 1873 production. This is a model in which the collector can specialize exclusively, and perhaps never run out of variations to acquire. Considerable variety is apparent in the Model 1873, in sights, magazines, finishes, markings, barrel lengths and weights, stocks, and even in screws, varying contours of wood and metal, knurlings, and *ad infinitum*. Export sales were considerable, and many of these arms experienced rough handling and those that survived are often in poor condition. Domestic sales have survived in a generally better state of condition, but the majority do show use, and often to a great degree. Perhaps the most famous of all Winchesters, the '73 was featured in the James Stewart film "Winchester '73." The Model boasts a production record covering more years (about 50) and more guns (over 720,000) than most of the company's other lever action models. Those under No. 525900 (approx.) made prior to December 31, 1898.

Rifles: Standard with 24" barrel, round or octagon. Buttplate of the crescent type. Cap on front of forend; the magazine tube attached to barrel with small band. Adjustable, open style sporting rear sight.

Carbines: Standard with 20" round barrel, and two barrel bands. Buttplate of distinctive curved profile. Saddle ring mounted on the left side of the frame. The rear sights of adjustable carbine type (compare with Rifle).

Muskets: Standard with 30" round barrel, 27" magazine. Three barrel bands usually present, the buttplate of carbine style, and the sights of adjustable musket type.

Major variations are:

Early First Model 1873, the dust cover with guide grooves is mortised in forward section of the frame; checkered oval thumbrest is separately affixed (very earliest is round thumbrest and worth premium). Note two screws on frame above trigger, lever latch fits into lower tang with threads, upper lever profile curves away from trigger; serial range from 1 to about 1600 (serials under 100 worth 30 percent to 50 percent premium).

Rifle:
5K-036   Values—Good **$2,250**   Fine **$8,500**

Carbine:
5K-037   Values—Good **$3,500**   Fine **$10,000**

Musket: None known to be produced.
(Note: On many, serial numbered 1 through approximately 600, Model 1873 markings are hand engraved and found on the lower tang with the serial number. This feature worth a premium in value.)

Late First Model 1873, the dust cover mortised as above (oval thumbrest is checkered on the cover itself and variations of that oval panel occur and fetch premiums), trigger pin appears below the two frame screws above trigger, improved type lever latch (the threads not visible) became standard as did the trigger block safety and the added profile to the lever behind trigger (to engage newly added safety pin); serial range about 1600 to 31000 (serials under 100 worth 30 percent to 50 percent premium).

Rifle:
5K-038   Values—Good **$1,750**   Fine **$6,500**

Carbine:
5K-039   Values—Good **$2,250**   Fine **$9,500**

Musket
5K-040   Values—Good **$2,250**   Fine **$9,000**

Second Model 1873, same as above but dust cover slides on center rail on rear section of top of the frame, the rail secured by screws; serial range about 31000 to 90000. On later Second Models, serrations on rear edges (for finger hold) replaced the checkered oval panel on the dust cover.

Rifle:
5K-041   Values—Good **$1,250**   Fine **$3,750**

Carbine:
5K-042   Values—Good **$1,500**   Fine **$5,000**

Musket:
5K-043   Values—Good **$1,250**   Fine **$4,000**

Third Model 1873, same as above but the dust cover rail is a machined integral part of the frame, no longer present are the two frame screws and pin formerly located above the trigger, and screws on lower tang are located much more rearward than previously; serial range about 90000 to end of production. Serrated rear edges on dust cover.

Rifles:
5K-044   Values—Good **$875**   Fine **$3,000**

Carbine:
5K-045   Values—Good **$1,250**   Fine **$4,500**

Musket:
5K-046   Values—Good **$1,100**   Fine **$2,750**

5K-042 / 5K-045
Carbine

5K-041 / 5K-044
Rifle

5K-043 / 5K-046
Musket

5K-047
Model 1873 Caliber 22 RF

Model 1873 22 Rimfire Rifle, easily identified by the 22 caliber markings and the lack of a loading gate in the right sideplate. Chambered for 22 short and long rimfire cartridges, and loaded through the front end of the magazine tube. 24" or 26" barrels standard. Made c. 1884-1904 in a total quantity of 19,552, this was the first repeating rifle manufactured in America chambered for the 22 rimfire ammunition (although Winchester's initial advertising of this rifle in their 1885 catalog offered it in 22 W.C.F. (centerfire) it is believed that was a clerical error as none are known, or recorded made in that caliber). Made in rifle size only.

It appears that only this variant chambered for 22 rimfire was offered with a takedown feature (in the early Winchester advertisements). The barrel, magazine and forearm fastened together as a single unit and were attached to the frame by a single tapered iron cross-pin. Merely removing (knocking out) that pin separated the frame from the barrel unit "thus making the gun more easily packed in trunk or case" as their catalog stated. The system was found unsatisfactory and few were actually produced and sold. It is noted that some other receivers had been drilled to accept that taper pin, but were fitted with the barrel unit and that pin is in a permanently fixed position. Actual takedown models and others with merely frames showing the permanent pin have been observed in the serial ranges 155,000 to 180,000. Authenticated takedown models worth substantial increased value.

5K-047	Values—Good **$1,150**	Fine **$3,750**

1 of 1000 and 1 of 100 rifles, are among the ultimate rarities in Winchester collecting. In the Model 1873 only 136 "1 of 1000" rifles were made, and 8 "1 of 100". These are distinguished by the special marking found on the top of the breech. Confirmation of the series can be made through Winchester Museum records, in which the original arms are documented. The desirability of 1 of 100/1000 rifles has made them attractive for faking; and caution is suggested in making a purchase. Although the "1 of 100" is the scarcer rifle it seems that the "1 of 1000" is more eagerly sought after, hence values are apparently the same for these two great rarities, ranging from:

1 of 100:

5K-048	Values—Good **$40,000**	Fine **$90,000**
	Exc. **$225,000**	

1 of 1000:

5K-049	Values—Good **$37,500**	Fine **$85,000**
	Exc. **$200,000**	

Winchester Model 1876 Rifle

Model 1876 Rifle. Manufactured c. 1876-97; total production of 63,871.

40-60, 45-60, 45-75, and 50-95 calibers. Tubular magazine located beneath barrel. The frames similar in appearance to the Model 1873, but are noticeably larger.

Oil stained or (less common) varnished walnut stocks. Blued finish, with hammers and levers, casehardened; frames and buttplates also not uncommon casehardened.

Serial numbering in individual series from 1 on up; located on the lower tang. MODEL 1876 stamped on the upper tang. Winchester name and address marking on the barrel, with King's Improvement patent dates. Caliber markings usually are present on bottom of the brass elevator block and on the barrel at breech.

Often known as the "Centennial Model" due to its introduction in 1876, the '76 was designed to offer the shooter a large caliber lever action for big game. It is sometimes confused with the Model 1873, until comparing their frames and calibers. The limited production total and years of manufacture recommend the '76 as among the less common Winchester lever actions. Shooters who enthusiastically endorsed the model include one of the most revered of all American hunters— Theodore Roosevelt. An important recent study *The Winchester Model 1876 Centennial Rifle* by H.G. Houze (q.v.) includes much fresh information about the Model 76 and discusses misconceptions about its origin and evolution.

Rifles: Standard with 26" or 28" round or octagon barrel. The buttplate of crescent type. Like the 1873, the forend has a metal cap, and the magazine tube is attached to the barrel with a small band. Adjustable, open style sporting rear sight. Stocks usually straight; pistol grip types are not common.

Carbines: The standard having 22" round barrel, 18" forend with a distinctive forend cap set back to allow for bayonet attachment, one barrel band (with band spring), carbine type buttplate. Saddle ring mounted on the left side of the frame. The rear sights of adjustable carbine type.

Muskets: Standard with 32" round barrel, the magazine tube concealed beneath the forend and the forend tip identical to that on the carbine. One barrel band, with band spring. Carbine type buttplate. Sights vary but are generally of military type. Muskets in the Model 1876 are scarce.

Major variations are:

First Model 1876, was made without a frame dust cover, and is in the serial range 1 to about 3000.

Rifle:

5K-050	Values—Good **$1,750**	Fine **$6,500**

Carbine:

5K-051	Values—Good **$2,250**	Fine **$7,500**

Musket:

5K-052	Values—Good **$5,500**	Fine **$10,000**

Early Second Model 1876, has a dust cover on the frame, with the thumbpiece of a die-struck oval, the dust cover guide rail screwed to top of frame; serial range about 3000 to 7000.

Rifle:

5K-053	Values—Good **$1,250**	Fine **$5,000**

Carbine:

5K-054	Values—Good **$1,750**	Fine **$7,000**

Musket:

5K-055	Values—Good **$5,000**	Fine **$9,500**

5K-053 / 056 / 059
Rifle

5K-054 / 057 / 060
Carbine

Late Second Model 1876, lacks the oval thumbpiece on the dust cover, but has knurling at the finger grip section at rear, the guide rail as on Early Second Model; serial range of about 7000 to 30000.

Rifle:
5K-056   Values—Good **$1,100**   Fine **$4,000**

Carbine:
5K-057   Values—Good **$1,750**   Fine **$6,000**

Musket:
5K-058   Values—Good **$4,500**   Fine **$9,000**

Third Model 1876, same as Late Second Model, but the guide rail machined integral with the frame; serial range of about 30000 to end of production.

Rifle:
5K-059   Values—Good **$1,100**   Fine **$4,000**

Carbine:
5K-060   Values—Good **$1,750**   Fine **$6,000**

Musket:
5K-061   Values—Good **$4,500**   Fine **$9,000**

Northwest Mounted Police Carbines, form especially prized variations of the 1876 Carbine. Though appearing in various serial ranges from as low as about 8000, the two major types are in the serial range of about 23801 - 24100 and the range 43900 - 44400. Mounted Police '76 Carbines bear an NWMP stamp on the buttstock, and are in 45-75 caliber; barrel lengths of the conventional 22":

5K-062   Values—Good **$3,250**   Fine **$8,750**

1 of 1000 and 1 of 100 Rifles, are of even greater rarity in the '76 than in the '73 Model. Only 8 "1 of 100s" and 54 "1 of 1000s" were made in the 1876 series, all fortunately recorded in the Winchester shipping records. The identifying marking appears on top of the breech end of the barrel. Again, caution is recommended for purchasing one of these ultra-rarities, due to the possibility of spurious markings. As with the Model 1873, the "1 of 100" is the scarcer rifle, but values in the collectors marketplace are about the same for these two great prizes:

1 of 100:
5K-063   Values—Good **$50,000**   Fine **$95,000**
           Exc. **$250,000**

1 of 1000:
5K-064   Values—Good **$50,000**   Fine **$90,000**
           Exc. **$225,000**

Winchester Model 1886 Rifle

Model 1886 Rifle. Manufactured c. 1886-1935; total produced 159,994. (Those under No. 119193 (approx.) made prior to December 31, 1898).

Made in a variety of calibers from as small as 33 W.C.F. to as large as 50-110 Express; total of about 10 chamberings; 45-70 and 45-90 are worth 25 percent premium; caliber 50 is worth 100 percent premium. Tubular magazine beneath the barrel. The frame distinctively different from previous lever action Winchesters, and featured vertical locking bolts, visible when viewing the gun from top or bottom.

Prior to 1900 and serial 120,000 (approx.) the M.1886 was standard with case hardened frame, hammer, forend cap and buttplates. Hence, such information is not included in factory letters. Following that date/serial all major parts were blued and case hardening had to be custom ordered and was so mentioned in factory ledgers. Takedown models almost always blued and not so mentioned. Straight grain, oil stained walnut stock standard. Although various grades of wood were extra, records merely mention "fancy"; pistol grip stocks usually fitted with better grades.

Serial numbering was in an individual series from 1 on up; marked on the lower tang. MODEL 1886 on the upper tang of most of the production; variations exist primarily in the late production due to adding of Winchester name and trademark data. Barrel marking of Winchester name and address, and, in late series arms, 1884 and 1885 patent dates were also used. Calibers marked on breech of the barrels.

The Model 1886, dramatically different from predecessor lever actions, was the first repeating rifle of John M. and Matthew S. Browning design to be adopted by Winchester. Improvements on their creation were made by Winchester's own William Mason, and the result was a vast improvement

5K-065
1886 Rifle

5K-066
1886 Light Weight Rifle

5K-069
1886 Carbine

5K-071
1886 Musket

over the Model 1876. Chamberings were in the big game calibers, and a featured part of the '86 was its shorter and quite streamlined frame. Immediately received with great enthusiasm by shooters (even several African hunters), the new model could count among its converts Theodore Roosevelt.

Major variations are:

Rifle; 26" round or octagon barrel, crescent style buttplate. Steel forend cap; the magazine tube attached to the barrel by a small band. Adjustable Buckhorn style rear sights. Straight buttstock:
5K-065   Values—Very Good **$1,500**   Exc. **$4,750**
Extra Light Weight Rifle; 22" round "rapid taper" barrel; half magazine, rubber shotgun buttplate; 45-70 and 33 calibers only:

33 caliber:
5K-066   Values—Very Good **$1,200**   Exc. **$3,750**

45-70 caliber:
5K-067   Values-Very Good **$3,000**   Exc. **$6,000**

Takedown Model Rifles: which come apart at forward end of the breech:
5K-068   Values—Add 10 percent to 15 percent premium depending on model and overall condition.
Carbine; 22" round barrel; saddle ring on left side of the frame. Adjustable carbine style rear sights. Carbine style buttplate. Calibers 45-70 and 50 Express worth premium:
5K-069   Values—Good **$3,000**   Fine **$7,500**
Full Stock Carbine; as above but with forearm extending nearly to the muzzle (as on the Model 1876 Carbine); one barrel band:
5K-070   Values—Good **$4,000**   Fine **$11,500**
Musket; 30" round barrel, 26" forend (the tip of the Model 1876 Musket style), one barrel band. Military windgauge rear sights. Production quite limited, only about 350 produced; the '86 Musket is the greatest rarity of all Winchester lever action muskets:
5K-071   Values—Good **$5,000**   Fine **$17,500**

Winchester Model 71 Rifle

Model 71 Rifle. (Not illus.; about identical in contours to the Model 1886.) Manufactured 1935-1957; total quantity of about 47,254.

348 Winchester caliber. Tubular 3/4-length magazine beneath the barrel. The frame used was an improved version of that employed for many years on the Model 1886. (Note: Early specimens [approx. first 15,000] have long 3-7/8" tangs and will bring a premium value. Standard tang is 2-7/8".)

Plain walnut pistol grip stocks; the forend of semi-beavertail type. Blued finish.

Serial numbered in an individual series, from 1 to 47254; marking was on the bottom curve of the forward end of the frame. Two basic types of barrel markings were used, both identifying the model, and giving caliber, company name and address, and etc. Winchester developed the Model 71 as a

continuation of the Model 1886, with improvements to handle the 348 cartridge. Though a relatively modern rifle, the 71 has proven a quite popular item with collectors.

Standard model; plain walnut stocks, without pistol grip cap, or sling, or sling swivels. 24" barrel length:
5K-072   Values—Very Good **$600**   Exc. **$1,000**
Deluxe Model; checkered pistol grip stock and quick detachable sling swivels:
5K-072.5   Values—Very Good **$750**   Exc. **$1,250**
As above, but in 20" barrels:
5K-073   Values—Very Good **$850**   Exc. **$1,750**
Deluxe Model; checkered pistol grip stock; detachable swivels; 20" barrel:
5K-073.5   Values—Very Good **$950**   Exc. **$1,850**

Winchester Model 1892 Rifle

Model 1892 Rifle. Made c. 1892-1941; total production approximately 1,004,067. (Those under No. 165,432 (approx.) made prior to December 31,1898).

32-20, 38-40, and 44-40 were the major calibers; 25-20 added

in 1895; quite scarce in 218 Bee. Tubular magazine beneath the barrel. The frame a smaller version of the Model 1886.

Oil stained or (less common) varnished walnut stocks. Blued finish, with casehardening a special order detail.

5K-074
Rifle

5K-076
Carbine

5K-078
Musket

Serial numbering in an individual series from 1 on up; marked on the bottom curve of the forward end of the frame. MODEL 1892, Winchester, and trademark stamps appear on the upper tang, in four basic marking variants. Barrel marking of Winchester name and address, and, in late series arms, 1884 patent date, was also used. Calibers marked on breech of the barrel.

The 1892 was designed as a modern successor to the Model 1873, with the same chambering of 32, 38, and 44 W.C.F. as the major calibers—the latter chambering being one of the most desirable today. The rather sleek and short frame was a scaled down version of the Model 1886. The '92 was so well made, functional, and attractive that many specimens still do service today in the hands of hunters and shooters. Export sales of the '92 were substantial, and large quantities of arms were shipped to Australia, South America, and the Far East. But the major market was North America. Due to the high production total, and the lengthy manufacturing run of over 50 years, a wide range of variants will be observed in virtually every detail, from butt to muzzle. In "excellent" or "mint" condition caliber 38-40 and 44-40 will bring premiums of 50 percent more. A few various European copies were made of the '92. Most often seen

is a near identical, Spanish made c. 1920, carbine marked EL TIGRE. Value as a "curiosity" substantially less.

The major variations:

Rifle; 24" round or octagon barrel (worth premium), crescent style buttplate. Steel forend cap; the magazine tube attached to the barrel by a small band. Adjustable buckhorn type rear sights. Straight buttstock:
5K-074   Values—Very Good **$675**   Exc. **$1,750**

Takedown Model Rifle; comes apart at forward end of breech:
5K-075   Values—Add 15 percent to 20 percent

Carbine; 20" round barrel; saddle ring on left side of the frame. Two barrel bands. Rear sights of adjustable carbine type:
5K-076   Values—Very Good **$875**   Exc. **$3,000**

Trapper's Model Carbine; same as above but with barrel lengths of 14", 15", 16", or 18":
5K-077   Values—Very Good **$2,000**   Exc. **$6,500**
(Note: Federal firearms laws should be checked to ascertain the legality of short lengths under 16".)

Musket; 30" round barrel, 27" magazine, portion of which protrudes from the forend. Three barrel bands. Rear sights of military type. Modified shotgun style buttplate. Quite rare:
5K-078   Values—Very Good **$4,500**   Exc. **$10,000**

Winchester Model 53 Rifle

Model 53 Rifle. (Not illus.) Manufactured 1924-1934 (with a few assembled as late as 1941); total made about 15,110. Substantially identical to the Model 1892.

25-20, 32-20 cals; 44-40 worth 25 percent premium. 22-inch round barrel standard. Tubular half-magazine beneath the barrel. The frame was that of the Model 1892. Plain walnut stocks. Blued finish.

Marked on bottom curve of forward end of frame. MODEL 53 and accompanying markings stamped on left side of the barrel; company name and address stamp on right side. Trademark stamping on the upper tang.

The Model 53 was produced as the final form of the Model 1892 series; except for the 1892 carbine, which continued through 1941.

Rather than keep the 1892 rifle with variations as a part of the product line, Winchester developed the 53, in which was combined some of its predecessor's most preferred details. These were the 22" round barrel, the walnut stock of pistol grip or straight type (buttplate of shotgun type checkered steel, or of rifle style in a crescent shape), and the 25-20, 32-20, and 44-40 calibers. Still further adaptations resulted in a new model, the 65, brought out in 1933.

Standard model; plain stocks:
5K-079   Values—Very Good **$800**   Exc. **$1,600**

Takedown model; comes apart at forward end of the breech. Apparently more takedowns were made than solid frames:
5K-080   Values—Very Good **$850**   Exc. **$1,750**

Winchester Model 65 Rifle

Model 65 Rifle. (Not illus.) Made 1933-1947; total quantity of about 5,704. Substantially identical to the Model 1892.

25-20, 32-20 cals; 218 Bee worth 15 percent premium. Tubular

half-magazine beneath the barrel. The frame was that of the Model 1892. Plain walnut stocks. Blued finish.

Serial numbered within the range of the Model 1892; the

marking on bottom curve of forward end of the frame. MODEL 65 and accompanying markings on left side of the barrel; company name and address stamp on the right side. Trademark and caliber stamp also on the barrel.

Designed from the Model 53 rifle, the Model 65 employed the 1892 action, but differed from its predecessor primarily in having a greater magazine capacity, a pistol grip stock only, and a sight cover mounted on the forged ramp type front base. Among standard features were the 22" round barrel, shotgun style butt (with checkered steel buttplate), and the solid frame (no takedown variations were produced):

5K-081   Values—Very Good **$950**   Exc. **$3,000**

Winchester Model 1894 Rifle

Model 1894 Rifle. Manufactured c. 1894 to present. The total production to 1975 in excess of 3,000,000. (Those under No. 147684 (approx.) made prior to December 31, 1898).

25-35, 30-30, 32-40, 32 Winchester Special, and 38-55 calibers; the largest proportion in the 30-30 caliber. Tubular magazine beneath the barrel. The frame similar in appearance to the Model 1892, but quickly differentiated by the straight bottom contour of frame (lacks the vertical locking bolt device as on the '92).

Oil stained or (much less common) varnished walnut stocks. Blued finish, with casehardened levers, hammers, and buttplates for varying periods into the 20th century.

Serial numbering in an individual series from 1 on up; marked on bottom of the frame at forward end. MODEL 1894, Winchester, and trademark stamps appear on the upper tang, in four basic marking variants. Barrel marking of Winchester name and address, and after 100,000 serial range, 1894 patent date added. Above range of about 100,000 a longer marking adopted, without patent date. And still other variants of barrel stamps appeared, later in production. Calibers marked on the barrel near breech end.

The Model 1894 was Winchester's first lever action made for smokeless powder cartridges, and is decidedly the most successful centerfire rifle the company ever produced. The design was by John M. Browning, and from the beginning the '94 was eminently practical—a specimen of ultimate perfection in a lever action rifle. It is of no surprise that the model has experienced not a single major change over its long production run. The Model 94 continues today as the major model of centerfire rifle in the Winchester line.

Variations as follows:

Rifle; 26" octagon barrel; early production with casehardened hammer, lever, trigger, and buttplate; the balance blued. Crescent style buttplate. Steel forend cap; the magazine tube attached to the barrel by a small band. Adjustable buckhorn style rear sights:

5K-082   Values—Very Good **$650**   Exc. **$2,000**
Same as above, but with full blued finish; the earlier production arms generally more desirable than specimens with high serial numbers:
5K-083   Values—Very Good **$575**   Exc. **$1,400**
Same as above, but with round barrel:
5K-084   Values—Very Good **$475**   Exc. **$1,250**
Extra Light Weight Rifle; 22" to 26" round, rapid taper barrel, straight buttstock with shotgun style buttplate:
5K-085   Values—Very Good **$900**   Exc. **$3,250**
Takedown Model Rifle; comes apart at forward end of the breech:
5K-086   Values—Add 15 percent to 20 percent depending on caliber and condition.
Carbine; 20" round barrel; saddle ring on left side of the frame (standard through 1925). Rear sights of adjustable carbine type. Modified shotgun style buttplate (Calibers 30-30 and 32 Special tend to bring 15 to 20 percent less than values shown):
5K-087   Values—Very Good **$700**   Exc. **$2,250**
Same as above, but without saddle ring (post-1925):
5K-088   Values—Very Good **$425**   Exc. **$900**
Trapper's Model Carbine; with or without saddle ring; barrel lengths of 14", 16", or 18"(scarce, worth premium):
5K-089   Values—Very Good **$2,000**   Exc. **$6,000**
(Note: Federal firearms laws should be checked to ascertain the legality of short lengths.)

5K-082
Rifle

5K-087
Carbine

Winchester Model 55 Rifle

Model 55 Rifle. (Not illus.) Manufactured 1924-1932; approximately 20,580 produced. Substantially the same as the Model 1894.

25-35, 30-30, and 32 Winchester Special calibers. Tubular half-magazine beneath the barrel. Frame used was that of the Model 1894.

Plain walnut stocks. Blued finish.

Serial numbering was at first in an individual range (1 to about 2868); and subsequently was made concurrent with that of the Model 1894; the marking on bottom curve of forward end of the frame. Barrel marking type was as used on the late production of the Model 1894—a long legend, without patent dates. Caliber designation was on the breech end of the barrel. The MODEL 55 identification also appeared on the barrel.

Winchester management decided to discontinue a variety of Model 1894 rifles and to replace these with the Model 55 (and at the same time continue with the 1894 carbine). Standard on the new model was the 24" round barrel, altered sights, and shotgun type buttstock terminating in a buttplate of checkered steel.

Standard model; solid frame, plain stocks:
5K-090   Values—Very Good **$600**   Exc. **$1,250**
As above, but of takedown type; coming apart at the forward end of the breech (more often seen):
5K-091   Values—Very Good **$650**   Exc. **$1,400**

Winchester Model 64 Rifle

Model 64 Rifle. (Not illus.) Made 1933-1957; in a total quantity of about 66,783. Substantially the same as the Model 1894.

25-35, 30-30, 219 Zipper, and 32 Winchester Special calibers (25-35 and 219 dropped in 1941). Tubular 3/4-length magazine beneath the barrel. The frame used was basically that of the Model 1894.

Plain walnut pistol grip stocks. Blued finish.

Serial numbering was concurrent with the Model 1894; marked on the bottom curve of the forward end of frame. Caliber designation, MODEL 64, and Winchester name and address markings were on the barrel.

The 64 joined the Winchester product line as the successor to the Model 55. Design changes over its predecessor were in an increased magazine capacity, adoption of the pistol grip type stock, sight cover mounted on the forged ramp type front base, and use of only the solid type frame (no takedown variations). Lengths of barrels were from 20" to 26", the latter only in the 219 Zipper caliber. Buttstocks with checkered steel buttplates, of shotgun style.

Standard model; plain walnut stocks; chambered for 30-30 or 32 Special caliber:
5K-092   Values—Very Good **$350**   Exc. **$775**

Deluxe Model: checkered pistol grip stock and detachable sling swivels:
5K-092.5   Values—Very Good **$500**   Exc. **$1,000**
As above, but in 25-35 or 219 Zipper:
5K-093   Values—Very Good **$850**   Exc. **$2,500**

Deluxe Model in 25-35 or 219 Zipper:
5K-093.5   Values—Very Good **$950**   Exc. **$3,000**

Winchester Model 1895 Rifle

Model 1895 Rifle. Manufactured c. 1896-1931; total of approximately 425,881. (Those under No. 19871 (approx.) made prior to December 31, 1898).

30-03, 30-06, 30-40 Krag (later with "30 ARMY" markings), 303 British, 35 Winchester, 38-72, 40-72, 405 Winchester, and 7.62mm Russian calibers. Box magazine located beneath the frame.

Oil stained or (less common) varnished walnut stocks. Blued finish; casehardening a special order detail.

Serial numbered in an individual series from 1 on up; marked on the lower tang. Four basic types of upper tang stamping; the first with WINCHESTER and MODEL 1895; later types with patent data added and other minor changes. On left side of the frame (except on the Flatside variation), the Winchester name, address, and patent dates with variation mainly in the adding of dates. Calibers were marked on the barrel at breech, or on top of the breech area of the frame.

Another brainchild of the uniquely talented John M. Browning, the Model 1895 was the first box-magazine lever action rifle to be successfully produced. Chambering was for the new high powered smokeless ammunition, capable of handling any big game throughout the world. Due to the box magazine beneath the frame, the Model 1895 has a distinctive profile, unlike any other Winchester rifle. Thanks mainly to a substantial order from the Russian government, the major proportion of '95 production was in the musket configuration.

Major variations are:
Rifle; The Flatside Model, the frame sides without escalloping or fluting; standard barrel lengths vary according to caliber, and are usually round; crescent style buttplate. Solid loop lever construction. Two-piece magazine; sporting style rear sights. Serial range 1 to about 5000:
5K-094   Values—Very Good **$1,100**   Exc. **$4,000**

Standard production model; the frame sides escalloped; two-piece lever; one-piece magazine; serial range about 5000 to end of production; this was the configuration for most of the rifle production:
5K-095   Values—Very Good **$750**   Exc. **$1,800**

Takedown Model Rifle; comes apart at forward end of breech:
5K-096   Values—Add 10 percent to 15 percent

Carbine; 22" round barrel; standard calibers of 30-03, 30-06, 30-40 and 303 British. Escalloped sides to the frame. With or without

5K-094
1895 Flatside Rifle

5K-095
1895 Standard Rifle

5K-097
1895 Carbine

5K-103
1895 NRA Musket

5K-104
1895 Russian Model Musket

saddle ring. One barrel band; forend includes handguard over the barrel. Rear sights of adjustable carbine type. Modified shotgun style buttplate; serial range above about 5000:
5K-097   Values—Very Good **$800**   Exc. **$3,000**
Same as above, caliber 30-40 only, but with U.S. government markings:
5K-098   Values—Very Good **$1,750**   Exc. **$5,000**

Musket, Flatside Model; the frame sides without escalloping or fluting; 30-40 Krag caliber; 28" round barrel; two barrel bands. Rear sights of military type. Modified shotgun style buttplate. No handguard over barrel. Serial range below about 5000:
5K-099   Values—Very Good **$6,000**   Exc. **$17,500**

Standard Model Musket; As above, but the frame sides escalloped and has handguard over barrel. 30-40 Krag, 30-03, or 30-06 calibers standard:
5K-100   Values—Very Good **$1,100**   Exc. **$3,250**

U.S. Army Model; 28" barrel; 30-40 cal.; fullstock with handguard. Large US top of receiver with various inspector markings. Ordnance Dept. purchased 10,000 1898-99 to fill war needs. All rejected for reasons unknown; later accepted too late for war use. 100 field tested late 1899 in Philippines. 9900 in storage sold 1906 on commercial market. Believed most to Cuba and Central America. Specimens very scarce; most show hard use:
5K-101   Values—Very Good **$1,600**   Exc. **$4,500**

U.S. Army National Rifle Association Musket; The first type was basically the standard model Musket, but with 30" round barrel, and Model 1901 Krag-Jorgensen rear sight. The NRA Model had been accepted officially for competitive use by the National Rifle Association:
5K-102   Values—Very Good **$1,250**   Exc. **$4,000**

NRA Musket Models 1903 and 1906; (variations of the above) differed in having 24" barrel and a special buttplate. These were also NRA approved for military type competition, and were in 30-03 and 30-06 calibers respectively:
5K-103   Values—Very Good **$1,000**   Exc. **$4,000**

Russian Model Musket; Chambered for 7.62mm Russian cartridge, a total of 293,816 were made, on order from the Imperial Russian Government. Production was in 1915-16; various Russian Ordnance stamps are present. Clip guides were present on the receiver top:
5K-104   Values—Very Good **$900**   Exc. **$3,000**

NOTE: Values shown for various single shot rifles include their specified sights. If sights are lacking values are lessened 20 to 30 percent.

Winchester Single Shot Rifle

Single Shot (High Wall and Low Wall) Rifle. (a.k.a. Model 1885) Manufactured c. 1885-1920; the total production approximately 139,725. (Those under No. 84700 (approx.) made prior to December 31, 1898).

Calibers provide the greatest variety in the entire history of Winchester firearms. From 22 rimfire through a broad range up to 50 caliber centerfire. (Very scarce.) The more popular and desirable calibers, especially those for which ammunition is available, often bring higher values.

Oil stained or varnished (uncommon) walnut stocks. Blued finish on metal parts, with casehardened frame and buttplate to about 90,000 serial range; thereafter, full blued finish standard.

Serial numbered from 1 on up; marked on the lower tang.

High Wall and Low Wall arms numbered together in the same range. Barrel marking of Winchester name and address; on later production patent date of 1879 present, and still later, 1907 added. The upper tangs not marked until above the 100,000 serial range; then appeared WINCHESTER and patent and trademark data. On breech end of the barrel, the caliber designation was marked.

Winchester's first single shot rifle, the model was a John M. Browning design, first as a High Wall. The company's purchase of manufacturing rights from the Browning brothers (in 1883) launched the historic and lengthy association of Browning and Winchester. The Single Shot Rifle series offers a tremendous variety of features, in calibers, barrel lengths and weights,

5K-105
1895 Carbine

finishes, stocks, buttplates, trigger guards, sights, and in relatively minor areas of contours, knurlings, and so forth. The result is a field of vast opportunities for the collector, and not a few enthusiasts have as their speciality *only* the Single Shot Winchester rifles. Deluxe features, such as double set triggers, half-octagon-half-round barrels, pistol grip stocks, checkering, and etc., all add to values. Certain details are rare, and some are more desirable than others.

A basic differentiation of types is by frames—High Wall and Low Wall:

High Wall: The frame features high sides which conceal the breechblock and all of the hammer but the spur; production began with this model.

Low Wall: Features low sides, with the breechblock and hammer spur quite visible; first appeared at about the 5000 serial range.

Of still further note to collectors are the "thickside" and "thinside" frame contours—made in both the High Wall and Low Wall actions:

Thickside: Frames with flat sides. They do not flare out at the frame ends to meet the stocks. Thickside frames are more common in the Low Wall rifles, and are scarce in the High Wall.

Thinside: Frames with their sides milled out to a shallow depth, so the ends flare out to juncture with the stocks. Thinside frames are the standard in the High Wall rifles, and are scarce in the Low Wall.

Major production variations in types of Single Shots are as follows:

High Wall Standard Model Rifle; in a variety of calibers, the barrel lengths varying according to caliber but usually between 24" and 30". Octagon barrels far outnumber the round. Barrels were offered in weights graded from 1 (light) up to 5 (heavy). Crescent style buttplate. Stocks usually straight; the forends taper and have a knurl finial with ebony wedge inlay. Variety of sights, but usually of adjustable sporting type. Rimfire models tend to bring about 15 percent less.

Standard Model; with octagon barrel of light or medium weight in center fire calibers:
5K-105   Values—Very Good **$1,100**   Exc. **$2,750**

As above, in rimfire calibers:
5K-105.2 Values—Very Good **$900**   Exc. **$2,000**

Same as above; but with heavyweight octagon barrel:
5K-106   Values—Very Good **$1,200** Exc. **$4,000**

Standard Model; but with round barrel of light or medium weight:
5K-107   Values—Very Good **$950**   Exc. **$3,000**

Same as above; but with heavyweight round barrel:
5K-108   Values—Very Good **$1,200** Exc. **$4,000**

High Wall Musket, most often observed in 22 rimfire caliber (usually of 28" length), but calibers vary and lengths vary according to caliber; the larger calibers usually fetching stronger prices. Full length forends terminating within about 3" of muzzle. Military windgauge sights standard, but sight types show wide variance. Modified shotgun style buttplate. U.S. and Ordnance flaming bomb markings will be observed on muskets purchased by the government:

First Model; High Wall frame, the forend secured by two barrel bands (with band springs), no finger grooves on the forend:

22 caliber with standard (thinside) frame: Although never officially recognized by the factory, it became known as the WINDER MUSKET (First Model) after Lt. Col. C.R. Winder, Ohio National Guard, who was most associated with its development. Take-down variant known; very rare:
5K-109 Values—Very Good **$850**   Exc. **$2,250**

45-70 caliber with thickside frame:
5K-110 Values—Very Good **$1,750** Exc. **$3,500**

Second Model; (a.k.a Second Model Winder); Winder High Wall frame, one barrel band, finger grooves in forend, and the forend slim forward of the barrel band; made in 22 r.f. only: Takedown variation scarce; worth premium:
5K-111 Values—Very Good **$775**   Exc. **$1,400**

High Wall Schuetzen Rifle, first appeared on the market c. 1900 with features on a reasonably standard basis; but for many years previous such details as Schuetzen buttplates, elaborate finger levers, and triggers had been available special ordered. The newly-devised standard Schuetzen Model offered the following:

5K-110
1st Model High Wall Musket with Thickside Frame

5K-111
2nd Model High Wall Musket with Thickside (standard) Frame

5K-112
High Wall Schuetzen Rifle

5K-115
Low Wall Rifle

5K-117
Low Wall Carbine

5K-118
Low Wall Winder Musket

Frames of High Wall type; 30" octagonal No. 3 barrels, usually chambered for 32-40 or 38-55 caliber; double set trigger; pistol grip buttstock of deluxe wood, checkered, and with cheekpiece; Schuetzen spurs on the buttplate; palm rest may be present; target sights. Takedown type not unusual. These true Schuetzen Rifles are generally found above the 80000 serial range:
5K-112   Values—Very Good **$3,250**   Exc. **$7,000**

High Wall Schuetzen style rifles made below serial range about 80000, and not the full Schuetzen of later production:
5K-113   Values—Very Good **$2,500**   Exc. **$6,500**

Shotgun, High Wall frame only; 20 gauge, 26" round barrel. Straight grip buttstock, rubber buttplate of shotgun type. Manufactured mainly in the serial range 110000 - 115000, but also appeared before and after:
5K-114   Values—Very Good **$1,500**   Exc. **$4,000**

Low Wall Standard Model Rifle; in a variety of calibers, the barrel lengths varying according to caliber but usually between 24" and 30". Octagon barrels far outnumber the round. Barrels were offered in weights graded from 1 (light) up to 5 (heavy). Crescent style buttplate. Stocks usually straight; the forends taper and have a knurl finial with ebony wedge inlay. Variety of sights, but usually of adjustable sporting type.

Standard Model, with octagon barrel of light or medium

weight in rimfire calibers:
5K-115   Values—Very Good **$475**   Exc. **$1,000**

Same in centerfire calibers:
5K-115.2 Values—Very Good **$550**   Exc. **$1,500**

Standard Model, but with round barrel of light or medium weight:
5K-116   Same as Above

Low Wall Carbine, in standard calibers of 32-20, 38-40, and 44-40; 15", 16", 18"; and 20" round barrels. Saddle ring usually present, on left side of frame. Carbine style rear sights. Modified shotgun style buttplates. Centerfire or rimfire calibers same values:
5K-117   Values—Very Good **$3,850**   Exc. **$8,500**

Third Model, Low Wall, Musket; (a.k.a. Third Model Winder) peep sight, forend and barrel bands like the Second Model High Wall Musket (*q.v.*):
5K-118   Values—Very Good **$550**   Exc. **$1,000**

Low Wall Schuetzen style rifle; usually made below serial range about 80000, and not the true Schuetzen of high wall production. Feature such details as Swiss type buttplates, elaborate finger levers, special triggers, checkered pistol grip or straight select grain stock, cheekpiece, etc. Centerfire or rimfire calibers same values:
5K-119   Values—Very Good **$3,000**   Exc. **$7,000**

Winchester-Hotchkiss Bolt Action Rifle

Hotchkiss Bolt Action Repeating Rifle, a.k.a. Model 1879, Model 1883. Made c. 1879-99; total produced approximately 84,555.

45-70 government caliber. Tubular magazine of six-shot capacity within the buttstock.

Oil stained walnut stocks; straight grip standard. Blued

finish, with casehardened receivers and buttplates.

Serial numbered in an individual series from 1 on up; marked on the left side of the receiver. Also on left side of receiver are Winchester name and address markings, and various patent dates from 1860 to 1878.

Benjamin B. Hotchkiss, designer of the rifle bearing his name,

5K-120
1st Model Sporting Rifle

5K-120
Close-up Hotchkiss 1st Model

5K-122
1st Model Musket

sold the rights to this bolt action weapon to Winchester, in 1877. After several years of development, the Hotchkiss appeared on the market in 1883, for military and sporting use. This was Winchester's first bolt action rifle, and the first with a magazine located in the butt. Martially marked specimens command a premium. Classification is in three basic model types:

First Model (a.k.a. Model 1879); serial range from 1 to about 6419. Distinguishing features are the one-piece stock with safety and magazine cutoff device in button style unit on right side (located above trigger guard area).

Sporting Rifle, 26" round or octagon barrel, Winchester name and address marking usually on the barrel. Crescent style buttplate; horn or ebony forend tip. Adjustable leaf rear sights:

5K-120 Values—Good **$450** Fine **$950**

Carbine; 24" round barrel, saddle ring on left side of stock, one barrel band, carbine style buttplate, military windgauge rear sight:

5K-121 Values—Good **$575** Fine **$1,250**

Musket; 32" round barrel, cleaning rod under barrel, for angular or saber bayonet attachment, two barrel bands, steel forend tip, carbine style buttplate, military windgauge rear sight:

5K-122 Values—Very Good **$600** Fine **$1,400**

Second Model; serial range about 6420 to 22521. Identification by the safety on the left side of the receiver, at top; and the magazine cutoff on the top right side, to rear of the bolt handle.

Sporting Rifle, with basic features same as First Model Rifle, other than noted above:

5K-123 Values—Good **$450** Fine **$950**

Carbine; basically same as First Model arms, but having 22-1/2" round barrel; and a distinctive nickeled iron forend tip with hinged door covering compartment inside forend for cleaning rod:

5K-124 Values—Good **$650** Fine **$1,750**

5K-124
2nd Model Carbine

5K-124
Close-up Hotchkiss 2nd Model

5K-126
3rd Model Sporting Rifle

5K-128
3rd Model Musket

Musket; 28" round barrel; various other features continued from First Model Musket:

5K-125   Values—Good **$650**   Fine **$1,750**

Third Model (a.k.a. Model 1883); serial range about 22522 to 84555. Easily identified by the two-piece stock, separated by the exposed receiver.

Sporting Rifle; with basic features as on earlier models, other than noted above:

5K-126   Values—Good **$500**   Fine **$1,400**

Carbine; 20" barrel, saddle ring bar and ring on left frame, short forend fastened by single barrel band. *Very rare:*

5K-127   Values—Good **$1,800**   Fine **$4,500**

Musket; basically same as Second Model:

5K-128   Values—Good **$650**   Fine **$1,750**

Martially Marked Models. Reliable evidence and U.S. Ordnance reports clearly seem to indicate that all martially marked Model 1879 First and Second Type Hotchkiss carbines and muskets were made by the U.S. Springfield Armory. (One counter-theory has it that just the Second Style carbines were assembled at Winchester from parts supplied by Springfield.) All the actions (bearing the usual Winchester markings) and buttplates were supplied by Winchester with the Springfield Armory adding their own barrels, stocks, sights and mountings. Considerable dimensional differences are noted when these martial specimens are compared to Winchester-made non-martial counterparts. The guns are considered as Springfield Armory weapons.

All barrels have the Springfield proofmarks of VP, eaglehead motif and U.S. at breech, while the two Navy Models have additional markings of an anchor motif. The rifles are caliber 45-70 while carbines are caliber 45-55.

Inspector markings on the First Type Army muskets and carbines are ESA/1878 on the left side of the stock and on the Navy musket SWP/1879.

Inspector markings on stocks of the Second Type Army carbines and Navy muskets are both SWP over the dates 1880 or 1881, and are found on the left side of the butt near buttplate.

The Third Model Hotchkiss (1883) was entirely of Winchester manufacture. Quantity sold to the U.S. unknown.

First Model Army Rifle; 32-1/4" barrel. Quantity made 513:

5K-129   Values—Good **$1,500**   Fine **$4,000**

First Model Army Carbine; 24" barrel. Quantity made 501. Although fewer made than the rifle above, more have survived:

5K-130   Values— Good **$1,000**   Fine **$2,750**

First Model Navy Rifle; 28-3/4" barrel. Quantity made 1474:

5K-131   Values—Good **$750**   Fine **$2,000**

Second Model Army Carbine; (This style was not made in rifle form.) 24" barrel. Quantity made 400:

5K-132   Values—Good **$1,000**   Fine **$3,000**

Second Model Navy Rifle; 28-3/4" barrel. Quantity made 999:

5K-133   Values—Good **$850**   Fine **$1,600**

Third Model Army Rifle; Winchester manufacture:

5K-134   Values—Good **$700**   Fine **$1,800**

Winchester-Lee Straight Pull Rifle

Lee Straight Pull Rifle. Manufactured c. 1895-c. 1902; total production of about 20,000. (Those under No. 13390 (approx.) made prior to December 31, 1898).

6mm Lee (236) caliber. Round barrel of 24" (Sporting) and 28" (Musket) lengths. Clip fed box-magazine, located beneath the receiver. Five shots.

Oil stained walnut stock of semi-pistol grip type. Metal parts blued.

Serial numbered in individual series from 1 on up; marked on top of the forward end of the receiver. Receiver markings noted below under variations.

James Paris Lee was the designer of this early bolt action rifle, and the rights to manufacturing rifles were obtained by Winchester, mainly to fill orders from the U.S. Navy. The model designation used by the Navy was 1895—not to be confused with the Winchester Model 1895 Lever Action arms. Specimens of the military musket were also sold commercially, following delivery of U.S. Navy contract orders. Mechanically the Lees are intriguing with their bolt which pulls slightly up and then rearward, without the initial upward arc turn found on conventional bolt actions.

Sporting Rifle, marked on the receiver with Winchester name and address, and patent dates 1893, '94, '95, and '98. 236 U.S.N., caliber marking on the barrel. 24" rapid taper barrel. Pistol grip stock extending to about half length on the barrel, and featuring finger grooves on the forend. Shotgun style buttplate of steel. Adjustable sporting style rear sights. The total made about 1,700:

5K-135   Values—Very Good **$725**   Exc. **$1,450**

U.S. Navy Musket, Model 1895, the receiver marked with Winchester name and address, and patent dates 1893, '94, and '95. 28" barrel. Semi-pistol grip stock of nearly full length with two barrel bands, and cover over the breech end of barrel; government style sights. Carbine style buttplate of steel. Fitted with knife type bayonet:

5K-136

U.S. Navy and Marine Corps issue. Two contracts: 1898 for 10,000. Marked on top of receiver **U.S.N./anchor/serial/ N.C.T.** (inspector). Second contract 1899 for 5,000. Markings same except for inspector initials **W.B.W.** 1,800 of the first contract were issued to U.S.M.C. of which 623 to the 1st Marine Battalion, the first U.S. forces landed in Cuba and first to come under fire. The primary rifle of both services 1895-1900 until gradually replaced by the Springfield-Krag. The Lee saw much action with the Navy and Marines in the Spanish-American War and with various landing parties in lesser incidents immediately following, in the Philippines and the Boxer Rebellion. A large group known aboard the USS MAINE, 1898, when sunk in Havana. 34 recovered 1900 in surprisingly good condition. Serial numbers with supporting documents shown in many early Bannerman, N.Y. catalogs and "Winchester Book" (Madis.) Worth substantial premium:

5K-136   Values—Very Good **$950**   Exc. **$2,000**

Civilian sales, without anchor and N.C.T. markings; with or without bayonet fixtures; approximately 3,300 total:

5K-137   Values—Very Good **$800**   Exc. **$1,750**

Winchester Model 1890 Slide Action Rifle

5K-138

Model 1890 Slide Action Rifle. Made c. 1890-32; total production approximately 849,000. (Those under No. 64,521 (approx.) made Prior to Dec 31, 1898).

22 Short, Long, and Long Rifle (not interchangeable) and 22 W.R.F. 24" octagonal barrel. Magazine tube beneath the barrel.

Oil stained walnut stock; straight buttstock. Metal parts blued, except for casehardened frames until serial 97050.

Serial numbered in individual series from 1 on up; marked on the lower tang, and after No. 232328 also found on receiver extension secured to the barrel. Winchester name and address, patent dates, model and caliber markings standard on the barrel.

A joint creation of John M. and Matthew S. Browning, the Model 1890 was the first slide action Winchester. It replaced the rather slow-selling Model 1873 22, which had been the firm's only repeating rifle in 22 caliber. The Model 1890 proved a popular shooting gallery rifle, and became one of the best selling rimfire repeaters in Winchester history. Ironically a competitor arm to this model was Colt's Lightning slide action 22, brought out in 1887. The Brownings' design was of overall superiority, and a comparison of production figures reflects that fact dramatically.

Basic variants are:

First Model Rifle, in the serial range from 1 to about 15521; made in solid casehardened frame type only:

5K-138   Values—Very Good **$1,500**   Exc. **$3,000**

Second Model Rifle, in takedown type; the serial range from about 15522 to 326615; concealed locking lugs as in the First Model; add 50 percent premium if frame is casehardened:

5K-139   Values—Very Good **$400**   Exc. **$1,250**

Third Model Rifle, also in takedown, have locking lugs visible in notch at top of each side of the frame; serial range about 326616 to end of production:

5K-140   Values—Very Good **$350**   Exc. **$875**

Winchester Double Barrel Shotguns

Double Barrel Shotguns, Imported, Marked and Sold by Winchester.

From 1879 to 1884, Winchester bought double barrel, outside hammer, breechloading shotguns of varying grades from selected English gunmakers. The arms were for sale through the store maintained by Winchester in New York City.

At first the guns were not Winchester marked, but beginning c. 1879 the top ribs bore: Winchester Repeating Arms Co./New Haven, Connecticut U.S.A., along with the grade of gun. The locks bore the Winchester name and the gun grade. Advertised and marked were Match Gun and Class A, B, C and D. Stocks were of English walnut, checkered, and of generally good

5K-141

quality. The highest grade was the Match Gun; the lowest Grade D.

Total quantity of all types: About 10,000. Gauges: 10 and 12. Barrel lengths: 30" and 32". English makers represented: C.G. Bonehill, W.C. Scott and Sons, W.C. McEntree & Company, and Richard Rodman.

No definitive data yet compiled on these scarce doubles. The plainest grade "D" could possibly be scarcer than fancier grades. Values established by general scarcity and their degrees of quality.

In one of few known Winchester promotional brochures "Class D" offered with "best English *twist* barrels" while all other classes had "Laminated Steel Barrels" (with class "A" and the "Match Gun" having "*Fine* Laminated." Class "D" offered with under-lever while all others had top lever; all classes except "D" offered with rebounding hammers).

Class "A" (add approximately 25 percent premium for "Match Gun"). Their best grade with fanciest engraving and finest finish:

5K-141   Values—Very Good **$2,250**   Exc. **$7,000**

Class "B" "C" "D". Successively less embellishments and engraving with other differences as noted above:

5K-142   Values—Very Good **$1,500**   Exc. **$4,000**

Winchester Model 1887 Lever Action Shotgun

5K-143

Model 1887 Lever Action Shotgun. Manufactured c. 1887-1901; total production approximately 64,855 (Those under No. 63953 (approx.) made prior to December 31, 1898).

10 and 12 gauge. 30" and 32" barrels, with Riot Gun in 20" barrel. Magazine tube beneath the barrel. 5-shot capacity.

Oil stained or (less common) varnished walnut semi-pistol grip stocks. Blued finish, with casehardened frame.

Serial numbered in individual series from 1 on up; marked on bottom of the forward end of the frame; serials were later continued by the Model 1901 Lever Action Shotgun. Stylish WRA Co. intertwined monogram marked on left side of the frame. The lower tang bears Winchester name and address marking, with 1886 patent dates. 10 or 12 marked on breech end of the barrel after the 30000 serial range, to indicate gauge.

The rear sight a notch on top of the receiver; brass bead front sight. The buttplate of steel or hard rubber.

The Model 1887 was Winchester's first lever action shotgun, and was made for black powder loads. John M. Browning created this rather massive scattergun, and company executives hoped the lever action mechanism would catch the fancy of the millions of shooters already sold on Winchester lever operated rifles. However, the resemblance between rifle and shotgun was negligible; the large cartridge of the latter required a rather awkwardly oversized breech. The result was only a comparatively moderate success for the '87, soon to be confronted with stiff competition from such slide action shotguns as the Model 1893 and 1897 Winchesters. (Note: The company's only 10 gauge shotguns were in the Models 1887 and 1901.)

Although the 1887 was not the first repeating shotgun manufactured, it is claimed to have been the first successful one. Many of them were later cut down for use as protective weapons, express company and stagecoach guards and other various legitimate (and some not so legitimate) purposes. Unless there are valid supporting documents of a historic association and use (such as by a stagecoach driver, etc.) values considerably lessened.

Basic Variations are:

Standard Model Shotgun, 10 and 12 gauge, 30" and 32" barrels; 10 gauge standard in 32" length, and 12 gauge in 30":

5K-143   Values—Very Good **$800**   Exc. **$3,750**

Riot Gun, 10 and 12 gauge, with 20" barrel:

5K-144   Values—Very Good **$1,000**   Exc. **$4,250**

Winchester Model 1901 Lever Action Shotgun

Model 1901 Lever Action Shotgun. (Not illus.) Made c. 1901-20; total production of approximately 13,500. Substantially the same as the Model 1887.

10 gauge only. 32" barrel length standard; not made in a Riot Gun variation. Magazine tube beneath the barrel; 5-shot capacity.

Oil stained or (less common) varnished walnut semi-pistol grip stocks. Blued finish.

Serial numbering continued where the Model 1887 left off; running from 64856 on up; marked on bottom of the forward end of the frame. WRA Co. intertwined monogram on left side of frame. On top of the barrel the Winchester name and address marking, with 1886 and 1897 patent dates. MODEL 1901 and 10 on the barrel breech.

Rear sight a notch on top of the receiver; brass bead front sight. The buttplate of hard rubber; steel uncommon.

The Model 1901 was an improved version of the Model 1887, able to safely fire smokeless powder loads. Though much more difficult for the collector to locate than the '87, it is not unusual to find '01's still used in the field at this writing.

5K-145   Values—Very Good **$675**   Exc. **$2,000**

Winchester Model 1893 Slide Action Shotgun

Model 1893 Slide Action Shotgun. Made c. 1893-97; total production approximately 34,050.

12 gauge. 30" and (less common) 32" barrels. Magazine tube beneath the barrel. Five shots.

5K-146

Oil stained walnut stock, semi-pistol grip type; hard rubber buttplate. Metal parts blued.

Serial numbered in individual series from 1 on up; marked on the bottom of front end of frame. Numbering later continued by the successor arm, the Model 1897 Shotgun. Markings include Winchester name and address, patent dates, and model identification.

In this John M. Browning design Winchester produced its first slide action shotgun. Chambering was for black powder shells, and in 12 gauge only. The Model 1893 encountered stiff competition from a variety of double barrel guns then on the market, and it also experienced some mechanical problems. Production was limited, thus adding to the attraction of the type to collectors:

5K-146   Values—Very Good **$325**   Exc. **$1,200**

Winchester Model 1897 Slide Action Shotgun

5K-146
Model 1897 Trench Gun "U.S." marked

Model 1897 Slide Action Shotgun. (Not illus.) Produced c. 1897-1957; total quantity Of about 1,024,700. Very similar in contour to the Model 1893.

12 and 16 gauge. Barrel lengths vary according to gauge, but in 12 the standard length was 30", and in 16 the standard was 28". Magazine tube beneath the barrel. 5 shots. A variety of chokes available.

Oil stained walnut stock, straight or semi-pistol grip buttstock; buttplate usually of steel. Metal parts blued.

Serial numbering continued from where the Model 1893 left off; beginning with about 34151. The major marking was on the bottom of the front end of the frame. Markings include Winchester name and address, patent dates, model identification, and gauge.

Due to problems in the Model 1893 Shotgun with smokeless ammunition, the type was discontinued, and quickly replaced with the Model 1897. The new gun achieved instant popularity, and became the best selling slide action shotgun on the market. No other exposed hammer gun of its type has approached its success and fame. A number of Model '97s are still in field use at this writing.

Major collector variations are:

Standard Model "Field Grade" Shotgun, 12 or 16 gauge, solid frame:
5K-147   Values—Very Good **$350**   Exc. **$850**

Same as above, takedown type:
5K-148   Values—Very Good **$350**   Exc. **$850**

Trap Gun (so marked):
5K-149   Values—Very Good **$550**   Exc. **$1,000**

Pigeon Gun (so marked):
5K-150   Values—Very Good **$700**   Exc. **$1,450**

Riot Gun; solid frame and takedown types, 20" barrel:
5K-151   Values—Very Good **$650**   Exc. **$1,250**

"U.S." Marked Riot Gun:
5K-151.5   Values—Very Good **$850**   Exc. **$1,750**

Trench Gun; solid frame and takedown types, 20" barrel:
5K-152   Values—Very Good **$900**   Exc. **$2,250**

"U.S." Marked Trench Gun; with hand guard and bayonet lug:
5K-152.5   Values—Very Good **$1,000**   Exc. **$2,500**

U.S. Model 1917 Enfield Rifle by Winchester *See Chapter IX-A U.S. Issue Military Long Arms (9A-455)*

Winchester Handguns

Winchester attempted to move into the handgun market between 1876 and 1883. Word-of-mouth tradition, debunked by some, has it that it was as threat to keep Colt from the manufacture of lever action rifles. About 12 various type experimental revolvers were made, most 44 cal. One submitted to U.S. Navy for trial, another to Russian government. Extreme rarities, the few that have appeared on collectors' market brought prices in the mid five figures.

A Single Shot Winchester Pistol. Occasionally finds its way to collectors. For many years considered as Winchester "curiosa"

5K-170

and merely a "lunch box special", i.e. made by factory employees on their own initiative and time, there is evidence that Winchester seriously considered making the gun. 1919 dated, very detailed factory drawings and a letter of that same year to a Winchester dealer alluded to their production. All utilize the bolt action and shortened barrel of the Model 1902 boy's single shot rifle; blued finish. Large, flat, saw handle frame usual; iron type mentioned. Caliber 22RF. Walnut grips:

5K-170   Values—Very Good **$2,500**   Exc. **$4,000**

Walch Ten-Shot Double Hammer Percussion Revolver   *See Chapter VII-A "Percussion Revolvers" (7A-117)*

These unique pocket revolvers were made by the New Haven Arms Company (Oliver Winchester, President and major stockholder at the time) circa 1860-62; produced at the factory concurrent with the Henry rifle. They are directly related to earliest of Winchesters and only recently beginning to be recognized for their historic associations and origins.

Winchester Model 1898 Breech Loading 10 Ga. Cannon

Made c. 1898-1958; total quantity 18,400. Intended usage as a noisemaker: for salutes, sound effects in theatrical productions, starting yacht and other sporting events, etc. 12" tapered, blued

5K-171

steel barrel with Winchester markings; made to accept 10 gauge, black powder, BLANKS only and so marked. Heavy cast iron carriage with 3-1/2" iron wheels; black japanned finish. Each side high relief marked **W.R.A. Cº/TRADE MARK/MADE IN U.S.A.** 17 overall. Weight 13-1/2 pounds. Not serial numbered; an identification number on barrel and band. In 1930 made available with rubber tires and also with chromium finish; although scarcer, demand less and consequently do not usually bring as much as blued models.

(Note: Under license by Winchester-Olin the cannon was made available again in 1976 and is marked on left side of breech MFD. BY BELLMORE-JOHNSON TOOL Co., HAMDEN, CONN, UNDER LICENSE FROM WINCHESTER. Serial numbered.

5K-171   Values— Very Good **$800**   Exc. **$1,250**
5K-172   Nickel finish and rubber tires
           Values—Very Good **$675**   Exc. **$1,100**

Chapter VI

American Military Single Shot Pistols

T he collecting of single shot American military pistols, especially early flintlocks, has long been one of the major fields in American antique arms. In the earlier days of collecting, these single shots were one of the few American arms (along with Kentucky rifles) that attracted the dilettante and the connoisseur. For many years, the flint single shots were considered as one of the ultimate, classic specialties. That same aura exists today, and they have maintained a level of high attraction, as indicated by the general scale of values.

Similar to U.S. military longarms, the field is divided into basic types: (a) **Primary** and (b) **Secondary.** Although both are terms of convenience applied by writers of an earlier era, and are identical to the categories dividing martial longarms, it should be noted that they have distinctly different connotations as applied to handguns.

Pistols classified as Primary herein are either the product of a national armory (i.e., Springfield or Harpers Ferry) or made under direct U.S. contract with either official or unofficial "model" designations (e.g., Model 1816, Model 1819, etc.). Certain exceptions will be found in this Primary section such as the "flat lockplate" Waters pistol which might be more accurately termed as a "Secondary" handgun, but by both traditional usage and as a matter of preference for quick identification is included as Primary.

The Secondary classification is quite another matter, truly a "can-of-worms." For the most part this classification has been traditional in gun collecting, and the author felt obliged to follow suit for lack of a better substitute. A word of explanation, though, is decidedly in order. Contract 1807-1808 flintlock pistols by various makers have traditionally been classified as "Secondary" in most arms literature. They are now properly identified as true "Primary" arms. For the sake of expedience they continue listed here in their former category. Other arms in the Secondary section consist of a miscellany of American flintlock handguns of the late 18th and early 19th centuries that may be generally considered as military types, for private purchases by small militia groups or individual officers and men (as personal sidearms). Also included are the few known contract types of both state and other federal contracts of such makers as T. French, Evans and Miles.

HOLSTER PISTOL vs. HORSE PISTOL

"**Holster Pistol**" is the terminology in common usage to classify almost all large size, single shot flintlock and percussion handguns, those too bulky and heavy to be comfortably carried on the person. (Exceptions are noted for types such as those designed for naval service, fitted with steel belt hooks, etc.) The name is derived from the fact that the large size of the weapons necessitated carrying them in SADDLE HOLSTERS. Made in both single and double types, the large leather sheaths or cases, usually connected with a leather center section, were fastened to the forward section of a saddle. (Single holsters usually had a large pouch for accessories in place of the second holster.) WAIST or BELT type leather holsters were rarely fitted even for smaller belt or pocket size pistols. It was not until the middle of the 19th century, with the introduction of the Colt and other revolvers, that the fashion of carrying handguns in a holster at the waist became popular.

"**Horse Pistol**" is merely an idiomatic expression, derived from the manner in which those large pistols were carried...by horse. The term is occasionally encountered in 19th century literature as a synonym for "Holster Pistol." In collecting circles "Horse Pistol" is not in wide usage, while the general public is often seen to use the term to characterize any large size antique handgun...revolvers included.

The **Primary section** is listed in chronological order by model and year. The Secondary section is listed alphabetically. Both follow traditional guidelines that have been generally accepted by American collectors.

Primary American martial pistols are extremely well recorded, with considerable supporting documentary material available in the National Archives, and with most published reference works being quite explicit as to specifications and details. The pistols themselves conform quite closely to established data.

Quite the opposite is true with the **Secondary pistols**. The so-called 1807-1808 contract types conform to general specifications and dimensions whereas the noncontract pieces are merely suggestive of general styles in common usage during eras shown. It is essential to realize that many often used earlier works on American martial pistols, published c. 1930's to 1950's are still in popular use and widely referred to today! One cannot fault the authors for their information; obviously the mere fact that the titles are still in print is indicative of their importance. Some are regarded as milestones in arms collecting. However, in reviewing the Secondary sections of those works, their "looseness" is immediately apparent. A great many of the noncontract type guns are merely representative specimens of American-made holster pistols of various eras. Some later writers copied and perpetuated the inaccuracy. Although exacting dimensions and markings are listed for some individual pistols as if representative of quantities of identical types, many are often found to be merely one-of-a-kind. Without awareness of this fact, a neophyte collector might be led astray. Other "secondary" pistols cataloged here are more or less typical of general types and styles of specific makers.

The collector should be aware that dimensions, especially of the Secondary pistols, will vary slightly, with differences more often encountered on earlier pieces, especially those made prior to 1816. Contours of handles, most often on the contract types, vary considerably due to hand workmanship.

The group of arms most lacking information are the so-called 1807-1808 contract flintlock pistols. It would be a complete misnomer to apply the word "model" to them. They have long been considered among the rarest and most eagerly sought of American flintlocks, yet there has been surprisingly little in research published about them. Listed here are known types and specimens with dimensions. Early records indicate there were other Pennsylvania contractors for these arms; the situation is very much like that of the 1792 to 1807 contract rifles (q.v.). Quite a few makers other than those listed are known to have contracted for these pistols, but specimens have yet to be positively identified. They would include such makers as DeHuff, Jacob Dickert and Peter Gonter, Abraham Henry, Adam Leitner, Henry Pickel and Winner, Nippes and Steinman. Any authentic specimens attributed to these makers of the 1807-1808 contract type pistols (or, for that matter, other Pennsylvania made military pistols like them) would be considered extreme rarities and of great value.

Only three other guns qualify as "single shot U.S. martial pistols"—the famed Remington rolling blocks, Models 1865, 1867 and 1871, which are to be found in Chapter V, Remington Arms (q.v.).

Several other American single shot percussion pistols (muzzle-loading and breech-loading) are often found included as Secondary martial single shot pistols in other published guidebooks. The author has failed to find any reason for their inclusion in the martial category other than their large size and large caliber. Such arms have no specific documentation of either being officially or unofficially carried by any military groups, nor proven to have been privately purchased as personal sidearms by officers or enlisted men in any larger quantities than smaller caliber arms! As a matter of fact, a few published discussions of the subject by collectors trying to justify their Secondary martial classification seem to defy comprehension! Various arms, including the Perry breech-loading single shot pistol, the small and large size Lindsay superposed load pistols, and percussion conversions of flintlocks, often have appeared in this group. The author has chosen not to continue classifying these as Secondary since collectors have not pursued such arms in recent times as "Secondary Martials." Specimens are to be found listed elsewhere in this work (notably Chapter VII, American Percussion Pistols).

There are other American handguns with both Primary and Secondary Martial usage which are traditionally classified in other categories. Among these are Colonial and Revolutionary-made American handguns (see Chapter XVI), flintlock and percussion dueling pistols (see Chapter VII) Kentucky pistols (see Chapter XI) and New England flintlock pistols (see Chapter XII).

Not a few flintlock holster size pistols classified as "Secondary Martials" will be seen bearing foreign proofmarks on the barrels. Many American makers imported parts in large quantities and utilized them (most often barrels and locks) on their own products, thus finding manufacture easier, cheaper and quicker. No doubt these markings tend to make the arms less valuable than an entirely American made specimen. However, these pistols are quite eagerly sought after and are fine collectors' items. In some cases there is a very minor line of differentiation between an English made flintlock pistol and an American one with imported parts. Values for specimens are almost identical except where distinctive American features set them apart.

The machinations that occurred with arms made by U.S. musket contractors of 1798 and 1808 undoubtedly transpired with pistol makers also. This was likely more evident during wartime (e.g., War of 1812) when the need was great by both federal forces and private groups (e.g., those arming a privateer for sea duty). Temptations to divert contract production were likely prevalent. The reader is referred to Chapter IX for a discussion of this matter, equally applicable to early military handguns and serving as an insight to better understanding them.

U.S. martial pistols have long been popular and the guns valued relatively high in comparison to other American arms. The field has never lacked for its share of counterfeiters. As a matter of fact, martials have served as a magnet, attracting quite a few nefarious individuals; in a sense being their training ground for later ventures! Regrettably, some of the most notorious frauds have been perpetrated in the field of single shot flintlocks. It thus follows suit that the collector should be especially wary when acquiring rare specimens. The lack of definitive information and the great many variances that do occur have afforded the counterfeiter plenty of opportunities to deceive the unsuspecting and gullible. Spurious markings have been notable violations. Quite a few such deceptions were perpetrated in the 1920s and '30s, and hence, with such items now acquiring the patina of age and with a corresponding increase in discriminating buyers, they are often easily passed as original, merely by virtue of their background—which when traced is not always virtuous!

The matter of originality of the flintlock ignition system on an early martial pistol is a major evaluating factor. It is probably more important in this collecting field than with other American arms. As may be seen from the valuations in this chapter, the difference between an original flintlock and a percussion conversion is often considerable. Thus, one of the more important procedures in the acquisition of a flintlock specimen is establishing its originality. Reconverted—or restored—specimens are certainly not frowned upon as they formerly were, and have gradually become accepted as commonplace and "legitimate" (see Chapter III, "Reconversions" and also Chapter II). Values, however, do fluctuate greatly. These guns are in no less demand whether percussion or reconverted, but price-wise there are vast differences. In this area the collector is cautioned to proceed slowly and with great care.

Additional markings on martial pistols denoting state ownership or issuance to special units will increase value. New York, Massachusetts and North and South Carolina seem most encountered, although other states are known. As with longarms, the less encountered state markings bring proportionately greater prices; and all southern markings, even though more commonly seen than some northern ones, will by virtue of their possible "Secondary Confederate usage" bring considerably higher premiums.

As with most American guns, variations in either configurations, dimensions, or markings can and do appear. The most often observed are listed here. Such variations when found and established as authentic are usually valued on the basis of the type of gun on which they appear, the period, historical importance or association, and the general nature of the variation. No fixed rule exists for percentage of premium that values will increase. This subject is also discussed at greater length in the text accompanying American Military Longarms (Chapter IX) and is equally applicable to handguns.

BIBLIOGRAPHY

Important information concerning U.S. martial handguns may also be found in other books on American firearms. A few of the more important titles found listed in bibliographies elsewhere in this book are: The Virginia Manufactory Of Arms by

Cromwell; *United States Military Small Arms 1816-1865* by Reilly; *U.S. Martial Flintlocks* by Reilly; *Small Arms And Ammunition In The United States Service* by Lewis; *The Collecting Of Guns* edited by Serven; *U.S. Military Firearms* by Hicks; *Catalog Of The William M. Locke Collection*; *U.S. Naval Handguns 1808-1911* by Winter. *U.S. Military Arms: Dates of Manufacture from 1795* (Pocket Guide).

Chapel, Charles Edward. *U.S. Martial And Semi-Martial Single Shot Pistols.* New York: Coward-McCann, Inc., 1962. One of the early basic guides to the subject with some of the material superseded in the light of present day knowledge.

Gluckman, Arcadi. *United States Martial Pistols and Revolvers.* Buffalo, New York: Otto Ulbrich Company, 1939, with many reprintings to present time substantially identical and unchanged from first edition. A basic guidebook to the field.

*Hartzler, Daniel D. & Whisker, James B. *U.S. Martial Single Shot Pistols.* Bedford, Penna: Old Bedford Village Press, 1997. Photo chronicle of martial and semi martial pistols, U.S. & state, 1776-1845.

Jeska, Robert. *Early Simeon North Pistol Correspondence.* Plainwell, Michigan: Privately published by author, 1993.

Kalman, James M. and Patterson, C. Meade, *A Pictorial History of U.S. Single Shot Martial Pistols.* New York: Charles Scribner's Sons. Circa. 1950s. Full scale colored drawings of primary and secondary types with short accompanying text to each.

Meadows, E. S. *U.S. Military Holsters and Pistols and Pistol Cartridge Boxes.* Dallas, Texas: Taylor Publishing Co., 1987. Encyclopedic in coverage. Profusely illustrated.

North, S. & R. *Simeon North-First Official Pistol Maker of the United States.* Concord, New Hampshire: The Rumford Press, 1913. Reprinted by the Gun Room Press circa 1977. Much original source material from official records. Some of the information obsolete in the light of later studies.

Sawyer, C. W. *United States Single Shot Martial Pistols 1776-1871.* Old Greenwich, Connecticut: WE, Inc., 1971. Reprint of the original 1911 edition which was a pioneer in the field.

Smith, S. E. and Bitter, E. W. *Historic Pistols—The American Martial Flintlock, 1760-1845.* New York: Scalamandre Publications, 1985 (distributed by the Gun Room Press, N. J.). An important reference with much new material not covered elsewhere.

(*) Preceding a title indicates the book is currently in print.

VI-A: PRIMARY TYPES

1799 Flintlock Pistol by North & Cheney

Model 1799 Flintlock Pistol by Simeon North and Elisha Cheney of Berlin, Connecticut. Manufactured 1799 to 1802. Total made presumed 2,000 under two contracts.

69 caliber, smoothbore, 8-1/2" round barrel (slight variances); usual markings **V/O/P/US**. Made without sights. Overall length 14-1/2".

Steel ramrod with button shaped head; inserted into lower right side of frame. Distinctive features are the brass frame and lack of a forestock. Trigger guard and buttcap brass; iron backstrap. One-piece walnut handle although cherry wood reported on some first contract. Metal parts finished bright.

As the first official model of pistol adopted by the United States, the Model 1799 is recognized as one of the great prizes in collecting American firearms. It was patterned directly after the Model 1777 French pistol, which has a barrel 1" shorter, a breech noticeably rounded at its lower portion, and an extra barrel securing screw on the forward section of the frame. Numerous spurious specimens of the Model 1799 have been made over the past half century. Generally, the counterfeiter altered a M.1777 French pistol, but other clever forgeries known. In 1964 the M.1799 was reproduced and marked "REPLICA." A few occasionally turn up with those markings removed and falsely aged to tempt the unsuspecting bargain hunter. They're usually easily spotted, but extreme caution is urged before acquiring any M.1799.

Only within recent years have archival documents and studies of this model determined that there were two contracts for them. Each contract apparently created a slight

6A-001

manufacturing change that collectors choose to recognize and that has affected values. Although there may be a difference in the curvature of handles, the major means of recognition are markings. The first contract for 500 pistols is marked in an arched curve on the underside of the brass frame: **S. NORTH & E. CHENEY BERLIN.** Serial numbers on the small group of recorded specimens all under 500. They are properly valued at a 20 percent to 30 percent premium over the values shown below for the later contract.

Second contract for 1500 pistols bear near identical marks, similarly located, but the first initials "**S**" (Simeon) and "**E**" (Elisha) of the makers' names are noticeably lacking from the marking die. From study of the small number of extant specimens, they were numbered in their own series of 1 through 1500 (approx.).

6A-001	Values—Good **$25,000**		Fine **$65,000**

As above, altered to percussion:

6A-002	Values—Good **$15,000**		Fine **$37,500**

Model 1805 Flintlock Pistol

Model 1805 Flintlock Pistol. Made at Harpers Ferry Armory, Virginia. C. 1806-1808. Total produced 4,096.

54 caliber, smoothbore. 10-1/16" round barrel with iron rib below holding an iron ramrod ferrule. When present the front sight is brass, open type rear sight on tang. Overall length 16".

Wooden ramrod with swelled tip believed original issue, however, many found with steel ramrods with swelled tip and believed correct. Brass mountings. Lockplate has integrally

forged iron flashpan with fence. Metal parts finished bright.

Standard lock markings ahead of hammer: Spread eagle and shield over US. Marked vertically at rear HARPERS/FERRY over the date of manufacture (1805, 1806, 1807 or 1808). Marked on the barrel at breech: Serial number, eaglehead cartouche, and P proof. Inspector's markings on the left side of the stock near the sideplate.

The Model 1805 pistol was the first military handgun

manufactured by a national armory. Recent research indicates that the guns were numbered and issued in pairs; thus, of the total 4,096 manufactured the highest serial number would be 2,048 with each serial number used twice.

Production records for this model as first seen in the 1822 Report of the Chief of Ordnance (and subsequently used and reprinted in numerous books on U.S. Martial pistol collecting) seemed to indicate the manufacture of eight pattern pieces in 1806 with a total production for the balance in the years 1807 and 1808. A lengthy study of existing specimens (including the viewing of authenticated 1805 dated pistols and over 30 specimens of 1806 dated specimens) and the compilation of known dates and serial numbers clearly points to the fact that the 1822 records, although correct in total, are misleading when applied to actual markings on the guns themselves. The most plausible theory advanced to explain the confusion of quantities made and dated 1805 and 1806 has been that Harpers Ferry was then operating on a fiscal year basis (October 1 to September 30) and thus the first 300 pistols while actually manufactured in the calendar year 1806 and so dated do not appear in reports for that year, but rather show up for the fiscal year 1807 on their production records. The difference may also be explained in the light of a knowledge of the method of Ordnance Department record-keeping in which arms made at the end of the year and not actually delivered either physically or record-wise from the

6A-003

armory to the military storekeeper until the following year show up on Ordnance reports as being made in the latter year.

1805 Dated Specimens; Just eight pattern pistols made that year; extremely rare:

6A-003   Values—Good **$20,000**   Fine **$50,000**

1806 Dated Specimens; Approximately 300 estimated manufactured:

6A-004   Values—Good **$10,000**   Fine **$30,000**

1807 Dated Specimens; 2,580 estimated manufactured:

6A-005   Values—Good **$4,250**   Fine **$15,000**

As above; converted to percussion:

6A-006   Values—Good **$2,500**   Fine **$6,000**

1808 Dated Specimens; 1,208 made:

6A-007   Values—Good **$4,500**   Fine **$16,000**

As above; converted to percussion:

6A-008   Values—Good **$2,750**   Fine **$6,500**

Model 1808 Navy Flintlock Pistol

Model 1808 Navy Flintlock Pistol. Made by Simeon North, Berlin, Connecticut. C. 1808 to 1810. Total produced 3,000.

64 caliber, smoothbore. 10-1/8" round barrel (originally finished brown). Made without sights. Overall length 16-1/4".

Hickory ramrod with swelled tip. Brass mountings. Full walnut stock, pin fastened. Brass flashpan with fence on lock. Iron belt hook attached to left side of the stock and an iron backstrap extends from tang to the butt cap.

Standard lock markings: Spread eagle motif above U. STATES ahead of hammer; marked vertically at rear S. NORTH/BERLIN/CON. Barrel is unmarked. Inspector's marking also present on left side of stock near the sideplate and belt hook.

Significant as a War of 1812 era handgun, the Model 1808 Navy has a secure position in American manufacturing history

6A-009

due to the pioneer methods of production used in the series by Simeon North:

6A-009   Values—Good **$5,500**   Fine **$17,500**

As above; converted to percussion:

6A-010   Values—Good **$3,000**   Fine **$7,500**

Model 1811 and Model 1811 Transition Flintlock Pistols

Model 1811 and Model 1811 Transition Flintlock Pistols (a.k.a. Model 1810). Made by Simeon North, Berlin, Connecticut, c. 1811 to 1813. Total made (of both types) 1,156.

69 caliber, smoothbore. 8-5/8" round barrel; made without sights. Overall length 15".

Hickory ramrod with swelled tip. Brass mountings include the umbrella shaped butt cap, trigger guard and sideplate. Pin

6A-011

fastened full stock. In many respects this pistol is similar to the Model 1808 North, except for the shorter barrel and overall length, the larger caliber, and the lack of a belt hook. Lock has brass flashpan with fence. Finish bright on all metal parts.

Lock markings ahead of hammer: Spread eagle motif above U. STATES. Marked vertically at rear: S. NORTH/BERLIN/CON. Breech of barrel marked with proofmark V over an eaglehead and CT within an oval cartouche. Inspector's marking also present on left side of stock, near the sideplate.

A sizable quantity of the Model 1811 production was completed when North was directed to alter the method of fastening the barrel to the stock (for ease in disassembly) by utilizing an iron double strap barrel band designed by M. T. Wickham, the U.S. Inspector of Arms. Forends of stocks were shortened approximately 2" to accommodate the band with a small retaining stud added.

Model 1811 Flintlock Pistol; pin fastened bbl. Quantity 606. As described above:

6A-011   Values—Good **$4,000**   Fine **$12,500**

As above; converted to percussion:
6A-012   Values—Good **$2,500**   Fine **$6,500**
Transition Model 1811 (a.k.a. Model 1812 modification) with iron double strap barrel band. Quantity 550:
6A-013   Values—Good **$4,500**   Fine **$15,000**
As above; converted to percussion:
6A-014   Values—Good **$2,750**   Fine **$7,000**

6A-013

Model 1813 Flintlock Pistol, Army and Navy

Model 1813 Flintlock Pistol, Army and Navy. Made by Simeon North of Middletown, Connecticut, c. 1813 to 1815. Total made approximately 1,626.

69 caliber, smoothbore. 9-1/16" round barrel; made without sights. Overall length approximately 15-1/4".

Hickory ramrod with swelled tip; the opposite end fitted with a metal ferrule threaded for cleaning and ball removal attachments. Iron mountings. The front strap of the double barrel band is not fluted and the stock terminates flush with the front of that band. Iron backstraps inset into stock from tang to butt cap. Flat lockplate beveled at the front and slightly rounded at rear with brass flashpan without fence, tilts upward to rear.

Lock markings ahead of hammer: S. NORTH (in downward curve) over an American eagle motif with letters U and S at either side over bottom line MIDL$^{\underline{N}}$CON. (in upward curve). Breech of barrel marked P/US on left side and inspector marking H.H.P. above touchhole. Inspector's marking also present on left side of stock near the sideplate.

The original contract for the Model 1813 called for North, at his new Middletown factory, to produce a total of 20,000 pistols. Due to the large caliber and harsh recoil, the order was revised. More recent research indicates 1,000 of these handguns were delivered to the Navy (inspected by Edward Trenchard) and 626 delivered to the Army, of which 85 (i.e. if they were all accepted)

assembled at the end of production in 1813, were fitted with the earlier 1811 barrels and flat locks then on hand at the factory. That variant has often been termed a "Transitional Model." (Authentic specimens rare and worth a premium. Caution should be exercised in determining originality.

As a limited production type, the Model 1813 is in strong demand by collectors. The model has added historic importance as the first arms contract in which a gun maker agreed to provide a product having parts interchangeability. Navy models are fitted with a steel belt hook on the left side and will bring a premium:

6A-015

6A-015   Values—Good **$4,250**   Fine **$12,500**
As above; converted to percussion:
6A-016   Values—Good **$2,500**   Fine **$6,500**

Model 1816 Flintlock Pistol

Model 1816 Flintlock Pistol. Made by Simeon North of Middletown, Connecticut, c. 1817 to 1820. Total manufactured 19,374.

54 caliber, smoothbore. 9-1/16" round barrel; brass blade front sight on forward strap of the double barrel band. Overall length 15-1/4".

Hickory ramrod with swelled tip; the opposite end fitted with an iron ferrule threaded for cleaning and ball removal attachments. All iron mountings; barrel band is fluted on sides of both straps. The stock extends beyond the front of the barrel band about 1/2". An iron backstrap is inset into the stock from the barrel tang to the butt cap. The flat lockplate is beveled at the front and slightly rounded at rear; brass flashpan without fence tilts upward to the rear. Lockplate casehardened, all other iron

parts finished brown.

Two styles of lock markings are encountered: (a) Early type: S. NORTH (in downward curve) over an American eagle motif with U and S at either side over bottom line MIDL$^{\underline{N}}$CON. (in upward curve); (b) Later type: Identical to above with slightly smaller die stamps and change in the lower address line reading MIDL$^{\underline{TN}}$ CONN. Markings are often weak:
6A-017   Values—Good **$1,100**   Fine **$4,000**
As above; converted to percussion:
6A-018   Values—Good **$650**   Fine **$1,600**
Special bolster type percussion conversion; iron ramrod and iron swivels replace wooden ramrod; side of bolster marked A.W.:
6A-019   Values—Good **$800**   Fine **$2,000**

6A-017

6A-019

Model 1817 Flintlock Pistol

Model 1817 Flintlock Pistol (a.k.a. Model 1807). Made by Springfield Armory. Manufactured c. 1807-1808 (partially, incomplete only) and 1817-1818. Total made 1,000.

69 caliber, smoothbore. 10-3/4" round barrel (will vary slightly). Brass blade front sight on forward strap of barrel band. Overall length 17-1/2".

Hickory ramrod with swelled tip; opposite end fitted with a metal ferrule threaded for ball screw or wiper attachments. All mountings of iron. Double barrel band fastening the forestock is fluted on both sides of straps; stock extends a short length forward of the band; iron backstrap from tang to butt cap. Lockplate flat with beveled edge; integral forged iron flashpan with high fence. All iron parts finished bright.

Standard lock marking: SPRING/FIELD/1818 placed vertically at rear (1815 dated also; see below); American eagle and shield motif over U.S. ahead of hammer. At breech of barrel P/V and eaglehead proof marks. On the backstrap near breech the date 1818. Inspector's markings present on left side of stock near sideplate. A stock maker's stamping may also be found, on the grip's right front section; e.g., RC.

Quite a few of the second type (see below) are seen with locks dated 1815 (they will bring a slight premium) with the usual 1818 date on backstrap. They are completely correct this way. This seeming incongruity is often overlooked and left unmentioned by other references and has long lacked for an explanation. To understand the most plausible theory advanced (and the one which will quite likely be found acceptable), it is necessary to recount the background of this pistol and the machinations within the armory and the ordnance department during the era. Production of this massive pistol was halted c. 1807-1808 when the large 69 caliber was no longer found suitable (the smaller 54 caliber then being adopted for armory production at Harpers Ferry). The semi-finished parts consisting of approximately 400 locks, 300 barrels, 1,000 barrel bands and rough cut stocks were merely kept in storage at the armory.

In 1814 the Springfield Armory was directed to establish a rifle assembly line and commence production and manufacture of the Model 1803 (Harpers Ferry type) Half Stock Rifle. Due to problems encountered with making stocks, the project was halted in 1816, and such arms that were partially made, but not assembled, were shipped to Harpers Ferry. It is thought that the locks made for that Model 1803 Rifle (which it should be noted are about identical to both the second production, post-1814, Model 1803 Rifle as well as the second type 1817-1818 production of Springfield Pistol) were those on hand already marked and dated 1815, that were subsequently used for the Model 1817 Pistol.

In 1817 the pistol project was revitalized under the initiative of Colonel Robert Lee, the Superintendent of Springfield Armory, with the sanction of Colonel Decius Wadsworth of the Ordnance Department. There appears to be no valid reason for the manufacture of these arms other than to rid themselves of

6A-020
Type I

6A-022
Type II

old work on hand at the armory or possibly to merely keep skilled workers at projects. Correspondence shows neither the need nor exact intended use for such pistols; in Lee's words of February 17th "… We can make them of good quality suitable for the Navy—or perhaps the Cavalry." In May of 1818 the pistols were again mentioned with no specific use intended for them other than possibilities as naval boarding or cavalry arms.

With parts available and on hand the first lot utilized the approximately 400 locks remaining from 1807 production (Type I below). The balance of the arms (Type II) were made utilizing a group (unknown quantity) of already fabricated and marked locks left over from the Model 1803 Rifle manufacture with the balance of the locks newly made (or merely marked) to correspond to the date of manufacture of the remaining pistols. It is evident also that the guns were never issued, for an 1850 armory inventory showed all 1,000 of them still on hand.

Considered a highly desirable specimen by martial collectors, the Model 1817 was the first handgun made in quantity at Springfield Armory (only two others would follow, the Models 1855 and 1911). It appears in two distinct types:

Type I: With the earlier 1807 style lock having teat-like projection at rear of lockplate, curled toe of frizzen with pointed top of frizzen, spear point finial on frizzen spring; large gooseneck hammer. Approximately 400 made:

6A-020	Values—Good **$7,000**	Fine **$20,000**

As above; converted to percussion:

6A-021	Values—Good **$4,000**	Fine **$7,500**

Type II: Evenly rounded rear of lock without projection; frizzen has straight toe and evenly rounded top; long bulbous, rounded finial on frizzen spring; reinforced type, double neck hammer. Approximately 600 manufactured:

6A-022	Values—Good **$6,500**	Fine **$20,000**

As above; converted to percussion:

6A-023	Values—Good **$4,000**	Fine **$7,500**

Model 1819 Flintlock Pistol

Model 1819 Flintlock Pistol. Made by Simeon North of Middletown, Connecticut, c. 1819 to 1823. Total manufactured 20,400.

54 caliber, smoothbore. 10" round barrel; brass blade front sight; oval shaped rear sight on tang. Overall length 15-1/2".

This model marks the introduction of the swivel type steel ramrod, inspired by similar fixtures on contemporary British military pistols. All iron mountings. Barrel bands secured by long, narrow spring; distinctive profile to lower lip of band. Iron

backstrap inset into back of handle from tang to butt cap. Trigger guard riveted to trigger plate. Flat, beveled lockplate ahead of hammer; rounded at rear. A sliding safety bolt, unique to U.S. martial arms, present at rear of hammer. Brass flashpan, without fence, tilts upward to the rear. All iron parts finished brown.

Lock marking ahead of hammer: S. NORTH. (in downward curve) over American eagle/shield motif with letters U and S at either side over bottom line MIDL⊥ⁿ CONN. (upward curve). Date of production (most often encountered 1821 and 1822) marked at rear of lock. Barrel marked at breech: J/P/US. Inspector's marking present left side of stock near sideplate. (Note: there is a Belgian copy of this gun, apparently antique, but likely of a later period. Its origins unknown and <u>not</u> having any known U.S. association.)

6A-024   Values—Good **$1,000**   Fine **$3,500**
As above; converted to percussion:
6A-025   Values—Good **$650**   Fine **$1,400**

6A-024

Model 1826 Flintlock Navy Pistol

Model 1826 Flintlock Navy Pistol. Made by Simeon North of Middletown, Connecticut, c. 1826 to 1829. Total quantity manufactured 3,000.

54 caliber, smoothbore. 8-5/8" round barrel; brass blade front sight; oval shaped rear sight on tang. Overall length 13-1/4".

Swivel type steel ramrod with button shaped head. All mountings of iron. Barrel bands secured by long narrow spring. Iron backstrap on handle from tang to butt cap. Trigger guard riveted onto trigger plate. Made with a long steel belt hook attached to the left side of the stock; when absent, will detract slightly from value. The lockplate is flat and beveled forward of the hammer and rounded at rear. Brass flashpan, without fence, tilts upward to the rear. All iron parts finished brown.

Lock markings ahead of hammer: US/S. NORTH; dated at rear 1827 or 1828. Barrel marked at breech: US/ET/P (in oval cartouche). Inspector's marking present on left side of stock, near the sideplate.

6A-026

6A-026

6A-027

Basically a smaller version of the Model 1819 pistol, the Model 1826 can be quickly identified by the abrupt angle of the grip. The majority were evidently converted to percussion and specimens found in original flintlock are extremely scarce. This was the last model of U.S. martial pistol made by Simeon North:

6A-026   Values—Good **$3,750**   Fine **$10,000**
As above; converted to percussion:
6A-027   Values—Good **$1,500**   Fine **$4,000**

Model 1826 Flintlock Navy Pistol by W. L. Evans

Model 1826 Flintlock Navy Pistol by W. L. Evans, of Valley Forge, Pennsylvania. C. 1830-1831. Total quantity estimated at 1,000 or less.

These pistols are identical to the Model 1826 by Simeon North. Variations noted primarily in the lockplate markings. Standard style most often seen: W. L. EVANS/V. FORGE ahead of hammer; marked vertically at rear 1831/USN (also seen without the USN marks). Also encountered: US/W. L. EVANS ahead of hammer and dated vertically at rear 1830.

A third style of marking, with but two or three known specimens is stamped ahead of hammer with a small eaglehead over W. L. EVANS/E. BURG. The arm is classified as ultra rare, and its value would be commensurate with prototype or experimental martial handguns and considerably higher than the standard Evans reflected below:

6A-028

6A-028   Values—Good **$3,250**   Fine **$9,000**
As above; converted to percussion:
6A-029   Values—Good **$1,250**   Fine **$3,500**

Model 1836 Flintlock Pistols by Asa Waters & Robert Johnson

Model 1836 Flintlock Pistol by Asa Waters, Millbury, Massachusetts and Robert Johnson of Middletown, Connecticut. C. 1836 to 1844. Total quantity 41,000.

54 caliber, smoothbore. 8-1/2" round barrel; brass blade front sight; oval shaped rear sight on the barrel tang. Overall length 14".

Swivel type steel ramrod with button shaped head. All mountings of iron. The barrel band has a strap extension which joins the sideplate; an iron backstrap integral with butt cap extends along back of handle to tang. Trigger guard rivet fastened to the trigger plate. The lockplate is flat and beveled ahead of the hammer and round at rear; brass flashpan with fence tilts upward to the rear. Casehardened lockplate, hammer and frizzen; blued trigger and frizzen spring; all other iron parts finished bright.

Lock markings are noted in the variations below. Proof stampings are on the breech of the barrel, e.g., US/P, beneath which are inspector's initials. Inspector's markings present on the left side of the stock, near the sideplate.

An improved version of the Model 1826, this was the last U.S. martial pistol produced in the flintlock ignition system. Many collectors regard this as the best made, most attractive, and best performing of all U.S. military flint handguns. It was the standard issue handgun of the Mexican War and continued to see extensive use, converted to percussion, in the Civil War. A

6A-030

significant quantity of production was later altered (in the 1850s) to percussion (most federal conversions were cone type). This model is often found with state militia markings. A small premium may be added for Northern states, while those bearing Southern state markings (N. Carolina most often seen, they received 2,660 between 1837 and 1846; most were converted to percussion) will increase value 25 percent or more. The collector is cautioned to be very wary of spurious marked specimens.

A. WATERS/MILBURY, MS. marked specimens. Dated 1837 through 1843. Estimated quantity made 20,000:

6A-030   Values—Good **$850**   Fine **$3,000**

Identical to above; converted to percussion:

6A-031   Values—Good **$500**   Fine **$950**

A. H. WATERS & C°/MILBURY, MASS/1844 marked specimens. Estimated quantity made 3,000:

6A-032   Values—Good **$875**   Fine **$3,250**

Identical to above; converted to percussion:

6A-033   Values—Good **$500**   Fine **$1,000**

US./R. JOHNSON/MIDD^N CONN marked specimens. Bearing dates 1836 through 1844. Total estimated manufactured 18,000:

6A-034   Values—Good **$850**   Fine **$3,250**

Identical to above; converted to percussion:

6A-035   Values—Good **$500**   Fine **$1,000**

US Navy marked conversion. Special bolster type with naval anchor markings and inspector initials N.W.P. on top of breech:

6A-036   Values—Good **$1,600**   Fine **$4,000**

Variant eagle marking. The lock marked ahead of hammer only with an awkward eagle motif with shield on breast. No other maker's marking present. Usually the double necked hammer has a circular piercing (in place of the normal heart shape). Very little is known about this type. It conforms in every other respect to the standard 1836 and although possibly a developmental or prototype piece it may very well prove to be special militia contract. A number of specimens are known:

6A-037   Values—Good **$950**   Fine **$3,000**

6A-031 / 6A-033 6A-035
Various Conversions to Percussion

Model 1836 Percussion Conversions with Experimental Automatic Priming Devices

Although full details not known about quantities made or exact years of production, two rare types of side lug conversions to percussion of the Model 1836 Flintlock Pistol are known. Possibly "Pattern" or prototype.

Maynard Taped-Primed Conversion of Model 1836 Pistol. About identical in appearance (much smaller in size) to Maynard conversion of the Model 1840 musket (see 9A-267). Readily identified by the large device affixed to the center of the lock having a hinged door which swivels downward to open, revealing the "magazine" into which Dr. Maynard's unique narrow strip of varnished paper holding small amounts of fulminate (similar to the caps on a child's cap pistol) are inserted. When the uniquely contoured hammer is cocked, a pawl device rotates that roll of caps a short length in order that one of them will move upward to cover the nipple (eliminating the necessity

for a separate copper cap). The swivel door to the magazine marked: "EDWARD MAYNARD/PATENTEE 1845." Values estimated high four to low five-figure range.

6A-037.5

6A-037.5
Maynard Conversion

Gedney Patent Conversion with Self-Priming Hammer to Model 1836 Pistol

Little known about this unique system. Entire device contained in the hammer which is then fitted to a side lug converted standard Model 1836. Hammer marked: "PAT MARCH 15, 1859/MC PRIMING CO. NEW-YORK." George W.B. Gedney of New York City received patent for the device March 15, 1859; recorded that some of the locks and hammers were purchased by the U.S. government in very small quantities. Also reported (although unverified) that the noted post-Civil War (and later) military goods surplus dealers Francis Bannerman Company of New York at one time had a small quantity of these "Gedney" marked, unattached, loose hammers. Such unattached parts would be valuable, but not quite the same as if assembled

**6A-037.6
Gedney Conversion**

originally with the pistols. Authenticated specimens estimated in mid to high four-figure range.

6A-037.6

U.S. Navy Elgin Cutlass Pistol

U.S. Navy Elgin Cutlass Pistol. Made by C. B. Allen of Springfield, Massachusetts, c. 1838. Total quantity 150 on U.S. Navy contract.

54 caliber, smoothbore. 5" octagonal barrel to which is attached below an 11" Bowie type blade of 2" width. The blade is forged integral with the trigger guard and knuckle guard. Overall length approximately 17".

Serial numbered from 1 on up. Boxlock type frame marked on left side: C. B. ALLEN/SPRINGFIELD/MASS. Barrel marked along top: ELGIN'S PATENT. Other markings usually seen on side of barrel PM and CBA with date 1837.

The Elgin possesses many desirable collector features. It was the only combination gun (knife and pistol) ever issued by any of the U.S. military services (the imposing Bowie-type blade was made by N. P. Ames of Springfield); it was the first percussion handgun officially used by the U.S.; and it possesses a superb historical association as being specifically made to outfit the famed Wilkes-South Sea Exploring Expedition, having known use on one of the exotic islands of the South Pacific.

Smaller Elgin cutlass pistols by other makers are known, but not considered as martial weapons. See Chapter VII, American Percussion Pistols (Single Shot).

This Navy Elgin was accompanied by a larger leather sheath with wide German silver tip and throat piece, the latter holding the removable brass tipped steel loading rod. If the original sheath is present and complete and in sound condition, the value can be increased by up to $6,500. A partial or very poor conditioned scabbard does not alter the values shown below significantly:

6A-038 Values—Good **$11,000** Fine **$35,000**

6A-038

Waters Single Shot Percussion Pistol

Single Shot Percussion Pistol, a.k.a. "Flat Lock Waters." Made by A. H. Waters & Co., Millbury, Massachusetts. Made c. mid 1840s to 1849. Quantity unknown.

54 caliber, smoothbore. Round barrel, 8-1/2" long. Brass blade front sight; the rear sight of oval shape and located on the tang. Overall length 14".

This handgun represents an enigma to the student and collector and its inclusion in this section is purely arbitrary as it was not an officially adopted or issued arm. It most certainly is a distinct model highly deserving of a place in a martial collection. It is thought to be a transitional piece between the last flintlock handgun (the Model 1836) and the first adopted percussion handgun (the Model 1842), and very possibly the maker's attempt at obtaining government contracts. Although on first glance resembling a conversion to percussion of a Model 1836, it was originally made as a percussion piece and its most easily distinguishing feature is the flat, flush fitted lockplate.

Numerous variations are found on this model. The most often encountered has a side lug holding the nipple (others have been seen with the cone type nipple on the barrel as well as bolster type). Iron furniture of the Model 1836 style is usual, but numerous variations appear utilizing combinations of brass and iron. Numerous marking variations are seen; the most often

6A-039

6A-039

observed is A. H. WATERS & C◦/MILBURY MASS. in the center of the lock. The barrels often bear late 1840s dates; inspector initials and US markings have been observed on the barrels.

Values for this model are basically the same in all variations. Minor variations can cause slightly higher prices for the most specialized of collectors and only close search of the available studies in published works (both books and periodicals) will equip the reader with these nuances:

6A-039 Values—Good **$750** Fine **$1,500**

Waters "All Metal" Single Shot Percussion Pistol

Single Shot Percussion Pistol, a.k.a. "All Metal Waters." Made by A.H. Waters & Co., Millbury, Massachusetts, c. 1849. Quantity unknown; very limited.

54 caliber, smoothbore. 8 inch round barrel, faceted breech; brass blade front sight. Iron swivel ramrod. Overall length 12-5/8". Two-piece walnut grips

Another enigma for the collector (*see above Waters pistols*) and not determined to be an officially adopted arm. Wide variance in markings noted on surviving specimens; some with full WATERS, MILLBURY, etc., on right barrel facet and US with or without eagle motif and the letter P; others with no markings. A few specimens noted with decorative band of engraving around front of frame

6A-039.5

and hammer:
6A-039.5 Values—Good **$1,100** Fine **$2,750**

Model 1842 Percussion Pistol

Model 1842 Percussion Pistol. Made by Henry Aston and Ira N. Johnson, both of Middletown, Connecticut and the Palmetto Armory of Columbia, South Carolina. Made c. 1845 to 1852. Quantities as shown below.

54 caliber, smoothbore. 8-1/2" round barrel; brass blade front sight. Overall length 14".

Swivel type steel ramrod with button shaped head, the opposite end threaded for ball screw or wiper attachments. All brass mountings. Barrel band has a strap extension joining the sideplate. Backstrap forged integral with the butt cap and extends to the tang. Trigger guard is attached to the trigger plate by two spanner nuts, rather than the riveted construction as on earlier models. Lockplate flat with beveled edge. All metal parts finished bright excepting the blued trigger.

Lockplate markings noted below. Proof stampings on breech of the barrel, e.g., US/P, beneath which are inspector's initials. Date stamping on barrel tang. Inspector's marking on left side of the stock near the sideplate.
US/H. ASTON marked specimens (forward of hammer). Also marked vertically at rear MIDD^{TN}/CONN./(date).
Approximately 24,000 made. Dated from 1846 through 1850:
6A-040 Values—Very Good **$800** Exc. **$2,750**
US/H. ASTON & CO. marked specimens. Markings at rear identical to above with dates 1851 or 1852. Approximately 6,000 made:
6A-041 Values—Very Good **$900** Exc. **$3,000**
Naval marked specimens. Identical to above, but with naval anchor marks or other naval inspector markings usually found on top of barrel at breech:
6A-042 Values—Very Good **$2,250** Exc. **$5,500**
US/I. N. JOHNSON marked specimens. Marked vertically at rear MIDD^{TN}/CONN./(date). Johnson had been a partner of H. Aston & Co., but left to set up his own production facility. Total quantity made 10,000. Dated 1853, 1854 or 1855:
6A-043 Values—Very Good **$800** Exc. **$2,750**
PALMETTO ARMORYmarked specimens made solely for use by South Carolina militia. Quantity 1,000. Marked ahead of hammer in completely circular design PALMETTO ARMORY.S★ C. Stamped within the center of the circle a design of a palmetto tree. Marked vertically at rear COLUMBIA/S. C. 1852. Marked at breech of barrel V/P above palmetto tree motif; marked on side

of breech WM. GLAZE & CO.Tang of barrel dated 1853 and also marked S. C.

The Palmetto Armory was formed by William Glaze and Benjamin Flagg, the latter a former superintendent of the Asa Waters factory at Milbury, Massachusetts.

A well researched and documented study "The origin of the Palmetto Pistols" by L.F. Southard in issue No. 5, 2000 of "*Man At Arms*," submits strong evidence that Wm. Glaze did not manufacture the Palmetto M.1842 pistol (and by inference the M. 1841 Rifle or M.1842 Musket; 9A-295). With no background in arms mfg. (his primary occupation a jeweler, dealer in military goods and clock repairer) and possibly having strong political links, it appears he was awarded the pistol contract. Documents and physical evidence on the pistols give support to Southard's theory that Glaze acquired over-run and condemned parts from northern contractors Aston and Johnson. His machinery may only have been sufficient to finish and assemble components as well as convert flintlock arms. The most compelling evidence was Glaze's inability at outbreak of Civil War to gain consideration for a contract. Hardly likely at such a critical moment, given the great demand for weapons. A close reading of J.A. Meyer's "*Wm. Glaze & the Palmetto Armory*" (*see Biblio. Chap. X*) lends credibility to the theory. The subject is likely to receive more intensive study. Firearms of the Palmetto Armory continue to be important, rare and eagerly sought.

CAUTION: **A much sought after Southern made, pre-Civil War pistol, considered a Confederate handgun. A rash of spurious examples, made from standard 1842s which had their Northern markings removed and replaced with false Palmetto**

6A-040

marks, found their way to the collectors' market in the late 1950s. The collector is urged to exercise great care when acquiring a specimen. Consult *Confederate Handguns* (see *Bibliography, Chapter X*) for details and illustrations of the fine points:

6A-044   Values—Good **$3,000**   Fine **$8,000**

EXPERIMENTAL SPRINGFIELD ARSENAL-MADE MODEL 1842 PISTOLS WITH SELF-PRIMING SYSTEMS

On occasion the collector is afforded the opportunity to acquire an Experimental, Trial or Pattern firearm. Such pieces are decidedly known and are to be seen in catalogs of private collections and various museum collections. Exemplifying those types are the three examples illustrated here.

Maynard Patent Self-Priming Single Shot Model 1842 Type Pistol

Maynard Patent Self-Priming Single Shot Model 1842 Type Pistol. About identical to the standard production Model 1842 pistol; not merely a composite of altered or assembled parts. A distinct variant model, displaying many unique features. Lock fastened with one screw entering on left side on its forward section; second screw at the rear of the lock entering on right side. Unique shaped lock boldly marked behind hammer (vertically) **SPRING/FIELD/1845** over an eagle and "**US.**" Hinged door ahead of hammer reveals the magazine for inserting the roll of detonating tape primers; door marked **EDWARD MAYNARD/PATENTEE**. 1845 was the year Maynard was given arsenal trials of his automatic capping system and same year awarded contracts for a few thousand alterations of muskets only. The contract specifically mentioned that U.S. gov't was given right to Maynard improvements in the percussion lock "...[for] a number of muskets or *other small arms.*" Other arsenal markings may or

6A-044.5

may not appear on such guns to indicate they were a "Model." It is known that a few of these were made at the time. Values, depending on condition from the low-five to mid-five figures.
6A-044.5

Variant Maynard Patent Self-Priming Model 1842 Type Pistol

6A-044.6

Variant Maynard Patent Self-Priming Model 1842 Type Pistol. Similar to the preceding "Trial" or "Prototype" Model 1842 (6A-044.5) with prominent differences in lock shape and primer system. **SPRINGFIELD** marking similar with date **1846**. Lock fastened in same manner. Noticeable absence of the **MAYNARD** markings. Value range same as foregoing.
6A-044.6

Rupertus Automatic Priming System Conversion of Model 1842 Pistol

Rupertus Automatic Priming System Conversion of Model 1842 Pistol. Jacob Rupertus, Philadelphia patent no. 25-142 of August 16, 1849 Automatic Priming System Conversion of U.S. Model 1842 Pistol. Less than 100 believed produced with work accomplished circa late 1859 or very early 1860s. Rare.

A rotating drum was installed in place of the usual bolster and nipple at the breech of the barrel. The drum was operated by an arm attached to the tumbler of the lock. Top edge of lock plate was enlarged to accommodate a loading tube which carried the globular priming pellets which were fed into the rotating drum. When the hammer cocked, the drum rotated to the rear to receive pellet from the priming tube. Upon pulling the trigger, the drum rotated quickly to its upright position allowing pellet to be struck by the hammer and ignite the full charge. The system was given various trials, but not found suitable for

adoption, Rare. Value range is similar to that of the foregoing.
6A-044.7

6A-044.7

Model 1842 Percussion Navy Pistol

Model 1842 Percussion Navy Pistol (a.k.a. Model 1843 or Navy Box Lock Model 1843). By N. P. Ames, Springfield, Massachusetts and Henry Deringer, Philadelphia. Manufactured c. 1842-1847. Estimated total quantity of 2,000 and 1,200 respectively.

54 caliber, smoothbore. Round barrel, 6" long. No rear sight, small brass post or blade front sight found on a few standard production.

Swivel type steel ramrod with button shaped head. All mountings of brass. The single barrel band secured by a pin. Trigger guard and trigger plate are integral. No backstrap present; the butt cap is flat, round, and inset into the butt. A distinctive feature is the boxlock action. The barrel is browned with all other metal parts finished bright.

Lockplate markings noted below. Proof stampings on the breech of the barrel, e.g., USN/RP/P/(date). Inspector's markings present on the left side of the stock, on the stock flat.

The Model 1842 has the distinction of being the first U.S. martial percussion pistol produced and delivered under contract to the government. Interestingly, Ames made delivery of 300 pistols before the contract itself had been officially signed.

Early production of 300 pistols having raised lockplate with beveled edge on front; high rounded shape at rear terminating in a point. Lock marked: N. P. AMES/SPRINGFIELD/MASS, in center; U.S.N./1842, stamped vertically, at rear. Barrels marked US/P, on breech. Grip of slender dimension, a bit longer than later production, as is trigger guard strap:

6A-045   Values—Good **$3,250**   Fine **$8,000**

Standard model production; lockplate flat, fitted flush to stock. Marked centrally on lock: N. P. AMES/SPRINGFIELD/MASS. Stamped vertically, at rear USN/(1843, 1844 or 1845):

6A-046   Values—Good **$700**   Fine **$2,000**

Revenue Service model; AMES markings as above, but marked at rear of lockplate, vertically: U.S.R., over date 1843 indicating purchase by U.S. Revenue Cutter Service, forerunner of the modern day Coast Guard. Very rare: Exercise caution; examine marks closely; "U.S.N." known altered to "U.S.R." mostly on poor condition specimens to enhance value:

6A-047   Values—Good **$2,750**   Fine **$6,500**

Standard model, manufactured by Henry Deringer. Of an estimated total of about 1,200 pieces by this maker only 300 were believed accepted by the Navy. Basic marking variations are: DERINGER/PHILADEL^ in center of lock, often with US above. Barrels either devoid of markings, or with DERINGER/PHILADELA near breech and often with inspector markings RP at breech. Found with or without front and rear sights:

6A-048   Values—Good **$850**   Fine **$3,000**

Standard model, as above; with Deringer markings, but with USN-1847 vertically marked at rear of lockplate and P near breech. Quite rare:

6A-049   Values—Good **$1,000**   Fine **$3,500**

Standard model; with Deringer markings as noted above (with U.S.), but with very deep seven-groove rifled barrels. Believed less than 200 produced. Of historic significance as being the first handgun manufactured for the U.S. government with rifled barrels:

6A-050   Values—Good **$1,400**   Fine **$4,500**

6A-045
Early Production
Model 1842 Navy

6A-046
Standard Model
1842 Navy

Model 1855 Percussion Pistol-Carbine

Model 1855 Percussion Pistol-Carbine. Made by Springfield Armory c. 1855-1857. Total quantity manufactured 4,021.

58 caliber, rifled bore. 12" round barrel with faceted breech. Two-leaf rear sight graduated to 400 yards attached to tang; iron blade type front sight on wide base. Overall length of pistol 17-3/4"; overall length with stock attached 28-1/4".

Swivel type steel ramrod; button tip concave to accept minie type bullet. All mountings brass. Single barrel band secured by long, narrow spring. Sling swivels attached to barrel band and toe of attachable buttstock; lanyard ring mounted on butt cap. Trigger guard attached to trigger plate by two spanner nuts. Lock is fitted with Maynard self priming device; clean-out screw in the nipple bolster. All metal parts finished bright.

Pistols numbered on butt cap and attachable stocks numbered on underside of the wide brass yoke. These numbers, seen only in range of 1 through 20, believed to be assembly (batch) numbers. There is every likelihood that they

were assembled and had their stocks fitted (to verify that catches properly fitted guns) in groups of 20, then sent to military storekeeper for inventory and perhaps even issued, with matching numbers. No records exist verifying this. The guns are rarely encountered with matched numbers and this feature does not affect value. Important that condition of attachable stock generally matches that of gun.

Lockplate marking ahead of hammer: U.S./SPRINGFIELD; dated at rear 1855 or 1856 (earlier date brings small premium); hinged door of the Maynard primer unit marked with eagle/ shield motif. Breech of barrel marked with V and P proofs over eaglehead motif. Date on tang usually matches that on lockplate. Butt-plate of attachable stock marked U.S. on heel. Considerable care should be exercised in purchase of attachable (often termed detachable) shoulder stock as a great many modern, very well made, spurious specimens exist.

6A-051 and 6A-052

A novel design, the Model 1855 Pistol-Carbine was intended for use on horseback as a pistol and when on foot as a carbine. Field use soon demonstrated that the type was not completely satisfactory, and competition from Colt revolvers helped to hasten obsolescence. Inspired by the Model 1855 design, Colt brought out variations of shoulder stocked pistols, some of which were bought for cavalry issue. The Springfield Pistol-Carbine is one of most popular of U.S. martial firearms with collectors, and shares with Model 1817 Flintlock Pistol and Model 1911 Automatic distinction of being the only handguns made in quantity by Springfield Armory. Prices shown below are for parts individually as they are occasionally found and/or sold. Small added premium is often added for pistol and stock together. Many issued to 1st & 2nd U.S. Cavalry in west: Pistol only without attachable stock:

6A-051   Values—Good **$1,750**   Fine **$6,500**
Shoulder stock only:
6A-052   Values—Good **$1,750**   Fine **$6,500**

U.S. Navy Model 1861 Percussion Signal Pistol

U.S. Navy Model 1861 Percussion Signal Pistol. Manufactured at the U.S. Navy Yard, Washington, D. C. Fired a B. T. Coston cylindrical multi-colored flare, ignited by a percussion cap. The Coston flare was not propelled into the air. It burned while affixed to the pistol, which acted as the igniter and receptacle for it. The flares came in a series of 12 color combinations of red, white, green lights. Total quantity made estimated 1,000.

All brass construction. 9-1/2" overall. Usual three-line markings on left side of frame: U.S.N.Y.W. (Navy Yard Washington) or U.S.O.Y.W. (Ordnance Yard Washington) over inspector's initials over the date of manufacture (1861 through the early 1870s). Civil War dated specimens usually bring slightly higher values.

Removable sideplate. Variations noted in quality and markings; unmarked often seen. Also known pre-model development type with snub barrel, conventional trigger; trigger bow. (Extremely rare):

6A-053   Values—Good **$1,000**   Fine **$2,500**

6A-053
Standard Production Type

"Pre-Model Development Type"

U.S. Army 1861 Percussion Signal Pistol

U.S. Army Model 1861 Percussion Signal Pistol. Made by William Marston, New York, c. 1861. Total quantity estimated at 500.

All brass construction and very similar in contour to the Navy model described above with distinctive features which make it easily distinguishable from its Navy counterpart: Two-piece construction (seamed in center) and does not have the removable sideplate of the Navy model, but rather the entire left side removes; absence of hammer screw and the addition of a small retaining bolt just below the nipple; contour changes are also easily detectable.

Markings in three lines are found either on the underside of the frame (most often) or on the left side: U.S. ARMY SIGNAL PISTOL over the initials A.J.M. (for Major Albert J. Myer, the Chief Signal Officer) over the date 1861:

6A-054   Values—Good **$1,100**   Fine **$3,250**

6A-054

U.S. Army 1862 Percussion Signal Pistol

U.S. Army Model 1862 Percussion Signal Pistol. Manufactured by William Marston, New York, c. 1862. Total quantity manufactured estimated at 1,000.

All brass construction with two-piece walnut grips. Short, stubby "barrel" which holds the Coston multi-colored flare (available in numerous color combinations). Butt markings: A.J.M./U.S./ARMY SIGNAL PISTOL/1862:

6A-055

6A-055   Values—Good **$1,000**   Fine **$2,500**

Model 1869 Breech-Loading Pistol

Model 1869 Breech-Loading Pistol. Made at Springfield Armory, 1869. Total quantity less than 50. An experimental/trial gun; terminology "Model 1869" later applied for collector/researcher convenience.

Following the Civil War the Ordnance Board sought to develop for cavalry use, in the then ensuing Indian War, a large caliber, long cartridge for multi-ball loads. The Armory was directed to fabricate a pistol to use the .50-45-350 cadet cartridge.

6A-055.5

Field tested by the Cavalry with negative results, further development ceased.

The Armory utilized the receiver and breech block of the Model 1868 rifle; only the forward section (receiver ring) was altered by thinning down to lighten and marked on top DEC/1869. The breech block has standard rifle markings (*q.v.*) as does the standard Model 1863 Springfield musket lock. 9" unmarked barrel is chambered in the .50-70 c.f. Front sight blade. Rear sight a "V" groove cut in top of breechblock hinge.

An unaltered M.1868 rifle stock also utilized. The band spring on underside is forward of the iron rifle band. *Rarely mentioned* is fact that stock made in two parts; handle is separately affixed with no attempt made to match direction of the wood grain. Brass buttcap and backstrap.

Massive 18-1/4" overall; weight 4-1/2 pounds. Very rare. Extreme caution recommended on acquiring this model. A few authentic receiver units have shown up over the years (less barrels) undoubtedly tempting for the gun faker, and not a few clumsy and crude copies of this little known handgun have found their way to the collectors' market.

6A-055.5   Values—Very Good **$14,000**   Exc. **$30,000**

U.S. Navy Model 1882 (Very) Signal Pistol

U.S. Navy Model 1882 (Very) Signal Pistol. Manufactured at the U.S. Navy Yard, Washington, c. 1882 to 1884. Total estimated quantity approximately 100.

All brass construction. 7-1/4" overall; two-piece walnut grips; lanyard swivel at butt. Accepts a 4 gauge centerfire multi-color signal flare. Markings are found on the right forward side of the frame in three-lines: ORD. Dep. U.S.N.Y./1884/(inspector marks).

This most unusual firearm is often called a "Double Ender" or "Double Header," and is occasionally found included in arms-curiosa or oddity collections. The brass barrel which swivels a complete 360 degree circle is fastened on the underside in its exact center. A flare cartridge may be inserted in either the breech or the muzzle end of the barrel and loading of a second flare extracts the used flare:

6A-056

6A-056   Values—Good **$950**   Fine **$2,750**

U.S. Navy Model 1894 (Very) Signal Pistol

U.S. Navy Model 1894 (Very) Signal Pistol. Modifications performed at the U.S. Navy Yard, Washington, c. 1894. Invented 1877 by Lieut. Edward S. Very, U.S.N., the flare proved a major innovation in the use of flares for signals. His system allowed the flare to be propelled and ignite high in the air and thus be visible at great distance. It is still in use by most countries.

Basically this is the Model 1882 signal pistol modified by inserting a 9" round steel barrel (chambered for 10 gauge) inside the usual brass barrel and the addition of an extractor device at the right side of breech. Marked on right forward frame: MFD.

6A-057

ORD. Dep. W.N.Y. 1894 T.F.J. Equip Dep. A.D:

6A-057   Values—Good **$850**   Fine **$1,500**

U.S. Navy Model 1896 (Very) Signal Pistol

6A-058

U.S. Navy Model 1896 (Very) Signal Pistol, a.k.a. Mark I. Manufactured at the U.S. Navy Yard, Washington, D.C. c. 1896 to 1900. Total quantity estimated under 500.

Brass frame with spur trigger. 9" round, blued, iron barrel tips downward to load. Ten gauge. Two-piece walnut grips.

Marked on the right forward frame ORD. DEP. W.N.Y. 1898 with naval anchor and inspector initials E.C.P. Left frame marked EQUIP. DEP. MODEL 96and serial number. Variations in markings and dates likely.

The forerunner/prototype of the commonly encountered Remington Signal Pistol (*see Number 5E-065*) and closely similar. Most noticeable difference in contour on forward frame which is straight/unfluted. Very scarce.

Specimens undated or dated 1898 or earlier considered "antiques" and not subject to G.C.A. provisions; those dated 1899 or later are subject to provisions of the Gun Control Act as "curios or relics":

6A-058   Values—Good **$650**   Fine **$1,150**

U.S. Navy Mark II (Very) Signal Pistol

U.S. Navy Mark II (Very) Signal Pistol. Made at the New York Navy Yard. Period of manufacture believed early 1900s/pre-WWI. Quantity unknown; limited.

Very similar to the above Model 1896, but has fluted or "pinched" section on extreme forward frame; about identical to the Remington Mark III Pistol (*see 5E-065*).

Marked on left forward frame NAVY YARD, N.Y. Marked on barrel MARK II.

Reclassified by A.T.& F. from National Firearms Act and now subject to provisions of the Gun Control Act as a modern firearm

6A-059

as "curios or relics":
6A-059   Values—Good **$475**   Fine **$850**

U.S. Navy Mark III Signal Pistol   *See Chapter V-E, Remington Arms, Item 5E-065.*

Remington Rolling Block Single Shot Martial Pistols Models 1865, 1867, and 1871
See Chapter V-E, Remington Arms.

U.S. Arsenal-Made Powder Tester ("Eprouvette")

U.S. arsenal-made Powder Tester ("Eprouvette"). This arsenal-made apparatus is closely allied to firearms production and although not firing a projectile...is certainly an explosive device! Included here to illustrate various unusual types of allied items the collector may encounter (among which are numerous powder testers of various shapes, fashioned in the style of handguns). Powder testers were made to test the strength of a small portion (of a larger quantity) of blackpowder. This example represents the basic quadrant shape in which the force of the detonation compresses the large "V"-spring. The short "snub-nose" barrel at the bottom was filled with a small, measured amount of blackpowder; a lesser amount added to the external flash pan in front. It was then ignited with a heated coal, wire, slow-burning match or fuse. This example of iron with the arched brass graduated scale along the bottom is well marked in center (above the scale) SPRING/FIELD/1820/US. A rarity (that might also be classified "arms curiosa") for its U.S. government manufacture. Value likely in low to mid-four figures.
6A-059.5

6A-059.5

VI-B: SECONDARY TYPES

(See also New England Type Flintlock Pistols Chapter XII)

A Word About 1807-1808 Contract Pistols and an Insight to Contracts

Now clearly recognized as "Primary" arms, extensive research by James Wertenberger (A.S.A.C. Bulletin, Fall, 1990) revealed a fascinating insight to the contracts, the manufacture and the reasons for variations of these pistols (and by inference, what may have occurred with other contract arms.) Archives reveal that substantial contracts were given various makers for *STOCKS ONLY* for 1807-8 pistols and such stocks were then supplied by government to various pistol contractors (also to 1797 McCormick type; in 1814 to Tryon and some to S. North.) To date, records indicate quantities limited, but also show makers used more than single source for mountings and locks (as well as common sources), accounting for many variances …and why collecting is not an exact science!

More About Non-Contract, Large Holster-Size, Private Purchase Flintlock Pistols

There are quite a few large flintlock" holster" or "horse" pistols not known to have been purchased under government or state contract. Yet, because of their size and general appearance they have traditionally been considered "Secondary Martial Handguns" and most often found included in American military firearms collections. There are no hard and fast rules or guidelines. Many examples of those generic types are illustrated and described in this "Secondary" section, along with those termed "1807-1808 Contract" types. Privately purchased by militia officers (and others) they have always been popular with American military arms collectors. Although specific dimensions and markings are listed in the following descriptions, they are not necessarily identical on all similar pistols by those same makers. Many near-identical types may have been custom-ordered by the militia officer or had some custom feature (such as caliber or barrel length) that might differ...while others were imported from England by American gunmakers or merchants who often marked their name on the gun after acquiring it or, as has also been recorded, may merely have imported parts (i.e. loose barrels, possibly even loose mountings) which they then stocked here, in America. In recent years a few published works have added immeasurably to information about these non-contract secondary types, notably *Martial Single Shot Pistols* (Hartzler & Whisker, 1997); *Historic Pistols; The American Martial Flintlock 1760-1845* (Smith & Bitter, 1985); *U.S. Martial Flintlocks* (Reilly, 1986) (see Biblio).

Angstadt Contract Flintlock Pistol

Adam and Jacob Angstadt of Kutztown, Berks County, Pennsylvania, 1807-1808, Contract Flintlock Pistol. (Not illus.) Quantity unknown; very limited. (Maker's name often spelled Anstat, Ansted, Angsted or Anstead.)

54 caliber. 8-5/8" part round/part octagonal barrel; smoothbore. Hickory ramrod. Brass mountings. Gooseneck hammer. Full curly maple stock.

Barrel marks: ANSTED or ANSTAT; believed Anglicized versions of well known Angstadt name.

Extremely rare. Well known and regarded as Kentucky rifle makers.

The above described is the most often listed specimen of an Angstadt pistol and does not conform to the usual 1807-08. They are known to have delivered 103 pistols in 1810 that were accepted by the U.S. and a lot of 105 pistols without their name marked on them was mentioned as "unfit for service" c. 1810-1811. Although the above described gun is almost classic as a "Kentucky Pistol," it is quite probable that this gun is not the 1807-1808 contract pistol (as listed in prior works). It may be reasonably assumed that Angstadt made pistols which more closely conformed to the more classic 1807-1808 contract type and that marked specimens would be extreme rarities and worth considerably in excess of the value estimated here:

6B-001   Values—Good **$4,500**   Fine **$15,000**

As above; converted to percussion:
6B-002   Values—Good **$3,250**   Fine **$7,000**

C. Bird & Co. Flintlock Pistols

C. Bird & Co., Philadelphia, Flintlock Pistols; various types. (Not illus.) C. 1810-1820s.

Lockplate marking: C. BIRD & CO./PHILAD^A/WARRANTED. Barrels sometimes inscribed PHILADELPHIA. Gooseneck hammer; sporting type lock.

No known government contracts by this maker. Various types of Kentucky type pistols as well as martial style large holster pistols have been seen bearing markings similar to above. No definite pattern has been encountered. It is reasonably felt that the BIRD & CO. markings merely indicate the lock maker's (or agent's) name and that the guns are the product of various Pennsylvania makers. Values vary depending on size, quality of workmanship, type of wood (curly maple usually brings more). Should definite proof of government purchase or ownership be established, values would increase considerably over the ranges indicated below:

6B-003   Values—Good **$1,250**   Fine **$3,000**

As above; converted to percussion:
6B-004   Values—Good **$650**   Fine **$1,250**

William Booth Flintlock Pistol

William Booth, Philadelphia, Flintlock Pistol. (Not illus.) Made c. 1810-1820. Quantity unknown; very limited. No known government contract.

58 caliber. Approximately 8" round smoothbore all brass barrel. Full pin-fastened walnut stock with plain, uncapped butt. Although not illustrated, it is almost identical to that shown for

"Unmarked Secondary Martial Pistols" (q.v., figure A).

Sporting type lock marked ahead of hammer BOOTH; gooseneck hammer. Barrel marked PHILADELPHIA. Booth was listed as a Philadelphia maker c. 1798 to 1816:

| 6B-005 | Values—Good **$1,500** | Fine **$3,500** |

As above; converted to percussion:

| 6B-006 | Values—Good **$800** | Fine **$1,750** |

Bridgewater Flintlock Light Dragoon Pistol

Flintlock pistol styled identically to the 1807-1808 contract type. Believed made by James, Luke and Rufus Perkins, gunsmiths of Bridgewater, Massachusetts circa 1799-1812 (see also their flintlock muskets 9B-003). Quantity unknown; very limited.

6B-006.5

66 caliber with 8 3/4-inch round, smoothbore barrel. Full length, pin-fastened walnut stock with single ramrod pipe; gooseneck hammer. Brass mountings with long recurved brass sideplate. 15 inches overall.

Lockplate markings: **BRIDGWATER** at rear of lockplate in a vertical curve (specifically note: no "**E**" in spelling of Bridgewater) and an eagle (wings downward) over small "**US**" in oval panel, center of lock ahead of hammer. Barrel marked only with large numeral and letters "**21st L.Ds.**" believed to indicate a New England Militia "Light Dragoon" unit (numbers too high for a Federal unit). Other unit markings likely encountered.

| 6B-006.5 | Values—Good **$4,500** | Fine **$10,000** |

As above; converted to percussion:

| 6B-006.6 | Values—Good **$2,000** | Fine **$4,500** |

William Calderwood Contract Flintlock Pistol

William Calderwood of Philadelphia, 1807-1808 Contract Flintlock Pistol. Quantity unknown; very limited. Known contract for 60 pairs April, 1808. All 120 delivered

54 caliber. 10" round barrel; smoothbore.

Full length, pin-fastened walnut stock with two ramrod pipes. Brass mountings; double neck hammer (although gooseneck hammer is reported); wooden ramrod.

Lockplate marking ahead of hammer: CALDERWOOD/PHILA at rear marked vertically US over year of manufacture (1808 observed). Eaglehead and P proofmark at breech:

| 6B-007 | Values—Good **$11,000** | Fine **$27,500** |

6B-007

As above; converted to percussion:

| 6B-008 | Values—Good **$5,000** | Fine **$14,000** |

T. P. Cherington Flintlock Pistol

T. P. Cherington of Catawissa, Pennsylvania, Flintlock Pistol. (Not illus.) Made c. 1790s to 1815. No known government contracts. Quantities unknown.

This arm has been traditionally shown in many reference works on American martial pistols. Very likely it was merely one-of-a-kind and does not represent an example of any quantity manufactured piece. It is representative of a general style of American flintlock pistol that may be just as easily classified as a

"Kentucky Pistol."

The type shown for this maker, a large piece, with 12" smoothbore octagonal barrel, approximately 45 caliber. Brass mountings with iron trigger guard; gooseneck hammer; full length walnut stock with uncapped rudimentary bird's head style butt. Marked on barrel and lockplate T. P. CHERINGTON:

| 6B-009 | Values—Good **$2,000** | Fine **$4,500** |

As above; converted to percussion:

| 6B-010 | Values—Good **$1,000** | Fine **$2,500** |

Richard Constable Flintlock Pistol

Richard Constable, Philadelphia, Flintlock Pistol c. 1817-1830. (Not illus.) Quantity unknown.

Approximately 50 caliber. 10" round smoothbore barrel. Full length walnut stock pin-fastened; brass mountings; sporting type lock with gooseneck hammer. Wood ramrod.

Lockplate marking: R. CONSTABLE. Top of barrel PHILADELPHIA and having British proofs at breech.

Constable and other American makers often used imported

parts (mostly barrels from England). An example of a general type secondary martial pistol of large proportion in reasonably extensive use during the era. The name Constable is also well known in the manufacture of single shot pistols in the percussion period:

| 6B-011 | Values—Good **$1,400** | Fine **$3,250** |

As above; converted to percussion:

| 6B-012 | Values—Good **$800** | Fine **$1,500** |

Jacob Cooke Contract Flintlock Pistol

Jacob Cooke, Lancaster County, Penna. 1807-1808 Contract flintlock pistols. Contract for 100, 1808; records show 66 delivered, 1810.

54 caliber. 10" barrel marked on top J. COOKE with eagle and

P proof. Lock marked at rear US and SCHWEITZER (lockmaker) in center. (not illus) similar other 1807-8 types:

| 6B-012.5 | Values—Good **$14,000** | Fine **$35,000** |

Samuel Coutty Flintlock Pistol

Samuel Coutty, Philadelphia, Flintlock Pistol. Made c. 1781 to 1790s. Quantity unknown; very limited.

58 caliber. Brass or iron round or octagon smoothbore barrel approximately 7-3/4".

Full length walnut stock, pin-fastened (contours vary); brass mountings; gooseneck hammer; wooden ramrod.

Lock marking: **COUTTY** in script. Top of barrel marked **PHILADELPHIA** in script. Breech of barrel with proofmarks, PV and V.

No known contracts by this maker. The type is representative of those privately purchased by officers and in use during the last quarter of the 18th century. Listed as a private maker in the closing years of the Revolution and known to have made pistols for private sale as well as working as a repairman for the

6B-013

Commonwealth of Pennsylvania up to the 1790s:
6B-013   Values—Good **$3,750**   Fine **$9,000**
As above; converted to percussion:
6B-014   Values—Good **$2,250**   Fine **$4,000**

Henry Deringer Contract Flintlock Pistol

Henry Deringer, Philadelphia, c.1813 Contract Flintlock Pistol. Quantity unknown; very limited. At least 56. No actual contract information located.

54 caliber. 10" round iron barrel; smoothbore.

6B-015

Full, pin-fastened, walnut stock. Brass mountings. Wooden ramrod. Reinforced type double neck hammer. Flat, beveled edge lock with decided projecting teat at rear.

Lock marking ahead of hammer: H. DERINGER/PHIL^A (also marked only H. DERINGER). Breech of barrel with proofmark P enclosed in oval cartouche; others unmarked.

Variously reported as 1807-8 Contract, more likely State of Maryland contract. The product of Henry Deringer, who also created the famed percussion pocket pistol. This model usually found with two ramrod pipes, although variations are encountered. Handle contour and configuration changes are also evidenced due to hand workmanship:
6B-015   Values—Good **$5,500**   Fine **$15,000**
As above; converted to percussion:
6B-016   Values—Good **$3,000**   Fine **$6,500**

Ezra Dodge Flintlock Pistol

Ezra Dodge, New London, Connecticut (1766-1798) Flintlock Pistol circa 1780-1790. Quantity unknown; very limited; rare.

Large, solidly constructed holster pistol; 12-1/2" overall. Thick walled 7" octagon brass barrel; caliber 44. Matching brass lock plate with integral brass flashpan marked in deep sunken hallmark in center "DODGE" with small sunburst design each end. Pin fastened full walnut stock; plain brass trigger guard and butt cap; serpentine shaped, military style sideplate.

One other similar "DODGE" pistol with brass barrel and lock is known. Primarily a silver and goldsmith as well as a watch and clockmaker, Dodge's obituary, August, 1798, also described him as a "brass founder, gunsmith, locksmith, grocer (and) an

6B-016.5

ingenious mechanic."
6B-016.5   Values—Good **$5,500**   Fine **$10,000**

Drepert Marked 1807-1808 Contract Flintlock Pistol   *See John Guest.*

O. & E. Evans Contract Type Flintlock Pistol

Owen & Edward Evans, Evansburg, Pennsylvania, Contract Type Flintlock Pistol. Made c. War of 1812. Total quantity unknown; very limited. Copied very closely after the French Model An. XIII Flintlock Dragoon Pistol of c. 1804-1805.

69 caliber. 8-7/8" round smoothbore barrel.

Walnut half stock fastened with wide brass barrel band retained by narrow spring. All brass mountings with brass flashpan. Double necked reinforced type hammer. Iron ramrod with button tip.

6B-017

Lock marked ahead of hammer EVANS. Barrel marked at breech with P proofmark; also seen marked on underside PM and dated 1814.

O. and E. Evans made flintlock muskets under U.S. government contracts of 1798 and 1808 (q.v.). Very little is known about these pistols and few specimens have been observed.

Extreme caution is urged on the acquisition of this Evans pistol as not a few standard French Dragoon pistols have been reworked to resemble them:

6B-017   Values—Good **$6,500**   Fine **$17,500**

As above; converted to percussion:

6B-018   Values—Good **$3,500**   Fine **$7,500**

Thomas French Contract Type Flintlock Pistol

Thomas French, Canton, Massachusetts, Contract Type Flintlock Pistol. Very possibly made under Massachusetts State contract; War of 1812 period. Quantities unknown; very limited.

64 caliber. 10-5/8" round barrel; smoothbore.

Full pin-fastened walnut stock; brass mounting; gooseneck hammer; wooden ramrod. Flat, beveled edge lock with decided projecting teat at rear. Iron flashpan.

Lock marked ahead of hammer with eagle motif over oval panel U.S. over T. FRENCH. Stamped vertically at rear CANTON. Breech of barrel marked P.M. and P.C., the latter within a rectangular cartouche; also accompanied by year of manufacture, usually 1814. These marks are classic type encountered on Massachusetts contract pieces of the era.

Specimens are known without lockplate markings and will bring proportionately less.

Another distinct variant T. French manufactured piece is known (see illustration) with 10" round barrel having eagle over P proof in oval cartouche. Lock marked identically to above without the CANTON marking at rear. Believed made for naval use as specimens observed are fitted with belt hook. Note the close resemblance of this type to the McCormick pistol (q.v.) in both furniture and overall configuration:

6B-019   Values—Good **$11,000**   Fine **$30,000**

As above; converted to percussion:

6B-020   Values—Good **$5,000**   Fine **$12,500**

6B-019

6B-020

Martin Fry Contract Flintlock Pistol

Martin Fry, York, Pennsylvania, 1807-1808 Contract Flintlock Pistol. (Not illus.) Total quantities unknown. At least 58 pair known to have been contracted for of which most were rejected by government inspectors for poor workmanship.

About identical in contours and appearance to other known 1807-1808 Contract pistols listed in this section.

58 caliber. 10" round iron barrel; smoothbore.

Full pin-fastened walnut stock; brass mountings; wooden ramrod; reinforced type double neck hammer.

Lockplate marking vertically at rear M FRY/U S. Barrel marked US at breech with eaglehead and P proof in oval cartouche.

With less than a handful of known specimens, these are among the most rare of American military handguns. Although

6B-021

the maker's name is quite often spelled Frye in correspondence, it is quite interesting to note that the markings are quite definitely Fry on the guns themselves:

6B-021   Values—Good **$12,500**   Fine **$32,500**

As above; converted to percussion:

6B-022   Values—Good **$6,500**   Fine **$15,000**

T. Grubb Flintlock Pistol

T. Grubb, Philadelphia, Flintlock Pistol. (Not illus.) Made c. 1820-1830s. Quantity unknown. No known government contracts. A piece that is listed in other well known reference works and is merely representative of the general style and type of this manufacturer of which probably no two were alike. The gun may be just as easily classified as a "Kentucky Pistol."

Approximately 44 caliber; round or part round/part octagonal smoothbore barrel of brass; varying lengths 8-3/4" to 10". Full length walnut stock with horn tipped forend; silver or brass mounted; wooden ramrod; gooseneck hammer.

Barrel marking: T. GRUBB.

An arm that would be considered among the better made and more elegant of secondary U.S. martial flintlock pistols. Owners of these pieces were probably prominent officers, sea captains or men of wealth. Silver mounted specimens are worth premium values:

6B-023   Values—Good **$3,000**   Fine **$5,500**

As above; converted to percussion:

6B-024   Values—Good **$1,250**   Fine **$3,000**

John Guest Contract Flintlock Pistol

John Guest, Lancaster, Pennsylvania, 1807-1808 Contract Flintlock Pistol. Quantities unknown; very limited. Known to have contracted for (with Henry and Brong evidently as partners) 400 pairs of pistols in 1808; not fulfilled.

54 caliber. 10-1/4" round iron barrel; smoothbore.

Full pin-fastened walnut stock; brass mountings; wooden ramrod; reinforced type double neck hammer.

Lockplate marking: DREPERT forward of hammer; marked at rear U.S. Barrel marked in large script *I. GUEST* and at breech with eaglehead over P in oval cartouche.

From existing documents it appears that Guest was the main contractor with Drepert (a.k.a. Drepperd) of Lancaster, Pennsylvania, merely supplying the locks under sub-contract.

6B-025

See also "Sweitzer" Contract 1807-1808 Pistol which very likely was made by Guest:

6B-025	Values—Good **$12,500**		Fine **$32,500**

As above; converted to percussion:

6B-026	Values—Good **$6,500**		Fine **$15,000**

Halbach & Sons Flintlock Holster Pistols

Halbach & Sons, Baltimore, Maryland, Flintlock Holster Pistols. Made c. 1785 to early 1800s. Total quantity unknown; limited. No known military contracts.

Numerous variations by this maker are encountered. His distinctive trademark found on all his pistols is the unique and handsome, large brass butt cap which bears a massive spread winged American eagle (of very archaic, almost primitive appearance) executed in high relief and surrounded with a cluster of 13 stars.

Calibers vary approximately 50 to 65. Barrels round or part round/part octagon from 6" to 9" in length approximately and are of brass or iron; found with or without cannon turnings at muzzle. Frequently, but not always, barrels are seen bearing profuse Spanish proofmarks indicating they were imported.

Locks usually marked HALBACH or HALBACH & SONS (unmarked specimens bring about 20 percent less); gooseneck hammer.

Full walnut stock, pin-fastened. Another feature seen on almost all Halbachs is the large shell designed carving in relief around the tang of the barrel having a stippled or star-like design stamped into the wood on the raised carved section.

Values shown here are for larger sized specimens with brass barrels. Iron barrels tend to bring about 10 percent less and smallest specimens 10 percent to 20 percent less:

6B-027	Values—Good **$3,000**		Fine **$7,500**

As above; converted to percussion:

6B-028	Values—Good **$1,250**		Fine **$3,500**

6B-027
Iron Barrel

6B-027
Brass Barrel

John H. Hall Breech-Loading Flintlock Pistol

John H. Hall, Yarmouth, Maine, Breech-Loading Flintlock Pistols. C. 1810. Quantity unknown. Extremely rare.

50 caliber. Bronze barrel with bronze breechblock; iron barrel with iron breechblock. Barrel lengths 6" to 7" approximately. Full walnut stocks pin or key fastened.

6B-029
Bronze Barrel

6B-029
Iron Barrel

One of the rarest and most highly desired of all early American flintlock pistols. There are but four known bronze barreled specimens of which only one bears markings **JOHN H. HALL** in script on the barrel. There are two (a matched pair) known iron barreled specimens, each marked JOHN H. HALL/PATENT on the top of the breechblock. These show later features than the bronze specimens and one treatise on the subject speculates that they might have been the product of the Harpers Ferry Armory c. 1820.

Because of their extreme rarity, and the mere handful of known specimens, and the variances in each, only the broadest range of values is given for flintlocks. (See also Chap. 12-009 for additional data):

6B-029   Values—Good **$11,000**   Fine **$37,500**

Joseph Henry Contract Flintlock Pistol

Joseph Henry, Philadelphia, 1807-1808 Contract Flintlock Pistol. Quantities unknown; very limited. Recorded contracts for this maker indicate 150 pairs 1807 and 600 pairs 1808. Quantities delivered not known.

54 caliber. 10" round iron barrel; smoothbore.

Full pin-fastened walnut stock; brass mountings; wood ramrod; reinforced type double neck hammer.

Marked vertically at rear of lock and on top of barrel: J.

6B-030

HENRY/PHIL^A. Marked in center of lock U.S. Breech of barrel bears two oval cartouche proofmarks with eaglehead and P.

Variances have been noted in both markings and contours (of handle especially), but generally J. Henry pistols conform to this description and illustration. The key factors being the presence of U.S. markings or proofs or both.

These are quite clearly the product of Joseph Henry as correspondence concerning these is so addressed:

6B-030   Values—Good **$5,500**   Fine **$15,000**

As above; converted to percussion:

6B-031   Values—Good **$2,500**   Fine **$7,000**

U.S. Navy Contract 1812 Joseph Henry Flintlock Pistol. Same style as above with the addition of a 5 1/2-inch iron belt hook on left side, fastened by the rear lock screw. Lock marked *horizontally* in center "J. HENRY/PHILA." Small, deep stamped oval at breech with relief CT (indicating "contract"). Total of 230 pairs (460 pistols) recorded delivered to the Navy. (102 pairs, 1813; 128 pairs, 1814). Very few known; rare. Worth 50 percent to 100 percent premium.

6B-031.2

Joseph Henry Contract Types Flintlock Pistols

Joseph Henry, Philadelphia, Flintlock Pistols similar to the 1807-1808 contract types. Total quantities unknown; very limited. Strongly believed made for state militia contracts as well as private sale.

54 caliber (62 caliber also reported). 10" round iron barrel; smoothbore.

Full pin-fastened walnut stock; brass mountings; wooden ramrod. Locks with pronounced teat-like projection at rear and two deep vertical flutes; large gooseneck hammer. One or two ramrod pipes.

Numerous variations of markings: J. HENRY or J. HENRY/PHIL^A ahead of hammer; seen with or without PHIL^A vertically at rear of lock. Barrels found with or without Henry markings and also seen with just single P in oval proof.

Variants are also known with plain flat unfluted lock and double neck hammer with knob shaped plain wood uncapped butt:

6B-032   Values—Good **$4,500**   Fine **$10,000**

As above; converted to percussion:

6B-033   Values—Good **$2,000**   Fine **$4,500**

Naval Boarding Pistol Variant. About identical to above. Lock marked only "J.HENRY"; large deep struck "P" proof mark in oval at breech of barrel. Variant quickly recognizable by the long iron belthook on left side of stock, fastened in place by the rear lockscrew. Overall length 16-1/2 inches; brass mounted; single brass ramrod thimble. No U.S. Naval contract known for the pistol. Surmised that a small group were made by J. Henry of Philadelphia during War of 1812 era (a few authentic specimens are known) possibly on order by an American merchant ship's captain (or owner) or privateer. (Exercise caution to determine

6B-032

6B-032

belthook original to period of mfr. and not late addition!) Authentic specimens worth 20 - 30 percent premium.

6B-033.5

John Joseph Henry Flintlock Pistol

John Joseph Henry, Boulton, Pennsylvania, Flintlock Pistol. Made c. 1820s. Quantity unknown; very limited.

58 caliber. 8-3/4" part round/part octagonal barrel; smoothbore.

Full length pin-fastened walnut stock; brass mounted. Sporting style lock with decorative engraving; gooseneck hammer. Wooden ramrod.

Lock marked ahead of hammer: J. J. HENRY/BOULTON.

No known contracts for this type. Style privately sold for militia and/or officer use:

6B-034

6B-034   Values—Good **$2,500**   Fine **$5,500**

As above; converted to percussion:

6B-035   Values—Good **$1,250**   Fine **$2,500**

J. J. Henry 1826 U.S. Type Flintlock Pistol

6B-036

J. J. Henry, Boulton, Pennsylvania, Model 1826 U.S. Type Flintlock Pistol. Made c. 1836. Quantity unknown; limited numbers.

Fashioned very closely after the Simeon North U.S. Navy Model 1826 pistol, the major differences are in the more severe angle of the stock of the Henry, the lack of a belt hook and the markings. No known contracts for this pistol; believed made for militia use. 8-1/2" unmarked barrel.

Marked on lock ahead of hammer: J. J. HENRY/BOULTON:

6B-036   Values—Good **$2,750**   Fine **$5,500**

As above; converted to percussion:

6B-037   Values—Good **$1,000**   Fine **$2,500**

Hodgson Flintlock Pistol

Hodgson & Company, Baltimore, Maryland Flintlock Pistol. Circa 1790s (possibly earlier) to 1800/1802. Quantity unknown; very limited. No known military contracts. Merchants and hardware dealers of Baltimore (after 1800-1802 firm name changed to Hodgson & Thompson).

The handsome, silver-mounted brass barrel pistol typical of a type imported during the late 18th-early 19th century from England by various American dealers (see especially "Halbach & Sons" pistols 6B-027). 14-1/2 inches overall; 9-inch part octagon, part round brass barrel marked in bold script BALTIMORE. Caliber 60. Full walnut stock with checkered handle. Lock with gooseneck hammer bearing similar script makings HODGSON. Profusely engraved silver mounts; pineapple finial on trigger guard; silver hallmarks of Birmingham silversmith and date mark of 1798 clearly indicating the period of manufacture of the gun.

6B-037.5

Values shown here for a brass barrel specimen similar to above with usually encountered brass mounts (silver furniture/mountings worth premium of 20 to 30 percent).

6B-037.5   Values—Good **$3,500**   Fine **$8,000**

As above; converted to percussion:

6B-037.6   Values—Good **$1,450**   Fine **$3,500**

Robert McCormick Contract Flintlock Pistol

Robert McCormick, Philadelphia, Contract Flintlock Pistol. C. 1797-1800. Total quantity unknown; extremely limited.

64 caliber. 10-1/4" round barrel; smoothbore.

6B-038

Full length, pin-fastened, walnut stock with narrow brass band inset near forend tip to prevent splitting. Brass mountings; wooden ramrod with swell tip; large gooseneck hammer.

Lock marked vertically in slight arch at rear: UNITED/STATES. Marked ahead of hammer KETLAND/& C°. Barrel marked at breech with proofmark of eaglehead over P in oval cartouche and U.S. Stock often found stamped on left side McCORMICK.

Considered one of the most rare and desirable of early U.S. flintlock military handguns, the exact date of manufacture or delivery of these arms is unknown. It is possible that they pre-date the Model 1799 North & Cheney, but no conclusive evidence of this. They are believed to be the very limited quantity of "Ship's Pistols" supplied to the Navy by McCormick c. 1797-1800. The locks are obviously imported from England and are very probably part of the lot of 3,000 rifle locks purchased by the U.S. government in 1799 to 1800 (*see Secondary American Military Longarms, Chapter IX, 1792-1807 Contract Flintlock Rifles*):

6B-038	Values—Good **$16,000**		Fine **$40,000**
As above; converted to percussion:			
6B-039	Values—Good **$8,500**		Fine **$17,500**

McKim & Brother Flintlock Pistol

McKim & Brother, Baltimore, Maryland, Flintlock Pistol. (Not illus.) Made c. 1810-1830s. Quantity unknown; very limited. Very similar to the J. J. Henry, Boulton militia pistol (*q.v.*), but with plain wood knob shaped butt without butt cap.

No known government contracts for this type. It has been traditionally listed in other classic works on martial handguns, but represents merely a general type only by this maker whose every product undoubtedly differed.

54 to 60 caliber. Approximately 10" part round/part fluted barrel; smoothbore.

Full pin-fastened walnut stock; brass mounted; wooden ramrod; gooseneck hammer with sporting style lock.

Lockplate marked ahead of hammer: McKIM BROTHERS/BALTIMORE or McKIM &/BROTHER/BALTIMORE or Mc K BROS./BALTIMORE:

6B-040	Values—Good **$1,500**		Fine **$3,250**
As above; converted to percussion:			
6B-041	Values—Good **$750**		Fine **$1,500**

Meacham & Pond Flintlock Pistol (*formerly 6B-042 & 6B-043*) see: Tryon 6B-056

John Miles Large Military Type Flintlock Pistol

John Miles, Philadelphia, Large Military Type Flintlock Pistol. C. 1800-1810. Quantities unknown; very limited.

No known U.S. contracts for this maker, but Miles supplied 250 pairs of flintlock pistols to the State of Virginia under contract c. 1800-1801. It is very possible that these are the Virginia contract pieces. Their decided military appearance and the historical background of Miles and his early period combine to make this a highly desirable collectors' item.

58 to 62 caliber. 10" round barrel; smoothbore.

Full pin-fastened walnut stock with wide brass band inset near forend tip to prevent splitting. Reinforced type double neck hammer; brass mountings; wooden ramrod.

Lock marked ahead of hammer in an oval-like design: MILES (in downward arch) over PHIL^A (in upward arch). Barrels found with or without markings MILES PHILAD^A:

6B-044

6B-044	Values—Good **$12,500**		Fine **$35,000**
As above; converted to percussion:			
6B-045	Values—Good **$7,000**		Fine **$15,000**

John Miles—Various Flintlock Pistols

John Miles, Philadelphia, Various Types of Flintlock Pistols. C. 1800-1810.

Caliber 58 to 64 approximately. 8-1/2" to 10" round iron barrels.

Various styles of Miles made arms have been observed; none known made under contract. Sporting style locks with deep vertical flutes and projecting teats at rear; gooseneck hammers.

Two distinct styles shown here: (a) 9-1/2" brass barrel 58 caliber; marked at breech PHILAD^A and sunken P proof in oval. Lock marked with deep sunken banner-like design with raised

letters MILES. Modified bird's head butt with thin brass sporting type butt cap; (b) 9-1/4" round barrel 64 caliber; unmarked. Lock marked vertically at rear MILES/CP indicating ownership by the Commonwealth of Pennsylvania.

Both styles described herein would be considered rare and desirable as well as other similar Miles marked specimens. Their value range only:

6B-046	Values—Good **$4,000**		Fine **$8,000**
As above; converted to percussion:			
6B-047	Values—Good **$2,000**		Fine **$4,500**

6B-046
Style A

6B-046
Style B

J.P. Moore Flintlock Pistol   *See "Tryon New York" 6B-056*

Richmond-Virginia Flintlock Pistol   *See Virginia Manufactory Second Model Pistol.*

C. Robbins Model 1826-Type Flintlock Pistol

C. Robbins Model 1826-Type Flintlock Pistol. Circa 1826-early 1830s. Quantities unknown; very limited. The maker possibly from Tioga, New York or Pennsylvania.

Closely patterned after the Simeon North, Model 1826 Navy pistol (6A-026) with 9-inch unmarked barrel; 54-caliber smoothbore. Civilian/non-military style, flat lockplate 3-5/8 inches long, retained by single screw; marked in center C. ROBBINS; gooseneck hammer. Walnut stock with a sharp angle to handle. Iron mountings with single, wide iron barrel band. Most specimens viewed are fitted with a classic military type iron ramrod affixed to the muzzle of the barrel with iron swivels (some specimens fitted with wooden ramrod). None are known with iron belthooks. Presumed designed and sold for personal use by militia officers.

6B-047.5

6B-047.5	Values—Good **$1,750**	Fine **$3,000**

As above; converted to percussion:

6B-047.6	Values—Good **$850**	Fine **$1,750**

Rogers & Brothers Flintlock Pistol

Rogers & Brothers, Valley Forge, Pennsylvania, Flintlock Pistol. (Not illus.) Made c. 1814-1825. Quantity unknown; very limited.

A secondary martial pistol traditionally listed in number of other well known references on the subject, but felt to be merely an example of a militia or officer's type pistol of the general era. No known contracts. Pistol conforms to civilian or secondary private-purchase type, and could even be classified as a "Kentucky Pistol."

54 caliber. 8-1/2" part round/part octagonal barrel; smoothbore. Full length, pin-fastened artificially striped maple stock; checkered grip; brass mounted; sporting style engraved lock with gooseneck hammer.

Lock marked ahead of hammer ROGERS & BROTHERS/WARRANTED.

The Rogers Brothers are identified as John, Evan, and Charles, listed from 1805 to 1846 as hardware merchants in Philadelphia. Their Valley Forge gunsmith-gunshop operation began in 1814. It is very possible that only the locks were made or supplied by Rogers with the gun itself fabricated by other Pennsylvania makers:

6B-048	Values—Good **$1,400**	Fine **$3,000**

As above; converted to percussion:

6B-049	Values—Good **$750**	Fine **$1,500**

Schweitzer Brass Cannon Barrel Flintlock Pistol

Abraham Schweitzer (also found spelled Sweitzer). Lancaster, Pennsylvania. Large, contract type, flintlock holster pistol c. 1795-1798. Quantity unknown; very rare.

Heavy 9" brass cannon type barrel; part octagon/part round. 54 caliber. Full walnut stock, wedge fastened. Brass mountings.

Lock engraved in script SCHWEITZER (possibly the lockmaker, although flintlock Kentucky rifles are known by this maker). Barrels noted with different inscriptions (WISE and O. SIMPSON etc. possibly barrel makers only). Deep stamped liberty cap over P oval, sunken barrel proof may date it pre-1798; 2'nd deep sunken proof PG of Peter Getz, Lancaster, inspector of both U.S. and Penna. contract arms.

Liberty cap proof used by Pennsylvania discontinued 1798. Brass barreled American marked, proofed and military issued arms are unique. Significant to note that government records of military stores on hand Philadelphia May, 1781 show 93 brass

6B-049.5

barrel pistols in inventory, while 1793 returns at Philadelphia, indicate "…80 brass pistol barrels" on hand:

6B-049.5	Values—Good **$20,000**	Fine **$45,000**

John Shuler Contract Flintlock Pistol

John Shuler, Liverpool, Pennsylvania, 1807-1808 Contract Flintlock Pistol. Total quantity unknown; very limited. One contract for 150 pairs of pistols given to Shuler in 1808 and there are recorded deliveries of 191 pistols by him in 1809.

54 caliber. 9-5/8" round barrel; smoothbore.

Pin-fastened full walnut stock; brass mountings; wooden ramrod; reinforced type double neck hammer.

Lock marking ahead of hammer: US with date marked

6B-050

vertically at rear or only US marked vertically at rear. Top of barrel marked: SHULER.

An extremely rare and highly desirable early American military handgun:

6B-050   Values—Good **$12,500**   Fine **$35,000**
As above; converted to percussion:
6B-051   Values—Good **$7,000**   Fine **$15,000**

Daniel Sweitzer Contract Flintlock Pistol

Daniel Sweitzer & Co., Lancaster, Pennsylvania, 1807-1808 Contract Flintlock Pistol. Quantity unknown; very limited.

54 caliber. 10-1/2" round barrel; smoothbore.

Walnut pin-fastened full stock; brass mountings; wooden ramrod; reinforced type double neck hammer.

Lock marked forward of hammer: SWEITZER/& C°. Marked vertically at rear: US. Breech of barrel marked: CT and eaglehead within an oval cartouche. Other specimens observed with barrels marked *I. GUEST* (in script) with eaglehead and P in oval proof.

There is every possibility that these guns were the product of John Guest of Lancaster, Pennsylvania (*q.v.*) with the locks only made by Sweitzer. It has been specifically noted that in official correspondence dated 1808 to John Guest (and his partners) Tench Coxe (the purveyor of Public Supplies) mentions he has received a pistol "… without any person's name on it, except "Sweitzer" on the lock … I suppose this is to be your pistol (meaning Guest)."

6B-052

A handful of specimens are known which fit the Tench Coxe description, the only markings being those of SWEITZER/& C° on the lock and no barrel markings. These are attributed to either John Guest or his partner, Abraham Henry.

All Sweitzer or Sweitzer & Guest marked pistols are considered extremely rare and desirable American martial handguns:

6B-052   Values—Good **$12,500**   Fine **$32,500**
As above; converted to percussion:
6B-053   Values—Good **$7,000**   Fine **$14,000**

Smith & Hyslop Flintlock Pistol

Smith & Hyslop, New York City, Flintlock Pistol. (Not illus.) Made c. 1820-1830. Total quantity unknown; very limited.

No known government contracts. A handgun believed made only for private sale to militia units or officers and an example of a general style of secondary martial handgun. It has been traditionally listed in other previous works concerning American military handguns and is an example of a general type and style only.

58 caliber. 8-3/4" round barrel; smoothbore.

Walnut full stock pin-fastened with checkered grip; brass

mounted; sporting type lock with gooseneck hammer; wooden ramrod.

Lock marked ahead of hammer SMITH & HYSLOP/NEW YORK/WARRANTED. There is every possibility that only the locks were either made or sold by Smith & Hyslop as agents and that the pistol itself was fabricated by other New York gunsmiths:

6B-054   Values—Good **$1,250**   Fine **$2,500**
As above; converted to percussion:
6B-055   Values—Good **$650**   Fine **$1,150**

George W. Tryon Flintlock Pistol

George W. Tryon, Philadelphia, Flintlock Pistol. Made c. 1815-1830. Quantity unknown; limited.

Approximately 50 caliber. 8-1/2" to 10" round or part round/part octagonal iron or brass barrels. Barrels usually bear English proofmarks indicating their importation, but are also marked along top PHILADELPHIA or PHIL^.

Full, pin-fastened, walnut stock with brass mountings; sporting type lock with simple engraved designs; gooseneck hammer.

Marked ahead of hammer: TRYON or TRYON/PHIL^.

No known contracts for this piece. A typical example of a militia or officer's type privately purchased arm of the era. The maker has been found traditionally listed in other general references on secondary military handguns:

Other similar, often identical holster pistols with imported brass or iron barrels, many likely entirely British made specifically for the American export trade are encountered.

6B-056

Among the more often seen names are H. YOUNG/NEW YORK (hardware and military goods dealers); MEACHAM & POND/ALBANY (or G. POND & CO) and J.P. MOORE/NEW YORK. Markings and features have minor variances but they all may be considered as generic types. Values generally same for all: iron barrels tend to bring about 20 percent less than the values shown here for brass types:

6B-056   Values—Good **$1,100**   Fine **$2,750**
As above; converted to percussion:
6B-057   Values—Good **$850**   Fine **$1,400**

Virginia Manufactory 1st Model Flintlock Pistol

Virginia Manufactory First Model Flintlock Pistol. Made at the Virginia State Armory, Richmond, Virginia (*see American Military Longarms, Chapter IX, for details*) c. 1805-1811. Total made estimated at 2,208.

69 caliber; smoothbore. Barrel lengths vary from 12" to 12-1/2"; fastened at top of forend with double strap barrel band. Earliest manufacture prior to 1807 does not have the narrow band retaining spring. Contours, especially of the handle, will vary due to hand workmanship. Overall length approximately 17-1/2" to 18-1/2".

Iron mountings. Brass front sight brazed to lower strap of barrel band. Iron ramrod with bulbous or flattened ball shaped head. Flat lockplate with projecting teat at rear; iron pan with fence forged integral. Distinctive large gooseneck hammer.

Lock marked ahead of hammer: VIRGINIA (in large block letters) over **MANUFACTORY** in bold script. Marked vertically at rear: RICHMOND in curved arch over date of manufacture. Earliest dates will bring a premium value. Barrel markings P (either with or without an oval cartouche) and Virginia

6B-058

regimental number (e.g., REG. 4V) or county name.

The first model pistols are known to collectors as the largest American martial handguns. Rare and highly desirable collectors' item and considered a secondary Confederate weapon also:

6B-058   Values—Good **$8,500**   Fine **$27,500**
As above; converted to percussion:
6B-059   Values—Good **$4,500**   Fine **$10,000**

Virginia Manufactory 2nd Model Flintlock Pistol

Virginia Manufactory Second Model Flintlock Pistol, a.k.a. Richmond-Virginia Flintlock Pistol. Made at the Virginia State Armory, Richmond, Virginia, c. 1812-1815. Styled directly after the Harpers Ferry Model 1805 pistol. Total quantity made estimated at 4,252.

54 caliber; smoothbore. 10" round barrel with iron underrib. Overall length 15-1/2".

Walnut half stock wedge fastened on forend. Brass mountings. Swivel type iron ramrod with button head. Some of the earliest 1812-1813 production (but not all) were issued with wooden ramrods and an iron ramrod pipe brazed to the underrib; original specimens will bring a premium in value.

Lock marked ahead of hammer: VIRGINIA. Marked at rear: RICHMOND in curved arch over date of manufacture. Some specimens, made c. 1815, are marked only RICHMOND in curve ahead of hammer and dated 1815 vertically at rear (scarcer, and will bring premium).

Barrels are usually unmarked. Occasionally a Virginia regimental marking may be encountered and is worth a small premium. These arms are also considered secondary Confederate handguns:

6B-060   Values—Good **$6,000**   Fine **$17,500**
As above; converted to percussion:
6B-061   Values—Good **$4,000**   Fine **$9,000**
Cross-Index: "H. Young, New York" Flintlock Pistol (*see "Tryon"* 6B-056)

6B-060

Unmarked or Partially Marked Secondary Flintlock Martial Pistols

A

B

Unmarked or Partially Marked Secondary Flintlock Martial Pistols. Large military or holster-type flintlock pistols are occasionally seen on the collectors' market that are considered as "Secondary Martial." They were made by a great many well known, professional, as well as unrecorded, backwoods gunsmiths in varying degrees of quality, size and shape. Some are very much borderline cases; that is, either secondary martials or Kentuckys, and the reader will do well to see Chapter XI for further information about these latter.

After establishing their martial characteristics, these arms should be categorized as to (a) period (Revolutionary and Colonial arms are in a class by themselves, *see Chapter XVI*); earlier ones will generally bring higher values; (b) quality; a very important factor. Crude ones bring lower values, fine quality fetch higher prices in direct proportion to workmanship; (c) type of wood used, walnut the most often encountered while cherry, maple or curly maple will often bring higher values, the latter being the most desirable type; (d) styles of workmanship; that is, all American made or using imported parts. Very often KETLAND or other imported or merely WARRANTED marked locks are seen along with British proofed barrels; (e) similarity in appearance to other known U.S. or contract type arms; (f) any other identifying markings other than maker such as regimental marks, barrel proofmarks or dates. Prices reflected herein are merely a general range and can vary considerably:

6B-062   Values—Good **$750** to **$1,250**
             Fine **$2,000** to **$3,500**

As above; converted to percussion:

6B-063   Values—Good **$500** to **$850**
             Fine **$1,000** to **$1,750**

C

D

E

"H. Young, New York" Flintlock Pistol   *See Tryon 6B-056.*

Rare ca. 1928-1830s blue wool-covered leather saddle holsters for a pair of American flintlock "holster" pistols. See section "Holster Pistol vs. Horse Pistol" in this chapter. Shown in illustration with close-up of the original Portland, Maine maker's label of "JOHN ROUNDS/ HARNESS AND TRUNK MAKER." (N. Flayderman & Co., c. 1990)

Chapter VII-A

Percussion Revolvers

American percussion revolvers have long enjoyed a wide following in the collecting world, offering a number of attributes which make them extremely interesting pieces to own and study. The wide and diverse field affords the collector an opportunity to specialize in specific types (such as U. S. military handguns) or sizes (pocket, belt, or holster models), or the output (often varied) of specific manufacturers. As the listings in this chapter indicate, there exist quite a few models and variations of American manufacturers; all dating from the mid-19th century, with the height of their popularity reached during the Civil War.

Among the chief elements affecting both demand and value is the size of the guns themselves. It will be evident in studying the variety of types that many of the so-called "martial size" revolvers produced in quite large quantities often (as a matter of fact—generally) fetch higher prices than the so-called "pocket" or "belt" models that were frequently made in far fewer quantities. Many may be termed very scarce or even rare. This disparity is purely an anomaly, an eccentricity of the collecting field. The most cursory and simple explanation is that the larger martial sizes not only offer more in pure bulk but often are associated with the more "glamorous" or "romantic" uses that might have been put to them in their military or western frontier applications. Many of these large types are known to have been used and purchased by the government, primarily during the Civil War era, and hence there is justification for their greater demand and consequent value by virtue of directly associating them with specific regiments or units during known campaigns and engagements. For those revolvers that are merely priced for their size and general type, there is actually no justification for the value other than the pure traditional aspect that may be "time-honored" in American gun collecting. The subject has been discussed at length in Chapter II ("Demand" sub-section) and the reader will find those thoughts applicable here.

The author ventures the opinion that not a few small pocket models and their variations have been very much underrated merely because of "traditional" collecting patterns. As a matter of fact—quite the contrary should be the case. It is well known and firmly established that many of the "pocket" or "belt" sizes were carried as personal sidearms by countless numbers of officers and enlisted men during the Civil War; probably equal to quantities of privately purchased "martial" sizes. There is also no doubt that those smaller models were carried in the same large proportions by Americans heading west to the frontiers. Significant numbers of these pocket and belt models have appeared in fine collections bearing historical inscriptions and with known historical associations; many existing tintypes and photographs bear testimony to their ownership by military

men, frontiersmen, western emigrants and others to which a "romantic flavor" may be associated. Thus, taken in the light of the relative rarity as to quantities manufactured and the general evolutionary changes in American gun collecting, there is every likelihood that not a few of these smaller models will eventually narrow the gap in values with the larger martial-size calibers. Whether they ever equalize or exceed the gap remains to be seen. There is no doubt, however, that the disparity represents a completely unjustifiable phenomenon of arms collecting.

Two of the most often heard and misunderstood terms in the field of American revolver collecting are the designations **Navy Model** and **Army Model.** In their most simple application **Navy Model** or **Navy Size** refers to revolvers of 36 caliber more-or-less (often a 34 caliber or even a 38 caliber will be considered **Navy**) while **Army Model** or **Army Size** refers to revolvers of 44 caliber more-or-less (calibers 40 and 41, and 46 are also considered **Army.**) As far as can be determined, neither the U.S. Army nor the U.S. Navy standardized their handguns on either size and the terminology does not stem from governmental or military sources, but rather appears to have originated with the manufacturers themselves; Samuel Colt most likely was the first to utilize the terms. Subsequent generations of both manufacturers and collectors have come to use "Army" and "Navy" generically; both are part and parcel of the terminology and jargon of gun collecting.

There is strong evidence of the origin of the terms from Sam Colt's own broadsides and other documents relating to firearms promotions. His first widely sold pieces, the Colt Dragoons, made in the large 44 caliber and actually purchased in considerable quantities by the U.S. Army, became known and called by him as **Army Models.** When he produced his second type of 44 caliber, newly designed revolver, the so-called Model 1860, it was officially termed the **New Model Army.** In 1850, Colt marketed a piece that had been foremost in his mind for quite some time; a medium frame, medium bore revolver in 36 caliber, named shortly thereafter **Navy Model** (of 1851). Originally this medium frame revolver was designated within the factory prior to its production as the "New Ranger size pistol," a term which found very little favor and for reasons not fully known, was soon redesignated the **Navy Model.** Very possibly the new name was in honor of an earlier purchase, for test purposes, by the Navy; most certainly the Navy designation was given to distinguish it from Colt's larger **Army** size. From early correspondence concerning this medium frame 36 caliber model, it can be seen that most early quantity orders were nevertheless earmarked for the U.S. Army, regardless of the revolver's **Navy** name.

The calibers 36 and 44 were thus generally introduced in manufacturing and sales circles as **Army** and **Navy** size by Sam Colt, with some of the other contemporary manufacturers following suit. Although in all cases such terms were not originally used by those manufacturers, the present day collector has applied the terminology to all pieces in those two general sizes. It is firmly established that both the U.S. Army and the U.S. Navy purchased and issued considerable quantities of both 36 and 44 caliber revolvers of various American manufacturers.

The percussion revolver was the most widely owned, carried and used sidearm of the Civil War. Approximately 314,000 American-made revolvers of various manufacturers were then purchased under contract, while additional quantities were bought by the government on the open market through private arms agents. Although all the large 36 and 44 caliber types are generally known to collectors as "martial" revolvers, those pieces actually bearing government inspector markings or known to have been purchased under direct contract, are normally the ones that fetch higher prices because of their documented military use and association. In many cases this is an inequity as far as "rarity" factor is concerned and is created strictly by the time honored aspects of American arms collecting. Information concerning governmental purchases, contracts and markings will be mentioned as both a value guide and collecting reference.
CONVERSIONS TO BREECH-LOADING CARTRIDGE

In the immediate post-Civil War years through the late 1870s and likely into the early 1880s, quite a few percussion revolvers were altered/converted from muzzle-loading to breech-loading in order to accept the more "modern" self-contained rimfire or centerfire cartridge. It appears that only Colt Firearms Company and Remington Arms Company performed such work as a standard practice and under usually patented methods. Only a few other conversions are felt to be, and accepted as, "factory" conversions such as the Hopkins and Allen DICTATOR, or others listed in this book. All others are thought to be the work of individual gunsmiths and vary greatly in quality of workmanship and simplicity, or complexity, of operation. The majority of such conversions are usually quite crude; in such cases values are lessened 25 percent to 50 percent (and often more) from the percussion state. Demand is lessened accordingly. Experimental or patented conversions of known type, or well marked and of fine quality workmanship, could

fetch premium values if accompanied by substantiating documentary evidence as to origins. Quite a few Starr single action and double action revolvers and a few Whitney navies have been noticed over the years with a uniform method of conversion. To date no data has come to light about the origins of these conversions; demand and values for such pieces are considerably less than their percussion counterparts.

The reader is urged to consult Chapter II "Values and Conditions" for many factors that can affect and alter values from those reflected in this section on "Percussion Revolvers." Reference should also be made to "Condition Standards for Antique Firearms" as outlined in Chapter II before assigning a value to any specific revolver.

BIBLIOGRAPHY

Few books are specifically devoted to this subject, but treatment is quite good in several works published within the past 20 years, many of them still in print, and found in other bibliographies within this book, most notably Chapters IV, VI, and IX. A considerable amount of material in the following is of great significance to the field of American percussion revolvers: *Civil War Guns*, Edwards; *U. S. Military Small Arms 1816-1865*, Reilly; *Small Arms and Ammunition in the U. S. Service*, Lewis; *Revolving Arms*, Taylorson; *The Collecting of Guns*, Serven (Editor); and *U.S. Naval Handguns 1808-1911*, by Winter; *Firearms From Europe: Imported During the American Civil War [by the U.S. and Confederacy]* by Noe and Whisker; *Civil War Guns* by Edwards.

*McAulay, John D. *Civil War Pistols*. Lincoln, R.I.: Mowbray Publishers, 1992. Important information of U.S. Government and state purchases and issuance of all Civil War handguns; quantities, dates, markings.

Sellers, Frank M. and Smith, Samuel E. *American Percussion Revolvers*. Ontario, Canada: Museum Restoration Service, 1971. An important, authoritative, definitive guide to all American percussion revolvers including revolving rifles. Widely cited and used throughout the collecting field.

Thalheimer, R. *Percussion Revolvers of the U.S.* St. Louis, Missouri: Privately published, 1970. Large illustrations; small unauthoritative, text. Resembles an amateur scrapbook.
  (*) Preceding a title indicates the book is currently in print.

Adams Revolving Arms Co., New York   *See Massachusetts Arms Co.*
The Adams marking was used on revolvers made by the Mass. Arms firm.

Allen & Thurber   *See Chapter V, Ethan Allen.*

Allen & Wheelock   *See Chapter V, Ethan Allen.*

C. R. Alsop Navy Model Revolver

C. R. Alsop, Middletown, Conn. Navy Model Revolver. Made c. 1862-63; total quantity about 500.

36 caliber. Fluted or round type cylinders; 5 shots. 3-1/2", 4-1/2", 5-1/2", and 6-1/2" (worth premium) octagonal barrels. Note distinctive spur triggers, and hammer location at top center of frame.

Wooden grips with hump-shaped backstrap. Blued finish.

Serial numbered from 1 on up. C.R. ALSOP MIDDLETOWN CONN. and patent dates of 1860 and 1861 marked on barrel. C.H. ALSOP and patent date NOV 26th 1861 on cylinder. On left sideplate: PATENTED JANY. 21st 1862.

7A-001
First Model
(with fluted cylinder)

First Model Navy; identified by presence of safety device on right side of frame above the spur trigger. Approximately first 100 production specimens:

7A-001   Values—Good **$1,100**   Fine **$3,750**

Standard Model; lacking the safety device on frame:

7A-002   Values—Good **$850**   Fine **$3,000**

(Note: Premium placed on specimens having 5-1/2" or 6-1/2" barrels, and/or with attachable shoulder stocks.)

7A-002
*"Standard Model
(with round cylinder)"*

C. R. Alsop Pocket Model Revolver

C.R. Alsop, Middletown, Conn. Pocket Model Revolver. (Not illus.; its appearance substantially that of the 36 caliber Navy type.) Made c. 1862-63; total quantity about 300.

31 caliber. 6-shot round cylinder (5-shot known; rare). 4" octagonal barrel. Shares distinctive spur trigger and center location of hammer (at frame top) with its 36 caliber Navy counterpart.

Wooden grips with hump-shaped backstrap. Blued finish. Serial numbered from 1 on up. C.R. ALSOP MIDDLETOWN CONN. and patent dates of 1860 and 1861 marked on barrel. C.R. ALSOP and patent date NOV 26th 1861 on cylinder:

7A-003   Values—Good **$500**   Fine **$1,500**

See Chapter VIII-A for a history of the Bacon Arms Co. and the Bacon Mfg. Co.

Bacon Arms Co. Pocket Model Revolver

Bacon Arms Co., Norwich, Conn. Pocket Model Revolver. Made c. mid-1860s; total quantity of about 2,000.

31 caliber. 5-shot round cylinder. 4" round barrel. The solid frame featuring a spur trigger.

Wooden grips. Blued finish. (*See also PA-020*)

Serial numbered from 1 on up. Specific markings noted below. (Note: Some specimens marked: UNION ARMS CO. N.Y.) **First Model Revolver;** distinguished by the form of cylinder pin release, a button on left side of frame, which when pushed forward allowed the cylinder to be removed. About 1,000 made. Specimens generally found without markings other than serial numbers:

7A-004   Values—Good **$475**   Fine **$1,250**

7A-004

Second Model Revolver; the cylinder pin secured by a cross screw. Marked on the barrel: BACON ARMS CO. NORWICH, CONN. Approximately 600 made:

7A-005   Values—Good **$350**   Fine **$900**

As above, but bearing UNION ARMS CO. N.Y. markings:

7A-006   Values—Good **$375**   Fine **$950**

Bacon Mfg. Co. Pocket Model Revolvers

Bacon Manufacturing Co., Norwich, Conn. Pocket Model Revolvers. Made c. 1858-67; total quantity with Bacon markings about 1,400; total with markings of other firms about 1,900 (**Fitch & Waldo, B.J. Hart & Bro., Tomes, Melvain & Co., Union Arms Co., Western Arms Co. and Hopkins & Allen**). Occasionally unmarked.

31 caliber. 5-shot round or fluted cylinders. 4", 5", and 6" (rare) round or octagonal barrels. Bearing considerable resemblance to Pocket Model Manhattan revolvers, the Bacon differs primarily in most having a ball type loading lever latch and lacking intermediate stops on the cylinder periphery. Bacon

himself had left Manhattan (apparently with a design for an improved Pocket Model), and formed his own company.

Wooden grips. Blued finish. Simple engraving standard on frame and barrel.

Serial numbered from 1 on up. Barrels marked (in one line): BACON MFG. CO. - NORWICH, CONN. DEPOT 297 BROADWAY N.Y. Further details in variations noted below.

First Model Revolver; known as their "EXCELSIOR MODEL" having round cylinder with five panel roll scene (sporting scenes). The barrel shape octagonal. Less than 1,000 estimated made:

7A-007   Values—Good **$325**   Fine **$1,000**

7A-007

7A-008

Second Model Revolver; with fluted cylinder (no roll engraved scene), and round barrel. Approximately 3,000 made:
7A-008   Values—Good **$300**   Fine **$1,000**
Fitch & Waldo, N.Y. Established 1864, the company is known to have had about 100 revolvers of the round barrel, fluted cylinder type made by Bacon and marked FITCH & WALDO N.Y.:
7A-009   Values—Good **$400**   Fine **$1,250**
B.J. Hart & Bro., N.Y. About 600 round barrel, fluted cylinder Bacon revolvers were marked B.J. HART & BRO. NEW YORK:
7A-010   Values—Good **$400**   Fine **$1,250**
Tomes Son & Melvain, N.Y. About 100 round barrel, fluted cylinder Bacon revolvers were marked TOMES, MELVAIN & CO. NEW YORK:
7A-011   Values—Good **$450**   Fine **$1,400**
Union Arms Co., N.Y. About 700 round barrel, fluted cylinder Bacon revolvers were marked UNION ARMS CO.:
7A-012   Values—Good **$350**   Fine **$1,000**
Western Arms Co.; about 400 round barrel, fluted cylinder Bacon revolvers were marked with the legend WESTERN ARMS CO. NEW YORK or WESTERN ARMS CO./CHICAGO, ILL:
7A-013   Values—Good **$400**   Fine **$1,250**
Third Model Revolver; with round barrel and round, unfluted

7A-013.5
Third Model

cylinder; three-piece (Whitney type) loading lever. Less than 1,000 made. Marked BACON ARMS CO.:
7A-013.5   Values—Good **$375**   Fine **$900**
Hopkins & Allen, Norwich Conn.; continued production of Third Model Bacon Revolvers, having taken over the firm's factory in 1867. Barrels marked HOPKINS & ALLEN MFG. CO. NORWICH. CT. 31 caliber. 4", 5" & 6" barrels, 5 shots. Three piece (Whitney type) loading lever. Two variations:

> **Octagonal barrel model** (about 250 made):
> **7A-014**   Values—Good **$400**   Fine **$1,250**

> **Round barrel model** (about 1,000 made):
> **7A-015**   Values—Good **$375**   Fine **$1,100**

Bliss & Goodyear Pocket Model Revolver

7A-016

Bliss & Goodyear, New Haven, Conn. Pocket Model Revolver. Made c. 1860, in a total quantity of about 3,000.
    28 caliber. 6-shot round cylinder. 3" octagonal barrel. Featured a spur trigger, removable sideplate, and solid frame.
    Wooden grips. Blued finish; iron frame.
    Serial numbered from 1 on up. On top of barrel: BLISS & GOODYEAR - NEW HAVEN, CONN:
7A-016   Values—Good **$375**   Fine **$1,250**

Brettell & Frisbie Pocket Revolver

Frank Brettell and Joseph Frisbie, Allegheny, Penn. Pocket Model Revolver. Manufactured c. 1858; total quantity believed less than 50.
    31 caliber. 5-shot. 3-1/2" octagon barrel. Double action.
    Two piece walnut grips. Serial numbered. Resembles the second model Ells (*q.v.*).
    Markings on left side of hammer: BRETTELL & FRISBIE PATENTED FEB 10,1857. On right side of hammer: BRETTELL & W.B. POTTS, COL. O; and on top: EUREKA.

7A-016.4

7A-016.4   Values—Good **$2,250**   Fine **$4,250**

"Wm. Bryce & Co." markings on percussion revolver   *See Sharps, Chapter V-F (5F-072).*

Charles Buss Pocket Revolver

Charles Buss, Marlboro, N.H. Pocket Model Revolver. Manufactured c. 1855; quantity estimated less than 25.
    31 caliber. 6-shot. Part octagon/part round barrel of 4-1/2" (varies).
    Two piece walnut grips. Hand rotated knurled cylinder. Trigger guard acts as spring to hold cylinder lock. Serial numbered. Slight variances noted in configuration and details on all specimens.
    Markings on top strap: CHARLES BUSS MARLBORO N.H. PATENTED APRIL 25, 1854:

7A-016.6

7A-016.6   Values—Good **$3,500**   Fine **$7,500**

Butterfield Army Model Revolver

Jesse Butterfield, Philadelphia, Penn. Army Model Revolver. Made c. 1861-62; total quantity of about 640.

41 caliber. 5-shot round cylinder. 7" octagonal barrel. Hammer centrally located on top of the frame; the frame of solid type and of brass with a special disc priming mechanism fitted (with its loading aperture forward of the trigger guard).

Wooden grips. Blued finish; the frame left bright.

Serial numbered from 1 on up. On topstrap (above the cylinder) the marking: BUTTERFIELD'S PATENT DEC 11, 1855/PHILADA. One of the more unusual American percussion revolvers, the Butterfield was to have been made on a government contract, and in a quantity of 2,280. But the contract was canceled, and thus the limited production of only about 640; considered by collectors as a Secondary U. S. Martial handgun. **Standard model;** as described above; the cylinder stop of

7A-017

tear-drop shape:

7A-017 Values—Good **$2,500** Fine **$6,000**
Late production model, without marking and the cylinder having a round stop; about 50 produced:
7A-018 Values—Good **$2,750** Fine **$6,500**

Cochran Turret Revolver

Cochran Turret Revolver, made by C. B. Allen, Springfield, Mass., c. late 1830s. Total quantity produced believed less than 150.

36 caliber (some variation). 7-shot turret horizontally

7A-019

mounted and held in place by axis and the frame topstrap. Barrel part octagon-part round; standard lengths vary from 4-3/4" to 5".

One piece walnut bag type grips. Unusual frame construction, with saw-handle shape at top of grip; note underhammer configuration. Iron frame usual; specimens known with brass and German silver frames; worth premium.

Serial numbered from 1 on up. Usually marked on topstrap of frame: COCHRAN'S PATENT C. B. ALLEN SPRINGFIELD MASS.

This noble experiment is recognized by collectors as one of the distinct oddities in American arms development. Though by no means practical (partly due to the possibilities of the shooter himself being shot) the Cochran's early date and mechanical intrigue have always held a distinct fascination:

7A-019 Values—Good **$6,500** Fine **$17,500**

Colt *See Chapter V.*

J. M. Cooper Pocket Model Revolver

J.M. Cooper & Co., Pittsburgh, Penn. Pocket Model Revolver. Made c. 1850'S to 1864. From 1864-69 the company was located in Philadelphia. Total quantity of Pocket and Navy revolvers (they were serial numbered together) approximately 15,000.

31 caliber. 5- (and in late production) 6-shot cylinders, round and without roll scene. 4", 5", or 6" octagonal barrels. All revolvers distinguished by the double action mechanism, and their visual resemblance to the Colt Model 1849 Pocket.

One piece walnut grips. Blued finish.

Serial number ranges and markings noted on variations below.

Pittsburgh Made Revolvers:
First Model; serial range 1 to 100. The cylinder notches

7A-020

alternated from rectangular to oval and totaled 10 in number. Markings: MANFD BY J.M. COOPER & CO/PITTSBURGH PA/PATD APL 25, 1854/PATD JAN. 7, 1851/REISSD JULY 26, 1859. Gripstraps of brass:
7A-020 Values—Good **$475** Fine **$1,500**
Second Model; gripstraps of iron; made in a new serial number range of 1 to 900.

First variation bore same markings as the First Model, conventional cylinder notches (rectangular, between each chamber); about 100 made:
7A-021 Values—Good **$475** Fine **$1,400**

Second variation; serial range about 100 - 900. Barrel markings: MANFD. BY J.M. COOPER & CO PITTSH. PA PAT JAN. 7, 1851/REIS'D JULY 26, 1859 PAT APR 25, 1854 PAT SEPT. 4, 1860. Iron gripstraps:
7A-022 Values—Good **$375** Fine **$1,200**

Philadelphia Revolvers:
First Model; a new serial range, 1 to about 400, the barrel marking (in three lines, and including the legend: FRANKFORD PHILA. PA.) added two 1863 patent dates and dropped the 1859 date. Quickly recognized by the absence of nipple shield on recoil shield. Gripstraps usually of iron:
7A-023 Values—Good **$375** Fine **$1,200**

Second Model; serial number range about 400 - 11000. Made with nipple shield, and all but the first 100 specimens have the cylinder bolt on left side of the frame (had previously been on right). Barrel marking differs from previous production, by dropping of the word: ADDRESS. Gripstraps primarily of brass:

7A-024   Values—Good **$350**   Fine **$1,100**

Third Model; serial range about 11000 - 15000. Cylinder diameter increased (to match that of the Navy Model), and the number of shots increased from 5 to 6:

7A-025   Values—Good **$350**   Fine **$1,100**

J. M. Cooper Navy Model Revolver

J. M. Cooper & Co., Philadelphia, Penn. Navy Model Revolver. Made c. 1864-69. Total quantity of Navy and Pocket revolvers (serial numbered together) was approximately 15,000.

36 caliber. 5-shot cylinder, round and (except early production) rebated; without roll scene. 4", 5", or 6" octagonal barrels. All revolvers distinguished by the double action mechanism, and their visual resemblance to the Colt Model 1862 Pocket Navy.

One piece walnut grips. Blued finish.

Serial number ranges and markings as pointed out below. This model is considered by collectors as a Secondary U.S.

7A-026
Second Model Cooper

Martial handgun, although there are no known government contracts.

(Note: No 36 caliber revolvers known to have been made at the J.M. Cooper Pittsburgh factory.)

First Model (Philadelphia); serial range 1 to about 400; the barrel marking: ADDRESS COOPER FIRE ARMS MFG. CO. FRANKFORD PHILA. PA./PAT. JAN.7, 1851 APR. 25, 1854 SEP. 4, 1860/SEPT. 1, 1863 SEPT. 22, 1863 (three lines). Barrel lug of small size, and cut out on right side to allow for loading; the cylinder was not rebated and was longer than subsequent production. Gripstraps usually of iron:

7A-026   Values—Good **$600**   Fine **$1,600**

Second Model; serial number range about 400 - 15000. Made with rebated cylinders (and thus the front part of frame notched to accept the larger diameter). (Note: In the serial range about 500 - 1000 the length was shorter than standard production by 3/16"; these arms bring an added premium.) The standard models (having the 3/16" longer cylinder) also have a shortened bolster on the barrel, and the lug is cut out on both sides to allow for loading. Word ADDRESS dropped from First Model barrel marking. Gripstraps standard of brass:

7A-027   Values—Good **$525**   Fine **$1,500**

Dictator   *See Hopkins & Allen.*

H. E. Dimick, St. Louis   *See Metropolitan Arms Co.*

Eagle Co.   *See Eli Whitney (Navy Model Revolver); Chapter V.*

Elgar & Smith 9-Shot Revolver/Volley Gun/Pepperbox

Elgar & Smith, Mineral Point, Wisc. Percussion Revolver-Volley Gun-Pepperbox. Made c. 1855-56. Total quantity (with a 3-shot pistol & 3-shot rifle) likely less than 10. Very rare.

32 caliber. 9-shot consisting of three separate, triangular shaped chamber groups of 3 shots each; single nipple each group, thus firing 3 salvos of 3 shots each. Manually revolved. Cluster of 3 round 5-1/2" barrels slightly angled to give spread pattern to bullets. A very large handgun 12" overall weighing 4 pounds.

Silver finished brass frame marked with names of the inventors WM. ELGAR & R.M. SMITH / MINERAL POINT, WISC.

This unique oddity was given trials by both the Army and Navy in 1856. In both tests experienced officers missed all their targets!

7A-027.5

7A-027.5   Values—Good **$9,000**   Fine **$17,500**

Josiah Ells Pocket Model Revolver

Josiah Ells, Pittsburgh, Penn. Pocket Model Revolvers. Made c. 1857-59; total quantity of various types about 1,375.

28 and 31 calibers (various frame sizes). Round cylinders, generally 6-shot, but some 5. 2-1/2", 3" and 3-3/4" barrels, of octagonal shape on most variations. All Ells revolvers are of double action type.

Walnut grips. Blued finish.

Serial numbering for each variation had an individual range, beginning with 1. Markings and other special features as

7A-028
1st Model round frame

7A-028
1st Model (later) flat frame

7A-029
2nd Model

7A-030
3rd Model

indicated below. Explicit details of each of the variations may be found in *American Percussion Revolvers* by Sellers and Smith. The values indicated here are for the most commonly encountered variants; those types having smaller production will command higher proportionate values.

First Model Revolvers; distinguished by the open top frame and bar type hammer. Five variations of this first model total about 625. Earliest have round frames and deep grooved cylinders; 28 caliber only (worth premium). Later types are flat frame; 28 caliber in earlier production and 31 caliber later, and more commonly encountered size. 2-1/2" and 3" barrel lengths, 5- or 6-shot cylinders. Standard hammer markings of combinations of the following: J. ELLS; PATENT; 1854; ELLS PATENT; AUGUST 1, 1854; and APRIL 28, 1857:

7A-028 Values—Good **$350** Fine **$950**

Second Model Revolvers; distinguished by the solid frame construction, and the bar type hammer. 28 and 31 caliber. Total made of the four major variations was about 550. 3-3/4" barrel length, 5-shot cylinders. Standard hammer markings of either ELLS PATENT AUGUST 1, 1854, *or* ELLS PATENT AUGUST 1, 1854 APRIL 28, 1857:

7A-029 Values—Good **$350** Fine **$950**

Third Model Revolvers; identifiable by the spur type hammer striking from the right side (and operable either on single or double action)–often known as the "Sidehammer Model." Hammer marking: ELLS/PATENT AUG 1, 1854/APRIL 28, 1857. 5-shot, 31 caliber, 3-3/4" octagonal barrel. Total production about 200:

7A-030 Values—Good **$500** Fine **$1,400**

Ells Center Hammer Revolver

Ells Center Hammer Double Action Revolver.
6 shot, 31 caliber. Extremely limited production; made under his earlier patent of August 1, 1854. Rounded hammer not provided with a cocking spur; easily distinguished by its oversize brass trigger guard. Bold leaf and branch engraving apparently standard on frrames. Marked J. ELLS PATENT left side of 6" round barrel and "1854" on right side Rare:

7A-030.3 Values—Good **$5,500** Fine **$8,500**

7A-030.3

Harmon Fife Percussion Revolver

Harmon Fife, North Pembroke, N.H. Percussion Revolver. Made c. 1835.

Hand revolved. Specimens recorded in 25 caliber with 6-shot cylinder and 36 caliber with 7-shot cylinder.

Concealed (inside) hammer; trigger guard acts as main spring. Unmarked. Dimensions and contours vary due to hand workmanship. One-piece handle. Rather primitive and awkward in appearance.

Intriguing folklore surrounds this piece; thought by some to have been invented before Colt's revolver. Fife died in 1845; a quaint rhyming verse appears chiseled on his gravestone ending

7A-030.5

with the lines "… never had a lover …but invented the revolver":

7A-030.5 Values—Good **$3,000** Fine **$6,000**

James P. Fitch, N.Y.   *See James Reid, New York City, Chapter VIII.*

Fitch & Waldo, N.Y.   *See Bacon Manufacturing Co.*

Austin T. Freeman Army Model Revolver

Austin T. Freeman. Army Model Revolver. Manufactured c. 1863-64; by Hoard's Armory, Watertown, New York; total quantity about 2,000.

44 caliber. 6-shot round cylinder, the nipples recessed. Solid frame, 7-1/2" round barrel.

One piece walnut grips. Blued finish, with casehardened

lever and hammer.

Serial numbered beginning with 1. Standard frame marking: FREEMAN'S PAT. DEC 9, 1862/HOARD'S ARMORY, WATERTOWN, N.Y.

Considered a Secondary U. S. Martial handgun by collectors, although no U. S. contracts are known for this weapon. It is possible that some were acquired during the Civil War under state contracts.

A few variations appear on early specimens, such as exposed barrel threads on frame, number of frame screws, and spring retainers on center pin latches, and very narrow recoil shields; all these features will increase value over the standard specimen:

7A-031

| 7A-031 | Values—Good **$1,400** | Fine **$4,000** |

William Hankins Pocket Model Revolver

William Hankins, Philadelphia, Penn. Pocket Model Revolver. Manufactured c. 1860-61; total quantity about 650.

26 caliber. 5-shot round cylinder. 3" octagonal barrel. Wooden grips. Blued finish.

Serial numbered from 1 on up. Approximately half of production marked on the barrel: WM HANKINS/PHILA. PA.; balance of specimens found without markings. Some specimens bear marking: F.G. WHEELER NEW YORK who as a dealer sold Hankins revolvers. The revolver is important to the collector because Hankins joined with Christian Sharps, in 1861, to form a gunmaking partnership. (Note: A few cartridge revolvers also made on the same frame; these are scarce, but will rarely fetch

7A-032

the same values as the percussion model):

| 7A-032 | Values—Good **$675** | Fine **$2,500** |

B.J. Hart & Bro., N.Y. *See Bacon Manufacturing Co.; also see IXL, New York.*

Hopkins & Allen Dictator Model Revolver

Hopkins & Allen, Norwich, Conn. Dictator Model Revolver. Made c. late 1860s-early 1870s, total quantity in percussion about 1,000; in metallic cartridge conversions about 5,100.

36 caliber. 5-shot round cylinder; with roll engraved scene of five panel motifs. 4" round barrel.

Walnut grips. Blued finish.

Serial numbered from 1 on up. Top of the barrel marked DICTATOR. This model was basically a Bacon Manufacturing Co. product, adapted to firing the 36 caliber projectile. Most of the production was converted to fire 38 rimfire cartridges prior to shipment.

Standard model; percussion; about 1,000 made:

| 7A-033 | Values—Good **$400** | Fine **$1,250** |

Factory Conversion model; chambered for 38 r.f.; about 5,100 made:

| 7A-034 | Values—Good **$250** | Fine **$650** |

7A-033
Percussion

7A-034
Conversion

Hopkins & Allen Pocket Model Revolver *See Bacon Manufacturing Co. (7A-014 and 015)*

William Irving Pocket Model Revolvers

William Irving, New York City. Pocket Model Revolvers. Believed made by James Reid of New York City, (see James Reid Chapter VIII-A) under contract for W.W. Marston of New York City with all evidence pointing to William Irving as merely agent for both makers. The use of the "20 Cliff St." address by both Irving and Reid establishes a direct association. Made c. 1863-1864.

31 caliber. 6-shot round cylinders without decoration. Walnut grips.

7A-035
First Model

First Model, spur trigger, solid frame revolver. Frame of brass; stop slots at front section of cylinder; 3" octagonal barrel. Barrel marked: W. IRVING. Total production about 50; rare:

7A-035   Values—Good **$750**   Fine **$2,250**

Second Model, similar to the Whitney Pocket Revolver. Standard barrel length 4-1/2", marked: ADDRESS W. IRVING. 20 CLIFF ST. N-Y. Total production about 2,100; note that serial numbering began with 1000. Basic variation breakdowns were:

   Brass frame with either round or octagon barrel; about 600 manufactured:

   7A-036   Values—Good **$400**   Fine **$1,250**

7A-036
Second Model

Iron frame with round or octagon barrel; about 1,500 made:

7A-037   Values—Good **$375**   Fine **$1,200**

IXL Navy and Pocket Model Revolvers

IXL, New York City. Navy and Pocket Model Revolvers. Made c. 1857, the identity of the manufacturer is unknown. Production totals of basic types noted below; overall total approximately 1,000.

   Pocket Models in 31 caliber, and the Navy Model in 36. Cylinders round with deep recesses for the nipples. Standard barrel lengths of about 4" (Pocket) and about 7" (Navy). Wooden grips. Blued finish. All models are double action.

   The IXL N.YORK marking is found on the 31 caliber center hammer Pocket Model. Note that a considerable number of similar revolvers were made in England and in Continental Europe, but those considered here are regarded as of American manufacture.

   These revolvers have been found bearing the marking of B.J. HART/BROADWAY, hardware and sporting goods dealers who probably contracted for a small production run. On the more commonly found IXL this marking is worth a premium; on the scarce models of low quantity the Hart marking will probably bring the same price.

Pocket Model; the spurless hammer pivoting in the center of frame behind the cylinder. Large trigger guard and trigger. Marked IXL N. YORK on top of barrel; total made about 750:

7A-038   Values—Good **$375**   Fine **$1,250**

Pocket Model; the spurred hammer mounted on the right side of the frame; operates both single and double action. Unmarked other than by serial numbers; total made about 150. (Not illus.; closely resembles the Navy Model in appearance):

7A-039   Values—Good **$550**   Fine **$1,400**

Navy Model; the spurless hammer pivoting in the center of frame behind the cylinder. Large trigger guard and trigger. Unmarked except for serial numbers; total made about 50. (Not illus.; closely resembles the Pocket Model with spurless hammer but much larger):

7A-040   Values—Good **$1,250**   Fine **$3,750**

Navy Model; the spurred hammer mounted on the right side of the frame; operates both single and double action. Unmarked other than by serial numbers; total made about 50:

7A-041   Values—Good **$2,000**   Fine **$5,000**

7A-038
Pocket Model

7A-041
"Navy Model with spur hammer"

Benjamin F. Joslyn Army Model Revolver

Benjamin F. Joslyn Army Model Revolver. Made c. 1861-62; total quantity of about 3,000. Production was by the Joslyn Firearms Company of Stonington, Connecticut.

   44 caliber. 5-shot round cylinder. 8" octagonal barrel.

   Walnut grips, checkered. Blued finish, with case hardened loading lever and hammer.

7A-042

   Serial numbered from 1 on up. Barrel marking: B.F. JOSLYN/PATD. MAY 4, 1858. A distinctive feature of these unusual arms is their solid frame and side mounted hammer. **First Model;** often attributed in their manufacture to W.C. Freeman. Distinguished by the flat iron buttcaps and brass trigger guards. Estimated about 500 produced:

7A-042   Values—Good **$1,500**   Fine **$5,000**

Standard Model; made by the Joslyn Firearms Company. Most do not have buttcaps, (they appear again only on the latest production) and the trigger guards are of iron. About 2,500 produced:

7A-043   Values—Good **$1,400**   Fine **$4,500**

   100 Joslyn revolvers were purchased by the Navy and delivered by Oct. 1861. Apparently quite a few were in the 300 to 400 serial range, but serials in 1200 range also recorded. Some marked **USN** on butt strap; others with small anchor on

underside of barrel. Total of 1,100 recorded purchased on the open market through N.Y. dealer and from Joslyn Nov. 1861 through April, 1862. None known to have inspector or other state or U.S. markings. Almost all to Ohio, with majority issued to 5th and 6th Ohio Cavalry. A few small quantity issues to various Illinois, Indiana, Kansas and Minnesota units. Caution advised for specimens that might be found with martial marks.

Moses Kinsey Pocket Revolver

Moses Kinsey, Newark, N.J. Pocket Model Revolver.
Manufactured c. 1858-59; quantity estimated about 20.

33 caliber (31 also reported). 5-shot; side hammer; single action. 3-1/2" octagon barrel. Solid frame; spur trigger.

Two piece walnut grips. Slightly resembles the Colt Root model.

Markings on barrel: M. KINSEYS PATENT JUNE 8, 1858, NEWARK N.J.:

7A-043.5

7A-043.5   Values—Good **$2,000**   Fine **$4,500**

John Krider, Philadelphia;   *LeMat percussion revolver. See 10-012.*

V.G.W. Libeau Percussion Revolver

V.G.W. Libeau, New Orleans, Louisiana Pocket Size Double Action Revolver. Circa 1847. Quantity unknown; possibly prototype.

34 caliber, percussion 4-3/4" octagon barrel; 5-shot cylinder. Not serial numbered. Concealed folding trigger. Exceptionally small loading lever mounted on left side of barrel. Innovative spring devices for each nipple allow for use of incorrect, oversize percussion caps if standard size not available.

7A-043.8

Markings engraved in script on the back-action lock V.G.LIBEAU NEW ORLEANS 1847 with additional markings gold-inlaid on barrel NEW ORLEANS. Blued finish. Checkered, bag-shaped walnut handle.

Libeau was a recorded New Orleans gunsmith, listed in local directories from 1834 to mid-1840s; known mostly as maker of percussion derringers and halfstock percussion sporting rifles. This unique revolver possibly experimental (others might exist) and is included as an example of the type of "one-of-a-kind" revolver the collector might encounter while "making his rounds" in pursuit of this hobby. Valued on quality of workmanship, uniqueness of mechanism and maker's name, location and reputation (the "New Orleans" address adds to this revolver's desirability). Assuming condition is (at a minimum) "very good" and upward they can easily fall in the range of low to mid-five figures.

7A-043.8

London Pistol Company   *See Manhattan Firearms Mfg. Co.; Chapter V.*

Manhattan   *See Chapter V.*

W. W. Marston Pocket Model Revolver

W. W. Marston, New York City, Phenix, Union, or Western. Pocket Model Revolver; solid frame type. Made c. 1858 into the early 1860s; total production about 13,000.

31 caliber. 5-shot round cylinder; 6-shot on late production (some 5-shot cylinders fluted). Barrels octagonal, and in lengths from 3-1/4" to 7-1/2" (last model had round barrel). Colt type rammers on all but seventh type.

Walnut grips. Blued finish.

Serial numbered from 1 on up. Markings vary considerably, as pointed out in the variations noted below. Note similarity between the Marston revolvers and the First Model Whitney. The Union, Phenix, and Western markings were trade names only. *See also, Wm. Irving 7A-035 & 7A-036.*

7A-044
1st Type
(grips squared at juncture to frame)

7A-046
3rd Type
(grip rounded at juncture to frame)

First type production; serial range approximately 1 - 1050. Barrel marking: Wm. W. Marston/Phenix Armory/New York City . 5-shot round cylinder:

7A-044   Values—Good **$350**   Fine **$1,100**

Second type; serial range approximately 1050 - 1500. Identical to first type. Barrel marking: The Union/Arms Co. 5-shot round cylinder:

7A-045   Values—Good **$375**   Fine **$1,200**

Third type; serial range approximately 1500 - 4000. Barrel marking: The Union/Arms Co. 5-shot round cylinder (varies in rounded shape to the juncture of the grip where it joins frame):

7A-046   Values—Good **$350**   Fine **$1,100**

Fourth type; serial range approximately 4000 - 6000. Barrel marking as above; but cylinder is fluted:

7A-047   Values—Good **$350**   Fine **$1,100**

Fifth type; serial range approximately 6000 - 8500. Barrel marking as above; top of frame grooved (previous types had flat top frames). 5-shot fluted cylinder:

7A-048   Values—Good **$350**   Fine **$1,100**

Sixth type; serial range approximately 8500 - 10000. Barrel marking either The Union/Arms Co., or The Union Arms Co. (one line), or Western Arms Co. New York or Western Arms Co./Chicago, Ill. Top of frame grooved; 6-shot round cylinder:

7A-049   Values—Good **$375**   Fine **$1,200**

7A-047
4th Type Fluted Cylinder

7A-050
7th Type Round Barrel

Seventh type; serial range approximately 10000 - 13000. Barrel marking either the one line Union, or either of the Western legends. Top of frame grooved; 6-shot round cylinder, and quickly distinguished by the round barrel. The rammer of the Whitney type:

7A-050   Values—Good **$350**   Fine **$1,100**

W. W. Marston Navy Model Revolver

W. W. Marston, New York City, "Western Arms Co." or "Union Arms Co." Navy Model Revolver. Made c. late 1850s-early 1860s; total quantity about 1,000.

36 caliber. 6-shot round cylinders, either plain or roll engraved with same scene as on Whitney Navy revolver (cylinders believed made by Whitney). 7-1/2", 8", 8-1/2" round or octagonal barrels.

Walnut grips. Blued finish.

Serial numbered from 1 on up. Barrels bore markings of either the Union Arms Co. or the Western Arms Co. The Union and Western stampings were trade names, and not the names of known companies.

First Model Navy; serial range 1 - 200. Revolvers unmarked except for serials. Octagonal barrels:

7A-051   Values—Good **$850**   Fine **$3,250**

Second Model; serial range 201 - 500. Barrels marked with **UNION ARMS CO.** or **WESTERN ARMS CO**. stampings. Octagonal barrels:

7A-052   Values—Good **$900**   Fine **$3,500**

Third Model; serial range 501 - 1000. Barrels marked as above, but round in shape:

7A-053   Values—Good **$850**   Fine **$3,000**

7A-051

Massachusetts Arms Company

The fine quality revolvers of this well-known company have considerable historical significance. They represent the most important of Sam Colt's earliest competitors and were the subject of a milestone legal case in arms lore. Many famous names are seen among the company's incorporators in 1851; Horace Smith and Daniel Wesson (later to be S&W); Joshua Stevens (later J. Stevens Arms Co.); and J. T. Ames (Ames Mfg. Co.). The newly formed company commenced operations in buildings part of the Ames factory, with a revolver based on the large dragoon size pistol of Edwin Wesson (brother of Daniel) expanding the line to include a pocket model. Sam Colt sued for patent infringement in 1851 and won his case; an injunction issued to prevent any further violation. To make their subsequently redesigned hand-revolved guns acceptable and salable to the public they added the Maynard primer device, hoping the novelty of the automatic primer that did away with individual copper caps would catch the public's fancy. Neither that nor various complicated innovations for automatic revolving (such as the J. Stevens patent of 1854; see 7A-057/058) met with great commercial success. With the expiration of Colt's patent in 1857 the company utilized it to produce revolvers based on the patents of Robert Adams of England.

The Massachusetts Arms Company first entered the longarms market in 1855 with the manufacture of the Greene breech-loading carbine, most of which were sold to the U.S. government. With the outbreak of the Crimean War they filled a substantial contract for that same model for the British government. The first of their Maynard carbines followed in 1858-59 with large quantities of that model and other breech-loaders (Smith, Warner) made during the Civil War. The earliest of their Maynard sporting models were introduced during those war years. Made in many models and variations (see Chap. 14), that line was the mainstay of the company's business until 1890.

The original Mass. Arms Co. was dissolved in 1866 when wartime production declined. The company name was retained and continued by T. W. Carter who had been superintendant of operations. Once again taken over in 1876, retaining its name, it continued under the supervision of a former Springfield Armory employee.

Mass. Arms Co. Wesson & Leavitt Dragoon

Massachusetts Arms Co., Chicopee Falls, Mass. Wesson & Leavitt Dragoon Revolver. Made c. 1850-51. Total production of about 800.

40 caliber. The 6-shot cylinder unmarked (a few with floral and military etched designs will bring premium value). Round barrels standard 7-1/8" length.

Walnut grips. Blued finish with casehardened frame.

Serial numbered from 1 on up. Standard markings of: MASS. ARMS CO./CHICOPEE FALLS(topstrap), WESSON'S AND LEAVITT'S PATENTS (lockplate), PATENT NOV. 26, 1850 (barrel catch), WESSON'S/PATENT/AUG. 28, 1849 (bevel gear), and LEAVITT'S PATENT APRIL 29, 1837 (rear of cylinder). Comparison should be made with Edwin Wesson and Warner & Wesson Dragoon revolvers.

(Note: When factory installed loading levers present (very few so fitted), the revolver commands an added premium.)

Early Type; lacking marking on the barrel catch, and fitted with 6-1/4" barrel. Approximately the first 30 specimens produced:
7A-054   Values—Good **$2,250**   Fine **$6,500**

7A-054

*7A-054
(with loading lever)*

Standard Model; with full markings as noted in general description above. Customary barrel length 7-1/8", but 6-1/4" and 8" also used infrequently. Total of about 770 made:
7A-055   Values—Good **$2,000**   Fine **$6,000**

Mass. Arms Co. Wesson & Leavitt Belt Rev.

Massachusetts Arms Co., Chicopee Falls, Mass. Wesson & Leavitt Belt Model Revolver (a.k.a. Pocket Model). Made c. 1850-51. Total production of about 1,000.

7A-056

A diminutive edition of the Wesson & Leavitt Dragoon. Patterned identically to it; proportionately smaller in size and weight.

31 caliber. The 6-shot cylinder with full etched designs of floral patterns and stand of arms. Round barrels varying in length from 3" to 7" (the longest lengths usually bring a slight premium). Most specimens have broad scroll engraving on the lock.

Blued finish with casehardened frame and walnut grips.

Serial numbered from 1 on up. Standard markings MASS. ARMS CO., CHICOPEE FALLSon topstrap; WESSON'S & LEAVITT'S PATENT on lockplate; LEAVITT'S PATENT APRIL 29, 1837 on front of cylinder:
7A-056   Values—Good **$600**   Fine **$2,000**

Mass. Arms Co. Maynard Primed Belt Revolver

Massachusetts Arms Co., Chicopee Falls, Mass. Maynard Primed Belt Model Revolver, a.k.a. John Brown Model. Made c. 1851-1857. Total quantity about 1,000.

31 caliber. Cylinder 6 shots with floral and military etched designs; most specimens have a broad scroll design engraved on the lock. Round barrels varying in length from 3" to 7" (the longest lengths usually bring a premium).

Blued finish with casehardened frame.

After losing a landmark patent infringement case to Colt (see preceding description), Mass. Arms Co. redesigned their Wesson & Leavitt Belt Model Revolver. In order to remain in business and not infringe on Colt, they made this model hand-revolved with a cylinder release button placed inside the trigger guard, just ahead of the trigger and also added a Maynard automatic nipple priming device. Markings MASS. ARMS CO./CHICOPEE FALLSon topstrap; PAT. NOV. 26, 1850 on barrel; MAYNARD'S PATENT SEP.

7A-057

22, 1845 on door of Maynard primer. Design of American eagle and shield usually encountered also on the door of Maynard primer (other designs are known and will bring a premium value). It is known that 200 of this model were sold to the abolitionist John Brown for his use in 1857. First sent to a farm in Ohio, they were trans-shipped to him in Kansas, 1859.
7A-057   Values—Good **$850**   Fine **$2,750**

Mass. Arms Co. Maynard Primed Pocket Rev.

Massachusetts Arms Co., Chicopee Falls, Mass. Maynard Primed Pocket Model Revolvers. Made c. 1851-1860. Total quantity of various types about 2,500 - 3,000.

28 and 31 calibers. Cylinders with etched floral designs; 6 shots; finish primarily blued; walnut grips.

7A-058

7A-059

A number of intriguing variations (some quite rare) appear in the automatically revolved (hammer or trigger actuated) types. As they are all almost identical from outward appearances, the collector is urged to refer to the Sellers & Smith book *American Percussion Revolvers* for details of these variations. It should also be pointed out that many of these internal revolving mechanisms were converted from one system to another within the factory before being offered to the public.

Manually revolved, earliest type; with Maynard Priming device on frame; tiny size; 6" overall length; the barrels 2-1/2" or 3". Made in 28 caliber only. Hand-revolved cylinder; button release mounted inside the trigger guard. Marked MASS. ARMS CO./CHICOPEE FALLS and on primer door MAYNARD'S PATENT 1845. Total production about 900:

7A-058 Values—Good **$450** Fine **$1,250**

Automatically revolved cylinder type; larger frame size than early manual type. Made in 28 and 31 calibers with 2-1/2", 3", 3-1/2" octagon (scarce) or round barrels. Markings same as above and on backstrap PATENT/JAN. 2, 1855. Approximately 1,500 - 2,000 of 3 distinct variations with numerous lesser variations. (Note: Values are for the most often encountered types. If time and care is taken to carefully identify them, a few variants can bring considerably more):

7A-059 Values—Good **$450** Fine **$1,250**

Mass. Arms Co. Adams Patent Revolvers

Massachusetts Arms Co., Chicopee Falls, Mass. Adams Patent Revolvers. Made c. 1857-1861. Quantities as noted below.

31 caliber and 36 caliber; 5-shot cylinders; solid frame; loading lever mounted on left side of barrel; all with double action mechanism. Walnut grips. Blued finish. Sliding cylinder safety on right side of frame. Each size serial numbered from 1 on up in its own range. Markings as noted below. Manufactured in America but based on a well-known English design and English patents held by Adams and Kerr.

Pocket Model; 3-1/4" octagon barrel with lengthy markings MADE FOR ADAMS REVOLVING ARMS CO., N.Y./BY MASS. ARMS CO., etc. with patent dates 1853, 1856, 1857. Total of about 4,500 made:

7A-060 Values—Good **$450** Fine **$1,250**

Note: Approximately 200 of this model were made with 4-1/4" barrels (about 100 were round and 100 octagon):

7A-061 Values—Good **$650** Fine **$1,750**

Navy Model; 6" octagon barrel; marked on topstrap MANUFACTURED BY MASS. ARMS CO., CHICOPEE FALLS on left frame ADAM'S PATENT MAY 3, 1858; on right frame PATENT JUNE 3, 1856; on loading lever KERR'S PATENT/APRIL 14th, 1857. Total of approximately 1,000 made of which about 600 were

7A-060
Pocket Model

7A-062
Navy Model

purchased by the U.S. Government and bear U.S. inspector's markings on the checkered walnut grips. These latter pieces usually bring a premium of 25 to 50 percent:

7A-062 Values—Good **$850** Fine **$2,250**

Thomas J. Mayall Pocket Model Revolver

7A-062.5

Thomas J. Mayall Patent, Roxbury, Massachusetts. Combination Percussion and Breech-Loading Cartridge Pocket Model Revolver. Circa 1862. Quantity unknown. Very limited, two specimens thus far recorded.

Made under Mayall patent of November 25, 1862, the revolver had interchangeable cylinders for 32-caliber percussion or rimfire ammunition. Nose of hammer swivels to accommodate either a percussion cap or rimfire cartridge. Six-shot cylinders. Brass frame with center hammer; rack-and-pinion loading lever hinged and folds against underside of frame. Six-inch round barrel. Partial blued and silver finish. Unmarked.

It is quite possible the revolver was produced in small quantity. Included here as an example of the type of rarity possible for the collector to encounter and experience difficulty in evaluating. Factors necessary to consider would be inclusion of both cylinders and if any markings present. Its value as a revolver in merely "very good" condition without accessories or spare cylinder would likely fall in the low four-figure range. Estimated values with both cylinders in area of high four to low five-figure range. Illustrated here as a cased set with both cylinders and special adapters for cylinder conversion along with other essential accessories (and worthy of an additional premium of 50 to 100 percent–possibly greater).
7A-062.5

Metropolitan Arms Co. Navy Model Revolver

Metropolitan Arms Co., New York City. Navy Model Revolver (copy of the Colt Model 1851). Manufactured c. 1864-66; total quantity about 6,063.

36 caliber. 6-shot round cylinder, standard roll scene of the Battle of New Orleans (on pistols serial range 1800 on up); earlier guns had plain cylinders. 7-1/2" octagonal barrel.

One piece walnut grips. Blued finish, with casehardened frame, lever, and hammer.

Serial numbered from 1 to about 63, and continued then from about 1164 on up to about 7100. The 1100 numbers added are believed to suggest the firm was making more specimens then it actually was. Markings as noted below.

Research has indicated that the Metropolitan Arms Co. received its impetus when Colt's factory suffered substantial fire damage in February, 1864. Every Metropolitan Arms product was a copy of a Colt, so much so that it is sometimes difficult to tell one make from the other. Although there are collectors who specialize in the Metropolitan revolvers, the types are also important to the Colt enthusiast, since they are so closely allied in design. Considered by collectors as a Secondary U.S. Martial handgun, despite the fact that no U. S. contracts are known. It is speculated, in view of the fact that his address was shown on a rare Metropolitan label, that Orison Blunt of New York City was the originator of the Metropolitan line, and that the unmarked examples of Navy and Police models were made by the Blunt firm, subsequently turning production over to Metropolitan.

First Model Navy; serial range 1 - 63, 1164 - 1799. Do not bear markings, other than serial numbers. Plain cylinders. Loading lever 3/16" shorter on first 63 guns, and they command a slight premium:

7A-063   Values—Good **$1,000**   Fine **$3,500**

7A-063

H.E. Dimick Navy; about 300 of the First Model production were sold to the H.E. Dimick firm. Of this number about 100 were marked on the barrel top: MADE FOR H.E. DIMICK St LOUIS *or* H.E. DIMICK St LOUIS. Exercise caution in purchase as spurious specimens exist:

7A-064   Values—Good **$3,000**   Fine **$8,000**

Standard Model Navy; serial range about 1800-7100. Barrels marked: METROPOLITAN ARMS CO. NEW YORK Cylinders bear Battle of New Orleans roll scene:

7A-065   Values—Good **$1,250**   Fine **$3,750**

Metropolitan Arms Co. Navy Model Revolver

7A-066

Metropolitan Arms Co., New York City. Navy Model Revolver (copy of the Colt Model 1861). Manufactured c. 1864-65; total quantity believed less than 50. By virtue of caliber and type this Model would be considered a Secondary U.S. Martial.

36 caliber. 6-shot round cylinder, standard roll scene of the Battle of New Orleans. 7-1/2" round barrel.

One piece walnut grips. Blued finish, with casehardened frame, lever, and hammer.

Serial numbered within the range of the Metropolitan Model 1851, and in number series about 2300 - 2350. Barrel marking: METROPOLITAN ARMS CO. NEW YORK

This is an extremely rare gun, and seldom available to the collector. A major difference from the Colt Model 1861 is the pivoted type loading lever, rather than the rack and pinion design. Thus, a screw is present in the barrel lug of the Metropolitan, on which the lever pivots:

7A-066   Values—Good **$3,000**   Fine **$7,500**

Metropolitan Arms Co. Police Model Revolver

Metropolitan Arms Co., New York City. Police Model Revolver (copy of the Colt Model 1862 Police). Manufactured c. 1864-66; total quantity about 2,750.

36 caliber. 5-shot half fluted cylinder. 4-1/2", 5-1/2", and 6-1/2" barrel lengths.

One piece walnut grips. Blued finish, with casehardened frame, lever, and hammer.

Serial numbered from 1101 to about 3850. Markings as indicated below. Note that the major mechanical difference

7A-068

between the Metropolitan Police Model and the Colt Model 1862 Police was the use of a pivoted lever assembly on the former, rather than the rack and pinion style as on the latter.
Unmarked specimens; found in the serial ranges about 1100 - 1800 and 1950 - 2400. Total of approximately 1,150:
7A-067   Values—Good **$450**   Fine **$1,250**

Note: A few of the above sold to the Union Arms Company, and are so marked:
7A-068   Values—Good **$750**   Fine **$1,650**
Marked specimens; the barrel stamping reading METROPOLITAN ARMS CO. NEW-YORK. Found in the serial ranges about 1800 - 1950 and 2400 - 3850. Total of approximately 1,600:
7A-069   Values—Good **$650**   Fine **$1,650**

Metropolitan Arms Co. Percussion .44 Cal. Army Model. Exercise extreme caution. All known examples merely well worn Colt Model 1860's with spurious markings. Specialists and arms historians are convinced no such model was ever made.

Nepperhan Fire Arms Co. Pocket Revolvers

Nepperhan Fire Arms Co., Yonkers, N.Y. Pocket Model Revolvers. Made c. early 1860s. Total quantity about 5,000.

31 caliber. 5-shot round cylinder. Barrel lengths from 3-1/2" to 6", (4-1/4" standard), and of octagon shape.

Two piece walnut grips. Blued and casehardened finish.

Serial numbered from 1 on up. Barrel markings as follows: NEPPERHAN/FIRE ARMS CO./YONKERS, N.Y. (range 1 - 500); NEPPERHAN/FIRE ARMS CO. (range 500 - 4000); and NEPPERHAN F.A. CO. YONKERS, NY. (balance of production). Values for the most widely used marking. The other two less encountered marked arms will bring a slight premium. These revolvers are similar to the Bacon and Manhattan Pocket models, all of which featured removable sideplates on the frames:

7A-070

7A-070   Values—Good **$375**   Fine **$1,250**

Frederick Newbury Pocket Model Revolvers

Frederick Newbury, Albany, N.Y. Pocket Model Revolvers. Manufactured c. 1855-60; total quantity very limited, and in a variety of types. Many patents were issued, and each variation was distinguished for its impractical design. Of the different types known, only one is believed to have gone into production; the others probably being patent models or prototypes. Various barrel lengths.

Two piece walnut grips. Brass or iron frames. Iron parts believed to have been blued.

Sometimes serial numbered. Some specimens known marked. The Newbury is one of the rarest of American percussion revolvers, and specimens are seldom seen.

The so-called "Production Model"; bears barrel marking NEWBURY ARMS CO.ALBANY; marking on the snub hammer, NEWBURY; on cylinder PATD. APL 10.1860. Nipples concealed under hooded shield, which is stamped: PATD JUNE 12, 1855. Tip up barrel. Iron frame of solid type. 26 caliber. 6-shot:
7A-071   Values—Good **$4,500**   Fine **$8,500**
Last type Brass frame without top- or bottomstrap; unusual C-shaped trigger. Barrel marking: NEWBURY ARMS CO ALBANY. Cylinder marking the same legend, with varying spacing. On the bottom of each grip: NEWBURY. 26 caliber. 6-shot:
7A-072   Values—Good **$4,500**   Fine **$8,500**

7A-071
Production Model

7A-072
Last Type

Nichols and Childs Belt Model Revolver

Nichols and Childs, Conway, Mass. Belt Model Revolver. Manufactured c. late 1830s; total quantity limited about 25 total. Patented by Rufus Nichols and Edward Childs, April 24, 1838.

Approximately 34 caliber. 5 or 6 shots; mechanism similar to that of the scarce Wheeler (Collier) type revolvers. Cylinder revolved by pawl attached to the hammer; lever on left side of frame pushed cylinder forward forming gas seal on breech of barrel. Barrel lengths about 6" and vary.

Bag shape walnut grips.

7A-073

Marking on frame: NICHOLS & CHILDS/PATENT/CONWAY/MASS.

One of the rarest of American percussion revolvers, the Nichols and Childs was made contemporary with the Paterson Colt revolver, and appeared also in rifle form. Production is believed to have been on special order only and noticeable differences appear in specimens:

7A-073   Values—Good **$5,000**   Fine **$12,500**

North & Savage   *See Savage*

Albert Parker Pocket Model Revolvers

Albert Parker, Springfield, Massachusetts. Pocket Model Revolvers. C. 1840s. Quantities unknown; likely less than 10 of each type. Very rare.

31 caliber. 5 shot. 3-1/2" round barrel. Brass frame. Two types known; both have very similar profiles. Exposed mechanism (illus. here) and internal revolving mechanism (not illus.)

Markings on cylinder ALBERT PARKER/SPRINGFIELD/MASS/PATENT/SECURED/CAST STEEL/WARRANTED No U.S. or other patent is known:

7A-073.5

7A-073.5   Values—Good **$5,000**   Fine **$12,500**

J. Peck Pocket Model Revolver

Jeremiah Peck, New Haven, Connecticut Pocket Model Revolver. Patent May 16, 1854. Quantity unknown. Very limited, at least four specimens are known to date (each with variations).

7A-073.8

31 caliber. Six-shot round cylinder; varying length octagon barrels. Iron frame. Not serial numbered. A removable (two screw-fastened) cover plate on left side of frame variously marked in script and/or block letters J. PECK / NEW HAVEN. CT. U.S.A. Another example is known marked PECK & GRILLEY / NEW HAVEN / PATENTED 1854. Believed that Peck acquired (directly from Whitney Arms Co.) frame castings and square-back trigger guards of the Whitney Two Trigger Model and adapted them to his use. Peck's was a complicated mechanism (an early attempt to circumvent Colt's patent) in which the hammer was not connected to the rotating mechanism or cylinder locking device. An unusual "spring shield" covered nipples, preventing adjoining chambers from accidentally detonating when the revolver was fired.

7A-073.8   Values—Good **$2,750**   Fine **$5,500**

C.S. Pettengill Pocket Model Revolver

C.S. Pettengill, New Haven, Conn. Pocket Model Revolver. (Not illus.) Manufactured for Pettengill by Rogers, Spencer & Co., Willow Dale, New York; c. late 1850s. Total quantity about 425.

31 caliber. 6-shot round cylinder measuring 1.5", 4" and 5" octagonal barrel. Iron frames standard; brass frames rare; worth premium.

Two piece walnut grips. Blued finish; the brass left bright.

Serial numbered from 1 on up, but appear to be some duplication with variations. Markings as noted below under variations. This quite unusual hammerless revolver features a double action mechanism and a rather large frame. About identical in appearance to the 34 and 44 caliber models, but smaller in size.

First Model Revolver. Marked PETTENGILL'S PATENT 1856 and T.K. AUSTIN. Irregular shaped removable center pin under barrel fitted only with the front half of a trigger guard. What appears to be the rear half of that trigger guard is actually the trigger itself. Approximately 25 made.

7A-074   Values—Good **$2,500**   Fine **$4,500**

Second Model; has standard trigger guard. Also a removable center pin; the finial in shape of an acorn. Production estimated at approximately 100.

7A-075   Values—Good **$1,750**   Fine **$3,750**

7A-074
1st Model Pocket

7A-075
2nd Model Pocket

7A-076
3rd Model Pocket

Third Model; frame marked on top PETTINGILL'S PATENT 1856 and markings on bottom of frame change to RAYMOND AND ROBITAILLE / PATENTED 1858. It has the split-type loading lever. Production estimated at approximately 300.

7A-076   Values—Good **$900**   Fine **$2,500**

C S. Pettengill Navy or Belt Model Revolver

C.S. Pettengill, New Haven, Conn. Navy or Belt Model Revolver. Manufactured by Rogers, Spencer & Co., Willow Dale, New York; c. late 1850s. Total quantity about 900.

34 caliber. 6-shot round cylinder measuring 1.7". 4-1/2" octagonal barrel. Frames of iron.

Two piece walnut grips. Blued finish.

Serial numbered from the Pocket Model predecessor arms, with some overlapping of numbers. Marked PETTENGILL'S PATENT 1856 and RAYMOND & ROBITAILLE PATENTED 1858 This version of the Pettengill was an improved and more potent development from the Third Model Pocket revolver.

Early production revolver, with the split type loading lever assembly. About 250 produced:

7A-078

7A-077   Values—Good **$750**   Fine **$2,250**
Later production; the lever of the so-called solid type. About 650 made:
7A-078   Values—Good **$700**   Fine **$2,000**

C.S. Pettengill Army Model Revolver

C.S. Pettengill, New Haven, Conn. Army Model Revolver. Manufactured for Pettengill by Rogers, Spencer & Co., Willow Dale, New York; c. early 1860s. Total quantity about 3,400.

44 caliber. 6-shot round cylinder. 7-1/2" octagonal barrel. Loading lever assembly standard. Double action hammerless type frame.

Two piece walnut grips. Blued finish; the frame and lever casehardened.

Serial numbered from where the Navy Model range left off (about 1300) on up. Standard marking: PETTENGILL'S/PATENT 1856 and RAYMOND & ROBITAILLE/PATENTED 1858(through serial range about 3500); late production arms marked PETTENGILL'S/PATENT 1856 and PAT'D JULY 22, 1856 AND JULY 27, 1858.

The U.S. Ordnance Dept. contract for 5,000, Dec., 1861, was subsequently changed to 2,000, June, 1862 when the sample gun failed trials. After changes were made the total contract delivered and accepted between Oct. 1862 and Jan. 1863. The 3rd Michigan Cavalry were issued 500 of them. Other mounted outfits issued lesser amounts were the 3rd and 5th Missouri Militia; 1st Arkansas; 3rd Illinois; 3rd Kentucky.

Model as above:
7A-079   Values—Good **$1,450**   Fine **$4,500**
Same as above, but with government inspector markings:
7A-080   Values—Good **$1,750**   Fine **$6,000**

7A-079

Plant's Mfg. Co., Belt Model Revolver   *See Chapter VIII.*

Plant's Mfg. Co., Pocket Model Revolver   *See Chapter VIII.*

P.W. Porter Turret Revolver

P.W. Porter, New York City. Turret Revolver. Manufactured early in the 1850s; quantity limited. Patent issued in 1851.

41 caliber. 9 shots; the vertically situated turret revolved by movement of the finger lever, which also cocks the hammer. Priming automatic, and using the pill lock system. Barrel length of about 5-1/4".

Two piece grips. Iron frame. Note rammer situated below barrel; the hammer mounted on right side of frame.

Unmarked. One of the rarest of American firearms of the 19th century, the Porter is also one of the most unusual. Because of the location of the turret, sighting was offset to the left. A distinct

7A-081

disadvantage was the continual direction of certain of the turret's charges directly at the shooter:
7A-081   Values—Good **$8,000**   Fine **$20,000**

E.A. Prescott Pocket Model Revolver

E.A. Prescott, Worcester, Mass. Pocket Model Revolver. Made c. 1860-61; total quantity about 100.

31 caliber. 6-shot round cylinder. 4" and 4-1/4" octagonal barrels. Spur type trigger; single action mechanism.

7A-082

Two piece walnut grips. Blued finish, with brass frame left bright.

Serial numbered from 1 on up. Some specimens marked: E.A. PRESCOTT WORCESTER, MS./PAT'D OCT. 2, 1860Most of production unmarked except for serial number.

This is a very rare American percussion revolver, and is seldom seen:

7A-082   Values—Good **$775**   Fine **$2,500**

Protection Pocket Model Revolver

Protection. Pocket Model Revolver. Identity of maker as yet unknown, although some authorities attribute production to Eli Whitney; an 1859 advertisement by well known New York agent for many gunmakers of the period, Joseph Merwin, promoted this as "Beal's Protection" and may be a clue. Manufactured c. 1857-58; total quantity about 1,000.

28 caliber. 6-shot round cylinder, standard with roll engraved scene of a policeman and two burglars and a traveler with two highwaymen. 3-1/4" octagonal barrel.

Iron frame casehardened with blued barrel. (Brass frame reported in earlier editions possible, but none verified.) Walnut two piece grips.

Serial numbered from 1 on up. PROTECTION marked on the cylinder, between two roll engraved panels. An unusual and scarce revolver, brought into production at about the time Samuel Colt's master patents expired in 1857:

First Model; production through about serial number 650. Front of frame having squared shape; cylinder roll scene present:

7A-083   Values—Good **$500**   Fine **$1,250**

Second Model; lack cylinder roll scene, and have rounded contour at front of frame. About 450 made, above serial range 650:

7A-084   Values—Good **$450**   Fine **$1,200**

7A-084

James Reid Pocket Model Revolver   *See Chapter VIII.*

Remington   *See Chapter V.*

Rogers & Spencer Army Model Revolver

Rogers, Spencer & Co., Willow Dale, N.Y. (near Utica) Army Model Revolver. Made 1865. Total quantity estimated 5,800 based on serial numbers reported, of which 800 would have been civilian usage. That figure has been questioned.

U.S. Ordnance contract for 5,000 Nov. 1864. 1,500 delivered by end of April, 1865; balance by Sept. 1865. No records indicate issuance of the gun. In 1901, military goods dealers Francis Bannerman, N.Y. acquired almost the entire lot of them at Government sale, offering them to collectors through their catalogs over the next few years. That accounts for the fine to mint condition in which many specimens are yet seen.

44 caliber. 6-shot round cylinder. 7-1/2" octagonal barrel. Hinged type loading lever assembly. The frame of solid type, with the mechanism single action.

Grips of two piece walnut. Blued finish, with casehardened hammer and lever.

Serial numbered from 1 on up. Marked: ROGERS & SPENCER/ UTICA, N.Y. on topstrap over cylinder. Government inspector markings standard on grips (RPB) and certain metal parts.

Comparison should be made with the Freeman revolver, of which the Rogers & Spencer is an improved design. Prior to

manufacture of the Rogers & Spencer revolver, the company had produced the Pettengill percussion revolvers of Pocket, Navy, and Army sizes.

Standard model; totaling 5,000 made on contract for the U.S. government. Bear inspector marks on grips and various metal parts:

7A-085   Values—Very Good **$1,750**   Exc. **$4,250**

As above, but civilian production; lack government proof stampings. Total believed to be about 800:

7A-086   Values—Very Good **$1,500**   Exc. **$3,500**

7A-085

Jacob Rupertus Army Model Revolver

Jacob Rupertus, Philadelphia, Penn. Army Model Revolver. Manufactured c. 1859; total quantity a dozen or less.

44 caliber. 6-shot; mechanism featured pellet priming from a

primer device on the backstrap. Single nipple employed, mounted on breech in line with upper section of cylinder. 7-1/4" octagonal barrel; loading lever operates side to side, with lever beneath barrel and rammer on right side of barrel lug.

Two piece walnut grips.

May bear marking: PATENTED, APRIL 19, 1859 on top of frame.

A considerable rarity in American percussion revolvers, the Rupertus had a rather impractical priming mechanism, and proved to be difficult to manufacture, and no competition to the Colt, Remington, or other well designed handguns on the market:

7A-087   Values—Good **$5,000**   Fine **$15,000**

7A-087

Jacob Rupertus Navy Model Revolver

Jacob Rupertus, Philadelphia, Penn. Navy Model Revolver. Manufactured c. 1859; total quantity a dozen or less.

36 caliber. 6-shot; mechanism featured pellet priming as on the Army Model, with a single nipple employed in line with the hammer. Octagonal barrel; loading lever operating in side to side fashion.

One piece walnut grips. Note brass trigger guard and buttcap.

Unmarked.

A great rarity in American percussion revolvers, the Rupertus was primarily meant as a test run revolver, and since it was not given an enthusiastic reception was made only in

7A-088

quite limited quantity. Note the appearance of the cylinder, seemingly for metallic cartridges:

7A-088   Values—Good **$5,000**   Fine **$15,000**

Jacob Rupertus Pocket Model Revolver

7A-089

Jacob Rupertus, Philadelphia, Penn. Pocket Model Revolver. Manufactured c. 1859; total quantity a dozen or less.

25 caliber. 6-shot; mechanism featured pellet priming as on the Army and Navy models, with a single nipple employed in line with the hammer. Octagonal barrel, without loading lever. Iron or brass frame.

One piece walnut grips. Sheath style trigger and brass buttcap.

Unmarked.

One of the rarest of American percussion revolvers. It would appear that the standard barrel length was 3-1/8", but the scarcity of specimens makes a determination difficult:

7A-089   Values—Good **$3,500**   Fine **$7,000**

Savage and North Figure 8 Pocket Model Revolver

Savage and North Figure 8 Pocket Model Revolver (a.k.a. "Baby Savage Figure 8"). Mfg. by Edward Savage, Middletown CT, under the Henry North Patents. Circa mid-late 1850s. Quantity unknown. Rare.

28 caliber. Five shot. 3-1/2" octagon barrel. Blued finish. Walnut grips. Specimens observed with oval contour brass frames will likely bring slight premium over those with flat contour iron frame types.

Mechanically these pocket models function similar to the large Navy models and are made without the large trigger guard. Value range when available likely to be in the high four figure to mid-five figure range.

7A-089.5

7A-089.5

Savage & North Figure 8 Navy Model Revolvers

Savage & North, Middletown, Conn. Figure 8 Model Revolvers. Made c. 1856-59. Total quantity of various models about 500.

36 caliber. Round cylinder, 6 shots. Octagonal barrels of 7-1/8" length.

Two piece walnut grips with humpbacked profile. Blued finish.

Serial numbering somewhat confusing and more than one range was employed. Standard marking (either on barrel or frame): E. SAVAGE. MIDDLETOWN.CT./H.S. NORTH. PATENTED. JUNE 17th, 1856.

The North & Savage Company was formed late in the 18th Century, by Simeon North with Josiah Savage. The company became known under the North & Savage name in 1831. In 1859 the company was reorganized under the name Savage Revolving Fire-Arms Co. A number of variations have been identified in the Figure 8 revolvers, and the key ones are discussed here.

First Production Model; (not illus.) having round shaped brass frame, cylinder chamber mouths protruded to fit into breech end of barrel. Early type rammer lever assembly. Approximately 10 produced; *extremely rare:*

7A-090　　Values—Good **$6,000**　　　　Fine **$15,000**

Second Variation of the First Model; most often encountered variation. Chamber mouths chamfered, to fit over breech end of barrel (standard thereafter). Total production about 250, of which 100 were made on an Ordnance Department order (thus bear government inspector markings and will bring a premium value). Round shaped brass frame and early type rammer lever assembly:

7A-091　　Values—Good **$4,250**　　　　Fine **$11,000**

Second Model; a near twin to the Second Variation of First Model, easily distinguished by the round shaped iron frame and creeping type rammer lever. Marked on rammer housing: H. S. NORTH, PATENTED APRIL 6, 1858, and also marked as noted in introductory material. About 100 total production:

7A-092　　Values—Good **$4,000**　　　　Fine **$10,000**

Third Model; having brass frame with flat sides and round recoil shield. Creeping type rammer. More graceful hump on grip back, instead of the sharp type spur. Quite confusing in serial numbering. May possibly include a government contract for 300 specimens for Navy issue, but none known with inspector marks. Estimated total production between 100 and 400:

7A-091
First Model Variation

7A-092
Second Model

7A-093
Third Model

7A-093　　Values—Good **$4,000**　　　　Fine **$10,000**

Fourth Model; (not illus.) virtually identical to the Third Model, but the frames of iron, with flat sides. Total made about 50:

7A-094　　Values—Good **$4,500**　　　　Fine **$12,000**

Savage Revolving Fire-Arms Co. Navy Model

Savage Revolving Fire-Arms Company, Middletown, Conn. Navy Model Revolver. Made c. 1861-mid 1860s; total quantity about 20,000.

36 caliber. 6-shot round cylinder. 7-1/8" octagonal barrel. Hinged type loading lever assembly. Flat sided frames, fitted with a heart-shaped trigger/lever guard.

Two piece walnut grips. Blued finish, with casehardened hammer and lever, trigger guard and triggers.

7A-095

7A-095.2

Serial numbered generally with two sets of numbers. Standard marking on framestrap (above cylinder): SAVAGE R.F.A. CO./H.S. NORTH PATENTED JUNE 17, 1856/JAN. 18, 1859, MAY 15, 1860.

Most of the Savage Navy revolver production were made on government contracts, and inspector markings on the grips are often observed (worth premium). Bought under contract by both the Army and Navy. Total of government purchases was 11,984. Balance of sales were primarily to civilians. Specimens with U.S. Government Inspector markings worth a premium. Comparison should be made with the North & Savage Figure 8 revolvers, from which the Savage Navy evolved:

7A-095　　Values—Good **$950**　　　　Fine **$4,250**

U.S. Navy Contract. Only 800 Savage 36 caliber revolvers are believed to have been contracted by the Navy during the Civil War. Specimens are seen with small anchor marking stamped at the top of the barrel just ahead of the frame and inspector markings P (proved) over J.R.G. the initials of the Navy inspector, Captain John R. Goldsborough, USN in the center of the cylinder. Many of the vessels to which these Savage revolvers were issued are listed in *Civil War Small Arms of U.S. Navy,* by McAulay (q.v.) and worth consulting. Depending on condition, naval marked equipment specimens are worth premium values 25 percent to 50 percent greater that other government inspected specimens.

7A-095.2

Jacob Shaw Underhammer Pocket Revolver

7A-095.5

Jacob Shaw Underhammer Pocket Revolver. Made at Hinckley, Ohio under his patent of June, 1857. Quantity estimated at fewer than 50. Rare.

30-caliber. Octagonal 3-1/4" barrel; 6-shot; rosewood grips; blued finish. Marked JACOB SHAW, Jr. on left frame. The cylinder center pin is a 5-inch iron tube with a brass liner that is pulled outward and serves as a tube sight. The large trigger cocks the hammer and rotates the cylinder; smaller trigger at bottom of guard fires the gun.

The primary claim for Shaw's patent was the compactness of the design; hammer inside the frame between the grips strikes the nipple of the bottom chamber. The center-mounted barrel serves to keep size minimal. Overall, only 3-1/4 inches high by 5-1/2 inches long.

7A-095.5   Values—Good **$6,500**   Fine **$12,500**

C. Sharps & Co., Philadelphia, Penn. *See Chapter V.*

Shawk & McLanahan Navy Model Revolver

Shawk & McLanahan, Carondelet, St. Louis, Mo. Navy Model Revolver. Made c. 1858; total quantity 100.

36 caliber. 6-shot round cylinder. 8" round barrel.

Two piece walnut grips. Blued finish, with brass frame left bright.

Serial numbered from 1 on up. When present, marking found on backstrap: Shawk & McLanahan, St. Louis, Carondelet, Mo. Often erroneously regarded as Confederate revolvers, these arms were produced by Union sympathizers shortly before the Civil War began. The design inspiration obviously was the Whitney Navy revolver:

7A-096

7A-096   Values—Good **$6,000**   Fine **$14,000**

Springfield Arms Co.

The Springfield Arms Company was founded about 1850, and was intended to compete with the Colt revolver. Within about a year the firm was required to cease production due to legal pressures from Colt's attorneys. Chief designer for Springfield Arms was James Warner, and revolvers were also made under his name (*q.v.*). Similarity is noticeable between the products of Springfield Arms, James Warner, the Massachusetts Arms Co., Edwin Wesson, Wesson Stevens & Miller, and Warner & Wesson. The products of Springfield Arms and of Massachusetts Arms are particularly intriguing to the collector due to the considerable number of variations.

Detailed specifics are to be found in Sellers and Smith's *American Percussion Revolvers,* and variations can be judged and valued accordingly by the rarity of known quantities.

Springfield Arms Co. Dragoon Model Revolver

Springfield Arms Company, Springfield, Mass. Dragoon Model Revolver. Made c. 1851; total quantity about 110.

40 caliber. 6-shot round cylinder. 6" (early model) or 7-1/2" round barrels; means of barrel removal differs according to presence or absence of loading lever assembly.

Grip variations noted below. Blued finish.

Serial numbered from 1 on up. Topstrap marking: SPRINGFIELD ARMS CO. Despite the quite limited production, several distinct variations on the Dragoons have been noted by collectors.

First type; with grip and frame cast (of metal) together; 6" barrel length. Cylinder revolves by cocking of hammer:

7A-097   Values—Good **$3,750**   Fine **$10,000**

7A-097
First Type

7A-098
Second Type

7A-099
Third Type

7A-100
Fourth Type

Second type; as above, but having a protective shield around the nipples, the shield fitted with a safety gate which pivots to shield nipple from the hammer:

7A-098   Values—Good **$3,500**   Fine **$8,500**

Third type; lacks the nipple shield and safety device, and has a 7-1/2" barrel and attached, hinged type loading lever; grip of cast metal:

7A-099   Values—Good **$3,750**   Fine **$9,000**

Fourth type; as immediately above, but with wooden grip and military style iron buttcap:

7A-100   Values—Good **$3,500**   Fine **$8,500**

Springfield Arms Co. Navy Model Revolvers

Springfield Arms Company, Springfield, Mass. Navy Model Revolvers. Made c. 1851; total quantity about 250.

36 caliber. 6-shot round cylinder, with etched decoration. 6" round barrel. Hammer mounted at top center of frame. Two piece walnut grips. Blued and casehardened finishes.

Serial numbered from 1 on up. Marked SPRINGFIELD ARMS CO. (topstrap). The Navy specimens are basically a larger caliber version of the standard types of the Belt Revolver. Considerable similarity exists. Note that on the Navy the rammer lever assembly attaches to the barrel lug. The Navy Model is considered a Secondary U.S. Martial handgun, although no contracts are known to collectors.

Single Trigger Navy Model; the hammer revolving the cylinder. Besides standard topstrap maker's marking, WARNERS PATENT JAN. 1851 is on the frame. About 125 made:

7A-101   Values—Good **$1,250**   Fine **$3,750**

Double Trigger Navy Model; the forward trigger revolving the cylinder. Does not include the JAN. 1851 portion of the WARNERS PATENT marking. About 125 made:

7A-102   Values—Good **$1,400**   Fine **$4,000**

7A-101
Single Trigger Navy

7A-102
Double Trigger Navy

Springfield Arms Co. Belt Model Revolvers

Springfield Arms Company, Springfield, Mass. Belt Model Revolvers. Made c. 1851; total quantity about 350.

31 caliber. 6-shot round cylinder, with etched decoration. 4", 5", and 6" round barrels. Hammer mounted at top center of frame. When rammer lever assembly present, it is mounted on the cylinder pin.

Two piece walnut grips. Blued and casehardened finishes.

Serial numbered from 1 on up but more than one series believed used. Markings as indicated below.

Jaquith Patent Belt Model; marked JAQUITH'S PATENT 1838 on the frame, and SPRINGFIELD ARMS CO. on topstrap. No rammer assembly. About 150 made:

7A-103   Values—Good **$700**   Fine **$2,000**

Warner Patent Belt Model; similar to the above, but marked WARNER'S PATENT/JAN. 1851 and SPRINGFIELD ARMS CO. About 100 made:

7A-104   Values—Good **$625**   Fine **$1,750**

Warner Model; (not illus.), as above, but fitted with attached rammer lever assembly; single trigger. Only a handful made and *rare*:

7A-105   Values—Good **$1,250**   Fine **$2,500**

7A-103
Jacquith Patent Model

7A-104
Warner Patent Model

7A-106
Double Trigger Model

Double Trigger Belt Model; as above, but having two triggers, the front serving to revolve the cylinder (after hammer was cocked), and then releasing the hammer by coming into contact with the second trigger. Also note the groove on cylinder in line with the nipples. Production postdates Colt's victory in the

Mass. Arms trial, and these revolvers bear no markings other than serial numbers. Very similar in appearance to the double trigger Navy; major difference in variant shape of barrel lug just ahead of the cylinder. About 100 produced:

7A-106   Values—Good **$800**   Fine **$2,250**

Springfield Arms Co. Pocket Model Revolvers

Springfield Arms Company, Springfield, Mass. Pocket Model Revolvers. Made c. 1851; total quantity about 1525.

28 caliber. 6-shot round cylinder with etched decoration; the nipples set into the side portion. 2-1/2" round barrel. Hammer mounted at top center of the frame. Made without rammer lever.

Two piece walnut grips of bird's head type. Blued and casehardened finishes.

Serial numbered in a variety of groupings. Markings vary, but usually consist of one of the following: WARNER'S PATENT/JAN. 1851, *or* SPRINGF'D ARMS CO, *or* WARNERS PATENT/JAMES WARNER, SPRINGFIELD, MASS. A considerable amount of variation has been noted in the Springfield Arms Pocket series, as noted particularly in the Smith & Sellers book. Basic groupings are noted below.

Early Model; the cylinder automatically revolves by pulling back the hammer. Marked only WARNER'S PATENT/JAN. 1851, or with SPRINGF'D ARMS CO. or without marking. Distinguishing feature is the lack of a deep groove on the cylinder. Frames were rounded on all but approximately 25 pieces which were

flattened on sides. These will bring a premium value. Total quantity about 525:

7A-107   Values—Good **$350**   Fine **$850**

Ring Trigger Model; made without trigger guard, the ring trigger serving to revolve the cylinder, and then releasing the cocked hammer on engaging the second, conventional type, trigger. About 150 made; may or may not be marked:

7A-108   Values—Good **$550**   Fine **$1,400**

Double Trigger Model; with trigger guard; both triggers of conventional type. Marked WARNERS PATENT/JAMES WARNER, SPRINGFIELD, MASS. or not marked. About 350 produced:

7A-109   Values—Good **$475**   Fine **$1,250**

Last Model Revolver; the hammer used to revolve the cylinder which bears the deep groove at its rear. Marking: WARNERS PATENT/JAMES WARNER, SPRINGFIELD, MASS. which apparently indicates Warner's own manufacture of this last type. Total quantity produced about 500:

7A-110   Values—Good **$350**   Fine **$850**

7A-107
Early Model

7A-108
Ring Trigger

7A-109
Double Trigger

7A-110
Last Model

Starr Arms Co. D.A. 1858 Navy Revolver

Starr Arms Co., New York City. Double Action Model 1858 Navy Revolver. Made c. 1858-60, in a total quantity of about 3,000. All Starr revolvers were made at their factories in Binghamton and Yonkers, New York.

36 caliber. 6-shot round cylinder. 6" round barrel.

Walnut grips. Blued, with casehardened hammer, trigger, and lever.

Serial numbered from 1 on up. Frame marking: STARR ARMS CO. NEW YORK and STARR'S PATENT JAN. 15, 1856. The unusual Starr D.A. mechanism was by no means of the conventional type. The so-called double action is unique and may more aptly be termed 'self cocking' as the gun cannot be used on single action by manually pulling back the hammer alone. The Navy model is the most difficult Starr revolver to acquire, due to its limited production in comparison with the Army types.

Standard Navy; as above:

7A-111   Values—Good **$950**   Fine **$3,500**

Martially marked specimens; with inspector stampings on the grip (JT). Note that despite the government's purchase of a total of 2,250 specimens, Starrs are seldom found with inspector stampings:

7A-112   Values—Good **$1,400**   Fine **$4,500**

7A-111

Starr Arms Co. D.A. 1858 Army Revolver

Starr Arms Co., New York City. Double Action Model 1858 Army Revolver. Made c. late 1850s early 1860s; total quantity about 23,000.

44 caliber. 6-shot round cylinder, note nipples protruding from the back section. 6" round barrel.

Walnut grips. Blued, with casehardened hammer, trigger, and lever.

Serial numbered from 1 on up. Frame marking: STARR ARMS CO. NEW YORK and STARR'S PATENT JAN. 15, 1856. Inspector markings standard on both sides of grips.

Most Starr Double Action Army revolvers will be found bearing government inspector markings and only occasionally lacking them (indicating civilian sales). Unless they have a special feature such as rosewood or other grips, the civilian arms

7A-113

usually bring the same price as the martially marked specimens. (The revolver has been reproduced in recent years for the black powder shooters' market.)

7A-113   Values—Good **$800**   Fine **$2,250**

Starr Arms Co. S.A. 1863 Army Revolver

Starr Arms Co., New York City. Single Action Model 1863 Army Revolver. Made c. 1863-65; total quantity about 32,000.

44 caliber. 6-shot round cylinder, the nipples partially protruding from the back section. 8" round barrel.

Walnut grips. Blued, with case hardened hammer and lever.

7A-114

Serial numbering continued the range of the Double Action Model 1858 Army series, from about 23000 on up. Frame markings: STARR ARMS CO., NEW YORK and STARR'S PATENT JAN. 15, 1856. Inspector stampings on one or both sides of the grips on most specimens.

The Starr Single Action was designed as an improved and less costly successor to their D.A. Model 1858 Army. Next to Colts and Remingtons, this was the major model of revolving handgun bought by the U.S. government in the Civil War period. (The revolver has been reproduced in recent years for the black powder shooters' market.)

The majority of Starr Single Actions will be found bearing government inspector markings. Approximately 25,000 of them were purchased under contract. Civilian specimens, though scarcer, usually bring the same price, unless having special features such as fancy grips. Even though the Single Action was produced in larger quantities than the Double Action Army, it brings a higher price on the collector's market:

7A-114   Values—Good **$1,100**   Fine **$3,250**

Tomes Son & Melvain, N.Y.   *See Bacon Manufacturing Co.*

Union Arms Co., New York   *See Bacon Manufacturing Co. and W.W. Marston. Also see Metropolitan Arms Police Model Revolver.*

Aaron C. Vaughn Double Barrel Revolver

Aaron C. Vaughn, Bedford, Penn. Double Barrel Revolver. Made c. early 1860s; total quantity about 20 or less.

27 caliber. 14-shot round cylinder, the chambers in a staggered alignment. 5" octagonal barrel, with two bores, to line up with the double sets of chambers.

One piece wooden grips. Blued and casehardened finish. Serial numbered from 1 on up, and not otherwise marked.

One of the most rare and unusual of American percussion revolvers, the Vaughn was quite limited in production, in part due to its apparent infringement of the Walch patent covering use of a double hammer and special trigger mechanism. In firing the Vaughn the first backward movement of the trigger releases one hammer, and when the trigger was pulled further back, the

second hammer fell. Note the general similarity of overall shape to the Colt Navy:

7A-115   Values—Good **$9,500**   Fine **$22,500**

7A-115

John Walch Navy Model 12 Shot Revolver

John Walch, New York City. Navy Model Revolver. Made c. 1859-early 1860s in a total quantity of about 200. Manufactured

at the Union Knife Company, Naugatuck, Connecticut, for Walch, and by J.P. Lindsay.

36 caliber. 12-shot cylinder with six chambers, each taking a double load; total of 12 nipples (six in each of two concentric circles at breech); note raised sections over each charge area. 6" octagonal barrel.

7A-116

Two piece walnut grips, sometimes checkered. Blued finish.

Serial numbered from 1 on up. Standard marking WALCH/FIRE ARMS CO./N.Y. (left side of barrel), and PATENTED FEB. 8, 1859 (right side of barrel). (Note: Some specimens found without markings other than serials, or with markings in script; and some revolvers bear light scroll engraving on sides of the frame.)

The Walch mechanism is one of the more unusual in American percussion revolvers. A single action, each chamber held two charges, the front fired by the outer nipple and struck by the right hammer, which is released by the right trigger. The left trigger released the left hammer, which in turn struck the inner nipple, firing the innermost charge! The Navy Model is regarded by collectors as a Secondary U.S. martial handgun, although contracts are unknown:

7A-116   Values—Good **$3,500**   Fine **$12,500**

John Walch Ten Shot Double Hammers Pocket Revolver

John Walch, New York, Ten Shot Double Hammers Pocket Revolver. Made for Walch and partner J.P. Lindsay (*see Lindsay pistol 7C-020*) by **New Haven Arms Company, Oliver F. Winchester, President and Major Stockholde**r, 1860-1862. Made at the factory concurrent with the Henry rifle. Total quantity 3,000.

31 caliber. 10-shot cylinder with five chambers, each taking a double load; total of ten nipples (five in each of two concentric circles at breech); note the raised sections over each charge area. 3-1/4" octagonal barrel. Two piece walnut grips. Barrels marked on top: WALCH FIRE-ARMS CO. NEW-YORK/PAT'D FEB. 8, 1859. The Pocket revolvers differed from the Navy in the standard use of a single trigger. The mechanism was designed to allow for one hammer to fall first (the right one, to fire the foremost charge), followed by the left. Note also the spur trigger configuration. Some revolvers bear light scroll engraving on sides of the frame.

Some of the Walch Pocket Models were privately purchased and carried during the Civil War by Union officers and soldiers. One entire outfit, Company "I" of the 9th Michigan Infantry armed themselves with the gun, where it received favorable comment. Not all field reports were so laudatory.

The revolver is usually sought as an example of "arms curiosa" or a scarce pocket type. The Walch's significance as a

7A-117

directly related Winchester collector's item has not yet been reflected in the marketplace. That may be due to the slight attention ever paid to its origins.

Brass Frame Model: Blued barrel, frame left bright. Serial range 1 to 1500 reported (a second survey reports 2000 made):
7A-117   Values—Good **$1,000**   Fine **$2,650**

Iron Frame Model: Blued finish overall. Serial range 1500 to 3000 (prox.) (Second survey reports only 1000 made which would make it scarcer. However the market has not recognized the disparity.)
7A-117.5   Values—Good **$1,000**   Fine **$2,650**

Charles Warner Pocket Model Revolver

7A-118

Charles Warner, Windsor Locks, Conn. Pocket Model Revolver. About identical to James Warner 1857 type. Made c. late 1850s; total quantity about 600.

31 caliber. 6-shot round cylinder. 3" round barrel. Two piece walnut grips. Blued finish. Iron frame.

Serial numbered from 1 on up. Cylinder marked: CHARLES WARNER. WINDSOR LOCKS, CONN.

These small revolvers were extremely close in design and quality to the more common Pocket Model 1857 type by James Warner. It is felt that manufacture of the two types was done in separate facilities, due to identifiable differences of minor details. A major difference is the cylinder stop on the Charles Warner mounted on the topstrap, three grooved rifling and the complete absence of a small screw on the left side of the frame just above the point where the top of the grip meets the frame (this screw is found on the James Warner model):
7A-118   Values—Good **$350**   Fine **$1,200**

James Warner   *See Also Springfield Arms Co.*

James Warner Belt Model Revolver

James Warner, Springfield, Mass. Belt Model Revolver. Made c. 1851; total quantity estimated at several hundred.

31 caliber. 6-shot round cylinder with etched decoration (5-shot variation known; worth premium). 4", 5", or 6" round barrels (4" the standard length).

Two piece walnut grips. Blued finish.

Serial numbered from 1 on up using an alphabet-number system. No maker's name or address markings.

This early, solid frame revolver is attributed to James Warner, and is believed to have been his first revolving handgun made on a production basis. Revolution of the cylinder was caused by the trigger:

7A-119

7A-119   Values—Good **$650**   Fine **$1,600**

James Warner Side Hammer Pocket Model Revolver

7A-119.2

James Warner, Springfield, Mass. Side Hammer Pocket Model Revolver. Made circa late 1850s. Quantity estimated under 100. Rare.

28-caliber. Round 3-inch barrel. Brass frame. Six-shot cylinder. Barrel and cylinder blued; frame either silver or gilt finished. Walnut grips; spring-loaded cap box in butt. Specimens unmarked except for serial number underside of barrel

Mechanical operation is unique and unlike any of the other James Warner revolvers; identified as James Warner production from external physical characteristics. Cylinder pin enters from rear of frame. Spring-loaded slots at rear of cylinder engage the rotating mechanism.

7A-119.2   Values—Good **$2,500**   Fine **$4,500**

James Warner Pocket Model Revolvers

James Warner, Springfield, Mass. Pocket Model Revolvers. Made c. 1857-late 1860s; total production approximately 9,500.

Calibers, cylinders, barrels, serial numbers, and markings noted under separate descriptions below. All variations were 6-shot. Iron frame standard; brass frame known; very rare; worth premium.

Warner's Pocket Model was by far his most popular and best selling firearm. It is interesting to note that these Pocket Revolvers were brought out after the expiration of Colt's master patents in 1857. Warner had the dubious distinction of losing patent infringement suits on revolver production first in the percussion period, and later in the cartridge. Both instances forced him to stop production. See the Cartridge Revolver chapter for a Warner almost identical to this model, and chambered for metallic cartridges.

First Model; 28 caliber, 3" octagonal barrel (integral with the frame), marked JAMES WARNER SPRINGFIELD, MASS. U.S.A. on topstrap. Safety notches at rear of cylinder. Total made about 500:
7A-120   Values—Good **$350**   Fine **$950**

7A-121

Second Model; first variation, made in 28 caliber, with round barrels of lengths from 2-5/8" to 4". Marking as above, but including WARNER'S PATENT 1857 on cylinder. Safety notches on circumference of cylinder. Production limited to a few hundred:
7A-121   Values—Good **$325**   Fine **$800**

Second Model; second variation, made in 31 caliber; barrel lengths and markings as above. Production of about 9,000+:
7A-122   Values—Good **$325**   Fine **$750**

Warner & Wesson Dragoon Model Revolver

7A-123

Warner & Wesson, Hartford, Conn. Dragoon Model Revolver. Made c. 1849; total quantity limited to about a half-dozen.

40 caliber. 6-shot round barrel, with early type barrel catch.

Walnut grips, with military style brass buttcap. Blued and casehardened finish.

Lockplate marked: WESSON'S & LEAVITT'S PATENT On the topstrap: LEAVITT'S PATENT/MANd BY WARNER & WESSON HARd, Cf.

This is one of the ultra rare early American percussion revolvers. It was a product of Thomas Warner, who had been hired to complete revolvers begun by Edwin Wesson, but unfinished at the time of his death in 1849. Other than in the markings, the Warner & Wesson is just about identical to the massive Mass. Arms Co. Wesson & Leavitt Dragoon (*q.v.*) with most easily distinguishable difference being the high domed brass military type buttcap:

7A-123   Values—Good **$6,500**   Fine **$12,500**

Edwin Wesson Dragoon Model Revolver

Edwin Wesson, Hartford, Conn. Dragoon Model Revolver. Made c. 1848-1849; total quantity unknown; very limited.

45 caliber. 6-shot round cylinder. 7" round barrel, with early type barrel catch.

Walnut grips, with military type brass buttcap. Blued and casehardened finish.

On the topstrap: D. LEAVITT'S PATENT/MANUFACTURED BY E. WESSON, HARTFORD, CONN.

A highly prized pioneer effort at revolver production, the Edwin Wesson revolver's 'bevel gear' mechanism is thought to have been designed by William Henry Miller and Joshua Stevens while they were employed at Colt's factory, in 1848. Colt himself caught them working on a revolver of their design on his time, and they were promptly fired. When the manufacture of the Edwin Wesson guns was interrupted (due to his death), Thomas Warner was brought in to complete production. In 1850 manufacture moved to Chicopee Falls, Mass., being continued by the newly formed Massachusetts Arms Co.

7A-124

About identical to the Warner & Wesson Dragoon above, with the high-domed brass buttcap. Most noticeable difference is the rounded lock plate, versus flush-fitting of the Warner & Wesson, and the deep, flat recessed section on the right frame where the hammer is fitted (see close-up illustration.

7A-124   Values—Good **$6,500**   Fine **$12,500**

Wesson & Leavitt   *See Massachusetts Arms Co.*

Western Arms Co., New York and Chicago   *See Bacon Manufacturing Co. and W.W. Marston.*

F.G. Wheeler, New York   *See William Hankins.*

Whitney   *See Chapter V.*

Wright Pill Lock Turret Pistol

Wendell Wright, New York City, N.Y. Pill Lock Turret Pistol. C. 1854. Quantity unknown; likely less than 10. Very rare.

36 caliber. 5-1/2" part octagon/round barrel. 8-shot. Iron frame. Unique mechanism: lever inset in face of handle revolves turret and cocks hammer; what appears to be trigger is merely a finger rest; actual trigger is a squeeze bar on back of handle.

No markings present. Pistol covered by U.S. patent No. 11,917 issued Nov. 7, 1854:

7A-125   Values—Good **$7,500**   Fine **$17,500**

7A-125

Chapter VII-B

Percussion Pepperboxes

The generic term "pepperbox" is aptly applied to this distinct group of firearms, and will undoubtedly bring to mind to the antiquarian "…a small container with holes in the top used in sprinkling pepper on food" (per Webster's dictionary). Very likely this is the implement after which the handgun species was named. Although the neophyte gun collector, an occasional arms author, the Philadelphian (and this writer's mother) more often called them "pepperpots," that term is more accurately applied to a spicy soup or stew!

The origin of the word "pepperbox" as applied to firearms, is obscure. The nickname was more popularly adopted by the purchasers and users of these arms in the mid-19th century and came into wide popular acceptance by collectors of the 20th century, rather than being adopted by the gun manufacturers themselves. As attested to by advertising, instruction sheets and other literature of the era, the makers preferred to term their arms as "revolving pistols" or "repeating pistols."

The specific features that identify a "pepperbox" are subject to debate; and the "hard liners" are often diametrically opposed to the "soft liners" on the subject. The former's definition quite narrowly refers to a revolving, multi-barreled firearm in which each barrel is individually fired by a single stroke of the hammer, sometimes allowing that the barrels may be rigid, but the hammer itself may revolve. Both proponents agree that the barrel group must be arranged around a central axis. On the opposite end of the spectrum, the "soft liners" or "liberals" (if you will) are much more all-inclusive, allowing for any firearm consisting of three barrels or more which are arranged either around a central axis or superimposed, and which will fire individually or all barrels simultaneously. Thus, it is really up to the collector as to how narrow or broad he wishes to confine his activities and define his group of pepperboxes. The vagueness and absence of a clear-cut definition is best outlined in *Encyclopedia of Firearms* by Peterson (see Chap. IV Bibliography).

The pepperbox principle extends to the beginning of arms development in the 16th century, with the height of its popularity reached in the second quarter of the 19th century in America. The first American pepperbox patent was granted to the Darling Brothers of Massachusetts in 1836, and they are generally credited with introducing the system here. A major innovation following shortly thereafter, and of far reaching significance in the pepperbox's popularity, was the double action mechanism, invented and introduced by Ethan Allen (*q.v.*) of Massachusetts. The design permitted rapid firing while the sleeker contours of the gun (i.e., the flat bar type hammer *vs.* the tall projecting spur of the single action hammer of earlier specimens) allowed for better concealment and easier use.

Pepperboxes found very wide acceptance among the general public; their reliability and low relative cost kept them popular for many years simultaneous with the production of several makes of percussion revolvers. Their demise was generally brought about by the larger manufacture at lower prices of the percussion revolver as well as the fact that pepperboxes did have detrimental features: (a) Difficult to aim; (b) heavy trigger pull; (c) the hammer (on most models) was in direct line of sight; and (d) the larger sized models became unwieldy and noticeably muzzle heavy. Pepperbox popularity generally waned in the 1850s and by the outbreak of the Civil War their sales were overtaken and surpassed by the single barrel revolver.

Collecting these multi-barreled handguns has always had a reasonably large and quite devoted following. Although there are several collectors who confine themselves entirely to these types, few are the American collections of almost any style that do not at least have representative specimens included. Just as their popularity in the 1840s and 1850s was brought about by their relatively low cost, so too have they been highly popular in the collecting world in present day. As will be seen from the following listings, a great majority of specimens are still within the reach of the average collector; an extensive and varied grouping is possible with but a reasonable outlay of money. As with any arms specialty, though, there are great rarities of significant value that may also be encountered.

Within this section are the pepperboxes of all the major and lesser known American manufacturers; either completely identified and described or cross-indexed to other sections where they are included with the arms of larger makers. Most notable among these are the significant group by Ethan Allen (Allen & Thurber, Allen & Wheelock, etc.), to be found in Chapter V. As the leading manufacturer and innovator, the Allens played a major role in the development of the type and specimens form an integral part of any pepperbox collection. The reader is urged to review the material that prefaces the pepperbox section within the E. Allen chapter (*q.v.* Chapter V) as much of that information will be found useful and applicable to pepperboxes in general.

As with the Allens, serial numbers are often not a good method of judging the rarity or period of production. For the most part, such markings are manufacturing "batch numbers" and hence, low digits are not truly indicative of actual quantities made.

Barrel lengths vary considerably on models and types of most makers. Thus, exacting measurements are not always the best way to classify types. However, these do generally fall within known patterns and unless barrel lengths are abnormally long or short (and proven original, of course), this feature does not affect value nor demand appreciably, if at all.

A standard feature of many pepperboxes (and as will be noted in the descriptions) is the broad scroll and floral engraving motifs on frames and nipple shields. When engraving is standard, this is reflected in values shown for those respective specimens. On occasion, an elaborate, custom engraved pepperbox may be encountered; these are rare and as with many other American antique arms, the style, quality and profuseness of engraving and the condition of the gun will add considerably to the value. Each specimen must be judged on its own merits. The most often observed extra feature that will affect value is the use of grip material other than walnut. Ivory appears occasionally and, of course, will command an added premium. The subject is discussed at greater length in Chapter II to which the reader is referred.

Cased pepperbox outfits will be seen with a reasonable frequency. Some makes, e.g., Blunt & Syms, Robbins & Lawrence and Allens, are found more often than other types; all such cased outfits may be looked upon as scarce and highly desirable, with notable premiums added to the value. The reader is referred to Chapter II for further discussion of evaluating casings.

Other features which may be found on pepperboxes and which affect values are special or custom details such as removable daggers (may be found mounted in the center of the barrel cluster) and possibly belt hooks (affixed to the frame). As these desirable variances are susceptible to counterfeiting and forgeries, specimens should be given extremely close scrutiny in order to ascertain originality.

BIBLIOGRAPHY

(Note: Material on pepperboxes also appears in other books covering American firearms, listed in complete bibliographic data elsewhere in this book, notably Chapters IV and V. See also *The Collecting Of Guns,* edited by James E. Serven; *Ethan Allen, Gunmaker: His Partners, Patents And Firearms,* by Harold R. Mouillesseaux; *The Story Of Allen And Wheelock Firearms,* by H. H. Thomas; *Manhattan Firearms,* by Waldo E. Nutter; and *Ethan Allen and Allen and Wheelock,* by Paul Henry.

Dunlap, Jack. *American, British And Continental Pepperbox Firearms.* San Francisco: Recorder-Sunset Press, 1964. The standard guide to the subject. Profusely illustrated.

*Mowbray, Stuart C. *The Darling Pepperbox; The Story of Samuel Colt's Forgotten Competitors.* Lincoln, RI; Mowbray Pub. 2004. A story long overdue.

Winant, Lewis. *Pepperbox Firearms.* New York: Greenberg: Publisher, 1952. The pioneer work on the subject; of lasting significance.

(*) Preceding a title indicates a book is currently in print.

E. Allen; Allen & Thurber; Allen & Wheelock   *See Allen Firearms, Chapter V.*

Thomas K. Bacon Single Action Underhammer Pepperbox

Thomas K. Bacon, Norwich, Connecticut, Single Action Underhammer Pepperbox. Made c. 1852 to 1858. Estimated production 200.

31 caliber. Six-shot. 3" ribbed barrels scarce; 4" ribbed barrels standard; 5" barrels very scarce, worth premium; fluted barrels very rare. Finish blued.

Hammer on underside of frame with large curved finger spur for cocking. Engraved nipple shield. Walnut grips.

Serial (batch) numbered. Barrel marking: BACON & CO., NORWICH C-T and CAST STEEL. Scroll, floral engraving standard on frame and nipple shield:

Ribbed barrels:

7B-001   Values—Good **$450**   Fine **$1,250**

Fluted barrels. Bacon markings not present on all viewed specimens:

7B-001.5   Values—Good **$550**   Fine **$1,400**

7B-001
(with ribbed barrels)

7B-001.5
(with fluted barrels)

J. G. Bolen, New York, an agent for Allen Pepperboxes   *See Allen Firearms, Chapter V.*

Blunt & Syms Underhammer Pepperbox

Orison Blunt and John G. Syms, New York, Ring Trigger Concealed Underhammer Pepperbox. (Often erroneously called hammerless.) Made c. late 1830s to 1850s. Total produced of various types believed a few thousand.

Calibers vary from 25 to 38. Six-shot; fluted barrel ribs standard on production types (barrels with smooth, round shape and non-ribbed are quite rare and will bring a considerable premium). Barrel lengths as below.

Double action operation. Capping slots on right side of frame show considerable variances and do not affect values. Scroll and floral engraving standard on frames. Varnished walnut grips. Blued finish standard.

Serial numbers sometimes present. These arms are usually found without maker markings and just the letters R-C (and often a two-digit number) on the face of the muzzle of the barrels. The markings BLUNT & SYMS NEW YORK are occasionally

7B-002
Small Frame Bag Shape

7B-003.5
*Medium frame with
exceptionally deep flutes*

7B-005
Medium Frame Saw Handle

7B-002.5
*Scarce Variant with straight
non-fluted/ribbed barrels*

7B-004
Dragoon Size Bag Shape

7B-006
Dragoon Size Saw Handle

found on the frame and are considered quite scarce, commanding premium value of 20 percent to 50 percent.

Variances have also been noted in the shape of the muzzles with some having crowned muzzles which are scarcer, but premiums in values have not been noted.

Blunt & Syms were prominent arms dealers and probably manufacturers or assemblers of numerous types of percussion firearms. Their products appear to have been a combination of European made frames and mechanisms with U.S. produced barrel clusters. A great amount of variation appears in their arms with the major types classified as below. Excepting the Allen made pepperboxes, these Blunt & Syms are the type most often seen by the collector. Two major styles are encountered, each with their own graduated size frames. Barrel lengths vary and have not been found to play a role in valuations (unless outlandish or exceptionally long in length). Average sizes are given below:

BAG SHAPED HANDLE:

Small Frame Type: Approximately 25 to 28 caliber. Short barrel cluster 1-5/8" to approximately 2-1/4"; scarce size:
7B-002   Values—Good **$450**   Fine **$1,250**

Medium frame with straight, non-fluted or ribbed barrels. Very scarce:
7B-002.5 Values—Good **$550**   Fine **$1,500**

Medium Frame Type: 31 caliber; approximately 4" barrel cluster:
7B-003   Values—Good **$375**   Fine **$1,100**

Medium frame; six-shot. Bag shape handle. 3" exceptionally deep fluted barrels, giving each barrel a full rounded appearance vs. the usual fluted types. Rare:
7B-003.5 Values—Good **$850**   Fine **$2,000**

Dragoon Size: 36 caliber. Barrel group approximately 5" in length:
7B-004   Values—Good **$850**   Fine **$2,250**

SAW HANDLE TYPE WITH FLARED BUTT (Not made in small frame size):

Standard or Medium Frame: 31 caliber. Barrels average 4" length:
7B-005   Values—Good **$450**   Fine **$1,275**

Dragoon Size: 36 caliber; barrels 5" and 6" average length:
7B-006   Values—Good **$900**   Fine **$2,500**

B. & B. M. Darling Pepperbox Pistol

Barton and Benjamin M. Darling, Bellingham, Massachusetts and Woonsocket, Rhode Island, Circa 1836-1839 (possibly slightly later) Pepperbox Pistol. Quantity unknown; usually estimated slightly over 100. However, one specimen located with serial number 211 was cause to revise the estimate to slightly over 200. *Rare.*

30 caliber; 6-shot. Barrel cluster 3-1/4 inches long with fluted ribs. Single action with high spur hammer. Iron frame. Wood (occasionally tortoise shell) grips.

Frame markings: B. & B. M. DARLING / PATENT / (serial number). Light, simple decorative engraving standard on frame and hammer.

The Darling is among the most rare and sought after of all American production type pepperboxes. Most of the limited

production made at Woonsocket; very few made earlier at Bellingham.

The first American patent for a pepperbox was that received by the Darlings April, 1836, for a "Rotary Pistol with Six Barrels." It was later claimed that the Darlings invented revolving firearms (i.e. the barrel cluster, or cylinder, revolved upon cocking of the hammer) despite the fact that Samuel Colt's patent was granted seven weeks earlier. Much legend and myth evolved from such notions, especially in arms collectors' literature over the past half-century…and from folklore of the locales where the Darlings conceived and manufactured those same pepperboxes! Documentary evidence confirms that legal actions against the Darlings were taken by Allen and Thurber, who may have considered the

7B-007
American Made

7B-007.5
Swedish Made

Darlings a threat with their own earlier patent. The saga of the brothers and their innovative revolving handgun is skillfully examined in *The Darling Pepperbox: The Story of Samuel Colt's Forgotten Competitors* (2004) by S. C. Mowbray (q.v.).

A Darling pepperbox bearing only the markings "W. GLAZE / COLUMBIA, S.C. / PATENT 4" is known (the "4" apparently the serial number); others may possibly turn up. A known arms dealer (see 6A-044) Glaze likely acted as a retailer for the Darling brothers. One other Darling is known marked only with the unidentified name "GODDARD," its significance an enigma. Specimens with either of those markings are worthy of premium values over those indicated for "Darling" marked:

7B-007   Values—Good **$3,250**   Fine **$8,500**

Swedish Made So-Called "Darling" Pepperboxes. Quite a few brass framed and brass barreled four-, five- and six-shot percussion pepperboxes are seen on the collectors' market which were formerly considered to be the product of B. & B. M. Darling and have been so identified in considerable early arms literature (see illustration). Somewhat primitively styled and bearing markings such as J. ENGH; A.C.S.; A.I.S.; I.E.H.; A.S.S.; while others are unmarked. They have been identified and are now recognized as Swedish manufacture. A great many were evidently made for export with reasonable quantities sold in the United States during the era of their manufacture. They are certainly good collectors' items, but are not considered as American manufacture:

7B-007.5   Values—Good **$450**   Fine **$800**

W. Glaze, Columbia, S.C. marked Pepperbox   *See B. & B. M. Darling.*

Goddard Marked Pepperbox   *See B. & B. M. Darling.*

Hyde & Goodrich, New Orleans, markings on Allen Pepperbox   *See Allen Firearms, Chapter V.*

Lane and Read, Boston, markings on Allen Pepperbox   *See Allen Firearms, Chapter V.*

G. Leonard, Jr. Concealed Hammer Pepperbox

George Leonard, Jr., Charlestown, Massachusetts, Ring Trigger, Concealed Hammer Pepperbox. Made c. 1849 to 1850. Several hundred estimated produced.

31 caliber. Four-shot. Barrel lengths approximately 3-1/4".

Ring cocking trigger with a small outer curved trigger for firing. Barrels are stationary and must be unscrewed and removed for capping the nipples. The concealed striker within the frame revolves to fire each barrel.

Iron frame with broad scroll engraved motifs standard. Blued finish. Walnut grips with bag shaped handle.

Barrel marking: G. LEONARD. JR. CHARLESTOWN/PATENTED 1849. CAST STEEL. Serial numbered.

A former Allen & Thurber employee, George Leonard, Jr.

7B-008

held patents for pepperbox arms dated September 18, 1849 and July 9, 1850. In 1850, Leonard production was turned over to Robbins & Lawrence of Windsor, Vermont:

7B-008   Values—Good **$750**   Fine **$2,250**

Manhattan Firearms Company   *See Manhattan Firearms, Chapter V.*

S.W. Marston Double Action Pepperbox

7B-009

Stanhope W. Marston, New York, Ring Trigger, Bar Hammer, Double Action Pepperbox. Quantity unknown, very limited; rare. Made c. early 1850s.

31 caliber. Six-shot. Scroll and floral engraving on frame and nipple shield standard. Bag shaped handle with walnut grips.

Mechanism covered by the S. W. Marston Patent of January 7, 1851. None are known bearing maker's markings.

Distinguishing feature is necessity of pushing forward the trigger after firing to allow re-engaging of hammer. Maker should not be confused with the better known William W. Marston:

7B-009   Values—Good **$800**   Fine **$2,000**

William W. Marston Double Action Pepperbox

William Walker Marston, New York, Bar Hammer Double Action Pepperbox. Also known with following trade name markings: W. W. Marston, New York City; W. W. Marston Armory, New York; William Marston, New York City; Marston & Knox, New York; Sprague & Marston, New York; The Washington Arms Company; The Union Arms Company; and Phenix Armory. Made c. 1850s.

31 caliber. Six-shot. Barrel clusters average 4" and 5" in length, but will vary.

Bar hammer construction with double action mechanism. Iron frames and separately affixed nipple shields bear scroll and floral engraving as standard. Bag shaped handle with walnut grips. Ribbed barrels are most often encountered on all types except those marked UNION ARMS COMPANY which are generally seen with fluted barrels.

A great variance will be seen in both barrel and hammer markings. These include company names and addresses as listed above (all capital block letters); also present may be CAST STEEL while hammers may be marked PATENTED 1849 and/or NEW YORK and/or with a maker identification (e.g., W. W. MARSTON - NEW YORK 1854).

The most commonly encountered markings seem to be W. W. MARSTON and values indicated are for those so marked. Until a detailed study or statistical survey determines relative rarity of types or markings, only slight premiums may be added for other marking variations. See also listing of W. W. Marston in the percussion revolver section of this chapter for further insights into their production of arms and use of trade names:

7B-010   Values—Good **$425**   Fine **$1,100**
Small Frame With Straight, Unfluted Barrels. 6 shot; 28 caliber; 2-1/2" barrels completely flat (no flutes or ribs) marked

7B-010
Ribbed Barrel

7B-010
Fluted Barrel

7B-010.5
Straight Barrel

SPRAGUE & MARSTON/ NEW YORK and on the bar hammer W.W. MARSTON/ NEW YORK/ PAT. 1849. Engraved frame with nipple shield. Rare:

7B-010.5   Values—Good **$700**   Fine **$1,750**

William W. Marston Three Shot D.A. Pepperbox

7B-010.7

William W. Marston, New York, Bar Hammer Double Action Three Shot Pepperbox. Made circa 1850s. Quantity unknown. Rare.

44 caliber deeply rifled bores. Fluted 3-3/4" barrels. Blued finish. Walnut grips. Markings engraved on top of bar hammer WM MARSTON, PAT'D 1855 N.Y. Made under Marston's Patent 13,581 of September 18, 1855 in which its system was described as a "Target" mechanism. First pull of trigger brought hammer to half-cock and rotated the barrel group part way. Second pull completed rotation and fired gun. Most specimens are lightly engraved. Value range from mid to high four figures. Rare.
7B-010.7

Marston & Knox   *See W. W. Marston.*

North & Couch Hand Held and Animal Trap Pepperbox

Henry S. North and John O. Couch, New York City and Middletown, Connecticut, Combination Hand Held Pepperbox and Animal Trap Gun. Made c. 1860s. Referred to in the original 1859 Patent as a "Game-Shooter."

Both types six-shot. See calibers and barrel lengths below.

Designed primarily as an animal trap gun to be suspended from a tree limb or staked to the ground, these pistols could also be fired in the conventional manner when hand held. On both types there is a single nipple which fires all six barrels simultaneously. When used as a trap gun, a trip cord tied to a rod in the center of the barrel cluster acts as trigger:

7B-011
Disk Hammer

7B-012
Spur Hammer

Disk Hammer Type: 28 caliber. 1-3/4" straight, unfluted barrel cluster. Large circular disk with knurled edge acts as hammer. Markings when present: NORTH & COUCH, MIDDLETOWN, CONN. Narrow, rounded iron frame:

7B-011   Values—Good **$800**   Fine **$2,250**

Single Action Spur Hammer Type: 31 caliber. 2-1/8" fluted barrel cluster. Marking: NORTH & COUCH. ADDRESS J. D. LOCKE 197 WATER STREET. N.Y. Flat sided iron or brass frame:

7B-012   Values—Good **$1,000**   Fine **$2,750**

Onion & Wheelock   *See Chapter V-A, Ethan Allen.*

Pecare & Smith Ten-Shot Pepperbox

Jacob Pecare and Joseph Smith, New York, Ten-Shot Pepperbox with sheathed or shielded barrel. Made c. late 1840s to early 1850s.

28 caliber. Ten-shot barrel cluster standard with a stationary shield extending to the muzzle. Specimens are known without the shield and merely a narrow nipple shield; considered very rare and will bring premium. Standard barrel length approximately 4".

Semi-concealed hammer visible from top; trigger folds down for double action firing. Brass frame standard; specimens with iron frame very rare and will bring premium. Walnut grips.

Sheath marked: PECARE & SMITH'Sand PATENT 1849. Marking on the barrel cluster (under sheath): CAST STEEL. Decorative scroll engraving on the frame and barrel shield is standard. Serial numbered.

Pecare and Smith is one of the most sought after of all American pepperboxes. The distinctive shield design for the barrels was to prevent the cluster from being grasped and held by the assailed party, not allowing the shooter to fire. Very scarce:

7B-013   Values—Good **$2,250**   Fine **$6,500**

Variant ten-shot with nipple shield and ribbed barrels. Engraved iron frame with matching engraved nipple shield;

7B-013
Sheathed Barrels

7B-013.5
Ribbed Barrels

3-1/2" ribbed barrel cluster. 28 caliber. Markings identical above. Rare.

7B-013.5   Values—Good **$4,000**   Fine **$8,500**

Pecare & Smith Four-Shot Pepperbox

7B-014
Double Action

7B-014.2
Single Action

Jacob Pecare and Joseph Smith, New York, Four-Shot Double-Action Pepperbox without shielded barrel. Made c. late 1840s to early 1850s.

28 caliber and 31 caliber. Four-shot barrel cluster approximately 3-7/8" length.

Bar type hammer; trigger folds down for double action firing. Brass frame most often seen; iron frame rare and will bring premium. Walnut grips.

Barrels marked: PECARE & SMITH'S / PATENT 1849 / CAST STEEL. Decorative scroll engraving on frame is standard. Pin-type front sights on muzzle of each barrel.

7B-014   Values—Good **$1,000**   Fine **$3,250**

Single Action Variant immediately identifiable by its larger hammer with the high cocking spur projecting from its top. 31 caliber; engraved iron frame; cluster of four 4-inch barrels. Occasionally classified "experimental," likely merely a short (and rare) production. Specimens with serial numbers in the mid-two digit range known.

7B-014.2   Values—Good **$2,250**   Fine **$5,000**

Phenix Armory   *See W. W. Marston.*

J. Post Double Action Pepperbox

7B-014.5

Jacob Post, Newark, New Jersey, Ring Trigger, Concealed Hammer, Double Action Pepperbox. Made circa 1849-1850. Quantity unknown; very limited. Rare.

30 caliber. 6-shot. 3-1/2" ribbed barrels. Bold scroll and leaf engraved designs on frame. Bag shape handle; walnut grips. Closely resembles Blunt & Syms with distinctly different mechanism.

Markings on top of frame J. POST'S SELF-ACTING SET/PAT 1849. A slightly complicated, and possibly a bit harebrained system: to fire, the ring trigger had to be pulled to first "set" the gun, then pulled forward to release the hammer:

7B-014.5   Values—Good **$1,250**   Fine **$2,750**

Robbins & Lawrence Pepperboxes

7B-015
Fluted Barrel

7B-016
Ribbed Barrel

7B-016
Conventional
Trigger Valant

Samuel E. Robbins and Richard S. Lawrence, Windsor, Vermont, Ring Trigger Concealed Hammer Pepperboxes. Made c. 1851 to 1854. Improved versions of the George Leonard, Jr. patent. Total quantity estimated over 7,000.

28 and 31 calibers. Five-shot. Barrel clusters 3-1/2" and 4-1/2" and unscrew to load directly into the hinged breech section. Entire barrel unit hinged on bottom and tips down for capping.

Ring cocking trigger with small outer curved trigger for firing. Decorative scroll engraving is standard on the iron frame and breech of barrels. Finish: blued frame with browned barrels. Walnut grips.

Barrel marking: ROBBINS & LAWRENCE Co./WINDSOR, VT./PATENT. 1849. Early 31 caliber specimens have LEONARD'S PATENT. 1849 forming the last line of markings and will bring small premium. Serial numbered.

Two distinct types of barrel hinges are noted: (a) Securely affixed type; a traverse hinge pin secures barrel to breech and (b) prong type with a traverse screw acting as hinge pin. On this type, the barrel merely lifts off the gun, seemingly falling apart. Values the same for either type.

These Pepperboxes proved to be among the best selling and most popular type of their day and would have fared better without the rapid growing proliferation of Colt revolvers. A number of very rare variations are known among them including types with conventional triggers, brass frames and dragoon sizes; all of which will bring substantial premiums:

Fluted Barrel Type: 28 and 31 calibers. Five-shot:

7B-015   Values—Good **$550**   Fine **$2,000**

Ribbed Barrel Type: 31 caliber only. The most often encountered style:

7B-016   Values—Good **$550**   Fine **$2,000**

A. W. Spies, markings on Allen made Pepperbox   *See Allen Firearms, Chapter V.*

Sprague and Marston Pepperbox   *See W. W. Marston.*

Starr Arms Co. Double Action Pepperbox

Starr Arms Company, New York City (sales office) and Binghamton, N.Y. (factory). Percussion double action pepperbox. Quantity unknown; likely less than ten; circa 1856.

Eben Starr's first attempt at firearms manufacture under his U.S. Patent 14,118 of Jan., 1856 which illustrates a pepperbox of usual style: bag shape handle, large trigger bow, 6 individual round barrels clustered around a central axis. Hammer and nipple arrangement unique. It is known that five Starr pepperboxes (5 shot types) were submitted for trial by the U.S. Navy. They underwent tests at the Washington Navy Yard under the direction of Cmdr. John Dahlgren, Jan., 1857. Although he reported favorably on them, it is likely that Starr's D.A. 36 Navy revolver (7A-111) that was close to completion voided the possibility of a future for his pepperbox. None are believed to have been made commercially. Extremely rare; no known specimen

7B-016.5

Stocking & Co. Single Action Pepperbox

Stocking Company, Worcester, Massachusetts, Single Action Pepperbox with long extended, angular, cocking spur on hammer. Made c. late 1840s to early 1850s.

28 and 31 caliber. Six-shot. Barrel clusters vary from 4" to 6".

Iron frame and nipple shield bear decorative scroll engraving. Walnut grips. Trigger guard found with or without the extra finger spur projecting at rear. Blued finish.

Barrel marking: STOCKING & CO., WORCESTER and CAST STEEL WARRANTED, and often accompanied by a small eaglehead proofmark. Hammer also may be marked PATENT SECURED 1848.

Variants are known made without nipple shield and removable nipples (integral nipples standard) and are considered rare. Both types will bring premium values:

7B-017   Values—Good **$550**   Fine **$2,000**

7B-017
Without shield

7B-017
With shield and
spur trigger bow

Tryon marked Pepperbox made by Allen   *See Allen Firearms, Chapter V.*

Union Arms Company Pepperbox   *See W. W. Marston.*

Washington Arms Company Pepperbox   *See W. W. Marston.*

Young & Smith marked Allen Pepperbox   *See Allen Firearms, Chapter V.*

Unmarked Underhammer Pepperbox

7B-018

Unmarked, Underhammer, American Pepperbox. Circa 1840s. Classic New England underhammer style displaying features and workmanship typical of well-known Massachusetts and Connecticut makers of single shot underhammer pistols (*see Chapter VII-E*). Excellent workmanship. Likely less than 15 made. Serial numbered. Specimens observed and thus far recorded all under serial number 10.

28 and 31 calibers. Six-shot. 3-1/2" fluted, ribbed barrels which rotate automatically when hammer is cocked.

Maplewood handle entirely edged in brass. Very rare:

7B-018   Values—Good **$1,400**   Fine **$3,250**

Unmarked Primitive Pepperboxes

Unmarked primitive American Pepperboxes. Seldom encountered and usually quite primitive, (often crude) in construction, these ostensibly "homemade" percussion pepperboxes are often quite astonishing in their mere size and awkwardness as well as the often unique methods devised to allow them to operate. Some are one-of-a-kind, made by a back-country gunsmith, possibly a blacksmith. Others (as nos. 7B-019.2 / 7B-019.3 / 7B-019.4) were obviously made in very limited quantity. An occasional specimen has shown up through the years and the type is known and illustrated in both the Dunlap and Winant books about pepperboxes (see Biblio this chapter). All are deserving of inclusion in a representative pepperbox collection, if not a generalized American arms collection, as they represent an early attempt at revolving handguns and are contemporary with the early, popular pepperboxes of the well-known American firms whose pepperboxes were significant innovations upon introduction to the American market, and prior to production of Sam Colt's revolvers. There is little, if any, uniformity to them. The few types of which other specimens are known, vary when compared, clearly indicating their individual construction. Almost all are manually rotated. The few exceptions adapted for

mechanical rotation are seldom found to operate correctly!

Valuing these "primitive" types may present a minor stumbling block for the collector. Collecting in more recent years has seen a wider interest and audience for these oddities and "arms curiosa." When they are priced in a logical range, the occasional specimen has found a ready market when specimens have occasionally become available. Features to consider in determining a value are: (1) Type of material. Brass regarded by some to mitigate the crude construction; usually worth a premium. (2) Size; a feature may offer more show-stopping appeal. (3) Quality: a wide range of workmanship is encountered, from the most clumsy and coarse, to reasonably refined professional. (as with 7B-019.4 below). As a general guide the following might be found helpful:

7B-019 – Values as below: For small pocket or belt sizes in most primitive of workmanship

Values—Good **$275-$750**

Values—Very Good **$600-$1,750**

7B-019.1 – For the large, often massive sizes in correspondingly large calibers

Values—Good **$400-$800**

Values—Very Good **$750-$1,850**

The following illustrations and descriptions represent a broad cross-section of the general types the collector might encounter. All are manually revolved:

7B-019.2

7B-019.2 This truly massive pepperbox is a type of which a number of specimens are known and is illustrated and described in both classic references for American pepperboxes. Believed made in Pennsylvania. This specimen is ten inches overall and weighs 3 pounds! The cluster consists of four round 5-inch ribbed barrels, each a huge 69 caliber! An opening at the top of the narrow nipple shield allows the hammer to strike the nipple when in-line. A distinctive feature on this and others like it, is the rather awkward-looking iron handle.
7B-019.2   Values—Good **$650**   Fine **$1,250**

7B-019.3

7B-019.3 Apparently made by the same maker as above, with decided variance to the frame. Equally massive four-barrel pepperbox, 11 inches overall; weighs 2 pounds. Its four round, ribbed 4-1/2 inch barrels are each 60 caliber. The topstrap on the frame runs the full length of the handle to butt; one-piece walnut grips. Surprisingly, it is decorated with semi-primitive (decidedly original) scroll and vine-like engraving its full length.
7B-019.3   Values—Good **$500**   Fine **$1,000**

7B-019.4

7B-019.4 An example of the type that does display semi-professional work of a competent craftsman, and one that paid more attention to detail. Overall 7-1/2 inches, yet heavy for its size; weight 2 pounds. Cluster of four, thick-walled round and tapered 3-inch barrels; each 46 caliber. Wide nipple shield with a single round opening at top to line up with the nipple being fired. Oddly shaped round iron frame with well-made, separately affixed, iron trigger guard. Although the walnut handle is simply shaped (almost awkward appearing, with a very sharp drop), it is well fitted to the frame and reflects competent craftsmanship.
7B-019.4   Values—Good **$800**   Fine **$1,750**

7B-019.5

7B-019.5 Underhammer primitive four-shot percussion pepperbox. Overall 7-1/2 inches, and 30 caliber. The barrels are all bored from a single large round iron rod or bar from which the nipples project at breech end. The uniquely designed "cylinder stop" is merely a large, flat spring mounted at top of the handle with a small, hollow iron cone at its forward end which fits over the nipple to lock the barrels in place! To operate, the small lever at rear of spring lifts it upwards ("unlocking" the nipple!) allowing mechanical rotation. No provision is made for a trigger guard. Awkwardly shaped maple handle. Representative of the most primitive form!
7B-019.5   Values—Good **$450**   Fine **$750**

7B-019.6

7B-019.6 Brass frame and barrels, primitive four-shot pepperbox. Thick-walled 3-inch 38-caliber barrels with nipples mounted in-line at rear within deep recessed openings at breech of each barrel. Seven inches overall. Box-lock style frame with central-mounted hammer. A small, flat iron spring mounted on left frame acts as the cylinder stop, fitting into a recessed groove at the breech of each barrel as it comes in-line. Uniquely designed trigger is flat-mounted on underside of frame. When the hammer is cocked, the back section of the trigger opens just slightly (it is not hinged or downward opening). To fire, the rear section of the trigger is merely squeezed upward. One-piece maple handle.
7B-019.6   Values—Good **$750**   Fine **$1,400**

Chapter VII-C

Percussion Single and Multi-Barrel Pistols

This section, alphabetically arranged, covers American percussion single and multi-barreled pistols and includes a few miscellaneous types not classified elsewhere in this chapter, e.g., the superposed load Lindsays, three-barrel Marstons and Reuthe trap guns. Published data is lacking for many arms listed here, thus it is quite possible the collector will find variations not mentioned or otherwise described. Such handguns should be assessed for possible value changes on their individual merits with common sense serving as the best rule-of-thumb guideline.

The specifications and data presented are as complete and accurate as possible based on the limited published studies about many of them. The personal experience of the author and fellow collectors and dealers in buying, selling and trading them over a long period of time has also been considered. Omission of a specific gun does not necessarily indicate the item is a collector's rarity. However, it clearly signals that further investigation and research is required, quite possibly proving the piece to be valuable.

Dimensions listed in this section are average ones for the more standard manufactured types. Variations, when encountered, will for the most part be in barrel lengths and calibers; where such differences are slight, there is no appreciable price fluctuation, if any. However, where ungainly sized barrels are encountered of exceedingly long or bizarre lengths (varying greatly from the norm) or calibers show exceptional variances from standard, the gun should be re-evaluated on the basis of those rare features. Factors to consider are the maker's name, the importance of the style and type of gun, its condition, and most important its demand on the collectors' market.

Marking variations may also be seen that differ from those listed herein. Generally speaking they will not have a great significance on the lesser known or recorded types, unless such markings have some specific historical significance to the gun or the type as being competitively sought by highly specialized collectors.

Major contour changes, i.e., the shape of the frame or handle, would be considered variations of importance, and hence value fluctuations could be considerable, dependent on the make, quality, condition and demand for that particular type. For the lesser known and sought-after types, these variations may be of insufficient significance to affect value to the same degree as with arms of a major manufacturer such as Colt, Whitney or Remington. Thus, it is all very much a matter of the style of gun, the maker's name, and most important—the demand for it—as to how great a premium should be added for variations.

Wherever possible, approximate dates or era of manufacture have been given in order to place the arms in a historical perspective. Note that some of the dates shown here have likely missed their mark by five years or more; only future definitive treatises or biographies of the makers will shed light on the subject. Estimates of quantities produced are in the same category and have been offered only where reasonably reliable information was known.

Most of the handguns in this section are pocket and belt sizes, with a few of the large caliber so-called holster types included that are often found listed elsewhere as "secondary martial handguns." Such listings were made strictly on a "traditional" basis with the precedent established by earlier arms authors having no other rationale for so doing except the large size and caliber of the arms themselves and possibly the original manufacturer's hopes that these large arms would be adopted by the military! Such "martial" terminology has proven nebulous at best. Nomenclature is equally misleading as such guns have no greater validity termed "secondary martial" than smaller handguns of the same era. This subject is discussed at considerable length in the prefaces of Chapter VII and Chapter VIII.

Many factors can and do affect and alter values from those indicated in this section. Extra features not considered "standard" enhance values to varying degrees. Most often seen is the use of materials for grips other than the usual walnut wood. Of these ivory appears most often, although occasionally pewter, pearl, ebony or other exotic materials may be seen. As with most other American arms, many of these types also may be found as complete cased outfits, bearing presentation or historical inscriptions, or elaborately engraved. All such features would be considered scarce and in some cases rare; all affect demand and values significantly. The reader is referred to Chapter II where the subject is discussed at greater length.

BIBLIOGRAPHY

There are no specific published works devoted solely to these arms. Considerable material about various makers may be found in general books that appear in complete bibliographic listings throughout this work; notably Chapter IV and the numerous individual manufacturers discussed in Chapter V. The reader is also referred to the prefatory text of Chapter VIII

"American Metallic Cartridge Pistols" that discusses material directly applicable to the handguns discussed and described in this section. Further material on the Lindsay pistols may be found in the Baxter work listed below.

Baxter, D. R. *Superimposed Load Firearms 1360 to 1860*. Hong Kong, China: South China Morning Post Limited, 1966.

Dike, C. *Cane Curiosa—From Gun to Gadget*. Geneva, Switzerland: Published by author, 1983 (distributed by Rutgers Book Center, N.J.). Coverage includes a number of American guns. A noteworthy work.

(*) Preceding a title indicates a book is currently in print.

C. B. Allen   *See Elgin Cutlass Pistols.*

Allen and Thurber; Allen and Wheelock   *See Ethan Allen, Chapter V.*

American Standard Tool Company   *See Manhattan Firearms, Chapter V.*

See Chapter VIII-A for a history of Bacon & Co.

Bacon & Co. Single Shot Ring Trigger Pistol

Bacon & Company, Norwich, Connecticut, Single Shot Ring Trigger Pistol. Made c. 1852 to 1858. Quantity estimated 400.

31 to 36 caliber. Part octagon/part round barrels of varying lengths, average 3" to 6". Distinctive ring trigger; single action with shotgun style hammer. Walnut grips.

Barrel marking: BACON & CO. NORWICH, C-T. CAST STEEL Decorative broad scroll engraving standard on frame and backstrap:

7C-001   Values—Good **$275**   Fine **$700**

7C-001

Bacon & Co. All Metal Ring Trigger Pistol

Bacon & Company, Norwich, Connecticut, Single Shot, All Metal, Ring Trigger Pistol. Made c. 1852 to 1858; very limited production.

31 caliber. 2" and 2-1/2" round barrels. Single action shotgun type hammer; ring trigger. The all iron handle and bag shape iron grips are cast integral with the frame (removable on left side). A diminutive piece under 5" overall length. Unmarked:

7C-001.5   Values—Good **$300**   Fine **$700**

7C-001.5

Bacon & Co. Single Shot Bar Hammer Pistol

Bacon & Company, Norwich, Connecticut, Single Shot Bar Hammer Pistol. Made c. 1852 to 1858.

31 to 36 caliber. Part octagon/part round barrels of varying lengths; 3" to 6" average. Double action mechanism with conventional trigger and guard. Walnut grips; this pistol is also found in two frame sizes for either small or large calibers. Quantity estimated 150 large frame and 100 small frame.

Barrel marking: BACON & CO/NORWICH, CT.Decorative broad scroll engraving standard on frame and backstrap:

7C-002

7C-002   Values—Good **$200**   Fine **$600**

Bacon & Co. Single Shot, Single Action Pistol

Bacon & Company, Norwich, Connecticut, Single Shot, Shotgun Style Hammer, Single Action Pocket and Belt Size Pistol. Made c. 1852 to 1858. Although a common style, specimens by Bacon considered rare, only a few observed. Slight variances especially in shape of the rudimentary bolster with typical light scroll & hen-track engraving as on other Bacons.

Specimen measured was 34 caliber with 5" part octagon/part round barrel but others may vary in bore size and barrel length. Walnut grips.

Barrel marking: BACON & CO./NORWICH, CT.Serial

7C-002.5

numbers on frame under grips and barrel match:

7C-002.5   Values—Good **$300**   Fine **$700**

Blunt & Syms Single Shot Bar Hammer Pistol

7C-003

Blunt & Syms, New York City, Single Shot Bar Hammer Pistol. Made c. 1840s to 1850s. About identical to the "Bruce & Davis" (see 7C-012).

Caliber approximately 34 to 36. Part round/part octagon barrels, average 6", but will vary. Bar hammer with double action mechanism and conventional trigger and large guard. Bag shaped handle; walnut grips.

Barrel marking: B & S NEW YORK and CAST STEEL. Decorative broad scroll engraving standard on frame and backstrap:

7C-003   Values-Good **$200**   Fine **$650**

Blunt & Syms S.S. Side Hammer Pocket Pistol

7C-004

Blunt & Syms, New York City, Single Shot Side Hammer Pocket Pistol. Made c. late 1840s to 1850s.

Calibers vary approximately 31 to 36. Octagon barrels from 2-1/2" to 6". Single action mechanism; rounded iron frame. Walnut grips with flat butt.

Barrel marking: B & S NEW YORK. Decorative broad scroll engraving standard on frame and backstrap:

7C-004   Values—Good **$425**   Fine **$900**

Blunt & Syms Single Shot Side Hammer Pistol

7C-005
without forend

7C-006
with forend

Blunt & Syms, New York City, Single Shot Side Hammer Pistol. Made c. 1840s to 1850s.

Caliber approximately 36 to 44. Varying lengths octagon barrels averaging approximately 4" to 6"; ramrods mounted beneath. Single action; side hammer; bag shaped handle; walnut grips.

Barrel marking: B & S NEW YORK. Decorative broad scroll engraving on frame and backstrap is standard.

Made without forend; varying frame sizes and calibers:
7C-005   Values—Good **$300**   Fine **$850**

With iron forend; usually engraved with matching motifs. Note: this style occasionally observed in extra fancy grade with all German silver frame and matching German silver forend and will bring premium over values listed here:
7C-006   Values—Good **$400**   Fine **$1,200**

Blunt & Syms Single Shot Pistol

Blunt & Syms, New York City, Single Shot Pistol. (Not illus.) Made c. late 1830s to 1850s.

Caliber approximately 42. Round barrel, flat along top, averages approximately 4"; ramrod mounted below. Back action type lock; walnut half stock.

Barrel marking: B & S NEW YORK and CAST STEEL. Often found with markings not present in which case will bring approximately 20 percent less than values reflected herein:
7C-007   Values—Good **$250**   Fine **$650**

Blunt & Syms Ring Trigger Pistol

Blunt & Syms, New York City, Ring Trigger Single Shot Pistol.
Made circa 1840s to 1850s. Caliber approximately. 38 but will
vary. Barrel lengths 3" to 5". Engraved, rounded iron frame.
Centrally mounted shotgun-type single action hammer. Bag-
shaped handle with walnut grips.

Barrel markings: B & S/NEW YORK/CAST STEEL:

7C-008   Values—Good **$275**   Fine **$650**

7C-008

Blunt & Syms Double Barrel Pistol

Blunt & Syms, New York City, Double Barrel Pistol. (Not
illus.) Made c. late 1840s to 1850s. About identical to the Bruce &
Davis (See 7C-012).

Caliber approximately 36 to 44. Side-by-side barrels averaging
approximately 7-1/2"; ramrod mounted below. Double side
mounted hammers. Walnut grips. This style has been encountered
with both conventional triggers and (scarcer) ring type trigger;
latter style will bring approximately 25 percent premium.

Barrel marking: B & S NEW YORK and CAST STEEL:

7C-009   Values—Good **$350**   Fine **$850**

Blunt & Syms Dbl. Bbl. Underhammer Pistol

**Blunt & Syms, New York City, Double Barrel Underhammer
Pistol.** Made c. 1840s to 1850s.

Caliber approximately 34. Octagonal barrels mounted side-
by-side averaging approximately 4" length. Underhammer
designed to strike both nipples simultaneously. Ring trigger.
Walnut grips.

Barrel marking: B & S NEW YORK and CAST STEEL. Decorative
broad scroll engraving standard on frame and backstrap:

7C-010   Values—Good **$475**   Fine **$1,250**

7C-010

Blunt & Syms Target or Dueling Pistol

Blunt & Syms, New York City, Target or Dueling Pistol. (Not
illus.) Made c. 1840s and 1850s.

Caliber approximately 52. Octagonal barrels vary in length;
approx. 9" average; ramrod mounted below. Walnut half stock.

Barrel marking: B & S NEW YORK and CAST STEEL:

7C-011   Values—Good **$750**   Fine **$1,750**

Blunt & Syms Deringer   *See Percussion Deringers, Chapter VII-D.*

Bruce & Davis Double Barrel Pistol

7C-012

**Bruce & Davis, Webster, Massachusetts, (also listed at
Worcester or Boston); distributors, dealers or agents. Double
Barrel Pistol.** Made c. 1850s.

36 caliber. Side-by-side barrels varying from 3" to 6". Double
hammers operated by a single trigger. Walnut grips; blued
finish.

Marked along top in flute between barrels: BRUCE & DAVIS.

Bruce & Davis were Webster, Massachusetts, arms agents or
distributors. These guns are quite firmly believed to be the
product of Allen & Thurber (*see Chapter V-A*), although no
documentary evidence substantiates this. It differs from the
A&T only with the addition of a ramrod. Almost identical
specimens known (with slightly thinner, rifled barrels) marked
BLUNT & SYMS worth premium. Other specimens are known
marked "SPAULDING & FISHER" (see 7C-036).

7C-012   Values—Good **$375**   Fine **$850**

Wm. S. Butler Single Shot Pistol

William S. Butler, Rocky Hill, Connecticut, Single Shot Pistol. Made c. 1857.

36 caliber. 2-1/2" round barrel. Centrally mounted single action shotgun type hammer. All one-piece cast iron frame and long bag shaped iron handle made integral.

Relief markings cast in frame on right side: WM. S. BUTLER'S PATENT./PATENTED FEB. 3, 1857:

7C-013   Values—Good **$425**   Fine **$850**

7C-013

J. Cohn & S. W. Marston   *See Stanhope W. Marston.*

#7C-013.2 D. Coon Patent Burglar Alarm Gun has been reclassified in Chapter XVIII as the <u>Simon</u> Coon patent (see item #18-071).

Darling Single Shot and Double Barrel Pistols

Darling (so-called) Single Shot and Double Barrel Pistols. All brass frames and barrels bearing markings such as: J. ENGH; A. I. S.; I. E. H., etc. These have been attributed in other listings to Barton and Benjamin M. Darling of Massachusetts and Rhode Island. They have been since identified and are now recognized as of Swedish manufacture. (*Also see listing for B. & B. M. Darling in Pepperbox section of this chapter*):

7C-013.5   Values—Good **$200**   Fine **$375**

7C-013.5

Delong Single Shot "Mule Ear"

Lucius Delong, Chattanooga, Tenn. Percussion "Mule Ear" Single Shot Pistol Circa 1850-1860. Quantity unknown. Rare.

38 caliber. 5-inch barrel. 9 inches overall (other calibers and barrel lengths likely). A number of unusual features unique to this piece. Iron frame is cast as one piece with the iron handle (on the right side). Left side of the handle has a wooden grip covering. Only markings stamped into the iron (right) side of handle: L. DE LONG. The most noticeable feature lending individuality to this odd appearing handgun is the side mounted "mule ear" hammer which cocks horizontally by pulling outward on the top spur.

7C-013.7

Lucius DeLong operated in Chattanooga circa 1860-1890 under the trade name "DeLong & Son."

7C-013.7   Values—Good **$1,750**   Fine **$3,000**

Elgin Cutlass Pistols

Elgin Cutlass Pistols. Made by Morrill, Mosman and Blair of Amherst, Massachusetts and C. B. Allen of Springfield, Massachusetts. Manufactured c. 1837.

Invented and patented by George Elgin, the use of a knife attachment, although not unique to firearms, was in that 1830 era, inspired by the fame and lore surrounding the then popular legendary fighting knife of James Bowie. Much of the circumstances concerning the manufacture of the gun and the reasons that two manufacturers turned them out—apparently simultaneously—is still unknown. It has been established that the famed cutler N.P. Ames of Springfield, Massachusetts, made the Bowie type blades for C. B. Allen, and there is every reason to believe that he also supplied blades to Morrill, Mosman and Blair as is evidenced by the style of decorative etched and engraved designs that appear on many of those blades.

Some Elgins did make their way west. A provocative advertisement in the St. Louis "*Missouri Republican*" Dec. 3, 1838 offers rare insight about them: "LIFE GUARDS - Just received two

dozen of ELGIN PATENT Bowie Knives with pistol attached which will shoot and cut at the same time. For sale by L. Deaver."

Considerable variation occurs in these knife pistols, especially in the markings and decorative etched panels on the blades. Those most often seen are listed here.

Both makers produced the gun in at least two distinct sizes and there is apparently quite a wide variation from the "norm" in sizes also. Not a few spurious examples have been fabricated over the years, thus the collector is cautioned to give very close scrutiny before acquiring a specimen.

If the original matching leather sheath (brass or German silver trimmed) accompanies the pistol and is in reasonably sound and complete condition, a premium of approximately 15 percent to 25 percent may be added to the value. Sheaths that are in very poor condition or only fragmentary usually will not add any appreciable value.

C. B. Allen Manufacture. Distinguished by their round trigger guard and octagon barrel.

Large martial type; made with knuckle guard. *See American Military Single Shot Pistols, Chapter VI.*

Small size. Although considerably scarcer than a military model and undoubtedly less than 100 made, their values are not as high. Octagon barrels averaging approximately 4" to 5". Calibers 35 to 41 approximately. The knife blade overall approximately 7-1/2" to 10-1/2". Two distinct methods of fastening the blade have been observed: (a) Identical to that as on the large martial size and as shown in illustration herewith; (b) back of blade fastened in vertical slot under the forward section of frame by one or two screws.

Markings: C. B. ALLEN SPRINGFIELD, MASS. in various forms on top of barrel or side of frame. Occasionally the blade is seen with etched panels bearing the blade maker's markings (scarce, and will bring premium value) N. P. AMES - CUTLER, SPRINGFIELD and on the opposite side etched panel "ELGIN"S PATENT" in center. Less than 200 estimated produced:

7C-014   Values—Good **$5,500**   Fine **$14,000**

Morrill, Mosman and Blair Manufacture. Distinguished by their square back, pointed trigger guard and round barrel.

Small size. Round barrel approximately 2-7/8". Caliber 32 to

7C-014

7C-015

34. Knife length overall 7-1/2" to 8" and fastened into forward section of frame by one or two screws. Most specimens were apparently unmarked except for serial numbers. Authentic marked specimens either on frame, barrel or blade will bring premium value:

7C-015   Values—Good **$4,500**   Fine **$12,500**

Larger size. These might more aptly be termed "medium size" as they do not nearly approximate the large U.S. Navy martial style C. B. Allen cutlass pistol. Round barrel approximately 4". Caliber 31 to 36 with rifled bore (usually eight-groove). Knife length overall 8-3/4" to 9-1/2" approximately. The gun is usually unmarked except for serial number and CAST STEEL often found on top of the barrel. The blades are usually etched with an elaborate panel on the right side displaying an American eagle, cluster of stars, large urn with floral spray, and ELGIN'S PATENT in center. Panel on left side bears the two-line inscription MORRILL, MOSMAN & BLAIR/AMHERST, MASS. surrounded by leaf and branch motif. The condition of the etched panel affects values. The prices reflected here for "good" condition would be without any blade etchings or markings, while "fine" condition would clearly indicate blade etchings and markings all clear and easily visible:

7C-016   Values—Good **$5,000**   Fine **$14,000**

A.B. Fairbanks All-Metal Pistol

A. B. Fairbanks, Boston, Massachusetts, All Metal Pistol. Made c. late 1830s to 1841.

33 caliber. 3" part round/part octagon barrel average, with lengths to 10". Heavy, one-piece all cast brass frame and handle. The hammer and trigger of one-piece construction. Belt hook often present on left side of frame.

Barrel marking: FAIRBANKS BOSTON. CAST STEEL:

7C-017   Values—Good **$425**   Fine **$900**

7C-017

A.B. Fairbanks All-Metal Target Pistol

7C-017.2

A.B. Fairbanks, Boston, MA, All-Metal Target Pistol. Made circa late 1830s to 1841. Identical mechanical function as smaller pocket pistol above; just one moving part; hammer and trigger bar single unit hinged in center.

.36 caliber. 10-inch octagonal steel barrel. Heavy, one-piece, plainly engraved, cast brass frame and handle with pointed butt. Long tang sight adjustable for elevation. Hammer in the distinctive shape of a snake's head. Specimens thus far recorded unmarked. Quantity unknown; possibly less than 100.

7C-017.2   Values - Good **$650**   Fine **$1,750**

Robert H. Fauntleroy Single Shot Pistol

Robert H. Fauntleroy, New Harmony, Indiana, Single Shot Percussion Pistol. Made late 1830s; very limited production.

31 caliber. 2-1/2" octagon brass barrel cast integral with brass frame. Centrally mounted shotgun type hammer. Trigger guard acts as mainspring. Odd "button" type, round, two piece rivet fastened walnut grips. Unmarked; serial numbered:

7C-017.5   Values—Good **$600**   Fine **$1,200**

7C-017.5

H.C. Fay Breech-Loading Single Shot Pistol

7C-017.7

H.C. Fay, Lancaster, Massachusetts. Breechloading Single Shot Percussion Pistol. Made circa late 1830s under his U.S. patent of May 23, 1837. Quantity unknown; estimated less than 10. Rare.

31 caliber. Part round, part octagon 5-1/2" barrel (other calibers and barrel lengths possible), engraved iron frame. Two-piece bag shaped walnut grips. Unmarked. Barrel tilts downward to open breech, simultaneously cocking the concealed hammer. Loaded with a removable iron auxiliary chamber with integral percussion nipple at base. When barrel locked in firing position trigger folds down. Rear sight integral with the barrel latch. Note the similarity of the system to the Thomas McCarty pistol no. 7C022.5):

7C-017.7   Values—Good **$2,500**   Fine **$7,500**

B. Fowler, Jr. Single Shot Pistol

7C-018

B. Fowler, Jr., Hartford, Conn., Single Shot Percussion Pistol. Estimated date of manufacture c.1840s.

38 caliber. 4" part round/part octagon barrel with double set of silver band inlays on the octagon section. Brass frame with iron trigger guard. Varied shape, fancy German silver inlays in the bag-shaped maple wood handle.

Barrel marking: B. FOWLER, JR. and often accompanied by small stamped eagle motif and other decorative stamped leaf and star designs.

Unverifiable sources attributed manufacture to the Connecticut State prison. Until recently the story was thought to have no basis in fact. Definite proof has established that handguns were manufactured in the Connecticut State prison in the 1840s and thus it is possible that this gun was also made there. See *Percussion Underhammer Pistols, Chapter VII-E, "Hale & Tuller"*:

7C-018   Values—Good **$375**   Fine **$750**

Gibbs Breech-Loading Pistol

7C-018.3

Lucius H. Gibbs, Oberlin, Ohio. Breech-loading, single shot percussion pistol. Believe marketed through the "Gibbs Arms Company" of New York City (actual manufacturer not known). Quantity unknown; very limited. The action operated by an underlever which moved the barrel forward then tilted it upward to load. The identical pattern of Gibbs was used for his military carbine manufactured during the Civil War by the Brooks Company of New York (see 9B-054).

36 caliber. 5-1/2" octagon barrel. Top of frame marked L. H. GIBBS PATENT JAN. 8, 1856 (for "Improvement in Breech-Loading Firearms"). Walnut grips. Specimens likely to vary in both caliber and barrel lengths. Rare. Values estimated in high four to low five-figure range.
7C-018.3

Harrington Breech-Loading Volley Gun

7C-018.5

Henry Harrington, Southbridge, Massachusetts, Multi-Barrel, Breech-Loading Volley Gun. Patented 1837. Quantity unknown; very rare.

All specimens vary; usual is three shots. On exterior resembles a single brass barrel; actually drilled with three bores. Removable breech unit with three matching chambers, single nipple. All barrels fired simultaneously as a volley. Its theoretical advantage was rapid firepower and quick reloading especially if a spare breech unit accompanied the pistol.

A double-hammer seven-shot type is known, one hammer firing three chambers simultaneously, the second hammer firing remaining four chambers. Also known in rifle size.

Markings, when present: HENRY HARRINGTON, PATENT 1837/SOUTHBRIDGE MASS:

7C-018.5   Values—Good **$5,500**   Fine **$20,000**

William Hart Pill Lock Pistol

7C-018.7

William Hart, Fredonia, New York, Pill Lock Pistol. C. 1827. Quantity unknown; very limited; rare. An important and not often seen ignition system on American firearms and the immediate predecessor of the percussion system. Hart was granted one of earliest U.S. patents, February, 1827, for this gun. For further information on the unique Pill Lock ignition (often termed "Punch-Lock") see *Miller Revolving Rifles* (15-0090).

38 caliber; 3" round brass barrel and brass boxlock style frame. (Dimensions and caliber may vary). Walnut handle with stained grain to simulate "tiger" stripe wood grain.

Markings: right frame HART'S and left frame PATENT.

An ingenious mechanical system with but three moving parts and an automatic pan cover to keep the pill primer in place when carrying:

7C-018.7   Values—Good **$1,250**   Fine **$3,000**

Haviland & Gunn Single Shot Gallery Pistol

Benjamin Haviland & George P. Gunn, Ilion, New York, Single Shot Gallery Practice or Salon Target Pistol. Made c. 1870s.

17 caliber. 5" round barrel, octagonal at breech.

The entire gun—barrel, frame and handle—cast integral as one piece. Nickeled finish; casehardened hammer. Mainspring also acts as trigger guard. Usually unmarked. There is the possibility that they were made for Haviland & Gunn by Remington as one known specimen has been recorded with Remington markings (and would be worth a considerable premium):

7C-019

7C-019   Values—Good **$425**   Fine **$875**

Hellinghaus Single Shot Pistol

Frederick Hellinghaus, St. Louis, Missouri. Single Shot, Large Martial Size Percussion Holster Pistol. Made circa 1840-1847.

7C-019.1

Quantity unknown. Rare.

48 caliber. 6-1/2" barrel. 11-1/2" overall. (Other calibers and barrel lengths likely.) All brass, rounded frame.

Hellinghaus is known to have made a percussion double barrel shotgun once owned and carried by the famous frontiersman Kit Carson. Before relocating to St. Louis he was a working gunsmith at Baltimore, Maryland 1832 to 1835. He served with the Missouri Mounted Infantry Regiment through the Mexican War, afterward heading for the gold fields in California and continuing his trade as a gunsmith in Sacramento and later San Francisco from 1856 to 1857. Values estimated in high four to five-figure range:
7C-019.1

Hellinghaus Central Hammer, Concealed Trigger Pocket Pistol

Hellinghaus Center Hammer, Concealed Trigger Pocket Pistol. Frederick Hellinghaus, St. Louis, Missouri. Single shot percussion pocket pistol with centrally mounted hammer; percussion nipple mounted at extreme breech of barrel in-line with barrel. Folding trigger on underside of the iron frame opens when hammer is cocked. Walnut grips individually affixed to each side of the iron frame; bag shaped handle.

48 caliber (others likely). 4" and 6" octagon barrels recorded; marked F. HELLINGHAUS ST. LOUIS top of barrel. (See entry above for bio of this maker). Rare. Values estimated in high four to five-figure range:
7C-019.2

7C-019.2

Hero Pistol   *See Manhattan Firearms, Chapter V; also Iver Johnson, Chapter VII-C*

"K & R Patent" All Metal Gallery or Trap Pistol

Unidentified percussion, single shot gallery gun. American, circa 1850-1860. Quantity unknown; believed very limited.

Oddly designed all metal; 5-1/2" overall. Heavyweight brass, one-piece frame and handle; 2-1/2" round, two-step barrel; small 21 caliber. Deeply marked K & R PATENT at front of left frame; serial numbered on barrel. Single action, bar type hammer. Uniquely designed, rigidly mounted, inverted "T" fixture under spur frame. The long serpentine iron "rod" ahead of spur acts as trigger. Small threaded aperture underside of frame. Rare and unusual.

7C-019.3

7C-019.3   Values—Good **$650**   Fine **$1,250**

R. N. Lambert Cane Gun

Roger N. Lambert, Upton, Massachusetts and Lyme, New Hampshire, 1832 Patent Cane Gun. Quantity unknown. Specimens rare.

Earliest examples were believed manufactured by Ethan Allen at Grafton, Mass. (q.v.) and generally reported to have been Allen's first venture in arms making, pre-1836. Not enough specimens known or studied to differentiate between earliest examples made in Massachusetts and those believed manufactured later in New Hampshire.

The Lambert gun obviously enjoyed a modicum of public acceptance. Enough so, to find their way west. An advertisement in the St. Louis "*Missouri Republican*" April 24, 1834 made comment: "G. & J. ERSKINE have 6 Lambert Patent cane guns. Believed to be first of their kind offered in St. Louis."

7C-019.5

Measurements and contours of ivory knob-like handle vary. 41 caliber (approximately) 33" overall. Rosewood cane shaft with wide brass tip having swivel muzzle cover. Heavy turned ivory knob handle with silver ferrules pulls upward and then swivels forming a pistol-like grip. Concealed trigger and flat bar hammer. Flat iron action marked on side: LAMBERT'S PATENT.

7C-019.5   Values—Good **$2,000**   Fine **$5,500**

Lewis Single Shot Pocket Rifle

7C-019.8

Nelson Lewis, Troy, New York, Single Shot Percussion "Pocket Rifle" (a.k.a. "Buggy Rifle"). Made circa 1840s-1860s. Upstate New York gunmaker noted for quality single shot percussion rifles of all types. This "Buggy Rifle" is typical of similar types made by other American makers of percussion sporting and target rifles, but considerably scarcer and seldom seen, especially when complete with matching shoulder stock.

Calibers 31 to 36. Octagon barrels 11" and 12" (other calibers and barrel lengths likely); usual with false muzzle (as illus. here). Barrel blued; frame and lock casehardened. Walnut stocks with matching detachable walnut shoulder stock. Markings on barrel N. LEWIS MAKER TROY, NY. Quantity unknown; limited. All specimens will likely have slight variances. Values shown here for specimens with false muzzles (if muzzles lacking values approximately 15 to 20 percent less). Pistols made without provision for false muzzle approximately 10 to 20 percent less than indicated.

7C-019.8   Values—Good **$1,750**   Fine **$4,500**

Pistol only lacking shoulder stock:
7C-019.9   Values—Good **$750**   Fine **$1,500**

Lindsay Two-Shot Belt Pistol

7C-020

Lindsay Two-Shot Belt or Large Pocket Size Pistol. Made by Union Knife Company of Naugatuck, Connecticut, for the inventor John P. Lindsay. Made c. early 1860s. Less than 100 believed made.

41 caliber. Superposed loads (i.e., two complete charges, one on top of the other in the single barrel). The single trigger (usual, but also seen with double triggers) releases the double hammers in proper sequence for firing respective charges.

Oddly shaped, stepped-down contour full octagon barrel varying in length from 4-1/4" to 5-1/2". Brass frame with scroll engraved motifs standard. Blued barrel. Slight variations have been noted in contours due to hand workmanship. These are generally believed to be the earliest style of Lindsay handguns.

Barrel marked along top LINDSAY'S YOUNG AMERICA and on either left or right side of frame PATENT APPLIED FOR

7C-020	Values—Good **$1,500**	Fine **$4,000**

Lindsay Two-Shot Pocket Pistol

Lindsay Two-Shot Pocket Pistol. Made by Union Knife Company, Naugatuck, Connecticut, for the inventor c. early 1860s. Estimated quantity several hundred.

41 caliber superposed load. Same operating principle as above described Lindsay. Double hammers.

4" octagon barrel fluted in center along top. Scroll engraved frame and both sides at breech of barrel is standard on all specimens.

Marked in panel on right side of barrel LINDSAY'S/YOUNG AMERICA/MAN'F'D. BY/J. P. LINDSAY - MAN'FG CO./NEW-YORK. Marked under the barrel PATENT'D FEB. 8. 1859. PAT'D. OCT. 9. 1860:

7C-021

7C-021	Values—Good **$1,000**	Fine **$2,750**

Lindsay Two-Shot "Martial" Size Pistol

Lindsay Two-Shot Large or (so-called) Martial Size Pistol. Made by Union Knife Company, Naugatuck, Connecticut, for the inventor John P. Lindsay, c. early 1860s. Approximately 100 made.

7C-022

45 caliber; smoothbore. Superposed loads as on smaller sizes; single trigger operates the double hammers in proper sequence. 8-1/2" part round/part octagon barrel with blued finish. Frame and mountings of brass. Varnished walnut grips.

Barrel marked at breech: LINDSAY'S/YOUNG-AMERICA/PATENT'D OCT. 9, 1860 Serial numbered.

The Lindsay two-shot mechanism was also made in a military musket and is one of the distinct oddities in American arms collecting. Lindsay had been an employee of the Springfield Armory. His attempts at obtaining a government contract for the pistols were unsuccessful. Traditionally considered by collectors as a secondary martial handgun, there is no evidence of such usage:

7C-022	Values—Good **$2,250**	Fine **$6,000**

McCarty Breechloading Pocket Pistol

Thomas McCarty, Elmira NY, Single Shot Percussion, Breechloading Pocket Pistol. Patent March 11, 1837. Total quantity unknown; estimated less than 50.

32 caliber. part octagonal, part round 3 and 4 inch barrels. Bag shaped handle. Walnut grips each affixed to a thin brass backing plate. Specimens unmarked. Loading accomplished by use of an auxiliary chamber, termed a tube, about an inch in length with the percussion nipple affixed on the side, (and used for removing it from the barrel). Barrel tips upward for loading, swinging on side-mounted trunions; folding trigger. rare.

7C-022.5 Values—Good **$5,000**	Fine **$8,500**

7C-022.5

Manhattan Firearms Co.   *See Manhattan Firearms, Chapter V.*

S.W. Marston Two-Barrel Swivel Breech Pistol

Stanhope W. Marston, New York City, Two-Barrel Swivel Breech Pocket Pistol. Made c. 1850s. Quantity unknown; very scarce.

31 and 36 caliber. Frame sizes are the same for either caliber. Superposed, flat sided barrels vary in length from 3" to 4-1/2".

Ring trigger; bar hammer; double action; barrels manually revolved.

Brass frame with broad scroll engraving standard. Specimens are known with iron frame, considered very rare and are worth premium. A unique feature on these was the positioning of the sights. The small, open-style rear sight is affixed to the *left side of the frame*; bead-type front sights for each barrel mounted on *sides of the barrels* rather than the top.

Marked vertically on barrels either J. COHN & S. W. MARSTON-NEW YORK or S. W. MARSTON & COHN-NEW YORK Side of hammer marked PATENTED 1851, with opposite side marked NEW YORK.

Very little is known about the inventor or manufacturer of these scarce handguns:

7C-023   Values—Good **$950**   Fine **$2,750**

7C-023

W.W. Marston Single Shot Double Action Pistol

William W. Marston, New York, Single Shot Bar Hammer Double Action Pocket Pistol. Also known with the following trade or brand name markings: W. W. MARSTON; W. MARSTON & CO.; W. W. MARSTON ARMORY; WM. MARSTON; MARSTON & KNOX; SPRAGUE & MARSTON; THE WASHINGTON ARMS CO.; and THE UNION ARMS CO.

7C-024

Calibers 31 and 36. Part octagon/part round barrels varying from 2-1/2" to 5" are average lengths. Longer lengths have been observed and are worth small premiums.

Broad scroll engraved designs are standard on the iron frame. A great variety of markings are encountered both on hammer and barrel; these include company names and address (usually New York City) in large letters. Also present may be CAST STEEL and markings on hammer NEW YORK 1854 or others.

See also W. W. Marston in the revolver and the pepperbox sections of this chapter for further insights into the production and marketing of arms by this firm and their use of trade names.

Values are approximately the same for all types. Advanced specialists may pay premiums for specific markings. No data is available describing relative scarcity of any one type or mark:

7C-024   Values—Good **$200**   Fine **$550**

W.W. Marston Single Shot Single Action Pistol

William W. Marston, New York, Single Shot, Shotgun Style Hammer, Single Action Pocket and Belt Size Pistol. Found with a variety of markings of which Sprague & Marston, W. W. Marston, Marston & Knox and Washington Arms Company have been observed. Undoubtedly others similar to those mentioned for the bar hammer style will be encountered. Markings may also include NEW YORK 1864.

Calibers 31 and 36. Part octagon/part round barrels average 4" to 6" with longer lengths seen which will bring slight premiums. Bag shaped handle with walnut grips:

7C-025   Values—Good **$225**   Fine **$575**

7C-025

W.W. Marston Breech-Loading S.S. Pistol

William W. Marston, New York, Breech-Loading Single Shot Pistol. Made c. early to mid-1850s. Total produced estimated at approximately 1,000.

36 caliber; rifled bore. Part octagon/part round barrels vary from 4" to 8-1/2". Full octagon barrels also encountered and scarcer, although will not necessarily bring premium.

The mechanism is operated by lowering the lever allowing for breech-loading of the unique Marston patent leather base, paperboard bodied cartridge.

Barrel marking: W. W. MARSTON/NEW-YORK/PATENTED 1850. Barrels on brass framed specimens will bear additional marking CAST STEEL.

Iron frames have casehardened finish while brass frame models have silver plated finish; barrels blued on both types. Simple engraved floral and scroll designs are standard on both styles of frame. More elaborate engraving is occasionally encountered and will bring premium values. Varnished walnut grips.

7C-026

Traditionally considered by collectors as a secondary martial handgun, no documentary or other evidence exists to substantiate either its military use or government purchase.

Iron Frame Model:
7C-026   Values—Good **$1,250**   Fine **$3,750**

Brass Frame Model. (Estimated to be approximately 25 percent of total production):
7C-027   Values—Good **$1,400**   Fine **$4,250**

W.W. Marston Three-Shot Pocket Pistol

7C-028

William W. Marston, New York, Three-Shot Pocket Pistol With Superposed Barrels. Made c. late 1850s. Very rare.

31 caliber. Approximately 4" barrels. A rising type hammer striker successively strikes each of the three nipples (from top to bottom) as the hammer is cocked. Extremely limited production; although quantity unknown, possibly only 10 to 20 made.

Considerable variance has been noted in these handguns, the predecessors of Marston's more well known and widely produced breech-loading metallic cartridge model (*q.v.*). The production type of this percussion model was double action (specimens in single action known) with a rounded or snub-type hammer spur; walnut grips:

7C-028   Values—Good $3,750   Fine $8,500

Mass. Arms Co. Single Shot Pocket Pistol

Massachusetts Arms Co., Chicopee Falls, Massachusetts, Single Shot Pocket Pistol. Made c. late 1850s.

31 caliber. 2-1/2" to 3-1/2" part round/part octagon barrel standard; 6" rare; worth premium. Maynard primer mechanism on right side of frame. Centrally mounted hammer. Walnut grips.

Barrel marking: MASS. ARMS CO./CHICOPEE FALLS. The hinged door cover of the primer magazine marked: MAYNARD'S PATENT SEPT. 22, 1845. Decorative scroll engraving standard:
7C-029   Values—Good $950   Fine $2,750

7C-029

Mass. Arms Co. Double Barrel, Swivel Breech Pocket Pistol

Mass. Arms Co. Double Barrel, Swivel Breech Pocket Pistol. Made circa late 1850s.

Very small 22 caliber percussion manually revolved superposed barrels, bored from tapered flat bar. Same Maynard primer unit on right frame as on single shot. Noticeably different frame and handle. Walnut grips. Decorative scroll engraving at breech. Primer cover bears "MAYNARD"S PATENT" and date. Barrels unmarked. Very rare; possible experimental run or very limited production. Frame and handle adapted from the Mass. Arms Company earliest style pistol. (See 7A-058). Estimated value for authentic specimens in low to mid four figures.
7C-029.2

7C-029.2

Morrill, Mosman and Blair, Amherst, Mass.   *See Elgin Cutlass Pistols.*

Parker Four-Shot Pistol

7C-030

Parker, Springfield, Massachusetts, Four-Shot, Removable Chambers, Pistol. Made c. late 1840s, early 1850s. Quantity unknown. Extremely rare.

33 caliber. 4" part octagon/part round barrel. Breech contains removable magazine of four separate chambers (attached to frame at rear of grip) which are aligned for firing with the main barrel by cocking of hammer.

Markings: ALBERT PARKER/PATENT SECURED/SPRINGFIELD, MASS/1849:
7C-030   Values—Good $9,500   Fine $20,000

Percival & Smith Repeating Magazine Pistol

Orville B. Percival, East Haddam, Connecticut and Aza Smith, New York City, Repeating Percussion Magazine Pistol.

Patented 1850. Quantity unknown; very rare.

27 caliber. 9" round barrel. Two suspended brass chambers

(magazines) under barrel: front magazine holds 24 balls; rear magazine for loose powder and smaller inner chamber with priming pellets.

After cocking hammer, both chambers swivel upward 180 degrees allowing lead ball to fall into breech from front magazine and loose powder into chamber behind ball from rear magazine; primer pellet also seats itself.

Marked on sleeve at breech of barrel: SMITH & PERCIVAL PATENT/MFD BY H. SMITH NORWICH CT.

Made by Horace Smith in Norwich, Connecticut c. 1850 prior to his Smith & Wesson partnership. Exercise caution: modern copies are known:

7C-030.5

| 7C-030.5 | Values—Good **$11,500** | Fine **$30,000** |

Perry Breech-Loading Single Shot Pistol

Perry Patent Firearms Co., Newark, New Jersey, Breech-Loading Single Shot Pistol. Made c. 1854 to 1856. Total quantity estimated at a few hundred.

52 caliber; rifled bore. Round taper barrel approximately 6" average with variations to 28". Trigger guard acts also as lever for opening breech which pivots on an axis fitted crosswise through the frame. Accepts a paper-wrapped cartridge.

Finish blued; varnished walnut grips.

Breechblock marking: PERRY PATENT FIREARMS CO/NEWARK, N.J. and A. D. PERRY/PATENTED.

Very scarce American breech-loading handgun with the same style action also made in various longarms. A cane gun

7C-032

version utilizing this pistol size action was also made and buyers are cautioned to be wary that they are not acquiring a cane gun that has merely been cut down to pistol size (slight contour differences).

Traditionally classed as a secondary martial handgun by collectors, no evidence exists substantiating the military use or government purchase of these pistols.

First Type. (Not illus.) Trigger guard/loading lever follows the contour of the grip, extending to the butt, then curves upward sharply; distinctive oval notch on the rear of frame at junction where it meets grips; no guide screw on right frame (only the pivot screw):

| 7C-031 | Values—Good **$2,000** | Fine **$4,500** |

Second Type. (See illus.) Has shorter trigger guard/loading lever of a modified S-curve. Distinguished by the automatic percussion cap priming device; guide screw on frame forward of breechblock pivot screw; altered shapes of hammer and trigger; the grips are straight at top at juncture with frame. Most readily apparent feature is the projection at underside of butt through which the percussion caps are fed:

| 7C-032 | Values—Good **$1,850** | Fine **$4,000** |

Pratt Burglar Alarm and Animal Trap Gun

George Pratt, Middletown, Connecticut, Combination Double Barrel Burglar Alarm and Animal Trap Gun. Made c. 1880s to 1890s.

38 caliber. 4" cast iron barrels (with galvanized-like finish) mounted side-by-side. Cast iron hammers mounted horizontally in straight line to strike the horizontally mounted nipples. Flat, long swivel arm to release hammers mounted on top. Marked with patent date, DEC. 18, 1883. The entire gun unit fits into a circular base which allows it to swivel a full 360 degrees.

These are occasionally seen in their original pasteboard box with full labels for which premiums may be added:

| 7C-033 | Values—Good **$475** | Fine **$900** |

7C-033

Wm. Reid Breechloading Percussion Pistol   *See Rollin White.*

F. Reuthe Animal Trap Guns

F. Reuthe, Hartford, Connecticut, Animal Trap Guns/Pistols. Made c. late 1850s to early 1860s. Total quantities estimated at several hundreds.

Calibers 28 to 50 approximately. Octagonal barrels from 3-1/2" (single barrel types) to 5" (double barrels).

These novel arms of heavy all cast iron construction were designed solely as an animal trap gun and the existence of the

handle on some models is an enigma as the gun was not designed as a hand held defense weapon. The principle of operation on all models is identical with two long barbed arrow-like devices protruding from above or between the barrels which acted as the triggering device. Bait was affixed to these barbs and when animal tugged upon it, the arm discharged.

Markings cast in high relief (in varying styles) on most models: F. REUTHE'S PATENT MAY 12, 1857 or F. REUTHE'S PATENT HARTFORD, CONN.

Single Barrel Model; 3-1/2" barrel with screw-in type all cast iron handle with deep fluted motif. Approximately 28 caliber. Black enamel finish:

7C-034   Values—Good **$550**   Fine **$1,250**

Double Barrel Model. Variations of these are found usually in the larger approximately 50 caliber. Encountered with the cast iron fluted design handle or with large iron ring rigidly attached at breech of barrels to which is affixed a long swivel type iron rod and hook used to fasten the trap to a tree or stake in the ground. Black enamel finish:

7C-035   Values—Good **$675**   Fine **$1,500**

7C-034
Single Barrel

7C-035
Double Barrel

7C-035
Variant Double Barrel

Rupertus Straight Line S.S. Pocket Pistol

Jacob Rupertus, Philadelphia, Penna, "Straight Line" Single Shot Pocket Pistol. C. late 1860s. Quantity unknown. Likely under 500. (*See chapter VIII-A also.*)

36 caliber. Octagon breech with round barrels 3-1/2" to 4-1/4". Iron frame. Walnut grip. Central mounted hammer.

Values shown are for unmarked examples as normally encountered. Marked specimens RUPERTUS/PAT'D rare and worth premium:

7C-035.2   Values—Good **$275**   Fine **$575**

7C-035.2

C. Sharps & Co., Philadelphia   *See Chapter V, Sharps Firearms.*

George Smith & Co. 3-Bbl. Animal Trap & Alarm Gun

George Smith & Company, New York City, Combination Three-Barrel Animal Trap and Burglar Alarm Gun. C. early 1860s. Quantity unknown; limited; scarce.

Cluster of three side-by-side 2-3/4" barrels with single, centrally mounted nipple which fires all three simultaneously as a volley. Caliber 34. Iron construction. Swivel device at rear with long, tapered, integral screw allows for mounting in many positions as well as a wide 120 degree traverse when attached to bait or other objects.

Marked on the flat, bar type hammer GEO. SMITH & CO. N.Y./PAT'D JUNE 11, 1861:

7C-035.4

7C-035.4   Values—Good **$850**   Fine **$1,750**

#7C-035.5 Smith, Torrey & Co. Percussion Alarm Gun has been reclassified in Chapter XVIII as item #18-075

Spalding & Fisher Double Barrel Pistol

Spalding and Fisher, Double Barrel Single Trigger Pistol. Made c. 1850s. Location unknown.

36 caliber. Side-by-side barrels of approximately 5-1/2", although other lengths are undoubtedly made. Double hammers operated by single trigger.

Walnut grips; iron frame; centrally mounted hammers; blued finish.

Marked in flute between barrels on top: SPALDING & FISHER.

Most likely arms agents or distributors. These guns are identical to the Bruce and Davis (*q.v.*) and quite strongly believed

7C-036

to be the product of Allen and Thurber (*see Chapter V 5A-009*):
7C-036   Values—Good **$375**   Fine **$850**

Sprague and Marston *See W. W. Marston.*

Stocking & Co. Single Shot Pistol

Stocking and Co., Worcester, Massachusetts, Single Shot Pistol. Made c. 1849 to 1852.

36 caliber. Part round/part octagon 4" barrel average length.

Rounded iron frame with broad scroll engraving standard. Long bag shaped handle; walnut grips. Distinctive feature is the long cocking spur extending from the rear of the bar type hammer (identical to that on the Stocking pepperbox, *q.v.*).

Barrel marking: STOCKING & CO./WORCESTER and WARRANTED CAST STEEL:

7C-037   Values—Good **$325**   Fine **$775**

7C-037

Stocking & Co. Single Shot, Single Action Pistol

7C-037.5

Stocking and Company, Worcester, Massachusetts, Single Shot, Shotgun Style Hammer, Single Action Pocket and Belt Size Pistol. (Not illus. looks about identical to Bacon [7C-002.5] and Marston [7C-025] with sharper angle to handle.) Made c. 1849 to 1852.

36 caliber. Part round/part octagon barrel in varying length.

Rounded iron frame both plain and simply engraved. Long bag shaped handle; walnut grips.

Barrel marking: STOCKING & CO./WORCESTER

7C-037.5   Values—Good **$225**   Fine **$575**

Uncle, Sam *See 7C-045; also 5C-023 and VIII-A Iver Johnson.*

Union Arms Company *See W. W. Marston.*

The Washington Arms Co. *See W. W. Marston.*

"Rollin White" Breech-Loading S.S. Pistol

7C-038

Rollin White, (attributed) Lowell, Massachusetts or James Reid, N.Y. Breech-Loading Single Shot Pistol Made c. 1862. Quantity estimated under 100.

28 caliber. Removable rectangular breechblock with single chamber. 2-1/2" round barrel. Walnut grips. Unmarked. Specimens are known both with and without trigger guard.

Formerly attributed to Rollin White by many earlier works, including this, firm evidence to positively identify this rare gun has been recently (with the 6th edition of this Guide) brought to light. A single marked specimen J. REID NEW YORK on top of frame, clearly points to that noted gunmaker (*see chapter VIII-A*):

7C-038   Values—Good **$800**   Fine **$2,250**

#7C-039 Wilson Percussion Alarm Gun has been reclassified in Chapter XVIII as item #18-076

Wurfflein Salon Pistol with Shoulder Stock

7C-039.5

William Wurfflein, Philadelphia, Percussion, Single Shot Salon (Target) Pistol with detachable shoulder stock. Made circa 1860s - 1870s. Quantity unknown; apparently limited. Scarce.

177 caliber. 4-inch round barrel; flat along top. Back action style lock marked "WURFFLEIN/PHILA." Barrel and trigger guard nickel finished. Walnut stock made in two grades: 1) plain uncheckered stock and spur trigger guard; often unmarked. 2)

Better quality; checkered stock and sides of spur guard. Worth small premium above values shown. Sold with the simple shaped dowel-type detachable iron shoulder stock with tapered tip that fits into butt of the handle. The pistol closely resembles the Philadelphia deringer pistols, some of which were also made by Wurfflein (see 7D-033). If stock is lacking, deduct 20 percent from values indicated.

7C-039.5   Values—Good **$650**   Fine **$1,250**

Yerty Patent Burglar Alarm and Animal Trap Gun

7C-040

Henry Yerty, Sidney, Ohio, All Brass Percussion Double Barrel Combination Burglar Alarm and Animal Trap Gun. A.k.a. "Horseshoe gun". Maker unknown; c. 1860s. Quantity unknown, likely very limited; rare.

32 caliber. Brass 2-1/4" octagon barrels made integral with a heavy, brass, horseshoe shaped frame. 6-1/2" overall. The hammers and internal parts only are steel. The tall, tapered, vertical center post intended to fit over a pin, allowing gun to rotate in line with target. Hammers tripped by cord attached to slender rod between barrels.

Most specimens unmarked; when marked: YEARTY'S PAT. DEC. 30, 1866:

7C-040   Values—Good **$1,400**   Fine **$3,000**

Unidentified Single Shot Percussion Salon Gun

Unidentified Percussion Salon (or Saloon) or Gallery Gun. American. c. 1860s. Quantity unknown; limited; scarce.

Intended for indoor shooting/target practice at very short range. Sole propellant is the fulminate in a percussion cap. Projectile a small BB or single lead shot.

All brass construction. 4-1/2" barrel made integral with heavy brass frame and handle. Tiny bore 10 caliber. Rosewood grips. Nickel finish.

Markings PAT. APPLIED FOR on top of barrel:

7C-041

7C-041   Values—Good **$250**   Fine **$550**

Unidentified Rising Breech Percussion Breech-Loading Pocket Pistol

7C-042

Unidentified Single Shot Rising Breech, percussion Breech-Loading Pocket Pistol. Circa 1850. Quantity unknown. Very rare.

Engraved brass, spur trigger frame with 2" part octagon/round barrel. Smooth bore 28 caliber. Walnut grips. Overall 6-1/2". No maker markings.

Unique breech-loading system: the vertical rising breech block loads from front; percussion nipple at rear face of block. Gun displays qualities of an highly accomplished gunmaker. Fine example of the great era of experimentation and development of breech-loading systems. With but single recorded recent sale, value shown very broad estimate:

7C-042   Values—Good **$2,500**   Fine **$4,500**

Unidentified Single Shot Percussion Pistol

Unidentified Percussion Pocket Pistol. Maker and quantity unknown. Circa 1850 to 1870.

Sturdy, inexpensively produced 36 caliber all brass construction. The 3" barrel cast integral with the frame; squat spur trigger. Central mounted hammer and nipple. Walnut two-piece grips fastened by simple wood screw. Only markings very small sized three digit serial or assembly number. 5-1/2" overall:

7C-043   Values—Good **$175**   Fine **$350**

7C-043

Unidentified Single Shot Percussion Pistols (various)

7C-044
"A"

7C-044
"B"

Unidentified Percussion Single Shot Pocket Pistols by various makers. Circa 1840s to 1879s.

A wide variety of these (often primitive) types are to be encountered. Many are likely one-of-a-kind, ostensibly made by backwoods gunsmiths or blacksmiths. Others will display qualities of a professional gunsmith, possibly produced in small quantities. Valuation primarily based on quality of workmanship. Also considered are: materials used (i.e. brass or iron), general appearance, size and caliber, condition …or occasionally, their unique mechanical features as "arms curiosa." Illustrated are examples of typical primitive and semi-primitive styles a collector might encounter.

A: Just a single 3" octagon barrel in which the solid breech end is hollowed out to enclose the centrally mounted hammer. Both the top strap and bottom strap of the handle are forged integral with the octagon frame, merely extensions of it. Elongated, bulbous shaped trigger; made without trigger guard. Single action shotgun style hammer. Caliber 56. Construction about as simple as will be found yet displays good craftsmanship.

B: Seldom seen this large pistol might be termed "belt model"; 10" overall with 5-1/2" octagon / round barrel; caliber 44. Boxlock type action with iron frame. Not fitted for trigger guard. Bag-shaped handle with walnut grips.

Values reflect the broad general range for types (unless some special feature places a specimen "far and above the crowd"):

7C-044   Values—Good **$100 to 200**   Fine **$175 to $375**

Unidentified, Center-Hammer Percussion Pocket Pistols

Unidentified Single Shot, Center-Hammer Percussion Pocket Pistols. Both types made in large quantities over a lengthy period circa late 1850s through 1880s. Caliber 31 usual (others known). All are unmarked. Varying barrel lengths 2-5" overall.

Very popular handguns, sold over a long period of time and widely advertised (and illustrated) by many of the most well-known dealers in their catalogs of the era.

"Type A" illustration from the 1876 edition of the notable Pittsburgh firearms dealer J. Bown & Company. This little pocket pistol possibly made by Manhattan Firearms Co. or Iver Johnson (*q.v.*) is captioned "UNCLE SAM PISTOLS" in their catalogs; advertised in three barrel lengths and in a "Premium Class" model named "PRINCE" with full nickel plate.

Specimens not observed with those actual markings. Round barrels standard. Bown & Company catalog directed their advertising towards youngsters with the inducement: "Boys, this is the best and cheapest pistol you ever saw for the money. Only cost you 80, 90 cents and $1.00."

"Type B." Maker unknown. Commonly encountered and seen in numerous catalogs, most of which preface descriptions with captions naming it an "AMERICAN SINGLE BARREL POWDER AND BALL PISTOL." Various illustrations depict it both with part octagon / round or full round, tapered barrels. Blued finish apparently standard.

Values usually in same range for both types:

7C-045   Values—Good **$75**   Fine **$175**

7C-045
"A"

7C-045
"B"

Pair of percussion gambler's pistols in their unique holsters and belt made to be carried in the small of the back. Matched pair of single-shot, belt-sized pistols with brass 4-inch octagon barrels; brass mountings and silver inlays on the walnut stocks. Guns each marked by noted maker of "Kentucky" rifles William Drepard of Lancaster, Pennsylvania. (*N. Flayderman & Co. Catalog No. 86 of November 1970*)

Chapter VII-D

Percussion Deringers
(Henry Deringer and His Imitators)

A fascinating collecting field and one surrounded with much lore is that of the small deringer percussion pistols, or as they are so often known, the "Philadelphia deringers." Mere mention of the name conjures up visions of miners in the California gold fields and gamblers aboard Mississippi steamboats. There is no doubt that these potent pocket pistols were an integral part of the American scene in those as well as other romanticized eras in mid-19th century America. There is also a somewhat morbid fascination for deringers since they often played leading roles, widely reported in the news media of the day, in quickly settling (sometimes terminally) arguments, figuring in not a few sensational homicides. The most noted and tragic of these was the assassination of President Abraham Lincoln. The arch villain, John Wilkes Booth, fired the fatal shot from one of Deringer's small pocket pistols (it had a 2" barrel and cap box in its butt). The gun was recovered that very evening from the President's box at the Ford Theater in Washington, was fully identified in the subsequent trial of the conspirators, and later was featured as part of a National Park Service exhibit at the Ford's Theater.

The originator of these distinctly designed small pocket pistols, Henry Deringer, is unique in the history of American arms as being the only maker whose name became a common noun in the English language. The word is interchangeably used as a generic term for all small, short barreled percussion and cartridge pistols. Although Webster's dictionary defines these as "… a small, short-barreled pistol of large caliber," it would be more accurate to say that they are small, short barreled percussion or cartridge pistols of any caliber as the term has come to encompass a great many small caliber types also.

Considerable commentary and much discussion has surrounded the spelling of the inventor's name vs. the generic use of it, i.e., **Deringer vs. derringer**. Henry Deringer spelled his name with one "r" and his guns were so marked. The use of the double "r" (i.e., derringer) has been quite thoroughly established as being merely a misspelling of the maker's name as reported in the press and by popular writers of the day, all of whom mentioned the gun liberally in their editorials, news accounts or fictionalized stories. As a matter of fact, the misspelling was in such wide common usage that some of Henry Deringer's own sales agents even resorted to it in their advertisements of his products! The *Magazine Of Antique Firearms* (among the earliest devoted to the subject) took an incorrect stab at the issue when it claimed in its April, 1911 issue, that Henry himself "…was very particular to make

people…discriminate between pistols marked Deringer (and) Derringer…as to prevent him from prosecuting them for using his name." Likely not the first attempt to resolve the issue, there's little doubt that played a large role in perpetuating the fiction.

A few present day writers and a whole host of collectors have practically made a fetish of explaining the spelling difference of this word, contending that it must be spelled with two "r's" and a lower case "d" (i.e., derringer) when using the word generically or for guns other than those made by Henry Deringer. It may be emphatically stated that no such "rules" or

Philadelphia
RIFLE MANUFACTORY.
HENRY DERINGER,
INFORMS his Customers and the Public in general, that he has on hand and intends to keep, at his Military Store, No. 374, north Front-street, an assortment of RIFLES, MUSKETS, FOWLING PIECES, PISTOLS, SWORDS, CUTLASSES, BOARDING, PIKES, BOARDING-AXES, &c. &c. of every description.

Orders from any part of the United States shall receive immediate attention, and will be executed with punctuality on the shortest notice and lowest terms, where articles of the above description will be repaired at low rates.

N. B. By writing to me I will send a specimen of Workmanship to any part of the United States.   H. D.
Aug. 26 - ifdpw6mcpf6m

Earliest known advertisement by Henry Deringer; from Philadelphia newspaper circa 1812.

"etiquette" exists and that even though Webster's dictionary uses the double "r" as it is applied in present day terminology, either spelling is permissible, acceptable and correct. It is all a matter of preference!

Born in Easton, Pennsylvania of German parents in 1786, young Henry was first apprenticed to a local gunsmith and is known to have then worked at the Virginia Manufactory in Richmond. By age 21, he returned, in 1808, to Philadelphia, commencing business as a gunmaker in 1809. As witnessed by this circa 1812 advertisement from a Philadelphia newspaper, he quickly engaged in the weapons trade. Many of those firearms and edged weapons advertised were likely the products of others, merely sold by Deringer as an agent in his "Military Store." His business grew rapidly. By 1813, he was already fulfilling quantity orders for various state contracts for flintlock muskets, soon followed by larger orders for rifles and muskets by the U.S. Government. Concurrently, with those contracts, he expanded his line of arms for civilian markets to include a wide range of handguns and even the occasional "Kentucky" rifle. Henry Deringer made quite a few pocket and belt pistols prior to 1850 on the general style of his famed and widely copied small percussion deringer. Every indication suggests that unique design did not become widely manufactured or popular until about 1852. Deringer was by then 66 years of age. No evidence exists that these arms—so dearly beloved to the California trade—were available or sold to the initial rush of gold miners in California in 1849 and 1850. Thus, the general era of Henry Deringer's small pocket pistols was about 1852 through 1868, ceasing with his death at the ripe old age of 82. Some of his imitators continued making them through the 1870s.

Deringer's pocket pistol generally evolved from considerably larger sizes he made in the 1830s and 1840s. In keeping with the tempo of the times, the type achieved wide popularity as a short range arm for self defense, gaining its greatest footholds and widest favor throughout the American South and West, especially in those areas that were heavily settled, but short on law and order; places where the prudent citizen and businessman found it desirable (if not mandatory) to be inconspicuously armed.

Henry Deringer's own production was fairly limited. It should be recalled that he was in his 70s during most of the era of production. His workmen at a later date recollected that he was at that time a very wealthy man apparently conducting business for his own pleasure. The great demand for these pistols led not only to many competitors, but also to imitators and counterfeiters. Thus there grew, from this one style of pistol, a whole host of identical and near identical handguns with many of them bearing spurious markings imitating Henry Deringer's own. It was not uncommon for dealers or agents to advertise their franchise or offering to the public of the only "… original derringer" in their respective locales. A few imitators copied the Henry Deringer markings as unscrupulously as the guns themselves, thus leaving for the collector a very difficult decision as to whether the gun is the product of the originator or that of an imitator (both, by the way, are still good collectors' items today!). Others merely copied his name, deviating from both marking style and contours sufficiently to immediately identify their product as a contemporary imitation. The mere fact, however, that they are copies does not in itself indicate any lack of desirability for them as collectors' items. The word, a disparaging one to be certain, in the collecting world, may very well tend to overshadow the importance of a specimen. In many cases the copies (both with spurious Henry Deringer markings as well as the honest marking of the actual maker) will fetch as much and more than the authentic Henry Deringer product. It was generally believed that no infringements were made of Henry Deringer's handguns, on which his name was fraudulently marked, prior to 1850. An article in *Man at Arms* (No. 5, 2000) by D.E. Eberhart reproduced an advertisement from the Washington, D.C. *Globe* newspaper of June 4, 1836 in which Deringer accused one Joseph Smith of Tennessee of having made such a pair spuriously marked with his name, offering a $100 reward to anyone furnishing "Proof that shall convict the man or men who are practicing fraud on the public in his name." Thus it seems that Henry Deringer's pistols had achieved notoriety earlier than formerly presumed.

As will be seen in the description of Henry Deringer's guns, there was a tremendous variety in barrel lengths and sizes. This large variety of arms is not seen among the products of his imitators, but their guns, too, will decidedly vary one from the other. That fact plays no major role in generally evaluating them. The imitators' arms, like the Henry Deringer products, remain more or less constant in size and generally fall into the tiny and medium models. They are classified by those general categories and not by exact barrel length graduations. An advanced specialist might be more precise in his taste, seeking exact barrel lengths to fill gaps in a collection, but for the purposes of identification and evaluation the preceding will hold true.

Many gun dealers, jewelers, and agents throughout the United States—most notably those in the South and West—stocked and sold deringer pistols; their names may often be found stamped on the top of barrels along with those of the makers. By far, the majority of agents' names are found on Henry Deringer's guns. Such markings, when authentic, will add to the value of a gun. A general rule-of-thumb would be an increase of approximately 25 percent, varying considerably with both the condition and quality of the gun as well as the agent's name and location. See further data regarding this and spurious markings, discussed with the products of Henry Deringer.

An extensive and comprehensive listing with accompanying details of all the well known, and many of the lesser known, Deringer makers is found in Volume 1 of *The Deringer in America*, by Wilson and Eberhart (q.v.). In assessing such items value-wise, comparisons may be made with known types. The mere fact of a rare name is not sufficient in itself to place the gun in a premium price category. Key factors to take into account are the quality of the gun, the type of marking, the gunsmith's name, and the area in which he worked (Southern or Western makers will usually bring premiums over Eastern makers). In many instances, American makers of large percussion dueling, target and holster pistols occasionally made small deringer type arms. Although they may be rare as collectors' items, they are valued in accordance with the general characteristics previously noted. It should also be noted there were European imitators, and such guns were often made solely for the American market. It is therefore important when viewing an "unknown" or unlisted deringer to disassemble and inspect it for markings that might appear inside the lock or on the underside of the barrel. If foreign proofmarks are seen, and no other markings present, the entire gun was likely made abroad (and not merely the barrel). The pistol may be considered a good collectors' item, but is valued considerably less than a deringer of American make. In reality, such guns are usually just as rare and fine as any American made piece, and should bring the same value. Traditionally, on the collectors' market, they simply do not fetch the same prices, there being an apparent and unfair stigma attached to their foreign manufacture.

Deringers Versus Belt Pistols

A whole host of small American made pistols—notably those by Pennsylvania makers, the so-called "Kentucky Pistol" makers—are marginal as far as being called "deringers." They are generally proportioned as the deringer, but contour-wise they often stray considerably from the "true" deringer's bird's head butt. Thus it is very much a matter of being in the "eye of the beholder" as to whether they wish to call them "Kentucky Belt Size Pistols" or "deringers." The terminology is strictly one of convenience with no hard and fast rules placing them in either category. Such items are usually one-of-a-kind.

The deringers listed in this chapter, although all hand-crafted, are considered produced in quantity, however limited that might be, and conforming to the general proportions indicated. Bores are generally in the area of 41 caliber, although they will be found to vary. Caliber does not seem to play any role in evaluating, except in the case of extreme sizes. The majority of imitators' guns are the smaller and medium sizes, generally running 2-1/2" to 3" in barrel lengths and overall lengths of about 6" to 7". Smaller types are usually not fitted with ramrods, whereas larger sizes are often found so fitted. The collector is urged to be careful of placing any great emphasis on numbers that might appear on deringers. As will be found with a great many other American made arms, they are usually not serial numbers, but indicate batch or manufacturing group numbers. For the most part, finishes are browned barrels with either plain or casehardened locks and hammers, although such finishes vary.

It appears from reading early accounts that Henry Deringer's products and probably those of most of his imitators were made and sold in pairs. The frequency in which they occur today as matched pairs is quite small, and hence, premiums may be added to values when they are so encountered. The reader is referred to Chapter II where this subject is discussed at greater length.

Cased pairs of deringers are choice collectors' items and are occasionally seen with either Henry Deringer made guns or those of his imitators. It is essential before evaluating such guns that the originality of the case be established. The reader is warned that there has been considerable skullduggery in this field in the past two decades. The subject is also treated at further length in Chapter II.

The use of wood or material other than walnut for stocks on deringers is quite rare and seldom encountered. There are some specimens known stocked in solid ivory and a few with all brass stocks. Both materials not only enhance the appearance of the guns on which they are used, but increase values considerably. A 50 percent increase would be a minimum figure and a 100 percent to 200 percent or more increase may even be in order. Here again, the collector should proceed with caution, for spurious, modern made stocks of such exotic materials are not unknown.

A variant feature most often encountered on deringers which will increase values is the use of precious materials such as gold and silver for mountings. The former is quite rare and seen on but a handful of specimens. The use of silver, though, is seen with a reasonable degree of frequency and increases value

approximately 25 percent to 40 percent. There is, of course, no hard and fast rule; a truly exceptional specimen or matched pair might very possibly exceed that percentage.

The following are some other makers and dealers of deringer type pistols that are known or have been reported:

Canfield & Brother, Baltimore
Henry Folsom, St. Louis
A. G. Genez, New York City
T. F. Guion, New Orleans
William Hahn, New York City
Hawes & Waggoner, Philadelphia
Louis Hoffman, Vicksburg, Mississippi
Klepzig & Company, San Francisco
A. Linde, Memphis, Tennessee
H. G. Newcomb, Natchez, Mississippi
David O'Connell, New York City
Seaver, New York City (known hardware merchants)
E. R. Sieber, Nashville, Tennessee
R. J. Simpson, New York City
A. W. Spies, New York City (known agents)
S. Sutherland, Richmond, Virginia
J. G. Syms, New York City

BIBLIOGRAPHY

Information about deringers may also be found in *The Collecting Of Guns*, edited by James Serven, to be found listed in other bibliographies within this work.

Eberhart, D. *The Henry Deringer Study; A Comparative Analysis Of The Percussion Deringer*. Monograph reprint of article in American Society of Arms Collectors Bulletin 76. Fall, 1997.

*Kirkland, Turner. *Southern Derringers Of The Mississippi Valley*. Union City, Tennessee: Pioneer Press, 1972. Includes Henry Deringer made pistols with southern agents' markings as well as those of southern manufacture.

Parsons, John E. *Henry Deringer's Pocket Pistol*. New York: William Morrow and Company, 1948, 1952. Highly detailed, authoritative study of Henry Deringer's product as well as those of his imitators with considerable lore surrounding the subject.

*Wilson, R. L. and Eberhart, L. D. *The Deringer in America. Volume I: The Percussion Period*. Lincoln, R.I.: Andrew Mowbray, Inc. Publishers, 1985. A standard reference for the subject. Extensive coverage. Volume II, 1993, devoted almost entirely to cartridge types, but does have additional important percussion era data.

(*) Preceding a title indicates the book is currently in print.

HENRY DERINGER'S PISTOLS

Henry Deringer Percussion Pocket Belt Pistols

Henry Deringer, Philadelphia, Pennsylvania, Pocket Pistols (and others). Popularly known as the Deringer Pistol, a.k.a. "Deringer derringer." Made c. late 1830s to 1868.

Earliest Henry Deringer Percussion Pocket & Belt Pistols

Very little specific detail has been known about Henry Deringer's earlier percussion handguns; those that led to the development of the easily recognized quintessential "Deringer." The anomaly was placed in clear perspective by the author of

"The Deringer in America" (L. D. Eberhart; q.v.). His article in "Man at Arms" (No. 5, 2000) is the first survey to delineate and illustrate those predecessors. It is noted that the checkered, bag shape walnut handle is usual on all types. The date of the

7D-000.5
First Style

7D-000.6
Square Guard Style
(oct / round barrel)

7D-000.6
Square Back Guard Style
(flat top barrel)

7D-000.7
Round Guard Style

introduction of the bird's head butt is yet to be determined; the early to 1840s is probable. There is considerable variation in all early specimens and none are known to bear the familiar **P** with sunburst barrel proofmark, introduced sometime after 1836.

First Style; belt size. Possibly as early as 1825 (according to a direct quote of Henry Deringer). 8-1/2 inches overall; 4 inch round barrel; 45 caliber. Bar type side lock marked **H. Deringer/PhiladA** with engraved border and slight leaf and branch engraved motif. Walnut full stock with horn forend tip; fitted with wooden ramrod. Iron mountings; German silver wedge escutcheons. Very rare.

7D-000.5 Values—Good **$2,500**   Fine **$7,500**

Square Back Trigger Guard Style. Likely the earliest introduction of the familiar back action lock. Manufactured in very small quantity until approximately 1835; beginning to display the development towards the ultimate design. On the few specimens recorded, the square back (iron or German silver) trigger guard is common to all; stocks full to muzzle; one specimen noted, almost to muzzle; bag shape handles; German silver forend tips. Sizes vary overall 6 to 8 inches; barrels vary,

part round/octagon or more fully developed round and flat on top. Engraved locks marked **Deringer/Phila**. All trigger guards with pineapple finials. Rare.

7D-000.6 Values—Good **$2,500**   Fine **$5,500**

Round Trigger Guard Style. Period of manufacture from about 1835. Similar to above with round iron trigger guard on specimens thus far surveyed. Barrels round, flat along top; about 4" usual; 8-1/2" overall. Stocks 3/4 length with german silver forend tip and wedge escutcheons; fitted with wooden ramrod. Engraved back action lock marked **Deringer/Phila**.

7D-000.7 Values—Good **$1,250**   Fine **$2,500**

The "Classic" Deringer of the Post-1850s

Although total quantity is unknown, a reasonable approximation may be made from the maker's own testimony, c. 1866. Deringer then advised that he had made 1,280 pairs over the five-year period, 1861 to 1866 (production had obviously fallen off considerably during the Civil War with little need for them then), and a total of 5,280 pairs over the entire decade from 1856 to 1866. Thus, it might be reasonably estimated that at least 15,000 or more Deringer Pocket Pistols were produced.

Triggerguard finial details for various periods of Henry Deringer pistol manufacture.

Note: Due to hand-engraved nature, details vary on specimen pistols.

#1

Circa 1820-30
Found on large pistols and some very early pocket pistols. Fitted in iron; guns will have large size address stamp, as found on Deringer rifles.

#2

Circa 1830-35
Coat size and pocket size pistols, in iron or coin silver, plain or lightly engraved. Barrel breech and lock marking same as in #1.

#3

Circa 1830-35
On earliest type pocket size Deringers, which are barrel breech and lock marked as the pistols with styles #1 and #2. There will be no cap box or butt cap cover on these pistols.

#4

Circa 1835-45
Tip of this finial sometimes squared off. Usually accompanied by forend caps, ramrods, and butt-cap boxes with covers. Locks and breeches with standard small-size maker marking, and sunburst and P.

#5

Circa 1845-48
A rarely observed early style pineapple finial; specimens will be fitted and marked generally as pistols noted in #4.

#6

Circa 1848-50
The finial rather sparsely engraved.

#7

Circa 1850-70
Through end of production, this pattern is the most often observed. Smallest size pistols will only have the pineapple and several leaves forward of the triggerguard.

Note: Pistols represented by figures 5, 6, and 7 will generally have the P marking within a sunburst on barrel breech. About 3% of Henry Deringer pistols observed by the authors were mounted in iron, about 1% in gold, about 10% in silver, and the balance in German silver.

Finial illustrations and data from *Deringer In America, Volume II* with permission of the authors.

No better description may be had, and one that shows the great variance of specimens, than that from Deringer's own words as taken from court testimony in the famous case for infringement of trademark brought by Henry Deringer's Estate against A. J. Plate of San Francisco, 1868:

"It is a single barrel pistol with a back action percussion lock, patent breech, wide bore and a walnut stock. It varies in length of barrel from 1-1/2" to 6" for the ordinary pistol and from 6" to 9" for the dueling pistol. It is commonly mounted with German silver. The barrels used are all rifled. The locks vary in size in proportion to the length of the barrels. On the lockplates and breech of such pistols the words DERINGER-PHILADEL[A] are stamped. The stamps being the same which has been used from the first manufacture of these pistols, and by which, they are known everywhere."

Calibers vary, but usually are approximately 41; larger for medium and dueling sizes. Barrel lengths vary considerably with but 1/8" intervals between sizes, leading to a large variety. Barrel shapes are standard; generally round with flat tops and crowned muzzle; patent breeches of semi-octagonal shape. Seven-groove rifling is standard. Finish on the barrel is simulated damascus (browned with a copper streaking). Locks

are casehardened with other iron parts blued. Stock varnished with checkered grip.

All Deringer made guns have two-piece iron barrels with the tang and breech plug screwed into the barrel. Many of the imitations (including the Slotter, *q.v.*) are made of steel and are one-piece with the breech joint being simulated.

Standard mountings are engraved German silver including the trigger guard, sideplate, flash plate (just below the nipple bolster), the wedge escutcheons on forend, the shield shaped escutcheon on back of the handle, tear shaped cap on bottom of butt and (when present) cap box in butt and forend tip.

Markings on both breech of barrel and the scroll engraved lockplate: DERINGER/PHILADEL[o]. Left side of breech most often seen marked with P encircled by a sunburst motif. Inlaid German silver bands quite often seen at breech of barrel. Occasionally these bands were of silver or gold, and depending on condition and size of specimen, premium may be added. Agent markings (as noted below) may also be seen on the barrels. Single set trigger rare and also worth premium.

Smallest measurements of the pocket sized models are approximately 3-3/4" overall, while the dueling types may measure as large as 15" overall. These post-1850 types are usually characterized by the bird's head styling of the butt. It's pronounced on the smaller sizes, becoming less conspicuous, but recognizable, on most of the larger sizes. Unusual variations and anomalies are occasionally encountered. Oddly shaped or sized specimens, likely produced on special order, such as large belt size, with normal small lock and out-sized, massive handle, add to the fascination of collecting arms of this famous maker.

Small Pocket Sizes. Barrel lengths overall approximately 1-1/2", 2-1/2" to 3". Very tiniest sizes will bring slight premiums. Not fitted for ramrods:

7D-001   Values—Good **$850**   Fine **$2,250**

Medium Pocket Sizes. Barrel lengths approximately 3-1/2" to 6". The larger sizes very often fitted with ramrods:

7D-002   Values—Good **$900**   Fine **$2,750**

Dueling Size Pistols. Barrel lengths approximately 7" to 9". Fitted with ramrods. Very scarce:

7D-003   Values—Good **$1,450**   Fine **$5,500**

Agents Markings. In some instances the Deringer factory marked the name and address of the dealer or agent for whom the guns were made along the top of the barrel. Such markings are quite desirable and enhance both the interest and value of the specimen guns. An approximate 25 percent premium is not out of line for such markings and rare or seldom encountered marks may be increased proportionately. Regrettably the modern day

Although neither the largest or smallest Henry Deringers, these two ideally demonstrate the great disparity that will be found in this model (top gun 11" overall, bottom gun 5" overall).

counterfeiter is also aware that Deringers can be "improved" upon. Dies very closely approximating some of the original agents' markings (most notably those in California) were made and a number of original Henry Deringer specimens had the added agents' markings placed upon them. The collector is thus cautioned to give close scrutiny to all agent-marked pieces to ascertain originality. Generally it has been found that they were authentic Henry Deringer made guns with merely the agent markings being spurious. Chapter III (Markings and Numbers) discusses the subject at greater length.

Some of the more well known and recorded agent markings:

MAN^D FOR HYDE & GOODRICH AGENTS N. O.(these will predate 1861)

MAN^D FOR W. C. ALLEN & CO. SAN FRANC^C CAL^a (very scarce)

MAND FOR F. H. CLARK & CO. MEMPHIS. TENN.

MADE FOR A. J. PLATE SAN FRANCISCO(apparently only 54 pairs so marked with others bearing this marking being the work of Slotter & Company, q.v.)

MAND FOR W. H. CALHOUN AGENT NASHVILLE, TENN.

MAND FOR A. J. TAYLOR & CO. SAN FRANCo CALa

WOLF & DURRINGER LOUISE KY AGENTS

MADE FOR L. SWETT & CO. VICKSBURG, MISS.(very scarce)

LULLMAN & VIENNA MEMPHIS, TENN.

C. CURRY SAN FRANC^O CAL^a AGENT (best known of Henry Deringer's agents in California, c. 1856 to 1863)

N. CURRY & BR^o SAN FRANC^o CAL^a AGENTS. (Brothers of C. Curry, took over the business; c. 1863 to 1868)

J. A. SCHAFER, VICKSBURG, MISS. (very scarce)

MAN^D FOR J. B. GILMORE (of Shreveport, Louisiana)—(very scarce)

MADE FOR M. W. GALT & BR^R. WASHINGTON, D.C. (very scarce)

Misspelled Markings. Quite a few Deringer imitations are encountered bearing markings approximating those of Henry Deringer, but purposely misspelled. Most often seen are DERRINGER, DEERRINGER, BERINGER and DERINGE. Origin of these pieces is unknown and it is likely that some are of European manufacture made for the American trade. Generally their quality is considerably under that of Henry Deringer or many of the other Deringer imitations.Unmarked Deringer infringements usually worth 20 to 40 percent less than the values reflected below:

7D-004   Values—Good **$550**   Fine **$950**

HENRY DERINGER'S COMPETITORS AND IMITATORS

The following makers are arranged alphabetically. Their guns are all closely fashioned and styled after the pocket pistols made by Henry Deringer of Philadelphia. Some are in direct imitation of him, while others are merely after his style, but with the maker's own innovations.

NOTE: Dimensions, caliber and, in many instances, markings, are those from viewed or reliably reported examples. There may be considerable variance in these features, especially on specimens by the scarcer and lesser-known makers.

W. Afferbach Pocket Pistol

William Afferbach, Philadelphia. (Not illus.) Styled very closely to that made by Henry Deringer. C. 1850s. Very scarce.

Approximately 41 caliber. Barrel marking: W. AFFERBACH PHILA:

7D-005   Values—Good **$950**   Fine **$2,000**

B. Auer Pocket Pistol

B. Auer, Louisville, Kentucky. Styled similar to the Henry Deringer c.1850s. Very scarce. Limited quantity.

Caliber 60 but will vary. Varying length octagon barrels; 4" average. Long iron tang extends 3/4-length back of handle.

Walnut stock with checkered handle; German silver sideplate, flash plate and wedge escutcheons; engraved iron trigger guard; pewter forend tip.

Lock marked in hand engraved script B. Auer:

7D-006   Values—Good **$1,100**   Fine **$2,250**

7D-006

T. Bailey Pocket Pistols

Thomas Bailey, New Orleans, Louisiana. Small pocket pistol with distinctive wide, flared, flat butt. Circa 1850s; possibly French or Belgian manufacture imported by Bailey. Directories indicate he was in business c. 1850s until 1863 when, for unknown reasons he emigrated to Great Britain. Caliber 52 smoothbore. 3" octagon barrel with imitation damascus twist / striped finish; deeply marked in bold script on top "T. BAILEY. NEW ORLEANS." Barrel may have had foreign proof marks (difficult to discern on known specimen). Walnut stock with engraved iron mounts. Specimens scarce.

7D-006.5   Values—Good **$1,250**   Fine **$2,750**

7D-006.5

F. Beerstecher Superposed Load Pocket Pistol

Frederick Beerstecher, Philadelphia, Two-Shot Superposed Load Pocket Pistol. Made c. 1850s. Very limited quantity. Rare.

Approximately 41 caliber. Barrel lengths vary; approximately 3" average. Loaded with two full charges, one on top of the other. The unique and distinctive features are the double bolsters with two nipples and the massive double strikers on the head of the hammer; the forward striker is hinged to selectively fire first the top, then the lower load.

Variations have been noted in minor contours and mountings. These arms were very probably made for Beerstecher by other Philadelphia gun makers.

Usual markings: F. BEERSTECHER'S/PATENT 1855 on the lock and LEWISBURG PA and PATENT 1855 on the barrel.

The gun is also known in large deringer or belt size with a full side lock and more simply shaped three-quarter length stock

7D-007

with bird's head butt, without butt cap or other ornaments. Marked only F. BEERSTECHER on lock (this variant presumably the patent model):

7D-007   Values—Good **$5,500**   Fine **$12,000**

Frank J. Bitterlich Pocket Pistols

Frank J. Bitterlich, Nashville, Tennessee. Distinctly styled Deringer type pocket pistols. Made c. 1854 to early 1860s.

Pocket size arms of approximately 41 caliber. Octagon barrels of various lengths. Mountings are usually of German silver and are plain, unengraved. Markings on both barrel and lockplate: FR. J. BITTERLICH/NASHVILLE, TENN. or FR. J. BITTERLICH &

**7D-008(a)
Square Butt**

**7D-008(b)
Bird's-Head Butt**

CO./NASHVILLE, TENN.

Bitterlich made both styles described below for Frederick G. Glassick of Memphis, Tennessee and both types are also found marked: F. GLASSICK & CO./MEMPHIS, TENN., on either the barrel or the lock. On a relative rarity scale, the Glassicks have been rated as being seen slightly more often than the Bitterlich marked specimens. Generally prices have been about the same for either type marking with only highly advanced specialists willing to pay premiums for the scarcer type.

There is every likelihood that Bitterlich also made these style deringers for William S. Schneider (Schneider & Company of Memphis, Tennessee, *q.v.*) and later the firm of Schneider & Glassick of Memphis, Tennessee (*q.v.*). The arms of both those firms, although similar, have notable differences in styling.

Bitterlich deringers are easily distinguishable by their (a) uniquely shaped locks with a pronounced double curve on the underside between the hammer and bolster; (b) barrels fastened by a screw from the underside of the forend with a large German silver screw escutcheon plate made in floral shape.

Often a plain, simple line engraving borders the edges of the hammer and a double broken line engraving edges the front section of the lock. The hammer screw most often seen is uniquely rectangular shaped.

Bitterlich deringers are made in two distinct styles: (a) Square/flat butt which is somewhat scarcer and will bring a small premium; (b) bird's-head butt:

7D-008   Values—Good **$2,000**   Fine **$4,500**

Blunt & Syms Pocket Pistol

Orison Blunt and Wm. J. & Samuel R. Syms, New York City. All metal frame and forend pocket pistol fashioned directly after the Henry Deringer type. Made c.1850s.

Caliber 50; 3" round deringer-type barrel, flat along top (lengths may vary). Six-groove bore. Entire frame, forend and grip straps integral cast of German silver with hand engraving on forend simulating wedge, wedge escutcheons and forend cap of the deringer-type pistol. Matching engraved German silver trigger guard. Two-piece checkered walnut grips on the short bag-shaped handle. Scroll engraved back action lock and hammer. Displays excellent quality workmanship. Is distinctly styled after the Philadelphia deringer and differs from the large belt and pocket size Blunt & Syms iron frame and forend pocket pistols (*see Chapter VII-C*).

7D-009

Marked on top of barrel: BLUNT & SYMS (in semi-circular arch) /NEW YORK:

7D-009   Values—Good **$850**   Fine **$2,000**

R.P. Bruff Pocket Pistol

R. P. Bruff, New York City. Pocket pistol fashioned very similar to the Henry Deringer type. Made c. 1850s to 1860s.

Caliber 41. Barrels approximately 2-1/2" to 3", although other longer lengths (worth premium) have been observed. German silver mounts; checkered walnut stock. Barrel marking: R. P. BRUFF (in semi-circular arch)/N.Y. and further along the barrel CAST STEEL. Scroll engraving standard on various parts and mountings:

7D-010   Values—Good **$650**   Fine **$1,250**

7D-010

Jesse S. Butterfield Pocket Pistol

Jesse S. Butterfield, Philadelphia. Pocket pistol fashioned after Henry Deringer style, fitted with patented priming mechanism. Made mid to late 1850s. Quantity very limited. Rare.

Caliber approximately 41. Barrel lengths 2" to 3-1/2".

German silver engraved mountings. Most stocks have a slight relief lip carved at the extreme tip of forend. Most easily distinguished feature is the unique pellet priming system built into the forward section of the lock with a large knurled knob removable cap on the underside for inserting supply of primers.

Lockplate marking: BUTTERFIELD'S/PATENT DEC 11. 1855.

Butterfields are among the most sought after of all variations of deringer pistols:

7D-011   Values—Good **$5,500**   Fine **$12,500**

7D-011

F.H. Clark Pocket Pistols

F. H. Clark & Co., Memphis, Tennessee. Pocket pistols fashioned very similar to the Henry Deringer style. Made c. 1850s to 1860s. A well known southern firm; although primarily jewelers, they carried a very large gun and sporting goods line. They were also agents for Henry Deringer of Philadelphia and many of his pistols are found with the dual markings: MAND FOR F. H. CLARK & CO. MEMPHIS, TENN. (*q.v.*).

Other non-Henry Deringer made pistols are encountered marked F. H. CLARK & CO./MEMPHIS on the barrel which were either made by Clark or for them by another (unknown) southern maker. Generally styled after the Henry Deringer Pocket Pistol, they may be most easily recognized by the use of a German silver cap on the forend, plain unengraved German silver mounts, either simple oval or fancy shaped barrel wedge escutcheons. Barrels that are often (but not always) fastened by a screw from the underside, entering through the finial of the trigger guard. Most specimens also are fitted with wooden ramrods.

Caliber approximately 41. Barrel lengths vary from 3-1/2" to 5":

7D-012   Values—Good **$1,750**   Fine **$4,500**

7D-012

R. Constable Pocket Pistols

Richard Constable, Philadelphia. A well known, respected gunmaker circa 1817 to 1851 with an extensive line of handguns of various sizes and types, from deringers to dueling pistols and longarms. Deringers will vary in size, calibers and mountings. Illustrated is the typical style fashioned after the Henry Deringer.

41 caliber; 3-1/2" octagon barrel (others known with the deringer-style barrel i.e. round with flat top); back action lock, seen with both script and block letter markings, "R. CONSTABLE—PHILADELPHIA" on barrel or lock (or both). Walnut stock with horn forend tip; checkered bag shaped handle:

7D-013   Values—Good **$875**   Fine **$2,000**

7D-013

J. Deringer Markings   *See Slotter & Company.*

Moses Dickson Pocket Pistol

7D-013.5

Moses Dickson, Louisville, Kentucky Pocket Pistols of various typed fashioned after those made by Henry Deringer. Circa 1848-1860 (later relocating and working 1860-1867 in Liberty, Missouri). Type illustrated and described here closely fashioned

after Philadelphia style deringers; others known with octagon barrel, full stock and longer arched handle; the long back action lock straight rather than curved as shown here.

38 caliber. Approximately 4-1/2" barrel (both round with flat top and octagon types). overall length 8-1/2". Curved and engraved back action lock (straight types also used) marked M. DICKSON; barrel markings LOUISVILLE KY. 3-1/4" length walnut, checkered handle (also full stock with longer arched handles, as shown); engraved German silver mountings with matching forend tip and fancy shaped wedge escutcheon; wooden ramrod. (Note: British proof marks observed on specimen with the longer arched handles and octagon barrels; values approx. 20 to 30 percent less than shown):

7D-013.5   Values—Good **$2,000**   Fine **$4,000**

H.E. Dimick Pocket Pistols

Horace E. Dimick & Co., St. Louis, Missouri. Pocket pistols fashioned very closely after the Henry Deringer type. Made c. 1850s to 1860s.

Caliber approximately 41; barrels 3" to 4". Lockplate usually plain, unengraved, with a simple scroll engraving on the hammer; some specimens have been noted with engraving of a large American eagle with upraised wings on the lock and will bring a premium. Other specimens encountered with very narrow line engraving bordering edge of lock while others have been reported with scroll type deringer style lock engraving.

Barrel marking: H. E. DIMICK in very small letters, occasionally followed by ST. LOUIS; also seen marked H. E. DIMICK & CO.

Dimick arms are found with barrels either fastened by screw from underside of forend or by the usual barrel wedge with oval escutcheon plates.

The arms of this maker have a special appeal due to his reputation in supplying the frontier trade during an important era of American westward expansion:

7D-014   Values—Good **$2,000**   Fine **$4,250**

**7D-014
(screw fastened
barrel)**

**7D-014
(wedge fastened
barrel)**

J. Drepperd Pocket Pistols

7D-014.5

John Drepperd, Lancaster, Pennsylvania. Pocket Pistols of small belt size not directly styled after the Henry Deringer. Made circa 1840s-1850s. Quantity unknown; rare.

A prolific maker of Kentucky rifles, this small handgun is listed here an example of the small, pocket handgun much in vogue during the era and often classified by the collecting world as "deringer." Especially desirable due to its maker's name and reputation for fine Kentucky rifles and the pistol's classification as a "deringer.".

Dimensions, calibers and quality will vary. This example 7" overall; 4" octagon brass barrel; 36 caliber. Marked both barrel and lock "DREPPERD—LANCASTER."Walnut stock; engraved brass trigger guard. Values dependent upon "Kentucky" riflesmith's name and quality of craftmanship; estimated in low to mid four-figure range:
7D-014.5

G. Erichson Pocket Pistols

G. Erichson, Houston, Texas. (Variously listed as G. Erichson or H. Erickson.) (Not illus.) Circa unknown, probably 1850s. Possibly only a dealer. Pocket pistols patterned very closely after Henry Deringer style.

45 caliber; 3-1/4" barrel on specimen viewed. Plain,

unengraved lock marked G. ERICHSON/HOUSTON/TEXAS.

Distinctively shaped hammer having deep fluted design along front edge; forend of stock with relief carved lip at tip. Rare:

7D-015   Values—Good **$4,000**   Fine **$9,500**

J.E. Evans Pocket Pistols

J. E. Evans, Philadelphia. Pocket pistols styled very closely after the Henry Deringer. Made c. 1850s to 1860s.

Approximately 41 caliber. Barrels vary from 2-1/2" to 3". German silver mountings; walnut stock with checkered grip. Barrel marking: J. E. EVANS PHILAD^. Scroll engraved designs standard on mountings and locks:

7D-016   Values—Good **$850**   Fine **$1,750**

7D-016

Reese Fitzpatrick Pocket Pistols

7D-016.2

Reese Fitzpatrick, Natchez, Mississippi Pocket Pistols generally styled after those of Henry Deringer circa 1840s-1860s. Before relocating to Natchez, Fitzpatrick had been in business in Baton Rouge, Louisiana (1829-1840) working as a gunsmith, located very close to noted Louisiana maker Daniel Searles. Handguns bearing both names are known, clearly indicating that they were in business together (at least for a short time) during those years. Searles is best known for having made Bowie knives on order for Rezin Bowie, brother of the legendary Jim Bowie. (Due to that association, Fitzpatrick's name is often seen mentioned as the man who made Jim Bowie's famous first knife, a legend that has since been conclusively disproven). Quantity unknown.

41 caliber. 4" inch barrel marked R. FITZPATRICK, NATCHEZ, MISS. 7-1/2" overall. Caliber and dimensions likely to vary. Walnut 3-1/4" length stock with bird's-head butt (not checkered); back action lock. Specimen viewed with profusely engraved and detailed, including the barrel tang, lock and silver mountings (worth premium). Rare:

7D-016.2   Values—Good **$4,500**   Fine **$9,000**

Charles Foehl Pocket Pistols

Charles Foehl, Philadelphia. Pocket pistol fashioned closely after the Henry Deringer. Apparently learned the gunmaking trade while working for Henry Deringer. Business directories show him active but a few years commencing 1868.

44 caliber. Short 1-1/2" barrel; just 4-1/2" overall. German silver mountings.

Marking: CHAS FOEHL/PHILA:

7D-016.3   Values—Good **$1,150**   Fine **$2,500**

7D-016.3

G.D.H. Gillespie Pocket Pistols

George D.H. Gillespie, New York City. Pocket pistol styled closely after the Henry Deringer. c. 1850s to 1860s.

Various contours noted with calibers varying from 41 to 50. Barrel lengths approximately 3-1/2" to 4-1/2". On specimens shown all mountings were German silver with only the trigger guards engraved.

Markings vary. Some found with die stamped small letters GILLESPIE on both lock and barrel. Others with only hand engraved markings: GILLESPIE on lock.

Gillespie known to have been a hardware merchant on Warren Street, New York who also handled firearms. Believed he handled the product of other New York State makers including Daniel O'Connell:

7D-016.5   Values—Good **$800**   Fine **$1,750**

7D-016.5

Frederick Glassick, Memphis, Tennessee   *See Bitterlich.*

J. C. Grubb Pocket Pistols

Joseph C. Grubb (Grubb & Co.) Philadelphia. Pocket pistol styled generally after the Henry Deringer type. Made c.1850s to 1860.

41 caliber. Varying barrels; approximately 4". German silver furniture with engraved iron trigger guard and ramrod pipe. Lock marked: J. C. GRUBB. Scroll engraved standard on trigger guard, lock and hammer:
7D-017   Values—Good **$850**   Fine **$1,500**

7D-017

Louis Hoffman Pocket Pistols

Louis Hoffman, Vicksburg, Mississippi. Circa 1853-1870. Pocket pistols generally styled after those of Henry Deringer. A well-known gunmaker and merchant, handling firearms of many other manufacturers; in business until early 20th century in Vicksburg. He made deringers as well as importing others from Europe on which he marked his name. Specimen illustrated typical of his workmanship.

50 caliber. 3-3/4" octagon barrel marked on breech LOUIS HOFFMAN / VICKSBURG. Simply engraved, curved back action lock marked L. HOFFMAN. 6-3/4" overall. Checkered walnut stock with fluted carving on tip of forend. German silver mounts. Values shown are for Hoffman/Vicksburg made specimens. Those bearing his name with foreign proof marks

7D-017.3

indicating their importation and custom order by himself approximately 30 percent less values:
7D-017.3   Values—Good **$4,000**   Fine **$7,500**

Joseph Jacob Pocket Pistols

7D-017.5

Joseph Jacob, Philadelphia. Pocket pistols styled after the Henry Deringer. c.1860 through 1870s.

46 caliber. 3" barrel with gold band inlays at breech and gold clean-out vent. Sterling silver mounts.

Barrel markings: J. JACOB PHILA

Display very fine, well above usual quality, with profuse engraving all mounts, tang and breech:
7D-017.5   Values—Good **$1,400**   Fine **$2,250**

Kirkman & Ellis Pocket Pistols

John Kirkman and James Ellis of Nashville, Tennessee; partners of a hardware firm of Nashville, Tennessee circa 1853 (possibly earlier) to 1857. Quantity unknown; scarce. Not known to have manufactured pistols. Deringer styled handguns bearing their name. Those that have been viewed are invariably of poor quality and somewhat awkward in their styling.

38 caliber. 4-1/2" octagon barrel. Simply engraved lock marked KIRKMAN & ELLIS. (Other markings are reported including H & J KIRKMAN and similar; some include the city

7D-017.6

name "NASHVILLE." others omit it):
7D-017.6   Values—Good **$600 to $900**   Fine **$2,000**

Peter Kraft Pocket Pistols

7D-017.8

Peter W. Kraft, Columbia, South Carolina. Pocket pistols styled after Henry Deringer type. Circa 1840s-1860s. Maker of fine percussion firearms including dueling pistols; also large dealer in swords, edged weapons and firearms of various manufacturers. Deringers likely to vary in size and caliber.

41 caliber. 3-1/2" round barrel; flat along top, 7-1/2" overall. German silver furniture with a pineapple styled finial on trigger guard. Barrel bears large markings P. W. KRAFT, COLUMBIA S.C. Scroll engraving on the back action lock and hammer:
7D-017.8   Values—Good **$3,500**   Fine **$6,500**

John H. Krider Pocket Pistols

John H. Krider, Philadelphia. One of the "old line" Philadelphia gunmakers and large arms and sporting goods merchants from 1826 to 1876. They both made and were agents for a wide range of firearms, including those fashioned identically after the Henry Deringer and other similar, small pocket pistols with full side locks.

Bird's-head butt style identical to Henry Deringer (not illus.). 41 caliber with 3-1/2" round barrel; flat along top. Checkered walnut handle; German silver mountings. Markings "JOHN KRIDER—PHILADELPHIA" on barrel.

Bag shaped handle style (illus. here); 7" overall; 4" round barrel, flat along top. Marked "PHILADELPHIA;" lock marked "JOHN KRIDER." Illustrated here a custom model profusely engraved. Silver mounts; unique concealed cap box in the lower

7D-018
("Custom Model")

handle; cap box cover almost full length of backstrap of handle; lifts upward exposing cavities for caps and bullets. (Scarce variant worth 50 percent or larger premium.) Valued below (not illus.) is bird's-head butt style, direct copy of H. Deringer:

7D-018   Values—Good **$875**   Fine **$1,750**

V. G. W. Libeau Pocket Pistol

7D-018.5

V. G. W. Libeau, New Orleans. Pocket pistols styled similar to the Henry Deringer type with noticeable variances. Circa late 1840s, possibly to mid-1850s. Limited production. Specimens will vary.

54 caliber with 5-1/2" octagon barrel. Overall approx. 10". Walnut stock with cap box marked LIBEAU on the engraved back action lock. Rare:

7D-018.5   Values—Good **$3,000**   Fine **$7,500**

A. Frederick Lins Pocket Pistols

A. Frederick Lins, Philadelphia. Pocket pistols styled very closely after the Henry Deringer. Made c. late 1850s to 1860.

Approximately 41 caliber. Barrels 2-1/2" to 3" approximately. Marked on top: A. FRED^K LINS. PHILAD^A:

7D-019   Values—Good **$875**   Fine **$1,750**

7D-019

C. Lohner Pocket Pistol

C. Lohner, Philadelphia. Pocket pistols styled generally after the Henry Deringer type. Circa 1850s. Varying sizes. 44 caliber. 5" round barrel (flat along top). Walnut stock with short bag-shaped checkered handle. German silver furniture with engraved iron trigger guard and ramrod pipes. Found also with single set triggers. Scroll engraved lock and hammer.

Marked on barrel: C. LOHNER.

7D-020   Values—Good **$775**   Fine **$1,600**

7D-020

J. P. Lower   *See Slotter & Company.*

A.R. Mendenhall Pocket Pistol

A.R. Mendenhall, Des Arc, Arkansas. c.1850s to 1860s. Pocket pistols styled after Henry Deringer. During the Civil War Mendenhall is shown listed as a gunsmith at the Confederate Ordnance Dept., Arkadelphia, Arkansas.

46 caliber. 3" barrel. Silver mounts. Very well made, with mountings and lock usually undecorated. Forend of stock usually has the distinctive flare.

Barrel marked A.R. MENDENHALL with or without DES ARC, ARK:

7D-020.3

7D-020.3   Values—Good **$3,750**   Fine **$7,000**

Murphy & O'Connell Pocket Pistols

7D-020.5

John Murphy and Daniel O'Connell, New York City. Pocket pistol styled similar to the Henry Deringer type; made c. 1858.

Caliber approximately 46; 3-1/2" octagon barrel. Engraved lockplate. German silver mountings; removable wooden ramrod.

Markings MURPHY & O'CONNELL appear on both the barrel and lock.

These makers actually listed themselves in New York City Business Directory as "manufacturers of Deringer pistols." Very rare:

7D-020.5   Values—Good **$1,000**   Fine **$2,250**

R. Myers Pocket Pistol

R. Myers, (location unknown). Very well made pocket pistol closely styled after the Henry Deringer.

38 caliber deep rifled. Unusually long 4-1/2" barrel (likely will vary). Plain, unengraved lock and iron trigger guard; other mounts german silver. Barrel fastened with screw from underside of forend.

Marked on breech and lock R. MYERS:

7D-020.7   Values—Good **$850**   Fine **$1,400**

7D-020.7

Stephen O'Dell Pocket Pistols

Stephen O'Dell, Natchez, Mississippi. Pocket pistols generally styled after the Henry Deringer, but with workmanship distinctive to this maker.

Caliber 34 to 44. Round barrels approximately 2" to 4" and usually with gold band inlays at breech. Distinctive shaped bolsters with deep fluting and often gold clean-out vent.

Walnut stock with bag shaped handle (bird's head butt not evidenced); German silver furniture; oval wedge escutcheons and forend tip. Larger models fitted with wooden ramrod.

Markings vary and are found both hand engraved or stamped. Usually S. O'DELL on lock or barrel or both. Markings NATCHEZ often accompany the maker's name.

A very important maker noted for fine rifles and many of his

7D-021

arms were carried by emigrants during the era of westward expansion:

7D-021   Values—Good **$3,000**   Fine **$6,500**

Robertson Pocket Pistols

Robertson, Philadelphia. Pocket pistols styled generally after the Henry Deringer type. Also noted with larger, heavier shaped forends having double wedges and escutcheons and double ramrod pipes; fitted with wooden ramrod.

Approximately 41 caliber. Barrel lengths vary 3" to 4-1/2". Marked: ROBERTSON, PHILA.:

7D-022   Values—Good **$850**   Fine **$1,250**

7D-022
(double wedge)

7D-022
(single wedge)

Schemann & Wirsing Pocket Pistol

Schemann & Wirsing, Cincinnati, Ohio. Pocket pistol c. mid-1850s to mid-1860s. Business directories show them variously listed as Schemann & Co., Schemann & Wirsing and Wirsing & Schemann; also T. & A.F. Wirsing, thus it is possible that any variation of these markings could occur on a pistol styled very generally after the Henry Deringer.

42 caliber. 2-1/8" barrel. Profuse engraved full side lock and iron trigger guard; other mountings German silver. Walnut stock with checkered handle and fluted shell design on underside of butt.

Marked on barrel: SCHEMANN & WIRSING CIN, O.:

7D-022.5   Values—Good **$1,150**   Fine **$2,500**

7D-022.5

E. Schmidt & Co. Pocket Pistol

7D-023

E. Schmidt and Company, Houston, Texas. Pocket pistol fashioned very closely after the Henry Deringer style. Made c. 1850s.

Approximately 45 caliber. 2-1/2" barrel, but undoubtedly specimens will vary. Those noted had single gold band inlay at muzzle and double gold band inlays at breech. Plain, unengraved German silver mountings with oval wedge escutcheons on forend. Checkered walnut stock. Plain, unengraved lock and hammer.

Barrel marking: E. SCHMIDT & CO. HOUSTON

7D-023   Values—Good **$4,000**   Fine **$9,500**

Schneider & Co. Pocket Pistols

7D-024
(Square Butt)

7D-024
(Bird's-Head Butt)

Schneider & Co., Memphis, Tennessee. Distinctively styled pocket pistols probably made by F. J. Bitterlich of Nashville, Tennessee (*q.v.*). Made c. 1850s to 1859.

Easily recognizable by their distinctive styling of locks, barrels and butt shapes identical to the Bitterlich made types. The notable differences are the method of fastening the barrel which is with a traverse wedge through the forend and two oval escutcheons plates for same.

Two styles were made: (a) Bird's-head butt identical to the Bitterlich, but with wedge fastened barrel; (b) square/flat butt type identical to the Bitterlich, but with wedge fastened barrel and a distinctive sheath or spur type trigger. This type is believed scarcer, but both styles bring approximately the same values. Barrel marking: SCHNEIDER & CO./MEMPHIS, TENN:

7D-024   Values—Good **$2,250**   Fine **$4,250**

Schneider & Glassick Pocket Pistols

Schneider & Glassick, Memphis, Tennessee. (Not illus.) Distinctively styled pocket pistols probably made by F. J. Bitterlich of Nashville, Tennessee. Made c. 1859 to 1862.

Both the square butt, spur trigger type with octagon barrel (as illustrated for 7D-024) and the bird's-head butt style of the F.J. Bitterlich (7D-008 with octagon barrel) styles are known. Each

with barrel markings: SCHNEIDER & GLASSICK, MEMPHIS, TENN. on barrels. Both types are the least often seen of the Bitterlich-Schneider-Glassick types and both with these dual name markings are rare:

7D-025   Values—Good **$2,500**   Fine **$4,500**

Slotter & Co. Pocket Pistols

Slotter & Co., Philadelphia. Formed by Henry Schlotterbeck (a former workman of Henry Deringer), his brother Frederick and two other former Henry Deringer employees. Pocket pistols fashioned identically after the Henry Deringer type. Made c. 1860 to 1869.

Calibers vary, but usually about 41. Barrel lengths generally 2-1/2" to 3-1/2". Engraved German silver mountings fashioned very closely after those of Henry Deringer. Barrel finishes also styled similar to the Henry Deringer, but do not retain the same

7D-026
Smallest size with pointed butt.

7D-026

copper streaking achieved on the original product. Varnished walnut stock; checkered handle.

Markings on earliest specimens are an almost exact duplication of the original: DERINGER/PHILADEL^A on both the engraved lock and barrel. Approximately 428 pairs of these were made with dual markings on barrel MADE FOR/A. J. PLATE/SAN FRANCISCO; others also known with the agent marking MADE FOR/R. LIDDLE & CO./SAN FRANC° CAL^A. Later specimens marked SLOTTER/& C°. PHIL^A; barrels also marked STEEL or WART STEEL. Other specimens seen marked either J. P. LOWER on the barrel or lock or (after 1866) J. DERINGER/PHILADEL^A on top of breech; both of these markings are sometimes accompanied with dual barrel markings SLOTTER/& CO. PHIL^A.

Slotter copies were in direct imitation of the Henry Deringer pistol attributable to the fact that most of the workmen had been in Deringer's prior employ. The smallest Slotter is easily distinguished by its exaggerated/pointed shape of the bird's head butt. When Deringer finally determined that it was Slotter who was flagrantly infringing upon his style and name, he brought suit for damages. The result, documented in the court case of *Deringer vs. Plate* is an important source of information on both the genuine and contemporary copies of the Deringer pistol.

Other details to note in determining a Slotter made piece from the original Henry Deringer product are the use of solid steel barrels (rather than iron) with the breech plugs often made as one piece (the joint merely being simulated in the finishing); larger size of sideplates; varying engraving styles; front sight usually of brass and rifling usually of five grooves.

John Deringer, a tailor by trade, was brought into the Slotter firm merely for the use of his name on their Deringer copies; this deceitful practice proving to be an intriguing bit of present day collectors' and deringer lore. J. P. Lower, after 1875, was a well known Denver, Colorado, arms dealer. During the era of manufacture of these deringers he was merely a clerk for J. C. Grubb, a large Philadelphia arms dealer; his name was likely used merely to deceive Henry Deringer and the public as to who was the actual manufacturer. (*See also Uhlinger Revolvers, Chapter VIII*):

7D-026   Values—Good **$950**   Fine **$2,250**

Spang & Wallace Pocket Pistol

Spang & Wallace, Philadelphia. Percussion pocket pistols fashioned generally after the Henry Deringer type. Made c. 1850s to 60s.

36 caliber (will vary). Round barrels (flat along top) varying in length; 5-1/2" illus. Scroll and leaf engraved motifs on lock and hammer. German silver furniture.

Lock marked: SPANG & WALLACE, barrel marked: SPANG & WALLACE/PHIL^A:

7D-027   Values—Good **$850**   Fine **$1,400**

7D-027

C. Suter Pocket Pistols

C. Suter, Selma, Alabama. (Not illus.) Pocket pistols fashioned very closely after the Henry Deringer style. Made c. 1850s.

Approximately 41 caliber. Barrel lengths vary 2" to 4-1/2". German silver mountings; walnut stock with checkered handle.

Barrel wedges usually accompanied by oval German silver escutcheons. Larger specimens usually fitted with wooden ramrods and have German silver forend tips. Considerable variances have been noted by this maker:

7D-028   Values—Good **$2,250**   Fine **$4,500**

I.F. Trumpler Pocket Pistols

I. F. Trumpler, Little Rock, Arkansas. Pocket pistols styled after the Henry Deringer type. Made c. 1850s to early 1860s.

Approximately 41 caliber. Distinct features are the high hammer, very narrow trigger guard and trigger plate, unusually shaped forend cap. Marked on barrel: I. F. TRUMPLER L ROCK,ARK. Rare:

7D-029   Values—Good **$3,750**   Fine **$7,000**

7D-029

Edward K. Tryon Pocket Pistols

7D-030

Edward K. Tryon & Co., Philadelphia. Pocket pistols fashioned very similarly after the Henry Deringer type. Made c. 1860 to 1875.

Approximately 41 caliber. Barrel lengths are from 2" to 4" and marked: TRYON PHILADᴬ.

Original Tryon advertising offered these pistols in varying lengths and three grades of quality from common steel barrels to twist barrels to those with extra mountings and fancier engraving. Prolific makers; varying contours noted. Tryon also imported derringer infringements from Belgium, (with LGE proof marks in a small oval cartouche) and from England, bearing standard British proof marks. Proofs are found either at the breech end of the barrel and easily viewed or often on the undersides of the barrel needing removal to be seen. Values here for Philadelphia-made specimens by Tryon. Imported specimens usually worth 25 percent less.

7D-030   Values—Good **$850**   Fine **$1,400**

Tufts & Colley Pocket Pistol

Tufts & Colley, believed to be of New York City. Pocket pistol of fine quality styled very closely after the Henry Deringer type. Made c.1850.

44 caliber; 3-1/2" barrel (but will vary). Engraved lock and hammer. Walnut stock made without provision for ramrod; checkered handle; engraved German silver furniture.

Marked on lock: TUFTS/ & COLLEY. Marked on barrel: DERINGER / PATTrᴛ

7D-031   Values—Good **$900**   Fine **$1,650**

7D-031

Wallis & Birch Pocket Pistols

Wallis & Birch, Philadelphia. (Not illus.) Pocket pistols styled very closely after the Henry Deringer type. Made c. 1850s.

41 caliber. Barrel lengths approximately 2-1/2" to 3". Marked: WALLIS & BIRCH PHILA.:

7D-032   Values—Good **$875**   Fine **$1,650**

A. Weisgerber Pocket Pistol

A. Weisgerber, Memphis, Tennessee c. mid-1860s to 1870s. Pocket pistols closely styled after Henry Deringer (as illus.) with others known with bag shaped handle.

44 caliber. 3" full octagon or round with flat top. It is thought that many of his locks and barrels were acquired from Bitterlich (*q.v.*)

Marked on barrel A WEISGERBER (or A.WEISGERBER & CO.)/MEMPHIS, TENN.

7D-032.5   Values—Good **$4,500**   Fine **$9,000**

7D-032.5

Andrew Wurfflein Pocket Pistols

Andrew Wurfflein, Philadelphia. Pocket pistols styled very closely after the Henry Deringer type. Made c. 1850s to 1860s.

41 caliber. Barrel lengths average 2-1/2" to 3". Markings: A. WURFFLEIN/PHILᴬ. Scroll engraving standard on mountings and locks.

7D-033

7D-033

Andrew was the first of that name to make Deringers (c. 1845-1870s) followed by his son William Wurfflein (c. 1870-1910). Deringer pistols also encountered marked J. WURFFLEIN, the product of John Wurfflein (c. 1840s-1867) whose exact association with Andrew and William is unknown, although there apparently was a family relationship.

Illustration depicts two varying style Andrew Wurfflein deringers:

7D-033   Values—Good **$875**   Fine **$1,750**

Wirsing & Schemann   *See Schemann.*

Cased pair percussion dueling pistols by Henry Deringer of Philadelphia. The 9-1/2" barrels also bear the marking of the dealer or agent that originally sold the outfit "MAN'D FOR A. MIL SPAUGH/ WASHINGTON, LA." Extremely rare.
(N. Flayderman & Co., c. 1970)

Chapter VII-E

Percussion Underhammer Pistols

Little explanation is needed to amplify the distinctive appearance of these uniquely designed antique arms. The word "underhammer" says it quite succinctly! The system of placing the hammer on the underside of the barrel originated during the flintlock era and the first specimens of these types were believed made in Europe. American made flintlock underhammers are extremely rare and most would be classed as one-of-a-kind, with none produced in quantity by any single maker.

The arms listed in this chapter, although not considered "mass produced" in the true sense of the word, represent examples by known makers who generally produced a number of specimens (quantities usually limited) of almost identically appearing guns. Often considerable variance exists in the handguns of these listed makers (barrel lengths and calibers being the most often noted), but they will all generally conform stylistically to those illustrated and described. The difference in calibers and barrel lengths will rarely alter the value of the piece. An unusually long barrel would be the exception to this rule; adding both interest and a value premium in many cases.

The system of placing a hammer on the underside of a barrel appeared on both handguns and longarms. Handguns, however, are treated individually herein for they seem to have been made in considerably larger quantities and are more conforming stylistically, whereas the longarms tend to be more individualistic or one-of-a-kind, varying considerably one from the other.

A term used interchangeably to describe underhammer handguns and one by which they are often better known, is *Bootleg* pistol. As the name suggests, the sleek, unencumbered design of the majority of these arms seemingly allowed them to be carried with great ease (for concealment and access) in the top of a man's leather boot. Obviously, though, they could just as easily be quickly drawn, and concealed, in a belt or a pocket. Although this same "bootleg" terminology was applicable to other pistols with conventional side hammers, modern day gun literature and collectors have by common acceptance and usage made the term "bootleg" synonymous for underhammer pistols. Occasionally these underhammers will be seen referred to as "whipsocket pistols", terminology not in popular usage today.

The practicality of the underhammer gun, and its popularity in reasonably widespread manufacture and sales, is further apparent from three other features unique to the type: (a) The extremely simple construction both mechanically and externally, quite often made without an encumbering trigger guard, while in other instances, the trigger guard acts in the dual capacity of mainspring; (b) Affords the shooter, especially on the heavy barreled target types, a much clearer line of sight with no obstructions to interfere with aiming; (c) A decided safety factor in lessening the possibility of exploded pieces from the percussion cap striking one's eye during ignition.

As will be obvious from reviewing the following descriptions, the underhammer pistol found its greatest popularity—and subsequently its widest production—in the New England area. Massachusetts and Connecticut makers, by far, produced the greatest quantities. The style caught hold principally in the New England and New York area, although isolated specimens are known to have been produced in other states. The general era of their manufacture, sales and use was from the mid-1830s to the commencement of the Civil War.

Considerable variation and individuality are found among these underhammer pistols. A general discussion and guide to evaluation of those other than the makers individually listed is found under the last heading "Unmarked or Otherwise Unidentified Types."

A few features common to most of the underhammers of the types listed herein (and features to be considered when evaluating them) are: (a) Calibers average from 31 through 36; differences in bore sizes do not usually influence values; (b) Walnut grips more or less standard unless otherwise indicated. Many makers used various types of wood for stocks. When pistols are found with maple, cherry or curly maple, etc. (not otherwise listed as standard), premiums in most cases may be added. Plain maple or cherry will fetch but small additional premiums at best; a 15 percent to 20 percent premium may be added for curly maple, especially if the wood grain has the desirable pronounced tiger stripe.

A large majority of the known quantity makers of stylistically similar underhammers are listed here, but others will undoubtedly be encountered. A general guideline to evaluating those other types is to compare them price-wise to similar underhammers described and illustrated herein. Prices are more or less comparable for quality, style, type of wood used, name of maker and area in which he worked.

Likely many of these underhammer pistols were made and sold as matched pairs. The frequency in which they are found today, however, is extremely small and a premium may be added to the value of them when they are so encountered. Merely placing two guns of the same type together to make a pair does not necessarily mean that they are truly that. They must match just about identically in every feature and most important—condition. The fact of finding a reasonably well known maker in a matched pair in just mediocre condition would not necessarily increase their values any more than they would be worth individually. However, a choice conditioned pair, identically matching, would certainly be worth a premium of 20 percent to 40 percent. Obviously, underhammer pistols with exotic materials utilized in their decoration such as silver in place of brass, or containing several very fine quality silver or brass inlays in the wood, are worth increased prices and premiums should be added accordingly.

A feature quite commonly encountered on the Massachusetts and Connecticut made underhammers is the use of a small American eagle and shield motif with the markings. There is no explanation for this; evidently the motif was merely popular with the makers of the area and in no way indicates any military usage or association.

BIBLIOGRAPHY

Logan, Herschel C. *Underhammer Guns.* Harrisburg, Pennsylvania: The Stackpole Company, 1960. The classic reference to the subject encompassing longarms and handguns, American and European. Over 300 types are illustrated.

(*) Preceding a title indicates book is currently in print.

E. Allen, Allen & Thurber   *See Allen Firearms, Chapter V.*

Anderson (so-called) Unmarked Underhammer Pistol

Anderson (so-called) Unmarked Underhammer Pistol.
Approximately 45 to 48 caliber. 4" to 5" part octagon/part round barrel. All steel saw-handle shaped frame. Walnut grips with flared butt.

Although a study in the 1950s concluded these were made in Anderson, Texas, and the terminology "Anderson Pistol" found its way into popular collector usage, the lack of supporting documentary or other substantial evidence in the 50 intervening years has failed to show any credible Texas background (or value!) to this well made underhammer. The similarity to handguns of Blunt & Syms of New York (*q.v.*) strongly suggests manufacture by that firm:

7E-001   Values—Good **$325**   Fine **$850**
Identical to above with bag shape handle. Calibers will vary 36 to 41; part octagon/round barrel 5", will vary. Walnut grips. Invariably found unmarked. Specimens known marked POCKET RIFLE/CAST STEEL worth 25 percent premium:
7E-001.5   Values—Good **$325**   Fine **$850**

7E-001
Flared Butt

7E-001.5
Bag Shape Handle

Andrews, Ferry & Co. Underhammer Pistol

Andrews Ferry & Co., Stafford, Connecticut. (Robert D. Andrews of Stafford had been granted a U.S. patent in 1837 for attaching knives to pistols.)

36 caliber. 3" part octagon/part round barrel.

Marked on topstrap ANDREWS FERRY & CO.It is not known whether they were manufacturers or agents. The guns are identical to the Gibbs-Tiffany (*q.v.*) and other Massachusetts-Connecticut made bootlegs of the same area:
7E-002   Values—Good **$475**   Fine **$1,100**

7E-002

Andrus & Osborn Underhammer Pistol

Andrus & Osborn of Canton, Connecticut.
25 caliber. 3-1/2 to 6" part round/part octagon barrel with small star inlays or simple engraved lines on topstrap.

Marked on barrel: ANDRUS & OSBORN/CANTON CONN.with eagle motif also and CAST STEEL near breech:
7E-003   Values—Good **$475**   Fine **$1,100**

7E-003

P. or W. Ashton Underhammer Pistol

Peter H. and William Ashton of Middletown, Connecticut.
28 to 38 caliber. 4" and 5" part octagon/part round barrels bearing markings W. ASHTON or P. H. ASHTON or W. A./MIDDL^N, CONN. Most easily recognized and distinctive feature of their product was the use of two-piece walnut grips fastened by a very large screw through center of handle. Considerable variances have been noted in contours of the guns themselves, although most specimens closely resemble that illustrated here:

7E-004

7E-004   Values—Good **$275**   Fine **$675**

Babcock Underhammer Cane Gun

Moses Babcock, Charlestown, Massachusetts.
52 caliber. Approximately 27" round barrel (overall length approximately 33" but will vary) wooden handle set at sharp right angle to the round iron frame. The entire barrel, frame and handle are painted in a simulated wood grain finish. Concealed trigger snaps open when underhammer is cocked.
Marked on hammer: M. BABCOCK/CHARLESTOWN:

7E-005

7E-005   Values—Good **$900**   Fine **$2,500**

Bacon & Co. Underhammer Pistol

Bacon & Co., Norwich, Connecticut.
34 caliber. 4" and 5" part octagon/part round barrels standard. 3" barrel scarce; 6" rare; both worth premiums. Estimated quantity made 500. Rounded all iron frame with broad floral and scroll engraving standard.
Barrel marked: BACON & CO./NORWICH, CONN./CAST STEEL:

7E-006

7E-006   Values—Good **$300**   Fine **$875**

T. Barns Underhammer Pistol

T. Barns (or "Barnes"), Greensburg, Indiana. Likely the same T. Barnes later listed at nearby Franklin, Indiana, maker of half-stock perc. rifles. c. 1850s.
25 caliber. Part-octagon, part-round 11-inch barrel (calibers and bbl. lengths likely to vary). Brass pin-type front sight; open sight mounted at top corner of the walnut handle. Brass mounts. Barrel marked T BARNS / GREENSBURG IA. Few known examples; rare.

7E-006.5

7E-006.5   Values—Good **$750**   Fine **$1,750**

W. Billinghurst Underhammer Pistol

William Billinghurst, Rochester, New York.
30 to 38 caliber. Varying weights and lengths of barrels generally 12" to 18"; usually part octagon/part round with plainer grades full octagon.
Marked W. BILLINGHURST/ROCHESTER, N.Y.

Famed gun maker noted for fine quality percussion target rifles, Billinghurst also made a few heavy barreled underhammer "buggy rifles" or pistols with detachable, skeleton type shoulder stocks. No two are identical, but all follow the general pattern of that illustrated. When made with

7E-007

(and still accompanied by) an original false muzzle, a premium of approximately 25 percent to 35 percent may be added to value. Telescopic sights and accessories and cased outfits will also increase values proportionately. Very fancy engraved and presentation types are also known and will bring premium values. Made in three frame sizes (largest shown); the smallest of approx. belt size usually brings about 20 percent less:

Pistol With Original Detachable Stock:
7E-007   Values—Very Good **$3,500**   Exc. **$8,000**
Pistol Only, Lacking Stock:
7E-008   Values—Very Good **$2,000**   Exc. **$4,500**

Blunt & Syms Double Barreled Underhammer Percussion Pistol

See Blunt & Syms in Sections B & C, this chapter.

B. M. Bosworth Underhammer Pistol

B. M. Bosworth, Warren, Rhode Island.
    38 caliber. 5-7/8" part octagon/part round barrel.
    Heavy brass frame cast integral with the brass handle which is hinged at top of left side, thus making the entire handle a compartment for accessories. Deeply marked in center left side of frame in arched design B. M. BOSWORTH over a small sunburst-like motif:
7E-009   Values—Good **$575**   Fine **$1,150**

7E-009

D. Brown Underhammer Pistol

D. B. Brown, Southbridge (later, Cambridge), Massachusetts. Circa 1850s. Underhammer pistol.
    31 caliber. 5-1/2" part-octagon, part-round barrel with blade-type front sight. Open rear sight at top corner of handle affixed to the long tang. Sharply angled one-piece walnut handle; brass mounts.
    Marked on upper tang D. BROWN / SOUTHBRIDGE MASS Also marked left side of barrel at breech CAST-STEEL. Specimens likely to vary on barrel lengths and calibers. Very few examples recorded; rare.

7E-009.5

7E-009.5   Values—Good **$650**   Fine **$1,450**

S. W. Card Underhammer Pistol

S. W. Card. Location unknown.
    34 caliber. 7-3/4" part octagon/part round barrel. Rounded iron frame. Bag shaped handle with walnut grips.
    Barrel markings S. W. CARD and CAST STEEL:
7E-010   Values—Good **$400**   Fine **$850**

7E-010

M. Carleton Underhammer Pistol

M. Carleton, Haverhill, New Hampshire.
    30 to 34 caliber. 3-1/2" to 7-3/4" part octagon/part round barrel.
    Unique design, patented action. Hammer cocks horizontally; pulling backward towards trigger. Entire trigger guard also serves as mainspring.
    Barrel marked: M. CARLETON & CO./PATENT

7E-011

7E-011   Values—Good **$475**   Fine **$1,250**

Case Willard & Co. Underhammer Pistol

Case Willard & Co., New Hartford, Connecticut.
    31 caliber. 3" part octagon/part round barrel.
    Curly maple handle, all brass edged; pointed butt.
    Topstrap marked: CASE WILLARD & CO./NEW HARTFORD, CONN.:
7E-012   Values—Good **$450**   Fine **$950**

7E-012

J. Caswell Underhammer Pistol

Jedediah Caswell, Manlius, New York.

A diminutive, delicate piece. 2" tapered octagon barrel just 18 caliber. 7" overall. Peep sight in tang. Sizes likely will vary. Unique shaped, concealed trigger opens when hammer is cocked. It is believed that this is the mechanism for which Caswell was granted one of the earliest U.S. Patents in 1828, before a patent numbering system was established.

Bold markings J. CASWELL on each side of the barrel:

7E-012.5   Values—Good **$575**   Fine **$1,250**

7E-012.5

A. Davis, Jr., Underhammer Pistol

A. Davis, Jr., Stafford, Connecticut. (Not illus.)

31 caliber. 7-3/8" part octagon/part round barrel. Curly maple handle all brass edged; pointed butt. Topstrap marked A. DAVIS, JR./STAFFORD, CONN.

About identical to the Case Willard, the Gibbs Tiffany and Ruggles (*q.v.*):

7E-013   Values—Good **$475**   Fine **$1,100**

J. Demeritt Underhammer Pistol

J. Demeritt, Montpelier, Vermont.

27 caliber. Octagon and part octagon/part round barrels of varying lengths.

Considerable variations have been noted on specimens by this maker. Almost all are of very small caliber and extremely delicate in proportions. The most notable features are the stag horn handles. Although no two are alike, all have displayed fine craftsmanship. Values vary considerably with size and workmanship.

Usually marked on the barrel or frame J.

7E-014

DEMERITT/MONTPELIER/VERMONT

7E-014   Values—Good **$950**   Fine **$2,000**

D. S. Ebersol Underhammer Pistol

7E-014.5

Daniel S. Ebersol, Ottawa, Illinois. Circa 1850s Underhammer Pistol.

41 caliber. 3-3/4" part-octagon, part-sixteen-sided barrel. Sharply angled walnut handle with pointed butt entirely edged in brass. Closely fashioned after many of the New England underhammers.

Marked at breech of barrel in a triangular fashion surrounded by star motif D. S. EBERSOL and also CAST STEEL. Specimens likely vary in barrel length and caliber. Ebersol listed maker circa 1850s; later in partnership with David Krouse (same location). Scarce.

7E-014.5   Values—Good **$650**   Fine **$1,500**

Gibbs Tiffany & Co. Underhammer Pistol

Gibbs Tiffany & Co., Sturbridge, Massachusetts.

Caliber 28 to 34. 3" to 8" part octagon/part round barrels. Walnut handle usually standard, but curly maple quite often seen and will bring a small premium value. Handles edged in brass; pointed butt.

Topstrap marked GIBBS TIFFANY & CO./STURBRIDGE, MASS. with small eagle motif. Barrel usually also marked E. HUTCHINGS & CO./AGENTS-BALT'O. Scarce markings GIBBS & CO/STURBRIDGE, MASS and MADE FOR ROGERS BROS. & CO., 52 MARKET ST. PHILAD. bring premium.

One of the most well known and often encountered of all

7E-015

New England underhammer pistols:

7E-015   Values—Good **$475**   Fine **$1,150**

J. Graves Underhammer Pistol

Joseph Graves, Bangor, Maine.

31 caliber. Various barrel lengths 5" to 8" part octagon/round. Believed to have worked for noted, early Bangor maker William Neal. Note the close similarity in style to pistols of that maker.

Barrel markings (very scarce) JOS. GRAVES/BANGOR/ME.:

7E-015.5   Values—Good **$600**   Fine **$1,275**

7E-015.5

H. J. Hale Underhammer Pistol

7E-016
Pointed Butt

7E-016
Bulbous Handle

H. J. Hale of Bristol, Connecticut and Worcester, Massachusetts.

31 caliber. 5" and 6" part octagon/part round barrels.

Considerable variance has been found in the products of Hale, one of the more prolific underhammer makers. Many are about identical to the Gibbs Tiffany (*q.v.*) with pointed butt, while others have the rounded butt with some encountered with a very odd appearing bulbous shaped handle (worth a premium for its odd shape). Other unique, likely one-of-a-kind underhammers by the same maker are known; most notably a specimen on which the bulbous handle is fashioned integrally with a full-length shoulder stock and an overall length of 21 inches (and worthy of a substantial premium).

Markings usually H. J. HALE/WARRANTED/CAST STEEL or H. J. HALE/BRISTOL/CONNECTICUT; these latter scarcer and will bring a slight premium.

Some of these occasionally bear a U.S. martial-like marking which is believed to be purely decorative and patriotic with no military connotation or association:

7E-016   Values—Good **$450**   Fine **$950**

Hale & Tuller Underhammer Pistol

Hale & Tuller, Hartford, Connecticut. Believed made in the Connecticut State Prison, Hartford County, Connecticut c.1837 to 1840. Quantity unknown.

44 caliber. 6" round tapered barrel. Walnut handle with pointed butt about identical to the Gibbs Tiffany (*q.v.*).

Barrel marked HALE & TULLER/HARTFORD/CONNECTICUT.

Original manuscript contracts dated 1837 and 1838 between William Tuller of Hartford and Amos Pilsbury, the warden of the Connecticut State Prison were recently discovered. These contracts provided for the setting up, manufacturing and contract for the labor of convicts to manufacture firearms within the walls of the Connecticut State Prison. Tuller was a Hartford tinware and stove merchant; he is not known to have been a gunmaker. It is strongly surmised that he formed a partnership

7E-017

with the gunsmith H. J. Hale, with the latter most likely overseeing the manufacture of the arms themselves. The full story will hopefully, one day be told and shed an intriguing sidelight into New England gunmaking:

7E-017   Values—Good **$500**   Fine **$1,250**

J. J. Henry Underhammer Pistol

7E-017.5

J. J. Henry, Boulton, Pennsylvania.

32 caliber. Various barrel lengths (part octagon/part round). Distinctive walnut handle with grip set at sharp 90 degree angle; pointed butt. German silver mountings.

Marked J.J. HENRY at rear of topstrap and CAST-STEEL on barrel. A noteworthy name in early American arms making, the various members of the Henry dynasty produced an impressive number of American military contract and civilian longarms and pistols (qv) over a lengthy period of the 19th century. These underhammers were believed produced only for a short period of about four years circa 1830s and often encountered lacking markings. Scarce:

7E-017.5   Values—Good **$650**   Fine **$1,500**

D. H. Hilliard Underhammer Pistol

D. H. Hilliard, Cornish, New Hampshire.
34 caliber. 10" to 12" part octagon/part round barrels.

7E-018

Distinctively shaped handle with large knob-like butt.

A fine and noted riflesmith, these long barrel underhammers were made strictly as target pistols. They are quite often seen with tiny rear peep and hooded front sights. Occasionally they are found with "Remington" marked barrels also. Specimens may be encountered with shorter 4-inch, 5-inch octagon/round barrels and rifled bores as small as 28 caliber. Values of such pocketsize specimens approximately 10 percent to 20 percent less than shown.

7E-018   Values—Good **$775**   Fine **$2,000**

J. Jenison & Co. Underhammer Pistol

J. Jenison & Co., Southbridge, Massachusetts.
28 caliber. 4" part octagon/part round barrel.
Topstrap marked J. JENISON & CO./SOUTHBRIDGE, MASS.

About identical to the Gibbs Tiffany (*q.v.*) with handle edged in brass and pointed butt. Specimens have been observed with the unusual use of oak wood for their handles:

7E-019   Values—Good **$600**   Fine **$1,400**

7E-019

Nicanor Kendall Underhammer Pistols

Nicanor Kendall, Windsor, Vermont.
Calibers from 31 to approximately 41. Part octagon/part round barrels from 4" to 10".

Size, contours, type of wood used for handles will all affect price.

Markings usually N. KENDALL/WINDSOR, VT.

A very well known riflesmith noted for his underhammer rifles and shotguns, but also a prolific maker of underhammer pistols in both small pocket or "boot" sizes as well as large heavy target types. His handguns do not have the "mass" produced qualities of most of the other makers listed here and vary considerably one from the other. Generally they may be said to

7E-020

be rather bulky in appearance and some even quite awkward. Most use brass trim and many have curly maple handles. Many of the Kendall underhammers were made within the Vermont State Prison at Windsor, it being common practice at the time to contract for convict labor:

7E-020   Values—Good **$650**   Fine **$1,750**

Malcolm Long Underhammer Pistol

Malcolm Long, Bangor, Maine (not illus.). Well-known gunsmith both before and after the Civil War with a very commendable war record. His pistols are the identical style of other Bangor makers as Graves, Ramsdell, Neal and valued

similarly. Known to have made larger size also (20" overall with 12" barrel, etc.) which are worth premium. Marked W.M. LONG/BANGOR, ME:

7E-020.5   Values—Good **$650**   Fine **$1,450**

Mead & Adriance Underhammer Pistol

Mead & Adriance, dealers of St. Louis, Missouri. (Not illus.) Made by E. Allen of Grafton, Massachusetts. (*See E. Allen Firearms, Chapter V.*) Specimens marked MEAD & ADRIANCE on barrel alongside POCKET RIFLE / CAST STEEL / WARRANTED on barrel worth approximately 25 percent to 50 percent premium over the E. ALLEN markings and sought after for their Western associations.

Their frequent advertisements in the "*Missouri Republican*" often mentioned fact of selling "E. Allen, Grafton" guns. Jan. 27, 1838 issue offered "...the Celebrated Mississippi Rifle Pistol" (Allen's 5A-001). Jan. 11, 1837 issue announced three dozen of them were "...highly recommended by all who have used them as excellent for sportsmen and for defense."

7E-021   Values—Good **$750**   Fine **$1,850**

William Neal Underhammer Pistol

William Neal, Bangor, Maine. Well known Bangor maker first listed there in 1843, it is very likely that he trained C.V. Ramsdell, Joseph Graves and Malcolm Long (*q.v.*) as their underhammers bear such a close resemblance to Neal's distinctive styling.

7E-022

31 caliber. Barrel lengths vary considerably, averaging 5" to 8"; part round/part octagon.

Distinguished by the rather thick, heavy one-piece walnut saw-handle grip.

Barrel marked WM. NEAL/BANGOR/ME:

7E-022   Values—Good **$775**   Fine **$1,850**

S. Osborn Underhammer Pistol

S. Osborn, Canton, Connecticut. (Not illus.)
34 caliber. 7-3/4" part octagon/part round barrel. Walnut handle edged in brass; pointed butt. About identical to the Gibbs Tiffany (*q.v.*).

Topstrap marked S. OSBORN/CANTON, CONN. and also with small eagle motif:

7E-023   Values—Good **$475**   Fine **$1,150**

"Pocket Rifle" marked underhammer Pistol   *See Anderson.*

H. Pratt Underhammer Pistol

H. Pratt, Roxbury, Massachusetts.
31 caliber. 8-1/2" octagon barrel. Brass sideplate. Trigger guard also serves as mainspring. Walnut handle with modified bird's head butt.

Marked on top of frame H. PRATT'S/PATENT:

7E-024   Values—Good **$750**   Fine **$1,750**

7E-024

Quinabaug Rifle Mfg. Co. Underhammer Pistol

Quinabaug Rifle Manufacturing Co., Southbridge, Massachusetts.
31 caliber. Part octagon/part round barrels vary from 3" to 8". Walnut or curly maple handles standard with the latter bringing a small premium. Handles edged in brass; pointed butt.

Marked on topstrap QUINABAUG RIFLE M'G CO/SOUTHBRIDGE, MASS. with American eagle motif. Also marked on barrel E. HUTCHINGS & CO./AGENTS/ BALT'O.

Very likely the product of Gibbs Tiffany (*q.v.*), although records indicate this name was one used by Nathaniel Rider & Co. of Southbridge, Massachusetts:

7E-025

7E-025   Values—Good **$675**   Fine **$1,450**

C.V. Ramsdell Underhammer Pistol

Charles V. Ramsdell, Bangor, Maine.
31 caliber. Various barrel lengths 4" to 7" part octagon/round. A well known Bangor maker, it's thought that he may have had his apprenticeship with the early Bangor maker William Neal (*q.v.*). Note the very close similarity in style and profile to pistols of that maker.

Marked C.V. RAMSDELL/BANGOR, ME on barrel:

7E-025.5   Values—Good **$675**   Fine **$1,400**

7E-025.5

Nathaniel Rider & Co. Underhammer Pistol

Nathaniel Rider & Co., Southbridge, Mass.
31 caliber. 2-3/4" part octagon barrel. A very tiny, delicately made piece, just 6" overall. Maple handle edged in brass. Its very small size is the feature that fetches the below listed value. Standard size specimens approximately 20 to 25 percent less.

Marked on top strap NATH'I RIDER & CO/SOUTHBRIDGE, MASS. and small eagle design:

7E-025.8   Values—Good **$675**   Fine **$1,400**

Variant Rider and Co. underhammer pistol with heavier, wider flat butt about identical to the D. BROWN, Southbridge, Mass. underhammer No. 7E-009.5 (*q.v.*), suggesting a business alliance

7E-025.8

between them. "RIDER & CO." markings identical above.

7E-025.9   Values—Good **$675**   Fine **$1,400**

A. Ruggles Underhammer Pistols

A. Ruggles, Stafford, Connecticut.
31 or 34 caliber. Part round/part octagon barrels varying 3" to 8".

7E-026
(earliest form)

7E-027
(classic style hammer)

Variation of markings are seen. Usually A. RUGGLES/STAFFORD/(CONN.)on topstrap in either two or three lines and occasionally accompanied by an eagle motif. Agent's markings may also be encountered on the barrel and will bring a small premium: E. HUTCHINGS & CO./AGENTS-BALT. MD.

A prolific maker, two distinct styles are the most often encountered, each with variations:

(A) "U" shaped semi-circular (almost tube-like) hammer; curly maple handle with flat sides having beveled edges; pointed butt; brass edged handle. Usually small decorative brass inlays in varying shapes and decorative wire inlays are found on the wood handles. This style is the earliest form made by Ruggles; believed circa 1829-1830. Earlier specimens produced as early as 1828 are assumed larger, relatively more crudely constructed and marked only "A. RUGGLES" and likely to bring a modest premium.

7E-026   Values—Good **$600**   Fine **$1,275**

(B) Classic form of hammer; curly maple rounded handle edged in brass; pointed butt. Specimen shown has a unique extra long trigger which will bring a premium:

7E-027   Values—Good **$475**   Fine **$1,000**

D. D. Sacket Underhammer Pistol

D. D. Sacket, Westfield, Massachusetts.
34 to 36 caliber. 3" and 4" part round/part octagon barrels. Topstrap bears variations of the markings D. D. SACKET/WESTFIELD/ CAST STEEL and small eagle motif.
Two types of handles, each edged in brass, are seen:

Pointed Butt:
7E-028   Values—Good **$675**   Fine **$1,450**
Bulbous Rounded Butt:
7E-029   Values—Good **$675**   Fine **$1,400**

7E-028

7E-029

Shaw & Ledoyt Underhammer Pistol

Shaw & Ledoyt, Stafford, Connecticut.
31 caliber. Part round/part octagon 2-1/2" to 3-7/8" barrels. Brass edged handle; pointed butt.
Topstrap marked SHAW & LEDOYT/STAFFORD. CONN.with small eagle motif:
7E-030   Values—Good **$625**   Fine **$1,450**

7E-030

A. Spalding Underhammer Pistol

Abel Spalding, Buckfield, Maine. (Not illus.)
44 caliber. 13-1/2" barrel; likely other lengths and calibers. Maple handle, very pointed at butt (similar "Sacket" above and others shown here): brass edged. Rare.

Barrel marked A. SPALDING BUCKFIELD, ME.:
7E-030.5   Values—Good **$875**   Fine **$1,650**

A. W. Spies Underhammer Pistol

7E-031

A. W. Spies. Well known New York City dealers and agents. Their markings found on engraved iron frame, saw-handle underhammers made by E. Allen of Grafton, Massachusetts. (*See Allen Firearms, Chapter V.*)

Markings: A. W. SPIES MISSISSIPPI POCKET RIFLE (worth premium) or A. W. SPIES POCKET RIFLE or POCKET RIFLE/CAST STEEL/WARRANTED. Values about identical to the E. Allen pocket rifle (*q.v.*). (About Identical/Gibbs-Tiffany, Socket, rider and other similar):

7E-031   Values—Good **$575**   Fine **$1,275**

A.B. or Peter Steiner Underhammer Pistol

A.B. or Peter Steiner of Bushkill, Pennsylvania.
36 caliber. 6" part octagon/round barrel. Maple handle must be removed in order to see markings on side of frame STEINER in large letters:
7E-031.5   Values—Good **$500**   Fine **$875**

7E-031.5

A. Thresher Underhammer Pistol

A. Thresher of Stafford, Connecticut (not illus.)
31 to 34 caliber; 4" to 6" barrel usual. About identical to Gibbs Tiffany and N. Rider type with pointed butt.

Barrel marked A. THRESHER/STAFFORD, CON. (note only single "N"). Scarce:
7E-031.6   Value—Good **$625**   Fine **$1,275**

Turner, Lull & Co. Underhammer Pistol

Turner, Lull & Co., Woodstock, Vermont.
38 caliber. 11" part octagon/round barrel; likely will vary. A large proportioned, heavyweight type. Maple stock with brass mountings; few inlays.
Barrel marked TURNER, LULL & CO/WOODSTOCK, VT.
7E-031.7   Values—Good **$750**   Fine **$1,600**

7E-031.7

B.C. Wood Underhammer Pistol

Barry C. Wood, Painted Post, New York.
44 caliber, smoothbore. 9" round barrel. Rifled and octagon barrels also likely. Trigger guard also acts as mainspring. Long, slender, curved walnut handle.
Barrel marked B.C. WOOD/P. POST, N.Y:
7E-031.9   Values—Good **$650**   Fine **$1,400**

7E-031.9

UNMARKED OR UNIDENTIFIED TYPES

Illustrated here are four examples of rather primitive, awkward, unmarked underhammers representative of a very large group of similar arms that may be encountered on the collectors' market. They are usually all one-of-a-kind and vary greatly in size, caliber, quality of workmanship and, of course, appearance. The cruder, primitive appearing and homelier specimens as are these illustrated may be generally priced in the value range shown below. If markings appear on the gun which can be identified as to maker and locality, values may be increased approximately 20 percent to 50 percent or more. Pistols that

7E-032

7E-032

7E-032

7E-032

display pleasing proportions and excellent quality workmanship on a par with those shown in the previous listings in this chapter, but are unmarked, will generally bring 20 percent less than comparable marked specimens. There are obviously many exceptions to this rule and each must be judged on its own merits.

It is possible that some of these "unmarked" types bear maker markings on the sides of the frame underneath the handle. On the better quality "bootlegs" especially, it may be auspicious to check that feature.

Values for unmarked types of awkward proportions, not displaying fine quality craftsmanship similar to those illustrated here:

7E-032   Values—Good **$375**   Fine **$775**

Western gambler's special vest fitted for uniquely designed pair of under-hammer percussion pistols and small Bowie knife. Unmarked American "Bootleg" pistols, almost matched with slightest variances: one has 5-inch brass barrel, the other a 4-1/2" iron barrel. Silver inlays on the flared butts. The leather and white linen vest custom-designed for these guns only.
(*N. Flayderman & Co. Catalog No. 86 of November 1970*)

Original green silk parade flag of the famous New York 69th Infantry Regiment…(of the Civil War "Irish Brigade"). Illustrated here with six cased sets of percussion pistols: *(Top Left)* pair English belt pistols c 1840; *(Center)* London Colt Model 1862 "Police" 36-caliber revolver #34522; "New York" barrel address; British proof marked barrel and cylinder; *(Right)* Pair American percussion dueling pistols c. 1850s. *(Bottom Left)* Allen & Thurber six-shot 31-caliber pepperbox with extra markings of their New York agent "J. G. Bolen, N.Y." on hammer and full label on inner lid of case. *(Center)* A pair of large English double-barrel holster pistols c. 1860-1865 with rifled bores by "Isaac Hollis & Sons, London. *(Right)* A pair of classically styled pocket pistols by Henry Deringer of Philadelphia c 1850s-1860s. Also illustrated are classic examples of both American and Sheffield Bowie knives c. 1840-1860s.

OPPOSITE PAGE: Unique revolving percussion 8-chamber "Fire Extinguisher Gun" invented by William Mont Storm, patented 1855. Intended to fire a special cartridge in the form of a paper-wrapped cake of nitrate of soda, sulfur and charcoal into a fire, the combustible mix igniting, thereby generating a gas to extinguish the fire! Illustrated *(above)* a pre-revolutionary pair of American silver-mounted flintlock pocket pistols marked "PERKIN, Fecit N. York" and a pair of American pill-lock, all brass pocket pistols by William Hart of Fredonia, NY c. 1830. The small cartridge handguns at bottom *(L/R)*. Three-barrel 22-caliber deringer with sliding knife blade by Wm. Marston, N.Y. c. 1858-1864; (2) Engraved four-barrel 30-caliber rimfire pepperbox by C. Sharps & Company Philadelphia c. 1860s; (3) Engraved three-barrel 32 rimfire deringer by Wm. Marston from N.Y. c. 1864-1872; (4) "Model No. 1 Knuckle-Duster" 32 rimfire 5 shot revolver with barrel made by James Reid of Catskill, N.Y. c. 1875; (5) Engraved "New Model Knuckle-Duster" five-shot 32 rimfire revolver also by James Reid c. 1883.

BELOW: Swivel-breech, double-barrel (over/under) percussion Kentucky rifle by Peter Smith of Pennsylvania; c. 1840. Exceptional use of eagle and dove motifs, along with extensive silver and brass inlays and mountings.

(As illustrated in *Steel Canvas; The Art of American Arms*, with permission of the author)

Historical, silver-mounted percussion half-stock "Kentucky" rifle made c. 1850s for Major Robert Anderson, Union hero of the Civil War, by Daniel Searles, of Baton Rouge, Louisiana. Searles is best known for the knives he made for Rezin (and Jim) Bowie. The sideplate is also richly engraved and inscribed with Anderson's name. Illustrated here with a Henry Deringer percussion belt-size pistol with barrel markings indicating it was specifically made for Hyde & Goodrich, New Orleans, merchants and agents for Henry Deringer and importers of weapons. Illustrated with three Bowie knives and a gambler's push-dagger, all with New Orleans maker or importer markings.

(As illustrated in *Steel Canvas; The Art of American Arms*, with permission of the author)

Historical, ornately engraved and gold-inlaid Massachusetts Arms Company 31-caliber percussion pocket revolver made for and owned by Cadwalader Ringgold, a distinguished U.S. naval officer (retired as admiral in 1866). The Massachusetts state seal is engraved on the hinged door of the Maynard tape primer unit (ahead of hammer); an etched floral and military scene decorating the cylinder. Gold-plated brass trigger guard and gold inlays on barrel. It is recorded that approximately 200 of this same model (plain undecorated) were sold to the abolitionist John Brown for his use in 1857 in "Bleeding Kansas." (The use of a mirror to depict both sides accounts for the smaller, reverse side of the gun.).

(As illustrated in *Steel Canvas; The Art of American Arms*, with permission of the author)

New England-made flintlock, half-stock rifle of exceptional quality; attributed to noted gunmaker Silas Allen of Shrewsbury, Massachusetts (1750-1834). Silver and brass mountings with silver wire inlays on the handsome curly maple stock. New England made rifles of this type were seldom embellished as elaborately.

(As illustrated in *Steel Canvas; The Art of American Arms*, with permission of the author)

Cased sets of matched pairs of percussion pistols by Henry Deringer of Philadelphia c 1850s-1860s. *(Left)* Pistols 8 inches overall. In addition to the "Deringer" markings, the barrels also marked "WOLF & DURRINGER, LOUISVILLE, KENTUCKY," agents for Henry Deringer. Silver-mounted. *(Right)* Slightly smaller in size with solid gold mountings and silver trigger guards. Both cases are a classic style used by Henry Deringer; of wooden construction and entirely covered in black leather with deep crimson velvet recessed contour-shape linings to match the pistols. *(Center)* Extremely rare, solid ivory-stocked pair by Henry Deringer. The ivory stocks and case attributed to design and work of Tiffany & Company of New York. 4-1/2 inches overall, representative of the smallest size produced by Henry Deringer.

(As illustrated in *Steel Canvas; The Art of American Arms*, with permission of the author)

Percussion half-stock target rifle by one of New England's finest gunmakers, John S. Dutton of Jaffrey New Hampshire c. 1850s. Made for George F. Ellsworth, whose name is engraved on an eagle inlay on the left side of the butt. 42-caliber with detachable false muzzle on the 31-inch octagon barrel. Illustrated here surrounded with a unique collection of original manuscript notebooks (dated 1858-78), all kept by that gunsmith John Dutton, with his personal notes and drawings on how to make and decorate rifles. The double patchbox of this rifle was a trademark of Dutton's.

(As illustrated in *Steel Canvas; The Art of American Arms*, with permission of the author)

British-made Webley, "Long-Spur" single-action percussion revolver made for the American trade; imported, embellished and inscribed by noted American arms dealers during the Civil War on the order of U.S. Navy Admiral David G. Farragut for presentation to an equally famous Civil War Navy officer Admiral David D. Porter. 44-caliber percussion. Gold inlaid on right side of barrel "CAPT'N D. D. PORTER, FROM CAPT'N D. G. FARRAGUT 1862"; left side similarly gold inlaid in old English style letters: "EVANS & HASSALL. 418 ARCH STREET, PHILADELPHIA" well-known military goods dealers from whom the set was acquired and commissioned to ornately embellish. The cylinder is similarly gold inlaid with figures of Union Army and Navy officers in combat positions. The custom wooden case also bears a silver plaque inscribed with the monogram initials of both officers. The outfit is believed presented to commemorate the Union's capture of New Orleans in March of 1862.

(As illustrated in *Steel Canvas; The Art of American Arms*, with permission of the author)

A unique caliber, barrel length and number. Custom engraved single-action Colt revolver built by Colt to commemorate the appraisal by Norm Flayderman, of the Colt Museum Firearms Collection of the State of Connecticut in 1974 (and so inscribed on the left side of the barrel). Serial-numbered NF-1; made in 44-caliber rimfire with original 6 1/2-inch barrel even with the special slanted early style barrel address (the only Colt single action produced in that post-WWII era with those unique features). Elegantly engraved and gold inlaid with both the Colt name and trademark as well as the logo and trademark of N. Flayderman & Co. Scrimshaw-carved ivory grips also bear both the Colt and N. Flayderman logos. Encased in a special book-type casing (similar to those used a century earlier by Sam Colt himself) gold embossed on cover and spine "In commemoration of the appraisal of the Colt firearms collection of the State of Connecticut April, 1974." ILLUSTRATED WITH A UNIQUELY DECORATED PRESENTATION WINCHESTER MODEL 94 CARBINE; factory engraved and gold inlaid on sides of frame with trademarks of Winchester Arms Co. and N. Flayderman & Co.; inscribed plaque on buttstock: "Made for Norm Flayderman by WINCHESTER as a memento of his appraisal of the WINCHESTER GUN MUSEUM December, 1971." A unique feature, considered an extreme rarity on modern Winchesters is the signature (on the trigger plate) of the factory engraver. Deluxe walnut stocks; caliber 30.

Owned and carried by the legendary Texas Ranger who tracked down and terminated the careers of the notorious "Bonnie and Clyde." Factory engraved Colt single-action revolver (serial #180260) with 4 3/4-inch barrel and handsome pearl grips with high-relief carving of an eagle's head. The revolver was originally owned and used by William H. Ford in a fatal shooting in Texas and subsequently acquired by Frank Hamer whose Texas Ranger career had begun in 1906 at age 22. The historic Colt revolver was accompanied by documents written personally by Hamer stating: "this weapon has been carried by me for a number of years while in the services as a peace officer." Illustrated here with a popular biography of Hamer's distinguished career.

(As illustrated in *The Peacemakers; Arms and Adventure in the American West*, with author's permission)

A favorite gun of the popular star of many early Western movies, Wild Bill Elliott. Highly ornate Colt single-action 45-caliber revolver (serial #350594) entirely covered with an abundance of cattle brand motifs by the well-known engraver Cole Agee. Chrome-plated finish (as occasionally seen on handguns used in films) with silver-mounted ivory grips. Elliott's film career in Westerns began in 1927 and continued through to 1954.

(As illustrated in *The Peacemakers; Arms and Adventure in the American West*, courtesy of the author)

Converted by a gunsmith in Montana Territory c. 1870s. Standard Sharps Civil War cavalry issue carbine altered to a classic style "Buffalo Rifle" by A. B. Charpie of Helena, Montana Territory, whose name and markings appear on the heavyweight 24-inch octagon barrel; caliber 50 centerfire; overall weight 11-1/2 lbs. Illustrated here with a Sheffield, England-made Bowie knife of the same era made for and bearing the markings of the well-known Denver, Colorado gunsmith and arms merchant John P. Lower & Son; also leather cartridge belts bearing brass buckles sold by Lower and the equally noted Denver gunsmiths and arms dealers Carlos Gove & Sons.

(As illustrated in *The Peacemakers; Arms and Adventure in the American West*, with author's permission)

OPPOSITE PAGE, TOP: Model 1874 Long Range Target Rifle No. 1 made by Sharps Rifle Company, Hartford, Connecticut with special order ornamentation by the noted arms engraver L. D. Nimschke. Factory shipping records (still in existence) indicate this was a special order rifle that had been tested for perfection by the factory superintendent himself. The rifle was given as a shooting prize to W. L. Ellison of Kansas City, Missouri in February of 1879. Shown here with close-up detail with its long-range Vernier tang rear sight yet intact.

OPPOSITE PAGE, BOTTOM: The most elaborately decorated, ornate rifle known by famous Philadelphia gun-maker Henry Deringer c. 1830s. Tastefully fitted with delicately engraved and pierced silver patchbox accompanied with numerous matching silver engraved inlays on both sides of the stock. Full-length curly maple stock has a compartmented cheekpiece inlay containing original removable brass compass in a specially fitted housing. Deringer markings inlaid in gold on the lockplate.

(As illustrated in *The Peacemakers; Arms and Adventure in the American West*, with author's permission)

Matched pair of presentation, engraved, ivory-grip MANHATTAN 36-caliber percussion, 5 shot-revolvers with 6 1/2-inch barrels. Each handsomely inscribed along their backstraps: "to G. W. France Acting Assistant Surgeon, U.S.A. / from Attendants of U.S. Gen. Hospital No. 11." Illustrated here with a Civil War Army issue Hospital Steward's (Corpsman) medicine case as worn on a waist belt. Dr. France served as a surgeon at a Prisoner-of-War camp outside Nashville during the Civil War; following cessation of hostilities he continued duty 1865 to June, 1866 at Army posts in Oregon Territory.

Presentation-inscribed Metropolitan Arms Company, New York. 36-caliber; 5-shot percussion revolver with 4 1/2-inch barrel. Serial #2086. About identical to the Colt Model 1862 "Police Model" revolver. Original, profuse factory engraving and ivory grips. Uniquely inscribed along the top of the barrel in two lines (in place of the usual maker markings): "PRESENTED TO HON. E. C. STACEY BY CO. C. 2'D REGT MINN. CAL'Y JAN 1, 1864." Edwin Clark Stacey, an attorney, played an active role in politics of Minnesota Territory and was later elected a judge. The 2nd Minnesota Cavalry saw service in the notorious Minnesota Indian uprising and also service against Indians in the Dakotas and the West.

Large Civil War-era Starr Arms Company, New York, single-action Model 1863 percussion 44-caliber revolver; an example of very earliest production with extremely low serial #15; entirely unmarked and with a distinct civilian-type blued finish (versus the less brilliant, somewhat duller, most often encountered military blued finish). Checkered one-piece ivory grips. Cased in original factory walnut box with red velvet compartment type lining, and original accessories and literature. Note: The great bulk of production of Starr revolvers was acquired by U.S. Army for military issuance during the Civil War.

Eight fine examples of the classic American "Kentucky" rifle… an indigenous American firearm and representative of the most handsome of all early American arms. Illustrated here from top down:

(1) Percussion Kentucky rifle c. 1830-40 attributed to J. Albright of Northumberland County, Pa.

(2) Percussion Kentucky rifle c. 1830-40 with handsomely fashioned, massive American eagle finial on its elegant patchbox. Signed "J. W." attributed to John Workman of Northumberland County, Pa.

(3) Gracefully designed, Kentucky percussion rifle by noted maker "John Shell 1860" (of Dauphin County, Pa.) whose name is engraved on the 39-inch octagon barrel. All the brass mountings and numerous inlays are profusely scroll engraved.

(4) 18th century flintlock Kentucky flintlock, full-stock rifle with relief-carved stock. Attributed to Wolfgang Haga of Reading, Berks County, Pa. A fine example of that maker's styling and workmanship and representative of the "Golden Age" era with classic, high-relief carving on the buttstock.

(5) Flintlock, fullstock Kentucky rifle attributed to Simon Miller of Hamburg, Pennsylvania (c. 1820-1830) who has been termed as "one of Pennsylvania's best riflesmiths." Numerous silver inlays on forend and left side of butt.

(6) Rare flintlock fullstock Kentucky rifle c. 1800-1820. Attributed to C. or J. Vogler of Salem, North Carolina. The distinctive design of the patchbox with its huge eagle and American shield on its breast is striking.

(7) Lavishly inlaid Kentucky full-stock percussion rifle c. 1830s. Attributed to George Spangler of Liverpool, Pa. whose initials are engraved on the 41-inch barrel. Markings on the lock of well-known Philadelphia arms merchant and gunmakers "Tryon."

(8) Profusely inlaid, Kentucky percussion rifle c. 1830-40. An inlaid plaque on the 35-inch barrel inscribed with name of maker (or owner) "Wm. Reed." Pronounced tiger-striped-grain full curly maple stock handsomely embellished with 30 varied-shape inlays fill both sides of the stock and along forend; incised scroll carving fills left side of butt.

Plant's Manufacturing Company, New Haven, Conn. Front-loading, cup-primed, large-frame "Army" revolver with interchangeable 6-shot cylinders for 42-caliber cup-primed metallic cartridges and/or muzzle-loading percussion cartridges. 6-inch octagon ribbed barrel; silver-plated brass frame. Marked "MERWIN & BRAY, NEW YORK" on barrel, the agents and financiers for Plant Manufacturing Co. Accompanied with its factory-supplied paperboard box with original label specifying "Directions for Use" and accessories…and even the original Merwin & Bray, January 1865 dated bill of sale.

The height of elegance of a Kentucky flintlock rifle! Georgia-made full-stock flintlock rifle elaborately embellished with elegant silver mountings, an exceptionally ornate, delicately fashioned and engraved open-work patchbox and sideplate with accompanying matching inlays. Made c.1830 by Wiley Rover Higgins of Monroe County (later Macon County) Georgia for Dr. J. A. Davis; both names so inscribed. Representative of the height of ornamentation encountered on this indigenous form of American rifle.

(As illustrated in *Steel Canvas; The Art of American Arms*, with permission of the author)

An exceptional cased pair of ornately embellished, silver grip Colt Model No. 3 Deringers, caliber 41 rimfire, made for the British market with English proofed barrels also marked with the name "Thornhill / London" the British arms dealer that contracted for their decoration. Profusely engraved with most elaborate scroll and floral motifs and fitted with a remarkable pair of solid silver grips, each high-relief decorated with chiseled and engraved scroll designs and double-headed imperial eagle monograms combined with intertwined letters denoting an apparent royal crest. Cased in a custom-fitted, silver-embellished rosewood box; blue velvet lined in the recessed contour French manner and accompanied with numerous accessories, including a matched relief-engraved silver oil canister with matching eagle motifs.

Chapter VII-F

Dueling and Dueling Pistols Percussion Target and Belt Pistols

About Dueling And Dueling Pistols

Throwing Down A Gauntlet

What constitutes an American dueling pistol…or, for that matter, any "dueling pistol?" How might it differ from a large "holster pistol," "horse pistol," "target pistol" or "officer's pistol?" It's a cloudy subject, at best, and a question that may not be easily resolved to everyone's satisfaction. The initial intention was to add explanatory commentary about dueling to this chapter. At first glance, a simple, unassuming explanation was envisioned. However, with ever-increasing curiosity, as the subject was examined, skepticism heightened accordingly. It became evident that the topic could be a veritable quagmire, expanding beyond the modest parameters for this chapter.

The conclusions drawn from the following discussion are likely numbered among the earliest attempts (if not the initial salvo!) to question and provide a logical rationale to understand "dueling" and "dueling pistols." Ostensibly, both subjects have

To the Public.

Whereas MARCUS GILLIAM, has by means the most base and false, tryed to destroy my reputation; and would not concede to any efforts that have been made by my friends to have the matter investigated; and at the same time declined to say that he was of opinion that I was guilty of the act, which has according to report, been laid to my charge; he has also refused to give me the satisfaction that an injured person has a right to require. I therefore pronounce him a *liar*, a *base slanderer* and a *coward*.

WM. NOBLE.

Petersburg, March 12, 1825.

To the Public.

The circumstances attending the loss of my Pocket Book were so strong, and so fully warranted my suspicions, as to convince me and every friend with whom I advised, that I could not, with propriety, accept the invitation contained in the note of William Noble. The ground of my refusal was, that I did not believe him to be a gentleman, which was distinctly stated to his friend who handed me the note. A regard to public opinion alone induces me to take this notice of an unprincipled vagabond & scoundrel.

Marius Gilliam.

MARCH 14th, 1825.

PUBLICLY CHALLENGED TO A DUEL. The proper and public manner to challenge a transgressor to a duel. Broadsides such as these were "posted" in a public place, the act of which could hardly be ignored by the party thus disgraced. Petersburg, Virginia. March, 1825: Two days later the fellow challenged publicly posts his refusal to the duel (highly unusual) naming, in turn, his adversary "…an unprincipled vagabond & scoundrel." A duel side-stepped…or a more bitter one in the offing?

Gen'l ALEXANDER HUNTER

Having grossly insulted me and used ungentlemanly language in the presence of LADIES, for
which he refuses to render the satisfaction due
to a gentleman,

I NOW POST HIM

A BASE LIAR!
A POLTROON!!
AND A
COWARD!!!

BENJAMIN BRADY.

Washington, December 20, 1834.

PUBLICLY "POSTING" THE GENERAL FOR HIS UNGENTLEMANLY BEHAVIOR. Tantamount to an open challenge to a duel to be read by his fellow citizens in Washington, D.C. No self-respecting gentleman (or military officer) could ignore this base insult and his honor remain unblemished.

been taken for granted by historians, collectors and the public at large as historical fact. These remarks venture to step into that breach and approach the subjects from a rational and questioning viewpoint. In offering this alternate perception of dueling, it clearly becomes subject to challenge. For an energetic researcher it affords potential for a sensible resolution to what has unmistakably been a long-standing enigma. Resolving that inaccuracy will add substantially to the literature of firearms and American folklore. It's a topic overdue for serious, unemotional inquiry…just waiting to be tapped. Optimistically, these remarks will offer incentive for that investigation.

The Practice Of Dueling In America (and the casual approach to the facts)

A much-abused subject, dueling in 19th century America has spawned a vast treasury of legend and folklore, all too often contradictory and aggrandized. The wide gap between perception and reality has been further magnified, often altered, by time and re-telling. Dueling is undeniably a subject that fascinates our collective imagination and clamors for attention! Before probing the essentials requisite of "dueling pistols," it is relevant to offer introductory comment about the time-honored "gentlemanly" practice itself. Regardless of the vast wealth of literature extant about dueling, it is strikingly apparent that many of the very basics of the custom have escaped most portrayals and narratives of the subject, commonly termed in earlier literature "single combat."

It is regrettable that there has been such a great propensity to accept, unquestioned, most dueling accounts (almost without exception), merely because they appeared in print over a century and half ago. There is an obvious willingness to believe that newspaper and other literature of earlier centuries must be accurate and more honest than any published in more recent eras; the reverse is likely true. With a subject as sensation-laden as dueling, its melodramatic traits made it all too easy to yield to temptation and report the exciting or lurid details that were most promising to capture the reader's attention. Assuming that the initial account of a duel may have been observed by the person who wrote that first "eye-witness" news story (rarely the case), it was common practice…as a matter of fact, virtually universal practice…that all newspapers acquired many of their stories, often weeks old, from other newspapers; not merely reprinting them word-for-word, but all too often tailoring those stories to suit their own reportorial style and personal fancies. Rarely was a reporter's by-line used in a news report. That very anonymity made for a wide range of obvious abuses. Caution and confirmation of facts were decidedly not watch-words. Those same legendary, anonymous and hearsay sources remain in use down through the past centuries to present-day, still ripe for embellishment. Dueling stories, of all eras…from the period they allegedly took place to current times, rarely supply sources. My own cursory research has seldom found many to have been conducted as reported…if at all. Of equal importance with those sources, is knowledge of the context in which the dueling account was related. Stories based on oral tradition are notoriously unworthy and prone to abuse. Rarely are they valid or hold up under scrutiny. The subject is rife with fictitious reports, distortions and spurious quotations. For many who chose to write about dueling, the subject proved too tempting not to embellish…especially so as there was little likelihood of contradiction.

The practice of dueling to defend one's honor or take revenge for a real or imagined slight, was a somber part of the American scene, particularly in the pre-Civil War years. Although observed in all sections of America and by officers of various branches of the military, the vast majority of such contests took place in the South and Southwest and by mid-century, in California. Duels in America, that is, those conducted under a *formalized set of rules*, were fought almost exclusively with firearms. Handguns were the usual weapon of choice; infrequent encounters are noted with rifles or shotguns, or an occasional motley assortment of less conventional weapons (many of them merely fabrication and magnified by time). Most duels arranged under such precepts were customarily fought between men of equal standing, those who would have considered themselves the upper strata of society. They were often carried out under loosely interpreted, vaguely defined rules of etiquette taken from the more rigid English and Irish codes, with substantial American modifications to suit the particular circumstances and social standing of the principals.

The most cursory examination of dueling reveals how remarkably widespread was its practice; enough so that laws were almost universally passed against the custom. Many states, as well as the federal government, administered oaths to elected and public officials to affirm that they had never engaged in, would not engage in, nor would be party to such contests. It is important here to qualify my terminology "remarkably widespread": the reading of most dueling accounts and dissertations, especially those of the latter 19th century to present day, would have the reader believe that a duel was taking place just about around every corner with a frequency almost beyond conception. The impression was also conveyed that participants in certain larger Southern cities were practically lining up to wait their turn to use special locales, popularly chosen or specifically set aside, for duelists to utilize. Although there were a few such "customary" dueling grounds, the actual recorded duels at such "grounds" were more modest than readers have been led to believe.

Lorenzo Sabine (1803-1877), a highly regarded American historian, in his *"Notes on Duels and Duelling…With Preliminary Historical Essay"* (1855), possibly the very first credible study of dueling and rational examination of the subject, placed it neatly in perspective:

"In the United States, as in England, killing in a duel is murder; but here, as there, *opinion* is superior to *law*. Bennett,[1] as far as I have been able to ascertain, is the only person who has been executed for taking the life of a fellow-man in single combat since we became a free people. In some States, the parties have seldom been held even to answer; in others the inquiry in the courts has been confined to the single question of '…the fairness of the fight;' and this point determined in favor of the survivor, acquittal has followed as a matter of course. In one State, we find the judge of a court on the dueling ground as a principal; and another, the ex-governor is there as a second; in a third, we read of principals and seconds, attended by an immense concourse in carriages, on horseback, and on foot…on their way to the appointed spot, without hindrance…[in other cases] the judicial records show the mockery of a sentence against the parties who had completed their arrangements for a mortal strike, of a fine of one dollar and an imprisonment of one minute. Yet in these states there are not only statute laws, but constitutional provisions in the book adverse to this relic of the Dark Ages."

Sabine's *Notes on Duels and Duelling* should be required reading for any student of the subject. Of the many American duels cited, some were merely named, while others were described in protracted detail. Immediately apparent is the frequency that such recourse was taken by U.S. senators, congressmen and legislators of all states; the very same that passed laws prohibiting dueling! Sabine's coverage of laws and oaths of office pertaining to dueling make fascinating reading. Whether the public approved of dueling or abhorred it, there is little doubt that the subject held great attraction for many of them. Feature stories, most by anonymous authors, appeared frequently in the press and periodicals. Sources are rarely offered.

Defining "Duel" And "Dueling"

It is essential that the term *duel* be defined and distinguished from merely a fight or encounter between two individuals. Primary definitions of duel: "…a prearranged combat between two persons fought with deadly weapons according to an accepted code of procedure" or "a formal fight between two persons armed with deadly weapons; prearranged and witnessed by two others called seconds, one for each combatant" (from *Random House* and *Webster's* dictionaries, respectively). Other dictionaries and references differ only slightly, but make obvious that the *duel* is an orderly, ritualistic affair not arrived at carelessly.

The secondary definition of *duel* covers its broadest possible interpretation: "any contest between two persons or parties" or "any contest or encounter suggesting such a fight, usually between two persons." Hence, that might indicate a wide host of contests, such as a "verbal duel…judicial duel…a scholarly duel." It is in its secondary connotation that the terminology is most often employed, and where much illogical and distorted (often fictitious) dueling stories are hatched.

Overworking The *Code Duello*

Repeatedly encountered in dueling literature is the phrase *code duello*. It is requisite to recognize that the terminology is a generalized or generic term to indicate the adoption of *some* established or negotiated rules, along general principles, that two duelists and their seconds agree upon to conduct a formalized duel in America. Among its earliest usage, it may have indicated the *Irish Code of Honour* of 1777, one of the important published works on dueling, in which etiquette is precisely defined; subsequently improved and modified by *"The British Code of Duel [and] the Laws of Honour and Character of Gentlemen,"* 1824. The impression is often given in modern dueling literature that *code duello* indicates a specific set of rules, one that the writer is smugly aware of…and of which the reader should be cognizant! It is noted that on occasion, duels were never fought because the principals or their seconds were unable to agree on the very rules by which they were to be conducted.

Thoroughbreds Only, Please

In Europe, dueling, in its earlier eras, was almost exclusively the practice of the landed gentry. The bourgeoisie and the proletariat were generally not considered qualified (but that was soon to be modified). In the British social system, where (prior to the Industrial Revolution) one's blood counted more than his bank account, rules governing duels were apparently more closely observed. In some of its codes, even the seriousness of the offense and the acceptance of an apology to avert a duel had a ranking and a protocol. Countless breaches of behavior and deportment could precipitate a duel. Physical blows and questioning one's parentage, as serious as they were, did not appear to be as base or amoral as bedding down a lady of high birth. The various offenses were clearly enumerated in the best-known and most often-cited *"British Code of Duel…to the Laws of Honor and Character of Gentlemen"* (1824) from which the very few published, *obscure* American codes followed. The frequent and lofty use of "gentleman" unmistakably implied that such a person was of good breeding and social standing, well-mannered and, possibly, one who did not work for a living. Dwelling greatly on definition, the lengthy index of the "Contents" of that British code markedly (if not extravagantly) emphasize such topics as "Hereditary Dignity…Good Breeding…Who is a Gentleman…Assumed Gentility…Legal Privileges of Gentlemen…" That code clearly indicates that pistols were the weapons to be used; the sword, although then outdated, could be chosen if desired. Rules were specific but left room for variances and changes at the discretion of the seconds; a review of them makes heavy reading. It is obvious that if such a manual were to have been adopted by Americans, few would have the patience to read it…even less would have been likely to guide themselves by it in an affair of honor.

With the passage of time it is clear that in England and likely much of Europe, the exclusivity of dueling and confining the practice only to the "landed gentry" became subject to considerable modification. The widespread development and advance of the Industrial Revolution, along with a simultaneous growth of an increasingly important and wealthy middle-class, accompanied a corresponding change in attitude towards what constituted the very terminology of "gentleman." Its definition grew by increments to encompass "gentlemen" not solely by their nobility of birth but also by their conduct and deportment in a broad cross-section of roles as merchants, engineers, doctors

---

1. Sabine refers to a duel fought in Illinois in 1820 in which William Bennett was indicted, tried and convicted of murder for killing his opponent in a duel with firearms and executed by hanging for the infraction.

and lawyers, etc. There was a decided change of sentiment and judgment as to exclusiveness and selectivity.

Some writers have maintained that few men participated in a duel seeking satisfaction from the death of their opponent; rather, the duel itself offered the opportunity to risk one's life by proving one's honor and enhanced reputation. That may have had validity in some duels, but could hardly be accurate as a generalization. As D. D. Bruce in *Violence and Culture in the Antebellum South* (1979) observed, dueling made men careful, compelling them to be thoughtful and respectful of their choice of words. The duel acted as a strong deterrent to impugning another gentleman's reputation; its mere threat was preventative. "Insults…were probably the major single cause of violence in polite society." Such personal affronts were intolerable and could not be ignored, especially among gentlemen, as they were directly aimed at a person's character and "his fitness to be a part of a community of well-bred men." A decided distinction was made between authentic duels and common physical violence.

A "*Code Duello*" Custom-Made For Americans

South Carolina Governor John Lyde Wilson's *Code of Honor; or Rules for the Government of Principals and Seconds in Dueling*, first published in 1838 and reissued at various times to 1883 (and possibly later), contrast the American view of dueling to that of Europe. It is *significant* that it is the most often mentioned of the two American codes yet to surface with even a modicum of frequency. Invariably it is accorded the status of the American counterpart to the widely known British codes; an importance clearly overemphasized by one and all. Circulation and recognition of American Codes were significantly less than credited. The most telling observation attesting to that fact was made by Sabine in his 1855 landmark reference *Notes on Duel and Duelling* where he asserted (italics added):

> "*I am not aware that American duellists have ever adopted a written code or that rules among them are entirely uniform.* Certain points, however, are well established. I suppose for example, that in a duel upon a mere question of honor, and exchange of shots, whether with or without effect, is sufficient; while a combat of positive wrong or deep injury may be and ordinarily should be, continued until the aggressor offers satisfactory explanation or apology, or until the fall or disability of one of the parties…it seems well settled that the challenged, in the matters of weapon, time and distance, shall be governed by usage between gentlemen; and that propositions to sit across a cask of powder, to jump from a precipice or a building, to meet at midnight, at a lone or distant spot, without friend or surgeons, may be rejected by the challenger."

Governor Wilson, a man who had engaged in numerous duels, specifically stated in the preface to his "*Code*": "I believe that nine duels out of ten, if not ninety-nine out of one hundred originate in the want of experience of the seconds." That clearly implied that any *code duello* observed for an American duel was most likely improvised at the whim of the participants or their seconds; if followed at all. Wilson suggested that guidelines or general ground rules for dueling had been observed for many years; the governor was merely codifying what was accepted practice. He also noted that "the old notion that the party challenged was authorized to name the time, place, distance and weapon, has been long since exploded; nor would a man of chivalric honor use such a right, if he possessed it."

After the fashion of the British code, the use of the word *gentlemen* is prominent in Wilson's code, though he did not dwell upon the matter as excessively. That *gentlemen* fought only other gentlemen and equals, and never anyone below their station in life is implicit. Wilson stressed the importance of that point, advising that upon receiving a challenge, or "a note from a stranger, you have a right to a reasonable time to ascertain his standing in society, unless he is fully vouched for by his friends [before replying]." Of course, such elevated status and good breeding as *gentleman* implies, had an understandably different interpretation and application in America, than that perceived in Britain. The French historian Alexis de Tocqueville, an astute observer of the American scene of the early nineteenth century and author of the oft-quoted "*Democracy in America*" (1835) noticed that difference; America's "common man" was of generally middle-class heritage and democratic principles, which made for the lines separating social levels in America much less distinguishable than that of Britain. Considering the broad range of Americans that reportedly engaged in such "individual battles," even those class distinctions may have been too restrictive.

Occasionally rearing its imposing title *The Code of Honor: or, the Thirty-Nine Articles;… Showing the Whole Manner in Which the Duel is to be Conducted; With Amusing Anecdotes, Illustrative of Dueling* is a second American dueling code also unknown to Sabine in his 1855 study. Published by William Taylor and Co. of Baltimore in 1847, the author's name, given only as "By A Southron," is yet to be identified. That code, occasionally quoted by 20th century authors on dueling (invariably leaving out the latter part of that title "…*With Amusing Anecdotes*"), apparently received but the slightest circulation in its day. Yet when mentioned by present-day authors, it is accorded the tacit status of having received wide circulation and recognition in its day…additional insight to the reliability of modern day dueling treatises. A further measure of the reputability of that anonymously authored "code's" recognition (and fresh evidence of the authenticity of contemporary dueling stories) is revealed by "A Southron's" specious accounts of duels that never happened!

Thus, it becomes apparent that formalized dueling codes, i.e. the *code duello* in the United States, were improvised and tailored by the combatants for the individual duel, taking into account some generally understood precepts of "gentlemanly" behavior and conventional, local customs. And, those improvised, impromptu rules obviously made for an unmitigated miscellany of dueling formats. Their vagueness and ambiguity ceded a virtually bottomless supply of fresh fuel for the creative writing talents of the host of reporters, dueling aficionados, dilettantes and devotees possessing literary talents and a ready pen-in-hand…through the ages.

Pistols "Sanctioned" For Duels

Bearing in mind the foregoing commentary on the American conception of a *code duello*, it becomes readily understandable that the specifics of firearms that might be chosen for weapons was likely to be generalized, if not dubious… and they were!

The "*British Code of Duel*" (1824) merely stated: "Projectile weapons are consonant to the principle of duel, as relates to guarding against the false pride of strength or agility…In the use of pistols, their examination requires care; as superior excellence is attributed to some…it is obviously proper that those of the same degree of excellence should be used by both parties." Nowhere in that widely known and obviously well-circulated work are specifics revealed for the firearms that might be used other than alluding to the general type of ignition of the pistol in its instructions for the seconds "…To examine the pistols and see that they are perfect even to the flint, that preclude mis-fire; and then to load them equally in the presence of each other." From practical experience in personally viewing and handling antique English handguns customarily considered as "dueling pistols," they are invariably fitted with long (approximate 8-inch to 10-inch) smoothbore barrels with a wide range of calibers. Rifled bores were not prohibited, although they apparently were occasionally utilized (as was often the case on the continent).

Governor Wilson's 1838 *Code of Honor or Rules for the Government of Principals and Seconds in Duelling* specifically dealt with the subject. Its section "Arms and the Manner of Loading and Presenting Them" states: "The arms used should be smooth-bore pistols, not exceeding 9 inches in length with flint and steel. Percussion pistols may be mutually used if agreed on, but to object on that account is lawful." The *"Code"* continued with instructions for loading, the manner of presenting pistols to participants and fighting positions with the pistols. Regardless of the suggestion for the use of "smooth bore pistols" it is well recorded that many with rifled bores of varying calibers were chosen by a wide cross-section of duelists… as were others with set triggers (often termed "hair triggers").

A later, almost unknown 1873 New Orleans reprint of Wilson's code (Clark & Hofeline, Printers) tersely stated: "The arms used should be smoothbore pistols not exceeding 9 inches in length." An equally obscure 1883 New Orleans revised edition (Brandao & Co., Printers) provided the identical description of the pistols. Both New Orleans printings noted how the pistol was to be held in "…the fighting position, with the muzzle down and the barrel from you, for although it may be agreed that you may hold your pistol with the muzzle up, it may be objected to as you can fire sooner from that position and consequently have a decided advantage, which ought not to be claimed and should not be granted."

A footnote reminds: "Every gentleman is expected to be familiar with the weapon, [such decidedly was not the case in many duels!] which is less deadly than the rifled pistol, the rifle or the shotgun." Revealing obvious inconsistency even in the printed codes, those footnoted suggestions, regardless of their practicality were seldom adopted in practice. It is just such instructions that were repeated by latter-day authors and students, omitting mention of the accompanying footnotes and suggestions, that were ultimately repeated through the ages as if inclusive with the very *"code"* itself! Thus, there is not merely ambiguity in the printed codes but outright perversions of them by later reporters and authors. The influence of American dueling "codes" was negligible; to strengthen that conclusion (and with the reader's indulgence) it is relevant to restate: *All the various imprints of Wilson's and other so-called dueling codes were highly unlikely to have been universally observed…nor were most of them even known to but a limited audience!* As for the pistols chosen by duelists, there is very little in period literature or news reports regarding their specifics. The preponderance of details about those handguns is to be found in 20th century dueling and firearms works, almost all of which are heavily weighted with assumptions offered as accepted fact, yet usually lacking in reliable references or substantiation!

Defining "Dueling Pistol"

In much the same manner as they embroidered the practice of dueling…a wealth of misconception, myth and unverified vague tradition flourished alongside the characterization and history of the *"dueling pistol."* It is apparently customary for collectors, historians and authors to believe there is a "hard and fast" authoritative definition of exactly what constitutes a dueling pistol. It became evident upon examining the subject that no such generally sanctioned rendering, contemporary to the era of their

usage, nor concurrent with modern arms collecting literature, was or has been arrived at by a general consensus. Other than the single, broad qualifying feature of a "smooth-bore barrel" (i.e. without rifling) neither the recorded American code …nor the more widely recognized British code, contained further qualifying features for the pistol. It is obvious that there was, indeed, broad latitude as to the type handgun British or American duelists might choose to employ. Thus, the enigma: Did many well-known American and British gunmakers devote some of their manufacturing and sales energies to the development of a style of handgun whose features were *peculiar to and designed specifically for the* practice of dueling, as many authors have proclaimed or would have you believe? Or, was the handgun that emerged to be "traditionally" accepted by arms historians and collectors as the "classic" dueling pistol merely the result of normal evolutionary innovations and improvements in all firearms and advances in industrial and manufacturing techniques…*the result of numerous influences, dueling merely being one among many?* Those questions have apparently never been posed. They are deserving of deeper investigation and resolution. Resorting to the threadbare analogy of "which came first, the chicken or the egg?" reduces the dilemma to its essentials and likely best expresses the quandary.

On reviewing the subjects *"dueling pistols"* and *"dueling"* in a generous cross-section of antique arms literature, it becomes apparent that most treatises and discourses describing the development and evolution of *"dueling pistols"* are ostensibly predicated on theory and assumption, if not outright conjecture. Many writers, including those of the earlier nineteenth century, reached plausible, reasoned conclusions that almost every innovation introduced on a particular style of large, non-military handguns was designed specifically as a result of…and for the sole benefit and use by those engaged in the practice of dueling. However, there does not appear to be solid documentary evidence to substantiate such common and deep-rooted beliefs. Those conclusions and explanations appear to be based more on the allure, imagery and the romanticized aura surrounding dueling, and are often in contention with one another. The assumption that they were designed solely for dueling…and therefore should be made more accurate, possess better balance and be easier to handle than any normal handgun of those respective eras, appears tenuous at best…merely presumptions taken on faith from some earlier writer, news reporter or weapons specialist's article which, by virtue of time, became deep-rooted in arms lore. There is *no doubting* those same handguns commonly termed "dueling pistols" were used in such contests…or *that some innovations popularly attributed to their development may be feasibly and reasonably granted them.* Lest I be castigated for demeaning the widely admired, if not awe-inspiring dueling pistol, it cannot remain unsaid (and reiterated here) that the subject of dueling did decidedly play a role in the early development of some of these pistols…and was obviously instrumental in naming the entire genre. Printed and documentary evidence exists that well-known, widely recognized British gunmakers (notably Rigby, Wogdon and Manton) recommended, developed and adopted certain innovations they asserted were designed specifically for dueling pistols. The actual term "dueling pistol" was apparently in common usage, although used sparingly for an advertisement or printed label of a British gunmaker or merchant in the early 19th century. The same use of those words "dueling pistol" is rarely observed in advertisements by an American firearms merchant or gunmaker. Should a concerted effort be made, it is likely that other indication of use of the terminology will surface. However, the very fact that the practice of dueling was frowned upon by society in general (even though widely practiced) and that it was generally prohibited by legislative statute and a miscellany of (governmental) ordinances, would ostensibly preclude gunmakers from devoting their special talents to fabricating weapons designed expressly for such purpose. Nor would it be thought prudent to be noted for promoting and trafficking in weapons exclusively intended for their clientele to use for unlawful purposes; all the foregoing to the detriment of other "common" handguns (excepting specific target types) that were more likely to be employed in potentially life-threatening situations. And further: it is seemingly inconsistent to infer that a dueling pistol, by virtue of its implied use, required greater accuracy (or as some have implied, *less accuracy*!) or ease of handling than any other form of large handgun. Improvements, changes and innovations on all types of firearms are more reasonably attributed to normal technical and manufacturing innovations, fashion trends, cost of production and selling price. Thus, the origins and accuracy and very definition of "true dueling weapon" are dubious.

It is justly logical to conclude that there is no fundamental difference to large size, single shot, flintlock or percussion handguns that may have been sold in their day as officer's pistols...holster pistols...target pistols...or dueling pistols! The vagueness of terminology has the earmarks of belonging solely in the eye of the beholder...or the gunmaker...or arms scholar...or just as plausibly, the creative writer of both earlier and current eras. Of all those various named handgun categories, none has aroused as much interest nor bequeathed such a legacy of disputable and uncertain arms lore as those said to have been specifically designed and purchased for...or actually used in a formalized duel. There is an obvious aura and wide range of fascination...from the valorous to the macabre, surrounding the practice of dueling and those handguns generally considered to have been specifically designed for that deliberate intent. With the passage of time and the many early and repeated usages of the terminology in the general literature of America and Britain, (especially firearms treatises) the "dueling pistol" has become a unique, yet indeterminate entity. An examination of firearms literature specifically dealing with dueling pistols clearly reflects a wide disparity among authors as to the attribution and development of innovations, modifications and technical improvements in handguns said to be specifically designed for, and unique to dueling. Risking redundancy: A significant flaw, apparently inherent with such studies is the almost complete lack of documentation in the form of footnotes alluding to valid sources. Also lacking are direct quotations from gunmakers, merchants, duelists or others contemporary to the fabrication of those same dueling firearms. All too often such treatises, laboring under the guise of accuracy, do not include even a sparse bibliography of published references utilized by the writer for their sources.

In view of preliminary rational study and personal experience in handling many of these same pistols, accompanied with an awareness of the diverse personalities that originally owned...or were presented with them, it is reasonably

concluded that the term "dueling pistol" is fundamentally *generic*, to include handguns of varying configurations, designed for a variety of roles and functions...in similar manner to the collective terminology "pepperbox" (Chapter 7-B)... "deringer" (7-D)... "bootleg pistol" (7-E); or even the unseemly "Saturday Night Special" (8-A). It is suitably comparable to other eponymous names embodied early in the formal and informal history of firearms...and subsequently the jargon of firearms collecting. The significant, and most notable, dissimilarity was the mystique and sense of fearlessness, if not chivalry, that accompanied the "dueling" pistol. Its very name carried with it a certain poignancy and aggressive spirit...much as the legendary terminology *"Bowie Knife"* is all-embracing and entered the language in a similar manner. And that subject, too, has proven equally contentious as to the origins of its name! Thus it becomes evident that this genre of handgun had captured the imagination and fascination (if not morbid curiosity) of the gunmaker, arms merchant and the consumer (who was not necessarily a duelist!) of their day... and the popular writer and collector of present day, allowing the terminology permanent residency in the language.

Further demonstration of the incongruity of the terminology "dueling pistol" and confirmation that the nomenclature was generic and merely a term of convenience is apparent when viewing the below illustrated cased and matched pair of fine quality American percussion pistols of the type normally considered and classified as "duelers:"

Made by, and fully marked, "G.B. EVANS – PHILADELPHIA" and representative of the best of the American arms maker's craftsmanship, each pistol bears a large, silver plaque inset on its left side engraved with the lengthy inscription: *"Presented to General Edward S. Salomon. Declared by the vote of his fellow citizens as the most popular Soldier of Cook County* [Illinois] *at the Fair of the Chicago* [Military Training League], *September, 1867."* Each is 17 inches overall with 10-inch octagon barrels; caliber 48 smooth-bores. Breech of barrels, barrel tangs, sidelocks and hammers are profusely scroll engraved. Walnut halfstocks with checkered handles. Guns are fitted with single set triggers (i.e. "hair triggers"). General Salomon had earlier led the 82nd Illinois Infantry Regiment through many heated battles of the Civil War including Gettysburg. In 1870 he was appointed by President Grant as the governor of the Territory of Washington.

Pair of American "Dueling" pistols by G.B. Evans of Philadelphia. Presented to General Edward Salomon by the citizens of Cook County, Illinois 1867.

Pair of American "Dueling" Pistols by Simeon North of Connecticut. Presented by the state of Connecticut to U.S. Navy Commodore Thomas MacDonough for his 1814 victory over the British-North.

Should that fine set not prove the point, this spectacular pair by one of America's best known early arms makers, Simeon North of Connecticut further supports the contention that the terminology "dueling pistol" is merely generic: In the collections of the Smithsonian Institution in Washington D.C. is this historical matched pair of elegantly embellished, gold mounted and engraved flintlock, half-stock 54-caliber smoothbore pistols; locks marked "S.NORTH/MIDDLETOWN/CONN." Their 10-inch barrels each engraved: "VOTED BY THE GENERAL ASSEMBLY OF THE STATE OF CONNECTICUT TO COMMODORE THOMAS MACDONOUGH [sic]". The pistols were presented by the governor and legislature of the state of Connecticut circa 1817 to honor a native son, U.S. Naval Commodore McDonough's capture of an English squadron on Lake Champlain on Sept. 11th 1814.

Also on record is a near-identical Simeon North set of flintlock pistols, made on order of the General Assembly of Connecticut and presented by the governor to U.S. Naval Commodore Isaac Hull to commemorate the escape of the U.S.S. Constitution from a British squadron while on her passage from Chesapeake Bay to Boston during the War of 1812.

Other so-called "duelers" are known and recorded having belonged to, being presented to or purchased by citizens and officers with no known record of having engaged in a duel or any proclivity for doing so. Were such pistols as those illustrated and described here (or many others similarly owned and presented), all of which are categorized under the general terminology "dueling pistols," to have been specifically designed (and in the public's concept, uniquely adapted) for dueling, they would hardly have been found suitable for an organizational, governmental (or other) presentation to a public figure or national hero! Nor would they have been wielded only incidentally by ordinary citizenry for the more conventional roles of a handgun.

Having ventured into relatively unexamined territory (and possibly belabored the subjects to the dueling devotee's vexation) it is essential to recognize that these large single shot, non-military flintlock and percussion handguns are invariably representative of the best of the American gunmaker's craftsmanship and artistry. The mere fact that *"dueling pistol"* has been the traditional, *generically* applied nomenclature to describe and classify a broad range of styles and types...to the detriment of their other, possibly more urgent functions...is imperative to cite and recognize. There is but slightest likelihood (if any) that there were the multitudes of "gentlemen" (English or American) seeking uniquely designed handguns with which to engage in duels, as might appear to have been indicated in dueling (and firearms) literature. Consequently, the marketplace for such narrowly specialized "dueling pistols" was relatively small. Judging from the great many gunmakers on both sides of the Atlantic known to have produced "dueling pistols" and the specimens yet surviving of those same type handguns, it becomes further obvious that the purposes for which they were actually designed were multifold...and their generic name merely being all-embracing. There is no doubting that the inspiration for some innovations or improvements in these handguns was influenced by dueling. However, there is every reason to believe that the trade for which they were sold was generalized and that the great majority of buyers were men who were neither duelists nor preparing for the eventuality of a duel. Thus, the conclusion, that the wide spectrum of uses for which these handguns were designed, purchased and put to use (dueling included) lends them considerably greater significance than the narrowly confined designation "dueling pistol" to which they have been limited.

Perhaps the entire subject and foregoing may have been placed in its clearest perspective by Colonel William Orbelo, well-known arms author and collector of American dueling pistols. When asked what was the difference between a target pistol and a dueling pistol, he candidly answered: *"....The target!"*

Evaluating Dueling Pistols

Valuing "duelers" is often a vague undertaking. Greater price fluctuations will be seen in these handguns than in most other areas of American arms collecting. Quite a few long-experienced collectors infer that American "duelers" are underrated in proportion to their relative scarcity. The often "romanticized" and envisioned uses for which they may have been designed or put to actual use...especially that of defending one's honor (however fictionalized) in a long-gone chivalrous era, merely adds to their aura. When these pistols are priced logically, a strong demand exists for them...and they sell readily. It has frequently been observed that collectors and traders unfamiliar with "duelers" tend to evaluate them solely on their scarcity and seeming "romantic" allure of dueling...and thus price them unrealistically. Sufficient examples survive for a collector to assemble a fine and varied selection of these "duelers" by American gunmakers.

A feature that decidedly affects values is the matter of origin of the entire gun and its components; i.e., whether production was entirely American or merely assembled from imported parts by American makers. The subject requires considerably greater discussion and the author will merely comment on facets of the market that he has personally observed and as generally practiced by most buyers and sellers. In contemplating acquisition of a "dueler," the basic approach is to remove the barrels and inspect their undersides for proofmarks. As a general rule, barrels that are completely unmarked or unproofed are normally considered American manufacture; such guns are usually taken for granted to be American make. There is every possibility that such barrels could have been imported without being proofed in their countries of origin, but as such a practice has yet to be substantiated, the American collectors' market has accepted specimens as their own. Should the barrels, on removal, display foreign proofmarks (invariably British), then for reasons never clearly defined, and which must be attributed to a quirk of the collectors' market (originating in traditional patterns of collecting), values are lessened somewhat as compared to a so-called "pure" American make. A decrease in value of 15 percent to 20 percent would be about average for such weapons, providing, of course, that other features clearly point to American manufacture. The subject has never been properly addressed. With the case of British barrels, the author hazards the conjecture that the mere fact that the proofs appear on the underside of the barrel would indicate it was either ordered by the American maker, or at very least, specifically intended for that export market.

After establishing the origin of a particular gun (either in part or in full), values are then basically dependent upon (a) quality of workmanship, (b) maker's name and consequent fame, origins and geographic location, and (c) condition; in that general order.

After viewing many of these types, it is obvious that a wide range of workmanship and quality exists, which in most cases (but not all) serves as the prime requisite for establishing values. Specimens will be seen within a broad spectrum of embellishments and other features from workmanship and quality of the stock woods to the types of fittings and furniture (i.e., iron, brass, German silver, silver or even possibly gold), forend caps (horn, silver, pewter, etc.), barrel work (gold inlays, silver bands, engraving, shapes, etc.) and, of course, engraving and other decor on the lock and furniture.

The second determinant in evaluation—maker's name—plays a significant role and is basically divided into the major categories of (a) Northern and (b) Southern, with a sub-category, viewed much less frequently, of Western makers. The general rule-of-thumb for evaluation places a premium on all Southern pieces by virtue of the fact that they are pre-Civil War and normally classified as "secondary" Confederate martial handguns, possibly carried by a Southern officer or enlisted man during his wartime service. The likelihood of such Southern-made arms being carried is greater than those for Northern pieces (due to the sparsity of weapons in the South at the outbreak of hostilities). And, in gun collecting, all Southern arms have greater romantic attributes! Any historical association attached to a dueler, either by virtue of its original owner or maker or known usage, will add immeasurably in value. Attributions should be well substantiated and documented and not merely "word of mouth" or as more affectionately known among seasoned gun traders—"Aunt Marys."

A few makers are noted whose duelers are more often seen on the collectors' market than others; most prominent is **Richard Constable** of Philadelphia whose guns are highly regarded for their excellent quality. **Henry Deringer**, of course, was a well known maker of dueling types as were **Mullin** of New York and **Happoldt** of Charleston, South Carolina. A great many American makers advertised the availability of duelers, but evidence points to their production in but very limited quantities; specimens are decided scarcities on the collectors' market. Occasionally very large similar types, that is, generally patterned after British duelers of the period, are found with iron ramrods and swivels affixed beneath the barrel. Features of that nature normally classify these as "holster pistols" rather than duelers, but they would be comparable value-wise.

The majority of these pistols (just like deringers) were originally made and sold as pairs, but over the years many became separated (especially if uncased) and are most often observed as single specimens. To be properly evaluated as an uncased, matched pair, they must be truly that; matched in markings and finishes, size and condition. When meeting these requisites, a percentage should be added to the total of individual values. That percentage is very much subject to wide fluctuations with no clear cut easily applied guidelines. Generally, the finer the condition, the larger the percentage. For instance, a pair in mediocre condition might be worth only the sum of the two pistols, whereas a pair rated fine to excellent would be worth a premium of 20 percent to 30 percent and a mint or "factory new" pair might command a premium of 50 percent to 75 percent. Such estimates are merely examples, not intended as inclusive guideposts; the observation is strictly "seat of the pants."

Made and sold cased, including a complement of accessories: When found in a complete state, the outfits are quite often in fine condition (it is unusual for *original* cased sets to be found heavily used and in worn condition) and prices, of course, may be considerably increased; with 50 percent to 100 percent not being unreasonable for those in excellent to almost new condition. It is important to determine that the case is authentic and the general condition matches those of the pistols. The accessories, or at least the important ones, should be intact. Shown here a fine complete set by J.E. Evans and (for size comparison) a pair of small belt size (or large deringer) pistols by John Krider, both noted Philadelphia makers.

Features such as full side locks or back action locks have not been a determinant of value. No noticeable preferences exist for one style over the other, or a lack of interest in one type. Size, though, is important in determining so-called "duelers." Those with barrels under about 8" and proportionately smaller throughout are generally not considered "duelers" and consequently will bring lesser values. This last statement is a generalization and will not hold true in every instance. Maker and quality are still key factors.

The two specimens here, illustrate general styles that might be encountered and are not representative of all types. The back action lock pistol was made by **Norris and Brother** of Baltimore, Maryland (and so marked); measuring 17" overall with a 10-1/2" octagon 54 caliber barrel. It displays fine quality workmanship including an engraved hammer, lock, breech and furniture, and very closely follows the British style popular during the 1830 to 1840 era. The second gun with the full side lock was by the well-known **H. E. Dimick and Company**, St. Louis, and although generally following the style of English duelers of the era, possesses distinct American characteristics, most notable in the unusual use of the part round, part octagon 11" barrel (48 caliber) and double set triggers.

The prices indicated are general guideposts only, to be tempered by the factors of quality, maker's name and condition. An approximate 25 percent to 50 percent (or more) premium may be added for Southern or Western makers. A notable exception to this rule-of-thumb are the pistols (very few known) of the noted **Hawken** of St. Louis whose arms (mostly rifles) are in such great demand and highly prized examples of western Americana that values would be considerably in excess than those described here. It is thus very much up to the collector to research the importance of each piece.

7F-001

7F-001

American Percussion Dueling Pistol: Northern Maker; good quality; usually engraved with scroll and floral designs; iron, brass or German silver furniture of good quality:

7F-001   Values—Good **$1,100**   Very Good **$2,000**
                    Exc. **$3,750+**

Matched Pair American Percussion Dueling Pistols as described above:

7F-002   Values—Good **$3,000**   Very Good **$5,000**
Exc. **$10,000+**

Cased, Matched Pair American Percussion Duelers (as described above) With Accessories:

7F-003   Values—Very Good **$9,500**   Exc. **$17,500+**

Belt Pistols

7F-004
"A"

7F-004
"B"

7F-004
"C"

It's often a very fine line that separates a "belt pistol" from a deringer; both being terms of convenience (*See Chapter 7D*).

A fair number of American "belt" sized pistols with barrels generally between 4" and 8" in length are seen on the collectors' market. Although each must be treated individually and valued accordingly, it is possible to discuss them in broad terms and set forth general price ranges for most. As with duelers, key evaluating features are (a) quality, (b) maker's name and (c) condition.

The specimens illustrated here are: **(A)** Long barreled belt sized pistol made by a St. Louis gunsmith of the 1840-1860 era and so marked: approximately 8" barrel, 46 caliber rifled bore, a highly desirable piece because of its Western association. Quality-wise the pistol does not nearly approximate the workmanship of fine Eastern makers of duelers and has simple, almost primitive features. The same gun found unmarked or with names of lesser known Eastern makers of no special historical significance or association would bring half the price. Quality and name are thus dominant factors in affecting demand as well. **(B)** "Belt" sized percussion pistol by the well known maker (and so marked) TRYON PHILADELPHIA; 6" octagon barrel with iron ramrod and swivels mounted below walnut stock; brass furniture; the classic example of a well made, popular and widely sold arm of its day by a noted—and prolific—maker. **(C)** Primitively made American belt pistol with 4" octagon barrel; 32 caliber unusual box lock action. The key features of the gun are the maker's markings (unidentified) and deep American eagle and shield motif stamped on the lock. Without those features the gun would have but small demand and attendant value. In this particular case the markings and the eagle motif make it a highly desirable piece doubling the normal value.

The broadest general price ranges for belt sized percussion American pistols found singly and of only simplest construction with no fancy embellishments and lesser known makers' names:

7F-004   Values—Good **$575**   Very Good **$1,000**
Exc. **$1,750+**

Broad general price ranges for these same types of finer quality construction, with no fancy embellishments and identifiable, more well known makers' names:

7F-005   Values—Good **$725**   Very Good **$1,500**
Exc. **$2,500+**

Premium values of 20 percent to 50 percent may be added to the above arms if found with Southern or Western makers names.

Chapter VIII-A

Metallic Cartridge Revolvers Pepperboxes, Single and Multi-Barrel Pistols, "Spur Triggers"

This chapter lists almost every known make and style of American handgun traditionally recognized as "antique collectors' guns" for one or more of the following reasons: Historical significance, period of manufacture, appearance, mechanical operation or makers' name. It would be impossible to list every known American metallic cartridge handgun in a work such as this; nor is there any need to do so. Many late 19th and early 20th century handguns have little collector interest or value and an attempt to list them all would be impractical here. However, the omission of a certain handgun does not necessarily place it in this aforementioned category. Furthermore, there are undoubtedly gaps, possible inconsistencies and likely some contradictions in these listings, for many of the subject guns have never been covered by detailed studies. Occasionally specimens will be encountered varying in dimensions from those listed and sometimes even in contours. This prefatory text is intended to provide the reader with sufficient facts to allow for the general identification of all types of cartridge handguns, whether they are individually described or not.

For practical purposes, these arms are catalogued under the major classification "Metallic Cartridge Pistols," alphabetically arranged (excepting automatics, which are described in their own sub-section). Although many merit their own sub-groupings, constituting specialized fields of collecting in themselves (e.g., deringers, pepperboxes, small bore and large bore revolvers, etc.), it was felt that a single grouping best served the purposes of this book. The inclusion of certain arms and exclusion of others has been purely arbitrary by the author, but is more or less based on traditional arms collecting patterns.

No definitive body of data is available for many of these makes and types. Descriptions largely reflect the basic, most often encountered, dimensions and styles of the handguns listed. When variations are encountered, it will be the reader's task to assess possible increases in value based on individual rarity and importance. The subject is discussed at greater length in Chapter II.

Undoubtedly the majority of variations observed will be in barrel lengths. As a general rule minor fluctuations of less than an inch will not affect values. In instances where arms are listed with barrels of 3" or 4" and are found by the reader with an inch or so longer or shorter, it may be generally stated that prices will remain constant or, at most, are affected but slightly— providing an interested buyer is found! That same gun, however, standard as a 3" or 4" model, when located with bizarre lengths of 8" or 10", may then be re-evaluated in the light of its demand (especially by maker's name) and desirability, as well as oddity value. Premiums may be placed accordingly. By rule-of-thumb, the premium increases in direct proportion to the make of the gun and the demand for it. Other variations to watch for are in the shape of barrels (guns listed as being standard with octagon barrels may be found with round or part round/part octagon and vice versa), cylinders listed as standard fluted might be found round, grip and handle shapes may vary, as at times will occur in calibers. All of these features should be assessed value-wise on the basis of the importance of the gun on which they appear; values increasing proportionately greater on the more well known makes. On a quite insignificant make or type of weapon, a variation might not affect value at all.

Wherever possible, estimates have been given for quantities believed produced. Such figures are certainly subject to error, correction and updating; they are offered as general guidelines to aid in establishing relative rarity. Known and/or approximated dates of manufacture are included in order to place the guns in an historical perspective.

The American metallic cartridge handgun made its first appearance in mass produced form in 1857 with the Smith & Wesson Model 1, 1st Issue, 22 caliber rimfire revolver (q.v.). The development of the metallic cartridge, its many experimental configurations, the various types that evolved, and the guns made to accept them constitute a fascinating study for the student. The field also offers tremendous potential for the collector to accumulate an intriguing cross-section of American arms of the golden era of cartridge experimentation—that of the third quarter of the 19th century. For greater insight to these arms, the reader is referred to such well known books on cartridge development as the widely referred to *Cartridges* by Herschel C. Logan, *The American Cartridge* by Charles Suydam, and *Cartridges For Collectors* by Fred Datig.

DERINGERS

The generic term "deringer" or "derringer" as applicable to metallic cartridge handguns has a different connotation than that for the percussion pocket pistol (*see Chapter VII, Section D Henry Deringer and His Imitators*). Percussion deringers were invariably large bore (averaging about 41 caliber), single shot, small sized pocket pistols styled generally (if not identically) after the product of Henry Deringer of Philadelphia. However, "deringer," when applied to cartridge handguns, covers quite a mixed bag of styles, types and sizes. While the Webster's definition is "… a small, short-barreled pistol of large caliber," it may be categorically stated that the manufacturer of the era of the 1860s through 1900, as well as the present day collector, allows the term a much broader coverage. Major manufacturers such as the Remington Arms Company used the word "derringer" to describe and advertise their various pepperboxes (of four and five barrels) as well as their famed double barrel over/under pistol. Other makers freely used the word (spelled either with a single or a double r) to describe a whole host of single and double barrel pistols of varying calibers. By an evolutionary process, the present day collector has generally come to accept any of the small single and double barreled metallic cartridge handguns as "deringers" regardless of caliber. Interestingly enough, the four- and five-barreled pistols actually termed "deringers" by many manufacturers of their day, are rarely called "deringers" currently, but better known as "pepperboxes," use of which is retained here. It should be noted that the authors of the recently published *Deringer In America, Volume 2, Cartridge Period* (see bibliography) have chosen to include cartridge pepperboxes as "deringers." Only time will tell if the jargon of the collecting world chooses to revert to its original 19th century terminology for those multi-barreled handguns.

As a further indication of the present day use of the term in its application to handguns of very small caliber, note the issuance c. 1950s by the Colt Firearms Company of their "4th Model Single Shot Deringer," a direct descendant of the Colt 41 caliber model of the 19th century, but in small 22 caliber rimfire—and actually termed by them "Deringer."

DERINGER vs POCKET PISTOL

The individual and/or interchangeable use of these terms is often a matter of personal preference in current collector terminology. In earlier editions of this Guide most of the small single shot metallic cartridge handguns were termed "Pocket Pistol" based on traditional collector nomenclature. With the growth of the hobby and the publication of research papers and treatises, "deringer" has become the more generally accepted generic term and is now reflected in this edition of the Guide. The recently published major work in this field, *Deringer In America, Volume II, The Cartridge Period*, has defined the cartridge deringer as "...any small, concealable, breech-loading pistol, excluding revolvers and automatics." Yet, to demonstrate the elusiveness of a perfect description for these small American handguns, and the difficulty in neatly classifying all weapons, how to explain the fact that one of the well-known makers of the day, James Reid, boldly marked on the barrel of one of his five-shot revolvers (#8A-154) REID'S DERRINGER?

As for the spelling of the generic term "deringer," that is a matter of personal preference; no hard and fast rules state whether "deringer" or "derringer" is correct. The subject is discussed in greater detail in the chapter dealing with Henry Deringer's pistols (Chapter VII, Section D).

The breechloading metallic cartridge deringer was a logical development from the percussion pocket pistol of the same caliber. The very caliber used in those earliest cartridge models was 41 rimfire, the same as the standard bore size of Henry Deringer's pistol. Note the common terminology in use for that metallic cartridge: "41 Deringer." The first of the pocket sized so-called "deringers" of large caliber was the all metal Moore (c. 1864), followed by the National Arms Company "No. 2 Type," both of which were subsequently taken over by Colt and manufactured by them. These served as the inspiration for a whole host of similar small sized guns with 41 caliber bores which the purist-collector likes to think of as the only "true" deringer. There is no doubting, though, that the smaller calibers too, constitute a very important segment of arms and deringer collecting, offering an interesting potential to the collector.

A very common error often committed when listing deringers is in caliber size. Not a few previous listings and guidebooks describe guns that are identified herein as made only in 41 caliber as also being made in 38 caliber (and even occasionally in 44). Although it is possible that a few of these arms were made in calibers other than 41, it will generally be found that the error occurred in hasty bore measurements. Many of those single shot deringers produced in 41 when measured with a bore gauge at the muzzle appear to be 38 caliber and, without actually checking their chamber with a cartridge, some authors and researchers have hastily listed them as 38. This very same error is commonly encountered with arms of 32 caliber that often measure but 30 at the muzzle.

UNMARKED DERINGERS

The collector will encounter quite a few variously styled, shaped and sized unmarked, single shot "deringer" type pistols on the antique arms market. Complete listings of these arms have yet to be made. There now appears to be sufficient interest in them to allow such a survey. The majority are usually spur trigger, iron frame (brass occasionally seen, but to a lesser degree), bird's-head butt style with round or part round/part octagon barrels that swing sideways to load; most are in the small calibers of 22 and 32 rimfire. Value-wise they may be compared to similar appearing, marked, fully identified pieces listed in this chapter, but with the absence of any markings they should be priced approximately 25 percent to 50 percent less, depending on the quality of workmanship and condition. The largest calibers, either 38 or 41 rimfire, may be equally compared to similar appearing specimens and priced approximately 25 percent to 35 percent less. When such pieces are seen with unidentified markings, or merely trade names (to the complete exclusion of a manufacturer's name), they may be priced relative to pieces of a similar style by the lesser known makers covered in this listing.

"SECONDARY MARTIALS"- A MISCONCEPTION

The term "Secondary Martial" as applied to certain cartridge revolvers is quite nebulous. The author has conscientiously avoided separately categorizing these handguns feeling that the terminology is inaccurate. The introduction of this phraseology in earlier works on American arms and its continued use in later literature, is not in general acceptance by present day collectors. The poignant fact is that such arms have no record whatsoever of secondary American military usage as do the earlier single shot flintlocks and percussion handguns and a great many of the longarms. It is true that a number of these revolvers could have been (and probably were) carried as individually purchased arms by officers and men in the military service, but likely no more so than a smaller caliber piece (see discussion of this in Chapter VII of American Percussion Pistols, Section A, Revolvers).

OTHER FACTORS AFFECTING VALUE

As is true for almost all other arms—especially handguns—there are other factors that will affect value. Foremost among these is the use of exotic materials for grips; most often seen on the metallic cartridge handguns are ivory and pearl. Engraved arms in varying degrees of quality and profuseness are known, as are presentation, historically associated guns and, of course, cased sets. All these factors and their effect on values are discussed at length in Chapter II, to which the reader is referred.

Many of these cartridge handguns were originally sold packaged in labeled factory pasteboard cartons often with printed "DIRECTIONS FOR USE" included. Depending upon the condition of the carton and its labels, values of boxed handguns are enhanced considerably; usually doubling prices, greater; rarity of the gun being the determining factor for the percentage of increased value. In most instances the boxed pistol is observed in extremely fine, often mint condition. A well-worn handgun yet retaining its original box, would likely be regarded an anomaly, the box apt to be valued individually from the gun.

THE HUMBLE SPUR TRIGGER REVOLVER
The Wraps Removed...Long-Awaited Recognition

Their day was long overdue! It has become increasingly apparent by the numbers of them appearing in displays of well-known collectors and dealers at antique arms shows, in advertisements and articles in the arms press, that the long forsaken, if not ubiquitous American *Spur Trigger Revolver* has, by virtue of time and antiquity, emerged from the fringes of the antique arms field...and been wholeheartedly welcomed into the collecting fraternity! It cannot pass unnoticed that the observation that "[these revolvers] *are unique in that they have almost no historical significance!*" made by Donald Webster a half-century ago in *Suicide Specials*, the first work to recognize this genre of handguns...has reversed itself! These small pocket handguns have long labored under the derisive terminology "Suicide Specials," a neat little term (if somewhat grim) synonymous with "Saturday Night Specials" coined in the immediate post-World War II era to describe an all-inclusive, wide cross-section of inexpensive, small-sized pocket revolvers...both the spur trigger, single-action types as well as double-action, solid frame and top-break styles...produced mainly during the latter 19th century. For the collector of antique arms, the foreboding terminology was reserved almost exclusively for spur trigger pocket revolvers...and those are the type that are discussed and valued here. Among features proven to make them attractive are the price ranges in which the majority are to be found. Those values were relatively static through to the sixth and seventh editions of this Guide, with but modest increases following. The values reflected here are convincing indicators of the attention now paid to them. Concurrent with heightened collecting interest and activity, there has been a noticeable increase in serious research studies devoted to them. Extensive projects have been underway (some nearing completion) that, when published are likely to further those stirrings.

As for the time-worn, ill-suited terminology "Suicide Specials"...it is not merely undeserved...but inaccurate as well. The commonly held perception, one generally taken for granted, implied that all of these spur trigger, single-action revolvers were not merely inexpensive handguns, but were all, across-the-board, of inferior quality. That assumption has since been disproved. Technical studies within recent years have clearly established that there is a wide range of skilled construction among them, with many displaying quality on a par with similar handguns of the best-known names in the industry. Hence, in deference to their rising popularity as significant collectible firearms, collectors and arms students are in accord that the demeaning "Suicide Specials" is as inappropriate as it is unmerited to describe and name these pocket handguns. A catchword name for them has yet to surface. By general consensus *"Spur Trigger Revolvers"* appears to be front-runner with "American Spur Trigger Trade Name Revolvers 1869-1898" (shortened to merely *"Trade Name Revolvers"*) a close runner-up. Almost all embody the following features: small, pocket-size, single-action revolvers distinguished by their solid, spur trigger frame; cylinders generally locked into frame by a removable center pin. Obviously, there are numerous variations within those qualifications, while the many examples of these same style revolvers by the larger well-known American manufacturers (such as Colt, Remington, S&W, etc.) are generally considered as specific named "models" of each respective gunmaker. A majority of these spur trigger types were manufactured under "Trade Names," i.e. arbitrarily chosen names by the manufacturer or the merchant exclusively retailing them to distinguish the revolver and/or enhance it salability. Those trade names were very often the only markings that appeared on many of these "spur trigger revolvers." They were produced by approximately 25 different manufacturers, of which only six have been estimated to have marked their company name on the little handguns along with the "Trade Name."

Manufacturing variations, often the objective in collecting, are plentiful on these small handguns. It has often been the provocative, if not amusing character of those same "Trade Names" which were the fascination and attraction for collecting them. Thus far over three hundred "Trade Names" been recorded (representative of all letters of the alphabet except "Z"...and that's bound to show up, too!)...with new ones continually coming to light. A brief survey includes such romantic, humorous and even ominous sounding markings as: ALERT, AMERICAN BOY, ARISTOCRAT, BANG UP, BIG BONANZA, BLOODHOUND, BLUE JACKET, BRUTUS, BUFFALO BILL, BULLDOZER, CAPTAIN JACK, DEAD SHOT, DEFENDER 89, DEFIANCE, EARTHQUAKE, ELECTRIC, FAULTLESS, GUARDIAN, HALF BREED, HERO, LIBERTY, LITTLE GIANT, LONG TOM, MARQUIS OF LORNE, MONARCH, PARALYZER, PATRIOT, RANGER, ROBINHOOD, SUCCESS, SWAMP ANGEL and TRAMP'S TERROR!

For the aficionado, classifications are best made by butt style (the bird's-head is most common), method of retaining the center pin, fluted or straight cylinder, sights, octagon or round barrel, types of sideplates, etc.

Methods for identification of actual manufacturer are vague and often nebulous. The recognition of patent date markings frequently is a key factor. Other means are the special features common to many types, e.g., cylinder pin latches or special styling features. Frequently identification is a complex subject, the great obstacle being the obscurities surrounding many of the lesser known makers.

These solid frame, spur-trigger "Trade Name" revolvers fall within general price ranges; a few specific features drastically affect both demand and value. Mechanical condition plays a highly important role. Mostly inexpensive guns, they are often extremely difficult and too costly to repair in proportion to their value; hence, with the more common types, mechanical functioning and completeness is basic to value. Condition is of equal significance. Unless the trade name is unusual or rare, the condition should be in finest grades to bring appreciable values.

Special features do affect demand and values just as with all other American guns. Most often seen are grips (either pearl or ivory) which increase value but a few dollars at most, unless

8A-001

8A-001

8A-001

8A-001

elaborately engraved or carved. Quite a few Spur Triggers were made with simple scroll and floral engraving. In such instances the designs will rarely increase values any appreciable amount, if at all. On occasion, however, a few of these handguns were made with elaborate decorations representative of the highest degree of the engraver's art. Specimens must be judged on their artistic merits, although rarely achieving values commensurate with the same engraving when found on more well known makes such as Colt or Smith & Wesson. Although wooden cased outfits are seldom encountered (in any event failing to command any exceptional value), boxed specimens are often seen, and if in fine condition and fully labeled, are highly desirable. Boxes usually are of heavy pasteboard and bear labels with illustrations of the gun, trade names and directions for use, etc. If the box is complete, clean and sound, values for the gun should at least double.

A general guide to Spur Trigger Revolver prices is:

(a) Commonest styles with well known names, in plain grades (or simply engraved where standard) with hard rubber or walnut grips (or whatever is standard issue). Mechanically complete and correctly functioning; **in excellent to factory new condition**. Approximate price range:

8A-001 $150 to **$350**

(b) Identical to above, but with the less often encountered trade names; **in excellent to factory new condition**. Approximate price range:

8A-002 $175 to **$425**

(c) Identical to above, but with rarely encountered trade names. **Excellent to factory new condition:**

8A-003 $250 to **$550**

Although inexpensive guns and, until recently, a rather insignificant field of arms collecting, these revolvers of lowly status have acquired increased interest in recent years; hence both their demand and values have risen accordingly. Condition is still a highly important factor in their values as is mechanical functioning. However, collectors do seem to be willing to settle for lesser states of condition than previously reported and prices should be revised downward as condition diminishes.

Alternate sources of information about these revolvers are the many original (and reprint) catalogs of the sporting goods, hardware and general gun dealers circa 1870-1910 that sold these popular handguns. Numerous listings and details about them are to be found in them.

BIBLIOGRAPHY

Information concerning American metallic cartridge handguns may be found in several other books covering American firearms appearing in complete bibliographic listings elsewhere in this book, notably in Chapter V concerning each of the individual manufacturers involved in cartridge handgun production (*q.v.*). Other books listed in Chapter IV of interest concerning this subject are: *The Gun Collectors Handbook Of Values* by C. E. Chapel, *Civil War Guns* by W. B. Edwards, *History Of Firearms* by H. B. C. Pollard, *Ten Old Gun Catalogs* compiled by L. D. Saterlee, *The Collecting Of Guns* edited by James E. Serven, *Revolving Arms* by A. W. F. Taylerson, *The Catalog Of The William M. Locke Collection, Henry Deringer's Pocket Pistol* by John E. Parsons, *Pepperbox Firearms* by Lewis Winant and *American British And Continental Pepperbox Firearms* by Jack Dunlap, and, in Chapter VII-A *Civil War Pistols* by J.D. McAulay.

*Bogut, Lionel. *All About Southerners: The History and Details of the .41 Caliber Rim Fire Southerner Derringer*. Lincoln, RI: Mowbray Pub. 2004 Details of that popular derringer in all its many variations and markings with interesting comments about fakery.

Bowen, Taylor G. *James Reid & His Catskill Knuckledusters*. Lincoln, Rhode Island: Mowbray Publishers, 1989. Significant study of these famous firearms oddities and their many variations and biography of their maker.

Carder, Charles E. *Revolvers and Pistols from Hopkins & Allen Mfg. and Arms Companies*. Delphos, Ohio: Avil Onze Pub. Co., 1998.

*Carder, Charles E. *Hopkins & Allen Safety Police Revolvers*. Delphos, Ohio: Avil Onze Pub. Co., 2005. Popularly manufactured double actions made circa 1885-1909; details and variations with history of H&A.

*Eberhart, L.D. & Wilson, R.L. *The Deringer In America...Volume II, The Cartridge Period*. Lincoln, Rhode Island: Mowbray Publishers, 1993. Most detailed guide to the subject; companion to Volume I covering percussion deringers (*q.v.*).

Fors, W. Barlow. *Collector's Handbook U.S. Cartridge Revolvers 1856-1899*. Chicago: Adams Press, 1973. Listings of brand names and patents; histories of various manufacturers.

*Goforth, W.E. *Iver Johnson Arms & Cycle Works Handguns 1871-1978*. Chino Valley, California: Blacksmith Corporation Pub., 1992.

Koch, R. W. *The FP-45 Liberator Pistol 1942-1945:* Arcadia, Calif. Privately published, 1974. Story of WWII secret production of single shot pistol for resistance forces.

*Laidacker, John S. *Developmental Cartridge Handguns In .22 Calibre As Produced In The U.S. And Abroad From 1855 To 1875*. Millville, Pennsylvania: Privately published by author, 1994. Also includes .22 handguns made before turn of century. Almost 400 pistols shown and described in detail. Important collector information.

*Layman, George. *The British Bulldog Revolver: The Forgotten Gun that Really Won the West!* Woonsocket, RI: Mowbray Pub, 2006 One of the most widely manufactured revolvers of its day by both British and American manufacturers.

Phelps, Art. *The Story Of Merwin, Hulbert & Co. Firearms*. Rough & Ready, California: Privately published by author, 1991. Revised second edition, 1992 Santa Ana, CA. Graphic Pub.

Sell, DeWitt E. *Collector's Guide To American Cartridge Handguns*. Harrisburg, Pennsylvania: Stackpole Company, 1963. Alphabetical listing of all known makers and their models from the 19th century to present; revolvers and automatics.

Sell, DeWitt E. *Handguns Americana*. Alhambra, California: Borden Publishing Company, 1972. 19th-20th century cartridge revolvers and automatics; corporate histories of most well known makers.

*Sellers, Frank M. *Baby Hammerless Revolvers*. Alstead, NH; Self published 2004. All about the series of curious, tiniest American revolvers that have always piqued collectors' fascination, and their variations.

Suydam, Charles R. *U.S. Cartridges and Their Handguns 1795-1975*. North Hollywood, California: Beinfeld Publishing, Inc., 1977. Well researched study of the handguns along with the standard, rare, and unusual cartridges they used.

Webster, Donald B., Jr. *Suicide Specials*. Harrisburg, Pennsylvania: Stackpole Company, 1958. The pioneer work on the subject. Lengthy and detailed alphabetical listings by both manufacturer and trade names.

---*Fifty Years Of Gunmaking: The Story Of The Hopkins & Allen Arms Co.* Canton, Conn.: Armsco Pub., c.1997.

(*) Preceding a title indicates the book is currently in print.

Aetna Arms Co. Pocket Revolver

Aetna Arms Company, New York, Pocket Revolver. Made c. 1869 to 1880. Total quantity estimated about 6,000.

22 caliber rimfire. Seven-shot. 3-1/8" octagon barrel. Brass spur trigger frame. Blued or plated finish. Walnut or rosewood grips; bird's-head butt.

Barrel marked: AETNA ARMS CO. NEW YORK

Numerous minor variations have been observed in barrel catches, ejectors and other parts. The name ALLING is occasionally encountered in place of the usual Aetna markings and will bring small premium. Except for the octagon barrel, the gun is a very close copy of the Smith & Wesson 1st Model, 3rd Issue:

8A-004

8A-004   Values—Very Good **$225**   Exc. **$575**

E. Allen, Allen and Wheelock, etc.   *See Chapter V-A, Allen Firearms.*

All Right Firearms Co. Palm Pistol

All Right Firearms Co., Lawrence, Massachusetts, Little All Right Palm or "Squeezer" Type Pistol. Made c. late 1870s. Total quantity estimated at several hundred.

22 caliber rimfire (although originally advertised in 22, 30, and 32 rimfire calibers, none but the 22 is known and should either 30 or 32 be found, it would be considered an extreme rarity and worth considerable premium). Five-shot. 1-7/8" barrel is standard, but also known in 2-3/8" barrel (rare, and will bring premium).

Sliding trigger fits in a tube on top of the octagonal barrel and when pulled rearward, cocks and fires the revolver, simultaneously revolving the cylinder. Usual finish nickel plated. (Blue rare).

Profuse markings in relief designs on the hard rubber grips: ALL RIGHT FIRE ARMS CO., MANUFACTURERS LAWRENCE, MASS. U.S.A. and also LITTLE ALL RIGHT.

8A-005

The inventors of this unique appearing arm were Edward Boardman and Andrew Peavey of Lawrence. (Peavey, earlier in Maine, patented a knife-pistol [*q.v.*]) Their patent was issued January 18, 1876. The term "Little All Right" was registered as a trademark on April 18, 1876. Although originally classified under the Federal Gun Control Act as a "curio and relic," the gun has since been declassified as not subject to the G.C.A. regulations and is considered as an "antique":

8A-005   Values—Very Good **$1,250**   Exc. **$2,750**

Alling   *See Aetna.*

American Arms Co. Double Barrel Deringers

American Arms Co., Boston, Massachusetts, Swivel Breech, Double Barrel Pocket Pistols. Made c. 1866 to 1878. Total quantity estimated at under 5,000.

Calibers and barrel lengths as below. Superposed barrels manually rotated for loading and firing.

Brass frame with silver plated finish; barrels blued. Rosewood grips with either square shaped or bird's-head butt.

Barrel markings: AMERICAN ARMS CO. BOSTON MASS. and WHEELER'S PAT. OCT. 31. 1865 - JUNE. 19. 1866 on the opposite barrel. Earlier production omitted the word WHEELER'S

Although barrel lengths on various models listed below are the same, overall dimensions and frame sizes are increased with the larger calibers.

Combination Calibers 22 Rimfire in One Barrel and 32 Rimfire in The Other; the most commonly seen model. Square butt, 3" barrels standard. Estimate quantity 3,000. (Bird's-head butt very rare; worth premium):

8A-006   Values—Good **$275**   Fine **$850**

22 Rimfire in Both Barrels; very rare; estimated quantity 50:

8A-006.5   Values—Good **$850**   Fine **$2,750**

32 Rimfire in Both Barrels With Square Butt; 3" barrel standard (shorter barrel will bring a small premium). Quantity made together with bird's-head butt below estimated 1500:

8A-007   Values—Good **$375**   Fine **$950**

32 Rimfire in Both Barrels With Bird's-Head Butt; 2-5/8" barrel standard; 3" barrel will bring small premium: Estimate quantity 1500.

8A-008   Values—Good **$375**   Fine **$950**

38 Rimfire in Both Barrels; although reported in that caliber, with bird's-head butt and 2-5/8" barrels, it is likely that former

8A-006 / 006.5

8A-007 / 008 / 009 / 010

measurements were erroneous, caliber actually being 41 rimfire. Premium values of 100 percent and more if found in 38 rimfire:

8A-009

41 Rimfire Both Barrels; made only with square butt. 2-5/8" barrel standard. Quantity estimate under 400:

8A-010   Values—Good **$500**   Fine **$1,750**

American Arms Co. Top-Break Revolvers

8A-011

American Arms Company, Boston, Massachusetts, Single Action and Double Action Top-Break Revolvers.

Spur trigger models made only in 38 caliber, single action. Double action models made in 32 caliber and 38 caliber.

Distinguishing feature is the manually operated extractor which appears as a split ring on the back of the cylinder. Cylinder has narrow double flutes between each chamber.

Barrel marked: AMERICAN ARMS COMPANY, BOSTON, MASS. and patent dates.

Although bearing the same name as the company previously listed which made the manually revolved double barrel deringer type pistols, this firm was not believed to have had any affiliation with them:

8A-011   Values—Very Good **$175**   Exc. **$450**

American Arms Co. Top-Break Revolver

American Arms Co., Boston, Massachusetts, unique locking device Double Action Top-Break Revolver.

32 caliber and 38 caliber centerfire. 3-1/4" round ribbed barrel; fluted cylinder; double cylinder locking notches (variations noted).

Embodying many distinctive and unique features, this "top-break" constitutes a decided "firearms oddity." Rocker type push bar latch on top of the humped back frame locks and releases trigger; unique small sliding switch in center of circular sideplate on left frame allows for single or two-stage trigger pull; depressable button latch in center of topstrap locks cylinder in place when opened for loading and unloading.

Finish nickeled; hard rubber grips with company monogram at top.

8A-012

Barrel markings: AMERICAN ARMS CO. BOSTON/PAT. MAY 25, 1886. Markings on topstrap: PAT'S PENDING or PAT'S MAY 25 '86/MAR 11 '89/JUNE 17 '90. As this revolver was susceptible to mechanical failure, and repairs were difficult, values shown here are for those in excellent working order. If otherwise, up to 50 percent less than shown.

8A-012   Values—Very Good **$275**   Exc. **$575**

"American Bulldog" Marked Revolver   *See Iver Johnson 8A-068.9*

American Standard Tool Company   *See Chapter V-C, Manhattan Firearms (5C-022/023).*

Babcock Marked Single Shot Pistol   *See T. J. Stafford.*

Baby Hammerless & New Baby Pocket Revolvers

Baby Hammerless & New Baby Pocket Revolvers. The smallest American double action revolvers. First made 1896-1897 by The Columbian Firearms Manufacturing Company of Philadelphia under the patents of Charles Foehl and Charles Weeks; 1897-1916 by Henry Kolb of Philadelphia; 1916-1938 by R.F. Sedgley, Inc. of Philadelphia; none of whose names appeared on them. The closest to maker identification were the K and S that appeared on the hard rubber grips. The earliest by Columbian Firearms Co. are worth a small premium. However as most were apparently fitted with pearl grips, easy identification is unlikely. Quantities made are unknown, but were quite substantial.

The tiniest of the 22s measured but 3-11/16" overall with a 1-1/4" barrel, and weighed slightly less than 4-1/2 ounces. The largest of the 22 caliber top breaks merely 4-7/16" overall; weighed a bit less than 7-1/2 ounces.

Listed here for the first time anywhere are seven basic types. Over 20 models were made and likely over 50 variations (not including grips, markings, finishes, etc.). Their semi-miniature size makes this diminutive handgun a fascinating arm to collect. All production was batch numbered 1 to 1000. All models have folding triggers. Publication in 2004 of *Baby Hammerless Revolvers* by Sellers greatly expands the horizons for assembling an even larger number of variants for these intriguing little revolvers.

The two most basic types are **bird's-head butts** (made prior to 1910) and **square butts** (made 1910 and later). Those revolvers marked MODEL 1910 merely indicate the change over to the slightly larger square butt type; later model markings (i.e. Model 1911, Model 1916, Model 1918, Model 1921, etc.) merely indicate the year of manufacture.

BABY HAMMERLESS markings (often with patent dates and Model year) are found on the topstrap over cylinder on all solid frame models. NEW BABY markings are found on the barrel of topbreak/tip-up types. ("New Baby's" were not made by Sedgley).

Grips are usually hard rubber, but pearl is quite commonly seen; worth 10 percent premium. Nickel finish most common; blue very scarce and worth 25 percent premium. *Mechanical condition, most important!* Values shown here are for specimens in perfect working order. If broken, as is quite common, values lessen by 40-50 percent. Note: Values shown here are for higher ranges of condition of "Excellent" and "Near Mint" and diminished considerably if less than "Excellent".

FIRST TYPE WITH BIRD'S-HEAD BUTT:

8A-012.1

Small solid frame, six-shot 22 rimfire Short. Smallest of the group. 3-11/16" overall; 1-1/4" barrel. PATENTS PENDING markings often seen:
8A-012.1 Values—Exc. **$150**   Near Mint **$300**

8A-012.2

Small frame tip-up NEW BABY. 22 rimfire Short. 4-7/16" overall. 2" barrel:
8A-012.2 Values—Exc. **$175**   Near Mint **$350**

8A-012.3

Large solid frame 32 centerfire. With or without loading gate. 5" overall. 1-3/4" barrel. (Specimens marked WESTERN ARMS CO or KONQUEROR" (sic) or SPECIAL MODEL, etc. are worth 25 percent premium:
8A-012.3 Values—Exc. **$190**   Near Mint **$325**

Large solid frame eight-shot 22 rimfire. (Not illus.) Looks about identical above. Very scarce:
8A-012.4 Values—Exc. **$450**   Near Mint **$600**

MODEL 1910 AND LATER SQUARE BUTT TYPE:

8A-012.5

Small frame six-shot 22 rimfire Short. Overall 4-1/16". Barrel 1-3/8":
8A-012.5 Values—Exc. **$150**   Near Mint **$300**

8A-012.7

Small frame EJECTOR MODELCal. 22 Long rimfire. A very narrow slot cut on the front right side of frame allows the entire cylinder to be quickly removed for extraction and reloading when the spring retained centerpin is partially withdrawn. Marked also on topstrap EJECTOR MODEL:
8A-012.7 Values—Exc. **$175**   Near Mint **$300**

8A-012.6

Large frame. Five-shot 32 centerfire. 4-1/2" overall. 1-11/16" barrel or 8 shot caliber .22 long RF:
8A-012.6 Values—Exc. **$225**   Near Mint **$400**

8A-012.8

Small frame Tip-up/Topbreak NEW BABY. Six-shot 22 rimfire. Overall 4-3/4". Barrel 2":
8A-012.8 Values—Exc. **$200**   Near Mint **$350**

THOMAS K. BACON, FIREARMS MANUFACTURER

Thomas K. Bacon (1813-1873) was directly associated with three companies bearing his name. Two of those companies were in business simultaneously, often lending confusion to the collector trying to distinguish the sequence in which Bacon arms were produced. The well-researched articles in the 1982-83 issues of the *Bulletin of the American Society of Arms Collectors* by Lowell J. Wagner are credited for finally placing the arms of this maker in proper perspective.

A machinist by trade, it is believed that Bacon's first employment in the gun industry was with Ethan Allen in the mid-1840s, although their association likely started earlier. Located in Grafton, Massachusetts in 1840, Bacon was known to have purchased real estate from Ethan Allen in that year, remaining there until 1842 when he relocated to Norwich, Connecticut, the very same year that Ethan Allen moved to that manufacturing town. Allen and Thurber record books show Bacon manufacturing "cones and trigger guards" for Allen in 1846, while the Norwich business directory of that same year listed Bacon at his own "armory." Although Allen left Norwich in 1847, it is clear that Bacon remained on, forming the first of the companies bearing his name, **Bacon & Company**, sometime between the years 1847 and 1850. He remained in business producing handguns under that name until 1857, the company's products including underhammer pepperboxes and single shot pistols (Bacon called them "Undercocks") and single shot bar hammer and ring trigger percussion pistols. Production

quantities were likely quite small as indicated by records showing their total employees to have been but fourteen.

Although yet unproven, Bacon is believed to have planned production of percussion revolvers of his own design. Likely encountering difficulty with financing such an enlarged undertaking, production at "Bacon & Co." ceased with Thomas Bacon finding employment almost immediately as superintendent of the recently established (1856) Manhattan Firearms Company of Norwich, Connecticut. His association with Manhattan was short-lived, leaving in 1858 after but one year, to form his second firm **Bacon Manufacturing Company.** (Manhattan subsequently sued Bacon to prevent his forming the new company to manufacture revolvers, Bacon having earlier agreed when originally employed, not to compete against Manhattan for 20 years. The contract, however, had never been executed and the lawsuit was dropped.)

Bacon, along with a few other revolver manufacturers lost a patent infringement suit brought by Smith & Wesson in 1862 (see chapter V-G S&W). **The arms remaining on hand at their plant or in a semi-state of manufacture were required to be additionally marked with the Smith & Wesson patent date.** It is believed only 1,124 of the large Navy model then in production were so marked with the S&W/Rollin White PAT.APRIL 3, 1855 on the cylinders only, to identify them. Such markings add to their collectibility for S&W collectors and usually adds a premium of 20 to 40 percent to the values.

Bacon Manufacturing Co. firearms were made in Norwich with Thomas Bacon supervising production until 1863. By then, Charles Converse, the largest shareholder and landlord of the factory, became displeased with Bacon's managership, taking personal control and forcing Bacon out of the company by October, 1863. Bacon Manufacturing Co. continued operations under that name until 1868, making percussion and cartridge revolvers, single shot cartridge pistols and a pepperbox. The latter two years saw extremely little business. With the demise of Bacon Manufacturing Co., its former manager and chief shareholder Converse, along with four other Bacon employees formed the Hopkins & Allen Manufacturing Company in May, 1868. Among the original stockholders were Samuel Hopkins and Charles W. Allen. H & A purchased the assets of Bacon Manufacturing Co., commencing manufacture of firearms with the equipment and remaining parts from Bacon Manufacturing Co. H & A remained in business until 1915.

Following his forced departure from Bacon Manufacturing Company, Thomas Bacon in late 1863 or early 1864 formed a third firm **Bacon Arms Company,** with operations continuing in Norwich. For reasons yet undetermined, he resigned and sold his interests in the firm December, 1865. Very little is known of him following that venture. Norwich directories for 1866 and 1867 list him variously as "pistol maker" and "pistol manufacturing," the 1868 directory shows him as "inventor," while 1869-1870 editions list him as an "agent" for an unknown product. Directories prior to his 1873 death merely list his name with no occupation indicated.

The Bacon Arms Company continued in operation until 1888, the longest of the three Bacon firms. In addition to the many arms listed here, they also manufactured many inexpensive spur trigger revolvers with names such as BONANZA; PENETRATOR; EXPRESS; RELIABLE and CONQUEROR. They also made a sidehammer single shot 12 gauge shotgun; this latter arm was still in production in 1888 when the firm closed down, its assets being purchased by the Crescent Arms Company who continued production of the shotgun at the Norwich plant.

Bacon Mfg. Co. Navy Model Revolvers

Bacon Manufacturing Co., Norwich, Connecticut, so-called "Navy Model" Revolvers. Made c. early 1860s. Total quantity estimated 900.

38 caliber rimfire. Six-shot. 7-1/2" octagonal barrel. Single action. Large size iron frame; spur trigger; square butt. Finish blued. Walnut grips.

Barrel marking: BACON MFG CO NORWICH CONN.

Bacon's hopes for this handgun being adopted by U.S. government for military service never materialized. They are the largest of the metallic cartridge Bacon firearms produced and have been traditionally considered as "Secondary Martial" handguns by collectors. At least four distinct variations exist and experimental types are also known. They are found only with the Bacon Mfg. Co. markings and not with other trade names as has been indicated by other listings. Cylinder marked PAT. APRIL 3, 1855 indicating the Smith & Wesson / Rollin White patent date (see Introductory "Bacon Firearms" text); worth premium of 20 to 40 percent.

**8A-014
Variant**

Cylinder must be removed for loading. In place of the hinged lever under barrel it has a short projecting cylinder pin, held in place by a small push-button latch on its underside. Believed an evasion of the Smith & Wesson patent. The marketplace yet to determine a firm valuation. A premium of 15 to 30 percent likely. **8A-013.5**

Variant of First Type. Estimated quantity 150. Unique cylinder with removable knurled edge disc at rear fitted onto the extended cylinder ratchet. Believed to be an evasion of the Smith & Wesson patent in order to avoid a patent infringement suit:

8A-014   Values—Good **$800**   Fine **$2,250**

**8A-013
1st Type**

First Type. Estimated quantity 400. Cylinder must be removed for loading by withdrawing the jointed/hinged lever under barrel which acts both as a center pin and ejector rod for spent cartridges. Quite often found with scroll engraving on frame which will not significantly increase price:

8A-013   Values—Good **$650**   Fine **$2,000**

Variant of First Type. Quantity unknown; very limited. Presumed the scarcest of these large Bacon "Navy Models."

**8A-015
2nd Type**

Second Type. Estimated quantity 325. Swing-out cylinder with removable iron rod ejector under barrel. Bears additional markings on side of barrel C. W. HOPKINS/PATENTED MAY 27, 1862. The cylinder is also marked PAT. APRIL 3, 1855. on those taken over by Smith & Wesson:

8A-015   Values—Good **$800**   Fine **$2,250**

Bacon Mfg. Co. Swing-Out Cylinder Revolver

Bacon Manufacturing Company, Norwich, Connecticut, C. W. Hopkins Swing-Out Cylinder Revolver. Made c. early to mid-1860s. Total quantity estimated at several hundred.

Caliber 32 rimfire. Six-shot. 4" octagon barrel. Blued finish. Walnut grips.

Barrel markings: BACON MFG. CO. NORWICH CONN.on

side and C. W. HOPKINS, PATENTED MAY 27, 1862 on opposite side. These are also occasionally seen with markings UNION ARMS CO. N.Y. or WESTERN ARMS CO. NEW YORKas made by Bacon for other dealers or agents using trade names. Slight premiums may be added for these latter two markings.

This scarce spur trigger revolver (almost identical in contour to the 38 caliber "Navy" model, but in diminutive size) had the unusual feature of a cylinder swinging to the right for loading and an ejector rod secured beneath barrel:

8A-016

8A-016   Values—Good **$300**   Fine **$950**
Small Frame Model. Calibers 22 and 25 rimfire. (Not illus.) Same profile as the 32 cal., but smaller overall. 2-1/2" barrel. Very

scarce:
8A-016.5   Values—Good **$450**   Fine **$1,200**

Bacon Mfg. Co. Removable Trigger Guard Pocket Revolver

Bacon Manufacturing Co., Norwich, Connecticut, Removable Trigger Guard Pocket Revolver. Made c. early 1860s. Total quantity estimated 300.

32 caliber rimfire. Two noticeably different frame sizes with cylinders for 32 short rimfire and 32 long rimfire. Six-shot. 4"

8A-017

octagon barrel. Unusual design of trigger guard which unscrews, acting as lock for center pins; cylinder must be removed for loading. Blued finish. Walnut grips; square butt, short frame worth premium.

Barrel marking: BACON MFG. CO. NORWICH, CONN./DEPOT 297 BROADWAY, N.Y. These are occasionally found unmarked and values are usually 10 percent to 20 percent less than indicated for such specimens.

Production of this model was cut short by action of Smith & Wesson for infringement on their control of the Rollin White bored-through-cylinder patent. Specimens in 22 caliber rimfire with 2-1/2" barrel very rare will bring premium: exercise extreme caution; spurious example reported:
8A-017   Values—Good **$225**   Fine **$900**

Bacon Mfg. Co. Pocket Revolver

Bacon Manufacturing Co., Norwich, Connecticut, Pocket Revolver. Made c. early 1860s. Total quantity limited.

32 rimfire six-shot with 4" to 6" octagon barrel. Spur trigger; square butt. Blued finish. Walnut grips.

Barrel marked: BACON MFG. CO. NORWICH, CONN. Occasionally seen marked WESTERN ARMS CO., NEW YORK or UNION ARMS CO. NEW YORK (NY often omitted); worth small premiums. This model often found unmarked; values approximately 10 percent to 20 percent less than shown herein for such specimens. Rare variation also known with Hopkins swing-out cylinder feature with patent markings; will bring premium.

Judging from the scarcity of this model, it would appear that production was cut short quickly by action of Smith & Wesson due to infringement of their Rollin White patent:

8A-018

8A-018   Values—Good **$175**   Fine **$475**
Small Frame Model. Calibers 22 and 25 rimfire. (Not illus.) Same profile as 32 caliber, but smaller overall. Seven-shot. 2-1/2" octagon barrel. Rare:
8A-018.5   Values—Good **$350**   Fine **$850**

Bacon Arms Co. Pocket Revolver

8A-019

Bacon Arms Company, Norwich, Connecticut, Pocket Revolver. Made c. mid-1860s. Total quantity estimated 1,000.

32 caliber rimfire. 4" round barrel. Five-shot; semi-fluted cylinder. Spur trigger; rounded iron frame. Blued finish. Walnut grips; bird's-head butt most often seen. Variations noted include square butt and non-fluted cylinder.

Barrel marked: BACON ARMS CO., NORWICH, CONN. Marking variations may be encountered with the additional legend CAST STEEL or the abbreviation CT. in place of CONN.

Mounted on the barrel is removable ejector rod:
8A-019   Values—Good **$175**   Fine **$475**

Bacon Arms Co. Pocket Revolver

Bacon Arms Company, Norwich, Connecticut, Pocket Revolver. Made c. late 1860s. Total quantity estimated at a few hundred.

32 caliber rimfire. 4" round barrel. Five-shot straight, unfluted cylinder. Rounded iron frame; spur trigger. Blued finish. Walnut grips; square butt.

Barrel marking: BACON ARMS CO., NORWICH, CONN. Variations may be encountered with the additional legend CAST STEEL and the abbreviation CT. in place of CONN.

These were a continuation of the percussion revolvers (*q.v.*) of the same shape, but were made as cartridge revolvers, not conversions:

8A-020

8A-020	Values—Good **$185**	Fine **$475**

Bacon Arms Co. Pepperbox Revolver

8A-021

Bacon Arms Co., Norwich, Connecticut, Pepperbox Revolver. Made c. late 1860s. Total quantity estimated 1,000.

22 caliber rimfire. Six-shot. Barrel cluster of 2-1/2" length. Iron frame; spur trigger. Blued finish usual, but also common in silvered frame with blued barrels or entirely silver finish. Rosewood grips, square butt.

Barrel marking: BACON ARMS CO. NORWICH, CONN.with or without PATENTED MAY 29, 1860. (Unmarked specimens often encountered; values slightly less than those shown here.)

Barrel cluster must be removed for loading and spent cartridge ejection. *See also Governor.*

Standard Type As Described Above:
8A-021   Values—Good **$550**   Fine **$1,400**
Variant With Loading Port on Right Side of Frame; *very scarce, be wary of spurious alterations. Although the variant is reported in various reference works, almost all specimens viewed have been regarded as later era, non-factory alterations. If proven authentic, specimens would be valued at double for the standard type.*
8A-022

Bacon Mfg. Co. Single Shot Pistols

Bacon Manufacturing Company, Norwich, Connecticut, Single Shot Pistols. Made c. early to mid-1860s. Total quantity estimated 2,400.

32 caliber rimfire. 4" or 5" octagon barrel pivots to right for loading. Iron frame; spur trigger. Blue finish. Walnut grips; square butt. Brass frame variants are known; rare; worth premium values.

High Standing Recoil Shield Type, a.k.a. Large Frame Type. Caliber 32 long rimfire. Estimated quantity 1,600. Most often encountered style. Small lip protrudes from botttom, breech of bar.

Barrel marking: BACON MFG. CO. NORWICH, CONN. Occasionally found with no barrel markings present; such specimens will bring approximately 10 percent to 20 percent less than values indicated here. Encountered with and without extractor device; values apparently the same for either. rel fits into notch on recoil shield. Plain, unengraved frame. Bold size marking on barrel approximately 1/16" high:
8A-023   Values—Good **$175**   Fine **$475**
Flush Fitted Recoil Shield Type, a.k.a. Small Frame Type. Caliber 32 short rimfire. Estimated quantity 800. Noticeably lighter weight construction and thinner grips. Found in 6" barrel length also. Broad scroll engraving standard on frame. No lip on breech of barrel; breech variations encountered. Very tiny barrel markings; letters only 1/32" high:
8A-024   Values—Good **$250**   Fine **$550**
Variant Small Brass Frame Type. Caliber 32 short rimfire. Breech of barrel has short protruding center section which fits dovetail fashion into matching mortise on frame. Tiny letter barrel markings:

8A-023
High Standing
Recoil Shield

8A-024
Flush Fitted
Recoil Shield

8A-024.5
Variant
Small Frame

8A-024.5	Values—Good **$375**	Fine **$725**

C. H. Ballard Single Shot Deringer

C. H. Ballard, Worcester, Massachusetts, Single Shot Deringer. Made c. 1870. Total quantity estimated at few thousand.

41 caliber rimfire. 2-13/16" part octagon/part round barrel; tips downward to load. Brass frame with silver plated finish; barrel blued or plated. Walnut grips; bird's-head butt.

Barrel markings on top: BALLARD'Sand usually on left side of barrel: C. H. BALLARD & CO/WORCESTER MASS/PAT'D JUNE 22, 1869.

Brass Frame Model:
8A-025   Values—Good **$600**   Fine **$1,750**
Iron Frame Model: (Found irregularly scattered throughout brass frame production.) Bears only the top barrel markings BALLARD'S
8A-026   Values—Good **$700**   Fine **$2,000**
30 Caliber R. F. Ballard:
Noticeably smaller brass frame is flat, lacking the distinctive flare around the recoil shield and breech area; other design differences. 3-1/8" part octagon/round barrel also of slender

8A-025
41 Caliber

8A-026.5
30 Caliber

proportions; unmarked. Checkered walnut grips. Very rare.
8A-026.5   Values—Good **$3,500**   Fine **$5,000**

Billings Vest Pocket Single Shot Deringer

Charles E. Billings, Hartford, Conn., Vest Pocket Single Shot Deringer. (Not illus.) Made c. 1865 to 1868. Quantity unknown. Very rare.

32 caliber rimfire. 2-1/2" round barrel. Blued finish. Large size handle with walnut grips.

Barrel marking: BILLINGS VEST POCKET PISTOL PAT APRIL 24, 1866.

Very similar in outline to the Remington-Rider Deringer, but entirely different mechanically with a rolling block type action:
8A-027   Values—Good **$2,000**   Fine **$4,500**

Billings Combination Bowie Knife-Pistol

Charles E. Billings, Hartford, Conn. Combination Bowie Knife-Pistol. Quantity unknown. Possibly experimental or prototype. The patent issued for this September 22, 1868 titled it "Pistol and Sword," and patent drawing illustrates the invention with a clip point Bowie knife blade and hilt identical to illustration. Rare.

32-caliber rimfire. Brass hilt with black ebony grips. Fashioned integral with a 12-inch Bowie knife blade (17" overall). Single-shot pistol is built into the handle with the 4-inch brass barrel inset within the edge of the handle (hinged at its muzzle and made integral with the upper cross guard). Barrel opened by latch inset at the top of the pommel. Hammer also inset at pommel is manually cocked for firing; the trigger, a small button at bottom of handle. Marked CHARLES E. BILLINGS on pommel and HARTFORD, CONN.at center of cross guard. Accompanied with its silver-mounted, embossed leather sheath. No known sales; value estimated in mid- to high five figures. As a young man in the 1850s, Charles Billings was employed by Sam Colt. By 1865 he had become president of the Roper Repeating Rifle Company (*see Chapter XV Revolving Rifles.*) and

8A-027.5

8A-027.5

in 1869 formed a partnership with Christopher Spencer (noted inventor of the Spencer Repeating Rifle) as "Billings & Spencer," manufacturing mostly parts for other mfrs.
8A-027.5

Bismarck Pocket Revolver

8A-028

Bismarck Marked Pocket Revolver. Maker unknown. Quantity unknown; very limited. c.1870s.

22 caliber rimfire; Seven-shot. 3" round ribbed barrel. Brass frame finished in the bright; spur trigger; bird's-head butt; rosewood grips with very low placement of grip screw; plated barrel and straight, unfluted cylinder. A direct infringement on the S&W Model 1, 3rd Issue revolver with 2nd Issue style cylinder.

Barrel marked on top BISMARCK:
8A-028   Values—Very Good **$175**   Exc. **$450**

F. D. Bliss Pocket Revolver

8A-029

F. D. Bliss, New Haven, Connecticut, Pocket Revolver. Made c. 1863 to 1864. Total quantity estimated at 3,000.

25 caliber rimfire. Six-shot. 3-1/4" octagon barrel. Spur trigger. Blued finish. Walnut, rosewood or checkered hard rubber grips; square butt.

Barrel marking: F. D. BLISS NEW HAVEN CT

A distinguishing feature is the removable plate at rear of cylinder, not unlike versions made by Remington of their percussion revolvers. Bliss was earlier in partnership with Alfred D. Goodyear in the manufacture of percussion revolvers. After the dissolution of their business, Bliss continued manufacturing arms with this small revolver which was based on the pattern of the earlier percussion model.

Early variants (very rare) with all brass frames are known and will bring a considerable premium over the prices indicated here. An automatic ejector variant is also known (in 22 caliber rimfire and on the brass frame) with extracting mechanism built onto the hammer. Extremely rare and also worth considerable premium over values indicated here:

8A-029   Values—Good **$250**   Fine **$850**

Bonnie Blue 22 Blank Deringer

Bonnie Blue 22 Blank Deringer made by Hopkins & Allen of Norwich, Connecticut c.1870s. Quantity unknown. Very scarce.

Caliber 22 Rimfire blank. Intended as a noise-maker only. Barrel not bored out. Only two moving pieces. Hammer and breech block single unit. Iron frame and barrel.

Although unmarked, the name BONNIE BLUE is that under which it was advertised. It very likely had other names applied, especially by collectors of recent vintage, such as "Fourth of July Pistol." Considered among the scarcest of the Hopkins & Allen deringers:

8A-029.5

8A-029.5   Values—Good **$175**   Fine **$325**

Boom Pocket Revolver

Boom marked Pocket Revolver. Made by C. S. Shattuck of Hatfield, Massachusetts c.1880s. Quantity unknown; limited.

22 caliber rimfire. Six-shot. 2-1/8" octagon barrel. Iron frame; spur trigger; bird's-head butt; rosewood grips. Nickeled finish.

Barrel marked BOOM on top, and PAT. NOV. 4.1879 on side.

Collectibility based on the distinctive, unique swing out cylinder. *See also "Shattuck Pocket Revolver"*:

8A-030   Values—Very Good **$325**   Exc. **$750**

8A-030

Boss Single Shot Blank Deringer

Boss marked Single Shot Blank "Deringer." Invented by L. Holt & J.C. Marshall, Springfield Massachusetts. Manufactured by Dexter Smith (son of Horace Smith of S&W). Distributed by Buckland Brothers, wholesale jewelers of Springfield, c.1870s. Formerly believed to have been made by Hopkins & Allen. Quantity unknown; likely few hundred; quite scarce. Patented April 22, 1873.

Although intended strictly as a 22 Rimfire blank noise-maker pistol, it does accept a 22 Short cartridge and likely would be quite dangerous if fired as barrel is much larger smooth bore caliber. Extremely simple mechanism; hammer and trigger one-piece. Nickname, with others of their type "Fourth of July pistol."

All iron; marked on top of breech BOSS:

8A-030.5   Values—Good **$200**   Fine **$475**

Brass frame made without trigger guard. 2" barrel marked on top 1776 and on side PAT.APR.22,73. Scarcer:

8A-030.6   Values—Good **$200**   Fine **$475**

8A-030.5

8A-030.6

C.C. Brand Single Shot Holster Pistol

8A-030.8

Christopher C. Brand, Norwich, Connecticut Single-Shot Breech-Loading Pistol. Patented (September 23, 1862). Large holster size; made circa mid-1860s. Quantities unknown; likely less than 50. Rare. (See also 9B-040 Brand Breechloading Carbine and 18-001 Brand Whaling Gun.)

Large "martial" size handgun; caliber 52 Spencer rimfire. 8-1/2" round barrel; steel frame, blue and casehardened finish. Unmarked. Walnut grips. Serial numbered. When small latch at top of backstrap is activated, it pivots a toggle joint allowing breechblock to open rearward in groove along backstrap for loading. Presumed that Brand made these odd handguns hoping to secure a U.S. Gov't. contract during the Civil war; without success. Value estimated in the mid- to high four-figure range. **8A-030.8**

H.A. Briggs Single Shot Deringer

Horace Briggs, Norwich, Connecticut, Single Shot Deringer. Circa 1850s. Made by D.B. Wesson, Norwich, Connecticut. Total quantity likely well under 500. *Rare:*

22 caliber rimfire. 4" part round/part octagon barrel. Blued finish. Walnut grips; square butt.

Marked on left side of frame: H. A. BRIGGS/NORWICH. CT. (most found unmarked).

The breech action is similar to the well known Flobert type:

8A-031   Values—Good **$1,250**   Fine **$2,750**

8A-031

"BRITISH BULL DOG" Marked Revolver   *See Iver Johnson 8A-068.8 and Forehand & Wadsworth 8A-061*

Brooklyn Arms Co. Pocket Revolver

Brooklyn Arms Co., Brooklyn, New York. Slocum Front-Loading Pocket Revolver. Made c. 1863 to 1864. Total quantity estimated at over 10,000.

32 caliber rimfire. Five-shot. 3" round barrel. A unique design with individual chambers in the form of sliding tubes within cutouts on the cylinder. Chambers slide forward one at a time over a fixed rod on right side to expose, load and eject.

Brass frame silver plated; barrel and cylinder blued or plated. Walnut grips; irregular, almost bag-like shaped, handle.

Barrel marked: B. A. CO. PATENTED APRIL 14, 1863. Decorative scroll engraving standard on frame.

The Slocum was another attempt at circumventing the Rollin White bored-through-cylinder patent controlled by Smith & Wesson.

Separate Chambers Style as Described Above:
8A-032   Values—Good **$350**   Fine **$950**
Variant With Standard Straight Unfluted Cylinder; 32 rimfire, six-shot. 3" round barrel completely unmarked. Brass frame, spur trigger and identical decorative scroll engraving. Distinctive flat butt flared slightly at rear. Walnut grips. Estimated under 100 manufactured:
8A-033   Values—Good **$450**   Fine **$1,250**
Small Frame Model 22 Rimfire. Seven-shot. 2-1/2" round barrel; straight cylinder. Square butt. Iron frame made without backstrap; has cutout on recoil shield and channel on frame to allow loading of cartridges. Noticeably different frame profile than the above two models. Specimens observed all unmarked. Design attributed to Frank Slocum and mfr. by Brooklyn Arms Co. Circa 1860s. Quantity estimated under 150. Rare.
8A-033.5   Values—Good **$775**   Fine **$1,750**

8A-032
Separate chambers

8A-033
Straight cylinder

8A-033.5
Small frame .22

Brown Mfg. (& Merrimack Arms Co.) Southerner Deringer

Brown Manufacturing Company and Merrimack Arms Company, Newburyport, Massachusetts, "Southerner" Deringer. Made 1866 to 1873. Total quantity estimated 16,500.

41 Rimfire. 2-1/2" octagon barrel pivots sideways to load. Extractor mounted under barrel at breech. Barrels blued; iron frames blued or casehardened; brass frames silver finished. Walnut or rosewood grips. Interesting to note that for the large estimated quantity made, the great majority of specimens that appear on the collectors' markets show considerable wear.

Large marking SOUTHERNER on barrels. Maker marks as shown below. A few second quality frames marked IMPERFECT; rare; worth premium.

Made by and marked on side of barrel: MERRIMACK ARMS & MANUFACTURING CO/NEWBURYPORT, MASS/PATENTED APRIL 9, 1867. Quantity estimated 6500. Made 1866-1869. Serial number range 1 to 6500:

8A-034 / 034.5

Brass frame. Estimated at 70 percent of production: Approx. 6,500:

8A-034   Values—Good **$300**   Fine **$950**

Iron frames. Although estimated at 30 percent of production (same as Brown) they are seen with much less frequency. Serial range 1950 to 4500:

8A-034.5   Values—Good **$375**   Fine **$1,100**

Made by and marked: BROWN MANUFACTURING CO/NEWBURYPORT, MASS/PAT APR.9, 1869. Made 1869 to 1873. Quantity estimated 10,000. Serial range 1 to 10,000:

Brass frame. Estimated 70 percent of production: Approx 10,000:

8A-035   Values—Good **$300**   Fine **$950**

Iron frame. Estimated 30 percent of production; serial numbers appear throughout entire range:

8A-035.5   Values—Good **$375**   Fine **$1,100**

8A-036

Bag handle variant; special long bag shaped handle with rounded butt. 2-1/2" or 4" octagon barrel. Found only in the brass frame model made by Brown:

8A-036   Values—Good **$1,250**   Fine **$3,500**

W.H. Brown Pocket Rifle

8A-036.5

William H. Brown, Worcester, Mass. Single Shot, Breechloading "Pocket Rifle" or "Buggy Rifle." Patented March 4, 1862 and manufactured same era. Quantity unknown; limited.

22 rimfire with round 22-inch barrel (usually blued). Underlever opens down and forward; barrel slides forward for loading. Nickeled brass frame. Detachable skeleton-style iron

stock. Usually unmarked. (Note: shorter barrels as well as pistols not adapted for shoulder stock possible to encounter.) Values for pistol accompanied with stock:

8A-036.5   Values—Very Good **$1,500**   Exc. **$3,500**
Pistol only, lacking stock:
8A-036.6   Values—Very Good **$750**   Exc. **$1,750**

Chafee Alarm Gun. *Was 8A-036.5; See 18-079*

G. & J. Chapman Pocket Revolver

G. and J. Chapman, Philadelphia, Pennsylvania, Pocket Revolver. Made c. 1860. Total quantity unknown; limited.

32 caliber rimfire. Seven-shot. 4" round barrel. Brass frame. Barrel and cylinder blued. Walnut grips; bird's-head butt.

Marked on frame or backstrap: G & J CHAPMAN/PHILADª/PATENT APPLIED FOR/1861. Specimens also encountered unmarked. Very scarce:

8A-037   Values—Good **$900**   Fine **$2,500**

8A-037

Chicago Firearms Co. Protector Palm Pistol

8A-038

Chicago Firearms Co., Chicago, Illinois, Protector Palm Pistol. Made c. 1890s. Total quantities estimated 12,800.

32 caliber extra short rimfire. Squeezer type pistol with rotary chambers. Nickel plated finish standard; blued finish quite scarce and will bring a premium value; estimated 1000 blued; fall in serial range 3700 to 5400. Hard rubber "grip" plates with pearl or ivory occasionally encountered and will bring premium.

Marking on sideplate: CHICAGO FIREARMS CO., CHICAGO, ILL. and THE PROTECTOR, with patent dates.

The matching, checkered, hard rubber grip pad (as shown) standard. Approximately 1000 made without pad or any provision for same; scarce; worth small premium.

A supplementary device known as a "double ring finger guard" was available for the gun, fitting over the muzzle of the barrel. Nickel finished. Marked JOHN T. NORRIS / SPRINGFIELD, OHIO. If authentic will be worth premium of 100 to 150 percent. Caution is suggested on this accessory as very well made spurious examples are known.

Originally classified as a "curio and relic" under the Federal Gun Control Act and subject to its provisions, this arm has since been declassified and is considered as an "antique":

8A-038   Values—Very Good **$1,100**   Exc. **$2,000**

William J. Christy Pepperbox

8A-038.5

William J. Christy, Philadelphia, Pennsylvania. 4-barrel Pepperbox c. 1866. Quantity unknown. Extremely rare.

32 Rimfire. Cluster of four 3-1/4" barrels. Extremely intricate, complicated mechanism. Barrels swivel for loading and simultaneously cock hammers which have various adjustments for firing. Trigger safety guard. Marked on top of brass frame W.J. CHRISTY/PAT 1866.

To date, but one elaborately engraved, silver finished specimen with relief carved ivory grips has been recorded (illustrated here). The Pepperbox is not valued here.
8A-038.5

Colt Firearms Company   *See Chapter V-B, Colt Firearms.*

"C.K." marked Single Shot 22 Deringer   *See "O.K." Deringer.*

Columbian Firearms Mfg. Co.   *See Baby Hammerless.*

"Comet" marked Spur Trigger 22 Cal. Revolver   *See Prescott Pistol Company Revolvers.*

D.D. Cone 22 and 32 Rimfire Revolvers   *See Uhlinger.*

Connecticut Arms Co. Pocket Revolver

8A-039
Standard

8A-039
Late Variant

Connecticut Arms Co., Norfolk, Connecticut, Cup Primed, Front Loading Pocket Revolver. Made c. mid-1860s. Total quantity estimated at least 2,700.

28 caliber cup primed cartridge. Six-shot. 3" octagon barrel. Brass frame; silver plated finish. Steel parts blued. Walnut grips; square butt.

Barrel marked: CONN. ARMS CO., NORFOLK, CONN.with single line 1864 patent dates on cylinder.

This front-loading revolver features a hook type ejector on the right side of frame. It is one of the various handguns made which attempted to circumvent the Smith & Wesson controlled bored-through-cylinder patent of Rollin White. A scarce, late variant is occasionally seen with a large knob tip on the ejector lever and two-line patent dates (1864 and 1866) on cylinder and will bring a premium:
8A-039   Values—Good **$250**   Fine **$650**

Connecticut Arms & Manf. Co. S.S. Deringer

8A-040

Connecticut Arms and Manufacturing Co., Naubuc, Connecticut, Hammond Patent Single Shot Deringer; a.k.a. "Bulldog." Made c. 1866 to late 1880s. Total quantity estimated 8,000.

44 caliber rimfire with 4" octagon barrel standard. Also known in 50 caliber rimfire with 6" barrel, but rare and will bring considerable premium. Breechblock pivots to left for loading. Iron frame with casehardened finish; barrel blued; a few known with original nickel finish and extra markings on side of barrel BULL_DOZER Rare; worth premium.

Marked: CONNECTICUT ARMS & MANF. CO. NAUBUC CONN. PATENTED OCT 25, 1864.

Other variations are known such as longer barrel, a line throwing pistol, a target model with 12" barrel caliber 32 rimfire, a pistol-carbine caliber 44 smoothbore and caliber 22 rimfire types both with and without attachable wire type shoulder stocks. All considered rare and worth premium:

8A-040   Values—Very Good **$475**   Exc. **$1,500**

Continental Arms Co. Pepperbox

8A-041

Continental Arms Co., Norwich, Connecticut, Pepperbox known as the "Ladies Companion." Patented by Charles A. Converse and Samuel S. Hopkins. Made c. late 1860s. Total

quantity estimated 800. Manufactured by Bacon Manufacturing Co. and marketed under this name to avoid confusion with a similar pepperbox by Bacon Arms Co.

22 caliber rimfire. Five-shot. Barrel cluster of 2-1/2" length. Iron frame; blued finish. Rosewood grips; square butt.

Barrels marked: CONTINENTAL ARMS CO. NORWICH CT. PATENTED AUG. 28, 1866.

This unusual design features a shield which encircles the barrel cluster, causing the illusion of the barrel group having a cylinder at its breech. A loading gate cut-out is present on the frame, but no ejector device was provided. Also known in very rare brass frame variation which will bring a considerable premium. Manufactured in their very last years by Bacon Mfg. Co. of which Charles Converse was president:

8A-041   Values—Good **$550**   Fine **$1,600**

F. Copeland Pocket Revolvers

Frank Copeland, Worcester and Sterling, Massachusetts, Pocket Revolvers.

22 caliber rimfire; Worcester, Mass. manufacture. c.1860s. Seven-shot. 2-1/4" to 2-7/8" octagon barrel. Straight, unfluted cylinder with notches on front. Brass frame; spur trigger; bird's-head butt; walnut or rosewood grips. Early type shown, later variations have forward section of frame in contours of the 32 caliber Sterling, Mass. production.

Values here for unmarked specimens (most often found). When barrel marked F. COPELAND, WORCESTER, MASS.worth 30 percent premium:

8A-042   Values—Good **$185**   Fine **$500**
Ten-Shot 22 Rimfire. Rare oddity of which under 100 estimated made. Small *iron* frame with elnlarged front of frame to accept the ten-shot cylinder. 2-1/2" unmarked octagon barrel:
8A-042.5   Values—Good **$1,250**   Fine **$3,000**
32 Caliber Rimfire. Sterling, Mass. manufacture. c.1870s. Five-shot; semi-fluted cylinder; 2-3/4" octagon barrel; iron frame; spur trigger; bird's-head butt. Nickeled finish.

Marked on barrel: F. COPELAND, STERLING. MASS. (another known mkd HORNET):
8A-043   Values—Good **$175**   Fine **$475**

8A-042
22 Caliber

8A-042.5
Ten-Shot 22 Caliber

8A-043
32 Caliber

F. Copeland Pocket Rifle

Frank Copeland, Sterling, Massachusetts, Single Shot "Pocket Rifle." (Not illus.) Made late 1860s or 1870s. Very limited quantity.

32 caliber rimfire. 14" part octagon/part round barrel (other lengths likely). Odd dropping block action. Square butt.

Rosewood grips with matching short forend. Made to accept a Stevens type, detachable, skeleton stock.

Marked: F. COPELAND MAKER/STERLING, MASS. USA.

Values shown for gun only. If accompanied by original stock add premium:

8A-043.5 Values—Good **$750**   Fine **$1,650**

Cottrell Flashlight Gun

Cottrell's Flashlight Gun. S. P. Cottrell & Son, Buffalo, New York. Combination flashlight-revolver. Made circa 1920s. Quantity unknown. Rare.

An intriguing example of "firearms curiosa," pairing a firearm with a utilitarian device. A conventional appearing but specially devised two cell, nickel plated flashlight. Uniquely wired and internally designed for the unmarked, oddly shaped, seven shot 22 RF revolver rigidly fitted within the forward section. 3-3/4" overall; muzzle of the 1-1/2" barrel above and flush with lens.

Markings on body of flashlight S.P. COTTRELL & SON,NY/PAT. U.S. JUL. 10, 1923 and PAT. CAN. DEC. 26, 1922. Cottrell advertising literature claimed that "...aiming is unnecessary as the bullet must

8A-043.7

travel to center of light. The most practical disposal defense arm ever invented." Rare. (Collectors should verify if these unique arms are subject to the provisions and restrictions of the National Firearms Act before attempting acquisition or disposition.)

8A-043.7 Values—Very Good **$2,750**   Exc. **$4,000**

Cowles & Son Single Shot Deringer

Cowles and Son, Chicopee, Massachusetts, Single Shot Deringer. Made c. 1865-1876. Total quantity estimated at 3,600.

22 caliber rimfire or 30 caliber rimfire. 3-1/4" part-round, part-octagon barrel pivots sideways to load. Brass frame with silver plated finish. Barrel blued. Walnut or rosewood grips; bird's-head butt. Scarcer are the two flat butt variants with milled and/or round frames.

Barrel marked: COWLES & SON, CHICOPEE, MASS. Rare variant markings, all forerunners of Cowles & Son, are known W.W. COWLES, DEANE & CO, CHICOPEE, MASS (c. 1869; estimated quantity 100) and SMITH & DEANE (c. 1869; estimated quantity 50 or less). Premiums should be added to shown values for these:

8A-044

8A-044 Values—Good **$225**   Fine **$650**

Silas Crispin Revolver

Silas Crispin Revolver. Made c. late 1860s. Total quantity unknown; very rare.

8A-045

Unique 32 caliber cartridge with a belted rim. Six-shot. 5" octagon barrel. Distinctive split cylinder. Iron frame; blued finish.

Reported frame marking: SMITH ARMS CO., NEW YORK CITY. CRISPIN'S PAT. OCT. 3, 1865 while others are completely unmarked.

This rare and unusual arm was made to circumvent the Smith & Wesson owned Rollin White patent. It fired a unique cartridge which proved rather dangerous to load. Only a few specimens are known and they are highly prized pioneer efforts in the development of metallic cartridge handguns in America. Considered as an experimental rather than production piece:

8A-045 Values—Good **$8,000**   Fine **$20,000**

O.S. Cummings Pocket Revolver

O. S. Cummings, Lowell, Massachusetts, Pocket Revolver. Made c. 1870 to 1880. Total quantity made estimated 1,000. Identical to Smith & Wesson 1st Model, 3rd Issue revolver (*q.v.*).

22 caliber rimfire. Seven-shot. 3-1/8" round ribbed barrel. Iron frame; spur trigger; nickeled finish overall. Rosewood or walnut grips; bird's-head butt. Often encountered with markings lacking or defaced; value 20 to 40 percent less.

Barrel marked: O. S. CUMMINGS, LOWELL.

8A-046 Values—Very Good **$250**   Exc. **$575**

8A-046

Cummings & Wheeler Pocket Revolver

Cummings & Wheeler, Lowell, Massachusetts Pocket Revolver. Made circa 1870 to 1880. Total quantity unknown. Patterned very closely after the Smith & Wesson 1st Model 3rd Issue revolver (*q.v.*). Although similar to the O.S. Cummings above, has a distinctly different grip contour and other noticeable differences including the longer cylinder flutes.

22 caliber rimfire. Seven-shot. 3-1/2" round ribbed barrel. Iron frame; spur trigger; nickeled finish. Rosewood or walnut grips; bird's-head butt.

Marked around the rear of the cylinder: CUMMINGS & WHEELER. LOWELL, MASS:

8A-047

| 8A-047 | Values—Good **$300** | Fine **$650** |

C.N. Cutter Pocket Rifles and Pistols

8A-047.2

Charles N. Cutter, Worcester, Mass. (1877-1886). "Pocket Rifle" a.k.a. "Buggy Rifle." Patented breechloading firearm July 10, 1877 (with Frank Wesson, for whom he worked before striking out on his own in 1880). Quantity unknown; made circa 1880-1886.

32-caliber centerfire (other calibers likely); octagonal 18 and 20-inch barrels (other lengths likely) are blued; iron frames nickel finish. Center hammer with extracting lever on right side. Serial numbered and marked (top of breech) C.N. CUTTER. With detachable walnut buttstock (as shown) and matching forend (necessary to verify if subject to provisions of G.C.A.):
8A-047.2 Values—Very Good **$1,400** Exc. **$3,000**
Pocket rifle only, lacking stock:
8A-047.3 Values—Very Good **$600** Exc. **$1,250**
Pistol not adapted for stock. Barrel lengths 7 or 8 inches (others possible):
8A-047.4 Values—Very Good **$550** Exc. **$1,250**

Daigle Repeating Cane Gun

Marcelin Daigle; Houma, Louisiana. Repeating Cane Gun. Patent No. 139,305 of April 10, 1877. Maker possibly Julian Saget of New Orleans. Quantity unknown. Very Rare.

Caliber .22 rimfire. Ball or knob shaped, composition handle on 26" metal shaft with painted finish simulating wood. 34" overall. Shaft contains side-by-side barrel and magazine tube which holds twenty cartridges which are loaded from breech. Pulling rearward on handle exposes breech, allowing cartridge from magazine to enter carrier in line with chamber. Pushing forward on handle, chambers and fires cartridge

8A-047.5

simultaneously. Repeating the motion, extracts spent round and readies next one for firing.

Markings on silver plated ring at base of handle: Magazine Cane Gun-J. Saget/M. Daigle Patented April, 1877.
8A-047.5 Values—Very Good **$6,000** Exc. **$11,500**

"Dead Shot" 22 Caliber Pocket Revolver

Dead Shot Marked Pocket Revolver. Made by Bacon Arms Co. (*q.v.*) Norwich, Connecticut c. 1869-70s. Quantity estimated less than 1,000.

22 caliber rimfire. Six-shot. 3" round barrel. Iron spur trigger frame. Blued finish. Walnut grips; square butt.

At the expiration of the Rollin White patent, Bacon Arms Co. altered pepperboxes and pepperbox parts then in production, turning them into revolvers. They merely cut the front of the frame and shortened the barrel cluster to revolver cylinder length, added a new section of frame and topstrap (pinned), marketing them as small pocket revolvers.

Marked on topstrap: DEAD SHOT:

8A-047.5

| 8A-047.5 | Values—Good **$125** | Fine **$375** |

"Defender" Knife-Pistol   *See U.S. Small Arms Co.*

Deringer 22 Caliber Pocket Revolver

Deringer, Philadelphia, Pennsylvania, 22 Caliber Pocket Revolver. Made c. 1873 to 1879. Total quantity estimated at 6,900.

22 caliber rimfire. 3" barrel tips up to load. Six-shot.

Brass or iron frame. Silver or nickel plated finish. Barrel and cylinder either blued or plated. Walnut grips; bird's-head butt.

Barrels marked on side: DERINGER RIFLE & PISTOL WORKS PHILA. PA. with other markings as noted below. Serial numbered from 1 on up. The correct serial number is that on the grip frame; other numbers are merely the last two or three digits of that grip serial.

Although Henry Deringer died in 1868 and production of his percussion deringer pistols ceased approximately in that era, his relatives carried on his business for a short period with the manufacture of metallic cartridge revolvers.

First Model. Octagonal, ribbed barrel with flat sides at breech. Straight, unfluted cylinder with extension ratchet protruding from rear (which fits into recoil shield); early type barrel latch near the extreme front of frame. Barrel marked on top: DERINGER PHILADA. PAT^D JUNE 3, 1873. Approximately 400 made:

8A-048   Values—Good **$185**   Fine **$425**

Transitional Model. (Not illus.) Has appearance of Second Model with fluted cylinder, but retains the extension ratchet of First Model:

8A-048.5   Values—Good **$200**   Fine **$550**

8A-048

8A-049

Second Model. Round ribbed barrel with fluted sides at breech; semi-fluted cylinder with ratchet near flush with rear of cylinder; later style barrel latch at center of under-frame. Barrel marked on top: DERINGER PHILADA. Approximately 6,500 made:

8A-049   Values—Good **$150**   Fine **$375**

Deringer 32 Caliber Pocket Revolver

8A-050

Deringer, Philadelphia, Pennsylvania, 32 Caliber Pocket Revolver. Made c. 1874 to 1879. Total quantity estimated at 4,000.

32 caliber rimfire. 3-1/2" round barrel tips up to load. Also made in 2-3/4" length (very scarce) and will bring premium. Five-shot.

Brass or iron frame silver or nickel plated; barrel and cylinder plated or blued. Walnut grips; bird's-head butt.

Barrel marking on top: DERINGER PHILADA; marked on side: MANUF'D AT THE DERINGER RIFLE & PISTOL WORKS PHILA. PA.

Serial numbered from 1 on up; correct serial is that on the grip frame while other numbers are merely the last two or three digits of the grip serial:

8A-050   Values—Good **$150**   Fine **$375**

E. L. & J. Dickinson Single Shot Deringer

E. L. & J. Dickinson, Springfield, Massachusetts, Single Shot Deringer. Made c. 1863-1868. Total quantity estimated at under 1,600.

32 caliber rimfire. 3-3/4" octagon barrel (will vary slightly). Unusual manual ejector rack and pinion operated with folding lever on underside of barrel.

Brass frame, silver plated; iron parts blued. Walnut grips; square butt.

Barrel marking: E. L. & J. DICKINSON SPRINGFIELD MASS.

32 Caliber Model As Described Above:

8A-051   Values—Good **$300**   Fine **$800**

8A-051

22 Caliber Rimfire Variant: 3-3/4" barrel. Rare:

8A-052   Values—Good **$750**   Fine **$1,750**

"Dictator" Revolver   *See Chapter VII-A Hopkins & Allen.*

J. B. Driscole Single Shot Deringer

J. B. Driscole, Springfield, Massachusetts, Single Shot Deringer. Made c. 1870s; possibly late 1860s. Total quantity estimated as low as 200.

22 caliber rimfire. 3-1/2" octagon barrel pivots downward for loading. Brass frame with silver plated finish; barrel blued. Walnut grips; square butt. Unusual trigger-like locking latch release under breech of barrel.

Barrel marking: J. B. DRISCOLE:SPRINGFIELD MASS.:

8A-053   Values—Good **$375**   Fine **$1,250**

8A-053

Duplex (Marked) Two-Barrel Revolver   *See Osgood Gun Works.*

Eagle Arms Company 30 Caliber and 42 Caliber Cup-Primed Revolver
See Plant Manufacturing Company.

Eagle Co. Caliber 22 Rimfire Spur Trigger Revolver   *See Whitney Arms Company, Chapter V-J.*

Eagle Co. "Electric Hammerless" Revolver

Eagle Mfg. Co., Norwich, CT "Electric Hammerless" Revolver made by Otis Smith of Rockfall, CT. Made c. 1880s-1890s. Total quantity estimated a few hundred. Scarce. (Not illus.)

Caliber 32 S&W Short. 5-shot, 3-inch round barrel with rib made integral with frame. Nickel finish. Hard rubber grips with eaglehead design at top.

Marked EAGLE MFG CO. NORWICH, CT. U.S.A.on barrel and ELECTRIC HAMMERLESS on left side of barrel. Cylinder pin latch is made to give the appearance of a tip-up hinge when it is actually a solid frame (apparently typical of Otis Smith products).

8A-053.5   Values—Very Good **$250**   Exc. **$600**

Eclipse Single Shot Deringer

Eclipse Single Shot Deringer made by Iver Johnson of Worcester, Massachusetts and their predecessors Iver Bye & Co. of Worcester c. 1870s to 1887. James Bown & Company of Pittsburgh, although claiming to manufacture the gun were merely distributors.

Calibers 22 and 32 rimfire. Examples in 25 Stevens known (very rare; worth premium). Iron frame, spur trigger, bird's-head butt. 2-1/2" part round/octagon barrel pivots sideways to load. Nickel finish. Walnut grips.

Barrel marked on left ECLIPSE (unmarked specimens valued 30 to 40 percent less). Examples known marked TIGER made for J.H. Hall of Nashville, Tennessee, very scarce; worth premium.

22 caliber rimfire. Approximately 15,000 made:

8A-054   Values—Very Good **$175**   Exc. **$450**

8A-054

32 caliber rimfire. Approximately 2,000 made:

8A-054.5   Values—Very Good **$200**   Exc. **$500**

1876 Single Shot Deringer

8A-054.8

1876 (marked) Single Shot Deringer. c. 1875-1876. Made by (or for) Hyde and Shattuck, Springfield, Massachusetts. Estimated quantity 100.

22 rimfire. 2-3/4" barrel with ejector pivots sideways to load. Brass frame; nickel finish; walnut grips. Likely made to sell during Centennial celebrations of the Declaration of Independence. A very rare piece, and although none observed, it is possible that specimens could turn up unmarked or with variant markings.

Large numeral markings on left side of barrel 1876:

8A-054.8   Values—Good **$450**   Fine **$1,100**

James P. Fitch, New York City   *See James Reid Pocket Revolver, Model 2.*

FOREHAND AND WADSWORTH REVOLVERS

Sullivan Forehand was first employed by Allen & Wheelock in 1860 in an administrative capacity. He subsequently married Ethan Allen's daughter and their two sons were later to enter, with their father, in the firearms business.

Henry C. Wadsworth, while an officer in the Union army during the Civil War, also married one of Ethan Allen's daughters. Upon his discharge at the end of the war, he joined the Allen firm. In 1865 the firm name was changed to Ethan Allen & Co. to reflect the new partnership formed by E. Allen and his sons-in-law, Forehand and Wadsworth.

Following Allen's death in 1871, the firm was continued by Forehand and Wadsworth, undoubtedly with the same line of guns that were currently in production with the markings on a few pieces subsequently changed to reflect the new management. The entire Forehand and Wadsworth story has yet to be told.

Forehand and Wadsworth continued operations until Wadsworth's retirement in 1890. The company changed its name to the Forehand Arms Company under which it operated until 1898 with the death of Sullivan Forehand. The heirs are believed to have continued manufacturing operations until 1902 when taken over by Hopkins and Allen who continued to manufacture many of the same models changing only the markings.

The following listings are the more well known and popular collectors' F&Ws. There are other models bearing their name—especially in the double action (hammer and hammerless) types which are in mild demand and which may be generally categorized as "Suicide Specials." Listings for such pieces and price ranges are generally comparable to other similar types discussed in broad terms in the prefatory text to this chapter.

Forehand & Wadsworth Single Shot Deringer

Forehand and Wadsworth, Worcester, Massachusetts, Single Shot Deringer. a.k.a. "Muff Pistol." Made c. 1871 to 1890. Total quantity estimated up to 2,000.

22 caliber rimfire. 2" and 2-1/2" part round/part octagon barrel pivots sideways to load. Iron frame with silver plated or nickeled finish; blued or plated barrel. Walnut grips; bird's-head butt.

The barrel is marked: FOREHAND & WADSWORTH - WORCESTER Two variations of barrel lock.

One of the smallest American deringers made:
8A-055   Values—Good **$300**   Fine **$775**

8A-055

Forehand & Wadsworth Large Frame Single Shot Deringer

Forehand and Wadsworth, Worcester, Massachusetts single shot large frame deringer. Made c. 1871-1890. Quantity estimated 1500.(Not illustrated). Although similar profile to above, frame noticeably larger, rounded and with deeper cut on recoil shield. Quantity likely less than estimated. Specimens are seen with much less frequency than above.

22 Rimfire. 3" and 4" (scarce) part octagon/round barrel (varies slightly); pivots sideways to load.

Barrel marked FOREHAND & WADSWORTH/WORCESTER, MASS PAT MCH 7, 1865:
8A-055.5   Values—Good **$250**   Fine **$600**

Forehand & Wadsworth Single Shot Deringer

Forehand and Wadsworth, Worcester, Massachusetts, Single Shot Deringer. Made c. 1871 to 1890. Total quantity estimated under 1,000.

41 caliber rimfire. 2-1/2" barrel; round at muzzle, relief ring turned in center, rounded at rear with flat sides. Barrel pivots sideways to load. Rounded iron frame; spur trigger. Blued finish. Walnut grips; bird's-head butt.

Barrel marked on left side: FOREHAND & WADSWORTH/WORCESTER. MASS./PAT. MCH. 7, 1865 Scarce:
8A-056   Values—Very Good **$600**   Exc. **$1,450**

8A-056

Forehand & Wadsworth Old Model Army

Forehand and Wadsworth, Worcester, Massachusetts, Old Model, Single Action Army Revolver. Made c. mid-1870s. Total quantity estimated under 1,000.

44 caliber Russian centerfire. Six-shot. 7-1/2" round barrel. Finish usually nickel; blue will bring premium. Walnut grips.

Barrel marking: FOREHAND & WADSWORTH, WORCESTER, MASS. U.S. PAT'D OCT 22 '61, JUNE 27 '71, OCT 28 '73

8A-057

This large handgun has been traditionally classed by collectors as a "Secondary Martial," however, there is no evidence to support the fact that it was purchased or used by the government. A number of these are known with a deeply stamped standing bear on the frame. Collector legend has attributed the mark to California militia and it tended to fetch a premium price because of the military association. More recent evidence indicates the marking is likely that of a California gunmaker or dealer. The State historian confirmed the bear device was not insignia of California militia or State Guard units at any time during the 19th century.

8A-057   Values—Good **$1,100**   Fine **$3,000**

Forehand & Wadsworth New Model Army

8A-058

Forehand and Wadsworth, Worcester, Massachusetts, New Model Single Action Army Revolver. Made c. late 1870s to

1880s. Total quantity estimated at under 1,000.

44 caliber Russian centerfire. Six-shot. 6-1/2" round barrel. Finish usually nickel; blue will bring premium.

The New Model is quite similar to its predecessor except for barrel length, the adoption of a safety notch in the hammer, the use of a side mounted ejector on barrel and frame, and the presence of an exposed type cylinder pin. This also has been traditionally classified as a "Secondary Martial" handgun, although there is no substantiating evidence to indicate such usage:

8A-058   Values—Good **$1,275**   Fine **$3,250**

Forehand & Wadsworth Side Hammer 22

Forehand and Wadsworth, Worcester, Massachusetts, Side Hammer 22 Caliber Rimfire Revolver. Made c. 1870s. Quantity estimated at approximately 1,000.

22 caliber rimfire. Octagon barrels vary 2-1/4" to 4". Seven-shot. Iron frame; spur trigger. Blued or nickel finish. Walnut grips; bird's-head butt. Found with or without the rolled cylinder scene designs.

Virtually identical to the E. Allen & Company (8th Issue) 22 Rimfire Revolver (*q.v.*) except for the barrel markings FOREHAND & WADSWORTH with patent dates:

8A-059

8A-059   Values—Good **$150**   Fine **$400**

Forehand & Wadsworth Center Hammer

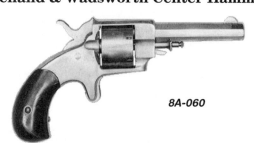

8A-060

Forehand and Wadsworth, Worcester, Massachusetts, Solid Frame Center Hammer Spur Trigger Revolvers. Made c. 1870s. Quantity estimated at a few thousand.

32, 38 and 41 caliber; all rimfire. Octagon barrels 3-1/2" and 4" usual but may vary. Iron frame. Blued or nickel finish. Rosewood or walnut grips; bird's-head butt.

Barrel markings: FOREHAND & WADSWORTH, WORCESTER, MASS. U.S. with 1861/1871 patent dates. 32 caliber size usually marked TERROR; 38 caliber size usually marked BULL DOG (BULL DOZER also known; scarce); 41 caliber size marked SWAMP ANGEL. Considerable variation exists on this model with names often appearing in caliber sizes other than those listed.

Distinctive and unique feature is the ejector rod contained within the centerpin; quickly removable by merely depressing the spring latch below centerpin:

8A-060   Values—Good **$100**   Fine **$350**

Forehand & Wadsworth "Russian Model"

Forehand & Wadsworth, Worcester, Mass. The last of the center-hammer, spur-trigger revolvers made by F&W. Made 1888-1891. Estimated quantity 18,000. 32 rimfire estimated as almost entire quantity; 38 rimfire rare, seldom seen (and worth premium). Five-shot semi-fluted cylinder. Sold with both round or octagon barrels. Bold markings RUSSIAN MODEL .32 on top strap over cylinder (or "38" if that caliber). FOREHAND & WADSWORTH markings on barrel (some observed adding WORCESTER, MASS.). Serial numbers located beneath barrel, rear of cylinder and underside of the square butt. Hard rubber grips with F&W monogram. Plain nickel finish standard.

8A-060.5

8A-060.5   Values—Very Good **$125**   Exc. **$200**

"BRITISH BULL-DOGS"

The Enigmatic Handgun that Helped "Win the West" Emerges from Obscurity

A notable example of evolving trends in the collecting of American antique firearms is the story of these American-made counterparts (directly appropriated infringements) of the English designated, originated and produced "BULL DOG" revolver. The solid-frame, double-action, easily concealable handgun, combined with a modest retail price and formidable firepower, assured its almost immediate world-wide success with its introduction in 1872.

The "BULL DOG" trade name, in view of its marked prevalence on innumerable handguns, is veritably ingrained in the jargon of the antique arms collecting market. Yet, in spite of the many and diverse examples of the British, Belgian and other European and American infringements often available in past years, the small handguns have been overlooked (if not contemptuously ignored) as conventional collectibles and for historic significance. In that respect, they are not unique, as witnessed by many other later 19th century firearms that, with the accrual of age and attainment of antiquity, are gradually accepted into the mainstream of "antique" collecting. The passage of time, aided by the publication of articles in the gun press have brought these once disregarded handguns to gradual recognition and, ultimately, the deserved welcome into the world of antique arms collecting. The "BRITISH BULL-DOG" revolver (especially those by F&W and Iver Johnson) is now classified by collectors as an authentic antique American firearm, and one that played a visible role in the saga of the American West. The recent study *The British Bulldog: The Forgotten Gun That Really Won the West* (G. J. Layman, 2006; q.v.) thoroughly established that despite the anomaly of its "BRITISH BULL DOG" name, this "little fistful of double-action repeating firepower" was a widely carried, dependable handgun during that stirring era...and one much underrated and undervalued as a genuine relic of our Western heritage.

Introduced to the English home market in 1872 (in caliber 44 Webley) by the noted gunmakers PHILIP WEBLEY & SON OF BIRMINGHAM, the small revolver (named merely "BULL DOG") almost instantly became the best selling handgun in Great Britain. By 1874 the British market had expanded to the United States and Europe, offering arms makers of those countries serious competition in their own home and export markets. In America, by virtue of the BULL DOG's low price and reliability, it achieved almost instantaneous success, from coast to coast; its reception in the Western states especially enthusiastic.

Belgian gunmakers were the first to sense the immense popularity and enthusiastic market for the little revolver. They quickly geared up to manufacture similar, near identical infringements of the Webley to cash in on that stunning response, especially by the American market. By 1879 over one hundred (estimated) Belgian firms were manufacturing duplications and knockoffs of the notable English prototype. Belgians are credited with being the first to actually mark their guns "*BRITISH* BULL DOG" (with various spellings and hyphenations). Priced at half the cost of the Webley, their revolvers proved especially popular. By 1880 "BULL DOGs" were available in other calibers (including 32 and 38 S&W as well as 450 and 45 Webley). Acutely aware of the competition and the sizable segment of their home market those foreign made "BULL DOGs" had captured, FOREHAND & WADSWORTH designed their own improved "British Bull Dog Pocket Revolver." Commencing production in 1879, it soon exceeded in popularity that of its English originator!

Dogged by a floating hyphen (the analogy was inevitable). There is reason to believe the many spelling variations of the "Bulldog" markings observed on the various revolvers may be misprinted. The reader's indulgence is requested to overlook such inconsistencies. Where spelling of the word (s) is significant for identification, the following descriptions endeavor to specify the exact markings as they appear on the respective revolvers. Also note: the manufacturers' or dealers' advertising for those very same handguns often differed from the actual marking on the gun!

Until the latter 1990s and the turn of the 21st century, the collector's scene for these "BULL DOGs" was not generally found at antique gun shows or arms fairs. Rather, that marketplace was developed by the newly emerging, flourishing field of Cowboy Action Shooting, in which the use and competition shooting of those actual firearms used in the era of the American West is the name of the game. Participants in that shooting sport were the first to perceive and popularize the historic significance of the "BRITISH BULL DOG." That recognition nurtured a newly emerging market for original specimens of the sturdy little revolver, which became a favorite "shooting iron" in many of their "Pocket Gun Side Matches." The enthusiasm of those Cowboy Action Shooters ultimately alerted and transposed to the antique arms collecting field, whose market and attendant values were reflected accordingly. Thus extricated from unmerited obscurity by the keen attention paid to them by the shooting crowd, these American-made "BULL DOGs," relatively slow-starters in the world of antique arms collecting (and despite the seeming anomaly of its name!), have achieved due recognition as a venerable and legitimate historical artifact.

Forehand & Wadsworth Double Action "British Bull-Dog" Revolver

Forehand & Wadsworth, Worcester, Massachusetts, Solid Frame, Double Action "BRITISH BULL-DOG" Revolver. Made circa 1879-1890. Total quantity 114,000. Calibers 32 S&W centerfire (7 shot); 38 S&W centerfire (6-shot); 44 Webley centerfire (5-shot). Manufactured with two different frame profiles as shown below; all models with 2-1/2" "oblong" barrels

8A-061
First Issue

8A-061.2
Second (and later) Issues

(i.e. round and flat along the top). Unless otherwise indicated, all models are marked BRITISH BULL-DOG on top strap of frame over the cylinder. Frame sizes will vary slightly with each model dependent on caliber; larger calibers being somewhat heavier in size. A *key feature* to differentiate this F&W "BULL-DOG" from the British Webley and European copies is the absence of European proofmarks (except on a very few pirated copies!) Bird's-head butt standard on all models; checkered hard rubber grips apparently standard all models (colorations of the hard rubber vary with later issues). Also common to all variants is the prominent mushroom-shaped tip of the center pin, which is manually pulled outward and swivels to the left to operate as an ejector rod for cartridges. It is apparent from statistical surveys of F&W "BULL-DOGS" that **caliber 32 S&W is the most commonly encountered (and valued approximately 25 percent less). Values shown are for the larger two calibers.** In some instances, where indicated the 44 caliber is extremely scarce, if not rare, and worth a premium value (where shown).

FIRST ISSUE: Easily identifiable by the distinctly different profile to the upper section of the frame (the area where hammer located); note the very curved, deep, crescent-shaped profile which distinguishes it from all other variations and "issues." Manufactured late 1879 through early 1880. Total quantity estimated between 800 and 1000 with serial numbers falling within that range (numbers overlap those of Second Issue). The *only external markings* on the gun are BRITISH BULL DOG. (NOTE: "BULL DOG" two words, not hyphenated). Serial numbers under left grip, on frame and front of cylinder. Caliber 44 rarely encountered; worth premium of 40 percent or more.

8A-061   Values—Very Good **$300**   Exc. **$450**

SECOND ISSUE: *Major distinguishing feature of this issue and all other following F&W "BULL-DOG" types is the different profile to the upper frame as seen in illustration; the deep-cut*

crescent profile of First Issue is modified to a lower, long, semi-squared profile. Manufactured circa 1880-1881; serial number range 850 to 18,300 (lower serials overlap First Issue). Only markings "BRITISH BULL-DOG" (now hyphenated) and also marked on front, left side of frame with a small bulldog's head motif and marking TRADE MARK (respectively) above and below the dog head.

8A-061.2   Values—Very Good **$275**   Exc. **$350**

VARIANT SECOND ISSUE: Mfd. 1880-1881; serial range 13,000 to 18,000; marking on top strap above cylinder changed from "BRITISH BULL-DOG" to "INDIAN BULL-DOG."

8A-061.3   Values—Very Good **$200**   Exc. **$325**

THIRD ISSUE: Identical frame profile of Second Issue with BRITISH BULL-DOG and markings of the dog head TRADE MARK with the addition FOREHAND & WADSWORTH and a Maltese cross trademark along the top of barrel. Manufactured 1881 to early 1887. Found in serial number range from 21,000 through 84,000.

8A-061.4   Values—Very Good **$200**   Exc. **$300**

VARIANT THIRD ISSUE: Markings INDIAN BULL-DOG on top strap (in place of "BRITISH BULL-DOG") also retains the F&W/doghead/trademark marking of Third Issue. It was offered as an option to buyers by F&W circa 1882 to 1885; usually encountered in serial range 18,000 to 22,000.

8A-061.5   Values—Very Good **$275**   Exc. **$350**

FOURTH ISSUE: Identical to Third Issue type: marked FOREHAND & WADSWORTH *only*, with the elimination of the bulldog head motif and "TRADE MARK" on the left, forward side of the frame. Mfd. 1887-1890 (although advertised by various dealers as late as 1896). Usually encountered in serial range 79,000 through 114,000.

8A-061.6   Values—Very Good **$175**   Exc. **$250**

Forehand & Wadsworth Double Action

8A-061.12

Forehand and Wadsworth, Worcester, Massachusetts, Solid Frame Double Action Revolver. Revolver shown is also known as the "First Model" of this solid frame type which was made in a few variants and is distinguished by its bird's-head butt (later variants with square butts) and its center pin (with mushroom-like knob top) which pulls out and swivels to operate as an ejector.

32 caliber rimfire. Six-shot. Blued or nickel finish. Distinctive contour caused by odd hump on back of frame; bird's-head butt.

Marked on topstrap over cylinder: FOREHAND & WADSWORTH/DOUBLE ACTION NO.32/WORCESTER, MASS. Left side of barrel: PAT'D JUNE 27 '71 -OCT. 28 '73

8A-061.12 Values—Good **$75**   Fine **$200**

"Fourth of July Pistol" *See Hopkins & Allen.*

Gage Single Shot Pocket Rifles and Pistols)

8A-061.15

James E. Gage, Rochester and Ontario, New York (1872-1895) and Concord, N.H. (1895-1924). Breechloading pistol under patents of 1884 and 1889. Quantity unknown; very limited; few specimens recorded.

22 and 32 caliber rimfire. Uniquely designed breech swivels left to expose chamber of barrel. Blued. Specimens recorded both unmarked or with J E GAGE CONCORD NHon top of frame. "Pocket Rifle" (a.k.a. "Buggy Rifle") with 15-inch to 20-inch barrels. Skeleton type detachable steel stock with novel attaching device, which merely clamps to butt of pistol (without screws).

Before acquiring or disposing of these pocket rifles, check their classification under the Gun Control Act to verify if subject to provisions of that act.

8A-061.15 Values—Very Good **$1,250** Exc. **$2,750**

Pocket rifle, only lacking the stock:
8A-061.16 Values—Very Good **$600** Exc. **$1,250**
Pistol only not adapted for stock; 7-inch and 10-inch barrels:
8A-061.17 Values—Very Good **$500** Exc. **$1,250**

"Gem" Pocket Revolver

Gem Marked Pocket Revolver. Made by Bacon Arms Company, Norwich, Connecticut. Patented by A. L. Sweet with half interest in patent assigned to the Bacon firm. Made c. late 1870s to early 1880s. Total quantities limited. Advertised as "THE LADIES PET...an appropriate present to make any lady. Can be carried on a fob or vest (by men)...an ornament to any room!"

Its desirability and value based on its tiny size. The smallest American antique revolver made. Just 3-7/8" overall.

22 caliber rimfire. Five-shot. 1-1/4" octagon barrel. Rounded iron frame; spur trigger; plated finish; usually engraved with decorative scroll designs. Walnut or ivory grips; bird's-head butt.

8A-062

Barrel markings on top: GEM and often the 1878 patent date; others also include 1881 patent date:
8A-062 Values—Very Good **$750** Exc. **$2,250**

Gem Blank Cartridge Pistol

8A-062.3

Gem Blank Cartridge Pistol (unmarked); single shot "deringer type;" caliber 22 rimfire blank cartridges. Manufacture attributed to Iver Johnson Company of Fitchburg, Mass. (q.v.) circa 1880s-early 1890s. Quantity unknown; estimated as "very large."

An 1890 dated advertisement by Boston dealer Lovell Arms. Co. stated "It has become so popular that the demand for them last year far exceeded the supply...the Gem Pistol unrivalled for celebration purposes. It is the standard 'Fourth of July' pistol of the country. ...A ball cartridge cannot be used [it.]" Illustration here from their 1890 catalog:
8A-062.3 Values—Good **$175** Exc. **$325**

"Gem" Marked Single Shot Spur Trigger 22 Caliber or 30 Caliber Rimfire Deringer
See Stevens Arms Company, Chapter V-H.

Abram J. Gibson S.A. Belt Revolver

Abram J. Gibson, Worcester, Massachusetts Solid Frame, Center Hammer, Single Action Belt Revolver. C. 1860-1861.

8A-062.5

Quantity unknown; likely under 100.

32 rimfire. Seven-shot. Heavy brass frame with silver finish. 5" octagon barrel. A recoil plate at rear of cylinder pulls outward to left exposing rear of cylinder for loading; the recoil plate also partially revolves, acting as a safety to prevent hammer from striking rim of cartridge. Made under Gibson patent 30,309 of Oct. 9, 1860.

Maker markings not present. Matching two-digit serial numbers on every major, and some minor, parts.

Although Gibson known to have been involved with patents utilized in making Pond revolvers, this large handgun clearly evidences many features of the large Prescott 38 Navy revolver:

8A-062.5   Values—Good **$800**   Fine **$2,250**

Abram J. Gibson 3 Shot Pistol

Abram J. Gibson, Worcester, Massachusetts. Three shot folding barrel pistol a.k.a. "ELEPHANT GUN", likening its appearance (especially when barrel folded downward) to an elephant's trunk. Patented 1860. Quantity unknown. Very limited.

22 RF. 3 shots. 5-1/4" open; 3" octagon barrel marked A.J. GIBSON WORCESTER, MASS. Less than 3" with barrel folded for convenience in carrying. Barrel claimed to render the long curved trigger immobile when folded, but could lead to dangerous discharge. Unique 3 chambers merely a round cylinder halved; brought into line manually. Very rare arms curiosa.

8A-062.6   Values—Good **$5,500**   Fine **$15,000**

8A-062.6

8A-062.6

Governor Pocket Revolvers

Governor Marked Pocket Revolver. (Not illus.) Made by Bacon Arms Company, Norwich, Connecticut c. 1870s - early 1880s.

Calibers 22 rimfire and 30 rimfire. Octagon barrels of varying lengths. Iron frame; spur trigger. Blued or nickel finish. Walnut grips; bird's-head butt.

Marked on topstrap: GOVERNOR

Bacon's second style of small inexpensive pocket revolver. Many variations encountered. This revolver was first thought to have been made from Bacon Arms Company pepperboxes. Such pieces are now identified as the "Dead Shot" revolver (q.v.). The Governor correctly belongs with the "Suicide Specials" type:

8A-063   Values—Very Good **$125**   Exc. **$350**

W. L. Grant 22 Rimfire and 32 Rimfire Pocket Revolvers   *See Uhlinger.*

Gross Arms Co. Pocket Revolver

Gross Arms Company, Tiffin, Ohio, Pocket Revolver. Made c. 1864-1866. Total quantity estimated at several hundred.

25 caliber rimfire (most commonly encountered) and 30 caliber rimfire (scarce and worth premium). Seven-shot. 6" barrel. Blued finish. Walnut grips. Barrel variations noted.

Marking: GROSS ARMS CO., TIFFIN, OHIO and GROSS PATENT 1861 TIFFIN OHIO.

Charles B. and Henry Gross were among the earliest U.S. manufacturers of metallic cartridge handguns. The latter brother had been active with Gwyn and Campbell in the carbine production (q.v.). A great many variations occur in this very

8A-064

scarce gun. They are basically in barrel lengths, barrel catches and caliber. Prices are generally the same for all types:

8A-064   Values—Good **$800**   Fine **$2,250**

Hammond "Bulldog" Derringer   *See Connecticut Arms Co. (8A-040).*

Harrington and Richardson   *See Frank Wesson Arms, Chapter V-I.*

Holey Manufacturing Company   *See Reid 22 Caliber Pocket Revolver, Model 1.*

Hood Firearms Co. Pocket Revolvers

Hood Firearms Company, Norwich, Connecticut, Pocket Revolvers. Made c. late 1870s to 1880s. Quantities estimated at several thousand.

Calibers 22 rimfire to 41 rimfire. Five-shot. Varying barrel lengths, 3-1/2" octagon average. Iron frame; bird's-head butt. Blued or nickel plated finish. Walnut grips.

Barrel marking: HOOD FIREARMS CO. NORWICH, CONN.

Although classified generally as "Suicide Specials," this firm very likely made more styles and different trade names than any other company producing that type of weapon. A key to identifying their products is the inclusion of the patent date February 23, 1875—the primary Hood patent covering the cylinder pin release; also the patent date April 6, 1875 and March 14, 1876.

8A-064.2

8A-064.2   Values - Very Good **$150**   Exc. **$350**

C. W. Hopkins   *See Bacon Manufacturing Company.*

HOPKINS AND ALLEN

Hopkins and Allen were major American arms makers c. 1868 to 1915 in Norwich, Connecticut. Manufacturers of a large line of "Suicide Special" spur trigger revolvers as well as some larger models, rifles and shotguns, they laid claim to being the "largest manufacturers of high-grade, popular priced firearms in the world." A majority of their products were sold to distributors and bore trade names other than their own. Some of the more popular were BLUE JACKET (a series of varying size rimfire spur trigger types) and their XL series Nos. 1 through 8 (rimfire calibers 22 through 41) as well as names such as CAPTAIN JACK, MOUNTAIN EAGLE, RANGER, etc. Their products are often identified by the patent date. March 28, 1871; April 27, 1875; May 27, 1879 usually seen either singly or in tandem.

H&A Mfg. Co. were successors to Bacon Mfg. Co. (*q.v.*) purchasing the assets of that company when it ceased operations 1868, utilizing their machinery and remaining parts. Charles Converse, a major stockholder and superintendent of Bacon Mfg. Co. along with Charles W. Hopkins, Samuel S. Hopkins

and Charles W. Allen were major principals in formation of H&A. In 1874 Charles Converse, then a 50 percent owner of H & R became disenchanted with the business and sold his shares to Joseph Merwin, an arms dealer in New York City. Although the company continued operations as H & A, they then commenced manufacture of a line of single and double action revolvers under patents owned by Joseph Merwin (and his various partners) with trade name Merwin, Hulbert & Co. (*q.v. 8A-076.5 et al*). The company also were successors to Forehand & Wadsworth, 1902 (*q.v.*).

A few of the more important and valuable Hopkins and Allen revolvers are described herein. The majority of the smaller revolvers are not listed and are priced comparable to those discussed in the "Spur Triggers" category.

Also see Pointer, XL Deringer, XL Vest Pocket and XPERT Single Shot Deringers and Chapter VII A-034 **Dictator**.

The publication of "*H & A Revolvers and Pistols*" by C.E. Carder, 1998 is a most important guide to this relatively new field.

Hopkins and Allen 22RF Pocket Revolver

Hopkins and Allen, Norwich, Connecticut, Pocket Revolver. Made circa late 1860s. Small quantity estimated.

22 caliber rimfire. Seven-shot. 3" part octagon/part round barrel. Early type center pin with button type latch. Iron frame; spur trigger; bird's-head butt. Rosewood grips.

Marked on cylinder HOPKINS & ALLENS MFG. CO., NORWICH, CT. Among the first of a very long line of pocket revolvers, most of which were marked with trade names:

8A-064.5

8A-064.5   Values—Good **$150**   Fine **$425**

Hopkins and Allen 32RF Pocket Revolver

Hopkins and Allen, Norwich, Connecticut, Pocket Revolver. Made c. late 1860s. Small quantity estimated.

32 caliber rimfire. Six-shot. 3" part octagon/part round barrel. Rounded iron frame; spur trigger; square butt. Cylinder removes to load. Rolled cylinder scene of hunter with dogs. Made from parts acquired from Bacon Mfg. Co.

Marked on barrel HOPKINS & ALLEN MFG CO/NORWICH,CT This 32 rimfire and the above 22 rimfire revolver were the first of the long line of metallic cartridge Hopkins and Allens; 32 rimfire believed to precede the 22 rimfire:

8A-064.7

8A-064.7   Values—Good **$165**   Fine **$450**

Hopkins and Allen "CZAR" Pocket Revolver

Hopkins and Allen, Norwich, Connecticut, "CZAR" Pocket Revolver. Made 1878 to 1900. Quantity unknown; estimated as very large.

22 and 32 caliber rimfire (the latter discontinued 1884). Seven shot. 3-1/2" octagon barrel. Semi-fluted cylinder. Plain nickel finish. Marked CZAR on top strap over cylinder and PAT. MCH 29, 71 and MAY 27, 79 on barrel; *none* are know to have H & R markings. Serial numbered at rear of cylinder; inside frame and underneath barrel. Square butt. Hard rubber grips standard (many types optional and worthy of premium).

This "CZAR" was without doubt the most widely advertised of the H & A pocket pistols, but yet, the least seen; surviving specimens scarce. Likely no other inexpensive spur trigger revolver of its type was promoted with as much "hype." Among the many wild claims for it: "The Czar kills farther than an ordinary revolver will shoot…it is a dead shot at a hundred yards…the barrel is rifled as carefully as a Creedmoor Rifle" are typical. Its popularity even spawned knock-offs, indicated by the warning: "Caution. Several unprincipled scalawags offer a cast iron imitation of the Czar for a less price. Beware of them." It is also likely that no other inexpensive spur trigger revolver was offered with so many options commonly available,

8A-064.8

including engraving, gold and silver plating (or combination of both) and even an interchangeable 8-inch octagon target barrel which "…can be changed in an instant." Some outstanding and handsome examples of the "CZAR" are known (and very scarce, too). It was even offered as a special "CZAR POCKET RIFLE" with that 8-inch barrel and a detachable skeleton type, iron rod shoulder stock that screwed onto the butt. Such pieces depending on their elaborateness and quality are valued proportionally higher than the standard plain, nickeled model which is valued here:

8A-064.8   Values—Good **$135**   Fine **$225**

Hopkins and Allen Army, Navy and Police Revolvers

Hopkins and Allen, Norwich, Connecticut, Army, Navy and Police Revolvers. Made c. late 1870s to early 1880s. Total quantity estimated at several hundreds.

Calibers and barrel lengths as below. Six-shot. Nickel plated or blued finish. Walnut grips; square butt.

Barrel marking: HOPKINS AND ALLEN MFG. CO., PAT. MAR. 28, '71, APR. 27, '75.

**8A-065
Navy Model**

**8A-066
Army Model**

Collectors consider the XL Army and Navy as the finest quality handguns made under the Hopkins and Allen name. They were their only revolvers that could be rated as serviceable for military use; they are traditionally classed as "Secondary Martial," but no evidence of their actual military or government purchase is known.

Navy Model. Markings on topstrap XL NAVY. Caliber 38 rimfire. 6-1/2" round barrel:

8A-065   Values—Good **$600**   Fine **$1,650**

Army Model. Marked on topstrap XL NO. 8. Caliber 44 rimfire and 44-40 centerfire. Barrel lengths 4-1/2", 6", and 7-1/2":

8A-066   Values—Good **$900**   Fine **$2,400**

Police Model. Marked on topstrap XL POLICE. Caliber 38 rimfire. 4-1/2" barrel (other lengths possible), walnut grips: Scarcer than Army or Navy model but value usually less:

8A-066.5   Values—Good **$500**   Fine **$1,250**

**8A-066.5
Police Model**

Hopkins & Allen Arms Co. Vest Pocket Deringer

Hopkins and Allen Arms Company, Norwich, Connecticut, Vest Pocket (full factory name "New Model Vest Pocket Derringer) Deringer Pistol a.k.a. "Parrot Beak". Made 1911 to 1915. Total quantity estimated at under 1,400.

22 caliber rimfire. 1-3/4" barrel pivots downward for loading. Folding trigger; hammerless. Scroll engraving and nickel finish standard; plain unengraved specimens and blue finish very scarce; worth premium. Pearl grips with H&A round gilt

8A-067

medallion standard (a few known without medallion); ivory very scarce. The buyer should exercise extreme caution in acquiring this piece. Very well made modern fakes have been made recently in Europe. They usually do not have the pearl grips with the Hopkins & Allen gilt medallion inlaid in them but

that feature in itself is not sufficient to either condemn or identify an original model.

Marking: HOPKINS & ALLEN ARMS CO., NORWICH, CONN. U.S.A.:

8A-067   Values—Very Good **$1,400**   Exc. **$2,750**

"Hornet" marked Revolver   *See Prescott 8A-128*

Hyde & Shattuck Single Shot Deringer   *See Queen Single Shot Deringer.*

W. Irving, New York City, Revolver   *See James Reid.*

"Invisible Defender"   *See Shattuck Arms Co.*

W. Irving Single Shot Deringer

W. Irving Single Shot Deringer. Made c. 1862-64 by James Reid of N.Y. City for W. Irving of N.Y. City who operated his own retail establishment as well as acting as Reid's agent.

22 caliber rimfire. 2-3/4" part octagon/round barrel pivots sideways to load. (Full octagon barrel known, very rare; worth premium; usually unmarked). Brass frame; spur trigger; square butt. (A transitional type with rounded butt known). About 50 percent of specimens marked W. IRVING. Quantity made less than 500:

8A-068   Values—Good **$550**   Fine **$1,250**

32 rimfire. 3" octagon barrel. Estimated quantity under 100. Rare.

Barrel marked W. IRVING NEW YORK:

8A-068.3   Values—Good **$700**   Fine **$2,000**

8A-068
22 Caliber

8A-068.3
32 Caliber

IVER JOHNSON REVOLVERS

The Iver Johnson firm was established in 1871 and has had continuous operation in manufacture of firearms to early 1993. Founded by a partnership of Iver Johnson and Martin Bye, both former employees of the pioneer New England arms maker Ethan Allen. Manufacture first commenced at Worcester, Massachusetts, changing to Fitchburg, Massachusetts in 1891. Martin Bye's share of the business was sold to Iver Johnson in 1883 and the firm's name was changed to Iver Johnson's Arms and Cycle Works by which it has been most widely known since. They were major American arms makers; around the turn of the century they probably produced more revolvers than any other manufacturer in the world. According to their company history their first handguns were percussion, single shot, spur trigger 30 caliber pocket pistols with nickeled frame, blued barrel, called the UNCLE SAM. None so-marked, or marked IVER JOHNSON are known. The pistol is about identical to the Manhattan Arms Co. HERO (5C-023) and may be one of the many unmarked types often seen.

Earliest production by Iver Johnson of spur trigger revolvers was almost entirely marketed under trade names only and did not bear Iver Johnson marks. They are credited with such names

as ECLIPSE, FAVORITE, TYCOON, ENCORE, etc. A majority of their guns were evidently marketed through the J. P. Lovell Arms Company of Boston.

Iver Johnson is credited with a tremendous production of double action revolvers and is most widely known for their owl-head trademark and design used on their grips. Most of these types bore their own company name. Their top-break double action, exposed hammer 32 caliber revolver has the dubious distinction of being the gun used by the anarchist Leon Czolgosc to assassinate President William McKinley on Sept. 6, 1901 while attending a public reception.

Demand for Iver Johnson revolvers on the collectors' market is limited mostly to: the small spur trigger revolvers with "cute" or intriguing names that are classified as "Spur Triggers" (discussed in the prefatory text), the various cutaway models which were ordered by dealers for demonstrator use in their retail establishments, and the below described "knuckler". There is very light collector demand for most double action types which are generally classified as modern or semi-modern arms.

See also Shattuck Double Action Revolver, Eclipse and Star Vest Pocket, and "Gem" Blank Pistol 8A-062.3.

Iver Johnson D.A. Revolvers with "Knuckle" Attachment

Iver Johnson, Fitchburg, Massachusetts, Double Action Revolvers with so-called "Knuckle" Attachment. Made c. 1904 to 1920s on special order at customer request only. Attachment is affixed to four top-break double action models only: The

hammer and hammerless models of the "small frame" 32 centerfire and "large frame" 38 centerfire. Total made approximately 6,000. Serial numbered in special series 1 on up. Revolvers with usual Iver Johnson marks; the attachment, affixed by three screws, marked PAT,MAY 10,'04. Serial numbers on attachment and gun match and should be under 6000.

Iver Johnson acquired the patent from Harrington & Richardson who never utilized it. The inventor, George C. Bourne of Worcester, Massachusetts received a royalty of 50 percent from Iver Johnson on each attachment sold.

Both the inventor and Iver Johnson claimed the attachment's use only as a "grip adaptor...to allow a more firm grip when fired." It's obvious from appearance and when held that its dual use as a "knuckler" was easily visualized and therein lies its major interest and value as an arms oddity for the collector. With production on a special order basis and fact that a great many were believed made for the South American market, specimens are scarce:

8A-068.5

8A-068.5	Values—Very Good **$400**	Exc. **$700**

Iver Johnson "Petite Hammerless" D.A. Revolver

8A-068.6

Iver Johnson, Fitchburg, Massachusetts "Petite Hammerless" Revolver. One of smallest American double action revolvers. Made less than 1 year, 1908. Although quantity of factory sold pieces estimated at less than 100, it is believed that factory employees assembled parts left over when production halted and thus possibility that total of approximately 300 were built. Surviving examples rare.

About identical to the Baby Hammerless revolvers (*q.v.*) it varies mostly in its internal mechanism (for which a patent was granted). As springs were not treated properly the gun broke down quite often; it apparently was unsafe for smokeless cartridges and was taken off the market.

22 Short rimfire. Six-shot. 3-15/16" overall. 1-1/4" barrel. Nickel finish. Hard rubber grips with fancy relief designs of letters I.J. that may be read in normal position and inversely. Not available with pearl or ivory grips.

Topstrap marked I.J. PETITE/HAMMERLESS.

Although it has been stated that this "Petite" was smaller than the "Baby Hammerless", the claim is only partially correct. It's about the same size as the Model 1910 "Baby" (8A-012.6) which is the largest of that line.

8A-068.6	Values—Very Good **$750**	Exc. **$1,750**

Iver Johnson Cutaway Salesman Demonstrators

8A-068.7

8A-068.7

Iver Johnson, Fitchburg, Massachusetts. Cutaway salesman demonstrator double action top-break revolvers. Factory name "CUT OPEN."

On special order they produced two known types with various size and shaped openings to expose the interior workings of: (1) 32 cal. with 3" barrel. Cutaway both sides. c. 1890-1910. Quantity about 75; worth premium. (2) 38 cal. Model 1910; 3-1/2" barrel; cutaway left side only. C prefix on serial numbers. Quantity about 250:

8A-068.7	Values—Very Good **$350**	Exc. **$675**

Iver Johnson "British Bull Dog" D.A. Revolver

Iver Johnson Fitchburg Massachusetts "British Bull Dog" Double Action Revolver. Made 1878-1882 (offered as late as 1884 in noted western dealer's catalog). Estimated quantity 5,000. 38 S & W centerfire (with 2-1/2" round barrel); 44 Webley centerfire (with 2-3/4" round smooth-bore barrel) with simulated rifling grooves at muzzle).

Marked only BRITISH BULL DOG on topstrap over the five-shot, semi-fluted cylinder. (Note: BULL DOG two separate words without hyphen.) Nickel finish only. Checkered hard rubber grips; bird's-head butt. Considered among the scarcest of the Iver Johnson solid frame D. A. revolvers, it was also among their very first of that type based on the 1878 patent of Johnson & Bye. See also the F & W "British Bull Dog" (8A-061.5) for historical significance of these "Bulldogs" and their collectability:

8A-068.8

8A-068.8   Values—Very Good **$375**   Exc. **$550**

Iver Johnson "American Bull Dog" D.A. Revolver

Iver Johnson Fitchburg Massachusetts "American Bull Dog" Double Action, Solid Frame Revolver. Made 1883-1884; estimated quantity 3,900 total for three sizes: large, medium and small frame; all with overlapping serial numbers.

32, 38, 44 centerfire. 2-1/2" round barrel standard. Only markings AMERICAN BULL DOG on topstrap over the fluted five-shot cylinder. (Note: BULL DOG two words, not hyphenated.) Mottled black and red hard rubber grips with large, relief design of open winged American eagle over shield; square butt. The 44 caliber scarce; worth 30 to 50 percent premium.

8A-068.9

Note: There were later, redesigned models of the AMERICAN BULL DOG with modified frames and octagon barrels; made 1885-1897. They are seen with variant markings and trademarks not found on these earliest types valued here:

8A-068.9   Values—Very Good **$375**   Exc. **$550**

Keno Single Shot Deringer

Keno Single Shot Deringer. Made by Hyde & Shattuck, Springfield, Massachusetts, c.1870 to 1880s. Quantity unknown, limited. Very scarce.

22 caliber rimfire. 2-1/2" round two-step barrel pivots sideways to load. Brass frame. Barrel with blued or nickeled finish. Walnut grips; bird's-head butt.

Barrel marked on left side: Keno:

8A-069

8A-069   Values—Good **$250**   Fine **$650**

King Pin Single Shot Deringer

King Pin Single Shot Deringer. Made by Hyde & Shattuck, Springfield, Massachusetts, c. 1870 to 1880s. Quantity unknown, limited. Very scarce.

22 caliber rimfire. 2-1/2" round two-step barrel pivots sideways to load. Quickly distinguished by its all brass frame and matching all brass barrel. Walnut grips; bird's-head butt.

Barrel marked on left side: King Pin:

8A-070

8A-070   Values—Good **$325**   Fine **$675**

Kinsey Single Shot Deringer

Moses Kinsey, Newark, New Jersey, Single Shot Deringer. Made c. 1865-1870. Quantity unknown; very limited; rare.

22 rimfire. 3-1/2" round two-step tip up barrel; blued finish. Brass frame; spur trigger. Unique barrel locking device. Walnut grips. Square butt.

Barrel marked M. KINSEY'S PATENT/NEWARK, N.J:

8A-070.5

8A-070.5   Values—Good **$850**   Fine **$2,000**

Lee Single Shot Deringer

James Paris Lee, Milwaukee, Wisconsin, Single Shot Deringer. Circa 1862. Quantity likely less than 100.

32 rimfire. Brass frame with silvered finish. 3-1/2" barrel (likely will vary). Pivots sideways to load; blued finish. Automatic extractor similar to Allen & Wheelock. Walnut grips. Square butt. Unmarked except for serial number. Rare.

The first patent granted to Lee who is best known for his many patents on breech-loading rifles made by Winchester,

8A-070.7

Remington and Sharps:
8A-070.7   Values—Good **$1,150**   Fine **$2,500**

Liberator WWII Pistol For Resistance Forces

Liberator single shot World War II pistol made by General Motors at Anderson, Indiana, 1942 under plans of the Joint Psychological Warfare Committee of the U.S. War Department. Quantity 1,000,000.

Caliber 45 ACP. 4" barrel of steel tubing; zinc hammer; frame/handle non-corrosive steel; folded seams. Hollow handle held 10 separate cartridges. No maker markings.

Official designation "FP-45" to confuse enemy intelligence ("FLARE PROJECTOR-45 CAL" later "FLARE PISTOL KIT-45"). Highly classified "Secret" project, the guns were designed to aid underground and resistance forces in Europe and Asia; most for air drop to clandestine units. The guns represent a tribute to American ingenuity, being designed, and the entire contract filled, in but a few months. The O.S.S. eventually received about half of them, most to the Asian theater.

Also thought that great majority of entire production scrapped after war; specimens scarce. Unsubstantiated rumor of manufacture in 9mm; specimen if authentic would be worth considerable premium. Not subject to the NFA but is a "firearm" as defined by GCA and should be handled accordingly.

8A-070.8

The name "LIBERATOR" by which it is most well-known and "WOOLWORTH GUN" are those used in the official O.S.S. manual. When found with its original paperboard box and instruction sheet, 25 to 50 percent premium:
8A-070.8   Values—Very Good **$1,150**   Exc. **$2,500**

Liddle & Kaeding Pocket Revolver

Liddle and Kaeding, San Francisco, California, Pocket Revolver. (Not illus.) Made c. 1880s. Total quantity estimated at several hundreds. This is merely a Forehand and Wadsworth piece bearing the markings of these California dealers.

32 caliber rimfire. Five-shot. 3-1/4" octagon barrel. Iron frame; blued finish. Walnut grips.

Marking on topstrap: LIDDLE & KAEDING, SAN FRANCISCO, CAL.:
8A-071   Values—Good **$325**   Fine **$650**

H.C. Lombard & Co. Single Shot Deringer

H. C. Lombard and Co., Springfield, Massachusetts, Single Shot Deringer. Made c. 1860s. Total quantity estimated under 1,000. Identical to the Morgan and Clapp (*q.v.*).

22 caliber rimfire. 3-1/2" octagon barrel pivots to right for loading. Brass frame silver plated. (Standard frame shown; very early production noticeably thicker in center, straight rather than angular shape to front of frame; thicker hammer. Scarce; worth premium.) Barrel blued; spur trigger. Walnut grips; square butt.

8A-072

Barrel marked: H. C. LOMBARD & CO., SPRINGFIELD, MASS:
8A-072   Values—Good **$200**   Fine **$575**

Lowell Arms Company   *See Rollin White Arms Co.*

J. P. Lower 22 Rimfire and 32 Rimfire Pocket Revolvers   *See Uhlinger.*

Maltby, Henley & Co.   *See Spencer Safety Hammerless; also see Otis A. Smith Company.*

Manhattan Firearms Company   *See Manhattan Firearms, Chapter V-C.*

Marlin Single Shot Pistols and Revolvers   *See Marlin Firearms, Chapter V-D.*

Marble Game Getter

Marble Safety Axe Company/Marble Arms and Manufacturing Company, Gladstone, Michigan, "Game Getter". Folding stock pistol with rifled barrel over smooth bore barrel; tip up to load. Invented by William Marble based on his 20 years experience in the Northwoods as trapper and timber cruiser, as an all-purpose, easily carried firearm that could dispatch at reasonable distance anything swimming, walking or flying in the woods.

NOTE: Values shown are for specimens with 18" barrel and attached folding stock which are traded under provisions of the G.C.A. and treated as any post-1898 handgun. If the shoulder stock is lacking, or it has a barrel under 18", it is then subject to the provisions and restrictions of the N.F.A. and collectors should not attempt to acquire or dispose of specimens without complying.
Model 1908. Made 1908 to 1914. Quantity estimated 8,500 to 9,999. Serial numbered in range 1 to 9999. Although the company apparently stated in a 1972 letter that serial range began at No. 1500 and other reports mention No. 700, with other three digit specimens known, there's strong likelihood the range began with No. 1.

Caliber 22 rimfire over 44-40 centerfire shot or round ball 410 added in 1915. 12", 15", 18" over/under barrels. Blued or nickel finish; tubular type folding stock.

Marked on barrel: MANUFACTURED BY THE MARBLE SAFETY

**8A-072.7
Model 1921**

AXE COMPANY, GLADSTONE, MICHIGAN, USA.

Type I. Checkered hard rubber grips with Marble logo; folding peep sight behind hammer at rear of frame:
8A-072.5 Values—Very Good **$1,250** Exc. **$2,250**

Type II. As above; furnished without folding peep sight with blank aperture:
8A-072.6 Values—Very Good **$1,100** Exc. **$2,000**
Model 1921. Made 1921 to 1942. Quantity estimated 11,000. Serial numbered in range 10001 to 20,000 approx.

Caliber 22 rimfire over 44-40 centerfire shot or round ball or 410 gauge shotgun (2" shell and later 2-1/2"). Barrels 12", 15", 18". Rolled sheet metal folding stock. Handle redesigned to conventional profile with no provision for the folding peep sight. Walnut grips.

Barrel marked MARBLE'S GAME GETTER GUN, MARBLE ARMS & MANUFACTURING COMPANY, GLADSTONE, MICHIGAN, USA:
8A-072.7 Values—Very Good **$1,100** Exc. **$2,000**

Wm. W. Marston Three-Barrel 22 Deringer

William W. Marston, New York City, Three-Barrel Deringer Caliber 22 Rimfire. Made c. 1858 to 1864. Total quantity estimated about 1,500.

3" superposed barrels tipping downward to load. Brass frame, silver plated; barrels blued. Outside mounted firing indicator on right frame. Walnut grips; square butt. Broad floral and scroll decorative engraving standard on frame, although very elaborate engraved specimens are known and will bring premiums.

Markings as indicated are standard, but vary in style: WM. W. MARSTON/PATENTED/MAY 26. 1857/NEW YORK CITY.
Three-Barrel Model Made Without Knife As Described Above. Estimated quantity 300. Usually found in serial range 800 to 1100. Although scarcest style, usually bring less than type with knife blade.
8A-073 Values—Good **$875** Fine **$2,750**

8A-074

Retractable Knife Blade Model. A sliding knife blade with flat spring clip locking it into position mounted on left side of barrels. "Clip point" or "Bowie" shape blade earliest production; estimated quantity 800. Usually found in serial range 1 to 800. Rounded or spear point blade late production. Estimated quantity 400. Usually found in serial range 1100 to 1500. Values generally same.
8A-074 Values—Good **$1,750** Fine **$4,250**

Wm. W. Marston Three-Barrel 32 Deringer

William W. Marston, New York City, Three-Barrel Deringer Caliber 32 Rimfire. Made c. 1864 to 1872. Total quantity approximately 3,300.

3" superposed barrels pivot downward to load; 4" barrels scarce; worth premium. Made without sliding knife blade attachment, but with an extractor device. Brass frame with silver plated finish; barrels blued. Firing indicator on right side of frame. Walnut or rosewood grips; square butt.

Marked on left side of barrel: WM. W. MARSTON/PATENTED/MAY 26. 1857/NEW YORK CITY with some specimens bearing additional markings IMPROVED 1864. Decorative scroll engraving apparently standard only on the first fifty pistols, and these (and any engraved specimen) will bring a premium in value:
8A-075 Values—Good **$750** Fine **$2,000**

8A-075

Mayall Patent Combination Pers. / Ctge. Revolver *See 7A-062.5*

Merrimack Arms Manufacturing Company, Newburyport, Massachusetts
See Brown Manufacturing Company.

Merwin & Bray Single Shot Deringers

Merwin & Bray, New York City, Single Shot Deringers. Circa 1859-1866. The firm were firearms and sporting goods dealers **(see the following commentary and history of Merwin, Hulbert & Co. for details.)** The deringers are believed to have been manufactured by Bacon Mfg. Company of Norwich, Conn. (q.v.). Total quantity both calibers estimated at 4,100. *(See also: Plant Front Loading Revolvers, calibers 30 and 42 for Merwin & Bray marked revolvers.)*

32 caliber or 22 caliber rimfire. Octagon barrel pivots to right for loading. Brass frame (iron frame rare; worth premium) silver plated; barrel blued. Spur trigger. Walnut grips; square butt.

Barrel marking: MERWIN & BRAY NEW YORK

Other markings: J.P. LOWER(very scarce) and A. WURFFLEIN PHILA (rare) known and worth premium.

8A-076
32 Caliber

8A-076.5
22 Caliber

32 caliber rimfire. 3-1/2" barrel:

8A-076	Values—Good **$150**	Fine **$475**

22 caliber rimfire. 3" octagon barrel marked as above. Smaller proportion than 32 caliber with sharper drop/angle of handle to frame:

8A-076.5	Values—Good **$275**	Fine **$650**

Merwin, Hulbert & Co. Revolvers

The history of Merwin, Hulbert & Co. and the cataloging of their firearms for easy identification reflect the customary, slow-evolving (often erratic) selective pattern evidenced in many other areas of collecting antique arms. Merwins are typical of firearms once considered on the periphery of "antique," possessing but minimal collector interest (and consequent values). With the passage of time and the publication of thought-provoking (if not eye-opening) information those same guns acquired the patina of antiquity, along with a following of devotees. Comparatively "late starters," firearms marked "Merwin, Hulbert" were largely overlooked by a broad segment of the collecting world. With increasing collector interest in American firearms of the latter nineteenth century and the coincidental publication in 1991 of the primary work *"The Story of Merwin, Hulbert & Co. Firearms"* (A. Phelps) as the stimulus for recognition, these revolvers slowly became much sought-after collectibles...their values rising (and continuing to do so) commensurately. The attractive book, with its remarkably profuse and detailed illustrations of an extensive collection of plain and fancy engraved specimens, along with the liberal use of patent drawings and illustrations from original Merwin, Hulbert catalogs, had been long awaited. Unexpectedly, it was imprecise in offering a correct history of the company...or cautiously classifying their firearms and numerous variants in a clear and comprehensive arrangement...i.e. one that would facilitate its use by the casual collector or dealer, as well as by the advanced specialist! In the years following the publication of that work, a Merwin, Hulbert Collector's Association was organized in the late 1990s...and there have been various attempts to codify all models and variants of their firearms. Articles about these revolvers have appeared with greater frequency in the arms press, yet they still lack for a much-needed, detailed, comprehensive handbook or directory.

As Merwin, Hulbert revolvers are now significant valuable collectibles, easily affirmed by the prices many of them command, the reader is due an explanation as to why they had yet to be categorized in greater detail, as with guns of

competitive makers. They represent the single instance in compiling this work where such remarks were deemed expedient...and for which the collector's indulgence is sought: Commencing with the sixth edition in 1994, through to this ninth edition I accumulated a vast file of correspondence with various specialist collectors (including the author of the prior-named 1991 work) in an attempt to organize and catalog them in order that they may be better understood and identified. That file of material, increasingly voluminous in the interims between editions, became ever more contradictory, conflicting...and occasionally illogical! For example, where one authority was of the opinion that major variants on certain models (such as "flutes" on cylinders or "scoops" on frames...or solid versus folding hammers on other models) made for significant differences and should be established as distinct variations (with commensurate alteration in values), others attached little importance to them, finding them neither worthy of mention nor having impact on values. There remain various schools of thought as to the importance of certain manufacturing variations encountered on Merwin, Hulberts. Only the marketplace will eventually sort out and solve the dilemma.

Merwin, Hulbert revolvers had a unique method of mechanical operation, primarily adapted to their loading and extracting. Their system was used on a large majority of their revolvers. The firm actively sought U.S. government contracts for those revolvers, none of which ever materialized. Their large-caliber handguns have traditionally been considered "Secondary Martial" handguns, but no evidence exists to substantiate actual military purchases or issuance. A few other Merwin, Hulberts of smaller pocket size, spur trigger, single-action and lesser sized double-action revolvers (none of which are listed here) are also slowly finding their way into the mainstream of collector recognition. Numerous marking variations (especially on the larger single and double action Merwins) are encountered. Occasionally large frame markings will be encountered **"CALIBER / WINCHESTER / 1873"** which may tend to confuse collectors to conclude that there is an association with the Winchester Co. Those marks merely indicate the revolver was chambered for the popular 44-40 caliber! The same model revolvers occasionally encountered marked **"CHAROLA y ANIT"** are almost exact copies of the Merwins that were made in Spain. They are collectible as antiques and generally bring about half of what the similar Merwin, Hulbert is valued.

The following re-classification, arrived at with the determined assistance of highly respected arms scholars, represents the first endeavor to place the quandary in a more understandable light. Quite a few other Merwin, Hulberts in the smaller pocket size, spur trigger, single action and other lesser double-action revolvers are also slowly finding their way to mainstream collector recognition to join the primary categories discussed and evaluated here.

WHAT'S IN A NAME?

In view of the foregoing, this appears the opportune time to narrate what has generally been agreed upon as historical background for the manufacture and naming of the Merwin, Hulbert & Company line of firearms. Periodically, attempts have been made to correct misleading evidence about the chronology of the company; however, it's clear that the corrected information has not found its way to all quarters. Despite information to the contrary, it is well established that Joseph Merwin, the prime mover behind Merwin, Hulbert & Company *was not an inventor of the revolver that bears his name, nor an inventor of any firearm or firearm improvement* (at least, one that can be documented!). Nor was Merwin, Hulbert & Company the actual manufacturer of the firearms that bear those names, but rather a group of New York City firearms and sporting goods dealers who owned a major, if not controlling, interest in **Hopkins & Allen**, a noted firearms manufacturer in

Norwich, Connecticut. All Merwin, Hulbert revolvers were made by Hopkins & Allen at that Connecticut factory. Quite a few revolvers will be observed bearing dual markings of Hopkins & Allen alongside Merwin, Hulbert. Those dual markings are found on much of the earlier manufacture; the H&A marking was eliminated on those later manufactured (See *Hopkins & Allen Revolvers* by C. Carder.).

Scholarly research by Merwin collectors disclosed that Joseph Merwin opened his gun store in New York City in 1859, with Edward Bray as a partner. Bray withdrew in 1866; by 1867 Merwin had taken on a new partner, Charles H. Simkins; the company name changed to "Merwin & Simkins." That name was quickly altered to "Merwin, Taylor & Simkins" when a second partner, Charles Taylor, joined the firm; the short-lived company existed but a year. Forming a new venture with William A. Hulbert in June 1869 (approx.), their new company was named "Merwin & Hulbert." Three years later Hulbert's elder half-brother joined the firm, the name modified to "Merwin, Hulbert & Co." Although Joseph Merwin died in 1879, they continued under that same name until early 1892, reverting to merely "Hulbert Brothers & Co."

It appears that Joseph Merwin (and subsequently, Merwin, Hulbert & Co.) owned 50 percent (possibly more) of the stock of Hopkins & Allen, and a seat on its board of directors. They were *the sole marketing agency* for Hopkins & Allen (that fact may possibly be subject to modification with further research). There is more to the Merwin Hulbert story; it continues to be an enigma for arms students, and data about the firm continues to be confusing, often frustrating. Their revolvers, though, have been considered by some authorities the equal of Colts for quality and, in certain features, perhaps superior…and deserving of the increasing popularity only recently acquired.

Merwin, Hulbert & Company Large Frame Single Action Revolvers

Merwin Hulbert & Company, New York City; manufactured by Hopkins & Allen, Norwich, Connecticut. Large Frame Single Action Revolvers (a.k.a. "Army Revolver"). Made c. 1876 to 1880s. Total quantity estimated at several thousand.

Caliber 44-40, 44 Merwin & Hulbert, 44 Russian. 3-1/4" and 7-inch barrels, with fractional differences in both barrel and cylinder lengths depending on the variation. Butt styles vary. Nickel-plated finish standard. Black hard rubber grips standard, with mottled colors; ivory or pearl grips bring premiums.

Barrel markings: MERWIN HULBERT & Co. NEW YORK, U.S.A. is usual on barrel (followed by long series of patent dates from Jan., 1874 to March, 1877) and THE HOPKINS & ALLEN Manufacturing Co. Norwich, Conn. U.S.A.(usually on left side of barrel). Markings similar and slightly varying on short-barrel revolvers, which included "POCKET ARMY" markings on right side of frame. Numerous marking variations. Revolvers chambered for caliber 44-40 marked on side of frame: CALIBRE / WINCHESTER 1873. Revolvers chambered for 44 Merwin & Hulbert marked CALIBRE / .44 M & H; those chambered for 44 Russian marked RUSSIAN / MODEL.

Early Models With Square Butt; open top (made without topstrap); scoop type cylinder flutes standard; wedge in front of cylinder pin housing below barrel. Many minor variations provide wide range of collectibles within this model.
8A-077 Values—Very Good **$1,750** Exc. **$5,500**

8A-079
Late Model Single
Action with Topstrap
and Scooped Cylinder

8A-080
Late Production
With Topstrap
& Bird's-Head Butt
("Pocket Army Variant")

8A-077
Early Large Frame
Single Action, Open Top

Early Model with Bird's-head Butt; open top (made without topstrap); scoop type cylinder flutes standard; wedge in front of cylinder pin housing below barrel. (Not illus.) Markings as above.

8A-078   Values—Very Good **$1,250**   Exc. **$3,250**

Later Production with Topstrap and Square Butt; conventional fluted cylinder standard; early scooped cylinders will bring slight premium.

8A-079   Values—Very Good **$1,000**   Exc. **$3,000**

Later Production with Topstrap and Bird's-head Butt; conventional fluted cylinder standard; early scooped cylinders will bring slight premium. Same gun with 3-1/2" barrel with markings on side POCKET ARMY valued at 20 to 40 percent premium.

8A-080   Values—Very Good **$1,250**   Exc. **$3,000**

Merwin, Hulbert & Company Large Frame Double Action Revolvers

Merwin Hulbert & Company New York; Manufactured by Hopkins & Allen. Large Frame Double Action Revolvers. Made c. 1880s. Quantity estimated at several thousand. Calibers 44-40, 44 M & H, 44 Russian. 3-1/4", 5-1/2", 7-inch round or ribbed barrels (Fractional differences in barrel and cylinder lengths). All double-action M & H revolvers are later production and have topstraps. Scooped cylinder flutes rare; serial numbers on these models should be checked for matching. Nickel finish and hard rubber grips standard. NOTE: The earlier square butt style valued at a slight premium over bird's-head type.

Markings same as above single actions with only the patent line different: PAT. APR. 17. 77 JUNE 15. 80. MAR. 14. 82. JAN. 9. 83. on top of barrel in single line with either company markings on left side of barrel. Other markings same as on single-action model. Extra barrels more often encountered on these double actions; a matching number set commands a substantial premium. Folding hammers frequently encountered on double actions (do not affect values) with markings Pat'd. / JAN. 27. 85 either on folding spur or on body of hammer.

Large Frame Double Action with Round Barrel

8A-081   Values—Very Good **$850**   Exc. **$1,250**

Double Action as above with Ribbed Barrel

8A-082   Values—Very Good **$950**   Exc. **$2,000**

Double Action Large Frame as above "POCKET ARMY." Short, round or ribbed, barrel marked "POCKET ARMY" **(the markings if present on long barrels, do not command a premium if present).**

8A-083   Values—Very Good **$1,100**   Exc. **$2,250**

8A-081
Large Frame
Double Action Model
with Topstrap and
Fluted Cylinder

8A-082
Double Action
with Ribbed Barrel
Bird's-Head Butt

Merwin, Hulbert & Company Medium Frame Spur Trigger, Single Action Revolvers

Merwin Hulbert & Company New York City. Manufactured by Hopkins & Allen. Medium Frame Single Action Revolvers. Made late 1870s to 1880s. Quantity unknown; estimated at several thousand.

Caliber 38 centerfire. Five-shot scooped or fluted cylinder. 2-3/4, 3-1/2", 4-inch, 5-1/2" round barrels with ribs. Nickel finish standard. Hard rubber grips standard with dog's head design at top of the earlier production grips; checkered or stippled design on later grips. Flat butt on early production;

both flat and bird's-head butt on later mfr. Values usually same for both types; slight premium possible for earlier flat butt.

Markings MERWIN HULBERT & Co. NEW YORK, U.S.A.or HOPKINS & ALLEN MFG. Co. NORWICH, CONN. U.S.A.on top of barrel rib followed by series of six patent dates from JAN. 24 (1874) through to MAR. 6. 77. When Hopkins & Allen markings used on barrel, the MERWIN HULBERT & CO. / NEW YORK U.S.A. appears on left side of frame and .38 CAL on right frame. Marking variations are encountered.

8A-084
Merwin Hulbert
"Earliest Production"

8A-084.1
Second Style
Early Production

Earliest production: Has exposed cylinder pin; scoop cylinder flutes; the recoil shield on right frame has a semi-circular scooped out area to allow for loading cartridges. 3-1/2" barrel; square butt. Estimated a few thousand made.

8A-084   Values—Very Good **$650**   Exc. **$1,250**

Second style of early production: Exposed cylinder pin, scooped cylinder flutes; an added loading gate (in place of the recoil shield cut-out) on right side of frame slides downward for loading. 3-1/2" barrel. Square butt; estimated a few thousand manufactured.

8A-084.1   Values—Very Good **$550**   Exc. **$1,100**

Later production: Covered (enclosed) cylinder pin; scooped or regular flutes; downward sliding loading gate; various barrel lengths. Flat or bird's-head butt. A few thousand estimated manufactured (listed in earlier editions as 8A-084.7).

8A-084.2
Later Production

8A-084.2   Values—Very Good **$500**   Exc. **$900**

Merwin, Hulbert & Company Medium Frame Double Action Revolvers

Merwin, Hulbert & Company, New York City; mfd by Hopkins & Allen; Medium Frame Double Action Revolvers. Made c. 1880s. Total quantity estimated a few thousand.

Calibers 32 Long and 38 centerfire. 3-1/2" to 6-1/2" round barrels with ribs. Nickel finish and hard rubber grips standard. Flat or bird's-head butts.

Barrel markings MERWIN HULBERT & CO. NEW YORK U.S.A. and PAT. APR. 17. 77 JUNE 15. 80 MAR. 14. 82 JAN. 9. 83 standard. The Hopkins & Allen markings seldom found on this model. Many variances noted. Extra barrels with matching numbers will add 25 to 50 percent to values. Small premium for folding hammers.

38 Caliber, 5 Shot, Flat Butt. Longer barrels will add slight premium.

8A-085   Values—Very Good **$650**   Exc. **$1,250**

38 Caliber, 5 Shot, Bird's-Head Butt. Longer barrels will add slight premium.

8A-085.2   Values—Very Good **$750**   Exc. **$1,500**

32 Caliber, 7 Shot, Flat Butt. Marked .32 CAL. 7 SHOT on left side of frame. Scarce. (Not illus.)

8A-086   Values—Very Good **$850**   Exc. **$1,600**

32 Caliber, 7 Shot, Bird's-Head Butt. Marked .32 CAL. 7 SHOT on left frame. Scarce. (Not illus.)

8A-086.2   Values—Very Good **$950**   Exc. **$1,750**

8A-085
Medium Frame
Double Action
Flat Butt

8A-085.2
Medium Frame
Double Action
Bird's-Head Butt

Merwin, Hulbert & Company Small Frame Double Action Revolvers

Merwin, Hulbert & Company Small Frame Double Action Revolvers. Merwin, Hulbert & Company New York City. Mfd by Hopkins & Allen. Small Frame Double Action Revolver. Made c. 1880s. Total quantity estimated at several thousand.

Caliber 32 Short Centerfire. 3-inch round barrel with rib. Nickel finish and hard rubber grips standard. Flat butt standard. Many variants noted in measurements and mechanisms. A definitive study in the future will undoubtedly isolate the scarcer types. Currently, no apparent value differences yet noted.

Barrel markings identical to those mentioned above for the "Medium Frame" Double Action models. Not usually encountered with Hopkins & Allen markings. Extra barrels with matching serial numbers will add 25 to 50 percent premium to values. Small premiums often added for folding hammers. (NOTE: Listed in earlier editions as 8A-085.1).

8A-087   Values—Very Good **$350**   Exc. **$750**

8A-087
Small Frame
Double Action

Merwin, Hulbert & Company Solid Frame Double Action Revolver

Merwin, Hulbert & Co. New York City. Mfd. by Hopkins & Allen. Solid Frame Revolver. Made c. 1870s – 1880s. Quantity estimated a few thousand. (Not illus.)

Calibers 32 rimfire and centerfire, and 38 centerfire. 2-1/2" to 6-inch barrels. Other calibers and barrel lengths possible. These are standard Hopkins & Allen revolvers usually in their XL series, but bear MERWIN HULBERT & CO. U.S.A.markings on top of barrel or topstrap over cylinder. H & A markings not usually applied. Small premium added for specimens with folding hammer.

8A-088.5   Values—Very Good **$300**   Exc. **$600**

Merwin, Hulbert & Company Spur Trigger 22 Revolver

Merwin, Hulbert & Co. New York City. Spur Trigger .22 Caliber Single-Action Revolver. Makers unknown. Made c. 1870s – 1880s. Quantity estimated at a few thousand. Almost identical in appearance and operation to the Smith & Wesson Model One, Third Issue Revolver. (q.v.)

22 Caliber Short Rimfire. 3 1/2-inch round tip-up barrel with rib. 7-shot fluted cylinder. Nickel finish and walnut grips standard (hard rubber, ivory and other materials also used (fancier types worth premium). Barrel markings MERWIN, HULBERT & CO.standard without patent dates. Other markings observed include SMITH & WESSON MODEL MERWIN HULBERT & CO. N.Y. worth small premium.

Numerous differences observed on these small revolvers (including specimens with squared vs. rounded tops of grips),

8A-089

which apparently preclude their manufacture by just one maker. Believed that these were supplied to M & H by various mfrs.

8A-089   Values—Very Good **$350**   Exc. **$850**

Minneapolis Firearms Co. Palm Pistol

Minneapolis Firearms Company, Minneapolis, Minnesota, The Protector Squeezer Type Palm Pistol. Made c. 1891 to 1892. Total quantity estimated at 3,000. Actual production was by James Duckworth, Springfield, Massachusetts.

8A-090

32 caliber centerfire. Seven-shot. 1-3/4" round barrel. Rotary chambers which must be removed for loading. Nickel plated finish standard; blue finish very scarce and worth premium. Hard rubber side plates; pearl or ivory worth premium. No grip pad on back lever, nor provision for same.

A turn of century Iver Johnson catalog recommended the squeezer as "specially adapted to bicyclists' use."

Markings on obverse sideplate THE PROTECTOR MINN. FIRE ARMS CO. and reverse plate PATENTED MARCH 6, 1883.

Somewhat smaller than the Chicago Palm Pistol and not as elaborately made. The patent date refers to that received by James Turbiaux of Paris, France, the inventor.

Originally classified as a "curio and relic" under the Federal Gun Control Act and subject to its provisions, this arm has since been declassified and is considered as an "antique":

8A-090   Values—Very Good **$1,200**   Exc. **$2,500**

Mohawk Manufacturing Company Pocket Revolver

Mohawk Manufacturing Company, Mohawk, N.Y. mid-1870s. Founded by a consortium of local businessmen. Made circa 1870-1878. Quantity unknown; estimated at a few hundred.

Spur trigger 5 shot 32RF revolver closely fashioned after the S&W Model 1-1/2 Second Issue (q.v.) except solid frame. Nickel or blued finish; rosewood grips; bird's head butt.

3-1/2" ribbed barrel marked Mohawk Mf'g Co. Mohawk. N.Y. Unique feature is spring loaded cylinder lock pin between barrel and ejector with spring inside the ejector; automatically returns center pin.

Company dissolved 1878; machinery moved to "ROME REVOLVER & NOVELTY WORKS" Rome, N.Y. Identical guns known with their markings. (See 8A-157.7).

8A-090.5

8A-090.5   Values—Very Good **$225**   Exc. **$550**

Monarch Marked Two-Barrel Revolver   *See Osgood Gun Works.*

Monitor marked 22 Rimfire and 32 Rimfire Spur Trigger Revolvers
See Whitney Arms Company, Chapter V-J.

Moore's Pat. Firearms Co. Front Loading Rev.

Moore's Patent Firearms Company and the National Arms Company, Brooklyn, New York. Front Loading Teat-Fire Revolver. Made c. 1864 to 1870. Total quantity estimated about 30,000.

32 caliber teat-fire (special cartridge designed by Daniel Moore and David Williamson). 3-1/4" barrel. Six-shot. Brass frame with silver plated finish; barrel and cylinder blued. Walnut or gutta percha grips; bird's-head butt. Markings as indicated below.

An attempt to circumvent the Rollin White patents, the Moore was one of the most successful competitors to Smith & Wesson. It is believed that their strong sales was one reason for Colt's purchase of the National Arms Company (Moore's successor) in 1870. At least six distinct variations are known; basic types and values shown below.

Without Hook Extractor; barrel marking MOORE'S PAT. FIREARMS CO. BROOKLYN, N.Y. Cylinder marked: D. WILLIAMSON'S PATENT/JAN. 5, 1864. Has small hinged swivel

8A-093

gate on right side of barrel lug ahead of cylinder. Estimated quantity made 20,000:

8A-091   Values—Good **$300**   Fine **$625**

Identical to Above; barrel markings NATIONAL ARMS CO., BROOKLYN, N.Y. Estimated quantity made 5,000:

8A-092   Values—Good **$300**   Fine **$675**

With Hooked Extractor Mounted on Right Side of Frame; barrel marking only NATIONAL ARMS CO. BROOKLYN, N.Y. Cylinder marked D. WILLIAMSON'S PATENT JUNE 5 - MAY 17, 1864. Estimated production 7,000:

8A-093   Values—Good **$350**   Fine **$750**

Moore's Patent Firearms Co. S.A. Belt Revolver

Moore's Patent Firearms Company, Brooklyn, New York, Single Action Belt Revolver, a.k.a. "Seven Shooter." Made c. 1861 to 1863. Total quantity estimated at 5,000 to 8,000.

32 caliber rimfire. 4", 5", and 6" octagonal barrels. Seven-shot cylinder. Removable ejector rod mounted under barrel. Barrel and cylinder swing to right for loading. Brass frame and handle with decorative broad scroll engraving standard; silver plated finish. Cylinder and barrel blued. Walnut grips; square butt.

Barrel marking: D. MOORE PATENT SEPT. 18, 1860 Barrels bearing additional markings MF'D FOR SMITH & WESSON BY MOORE'S PATENT FIREARMS CO.(valued at 20 to 40 percent premium).

A very popular competitor to the Smith & Wesson cartridge revolvers, the Moore had a short life due to its loss of an infringement suit brought by Smith & Wesson. Quite a few of

these were known to have been privately purchased by Union officers and enlisted men and carried during the Civil War:

8A-094   Values—Good **$450**   Fine **$1,400**

8A-094

Moore's Patent Firearms Co. No. 1 Deringer

Moore's Patent Firearms Company and the National Arms Company, Brooklyn, New York. All Metal No. 1 or First Model **Deringer.** Made by Moore c. 1860 to 1865 and by National c. 1865 to 1870. Total quantity estimated approximately 6,000 equally divided between Moore and National.

41 caliber rimfire. 2-1/2" barrel twists sideways to load (2" barrels very scarce, will bring premium). Brass frame with silver plated finish (Moores are known in iron, very rare, will bring premium); barrel either plated or blued. Decorative broad scroll engraving on frame and breech of barrel is standard. Distinct variations may be noted in contours especially of the trigger area in the early Moore production.

The Moore is of importance to the collector as it was the first of the large caliber metallic cartridge deringer pistols. The National Arms Company succeeded Moore in 1865 and was in turn purchased by Colt Firearms Company in 1870. Colt brought some of the workmen from National to his Hartford plant, and for a short time, continued production of this all metal deringer as well as the National No. 2 Model (*q.v.*), actually marketing them under the Colt name with design improvements.

Earliest Production; marked PATENT APPLIED FORalong top of barrel; removable sideplate and barrel release button on left side of frame; and straight trigger sheath:

8A-095   Values—Good **$2,000**   Fine **$7,500**

8A-095
Earliest Production

8A-097
Standard Production

Early Moore Markings; D. MOORE PATENTED FEB. 19, 1861 along top of barrel. Release button on right side of frame; curved trigger sheath:

8A-096   Values—Good **$1,250**   Fine **$3,000**

Standard Moore; markings MOORES PAT. F.A. CO. BROOKLYN N.Y. Markings along top of barrel. Release button on right side of frame A very scarce variant has large arrows engraved at each side of barrel markings D. MOORE PATENT FEB.24,1863

(worth premium):

8A-097   Values—Good **$575**   Fine **$1,400**

National Arms Standard Production; barrel marked NATIONAL ARMS CO. BROOKLYN, N.Y. with underside of barrel marked PAT FEB 24 1863:

8A-098   Values—Good **$575**   Fine **$1,400**

Iron Frame National; markings as above:

8A-099   Values—Good **$775**   Fine **$1,750**

Morgan & Clapp Single Shot Deringer

Morgan and Clapp, New Haven, Connecticut, Single Shot Deringer. Made c. 1864 to 1866. Total quantity estimated 500.

30 caliber rimfire (.22 and 30 RF both scarce; worth premium). 3" octagon barrel (with slight variations not affecting values) pivots to right for loading. Two shapes to brass frame (identical to 8A-076 & 8A-076.5 [*q.v.*]) both rounded and flat. Barrel blued. Spur trigger. Walnut grips; square butt.

Barrel marking: MORGAN & CLAPP NEW HAVEN CT.

8A-100

8A-100   Values—Good **$200**   Fine **$475**

Mossberg Brownie Pepperbox

O.F. Mossberg & Sons, New Haven, Connecticut, Four-Barrel Pepperbox c. 1919 to 1932. Quantity 37,000. Although

8A-100.5

resembling a semi-auto pistol the 2-1/2" barrel block has four bores with revolving firing pin in frame; top breaks for loading. The first firearm made by the New Haven firm.

22 rimfire. A thin, removable 3" steel bar that acts as ejector fits in a narrow slot at the top of left frame; rarely, if ever, intact. (Values shown are without ejector). Walnut grips with series of narrow, vertical incised lines.

Barrel marking left side: O.F. MOSSBERG & SONS/NEW HAVEN, CONN. U.S.A. and BROWNIE left frame. Right side of barrels: PAT.JULY 27,1920. Earlier markings up to about serial range 2,500 marked on right "PAT. APPL'D FOR"indicating manufacture circa 1919 to early 1920 before issuance of the patent, worth 25 to 50 percent premium. The "Brownie" is invariably found in quite worn condition; excellent or better specimens quite scarce. (*see also "Invisible Defender" 8A-167.4*):

8A-100.5   Values—Good **$175**   Fine **$350**

National Arms Company, Brooklyn, New York, 32 Caliber Teat-Fire Revolver and 41 Caliber Single Shot Deringer   *See Moore's Patent Firearms Company.*

National Arms Co. Large Frame Teat-Fire Rev.

National Arms Company, Brooklyn, New York, Large Frame Teat-Fire Revolver. Made c. mid-1860s. Total quantity unknown; very limited; rare.

45 caliber teat-fire (special cartridge designed by D. Moore and D. Williamson). 7-1/2" barrel. Six-shot. Brass frame, silver plated finish; barrel and cylinder blued. Walnut grips; bird's-head butt.

Barrel marking: NATIONAL ARMS CO., BROOKLYN, N.Y.:

8A-101

8A-101   Values—Good **$4,500**   Fine **$20,000**

National Arms Co. Single Shot No. 2 Deringer

National Arms Company, Brooklyn, New York, Single Shot No. 2 Deringer Pistol. Made c. 1865 to 1870. Total quantity estimated at 12,000.

41 caliber rimfire. 2-1/2" barrel twists sideways to load. Also made in 2" barrel, will bring premium. Made with or without knife blade extractor. Walnut grips; bird's-head butt. Decorative broad scroll engraving standard on frame and breech of barrel.

Top of barrel marked: NATIONAL ARMS CO. BROOKLYN, N.Y.

8A-102

Purchased by Colt in 1870 who continued manufacture and production of this model under their own name. *See details with description of Moore No. 1 Deringer.*

Made in both iron and brass frames with the latter believed just slightly scarcer. Values about the same for both:

8A-102   Values—Good **$475**   Fine **$1,250**

Newbury Arms Co. Single Shot Deringers

Newbury Arms Co., New York City, Single Shot Deringer (the Albany address often seen for this firm is that of their patent attorney). Made circa mid-1860s. Similarities in workmanship tend to point to James Reid as maker. Quantities unknown; estimates as high as 700 due to recorded serial numbers. Specimens very rare and only few known. Production likely considerably less.

8A-103

22 rimfire. Brass frames with several variations including with and without small lip/overhang on recoil shield and both straight and indented contour to top of grips where they join frame. 1-5/8" to 2-1/4" part octagon/round barrels. Rosewood or walnut grips; bird's-head butt. Almost all specimens unmarked except for serial numbers.

Made without ejector (not illus., identical profile 8A-103.5):
8A-103   Values—Good **$650**   Fine **$1,750**

Made with ejector; a most unusual arrangement appearing as a long, thin, flat bar with rounded protrusion on forward

end, inset on left side of barrel. Serial numbers thus far recorded all under 200 Rare:
8A-103.5 Values—Good **$1,150**   Fine **$2,500**

Newbury Arms Company Large Frame S.S. Deringer

8A-103.8

Newbury Arms Company, New York City, Large Frame Single Shot Deringer. Made circa mid-1860s. Quantity unknown; likely well under 100. Rare.

32 rimfire. Brass frame; square butt. 5" octagon barrel (lengths likely will vary); pivots sideways to load. Circular device on side of recoil shield is barrel lock. Has distinctive Newbury patent ejector with long, flat bar lever, manually operated from front of frame.

Markings on left side of barrel: F.D. NEWBURY; on right side of barrel: F.D. NEWBURY ARMS CO.
8A-103.8   Values—Good **$1,400**   Fine **$3,000**

Newbury Arms Company Single Barrel 2-Shot Deringer

Newbury Arms Company, New York City, Single Barrel Two Shot Deringer. a.k.a. "Double-Ender." Made circa 1860s. Quantity unknown. Very rare.

Made on a specially adapted, large brass frame of the above Deringer (*8A-103.8*). Special 3" thick-walled octagon barrel cal. 25 RF swivels 360 degrees and is chambered at each end. Operates on same principle as the Perry & Goddard (*8A-107*) on theory that it could be more rapidly fired by simultaneously expelling the empty cartridge case. Barrel markings include both **NEWBURY** name and **ALBANY** (N.Y.) address of the firm's patent attorney. Single specimen known, possible prototype. Estimated value for others in mid-high four figures.
8A-103.9

8A-103.9

O.K. Single Shot Deringer

O.K. Single Shot Deringer. Made by Marlin Firearms Co., New Haven, Connecticut, c. 1863-1870. Quantity estimated 800.

All earlier editions of this *Guide* list this deringer as "maker unknown." Recent research clearly shows this to be the product of Marlin.

22 rimfire. 2-3/4" part round/octagon barrel swivels sideways to load. Brass frame; *square butt* which distinguishes it from the commoner type Marlin "O.K." models. Walnut grips.

8A-104

Barrel marked on top: O.K. When J.M. MARLIN/NEW HAVEN markings also present, worth premium. (See 5D-002.)

Markings C.K. often observed on this deringer; merely the result of the marking die having been chipped or broken:

8A-104   Values—Good **$250**   Fine **$725**

Osgood Gun Works Duplex Revolver

Osgood Gun Works, Norwich, Connecticut, Duplex Nine-Shot Two-Barrel Revolver. Made c. 1880s. Total quantity estimated at several hundred.

22 caliber, eight-shot cylinder and 32 caliber rimfire single shot center barrel. 2-1/2" round superposed barrels, the lower one acting as center pin also. Blued or nickel plated finish. Walnut grips.

Barrel marking: OSGOOD GUN WORKS - NORWICH, CONN. and also DUPLEX (usually on barrel catch).

A unique metallic cartridge revolver classed also as a "freak" or oddity. The Duplex featured a hammer striker which pivoted for selectively firing either the revolver or the single-shot center barrel. Barrel pivots downward for loading. A few specimens are also known marked MONARCH; these are invariably

8A-105

encountered with profuse scroll engraving and fancy (pearl, etc.) grips. Worth premium in value:

8A-105   Values—Very Good **$625**   Exc. **$1,450**

Paragon marked Spur Trigger Revolvers (32/38/41 Rimfire)   *See Prescott Pistol Company Revolvers.*

A.J. Peavey Clasp Knife-Pistol

Andrew J. Peavey, South Montville, Maine, Combination Clasp Knife and Pistol. Made c. late 1860s.

22 caliber rimfire. The inventor claimed it could also be used as an alarm gun. Heavy all brass construction with short breech-loading barrel concealed within the handle. Folding single edged knife blade. Concealed trigger snaps open when the oddly shaped hammer (which resembles a second folding knife blade when closed) is cocked.

Peavey filed two patents for his knife pistol. The earlier one described a percussion type of which no specimens have been located. The gun has been declassified by the A.T.& F. Bureau, Department of Treasury from its former classification as "curio or relic" and is no longer considered an NFA weapon, but

rather as an antique and therefore not subject to the Gun Control Act regulations.

First type (a.k.a. "Hook Hammer"). No maker marks present; serial numbered. Distinguished by prominent arched contour to end of hammer which passes through slot at breech of barrel to strike cartridge directly:

8A-106   Values—Good **$2,750**   Fine **$5,000**

Second Type. Flat hammer profile; strikes a pivoting combination extractor-striker which in turn strikes cartridge. Early (scarce) markings A.J. PEAVEY PAT/SEP, 65. Usual markings A.J. PEAVEY/PAT SEPT 5, 65 & MAR 27, 66. All markings on left side of hammer. Serial numbered:

8A-106.5   Values—Good **$2,500**   Fine **$4,500**

8A-106
First Type

8A-106.5
Second Type

Perry and Goddard Single Bbl. 2-Shot Deringer

Samuel M. Perry and Emerson Goddard, Brooklyn, New York, Single Barrel Two-Shot Deringer. Made by Renwick Arms Company, New York City; a.k.a. Double Header Pistol or Perpetual Revolver. Made c. late 1860s. Total quantity estimated 25. Very rare.

Differences noted on all recorded specimens; all display very high quality workmanship. Calibers 41 and 44 rimfire. Barrels 2-11/16" but variances likely; post type sights at each end. Trigger sheaths both straight and curved. Iron frames. Finish full blue, full silver or combination of both. Butt shape either

8A-107
Bird's-Head Butt

**8A-107
Arched Butt**

bird's-head or arched; gutta percha grips. Engraving on frames and barrels standard.

Barrel swivels complete 360 degrees and may be loaded at either end, the theory being that for rapid firing it could be speedily reloaded and fired while simultaneously expelling "the empty cartridge shell from the muzzle in advance of the ball!"

Top of barrel marked in oval panel: DOUBLE HEADER/E. S. RENWICK/MANUFR./NEW-YORK/PAT. JUNE 21, 1864:

8A-107   Values—Good **$9,500**   Fine **$25,000**

The Phenix   *See James Reid Pocket Revolver Model 2.*

Plant's Mfg. Co. Front-Loading "Army" Rev.

Plant's Manufacturing Company, New Haven, Connecticut, Front-loading, Cup-primed, Large Framed Army (so-called) Revolvers. Made c. mid-1860s. Quantities as below:

42 caliber cup-primed cartridge. Six-shot. 6" octagonal ribbed barrel. Spur trigger frame. Walnut or rosewood grips. Serial numbered in sequence 1 through slightly over 8,000. Markings as below.

Merwin and Bray were agents and financiers for the Plant revolvers, all of which were intended to circumvent the Rollin White bored-through-cylinder patents controlled by Smith & Wesson. The intriguing design of the Plant (invented by W. C. Ellis and J. H. White) featured a combination of front-loading, and an exchangeable cylinder, allowing for firing metallic cartridge or muzzle-loading percussion. The cup-primed metallic cartridges also loaded from the front of the cylinder. Though not proving practical, Plants are quite prominent in the era of early metallic cartridge handgun manufacture in America. Occasionally the original spare interchangeable percussion cylinder is found with the 3rd Type Plants (usually on a cased

**8A-108
First Model**

**8A-110
Second Model**

**8A-112
Third Model**

set) and values may be increased approximately 25 percent or more when cylinder is present. In some instances the cup-primed cartridge cylinder will be found bored completely through to accept a breech-loading rimfire cartridge. This was usually a later alteration and will detract from value approximately 25 percent.

Government records have yet to reveal any contract purchase of these pistols. A Merwin & Bray advertisement in Harper's Weekly, May 6, 1865 (and other issues) states the revolver was "...officially adopted by the U.S. Revenue Service." (Be wary of any so-marked specimens). The gun was privately purchased and carried during the Civil War as a personal sidearm.

First Model, Brass Frame. Very much resembles an oversize Smith & Wesson Model 2 Army (*q.v.*). 6" octagon ribbed barrel hinged at top; lifts upward, with cylinder removable, for loading. Ejector rod rigidly fixed in lug below barrel. Rounded all brass frame with silver plated finish. Barrel and cylinder blued. Barrel marked PLANT'S MFG. CO. NEW HAVEN, CT.on top. Marked on side M & B (Merwin and Bray). Cylinder marked PATENTED JULY 12, 1859. Less than 100 believed made:

8A-108   Values—Good **$1,150**   Fine **$3,000**

First Model, Iron Frame. Identical to above. Most often encountered style. Markings identical with addition on side of barrel M & B/N.Y. Estimated quantity made 150:

8A-109   Values—Good **$1,150**   Fine **$3,000**

Second Model, Rounded Brass Frame. 6" octagon ribbed barrel screws into frame. Ejector housing and ejector with round knob handle affixed to right frame behind cylinder. Barrel marked: PLANT'S MFG. CO. NEW HAVEN, CT.on top and MERWIN & BRAY, NEW YORK on frame ahead of cylinder. Cylinder marked: PATENTED JULY 12, 1859 & JULY 21, 1863. Very scarce. Quantity estimated under 50:

8A-110   Values—Good **$1,400**   Fine **$3,500**

Second Model, Rounded Iron Frame. Identical to above. Quantity estimated 350:

8A-111   Values—Good **$950**   Fine **$2,500**

Transition Model: (Not illustrated) Iron frame; flat, with contours of 3rd model (below) except front of frame and barrel lug retain the longer shape of the 2nd Model. Quantity estimated 100:

8A-111.5   Values—Good **$900**   Fine **$2,500**

Third Model. Similar contours to 2nd model with BRASS, flat frame having squared front. Estimated quantity 7,300. Serial range 700 to 8,000 approximately. Small projection on cylinder face after serial 2100 approx. for support allows center pin to pass through; narrow cut-out on right frame allows cylinder to enter.

Type I. Standard (or heavy) Frame: Serial range 700 to 6800 approx. (as illustrated). Sight groove along top strap is full length. Earlier production (worth slight premium) serials 700 to 2100 approx. Face of cylinder is flat (without projection or frame cut-out. Forward lower frame 3/4". A few known with iron frames in serial 6500 range; very rare; worth premium):

8A-112   Values—Good **$400**   Fine **$1,400**

Type II. Light Frame: Serial range 6800 to 8000 approx. Although profile about identical, frame is noticeably thinner and narrower with shorter (9/16") forward, lower frame; sight groove on top strap is scooped out (pinched both ends). Barrel also lighter and thinner; narrow ejection groove on frame:

8A-112.5 Values—Good **$425**   Fine **$1,500**

Plant's Mfg. Co. Front Loading Pocket Revolver

Plant's Manufacturing Company, New Haven, Connecticut, Front Loading, Cup-Primed Pocket Revolver. Made c. mid-1860s. Total quantity estimated at 20,000. Although known to collectors as the Pocket Model Plant and an almost identical version of the large frame Plant (Third Model) Army, but in diminutive size. Production of these arms was by the Eagle Manufacturing Company of New York City with Plant's Manufacturing Company, New Haven as the sales office.

30 caliber cup-primed. Five-shot on most; 6 shot on Eagle Arms Co. 3-1/2" octagon ribbed barrel. Brass frame, silver plated finish with barrel and cylinder blued. Spur trigger. Rosewood or walnut grips; square butt. Various barrel markings encountered: EAGLE ARMS CO., NEW YORK or MERWIN & BRAY FIREARMS CO., N.Y. or REYNOLDS, PLANT & HOTCHKISS, NEW HAVEN, CONN. (this latter brings a slight premium). Cylinder marked PAT. JULY

8A-113

12, 1859 and JULY 21, 1863. The markings A. L. IDE of Springfield, Illinois gunsmith and dealer, circa mid-1860s, noted on a few specimens (also on a few S & W Model 2 "Armies") and may tend to bring a premium. Quite a few variations have been observed, most relatively minor, in hammer profiles, center pins, trigger sheaths, angle of handle:

8A-113   Values—Good **$225**   Fine **$650**

Pointer Single Shot Deringer

Pointer marked Single Shot Deringer. Made by Hopkins & Allen of Norwich, Connecticut c.1870s to 1890. Although unmarked by H&A the gun does appear on their advertising literature of the era along with their revolvers and specifically states that they are "… made at one factory." Estimated quantity 1000.

22 caliber rimfire (also advertised in 30 caliber rimfire, but specimens have not been viewed and would be considered rare and worth premium). 2-3/4" round barrels swivels sideways to load. Made without ejector. Brass frame; spur trigger. Nickel frame with blued barrel standard. Walnut grips.

8A-114

Barrel marking: POINTER:

8A-114   Values—Very Good **$225**   Exc. **$575**

Polhemus "Little Pal" Knife-Pistol

8A-114.5

L.E. Polhemus Mfg. Co., Miami, Arizona. Combination single shot pistol and folding knife. Circa 1925. Quantity 30.

22RF. 1" barrel. Bolt action. Marked on left side of frame L.E. POLHEMUS MFG. CO./ USA, MIAMI, ARIZ./ PAT. APL'D FOR and on right "LITTLE PAL/ MODEL 23/.22 SHORTS ONLY. Two folding knife blades also with Polhemus markings.

The pistol is not permanently joined to the knife and is provided with means to be detached from it. The gun was intended as an utility tool for outdoorsmen, but was quite impractical. Very rare:

8A-114.5 Values—Very Good **$2,500**   Exc. **$5,500**

Lucius W. Pond S.A. "Army" Revolver

Lucius W. Pond, Worcester, Massachusetts, Single Action Large Frame Army (so-called) Revolver. (Not illus.) Made c. 1861 to 1863. Total quantity unknown. Extremely rare with but two or three known specimens.

44 caliber rimfire. Six-shot. 7-1/4" octagon barrel tips upward for loading; hinged at rear of topstrap on recoil shield. Brass frame with plated finish; barrel blued; spur trigger. Walnut grips; square butt. Brass handled screwdriver fitted in underside of butt.

The few known specimens are all unmarked.

Traditionally considered by collectors as a "Secondary Martial" handgun. There is no evidence that they were purchased or issued by the government. The gun has been listed in other works as if it were a widely produced, rather commonly encountered type. It is, in fact, extremely rare with a very limited production as noted:

8A-115   Values—Good **$8,500**   Fine **$25,000**

Lucius W. Pond S.A. Pocket or Belt Revolver

Lucius W. Pond, Worcester, Massachusetts, Single Action Pocket or Belt Size Revolver. Made c. 1861 to 1870. Total quantities estimated at several thousand.

32 caliber rimfire. Six-shot. 4", 5", and 6" octagonal barrels; lift upward to load; hinged at rear of topstrap where it joins recoil shield. Spur trigger; square butt; small screwdriver fitted into the underside of butt.

A direct infringement on the Rollin White patent under control of Smith & Wesson, Pond lost a suit brought by Smith & Wesson which caused cessation of production. The arms remaining on hand at their plant (4,486 of them) were additionally marked on the barrel MANUF'D FOR SMITH & WESSON PAT'D APRIL 5, 1855. These markings usually add approximately 20 to 40 percent premium for their increased interest and Smith & Wesson association.

Quite a few variations have been noted in this model, most notably in barrel latches. Major varieties only are described here.

8A-116

Brass Frame Pond. Small round button latch on left forward frame (a later and rare variant has the topstrap and barrel lug only of brass with the frame of iron and will bring a substantial premium):
8A-116   Values—Good **$350**   Fine **$950**
Iron Frame Pond. Barrel catch a small button on left frame (scarce variant has long recessed bar with spring on left forward frame which acts as barrel release and will bring a small premium):
8A-117   Values—Good **$275**   Fine **$850**

Lucius W. Pond Front Loading Separate Chambers Revolvers

8A-118

Lucius W. Pond, Worcester, Massachusetts, Front Loading Separate Chambers Revolvers. Made c. 1863 to 1870. Total quantity estimated at several thousand.

22 caliber rimfire and 32 caliber rimfire. Other details as noted below. Brass frame with silver plated finish; spur trigger. Barrel and cylinder blued. Walnut or rosewood grips; square butt.

Barrel marking: L. W. POND, WORCESTER, MASS. PAT'D SEPT. 8, 1863, PAT'D NOV. 8, 1864.

The Pond's unusual feature of front loading cylinder utilizing removable individual steel chambers was an attempt to circumvent the Rollin White patent under control of Smith & Wesson.

22 Caliber Rimfire Model. Seven-shot. 3-1/2" barrel. Approximately 2,000 estimated made:
8A-118   Values—Good **$450**   Fine **$1,200**
32 Caliber Rimfire Model. (Not illus.) Very similar in contour to above with larger overall dimensions and different cylinder pin release catch. 4", 5", or 6" octagon barrel. Six-shot. Approximately 5,000 estimated made:
8A-119   Values—Good **$450**   Fine **$1,200**

E.A. Prescott S&W Style Pocket and Belt Revolvers

E.A. Prescott, Worcester, Massachusetts, Smith & Wesson Style Pocket and Belt Size Revolvers. Circa 1861 to 1863. Quantity estimated at few hundred.

22 rimfire and 32 rimfire. Brass frames; spur trigger. Octagon ribbed barrels. Walnut or rosewood grips; square butt. Barrel and cylinder blued.

Barrel marking: E. A. PRESCOTT, WORCESTER, MASS. PAT. OCT. 2, 1860.

Both models are quite scarce and believed to be the earliest forms of Prescotts. Both are extremely close in appearance to Smith & Wesson revolvers, but are easily and quickly distinguished by their solid brass frames with non-hinged barrels.
22 Caliber Size; seven-shot. 3-1/8" barrel (will vary slightly). Closely patterned after the Smith & Wesson Model 1, 2nd Issue; often encountered without marker's markings:
8A-120   Values—Good **$375**   Fine **$1,100**
32 Caliber Model; six-shot. 5-3/4" barrel (will vary slightly). Closely patterned after the Smith & Wesson Model 2 Army;

8A-120

8A-121

marker's markings usually present:
8A-121   Values—Good **$450**   Fine **$1,400**

E.A. Prescott Single Action "Navy" Revolver

E.A. Prescott, Worcester, Massachusetts. Single Action Navy Model (so-called) Revolver. Made c. 1861 to 1863. Total quantity estimated at a few hundred.

38 caliber rimfire. Six-shot cylinder. 7-1/2" octagon barrel

(vary slightly), but also known with 6-1/2" and 8-1/2" lengths. Barrels and cylinders blued; silver plated on (or nickeled) brass frame models and blued on iron frame. Walnut grips; square butt. Earlier models with locking notches forward on cylinder;

later production with locking notches at cylinder rear.

Barrel marking: E. A. PRESCOTT, WORCESTER, MASS./PAT. OCT. 2, 1860.

Prescott revolvers were infringements on the Rollin White patent. Manufacture of this model and other Prescotts was halted through legal action by Smith & Wesson. Traditionally classed by collectors as "Secondary Martial" handguns. Prescott advertised in popular periodicals that "...by recent experiments made in the Army these revolvers were pronounced the best and most effective weapons in use." Possibly overstating the case, the company did sell 400 of them to the state of Kansas, March, 1862. Kansas, in turn, offered to sell them to U.S. Federal forces then in the state. A U.S. Ordnance report on the pistol gave it praise, but declined to accept them "...as entirely too small to be efficient in the field." The guns are believed to have remained in Kansas and likely were issued to Kansas militia forces. None are known with identifying markings. Quite a few of this model were privately sold to Union military men for personal use during the war years.

**8A-122
Navy Model**

Although iron frame model much scarcer, the brass frame has been more popular and values about the same:

Brass frame Model; most often encountered:
8A-122   Values—Good **$650**   Fine **$1,650**

Iron frame Model; approximately 25 percent production (200 pieces approximately) estimated with iron frames:
8A-123   Values—Good **$725**   Fine **$2,000**

E.A. Prescott Single Action "Army" Revolver

E.A. Prescott, Worcester, Massachusetts, Single Action Army Model (so-called) Revolver. Made c. 1861 to 1863. Quantity unknown. Extremely rare. Closely resembles the Prescott "Navy" above but much larger frame and overall size.

44 caliber rimfire. six-shot. 9" octagon barrel. Extractor rod and loading gate on right side.

Barrel markings E.A. PRESCOTT, WORCESTER, MASS / PAT OCT. 2, 1860:

8A-123.5   Values—Good **$9,000**   Fine **$22,500**

**8A-123.5
Army Model**

E.A. Prescott Pocket Model Revolvers

E.A. Prescott, Worcester, Massachusetts, Pocket Model Revolvers. Made c. 1862-67. Total quantity estimated at several hundred of each of the various styles.

Numerous variations may be found in the arms of this maker. Barrel lengths average 3" to 4" but will vary considerably, as do the shape of frame plates, center pins and their locking arrangements.

Barrel markings: E. A. PRESCOTT WORCESTER, MASS. PAT. OCT. 2. 1860.

Basic styles are:

Long Frame Style; 32 rimfire. Six-shot; noticeably longer handle and grips; flat butt; cylinder locking notches on front. Split-type cylinder pin with blade locking device on underside of pin itself. Iron or brass frame; values apparently the same for each.

**8A-124
Long Frame 32 Rimfire**

**8A-127
Bird's-Head Butt**

**8A-126
Short Frame**

**8A-128
Humped Frame
Variant with Square Butt**

Irregular shaped sideplate standard; round sideplate scarce and worth premium:

8A-124   Values—Good **$200**   Fine **$625**

Long Frame Style; 22 rimfire. Seven-shot. (Not illus.) Same profile as the 32 caliber model but smaller overall proportions. Iron or brass frame; values apparently the same for each. Full octagon barrel standard. Part round /part octagon barrels rare and worth premium. Usually encountered without maker's markings; marked specimen worth premium:

8A-125   Values—Good **$275**   Fine **$675**

Short Frame Style; 32 rimfire. Six-shot. Shorter handle and grips; flat butt. Cylinder locking notches at rear. Latch for center pin on front of frame. Irregular shaped sideplate. Brass or iron frame; values the same for each:

8A-126   Values—Good **$200**   Fine **$625**

Bird's-Head Butt Style; 32 rimfire. Six-shot. Spur trigger; brass frame only. Cylinder locking notches on front. Other features similar to the long frame type:

8A-127   Values—Good **$200**   Fine **$650**

Humped Frame Style; 22 rimfire. Seven-shot. Brass frame.

8A-129
Humped Frame
Variant with Bird's-Head Butt

Octagon barrel 3" to 4" standard. Usually encountered without maker markings or trade names such as "Hornet" (Prescott markings worth premium over values shown):

Square Butt; early type. Retains features of blade latch on cylinder pin; cylinder locking notches on rear. Very scarce:

8A-128   Values—Good **$275**   Fine **$750**

Bird's-Head Butt Style. With later type center pin as usually encountered on the Hatfield production:

8A-129   Values—Good **$200**   Fine **$675**

Prescott Pistol Company Magazine Deringer

8A-129.5

Prescott Pistol Company, Hatfield, Massachusetts, Magazine Deringer. Made c. 1875. Quantity unknown; likely less than 100. Very rare.

32 rimfire. 4-3/8" round, ribbed barrel. The lower "barrel" actually the magazine, holding six cartridges. Top break action; when opened automatically ejects spent cartridge and in closing self-loads new cartridge into chamber. Bird's-head butt.

Barrel marked PRESCOTT PISTOL COMPANY, HATFIELD MASS. (or unmarked):

8A-129.5   Values—Good **$3,750**   Fine **$9,500**

Prescott Pistol Company Revolvers

Prescott Pistol Company, Hatfield, Massachusetts, Single and Double Action Pocket Revolvers. Made c. 1873-1875. Quantities limited. Estimated at few hundred each. These revolvers were made after the expiration of the Rollin White patents and thus are not considered infringements. Although on outward appearance they may be mistaken for "suicide specials" their collectibility is based on much better than average quality and their manufacture by Prescott. Although few of them carry the Prescott name, they are identifiable to their Prescott origin from various manufacturing features and the fact that an occasional original boxed specimen has been seen bearing the Prescott Pistol Company markings.

Open Top Model; 32 rimfire. Five-shot. Spur trigger. 3-1/2" barrel. Brass frame. Nickeled finish. Bird's-head butt. Walnut grips. Numerous features clearly show this to be Prescott manufacture and closely patterned after the Colt Open-Top 22 revolver in style. Unmarked:

8A-130   Values—Very Good **$425**   Exc. **$1,250**

Smith & Wesson Top Lock Model; 32 rimfire. Five-shot. Brass frame, spur trigger, round sideplate. Cylinder locking mechanism on topstrap identical to S&W style. Unmarked:

8A-131   Values—Very Good **$250**   Exc. **$700**

Star Model; Five-shot. Brass frame; spur trigger; nickeled finish; bird's-head butt; walnut grips. Octagon barrels all calibers. Prescott markings not present but they all have trademark of a large 5-pointed star stamped on the topstrap over the cylinder accompanied by No. 32/No. 38/ No. 41. Boxed/labeled specimens that have been viewed do bear the Prescott label as

8A-130
Open Top Model

8A-131
S&W Top Lock Model

8A-132
Star Model

well as the word Star for their model name. Although 41 caliber is the most commonly encountered, traditional collecting patterns cause it to bring the higher price:

8A-136
Paragon

8A-139
Double Action

32 Caliber Rimfire:
8A-132   Values—Very Good **$175**   Exc. **$425**

38 Caliber Rimfire:
8A-133   Values—Very Good **$175**   Exc. **$425**

41 Caliber Rimfire:
8A-134   Values—Very Good **$325**   Exc. **$675**

Comet Model; 22 rimfire (not illus.). About identical to the Star Model above but smaller overall proportions. Brass frame; Seven-shot 2-1/2" octagon barrel; marked COMET on topstrap:
8A-135   Values—Very Good **$250**   Exc. **$550**

Paragon Model; distinctive humped shaped brass spur trigger frame. 2" to 3" octagon barrels. Nickeled finish. Bag-shaped handle; walnut grips. Marked on topstrap PARAGON and No. 32/No. 38/No. 41:

32 Caliber Rimfire:
8A-136   Values—Very Good **$200**   Exc. **$450**

38 Caliber Rimfire:
8A-137   Values—Very Good **$200**   Exc. **$450**

41 Caliber Rimfire:
8A-138   Values—Very Good **$375**   Exc. **$750**

Double Action Model; 38 rimfire. Five-shot. 2-1/2" and 4" octagon barrels; other lengths possible. Heavy appearing, all brass, solid frame and bag shape handle with dome shape butt cast integral. Nickeled finish. Barrel marked: PRESCOTT PISTOL CO. HATFIELD, MASS. (some specimens have been noted marked only UNION .38; although probably scarcer such specimens will tend to bring less than values shown here). With the passage of time, this little handgun has gained interest as another American infringement on the popular English-made Webley "BRITISH BULLDOG," circa 1870s-1880s, which found much favor in America and widely copied by Forehand & Wadsworth (see 8A-061 for the story). This Prescott closely resembles the Bulldog with variances; noticeably, its brass frame.
8A-139   Values—Very Good **$175**   Exc. **$600**

Prescott Pistol Co. Single Action 44 Revolver

8A-139.5

Large, heavy (2-1/2 pounds) single action is conspicuous by its brass frame. Caliber 44 C.F. Semi-fluted 6 shot cylinder.

7-1/4" round, ribbed barrel marked on top PRESCOTT PISTOL CO. HATFIELD MASS. Latch at top of the rearward swiveling loading gate locks in small round aperture on recoil shield. Nickel finish; walnut grips. Not serial numbered. 13" overall. Very rare.

Although there are similarities to the F&W "Old Model Army" (8A-057) and the United States Arms Co. Single Action (8A-186), numerous differences are quickly recognizable when compared. (Button tip of the round center pin is lacking.) One other specimen, elaborately engraved with relief carved ivory grips, silver plated frame and blued barrel and cylinder is recorded in cal. 44 rimfire.
8A-139.5   Values—Very Good **$12,500**   Exc. **$20,000**

Protector Pocket Revolver   *See Jacob Rupertus.*

Queen Single Shot Deringer

Queen Single Shot Deringer; made by Hyde & Shattuck of Hatfield, Massachusetts. c.late 1870s. Quantity estimated 900.

22 caliber rimfire. 2-3/8" part octagon/part round barrel swings sideways to load. Distinctive "sway-back" frame exposes most of hammer. Barrel blued or nickeled plated. Brass frame; spur trigger; bird's-head butt.

Marked on left side of barrel QUEEN. (Note: some specimens occasionally encountered marked HYDE & SHATTUCK and are worth premium over values indicated here):
8A-140   Values—Good **$425**   Fine **$950**

8A-140

JAMES REID, NEW YORK CITY AND CATSKILL, NEW YORK

James Reid (1827-1898) best known for his dual purpose "Knuckleduster" pistols was active as a gunmaker in New York City 1861-1865 (possibly earlier) and Catskill, New York 1868-1883. The first classification of his unique handguns appeared in the November, 1952, issue of *The Gun Collector*, remaining the basic reference to them until the recent publication of the exhaustive study by Taylor G. Bowen, *James Reid and his Catskill Knuckledusters,* which greatly amplified the Reid story.

Born in Belfast Ireland and receiving his early factory experience there and later in Glasgow, Scotland, Reid immigrated to New York in 1857. Utilizing his mechanical abilities and experiences with machinery and tools, he is found listed in 1862 in New York City directories as the "James Reid Manufactory" and by 1863 as "Pistolmaker." His first known product c. 1860-1861, of which but one marked specimen is thus far known, was a percussion, breech-loading, single shot pocket pistol (*see 7C-038*). Reid brought out his 22 caliber cartridge revolver in 1861, quickly followed, in 1862, with his "No. 2" model in 32 caliber. It has been reasonably established that simultaneous with the production of these revolvers, Reid also produced (c. 1862) the small single shot cartridge deringer bearing the name W. IRVING (8A-068), an agent and dealer and whose address at 20 Cliff Street, New York, was the same that Reid used to advertise these revolvers. By year's end, 1862, Reid's business was prospering. In a seemingly obvious attempt to circumvent the Rollin White patent and avoid legal entanglements, Reid devised a dual ignition, combination percussion-cartridge, system for which he was issued a patent in April, 1863. Production on those revolvers commenced immediately running through to 1865.

A great demand for personal handguns was created by the Civil War. In 1863 Reid is believed to have curtailed production to fill (or sub-contract) an order for fellow New York arms maker W.W. Marston for approximately 2000 percussion 31 caliber pocket model revolvers. Those pistols bore the markings of W. IRVING 20 CLIFF STREET N.Y. (*see 7A-036 and 037*); all evidence indicating that Irving was an agent for both makers.

Illness in Reid's family created the necessity to move from New York City to a more healthful environment. Choosing Catskill, New York, north of the city in the Catskill Mountains, for its clean air and surroundings, Reid moved his family there first in late 1865, eventually relocating his manufactory as well. When production ceased in New York City in 1865 his entire work force numbered but nine men and one boy.

In the three year hiatus of his gunmaking activities, 1865-1868, Reid's main business and source of income was from the operation of a grist mill on his new property, a business he continued and ran simultaneous with his gunmaking.

See also Rollin White percussion, breech-loading pistol (7C-038)

Trial examples of Reid's first, most profitable and most famous "My Friend" knuckleduster were made at the New York factory prior to his receiving the patent granted for them at year's end, 1865. Gun manufacturing resumed in Catskill in late 1868 with that "Knuckler." It was well received and sales were brisk. This 22 turned out to be his most successful pistol, made over the longest period, with the total quantity produced over 50 percent of his entire 25-year output. By 1870, under full production he reached a high point of employment with 12 men! Two severe, lengthy economic depressions in the United States, commencing 1873 through the 1880s created great hardships. By 1880 Reid's entire work force consisted of just his three sons, one old hand and a boy helper. The highly competitive market and the introduction of double action revolvers added to his increasing financial predicament. He brought out six new models between 1882 and 1884 in an attempt to attract a broader market, to but slight avail. None generated any appreciable business and merely allowed him to keep his factory limping along. By 1883 all production ceased.

Although his total output was never large, his handguns were not only unusually styled, but were quality products as well. The demise of his business was apparently due to the very poor financial climate in America during the 1870s and 1880s with one depression following closely on the heels of another. In 1884 Reid relocated to West Troy, New York, where he took employment as a machinist.

KNUCKLEDUSTER is a 20th century collector's "Term of Convenience" to describe Reid's dual purpose pistols...obviously derived from "Knuckler" which, with "My Friend," were the original terminology used to advertise them. The MY FRIEND marking, so prominently seen on various models, has obscure origins; Reid's choice of that name is strictly speculative by today's researchers.

NOMENCLATURE. James Reid assigned "No. 1" and "No. 2" to describe his first two revolvers. The word "Model" was not used. Nomenclature used here, for all subsequent pistols is that assigned by the pioneer study published in 1952 and the detailed treatise in 1989. Quite a few interesting variations other than shown here, are to be found in Reid pistols.

REID SERIAL NUMBERS began with No. 1 on his 22 caliber "No. 1" revolver and were carried through consecutively on all subsequent models to the end of production at approximately No. 18600. New York City production ended at approximately No. 3500. It is important to understand that serial numbers were stamped in sequence in batches. For instance, after a small run of one caliber Knuckledusters, production would switch to another model or another caliber, serials would merely continue from where the last model or caliber left off.

James Reid Pocket Revolver Model 1

James Reid, New York City, Pocket Revolver Model 1. Made 1861-1864 New York City. Estimated production 880, which appear in approximate serial range of No. 1 to 2650.

22 caliber rimfire. 3-1/2" octagon barrel. seven-shot cylinder. Iron frame standard with blued or silver finish; brass frames rare and worth premium; combination of iron frame and brass parts (such as loading gate, escutcheon plate, etc.) also rare; worth premium. Three frame variations: earliest, and most common, known as "High Hump" (as shown here) with noticeable bump on top of frame (into which loading gate pivot screw fastens). Later, very scarce style "Straight Line" frame has no hump,

8A-141

merely slight bulge at rear of top strap. Third style frame also scarce, without the small circular inspection plate on left frame with hammer screw. Barrel and cylinder also blued or silvered. Few rare variants are known with rounded butts.

Barrel marking: J. REID. NEW YORK. Variant markings: JAMES P. FITCH. N.Y. PHOENIX REVOLVER or WM. IRVING, NEW YORK scarce and worth premium; HOLEY MFG. CO, LAKEVILLE, CONN rare and worth premium.

Model No. 1 also known with ejector rod on right side of barrel; scarce and worth premium:

8A-141   Values—Good **$300**   Fine **$1,100**

James Reid Pocket Revolver Model 2

James Reid, New York City, Pocket Revolver, Model 2. Made c. 1862-64. Total quantity estimated at 1,200. Specimens fall in approximate serial range 400 to 2870.

32 rimfire. 4" to 7" octagon barrels. Seven-shot cylinder. All frames are iron; blued or silver finish; barrels and cylinders blued. Upward swiveling loading gate. "High Hump" frame found on early production and likely a bit scarcer than the "Straight Line" frame as shown here. Values same. Earlier productions had many simple scroll engraved frames and worth slight premium. Made both with and without a push rod ejector with loop housing on right forward frame; worth 10 percent premium. Ejector rod often lacking due to poor method of fastening. Other variants of this model known. Walnut grips. Advertisements in *Harpers Weekly* during 1862 offered the gun as the "Army Cartridge Revolver." However, there are no known government or state purchases on record.

Barrel marking: ADDRESS. W. IRVING. 20. CLIFF ST. N.Y. or JAMES P. FITCH. N.Y. PHOENIX REVOLVER or THE PHENIX (sic).

8A-142
With Ejector
"Straight Line Frame"

8A-142
Without Ejector
"High Hump Frame"

The barrel marking: J. REID NEW YORK rarely encountered and worth premium:

8A-142   Values—Good **$300**   Fine **$1,100**

James Reid Pocket Revolver Models 3 and 3A

James Reid, New York City, Combination Metallic Cartridge and Percussion Pocket Revolver Models 3 and 3A. Manufactured 1863.

Dual ignition; combination percussion 31 caliber with removable nipples to "quickly" convert to 32 rimfire. 6-shot. Octagon barrel 3-1/2" to 8" (rare length). Upward swiveling loading gate Iron frame standard.

8A-143
Model 3

8A-143.5
Model 3A

Key identification between this model and models 4 and 4A is manner cylinders are removed for cleaning. Model 3 removed in conventional way by removing center pin. Models 4 and 4A require wrench to loosen barrel and partially unscrew to remove cylinder.

Basic visual difference: Models 3 & 3A no barrel threads visible between front of cylinder and frame. Models 4 and 4A barrel threads in clear evidence between front of cylinder and frame.

Barrel markings: J. REID N.Y. CITY/PATD. APL.28,1863.

Finish: Cylinder and barrel blued; frame either blued or silverplated.

Model 3. Estimated quantity made 120. Found in approximate serial range 1900 to 2130. Loading lever and plunger mounted below barrel:

8A-143   Values—Good **$550**   Fine **$1,500**

Model 3A. Estimated quantity made 220 which appear in approximate serial range 1950 to 2230. Intended for sale primarily as cartridge/rimfire revolvers although the dual ignition threads for percussion nipples are found both intact and removed in chambers of cylinder. Brass frames are known in this model; very rare; worth premium:

8A-143.5   Values—Good **$475**   Fine **$1,275**

James Reid Pocket Revolver Models 4 and 4A

James Reid, N.Y. City, Dual Ignition Revolver Combination 32 Metallic Cartridge and/or 31 Caliber Percussion Models 4 and 4A. Made 1863-1865.

See Model 3 above for major distinguishing feature. Barrel 3-1/2" to 8" (rare). Iron frame; loading gate on right swivels upward. Finish: blue cylinder and barrel; blue or silver finished frame. Rosewood grips.

Barrel marking: J. REID N.Y. CITY/PATD.APL.28.1863.

Model 4. Estimated quantity made 1,070 found in serial range 2230 to 3500. Loading lever and plunger mounted under barrel;

8A-144
"Model 4"

removable nipples:

8A-144   Values—Good **$400**   Fine **$1,000**

8A-145
"Model 4A"

Model 4A. Intended primarily for use only with metallic cartridges. Made without loading lever and button tip center pin. Although intended for use with metallic cartridges the nipple threads in chambers of cylinder were kept intact (except for handful of very last production) to avoid infringement of the Rollin White patent. Estimated quantity made 50, found in serial range 2335 to 3470:

8A-145   Values—Good **$425**   Fine **$1,000**

James Reid 22 Cal. Knuckle-Duster Revolver

James Reid, Catskill, New York, Knuckle-Duster Revolver 22 Caliber Rimfire. Made c. 1868 to 1882. Total quantity estimated 10,690. Found in serial range 3500-17715.

Seven-shot. All metal construction. Brass frames are silver plated; iron frames blued. Safety device appears on frames through to approximately Serial No. 10000.

Left side of frame marked MY FRIEND underneath cylinder (and will bring slight premium); later production marking changed to MY FRIEND PATD. DEC. 26, 1865 over the cylinder. Broad scroll engraving standard on frame, varies considerably.

One of the most distinctive appearing American revolving cartridge handguns, the frame acts also as a set of knuckles for hand fighting. More of this model were made than any other Reid firearm; over 50 percent of total production. Also widely known and often termed in advertising of its era, a "Knuckler," (but not so marked on the gun).

8A-146

Brass Frame Type; most often encountered. Estimated quantity made 9,900. Many center pin variations:

8A-146   Values—Good **$700**   Fine **$1,650**

Iron Frame Type; made towards end of production 1881-1882. Estimated quantity made just 270 in serial range 17373 to 17715. *Rare:*

8A-147   Values—Good **$950**   Fine **$2,250**

James Reid 32 Cal. Knuckle-Duster Revolver

James Reid, Catskill, New York, Knuckle-Duster Revolver Caliber 32 Rimfire. (Not illus.) Made c. 1870 to 1882. Total quantity estimated 3,100 in serial range 6570 to 17900. About identical in contour to the 22 caliber model, but larger in size.

Five-shot. All metal construction. Brass frame type, silver plated; iron frame blued.

Left side of topstrap marked: MY FRIEND PATD. DEC. 26, 1865. Broad scroll engraving standard on frame.

Early production style with brass frame; safety device on underside of frame and trapdoor in butt secured by a screw

(allows access for adjusting mainspring tension). *Very scarce:*

8A-148   Values—Good **$900**   Fine **$2,000**

Standard brass frame model; made without safety device. Has removable plate on left side of frame allowing for access to mainspring. Approximately 2,900 brass frame models made (includes the early production):

8A-149   Values—Good **$850**   Fine **$1,750**

Iron frame model; manufactured towards end of production in approximately 17000 serial range. Approximately 170 made:

8A-150   Values—Good **$1,150**   Fine **$2,750**

James Reid 41 Cal. Knuckle-Duster Revolver

James Reid, Catskill, New York, Knuckle-Duster Revolver Caliber 41 Rimfire. Made c. 1870 to 1872. Total quantity estimated about 150 in serial range 6000 to 9000. About identical in contour to smaller caliber models, but larger overall size and note the length of cylinder in proportion to frame.

All metal construction. Five-shot with each chamber rifled. Brass frame silver plated. Safety device standard as is trapdoor in butt for access to mainspring adjustment screw.

Topstrap marked: J. REID'S DERRINGER/PATD. DEC. 26, 1865 Scroll engraving standard on frame:

8A-151   Values—Good **$6,500**   Fine **$20,000**

8A-151

James Reid Model No. 1 Knuckle-Duster

James Reid, Catskill, New York, Model No. 1 Knuckle-Duster With Barrel; a.k.a. 3" Barrel Knuckle-Duster. (Not illus.) Made 1875. Total quantity estimated at 250. Serial number range 11833 to 12019. Identical to Model No. 2, but longer barrel.

32 caliber rimfire. Five-shot. 3" round barrel; post type front

sight. All metal construction. Brass frame engraved and silver plated.

Left side of topstrap marked: MY FRIEND PATD. DEC. 26, 1865. Scroll engraving standard on frame:

8A-152   Values—Good **$1,850**   Fine **$5,000**

James Reid Model No. 2 Knuckle-Duster

8A-153

James Reid, Catskill, New York, Model No. 2 Knuckle-Duster With Barrel; a.k.a. 1-3/4" Barrel Knuckle-Duster. Made 1877. Total quantity estimated about 100. Most specimens fall in the 13330 to 14430 serial range.

32 caliber rimfire. Five-shot. 1-3/4" round barrel; blade type front sight. All metal construction. Brass frame, silver plated.

Left side of frame marked: MY FRIEND PATD. DEC. 26, 1865. Also marked on barrel and on cylinder: MY FRIEND. Scroll engraving standard on frame:

8A-153   Values—Good **$2,000**   Fine **$5,000**

James Reid Model No. 3 Deringer

James Reid, Catskill, New York, Model No. 3 Deringer With Octagon Barrel; a.k.a. All Metal Revolver. Made 1882. Total quantity estimated about 75. Specimens fall in serial range of 17715 to 17790.

41 caliber rimfire. Five-shot semi-fluted cylinder. 2-7/8" octagon barrel. All metal construction. Iron frame silver plated.Profuse engraving entire frame and handle is standard.

Barrel marking: REID'S DERRINGER

8A-154

8A-154   Values—Very Good **$2,000**   Exc. **$5,000**

James Reid Model No. 4 Deringer

James Reid, Catskill, New York, Model No. 4 Deringer With Barrel; a.k.a. Reid's Extractor. Made 1882. Total quantity estimated at about 125. Most specimens fall within serial range 17790 to 17930.

41 caliber rimfire. Five-shot semi-fluted cylinder. 2-7/8" octagon barrel. Brass frame with silver plated finish. Combination type loading gate and cartridge extractor on right side of frame (the Reid's patent "extractor" from which the markings are abbreviated). Rosewood grips.

Barrel marking: REID'S EX'TR.:

8A-155

8A-155   Values—Very Good **$1,600**   Exc. **$4,750**

James Reid New Model Revolver

James Reid, Catskill, New York, New Model Revolver. Made c. 1882-83. Total quantity estimated about 250. Serial number range 17990 to 18240.

32 caliber rimfire. Five-shot semi-fluted cylinder. 2-1/2" round barrel. Brass frame with silver plated finish. Combination type loading gate and cartridge extractor on right side of frame. Rosewood grips.

Barrel marking: REID'S NEW MODEL .32 Marked on right side of frame: REID'S SHELL EXTRACTOR

8A-156

8A-156   Values—Very Good **$600**   Exc. **$1,500**

James Reid New Model Knuckle-Duster

James Reid, Catskill, New York, New Model Knuckle-Duster Revolver; a.k.a. "Protector." Made 1883. Total quantity estimated about 360. Specimens fall within serial number range approximately 18240 to 18600.

32 caliber rimfire. Five-shot semi-fluted cylinder. 2" round barrel. Spur or knob type hammer.

The silver plated iron frame in appearance is a partial reversion to the knuckle-duster type design. Knurled cylinder pin. Scroll engraving on handle and trigger sheath is standard. Encountered with and without loading groove on right frame.

8A-157

Barrel marking: REID'S NEW MODEL .32 MY FRIEND

8A-157   Values—Good **$1,250**   Fine **$3,750**

Remington Arms Company   *See Chapter V-E, Remington Arms.*

Renwick Arms Company   *See Samuel Perry and E. Goddard.*

Reynolds, Plant and Hotchkiss Marked 30 Caliber Cup-Primed Revolver
See Plant's Manufacturing Co.

Rodier Single Shot Deringer

Louis C. Rodier, Springfield, Massachusetts, Single Shot Deringer. Made circa mid-1870s. Quantity estimated less than 1000; examples quite scarce.

22 rimfire. 2-3/4" round barrel (will vary). Iron frame. Blued finish. Walnut grips. Very simple construction; only two moving parts. The hammer, breech block and firing pin one solid single unit. Markings: "RODIER PAT. SEP. 15 74" on barrel:

8A-157.5   Values—Good **$275**   Fine **$650**

8A-157.5

Rome Revolver Works Pocket Revolver

Rome Revolver & Novelty Works, Rome, New York, circa 1878-1908 (not illus.). Quantity not known; extremely limited with few known specimens (actual production of revolvers by that company ceased in the mid-1880s and company name reverted to merely "Novelty Mfg. Co."

Spur trigger, five shot, caliber 32 rimfire revolver. About identical (with very few minor variations) to the MOHAWK MFG. COMPANY REVOLVER; see 8A-090-5.

The Rome Revolver Works had purchased the remaining stock of machinery of the failed Mohawk Company and was equally unsuccessful in the venture:

8A-157.7   Values—Very Good **$275**   Exc. **$600**

Jacob Rupertus Pepperbox

Jacob Rupertus, Philadelphia, Pennsylvania, Pepperbox. Made c. 1860s. Total quantity estimated at 3,000.

22 caliber rimfire. Eight-shot. 2-1/2" (earlier) and 3" tapering barrel cluster. Brass frame. Walnut grips. Barrels blued.

Marked: RUPERTUS PAT. PISTOL MFG. CO. PHILADELPHIAon butt on earlier specimens; same marking on left side of frame on later production.The 3-inch variant usually marked on left frame in circular motif: "RUPERTUS PATENT JULY 19TH, 1864." There are a few recorded entirely unmarked.

Patented July 19, 1864, this spur trigger, single action Pepperbox has converging, tapered barrels (for lightening overall weight) and a rotating breech piece with loading gate that also acts as a safety. A removable ejector rod is mounted in

8A-158

the center of the barrel cluster:
8A-158   Values—Good **$700**   Fine **$2,000**

Jacob Rupertus Single Shot Deringer

8A-159

Jacob Rupertus, Philadelphia, Pennsylvania. Single Shot Pocket Deringer. Made c. 1870s to 1880s. Total quantity estimated approximately 2,000. Calibers and barrel lengths as below. The part round/part octagonal barrel twists or rotates sideways for loading. Iron frame; spur trigger; blued finish. Walnut grips with squared butt.

Marked on barrel: RUPERTUS PAT'D. PISTOL MFG. CO. PHILADELPHIA.

22 Caliber Rimfire; 3" barrel average length. Estimated quantity made 500:
8A-159   Values—Good **$250**   Fine **$600**
32 Caliber Rimfire; 4" or 5" barrel average. Estimated quantity made 1,000:
8A-160   Values—Good **$250**   Fine **$550**
38 Caliber Rimfire; 5" barrel. Estimated quantity made 1,000:
8A-161   Values—Good **$250**   Fine **$550**
41 Caliber Rimfire. Previous listings in 41 rimfire likely incorrect measured 38 rimfire size. Specimens in 41 rimfire if found would be very rare. Estimated values:
8A-162   Values—Good **$1,500**   Fine **$3,750**

Jacob Rupertus Double Barrel Deringer

Jacob Rupertus, Philadelphia, Pennsylvania, Double Barrel Deringer. Made c. 1870s or early 1880s. Total quantity estimated at 100.

22 caliber rimfire. 3-1/8" side-by-side mounted round barrels. About identical in appearance to the single shot model except for the barrels. Iron frame, spur trigger. Overall blued finish. Walnut grips; squared butt.

Marking: RUPERTUS PAT'D. PISTOL MFG. CO. PHILADELPHIA

An unusually designed handgun, the firing pin is adjustable for selectively striking either barrel with the single hammer. Two

8A-163

variations of the firing pin have been noted (a) mounted in frame (b) mounted on hammer; both equally rare:

8A-163   Values—Good **$950**   Fine **$2,500**

Jacob Rupertus Spur Trigger Revolvers

8A-164

Jacob Rupertus, Philadelphia, Pennsylvania, Spur Trigger Revolvers. Made c. 1870s to 1880s. Dimensions and quantities as below.

Iron frames; spur triggers; plated or blued finish. Walnut grips; bird's-head butt.

22 Caliber Rimfire; (illustrated) seven-shot; straight unfluted cylinder with small locking notches on forward edge; 2-3/4" round barrel marked on top EMPIRE PAT. NOV. 21. 71 and along

side J. RUPERTUS. PHILA. Specimens also found with the marking PROTECTOR ARMS CQ Estimated quantity made 1,000:

8A-164   Values—Good **$125**   Fine **$375**

32 rimfire or centerfire. Five-shot with semi-fluted cylinder. 2-1/2" to 3" round barrel; markings as above. Estimated quantity made 1500:

8A-164.5   Values—Good **$125**   Fine **$350**

38 rimfire or centerfire. Five-shot with semi-fluted cylinder. 2-7/8" round barrel; markings as above and often EMPIRE No. 1 on topstrap. Estimated quantity made 1500:

8A-164.6   Values—Good **$125**   Fine **$350**

41 Caliber Rimfire; five-shot with semi-fluted cylinder. 2-7/8" round barrel. Barrel markings along top EMPIRE 41, and on side J. RUPERTUS PHILA. PA. Estimated quantity made several hundreds. In general contours, similar to the 22 caliber model, but larger. Basic differences in semi-fluted cylinder and variances in cylinder pin:

8A-165   Values—Good **$300**   Fine **$750**

Francis Schopp Two Shot "Harmonica" Pistol

Francis Schopp Two Shot "Harmonica" Pistol. Patented 1865 by Francis Schopp, New York City. Quantity unknown. Very rare.

Silver plated iron, spur trigger frame. Caliber 30 RF. 2-1/2" round barrel. 6" overall. Blued finish to the two chamber "harmonica" bar. Only markings **NEW YORK** on left side of barrel.

Displays very fine workmanship of highly accomplished gunmaker; also profusely engraved in the same professional manner.

Cocking the hammer moves the spring-loaded two chamber bar to the right to bring first shot in line. After firing, hammer brought to half-cock and bar manually moved to left, after which, hammer may be brought to full cock to fire. Twin firing pins to strike top and bottom of cartridge simultaneously insure

8A-165.5

ignition. With only a single recorded recent sale, values shown are broad estimate:

8A-165.5   Values—Very Good **$3,500**   Exc. **$6,000**

"1776" Marked Single Shot Deringer   *See "Boss."*

C. Sharps & Company   *See Chapter V-F, Sharps Firearms.*

Sharps & Hankins   *See Chapter V-F, Sharps Firearms.*

C.S. Shattuck Pocket Revolver

C. S. Shattuck, Hatfield, Massachusetts, Pocket Revolver. Made c. 1880s. Total quantity estimated at a few thousand.

32 caliber rimfire (calibers 22, 32 centerfire, 38 and 41 very scarce and will bring premiums). Five-shot. Spur trigger; nickeled finish. Checkered black rubber grips; square butt.

Barrel marked: C. S. SHATTUCK HATFIELD, MASS. PAT. NOV. 4, 1879. (*See also "BOOM" revolver 8A-030*)

Although in outward appearance a "Suicide Special," their collectibility is based on the distinctive, unique swing-out cylinder. Some specimens are seen with special hard rubber

8A-166

grips having high relief portrait on left side of Abraham Lincoln and on right side James A. Garfield, the two assassinated presidents; a rather macabre commemoration of their demise. Such grips if in excellent condition will add approximately 25 to 50 percent premium to the value:

8A-166   Values—Very Good **$200**   Exc. **$475**

C.S. Shattuck Patent Double Action Revolver

C.S. Shattuck, Hatfield, Massachusetts, Patented Double Action Revolver. Likely made by Iver Johnson Company (*q.v.*) c. 1880s. Quantity made unknown; very limited. Shattuck named this the **PATENT SWING CYLINDER REVOLVER**, but the gun was not so marked.

32 and 38 caliber centerfire (41 and 44 centerfire also; will bring premiums). Six-shot. Nickeled finish. Checkered black rubber grips (many with dog's head design common to Iver Johnson); square butt.

Usual markings: patent dates NOV. 4, 1879/MARCH 6, 1883 only (one reported specimen with Iver Johnson and Co Makers marks); other markings reported.

8A-166.5

Collectability based on the distinctive, unique swing-out cylinder:

8A-166.5   Values—Very Good **$250**   Exc. **$550**

C.S. Shattuck Arms Co. Unique Palm Pistol

C. S. Shattuck Arms Company, Hatfield, Massachusetts, Unique Squeezer Type Palm Pistol. Made c. 1907 to 1915. During years 1907 to 1909 production was by O. F. Mossberg at Chicopee Falls, Massachusetts, but specimens have not been observed bearing their markings. Total quantity estimated at several thousand.

Classified under the Federal Gun Control Act as a "collectors' item" and considered as a "curio and relic," it must be handled as per provisions of the act.

FIRST TYPE: Possibly pre-production or prototype. Caliber 22 RF. Blue finish. Same size as 22 Cal. standard model. Design conforms almost exactly to the Patent drawing; ejector fitted to the barrels. Swivel for a lanyard or fob affixed to rear of frame. Unmarked. Extremely rare. Estimated range of value in mid to high four figures.
8A-166.8

Standard Production:

Calibers 22 RF and 32 RF. Calibers 25 rimfire and 30 rimfire rare and will bring a premium. Four-shot; firing pin revolves to strike each barrel individually. 1-1/2" barrel cluster, pivots downward for loading. The bottom of the handle is squeezed upward for cocking and firing. Iron frame. Nickel finish standard; various combinations of blue/nickel and blue with casehardened frame are known and bring premium.

Marked on left side of frame: UNIQUE/C. S. SHATUCK ARMS CO./HATFIELD, MASS. This little arms oddity is unique in another way. It appears that the toolmaker misspelled the company name on the marking die. On all specimens observed thus far, it is found that the "Shattuck" name is spelled with a single "T," vs. the double "T" on all other arms. Considerable checking, research and correspondence was engendered by that seemingly minor point. The potential of a variant with both "T's" unlikely to affect the value, but would sure clear up a controversy.

A very rare variation is known with differing action and frame contour; marked INVISIBLE DEFENDER. Worth premium value.

22 rimfire. 1-3/8" steel barrels:
8A-167   Values—Very Good **$1,250**   Exc. **$2,250**
32 rimfire. Steel or brass barrels:
8A-167.3   Values—Very Good **$1,400**   Exc. **$2,750**

*8A-166.8
First Type*

*8A-167
Standard
Production*

*8A-167.4
"Invisible
Defender"*

"**INVISIBLE DEFENDER**" marked variant. Very obvious design and contour differences. Cal. 22 RF. Only markings in two lines on side of barrels "**INVISIBLE DEFENDER**." Shattuck advertising literature has identified this variant as their production. Of added interest is an early undated, pre-WW I advertisement for this pistol stating "**MANUFACTURED BY**

O.F. MOSSBERG, CHICOPEE FALLS, MASS." The gun has many of the design features seen in Mossberg's 4 barrel "**BROWNIE**" (*see item 8A-100.5*). Oscar F. Mossberg earlier worked for Shattuck.

8A-167.4   Values—Very Good **$3,500**   Exc. **$5,750**

Slocum Revolver   *See Brooklyn Firearms Company.*

Smith Arms Company, New York   *See Silas Crispin.*

Smith & Wesson, Springfield, Massachusetts   *See Smith & Wesson, Chapter V-G.*

OTIS A. SMITH

Otis A. Smith Company, Rockfall, Connecticut; held many patents for spur trigger and double action pocket revolvers; manufacturers of very large quantities of same; circa 1870s to 1890s.

Calibers 22 through 41 rimfire and centerfire. Made extensive line of handguns and although usually classed by collectors as "Suicide Specials" quite a few models were of excellent quality and are due better recognition than they have had. Values generally in the "Suicide Special" price ranges with the larger calibers and finer made pieces bringing premiums of 25 percent to 75 percent depending on appearance, quality and condition.

Many of their spur trigger revolvers are similar in appearance to the Hopkins and Allen or Bacon models. These better types are quite often marked only No. 32, No. 38, No. 41 or No. 44 (referring to caliber) with no makers names or markings otherwise appearing. They are often found with hard rubber grips with the intertwined initials O.A.S. or U.S. Arms Co.

Their double action revolvers of various types were marketed under names such as Smith, Columbian, Maltby-Henly. One of their most widely used trade names was "U.S. Arms Co." and oftentimes their monogram was used on grips only.

Otis A. Smith Pocket Revolver

Otis A. Smith Company, Rockfall, Connecticut, Pocket Revolver. Made c. 1880s. Quantity estimated at a few thousand.

32 caliber centerfire. Five-shot. 3-1/4" round ribbed barrel. Nickel finish. Sliding rod under barrel pushes manually to eject.

Marked on barrel: SMITH'S PATENT MODEL 1883 SHELL EJECTOR/OTIS A. SMITH MANUFACTURER, ROCKFALL, CONN. U.S.A. Marked on topstrap: PATENT DECEMBER 1881/32-100 (others marked "New Model," "Newest Model" etc.) CALIBER Checkered hard rubber grips with Smith monogram initials.

Collectibility based on its distinctive brass construction (cylinder only is steel) and unique "T" shaped barrel latch

8A-167.5

containing floating firing pin. An American arms oddity:

8A-167.5   Values—Very Good **$200**   Exc. **$450**

Charles E. Sneider Two-Cylinder Revolver

8A-168

Charles E. Sneider, Baltimore, Maryland, Two-Cylinder, Fourteen-Shot Revolver. Made c. mid to late 1860s. Quantity unknown; very limited. Extremely rare.

22 caliber rimfire. Two individual seven-shot cylinders. 2-3/4" octagonal barrel pivots downward to remove cylinders and load. Cylinders arranged in alignment; one facing shooter, the other facing the muzzle. After forward cylinder fired, cylinder pin rotated to allow for firing second cylinder. Brass or iron frame; spur trigger. Walnut grips; square butt. Value only estimated with no known recorded recent sales. Some specimens marked in script on barrel: E. SNEIDER PAT. MARCH 1862.

8A-168   Values—Good **$8,500**   Fine **$25,000**

Southerner Deringer   *See Brown Manufacturing Company.*

Spencer Safety Hammerless Revolver

Spencer Safety Hammerless Double Action Revolver. Made by Otis Smith of Conn.; Maltby, Henley and Company, New York, New York were agents, c. 1890s (*see also Otis A. Smith*). Total unknown. Estimated at few thousand.

32 caliber centerfire. Five-shot. 3" round ribbed barrel.

Marked on barrel: SPENCER SAFETY HAMMERLESS PAT. JAN. 24, 1888 & OCT. 29, 1889.

Its distinctive all brass construction (i.e., brass barrel, frame and trigger guard all made integral with only the cylinder of steel) classifies this as an American arms oddity.

It is estimated that 75 percent of the total produced were all-brass construction (the feature which has made them most desirable). The remaining 25 percent (approx.) of production were of all-iron construction. Although much scarcer, due to the vagaries of the collecting marketplace, that iron type will bring (possibly) about the same as the brass model and often quite a bit less (subject to change with passage of time and increasing popularity of guns of the era). Three minor variations observed in the profile of rear of frame and position of the safety are yet to be reflected in their values.

8A-169   Values—Very Good **$175**   Exc. **$550**

Spencer Safety Hammerless "Model 1894" Revolver

22 caliber. Generally similar in profile to above. Smaller in size and all iron construction only. Seven shots. 2-1/2" octagon barrel; safety inset at top of backstrap. Quantity unknown; very limited. Scarce.

8A-169

Marked at top of barrel SPENCER SAFETY HAMMERLESS / PAT. OCT. 29. 89. CAL 22, MODEL 1894...or MALTBY, HENLEY & CO. NEW YORK USA with the identical patent dates and MODEL 1894 as above. Valued in range of 20 to 30 percent premium over larger 32-caliber all-brass model.

8A-169.5

Springfield Arms Co. Pocket Revolver

Springfield Arms Company, Springfield, Massachusetts, Pocket Revolver. Made c. 1863. Total quantity estimated approximately 6,000.

30 caliber rimfire. Five-shot. 3-1/8" octagon barrel. Brass spur trigger frame with silver plated finish; iron parts blued. Walnut grips; square butt.

Barrel marked: SPRINGFIELD ARMS CO. MASS.

A lawsuit by Smith & Wesson (for infringement on their Rollin White patent) cut short the production of this model. In 1863, 1,513 of them were turned over to Smith & Wesson as part of a settlement. Barrels bearing the additional markings indicating manufacture for Smith & Wesson will bring approximately 20 to 40 percent premium:

8A-170   Values—Good **$175**   Fine **$425**

8A-170

T.J. Stafford Single Shot Deringer

T. J. Stafford, New Haven, Connecticut, Single Shot Deringer. Made c. early 1860s. Total quantity estimated at 2100.

22 caliber rimfire. 3-1/2" octagon barrel tips downward to load. Brass spur trigger frame, silver plated finish; barrel blued or plated. Rosewood or walnut grips; square butt.

Barrel marked: T.J. STAFFORD, NEW HAVEN, CT. Early production (serials under No. 300) marked on butt PATENT APPLIED FOR and may fetch small premium. Later production marked on butt PATENTED / MARCH 19, 1860. Engraved specimens often encountered and worth premium.

Based on the Babcock patent, this pistol may occasionally be found listed elsewhere as a "Babcock." If seen with such markings, and proved to be authentic, a considerable premium

8A-171

may be added. The Stafford was also made in a larger frame size with 6" barrel chambered for 38 caliber rimfire. Considered rare, this too will bring a considerable premium:

8A-171   Values—Good **$250**   Fine **$650**

"Star" (marked with 5-pointed star trademark) Spur Trigger (32/38/41 Rimfire) Revolver   *See Prescott Pistol Company Revolvers.*

Star Vest Pocket Single Shot Deringer

Star Vest Pocket Single Shot Deringer. Made by Iver Johnson. Circa 1870-1890. Quantity unknown; estimated at a few thousand.

22 caliber rimfire 2" to 4" part octagon/part round barrel (2-1/2" standard); swivels sideways to load. Iron frame; nickeled finish. Bird's-head butt; rosewood grips.

Barrel marked: STAR VEST POCKET:

8A-172   Values—Good **$200**   Fine **$525**

8A-172

Eben T. Starr Single Shot Deringer

Eben T. Starr, Yonkers, N.Y. Single Shot Deringer; Manufactured by Merrill Patent Firearms Mfg. Company, Baltimore, Maryland, 1864-1869. Total quantity estimated at 800.

41 caliber rimfire. 2-3/4" round barrel tips downward for loading; manual extractor. Brass spur trigger frame with silver plated finish; barrel blued or plated. Checkered walnut grips.

Marking on left sideplate: STARR'S PAT'S MAY 10 1864.

A few very early made specimens have part octagon/part round barrels and are completely unmarked. Considered rare, they will bring a premium over values indicated here:

8A-173

8A-173 Values—Good **$1,100** Fine **$2,400**

Eben T. Starr Four-Barrel Pepperboxes

Eben T. Starr, Yonkers, N.Y. four barrel pepperboxes. Made by Merrill Patent Firearms Mfg. Company, Baltimore, Maryland, 1864-1869. Total quantity estimated at slightly over 2,000 of which approximately 1,500 were 4th and 5th models.

32 caliber rimfire. Four-shot. 2-1/2", 2-3/4" to 3-1/4" barrel cluster; tip forward for loading. Outside mounted hammer; button type trigger. Brass frame with silver plated finish; barrels blued. Walnut grips.

Marking: STARR'S PAT'S MAY 10. 1864 either on one line on left side of forward frame or in circular design on left sideplate (on 1st Model found on forward frame). Serial numbers are combination of letters and digits, possibly manufacturing batch numbers and hence, are not means of determining quantities or period of manufacture.

Six basic models of Starrs have been identified; minor variations within those same models. Starrs may be basically identified and relative rarity established by two major features: (a) those with outside springs and short, fat grips, (b) those with inside springs and longer, thin grips. Models 1 through 4 all have the short, fat grip.

8A-175
Second Model

Transition Variation: Same as Second Model above, but breech of barrels are recessed and fit into the recoil shield, cartridge rims no longer visible.

8A-175.5 Values—Good **$950** Fine **$2,500**

Third Model. Rounded standing breech; only vertical firing pin retaining spring visible on right side frame (variant with only horizontal barrel release spring visible on right frame):

8A-176 Values—Good **$650** Fine **$1,600**

Fourth Model. Rounded breech with neither spring visible on right frame. 65 to 75 percent of production estimated this model:

8A-177 Values—Good **$650** Fine **$1,600**

Fifth Model. As above with noticeably longer and thinner grips; convex, checkered front of button trigger. Second most often encountered.

8A-178 Values—Good **$600** Fine **$1,500**

Sixth Model. As above with shorter frame; long, thin grips often checkered; usually short, 2-1/2" barrels:

8A-179 Values—Good **$700** Fine **$1,850**

8A-174
First Model

8A-176
Fourth Model

8A-178
Fifth Model

First Model. Fluted (or dished) standing breech; long narrow barrel release spring horizontally mounted on right side of frame; short narrow vertically mounted firing pin retaining spring on right side of frame just ahead of hammer. Breech end of barrels not recessed to fit into recoil shield, hence the rims of cartridges visible when loaded. Variations are noted in barrel and frame length; smooth front on button trigger. Some specimens have spring raised barrel:

8A-174 Values—Good **$1,250** Fine **$3,500**

Second Model. Flat standing breech; both springs as noted above on right side of frame:

8A-175 Values—Good **$750** Fine **$2,000**

Stevens Single Shot Pistols *See Stevens Arms, Chapter V-H.*

L.B. Taylor Single Shot Deringer

L. B. Taylor & Company, Chicopee, Massachusetts, Single Shot Deringer. Made c. 1868-1870. Total quantity estimated at 1,800.

32 caliber rimfire. 3-1/2" octagon barrel. Brass spur trigger frame with silver plated finish; barrel blued. Walnut grips; square butt. Rare and worth premium in 22 rimfire.

Barrel marked: L. B. TAYLOR & CO. CHICOPEE MASS.

The very bulky appearing forward frame houses the bar type latch which depresses to allow barrel to open:

8A-180

8A-180   Values—Good **$350**   Fine **$950**

J.C. Terry Single Shot Deringer

Jabez Carlos Terry, Springfield, Mass. Single Shot Deringer. Made c. 1860s. Total quantity estimated at under 700.

22 caliber rimfire. 3-3/4" round barrel. Hammer also serves as breechblock. Silver plated brass frame; barrel blued. Walnut or rosewood grips.

Marked along backstrap or butt: J. C. TERRY/PATENT PENDING:

8A-181

8A-181   Values—Good **$750**   Fine **$1,850**

"Tiger" Marked Single Shot Deringer *See "Eclipse."*

Wm. Uhlinger Pocket Revolvers

William P. Uhlinger, Philadelphia, Pennsylvania, Pocket Revolvers. Made c. 1861 to 1865. Total quantity estimated about 10,000 in all variations.

Uhlinger bought the tools and stock-in-process of William Hankins when Hankins entered into partnership with Christian Sharps in 1861. The three basic "models" made by Uhlinger, in order of their production: (a) Long cylinder 22 caliber, (b) 32 caliber, (c) short cylinder 22 caliber. A number of variations occur on all three models, none of which apparently affect values.

To avoid detection by Smith & Wesson (as these revolvers were an infringement on the Rollin White patent owned by them), Uhlinger made these pistols under the following trade names:

D. D. CONE/WASHINGTON, D.C. A patent attorney who, as far as is now known, did not market any of these arms.

W. L. GRANT. No known association has been established for this name. The only individual/firm so named yet located was a dry goods merchant in Camden, New Jersey.

J. P. LOWER. After 1875 a very well known arms dealer in Denver, Colorado; but, during period of manufacture of these arms, he was merely a clerk for a large Philadelphia arms dealer, J. P. Grubb.

W. P. UHLINGER/PHILA. PA. The actual maker of these arms and whose markings are extremely scarce on them.

The models as listed below are evaluated for Cone, Grant or Lower markings which are all about the same. Uhlinger marks will bring approximately 50 to 100 percent premium over those listed. Unmarked specimens are very often encountered. It has been estimated, approximately 50 percent of production were completely unmarked other than serial number. Such specimens, although worth the same as marked ones, usually tend to bring about 10 percent less.

8A-182
22 Model

Long Cylinder (1-3/16") 22 Caliber Rimfire Model. Six-shot. 2-3/4" or 3" octagon barrel. Square butt. Iron frame. Rosewood or walnut grips. Blued finish. Very scarce:

8A-182   Values—Good **$275**   Fine **$675**

Short Cylinder (1") 22 Caliber Rimfire Model. Six-shot. 2-3/4" or 3" octagon barrel. Iron frame standard; also known in brass frame, but very rare and will bring considerable premium:

8A-183   Values—Good **$250**   Fine **$625**

8A-184
32 Model

32 Caliber Rimfire Model. Six-shot. 5", 6", or 7" octagon barrel. Walnut or rosewood grips. Plated or blued finish. Iron frame standard; brass frame very rare and will bring considerable premium:

8A-184   Values—Good **$275**   Fine **$750**

"Uncle Ned" Single Shot Blank Gun

"Uncle Ned" Single Shot Blank Gun. Maker and quantity unknown. Estimated period of manufacture last quarter of 19th century.

Caliber 22 RF Blank. Iron frame, spur trigger. Low quality workmanship; very inexpensively produced. Intended strictly as a noisemaker. Only markings UNCLE NED on side of the short octagon barrel which is cast as one piece integral with the frame. Bird's-head butt; crude wood grips fastened with a simple wood screw. Possible that this blank pistol could be encountered with other names applied.

8A-184.5   Values—Good **$185**   Fine **$350**

8A-184.5

Uncle Sam   *See Iver Johnson.*

Union Single Shot Deringer

Union Single Shot Deringer, made by Norwich Falls Pistol Co., Norwich, Connecticut. Made c. 1880s. Total quantity estimated at 3,100.

22 caliber rimfire. 2-3/4" round barrel swings sideways to load. Iron frame, spur trigger. Nickeled finish. Bag-shaped handle with rosewood or walnut grips.

Barrel marked: UNION:

8A-185   Values—Good **$250**   Fine **$550**

8A-185

Union Arms Company   *See Bacon Manufacturing Co.*

Union Firearms Co., Toledo, Ohio; Automatic Revolver   *See Semi-Automatic Pistols, Chapter VIII-B.*

Union 38 marked Solid Frame Double Action Revolver   *See Prescott Pistol Company Revolvers.*

"Unique" Squeezer Pistol   *See C. S. Shattuck Arms Company.*

U. S. Arms Company; Spur Trigger and Double Action Revolvers   *See Otis A. Smith.*

United States Arms Co. Single Action Revolver

United States Arms Company Single Action Revolver. Made by the Otis A. Smith Company of Connecticut circa 1870s. Quantity unknown. Very limited production.

Combination caliber 44 rimfire or 44 centerfire. Note the unique rigidly mounted double strikers on the face of the hammer. 7" round, ribbed barrel. Unique design side rod ejector locks in place on the oversized center pin; unusual spring retained loading gate. Rosewood grips.

Marked on top of barrel: UNITED STATES ARMS COMPANY—NEW YORK. On topstrap No. 44:

8A-186

8A-186   Values—Good **$2,500**   Fine **$9,000**

U.S. Small Arms Co. Knife-Pistol

U.S. Small Arms Company DEFENDER and HUNTSMAN combination knife-pistols. Invented by L. L. Rogers of Boston,

8A-186.4
"Defender"

8A-186.4
"Defender"

Mass., 1916 who is believed to have made a few of earliest **DEFENDER** types. Almost entire production by U.S. Small Arms Co., Chicago c. 1920-1930. All models caliber 22 RF.

These are subject to the provisions and restrictions of the National Firearms Act. Collectors should not attempt to acquire or dispose of specimens unless complying with those provisions.

Early manufacture by L. L. Rogers (attributed). Workmanship and quality visibly better than later production. Smallest model; only 3" overall, closed. German silver construction. Only the tiny 3/4" barrel, the trigger and the two folding blades (1-7/8" and 1-1/2"; may vary) are steel. Larger blade marked DEFENDER/PATENT APL'D FOR Very rare.

8A-186.3

DEFENDER model by U.S. Small Arms Co. Quantity unknown; considerably less than the **HUNTSMAN**. Markings and dimensions about identical to above. All iron/steel construction and the trigger folds flush into the body. Advertising literature of the period termed this as "Pocket knife size." Very scarce, if not rare:

8A-186.4

HUNTSMAN model by U.S. Small Arms Co. Although quantity unknown, it's said to be "the most widely sold knife-pistol of the period." Advertised as the "**JACKNIFE** size," 4" overall, closed. All iron/steel construction. 1-1/8" barrel tips downward to load. Folding trigger automatically cocks hammer; single 2-3/4" folding blade. Marked **PATENTED** on top of barrel; left side often marked **U.S. SMALL ARMS CO./CHICAGO, ILL:**

8A-186.5

8A-186.5
"Huntsman"

Victor 22 Blank Revolver

Victor Patent Cast Iron Seven Shot Revolver. Fires blank 22 cal. Rimfire cartridges only. Made c. 1880s to 1900. Almost identical to toy cap pistols; might also be termed a "Fourth of July Pistol." Note the narrow cylinder for those short blank cartridges. Cast Iron construction of frame, barrel and handle (integral as one-piece). Double action operation. Nickel finish. Markings cast in relief at top VICTOR PATENT APPLIED FOR Quantity mfd. unknown; maker unknown, possibly Hopkins & Allen or Harrington & Richardson (the latter made a series of revolvers with "VICTOR" markings).

8A-186.8   Values—Good **$100**   Fine **$185**

8A-186.8

James Warner Single Shot Deringer

8A-187

James Warner, Chicopee Falls, Massachusetts, Single Shot Deringer. Made c. mid-1860s. Total quantity estimated 25. Very rare.

41 caliber rimfire. 2-3/4" round barrel. Brass frame. Blued barrel. Walnut grips; bird's-head butt. The wide breechblock is hinged on left side and lifts upward exposing chamber; identical in principle to the Warner Cavalry Carbine (*q.v.*). Elaborately engraved specimens worth a premium.

All specimens observed are unmarked:

8A-187   Values—Good **$8,000**   Fine **$25,000**

James Warner Pocket Revolver

James Warner, Springfield, Massachusetts, Pocket Revolver. Made c. late 1860s. Total quantity estimated at approximately 1,000.

30 caliber rimfire. Five-shot. 3" round barrel; cylinder pin also acts as ejector. Iron frame. Overall blued or plated finish. Walnut grips.

Markings: WARNER'S PATENT 1857 and often seen with additional marking PATENT APRIL 3, 1855 indicating the Smith & Wesson patent infringement; will add a premium of 20 to 40 percent to the value.

Although it appears to be a conversion of a Warner percussion revolver, this handgun was made as an original

8A-188

breechloading metallic cartridge revolver. The frame includes a loading gate:

8A-188   Values—Good **$225**   Fine **$575**

Werner Double Barrel Knife-Pistol

8A-188.3

Daniel Werner; St. Louis, Missouri Double Barrel Knife-Pistol. Patent No. 82,908 of Oct. 6, 1868. Maker and quantity unknown. Very rare.

Caliber 30 Short rimfire. Side-by-side 3" barrels slide forward to load; flat spring latch on top. Silver plated frame with horn side plates. Two vari-sized folding knife blades. Double hammers and triggers. 6-1/2" overall:

8A-188.3   Values—Very Good **$4,500**   Exc. **$7,000**

Wheel-Spoke (so called) Pistol

8A-188.5

Wheel-Spoke (so called) Pistol (a.k.a. Spoke Pistol). Maker unknown. c. early 1850s. Quantity unknown; very small.

22 rim fire. 6 shot. Brass frame and brass octagon barrel (iron also known). Unique vertical turret, manually revolved.

Only three chambers of the spoke-like barrels can be loaded at any one time. The bullet's path when fired is quite convoluted, passing from the chamber, through a hole in the center axis, then through the opposite empty (!) chamber until finally entering the breech of the barrel and passing through it. Very rare:

8A-188.5   Values—Good **$4,000**   Fine **$8,000**

Frank Wesson Handguns   *See Frank Wesson Arms, Chapter V-I.*

Wesson and Harrington Revolvers   *See Frank Wesson Arms, Chapter V-I.*

Western Arms Company, New York   *See Bacon Manufacturing Company.*

Rollin White Arms Co. S.S. Pocket Pistol

8A-189

Rollin White Arms Company, Lowell, Massachusetts, Single Shot Pocket Pistol. Made c. 1861-1864. Total quantity estimated about 3,000.

Octagon ribbed barrels (calibers and lengths as below). Brass spur trigger frame with silver plated finish or iron frame with blued finish. Walnut grips; square butt. Unique breech swivels to right for loading; large bar type manual ejector on side.

Marked ROLLIN WHITE ARMS CO. LOWELL MASS. PATENTED APRIL 13, 1858.

32 Caliber Rimfire; 3" barrel; most often seen size:
8A-189   Values—Good **$375**   Fine **$1,250**

38 Caliber Rimfire; 5" barrel; considerably larger frame. Estimated quantity made 200 to 300; very scarce:
8A-190   Values—Good **$600**   Fine **$1,500**

Rollin White Arms Co. Pocket Revolver

Rollin White Arms Company, Lowell, Massachusetts, Pocket Revolver. Made c. 1860s. Total quantity estimated at about 10,000.

22 caliber rimfire. Seven-shot. 3-1/8" octagon barrel. Brass

8A-191
First Type

spur trigger frame with silver plated finish; barrel and cylinder blued. Walnut grips; square butt.

Barrel marking: MADE FOR SMITH & WESSON BY ROLLIN WHITE ARMS CO., LOWELL, MASS. or merely ROLLIN WHITE ARMS CO. LOWELL, MASS. or LOWELL ARMS CO., LOWELL, MASS.

The Rollin White Arms Company was formed by Rollin White in 1861 to manufacture revolvers to meet the demand which Smith & Wesson could not fill during the Civil War. Their entire production was marketed by Smith & Wesson through their normal dealers. The firm name was changed to Lowell Arms Company in 1864 (Rollin White's association with it was terminated) following a change in management. Approximately 5,000 revolvers were made by the Rollin White Arms Company with the balance of approximately 5,000 made by Lowell Arms Company c. 1864-1865. Values about identical for all three markings, although S&W collectors may pay 15 to 30 percent premiums for those bearing S&W markings. Premiums are debatable for S&W markings and usually less than those of other makers whose revolvers were infringements. Rollin White made many more of these, under contract and by agreement with S&W, than those other makers and these Rollins are more commonly encountered with "S&W" markings.

8A-192
With ejector
and loading gate

8A-191   Values—Good **$225**   Fine **$500**
Variant with ejector. Has special designed ejector mounted on right forward section of frame and a narrow swivel loading gate with loading slot on right frame behind cylinder. Extra markings on right forward frame: PAT. APRIL 2, 1867:

8A-192   Values—Good **$275**   Fine **$625**

E. Whitney or Whitneyville   *See Chapter V-J, Whitney Arms.*

Williamson Single Shot Deringer

8A-193

Williamson Single Shot Deringer, David Williamson, New York City, inventor; made by Moore's Patent F.A. Co. and National F.A. Co. of Brooklyn, New York c. 1866-1870. Although serial numbers as high as 20,000 range, believed considerably less manufactured; likely under 10,000.

41 rimfire and also accepts an auxiliary/adapter percussion chamber. 2-1/2" barrel slides forward for loading. Scroll engraving standard on the silver finished brass frame and trigger guard (gold finish scarce). Barrel blued and if scroll engraved is scarce and worth premium. Walnut stock with checkered handle; tiger stripe maple stock scarce, worth premium.

Marked on side or top of barrel WILLIAMSON'S PAT. OCT.2, 1866 NEW YORK with large arrow design on one or both sides of barrel.

Although substantial quantities produced, the gun is scarce. A great many are seen with handles and grips broken, cracked or repaired. It's quite possible that structural weakness led to many being discarded and the high rate of attrition. When found with the auxiliary chamber, premium of approximately 10 percent may be added to value. Extreme caution is urged as the majority of such chambers are probably of modern manufacture:

8A-193   Values—Good **$450**   Fine **$1,250**

W. Wurfflein Single Shot "Gallery and Target" Pistol

William Wurfflein, Philadelphia, Pennsylvania, Single Shot Gallery and Target Pistol. Made c. 1884 to 1890's. Total quantity estimated at several hundreds. Action same as rifle (*see 14-042*).

8A-194

22 RF and S&W 32, 38 and 44 centerfire. Also advertised with "Shot" barrels in various calibers and gauges. Part round/octagon 10" barrel tips down for loading. Iron frame. Blued finish. Plain or checkered walnut grips. Projecting finger spur at rear of trigger guard. Available with extra barrels and sights.

Barrel marked: W. WURFFLEIN PHILAD'A PA. U.S.A. PATENTED JUNE 24th, 1884.

Often found equipped with a detachable shoulder stock and when present will add premium of 25 percent to 50 percent to value. Also sold with extra interchangeable barrels in varied calibers and lengths. If accompanying gun and matching condition, worth premium of 20 to 40 percent.

8A-194   Values—Very Good **$750**   Exc. **$1,750**

XL Derringer Pistol

XL Derringer Pistol. Made c. 1870s. Total quantity estimated at 2,000.

41 caliber rimfire. 2-9/16" octagon barrel. Iron or brass frame (the latter slightly scarcer and will bring small premium). Barrel swings sideways to load. Frames usually plated with barrels blued, but overall plating not unusual (full blue very rare). Fluted sides to frame. Rosewood grips.

Top of barrel marked: XL DERRINGER. Left side of barrel marked: PAT. APR. 5, 1870.

8A-195

Made by Hopkins & Allen of Norwich, Connecticut. Although the gun does not bear H&A markings, it does appear in their advertising literature along with their marked revolvers and specifically mentions that they are all "… made at one factory." The patent date that appears on it is for the Marlin Ejector used on the gun and for which a royalty was very likely paid to Marlin:

8A-195   Values—Good **$450**   Fine **$950**

XL Vest Pocket Single Shot Deringer

XL Vest Pocket, Single Shot Deringer. Made by Hopkins & Allen, Norwich, Connecticut. Circa 1870-90s. Although the H&A markings do not appear on the gun, the piece is shown on their advertising literature along with their line of revolvers and it is mentioned that they "… are made in one factory." Quantity estimated at 1,500.

22 caliber rimfire. 2-1/4" round two-step barrel, swivels sideways to load. Iron spur trigger frame; plated finish. Walnut grips; bird's-head butt.

Barrel marked: XL VEST POCKET:

8A-196

8A-196   Values—Good **$275**   Fine **$575**

XL Single Shot (Marked) Deringer

XL Single Shot (Marked) Deringer. (Not illus.) Made by Hopkins & Allen, Norwich, Connecticut c. 1870-80s. Very similar to above XL Vest Pocket in contours and slightly larger. Quantity likely less than 500.

22 and 30 caliber rimfire. Part round/octagon barrel. Iron spur trigger frame; nickel plated finish; walnut grips; bird's-head butt.

Barrel marked: XL SINGLE SHOT 22 CAL. Estimate 400 made:
8A-196.5   Values—Good **$450**   Fine **$1,250**

Barrel marked: XL SINGLE SHOT 30 CAL. Estimate just 100 made:
8A-196.6   Values—Good **$600**   Fine **$1,400**

XPERT Single Shot Deringer

8A-197

XPERT Single Shot Deringer. Made by Hopkins & Allen. Made 1880's. Quantity estimated at 4,000.

22 caliber and 30 caliber rimfire (scarcer worth 20 percent premium). 2-1/4" barrel (with longer barrels up to 6" encountered). 2-1/4" round barrel. Long, narrow breechblock swivels outward to left for loading. Nickeled finish. Bird's-head butt; rosewood grips.

Barrel marked: XPERT-PAT.SEP.23.1878 or XPERT PAT APPLIED FOR (scarce, worth premium):
8A-197   Values—Very Good **$325**   Exc. **$750**

XPERT "Pocket Rifle"

8A-198

XPERT "Pocket Rifle" variation of the above deringer by Hopkins & Allen circa mid-1870s to 1890s. Same small frame with long 7-1/2" barrel standard (up to 12" reported). Calibers 22 and 30RF. a.k.a to collectors as "Bicycle Rifle." Sold with simply constructed, wire type, half skeleton stock (illus.) or full skeleton style with screw into threaded hole at bottom of backstrap. H&A advertised the little gun "...equal to any rifle of short range. It will bring down a squirrel from out of the tallest tree, and is unequalled for target practice." Values for gun with stock. (must first verify if subject to provisions of NFA or GCA):
8A-198   Values—Very Good **$850**   Exc. **$1,400**

Unidentified Double Barrel Pocket Pistol

Unidentified Double Barrel Pocket Pistol. Circa 1860s. Maker and quantity produced unknown. Rare.

Iron spur trigger frame. Side-by-side 5" round barrels with center rib. Depressing large button underside of frame allows barrels to tip downward for loading. Caliber 32 RF. Silver plated finish. No maker markings; displays quality workmanship of professional gunmaker with some features that may indicate fabrication by Prescott of Worcester, Mass.

8A-199

Cleverly designed, intricate mechanical operation. The double hammers fired by single trigger. When both at full cock, a light pull of trigger fires right barrel; more forceful pressure then fires left barrel. If trigger pulled too hard when both hammers at cock, barrels will fire in sequence.

Only single recorded, recent sale. Values shown are very broad estimate:

8A-199   Values—Very Good **$1,750**   Exc. **$3,000**

Unidentified Single Shot Deringer

8A-200

Unidentified Single Shot Deringer. Although maker and quantity unknown, the handgun displays workmanship of a highly accomplished, professional gunmaker. A possible attribution is the Newbury Arms Co. of New York. Manufacture circa 1860s.

Caliber 30 RF. Brass spur trigger frame with a distinctive projecting lip on the upper recoil shield which covers breech of the barrel. Fine quality, professional, floral engraving on frame. 3-1/8" octagon barrel swivels sideways to load. Bird's-head butt; rosewood grips. 5-1/2" overall. Rare:

8A-200   Values—Good **$1,500**   Fine **$3,000**

Page from Merwin, Hulbert & Co. catalog of 1887.

Chapter VIII-B

Semi-Automatic Pistols

Although Americans played major roles in the origin and development of the semi-automatic handgun, these inventors found wider acceptance for their ideas in Europe than at home. Reasonable quantities of semi-automatics were made in the United States during their early period of development, but it is somewhat of an anomaly that subsequent to their introduction near the turn of the century almost all major innovations, and the greatest quantity of manufacture, took place in Europe. Thus, any collector devoting specific attention to this type handgun will certainly have a preponderance of foreign made pieces in his arms group. By far the greatest rarities in the automatic field and those generally bringing the highest values are the foreign made pieces, particularly European. As attested to by this section, the number of American manufacturers for semi-automatics was relatively limited.

A milestone in the development of firearms was the practical application of the "self" or "auto" loading system, generally attributed to the American engineer, Hiram Maxim, whose first patent was granted in 1883. Much of his later work was completed in England (later he became a British citizen) where these arms developments were given wider support and acceptance. Hugo Borchardt of Connecticut, often referred to as the "father" of the Luger pistol, also found much greater interest for his inventions in Europe; the Borchardt semi-automatic pistol was first produced in Germany. A third American, John M. Browning, decidedly one of America's greatest arms inventors, also found far greater interest and reception for his ideas abroad. It is true that after Browning's initial 1897 patent for a selfloader his ideas were found receptive by Colt Firearms (q.v.) and that his innovations were utilized by both that American firm and the Fabrique Nationale d'Armes de Guerre

of Belgium (the famed "FN" trademark). But it may be generally said that far greater interest and reception was found for Browning's ideas in Belgium than in his homeland.

The preponderance of American automatics were made by Colt with most, but not all, based on Browning patents. There can, of course, be few pistols in the world to equal the fame of the Colt Model 1911 45 still in use by the U.S. armed forces. In recent years many American makers have entered the field increasing the quantity of semi-automatics made here, but domination is still by Europeans with Germany having played a major role in the development, manufacture, use and military issuance of such arms.

This section, alphabetically arranged, lists the bulk of American pistols generally considered as "semi-automatics" (or auto-loading or self-loading), all of which are commonly referred to (even by most manufacturers in their literature) as merely "automatics."

The collector should familiarize himself with the Gun Control Act of 1968 before buying, selling or trading weapons of these general types. Most will fall in the "modern" gun category and be thusly treated by federal, state and local laws. Collectors should certainly be aware of the ramifications of same.

Unless of extreme rarity (like the Grant-Hammond) the singularly most important factor in determining values in most automatics is condition. Many specimens are desirable in only "excellent" or close to "factory new" with the lower grades of condition displaying sharp price decreases.

As with other American arms it is quite possible to find examples with extra fancy embellishments such as engraving, custom grips, etc. and premiums may be added accordingly. As always, originality is a key feature.

BIBLIOGRAPHY

(Note: Some material about American automatics may be found in several books having general coverage and appearing in complete bibliographic listings elsewhere in this book, such as: *Collectors' Guide To American Cartridge Handguns* by DeWitt Sell; *Handguns Americana* by DeWitt Sell; *The Collecting Of Guns* edited by James E. Serven; and *Savage & Stevens Arms & Collector's History* by Kimmel; U.S. Military Match and Marksmanship Automatic Pistols by Jenkins; see Colt Chapter.)

Carr, James R. *Savage Automatic Pistols*. Privately published by the author, c. 1970. Detailed study of the arms of that maker.

*Dance, Tom. *High Standard. A Collector's Guide To The Hamden And Hartford Target Pistols*. Lincoln, R.I.: Mowbray Publishers, 1991.

Johnson, Melvin Jr. and Haven, Charles T. *Automatic Weapons Of The World*. New York: William Morrow & Co. 1945. General coverage of handguns and longarms of the world with most American models illustrated and discussed.

*Meadows, E.S. *U.S. Military Automatic Pistols 1894-1920*. Vol. I, Moline, Illinois: Ellis Pub. 1993.

*Petty, C. E. *High Standard Automatic Pistols 1932-1950*. Charlotte, North Carolina: Published by author, 1976. Reprinted 1989, Gun Room Press, Highland Park, N.J.

*Spacek, J.V., Jr. *High Standard Autoloading Pistols 1951 to 1984*. Berlin, Conn.: Privately published by author, 1993.

Stern, Daniel K. *10 Shots Quick—The Fascinating Story Of The Savage Pocket Automatics*. San Jose, California: Globe Printing Company, 1967. Detailed study of the arms of that maker contains material not in the above referenced Carr work on the same subject.

Wilson, R. K. *Textbook Of Automatic Pistols 1884-1935*. Plantersville, South Carolina: Small-arms Technical

Publishing Company, 1943. Reprinted by Stackpole, 1976. Broad detailed coverage of automatic handguns of the world. Most American arms included.

(*) Preceding a title indicates the book is currently in print.

Colt Automatics   *See Colt Firearms, Chapter V-A.*

Davis-Warner Automatic   *See Warner Arms Company.*

Fiala Arms Co. Target Pistol

8B-001

Fiala Arms Company, New Haven, Conn. and New York City (Fiala Outfitters) Target Pistol. Made 1921-26 by the Page Lewis Arms Company of Massachusetts. Named for Major Anthony Fiala, N.Y. National Guard; commanded machine gun company Mexican Border War, 1915; sportsman; earlier member of 2 Arctic explorations.

22 caliber rimfire. Ten-shot magazine. Interchangeable barrels of 3", 7-1/2" and 20".

Finish blued. Walnut grips.

Frame marked: FIALA ARMS AND/EQUIPMENT CO. INC./NEW HAVEN CONN./PATENTS PENDING on most specimens with others having markings of the Fiala Arms Company, New York and a few noted bearing markings of BOTWINICK BROTHERS

(Bridgeport, Connecticut hardware dealers), SCHALL or COLUMBIA (believed trade names of Hartford Arms Company).

In design the Fiala appears to be quite similar to the Colt Woodsman. It is, however, not semi-automatic, but must be manually operated to eject, load and cock for each shot. It was originally sold in a small leather covered trunk type case with plush lining fitted for three interchangeable barrels, a detachable wooden shoulder stock and cleaning accessories. It is most desirable and in demand in that complete condition. Classified with its detachable stock under the federal Gun Control Act as a "curio and relic" and thus, licensed collectors may acquire or dispose of them subject to the provisions of that act.

Complete outfit with three barrels, stock, case:
8B-001   Values—Very Good **$1,250**   Exc. **$2,750**
Pistol only with one barrel:
8B-002   Values—Very Good **$300**   Exc. **$750**

Grant Hammond Military Automatic Pistol

8B-003

Grant Hammond Manufacturing Corporation, New Haven, Connecticut, Large Military Automatic Pistol. Made c. 1917. Very limited production for U.S. government trials only and not believed made for the commercial market. Very rare.

45 caliber. Eight-shot magazine. 6-3/4" barrel. Blued finish. Checkered walnut grips.

Markings on right side of slide: GRANT HAMMOND MFG. CORP. NEW HAVEN. CONN. U.S.A. Left side of slide: PATENTED MAY 4, 1915 OTHER PATENTS PENDING. Marked on top of slide: HAMMOND.

A distinctive and novel feature was the automatic ejection of the clip after the last round was fired, thereby allowing for quicker insertion of a fresh full clip. The bolt operates somewhat similar to the Japanese Nambu:
8B-003   Values—Very Good **$12,000**   Exc. **$27,500**

Harrington and Richardson Pocket Automatics   *See Frank Wesson, Wesson and Harrington, Harrington and Richardson Arms, Chapter V-I.*

Hartford Arms & Equip. Co. Target Pistol

Hartford Arms and Equipment Company, Hartford, Connecticut, Target Pistol. Made c. 1929 to 1930. Quantity unknown; very limited.

22 caliber rimfire. Ten-shot magazine. 6-3/4" barrel. Blued finish. Hard rubber grips.

Marked on left side of frame: MANFD. BY/THE HARTFORD

ARMS & EQUIP. CO./HARTFORD, CONN./PATENTED/22 CAL./ LONG RIFLE.

About identical in appearance to the High Standard Model B and very similar in appearance to the Colt Woodsman. Production was very limited; the company was acquired by High Standard in 1932. A few variations are known as listed below:

Early production model. As described above and semi-automatic in operation:

8B-004   Values—Very Good **$300**   Exc. **$700**

Manually operated model. Slide must be manually activated to eject, load and cock for each shot. Regular ten-shot magazine:

8B-005   Values—Very Good **$200**   Exc. **$550**

Single shot pistol. Made without magazine or provision for same:

8B-004

8B-006   Values—Very Good **$200**   Exc. **$500**

High Standard Target Automatic

High Standard Manufacturing Corporation, Hamden, Connecticut, Target Automatic. Prolific makers of American semi-automatic target pistols. Almost their entire series of arms is considered and classified as "modern" and hence, not within the scope of this work.

The firm acquired the Hartford Arms and Equipment Company (*q.v.*) c. 1930 and commenced its long line of

8B-008

semi-automatic pistols with the High Standard Model "B" (introduced about 1930 and discontinued 1942) which is very closely patterned after the Hartford automatic.

The Model B has a collector's value as a descendent and associated with the Hartford and the Fiala and also as the first model in the long series of High Standards. It has further interesting military association as a number of them were sold to the U.S. Army Ordnance Department for firearms training purposes in World War II.

22 caliber rimfire. 4-1/2" and 6-3/4" barrels. Ten-shot magazine. Blued finish. Checkered hard rubber grips with HS monogram.

Marked HI-STANDARD/MODEL "B" on left side of slide with company name, address and patent on left side of frame: Civilian Model:

8B-007   Values—Exc. **$300**   Factory New **$750**

Identical to above, but U.S. government markings PROPERTY OF U.S. on right side of frame and Ordnance Department crossed cannon insignia stamped below:

8B-008   Values—Exc. **$650**   Factory New **$950**

Ithaca Gun Company, Inc. Model 1911A1 45 Caliber Automatic   *See Colt Firearms, Chapter V-B.*

Phoenix Pocket Automatic

Phoenix, Lowell, Massachusetts, Pocket Automatic. Made c. 1920. Quantity unknown. Very limited.

Caliber 25. 2-1/4" barrel. Six-shot magazine. Blued finish. Checkered hard rubber grips.

A small pistol about the same size as the Colt 25 auto. Blow-back type action with retractor spring on top of barrel as with European pistols of the era, of which it is a direct copy. Company name and address on left side of slide. Reported in 32 caliber, but specimens not verified:

8B-009   Values—Very Good **$300**   Exc. **$650**

8B-009

Reising Arms Co. Target Pistol

Reising Arms Company, Connecticut, Target Pistol. Made c. early 1920s. Quantity unknown; limited.

Caliber 22 rimfire. 6-1/2" tip-up barrel. Twelve-shot magazine. Hard rubber grips with relief designs of bear's head and markings: REISING-IT'S A BEAR.

Marked on right side of slide: PAT'D MAY 16 '16 OCT 29 '21/OTHER PATENTS PENDING.

Exposed hammer; follows closely in design to the Mannlicher military Model of 1901. Well made, but stiff competition by Colt's

8B-010

Woodsman auto caused its demise. The invention of the noted gun designer Eugene G. Reising, it has been variously described as manufactured by the New Haven Arms Company of New Haven, the Reising Manufacturing Company of Hartford, the Reising Arms Company of Waterbury, Connecticut and the Reising Arms Company of Hartford, Connecticut! The author leaves it to a more diligent researcher to resolve the problem:

8B-010   Values—Very Good **$300**   Exc. **$750**

Remington Automatics   *See Remington Firearms, Chapter V-E.*

Remington Rand, Inc. Model 1911A1 45 Caliber Automatic   *See Colt Firearms, Chapter V-B.*

Remington-U.M.C. Model 1911 45 Caliber Automatic   *See Colt Firearms, Chapter V-B.*

SAVAGE MILITARY & POCKET AUTOMATICS

Savage Arms Company, Utica, New York. Various model military and pocket automatics.

Founded by Arthur W. Savage (1857 to 1938), an Englishman born in Kingston, Jamaica, British West Indies, educated in England and having an amazingly varied early career prior to his venture in gun making. His experiences included work for a famed London periodical, mining and cattle raising in Australia, coffee planting in Jamaica and the management c. early 1890s of a railroad in upstate New York. His first gun designs submitted c. 1891 were for an improvement in the British service rifle of the era. Continuing his arms interest, he formed the Savage Arms Company in 1894 to manufacture his newly designed lever action rifle (which ultimately became the famed Model 99). Savage managed the company until about 1911 or 1912, moving to California where he engaged in other manufacturing enterprises. Second only to Colt, Savage Arms Company was the most prolific American maker of automatics of the early era.

The original design for the Savage automatic is that of E. H. Searle of Philadelphia whose first two patents were filed 1903 and 1904 and both granted on November 21, 1905. Financial backing for Searle is believed to have been by W. D. Condit, a Philadelphia financier, who was attributed with the promotion and sales of the design to Savage c. 1905-1906. The latter's original interest in the weapon and its manufacture was created by the possibility of competition with other manufacturers in the U.S. Army tests to adopt a standard service automatic and the possible lucrative contracts that might follow. Although unsuccessful in acquiring adoption of the Savage in the government trials c. 1907 through 1911, the first military version of the automatic spawned the popularly accepted pocket models that were made and marketed for many years.

Savage also produced approximately five each of Military Model 1910 and Military Model 1911 automatics in 45 caliber in attempts to compete with Colt. These are very similar in appearance to the below Military Model 1907 with variances in slides and safeties. Very rare; worth premiums.

A few Savage automatics were made in very small 25 caliber size. All such specimens are considered extremely rare.

Military Model 1907; 45 caliber. Made c. 1907 to 1911. Total quantity estimated at 300. Eight-shot magazine. 5-1/2" barrel. Checkered walnut grips. Blued finish. Serial numbered (on the bottom of the slide under hammer) 1 to 290 with approximately the first ten prototypes unnumbered. Marking on slide: MANUFACTURED BY SAVAGE ARMS COMPANY IN UTICA N.Y. U.S.A. NOV. 21, 1905. CAL .45. The complete disbursement of all 300 Savages estimated made is not known; a number of them obviously were the first ones submitted for government testing in the trials of 1907, subsequent to which the government purchased 200 Savage 45s issued to the U.S. Cavalry for field trials c. 1908 to 1909.

Undoubtedly others were made for replacements for those that failed, possibly accounting for the balance. After completion of government testing, Savage purchased their arms back from the government c. 1912, reconditioned them (refinishing many) and sold them c. 1922 to the general public with the firm of E. K. Tryon of Philadelphia apparently acquiring the majority of them and in turn reselling them.

8B-011

Military Model as above, original finish:
8B-011   Values—Very Good **$5,500**   Exc. **$12,500**

Identical to above; Tryon Co. refinished:
8B-012   Values—Very Good **$4,000**   Exc. **$8,000**

Model 1907 32 Caliber Pocket Auto; open hammer. Made c. 1907 to 1926. Total quantity estimated at 209,791. Ten-shot magazine. 3-3/4" barrel. Blued finish. Hard rubber grips with circular panel in center having raised Indian head design and legend SAVAGE QUALITY. Serial numbered from 1 on up. Standard slide marking: MANUFACTURED BY SAVAGE ARMS CO./UTICA. N.Y. U.S.A. PAT. NOV. 21. 1905. Caliber markings vary as noted below. The pocket sized 32 was a natural evolution from experiments with the military 45 caliber model and was Savage's first production automatic for civilian sale. Quite a few variations have been detailed in the two reference works on the subject (*see bibliography*) some of which can affect values.

Early Production Types. Serial range through approximately 10980. Distinctive feature are the all metal checkered grips

8B-013

with the same circular panel having raised Indian head design and SAVAGE QUALITY as noted above. Serial number on bottom of frame forward of trigger guard. Three basic variations of this type. Markings in large letters CAL 32 to right of the two-line address marks:

8B-013   Values—Very Good **$225**   Exc. **$400**

Mid-Production (or so-called "Common" Production). Serial range approximately 10981 through 184600. Hard rubber grips with trademark design as above. Bright blue finish, but not of the high luster as noted on the early production above. Serial number first at bottom of frame forward of trigger guard and later after range 19500 on forward flat of frame. Eight basic variations are detailed in this group. Slide markings as noted above with addition CAL. 32. in small letters to right of the two lines or of two different styles adding CAL 32 at end of first line and 7.65mm at end of second line:

8B-014   Values—Very Good **$200**   Exc. **$300**

Late Model 1907. Serial range from approximately 184601 to 229800. Two basic variations identified. Blue not of the bright quality and on later specimens appears as a dull black. Hard rubber grips as above. Two-line markings with CAL 32 at end of first line and 7.65mm end of second line. Most distinctive feature is the spur type hammer on the last group of these manufactured c. 1919-1920; approximately 26,400 of them from Serial No. 203400 to 229800:

8B-015   Values—Very Good **$200**   Exc. **$300**

Model 1907 380 Automatic. Made c. 1913 to 1915 (approximately 8,000) and later from 1919 to 1920 (approximately 1,849). Total quantity estimated made 9,849. Identical in contour to the 32 caliber model with same production variances as noted for that type commencing with the later so-called "common" type. All models with hard rubber grips having same Indian head and SAVAGE QUALITY motif and the later style slide markings. Serial numbered in its own range commencing with approximately 2000 up to approximately 10000 and in the later series 13901 to 15749. The presence of a "B" affixed to the serial number indicates the larger 380 caliber. The last styles of this model also have the spur type hammer (made 1919 to 1920). Earlier specimens have only the CAL 380 marked in two lines to right of the usual company name and address. Later have CAL .380 at right of first line and 9.m/m at right of bottom line:

8B-016   Values—Very Good **$200**   Exc. **$425**

Model 1915 32 Caliber Hammerless, Grip Safety Auto. Made c. 1915 to 1916. Total quantity estimated 6,500. Ten-shot magazine. 3-3/4" barrel. Bright blued finish. Hard rubber grips with monogram as above. Serial numbered in range 103000 to 136500. Standard slide markings in italics *SAVAGE ARMS CO. UTICA. N.Y. U.S.A. CAL 32./PATENTED NOVEMBER 21. 1905 - 7.65mm.* Marked in very large letters on left side of frame above grips SAVAGE. Major distinguishing features are the grip safety and the shrouded hammer. Serial numbers and production were from the regular run of the Model 1907:

8B-017   Values—Very Good **$250**   Exc. **$500**

8B-017

Model 1915 380 Caliber Hammerless, Grip Safety Auto. Made c. 1915. Total quantity estimated at 3,900. Identical in contour to the above 32 caliber. Serial numbered in range 10001 to 13900 (with a few earlier numbers noted). Slide markings: SAVAGE ARMS CO. UTICA. N.Y. U.S.A. CAL .380/PATENTED NOV. 21, 1906-9.m/m.:

8B-018   Values—Very Good **$350**   Exc. **$700**

8B-019

Model 1917 32 Caliber Automatic. Visible spur type hammer. Made c. 1920 to 1926. Total quantity estimated from 27,000 to 30,000. Ten-shot magazine. 3-3/4" barrel. Dull blue-black finish. Checkered hard rubber grips with oval panel at top having raised design of Indian holding rifle and legend SAVAGE QUALITY. Serial numbered in range 229800 to 259472. Markings on top of slide SAVAGE ARMS CORP. UTICA. N.Y. U.S.A. CAL 32./PATENTED NOVEMBER 21, 1905-7.65m-m. Quickly distinguished by the redesigned shape of the handle (gently sloping at back) and the new style hard rubber grips that are wide at the bottom and tapering towards top. Later production has markings on side of frame SAVAGE MODEL 1917:

8B-019   Values—Very Good **$200**   Exc. **$350**

Model 1917 380 Caliber Automatic With Visible Spur Type Hammer. Made c. 1920 to 1928. Total quantity estimated at 14,223. Identical in configuration to the above 32. Serial numbers from 15750 to 29972. Same distinctive features as noted for the 32 caliber model. Slide markings identical as above, but with CAL. 380. and 9m-m at right side of top and bottom lines respectively:

8B-020   Values—Very Good **$250**   Exc. **$550**

Singer Manufacturing Company Model 1911A1 45 Caliber Auto   *See Colt Firearms, Chapter V-B.*

Smith & Wesson Automatics   *See Smith & Wesson Firearms, Chapter V-G.*

Springfield Armory Model 1911 45 Caliber Automatic   *See Colt Firearms, Chapter V-B.*

Union Firearms Co. Auto Pistol & Auto Revolvers

Union Firearms Company, Toledo, Ohio. Automatic Pistol and Automatic Revolvers. Made c. 1903 to 1913. Total quantity unknown; limited.

Very little has been recorded about this firm, although they apparently devoted most of their energies to the manufacture of shotguns. It is believed that they were sold to the Ithaca Gun

8B-021

8B-022

Company in 1913.

Markings: UNION FIREARMS CO. TOLEDO OHIO.

Automatic Pistol. Caliber 32 S&W (a few known in 38 and worth premium). Approximately 4" barrel. Blued finish. Somewhat resembles the German Luger. Has been noted that it was of "relatively poor manufacture":

8B-021   Values—Very Good **$950**   Exc. **$2,250**

Automatic Revolver. Closely patterned after the British Webley-Fosbery. Utilizes the recoil of a fired cartridge to revolve the cylinder and cock hammer. Cylinder has deep zig-zag grooving. Caliber 32. Six-shot. 3" barrel. Marked on right side of frame UNION FIRE ARMS CO/TOLEDO. O. LEFEVER PAT

8B-022   Values—Very Good **$1,200**   Exc. **$2,750**

Union Switch and Signal Company Model 1911A1 45 Caliber Automatic

See Colt Firearms, Chapter V-B.

Warner Arms Corp. Pocket Automatic

Warner Arms Corporation, Brooklyn, New York (but also listed for Norwich, Connecticut), Pocket Automatic. Made c. 1910 to 1913. Total quantity unknown.

32 caliber. Blued finish. "Blow forward" action.

Marked: THE WARNER ARMS CORPORATION, BROOKLYN, NEW YORK, U.S.A., along with German mfr.'s markings; with company monogram W.A.C. on hard rubber grips.

This is a German made Schwarzlose Model 1909 pistol merely imported and marked for the Warner Corporation who distributed it in the United States prior to World War I. Similar "Warner" markings are found on Belgian made and imported "Melior" pocket automatics (copies of "FN" Browning Model 1900):

8B-023   Values—Very Good **$250**   Exc. **$500**

8B-023

Warner Arms Corp. (Davis-Warner) "Infallible"

Warner Arms Corp. (Davis-Warner Arms Co.) "The Infallible" or (later) "Infallible." "The Infallible" was originally patented in 1914 and produced in limited quantities c.1914-1920.

Caliber 32, blued finish. Early specimens bear only the JULY 28, 1914 patent date and a NORWICH, CONN. address. Later examples show some minor machining differences, bear an additional patent date of MARCH 9, 1915 and were manufactured in Assonet, Massachusetts by the Davis-Warner Arms Co.:

8B-024   Values—Very Good **$200**   Exc. **$350**

8B-024

Chapter IX

American Military Longarms

Although perennially among the most popular fields of American arms collecting, and one about which there is a wealth of available literature, there yet remains much to be explained and published about American military longarms; particularly of the earlier periods. The field is one which has long enjoyed a wide following of devotees and offers any number of possibilities for specialization. The four most important factors which have attracted collectors have been the (a) quantities available, (b) the many basic models and variations of each, with issuance over a lengthy period of time, (c) the generally moderate and low price structuring, (d) great historical associations with events in American history.

As earlier discussed in Chapter II, there had been a decided eccentricity in the market place regarding longarms vs. handguns, especially so in the American martial field. A great many of the early flint longarms, particularly those dating prior to 1812, literally went begging for a market for many years while their counterparts in handguns were readily snapped up. That gap has gradually been closing over this past decade, a fact quite evident of late where the general scarcity, if not rarity, of most early pieces has been more widely recognized. Influenced also by an influx of new collectors, the field of martial longarms has shown a very healthy and steady growth and undoubtedly will continue to do so.

This chapter is divided into two major segments: (a) **PRIMARY** and (b) **SECONDARY** types. These are purely terms of convenience and in no way reflect on the status of the arms, especially those within the latter section. A classic example is the Spencer carbine, certainly one of the most important cavalry weapons ever issued by the U.S. forces and found in the "Secondary" section, while a piece like the Model 1840 flintlock musketoon, very likely never made for issuance, is found as a "Primary" weapon. The author has followed the general categorizing of longarms that has been established and utilized by most previous authors and collectors in the field. Division into two major sections has been found easiest to use for quick reference and identification.

Items listed in the **PRIMARY** section are all arms made at the national armories of Springfield and Harpers Ferry, and also include other weapons either officially designated as standard "U.S. Models" or traditionally known and termed as such by collectors. Exceptions are the contract pieces of several makers (i.e., contracts 1798, 1808 and 1861) on patterns supplied to them by the U.S. armories and generally following the officially adopted arm.

The **SECONDARY** classification is sub-divided for ease of identification into **muzzle-loading** and **breech-loading** categories and is composed of arms made for and issued to federal forces and to militia organizations; these are generally items which fit in the catchall term "military longarms." The largest group are to be found in the **breech-loading** section consisting of the many carbines of the Civil War era. For convenience they have been alphabetically arranged, again following a traditional method of classification.

The author by no means wishes to imply that the divisions into either classification or sub-categories indicates collecting patterns for those weapons; that is decidedly not the case. The listings here are strictly a matter of preference for quick identification.

Other weapons may be observed that are not found listed here and that by general configuration, or markings, or known historical backgrounds properly should be classified as "martial longarms." Such arms, many of which may be rarities, are generally not listed or recorded and very possibly may be experimental or trial pieces submitted for federal or state approval, but never accepted and hence, never manufactured in quantity. Their values are very much dependent upon the maker's name, the type and configuration, the period of manufacture, and any possible historical association. The Deringer and J. J. Henry (South Carolina contract) flintlock rifles listed in the **SECONDARY** section are general examples of this type. Similar products of other makers are sometimes found and they may be generally priced in this same range. A factor of importance in determining such values is, of course, *Demand*; the reader is referred to Chapter II for a general discussion of that subject. The mere fact that the item is unique or rare, unusual or interesting, is not in itself sufficient to place it in the higher plateaus of value.

The collecting of U.S. martial longarms, like many other specialties in antique weapons, encompasses several areas which are still very much an inexact science! A great deal of data remain to be learned and studied about them, as witness the introductory text of the sections dealing with the Model 1795 flintlock muskets and what is hoped will be the death-knell to the non-existent Model 1808. Prices are based on what has generally been accepted as the most accurate information about various makers. This proviso is especially applicable to those early pieces of the pre-Model 1812 era. In some instances an early model manufactured during various years in differing quantities will show price variations for each of the varied date markings; whereas other models having similar quantity differences between years will show no appreciable price difference. This merely reflects the eccentricity of the collectors' market as it currently exists. There is no doubt that with the passage of time such statistical differences will alter values accordingly. The author can only reflect the state of the present market.

Quite a few American-made guns classified as martial weapons are not to be found listed in this or any of the more popular books on U.S. martial longarms. The majority of such pieces are odd breechloaders of the general era 1865 to 1875, though not to the complete exclusion of other periods. Many are individual hand-crafted pieces made on an extremely limited production basis (less than ten) for submission to the various U.S. government trials (mostly of the post-Civil War era) for adoption as standard U.S. service weapons. Many famous as well as lesser known inventors and manufacturers submitted specimens of their arms for U.S. testing. These are considered highly desirable collectors' items, but values are very much tempered by the demand current at the time on the collectors' market and each must be assessed on an individual basis. Values will be dependent upon known background information, maker and markings, general configuration, and type. It has for instance, been a general rule-of-thumb that experimental and trial carbines have always had greater demand and fetched higher prices than the same type of weapon in musket or rifle size. Such is merely an eccentricity of the market and one that very much indicates how the demand factor operates. Two basic books, *The Breechloader In The Service 1816-1917* by Fuller and *Digest Of U.S. Patents Relating To Breech Loading And Magazine Small Arms 1836-1873* by Stockbridge (*see bibliography*), quite adequately cover these weapons and the collector will find them extremely helpful in identifying experimental and trial types.

Original arsenal-made **Model** or **Pattern** guns are distinct rarities and quite valuable pieces which must be treated as individual entities value-wise. Specimens are seldom encountered, but the reader should be aware of their existence. These were the original pre-production and/or sample guns made at Springfield or Harpers Ferry to the most exacting specifications and were used by the U.S. government inspectors for verifying the dimensions of a contractor's piece as well as serving as the sample gun which the contractor copied for his own production. Information about such weapons is sketchy at best. Their existence, however, is quite well known and specimens of several different types have appeared on the collectors' market over the years. Examples are readily identifiable by the special markings, either MODEL or M present on almost every part of the gun, and usually with matching serial numbers. In almost all instances specimens are in unused, unissued condition. Values are in the many thousands of dollars each.

INTERCHANGEABILITY

A significant attempt was made during the War of 1812, with the increased need for arms, to improve and set standards for the inspection and accurate gauging of parts to achieve interchangeability. Not until the 1830's were arsenal-made inspector gauges (actually termed "VERIFYING GAUGES") supplied for the Type III Model 1816 musket, although hand fitting continued on many contractor arms. First full interchangeability was achieved for the M. 1819 Hall flintlock rifle by Harpers Ferry and Simeon North in the 1830's on the M. 1840 and M. 1842 percussion musket. The use of accurate gauges and "Model" (or "pattern") guns supplied by both arsenals became widespread in the 1840's through 1850's. It was not until the Civil War that the practice was universal for contract arms.

Illustrated here is a set of "verifying gauges" made at Springfield for inspector / contractor use on each individual part of the model 1841 rifle. Such sets (and individual gauges) are quite rare, although occasionally offered on the collector market.

The matter of *mixed dates* on longarms has always been a controversial subject and there is no simple answer. It should be realized that during their active life many martial guns underwent various alterations, modifications and parts interchanges, especially in wartime. Ordnance reports and arsenal inventory records indicate the reassembly of many weapons in order to make them serviceable. This was most evident with the 58 caliber percussion Model 1861/1863 muskets, and the subject is discussed further in the prefatory text to those models. There is no positive guide to assist in evaluating weapons where barrel dates do not match those of locks or other parts. Evaluation must be made on an individual case-by-case basis. The only general rule-of-thumb which is applicable concerns **dates within one year of each other** for which there is little or no concern nor value differential; a one year date difference is generally accepted by most parties as being "as issued." It is certainly possible that demand for such a piece might be lessened slightly, but only on the part of the most "purist" of collectors. Where dates differ a few years or more, the piece must be judged on total appearance and originality and a very close inspection should be made to verify when the marriage of parts was made—then, during its period of use—or now! If the piece has not been tampered with and is apparently in original condition and otherwise meets specifications, and the dates are of reasonable proximity, then it may very well bring about the same, or just slightly less, than a matched date specimen. The demand factor though would be very likely lessened and the arm could easily be found unacceptable by more advanced collectors. If the gun is proven to be of recent assembly, although of all original period parts, it still has a collectibility and value, but certainly to a much lesser degree, and very likely would be worth half of what that same specimen in original condition would bring. The demand factor, too, is lessened greatly and the weapon would be in the "bargain hunter's" category, considered hardly a desirable investment by any but the most elementary novice seeking a low priced example of that general model. The collector should be aware that over the years as various models became obsolete, they were sold on the open market to private individuals. Not only were entire guns sold, but parts as well, and thus a number of very strange appearing pieces that have since acquired a genuine age patina are occasionally observed being offered as "rare variants." The subject as it is applicable to later weapons is discussed in the prefatory text accompanying the "trap-door" Springfield rifles listed in this section.

There is definitive proof that a number of *composite pieces* are completely original and it is really up to the discriminating collector armed with the proper facts, specifications, and his own good judgment to eliminate the modern marriage from the original period assembled arm. The War Department in 1812 issued bulletins to the effect that stocks and older pattern parts on hand both at the armories and in various contractors' plants were to be used on pieces then under current manufacture until such parts were either disposed of or used up. This accounts for many mixed arms until the Model 1816 was approved and adopted. Thus, determining the originality and appearance of an early arm is very often a matter of the discerning eye.

There are decided, although slight, *variations in measurements* that appear in this book, in contrast with preceding publications. Such measurements normally are slight variances in barrel length dimensions; usually fluctuating no more than 1/4" at most. It is well established that these variances do exist on the weapons themselves and there was an allowable tolerance given during the period of manufacture. The variances are 1/2" or sometimes more on the early flintlock muskets. The key to identification of the originality of a piece is not whether it measures within that 1/4" or 1/8" that might differ from one gun or one author's description to another, but rather what is the general condition and appearance of the piece, especially at the muzzle of the barrel (the distance of the sight and bayonet stud from the muzzle is a key feature.) This lack of uniformity, especially noted with early contractors' arms, was often a subject of comment in official correspondence of the era.

Occasionally a *highly embellished and elaborate flintlock* musket is observed which may include such decoration as fancy brass or silver inlays in the stock (generally in the shape of eagles over banners, large stars, etc.) or other deluxe designs and engraving on the barrel and furniture. These are highly desirable collectors' items and regardless of the model on which they appear, either by a national armory or a contractor, there is little likelihood that the decoration was by the maker whose name appears on the lock. Normally embellishment was during the era of issuance by private gunsmiths on custom order from a military group or organization for presentation purposes; most likely as a target shooting prize. Specimens have also been noted with inscriptions of presentation as a testimonial of esteem for an officer or enlisted man by his comrades-in-arms. Apparently no rigid pattern or style existed and examples are encountered in various degrees of elaborateness and inscriptions. At times the name of the gunsmith responsible for the work is found marked on the metal. Values are very much dependent on condition, quality of workmanship, degree of elaborateness, and historical association, if any, based on documents or inscriptions. Each gun must be treated as an entity in itself since no two are identical. Values at a minimum, should be increased at least 50 percent from standard models, and may reach considerably in excess of that.

Unusual or *experimental conversions* of muzzle-loading U.S. longarms to breechloaders, or guns with experimental priming systems, may be occasionally observed. The well known, standard issue types are illustrated and discussed within this chapter. Specimens encountered which are not described herein are well worth further investigation; in many instances they may be determined great rarities, especially those having automatic priming systems. Such specimens are often unique—trial or experimental pieces—and their values fluctuate considerably based on historical association, maker and the type of basic weapon.

A number of *other variations* and special features may be seen on martial longarms that are not found listed here. Occasionally guns not normally adapted to accept a bayonet will be found with special fittings and studs for socket or sword type bayonets, long range or other special sights may be present, special barrel lengths are known, and so forth. Each of these features must be weighed individually when assessing values. The increase will be proportionate to the type of gun involved, condition, and the general period of the weapon.

Sporting variations of arms usually considered to be solely military are sometimes found on the collectors' market. Those that most quickly come to mind are Spencers, Burnsides, Gallagers and Perrys. Many others are also known. In some instances gun makers produced large quantities of arms for public sale on the identical principle and appearance of the military models (Maynard was undoubtedly the most prolific) with added sporting features and varying barrel lengths and calibers. Some of these are discussed in Chapter XII, while others rarely found are merely mentioned here. For instance, Joslyn and Gallager are also known as sporting rifles, and as such they are very rare, but the demand for them is minimal at best. Although they certainly are worth in excess of their more often seen military counterparts, the proportionate increase in value is often slight. Of course, highly elaborate or fancy embellished specimens of these arms would be considered in a class unto themselves and have values commensurate with the quality of the embellishments and condition.

A wide variety of arms were submitted by American gun makers for official tests early in the Civil War, in hopes of acquiring federal or state contracts. The better known types will be found listed in this chapter, but it is still possible to encounter a piece as yet unknown. Values may be generally applied to them as on the more rare pieces found herein, but added research usually will be required.

Often confusing to the collector is the cartridge terminology applied to weapons used late in the Civil War and in the years immediately following. Most terms apply to the popular Spencer cartridge which was used in many other breech-loading weapons of that era—the 56-56, the 56-52 and the 56-50. A general discussion simplifying these terms will be found in the prefatory text accompanying the Spencer rifles and carbines in the **SECONDARY** section of this chapter.

Extra markings denoting state ownership or issuance to special units usually increase the value of the gun on which they appear. New York, New Jersey and Massachusetts seem to be the most often seen extra markings on flintlock muskets, although almost all other state marks can and do appear on various pieces. The lesser encountered state marks bring the proportionately greater price increases; by the same token, all southern state markings even if more common will bring higher values by virtue of their possible "Secondary Confederate" usage. Company or regimental marks may also be seen on stocks or barrels (most often viewed on Pennsylvania and Virginia arms) and will command an added premium. All such markings should be carefully inspected and verified for originality.

Important insights to the American firearms industry in the first half of the 19th century, especially with regard to the manufacturing of martial longarms, may be gleaned from reading the section on Whitney (Chapter V-J). The experience of that maker in capitalizing on surplus and imported parts and marketing them as "good and serviceable arms" to others than the federal government was undoubtedly the identical vehicle of other arms manufacturers of those same years. The practice very likely accounts for certain heretofore unclassified and odd-ball variations that appear with reasonable frequencies on the collectors' market. It is significant to understand that military outfitters, commission agents and various other commercial enterprises, as well as gunmakers, were engaged in the firearms trade; usually very brisk in time of war. Catalogs and advertisements of those eras, the Civil War especially, are important tools to gain a further understanding of the traffic in those weapons; the 1864 illustrated catalog of the prominent N.Y. military outfitters Schuyler, Hartley & Graham the most notable example. Offered for sale to the general public by that catalog were obsolete as well as then-modern, up-to-date, U.S. military firearms. Pre-Civil War catalogs are but seldom seen, while those in the post-war to 1900 eras are common enough to make today's collector aware of what military firearms, obsolescent and current, were available for private purchase by military personnel and sportsmen. Thus, arms thought to be made solely to fill a military contract were often seen to be sold simultaneously to the public at-large. That fact may possibly account for the occasional fine conditioned specimen lacking usual government inspector markings; the rationale will be applicable to earlier flintlock firearms also. Although redundant, the author feels it necessary to again remind the reader that although a gun maker of the 19th Century may have assembled or otherwise produced an apparently odd "variant" firearm, the collector must exercise the most careful judgment to distinguish between the genuine antique piece and that which may be a spurious modern composite. It is in this area that the credibility gap is greatest and in which the gullible often fall prey.

QUAKER GUNS

This term, and guns to which it is applied, has taken on a life of its own in more recent years. Although defined in the dictionary as "...a dummy gun as on a ship or fort; so-called in allusion to Quakers opposition to war," it is rarely seen mentioned in any arms book, and then only as it applies to artillery and the use of logs in a fortress, etc. to give an enemy the false impression there was greater firepower than was the actual case.

As it applied to antique firearms, the terminology was coined in the late 19th century by dealers in Civil War and other military surplus to describe various obsolete rifles and muskets, acquired in generous quantities at government auctions, which were found commercially profitable to alter, shorten and lighten for sale to the then common Boys Brigades and cadet and military academies. Alterations were often well done and some are hawked to the unsuspecting collector as rare variations. Among the more flagrant, and amusing, are those with wooden barrels, most often seen on models 1842 and 1861/63 muskets. Slick pitchmen, with fast talk and fancy footwork, have been known to palm these off as Civil War rarities; their actual worth being parts value only. The famous Bannerman & Sons, New York stated in their 1907 catalog "...in 1889 we invented this gun for use in academies" in their description of a M. 1863 shortened, two-band musket with a wooden barrel that was attached to the original iron breech with nipple. "QUAKER" was more often substituted by "CADET", a catch-all for most altered, lightened guns.

BIBLIOGRAPHY

Important information concerning U.S. martial longarms may also be found in other books on American firearms. A few of the more important titles found listed in bibliographies elsewhere in this book are: *The Rifle In America* by Sharpe; *The Collecting Of Guns*, edited by Serven; *Our Rifles*, by Sawyer.

Ball, R.W. *Springfield Armory Shoulder Weapons 1798-1968*. Dubuque, Iowa: Antique Trader Books, 1997.

Batha, Thomas D. *U.S. Martial .22 Rifles*. Tucson, Arizona: Excalibur Publications, 2000.

Baumann, K. *Arming The Suckers 1861-1863*. Dayton, Ohio: Morningside Publishers, 1989. (Illinois nickname "The Sucker State" in 19th century.) All regiments and their (often odd civilian types) issue weapons.

Behn, Jack. *45-70 Rifles*. Harrisburg, Pennsylvania: The Stackpole Company, 1956 (Second Printing 1972, The Gun Room Press, Highland Park, New Jersey). Devoted entirely to all American guns, sporting and military, made to accept the 45-70 cartridge.

Benton, Captain J. G. *A Course Of Instruction In Ordnance And Gunnery Composed And Compiled For Use Of Cadets Of The U.S. Military Academy*. New York: Van Nostrand, 1861. A great wealth of important data and specifications of arms, equipment and other ordnance material in use by U.S. Army at mid-nineteenth century.

*Bilby, Joseph *A Revolution in Arms: A History of the First Repeating Rifles* Yardley, PA. Westholme Publishing, 2005. Primarily story of the Henry and Spencer rifles/carbines of the Civil War.

Blanch, H. J. *A Century Of Guns: A Sketch Of The Leading Types Of Sporting And Military Small Arms*. London, England: John Blanch & Son, 1909 (with two or three reprints c. 1950s/1960s). Contains great many odd breechloaders and conversions to breechloaders (European and American) of the Civil War and post-war eras.

*Brophy, William S. *Springfield 1903 Rifles*. Harrisburg, Pennsylvania: The Stackpole Company, 1985. Definitive. A standard reference for the subject.

*Brophy, William S. *Krag Rifles*. North Hollywood, California: Beinfeld Publishing, Inc., 1980. First comprehensive work detailing evolution and variations of this famed bolt action American military rifle.

Brophy, William S. *The Springfield Armory 1896-1948*. Lincoln, R.I.: Man-at-Arms Books, 1991. Year by year account from official records.

Brown, Stuart E. Jr. *The Guns Of Harpers Ferry*. Berryville, Virginia: Virginia Book Company, 1968. Detailed photographic and textual coverage of the longarms and handguns made at Harper Ferry Armory.

Buckeridge, J. O. *Lincoln's Choice*. Harrisburg, Pennsylvania: The Stackpole Company, 1956. The development, acceptance and use of the Spencer repeating carbine.

*Campbell, Clark S. *The '03 Springfield*. Beverly Hills, California: Fadco Publishing Company, 1957. Reprints 1971, 1978 by Riling Arms Book Company, Philadelphia. Retitled *The '03 Springfields*. Classic guide for this famed rifle.

*Canfield, B. *A Collector's Guide to the '03 Springfield*. Lincoln, R.I.: Andrew Mowbray, Inc., 1989. Retitled and enlarged as: *An Illustrated Guide to the '03 Springfield Service Rifle*, 2004. A standard reference.

*Coates, E.J. & Thomas, D.S. *Introduction to Civil War Small Arms*. Gettysburg, Pennsylvania: Thomas Publications, 1990. General coverage; good information on imported arms; good illustrations on ammo used with each arm.

Coggins, Jack. *Arms And Equipment Of The Civil War*. Garden City, New York: Doubleday and Company, 1962. Short, informative section on longarms of cavalry and infantry.

Colvin and Viall. *United States Rifles and Machine Guns*. New York: McGraw Hill, 1917, 1928. Reprint, Prescott, Arizona: Wolfe Publishing Co., 1984. Detailed account of manufacture of the M1903 with fine drawings of all parts; also the modified Enfield rifle.

Cromwell, Giles. *The Virginia Manufactory Of Arms*. Charlottesville, Virginia: University Press of Virginia, 1975. Excellent, highly detailed coverage of all handguns, longarms, edged weapons produced.

Crossman, E. C. *Book of the Springfield*. Georgetown, South Carolina: Small Arms Technical Publishing Company, 1951. Well known work on the subject.

Edwards, William B. *Civil War Guns*. Harrisburg, Pennsylvania: The Stackpole Company, 1962 (reprint 1975, Book Sales, New York). Story of Federal and Confederate small arms; design, manufacture, identification, procurement, issue, employment, effectiveness and post-war disposal. A classic in its field. Heavily referred to.

Ferris, C.S. & Beard, J. *Springfield Model 1903 Service Rifle Production & Alterations 1905-1910*. Arvada, Colorado: Private published monograph, 1996.

*Frasca, A.J. & Hill R.H. *The 45-70 Springfield*. Northridge, Calif: Springfield Publishing Co., 1980. Detailed coverage from Model 1865 Allin through all variations of the trapdoor including experimentals and prototypes.

*Frasca, A.J. *The 45-70 Springfield; Book II; Caliber .58, .50, .45 and .30 Breech Loaders in U.S. Service 1865-1893*. Springfield, Ohio: Frasca Publishing, 1997.

Fuller, Claud E. *The Breech-Loader In The Service 1816-1917. A History Of All Standard And Experimental U.S. Breech Loading Magazine Shoulder Arms*. Topeka, Kansas: Arms Reference Club of America, 1933. Reprint, New Milford, Connecticut, N. Flayderman & Co., Inc., 1965. A significant and dependable reference. Often the only source of identification of trial and experimental American breechloaders.

Fuller, Claud E. *The Rifled Musket*. Harrisburg, Pennsylvania: The Stackpole Company, 1958. Highly detailed coverage U.S. Model 1861 and 1863. 58 caliber muskets and all the varied contractors of same.

*Fuller, Claud E. *Springfield Shoulder Arms 1795-1865*. New York: Francis Bannerman Sons, 1930. Reprint Glendale, New York: S&S Firearms, 1968. Classic reference. Highly respected; heavily referred to.

Gluckman, Colonel Arcadi, U.S.A. Retired. *United States Muskets, Rifles And Carbines*. Harrisburg, Pennsylvania: Stackpole Company, 1959. Revised and retitled *Identifying Old U.S. Muskets, Rifles And Carbines* by same publisher, 1965. A basic guide for the field. Should be used in conjunction with more recent studies on the subject.

* Hartzler, Daniel D. & Whisker, James B. *The Southern Arsenal; A Study of the U.S. Arsenal at Harpers Ferry*. Bedford, Penna: Old Bedford Village Press, 1996. Wealth of new detail on this important ordnance facility; fine illustrations.

*Hartzler, Daniel D. & Whisker, James B. *The Northern Armory; The U.S. Armory at Springfield, Mass. 1795-1859*. Bedford, Penna: Old Bedford Village Press, 1996. A new look at the most famous U.S. Armory and their guns; fine, profuse illustrations.

*Hartzler, D.D., Yantz, L.W., Whisker, J.B. *U.S. Rifle-Musket Model 1861 As Manufactured By The Armory At Springfield And Various Contractors*. Rowe Publications, 2001.

*Hassell, Col. J.A. *Warner Civil War Cavalry Carbines*. Gettysburg, Pa.: Thomas Publications, 1998. Monograph.

*Hicks, Major James E. *Notes On United States Ordnance* (Volume I) *Small Arms 1776-1940* (Volume II) *Ordnance Correspondence Relative To Muskets, Rifles, Pistols And Swords*. Mount Vernon, New York: Privately published by the author, 1940. Two extremely important references for the collector of military longarms. Exceptional detailed line drawings, Volume I. Both volumes with wealth of original documents from the U.S. archives pertaining to contracts. Basic source of research information. Volume I has since been reprinted as *U.S. Military Firearms 1776-1956*, published LaCanada, California by James E. Hicks & Sons, 1962.

*Hicks, Major James E. *Nathan Starr Arms Maker 1776-1845*. Mount Vernon, New York: James E. Hicks, 1940, with modern reprint; publisher unknown. Although concentrating basically on Starr swords, coverage also of the M1817 rifle, M1816 musket and experimental carbine.

*Hosmer, Richard A. *The .58 and .50 Caliber Rifles and Carbines of the Springfield Armory 1865-1872*. Tustin, CA: North Cape Pub., Inc. 2007 Paper covers.

*Hull, E. A. *The Burnside Breech Loading Carbines*. Lincoln, R.I.: Andrew Mowbray, Inc., Publishers, 1986. Model-by-model examination of important Civil War cavalry weapon.

*Hull, Edward A. *Providence Tool Co. Military Arms*. Milton, Florida: Santa Rosa Printing, 1978, 1979. American and European as well as conversations and sporting types of Peabody & Peabody-Martini arms.

Huntington, R. T. *Hall's Breechloaders*. York, Pennsylvania: George Shumway Publisher, 1972. Basic reference all models; well researched.

Jordan, G., Editor. *Merrill Single Shot Breech-Loading Percussion Carbines From The Collection Of W.D. Moore*. Baton Rouge: private printed by Editor, c. 1999. Monograph.

Koury, Michael J. *Arms For Texas*. Fort Collins, Colorado: The Old Army Press, 1973. Study of weapons of the Republic of Texas including discussions of the Model 1816 and 1841 Tryon muskets and rifles.

Lewis, Berkeley R. *Small Arms And Ammunition In United States Service*. Washington, D.C.: Smithsonian Institution, 1956. Classic work on the subject; heavily referred to.

Lord, Francis A. *Civil War Collector's Encyclopedia*. Harrisburg, Pennsylvania: Stackpole Company, 1963. Broad coverage of arms, uniforms, equipment of both North and South. Subsequent Volumes Two, Three and Four privately published by the author c.1975.

Lustyik, Andrew F. *Civil War Carbines: From Service to Sentiment*. Aldeo, IL: Gun Report Pub., 1958 Paper cover monograph, by noted carbine authority.

Madaus, H. Michael *Warner Collector's Guide to American Longarms*. New York, N.Y.: Warner Books, 1981. Well written; much good information not found elsewhere.

Mallory, F.B. *The Krag Rifle Story*. Silver Springs, Maryland: Springfield Research Service, 1979. Historical and technical aspects of Krag story; American and European models. Detailed descriptions; data on sights, bayonets, accessories.

*McAulay, John D. *Carbines of the Civil War 1861-1865*. Union City, Tenn: Pioneer Press 1981. Wealth of important detail on actual procurement and government contracts for 19 different model carbines. Good source for historical data.

*McAulay, John. *Carbines of the U.S. Cavalry 1861-1905*. Lincoln, R.I.: Andrew Mowbray Publisher, 1996. Valuable information, especially on issuance, use, makers.

McAulay, John D. *Civil War Carbines—Vol. II—The Early Years*. Lincoln, R.I.: Mowbray Publishing Co., 1991. Important coverage of those made pre-Civil War.

*McAulay, J. D. *Civil War Breech Loading Rifles*. Lincoln, R.I.: Andrew Mowbray, Inc., 1987. Survey of these innovative infantry arms.

*McAulay, John D. *U.S. Military Carbines from the Civil War and Indian Campaigns to the Spanish-American War and Philippine Insurrection*. Woonsocket, RI: Mowbray Pub, 2006.

*McAulay, John D. *Rifles of the U.S. Army 1861-1906*. Woonsocket, RI: Mowbray Pub, 2003

Marcot, Roy M. *Spencer Repeating Firearms*. Irvine, California: Northwood Heritage Press, 1983. Highly recommended as the last word on Spencer. Standard definitive reference. Much on Roper Arms also.

*Moller, G. D. *Massachusetts Military Shoulder Arms 1784-1877*. Lincoln, R.I.: Andrew Mowbray, Inc., 1988. First detailed, authoritative account of these widely produced, multi-style muskets and rifles.

Moller, George D. *American Military Shoulder Arms*. Vol. I. *Colonial & Revolutionary War Arms*. Vol. II. *From 1790s to End of Flintlock Period*. Niwot, Colorado: University Press of Colorado, 1993. Major works on the subjects. Vast amount of information not to be found elsewhere; fine illustrations.

Nehrbass, Arthur F. *U.S. Military Flintlock Rifles 1803-1840* and *Early U.S. Rifle Manufacture*. Unpublished manuscripts in possession of the author. Jacksonville, Florida, 1976.

Norton, Brigadier General Charles B. *American Breechloading Small Arms: A Description Of Late Inventions, Including The Gatling Gun And A Chapter On Cartridges*. New York: F. W. Christern, 1872. Detailed discussion; superb illustrations. Early inventions in field of breechloaders including Remington, Peabody, Ward-Burton, Springfield, Joslyn, etc., as well as handguns.

Norton, Brigadier General Charles B. *American Inventions And Improvements In Breech-Loading Small Arms, Heavy Ordnance, Machine Guns, Magazine Arms, Fixed Ammunition, Pistols, Projectiles, Explosives, etc.* Boston, Massachusetts: Osgood & Company, 1882. Includes some information on the earlier 1872 edition and greatly expanded, including later developments of Peabody-Martini, Hotchkiss, etc.

Pech, G., Newell, B. and Wright, J. *Henry of Boulton—A Pennsylvania Gunmaking Family and its Firearms*. Nazareth, Pennsylvania: 1988.

Peterson, H. L. *The Fuller Collection of American Firearms*. National Park Service: Published by Eastern National Park and Monument Association, 1967. Catalog of the noted Claude E. Fuller collection of antique American military shoulderarms. 355 weapons from colonial through World War I eras.

*Poyer, J. & Riesch, C. *The 45-70 Springfield*. Orange, Cal.: North Cape Publishers, 1991. Very brief survey; not well reviewed.

*Poyer, J. *The American Krag Rifle and Carbine*. Tustin, CA: North Cape Pub: 2002.

Reilly, Robert M. *United States Martial Flintlocks*. Lincoln, Rhode Island: Andrew Mowbray, Inc. Publishers, 1986. A highly important, comprehensive history of American flintlock longarms and handguns (mostly military) c. 1775 to c. 1840. Fine profuse illustrations. A companion work to his 1970 book.

*Reilly, Robert M. *United States Military Small Arms 1816-1865*. Baton Rouge, Louisiana: The Eagle Press, Inc., 1970. A classic guide. One of most often used and referred to works on the subject.

*Rentschler, Thomas B. *Cosmopolitan and Gwyn & Campbell Carbines In The Civil War*. Lincoln, R.I.: Andrew Mowbray Publishers, 2000.

Scarlata, Paul S. *Collecting Classic Bolt Action Military Rifles*. Woonsocket, RI: Mowbray Pub: 2001, Reprint 2005

Schmidt, Peter A. *Hall's Military Breechloaders*. Lincoln, R.I.: Andrew Mowbray Publishers, 1996. Remarkable technical details, fine history of these famous models.

*Schmidt, Peter A. *U.S. Military Flintlock Muskets and their Bayonets; The Early Years 1790-1815*. Woonsocket, RI; Mowbray Pub: 2006. Coverage of the early Charleville Patterned Muskets, and the contracts of 1798 and 1808 and other important reference material for the collector. Also see Volume II, The Later Years; 1816 Through the Civil War, 2007

Schofield, Robert D. and Nehrbass, Arthur F. *U.S. Muskets and Rifles 1792-1812*. Unpublished manuscript in possession of authors. Hyde Park, New York and Jacksonville, Florida, 1976.

Shields, Joseph W. Jr. *From Flintlock To M1*. New York: Coward-McCann, Inc., 1954. Chronological development of U.S. military longarms with excellent illustrations.

Shockley, Col. P.M. *The Trap-Door Springfield in the Service*. Adelo, IL; Gun Report Pub; 1958. Monograph; paper covers important early material on this famous Springfield.

Smith, Merritt R. *Harpers Ferry Armory and the New Technology*. Ithaca, N.Y.: Cornell University Press, 1977. Highlights major problems of American technical innovation; interchangeable manufacture.

Stockbridge, V. D. *Digest Of Patents Relating To Breechloading And Magazine Small Arms (Except Revolvers) Granted In The U.S. From 1836 To 1873 Inclusive.* Washington, D.C.: Patent Office, 1874. Reprinted New Milford, Connecticut, N. Flayderman & Co., Inc., 1963. Important reference and often the only source of identification of odd experimental and trial U.S. longarms. Classified and arranged according to the movement of the principal parts for opening and closing the breech.

*Todd, Frederick P. *American Military Equipage 1851-1872.* Providence, Rhode Island: Company of Military Historians, Volume I, 1974; Volume II, 1977; Volume III, 1978. Reprint 1981 by Scribner Book, N.Y., all three Vols. in one binding. Although heavily devoted to accoutrements, uniforms, equipment, contains excellent section on firearms; especially good on imported European arms for Civil War use.

U.S. Government. *Reports Of The Chief Of Ordnance.* Various years covering entire nineteenth century. Issued annually with (and part of) the *Report Of The Secretary Of War, Being Part Of The Message And Documents Communicated To The Two Houses Of Congress, etc.* Published Government Printing Office. Each annual edition containing wealth of highly definitive detail regarding American military longarms and handguns.

U.S. Army. *Ordnance Manual For The Use Of Officers Of The United States Army.* Editions of 1841, 1850 and 1861. Published Government Printing Office, Washington, 1841, 1850, 1861. Wealth of important detail regarding arms and accessories. Basic research material.

*Waite, M. D. & Ernst, B. D. *The Trapdoor Springfield.* North Hollywood, California: Beinfeld Publishing, Inc., 1979. Comprehensive study of the ordnance trials, evaluations and evolution of the many variations of this well-known arm.

Wasson, R. Gordon. *The Hall Carbine Affair.* New York: Privately printed Pandick Press, 1941. Reprint by Pandick Press, 1948. Story of the J. P. Morgan purchase of surplus Hall carbines and subsequent resale to the government.

*Whisker, J.B., Yantz, L.W., Hartzler, D.D. *U.S. Civil War Carbines.* Rochester, NY: Tom Rowe Pub, 2001.

(*) Preceding a title indicates the book is currently in print.

IX-A: PRIMARY

THE TWO MODEL 1795s AND A REQUIEM TO THE MODEL 1808

Gun collectors and authors appreciate neatly systematized, classified and codified antique firearms—especially U.S. military models. Not only does this make them easier to understand, but simplifying their identification places a minimal strain on the mental processes for pigeonholing weapons in their proper chronological order for both collection and evaluation purposes. For the most part, after 1816 U.S. military longarms fall into these neat, clear patterns. This is not the case with the pre-1816 muskets.

The traditional nomenclature for American military muskets c. 1795 to 1816 are purely terms of convenience applied by early 20th Century arms authors. In many cases the perpetuation of these terms has caused no ill effects and has facilitated the understanding and collecting of the arms themselves. Those same terms should certainly continue in usage having been widely accepted into the language of gun collecting. An attempt to rename or redesignate such arms would not only be an injustice, but most presumptuous on the part of the author.

However, the case of the so-called Models 1795 and 1808 is unique. Not only are the designations misnomers, but they are misleading, creating a lack of understanding and comprehension in that field and period. One can readily appreciate the situation when reading texts and guides to the subject which either ignore obvious inconsistencies or state them in such a way as to leave the reader decidedly puzzled.

For the author, the matter presented a most difficult problem; one that was agonized over at great length. The following material is neither the complete nor definitive guide to collecting U.S. muskets of the 1795 to 1812 era, but rather is the groundwork for a general understanding of the subject in simplified terms. This data should provide the seed for future definitive studies and at the very least, ought to alter the patterns and eradicate the false impressions in the collecting of early U.S. martial longarms. The limitations and scope of a work such as this, basically confined to identification and evaluation, does not allow for a discussion in detail of the history of early U.S. arms manufacturing and the multi-faceted story of the evolution and development of those arms.

Simply Stated: The designations Model 1795 and Model 1808 especially as applied to the arms of the national armories of Harpers Ferry and Springfield, are erroneous. No such terminology was used during the era of original manufacture nor in any subsequent government or official correspondence. That in itself, however, is not sufficient to alter their current-day collector usage. A more accurate account of these early pieces may be obtained by reading the "fine print" in quite a few prior published works about U.S. martial arms. It is necessary to read between the lines to understand the picture fully and to realize the perpetuation of the terms Model 1795, Model 1808 and Transitional Model 1795/1808, as ill-conceived and misleading.

A few basic facts bring the situation into clearer focus. In dealing with arms of the early eras, it must be understood that contradictions do occur, and will often be encountered. The arms just do not fall into the neat patterns and consistencies of the later mass-produced weapons. They were for the most part handmade, and in many cases under quite primitive conditions. The U.S. government and the ordnance section of the War Department in their infancy used methods for inspection and acceptance in the acquisition of these arms which were not as rigid nor well defined as in later years. Exigencies of war eras also allowed for deviation from the established norms. Lastly, and of great importance in understanding deviations and variations in arms other than those made at the national armories, or under direct U.S. contract, many makers produced weapons to meet requirements (often minimal and ill-defined) of individual states and militia groups or even to individual civilian purchasers; thus allowing for a wide latitude in production. For instance, it is well known that letters of marque were given by the U.S. government, officially sanctioning the private arming of American commercial vessels to prey upon British and other foreign enemy shipping during the War of 1812. Such licenses for privateering were acquired by individuals entering the venture on a purely commercial basis; their incentive being the booty to be divided from the capture of a ship and its sale. Such enterprises looked to the commercial arms market for equipment; obviously muskets were a part of the magazines of each privately armed vessel. It is further likely that many such ventures never bothered to get official sanction, adding to the total number engaged in privateering. Hence, a brisk private arms trade developed and there is every likelihood that many makers under contract to the U.S. government diverted some production to such privateers who were willing to pay a premium for quick deliveries.

The earliest procurement by the government of muskets was apparently in 1794. Documentary evidence states that such contracts were made for 7,000 muskets, "… to be manufactured in the United States" fashioned after the French Model 1763 style, then the greatest bulk of weapons in U.S. inventories. No documentary evidence exists detailing the makers of such muskets, nor quantities or dates of delivery. In all likelihood noticeably less were produced than the allotted amount. Fabrication was probably from parts supplied to contractors by the government, which in turn had purchased large quantities of parts both in Europe and America. No accurate information is available for the identification of these muskets. A few students of the subject have even advanced the theory that no such arms were ever delivered. There is every likelihood that a number of unmarked, early French style American-made muskets belong in this category.

In 1794 Congress provided funds for the construction (authorized earlier) of federal armories at Springfield, Massachusetts, and Harpers Ferry, Virginia, for the manufacture of small arms. Production began at Springfield in 1795 and at Harpers Ferry in 1800.

Springfield Armory records indicate 245 muskets were made in 1795 with a total of 3,152 made between the years 1795 and 1798. Exact identification of these weapons has not been made for they were neither dated nor marked as far as can be ascertained. Records indicate that the well known eagle motif die stamps for marking lockplates were not purchased until 1799 at which time five were acquired with an additional two die stamps bought the following year. This date accounts for variations in the eagle markings on Springfield locks.

The first production at Springfield was patterned directly after the French Model 1763 Charleville musket and is more aptly termed the "Charleville Pattern." It is interesting to note that ordnance correspondence of the era termed these arms as "Charleville Muskets" (when actually meaning Springfield-made pieces) or "Charleville Pattern" or "New Muskets Charleville Pattern," etc.

The first known Springfield muskets bearing markings were made in 1799. These bore the full Springfield lock marks with the eagle motif and were dated on the heel of the buttplate with the year of manufacture. The Springfield Model 1795 musket proceeded through various evolutionary changes (as will be found listed below) with no major model change made (especially as it applies to collectors' terminology) until the Model of 1812. Springfield's manufacture of the Model 1812 did not actually begin until 1814.

Harpers Ferry Armory produced its first muskets in 1800, five years after Springfield had been in operation. Though also known as the "Charleville Pattern," these were not identical to the production at Springfield, having considerable distinct differences. For collecting purposes, it is essential that classification be separate from the Springfield manufactured Model 1795. Harpers Ferry muskets evolved in four basic types from their inception in 1800 until 1816 and do not reflect the interim Model 1812 production as found in the Springfield arms. Judging from official correspondence and terminology of the era, these Harpers Ferry arms were still considered the "Charleville Pattern." No attempt was made to standardize the Harpers Ferry and Springfield muskets until c. 1816 with the introduction of the Model 1816 musket.

To clarify the issue: Using the old terminology, in general use until now, there is a Model 1795 Springfield and a Model 1795 Harpers Ferry—both of which are distinctly different, and both of which have evolved and developed variations along their own lines peculiar to each armory. In order to properly identify, classify and evaluate, the 1795s must be treated as two distinct models. They will be found so listed herein—and, it is hoped also by future writers.

In 1798, with strained relations between the United States and France, and the possibility of an outbreak of hostilities, contracts were given to a great many independent makers to produce a total of 40,200 muskets fashioned after the French Charleville pattern then produced at the Springfield Armory. The muskets of those makers are accurately termed the **U.S. Contract Muskets of 1798**—and not as occasionally called the "Model 1795 Contracts." It is not known if the various contractors were supplied with U.S. made Springfield muskets or French made Charlevilles as patterns; it could have been either. The 1798 contract arms show a generous variance in several features and dimensions. Of the various contractors, it is believed that six failed to make any deliveries, while others manufactured considerably less than anticipated. Probably not more than half of the 40,200 were actually delivered. Information concerning the contractors and the identification of their output is found listed below. Likely those same makers produced arms for private sale simultaneously. The presence of a "U.S." stamping would most clearly indicate federal purchase; but the absence of such a marking does not preclude sale to the U.S., as it must be clearly recalled that even Springfields were unmarked until 1799. Often these unmarked early arms of Charleville pattern are overlooked by the collector because of their lack of markings. Such pieces should be considered in a much clearer light as they have considerably more importance and respect due them than has been paid to date. There is a very strong likelihood that they may be of the earlier 1794 contract (for 7,000 pieces) as well as of the 1798 contract. The absence of markings on large quantities of arms of the 1790s era has not been fully explained. The reprisal theory does not hold water and most likely represents a lack of specifications on the contracts. The omission of markings merely meant the contractor had that much less cost involved in making dies and time spent in marking his products. The number of pieces submitted for government approval found to be of poor quality led to specifications for identifying manufacturers. The practice was probably not standard until at least after 1799 when Springfield first began marking their production.

With another war ensuing in Europe between England and France, and the eventuality that America might also be embroiled, the U.S. Congress with some foresight acted in 1808, giving authority to the War Department to procure war material in an "Act for Arming and Equipping the Militia." Contracts were given to 19 makers for a total of 85,200 muskets, of which approximately 50 percent appear to have been delivered. These were specifically contracted for "… arming and equipping *the militia.*" Some remained in federal armories until needed, while others were sent direct to the individual states for issuance to militia immediately upon delivery from the contractor. Those same contractors were simultaneously making muskets for private sale. Documentation in this area is extremely weak and practically non-existent; hence, manufacturing estimates and exact identification is speculative at best. Although the intent of this work is basically identification and evaluation, a certain amount of background and historical information is essential in order to understand and properly identify these types.

Essential to the understanding of these contract pieces is the fact that there was no Model 1808 supplied by the national armories as pattern pieces to the various contractors for use in making their contract arms. The most reasonable school of thought, and that now in popular acceptance by arms historians was succinctly presented by Schofield and Nehrbass (*see bibliography*) laying to rest the myth of the use of spare parts from earlier 1798 contracts leading to the so-called "Transitional Model 1795/1808" muskets. It has been reasonably substantiated that with but few exceptions (and each of these completely justified), the styles of muskets produced by the 19 contractors generally matched the pattern of the sample Charleville type musket received by them from either the Springfield or Harpers Ferry Armory. Most likely the contractor received the sample musket from the armory nearest to him; thus, a majority of the Northern contractors received Springfield Armory made "Charlevilles," while those located in Pennsylvania and southern areas received samples by Harpers Ferry. A few exceptions are justifiably explained by personal visits to arsenals out of their area by the contractors themselves.

There are two distinct styles of 1808 Contract Muskets, each based on the then-current evolutionary stages of the "Charleville" pattern made at Springfield or Harpers Ferry. Each of which had followed different lines of developmental characteristics.

As for a "Model 1808" of either Harpers Ferry or Springfield manufacture, *there never was such a gun.* The term was merely one of convenience coined in an earlier era of 20th century American arms research and perpetuated to present day. As further evidence of this, the features of the erroneously labeled Model 1808 Springfield actually appeared as an evolutionary improvement two or three years earlier.

In view of the foregoing, the author feels obliged to correct the distinct inaccuracy in nomenclature. In general agreement with students and historians closely associated with the field he has classified below the 1808 contract muskets as either *Harpers Ferry Style* or *Springfield Style*. A certain latitude must be observed in the collecting and understanding of early U.S. contract muskets. At the risk of redundancy, it is again brought to the readers' attention that contradictions exist. They are caused not only by the hand manufacture of the arms, but very likely on purpose by the individual contractors in their simultaneous production of arms under rather rigid federal contract and more loosely controlled private sales; their business and production machinations may only be surmised.

In summation, the author after careful consideration has separately categorized and identified evolutionary stages of the Charleville style flintlock musket as it developed from 1795 at the Springfield Armory and from 1800 at the Harpers Ferry Armory; treating each piece as a separate entity with its own major changes—to the complete exclusion of the so-called "Model 1808" musket which decidedly did not exist. The two major contract dates of 1798 and 1808 are treated as individual entities and not merely as sub-varieties of a U.S. "Model."

It is also recorded that the states of Pennsylvania and Virginia gave contracts in 1797 for their respective state militias. These also are treated as individual entities. A last category, and one which clearly points out the unlimited possibilities still available for research in this important field of collecting, is that of the so-called "independent manufacturers or otherwise unidentified contracts" describing and evaluating known firearms that constitute important collectors' items, but for which historical information as to origins is yet to surface.

Model 1795 Springfield Flintlock Musket

Model 1795 Flintlock Musket; Springfield Manufacture. Made at Springfield Armory, Massachusetts, c. 1795-1814. Total quantity approximately 80,000 to 85,000.

Specimens made prior to 1799 unmarked; none have been positively identified. Production from 1799 to 1814 generally divided into three major types as itemized below. Features common to all three types: All locks are flat with beveled edges and small projecting teat at rear. Because of hand workmanship, locks will vary slightly in configuration. Numerous styles of eagle markings viewed with eagles' heads facing left or right and apparently having no significance as to value. Barrel lengths vary 1/2" generally, 44-1/2" throughout with the first type (1799-1806) just slightly longer, approximately 44-3/4". 69 caliber all types; fastened by three barrel bands retained by springs. Barrel markings consistent throughout with P, small eagle's head and V across breech. Commencing in 1799 all buttplates of Springfield manufactured Model 1795 muskets were dated with year of manufacture. Locks were dated with year of manufacture commencing 1804.

The Model 1795 represents many firsts in U.S. martial arms: The first truly standardized and official model of musket made for the U.S. government; the first made by a U.S. arsenal; the first model of firearm made by the Springfield Armory. Although divided into three major classifications as listed here, there are sub-groups and variations which advanced collectors also recognize.

TYPE I: First marked style 1799 to 1806. Total quantity approximately 25,000 of which about 15,000 had socket bayonets brazed-on (permanently affixed). Most of these latter, if not all, were cut off and shortened later c. 1812-1813 (*see 33" barrel M1795*).

Lock markings c. 1799-1802: Marked forward of hammer with eagle over *U.S.* in script. Marked vertically at rear SPRINGFIELD in arch/curve. Lock markings c. 1802-1803: Marked forward of hammer eagle over *U.S.* in script. Marked horizontally at rear SPRINGFIELD in arch/curve. Lock markings c. 1804: Marked forward of hammer *U.S.* in script over eagle over SPRINGFIELD in horizontal curve. Marked in vertical curve at rear 1804. Lock markings c. 1805: Marked forward of hammer *U.S.* in script over eagle. Marked at rear SPRINGFIELD in slanted curve and dated 1805 vertically. Lock markings c. 1806: Marked forward of hammer *U.S.* in script over eagle over SPRINGFIELD in horizontal curve.

Hammer: Flat face; beveled edge; curled at top of spur (or top jaw guide). In 1804 the curl was eliminated and top of spur straight on all subsequent production.

Frizzen: Curled toe bottom of frizzen which in 1804 changed to straight shape.

Frizzen spring: C. 1799-1804 round pad with projecting teat. C. 1805-1806 spear point shaped.

Flashpan: Iron detachable type. C. 1799-1804 faceted/beveled shape. C. 1805-1806 (detachable) and continuing through to end of production. C. 1812 rounded shape.

Trigger guard: Long pointed finials top and bottom.

Stock: Long flutes approximately half length of comb on either side.

Bayonet lug: 1-1/4" from muzzle.

Sling swivels: One piece welded type without screw.

1799 dated specimens. Rare:

9A-001	Values—Good **$7,000**	Fine **$18,500**

As above, converted to percussion:

9A-002	Values—Good **$3,000**	Fine **$6,500**

1800-1803 dated specimens; most often observed:

9A-003	Values—Good **$2,750**	Fine **$6,500**

As above, converted to percussion:

9A-004	Values—Good **$1,400**	Fine **$2,750**

9A-001

9A-001
Type I

9A-007
Type II

1804-1806 dated specimens; very scarce dates:
9A-005   Values—Good **$2,750**   Fine **$7,000**
As above; converted to percussion:
9A-006   Values—Good **$1,400**   Fine **$3,000**
TYPE II: 1806-1809. Also known as Model 1795/1808, but a misnomer. Total quantity made approximately 10,000. There is a decided overlap in manufacture of this type with the following third type as noted by the years of production.

Lock marked *U.S.* in script over eagle and SPRINGFIELD in horizontal curve forward of hammer. Dated 1806 to 1809 horizontally at rear of lock with matching date at butt. Round detachable iron flashpan (key feature of identification). Hammer flat faced, beveled edge with straight spur (top jaw guide). Frizzen with straight toe; frizzen spring has spear point tip. Trigger guard semi-pointed on front finial, rounded at rear (another key feature for identifying). Sling swivels seen with and without screw. Stock flutes about one-third length of comb. Bayonet lug varies from 1-1/4" to 1-1/8" from muzzle:
9A-007   Values—Good **$1,500**   Fine **$4,500**

Identical to above; converted to percussion:
9A-008   Values—Good **$650**   Fine **$1,000**
TYPE III: c. 1808-1814. Quantity made approximately 45,000 to 50,000.

Lock marked *U.S.* in script over eagle and SPRINGFIELD in horizontal curve forward of hammer. Dated 1808 to 1814 horizontally behind hammer with matching date on heel of buttplate.

Two key features of identification are the integral forged iron rounded flashpan and trigger guard which is rounded at both ends. Hammer, frizzen and spring identical to second type. Sling swivels generally found with screws. Stock generally has flutes for quarter length or less of comb up to 1813. 1813 and 1814 dated muskets have stocks with thick wrists, very short flutes by comb and very slight cheek recesses on left side of comb:
9A-009   Values—Good **$1,250**   Fine **$4,500**
Identical to above; converted to percussion:
9A-010   Values—Good **$650**   Fine **$950**

Model 1795 Harpers Ferry Flintlock Musket

Model 1795 Flintlock Musket; Harpers Ferry Manufacture. Made at Harpers Ferry Armory, Virginia c. 1800-1815. Total quantity made approximately 70,000.

As discussed earlier in this chapter, the arms produced at Harpers Ferry proceeded along their own evolutionary development stages quite different from those made at Springfield.

There are no interim models (i.e., Model 1812) in Harpers Ferry production; the first major change being the Model 1816 as earlier referred to. There are, to be certain, many variations that do exist and are encountered in Harpers Ferry muskets. For practical purposes it is found that they are most easily divided into four major classifications or "types" for identification. Future studies will very likely sub-divide these types, however, they will suffice for purposes of this work. Production figures as indicated will also be found of use as an indicator of rarity and hence, value.

Although many prior works have stated that Harpers Ferry production did not commence until 1801, it has been quite thoroughly documented that earliest production was actually in the year 1800. Four known dated specimens with that date

have been verified. The misconception could have occurred through an incorrect tabulation by Colonel Bomford in his 1822 compilation of Harpers Ferry production records (which is the first official tabulation made) or by the method of military record keeping in which arms made at the very end of a year and not actually delivered either physically or record-wise from the armory to the military store keeper until early the following year, show up in ordnance reports as being made in that latter year.

Features common to all types of Harpers Ferry production: Locks with integral forged iron, rounded pans; frizzen with short straight toe (although a few curved ones have been noted); double necked flat, beveled edged hammer with a distinctive shape (peculiar to Harpers Ferry production) of the spur or top jaw guide—found on all variants through 1816; the back of the guide is gently curved and arches inward at its lower point where it meets the lower jaw of the hammer rather than being straight and flush fitted with it as found on Springfield production. Extreme tip of the spur or top jaw guide is evenly rounded having a profile that is bulbous. Stocks of Harpers Ferry Model 1795s deviate considerably from the Charleville

9A-011

9A-011

and Springfield Model 1795 style having much lower combs and without fluting along sides.

TYPE I: Generally styled after the French Model 1763 Charleville with 44" to 45" barrel. Lug for socket type bayonet under barrel near muzzle. One-piece welded sling swivels. Lock marked ahead of hammer with large eagle having large shield on breast; U.S. marked below. Marked vertically at rear HARPERS/FERRY/(date). The die stamps used were quite large and have a double line or shadow-like effect to each of the letters. Barrels usually proofed with eaglehead, P and U.S. All are serial numbered. Some small variations noted in early specimens in parts contours and configuration of buttstock. First year of production, date 1800; quantity unknown; worth considerable premium value over the price shown. Second year of production dated 1801; quantity made 293; also premium over value shown. Others dated 1802 (quantity made 1,472); 1803 (quantity made 1,048); 1804 (quantity 161); 1806 (quantity 136); 1807 (quantity 50). The lower production dates will also command a premium in value:

9A-011   Values—Good **$3,000**   Fine **$7,000**
Identical to above; converted to percussion:
9A-012   Values—Good **$800**   Fine **$1,750**

TYPE II: Similar to above. Bayonet stud moved to top of barrel near muzzle. Lock markings distinctly different with smaller, more detailed eagle and appreciably smaller shield on breast; the U.S. marks appear within the shield itself (a few early 1808 dated pieces still bear U.S. under eagle). HARPERS FERRY markings and date at rear of lock in smaller, neater block letters. Barrels continue serial numbering. Specimens dated 1808 (quantity made 3,051); 1809 (quantity made 7,348); 1810 (quantity made 9,400); 1811 (quantity made 10,000). Change over from Type II to Type III apparently occurred in 1812 and both Type II and Type III are observed with 1812 date also. Values remain constant for almost all dates with earliest bringing a very slight premium:

9A-013   Values—Good **$1,800**   Fine **$4,250**
Identical to above: converted to percussion:
9A-014   Values—Good **$600**   Fine **$950**

TYPE III: Similar to above. Serial numbering on barrels discontinued; trigger guard changed to rounded upper and lower finials. Eagle marking on lock made smaller. Stock strengthened and appears thicker and heavier than Type II. Production apparently unchanged 1812 through 1815. Specimens dated 1812 (quantity made 10,000); 1813 (quantity made 9,000); 1814 (quantity made 10,400); 1815 (quantity made 5,340):

9A-015   Values—Good **$1,800**   Fine **$3,750**
Identical to above; converted to percussion:
9A-016   Values—Good **$600**   Fine **$900**

TYPE IV: Identical to Type III, but 42" barrel with barrel bands proportionately spaced. Change apparently occurred to shorter length in 1814 with all of 1815 production apparently of 42" length:

9A-017   Values—Good **$1,750**   Fine **$3,450**
Identical to above; converted to percussion:
9A-018   Values—Good **$575**   Fine **$800**

1797 Ship Muskets

1797 Ship Muskets. (Not illus.) Often referred to in early naval correspondence and records, this musket is a variant of the 1795 Infantry Musket using the same mountings and lock. The arm was a distinct entity but not adopted as a "Model" and its specifications vague, at best. It continues to elude a neat, simplified classification.

The year 1797 marked the re-establishment of the U.S. Navy and the initial order and subsequent commissioning of its first three vessels (*Constitution, United States* and *Constellation*). It also marked the first known order for a specifically titled "ship's musket" to be part of the armament of those vessels.

Years of production believed to have been c. 1797 to 1819 and possibly later. Quantities unknown; 400 were ordered by the Secretary of War in 1797. Navy correspondence notes that "100 New Ship Muskets" received in Boston in 1798 and Springfield Armory inventory records 1,625 of them in 1810. Known manufactured at Springfield Armory and also in Philadelphia (contractors undetermined; possibly John Miles).

The following description, as yet incomplete, identifies in broadest terms a "ship's musket." Various ongoing research

projects on this model will likely result in more detailed, definitive identification.

An identifying feature on many is the almost combless buttstock (similar in style to the later Model 1816 type). 42" barrel with proportionately shorter stock and barrel band proportionately spaced. Locks generally Model 1795 (Type I) style; others known. Both pointed and rounded style trigger guards observed. It is believed a quantity made in 1818 era rebuilt from earlier muskets using old hardware and locks as stock dimensions and style are typical Model 1816 type. Barrels observed with post-1817 style proofmarks (raised P in sunken oval cartouche). Despite this and other seemingly definitive descriptions of the "Ship's Musket", most remain an enigma to properly identify...or, even fully understand. Some do fall within the guidelines given. Ambiguity surrounds identification of a large segment of "Ship Muskets"; many will not neatly fit exacting configurations as do most other U.S. issue arms (and, as collectors savor for guidelines). Regardless of official Navy mention of the muskets, it is suspected that in actual practice the manufacture or alteration of muskets to fit naval needs were very loosely interpreted. Considering the relatively small size of the navy and many vagaries that acquiring smallarms for that service were subject to, there is little doubt that there was a lack of standardization with their smallarms. Reading between the lines of literature on the subject is as important as reading the printed words themselves. Important, scholarly discussions of this historical arm are found in *"Boarders Away"* Vol. II (Gilkerson) and *"American Military Shoulder Arms"* Vol. II (Moller):

9A-019   Values—Good **$1,750**   Fine **$3,750**
Identical to above; converted to percussion:
9A-020   Values—Good **$575**   Fine **$950**

Model 1795 Springfield with 33" Barrel

9A-021

Model 1795 Springfield with 33" Barrel. Quantity made estimated approximately 7,000. Full stock fastened by two barrel bands (the lower and the upper double band of the standard 1795). Forward sling swivel mounted between the upper and lower band and held by a screw that passes through the forend wood and an iron stud brazed to the bottom of the barrel. Lower sling swivel mounted behind trigger guard plate on a stud that screws into the butt. Bayonet lug at top of barrel 1-5/8" from muzzle with all specimens viewed having a letter stamped into the lug.

These 33" muskets were originally First Type Model 1795s with full 44-1/2" barrels and bayonets brazed on. Although details are incomplete, it is known that c. 1815 after many years in armory storage or after being returned from the field for removal of the brazed bayonets, official orders were issued to shorten barrels by 4" (in other words, just cut off the brazed bayonets, barrel and all). For reasons unknown (and most likely in error) 12" of the barrel were cut off. A small lot of the shortened 33" muskets were sent to West Point for cadet use (correspondence indicates they were very much disliked) and about 1815 the balance of shortened guns were finished (that is, bands and bayonet studs were correctly installed) and the entire lot was sold privately as surplus. It appears that they were immediately resold by American agents to parties in South America and/or Africa:

9A-021   Values—Good **$2,000**   Fine **$5,000**
Identical to above; converted to percussion:
9A-022   Values—Good **$675**   Fine **$1,100**

U.S. (Federal) 1798 Contract Flintlock Muskets

Patterned directly after the French Model 1763 Charleville and the Model 1795 Springfield Armory manufacture flintlock musket, these 1798 arms are found with minor varying details and markings. There is every likelihood they were also made under state contracts as well as for private sales. The reader is urged to review the introductory text accompanying this chapter pertaining to the early development of American flintlock muskets and to bear in mind that contradictions can, and often, appear.

Markings listed here are those that have been seen and recorded. There is no hard and fast rule that these exact markings must appear on every piece; undoubtedly variations will occur as previously unrecorded specimens are brought to light. They may be comparatively valued with known specimens for other rare contracts. Placing an arbitrary value for an unknown/unmarked specimen yet to be recorded would be improper.

The 1798 U.S. contract muskets have features, contours and measurements about identical to those found listed for the earliest Springfield muskets of the 1799-1800 era (*q.v.*). The following are the known makers to whom U.S. government contracts were given and the information currently known about them. Considerable data herein will be found at variance with earlier published works regarding quantities known, made and delivered. This updated, revised information from archival material and Springfield Armory inventory reports of the early 19th Century is from *U.S. Muskets And Rifles 1792-1812* (*see bibliography*):

1. **Amasa Allen, Samuel Grant and Joseph Bernard** of Walpole, New Hampshire. Received contract for 1,500 and believed all were delivered. Markings unknown; very possibly unmarked.
9A-023

2. **Elijah Baggett** of Attleboro, Massachusetts. Received contract for 500; no recorded deliveries; no identified specimens located.
9A-024

3. **Thomas Bicknell**; location unknown. Received contract for 2,000 with records indicating delivery of 1,300 by 1801. Markings unknown; possibly unmarked.
9A-025

4. **Elisha Brown** of Providence, Rhode Island. Received contract for 1,000; recorded deliveries of 775 by 1801. Lockplate marked E. BROWN/1801/U.S. vertically at rear of lock:
9A-026   Values—Good **$2,000**   Fine **$5,000**
As above; converted to percussion:
9A-027   Values—Good **$650**   Fine **$1,100**

5. **Darius Chipman, R. Crofts, T. Hooker and J. Smith,** Rutland, Vermont. Completed delivery of 1000 gun contract 1799 to 1802. One known specimen attributed to them. Deeply marked at rear of lock in reverse curve "RUTLAND" with primitive, skeleton-like eagle in center.
9A-028   Values—Good **$3,000**   Fine **$8,000**

6. **Alexander Clagett** of Hagerstown, Maryland. Contract for 1,000 with recorded delivery of 600 by 1803. Markings unknown; possibly unmarked.
9A-029

7. **Joseph Clark** of Danbury, Connecticut. Contract for 500 with deliveries of 325 recorded by 1801. Lock marked DANBURY head of hammer. Few known specimens:
9A-030   Values—Good **$2,500**   Fine **$7,000**

As above; converted to percussion:

9A-031   Values—Good **$850**   Fine **$1,750**

8. **Nathan and Henry Cobb** of Norwich, Connecticut. Contract for 200 with all recorded delivered by 1801. Marked NORWICH vertically at rear of lock:

9A-032   Values—Good **$2,500**   Fine **$6,000**

As above; converted to percussion:

9A-033   Values—Good **$800**   Fine **$1,750**

9. **Matthew and Nathan Elliott,** Kent, Connecticut. Contract for 500 with recorded delivery of 235 by 1801. Marked KENT vertically at rear of lock or KENT horizontally ahead of hammer. On specimens observed stocks have been either of curly maple or walnut:

9A-034   Values—Good **$2,500**   Fine **$6,500**

As above; converted to percussion:

9A-035   Values—Good **$800**   Fine **$1,700**

10. **Owen Evans,** Montgomery County, Pennsylvania. Contract for 1,000. No records found pertaining to federal delivery; however specimens are known marked EVANS/U.S. at rear of lockplate indicating some were furnished on federal contract. It is known that deliveries by this same maker were made under State of Pennsylvania contract for same period (*q.v.*):

9A-036   Values—Good **$1,750**   Fine **$3,750**

As above; converted to percussion:

9A-037   Values—Good **$550**   Fine **$950**

11. **Richard Falley,** Montgomery, Massachusetts. Contract for 1,000 with recorded deliveries of 750 by 1801 and the entire contract of 1,000 pieces recorded in the Springfield Armory inventory in 1810. Marked with large eagle over US ahead of hammer; *FALLEY* in script along lower edge of lockplate just to the left of the frizzen spring; marked vertically in arch at rear MONTGOMERY/1799. (Other dates could appear):

9A-038   Values—Good **$2,500**   Fine **$7,000**

As above; converted to percussion:

9A-039   Values—Good **$950**   Fine **$2,000**

12. **Daniel Gilbert** of Mansfield, Massachusetts. Contract for 2,000 pieces with 875 recorded delivered by 1801. Lock marked ahead of hammer US (in intertwined letters) over D. GILBERT and dated vertically at rear:

9A-040   Values—Good **$2,500**   Fine **$6,500**

As above; converted to percussion:

9A-041   Values—Good **$800**   Fine **$1,250**

13. **William Henry II,** Bethlehem, Pennsylvania. Contract for 500 with 252 recorded delivered by 1801. Marked US ahead of hammer and vertically at rear HENRY (*see also Pennsylvania contracts*):

9A-042   Values—Good **$2,250**   Fine **$6,500**

As above; converted to percussion:

9A-043   Values—Good **$800**   Fine **$1,250**

14. **Joshua Henshaw,** Middlebury, Vermont. Delivered either 677 on contract to him, or total 1677, including 1000 muskets of contract taken over from Jonathan Nichols. Markings MIDDLEBURY on sideplate believed this maker. Known specimen with unmarked lock; barrel US / 1799 / Pw:

9A-044   Values—Good **$2,750**   Fine **$7,000**

15. **Gordon Huntington, John Livingston, Josiah Bellows and David Stone** of Walpole, New Hampshire. Contract known for only 500 pieces, yet 608 recorded delivered by 1801, and 1,005 recorded in Springfield Armory inventory of 1810. Marked with large eagle center of lock and vertically at rear WALPOLE/NH. Sideplate marked G. HUNTINGTON & Co. on the single specimen thus far recorded. Rare:

9A-045   Values—Good **$2,750**   Fine **$8,000**

16. **Stephen Jenks and Hosea Humphries** of Providence and Pawtucket, Rhode Island. Contract for 1,500; recorded deliveries of 1,050 by 1801, and 1,275 listed in later U.S.

Treasury Department accounts. Lock markings US ahead of hammer and SJ at rear of lock:

9A-046   Values—Good **$1,750**   Fine **$3,750**

As above; converted to percussion:

9A-047   Values—Good **$650**   Fine **$1,000**

KETLAND & CO. - UNITED STATES markings: *See Item 10 under "Independent Manufacturers."*

17. **Adam Kinsley and James Perkins** of Bridgewater, Massachusetts. Contract for 2,000 pieces; recorded deliveries of 1,550 by 1801. Markings not known for this early contract; possibly unmarked; *see same maker for 1808 contract muskets.*

9A-048

18. **Robert McCormick** of Northern Liberties, Pennsylvania. Contract for 3,000. No recorded delivery but correspondence exists showing delivery by the U.S. government in 1799 of gun barrels, stocks, locks and ramrods "… for the purpose of being made up into muskets and which when completed he will deliver to the public store." Specimens known marked ahead of hammer with tiny eaglehead over US and vertically at rear of lock McCORMICK/99 (*see also Pennsylvania and Virginia contracts 1797 for same maker*):

9A-049   Values—Good **$2,500**   Fine **$7,000**

As above; converted to percussion:

9A-050   Values—Good **$950**   Fine **$2,250**

19. **Jonathan Nichols, Jr.,** Vergennes, Vermont. Contract for 1,000 pieces; assigned to Joshua Henshaw (*see Item 14*).

20. **Abijah Peck,** Hartford, Connecticut. Contract for 1,000; recorded delivery of 775 by 1801; total of 904 recorded in Springfield Armory inventory of 1810. Markings unknown; possibly unmarked.

9A-051

21. **William Rhodes and William Tyler** of Providence, Rhode Island; contract for 2,000 pieces. 950 recorded delivery by 1801. Markings unknown; possibly unmarked.

9A-052

22. **Mathias Schroyer** of Taneytown, Maryland. Contract for 1,000. Recorded delivery of 150 by 1801, and 640 pieces recorded as received at Harpers Ferry Armory by 1803. Markings unknown; possibly unmarked.

9A-053

23. **Amos and Ethan Stillman** of Farmington, Connecticut. Contract for 500. Recorded delivery of 525 by 1801. Marked on lock E. STILLMAN and on some an additional marking CT. This latter mark observed on barrel proofs and lock has often been believed to indicate the State of Connecticut ownership; however valid opposing theories hold that it merely indicates an abbreviation for the word "contract":

9A-054   Values—Good **$1,750**   Fine **$4,000**

As above; converted to percussion:

9A-055   Values—Good **$650**   Fine **$1,000**

24. **Thomas Townsey and Samuel Chipman** of Vergennes, Vermont. Entire contract for 1,000 recorded delivered. Markings not positively identified, but specimens observed marked VERGENNES on sideplate are tentatively attributed to this maker. Lock unmarked; barrel marked at breech U.S. with eagle over P in oval proof. Stock on observed specimen was maple. (*See also Henshaw, Item 14*):

9A-056   Values—Good **$2,500**   Fine **$6,500**

As above; converted to percussion:

9A-057   Values—Good **$900**   Fine **$1,750**

25. **Asa Welton** of Waterbury, Connecticut. Springfield Armory inventory of 1810 records 300 of these on hand. Observed markings WELTON ahead of hammer on lock or unmarked locks and WELTON marked on sideplate:

9A-058   Values—Good **$2,000**   Fine **$4,500**

As above, converted to percussion:
9A-059   Values—Good **$750**   Fine **$1,250**

26. **Nicholas White, Thomas Crabb, Jacob Mitzger and Christopher Barnhizle** of Frederickstown, Maryland. Contract for 1,000. Delivery of 235 recorded by 1801 and 540 recorded as received at Harpers Ferry Arsenal by 1803. Markings unknown; possibly unmarked.
9A-060

27. **Eli Whitney**—*see Whitney Arms, Chapter 5.*

28. **Eli Williams** of Williamsport, Maryland. Contract for 2,000. Recorded delivery of 224 received at Harpers Ferry Arsenal in 1803. Markings unknown; possibly unmarked.
9A-061

(See also **INDEPENDENT MANUFACTURERS OR OTHERWISE UNIDENTIFIED CONTRACTS** for other possible 1798 contract markings.)

Commonwealth of Pennsylvania Flintlock Muskets Authorized by Legislative Act of 1797

Styled directly after the French Model 1763 Charleville pattern. Authorization for 20,000 muskets for state militia issuance. Recorded placement of contracts totaling 19,000 pieces were made with total deliveries unknown.

Same general specifications are applicable to these arms as for the 1798 U.S. contract pieces (*q.v.*). Specifications in Pennsylvania laws mention requirement of barrel proofs and markings near breech and on lock of letters CP denoting ownership by the Commonwealth of Pennsylvania. It has been established that on Pennsylvania arms made prior to 1799 a deep sunken oval proof mark bearing a small liberty cap motif over P was used. This design was changed in 1799 to the eaglehead motif then in current U.S. usage by the national armory.

Very often these Pennsylvania muskets are observed with the CP markings as required; however, they are often seen without such markings indicating either loose inspection procedures or the possibility that some were privately sold. Values usually do not fluctuate and would be the same with or without the CP markings for each of the various makers. Occasionally Pennsylvania contract pieces are seen bearing divisional and regimental markings along the tops of the barrels. These decidedly add to the value of the piece and a premium should be placed on them.

All known contractors are listed below. Values are not assigned to pieces of which specimens have yet to be observed or are unknown:

1. **Melchior Baker** of Fayette County. Contract information not known. Lock marked vertically at rear M. BAKER/CP. Contract for 2000 muskets actually secured by Albert Gallatin (*see 9A-071*):
9A-062   Values—Good **$2,000**   Fine **$4,000**
As above; converted to percussion:
9A-063   Values—Good **$600**   Fine **$1,000**

2. **Peter Brong (or Brang)** of Lancaster. Contract for 500. Markings unknown.
9A-064

3. **Henry DeHuff** of Lancaster. Contract for 500. Markings unknown.
9A-065

4. **Jacob Dickert and Matthew Llewellin** of Lancaster. Contract for 1,000. Markings unknown.
9A-066

5. **Edward and James Evans** of Evansburg. Contract for 1,000. Markings unknown. Although documentary evidence has not been found, it is thought that these Evans were related to Owen Evans (below) and may have worked together as one firm and hence, all arms may have been marked as below.
9A-067

6. **Owen Evans** of Evansburg. Contract for 1,000. Marked vertically at rear of lock EVANS/CP. Other markings EVANS ahead of hammer and CP at rear:
9A-068   Values—Good **$2,000**   Fine **$4,000**
As above; converted to percussion:
9A-069   Values—Good **$650**   Fine **$950**

7. **John Fondersmith** of Lancaster. Contracts for 1,000. Markings unknown.
9A-070

8. **Albert Gallatin** of Fayette County. Contract for 2,000. Gallatin merely secured the contract. The muskets actually made by Melchior Baker (*see 9A-062*).
9A-071

9. **Jacob Haeffer** of Lancaster. Contract for 500. Markings unknown.
9A-072

10. **Abraham Henry and John Graeff** of Lancaster. Contract for 2,000. Markings unknown.
9A-073

11. **William Henry II** of Nazareth. Contract for 2,000. Three marking variations known: (1) W. HENRY ahead of hammer and CP vertically at rear; (2) W. HENRY, NAZ'H vertically at rear; (3) HENRY vertically at rear and CP ahead of hammer:
9A-074   Values—Good **$1,750**   Fine **$4,000**
As above; converted to percussion:
9A-075   Values—Good **$650**   Fine **$950**

12. **John and Samuel Kerlin** of Bucks County. Contracts for 1,000. Markings unknown.
9A-076

13. **Ketland & Co.** of London, England; contracts placed through Thomas and John Ketland, their Philadelphia office. Contract for 10,000 but no deliveries made. Locks with their markings undoubtedly from the large lot of 15,000 locks only which were purchased by the U.S. government in 1795 and were received in the following years and which were believed used in other federal contracts of 1798 (*q.v.*).

14. **Jacob Lether (Laether/Leather) and Kunrat Welhance** of York. Contract for 1,200. Marked LETHER & CO. ahead of hammer and CP at rear:
9A-077   Values—Good **$2,000**   Fine **$4,000**
As above; converted to percussion:
9A-078   Values—Good **$700**   Fine **$1,000**

15. **Robert McCormick and Richard Johnston** of Philadelphia. Contract for 1,000. Possibly defaulted. Markings unknown on Pennsylvania contract with McCORMICK/GLOBE MILLS marks believe made for Virginia contract pieces (*q.v.*).

16. **John Miles,** Northern Liberties, Philadelphia. Two contracts of 2,000 each 1798 and 1801. Lock markings at rear, stamped vertically MILES/CP. Also observed marked MILES/PHILAD:
9A-079   Values—Good **$2,000**   Fine **$4,000**
As above; converted to percussion:
9A-080   Values—Good **$650**   Fine **$1,200**

Miles Flintlock Musket. Identical to above, but with all brass mountings throughout. Two distinct lock markings have been observed: (A) On rear of lock, vertically MILES (in upward curve) over PHILA (in downward curve); all in small letters. (B) Marked forward of hammer MILES/PHILADA. These are often seen with S.N.J. (New Jersey) markings on the stock and Burl (Burlington County, N.J.) markings on the barrel accompanied with regimental marks. These may be earlier than identified here. Very rare:

9A-081   Values—Good **$4,000**   Fine **$10,000**

As above; converted to percussion:

9A-082   Values—Good **$2,500**   Fine **$4,500**

17. **Daniel Sweitzer** of Lancaster. Contract information unrecorded. Possibly only the lock maker. (*See "Sweitzer" marked martial pistol. 6B-052.*) Muskets known marked inside lock either SWEITZER & CO. or D. SWEITZER. Both types bear

CP markings at rear of lock outside. Liberty cap proof on barrel and also CP on breech:

9A-083   Values—Good **$2,000**   Fine **$5,000**

As above; converted to percussion:

9A-084   Values—Good **$750**   Fine **$2,000**

18. **Conrad Welshanse, Jacob Dolls and Henry Pickell** of York. Contract for 1,000. Markings unknown.

9A-085

(*See also* **INDEPENDENT MANUFACTURERS OR OTHERWISE UNIDENTIFIED CONTRACTS**.)

Virginia Manufactory and Virginia 1797 Contract Flintlock Muskets

9A-086

Virginia Manufactory 1st Model Flintlock Muskets, a.k.a. Model 1795 Type Musket.

An armory to manufacture arms for the State of Virginia was authorized by legislative act of that state in 1797. The facilities were erected in Richmond in 1801 with manufacture of a Charleville-French style (or Springfield Model 1795 type) musket commencing in 1802. Approximately 336 were estimated completed by the end of that year with each of the following years from 1803 to 1812 averaging from approximately 1,500 to 3,000 annually. The exact quantities manufactured are unknown, however, slightly over 21,000 are estimated made up to 1811.

Although generally following the Charleville or U.S. Model 1795 style, the Virginia Manufactory musket has many features unique to it. Most evident are the almost angular shape and extra long points or teats on top and bottom finials of the trigger guards and the combless buttstock (similar to the Harpers Ferry production Model 1795), but with a distinctive downward drop or "bend" to the butt.

Markings are identical on all models through to the end of production in 1821: ahead of hammer in large block letters VIRGINIA over script markings MANUFACTORY. Marked vertically in arch behind hammer RICHMOND over date of production.

Classified as a secondary Confederate weapon, especially when found as a percussion conversion, important information about it is to be found in "CONFEDERATE RIFLES & MUSKETS" (Murphy/Madaus) and "VA. MFTY. OF ARMS" (Cromwell), both giving much detail of variations and markings.

Virginia Manufactory muskets are usually found bearing county and regimental markings on barrels which will add premium to values.

As with the production of Harpers Ferry and Springfield Model 1795 muskets, changes in configuration of parts on the Virginia Manufactory muskets were evolutionary. There is no clear cut line of demarcation where one style ends and another begins, but rather they are found overlapping. (See also VIRGINIA MANUFACTORY, U.S. MODEL 1812 MUSKETS.) **1ST MODEL VIRGINIA MANUFACTORY MUSKET.** Production 1802-1809. Approximate quantity made 14,000. First year of production 1802 dated specimens (only 336 estimated made) will bring premium values.

Flat lockplate with projecting teat at rear; size 6-3/8" by 1-1/4"; integral forged iron flashpan; large, flat faced gooseneck hammer; curl to toe of frizzen. Barrel band springs located behind bands.

44" barrels standard with 42" barrels also common. Also made in 39" and 36" length with three barrel bands proportionately spaced. These latter two known as Artillery Model by collectors or as encountered in original period correspondence "Carbines" or "Short Muskets." They will bring premium values over standard musket. Made in shorter lengths both for economy reasons to use stocks that would not finish to the longer lengths and also to utilize standard barrels that had burst on proofing and necessitated shortening. Barrels marked with P proof (either with or without oval cartouche):

9A-086   Values—Good **$3,500**   Fine **$10,000**

As above; converted to percussion:

9A-087   Values—Good **$2,000**   Fine **$6,000**

Transitional Model: Manufactured 1810 to 1811. Estimated quantity made 7,100. About identical to above with noticeably smaller lockplate 6" by 1-3/16" and gooseneck hammer with rounded face. (Some double necked rounded face hammers are also encountered in late 1811 production on which toe or frizzen is straight.) Markings and other features identical to above with dates 1810-1811 and lockplates with few specimens observed 1812.

42" barrel is standard (a few encountered in 44") with 36" and 39" lengths as above which will bring a premium:

9A-088   Values—Good **$3,000**   Fine **$6,500**

As above; converted to percussion:

9A-089   Values—Good **$1,500**   Fine **$4,250**

1797 VIRGINIA CONTRACT MUSKETS

Robert McCormick of Globe Mills, Pennsylvania. Contract of 1799 for 4,000 muskets. 925 delivered by 1801. Standard Charleville-Springfield Model 1795 pattern. Two style lock markings observed with slightly different die stamp sizes. Each marked ahead of hammer McCORMICK and vertically in arch design at rear GLOBE/MILL; some observed with date. Virginia county and regimental markings believed stamped on all barrels and values here are for pieces so marked (if no county or regimental markings appear, values approximately 10 percent or 20 percent less):

9A-090   Values—Good **$3,250**   Fine **$10,000**

As above; converted to percussion:

9A-091   Values—Good **$1,750**   Fine **$3,500**

McCORMICK & HASLETT lock marking. James Haslett, foreman for McCormick is known to have assembled and completed 50 muskets following the bankruptcy and imprisonment of Robert McCormick. These 50 pieces were in addition to the 925 previously delivered and, although exact markings are unknown, it was recorded in original documents of the era that they were marked with the names of McCORMICK & HASLETT. No specimens located to date. Very rare.

9A-092

John Miles, Globe Mills, Pennsylvania. Took over the uncompleted contract of McCormick (purchased his machinery and material on hand). Delivered 3,025 muskets of the same pattern 1801-1802. Lock marked MILES vertically at rear. Barrel with Virginia county and regimental markings:

9A-093   Values—Good **$3,000**   Fine **$6,500**

As above; converted to percussion:

9A-094   Values—Good **$1,250**   Fine **$3,000**

James Haslett of Philadelphia, Pennsylvania. Contract of 1801 for 600 muskets. Delivery completed by 1802. Model 1795 type musket. Lock marked in very small letters HASLETT either ahead of hammer or vertically at rear. Virginia county and regimental markings on barrel:

9A-095   Values—Good **$3,000**   Fine **$6,500**

As above; converted to percussion:

9A-096   Values—Good **$1,250**   Fine **$3,000**

George Wheeler, Stevensburg, Culpepper County, Virginia. Contract c. 1800 for unknown quantity of muskets. 1,000 recorded delivered by 1803. Model 1795 style. Unmarked lock. Barrel marked in large block letters WHEELER'S. MANUFACTORY, also marked with Virginia county and regimental numbers. Rare:

9A-097   Values—Good **$4,500**   Fine **$12,500**

As above; converted to percussion:

9A-098   Values—Good **$3,000**   Fine **$5,750**

Independent Manufacturers or Otherwise Unidentified Contracts of the Charleville Model 1795 Springfield Style Flintlock Muskets

The following are known markings on American flintlock military muskets c. 1795 to 1808 that are as yet unidentified. This fact makes them no less important than those for which information has been recorded; it merely indicates that the field of collecting is indeed one very much in need of further diligent research. The following are listed alphabetically by lock markings:

1. PB marked ahead of hammer on lockplate with U.S. marked at rear of lock. Small crude Indian head marking inside lockplate. Unidentified; tentatively attributed to Peter Brang & Company of Lancaster, Pennsylvania Model 1795 type musket:
   9A-099   Values—Good **$1,500**   Fine **$3,000**

2. E. BUELL marked in vertical line at rear of lock and ahead of hammer eagle over MARLBOROUGH 1795 style musket with barrel bearing Liberty cap over P proof. Few specimens known:
   9A-100   Values—Good **$1,750**   Fine **$3,500**

3. CANTON in curved vertical line at rear of lock and marked ahead of hammer with large eagle over large U.S. Model 1795 style musket. Barrel with eaglehead over CT proof:
   9A-101   Values—Good **$1,750**   Fine **$3,500**

4. CASWELL & DODGE marked lockplate on 1795 style musket. Barrel dated 1807. Known to have worked in New Hampshire:
   9A-102   Values—Good **$1,750**   Fine **$3,750**

5. E.D. & CO. marked ahead of hammer with intertwined U.S. above it. Marked vertically at rear of lock 1800:
   9A-103   Values—Good **$1,500**   Fine **$2,750**

6. H.H. marked at rear of lock; intertwined U.S. ahead of hammer. Tentatively identified as Hosea Humphries of Pawtucket, Rhode Island; known to have been associated with Steven Jenks:
   9A-104   Values—Good **$1,500**   Fine **$2,750**

7. PICKELL marked forward of hammer on Model 1795 style musket. Other markings known of crude eagle over PICKELL forward of hammer and date 1807 at rear:
   9A-105   Values—Good **$1,750**   Fine **$3,500**

8. A. PRATT marked ahead of hammer with eagle motif stamped above it. Marked at rear in script U.S.:
   9A-106   Values—Good **$1,750**   Fine **$3,000**

9. SCITUATE/1800 marked vertically at rear of lock (in script). Marked ahead of hammer with archaic style eagle over U.S. Maker unknown; either Massachusetts or Rhode Island manufacture:

9A-107   Values—Good **$2,000**   Fine **$4,000**

10. UNITED STATES marked in slight arch in two lines vertically at rear of lock; marked inside lock KETLAND & CO. A desirable specimen; this musket could possibly be the work of other U.S. contractors of 1798 for whom no known specimens have been recorded. A fact not often mentioned is the large purchase of 3,000 musket locks (as well as 3,000 rifle locks) in 1795 from the Ketland firm in England and delivered over the following years. It is known that these locks were issued from public stores to various makers from time to time; the incompleteness of records does not testify as to which makers actually used them. There is no doubt though that they were utilized. Guns so marked are occasionally encountered on the collectors' market and are considered highly desirable:
    9A-108   Values—Good **$2,500**   Fine **$4,500**
    As above; converted to percussion:
    9A-109   Values—Good **$900**   Fine **$1,750**

11. **Unidentified Eagle** or U.S. marked Charleville-style muskets. Not a few early muskets will be found bearing various forms of eagle stampings or merely U.S. or other identifying features proving them to be American military arms, but no further identification as to maker. From the historical and collector viewpoints, they are desirable pieces. The possibility exists that some of these (especially those without the eagle motif) might represent specimens of the contract of 1794. The U.S. in those early formative years followed the English custom of issuing various parts to contractors for assembly; musket locks being the best known example (*see Item 10 above*) but barrels were also known to have been issued for fabrication and to complete arms. This practice continued side-by-side with the acquisition of 1798 contracts until approximately the year 1800. As traditional collecting patterns change and more material is developed in this field, the importance and consequently the value of this group will undoubtedly show increases. Values now for such weapons are normally less than those for specimens bearing maker's or other identifiable markings. Completely unmarked specimens will bring approximately 25 percent less than the values indicated here for those pieces bearing only U.S. or eagle markings:
    9A-110   Values—Good **$1,400**   Fine **$2,000**
    As above; converted to percussion:
    9A-111   Values—Good **$550**   Fine **$900**

Model 1803 U.S. Flintlock Rifle

9A-112

Model 1803 U.S. Flintlock Rifle. Made by Harpers Ferry Armory, Virginia, c. 1803-07; total quantity 4,023. Later production c. 1814-20; total quantity 15,703.

54 caliber. Single shot muzzleloader. Specifications called for 33" part octagon/part round barrels, but lengths vary from approximately 31-3/4" to 33-1/2"; in 1815 it was increased to 36". Blade front sight and open type rear sight. Barrel secured by sliding key to stock; note distinctive rib beneath barrel, having two ramrod ferrules. No provision for use with bayonet. The lock has an integral forged iron flashpan with fence at rear.

Brass mountings. Metal parts finished bright, excepting browned barrel, barrel rib, and ferrules (iron). Note Kentucky rifle influence on most parts. Steel ramrod with brass tip.

Walnut half stock with small cheekrest; brass patchbox on right side of butt.

Lockplate marking: (eagle motif)/US, forward of hammer. Behind hammer, HARPERS/FERRY/(date), marked vertically. Barrel marking at breech: US within oval/(eaglehead)/P within oval, proofmarks.

One of the key U.S. martial longarms. The Model 1803 was the only muzzle-loading flintlock rifle produced by either of the U.S. national armories. It saw extensive service during the War of 1812. The graceful lines and Kentucky rifle styling are important ingredients in the collector popularity of this first of the U.S. regulation rifles.

Model 1803, First Production 1803-1807; Total 4,023. Production records first seen in the 1822 Report of the Chief of Ordnance (and subsequently reprinted in various U.S. martial collecting books) seemed to indicate first manufacture in 1804. Authentic dated 1803 specimens (only a few known) clearly indicate that the 1822 records are misleading when applied to actual markings on the guns themselves. (*See full details and discussion*

with description of the Model 1805 Harpers Ferry flintlock pistol). Serial numbered from 1 on up.

Overall length about 47"; stock length about 26-1/2". A variety of rifling was used. Locks are dated with the year of manufacture. It has been asserted, but unsubstantiated, that this Model rifle, dated in first year of production was the type carried on the famed Lewis & Clark Western Exploring Expedition. More recent research ("*Man at Arms*" No.3, 1999) discloses that the guns were most likely U.S. Contract Rifles of the 1792-1809 type (*see 9B-001*).

"1803" dated specimens worth premium of 50 to 100 percent.

"1804" dates bring premiums of 25 to 50 percent:

9A-112 Values—Good **$6,000** Fine **$22,000**

As above; converted to percussion:

9A-113 Values—Good **$2,250** Fine **$5,000**

Model 1803, later production c. 1814-1820; total manufactured 15,703. Often termed (erroneously) the Model 1814 Harpers Ferry half stock. Due to exigencies of the War of 1812, production on this model was resumed in June, 1814. Those made (approximately 1,600) in that year were about identical to earlier production (only eagle marking different) and bring a premium. Barrel length increased to 36" in 1815 and apparently the balance of production to 1820 were this length. The stock was lengthened proportionally to 30-1/2" and rifling standard with seven grooves. Markings remain as described above with varying dates; the eagle stamped in center of lock is slightly smaller and the U.S. appears within the shield on the eagle's breast. Not serial numbered.

9A-114 Values—Good **$3,500** Fine **$10,000**

As above, converted to percussion:

9A-115 Values—Good **$1,250** Fine **$3,000**

Model 1807 U.S. Flintlock Carbine

Model 1807 U.S. Flintlock Carbine, a.k.a. "Indian Carbine." Made by Springfield Armory, c. 1807-1810; total quantity 1,202.

54 caliber smoothbore. Single shot muzzleloader. 33-3/4" round barrel.

Brass mountings. Metal parts finished bright. Wooden ramrod with trumpet shaped tip (specimens observed with iron ball puller devices attached to lower end and trumpet tip reinforced with horn tip). Iron flashpan forged integral with lockplate, rounded on bottom with flat face on outer edge and has 1/4" high fence. Hammer of earliest Springfield type with

curl at top of spur; frizzen has straight toe without curl; spear blade shaped tip on frizzen spring.

Full walnut stock to about 1/8" from muzzle; pin fastened; uncapped, but specimens observed with reinforcements at tip probably added later to prevent wood splitting.

Lock markings: US/(eagle motif)/SPRINGFIELD, between hammer and frizzen spring. Behind the hammer, the date, e.g., 1808. On breech of barrel: P/(eagle head)/V and US.

Of dual importance as the first official U.S. arsenal-made carbine and the only gun made in a national armory, under order

9A-116

of the Indian Dept., as gifts for friendly Indians. The "Model" gun only was made in 1807; first complete carbines were 1809, although parts/locks, etc. were being mfd. 1807-1809, thus accounting for a few "1808" dated specimens. Dates often mismatched on barrel and lock by one year, occasionally two, due to earlier parts mfr. Specimens in original flintlock extreme rarities; less than handful known.

9A-116　Values—Good **$12,000**　　Fine **$37,500**
As above, converted to percussion:

9A-117　Values—Good **$4,000**　　Fine **$8,500**
Cadet model; altered in 1830 to allow for bayonet attachment. Quantities not known, but have been estimated at approximately 25 percent of original production. In doing so the forward ramrod ferrule and a section of stock were removed, and a bayonet stud was added:

9A-118　Values—Good **$10,000**　　Fine **$35,000**
As above, converted to percussion:
9A-118.5　Values—Good **$4,000**　　Fine **$8,500**

1808 Contract Flintlock Muskets

Many details regarding the background of the 1808 contract arms are explained in the REQUIEM TO THE MODEL 1808 preceding this section. It is strongly suggested that before buying, selling or collecting these contract arms the reader refer to that material in order to understand their development and significance.

To briefly review the salient points: The U.S. War Department under authority granted by Congress in 1808 (and in preparation for a threatened war with Europe), contracted with 19 gun makers for a total of 85,200 muskets, of which only half were delivered. The major variances noted in both design and configuration of parts depends upon which samples were sent to the contractor; that is, either a product of the Springfield Armory or the Harpers Ferry Armory. It is felt that the Harpers Ferry samples were most likely those of c. 1803 manufacture (*see Harpers Ferry data*) while the Springfield samples were most likely the latest type made of the c. 1808 or 1809 production (*see Springfield Model 1795 data*). Hence, the samples submitted by the two armories reflected the then-current evolutionary features of their respective muskets. The previously advanced theory of utilization of "old parts" which accounted for so-called "transitional 1795/1808" types by these contractors does not hold credibility when viewed in this light.

The following listings refer to both federal and state 1808 contract muskets. An important feature in both collecting and identification, and one that accounts for many marking variations, is the fact that these same makers were selling almost identical guns to private individuals and organizations simultaneous with their production for the federal contracts. A poignant example and verification of this practice is the complaint of the Commissary General to the Secretary of War in 1813 about the duration contracts had been running and were as yet unfilled, specifically making note of the great many "… exceedingly defective and objectionable" arms being made while further objecting to the malpractice (if not illegality) of the sale to other buyers of muskets made and inspected under government contracts! The introductory text to this section discusses the subject at greater length.

It is quite apparent from existing records and correspondence that inspection on federal contract 1808 muskets was strict and therefore U.S. proofed and marked pieces quite closely follow the pattern (i.e., Springfield or Harpers Ferry) muskets supplied. On state contracts or those made for private sale, numerous variances occur, most frequently in markings. Another quite often noted variation in non-federal muskets are shorter barrel lengths of 42" and 43" (with bands proportionately spaced).

The general style of each contractor's arm is given in the following descriptions (i.e., Harpers Ferry or Springfield style). The reader is referred to those sections which describe the respective c. 1803 Harpers Ferry and c. 1808/1809 Springfield for physical appearance of each contractor's musket. Barrel lengths vary and are approximately 44" to 45" for federal contracts. In every case such pieces will bear U.S. markings of ownership and/or proofs indicating government purchase. These arms can also bear state markings (usually on barrel and occasionally on the stock) which will add varying premiums to their value (slight with New Jersey, New York, and Massachusetts markings, and higher with states such as Ohio, Delaware, and Maryland). The values indicated on the following items generally reflect the federally marked specimens for the more well known types. In such cases, the state contract pieces (that is, those bearing no U.S. markings) bring slightly less, 10 percent being a reasonable figure; for all the very scarce and seldom encountered markings state or federal, values would be about the same. A very scarce marking variant, seldom seen, would certainly be worth a premium for that same maker's often observed federal contract specimen.

It should be clearly understood that not all markings are yet known or listed, nor have any major in-depth studies been performed in order to acquire statistical information on types, variants and markings. Values reflected are based on the relative rarity and frequency with which the following pieces appear on the collectors' market.

A great deal of previously unpublished information regrading contractors' delivery figures appears throughout the following listings. All such data is based on original reports, correspondence, and the original Irvine account book covering 1808 contracts found in the National Archives. The material has been extrapolated from the Nehrbass and Schofield manuscript *U.S. Muskets And Rifles 1792-1812* (*see bibliography*).

Definitely, vagaries exist in the complete listing and identification of all muskets of this early era. That truth is quickly apparent from original research. Although a great many facts appear in original correspondence, those same facts are not often translated into the actual guns themselves as they are encountered and observed. The reader is again cautioned not to try to "pigeonhole" and neatly place every piece in a perfect category!!

1. **Joshua and Charles Barstow** of Exeter, New Hampshire. Contract for 2,500 with 2,375 believed delivered. Springfield pattern. Locks marked vertically at rear J. & C.B. Marked ahead of hammer *US* (in script) over small eagle over EXETER (the most commonly encountered style) or J&CB/EXETER vertically at rear with large eagle over US in oval ahead of the hammer (scarcer and will bring premium). Barrels also observed marked EXETER with proof marks:
   9A-119　Values—Good **$1,750**　　Fine **$3,000**
   As above; converted to percussion:
   9A-120　Values—Good **$600**　　Fine **$850**

2. **Asher and Pliny Bartlett** of Springfield, Massachusetts. Contract for 2,500 with 1,700 believed delivered. Springfield pattern. Marked ahead of hammer (eagle) /U.S./BARTLETT; dated at rear of lock. State contracts bear only BARTLETT ahead of hammer:
   9A-121　Values—Good **$1,750**　　Fine **$3,000**
   As above; converted to percussion:
   9A-122　Values—Good **$600**　　Fine **$850**

3. **Oliver Bidwell** of Hartford, Connecticut. Contract for 4,000 with 1,025 believed delivered. Springfield pattern. Four or five marking variations known; all seem to be on U.S. contracts. Lock marked ahead of hammer with eagle over O. BIDWELL and horizontally at rear U.S. over date. Others marked ahead of hammer (eagle)/O. BIDWELL/MIDDLETOWN with same markings at rear. Variant marking with merely eagle over MIDDLETOWN ahead of hammer and U.S. at rear:

   9A-123   Values—Good **$1,750**   Fine **$3,000**
   As above; converted to percussion:
   9A-124   Values—Good **$600**   Fine **$850**

4. **John, James and Nathan Brooke** of Chester County, Pennsylvania. Contract for 4,000. 1,379 believed delivered. Harpers Ferry pattern. Lock marked ahead of hammer with eagle over small oval panel bearing U.S. in center; marked vertically at rear BROOKE:

   9A-125   Values—Good **$1,750**   Fine **$3,000**
   As above; converted to percussion:
   9A-126   Values—Good **$600**   Fine **$850**

5. **Owen and Edward Evans** of Montgomery, Pennsylvania. Contract for 4,000 with 2,128 believed delivered. Harpers Ferry pattern. Federal contracts usually marked EVANS vertically at rear of lock and eagle over oval panel with U.S. in center ahead of hammer. State contracts usually marked only EVANS in small letters ahead of hammer. More state contract specimens have been observed than federal. All quite scarce:

   9A-127   Values—Good **$1,750**   Fine **$3,000**
   As above; converted to percussion:
   9A-128   Values—Good **$600**   Fine **$850**

6. **Thomas French, Blake and Adam Kinsley** of Canton, Massachusetts. Harpers Ferry pattern except with distinctive hammer having straight spur (or top jaw guide) as found on the Springfield musket. Contract for 4,000 with entire quantity believed delivered. Quite a few variant markings have been recorded and most were federal contracts. Most commonly observed marking: Ahead of hammer eagle with small oval panel below marked U.S. over T. FRENCH. Marked vertically at rear in arch CANTON over date. Other markings (which will bring varying premiums):

   9A-129   Values—Good **$1,750**   Fine **$3,000**
   As above; converted to percussion:
   9A-130   Values—Good **$600**   Fine **$850**
   (A) Identical to that described, but omitting the T initial in T. FRENCH and usually dated 1810:
   9A-131   Values—Good **$1,750**   Fine **$3,000**
   (B) Identical to that described, but inverted with T. FRENCH above the eagle motif:
   9A-132   Values—Good **$1,750**   Fine **$3,000**
   (C) Marked only FRENCH ahead of hammer; considered state contract. Very scarce:
   9A-133   Values—Good **$1,750**   Fine **$3,000**

7. **Daniel Gilbert** of North Brookfield, Massachusetts. Contract for 5,000 with 2,050 believed delivered. Markings not known; most likely of Springfield pattern. Rare.
   9A-134

8. **Frederick Goetz and Charles Westphall** of Philadelphia, Pennsylvania. Contract for 2,500 with 1,019 delivered. Harpers Ferry pattern. Two markings known: (A) Ahead of hammer with eagle over oval panel bearing small U.S. inside and vertically at rear G&W/PHILADᴬ; (B) Ahead of hammer with larger eagle clutching arrows over U.S. and WESTPHAL/PHILADᴬ vertically at rear. Both very scarce. Observed specimens all appear to be federal contracts with surcharge state ownership markings on some:

   9A-135   Values—Good **$1,750**   Fine **$3,250**

   As above; converted to percussion:
   9A-136   Values—Good **$600**   Fine **$900**

9. **William and John J. Henry** of Northampton County and Philadelphia, Pennsylvania. Contract for 10,000 with approximately 4,500 believed delivered. Harpers Ferry pattern. Most often seen markings: Ahead of hammer with small eagle over panel with U.S. inside and vertically at rear J. HENRY/PHILA. Markings variations (which will bring varying premiums) are occasionally encountered:
   (A) Identical to those described, but without the eagle ahead of hammer and bearing only small U.S.:
   9A-137   Values—Good **$1,750**   Fine **$3,000**
   (B) Large eagle and U.S. in oval ahead of hammer and W. HENRY/NAZRᵀᴴ vertically at rear:
   9A-138   Values—Good **$1,750**   Fine **$3,000**
   (C) Small eagle over oval with U.S. ahead of hammer; PHILA. on forward section of lock and W. HENRY/JR. vertically at rear:
   9A-139   Values—Good **$1,750**   Fine **$3,000**
   As above; converted to percussion:
   9A-140   Values—Good **$600**   Fine **$850**

10. **Steven Jenks and Sons** of Providence, Rhode Island. Contract for 4,000 with 3,925 believed delivered. Harpers Ferry pattern. Marked ahead of hammer with eagle and laurel leaf over small oval panel bearing U.S. in center. Federal contract specimens marked vertically at rear JENKS'S/R.I. and found with or without date. State contract specimens marked JENKS forward of hammer and date marked vertically at rear:
    9A-141   Values—Good **$1,750**   Fine **$3,000**
    As above; converted to percussion:
    9A-142   Values—Good **$600**   Fine **$850**

11. **Sweet and Jenks** of Providence, Rhode Island. Original contract for 3,000 was split evenly between them, each to make 1,500 individually. Delivery of 150 recorded for Jenks with marks presumably as listed above (Item 10). Delivery of 375 recorded for Sweet, but markings unknown with no specimens positively identified.
    9A-143

12. **Rudolph and Charles Leonard** of Canton, Massachusetts. Contract for 5,000 with 4,208 believed delivered. Harpers Ferry pattern except with hammer having straight spur (or top jaw guide) as on Springfield. Lock marked ahead of hammer with eagle over small oval panel with .S. in center over R.&C. LEONARD. Marked vertically in arch at rear CANTON over date. State contract markings R&C LEONARD ahead of hammer and marked vertically at rear in arch CANTON:
    9A-144   Values—Good **$1,750**   Fine **$3,000**
    As above; converted to percussion:
    9A-145   Values—Good **$600**   Fine **$850**

13. **John Miles** of Bordentown, New Jersey. Original contract for 9,200 (subsequently reduced in 1810 to 4,000) with 2,447 believed delivered. Miles defaulted on this contract with the balance of production and delivery made by John Kerlin, Jr. (*see INDEPENDENT MAKERS, Item 15*). Harpers Ferry pattern. Two styles of lock markings observed: Ahead of hammer with either a very small, upper section of an eagle over panel with U.S. in center, or with full design of eagle over U.S. in oval panel. Both types marked vertically at rear MILES:
    9A-146   Values—Good **$1,750**   Fine **$3,500**
    As above; converted to percussion:
    9A-147   Values—Good **$600**   Fine **$900**

14. **Rufus Perkins** of Bridgewater, Massachusetts. Contract for 2,500 with 225 believed delivered. Released from contract in

1813. Springfield pattern. Lock marked ahead of hammer with eagle over oval panel with U.S. in center over arched BRIDGEWATER, date (inverted stamping) marked at rear. Other marking variations known, but probably for muskets made for Indian Department, state contracts or private sales (*see SECONDARY U.S. MILITARY LONGARMS— "BRIDGE~WATER" FLINTLOCK MUSKETS*):

9A-148   Values—Good **$1,750**   Fine **$3,500**

15. **William and Hugh Shannon** of Philadelphia, Pennsylvania. Contract for 4,000 with approximately 1,100 delivered. Harpers Ferry pattern. Lock marked ahead of hammer with eagle over oval panel bearing U.S. in center; marked vertically at rear W & HS/PHILA. Rarely seen:

9A-149   Values—Good **$1,950**   Fine **$3,750**

As above; converted to percussion:

9A-150   Values—Good **$675**   Fine **$1,100**

16. **Ethan Stillman** of Burlington, Connecticut. Contract for 3,500 with 1,885 believed delivered. Springfield pattern. Marked ahead of hammer U.S./(eagle)/STILLMAN, the latter in an arched curve; date marked at rear. State contracts observed with markings S. CT./E. STILLMAN (in arched curve) ahead of hammer:

9A-151   Values—Good **$1,750**   Fine **$3,000**

As above; converted to percussion:

9A-152   Values—Good **$550**   Fine **$850**

17. **Elijah and Asa Waters and Nathaniel Whitmore** of Sutton, Massachusetts. Contract for 5,000 with 4,270 believed delivered. Springfield pattern. Locks on federal contracts marked ahead of hammer with eagle over panel with small U.S. in center over SUTTON. Seen with or without date at rear with variance known having eagle over U.S. in oval over MILLBURY ahead of hammer. Variations also observed on state contract: (A) SUTTON over date marked ahead of hammer; (B) MILLBURY over date marked ahead of hammer:

9A-153   Values—Good **$1,750**   Fine **$3,000**

As above; converted to percussion:

9A-154   Values—Good **$550**   Fine **$850**

18. **George Wheeler and Caleb Morrison** of Washington, Culpepper County, Virginia. Contract for 2,500 with 125 believed delivered. Harpers Ferry pattern. Markings unknown.

9A-155

19. **James Winner, Abraham Nippes and John Steinman** of Philadelphia Contract for 9,000 with 4,126 believed delivered. Harpers Ferry pattern. Lock marked ahead of hammer with eagle over oval panel with small U.S. in center; marked vertically at rear W. N. &S./PHILAD. Variant markings at rear of lock NIPPES/& CO. It is not known if this latter type marks were used on the WN&S contract or produced by others of the Nippes family for sale (but not contracted to) to the government:

9A-156   Values—Good **$1,750**   Fine **$3,000**

As above; converted to percussion:

9A-157   Values—Good **$550**   Fine **$850**

Independent Makers or Otherwise Unidentified 1808 Contract Type Flintlock Muskets

The following are known markings about which no further information is available. This fact does not make them less desirable nor important, but, as with the 1798 contract muskets, it clearly indicates that the field of collecting still offers a rich potential for the arms historian:

1. S. ALLEN marked on lock; Springfield pattern. Made by Silas Allen, famed New England maker, of Shrewsbury, Massachusetts:

   9A-158   Values—Good **$1,750**   Fine **$3,000**

2. L. B. & CO./ASHFORD with eaglehead above marked ahead of hammer. Maker unidentified; most likely of Ashford, Connecticut:

   9A-159   Values—Good **$1,950**   Fine **$3,250**

3. I. BROAD marked lockplate with small five-point star. Maker unidentified:

   9A-160   Values—Good **$1,750**   Fine **$2,750**

4. S. COGSWELL in arched curve marked ahead of hammer with two-line markings above the name SNY/ALBANY indicating manufacture for the State of New York. This same maker's name observed on other type of New York contract arms:

   9A-161   Values—Good **$1,750**   Fine **$2,750**

5. D. HENKELS (in arch) over PHIL^A marked ahead of hammer and date (1814 observed) marked vertically at rear:

   9A-162   Values-Good **$1,750**   Fine **$3,000**

6. MASS markings ahead of hammer. *See POMEROY, Item 8.*

7. H. OSBORNE marked on lockplate or barrel. Maker of Springfield, Massachusetts. Numerous variations observed; considerable inconsistency in his markings. The most often seen, distinctive marking on his arms (observed both on locks or barrels or both) a small eaglehead stamp (sometimes found horizontally or twice marked) marked in addition to H. OSBORNE or only SPRINGFIELD in block letters (and should not be confused with U.S. Springfield Armory production):

   9A-163   Values—Good **$1,750**   Fine **$2,750**

8. POMEROY marked ahead of hammer. A prolific maker of Pittsfield, Massachusetts, with entire production evidently devoted to numerous state contracts. Distinctive arm; all observed specimens with 42" barrel and locks with point (not teat) at rear and brass pans with fence. Identical specimens may also be encountered marked ahead of hammer (A) MASS, rare, worth premium, (B) SNY, (C) S.CT. All these latter attributed to Pomeroy. Value approximately the same for all variations:

   9A-164   Values—Good **$1,750**   Fine **$2,750**

9. A. PRATT with archaic type eagle motif marked ahead of hammer and *U.S.* in script at rear. Variant marking of same eagle ahead of hammer and vertical markings at rear A. PRATT over U.S. (in script). Probably Alvin Pratt of Sutton, Massachusetts:

   9A-165   Values—Good **$2,000**   Fine **$3,000**

10. S. CT. lock markings ahead of hammer. *See POMEROY, Item 8.*

11. SNY lock markings ahead of hammer. *See POMEROY, Item 8.*

12. SPRINGFIELD (in square block letters) marked ahead of hammer. *See H. OSBORNE, Item 7.*

13. UPTON marked in slanted vertical line at rear of lock with large primitive eagle over U.S. ahead of hammer; federally proofed. Maker unidentified:

    9A-166   Values—Good **$1,750**   Fine **$3,000**

14. L. WOOD marked on lockplate ahead of hammer with variant marking reported also bearing a five-point star in circle motif above name. Made by Luke Wood of Sutton, Massachusetts:

    9A-167   Values—Good **$1,750**   Fine **$3,000**

15. "IY", (formerly misidentified as the Roman numeral "IV") marked vertically at rear of lock with eagle over "U.S." in oval ahead of hammer, identical to that of the Miles contract (9A-146). Initials of JOHN YOUNG, Easton, Penna., musket of Kerlin, Young & Co. delivered against the defaulted Miles contract.

    9A-168   Values—Good **$1,500**   Fine **$2,500**

16. UNIDENTIFIED EAGLE MARKINGS. Not a few 1808 contract type arms have been encountered with various forms of American eagle stampings over U.S., or merely eagle motifs—or occasionally merely U.S. on their lockplates. Others are encountered completely unmarked, although most of this latter type bear some type of proofing or barrel marking identifying them as American. Until such time as definitive information is found either on the style of die stamps used or other peculiar features of these arms, they must remain "unidentified." They are, however, good examples of early American military muskets; many of them undoubtedly used during the War of 1812. They are no less important historically than the marked types, but their values are consequently less. Completely unmarked specimens will bring approximately 25 percent less than the values indicated here for those bearing only eagle—or eagle and U.S.—or just U.S. lock markings:

9A-169 Values—Good **$1,500**   Fine **$2,000**

As above; converted to percussion:

9A-170 Values—Good **$500**   Fine **$750**

Model 1812 U.S. Flintlock Musket

9A-171
Type I

9A-173
Type II

9A-175
Type III

Model 1812 U.S. Flintlock Musket. Made by Springfield Armory; c. 1814-1816. Total quantity approximately 30,000 all three types.

69 caliber, single shot muzzleloader. 41-1/2" to 42" round barrel secured by three barrel bands.

Iron mountings. Metal parts finished bright. Steel ramrod with button shaped head. Bayonet lug on top of barrel near muzzle. Iron flashpan forged integral with lock and having fence.

Walnut stock; oval cheek recess or cut-out on left side of butt; lowered profile of comb without the noticeable fluting or grooves on each side of comb as on earlier models.

Lockplate marked *U.S.* (in script) over eagle motif over SPRINGFIELD (in curved arch) forward of hammer. Date stamped at rear of lock. Barrel marked at breech P over eaglehead proof over V. Date marking on tang of buttplate.

The term "Model 1812" is a misnomer; actually only patterns for this style musket were made and accepted in 1812. Actual production did not start until 1814.

The Model 1812 (collectors' term of convenience) evolved during production of the last style Model 1795 Springfield; improvements and changes being made as production progressed. The U.S. Ordnance Department decided to standardize those changes and the so-called Model 1812 was the result. Due to the practice of using up out-of-date parts, the collector will encounter not a few specimens which do not conform precisely to the specifications as detailed above.

There was no Harpers Ferry production of this so-called Model 1812 (*q.v.*).

Major differences between the Model 1795 Springfield manufacture Type III and the Model 1812 are: Rear of lockplate evenly terminated in a point—and not the extended point or teat as on the Model 1795 (it should be noted that there are decided exceptions to this rule and that 1814 and 1815 dated specimens are seen with the teat as a carry-over of earlier parts). The lockplate 1/4" shorter and 1/16" wider than Model 1795; hammer rounded instead of flat; barrel 2-1/2" shorter than Model 1795; stock approximately 3" shorter; left side of stock butt has cheek piece cut out. As earlier mentioned, the War Department in 1812 noted the fact that considerable quantities of earlier pattern parts were on hand at the armories and issued instructions that such parts were to be used on pieces then under current manufacture until either supplies were exhausted or otherwise disposed of. Thus, not a few Model 1812s are of the Type I found with varying degrees of earlier features and parts.

TYPE I: As described above. All three band springs located behind bands. Approximate quantity 10,000. Very scarce:

9A-171 Values—Good **$1,750**   Fine **$4,000**

As above; converted to percussion:

9A-172 Values—Good **$550**   Fine **$1,100**

TYPE II: Identical to above with major distinguishing feature the small rectangular studs (in place of long narrow band springs) positioned forward of the barrel bands. Usually dated 1816 on lock. Approximate quantity 5,000 to 10,000. Although fewer made, it is the most often seen type. (Note: 1813 dated locks, if perfectly fitted, are also correct with 1816 dates on buttplate on this particular musket; one of few instances where correct. Evidently the armory was utilizing old parts in inventory.):

9A-173   Values—Good **$1,750**   Fine **$3,500**
As above; converted to percussion:
9A-174   Values—Good **$550**   Fine **$950**

TYPE III: As described above with the barrel band springs located forward of bands on middle and lower bands. Trigger guard shortened to approximately 9-1/4". Specimens generally dated 1816, 1817 and most often encountered 1818. Approximate quantity 15,000:

9A-175   Values—Good **$1,750**   Fine **$4,000**
As above; converted to percussion:
9A-176   Values—Good **$550**   Fine **$1,100**

U.S. Contract Muskets Model 1812

The following arms (not illus.) are listed here as they have traditionally appeared in many previous "guides" to this subject. One U.S. contract in 1815 mentions "New Pattern" (*see Henkels*) and an existing specimen has distinctive Model 1812 characteristics. The Whitney of this period predates the Model 1812 and certainly was not influenced by it. Some independent makers' muskets may have varying degrees of similarity to the 1812. Most arms traditionally listed as "Model 1812 Contract" were merely continuations of the 1808 contract, following the pattern of those muskets and not conforming to the specifically redesigned and designated Springfield Model 1812. Thus, most so-called "Contract 1812" types should be more aptly titled "Contract Muskets of the 1812 period." The fact that not even the U.S. Armory at Harpers Ferry made the Model 1812 would appear to add further weight to the opinion. The field has had extremely little research or published informative data and hence, inconsistencies and gaps of information occur. The following are those makers that are usually included in this grouping with notations made respecting their suggested actual attributions:

1. **Adam Carruth** of Greenville, South Carolina. Took over (November, 1816) the entire contract for 10,000 muskets originally given in February, 1815 to Elias Earle of Centerville, South Carolina. Recorded deliveries of 2,250 by December, 1821. Lock marked ahead of hammer A. CARRUTH and behind hammer U.S. over date. Variant marking known A. CARRUTH, GREENVILLE S.C. (most likely a state contract). 1818-1819 dates observed:

    9A-177   Values—Good **$4,000**   Fine **$7,000**
    As above; converted to percussion:
    9A-178   Values—Good **$2,250**   Fine **$3,750**

2. **Owen & Edward Evans** of Montgomery, Pennsylvania. Their 25 muskets known delivered in March, 1816 were made as partial payment due the U.S. Government for an original advance payment given to them on their 1808 contract (*q.v.*) There is every reason to believe these 25

muskets were identical in appearance to their 1808 contract arms. Values would be identical.

3. **Daniel Henkels** contract of February, 1815, to deliver up to 2,000 muskets. Contract was given partially to satisfy indebtedness of Winner-Nippes 1808 contract (*q.v.*) to the United States. Henkels was both executor and agent for Nippes. It is known that the musket was intended to follow a Joseph Henry musket except, "… the barrel to be furnished of the gauge of the New Pattern," this being the only mention known of an actual 1812 pattern in a so-called 1812 contract arm. Deliveries were probably in excess of 800.

    A positively identified specimen with key features of federal ownership and inspection is marked P over US on the 42" barrel while both barrel and stock bear markings of the government inspector George Flegel. Stock has typical Model 1812 features with thick wrist, low comb, cheek piece cutout on left butt and barrel band springs located forward of the two lower bands (as on the Type III). Lockplate is typical Henkels style with small projecting teat at rear, marked in small block letters in center D.HENKELS. There are other typical Henkels features but musket is distinct 1812 pattern. Very rare:

    9A-178.5 Values—Good **$2,000**   Fine **$3,750**
    As above; converted to percussion:
    9A-178.6 Values—Good **$600**   Fine **$1,100**

4. **John Joseph Henry** of Philadelphia, Pennsylvania. Reported contract of February, 1815 for 2,707 muskets. Henry was known to have supplied 1808 contract muskets well into the 1812 era. All known facts seem to indicate that if there was an 1815 contract, it was merely a continuation of earlier contracts, with some of the monies received by Henry to be used to satisfy debts owed the U.S. from earlier advances. Thus, there is every reason to believe that the muskets were identical in appearance to his 1808 contracts. Quantity delivered unknown.

5. **Eli Whitney** 1812 contract. *See Whitney Arms, Chapter V.*

Virginia Manufactory 2nd Model Musket

Virginia Manufactory 2nd Model Musket, a.k.a. Model 1812 Type Musket. (Not illus.) Made c. 1812-1821. Total quantity approximately 37,000.

Major distinguishing feature from 1st Type (*q.v.*) is changed configuration of lockplate which terminates in an even point at rear instead of the projecting teat; flat beveled edge hammer with double neck. Lockplate enlarged to 6-3/8" by 1-1/4". Markings identical to 1st Type; ahead of hammer VIRGINIA (in large block letters) over MANUFACTORY (in script); at rear marked vertically RICHMOND in arched curve over date of manufacture.

42" length standard, but also seen in 36" and 39" lengths (will bring premium values). *See 1st Model Virginia Manufactory for further details.* 60,000 flintlock muskets recorded in Richmond Arsenal inventory by C.S. Ordnance at beginning of Civil War;

assumed that majority of Va. Mfty. make. 50,000 issued in flintlock Apr.-Nov. 1861. Contracts later given to various private firms to convert those arms to perc. as they were recalled from field, then re-issued to both Virginia and C.S. gov't troops. Significant information about the many various alterations to percussion of this model, especially during the Civil War by the Confederate Government (*see Chapter 10-060*) and which will significantly affect the value of those percussion conversions, is to be found in an important article, "The Alteration of Virginia Mfty Weapons 1813-1863," by Giles Cromwell in issue no. 53 (Spring 1985) of the *Journal of the American Society of Arms Collectors.*

Early Style 1812-1815: Retains iron integral forged flashpan; pointed finials on trigger guard; band springs located behind band as on 1st Model. Approximate quantity over 14,000:

9A-179   Values—Good **$3,000**   Fine **$6,500**

As above; converted to percussion:
9A-180   Values—Good **$2,000**   Fine **$4,000**

Transitional or Interim Style c. 1816-1817: Identical to above, but trigger guard rounded at both ends and band springs located forward of center and lower bands. Approximate quantity 8,000:
9A-181   Values—Good **$2,750**   Fine **$6,000**

As above; converted to percussion:
9A-182   Values—Good **$2,000**   Fine **$4,000**

Late Style c. 1818-1821: Major distinguishing feature is the brass flashpan with fence. Also has rounded ends of trigger guard and band springs located forward of center and lower bands. Approximate quantity 14,000. Although more of these were produced than the "Interim" style above, specimens are more difficult to locate:
9A-183   Values—Good **$2,750**   Fine **$6,000**

**9A-183
Late Style**

As above; converted to percussion:
9A-184   Values—Good **$2,000**   Fine **$4,000**

Independent Makers of 1812 Muskets

A very weak field for research and data; very little is known about these arms and with the hodgepodge of parts that were used and allowable in that era (as per bulletin of War Department mentioned earlier), it is even possible that some of these pieces listed are in actuality duplications of 1808 types mentioned earlier:

1. **Elisha Buell** of Marlborough, Connecticut. 1812 type muskets observed marked ahead of hammer with eagle motif over MARLBOROUGH and vertically at rear E. BUELL:
   9A-185   Values—Good **$1,750**   Fine **$3,000**
   As above; converted to percussion:
   9A-186   Values—Good **$550**   Fine **$850**
2. **Lewis Ghriskey,** Philadelphia, Pennsylvania. Specimens known marked only GHRISKEY on lockplate:
   9A-187   Values—Good **$2,000**   Fine **$4,000**

As above; converted to percussion:
9A-188   Values—Good **$750**   Fine **$1,750**

3. **Osborne** of Springfield, Massachusetts. Muskets of 1812 pattern marked on lockplate H. OSBORNE and with and without SPRINGFIELD (in block letters). Distinguishing features seem to be lack of uniformity! *See also Osborne 1808 contracts for further details:*
   9A-189   Values—Good **$1,750**   Fine **$2,500**
   As above; converted to percussion:
   9A-190   Values—Good **$550**   Fine **$800**
4. **Asa Waters** of Sutton and later Millbury, Massachusetts. Although listed as an independent 1812 maker, these very probably are the same arms listed for Waters under 1808 state contracts (*q.v., Item 17*). 1812 variants if identified would be valued same approximate range as those listed for 1808 style.

Model 1814 U.S. Flintlock Rifle

9A-191

Model 1814 U.S. Flintlock Rifle. Made c. 1814-1817. Contract awarded in amount of 2,000 each to H. Deringer, Philadelphia, Pennsylvania and R. Johnson of Middletown, Connecticut. Amounts delivered unknown; believed to be considerably less than quantities contracted for. Although only 51 specimens were recorded as delivered in November, 1814, by Deringer, it is obvious from the number of specimens viewed over the years that quite a few more were manufactured and it is quite possible that some were sold to individual states. Variances have been noted in markings (especially on Deringer made pieces) and in minor parts. Usual lock markings: US/H.DERINGER/PHILADA or US/R.JOHNSON with or without MIDDLETOWN A variation of the Johnson contract that does not bear his name, marked only US on lock, is considered rare; worth premium.

Other contractors and state marked specimens are known (especially that by S. Cogswell of Troy, New York, made for New York state contract); all worth premium.

54 caliber single shot muzzleloader; rifled bore; 33-1/2" barrel. Although actually based on an improved Model 1803

Rifle the gun more closely resembles the following Model 1817 Common Rifle, being full stocked and with large oval iron patchbox. The most easily distinguished features are the part round/part octagon barrel secured by three barrel bands, held by *stud* type barrel springs; two relief finger ridges on the lower trigger guard plate with the sling swivel at its lower tip, and a raised cheekplate on buttstock. The brass flashpan is mounted at an inclined angle; the iron ramrod is brass tipped.

The short-lived Model 1814, still somewhat an enigma to arms historians, was the result of a design produced by M. T. Wickham (then U.S. Inspector of arms) submitted at the urging of Callender Irvine (Commissary General of Military Stores and in charge of arms procurement) to arm three additional regiments of riflemen raised for the War of 1812. The iron under-rib of the Model 1803 was eliminated (having been criticized as being "heavy and of no value except to support a ramrod") and its somewhat fragile stock was strengthened and made full length:
9A-191   Values—Good **$3,000**   Fine **$8,000**
As above; converted to percussion:
9A-192   Values—Good **$1,000**   Fine **$2,250**

"Navy Contract" Model 1816 Musket

So-called "Navy Contract" Model 1816 Musket with unique thick brass buttplate with high hump on heel. Identified as the Massachusetts Sea-Fencibles Musket. Found marked by Asa Waters and E. Whitney or (less frequent) Springfield. *See Chapter V, Whitney Firearms for full details.*

Model 1816 U.S. Flintlock Musket

9A-195

Model 1816 U.S. Flintlock Musket. Made by Springfield Armory c. 1816-1840 and by Harpers Ferry Armory c. 1816-1844. Largest production total of the U.S. flintlock muskets; over 325,000 made at Springfield and over 350,000 at Harpers Ferry.

69 caliber. Single shot muzzleloader. 42" round barrel; secured by three barrel bands.

Iron mountings. Metal parts finished bright, or browned, or combination; the lockplate casehardened; detachable brass flashpan without fence. Steel ramrod with button shaped head. Bayonet lug on top of barrel at muzzle.

Walnut stock, featuring a quite low, almost eliminated comb.

Lockplate marking: SPRING/FIELD/(date) *or* HARPERS/FERRY/(date), vertically behind hammer. Forward of hammer an American eagle motif above US or U.S. Barrel marked at breech: P/(eaglehead)/V.

Distinctive features of the Model 1816 include flat beveled lockplate with rounded rear section, forward bend at top of frizzen, low stock comb, flashpans of brass.

Variation in details will be observed in the Model 1816, especially on the earlier ones, due to the lack of exact conformity in production.

Earliest transitional Model 1812-1816. Generally conforms to Type I below, but has iron integral flashpan and flat beveled lockplate usually dated 1817. Variations have been noted in barrel bands and placement of stud for use of either 1812 or 1816 style bayonet:

9A-193   Values—Good **$1,750**   Fine **$4,000**
As above; converted to percussion:
9A-194   Values—Good **$600**   Fine **$900**
Model 1816 Musket, (a.k.a. Type I) Lower sling swivel fastened to a lug which passes through and upward on front of trigger plate. Trigger bow integral with trigger plate. Bandsprings forward of lower and center bands. Made 1819-1822.
9A-195   Values—Good **$1,750**   Fine **$3,750**
As above; converted to percussion:
9A-196   Values—Good **$600**   Fine **$850**
Model 1816 Flintlock Musket, Type II; a.k.a. "National Armory Brown" and erroneously as Model 1821 or Model 1822; made c. 1822-31; browned finish on all iron parts excepting lock; sling swivel moved from stud to bow of trigger guard; trigger guard riveted onto trigger guard plate.
9A-197   Values—Good **$1,750**   Fine **$3,250**
As above; converted to percussion:
9A-198   Values—Good **$600**   Fine **$850**
Model 1816 Flintlock Musket, Type III; a.k.a. "National Armory Bright;" made c. 1831-44. Features addition of a strengthening device of ball shape to front section of trigger guard bow (area of sling swivel). Bright finish standard. More of this type were converted to percussion than Type II, hence flintlock specimens are very scarce, if not rare:

9A-199   Values—Good **$2,500**   Fine **$7,000**
As above; converted to percussion:
9A-200   Values—Good **$600**   Fine **$900**
CONTRACT ARMS; identical to Springfield and Harpers Ferry arms. The following include makers supplying under direct U.S. contracts as well as sales to states for militia issuance and others manufactured for private trade:

J. Baker, Philadelphia; total quantity unknown, but very limited. Model 1816, Type III configuration. Marking forward of hammer: US/J. BAKER. Behind hammer: PHILᴬ/1837 (all known examples bear the 1837 date):
9A-201   Values—Good **$1,400**   Fine **$3,000**

As above; converted to percussion:
9A-202   Values—Good **$600**   Fine **$750**
P. & E. W. Blake, New Haven, Ct.; made by Whitney Arms Co. (*see Whitney Firearms, Chapter 5J-025*).

E. Buell, Marlborough, Ct.; total quantity limited, estimated at a few hundred only. Model 1816, Type I configuration. Markings of either American eagle motif over a curved MARLBOROUGHin center and E. BUELL stamped vertically behind hammer *or* American eagle motif above E. BUELL in center. Believed made for state contracts:
9A-203   Values—Good **$1,400**   Fine **$2,500**

As above; converted to percussion:
9A-204   Values—Good **$575**   Fine **$750**

A. Carruth, Greenville, South Carolina; approximately 3,031 made, c. 1818-22. Type I configuration. Lock marking of American eagle motif over curved A.CARRUTH in center and date (either 1818 or 1819) over US, stamped vertically behind hammer:
9A-205   Values—Good **$3,750**   Fine **$7,000**

As above; converted to percussion:
9A-206   Values—Good **$2,250**   Fine **$3,750**
Brooke Evans, Philadelphia; 10,000 made, c. 1821-25. Type I configuration. Lock marking of American eagle motif encircled by B. EVANS*VALLEY FORGE*; the date (either 1824 or 1825) marked vertically behind hammer:
9A-207   Values—Good **$1,500**   Fine **$2,500**

As above; converted to percussion:
9A-208   Values—Good **$575**   Fine **$750**
W. L. Evans, Evansburg, Pa.; 5,000 estimated made, c. 1825-30. Type II configuration. Lock marking (misspelled by die maker) W.L. EVENS/(American eagle motif)/V. FORGE in center; the date (usually 1826, 1827, or 1828) over US is stamped vertically behind hammer:
9A-209   Values—Good **$1,400**   Fine **$2,500**

As above; converted to percussion:
9A-210   Values—Good **$575**   Fine **$750**

W. L. Evans, Evansburg, Pa.; 1,500 made, c. 1832-33. Type III configuration. Lock marking of W.L. EVANS/(American eagle motif) /V. FORGE in center; and the date (either 1832 or 1833) over US vertically behind hammer:

9A-211   Values—Good **$1,400**   Fine **$2,750**

As above; converted to percussion:

9A-212   Values—Good **$575**   Fine **$750**

R. & J. D. Johnson, Middletown, Ct.; estimated 600 made, c. 1829-34. Type III configuration. Lock marking in center of American eagle motif, US above and JOHNSON (in an arc) below. Behind hammer marked vertically with the date (either 1831, 1832, 1833 or 1834) and MIDD^N CONN. in an arc:

9A-213   Values—Good **$1,400**   Fine **$2,750**

As above; converted to percussion:

9A-214   Values—Good **$575**   Fine **$775**

D. Nippes, Mill Creek, Pa.; estimated approximately 1,600 produced; c. 1837-40. Type III configuration. Lock marking in center US/D.NIPPES/PHILA. and the date (either 1837, 1838, 1839, or 1840) behind hammer, stamped vertically:

9A-215   Values—Good **$1,400**   Fine **$2,750**

As above; converted to percussion:

9A-216   Values—Good **$575**   Fine **$750**

H. Osborne, Springfield, Mass.; quantity unknown and found in all three types of configuration. Four variant lockplate markings observed all marked in center: (1) H. OSBORNE; (2) H. OSBORNE/SPRINGFIELD; (3) small horizontal eaglehead motif over SPRINGFIELD; (4) small horizontal eaglehead motif over H. OSBORNE/SPRINGFIELD:

9A-217   Values—Good **$1,400**   Fine **$2,500**

As above; converted to percussion:

9A-218   Values—Good **$600**   Fine **$750**

L. Pomeroy, Pittsfield, Mass.; 21,600 made; c. 1817-36. Made in Type I and Type III configurations. Lockplate marking of American eagle motif over L. POMEROY; date over US marked vertically behind hammer:

9A-219   Values—Good **$1,400**   Fine **$2,500**

N. Starr, Middletown, Ct.; 15,530 made, c. 1829-40. Type III configuration. Lockplate marking of US over sunburst over N.STARR (in an arc); behind hammer marked vertically; MIDD^TN/CONN./(date). Early specimens also have an 8-pointed star (or floral) motif beneath the date:

9A-220   Values—Good **$1,400**   Fine **$2,750**

As above; converted to percussion:

9A-221   Values—Good **$600**   Fine **$775**

Tryon Republic of Texas Musket. Contracted by G.W. Hockley, chief of ordnance of the Republic of Texas with Tryon Son and Company, Philadelphia, 1839. Total quantity 1,500 of which 860 were recorded delivered and paid for by Texas; whose records show 437 issued 1840 and 321 later issued for the Santa Fe Expedition. Recent research disclosed the balance of 640 were shipped to Tryon's agent in New Orleans, 1840; as payment not made, all returned to Tryon.

Not until outbreak of the Mexican War did Tryon succeed in selling those Texan muskets to the U.S. Records reveal all were delivered to the Frankford Arsenal, Phila. July 10, 1846 (only one month after first U.S. victory at Palo Alto) and shipped four days later to the U.S. Depot at Galveston. Texas Gov. Horton complained in letter Oct. 30, 1846 to the Frankford Arsenal that "...a portion of the arms (were) issued to three companies of Texas Volunteers in the service of the U.S." It is assumed Horton believed those Tryon muskets should have been used only for frontier service with Texas militia units. In either event, it is likely Texas outfits utilized most, if not all, 640 muskets. Surviving specimens very rare. Tryon not known to have any other state or U.S. contracts for flintlock muskets. Be cautious of spurious markings.

Lock markings TRYON/PHILAD'A vertically at rear; with large 5-pointed star with smaller star in middle over TEXAS in center. Barrel marked P over GF:

9A-221.5   Values—Good **$9,500**   Fine **$25,000**

As above; converted to percussion:

9A-221.6   Values—Good **$6,000**   Fine **$11,500**

A. Waters, Jr., Millbury, Mass.; 36,560 made, c. 1817-36. Types I, II, and III configurations.

Early production Waters, the lockplate marking a script US over MILLBURY, and the date (either 1817 or 1818) vertically behind hammer; about 5,000 produced:

9A-222   Values—Good **$1,500**   Fine **$2,750**

As above; converted to percussion:

9A-223   Values—Good **$600**   Fine **$750**

Second type Waters; the lockplate marking an American eagle motif above script US, and A. WATERS/(date) vertically behind hammer. About 10,000 made:

9A-224   Values—Good **$1,500**   Fine **$2,500**

As above; converted to percussion:

9A-225   Values—Good **$575**   Fine **$750**

Third type Waters; lockplate marking of US/A.WATERS in center and vertically stamped behind hammer; MILLBURY/(date); about 21,560 produced:

9A-226   Values—Good **$1,400**   Fine **$2,400**

As above; converted to percussion:

9A-227   Values—Good **$575**   Fine **$750**

E. Whitney, Jr., New Haven, Ct. (*See Whitney Firearms, Chapter V.*)

M. T. Wickham, Philadelphia, Pa.; about 16,600 made, c. 1822-37. Following lockplate markings will be observed: Early production, M.T.WICKHAM in an arc over PHILA. Later production, U.S. over M.T. WICKHAM (in arc); behind hammer PHIL^A/(date) marked vertically:

9A-228   Values—Good **$1,400**   Fine **$2,250**

As above; converted to percussion:

9A-229   Values—Good **$575**   Fine **$700**

Model 1817 U.S. Flintlock Artillery Musket

Model 1817 U.S. Flintlock Artillery Musket. Made by Springfield Armory and by Harpers Ferry Armory; c. 1817-1821. Total quantity 1,039 at Springfield and unknown at Harpers Ferry; limited.

The Harpers Ferry was a shorter version of the Model 1816 U.S. Flintlock Musket, and is distinguished by such features as: 36" barrel, 69 caliber, the stock (at 48-3/8" length) is about 5-5/8" shorter than the Model 1816, the lockplate and barrel tang markings as on the Model 1816 (*q.v.*), browned iron parts except for casehardening on the lockplate. All Harpers Ferry specimens

are basically of the Type I configuration of the Model 1816, with exceptions noted.

The Springfield version does not readily conform to a neatly defined pattern. Stocks are mostly of 1816 type with early parts used. Barrels that failed at the muzzle in proof testing were often used as were barrels from earlier models that were too narrow at breech to be used with the new brass pan locks of the 1816. Thus, in almost all cases, the Springfield artillery musket is composed of earlier iron pan locks and hardware and locks will be found bearing earlier dates. The

9A-230

barrel proof marks, however, are the type used after 1817. 200 of these muskets were made for cadet use in 1817. "Springfield" marked specimens are also known having the 1816 type lock with brass pan, in 36" barrel length but two bands, the top band with sling swivel affixed in same manner

as a British "Brown Bess;" scarce and worth premium; caution advised for spurious alterations:

| 9A-230 | Values—Good **$2,500** | Fine **$5,500** |

As above; converted to percussion:

| 9A-231 | Values—Good **$600** | Fine **$850** |

Model 1817 U.S. Flintlock Rifle

9A-232

Model 1817 U.S. Flintlock Rifle, a.k.a. "Common Rifle." Made c. 1817 to early 1840s; total quantity 38,200. Contracts awarded to H. Deringer, Philadelphia, Pennsylvania; and to R. Johnson, R. & J. D. Johnson, N. Starr, and S. North, of Middletown, Connecticut.

54 caliber rifled with seven grooves. Single shot muzzleloader. 36" round barrel, fastened with three barrel bands.

Iron mountings, finished brown, including barrel. Lockplate casehardened; separate attached brass flashpan without fence.

Steel ramrod with trumpet type head capped with brass tip. Not made for use with a bayonet.

Walnut stock; oval patchbox on right side of butt.

Lockplate markings as noted under variations below. Barrel marking at breech: US/P/(inspector initials); date marking on tang. US on tang of buttplate.

Based on pattern rifles made at the Harpers Ferry Armory, the Model 1817 Flintlock Rifle is unusual, being made solely by contractors. Quite a few of this model saw Civil War service. Most production was in the 1820s, as evidenced by date stampings on known specimens. The nickname "Common Rifle" dates back to the actual period of use of the gun and was used to differentiate it from the Hall's Patent *breech-loading* Model 1819 rifle produced and issued simultaneously.

H. Deringer Contract Arms. Total quantity 13,000. Some specimens appear with earlier features and mixed parts, most notably trigger plate without the pistol grip projection and the sling swivel mounted on trigger bow; or having the finger ridges of the predecessor 1814 rifle. These pieces were found acceptable under his U.S. contract. Three distinct lock markings are known, but prices have generally been the same for all types: (1) Large US over H. DERINGER over PHILAD^A in center of lock with date of manufacture marked vertically behind hammer; (2) identical to preceding, but the US is smaller size, about the same height as the other two lines; (3) two-line DERINGER/PHILADEL^A in very tiny letters identical to markings used on the boxlock Model 1842 Navy pistol:

| 9A-232 | Values—Good **$2,500** | Fine **$6,000** |

As above; in percussion:

| 9A-233 | Values—Good **$900** | Fine **$2,250** |

Original Percussion Specimens; 58 caliber; lock marking: US/DERINGER/ PHILADEL^A. Barrel breech marking only the letter P. Nipple bolster integral with barrel. Believed made by

Deringer in attempt to obtain contract orders, or to fill a state contract. Very limited quantity produced. It is obvious on inspection of the lockplate that it has been specifically made as percussion with no signs or provisions, or filled holes, indicating it once held flintlock parts:

| 9A-234 | Values—Good **$1,100** | Fine **$2,850** |

R. Johnson contract arms; total quantity 5,000; made c. 1821-23. Standard lockplate marking: R JOHNSON (in arc)/U (eagle motif) S/MIDD^N CONN. (upward arc). Date marking vertically behind hammer:

| 9A-235 | Values—Good **$2,000** | Fine **$5,500** |

As above; converted to percussion:

| 9A-236 | Values—Good **$875** | Fine **$2,200** |

Scarce variation; lock marking US/R.JOHNSON/MIDDLETOWN; no date stamping; believed to be used on earliest production:

| 9A-237 | Values—Good **$2,250** | Fine **$5,750** |

As above; converted to percussion:

| 9A-238 | Values—Good **$1,000** | Fine **$2,000** |

R. & J. D. Johnson contract arms; total quantity 3,000: made c. 1824-27. Two types of lockplate markings observed:

(1) U.S./R. & J.D.JOHNSON, in center; at rear marked vertically, (date)/MIDD^N CONN (in arc):

| 9A-239 | Values—Good **$2,250** | Fine **$5,750** |

(2) US./(eagle motif)/R. & J.D. JOHNSON (upward arc) in center; at rear section of lock, marked vertically, (date)/MIDD^N CONN. (in arc):

| 9A-240 | Values—Good **$2,250** | Fine **$5,750** |

As above; converted to percussion:

| 9A-241 | Values—Good **$850** | Fine **$2,000** |

Simeon North contract arms; total quantity 7,200; made c. 1824-29. Standard lockplate marking: U.S./S.NORTH, in center. At rear of lock, MIDLT^N/CONN/(date), stamped vertically:

| 9A-242 | Values—Good **$2,250** | Fine **$5,750** |

As above; converted to percussion:

| 9A-243 | Values—Good **$850** | Fine **$2,000** |

Nathan Starr & Son contract arms; total quantity 10,020; made on contracts awarded 1823 and 1840. Lockplate markings as follows:

(1) **1823 contract arms;** total made 4,020; U.S./N.STARR in center; (date)/MID^N CON. (in upward arc) at rear stamped vertically:

| 9A-244 | Values—Good **$2,250** | Fine **$5,750** |

As above; converted to percussion:

9A-245   Values—Good **$850**   Fine **$2,000**

(2) **1840 contract arms;** total made 6,000; N. STARR & SON (in semi-circular motif)/(Starr sunburst trademark)/U.S. in

center; MIDDT^N/CONN/(date) at rear stamped vertically:

9A-246   Values—Good **$2,250**   Fine **$5,750**

As above; converted to percussion:

9A-247   Values—Good **$850**   Fine **$2,000**

Model 1819 Hall U.S. Breech-Loading Flintlock Rifle

9A-248

9A-248

Model 1819 Hall U.S. Breech-Loading Flintlock Rifle. Made by Harpers Ferry Armory, under John H. Hall's patent; c. 1817, 1819, 1823-24, and 1827-40; total quantity 19,680.

52 caliber. Rifling extended to within 1-1/2" of muzzle, apparently to allow for muzzle-loading if necessary. Single shot breechloader; breechblock pivots upward for loading, and is released by lever device protruding through bottom of stock forward of trigger guard. 32-5/8" round barrel; three barrel bands.

Iron mountings, finished with brown lacquer, including barrel. Breech casehardened. Steel ramrod with button head end. Front sight doubles as lug for attachment of angular bayonet.

Walnut stock.

Breechblock markings as noted under variations below.

Earliest production of Hall breechloaders was in Portland, Maine, home of the inventor. It is known that he supplied 100 of his "improved" breech-loading rifles on U.S. Government order in 1817, but no known specimen has been positively identified. It is thought that they were similar to his sporting models then being made in Yarmouth and Portland, Maine (see *Hall's Breechloaders* by R. T. Huntington). His patented design led to the first breech-loading military arm produced in large quantities and adopted as a regulation weapon nationally. The Hall also became the first firearm successfully made with total

interchangeability of parts. Hall received a contract for 1,000 rifles in 1819—but by 1823 he had completed only 22 of them, by hand. These pieces (very rare and practically unknown) were not interchangeable with the balance of the 1,000 which were completed in the following year *and* it is believed that all were dated 1824. Barrel bands retained by springs until 1832 when they were changed to pin fasteners.

Numerous minor variations appear which can affect value slightly and a few very rare pre-production and experimental pieces exist. A large number of these were in the various Southern arsenals at the outbreak of the Civil War and were altered by Confederate states to percussion. Considerable discussion and illustration devoted to them in *Confederate Rifles*

9A-248
**Presented by Act of U.S. Congress
for Heroism in War of 1812**

& Muskets (Murphy/Madaus; q.v.) Various features, especially hammer contours, differ from regular U.S. conversions. Although none with "C.S." markings, certain features may identify them, thus possibly adding to their value considerably.

The Hall Model 1819 also bears the distinction of being the only gun presented by Act of Congress of the U.S. in lieu of a medal or other citation for gallantry in battle.

Fifteen Hall rifles, all of them of 1824 production, were awarded to Americans who, ten years earlier, during the War of 1812, as schoolboys mostly 15 years of age, had volunteered and were accepted for service with the U.S. forces during the siege of Plattsburgh, New York, in 1814. They performed heroically in the defense of a bridge against advancing British troops.

The Hall rifles presented were appropriately inscribed with a large silver plaque inset in the right butt commemorating the event and the recipient's name. A small shield-shaped plaque bearing the recipient's initials and date of the battle is inset at the wrist. Four specimens are known to still exist. An extremely rare and historic gun—the collector is urged to be wary before acquiring a specimen as spurious examples are known. Authentic Congressional presentation specimens (depending on condition) are valued in the mid to higher five figures.

First production type; all dated 1824, with breech marking: J. H.

HALL/H. FERRY/1824/U.S.:

9A-248   Values—Good **$4,000**   Fine **$8,750**

Second production type; bearing dates 1826 to 1838; the breech marking of J. H. HALL/H. FERRY/US/(date):

9A-249   Values—Good **$1,750**   Fine **$3,500**

Third production type; bearing dates 1837 to 1840; the breech marking of J. H. HALL/US/(date):

9A-250   Values—Good **$1,750**   Fine **$3,500**

As above; converted to percussion:

9A-251   Values—Good **$950**   Fine **$1,500**

Contract Model 1819 by Simeon North, Middletown, Conn.; c. 1830-36 total quantity 5,700. The North-Hall contract rifles are virtually identical; the main distinction is in the breechblock marking: U.S./S. NORTH/MIDL^TN/CONN./(date). The only difference otherwise is in the means of securing the barrel bands—North used band springs exclusively, whereas Harpers Ferry used either band springs or pinned the bands into position. Henry Deringer, R. & J. D. Johnson, and Reuben Ellis were also awarded contracts to make the Model 1819 Hall Rifle, but only North delivered on his commitments:

9A-252   Values—Good **$2,000**   Fine **$3,750**

As above; converted to percussion:

9A-253   Values—Good **$950**   Fine **$1,500**

Model 1841 Hall Breech-Loading Percussion Rifle

Hall U.S. Breech-Loading Original Percussion Rifle, a.k.a. Model 1841 Hall (correct name). (Not illus.) Made by the Harpers Ferry Armory, c. 1841-1842; total quantity 4,213. Configurations and dimensions generally identical to the Model 1819.

52 caliber. Single shot breechloader with identical action to Model 1819 Rifle, excepting the breechblock release of the so-called fishtail type like that seen on the Model 1840 Hall-North carbine, Type II; transition specimens having the old style spur release device. 32-5/8" barrel; three barrel bands, pin fastened.

Iron mountings, browned finish, including barrel. Breech finished in casehardening. Steel ramrod with button head end. Walnut stock.

Breechblock marking: H. FERRY/US/(date 1841 or 1842).

Made after Hall's death in 1841, his name was dropped from the breechblock marking. Many features of the Percussion Rifle will be seen as carried over from the Model 1819 Flintlock. Major differences other than the breech release which help identify this from a converted Model 1819 are: the rifling, which is 7-groove and extends all the way to the muzzle; the absence of the pistolgrip feature on the Model 1841; the lower sling swivel on rear section of trigger guard plate; and the use of an extended section of that plate to include the breechblock release lever (on Model 1819 a separate plate had been used):

9A-254   Values—Good **$1,750**   Fine **$4,000**

Model 1830 U.S. Flintlock Cadet Musket

Model 1830 U.S. Flintlock Cadet Musket. Made by Springfield Armory c. 1830-1831. Total quantity 307 (154 of 36" style and 153 of 40").

54 caliber smoothbore. Single shot muzzleloader. Made in two styles, 40-1/4" barrel or 36" barrel with stud for socket type bayonet on top near muzzle; fastened by three barrel bands. Steel ramrod with trumpet shaped tip.

Iron mountings; metal parts finished browned with small size casehardened lock 5-3/8" in length similar to those used on Model 1817 rifle marked with eagle over U.S. in center; vertically behind hammer SPRING/FIELD/1830. Barrel markings P proofmark in circular panel, eaglehead and V with tang bearing date 1830. A small serial number stamped at the extreme breech of barrel and on bayonet lug.

**Model 1816 Musket (top).
Shown for size comparison
with Model 1830 cadet (bottom).**

These arms were specifically designed for use of the cadets of West Point with the approval of the Secretary of War; the use of the Model 1817 artillery musket and other shortened standard arms having proved unsatisfactory:

9A-255 Values—Good **$14,000** Fine **$37,500**
As above; converted to percussion:
9A-256 Values—Good **$5,500** Fine **$12,500**

Model 1840 U.S. Flintlock Musketoon

9A-257

Model 1840 U.S. Flintlock Musketoon. a.k.a. Model 1839. Reportedly made by Springfield Armory, c. 1839-1843 but no known specimens authenticated. It is strongly believed that this model was never produced at all beyond the "model" marked pre-production pieces. The pattern models made at Harpers Ferry in 1839 (of which one is known to exist) is dated 1839. Correct nomenclature is "MODEL 1840" and it is so named in the 1840 Ordnance manual.

69 caliber smoothbore. Single shot muzzleloader. 26" round barrel, sometimes fitted with bayonet stud (for angular bayonet); two barrel bands.

Iron mountings. Metal parts finished bright. Iron ramrod with trumpet shaped end. Walnut stock of nearly full length.

Lock markings on the pattern piece: (Eagle motif) US, forward of the hammer. Behind hammer and reading vertically: HARPERS/FERRY/1839. On breech of barrel: V/P (eaglehead). The markings U.S.M. (indicating U.S. MODEL) appear on all major parts. Smaller parts such as lock screws, internal parts, etc. are marked merely with the letter M. The breech of barrel on the only known specimen also bears the word MODEL and

the serial No. 1. The Model 1840 shares with the Model 1807 the distinction of being the only two carbines of flintlock system made in a U.S. government armory.

The gun is similar in appearance to the Model 1840 flintlock musket but smaller proportioned and easily distinguished by the circular opening in the hammer. A key feature often overlooked is the smaller, scaled down lock 5-1/8" long by 1-1/16" high, considerably smaller than the musket lock. It also has a shorter trigger guard plate 8-5/8" overall. Most specimens viewed on the collector's market have the large musket size lock and there is considerable doubt that the Springfield Arsenal made them thusly, especially as the arm does not appear in otherwise accurate production tables of both armories. Reference material about them in printed works is sketchy at best, and often confusing.

The MODEL marked pieces are beyond the scope of this volume; the doubtful production of any known quantity further precludes the arbitrary evaluation of authentic specimens. Examples, if proven authentic, would be worth in the five-figure range. **9A-257**

Model 1840 U.S. Flintlock Musket

Model 1840 U.S. Flintlock Musket, a.k.a. Model 1835. Made by Springfield Armory; total produced 30,421 (of which 26,841 altered to percussion from 1849-51, and still more altered at later date).

69 caliber. Single shot muzzleloader. 42" round barrel; secured by three barrel bands. Its most quickly identifying feature is the unique, completely circular opening in the center of hammer (through which the screw for top jaw passes).

Iron mountings. Metal parts finished bright. Detachable flashpan of brass with fence at rear. Steel ramrod with trumpet-shaped head. Bayonet lug on bottom of barrel at muzzle.

Walnut stock, with a high comb.

Lockplate marking in center of American eagle motif over US; behind hammer, marked vertically: SPRING/FIELD/(date). The breech of barrel marked: V/P/(eaglehead). Inspector initial cartouche stamped on left side of stock, opposite lock.

The 1840 was the last standard production model of U.S. flintlock musket. It was originally designated the Model 1835, however, it went through numerous alterations in the five years prior to production in 1840 and has become generally accepted as the Model 1840. Considerable changes appear in this piece from the Model 1816 type, and it bears a resemblance to the French Model 1822 musket. Another readily identifiable difference from earlier U.S. models is the very narrow sideplate through which the two lock screws pass identical to the later Model 1842 percussion musket.

Caution to buyers: As the great percentage of these were converted to percussion, original flintlock specimens are considered rare. Not a few specimens have been restored to flintlock over the past 30 years—and extreme care should be taken when acquiring this model.
In original flintlock:
9A-258 Values—Good **$3,500** Fine **$7,500**
As above; altered to percussion:
9A-259 Values—Good **$550** Fine **$1,000**

9A-258

D. Nippes, contract Model 1840 Musket; 5,100 made, c. 1842-48. Lockplate marking D. NIPPES/US (forward of hammer); stamped vertically behind hammer: MILL/CREEK/PA. (date marking usually present in a fourth line):

9A-260	Values—Good **$2,250**		Fine **$4,750**

As above; converted to percussion:

9A-261	Values—Good **$575**		Fine **$800**

L. Pomeroy, contract Model 1840 musket; about 7,000 produced, c. 1840-46. Lockplate marking of American eagle motif above L. POMEROY in center, and (date, from 1840-1846) over U.S. vertically behind hammer:

9A-262	Values—Good **$2,750**		Fine **$5,500**

As above; converted to percussion:

9A-263	Values—Good **$600**		Fine **$950**

Conversions of U.S. Flintlock Muskets to Percussion Performed by U.S. Arsenals c. 1840s Through Late 1860s

9A-264
French Style
("side-lug")

9A-264
Belgian Style
("cone type")

Conversions of U.S. Flintlock Muskets to Percussion performed by U.S. arsenals c. 1840s through late 1860s.

With adoption and issuance of the more "modern" percussion ignition system for U.S. military arms, the final decision to cease all flintlock production was made in 1842. A six-year inventory ensued in which all arms held by National and private armories were classified into four major categories by their period of original manufacture and condition or suitability for use. By 1848 when reports were complete, the totals of muskets on hand were in excess of 700,000. Those in lowest category, over 100,000 pieces, which included all arms made prior to 1812 as well as later pieces considered unserviceable or damaged and not worth repairing, were ultimately condemned and sold on the open market to highest bidders. The remaining flintlocks were kept intact and eventually, over a lengthy period, a great many (exact quantity unknown) were altered to the percussion system.

Three basic types of conversions were performed:

(1) Officially termed the "French Style" but more commonly known to collectors as the "side lug" or "drum and nipple" conversion. All external lock parts were removed with threaded holes plugged, the flashpan cut and ground flush with lockplate, hence remnants of the pan are usually intact; a drum type bolster holding nipple merely threaded into the enlarged touch hole; the hammer resembles that of a civilian fowling piece. The earliest method used and performed through the early 1850s, and the one which lends itself the easiest for restoration in modern day to flintlock condition. This method believed all performed by private contractors.

(2) Officially termed the "Belgian alteration" and more commonly known to collectors as the "cone type" conversion. Second style; performed early 1850's. All external lock parts removed with screw holes plugged; the pan ground flush with lockplate (hence leaving remnants intact) and the small existing cavity in pan filled with brass to give it a level or squared off profile along top. The vent hole of barrel plugged with nipple screwed into threaded receptacle at top of barrel, set off center towards lock side; distinctive arsenal, military hammer. From existing records this method is the only one performed by National Armories.

(3) The "Bolster type" conversion. Last method used c. mid-1850's through to early Civil War; all believed performed by

private contractors. Lock altered as with "cone type" above with 2 distinct methods (with variations of each) of attaching the bolster with nipple:

(a) bolster merely brazed over the vent hole of flintlock barrel.

(b) breech of barrel removed by cutting-off and an entire new breech having the bolster made integral screwed into barrel.

For general collector purposes, it has been found that there is no value distinction made in any of the three above conversion types; i.e., one style is not worth more or less than the other when found on any particular U.S. musket. Some of the third or bolster type conversions are found on muskets that have also had their bores rifled and two-leaf rear sights added—and such specimens when encountered will bring a premium. These arms are of dual interest as the conversions usually denote they were performed early in the Civil War era for issuance to Union troops.

Specimens of a known contract to a private firm for conversions are often encountered and are treated as a distinct type:

Hewes & Phillips, Newark, New Jersey, percussion conversions c. 1861-62, on contract with the State of New Jersey and the U.S. government. Total number of alterations (from

9A-265
Bolster Type

flintlock to percussion) 20,000. The arms altered were generally the Model 1816 and Model 1835 (1840) muskets, of both contract makes and National Armory production. Bolster type alteration fitting a replacement breech with integral bolster into breech of barrel. Rifling of barrels was standard; exceptions noted below.

Identifying characteristics of these arms are as follows:

1st type; believed most supplied to State of New Jersey. Small bolster similar in shape to the 1855 Rifle Musket, with clean-out screw. Two types of 1861 style rear sight; three-groove

rifling, though some specimens noted smoothbore: total approximately 8,000 arms:

9A-264   Values—Good **$600**   Fine **$1,150**

2nd type; believed almost all supplied under contract to U.S. Easily distinguished by the large bolster, made without clean-out screw and marked on side of bolster H & P and usually bearing an 1861-63 date at top, breech of barrel. Barrel rifled; with sights as above. Approximately 12,000 so altered:

9A-265   Values—Good **$600**   Fine **$1,150**

Conversions to Percussion with Mechanical or Auto-priming Systems

A number of systems were devised to replace the need to manually prime percussion arms with the small and often difficult to handle percussion cap. Although one system, the Maynard tape primer was ultimately adopted and incorporated on almost all 1855 Model arms, a few others were converted from flintlock in varying quantities and issued on both experimental and regular basis.

9A-267
D. S. Nippes
Conversion with
Maynard Tape Primer

9A-266
Butterfield
Disc/Pellet Primer

(A) Butterfield disc or pellet primer. Consists of a distinctive appearing narrow, tubular magazine, vertically mounted in center of lock which holds a supply of tiny fulminate detonator discs. The discs are loaded from underside of magazine tube by removing the large brass knob cover. Internal mechanism fitted at top of lock allowed the discs to automatically release and cover the nipple by the action of cocking the hammer.

The U.S. government awarded Jesse Butterfield a contract to alter 5,000 arms to his automatic system in 1859. Although no records are available, there is every indication that the contract was unfulfilled and deliveries were very limited. The gun is a collector's rarity. The conversion has been observed on various models of U.S. flintlock muskets—both contract and National Armory types; it is most often encountered on the Model 1816. Variations of the disc priming tubes and methods of mounting them have been noted. The most often encountered is as illustrated. Bolsters are also specially designed and shaped for this conversion.

Locks usually bear their original markings with the addition on forward section of BUTTERFIELD'S/PATENT DEC. 11, 1855/PHILAD^A:

9A-266   Values—Good **$2,500**   Fine **$8,000**
(B) Maynard Type Primed conversion of U.S. Model 1840 muskets. Quickly recognized by the large box-like device mounted in the center of lock with hinged door which swivels downward to open retained by small pointed swivel catch in center. The bolster with nipple is extra long in length, specially made to fit the Maynard device. The hammer contour is also unique to this conversion with two styles noted. A tape or narrow strip of varnished paper, holding small amounts of fulminate at regular intervals (very much like a roll of caps for a

child's cap pistol of today) was the basis for the system. The roll of tape was inserted in the box-like magazine and when the hammer cocked a pawl or finger-like device rotated the tape, ejecting a short length of it containing the fulminate from top of magazine to cover the nipple. The Nippes alterations (see below) could be used either with tape or manually primed with single percussion cap. Although Springfield reportedly converted 300 to the Maynard system circa 1848, such specimens are unknown and their markings, if any, unverified. (An experimental pistol with the same system is known; see 6A-037.5.)
D. S. Nippes, Philadelphia. Conversion; c. 1848-1849. Two contracts for 1,000 each delivered by Nippes. Majority of arms used were Nippes own earlier Model 1835 (1840) flintlocks, but those bearing other makers' marks are known. Two markings on the magazine door are encountered: EDWARD MAYNARD/PATENTEE/1845 or MAYNARD'S PATENT/WASHINGTON/1845:
9A-267   Values—Good **$2,000**   Fine **$3,750**
(C) Maynard conversion by Frankford Arsenal, Philadelphia 1856-1859.

Remington Arms Co. completed contract for 20,000 Maynard primer locks and percussion bolsters, supplying all to Frankford

9A-268
Maynard
Conversion by
Frankford Arsenal

who then fitted them to various make M. 1816 (type II & III) muskets. Frankford also rifled the barrels and fitted long range leaf sights. Lock markings "REMINGTON'S/ ILION, N.Y. / (date) / N.Y." Dates 1856-58 usual. Rare variant markings on earliest production has "HERKIMER" in place of "ILION" dated "1855" (possibly only 50 so marked). Total muskets so-fitted 20,000, many seeing service in Civil War. Six hundred delivered to the U.S. Navy, 1857, others to the 6th U.S. Infantry, Fort Riley, Kansas, 1857 and many to N.Y. state outfits. Two thousand were converted for New Jersey and will bear N.J. markings at breech of barrel and stock.

9A-268   Values—Good **$875**   Fine **$1,850**

(D) Ward tape primed conversion. Easily recognized by the uniquely designed, almost awkward appearing hammer which has a swivel door on its upper section covering an inner receptacle for a roll of tape primers. Cocking the hammer operates an inner ratchet which ejects a short strip of tape containing the fulminate, thus covering the nipple. The bolster used with this hammer is uniquely shaped (see illustration) and a further means of identifying authentic specimens.

Ward conversions are found on M. 1812 and M. 1816 muskets of various makers. Although rifled bores were specified, examples studied are all smooth; uniquely designed short, single leaf rear sight and tall, brass cone type front sight

**9A-269
"Ward tape primed
conversion"**

usual (other types known). Right side of hammer marked **"J.N. WARD. U.S.A. / PATENTED JULY 1, 1856."** Serial numbers on various parts of hammer do not match on all specimens studied. Quantity made unknown. N.Y. contracted for 1200 in 1857 of which less than 300 believed delivered. 100 "SPRINGFIELD" muskets known fitted with Ward hammer by U.S. Arsenal same year. Rare.

9A-269   Values—Good **$2,400**   Fine **$4,500**

Model 1833 Hall-North U.S. Breech-Loading Percussion Carbine

9A-270

Model 1833 Hall-North U.S. Breech-Loading Percussion Carbine. Made by Simeon North, Middletown, Ct., c. 1834-39; total quantity 7,163.

52 and 58 caliber smoothbore. Single shot. The breechblock released by spur type latch mounted forward of the trigger guard with small sliding catch to hold the spur latch closed (may have been omitted on last 1600 produced); block pivots upward for loading. 26-3/16" round barrel; secured by two barrel bands. Combination 25-1/4" ramrod-bayonet mounted in the forend of stock. Two finger ridges behind trigger bow; sling ring below trigger plate.

Iron mountings and barrel, finished with brown lacquer; breech casehardened. Walnut stock, fitted with implement compartment on bottom of butt area.

Breechblock marking on this gun U.S./S. NORTH/MIDL^{TN}/CONN./(date, e.g. 1834). Note: Specimens with breech marking simply S. NORTH are rare and command added premium. Very rare and valued accordingly are pieces marked with an inlaid

gold medallion die struck: S. NORTH/MIDDLETOWN Standard barrel marking of inspector initials, e.g. NWP.

The Model 1833 Carbine is important historically as the earliest percussion weapon adopted officially by the U.S. (or any other) government, and the earliest breechloader so adopted. The bayonet device is also unusual and of special interest, quite in advance of its time (the 1880s):

58 caliber specimens; made in 1834; total of 1,028 produced. Most of these were sent west to arm the 1st U.S. Dragoons at Ft. Gibson, Arkansas Territory, subsequently seeing hard use in early western campaigns:

9A-270   Values—Good **$2,750**   Fine **$7,000**

52 caliber specimens; made c. 1836-39; total of 6,135 produced. The 2nd U.S. Dragoons were armed with these for their initial service in Florida (later replaced with Model 1836). A special order for 100 with 52 caliber rifled barrels was made for the state of Alabama in 1836, to arm an elite city of Mobile militia unit. Numbered 1-100 at top / rear of breech block and delivered without U.S. inspector markings; worth premium:

9A-271   Values—Good **$2,000**   Fine **$4,500**

Model 1836 Hall U.S. Breech-Loading Percussion Carbine

Model 1836 Hall U.S. Breech-Loading Percussion Carbine. Made by Harpers Ferry Armory, c. 1837-40; total quantity 2,020.

64 caliber smoothbore. Single shot. Breechblock mechanism operating as on Model 1833 (*q.v.*). 23" round barrel, secured by two barrel bands. Ramrod style bayonet of 22-1/4" length mounted beneath the forend.

Iron mountings and barrel, finished with brown lacquer; breech casehardened. Walnut stock; earlier production (about 50

percent) fitted with implement compartment on underside of butt area (omitted on late production) worth about 10 percent premium. An eyebolt inset through center of wrist of stock acts as sling ring.

Breechblock marking: J.H. HALL/U.S./1837.

Among special features to note (besides the large caliber) is the hole bored through the hammer, the integral bolster on the breechblock and the high fence, giving the illusion that this was

9A-272

a piece converted from flintlock; it is an original percussion gun. There were no flintlock Hall carbines made (except possibly experimentals) and the collector should be extremely wary when he is offered such a specimen. Issued to the 2nd U.S. Dragoons then serving in Florida campaign:

9A-272   Values—Good **$1,750**   Fine **$4,000**

Model 1840 Hall-North Breech-Loading Percussion Carbine, Types I and II

Model 1840 Hall-North Breech-Loading Percussion Carbine, Types I and II. Made by Simeon North, Middletown, Ct., c. 1840-43; total quantity 6,501.

52 caliber smoothbore. Single shot. Breechblock mechanism operating basically as on Model 1833 (*q.v.*), but with operating lever variations. 21" round barrel, secured by two barrel bands. Button head ramrod; sling ring on lower trigger plate.

Iron mountings and barrel, finished with brown lacquer; breech casehardened. Walnut stock.

Breechblock marking: US/S. NORTH/MIDL^TN/CONN./(date).

The major structural feature setting the Model 1840 off from its predecessors and successors was the operating lever, described in the value listings below.

Type I Carbine; total 500 made, delivered in 1840. Fitted with breech lever of L (or elbow) shape mounted on the trigger plate. Rare: (Variation with .52 rifled bore known; 1840 date only)

9A-273   Values—Good **$3,750**   Fine **$7,000**

Type II Carbine; total 6,001 made; features so-called "fishtail" operating lever:

9A-274   Values—Good **$1,750**   Fine **$3,750**

Variation of Type II, produced 1842-43; having 8-1/2" long sling bar and ring fitted to the lower barrel band and the area just above trigger on left side of the stock:

9A-275   Values—Good **$1,750**   Fine **$3,750**

9A-273
Type I

9A-274
Type II

Model 1842 Hall Breech-Loading Percussion Carbine

9A-276

Model 1842 Hall Breech-Loading Percussion Carbine, by Harpers Ferry Armory. Made c. 1842-43; total quantity 1,001.

52 caliber smoothbore. Single shot. Breechblock mechanism operating basically as on Type II Model 1840 (*q.v.*). 21" round barrel, secured by two barrel bands. 8-1/2" ring bar and ring on left side.

Brass mountings (vs. iron on all other Halls), finished bright. Barrel finished with brown lacquer. Casehardened breech.

Walnut stock.

Breechblock marking: H. FERRY/US/1842.

Trumpet shaped head of the iron ramrod; trigger bow affixed separately. From a historical standpoint, the Model 1842 is important as the last carbine to be manufactured at Harpers Ferry. All sent to the 1st U.S. Dragoons for service on western campaigns. Rare:

9A-276   Values—Good **$4,750**   Fine **$8,750**

Model 1843 Hall-North Breech-Loading Percussion Carbine

Model 1843 Hall-North Breech-Loading Percussion Carbine, a.k.a. Side Lever Hall. Made by Simeon North, Middletown, Ct., c. 1844-53; total quantity approx. 10,500.

52 caliber smoothbore. Single shot. Breechblock mechanism operating by release of a thumb lever located on the right side of the breech, a distinct departure from all other models of Hall carbines. 21" round barrel, secured by two barrel bands.

Iron mountings, finished in brown lacquer, as is the iron barrel. Casehardened breech. Walnut stock.

Breechblock marking on this gun: U.S./S. NORTH/MIDL^TN/

9A-277

CONN./(date). Inspector initials WAT sometimes marked on stock, at right cheekpiece area. Barrel marking of sub-inspector initials at breech; arms made post 1848 marked STEEL behind rear sight.

Among the outfits issued these were the 1st and 2nd U.S. Dragoons during their Mexican War service. Many Union cavalry regiments were armed with these M. 1843s throughout the Civil War. Quite a few outfits in Illinois, Missouri and Kansas were so equipped, while others such as the 4th Arkansas, 5th Iowa, 8th & 9th N.Y., 2nd Wisconsin and 1st Indiana are also known to have been issued them.

Standard model; as above:

9A-277   Values—Good **$1,500**   Fine **$3,250**

58 rifled barrel for Civil War use. At the outbreak of the Civil War 5000 Model 1843s, then considered obsolete, were in the

U.S. Arsenal in New York. In August, 1861, they were the focus of a scheme that was to become known as the "Hall Carbine Affair," a notorious Civil War procurement scandal that had the backing of the financier J.P. Morgan. Purchased from the government Arsenal in N.Y. at $3.50 each they were immediately resold (even prior to taking legal title) to U.S. forces under General John Fremont at St. Louis for $22.00 each. Before shipping to Fremont, carbine barrels were rifled to 58 caliber, the majority of the work by the well-known N.Y. gunmaker W.W. Marston. Although a contributing factor to Fremont's relief from command, all other parties were ultimately absolved.

Among cavalry regiments armed with these 58 rifled barrel Halls were the 2nd and 9th Illinois:

9A-278   Values—Good **$1,500**   Fine **$3,250**

Model 1841 U.S. Percussion Rifle

9A-279

Model 1841 U.S. Percussion Rifle, a.k.a. "Mississippi Rifle." Made at Harpers Ferry Armory, c. 1846-1855; total quantity 25,296, with contractors (see following) producing another 45,500. There is no conclusive evidence that the Springfield Armory made any of these other than "model" pieces; Springfield marked specimens should be viewed with great care.

54 caliber. Single shot muzzleloader. 33" round barrel, fastened by two barrel bands.

Brass mountings finished bright; blued screw heads; barrel is browned, and the lock is casehardened. Steel ramrod of trumpet head type, with brass tip; all iron after 1855.

Walnut stock; large patchbox on right side of butt.

Lockplate markings as noted below. Barrel marking of standard V, P, eaglehead, and date at breech; some barrels also marked: STEEL. US on tang of buttplate. Inspector initial marking on left side of stock, opposite lock.

Regarded by many collectors as one of the most handsome of all percussion U.S. military longarms, the "Mississippi Rifle" owes its name to the successful use of the weapon by a Mississippi regiment under command of Jefferson Davis, in the Mexican War. In its period of manufacture and use, military authorities even then regarded the Model 1841 as the best of its type.

Specimens which bear Mexican War era dates pre-1847 tend to bring a slight premium in value. Condition of rifling and bores has become more important than in previous years. Bores less important on lower grades; fine bores on upper grades tend to fetch premium values. This model was advertised as available for commercial sale in the 1864 catalog of the noted New York City military outfitters Schuyler, Hartley & Graham; described as the "U.S. or Mississippi rifle with or without sword bayonet" and nicely illustrated. This may account for the occasional specimen in choice condition lacking inspector marks on the stock.

(Note: Variations in sights will also be noted. Added premium in value for adjustable, long leaf sight with sliding wedge.)

Harpers Ferry production; lockplate marking: (eagle motif) /U S, forward of hammer. At rear of lock: HARPERS/FERRY/(date), marked vertically. Made without provision for bayonet; brass blade front sight, V-notch rear sight:

9A-279   Values—Good **$1,250**   Fine **$4,500**

Specimens adapted for the Snell patent saber bayonet; required slight modification at muzzle of two 1/2" slots at right angles to each other on right side at muzzle. Records indicate 1,646 bayonets of this type made at Harpers Ferry, 1855:

9A-280   Values—Good **$1,700**   Fine **$4,750**

Second style bayonet adaptation; saber type, requiring shortening of stock forend, fitting of lug to right side of barrel, and use of shorter type front barrel band. 10,286 bayonets of this type made at Harpers Ferry, 1855-57:

9A-281   Values—Good **$1,250**   Fine **$4,500**

Angular (socket) bayonet adaptation of 1859; identified by the combination front sight/bayonet lug and the (usually) turned down diameter of barrel at muzzle, *or* the turned down diameter with special stud mounted on bottom side of muzzle:

9A-282   Values—Good **$1,250**   Fine **$4,250**

Colt factory alteration; performed late in 1861, by reboring to 58 caliber, fitting Colt style folding leaf rear sight, and Colt bayonet lug (mortised and secured by rivets). In excess of 5,000:

9A-283   Values—Good **$1,250**   Fine **$4,250**

Alteration by national armories; c. 1855-60 total quantity 8,879. Rebored to 58 caliber, and ramrods replaced by all steel type having exaggerated trumpet head profile without brass tip:

9A-284   Values—Good **$1,250**   Fine **$4,500**

Contract arms, as follow: Identical to the Model 1841 Rifles made by Harpers Ferry; those differences to be noted are indicated in variations below.

Remington contract; by E. Remington, Herkimer, New York; c. 1846-54. Delivered 10,000 1850-54 (a few known with 1848 & 1849 dates believed to indicate that lockplates were made in advance of completed rifles). Lockplate marking: "REMINGTON'S / HERKIMER / N.Y." forward of hammer with "U.S. /(date)" at rear.

9A-285   Values—Good **$1,250**   Fine **$4,250**

N.Y. State alteration for saber bayonet. Contract issued to Remington May, 1861 to alter 5000 **Remington**-made M. 1841 rifles to accept Collins, Hartford (marked and dated "1861") brass hilt saber bayonets. Total delivered 3268 by Sept. 1861. (see below entry for balance). Caliber .54 unchanged. Only addition was short (slightly over 1/2") stud 4-1/2" from muzzle on right side stamped with 3 digits; front barrel band left unchanged. It appears from recorded specimens that re-assembly made without regard to lock and barrel dates. Known issued late 1861 in varying quantities to 13th, 20th, 28th, 45th, 55th N.Y. regiments.

9A-285.4 Values—Good **$1,250**   Fine **$4,250**

N.Y. State alteration for M. 1842 socket bayonet. Contract issues to F.H. Grosz N.Y. City gunsmith to alter 1600 **Remington** M. 1841 rifles. All delivered by Dec. 1861. Barrel muzzle turned down with small, square bayonet stud added at underside near muzzle; blade front sight repositioned behind turn-down area. Some known issued to Federal units and N.Y. 7th, 10th, 12th, 192nd regiments.

9A-285.6 Values—Good **$1,250**   Fine **$4,250**

Robbins, Kendall & Lawrence contract, made at Windsor, Vermont; c. 1845-48; total quantity 10,000. Lockplate marking ROBBINS/KENDALL &/LAWRENCE/U.S. forward of hammer; WINDSOR VT/(date), marked vertically at rear section of lock. (Note: Believed to be the only contract arms produced by this firm.):

9A-286   Values—Good **$1,250**   Fine **$4,250**

Robbins & Lawrence contract made at Windsor, Vermont; c. 1848-1853 total quantity 15,000. Lockplate marking:

ROBBINS/&/LAWRENCE/US, forward of hammer; WINDSOR VT/(date), marked vertically at rear section of lock.

9A-287   Values—Good **$1,250**   Fine **$4,250**

Tryon contract; by George W. Tryon, Philadelphia; c. 1846-1848. Details of exact contract date are not known. Total of 5,000. Lockplate markings ahead of hammer TRYON/US and vertically at rear PHILADᴬ/PA/(date):

9A-288   Values—Good **$1,250**   Fine **$4,250**

(Note: The reader will encounter in other published works mention of a REPUBLIC OF TEXAS marked Tryon contract 1841 rifle with variations of markings. There is considerable reason to believe that no such weapon was ever made for the infant Republic of Texas. The author has never had the opportunity to view or own a specimen he felt authentic. The collector is urged to pursue the subject in greater depth and give very careful consideration to a specimen before acquiring it. If proven original, such a gun would be worth a considerable value in the four to low-five figures.)

Eli Whitney Jr. contract. (*See Whitney Arms, Chapter V-J.*)

Palmetto Armory contract to the State of South Carolina; by Palmetto Armory, Columbia, South Carolina, c. 1853; total quantity 1,000. Made with machinery purchased from Tryon of Philadelphia (*q.v.*). Lockplate marking of palmetto tree encircled by: PALMETTO ARMORY S.C, forward of hammer. To rear of lock, marked vertically: COLUMBIA/S.C. 1852. Barrel marking V/P and palmetto tree, STEEL and W GLAZE & CO. On tang; 1853. SC on breech plug and on tang of buttplate. Not made for bayonet attachment. Caution: Beware of spurious specimens which are regular U.S. contract pieces that have been restamped with Palmetto Armory markings. Considered a secondary Confederate weapon. 500 of these recorded as destroyed at the Citadel college, Columbia, S.C. Feb. 1865 by General Sherman's forces. (*See also 9A-295 Palmetto M.1842 Musket and 6A-044 Palmetto M.1842 Pistol for further information on Palmetto Armory.*)

9A-289   Values—Good **$7,500**   Fine **$25,000**

Model 1841 U.S. Percussion Cadet Musket

9A-290

Model 1841 U.S. Percussion Cadet Musket. Made by Springfield Armory c. 1844 to 1845. Total produced 450.

.57 caliber, single shot muzzleloader. 40" round barrel secured with three bands. No rear sight. Documents in National Archives indicate that this model made with 31" and 34" barrels also (three band fastened). Specimens are known. Extreme caution advised with shorter lengths.

Iron mountings. Lock finish casehardened; all other parts browned. Bayonet stud under barrel at muzzle. Steel ramrod with trumpet shaped head.

Walnut stock with comb.

Lockplate of Model 1841 rifle-size and shape. Marked in front of hammer with American eagle motif over US; marked vertically at rear SPRING/FIELD/(date)—usually 1844. The barrel marked V/P/(eaglehead).

Easily distinguished by its scaled down size and special, small caliber bore. This model was specifically designed for use of the Corps of Cadets at West Point and was in use until 1856 when replaced by the Rifled variant of the Model 1851 Cadet (*q.v.*):

9A-290   Values—Good **$6,500**   Fine **$17,500**

Model 1842 U.S. Percussion Musket

Model 1842 U.S. Percussion Musket. Made by Springfield Armory and Harpers Ferry Armory; c. 1844-1855. Total produced about 275,000 (of which 172,000 at Springfield).

.69 caliber. Single shot muzzleloader. 42" round barrel; secured by three barrel bands.

Iron mountings. Metal parts finished bright. Steel ramrod with trumpet shaped head. Bayonet lug on bottom of barrel at muzzle.

Walnut stock with a comb.

Lockplate marking of American eagle motif above US (forward of hammer); behind hammer, marked vertically, either SPRING/FIELD/(date) *or* HARPERS/FERRY/(date). The breech of barrel marked V/P/(eaglehead); sometimes inspector initials also present. Inspector initial cartouche stamped on left side of stock, opposite lock.

9A-291

The first regulation model of musket made in the percussion ignition system at the national armories, the Model 1842 has other important distinctions as well. Last smoothbore U.S. arm made in 69 caliber, and the first U.S. weapon made at both Springfield and Harpers Ferry Armories being fully interchangeable in parts. Other than the shape of the lock, the Model 1842 U.S. Percussion Musket is about identical with its flintlock predecessor, the Model 1840 Musket.

Specimens which bear Mexican War era dates pre-1847 tend to bring a slight premium in value.

As above; by Springfield Armory; about 172,000 made:
9A-291   Values—Good **$950**   Fine **$2,750**
As above; by Harpers Ferry Armory; about 103,000 made:
9A-292   Values—Good **$950**   Fine **$2,750**

Model 1842 U.S. Rifled Musket; alteration by rifling barrels; work performed by the Springfield and Harpers Ferry Armories, c. 1856-1859; total quantity 14,182. Basically the same as the Model 1842 Musket, but features rifling. Slightly less than 10,000 were fitted with long range rear sights, the balance issued without them. Values tend to be the same:
9A-293   Values—Good **$1,100**   Fine **$3,250**

Model 1842 U.S. Percussion Musket Contracts

Model 1842 U.S. Percussion Musket, contract arms by B. Flagg, Asa Waters, and the Palmetto Armory. (Not illus.) (*See also "New Hampshire" marked M. 1842 type, number 9B-035.*)

These muskets are virtually identical to the production of the Springfield and Harpers Ferry Armories, with exceptions noted below.

Benjamin Flagg variation; lockplate marking of American eagle motif above U.S. (forward of hammer). Behind hammer, marked vertically B. FLAGG & CO./MILLBURY/1849. (Note: On some variants the date is marked horizontally.) Variations noted in these arms, such as in lockplate configuration:
9A-294   Values—Good **$1,100**   Fine **$3,500**

Palmetto Armory variation; Columbia, South Carolina. Lockplate marking of Palmetto tree, encircled by: PALMETTO ARMORY S*C. To rear of hammer: COLUMBIA/S.C. 1852. Various barrel markings: "W.GLAZE & CO." or "WM. GLAZE & CO." or "W.G. & CO". also proofs "P / V" with palmetto tree motif. Tang with date or "SC". Brass barrel bands; iron buttplate with either "SC" or "US" (indicating use of surplus US armory parts). Lug at top near muzzle for standard M. 1842 socket bayonet or on underside for U.S. surplus M. 1816 bayonets. Total made 6,000

for state of South Carolina contract. Considered a secondary Confederate arm.
9A-295   Values—Good **$3,250**   Fine **$6,500**
Palmetto Musket with rifled bore. Identical above with three groove shallow rifling and open type, fixed rear sight. Palmetto Armory alteration under S.C. contract February through August, 1861. All will have "1852" dates. Total quantity 3,700.
9A-295.2   Values—Good **$3,500**   Fine **$7,000**
Palmetto Armory Conversions of Flintlock M 1816 muskets. In 1851 the armory completed a contract with S.C. for conversion to percussion of about 6000 flintlock muskets (of various makes) then in state armories. Many will be found with "SO.CAROLINA" markings and are valued accordingly. Under 1861 S.C. contract Palmetto added shallow rifling and open rear sights to 1800 of those earlier bolster type conversions between Oct.-Dec., 1861. Values are for rifled specimens with S. CAROLINA markings. (*See also 9A-289 and 6A-044*).
9A-295.6   Values—Good **$2,250**   Fine **$3,750**
A.H. Waters variation; lockplate marking American eagle motif above US (forward of hammer). Behind hammer A.H. WATERS & CO./MILBURY MASS. Mountings of either iron or brass. Scarce:
9A-296   Values—Good **$950**   Fine **$3,250**

Model 1847 U.S. Artillery Musketoon

Model 1847 U.S. Artillery Musketoon. Made by Springfield Armory, c. 1848-59, total quantity 3,359.

69 caliber smoothbore. Muzzleloader. 26" round barrel; two barrel bands; bayonet stud (for angular bayonet) sometimes present on muzzle.

Iron mountings, finished bright, as is the barrel. Iron ramrod with trumpet shaped end. Walnut stock of nearly full length; sling swivel on lower barrel band and near toe of butt.

Lock markings: (eagle motif)/US, forward of the hammer. Behind hammer and reading vertically: SPRING/FIELD/(date). On barrel breech: V/P/(eagle head) and date. Inspector stamping on left side of the stock, opposite the lock. US on tang of buttplate.

Numerous alterations and parts interchange occurred with this model, leading to many composite specimens with mixed parts from other Model 1847's. Such arms are frequently encountered and are decidedly good collector's items. Their

9A-297

9A-297 Artillery

9A-300 Navy

values are slightly less than for specimens which conform to exact specifications.

Standard Model; as above:

9A-297   Values—Good **$1,500**   Fine **$4,750**

Altered from Cavalry Musketoon; iron ramrod swivels and ring bar removed (ramrod left intact), the tip of forend shortened (small section protruding ahead of upper band) in order to give clearance for socket bayonet. Bayonet stud added under muzzle; two types of sling swivels added: (A) On upper band and on stud ahead of trigger bow. (B) On lower band and underside of butt near toe. Some were also rifled (will bring a small premium) and have their ramrod changed to tulip head type (to fit minie bullet) and two-leaf rear sight. It is believed alterations were performed c. 1855-1860 when the cavalry received the New Model 1855 carbine as well as various breechloaders. Some were likely altered for Civil War artillery use:

9A-298   Values—Good **$1,250**   Fine **$3,750**

Altered from Sappers Musketoon; the unique bayonet guide and stud (and often barrel band and its unique guide) removed:

9A-299   Values—Good **$1,200**   Fine **$3,500**

So-called Navy Musketoon; as above, but quickly distinguished by its very narrow double strap top barrel band, completely different than any other found on the 1847s. The lower band is heavier and thicker than usual and found without the groove or fluting on the outside. Band springs are noticeably shorter and the iron sideplate has the configuration as seen on the cavalry carbine, although no provision is made for ring bar. A single screw fastens the lower trigger plate instead of the usual two screws. Most specimens observed are dated 1851:

9A-300   Values—Good **$2,000**   Fine **$4,750**

Model 1847 U.S. Sappers Musketoon

Model 1847 U.S. Sappers Musketoon, a.k.a. "Sappers & Miners." Made by Springfield Armory, c. 1847-1848 (250 manufactured), 1855 (80 made), and 1856 (500 made); total quantity 830 (of which 228 altered to Model 1847 Artillery).

Virtually identical to the Model 1847 Artillery Musketoon, except as follows: Lock datings 1847, 1848, 1855, and 1856 only. Lug for saber type bayonet mounted on right side of upper barrel band and double steel large type guides for bayonet affixed to right side of barrel near muzzle. Sling swivels on toe of buttstock and on lower barrel band. (Note: This arm is specially fitted for a unique brass hilted sword-bayonet made only for this model.) The collector is cautioned to take special care in the acquisition of this model as not a few regular 1847 Artillery Musketoons have been spuriously altered to resemble this desirable variation. *See Model 1847 Artillery Musketoon for reference to Sappers specimens altered to Artillery.*

Although usually reported as being first made in 1848, some of earliest production was actually in 1847 and original

specimens so dated are known. These are easily accounted for and the misimpression often caused by reported manufacturing dates is explained when the collector is cognizant of the method of Ordnance Department record keeping. Arms made at the very end of the year and not actually delivered either physically or recordwise from the armory to the Military Storekeeper until early the following year show up on Ordnance Reports as being made in the latter year:

9A-301   Values—Good **$2,500**   Fine **$6,000**

9A-301

Model 1847 U.S. Cavalry Musketoon

Model 1847 U.S. Cavalry Musketoon. Made by Springfield Armory, c. 1848-59; total quantity estimated from 5,804 to 6,703.

Virtually identical to the Model 1847 Artillery Musketoon, except as follows: The button head ramrod is fastened with iron swivels under the muzzle of barrel; all mountings of brass (finished bright); lacks sling swivels and in their place has a 9-1/4" ring bar and ring on left side; upper barrel band is

narrower and of straight configuration, and the stock extends 1/2" beyond it. Some specimens will be found rifled, and/or with two leaf rear sight of musket type. A premium should be added for the latter feature.

Standard model:

9A-302   Values—Good **$2,000**   Fine **$4,750**

Variation made as above but ramrod swivel replaced by sleeved chain device, the ramrod of greater length, and a retaining spring

9A-302

of spoon type inserted into stock. Specimens made in 1852 and later. (Note: Although these chain devices were supposed to replace the swivels, it has been the author's experience in seeing quite a few specimens over the years that almost no chain devices survived and hence are more rare intact than the swivels. Collector is cautioned to be aware of spurious alterations.):

9A-303   Values—Good **$2,750**   Fine **$6,500**

(Note: *See Model 1847 Artillery Musketoon for Cavalry specimens altered to Artillery.*)

9A-303
Chain Device for Ramrod

Model 1851 U.S. Percussion Cadet Musket

Model 1851 Cadet (top) shown for size comparison with Model 1842 Musket (bottom)

Model 1851 U.S. Percussion Cadet Musket. Made by Springfield Armory c. 1851 to 1853. Total production 4,000; almost all to various states for their military schools.

57 caliber. Single shot muzzleloader. 40" round barrel. Almost identical to the Model 1841 Cadet; the major distinguishing feature is the use of the Model 1847 Musketoon lock which is slightly smaller. Metal all finished bright.

Markings identical as shown for Model 1841 Cadet with dates as noted below. A few were produced at the end of 1851 and original specimens bearing that date have been observed. They are worth a slight premium in value. The occurrence of them is accounted for by the system of ordnance record keeping. (See explanation with 1847 Sappers Musketoon.)

It is known that 300 of this model were ordered for Virginia Military Institute under direct orders of President Zachary Taylor. Either 200 or 300 (quantity unresolved) were subsequently received. All were apparently dated 1851. Although recently published information (undocumented) states that VMI guns were finished brown, more thorough research clearly indicates that they were finished "bright" as standard. A proven VMI association and possible Confederate usage would be worth premium value. Although an Ordnance Dept. 1851 letter requests approx. 650 cadet muskets with "...barrels of reduced length for use of smaller cadets" armory

records do not reflect their mfr. or alteration. Collectors are advised to exercise caution and review the section "QUAKER GUNS" at beginning of this chapter.

1852 dated specimens. 2,840 produced:

9A-304   Values—Good **$650**   Fine **$1,750**

1853 dated specimens. 1,160 produced:

9A-305   Values—Good **$750**   Fine **$1,850**

Rifled Variation: Springfield records for 1857 indicate 341 cadets muskets (apparently from armory stock and not returns from the field) were rifled and fitted with long range rear sights. It is possible other smoothbore M.1851's still in arsenal stock were similarly altered in subsequent years:

9A-306   Values—Good **$875**   Fine **$2,250**

The Rifled Variation At West Point: Further study, discussions and statistical calculations by West Point Museum indicate it was unlikely that smoothbore M.1851's, as they were first produced at Springfield, 1851-53, were ever sent or issued at the Academy. There was no apparent need to replace the near identical, still serviceable M.1841 Cadet musket, still on hand in sufficient quantity. Thus, the first M.1851's sent to West Point (c. 1857-58) were the rifled variations, direct from arsenal stock. They were intended to replace and update the obsolete smoothbore and familiarize cadets with the improved rifled system recently adopted for army longarms.

Model 1855 U.S. Percussion Rifle-Musket

Model 1855 U.S. Percussion Rifle-Musket. Made by the Springfield and Harpers Ferry Armories, c. 1857-1861; total quantity 59,273.

58 caliber. Single shot muzzleloader. 40" round barrel fastened by three barrel bands; cleanout screw on bolster.

Iron mountings, with brass forend cap. All metal parts finished bright. Steel ramrod with tulip shaped end and swelled shank. Front sight doubles as lug for angular bayonet. Earlier models have a long range rear sight with large leaf and were made without patchbox. In 1859 the forend tip was changed to iron and the patchbox was added (worth premium).

Walnut stock.

Lock markings as indicated below, eagle motif on tape primer compartment lid. Barrel marking at breech:

V/P/(eaglehead). US on tang of buttplate. Inspector initials on left side of stock (opposite the lock).

This model proved one of the staple arms of the Civil War, and was the first U.S. martial arm firing the Minie bullet in 58 caliber.

Springfield Armory; lockplate marking U.S./SPRINGFIELD; date stamped at rear of lock behind hammer. Total made 47,115:

9A-307   Values—Good **$1,250**   Fine **$4,000**

Harpers Ferry; lockplate marking U.S./HARPERS FERRY; date stamped at rear behind hammer. Total made 12,158:

9A-308   Values—Good **$1,400**   Fine **$5,000**

Artillery Model (so-called); 33" round barrel; two-barrel bands. The collector is urged to be wary of such specimens. There is no record of the manufacture or alteration to such size or length in

9A-307

9A-307

otherwise detailed annual government reports. It is the author's opinion that such "models" are non-armory. The shortening could have occurred during the Civil War or later by parties as yet unknown. If proven original value should be at least 50 percent higher than rifle-musket. If not certain, value should be 25 percent to 50 percent less than the rifle-musket.

Whitney and so-called Confederate Whitney. (*See Whitney Arms, Chapter V.*)

See also discussion of "QUAKER GUNS" in text at beginning of this chapter.

Model 1855 U.S. Percussion Rifle

9A-309

Model 1855 U.S. Percussion Rifle. Made at Harpers Ferry Armory, c. 1857-61. Recent research (2003) places quantity manufactured at 8,700.

58 caliber. Single shot muzzleloader. 33" round barrel; two barrel bands. Lug on right side of muzzle for saber bayonet.

Iron mountings standard, although brass used on early production (see below). All metal parts finished bright; blued barrel bands observed occasionally on iron mounted arms; browned barrel standard on brass mounted arms. Steel ramrod of tulip-head type, with swelled shaft at point of engagement with forend cap.

Walnut stock; patchbox on right side of butt.

Lockplate marking: Eagle motif on lid of Maynard tape primer compartment; U.S./HARPERS FERRY, at forward section of lock; date marking at rear section. Barrel breech marking of V/P/(eagle head) proofs.

Recent research reveals that 3,544 were brass mounted through to mid-1859 when mountings were changed to iron of which 5,151 were so fitted. Research further disclosed that the capture and burning of the arsenal by Confederate forces in April, 1861; of the approximate 3,450 Model 1855 rifles then on hand and destroyed in the fire, approximately 2,800 of them were the brass mounted types. That clearly accounts for the scarcity of the brass mounted version.

Brass mounted specimens; early production; made prior to 1860. Long range type rear sight, graduated to 500 yards, standard. Front sight of early specimens offered attachable double ring crosshair type, secured by a set-screw; standard sight was of fixed type; very scarce:

9A-309   Values—Good **$3,750**   Fine **$10,000**

Iron mounted specimens; later production. Does not have special attachable front sight; long range style rear sight graduated to 400 yards or smaller two-leaf sight:

9A-310   Values—Good **$2,500**   Fine **$6,000**

Model 1855 U.S. Rifled Carbine

Model 1855 U.S. Rifled Carbine. Made by Springfield Armory, c. 1855-56; total quantity 1,020.

54 caliber. Single shot muzzleloader. 22" round barrel; one barrel band.

Iron mountings, with brass forend cap. Metal parts finished bright. Button tipped steel ramrod, affixed to muzzle by large,

oval, U-shaped iron swivel. Walnut stock of three-quarter length.

Lock markings: (eagle motif)/US, forward of the hammer. To rear of hammer and reading vertically: SPRING/FIELD/(date). On breech of barrel: V/P/(eagle head) and the date. US on tang of buttplate.

9A-311

Among the distinguishing features of this scarce carbine is the large sling ring mounted on the rear section of the trigger guard, the two-leaf rear sight, and the three-quarter length stock. Some examples were altered to 58 caliber, but values have been similar for either caliber. Of historical interest, this is the sole variant in the Model 1855 U.S. martial arms group made for manual priming, and thus lacking the Maynard tape system:

9A-311   Values—Good **$4,500**   Fine **$20,000**

9A-311
Close-up of Muzzle End of Barrel

Model 1858 U.S. Cadet Rifle-Musket

Model 1858 U.S. Percussion Cadet Rifle-Musket. (Not illus.) Made Springfield Armory, c. 1858-1860. Total quantity 2,501.

58 caliber. Identical in configuration to the Model 1855 Rifle-Musket, but slightly smaller. Barrel 38", stock shortened accordingly. Care should be exercised on acquisition to be certain the gun is not merely a Model 1855 rifle-musket spuriously altered.

Stock is 50" long. The butt is 1" shorter than the musket and forend 2" shorter than musket; buttplate smaller.

When placed side by side this Cadet model and the Musket have the same measurements from the nose, or front corner of the comb to the lower barrel band; below and above those points it differs as does band spacing. Locks and trigger guards identical.

Although termed a "Cadet" model because of its physical characteristics, this model was not issued at West Point. Very scarce:

9A-312   Values—Good **$1,400**   Fine **$4,250**

U.S. Navy Plymouth Pattern Percussion Rifle

9A-312.5

U.S. Navy "Plymouth" Pattern Percussion Rifle. Made c.1857-1858 at the Washington Navy Yard (D.C.) Total quantity approx. 55.

Made on the orders of Commander John A. Dahlgren, these were the trial and pattern rifles for what eventually became the U.S. Navy Model 1861 Percussion rifle, the so-called "Whitney-Plymouth." (*see #5J-041 Chapter V-J*).

The 69 caliber barrels (with the Model 1842 musket type bolster) were made by Remington and rifled at Harpers Ferry. The then obsolete M. 1842 musket locks (with HARPERS FERRY markings and dates of 1854 and 1855) were assembled into

complete rifles at the Washington Navy Yard and taken aboard the U.S.S. Plymouth for testing, May, 1858. Although Remington may have supplied the total 150 barrels ordered, it's not known how many rifles were actually assembled. Only 54 are accounted for in logbook of the U.S.S. Plymouth.

The rifle is closely similar to the Whitney model (*q.v.*) with differences as noted and has brass mountings. The sight is the standard Model 1842 Long Range musket type. 34" barrel with distinctive markings PLYMOUTH/PATTERN/1858. Very rare; but few recorded surviving specimens:

9A-312.5   Values—Good **$5,000**   Fine **$17,500**

Civil War 58 Caliber Rifled Muskets

Among the most widely produced of all American military longarms was the 58 caliber percussion rifled musket of the Civil War era. Over one and a half million were made—almost 800,000 of the Models 1861 and 1863 by the Springfield Armory, with the balance by 32 different private contractors. Even assuming a high attrition rate over the years and with many others altered for sporting purposes, a reasonably large quantity of these arms still exist on the collectors' market. The values reflected in the following listings are for complete specimens matching the configurations in which they left the armory or were delivered by the contractor. Most fine conditioned pieces and a great many showing varying degrees of use will conform closely to those specifications. However, it is important to realize that the arms were made and issued in tremendous quantities and were often subject to considerable repair, replacement and rebuilding, both by company armorers in the field and at supply depots and arsenals. This was the most widely used and popular infantry

weapon of the Civil War by the North and by the South, who captured them in sizable quantities. Quite a few specimens are seen with parts that do not match in date and are in varying degrees of mixed composition. Such composites are worth proportionately less than arms in the condition they left the arsenal. However, composite types do enjoy a healthy demand and (except for the ultimate "purist") will maintain values commensurate with "pure" pieces, possibly being affected slightly downward at most. It certainly would be true that a mint composite specimen or one in exceptionally fine condition would not bring the value of the same type in "as issued" condition, and that the collector might turn up his nose at such a piece for being of modern assemblage from original parts—thus pricing it downward accordingly. That same gun, though, in well-worn condition, having every appearance of use in that condition, would be about equally as desirable in value as that same piece, condition-wise, in "as issued" state.

The market for pieces less than mint or very fine condition is very much based upon overall soundness of the weapon and, in the medium and better grades, for condition of the bore also. Better bores do bring higher prices, since many arms find their way to shooters in black powder competition or Civil War reenacts, etc. For the lesser quality/conditioned pieces, bores are unimportant and the items enjoy a ready salability as the most widely used and classic infantry weapon of the Civil War. Thus, the matter of composite parts and their acceptability is very much in direct relationship to condition.

THE SO-CALLED "ARTILLERY" AND "CADET" MODELS

A major source of disagreement on the Model 1861/1863 muskets is the so-called **Artillery Model** or short two-band fastened musket with 33" barrel. The reader is urged to see the note regarding this and the author's opinion about it appended to the description of the Model 1855 U.S. percussion rifle-musket and a similar note appended to the description of the Model 1865 U.S. breech-loading Allin conversion (1st Model Allin). The latter is especially applicable in the case of the so-called **Artillery Model** and lends credence to the fact that if a 33" barreled model were original, it would conform more closely to the proper spacing of that short 1st Model Allin described. Much has been made of a single cryptic entry of a lot of 775 "SPRINGFIELD MUSKETS, SHORT, Cal .58" that appeared in a Springield Armory "Statement of Expenditures" for year ending June, 1866 under "ARMS REPAIRED." No other mention of shortened .58's in Armory records has turned up. There is strong possibility the term was used merely to indicate something other than a percussion M1861/1863 musket. It is not sufficient for a collector to rely on without further substantiation. A parting comment...*caveat emptor*.

When these 58 caliber muskets became obsolete, they were sold in large quantities (both as complete muskets and spare parts) on the surplus market, in the last quarter of the 19th Century. As with surplus military arms of later eras, it was necessary for the commercial dealers to find a suitable method to make them salable to a civilian population (collectors were not yet extant!). One means was sporterizing, and many were bored smooth, cut down, and then sold as inexpensive muzzle-loading fowling pieces. Many others found their way to the Colonial trade dealing with Africa and South America where muzzle-loading arms were in demand because of the minimum expense required to operate them (metallic cartridges were expensive even through the late 20th Century). A substantial group remained in the United States and were shortened and lightened for military academies and other cadet type school usage, and for parade use by the G.A.R. and many other quasi-military organizations. The 1889 Bannerman, N.Y., catalog offered the perfect example of an homogenized, composite Civil War musket: "**U.S. Springfield Cadet M.L. Rifle**...same as the Model 1862 rifle except has been lightened by having barrel shortened to 30", stock reduced in length and thickness and thin .45 caliber lockplate substituted for the heavy .58 caliber lockplate...metal reblued...the neatest and safest M.L. Cadet gun made." Quite a few specimens, altered for civilian use, and now approaching 100 years in age, have acquired the patina and character of genuineness. There is no doubting their antiquity and earlier U.S. manufacture, however, discretion must be exercised in acquisition. Not a few traders have been known to pass off such mongrels as rare variations or Confederate alterations to the uninformed novice or the gullible collector. See also discussion of "QUAKER GUNS" at beginning of this chapter.

Model 1861 U.S. Percussion Rifle-Musket

9A-313

Model 1861 U.S. Percussion Rifle-Musket. Made by the Springfield Armory, c. 1861-1862; total quantity 265,129. A substantial number also made under contract by various firms and are noted below.

58 caliber. Single shot muzzleloader. 40" round barrel; three barrel bands; cleanout screw on bolster.

Iron mountings. All metal parts finished bright (rear sight sometimes blued). Steel ramrod with tulip shaped end and swelled shank. Front sight doubles as lug for angular bayonet.

Walnut stock.

Lock marking: Eagle motif forward of hammer; U.S./SPRINGFIELD, beneath nipple bolster. Date (either 1861 or 1862) at rear section of lock. V/P/(eaglehead) on breech of barrel. US on tang of buttplate. Inspector initials on left side of stock (opposite the lock).

The Model 1861 was the standard musket in use during the Civil War, and as such is the nucleus of any collection featuring U.S. martial percussion longarms. A major improvement in its design over the Model 1855 predecessor was the elimination of the Maynard primer system. The hammer profile of Model 1855 style, however, was retained. Approximately 1,000,000 Model 1861 type muskets were manufactured during the Civil War

9A-313

period, and this model served as the pattern for most arms made for war use. Springfields (only) with 1861 dated locks tend to bring up to 25 percent premiums.

Standard model; as above:

9A-313   Values—Good **$900**   Fine **$3,000**

So-called Artillery Model; 33" barrel; two barrel bands. (*See note about identical type found on Model 1855 rifle-musket; also notes in text preceding this model.*)

By Alfred Jenks & Son, Bridesburg and Philadelphia, Pennsylvania. Total produced 98,464, c. 1861-65; one of the largest orders contracted for and delivered by an armsmaker during the Civil War. Lock markings as follows; eagle motif standard:

U.S./BRIDESBURG beneath nipple bolster. Date either beneath this marking (scarcer and worth slight premium) or at rear of lock:

9A-314 Values—Good **$850** Fine **$2,750**

U.S./PHILADELPHIA beneath nipple bolster. Date at rear of lock (1862). Although attributed to Jenks, may be made by John Rice of Philadelphia.

9A-315 Values—Good **$850** Fine **$2,750**

Eagleville contract; by Eagle Manufacturing Company, Mansfield, Conn., c. 1861-62, total quantity contracted for was 20,000, of which it is known 5,500 were delivered. Existing records imply that all 20,000 may have been completed but the relative scarcity of them seems to indicate the accuracy of the 5,500 figure. Lock marking with standard eagle motif, date 1863 at rear section, and U.S./EAGLEVILLE beneath nipple bolster:

9A-316 Values—Good **$900** Fine **$3,000**

Manton marked 1861 contract type. Definitive information proves these to be the product of E. Whitney. (*See Whitney Firearms, Chapter V-J.*)

William Mason contract; made in Taunton, Mass., total quantity of 30,000. Lock marking of standard eagle motif, date, and: U.S./W MASON/TAUNTON:

9A-317 Values—Good **$850** Fine **$2,750**

Millbury contract; made in Millbury, Mass., believed by A. H. Waters & Co. Lockplate marked with small eagle motif and U.S./MILLBURY to right of hammer, and the date to rear of hammer. Unusual detail of the eagle facing to the rear, and with wings downward in contrast to all other contract rifle-muskets. Quantity produced unknown; *scarce:*

9A-318 Values—Good **$900** Fine **$3,000**

James D. Mowry contract; made in Norwich, Conn., by Mowry. Total quantity 22,000; c. 1861, 1863-64. Lock marking of standard eagle and U.S./JAS D.MOWRY/NORWICH, CONN; and the date (usually 1864):

9A-319 Values—Good **$850** Fine **$2,750**

William Muir & Co., contract; made in Windsor Locks, Conn. Total quantity 30,000; made c. 1863-64. Lock marking of standard eagle motif above U.S., and to the right: W MUIR & CO./WINDSOR LOCKS, CT. At rear the date (either 1863 or 1864):

9A-320 Values—Good **$850** Fine **$2,750**

Sarson & Roberts contract; made in New York with most of the parts subcontracted by Alfred Jenks & Son, Philadelphia. Total quantity 5,140; made c. 1862-63. Lock marking of eagle motif to right of hammer; beneath nipple bolster—US/NEW YORK/(date):

9A-321 Values—Good **$850** Fine **$2,750**

Norfolk contract; made by Welch, Brown and Co., Norfolk, Conn., c. 1862-63; total quantity of 18,000. Lock marking of eagle motif and U.S./NORFOLK, to right of hammer. At rear of lock the date:

9A-322 Values—Good **$850** Fine **$2,750**

Norwich contract; made by Norwich Arms Co., Norwich, Conn., c. 1863-64; total quantity 25,000. Lock marking of standard eagle motif and U.S./NORWICH. to right of hammer. Date at rear of lock. Standard Model 1861 Rifle-Musket configuration:

9A-323 Values—Good **$850** Fine **$2,750**

Parkers' Snow & Co. contract; made by Parker, Snow & Company, Meriden, Conn., c. 1863-64; total quantity 15,000. Lock marking of eagle motif above U.S., and PARKERS' SNOW & CO./MERIDEN, CONN, to right of hammer; date at rear of lock, 1864. A variant of this musket bearing the same markings but with an 1863 dated lock is believed to be the product of the James

Mulholland contract of 1861, of which only 5,502 were delivered. Although definitive proof is not available, these 1863-dated specimens can bring a premium over the regular 1864-dated arms by this company. This musket has dual historical significance. It represents the first venture in firearms manufacturing by Charles Parker of Meriden, Connecticut. Originally a manufacturer of hardware, he soon, after the Civil War, in 1866-1867 formed what was to become the most famous of all American shotgun manufacturers, the famous "Parker Brothers" (see full story in Chapter XVII; see also "Triplett & Scott Carbine 9B-101):

9A-324 Values—Good **$850** Fine **$2,750**

Providence contract; believed to be by Providence Tool Co., Rhode Island. Limited quantity. Lock marking of standard eagle motif to right of hammer, and U.S./PROVIDENCE beneath nipple bolster. To rear of lock the date 1862. Possibly by contractor C.D. Schubarth, also of Providence:

9A-325 Values—Good **$850** Fine **$2,750**

Providence Tool Company contract; made in Providence, Rhode Island; c. 1862-65; total quantity 70,000 (one of the major contractors of muskets in the Civil War period). Lock marking of U.(eagle motif) S./PROVIDENCE TOOL CO/PROVIDENCE R I. At rear of lock the date:

9A-326 Values—Good **$850** Fine **$2,750**

Remington contract; by E. Remington & Sons, Ilion, New York; c. 1864-66; total quantity 40,000. Lock marking of eagle motif/U.S. to right of hammer, and REMINGTON'S/ILION, N.Y. beneath nipple bolster. Date marking at rear of lock; inspector's initials on forward lock:

9A-327 Values—Good **$850** Fine **$2,750**

E. Robinson contract; made in New York; c. 1863-65; total quantity 30,000. Lock marking of 12,000 arms delivered on contract of June, 1863, had eagle motif/U.S. and E. ROBINSON/NEW YORK, to right of hammer and beneath nipple bolster respectively; date marking at rear of lock. Later contracts were similarly marked excepting the E. ROBINSON legend was in an arc over NEW YORK; these bear 1864 and 1865 dates:

9A-328 Values—Good **$850** Fine **$2,750**

Savage Revolving Fire Arms Co. contract; made in Middletown, Conn.; c. 1862-64; total quantity 25,520. Lock marking of eagle motif/U.S. and SAVAGE R.F.A. CO/MIDDLETOWN. CON, to right of hammer. Date marking to rear of lock:

9A-329 Values—Good **$850** Fine **$2,750**

C.D. Schubarth and Co. contract; made in Providence, R.I.; c. 1862-63; total quantity 9,500. Lock marking of eagle motif and U.S./C.D.SCHUBARTH/PROVIDENCE to right of hammer. Date marking at rear of lock:

9A-330 Values—Good **$900** Fine **$3,000**

S. Norris and W.T. Clement contract; made in Springfield, Mass.; c. 1863-64; total quantity of eleven thousand. Lock marking of eagle motif/U.S. and S.N. & W.T.C./ FOR/MASSACHUSETTS, to right of hammer. Rear of lock marked with date. Production was on direct contract with the State of Massachusetts. (Note: The so-called "Artillery Model" is more often encountered with this contractor marking than others, usually with 31" barrel. Extreme caution should be exercised to authenticate legitimate specimens.) Standard model:

9A-331 Values—Good **$850** Fine **$2,750**

Trenton contract; by J.T. Hodge and A.M. Burton, at the Trenton Locomotive and Machine Co., Trenton, New Jersey; c. 1863-64; total quantity of 11,495. Lock marking of eagle motif and U.S./TRENTON to right of hammer; date at rear of lock:

9A-332 Values—Good **$850** Fine **$2,750**

Union Arms Company contract; made by Union Arms, New York City; c. 1862-63; total quantity estimated at about 300, although total contracts had been for 65,000. Lock marking of eagle motif/U.S. *and* U.A.CO./NEW YORK, to right of hammer. Date at rear of lock, and only 1863 has been observed. Note: Possibly manufactured for Union Arms by Parker, Snow, Brooks & Co., Meriden, Connecticut:

9A-333 Values—Good **$1,250** Fine **$4,000**

German contract; made in Suhl, Germany; c. 1861. Lock marked with distinct variant of the usual eagle motif and either US or U.S. on the extreme forward section of lock. Date 1861 at rear of lock. Of excellent workmanship; stocks of maple-like wood. Serial or batch number on all parts. Barrel markings sometimes present include small diamond panel with "g" in center proofmark and SUHL or CH FUNK/SUHL. Possibly imported by William Hahn, New York City, in 1862; estimated production of a few hundred:

9A-334 Values—Good **$1,250** Fine **$4,000**

Watertown contract; by Charles B. Hoard, Watertown, New York; c. 1863-65; total quantity of 12,800. Lock marking of eagle motif and U.S./WATERTOWN, to right of hammer. Date marking at rear section of lock:

9A-335 Values—Good **$850** Fine **$2,750**

Whitney contract; various markings. (*See Whitney Arms, Chapter V-J.*)

Windsor Locks contract; believed either by Dinslow & Chase or William Muir & Co., both of Windsor Locks, Connecticut. Total quantity unknown. Lock marking of eagle motif and U.S./WINDSOR LOCKS forward of hammer; date at rear section of lock. *Rare:*

9A-336 Values—Good **$1,150** Fine **$3,750**

Special Model 1861 Contract Rifle-Musket

Special Model 1861 Contract Rifle-Musket. Made by various contractors, c. 1861-65; total quantity in excess of 152,000. Manufacturers noted below under values.

58 caliber. Single shot muzzleloader. 40" round barrel, three barrel bands.

Iron mountings. All metal parts finished bright (rear sight sometimes blued). Steel ramrod with tulip shaped end, straight type shank. Front sight doubles as lug for angular bayonet.

Walnut stock.

Lock markings noted below. At barrel breech: V/P/(eagle head), and the date; on bolster an eagle motif. US on tang of buttplate. Inspector initials on left side of stock (opposite the lock).

Despite similarity in appearance to the Model 1861 Rifle-Musket, the differences between the regulation model and the Special Model are distinct. Parts are rarely interchangeable and the most immediate contrast is in the contour of the hammer and the lockplate. Source of the design is attributable to the Colt company, and the pattern was based on a British military musket of Enfield manufacture.

Amoskeag contract; made by the Amoskeag Manufacturing Company, Manchester, New Hampshire; c. 1862-65; total quantity 27,001. Lock marking of U.(eagle motif) S./AMOSKEAG M^FG. C^O/MANCHESTER, N.H. beneath nipple bolster. Date at rear section of lock:

9A-337 Values—Good **$1,100** Fine **$3,000**

Colt contract. (*See Chapter V-B, Colt Firearms.*5B-255.)

Lamson, Goodnow & Yale Co. contract; Windsor, Vermont and Shelburn Falls, Mass. Made c. 1862-64; total quantity 50,000. A distinctly different lock marking appears with each of the three

9A-337

years these pieces were manufactured. Locks dated 1862 are marked with small eagle/U.S. and L.G. & Y/WINDSOR-V^T. Locks dated 1863 marked identically except with large eagle motif and the words *WINDSOR V*^T are in italics. Locks dated 1864 lack the eagle motif and bear markings as above but in 3 lines, with U.S. added at the top line:

9A-338 Values—Good **$1,000** Fine **$2,750**

E.G. Lamson & Company, variation; by the Lamson firm of Windsor, Vermont (successor to Lamson, Goodnow & Yale). Made c. 1865; total quantity estimated at a few hundred. Lock marking of U.S./E.G. LAMSON & CO./WINDSOR V^T. forward of hammer. 1865 date marking at rear section of lock. Believed a means of using up leftover parts from earlier contracts, and the sales were primarily to states or to individuals; *scarce:*

9A-339 Values—Good **$1,150** Fine **$3,250**

Model 1863 Rifle Musket, Type I

9A-340

Model 1863 Rifle Musket, Type I. Made by Springfield Armory, c. 1863; total quantity 273,265.

58 caliber. Single shot muzzleloader. 40" round barrel; three barrel bands.

Iron mountings. All metal parts finished bright excepting casehardened lock; rear sights sometimes blued, as are occasionally barrel bands and some other parts. Steel ramrod with tulip shaped end, straight type shank. Front sight doubles as lug for angular bayonet.

Walnut stock.

Lock marking: Eagle motif to right of hammer; U.S./SPRINGFIELD, beneath nipple bolster. 1863, at angle, at rear section of lock. The nipple bolster bearing an eagle motif. Barrel breech marking of V/P/(eagle head) and the date 1863. US on tang of buttplate. Inspector initials on left side of stock (opposite the lock).

Origin of the Model 1863 Rifle Musket was a combination of improvements on the Model 1861 Rifle Musket, and features on the Special Model of 1861 Rifle Musket. Among distinctive details on the Model 1863 Rifle Musket Type I are the beveled contours on the hammer shank and the lack of barrel band retaining springs with split type bands. The addition of finishes such as casehardening and bluing is also a departure from previous U.S. martial longarm production, as observed in the Model 1855 and 1861 Rifle-Muskets:

9A-340   Values—Good **$900**   Fine **$2,750**
Contractor production; No known government contracts were given for the Model 1863. It is evident though that some of the 1861 contractors made modifications in their production to conform with this newer Springfield adaptation. Until details of this are fully known 1863 type variants in 1861 contract pieces may be generally valued as already stated.

Model 1863 Rifle Musket, Type II

9A-341

Model 1863 Rifle Musket, Type II, a.k.a. Model 1864. Made by Springfield Armory, c. 1864-1865; total quantity of 255,040.

The Type II is identical to the Type I, with the following exceptions: Lock date marking of either 1864 or 1865; single leaf rear sight (two leaf was standard on Type I); solid barrel bands secured by flat springs mounted in the stock; ramrods either of the tulip head type or the new design, knurled and slotted; cone shoulders rounded; and bluing eliminated on certain parts.

A historically important arm due to its widespread use in the latter part of the Civil War, this model is the last U.S. martial regulation arm of muzzle-loading design. Breechloaders had proven themselves during the four years of Civil War combat.
Standard model; as above:
9A-341   Values—Good **$900**   Fine **$2,750**
So-called Artillery model; 33" barrel; two barrel bands. (*See note about identical type found on Model 1855 rifle-musket; also notes in text preceding the Model 1861.*)

Model 1863 U.S. Double Rifle Musket

9A-342

Model 1863 U.S. Double Rifle Musket. Made by J. P. Lindsay, New York; total quantity about 1,000; c. 1863-64.

58 caliber muzzleloader. Superposed load; two full charges in the single barrel, one on top of the other, fired separately using double hammers, and a single trigger. 41-1/8" barrel, round with semi-octagonal breech having two percussion nipples. Three barrel bands.

Iron mountings. All metal parts finished bright. Steel ramrod with tulip shaped end. Front sight doubles as lug for angular bayonet.

Walnut stock.

Barrel marking at breech top: LINDSAY/PATENT'D. OCT. 9.

1860. US on tang of buttplate. Inspector initials (ADK) and those of sub-inspector, marked on left flat of stock in breech area.

Original design for this quite unusual arm was incorporated by the inventor in handguns (*q.v., Chapter VII*). Despite the confidence of the U.S. government, as expressed in a contract for 1,000 rifle muskets, the guns did not prove themselves in combat, and the somewhat involved system was not well received by units issued them, especially when both charges fired simultaneously. This unfortunate circumstance very likely reduced the number of surviving specimens, one of the several reasons for the Lindsay's desirability as collector's item.
9A-342   Values—Very Good **$2,500**   Exc. **$4,500**

Model 1863 Remington Percussion "Zouave" Rifle   *See Chapter V-E, Remington Arms.*

Breech-Loading Percussion Conversions From Muzzleloaders

Lindner Alteration

Lindner Alteration, From Percussion Muzzleloader to Percussion Breechloader. Altered by Allen & Morse, Boston, Massachusetts; c. 1861; total quantity of 100 made under contract for State of Massachusetts.

54 caliber. Alterations were performed using the Model 1841 Rifle. The system was based on Edward Lindner's patent of March 29, 1859. Rear section of barrel breech removed (4-1/2"), and replaced by pivoting breech section complete with nipple

bolster. A rotating sleeve mounted on the barrel serves to secure or release the pivoting breech section, which accepted combustible cartridges. Upper tang area replaced by larger and stronger section, and a floorplate also fitted. Combination bayonet stud/front sight added on muzzle, and near rear sight also added.

Marking on rotating sleeve: PATENTED/MAR. 29, 1859. Serial number marked under sleeve. All the altered rifles were specimens which had been produced by Robbins & Lawrence. (Note: Three specimens were altered by Amoskeag Manufacturing Company, as samples, prior to the Allen & Morse contract. These pieces, if authenticated, would be considered very rare and command premium values):

9A-343   Values—Good **$3,250**   Fine **$5,500**

9A-343

Merrill Alteration

9A-344

Merrill Alteration, from Percussion Muzzleloader to Percussion Breechloader. Altered by James H. Merrill, Baltimore, Maryland; c. 1861-62; total quantity 100 each of 3 models.

The Merrill breech-loading mechanism is described in data presented on the Merrill rifles and carbines (*q.v.*) and the

alteration should not be confused with those arms. Models known to have been utilized were primarily the 1842 Musket (they were rifled with long range rear sights attached simultaneously with their conversion) and the U.S. Model 1841 Rifle; other types known and classified as experimental. Lockplates retain regular maker marking with Merrill name and patent dates on lever.

Means of alteration was by replacing the original tang/breech plug with the Merrill breech mechanism (6" length), including attaching a latch for the lever on top of the barrel. Reinforcement screw to lockplate and bolster clean out screw were also added.

Model 1842 Musket; most often observed arm used for Merrill Alteration. Rare:

9A-344   Values—Good **$2,750**   Fine **$5,000**

Model 1841 U.S. Rifle; rare:

9A-345   Values—Good **$3,500**   Fine **$6,500**

Model 1847 Cavalry Musketoon; very rare:

9A-345.5   Values—Good **$3,500**   Fine **$7,000**

Breech-Loading Cartridge Conversions From Muzzleloaders

Miller Model 1861 58 Caliber Conversion

Miller Conversion to Breech-Loading, of U.S. 1861, 58 Caliber Rifle-Musket. Patented by William H. and George W. Miller, West Meriden, Connecticut, and altered by the Meriden Manufacturing Co., Meriden. Altered c. 1865-1867; quantity approx. 2,000. Records show Maryland militia, 1876, issued 50 and N.Y. dealers Schuyler, Hartley purchased 45 from N.Y. militia arsenal as surplus, c. 1880's.

58 rimfire cartridge. Conversion breechblock unit adapted to breech of barrel. Lifting upward on lug type latch released the breechblock allowing it to swing upward for loading. The firing pin angled through the block.

Marking on top of breechblock: W. H. & G. W. MILLER PATENT MAY 23, 1865/MERIDEN MFG. CO., MERIDEN, CONN. A number also present.

Mountings, finishes, and other details remain the same as for

9A-346

standard 1861 muskets. Lock markings most often encountered PARKERS' SNOW & CO/MERIDEN. CONN.

9A-346   Values—Good **$550**   Fine **$1,250**

Morse Centerfire Alteration

Morse Centerfire Alteration to Breechloader. Altered by Springfield and Harpers Ferry armories, c. 1860-1861; total quantity estimated at about 655.

The U.S. Model 1816 muskets already altered to percussion were the arms used for this breech alteration; rifled bores and

long range rear sights.

Patented by George W. Morse 1856 and 1858, the system required machining out a section of barrel breech, and installing the pivoting type breechblock; the nipple was removed and the top section of the bolster machined off; the front section of hammer was cut away, the remaining hammer served as a locking device for the breechblock. At half cock the breechblock is free to be pivoted upward manually. Forward lock retainer is by slotted, round head nut on outside. The hammer-cocking piece attached to an internal locking lever. When fired the locking lever struck the firing pin igniting the specially designed 69 caliber center-primed metallic cartridge.

The Morse is of great importance in firearms evolution, as the first U.S. breech-loading cartridge longarm.

Springfield Armory alteration; total known completed of 54 muskets:

9A-347   Values—Good **$5,000**   Fine **$17,500**

Harpers Ferry alteration; estimated at about 600 in various stages of production, but is unknown how many were completed at time of Confederate capture and burning of the armory. Judging by the frequency with which specimens appear on the market they are as rare as the Springfield marked pieces:

9A-348   Values—Good **$4,750**   Fine **$15,000**

9A-347

Mont Storm Conversions

Mont Storm Conversion to Breech-Loading, of U.S. Rifles and Rifle-Muskets. Patented by William Mont Storm, in July 1856 and altered at Harpers Ferry Armory; total quantity of 400, c. 1860-61.

58 rimfire. The breech similar in appearance to that of the Allin Conversion, of trap door type, with a small, rounded handle mounted on right side of breechblock.

On September 22, 1858 the U.S. Government purchased from Mr. Storm the right to alter 2,000 muskets to breech-loading under his assistance. It is known (per Ordnance Report of 1860/1861 by the Superintendent of Harpers Ferry) that a total of 400 rifles were so altered. These are strongly believed to have been the Model 1841 (so called "Mississippi" rifle). No specimen of that armory alteration is believed to survive; it is quite possible the entire production was lost when Harpers Ferry Armory burned in April of 1861.

Three specimens are known to the author of the Mont Storm breech alteration (58 rimfire) on Model 1863 muskets (specimen

9A-349

illustrated here). These were very likely used in the government trials of 1867. Values shown are merely estimates of what an authenticated Model 1841 specimen might bring on the collectors' market:

9A-349   Values—Good **$4,000**   Fine **$7,500**

Needham Conversion of M.1861/63 Musket

Needham Conversion to Breechloading of Model 1861/63 Percussion Rifle-Musket. Patented England, 1865 by inventors J & G Needham and in U.S. May, 1867. Conversion performed Trenton N.J. c. 1869. Quantity unknown; specimens encountered with reasonable frequency until very recent years.

9A-350

A fascinating story surrounds these breechloaders, the result of exhaustive research by arms historians Graham Burnside and Edward Hull. In the immediate post Civil War years, the Irish-American secret society, the Fenian Brotherhood, plotted to invade Canada and thus have a bargaining chip with England to gain independence for Ireland. After raising considerable funds, they purchased over 4,200 percussion, muzzleloading, M.1861 and M.1863 type rifle muskets, almost all of which were from Alfred Jenks & Son, contractors of the M.1861 "Bridesburg" musket; *q.v.* (assumedly that accounts for the preponderance of locks bearing that name and 800 from other sources.) The muzzleloaders were distributed to Fenian groups, 600 of whom crossed the Canadian border at Niagara, New York, June, 1866 and defeated a column of Canadian Volunteers at Ridgway, then beat a hasty retreat to thwart Canadian forces closing in on them. Arrested by U.S. authorities, their weapons (quantities unknown) were confiscated. They were soon released and through political machinations their weapons were returned! By 1867 they were reorganized. Their muzzleloaders by then obsolete and out-of-fashion, means were found to convert them to breechloaders, utilizing the Needham Patent. (It is speculated that the Needham was the most practical for the funds available...and rather ironic that it was by Englishmen.) Work was performed secretly in rented premises in Trenton, N.J. and *not* at the Bridesburg, Pa. works. Total of 5,020 converted. Thus armed with the Needhams and various and sundry other weapons, 200 Fenians again attempted, in May, 1870, to invade Canada, by way of Vermont. After a brief skirmish, all were captured, their leader arrested and all arms confiscated. There is reason to believe that those Needhams and all others the gov't could lay its hands on were seized. They were most likely included in the 1000 "breechloaders" both complete and in unassembled state and parts that were sold by the U.S. Arsenal, N.Y., 1871 to Schuyler, Hartley & Graham who assembled those incomplete muskets, selling both without differentiation. It is theorized that the method of affixing the striker to the hammer nose is a means of identifying the "true" Fenian type and that it will have a "V" cut splice under the mid band which is in accord with the 1870 description of officer at army Q.M. warehouse "(muskets of poorest quality ... stocks sawed in two as to fold and be packed in a small trunk or case.") By 1884 Needhams were advertised by name in catalog of Meacham & Co., St. Louis and were offered by the 1920's in the Bannerman, N.Y. catalogs where their Fenian use is specifically mentioned. Approximately 2500 Fenian Needhams were secreted along the border for the raid, some of which still turn up in those areas.

These "Bridesburg" (and a few "Springfield") marked Needhams were actually used twice by the Fenians in their invasion plans; once as muzzleloaders and again as breechloaders, and played a distinct role in a little known incident in American-Canadian-British relations. It is in that context, as well as their interest as an American breechloader, that they are valued. Only known use by any American military organization was the 1870 order from Schuyler, Hartley, N.Y. for 20 Needhams by the "Hibernia Rifles" of Newark, N.J. A few other orders for small quantities from towns in Georgia, Penna. and R.I. may have been for similar local militia.

Although caliber has invariably been listed as 58 rimfire, the hammer and breech giving that appearance, it is actually chambered for 58 centerfire. Conversion was accomplished by cutting away much of the breech end of the barrel and slicing through most of the front section of the lock. The breech block swings out to the right and forward, allowing for insertion of the cartridge; hammer strikes firing pin through a slot cut into the breech. Lock markings invariably BRIDESBURG, occasionally "NEW YORK" (rarely "SPRINGFIELD" which is not worth premium) with Civil War dates. Although Bridesburg was made under M.1861 contract they apparently were the only contractors to also use the stock and barrel bands of the M.1863, Type I (*also see note with 9A-340*).

9A-350   Values—Good **$750**   Fine **$1,250**

Peabody Conversion To Breech-Loading   *See Peabody Carbines and Rifles in latter part of this chapter—*
"Secondary American Military Longarms; Breech-Loading."

Phoenix Conversions of Model 1861/63 Muskets   *See Whitney Arms Co., Chapter V-J.*

Remington Rolling Block Conversions of Model 1861/63 Muskets
See Remington Arms Co., Chapter V.

Roberts Model 1861/63 Rifle-Musket Conversion

Roberts Conversion to Breech-Loading of U.S. Model 1861/63 Rifle-Muskets. Patented by Brigadier General B. S. Roberts, U.S. Army, 1867. Made c. late 1869-1870 by the Providence Tool Co., Providence, Rhode Island for the Roberts Breechloading Arms Company, New York City. Quantity 5,000.

Caliber 58 Roberts centerfire. Alteration made by cutting off breech of 58 percussion musket and inserting in its place the Roberts breech. To operate, a short lever extending at tang over wrist was raised which dropped the breech downward exposing the chamber. Cocking the hammer closed the breech.

Markings on side of breech ROBERTS' PAT. JUNE 11, 1867.

Mountings, finish and other details same as on standard 1861/63 arms converted.

Endorsed by the New York Trial board in 1867 and selected over the Allin, Berdan and others, the state contracted with Roberts to convert 10,000 muskets then in state armories; the contract signed in 1868. The Providence Tool Co. had already made 2,000 conversions for Roberts when, in 1869, the N.Y. legislature refused to appropriate funds for the contract. Roberts hurriedly found a buyer, the State of South Carolina, who purchased a total of 5,000 conversions in 1870 and armed all 13 of its National Guard regiments. The rifles were phased out between 1879 and 1890.

9A-351

Suffering heavy loss and breakage while in service, the survival rate was very low, hence examples, especially those in finer states of condition are very scarce.

The conversion has been encountered on the Model 1855 Rifle-Musket also. When found on American arms other than the Model 1861 Musket, a premium should be added to the value:

9A-351   Values—Good **$950**   Fine **$2,250**

Sharps Conversions of Model 1861/63 Musket   *See Sharps Rifle Co., Chapter V.*

Joslyn Breech-Loading Rifle

Joslyn Breech-Loading Rifle Made by Springfield Armory c. January to June 1865. Quantity made 3,007.

Until documentary evidence was found in 1972, this piece had generally been considered a post Civil War conversion of muzzleloader to breechloader. Substantiating material has proven this to be the first true breech-loading cartridge weapon to be made in substantial quantity by a National armory—and decidedly not an alteration.

The actions/breech units, identical to the Joslyn 1864 carbine actions (*q.v.*), were supplied by the Joslyn Firearms Company to the Springfield Armory in early 1865, where they were assembled on newly fabricated infantry rifles specially designed for this action. Although commonly listed as 56-50 rimfire and that Spencer cartridge fits, the correct cartridge is the 50-60-450 Joslyn rimfire made at the Frankford Arsenal. 35-1/2" round barrel (which is not a converted or sleeved musket barrel) three band fastened; uniquely shaped lock most likely altered from an 1863 type marked with eagle ahead of hammer, U.S./SPRINGFIELD on the forward section and 1864 at rear. The walnut stock is of original manufacture, designed specifically for the Joslyn breech, special shaped lock and smaller barrel. Serial numbered. Markings on breechblock: B. F. JOSLYN'S PATENT/OCT 8th 1861/JUNE 24th 1862. It is believed that some of these were issued to Union forces before cessation of hostilities in Civil War, but no record of these in actual combat use:

9A-352   Values—Good **$900**   Fine **$2,000**

9A-352

Conversions to 50-70 centerfire; Armory records indicate that 1,600 Joslyn rifles were converted by rechambering for the 50-70 cartridge (all found with mixed serial numbers). Firing pins were also altered to centerfire with the rimfire pin hole plugged. Records further indicate that the entire group of 1,600 were sold that same year and shipped to France for use in Franco-Prussian War. It is believed that most of the lot eventually were converted for civilian sales as shotguns (majority to Africa), hence surviving full military specimens very scarce:

9A-353   Values—Good **$900**   Fine **$2,250**

Allin Conversion Model 1865 Rifle

Model 1865 U.S. Breech-Loading Rifle, Allin Conversion, a.k.a. First Model Allin. Designed by Erskine S. Allin, Master Armorer, Springfield Armory. Made c. 1865. 5,000 altered at Springfield using the Model 1861 percussion musket.

58 rimfire cartridge. 40" barrel overall (from face of breech 37-3/4"). Breechblock released by thumb latch on right side, pivoted upward; firing pin within block.

The first use of the distinctive "trapdoor" breechblock easily recognizable by its shape and highly visible rack and pinion ejector system at right side of breech.

Breechblock unmarked. Lock marked ahead of hammer with eagle and U.S./SPRINGFIELD. All specimens dated 1865 at rear.

Mountings, finishes and other details same as on Model 1861 muskets with flat barrel bands:

9A-354   Values—Good **$1,500**   Fine **$3,500**

9A-354

Variations with shorter barrels: The collector is urged to be wary and exercise caution when encountering other barrel lengths of this 1st Model Allin, usually two-band fastened. The most often encountered has 32" barrel on which the two bands are in the same positions as the three-band model, leaving a considerable length of forend at top. The workmanship of shortening, the barrel placement and other features as well as lack of any mention in ordnance records seems to indicate these were performed by various firms late in 19th century to make them more saleable as surplus. These are often seen with the wood around the wrist and lock areas thinned down greatly, another distinct sign of their surplus alteration by civilian sales firms. There is one short model that is original and correct. Estimated production 270 and believed intended for cadet use.

36" barrel with two bands properly spaced indicating armory alteration. The stock is full proportioned at wrist and around the lock aperture but was shortened from the longer three-band length. The band spring slot was filled in and the upper forend thinned down in the area of the former band. Key features to identification:

1. The original inspector mark ESA in an oval cartouche appears near the lock screw.

2. An additional inspector mark SWP in a rectangular cartouche was added at the time of alteration/shortening.

3. The original midband which held the sling swivel was discarded and former top band was moved back on the thinned forend. The sling swivel and stud which held it was actually cut out of the former midband and brazed to the upper band.

Although rare, specimens seldom bring more than the standard 40" barrel type as "demand" is moderate, at best, and collectors are cautious due to many spurious examples:

9A-355   Values—Good **$1,500**   Fine **$3,750**

Allin Conversion Model 1866 Rifle

Model 1866 U.S. Breech-Loading Rifle, Allin Conversion, a.k.a. Second Model Allin "Trapdoor." Designed by Erskine S. Allin. Made c. 1866. Total of 25,000 altered at Springfield using Model 1863 percussion muskets.

50 caliber centerfire. 40" Civil War barrel (actual length to face of breech 36-5/8") bored to larger diameter with a liner tube of 50 caliber inserted and brazed. Three barrel bands with band springs.

9A-356

Changes from Model 1865 Allin included a lengthened bolt, a firing pin spring and stronger internal extraction system which dispensed with the rack and pinion type.

Breechblock marking 1866 over American eagle. Standard Civil War lock with Springfield markings usually dated 1863 or 1864.

Mountings, finishes and other details remained the same as on the Model 1863 muskets—all bright. Breechblock has original blackened finish caused in casehardening process by quenching in oil while the lock and hammer have the bright casehardening colors caused by quenching in water:

9A-356   Values—Good **$750**   Fine **$2,000**

Variations with shorter barrels. Refer to note about similar arms in Model 1865 First Type Allin. Similar alterations are often seen with the Model 1866. There is a 36" barrel, two band variant, assumed to be arsenal original. Information is tenuous at best, based on a single entry thus far located in the Springfield Armory report for Jan. 6, 1883: "Springfield B.L.R. musket Cal. 50 Model 1866 (Short). Ready for issue. Cleaned and repaired. 1,019 on hand." Promising, but not enough to be proof positive of exactly what the guns were or their particulars. Arsenal original specimens would be considered rare. Caution is advised before acquisition:

9A-357   Values—Good **$850**   Fine **$2,500**

"Officer's Sporting Rifle" of Model 1866 Allin

9A-357.5

"Officer's Sporting Rifle" of Model 1866 (Allin Conversion) (a.k.a. Second Model Allin "Trap Door") converted by Springfield Arsenal on custom order to "Sporting Models" for various officers. 50-caliber centerfire. It is also believed some were custom altered by U.S. Army Ordnance at Fort Leavenworth, Kansas. Quantities unknown; although approximately 100 estimated altered by Springfield Armory late 1860s-early 1870s.

Other than an original Springfield document "Register of Ordnance Stores Sold March 1869 through Dec. 1871" that actually lists a number of "Officer's Sporting Rifles" altered at the Armory (along with names of those who ordered them), very little has been officially recorded about these arms. It is apparent that all are likely to have variances (mostly minor) attributable to their custom order and the absence of an adopted, exact arsenal pattern. Significant sources of information about them and their background are *"General Custer and His Sporting Rifles,"* by C.V. Haynes, (1995). Basic alteration to the 1866 Allin rifle consisted of shortening the barrel and the full-length stock to a half-stock, utilizing either a single barrel band or (in its place) a barrel wedge; often adding a sporting type trigger guard, double set triggers, a metal forend cap; various sights and buttplates. When stocks were "sporterized" with their shortened forends, the buttstock was often reduced accordingly by narrowing its width to that of the "Cadet Rifle." Each example is judged on its own respective features. The origins of the few known examples of M1866 Allin Conversion "Officer's Sporting Rifle" are mostly credited to the Springfield Arsenal or other government ordnance works. There is also reason to believe that those large 50-caliber Allins were unlikely to have been available on the civilian surplus market. Although remote, the possibility remains that a "loose" 1866 Allin was converted during the era by a civilian gunsmith. Authenticated period specimens are great rarities and especially desirable for their probable Western associations. There is continuing, ongoing research on this rifle and the later 1868, 1870 and 1873 "Officer's Sporting Rifles" certain to add further details for their identification. Values are seen in the low to mid-five figures.

9A-357.5

Model 1867 U.S. Cadet Rifle

Model 1867 U.S. Breech-Loading Cadet Rifle. (Not illus.) Made c. 1867-1868 at Springfield Armory. Total production 424.

A scaled down version of the Model 1866 Second Model Allin "Trapdoor." 50 caliber centerfire. New, unlined 33" barrel.

Proportionately shorter stock (12-1/2" from center of buttplate to center of trigger); two-band fastened. Made without sling swivels; narrow trigger guard.

Two key identification features are breechblock and lock. Breechblock has blackened finish and underside has very noticeable, deep arched cut-outs at each side leaving a narrow flat ridge in center, marked 1866 over eaglehead. The lockplate is unique; specially made for this arm only and noticeably thinner than other Civil War lockplates. Markings are usual eagle and US/SPRINGFIELD, but bears 1867 date at rear.

Oval barrel bands with all mountings and barrel finished bright; casehardened lock. Rear sight same as on Model 1866 Allin. Slim shaft iron ramrod without stop (screw-in type) with head same as Model 1866. *Rare:*

9A-358   Values—Good **$2,500**   Fine **$7,500**

Model 1868 U.S. Cadet Rifle

Model 1868 U.S. Breech-Loading Cadet Rifle. This "Trapdoor" model appears in other published works on U.S. martial arms.

As far as can be ascertained there was no such model and earlier works probably misidentified the Model 1867 Cadet listed here.

Model 1868 U.S. Springfield Rifle

Model 1868 U.S. Springfield Rifle, a.k.a. "Trapdoor." Made by Springfield Armory, c. 1868-1872; total quantity 51,389.

50 centerfire cartridge. The breechblock pivoted forward; released by a thumb latch; design was also by Allin and served as the government standard for breech-loading single shot military rifles and carbines until the 1890s. 32-1/2" barrel, secured by two barrel bands and screw through tang. Rear sight of long range type with adjustable slide leaf; front sight on lug also serving as bayonet stud.

Iron mountings standard, finished bright. Cleaning rod not cupped at end (as had been standard on percussion ramrods), and is slotted; a shoulder 4" under the head engages an aperture formed in the upper end of ramrod groove. Walnut stock, oil finished. Civil War lockplates, barrel bands and other mountings still used.

Serial numbered on barrel and receiver. Lock marking of eagle and US/SPRINGFIELD forward of the hammer; dated 1863 or 1864 at rear. Breechblock dated 1869 or 1870 and also bears small eaglehead over crossed arrows over US. A small quantity, likely less than 200, were made at the end of 1868. A few low numbered specimens with 1868 dated breechblocks are known and worth a premium in value. Their occurrence is accounted for

9A-359

by the system of ordnance recordkeeping (*see explanation with 1847 Sappers Musketoon, 9A-301*).

This arm is readily identified from the Model 1870 with which it is often confused by two major features: (A) The length of the arch on the underside of breechblock is 1-7/8" (shorter than the 2-3/16" of Model 1870) and (B) the front of the receiver (i.e., the section into which the breech of the barrel is screwed) is 2-1/8" (longer than the 1-13/32" of the Model 1870):

9A-359   Values—Good **$750**   Fine **$1,500**

"Officer's Sporting Rifles" of Models 1868 and 1870

"Officer's Sporting Rifles" of Models 1868 and 1870 Springfield "Trapdoor" Rifles. 50 caliber centerfire.

Model 1868 U.S. Springfield "Officer's Sporting Model Rifle." Quantity unknown; extremely limited; made on custom order at Springfield Armory and possibly other ordnance works for officers in the field. Many were altered from "Cadet Rifles."

These altered Springfield "Trap Doors" are modified similarly to the early 1866 Allin Conversions "Officer's Sporting Rifles" (see 9A-357.5). Whether they are actually government arsenal alterations or the work was accomplished by some professional western (or other) gunsmith remains unknown. However, the fact that many were modified from Springfield Cadet Rifles, as specified in official U.S. Ordnance correspondence, suggests production at the National Armory. They are generally evaluated based on their established authenticity (often by a consensus of opinion of recognized authorities) as genuine antiques of the period (with an assumed western association). Both are rare, the 1870 more so. Values predicated on condition and general appearance; estimated in the low to mid-five-figure range.

9A-359.5

Model 1869 U.S. Cadet Rifle

Model 1869 U.S. Cadet Rifle, a.k.a. "Trapdoor." (Not illus.) Made by Springfield Armory, c. 1869-76. Total quantity 3,422.

50 caliber centerfire. Basically similar to the Model 1867 Cadet, but with standard Civil War Springfield marked locks bearing 1863-1865 dates.

29-5/8" barrel. Mountings similar to the Model 1867 and noticeably smaller than standard 50 caliber Trapdoors. No provision for sling swivels.

Has the improvements of the Model 1868 rifle; ramrod with single shoulder stop and forend tip with ramrod stop. Model 1868 type rear sight. Smaller buttplate. Serial numbered on barrel and receiver:

9A-360   Values—Good **$850**   Fine **$1,750**

Model 1870 U.S. "Trapdoor" Springfield Rifle and Carbine

9A-362 Carbine

9A-361 / 362

Model 1870 U.S. "Trapdoor" Springfield Rifle and Carbine. Made by Springfield Armory, c. 1870-1873; total quantity 11,533.

50 caliber centerfire. 32-1/2" barrel. Almost identical to Model 1868 with most noticeable distinguishing features: (A) The length of the arch on the underside of breechblock is 2-3/16" (longer than the Model 1868) and (B) the front of the receiver (i.e., the section into which the breech of the barrel is screwed) is 1-13/32"; shorter than the Model 1868 and same length as on the later Model 1873.

Breechblock marked either 1870 or Model 1870 (value same for either marking) over small eaglehead, crossed arrows and US.

Lock is standard Civil War type with Springfield markings and 1863-1865 dates:

9A-361 Values—Good **$700** Fine **$1,800**

Carbine: Identical action to above and markings same. Breechblock marked with 1870 date (and not word MODEL.) 22" barrel. Carbine half stock with long wrist and short comb (similar to that of the 1873 carbine) with single barrel band. Not fitted for cleaning rod or bayonet. Sling ring bar on left side opposite lock. Only 341 produced in 1871. *Very scarce:*

9A-362 Values—Good **$4,000** Fine **$10,000**

THE "TRAPDOOR" SPRINGFIELDS CALIBER 45-70

The following guns of clearcut historical and collector importance are listed in their chronological sequence as manufactured by the Springfield Armory. By so doing, other arms manufactured simultaneously have been taken out of their normal chronological order and will be found listed following this "Trapdoor" segment. This arbitrary decision was made in the interest of preserving the "Trapdoor" as a distinct and separate type.

The following arms are all identical in action and principle, composing the famed series of breech-loading Springfield Armory made longarms familiarly and fondly known as the "Trapdoors." This is the first time that any such detailed listing has been published. It is hoped that the nomenclature and model designations used here will supersede and update many incorrectly named and misunderstood models and variations of these highly popular collectors' items. The reader will note that in some cases the author has gone to considerable detail in explaining minor variances that often play important identifying roles and in describing major features to look for. The author's intent has been to avoid confusion in a subject that has begged for clarification.

The Model 1866 described earlier marked the beginning of the standard series of historic "Trapdoor" Springfields. Truly one of the guns which "won the West," the trapdoor in one form or another—and as the reader will see there are many variations—long served as the standard longarm for U.S. forces in most of the major Indian engagements, and in government forts and garrisons throughout America.

Despite the fact that successor arms were adopted within a few years of the last model Trapdoor, these weapons remained in service beyond the turn of the century and were the standard for the great majority of militia and volunteers who fought at the beginning of the Spanish-American War in 1898.

Quite a few collectors are "Trapdoor Springfield" specialists. Specific literature has fast developed around these romantic and historic arms, although none to date has categorized the field as you will find herein.

A few basic facts, common to all models, are omitted in each of the following descriptions as they would be redundant. Mention of them here will suffice: All of the following trapdoors were made at the Springfield Armory. All (except where noted in a few instances) are of 45-70 caliber. Lock markings are invariably the same throughout with the eagle motif ahead of the hammer, and forward of that U.S. over SPRINGFIELD. When lock markings vary or have extra features, this will be so noted.

Only on the Model 1888 Trapdoor with the ramrod-bayonet is the trigger guard made of one piece (i.e., the guard and the bow). On all other models (except in a few isolated instances where noted) trigger guards are of the Civil War style (i.e., two-piece construction with the trigger plate and trigger bow joined together by two locking nuts).

Stocks on all trapdoors are black walnut, oil finished. The inspector markings appear on the stock opposite the lock. From 1873 to 1877 the initials ESA (of the master armorer at Springfield, E. S. Allin) appear in an oval cartouche without date. From 1877 to 1878 the ESA initials are the same size and appear over the date either 1877 or 1878 in a larger oval cartouche. After 1878, the cartouche became square shaped and bears the initials SWP of Samuel W. Porter, Master Armorer, and the year of manufacture.

Only the ramrod-bayonet models are fitted for a butt compartment for cleaning tools (and shell extractor) with a corresponding trapdoor in the buttplate. All other rifles and cadet models do not have this feature.

All carbines except the Model 1873 are fitted in the butt with a compartment for three-piece cleaning rod and have a corresponding hinged door on buttplate.

High Arch Breech

Low Arch Breech

All cadet muskets have the old style 1873 stocks with the short 9" comb.

Regarding the matter of "high arch breechblocks," which is a key identifying feature on the early 1873s, it should be noted there were no conversions of this type to the low breechblock form (see illustrations). In other words, the 1873s fitted with high arch breechblocks were used that way until either destroyed, condemned, sold or returned to armory stocks. As far as can be determined, they were not altered. It is impossible to merely interchange or replace the high arch breech with the low arch form. They can be fitted if ground and filed, but there is no evidence that the government ever performed such alterations. The only common alterations were sight changes. As newer models were introduced, the variances and innovations they brought about did not cause modifications on the already existing types; rather, they were used as is or, if obsolescent, were sold or otherwise disposed of. Sights only apparently were updated, but not on all models; it depended very much on where the gun was used, stored and inventoried.

Breechblocks and tangs were finished by casehardening. On the Model 1873 high arch breechblocks, this casehardening finish will appear as black or very deep blue. Considerable quantities of these high arch breechblock M. 1873s were refinished by the arsenal during their period of use and hence may be observed in the color casehardened finish or even blued. All subsequent Trapdoor Springfields were originally color casehardened as they left the armory.

The 45-70s described here are as they left the armory. Not all of them (as a matter of fact, very few) will be found meeting these exact specifications; most have had some changes performed in the field during their lifetime—usually very minor and on sights only. As such, prices will not be affected to any degree. A major change would be a replaced stock or completely incorrect sight. Such pieces are certainly still good collectors' items, but should be priced downward accordingly.

Serial number ranges as indicated here are approximate only. There were definite overlaps in the production and assignation of numbers and in other instances complete blocks of numbers were very likely used for replacement receivers.

The collector should carefully scrutinize carbines to be certain that they are not merely rifles that have been altered and cut down in size. Quite a few such "carbines" were made over the years, some with no malice aforethought; others with larceny in mind. With careful inspection, it is possible in almost all instances to identify a rifle that has been shortened to carbine length. The key feature to observe is the ramrod channel on the rifle which has been filled in on the tip of the carbine forend. Occasionally an exceptionally fine wood fill-in repair is seen requiring extra scrutiny to detect. For the most part, the wood plug shows quite easily. More clever operators have added an entirely new piece of wood at the forend tip (that which protrudes ahead of the barrel band), thus eliminating the remnants of the rifle ramrod channel. In order to circumvent this sharp practice, merely slide the barrel band forward and expose the seam underneath where the wood has been spliced. Original Trapdoor Carbine ring bars have been on the market for years; hence, there was no problem in adding those to a rifle when changing to carbine appearance; the wood is the key difference.

Measurements given for barrel lengths are made from the muzzle to the face of the breech; thus, if measuring on the outside of the barrel, dimensions will vary slightly. All rifling in 45-70's is three-groove except in the long range rifle which was six-groove.

Bores and finishes play an important role in evaluating Trapdoor rifles; especially on the common types. For the very rare ones, these features would be secondary in importance. Not a few of the more common models are purchased by individuals using them for target shooting or hunting purposes; hence, oftentimes slight differences in condition, especially bores, will create or lessen demand and value for a particular piece.

A very common mistake made on the Trapdoor is the identification of a MODEL 1878 as seemingly indicated by markings on some breechblocks. No such type exists and these markings are merely very deeply struck Model 1873 dies that on first appearance with the naked eye appear to be the date 1878. Close inspection will prove the date to be 1873.

The "Model" designations shown herein consist of both the official terminology used by the armories and the Ordnance Department on the few basic types as well as unofficial, collector designations which have been applied to others over the years and are generally accepted as terms of convenience for the various configurations. The author has tried to indicate in all cases where the terminology originated and in some instances has updated nomenclature that was previously incorrectly applied not wishing to perpetuate what in some cases were pure myths.

Surplus Parts & The Civilian Market

Very large amounts of loose parts were sold either as surplus or obsolete by the government in the late nineteenth and early twentieth centuries. These parts have been in existence until relatively recent years; hence, it is possible to find all kinds of "married" and/or composite Trapdoors available. Almost all of these are quite easily recognized by even the most novice of collectors; it takes only the slightest discerning eye and discretion on the part of the buyer. Not a few complete arms were assembled by large surplus dealers around the turn of the century using condemned and obsolete Trapdoors to sell to private academies and militia groups. One of these types is mentioned and described as the "1883-1884 Lock Dated Trapdoor Rifles" in the following section, but others will be observed. Some of these have stocks which have been very thinned in the wrist and lock area to lighten them, while others have features not quite standard. All such non-armory issue or military issue weapons when so altered are valued for their shooting qualities and condition.

Another common type of alteration performed on surplus arms and strictly sold to the civilian market, usually for youngsters at a military school, is the so-called "U.S. Springfield Breech-Loading Cadet Rifle," one of the many titles used for it. One particular example is that advertised in the 1889 and later catalog of the famous Francis Bannerman of New York with the caption, "This is a regulation gun, made suitable for military academies by having the barrel shortened to 28 inches, the stock reduced in thickness and shortened in length, etc..." With a further 120 years of acquired age, many of these, and others like them, could pass or be palmed off, to the unsuspecting as original arsenal manufacture.

The Enigmatic "RGS" Inspector Marking

Among the many oddball variations of the 45-70 "trap-door" a few at first glance, have the appearance of arsenal assembly, complete with U.S. government style inspector marks "**RGS**" in an oval cartouche stamped on various parts of the stock. The marks are alleged those of "R.G. Shurtleff" an arsenal inspector. A fancy, large, script-like "R" is stamped in another area of the same stock. It has been reasonably established and is the consensus of those who specialize and write about the "trap-door" that the markings are NOT those of any U.S. or arsenal inspector but, rather, were applied by Bannerman's, N.Y. or Schuyler, Hartley & Graham of N.Y. (or similar) and are found only on rifles assembled and/or altered from surplus parts. "RGS" and his trail of broken hearts is discussed at length by A.T. Frasca in Issue No. 4, 1998 *"Man at Arms."*

Collectible Civilian "Trap Doors"

There is one group of arms, privately altered during the nineteenth century that does hold considerable interest, and value for the collector. These have yet to be completely identified and detailed, although not a few specimens have been observed over the years. Evidently quite a few surplus 45-70 Trapdoor rifles were purchased during the 1870s and 1890s by well known arms and sporting goods dealers and converted to sporting purposes. Some show evidence of very fine workmanship, while others are professional in their alteration, but very simply fashioned. It is fully documented that in 1883 a total of 300 Trapdoor Springfields were altered to sporting rifles by Whitney Arms Company, on order of the famed New York dealers Hartley and Graham. Their stocks were shortened to half length and checkered at the wrist and forend with a buffalo horn insert at the tip. Most had octagonal barrels added and sporting sights; calibers 45-70 and 40-65 are known. Other makers performed similar alterations. Such arms when proven authentic are quite desirable collectors' items and each must be taken on its own merits as to quality and condition in order to properly evaluate. A very general price range broad enough in scope to cover a majority of such weapons would be from $600 to $4,000, and is very much dependent on quality, condition and authenticity of its nineteenth century alteration. The conversion of Trapdoor Springfields to sporting rifles continues to the present day due to great popularity for black powder shooters.

Model 1873 "Trapdoor" Rifle, Carbine and Cadet Rifle

9A-363

9A-364

Model 1873 "Trapdoor" Rifle, Carbine and Cadet Rifle. Made c. 1873-1877. Total quantity approximately 73,000 all types.

Rifle barrel 32-5/8"; secured by two barrel bands. Long range type rear sight with adjustable slide leaf; front sight on lug also serves as stud for socket type bayonet.

Iron mountings standard. Finish blue throughout with casehardened breech and tang (oil quenched giving them a black or very deep blue color). Cleaning rod retains the wide, channeled and slotted head cleaning rod of the earlier 1870, but narrower in diameter with cannelures at lower end to improve finger hold.

Lockplate fits flush with stock and made without bevel. Two-piece trigger guard. High arched breechblock.

Serial numbered 1 to 80000 approximately with Carbines and Cadet Muskets also falling within this range. Lock marking: ahead of hammer eagle and US/SPRINGFIELD/1873. Until mid-1876 breechblock marking MODEL 1873 over eaglehead, over crossed arrows, over US. After mid-1876 marked U.S./MODEL/1873.

The Model 1873 was the first of the Trapdoor Springfields chambered for the 45-70 cartridge. The ordnance department had determined that standardization of U.S. small arms in 45 caliber (45-70 for long arms and 45 Colt for handguns) was advisable, effective 1873. Among other changes to note in the Model 1873 from earlier 50 caliber trapdoors: Pitch of rifling increased; weight reduction to 8-1/4 lbs.; hammer of more rounded contour; most screw heads rounded; rear sight made larger and moved forward and close to the lower barrel band; sight base graduated to 400 yards; leaf to 1,200 yards.

A feature that also helps identify these early 1873s is the flush sides or fit of the barrel at the point where it screws into the receiver; hence, the stock recess/channel is straight cut at that point whereas in later trapdoors the receiver was widened and there is a slight two-step cutaway in the stock.

The Model 1873 did not have barrel proof marks until approximately Serial No. 50000, after which an eaglehead and small V/P were used. Rifle has two-click tumbler. Comb of stock (known as the short comb) about 9" in length. Some of early hammers have coarse checkering without border. All stocks carry inspector markings of E. S. Allin, with script initials ESA in oval cartouche on left side opposite lock and P in oval below trigger guard on butt. Made without trapdoor in butt for cleaning tools.

The early 1873s (up to 1877) had breechblocks casehardened and quenched in oil which gave them a black look. After 1877 casehardening process used water to quench which gave the brilliant colors. During the lifetime of many of the early '73s, they were probably refinished with the later water quenching method.

Rifle: Production of rifles approximately 50,000:

9A-363   Values—Good **$750**   Fine **$2,000**

Carbine: Identical, but with 22" barrel and short carbine half stock fastened with single barrel band having stacking swivel. Blade type front sight fastened in base by pin; rear sight base graduated to 500 yards, sight leaf to 1,200 yards; no sling swivel on trigger guard; three-click tumbler; sling ring and bar on left side.

The original 1873 carbine as issued should have the short comb stock without compartment in butt for cleaning rod and no trap in buttplate. Many of these were restocked and their value

is considerably less (30 percent to 40 percent) when so found. Oftentimes restocked specimens will have the buttplate changed (to fool the buyer) to the solid type to give the impression of being correct. The collector should remove the buttplate to be certain no compartment exists underneath. Inspector markings always ESA in cartouche on stock. Approximately 20,000 made, but scarce in unaltered condition. Pre-1876 made carbines, falling below the serial range of approximately 43,700:

Worth premium of 20 to 50 percent depending on condition as they are considered typical of the model Colonel George Custer's 7th Cavalry was armed with prior to the battle at the Little Big Horn in 1876. (Of course, if the actual serial number can be documented explicitly to issuance to that famous cavalry unit, premiums easily reach five figures for historical significance; condition of secondary importance.)

9A-364   Values—Good **$3,000**   Fine **$7,000**

Cadet Rifle: Basically identical to the rifle, but with 29-1/2" barrel. Stacking swivel only on top band and made without sling swivels. Two-click tumbler; smaller buttplate. Same rear sight as rifle. Approximately 3,000 made:

9A-365   Values—Good **$675**   Fine **$1,500**

Cadet Rifle Variation: Identical to above, but has sling swivels as well as stacking swivel. These are merely "true" Cadets as above which when taken out of West Point service and replaced by later models were given or sold to military schools or organizations which required the use of slings:

9A-366   Values—Good **$500**   Fine **$950**

"Officer's Sporting Rifle" Modification of Model 1873 Rifle

"Officer's Sporting Rifle" Modification of Model 1873 Springfield "Trapdoor" Rifle.

Caliber 45-70 as above. Custom altered by the Armory at the special request of various U.S. Army officers to the Chief of Ordnance. (See No. 9A-357.5 and 9A-359.5 for information directly relating to "Sporting Rifles.") To avoid the time-consuming custom work the Ordnance Dept. decided to standardize the "Sporting Rifles," ultimately renamed and fabricated as the "Model 1875 Officer's Rifle" (9A-367). As these earlier "Sporting Rifles" were individually fabricated, numerous differences and variations are to be observed on all

specimens. Collectors urged to exercise utmost caution before acquiring a presumptive specimen; most that have been examined were modifications by commercial gunsmiths (and not of U.S. Armory origin). All such civilian-modified M1873 rifles, as long as conclusively established as alterations contemporary to use in the 19th century, would be regarded fine collector's items (valued for their appearance and quality of workmanship) but not the rare "Officer's Sporting Rifle." Confirmed examples by the National Armory are estimated valued in the lower 5 figures.

9A-366.5

Model 1875 U.S. "Trapdoor" Officer's Rifle

Model 1875 U.S. "Trapdoor" Officer's Rifle. Made c. 1875-1885. Total quantity 477.

26" barrel fastened by single barrel band. Three styles of rear sights used (Model 1873, 1877, 1879) depending on the period made. Front sight combination globe or peep. Upper section of stock wrist fitted with folding tang peep sight adjustable for windage and elevation.

Iron mountings standard; blued finish with casehardened mountings found on earlier issued guns. Wooden cleaning rod with nickel plated tips (brass tips on later production); small slot at end. Oil finished walnut stock with checkering at wrist and

forend. One small batch in 1881 and another in 1885 bore inspector marks on left side opposite lock with initials and date (either 1881 or 1885); otherwise majority do not bear inspector markings. All will have the P in oval marked on underside of butt just below the checkered area.

One of the highly desirable features of these rare and much sought-after arms is the original fancy scroll engraving on the lockplate, hammer, breechblock, receiver, barrel band, buttplate heel and trigger guard. Other special details were single set trigger and sporting nature of stock, including single ferrule under barrel and forend cap slotted to accept the cleaning rod.

9A-368

Not serial numbered, but a few are dated 1881 at the back of the receiver where numbers usually appear. Lock and breechblock markings same as regular guns of the same eras made; hence, will vary.

The Officer's Rifle was not issued, but was sold to Army officers for personal sporting use. One of the attractions of service in the American West was the excellent hunting and this model offered a quality rifle chambered for the standard military cartridge. **First Type Model 1875;** Has the high arch breech block and other features of the Model 1873 and, usually, finer quality engraving. Made c. 1875-1877. Quantity estimated 125:

9A-367 Values—Very Good **$12,000** Exc. **$37,500**

Second Type Model 1875; features of the Model 1877 and 1879 respectively with detachable checkered wood half pistol-grip. Made c. 1877-1881. Quantity estimated 252:

9A-368 Values—Very Good **$10,000** Exc. **$35,000**

Third Type Model 1875. Similar "Second Type;" stock protrudes 5/8" longer in front of barrel band; square profile to forend cap (instead of rounded); ramrod tip brass (and not plated); inspector markings "SWP/1885" on stock. Made 1885. Quantity estimated 100:

9A-368.5 Values—Very Good **$10,000** Exc. **$35,000**

Model 1877 U.S. "Trapdoor" Rifle, Carbine and Cadet Rifle

Model 1877 U.S. "Trapdoor" Rifle, Carbine and Cadet Rifle, a.k.a. Transitional 1873/1879. (Not illus.) Total quantity, all types, 25,500 approx. Made c. 1877-1878.

A source of confusion to the collector, the term Model 1877 is both official and unofficial. All three types still retain the breechblock marking MODEL 1873, however, the Carbine was actually renamed in official correspondence and literature as the **MODEL 1877**, while the present-day collector has applied Model 1877 as terms of convenience and differentiation to the Rifle and Cadet models.

Basic changes: The wrist of the stock in the carbine and rifle only (not in the cadet) was thickened and the comb lengthened 1-1/2" (to overall 10-1/2"); a compartment fitted in the buttstock of the carbine only for three-piece cleaning rod with trapdoor on buttplate. The 1873 date on lock was omitted on all three types.

A major change was in the breechblock which was made thicker and known as the "low arch" type. Other changes were made, but not incorporated simultaneously; hence, specimens encountered may vary and not include all newer improvements such as firing pin spring omitted; gas escape on receiver enlarged; rear of barrel rounded; hinge pin hole in breechblock elongated; breechblock and tang were color casehardened; extractor lug made higher; square corners on receiver rounded. To inject a note of confusion, the old high arch breech, but with M.1877 type markings as noted below, and even the old M.1873 sights are in evidence through serial 82000 approx.

The majority (all but the last 2,000 or so) of these 1877s still have the narrow receiver that is flush fitted with the barrel as on the 1873, and hence, the recess in the stock for the barrel and receiver does not have the two-step cut-away (except on the last 2,000 or so) and is a good quick visual check for identification.

Two types of 1877 rear sight: Stepped base or continuous curved base. Rifle and cadet sights marked R on side and graduated to 1,100 yards.

Inspector markings on all stocks are *ESA* in script over dates 1877 or 1878 within oval panel. Breechblock markings US/MODEL 1873 only (omitting the arrows and eaglehead). Serial number range 75000 to 115000. Barrel markings of eaglehead and large V and P.

Rifle production of approx. 20,000:
9A-369 Values—Good **$800** Fine **$1,800**
Carbine; approx. 4,500. 22" barrel with differences noted above; carbine half stock with single band; rear sight graduated to 1,200 yards and marked C; stacking swivel on barrel band. Quantity made 2,946:
9A-370 Values—Good **$3,000** Fine **$6,000**
Cadet Rifle; approx. 1,050. 29-1/2" barrel; about identical in contour to Model 1873 Cadet, but with transition features noted above. Still retain the short comb stock of the 1873. Quantity made 1,050:
9A-371 Values—Good **$1,000** Fine **$2,400**

Model 1879 U.S. "Trapdoor" Rifle, Carbine and Cadet Rifle

Model 1879 U.S. "Trapdoor" Rifle, Carbine and Cadet Rifle. (Not Illus.) Made c. 1879-1885. Total quantity all types approximately 160,000.

Barrel lengths and configuration about identical to the Model 1873. These are also a source of some confusion to the collector. There was no official designation Model 1879 and the breechblocks all bear the markings U.S./MODEL/1873. There are, however, basic changes in their design which constitute distinct and noticeable differences to the collector and consequently value differences.

Serial number ranges all types approximately 100000 to 280000.

Quickly distinguished from the earlier 1873s by the noticeably different, thicker, wider receiver. No longer flush with barrel, it is wider than the barrel and hence the inletting on stock is two-step at that point where receiver and barrel meet and fit into stock. Low arched breechblock.

Finished blue with color casehardening breechblock and tang. Markings ahead of lock with eagle and US/SPRINGFIELD.

Four forms of Model 1879 Buckhorn rear sight; ramrod has small button tip with cleaning patch slot below it. Sling swivels and stacking swivel. Two-piece trigger guard; straight grooved/corrugated trigger adopted in 1883; buttplate thickened in 1881. Carbine only has compartment in trapdoor at butt.

Barrel markings are eaglehead and large V and P. Inspector markings on stock in rectangular cartouche, with corners angled, and initials SWP with dates 1879 to 1885. Some observed with a star mark after the serial number. Its meaning is unknown and it should not affect value.

Rifle: Approximately 140,000 made:
9A-372 Values—Very Good **$500** Exc. **$1,250**
Carbine: Similar Model 1873 with changes noted above. Made without stacking swivel on barrel band. Approximately 15,000 made:
9A-373 Values—Good **$1,000** Fine **$2,500**
Cadet Rifle: Similar to Model 1873 Cadet with changes noted above, but still used the old style, short comb (9") stock without compartment in butt and narrower buttplate. Single stacking swivel only. Approximately 5,000 made:
9A-374 Values—Good **$600** Fine **$1,000**

Model 1880 U.S. "Trapdoor"

Model 1880 U.S. "Trapdoor" With Sliding Combination Ramrod-Bayonet. Made c. 1880. Total quantity 1,001.

Configuration similar to Model 1879. The Model 1880 differed in its unique sliding type triangular shaped combination ramrod-bayonet fitted in the stock forend. The breechblock marking is still US/MODEL 1873. This scarce model made for trial by government troops and was the first use of the sliding rod-bayonet on the trapdoor series; also has compartment in butt for tools.

Serial numbered in 154000 to 158000 range. Inspection mark

9A-375

and date on stock is 1881 on all specimens:

9A-375   Values—Very Good **$2,750**   Exc. **$4,500**

Model 1881 U.S. "Trapdoor" Shotgun

9A-376

Model 1881 U.S. "Trapdoor" Shotgun, a.k.a. "Forager." Made c. 1881-1885. Total quantity 1,376.

20 gauge; centerfire. 26" round, unmarked barrel with 3/16" high brass bead front sight. Forend fastens to barrel by screw on underside; no barrel band used.

Stock made from Civil War musket stock cut down to 28" (approximately) with the ramrod channel filled with wooden dowel and very slim forend. Action is Model 1879 type with receiver enlarged to take the 20 gauge brass shell; ejector stud not present in receiver and special extractor fitted. Casehardened breechblock with other parts blued.

Breechblock marked only *1881* in large slanting numerals. Lock is of first type 1873 with three-line markings including the 1873 date. Two-click tumbler. Carbine type trigger guard without provision for sling swivel. Seen with or without the grooved/corrugated trigger.

Inspector mark in rectangular cartouche with slanted corners SWP over dates 1881 to 1885. P proof in circle on underside of butt below trigger guard.

Serial numbered in its own series 1 to 1376.

Made for use by government hunters and scouts at western military outposts. They were issued at the rate of two per company. Last known issue was in 1906 in Alaska.

Caution should be exercised when acquiring this model. Quite a few other commercial alterations to shotguns were made from Springfield Trapdoors over the years utilizing surplus trapdoor parts. They appear in various gauges and calibers. Their value is minimal at best unless some unique historical association or background accompanies them:

9A-376   Values—Good **$1,500**   Fine **$3,000**

Model 1881 U.S. "Trapdoor" Marksman Rifle

9A-377

Model 1881 U.S. "Trapdoor" Marksman Rifle, a.k.a. Third Type Officer's Model. Made c. 1881. Total quantity 11 pieces.

Undoubtedly one of the rarest and most eagerly sought after of Springfield rifles with but four specimens recorded to date. Looks similar to the Model 1875 officer's model with chief distinguishing feature the checkered full pistol-grip half stock of fancy grade walnut with horn forend cap (Schnabel type); fastened by single barrel band. 28" round barrel. Hotchkiss style buttplate with trap for cleaning rod. Silver plate inset in pistol-grip (for presentation inscription). All parts engraved as on the Model 1875 Officer's Model.

Vernier tang peep sight inset in stock behind tang. Model 1879 Buckhorn rear barrel sight marked MR; removable globe front sight with spirit level. Not standard with set trigger. Hammer lightened. Usual Springfield markings with date 1881 at rear of receiver in place of serial number.

Only 11 of these were made to be given as second prize at national shooting matches.

There are commercially converted Trapdoor rifles with octagon barrels and checkered half stocks which are occasionally termed a Marksman Rifle. Such pieces have collector value and interest, but are not armory-made pieces and values are moderate at best and cannot be classified in the same category as this great rarity:

9A-377   Values—Very Good **$45,000**   Exc. **$75,000**

Model 1881 U.S. "Trapdoor" Long Range Rifle

9A-378

Model 1881 U.S. "Trapdoor" Long Range Rifle. Made c. 1881. Total quantity 151, plus 40 1879-1880.

Basically a Model 1879 (with same markings), but chambered for the 45-80-500 cartridge with 2.4" case. Six-groove rifling. Most easily distinguished feature is the shotgun style butt with Hotchkiss buttplate. Some specimens have uncheckered, walnut detachable pistol-grip.

24 of these were made with Sharps peep and globe sights (worth 20 percent premium), the balance have the Bull's Model 1879 Buckhorn sight with windage screw on right side. Barrels marked at top of breech HGR or HG in small letters and also bear usual V and P with eaglehead proof.

The Long Range falls in the serial range of 162000 to 162500.

Predecessors of this Long Range rifle were made: 20 in 1879 and 20 in 1880. They are found in serial range 110,000 to 132,000 but are not as easy to identify. Standard service type buttplate and some have the detachable plain pistol-grip. Most have the Bull's adjustable rear sight of earlier form. Key features are the six-groove rifling and the longer 2.4" chamber for the 45-80-500 cartridge. Some of these were made for the Army and militia Creedmoor teams. They are also encountered with tang peep sights.

9A-378   Values—Very Good **$9,500**   Exc. **$20,000**

Model 1882 Experimental U.S. "Trapdoor" Rifle

Model 1882 Experimental U.S. "Trapdoor" Rifle, a.k.a. Model 1882 "Short Rifle." Made c. 1882. Total quantity 52.

28" barrel with rear sight as on Model 1879, but marked 28 B on side of base; other markings as on M.1879. Full stock; two-band fastened. Iron mountings; blued finish with casehardened breechblock. Specimens appear in 197000 to 199000 range. Found in two basic variants:

First Type: Base of front sight serves as lug for socket type bayonet also. Has wraparound or bent type sling swivels to facilitate easy entry into cavalry rifle scabbard:

9A-379   Values—Very Good **$20,000**   Exc. **$40,000**

Second Type: Similar to above. Also with the wraparound/bent sling swivels, but fitted with sliding triangular combination ramrod-bayonet fitted in forend:

9A-380   Values—Very Good **$20,000**   Exc. **$37,500**

9A-380

Model 1884 U.S. "Trapdoor" Rifle, Carbine and Cadet Rifle

Model 1884 U.S. "Trapdoor" Rifle, Carbine and Cadet Rifle. (Not illus.) Made c. 1886-1891. Total quantity all types approximately 232,500.

Rifle barrel length 32-5/8". Blued finish with casehardened breechblock and tang. Socket bayonet standard.

Serial numbered in 300000 to 500000 range. Lock markings of eagle and US/SPRINGFIELD forward of hammer. Breechblock markings US/MODEL/ 1884. It is noted that in order to deplete old stock of "MODEL 1873" marked breech blocks, Springfield Armory used them on earliest production, through to early 1887, in assembly of this Model 1884, which makes for some confusion in the identification.

A feature of the Model 1884 is the Buffington rear sight; leaf style adjustable for windage and elevation, marked R on side. Other changes made over the years of production; bronze firing pin. Retains the standard two-piece trigger guard with grooved/corrugated trigger.

The cartridge for the Model 1884 had a 500 grain bullet rather than the 405 as previously employed.

Rifle: Total quantity rifles approximately 200,000:

9A-381   Values—Very Good **$500**   Exc. **$1,500**

Carbine: Similar to Model 1879 with 22" barrel; carbine half stock with single barrel band. Made c. 1886 to 1889.

Buffington rear sight has marking letter C on leaf; barrel band grooved on top to allow sight leaf to rest on it. Serial numbered in range 325000 to 480000. Markings as on rifle. Sling ring and bar on left side opposite lock. Approximate quantity made 20,000:

9A-382   Values—Good **$800**   Fine **$2,500**

Cadet Rifle: Similar to Model 1879 Cadet with 29-1/2" barrel. Major difference is the Buffington rear sight same as on rifle and new breech markings. Made c. 1888-1893. Two distinct variations encountered. Although many more of the second type were made, they are as scarce on the collectors' market as the first type and hence values about the same for either:

First Type: Two-piece carbine style trigger guard and stacking swivel only. 2,000 made in 1888; serial numbers in rifle range:

9A-383   Values—Good **$500**   Fine $**1,000**

Second Type: Have one-piece 1888 type trigger guards with stacking swivel and sling swivels. 10,500 made 1890-1893. Serial numbers in ranges to about 567000. These Cadets constitute the very last production of the famed trapdoors of all types:

9A-384   Values—Good **$450**   Fine **$900**

Model 1884 Experimental "Trapdoor" Rifle

Model 1884 Experimental "Trapdoor" Rifle with Ramrod-Bayonet. (*See illus. with Model 1888 also.*)

Standard 32-5/8" barrel. Standard markings and finishes. Made c. 1884. Total quantity 1,000.

Made with cover rigidly affixed over front sight and combination sliding round ramrod-bayonet in forend. They appear in the 320000 serial number range. Rear sight does not have the letter marking. Inspector's cartouche on stock bears 1885 or 1886 date. Compartment in butt for tools.

This is the predecessor of the commonly seen 1888 ramrod-bayonet model and looks very similar to it. The chief distinguishing feature is the latch that holds the rod bayonet; it is flat with short side "ears" that project outward, while the 1888 style is a wraparound or curved ears type latch. The round sliding rod-bayonet has four deep locking grooves which on this Model 1884 Experimental have a single square shoulder at each groove; the common 1888 has both shoulders of each groove

9A-385 Model 1888

9A-385 Model 1884 Experimental

with a more or less squared appearance. Breechblock still bears marking U.S. /Model/ 1873.

The production run was made for trial use and distribution was widespread. Survival rate is quite small. Very scarce:

9A-385   Values—Very Good **$6,000**   Exc. **$18,000**

Model 1886 Experimental "Trapdoor" Carbine

9A-386

Model 1886 Experimental U.S. "Trapdoor" Carbine, a.k.a. Experimental Model 1882 Third Type or Fourth Type; both are misnomers. Was officially termed in ordnance correspondence as "24" Barrel Carbine." Present-day collectors more accurately termed it the Model 1886 conforming to the year of manufacture. Total quantity 1,000.

24" barrel. Major distinguishing feature is the almost full stock with typical tapered, uncapped forend; fastened by single barrel band with bent or wraparound type upper sling swivel (to

facilitate sliding into saddle scabbard); lower sling swivel on butt. Sling ring and bar on left side. Has Buffington type Model 1884 rear sight marked XC on leaf. Most specimens appear in 325000 to 400000 range. Compartment in butt for cleaning rod (the sections of which are 1" longer than standard). A detailed study (*Man at Arms*, Nov. 6, 2000), indicates almost entire production issued (in varying quantities) to all cavalry regiments then on active service in the American West.

9A-386   Values—Very Good **$2,750**   Exc. **$5,750**

Model 1888 U.S. "Trapdoor" Rifle

9A-387 Model 1888 (standard issue)

Model 1888 U.S. "Trapdoor" Rifle, a.k.a. "Ramrod-Bayonet Model" and a.k.a. Model 1889. (*See illus. of Model 1884 Experimental also.*) Made c. 1889-1893. Total quantity approximately 65,000.

The 1888 differed from the Experimental Model 1884 with sliding ramrod-bayonet in having more effective cannelures on the rod bayonet (for more secure locking when in extended position); bayonet catch more secure (it has the wraparound appearance) and has *one-piece trigger guard;* grooved/corrugated trigger; trap and compartment in butt for tools.

9A-385 Model 1884 Experimental

Serial numbered in the approximate range 500000 to 565000.

The breechblock markings remained US/MODEL/1884 and are often a source of confusion to the new collector. The government actually called this in official correspondence the Model 1888.

The last of the U.S. Trapdoor single shot, big caliber, black powder longarms, the Model 1888 marked the end of an era and is a key-piece for any collector of Springfields:

9A-387   Values—Very Good **$750**   Exc. **$1,500**

Model 1888 Experimental U.S. "Trapdoor" Rifle

Model 1888 Experimental "Positive Cam" U.S. "Trapdoor" Rifle. (Not illus.) Made c. 1888. Total quantity 100.

Model 1884 type. Easily identified, but one must look very closely! Breechblock marked US MODEL 1888. The screw that retains the firing pin is on the side of the breech rather than underneath it, and although partially obscured by the thumb piece, it can be seen. The "Positive Cam" itself is part of the breech locking device; by a camming or wedging action a more firm lock was created for the breechblock, taking all loose play out of it. Although the camming parts can only be seen when disassembling the breechblock, the action is observable. When the breech latch thumb piece is raised, it moves inward or closer to the breech itself as it raises. Receiver also has an extra relief cut on right side for cam shaft clearance.

Inspector cartouche on stock dated 1888. Serial number of known specimens 400000 to 416000 range:

9A-388   Values—Very Good **$6,500**   Exc. **$15,000**

So-called Model 1890 U.S. "Trapdoor" Carbine

So-called Model 1890 U.S. "Trapdoor" Carbine. Alterations made by Springfield Armory c. 1890s.

There were no carbines manufactured after 1889 (the Model 1884s). The designation Model 1890 is purely a collector's term of convenience and represents Model 1873, Model 1877 and Model 1884 carbines that have a specific government alteration of front sight cover and special protector barrel band. The band has a high hump on top which acts as a buffer to protect the sight when it slips into the carbine boot. The front sight cover, a figure-8-shaped-device of sheet metal/spring steel, slides over the sight and is fastened to it with a pin that goes through the cover and the blade of the sight.

This alteration when found on a Model 1873 or Model 1877 carbine would affect the price downward making such models worth less than if in original unaltered state. The alteration when found on a Model 1884 carbine would not affect price.
9A-389

9A-389

Exp. 30 Caliber "Trapdoor" Springfields

Experimental 30 Caliber "Trapdoor" Springfields. (Not illus.) Made c. 1890-1894. Total quantity 15.

Rare arms with but a few known. They were used to develop the ammunition for the Krag rifle. Records indicate more barrels were made than complete rifles. Not serial numbered, but barrels had letter stamped on them, just forward of the receiver. They are seen both with and without the ramrod-bayonets. All actions had the positive cam locking latches (*see Model 1888 positive cam*) and receivers are wider than the 45 caliber models. Short Buffington type rear sight and special wooden hand guards on top of barrels:
9A-390   Values—Very Good **$25,000**   Exc. **$55,000**

Trapdoor Springfield Fencing Muskets

Trapdoor Springfield Fencing Muskets. Made at the Springfield Armory. Four basic types over various periods.

The Army did not wish to damage service issue rifles during bayonet practice. These specially designed pieces were produced to fill that requirement. Values shown are for muskets only without bayonets.

Type I: Model 1873 style. Quantity made 170 c. 1876-1877. Newly made with the same dimensions as the Model 1873 rifle, but without breech or lock. Rough finished stocks have barrels inlet only without receivers and with no inlet or aperture provided for lock. Unmarked. Used a socket type bayonet with a whalebone blade:
9A-391   Values—Very Good **$650**   Exc. **$950**

Type II: A Model 1884 type. Quantities unknown. Consists of standard 1884 rifle with hammer removed and tumbler and thumb piece/latch for breech ground flush with lockplate. Sling swivels and rear sight removed. Front sight blade ground flush. Socket type bayonet used with spring steel blade covered with leather and padded tip:
9A-392   Values—Very Good **$425**   Exc. **$650**

Type III: Model 1905 Fencing Musket. Quantity made 1,500 c. 1905-06. Similar to Type II, but shortened to 43-1/2", the same overall length as the Model 1903 rifle. Stud for socket bayonet on side near muzzle. Bayonet similar to Type II, but shorter:
9A-393   Values—Very Good **$475**   Exc. **$850**

9A-391
Type I

9A-394
Type IV

Type IV: Model 1906 Fencing Musket. Quantity made approximately 11-12,000 c. 1907-1916. Similar to Type III, but barrel filled with lead. Bayonet has two cross pieces with rings that slip over muzzle and fastened by two screws. Three style of bayonets (Model 1906, Model 1909, Model 1912) adaptable to this:

9A-394   Values—Very Good $325   Exc. $550

Metcalfe Experimental Ctg. Block Attachment

9A-395

Metcalfe Experimental Cartridge Block Attachment for Model 1870 and Model 1873 Rifles. Made at Springfield Armory 1873 and 1876.

Lt. Henry Metcalfe, an ordnance officer, designed a quick-loading attachment for the Trapdoor rifle. It consisted of a wood block containing eight or ten cartridges that attached to the right-hand side of the rifle just forward of the lockplate. Ammunition was issued in these blocks and they were carried on the waist belt by a special metal and leather carrier.

There were 100 Model 1870 rifles caliber 50-70 made in 1873 for the Metcalfe attachment and 1,008 caliber 45-70 Model 1873 rifles made in 1876 with this attachment.

The Model 1870 rifles were used in the 1873 trials, but no substantiation has been found to prove that the 1,008 Model 1873s manufactured in 1876 (estimated serial number ranges 60000 to 74000) were ever issued or used in any trial. It is believed most were taken apart at the armory, the standard parts used to make regular 1873s with the special Metcalfe parts either destroyed or disposed of at sale. Many of these Metcalfe parts appeared as surplus in large dealers' inventories many years ago; including stocks, lockplates and bars and were still available in quantity in the 1940s. Most of the Model 1873 rifles seen on the collectors' market with Metcalfe attachments have been assembled using these surplus parts. Values shown are for those later assembled guns. A specimen proved to be original would be very rare and worth at least two or three times values indicated here:

9A-395   Values—Very Good **$1,200**   Exc. **$2,500**

1883-1884 Lock Dated Trapdoor Rifles

1883-1884 Lock Dated Trapdoor Rifles. (Not illus.) Quite often seen on the collectors' market are U.S. Springfield marked trapdoor rifles caliber 45-70 with *lockplates* bearing dates 1883 and 1884. Such guns usually have five-groove rifling and are often seen with the Model 1868 type hammers (from the 50-70 model), Model 1873 stocks, receivers and breechblocks. Barrels, although marked with the usual V and P and eaglehead, but not always in the normal place. Many have casehardened barrel-bands and markings not normally observed on armory made trapdoors. It has been quite definitely ascertained that these guns are not the work of Springfield or any other government armory, but it is not known where or by whom they were assembled. The most plausible theory is that they were built from surplus parts by a number of well known arms and military goods dealers at the turn of the century. These pieces are valued mostly for their bore and exterior conditions for use by black powder shooters and are not categorized as an official martial arm:

9A-396   Values—Very Good **$300**   Exc. **$600**

Springfield Alteration of Spencer Carbine   *See Chapter IX-B: Secondary Military Longarms.*

Springfield Model 1870 Alteration of Sharps Carbines and Rifles
See Sharps Firearms, Chapter V-F.

Model 1870 Rolling Block U.S. Navy Rifle

Model 1870 Rolling Block U.S. Navy Rifle. Made by Springfield Armory on royalty agreement with the Remington Arms Company. Produced c. 1870-1871; total quantity 22,013. 50 caliber centerfire. 32-5/8" barrel (Springfield Model 1868

9A-397

Trapdoor Rifle type), secured by two barrel bands and screwed into frame. Rolling block action. Slide leaf style rear sight, folding rearward; blade front sight. Bayonet stud positioned on underside of barrel. Sling swivels on forward band and on front of trigger guard.

Iron mountings, finished bright; barrel blued; frame casehardened. Cleaning rod with knurled and slotted head, and shoulder to engage in rod cutout. Walnut two-piece stock.

Not serial numbered. Right frame marking: American eagle motif above USN/SPRINGFIELD/1870. Anchor motif stamped on top of barrel at breech. Inspector marks P/H.B.R. on left frame (an occasional specimen is seen without these latter markings).

The Navy Department ordered these arms in 1870, but of the total produced, the first 10,000 were rejected and subsequently sold commercially. They are quite scarce and generally bring a premium value. The Navy claimed the rear sight was too far back (it is just 1/2" in front of receiver, whereas accepted sight is 3-1/8" ahead of receiver); they usually do not bear anchor or

inspector markings. Sights on both styles are the same. They all went to France for issuance during Franco-Prussian War.

The Navy marked specimens may occasionally be encountered with bayonet stud ground flush and adapted to a socket bayonet. Believed altered by commercial surplus firm after the guns were officially disposed of. Such altered specimens are worth about 10 percent less. Value for U.S.N. marked and issued specimen:

9A-397   Values—Good **$800**   Fine **$2,000**

22RF Variant: Approximately 100 or less were converted by Winchester for the U.S. Navy in 1889 to 22 rimfire caliber for shipboard rifle practice. The 22 caliber barrel liner extends only two-thirds length of barrel; breech and extractor altered for the 22 cartridge. Additional barrel markings near rear sight No. (2-digit number) W.W.K. 1889. This conversion is the first known use of the 22 rimfire cartridge by a U.S. military organization:

9A-398   Values—Good **$2,500**   Fine **$5,500**

Model 1871 Rolling Block U.S. Army Rifle

9A-399

9A-401

Model 1871 Rolling Block U.S. Army Rifle and 1870 Trial Models. Made by Springfield Armory on royalty agreement with the Remington Arms Company. Produced c. 1871-1872; total quantity 10,001, plus experimental trial model rifle and carbine of 1870.

50 caliber centerfire. 36" barrel, secured by two barrel bands. Rolling block action. Sights, sling swivels and most other details same as on the Model 1870 Remington U.S. Navy rifle.

Iron mountings, finished bright; the frame color casehardened. Cleaning rod has double stop as on Model 1870 trapdoor. Walnut two piece stock.

Not serial numbered. Frame marking left side: MODEL 1871. Right side bears American eagle motif above U.S./SPRINGFIELD/1872. On tang REMINGTON'S PATENT. PAT. MAY 3d, NOV. 15th, 1864, APRIL 17th, 1868.

Known as the "locking action" as hammer went to half cock when breechblock was closed. Hammer spur and thumb piece

on breech are noticeably larger than on experimental Model 1870 below:

9A-399   Values—Very Good **$875**   Exc. **$1,800**

Model 1870 Trial or Experimental Springfield Rolling Block Army Rifle: Made 1870; total quantity 1,008. 50 caliber. 36" barrel. Similar to the Model 1871 above with major distinguishing feature markings on right frame of eagle motif over US/SPRINGFIELD/1870. No markings on left frame. Other distinguishing features are shorter hammer spur and thumb piece; single stop ramrod; does not have "locking action" of the Model 1871:

9A-400   Values—Good **$2,250**   Fine **$4,750**

Model 1870 Trial or Experimental Carbine: Total quantity 314. Identical action and markings to trial rifle with 22" barrel and carbine style forend noticeably different and longer (11-3/4") than Remington made forends. Long ring bar on left side with upper section affixed to receiver by screw that passes entirely through receiver from right side; lower ring bar affixed to short plate inletted into side of stock; very rare:

9A-401   Values—Good **$6,000**   Fine **$25,000**

Model 1871 Ward-Burton U.S. Rifle

Model 1871 Ward-Burton U.S. Rifle. Made by Springfield Armory, c. 1871; total quantity 1,011 rifles and 316 carbines.

50 caliber centerfire. Early bolt action mechanism; cartridge loaded directly into the opened breech; self cocking with closing

9A-402

9A-403

of bolt. Single shot. 32-5/8" barrel, secured by two barrel bands. Sliding leaf style rear sight, folding rearward; front sight doubled as lug for socket type bayonet. Sling swivels on forward barrel band and on front of trigger guard.

Iron mountings, finished in the white. Model 1868 trapdoor type ramrod with single stop. Walnut stock. Receiver blackened (oil quenched casehardened) and bolt bright.

Not serial numbered. Top of bolt marked: WARD BURTON PATENT DEC. 20, 1859-FEB. 21, 1871. Left side of breech marked

with American eagle motif, and US/SPRINGFIELD 1871.

One of the earliest of bolt action military arms put into service by the U.S. government, the Ward-Burton was basically a trial piece. It was not enthusiastically received by troops, and its limited production makes it a scarce piece for the collector:

9A-402 Values—Very Good **$1,250** Exc. **$3,000**

Carbine: Identical but 22" barrel, single barrel band fastening the short carbine stock; no provision for cleaning rod:

9A-403 Values—Good **$3,000** Fine **$5,500**

Model 1875 Lee Vertical Action Rifle

9A-404

Model 1875 Lee Vertical Action Rifle. Made by Springfield Armory c. 1875. Total quantity 143.

45-70 caliber. Martini type dropping block action with unique, centrally mounted hammer with tall top spur. To open breech (or eject spent case from chamber) the hammer must be struck a sharp blow from behind with the heel of the hand. The insertion of a round in the chamber allows the breech to automatically close. Hammer cocked in conventional manner for firing.

32-5/8" barrel fastened by two barrel bands. Iron mountings. All blued finish. Model 1873 trapdoor type rear sight. Front sight doubles as lug for socket type bayonet. Ramrod Model 1873 type

with large slotted, knurled head, with double stop. Stacking and sling swivels on upper band; sling swivel on trigger guard. Walnut stock.

Serial numbered 1 through 143 on internal parts. Upper tang marked U.S./PAT. MAR. 16, 1875. No barrel proof marks. Inspector marks ESA in oval on stock.

Invented by James P. Lee and made under his supervision at Springfield. The small amount of money appropriated for its manufacture ran out after only 143 were made. *A rare martial rifle:*

9A-404 Values—Very Good **$2,750** Exc. **$6,500**

Models 1878 and 1879 U.S. Army and Navy Hotchkiss Rifles and Carbines

See Chapter V, Winchester Firearms.

1882 U.S. Magazine Rifle, Chaffee-Reese

9A-405

Model 1882 U.S. Magazine Rifle, Chaffee-Reese. Made by the Springfield Armory, c. 1884; total quantity 753.

45-70 centerfire cartridge. Bolt action repeater, with cartridges fed through the butt. 27-7/8" barrel, secured by two barrel bands.

Iron mountings, blued finish. Sliding leaf style rear sight; front sight doubles as lug for socket bayonet. Button tip cleaning rod having two shoulder stops. Stacking swivel and sling swivel on upper barrel band; lower sling swivel on trigger guard. Walnut stock.

Not serial numbered. Left side of breech marked: US SPRINGFIELD, 1884. Barrel V, P, and eaglehead proof.

The cartridge feed mechanism does not have a spring and follower (such as the Spencer) and is often found with a section of the cartridge feed (2 movable racks and spring elevator) lacking. Value about 10 percent less. The internal feed mechanism, not visible, is usually intact.

Invented by General J. N. Reese and R. S. Chaffee, the rifle was approved for U.S. government service in 1882 by an Ordnance Board responsible for selecting a magazine repeater:

9A-405 Values—Good **$950** Fine **$2,750**

THE U.S. KRAG-JORGENSEN BOLT ACTION MAGAZINE RIFLES, MODELS 1892 THROUGH 1899

The first small caliber, smokeless powder, repeating rifle adopted by the U.S. government, the Krag-Jorgensen, was nearly identical to the standard bolt action military rifle of Denmark. Due mainly to the intricacies of the chemical make-up of smokeless powder, the U.S. was slow in adopting a rifle firing that type of ammunition. An advantage of the Krag (as it is more commonly known) was a cut-off which allowed for firing either single shot or as a magazine-fed repeater.

There are many features of Krags common to all models. These are listed here to avoid repetition with the following individual descriptions. Variances and distinguishing features between models are described to simplify identification.

All Krags are 30-40 caliber centerfire; all were manufactured at the Springfield Armory. They are bolt action operated; magazines hold five rounds of ammunition and are loaded from the right side through a large hinged loading gate. Blade type front sights set in a high stud near the muzzle are used on all models.

Unless otherwise noted, all rifles have sling swivels affixed to the lower barrel band and at the underside of the butt; stacking swivels are affixed to the top band.

Stocks of all models are walnut, oil finished, with wooden hand guards/barrel covers fitted from receiver to the lower band. There is marked variation in the hand guards; often they are a major feature of identification and differences will be noted.

Finishes are consistent throughout. All metal parts are blued with the receivers casehardened and having a dark grayish-mottled finish rather than brilliant colors. In the casehardening process, the receivers were quenched in oil which left a dark, almost black, coloration when in the mint state; whereas in the water quenching method, casehardening colors were brilliant.

A number of rear sight and hand guard changes as well as other lesser variations were made to Krags over the years of their issuance and use. It is quite rare to find any Krag in the exact original issued condition with regard to both sights and hand guards. The guns described here are the way in which they left the armory after manufacture. As the great majority of specimens found on the collectors' market were updated with sights and hand guards, it will be found, for most practical purposes, that values will not be affected to any great degree except to the most advanced Krag specialist. This is especially evident with these minor changes that are easily rectified and

restored to their original state. With the early and rare Krags that were altered to later modifications, values do change drastically especially as it is not possible to rectify the modifications. These features are discussed with the individual models.

The collector will note on the market many Krags not conforming to standard models described here. He is cautioned to look before he leaps! Quite a few may be seen with varied barrel lengths and other alterations which on first appearance may be taken as rare variations. A tremendous quantity of Krags were sold as surplus by the U.S. government in the early 1900s and post-World War I era and a few firms devoted their entire business activities to the alteration of Krags for mail order sales to the public, commencing in the 1920s. Some Krags were sporterized; that is, stocks cut down with all military parts stripped off to make them as light as possible. These specimens are easily spotted by even the neophyte collector and are valued solely as a mutilated military piece suitable for sporting purposes. Other Krags, however, still retain their military look, but have had modifications making them shorter and lighter in weight lending them an apparent "variant" appearance. Close inspection of the workmanship normally will show that it is distinctly non-armory in quality and will usually suffice to place the gun in the non-martial collectors' category. Large quantities of rifles were also altered to carbines by these military goods dealers and can be found in many variations. It is therefore quite important that such models be inspected carefully before acquisition, as they too are non-martial collectors' items and valued merely for their sporting use and condition.

A group of Krags made for the director of Civilian Marksmanship Sales to National Rifle Association members by the Benicia Arsenal in the 1920s possesses semi-martial collectibility. They are shortened Model 1898 rifles with Model 1899 carbine stocks and Model 1903 front sights. Considered interesting variations, their values would generally be considerably less than the true Model 1899 carbines.

The passage of time and accumulation of over a century of age have added to the Krag's historical importance. Their increasing popularity with American collectors is obvious by the numerous, well-researched, recent articles in the antique arms press and issuance of significant reference works specifically about these Krags.

Model 1892 Krag Bolt Action Rifle

Model 1892 Krag Bolt Action Rifle. Made c. 1894-1896. Total quantity 24,562.

30" barrel. Serial numbered 1 through 24562. Receiver marked on left side U.S. (year of manufacture 1894, 1895 or 1896) SPRINGFIELD ARMORY and serial number.

Many changes and improvements were made to the Model 1892 during its period of manufacture. Approximately the first 9,000 had serial numbers stamped on the gate, sideplate, carrier and follower. The great percentage of this model were armory converted to the Model 1896 in the years 1896 through 1902.
First Type: Solid wide upper barrel band and one-piece iron cleaning rod under barrel (fitted through forend of stock). Approximately 1,500 made (serial number range 1 to 1500). Inspectors markings on stock SWP/1894 within a rectangle having angled corners. Flat muzzle (uncrowned); extractor does not have hold-open pin; receiver not notched for hold-open pin. No compartment in butt, straight toe; flat buttplate without hinged door. Wooden hand guard fits only up to receiver and does not

cover it. Step type rear sight base. Receiver dated 1894 only. When first made the iron cleaning rods all had brass tips; just 300 of these were issued with that brass tip; the remaining unissued ones in

9A-406
(First Type)

the armory had brass tips removed and steel rods installed as replacements. Brass tips will bring an added premium.

Value in unaltered condition as described above, complete with cleaning rod:

9A-406   Values—Good **$5,500**   Fine **$22,500**

Second Type: About identical to above, but has double strap upper band (special style cut for the cleaning rod and not the same as on the Model 1896). Serial range 1500 to 24500. The date 1894 or 1895 will appear with the inspector markings on stock as well as on receiver. Still retains iron cleaning rod:

9A-407   Values—Good **$2,750**   Fine **$7,000**

Altered To Model 1896 Style: Nearly the entire production of Model 1892s were altered to 1896 style, but they retain their original 1894, 1895, 1896 receiver markings. Cleaning rod removed and slot filled with wood plug. Upper band replaced (has no hole or provision for cleaning rod). Butt has compartment for cleaning rod; trap-door in buttplate; curved toe. Has longer hand guard over barrel which covers the receiver; 1896 style sight; crowned muzzle; safety retained by

9A-407
(Second Type)

spring and plunger; hold-open pin on extractor and receiver notched for same. Value for altered Type I or II the same:

9A-408   Values—Good **$450**   Fine **$950**

Model 1892 Carbine: Although listed in some reference works, this gun never progressed beyond the prototype stage. Just two samples were built in 1894.

Model 1896 Krag Rifle

9A-409

Model 1896 Krag Rifle. Made c. 1896-1898. Total quantity approximately 62,000.

30" barrel. Model 1896 differed from Model 1892 in following features: Wood hand guard longer extending over the receiver; trap-door in butt which contained jointed cleaning rod; upper barrel band two-strap type; toe of butt has rounded contour; rear sight allows for elevation adjustment with leaf in down position and base has continuous curve instead of three-step contour. Receiver marking U.S. MODEL 1896 and SPRINGFIELD ARMORY

with serial number. Stock inspector initials bearing dates 1896, 1897, 1898.

Serial number range approximately 35000 to 110000. On early production the word MODEL does not appear before the date 1896. Many of the Model 1896 had rear sights and hand guards changed to later styles either by company armorers in the field or at the armory when repaired or rebuilt. When found altered, prices usually decrease by approximately 10 percent to 20 percent, depending on the alteration:

9A-409   Values—Very Good **$700**   Exc. **$1,400**

Model 1896 Krag Carbine

9A-410

Model 1896 Krag Carbine. Made c. 1896-1898. Total quantity 19,133. It was the Model 1896 Krag carbine that was carried by Teddy Roosevelt's 'Rough Riders' First U.S. Volunteer Cavalry, at the charge up San Juan Hill in the Cuban campaign in 1898.

22" barrel secured by single barrel band which has a thick, high hump at its top which acts as a guard for the rear sight. Sling ring mount on left side of stock opposite bolt. Compartment in butt for cleaning rod; trap-door in buttplate. Carbine type half stock with 7" hand guard covering receiver also. Flat buttplate with rounded toe.

Serial numbered approximately 35000 to 90000 range. Markings same as rifle. The rear sight, graduated for distance differently than the rifle, is also marked "C" to denote "carbine."

Collector should note that some specimens of the Model 1896 carbine were altered to conform to later changes found in the Models 1898 and 1899, however, breech markings continued to denote the Model 1896 year. Prices for alterations vary downward approximately 10 percent to 20 percent, depending on type of work performed:

9A-410   Values—Good **$1,000**   Fine **$2,750**

Variant Carbine: Known to collectors as the Model 1895 carbine and almost identical to above except dated 1895 and 1896 on the receiver without the word MODEL Made prior to the official adoption of the "Model 1896." Serial range 25000 to 35000. Thumb safety smaller; trap in butt not cut for oiler; no fillet at junction of body and heel of extractor (rounded in the Model 1896 and square shaped in this early variant):

9A-411   Values—Good **$1,100**   Fine **$2,750**

Model 1896 Krag Cadet Rifle

Model 1896 Krag Cadet Rifle. (Not illus.) Made c. 1896. Total quantity 404.

Barrel length and weight same as Model 1896 rifle; not scaled down in size. Distinguished by its one-piece cleaning rod under the barrel and utilizing the 1896 double strap upper band. Curved toe buttplate, but without trap at butt; made without sling swivels; lower band retained by spring.

These represent the last special rifles made for West Point cadet use. They were in service only until 1898 when replaced by the standard Model 1898. Survival rate of original specimens very small as most were altered to the Model 1896 standard rifles when returned to the armory in 1898. *Very rare:*

9A-412   Values—Good **$15,000**   Fine **$35,000**

Model 1898 Krag Rifle

Model 1898 Krag Rifle. Made c. 1898-1903. Total quantity 330,000.

30" barrel. Differed from the Model 1896 as follows: Seat of bolt handle flush with breech; sights; receiver markings U.S./MODEL 1898 and SPRINGFIELD ARMORY with serial number.

Found with four different models of rear sights and three styles of hand guards. In 1905 when all U.S. Army issued Krags were recalled and before being put into storage, all rear sights were changed to Model 1901 or Model 1902 types.

The last of the Krags, the Model 1898 represents the largest quantities produced. Serial range 110000 to 480000 (Note: Below

9A-413

serial number 152670 is considered "antique" under Federal Firearms law):

9A-413   Values—Very Good **$650**   Exc. **$1,400**

Model 1898 Krag Carbine

Model 1898 Krag Carbine. (Not illus.) Made c. 1898. Total quantity 5,000.

22" barrel. Identical to the Model 1896 carbine except with the Model 1898 action and markings identical to the 1898 rifle. Has ring bar and ring on left side, the last U.S. carbine equipped with that accessory. Serial range is mixed in with rifle serial numbers 125000 to 135000.

Most sought after of all Krag carbines. The Model 1898's popularity with collectors is mainly attributable to its limited production total and low survival rate in original form. Most were altered to conform to the Model 1899 and hence a number of other published sources show modified 1898 carbines, thus adding confusion to its identification.

Inspector markings in stock of original unaltered 1898 carbines will bear only 1898 dates. Those specimens identical in other respects to the Model 1899 carbine described herein, but with 1898 dated receivers are altered Model 1898 carbines and values should be the same as for the Model 1899. In original unaltered condition:

9A-414   Values—Good **$1,000**   Fine **$2,500**

Model 1898 Krag With 26" Barrel

Model 1898 Krag With 26" Barrel. (Not illus.) Made c. 1902. Total quantity 100.

In an attempt to make a single arm to satisfy both infantry and cavalry, a small lot of Krags with special 26" barrel lengths were made and subsequently issued to the Plattsburgh Barracks, New York, for trial. Standard 1898 actions and markings. Other identifying features: Model 1901 type rear sight, but specially manufactured for this group of rifles with a special leaf graduation to 2,100 yards; stock dated 1902 and does not have the lightening channel cut in the barrel bed of the stock (can only be seen when barrel disassembled). Serial number range 387000 to 389000. A standard Krag bayonet will not fit as the diameter of the muzzle is too large:

9A-415   Values—Very Good **$6,500**   Exc. **$15,000**

Parkhurst Clip Loading Attachment

Parkhurst Clip Loading Attachment on Krag Model 1898 Rifle and Model 1899 Carbine. Alteration by Springfield Armory c. 1901 in an attempt to try to equal the rate of fire of the Mauser rifle. Total quantity 200 altered (100 rifles, 100 carbines). 2,000 special clips also manufactured.

Parkhurst attachment is a steel block that is fitted into the right side of the receiver just behind the magazine cover. It is machined with a T-shaped slot into which the clip fits and has internal parts that strip clip when used. A guide lip is riveted inside the magazine well. Found in serial number range 288000 to 290000. Most of the guns to which this attachment was affixed were stripped for parts and receivers destroyed; hence, surviving specimens very rare. Most specimens viewed have been assembled from parts and are worth considerably less than the original valued here:

9A-416   Values—Good **$6,500**   Fine **$16,000**

9A-416

Model 1898 Krag Gallery Practice Rifle

Model 1898 Krag Gallery Practice Rifle. (Not illus.) 22 rimfire. Made c. 1906-1907. Total quantity 841.

30" barrels chambered for 22 rimfire cartridge. Externally identical to Model 1898 rifle. Receivers have standard Model 1898 markings with the addition of CAL. 22 in two lines to the right of the serial number.

Chambers have auxiliary extractor system that is pulled out by normal bolt extractor and snaps back when bolt is fully opened. Bore is offset (downward) at breech in order for the standard centerfire pin of the bolt to strike the rim of the small cartridge; bore is centered at muzzle. Receiver cut-away at right side to facilitate loading.

These Gallery Practice Models left the armory in two styles: (A) As merely barreled actions to be installed by company armorers in guns already in the field; (B) As complete armory assembled rifles. These latter are identifiable by the inspector markings on the right side of stock consisting of four large interwoven fancy script initials without a date. These tend to bring approximately 20 percent to 25 percent higher values than the first type which is valued here:

9A-417   Values—Very Good **$1,250**   Exc. **$4,500**

Pope Barreled Krag Variant: A 22 rimfire variant of the Krag is occasionally observed with no CAL. 22 receiver markings, no auxiliary extractor and the bore offset at the top of the breech. The markings STEVENS-POPE may appear at the top of the barrel forward of the hand guard. These arms are not government altered or purchased. They are strictly commercial products. The barrels only were sold by the Stevens Arms Company c. 1905 (and so advertised in their catalogs) when Harry Pope worked for them. A number of sales were made to National Guard shooting teams (New Jersey is known to have purchased some) and to private individuals who owned Krags. These pieces are certainly good collectors' items. The Stevens-Pope marked barrels tend to have a strong demand, but either type is usually priced in the same range as the 22 rimfire Krag Gallery Practice rifle.

9A-418

Model 1899 Krag Carbine

9A-419

Model 1899 Krag Carbine. Made c. 1899-1902. Total quantity approximately 36,000.

The Model 1899 was the last carbine of the Krag series and type made in greatest quantity. 22" barrel. Action identical to Model 1898 with exception of changed marking MODEL 1899. Differences from 1898: Stock 2" longer and barrel band moved forward 2". Sling ring bar omitted. When the Model 1896 or Model 1901 sights are used, the wooden hand guard has a large hump just ahead of the sight that serves to protect. When the Model 1898 or Model 1902 sight used, the hand guard is flat without hump. All rear sights have the letter C marked on them. Barrel band retained by band spring. The small, knurled straight cocking knob (as shown in illustration here) is found on some Model 1899 carbines only. This variant will not affect value:

9A-419   Values—Very Good **$750**   Exc. **$1,750**

1899 Philippine Constabulary Krag Carbine

9A-420

Model 1899 Philippine Constabulary Krag Carbine. Termed in official ordnance correspondence of the era the "M1899 carbine altered for knife bayonet." Total altered approximately 8,000 at the Manila Ordnance Depot, circa 1906, and the Springfield Armory and Rock Island Arsenal to 1916. Exact quantities of each unknown. Benicia Arsenal (previously reported) not believed to have performed any alteration to this model.

This specially designed rifle, which resembles a miniaturized *full stock* rifle, is assembled with the Model 1899 carbine action and a 22-inch barrel placed on a Model 1898 rifle stock, which has been shortened 8 inches (for a full length appearance) with wood filled in where it had been inletted and grooved. The forend and barrel band are also modified. The muzzle of barrel is turned down to accept the Model 1905 knife bayonet.

Springfield Armory-made pieces (will bring premium value) are identifiable by the three inspector initials (usually J.F.C.) in a rectangle on the left side of the stock; the same inspector markings that were used on Model 1903s of the period.

Rock Island Arsenal-made pieces were not specifically identified and original stock inspector markings were left intact.

The collector should exercise care in the acquisition of this model as many similar pieces were made in the 1920s-1930s by various mail order firms using surplus Krag parts. They usually can be identified by their crude workmanship, especially around the upper band area. They often used Model 1898 rifles with shortened barrels and non-issue front sights. Such pieces are not classed as martial collectors' items. The value for an authentic Constabulary Model:

9A-420   Values—Good **$600**   Fine **$1,750**

MODEL 1903 SPRINGFIELD RIFLES

The Model 1903 Springfield was developed after the German Mauser bolt action military rifle and evolved as the successor to the Krag series. Improvements of the "'03" (as it is more familiarly known) over its predecessors were in higher muzzle velocity (a superior rimless cartridge was adopted), more efficient mechanism, and a better magazine (clip fed). This famed arm was the standard U.S. rifle of World War I and was not succeeded until c. 1936, by the M1 Garand.

Except for the very earliest '03s (in caliber 30-03), all models are in caliber 30-06.

Features common to all '03s are listed here to avoid repetition while variations and distinguishing features between each model are described with the individual listings, to aid and simplify identification.

All '03s have oil finished, walnut stocks bearing inspectors' marks (cartouche) of many varieties, found on the left side opposite the bolt handle. All barrels are 24" as standard on 30-06 caliber models; exceptions are on the 30-03 caliber (very early models) and the special heavy barrel target models. Finishes vary and are so noted.

'03 Springfields, unlike Krags, have very few sight changes in service issued pieces. There are the early sights graduated for 30-03 ammunition and those for the 30-06 on all other pieces, excepting two varieties of Lyman sights used for the Model 1922 and Model 1922M1.

Listed herein are only arsenal made rifles as they left the armory *when newly made*. Modifications, rebuilds, etc. are only shown where of collector importance. There were many rebuilt 1903 Springfields—many of them arsenal re-worked after World War I and during and after World War II. Some were done in very large quantities. On such weapons barrel dates usually do not match serial number ranges; parts are mixed and refinishing is common. Values for such items are mostly for their shootability or sporterizing potential and are considerably less than for the "as issued" specimens. An arbitrary cut-off point was used in the following listings, including all models prior to World War II. The exclusion of '03s of later date was not intended to reflect on their lack of collectibility.

During World War II a Philadelphia firm made up a sizable mixed batch of rebuilt 1903 Springfields for drill-guns or so-called "blank guns." They were intended strictly for firing salutes with blank cartridges. Although standard service rounds apparently may be chambered, these rifles were not intended for firing and may be dangerous if so used. Some specimens have zinc cast parts—often observed in the sight leafs, the stacking and sling swivels, the buttplates and floor plates. Some barrels are unmarked; some rifles may bear early dated barrels on later numbered receivers; some barrels are S marked. All these "blank guns" were assembled using surplus barrels and parts, and what the maker was not able to find as surplus, he made by casting. Some arms are found with Model 1917 Enfield front bands and reinforcement bolts forward of the magazine well.

1903 Springfields, from their conception until 1941, were manufactured only by the U.S. arsenals at Springfield and Rock Island, Illinois. Manufacture was almost continuous at Springfield through-out the entire era while at Rock Island production was intermittent and ceased in 1918 with none made complete after that date. Springfield manufactured approximately three times as many '03s as Rock Island. Springfield production figures for 30 caliber '03 rifles of all types was 1,028,634, while Rock Island's total of assembled rifles was 346,779. Although the latter type is scarcer quantity-wise, specimens usually fetch less money than Springfield marked rifles due to the "magic" or "glamour" of the Springfield name in American arms history. The production of each arsenal's arms bore individual serial number ranges; Springfield Armory serials run from 1 to 1592000+; Rock Island's from 1 through 415000+ with many of the very high numbered receivers made as replacement parts rather than as completely assembled guns.

Serial number ranges above 800000 for Springfield arms (and 285506 for Rock Island arms) are the more desirable types for those acquiring '03s for shooting purposes. Under those serial ranges the receivers/actions are of questionable strength because of a single heat treating process causing some brittleness on many. It is not known which receivers fall in that category (exact numbers not recorded other than the fact that they fall below those serial ranges). In 1927 all '03s of Springfield manufacture under serial number 800000 and all Rock Island '03s under 285506 were taken out of service.

Although there are two distinct calibers in the 1903 Springfield (30-03 and 30-06), and several variations and distinct model changes, all receivers on all models (except for the 22 caliber types) bear identical five-line markings: U.S./SPRINGFIELD/ARMORY/MODEL 1903/(serial number). Rock Island pieces substitute its name for SPRINGFIELD. The only variance in markings appears in the style of letters (die stamps) up to approximately the 285000 serial number range. Small block letters were used for the markings with fancy script-like serial numbered digits. After the 285000 range, block letters are larger and the serial numbers are deeper stamped in block style.

During the year 1906, and running through their entire production into the 1940s, all barrels bore standard three-line markings near the muzzle behind the sight: S.A. (or R.I.A.) over the small flaming bomb device of the Ordnance Department, over the numerical designation for month and year of manufacture (i.e., 7-21 for July, 1921).

Stocks on all issued '03s until 1929 were the so-called "S" style; that is, with straight grip and grasping grooves along sides.

All 1903 Springfield rifles are five-shot.

Many lesser variations are found on the '03s (Rock Island Arsenal changes follow those of Springfield), some of them quite important to collectors. The reader is referred to the widely respected, classic work on the subject, *The '03 Springfields*, by Clark S. Campbell (*q.v.*).

Model 1903 Rod-Bayonet Rifle

Model 1903 Rod-Bayonet Rifle. Made at Springfield Armory, c. November, 1903, to January, 1905. Total quantity approximately 74,500 (with serial numbers commencing at No. 1). Production at Rock Island Arsenal c. May, 1904, to January, 1905, with total

9A-421

The rod-bayonet was carried under the barrel in a hole in the forend. Nose cap had plunger type latch for rod-bayonet in closed and open positions. Front sight blade type was set in a band type ramp. Rear sight was the Model 1902 Krag type mounted on a band type base. One-piece wooden hand guard ran from upper band to rear sight base. Narrow upper barrel band about the same width as lower band.

Survival rate of this model is extremely small; most were altered to accept the later Model 1905 knife-bayonet at which time Model 1905 type sights also installed.

Barrel is unmarked behind the front sight (later barrels after 1905 all marked). Barrel length 24.206"; stock length 41-3/8"; hand guard 18-1/4". Overall length 43-1/2". Bolt body bright while the bolt handle is blued. Extractor purple; receiver casehardened and quenched in oil, thus giving it a dark, mottled appearance. Barrel and mountings blued.

The buyer is cautioned to be very wary when acquiring this model as most were altered from their original condition. Attempts have been made in present day to restore most altered specimens as close as possible to original and such pieces are certainly good collectors' items, but their values are drastically different from an original specimen.

Original unaltered specimen:

9A-421	Values—Good **$14,000**	Fine **$30,000**	

Altered to Model 1905, but still in 30-03 caliber:

9A-422	Values—Good **$5,500**	Fine **$20,000**	

Altered to Model 1905 and in 30-06 caliber:

9A-423	Values—Good **$1,200**	Fine **$4,000**	

Restored to Rod-Bayonet, original condition:

9A-424	Values—Good **$2,500**	Fine **$6,500**	

estimated production approximately 18,000 rifles. There is, however, some confusion as to whether Rock Island actually made entire rifles or merely parts for 18,000 rifles with rod-bayonets, but which were assembled later as original 1905 or 1906 modifications. The buyer is cautioned to be especially wary on Rock Island pieces as many specimens appear to have been later collector assemblies rather than arsenal work.

Production of the Model 1903 Rod-Bayonet was halted under orders of President Theodore Roosevelt on January 4, 1905. He took an immediate dislike to the rod-bayonet when first observing the rifle, requesting that the more usable and utilitarian knife-bayonet be substituted.

Caliber for this early '03 was 30-03; using a 220-grain round nose bullet similar to that used in the Krag.

In 1904 the safety was changed from a Mauser type to the double shoulder type with spring and plunger.

Model 1903 Rifle With 1905 Modification

Model 1903 Rifle With 1905 Modification (new made and not an alteration of the Rod-Bayonet). (Not illus.) Made at Springfield, April, 1905, to November, 1906. Caliber 30-03. Barrel length 24.206". Stock length 40-1/4". Hand guard length 15-1/8" from sight base to upper band; overall length 43-1/2". A total of about 269,000 of these newly made pieces and altered guns from Rod-Bayonet Models were produced. Generally found below 270000 serial number range.

Differences in the 1905 modified rifles: ramrod-bayonet and latch for same were completely omitted; rear and front sight changed to Model 1905 type (with movable stud); double strap front band with bayonet stud and stacking swivel, swell added to the lower end of the shorter hand guard to protect rear sight. The Model 1905 knife-bayonet designed for this rifle.

Altered Rod-Bayonet rifles can be told from newly made pieces by the wood plug in the front end of stock (concealing the ramrod channel); serial numbers are below 74500; no barrel marking behind the front sight. New made barrels marked S.A. over flaming bomb ordnance insignia over 05 (1905).

Very few, if any, of these rifles were ever issued. An original specimen of the Model 1903 with 1905 alteration still in 30-03 caliber is very rare. Most were altered to 30-06. Rear sights of the 1905 modification are graduated to 2,400 yards and have a silver line above and below the peep sight aperture.

Original unaltered 30-03 as made in 1905:

9A-425	Values—Good **$5,000**	Fine **$20,000**	

Altered to 30-06 caliber:

9A-426	Values—Good **$950**	Fine **$3,500**	

Model 1903 Rifle Caliber 30-06 Altered From Model 1905

Model 1903 Rifle Caliber 30-06 Altered From Model 1905 and Rod-Bayonet Types. (Not illus.)

In 1904 the Germans developed a lightweight, pointed bullet for the 8mm Mauser rifle (the "Spitzer") which outperformed the U.S. 220-grain bullet so much that the Ordnance Department decided to develop a lighter, pointed bullet for the 1903 rifle which would be competitive with the Mauser. The new pointed bullet required shortening of the neck of the cartridge case by .070"; thus leaving the chamber of the early '03 rifles too long. This was corrected by setting the barrel back into the receiver .200" (or two threads); thus the barrel was 24.006" in length when altered. The new cartridge was adopted in October, 1906, and officially named the "Cartridge, Ball, Caliber 30, Model of 1906" or as is commonly known, the 30-06.

After adoption of this new cartridge, it was necessary to

modify all previously produced Model 1903 rifles to chamber the new round. From November, 1906, to early 1909 all '03 rifles, both the new ones in storage at the armory and those issued in the field, were altered. Only a very few rifles were overlooked, accounting for the collector rarity of the early Rod-Bayonets and the 1905 modifications.

In altering the Model 1905 types, the barrels were shortened .200" at breech and rechambered; rear sight base moved forward .200" and a new sight leaf, graduated to 2,700 yards was added. The hand guard and front end of stock both shortened .200" and front barrel band moved back this same amount. Simplest way to identify a Model 1905 altered rifle is to remove upper barrel band; if a plugged hole appears about 1/4" forward of the present upper band screw hole, it indicates the upper band was moved back .200" and thus the stock is a modified 1905 type.

Rod-Bayonet type 1903s that were returned for modification from the field did not receive the Model 1905 type alteration, but were altered directly to caliber 30-06 and also: Rod-Bayonet parts removed; front of stock plugged with wood and shortened to the '06 length and the 1905 type upper double barrel band fitted; a new '06 length hand guard installed; 2,700-yard 1905 type rear sight added; barrel set back .200" and rechambered; 1905 type front sight added. If the bore was pitted or worn, a new barrel of current manufacture was installed. Guns modified after February, 1908, had rear stock bolts to prevent splitting.

Dimensions of 30-06 caliber Model 1903 rifle are: Overall length 43-1/4"; stock length 40"; hand guard length from sight base to upper band 15-15/16"; barrel length 24.006". All guns, whether altered or newly made, conformed to these dimensions:

9A-427   Values—Good **$1,100**   Fine **$4,000**

Model 1903 Rifle Caliber 30-06 (c. 1907-10)

Model 1903 Rifle Caliber 30-06 as Manufactured From 1907 to 1910. (Not illus.) Approximate quantity 131,000. Also made during same period by Rock Island.

Serial number range approximately 269000 to 400000. Hand guard does not have spring clips or clearance cut in the swell ahead of sight (added in 1910). Windage knob approximately 7/16" diameter; stock has square corner alongside receiver ring on right side; trigger smooth and pointed; buttplate smooth; bolt handle not bent back; metal blued. Receiver casehardened and oil quenched giving a black or dark mottled appearance.

Made without stock bolts, with a single stock bolt added to specimens made after 1908 to prevent splitting. Barrel dates 1906 through 1909.

The survival rate of rifles of this era, in original condition as they left the armory, is quite small. Most were rebuilt by government arsenals during and after World War I and had Parkerized refinishes and updated. Such specimens worth considerably less than values reflected here:

9A-428   Values—Very Good **$1,250**   Exc. **$4,500**

Model 1903 Caliber 30-06 (c. 1910-1917)

Model 1903 Caliber 30-06 As Manufactured c. 1910 to 1917. (Not illus.) Approximate quantity manufactured 250,000. Serial range between approximately 385000 and 635000. Also made by Rock Island until November, 1913.

Stocks have a taper rather than square corner on right side by receiver ring; trigger serrated and thicker; buttplate checkered; bolt handle not bent back; metal parts blued; receiver casehardened as previous stock has a single (rear) bolt passing crosswise through it to prevent splitting; windage knob 9/16" diameter.

Survival rate "as issued" and in the better states of condition very low. Most were rebuilt and Parkerized in government arsenals at later dates. As issued:

9A-429   Values—Very Good **$1,250**   Exc. **$4,250**

N.R.A. and U.S. Ordnance Dept. proof mark (small flaming bomb) stamped on trigger guard indicating sale by Director of Civilian Marksmanship to National Rifle Association:

9A-429.5   Values—Very Good **$1,100**   Exc. **$3,500**

Model 1903 Caliber 30-06 (c. 1917-1921)

9A-430

Model 1903 Rifle Caliber 30-06 As Manufactured c. 1917 to 1921. Although some are of post-war manufacture, all these are generally considered as World War I arms by collectors. Quality of workmanship not as good as earlier peacetime specimens. Parkerized finish. Approximate quantity made 590,000. Serial number ranges approximately 635000 to 1225000. Barrel dates from 1917 through 1920. Also made by Rock Island February, 1917, to June, 1919. (Rock Island specimens usually bring about 15 percent less.)

Buttplates smooth; triggers of many were not serrated, but have the thick contour; receivers and bolts of guns below Serial No. 800000 (approximately) casehardened with those above that serial range double heat treated and considered stronger. Bolt handles bent rearward at approximate 800000 serial range also. For unknown reasons, the lower barrel bands were blued and not Parkerized. Two stock bolts to prevent splitting under receiver.

Although large quantities were manufactured in this era, clean, unaltered specimens are quite difficult to find. Many later rebuilt and put into storage after the war; many more were made into sporting and hunting arms after being sold as surplus:

1917-1918 dated:
9A-430   Values—Very Good **$1,250**   Exc. **$4,250**
1919 to 1921 dated:
9A-430.5   Values—Very Good **$875**   Exc. **$3,250**

Model 1903 Rifle (c. 1921-1927)

Model 1903 Rifle as Manufactured c. 1921 to 1927. (Not illus.) Approximate quantity manufactured 80,000. Serial number range approximately 1200000 to 1280000.

Rifles of this era similar to the World War I manufacture, but workmanship considerably better. All metal parts Parkerized. Many found with checkered buttplates and serrated triggers.

Stocks of the "S" type (same as 1917 to 1921 production) with grasping grooves and straight grips; swell of the hand guard made longer and larger. Barrels dated 1921 to 1927.

Manufacture of issue type '03 rifles ended in 1927. All production after that year was special target or sales guns. Manufacture of replacement parts continued until approximately 1943 including receivers and barrels.

Approximately 2,000 Rock Island marked receivers were sent to Springfield in an unfinished state during this period. They were finished by Springfield and numbered along with the Springfield marked receivers in the 1275000 to 1300000 range. Considered as curiosities and will bring a small premium.

Many '03 rifles were reassembled by arsenals and ordnance depots of the Army, Navy and Marine Corps. Such pieces are found with numerous combinations of parts, and although representative for specimens of the '03, they are worth considerably less than the unaltered types valued here:
9A-431   Values—Very Good **$1,000**   Exc. **$3,000**

Model 1903 Cutaway-Demonstrator

Model 1903 Cutaway-Demonstrator. Made by Springfield and Rock Island Arsenals for training and classroom instruction. Detailed information about their manufacture and quantities is sketchy, at best. The large majority made prior to WWI, with lesser numbers between wars. It is believed that a small quantity were fabricated at a few major ordnance depots.

Utilizing rejected and condemned parts unsuitable for issue, it is a full-size, mechanically functioning M.1903 rifle with numerous apertures, of varying size and shape, cut into every part in order that interiors may be viewed. Most bear pre-1916 barrel dates; receivers usually without serial number or with cutaway aperture in that area obscuring number.

Originality is generally established by the quality of workmanship. Those that reflect the high degree of quality

9A-431.5

typical of arsenal work usually adjudged authentic (no significant amount of spurious examples have been noticed).
9A-431.5   Values—Very Good **$1,500**   Exc. **$3,250**
WWII Model 1903 Cutaway-Demonstrator; same as above; most are Remington M.1903-A1 with early features of 1942, although M.1903-A3s known. All made from condemned guns:
9A-431.7   Values—Very Good **$900**   Exc. **$2,400**

Model 1903 A1 Rifle as Adopted 1929

9A-432

Model 1903 A1 Rifle as Adopted 1929.

The new A1 designation indicates the standard '03 with the full pistol grip stock without grasping grooves on side (or as the stock is officially known, the "C" stock). Checkered buttplates and serrated triggers were also used.

The only newly made Model 1903 A1 rifles assembled at the armory were for the Director of Civilian Marksmanship sales.

In actuality, these A1s are merely restocked 1903 rifles. It is quite difficult, if not impossible, to know which were actually made up for D.C.M. sales unless the original bill of sale still accompanies the piece and in such instances the gun certainly would be worth a premium over the value indicated herewith. These 1903 A1 types are found in many variations as rebuilt or merely restocked. All are worth approximately the same:
9A-432   Values—Very Good **$800**   Exc. **$2,500**

Model 1903 Rifle Stripped for Air Service

9A-433

Model 1903 Rifle Stripped for Air Service. Quantity made 910. Serial number range 857000 to 863000. Barrels dated in first half of year 1918.

The Ordnance Report for year 1918 lists and describes these pieces as "Stripped for Air Service." Other documentary evidence is not available, but it is believed that they were intended to be carried aloft by observation balloons and not for mounting aboard airplanes. They differ from the standard issue '03 as follows: Special stock (29") and hand guard (5-3/4") made specifically for this model resembling the standard stock, with entire forward portion of stock and hand guard eliminated; upper barrel band and sling swivels omitted; lower band solid (not split) and retained by wood screw from underside; rear sight leaf shortened and altered to open sight with square notch; front sight blade 1/10" wide; 25-shot extension magazine utilized. *Very rare:*
9A-433   Values—Very Good **$8,500**   Exc. **$20,000**

Model 1903 Mark I Rifle Modified for Pedersen Device

Model 1903 Mark I Rifle Modified for Pedersen Device. Total quantity 101,775. Manufactured c. 1919-1920. Found in serial number range approximately 1000000 to 1200000.

A modified '03 designed to take the "Automatic Bolt Model of 1918 Mark I" or as more commonly known—the Pedersen Device.

A standard bolt action 30-06, but when the special automatic bolt installed (and regular bolt removed), it becomes a 40-shot semi-automatic rifle using a small 30 caliber pistol type cartridge. Both the device and rifle were classified "Secret" until March, 1931. After manufacture, they were put in storage and stayed there until 1931 when almost all of the devices were destroyed and the rifles had their special triggers and magazine cut-offs removed and reclassified and carried on the books as standard '03s. Many were issued as "Standard" to National Guard units.

This special modified rifle bears an additional line marking on the receiver (making a total of six-line marking) MARK I just above the serial number. It differed from the standard '03 as follows: Oval slot cut through left receiver wall, acting as ejection port for Pedersen Device; trigger and sear assembly had extra lever to release firing pin in device; magazine cut had two locking shoulders machined to lock device onto rifle; cut-off spindle screw had turned down end; cut-off spindle had spring-loaded plunger and screwdriver slot at back end; stock has clearance cut by the ejection port.

Barrel dates on this model should be 1919 or 1920. A correct unaltered armory manufactured Mark I is difficult to encounter. Many Pedersen Devices have been rebuilt from burned and scrapped parts (after they were sold as surplus) and do not bring the values of an original "as issued" unrebuilt specimen.

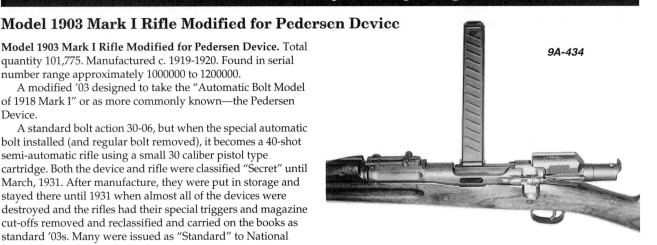

9A-434

As Issued (without device):
9A-434   Values—Very Good **$650**   Exc. **$2,000**
Mark I Rifle as above, but altered, with the special parts removed (usually triggers, magazine cut-offs and stock of later standard type). Considered as a rebuilt 1903 with Mark I receiver:
9A-435   Values—Very Good **$450**   Exc. **$850**
Pedersen Device without magazine:
9A-436   Values—Very Good **$11,500**   Exc. **$30,000**
Pedersen Device complete with one magazine:
9A-437   Values—Very Good **$12,500**   Exc. **$35,000**
Metal carrying scabbard for Pedersen Device:
9A-438   Values—Very Good **$3,500**   Exc. **$6,000**
Web pouch for spare magazines (quite commonly encountered):
9A-439   Values—Very Good **$10**   Exc. **$20**

Model 1903 Sniper Rifle

Model 1903 Sniper Rifle.

Selected '03 rifles were fitted with telescopic sights for use by Sharpshooters from 1907 to 1919. Ordnance Reports indicate that 25 were fitted with telescopic sights in 1906, but did not specify the type used. It is believed the scopes were made by the Cataract Tool and Optical Company. Specimens of rifles with sniper scopes fitted of that 1907 period, if proven original, would be worth considerably in excess of prices indicated here.

In 1911, 400 rifles were fitted with the Model 1908 Warner and Swasey telescopic musket sight of 6-Power magnification. These sights actually marked MODEL 1908 with the full Warner-Swasey markings as well. They were a prismatic scope, mounted offset to the left on a dovetail rail screwed to the left wall of the receiver. The scopes had a large oval soft rubber eye cup and external adjustment knobs for windage and elevations. They were graduated to 3,000 yards. They are invariably found with

9A-440

the scope numbers not matching the rifle numbers. Values for this Model '03 with scopes attached are approximately 30 percent to 50 percent more than for the Model 1913 scope with rifle as indicated below.

From 1914 to 1919 over 5,000 '03 rifles were fitted with the Model 1913 Warner-Swasey telescopic musket sights. These were similar to the Model 1908, but in lesser 5.2 Power. They also were fully marked.

When originally fitted to the '03 rifles, the scopes bore the serial number of the rifle (at the bottom of the dovetail of the mount on the scope) while the Warner-Swasey serial number is found on the left side of the scope body.

Many Model 1913 telescopic sights were sold separately as surplus equipment in the 1920s and '30s. A large portion of them were brand new and never bore '03 serial numbers. Others which were returned to armories for storage had the scopes detached and stored separately; hence, survival rate of matched serial numbers is extremely small (such pieces would bring a premium of at least double the price indicated here). Almost all specimens encountered will have mismatched number of scope to rifle:
9A-440   Values—Very Good **$3,250**   Exc. **$7,500**
Variant Sniper Scope: During World War II the U.S. Marine Corps issued some sniper rifles with Unertl 8-power 1-1/4" target type telescopes mounted on Model 1903 A1 rifles. Many were National Match Rifles. Quantity made is unknown, but U.S.M.C. marked Unertl scopes are seen with serial numbers in the 4000 range. Many of these scopes were sold separately as surplus in the 1950s and mounted on '03 rifles by individuals to give the appearance of sniper rifles. These generally can be

identified by the manner in which the wooden hand guard is cut to allow for the forward scope mount. Original issue type hand guards were professionally machine cut whereas the assembled pieces usually are hand filed for the cutaway for scope. Original specimens with scopes:

9A-441   Values—Very Good **$3,750**   Exc. **$8,500**

Model 1903 National Match Rifle (c. 1921-28)

Model 1903 National Match Rifle c. 1921 to 1928. (Not illus.) Quantity made approximately 18,000. Found in serial number range 1210000 to 1300000.

Rifles used at the National Matches prior to 1921 were standard '03 service rifles that were selected for their shooting qualities. In 1921 a special rifle was manufactured for use at the matches differing from the issue '03 as follows: barrel rifled with a double scrape cutter giving a smoother finish to the bore; bore dimensions held to closer tolerances and checked with a star gauge—the muzzle being marked (at its front end in approximately the 6:00 o'clock position with a star-like device of a small circle with four, six or eight rays emanating from it); bolt polished bright with camming surfaces honed for smooth operation; bolt runways in receiver polished; trigger pull set from 3-1/2 lbs. to 4-1/2 lbs.; deep checkered buttplate; serrated trigger; extractor bright; serial number hand etched on the bolt on many, but not all; stocks of many (but not all) also bore serial number stamped just forward of the rear sling swivel.

National Match rifles made for N.R.A. sales were drilled and tapped for a Lyman 48 rear sight; stock not cut for sight unless ordered with the rifle.

National Match rifles made after 1923 had a reversed safety specially made at the Armory. All stocks of these models were of the "S" type with straight grip and grasping grooves. Inspector mark DAL enclosed in rectangular cartouche. Some specimens will be found with the headless cocking piece (that is, without knurled knob).

National Match rifles, when no longer suitable for match shooting (bores not as accurate), were turned into the arsenal where their safeties were replaced with normal type and the pieces were carried on the books as the standard '03. Such specimens with the standard safety worth approximately 20 percent less than the values indicated here.

Specimens with very fine bores will usually bring a premium. Demand for specimens with shot-out or heavily worn bores will not be as strong nor worth as much as indicated here. Bores should be looked at and considered when pricing:

9A-442   Values—Very Good **$1,750**   Exc. **$4,000**

1903 A1 National Match Rifle (c. 1928-1940)

Model 1903 A1 National Match Rifle c. 1928 to 1940. (Not illus.) Quantity approximately 11,000. Found in serial number range 1285000 to 1532000.

Basically the same as preceding except with "C" type or pistol grip stock; no grasping grooves. Armory assembled National Match rifles of this era had bolts and stocks with matching numbers to receiver. Stocks will bear a P in circle proof or marking on underside of the pistol grip and most will have inspector marks on side of either D.A.L. enclosed in rectangular cartouche or S.A./SPG in square cartouche. Specimens are encountered with both regular and reverse type safeties and prices are same for each:

9A-443   Values—Very Good **$1,650**   Exc. **$3,750**

Model 1903 and 1903 A1 Rifle Type "S.S."

Model 1903 and Model 1903 A1 Rifle Type "S.S." (Not illus.) Quantity unknown, but estimated as quite large.

The "S.S." is an issue type rifle with a star gauged barrel. Made for sales to National Rifle Association members not wishing to pay the full price of the National Match rifle, but desiring a target grade barrel. Made in '03 and '03 A1 configurations. Many of these types privately assembled as the star gauge barrel and receiver could be purchased from the Armory by NRA members:

9A-444   Values—Very Good **$1,200**   Exc. **$2,750**

Model 1903 Style National Match Special Rifle

Model 1903 Style National Match Special Rifle. Quantity made 150, c. 1924. Identical to the '03 National Match, but with noticeably different buttstock configuration the same as the Model 1922 NRA; utilized large shotgun type steel buttplate; full pistol grip. Springfield Armory assembled pieces marked with the P in circle on the underside of pistol grip:

9A-445   Values—Very Good **$3,250**   Exc. **$8,000**

Variant with replacement stock: The stock only could be separately purchased by NRA members and used on any '03 or National Match. When found with such replacement stock, the P in circle inspector marking does not appear on underside of pistol grip and value considerably less:

9A-446   Values—Very Good **$1,500**   Exc. **$3,000**

9A-445

Model 1903 Style "NB" National Match Rifle

9A-447

Model 1903 Style "NB" National Match Rifle. Quantity made 195, c. 1925 and 1926. Made with the "B" type stocks which have service type, deep checkered buttplate and pistol grip with configuration having noticeably squared profile. The "B" stock had more drop than standard and was suitable for off-hand shooting only. It was also available separately from the armory and thus guns of other periods are often encountered with this type of stock. Armory assembled specimens will bear the P in circular proof on underside of pistol grip while separately purchased stocks privately assembled will not bear that marking.

A standard service rifle was sold to NRA members with this "B" stock on them and were called style "SB."
NB type; arsenal assembled with P in circle stock marking:
9A-447 Values—Very Good **$4,000** Exc. **$8,000**
As above; but with privately replaced stock lacking the P in circle marking:
9A-448 Values—Very Good **$1,400** Exc. **$3,000**
SB style; arsenal assembled with P in circle proof:
9A-449 Values—Very Good **$3,000** Exc. **$6,500**
SB style; privately assembled without stock proof:
9A-450 Values—Very Good **$1,600** Exc. **$2,750**

Model 1903 N.R.A. Sporter

9A-451

Model 1903 N.R.A. Sporter. Quantity made approximately 6,500 c. 1924 to 1933.

A match quality sporting type rifle for sales to NRA members. 30-06 caliber. Utilized a Model 1922 type half stock without grasping grooves; National Match quality action with star gauged barrel that had heavier contour of the 22 caliber barrel (same diameter at muzzle and breech, but thicker throughout); steel shotgun type buttplate and Lyman 48 receiver

sight. Bolt finished bright and usually numbered to correspond to receiver serial.

For sales only and not an issue item. Armory stopped manufacture 1933 as private industry was then making quality bolt action sporting rifles of same type. Stock bears P in circle cartouche on underside of pistol grip. Found in serial number range 1260000 to 1445000:
9A-451 Values—Very Good **$1,750** Exc. **$4,000**

Model 1903 N.B.A. Sporter

Model 1903 N.B.A. Sporter. (Not illus.) Quantity made 589, c. 1925 to 1926. 30-06 caliber. For sale to NRA members. Barrel, action and sights identical to NRA sporter and fitted on "B" type stock. Buttplate deep checkered service type. Stock marking P in

circle on underside of pistol grip. Serial number range 1267000 to 1275000. Basic difference is the grasping grooves on sides of stock and the "B" or squared profile at bottom of pistol grip:
9A-452 Values—Very Good **$3,250** Exc. **$6,000**

Model 1903 Heavy Barreled Match Rifles

9A-453

9A-453

Model 1903 Heavy Barreled Match Rifles. Quantity made 566, c. 1922 to 1930.

Made in many variations and configurations. Most commonly encountered are the style "T" with the NRA type stocks. Barrels measure .860" at muzzle and 1-1/4" at breech; made in three lengths, 26", 28", and 30". Lyman 48 rear sight; Winchester globe front sight set on modified B.A.R. front band; telescope blocks fitted to receiver and barrel. Some have adjustable hook type buttplates, set triggers, Garand speed locks and cheek pieces (and such features will bring premiums).

Least common of these Heavy Barreled guns are the **International Match** rifles which are worth double values indicated here for the standard Heavy Barreled pieces. These are seen with numerous variant features which were changed yearly at individual request of the shooters for whom they were made. Generally they have palm rests, double set triggers, adjustable hook buttplates, adjustable forward sling swivels and beaver-tail type forends. Some are seen with checkered pistol grips, Swiss style butts, thumb and finger rests, Garand speed locks, varying barrel weights and sights. The telescopic sights used generally were the Winchester 5A. They all may be considered extremely scarce, if not rare.

Another variant encountered is the **1922 Match Springfield** which has the NRA type stock with grasping grooves, 24" barrel with service type front sight mount and small base that is integral with barrel; telescope blocks on barrel.

Values indicated are for more often encountered heavy barreled match rifles without special accessories:

9A-453   Values—Very Good **$4,500**   Exc. **$11,000**

Model 1903 22 Caliber Gallery Practice Rifle "Hoffer-Thompson"

Model 1903 22 Caliber Gallery Practice Rifle "Hoffer-Thompson." (Not illus.) Quantity made 15,525, c. 1907 to 1918 with 7,313 replacement barrels manufactured 1920 and 1921.

Differed from standard issue '03 as follows: barrel bored and rifled to 22 caliber and chambered for the Hoffer-Thompson cartridge holder; rear sight graduated to 2,400 yards (was the M.1905 sight graduated for the 30-03 cartridge); mainspring shortened; stocks generally found without cross bolts and not marked with the P in circle on underside of pistol grip; receivers of rifles made after 1910 usually bear extra marking .22 at top of bridge.

Survival rate quite small; as most apparently destroyed or broken down for parts after World War I.

Ammunition used was 22 caliber rimfire short with black powder (very corrosive and ruined many bores). The small 22 rimfire cartridge loaded into a steel cartridge holder which resembled the 30-06 round. Five of these cartridge holders are placed into the magazine and rifle operated in same manner as the 30 caliber. Markings and finish identical to the issue 1903 and configuration externally identical:

Dated 1907-1908 with birchwood upper hand guard:

9A-454   Values—Very Good **$2,200**   Exc. **$4,500**

Dated 1910-1918 as described:

9A-454.5   Values—Very Good **$1,800**   Exc. **$4,000**

Model 1917 U.S. Magazine Rifle

9A-455

Model 1917 U.S. Magazine Rifle, a.k.a. Model 1917 Enfield. Made by Winchester Repeating Arms Co. and Remington Arms U.M.C. Co., c. 1917-18; total quantity 2,193,429. Breakdown as follows: Winchester, 465,980; Remington, Ilion, N.Y., 545,541; Remington, Eddystone, Pa., 1,181,908.

30 centerfire caliber. 26" barrel, secured by two barrel bands and screwed into breech. Stacking swivel on upper band; sling swivel on lower band; lower swivel on bottom of buttstock. Rear sight having sliding peep aperture, mounted on back section of breech (near eye); graduated to 1,600 yards, and adjustable only for elevation. Hand guard running most of length of barrel. Bayonet stud on forward barrel band.

Metal parts with dark, blue-black finish. Oil stained walnut stock; note semi-pistol grip and straight comb.

Serial numbered. Breech at forward section marked: U.S. MODEL 1917 (REMINGTON *or* WINCHESTER) and serial number.

To meet the considerable needs of U.S. forces for the World War I effort, the Remington and Winchester arms companies were pressed into service using equipment on which had been produced Enfield rifles for the British government. Modifications as follows were made to the British model: Chambering for the 30 caliber rimless cartridge, alteration of the bolt to accept that ammunition, and increase of magazine size. A distinctive design feature of the Model 1917 Enfield was the bend in the bolt handle, and still another detail was the stock profile in the butt area. No cocking piece is visible on the bolt, as appears on the Model 1903 Springfield series. WWII reconditioned and Parkerized Enfields worth about 50 percent less than values below. Values are for EDDYSTONE made rifles; REMINGTON marked worth 10 percent premium; WINCHESTER marked 20 percent premium.

9A-455   Values—Very Good **$450**   Exc. **$1,150**

Model 1922 22 Caliber Rifle

Model 1922 22 Caliber Rifle. Quantity made 2,020, c. 1922 to 1924.

Walnut half stock without hand guard. Stock known as the Model 1922 or the "NRA" stock. Large, checkered steel shotgun type buttplate. Chambered for 22 rimfire long rifle cartridge. 24-1/2" barrel .060" larger in diameter at lower band than the issue '03 rifle. Five-shot detachable clip magazine protrudes 5/8" below the floor plate. Double firing pin on bolt striking both top

9A-456

and bottom of the cartridge; cocking piece is headless (without knurled knob); bolt throw 3-1/4"; Lyman 48B rear sight with standard issue type '03 front sight; sling swivels on barrel band and butt of stock.

Receiver markings in six lines U.S./SPRINGFIELD/ARMORY/MODEL OF 1922/CAL. 22/(serial number). Barrel marked behind front sight in three lines S.A./(flaming bomb device)/(date). Serial range 1 to 2020.

Two distinct types: (A) For service issue with grasping grooves in sides of stock; barrel not tapped for scope blocks; (B) for NRA sales made without the grasping grooves in stock and barrel is tapped for scope blocks. Finish blued on both types; bolt handle and body finished bright.

Survival rate quite small; most modified into later M1 or M2 types in which case marking M1 stamped into receiver after words MODEL of 1922 and letter A stamped after the serial number. When M2 bolt, magazine and stock were installed, the marking M2 stamped after Model of 1922 and letter A stamped after serial number.

Issue type:
9A-456	Values—Very Good **$1,850**	Exc. **$3,750**

NRA sales type:
9A-457	Values—Very Good **$1,500**	Exc. **$3,250**

Altered to either M1 or M2:
9A-458	Values—Very Good **$850**	Exc. **$1,500**

Model 1922 M1 22 Caliber Rifle

9A-459

Model 1922 M1 22 Caliber Rifle. Approximate quantity made 20,000, c. 1924 to 1933. Serial number range 1 to 21000.

Configuration about identical to Model 1922. Major distinguishing feature is the single firing pin that strikes the top of cartridge rim; clip magazine flush fitted with floor plate. Lyman 48C receiver sight.

Made in two styles: (A) Issue type having the "B" type stock (as illustrated) with grasping grooves and deep checkered service type buttplate; barrel and receiver not drilled and tapped for scope and Parkerized finish; (B) NRA sales model with the N.R.A. type stock and barrel and receiver drilled and tapped for scope blocks and with blued finish. All bolts on both types were bright with the receiver serial number etched on them. Mismatched numbers should be priced downward accordingly.

Two types of receiver markings are encountered—each identical in value, either U.S./SPRINGFIELD/ARMORY/MODEL OF 1922/M1 CAL. .22/(serial number) up to approximately serial

number 9000 when changed to accommodate holes for rear scope block, the last three lines changed to read M1922M1/CAL. .22/(serial number).

Survival rate of the NRA model quite high, however, a large percentage of the issue types were modified to M2 style in which case the receiver markings were changed by adding a second digit 1 after the 1922M1 marking, changing it to read Model 1922M11 with the letter B stamped after the serial number.

Unaltered Model 1922M1 service type:
9A-459	Values—Very Good **$1,000**	Exc. **$2,500**

Altered to M2:
9A-460	Values—Very Good **$550**	Exc. **$1,100**

NRA sales type; unaltered:
9A-461	Values—Very Good **$800**	Exc. **$1,750**

NRA sales type altered to M2:
9A-462	Values—Very Good **$675**	Exc. **$1,000**

U.S. Rifle Caliber 22 M2

U.S. Rifle Caliber 22 M2. Quantity made approximately 12,000. Serial number range approximately 1 to 22000 which includes

the M2A1. (A sub-caliber, stockless, 22 caliber barreled action, mounted on anti-tank guns for gunnery practice.)

9A-463

Markings on receiver in five lines U.S./SPRINGFIELD/ARMORY/CAL. .22M2/(serial number). Bolts are all finished bright and numbered to correspond with receiver. Parkerized finish to barrel and receiver. 24-1/2" barrel.

Major differences from M1922M1: Firing mechanism in bolt changed to give faster lock time; knurled cocking knob added; bolt throw shortened to 1-3/4"; magazine modified to improved feeding; extractor claw reshaped; latch mechanism omitted from locking lug on bolt; butt of stock has less drop; pistol grip reshaped; head space adjusting mechanism installed in locking lug after approximately 3,800 were produced. Four collector variants:

1st Type; total quantity 3,800. Made without the adjustable head space mechanism on locking lug of bolt; M2 type stock. Survival rate of original unaltered specimens quite low as most were replaced with later type bolt:

9A-463   Values—Very Good **$900**   Exc. **$2,250**

2nd Type; Adjustable head space mechanism found in locking lug of bolt; M2 type stock. Often encountered style:

9A-464   Values—Very Good **$600**   Exc. **$1,100**

3rd Type; as above with head space mechanism; NRA type stock; barrel drilled and tapped for scope blocks. Issued to R.O.T.C. units and not sold until after WWII as surplus. *Scarce:*

9A-465   Values—Very Good **$950**   Exc. **$2,250**

4th Type; head space mechanism in bolt; M2 type stock; not drilled or tapped for scope blocks. All were made 1942 to 1943 and have barrels 1/2" shorter (24"). Often encountered style:

9A-466   Values—Very Good **$625**   Exc. **$1,000**

Arsenal rebuilt for D.C.M. sales. Mixture of parts; patched stocks, valued as shooters:

9A-467   Values—Very Good **$550**   Exc. **$800**

Model 1922 International 22 Cal. Heavy Barrel

Model 1922 International 22 Caliber Heavy Barrel Rifle. (Not illus.) Quantity made 12. Circa 1924. Made for the International Rifle Team as a match for their 30-06 caliber rifles.

30" heavy barrels; 22 caliber rimfire. Set triggers; palm rest; adjustable hook type buttplate. Serial numbers all appear in the high 1900 and low 2000 number series.

Blue finish; markings same as Model 1922. Half stock known as the International Type, with hook buttplate, beaver-tail forend, adjustable forward sling swivel and checkered pistol grip. Single shot only:

9A-468   Values—Very Good **$22,500**   Exc. **$45,000**

Complete kit of accessories for the Model 1903 Springfield Mark I Rifle modified for the Pederson device (see items 9A-434 through 439).

IX-B: SECONDARY

Muzzle-Loading

FLINTLOCK

U.S. Contract Flintlock Rifles, c. 1792-1809

9B-001
Made by Gumpf

9B-001
Made by J. Dickert

9B-001
Made by DeHuff

U.S. Contract Flintlock Rifles, c. 1792-1809. Various makers. Total quantities delivered by various makers under contract of 1792 estimated at 1,500; quantities delivered by various makers under contract of 1794 estimated at 2,000.

To arm a battalion of riflemen created in 1792 by presidential decree, the government placed orders with established Pennsylvania gunsmiths. The quantities in which total deliveries were made over the approximate 17-year period would seem to indicate that more than one battalion was so equipped and possibly single rifle companies within other regiments were issued such rifles. There is strong evidence to indicate it was the 1792 Contract rifle that was carried on the historic Lewis & Clark Western Exploring Expedition 1803-1806, and not the 1803 Harpers Ferry Rifle as most often mentioned.

There is every likelihood that these rifles represent the first federal procurement of arms. The purchase of these rifles was in small, intermittent lots of 50 to 100 from various makers until 1807 at which time small quantity contracts were actually let for them.

Documentary evidence is slight and references to these rifles are sketchy, but sufficient to prove the existence of recorded makers and some deliveries. Although no known patterns were supplied by the government, it has been reasonably established from existing specimens and official correspondence that the guns followed a general style with characteristics common to most, if not all of them. An 1807 letter of Tench Coxe (Purveyor of Public Supplies) mentions some specifications. As so little has ever been written about these rifles, and illustrations have not appeared previously of them, it is quite possible that other rifles, especially those of the earliest types before the turn of the century, were supplied that did not hold to these general characteristics, and therefore remained yet to be discovered! Surviving specimens are extremely rare.

It is also known from correspondence that some of these rifles were purchased without locks from the makers with same being furnished by the government. It is further known that 3,000 English made rifle size locks were purchased by the U.S. government in 1800 from Thomas Ketland & Company of London, England with at least 1,550 of them received that year. It is believed that those locks bore the markings UNITED STATES as well as those of KETLAND & CO, but to date no rifles that may be considered as part of these purchases or contracts have been recorded (the locks possibly used in the McCormick, Philadelphia Naval pistol of the same era).

Official correspondence also mentions some of these rifles were supplied to the U.S. Indian Department for use as gifts to friendly Indians, while other correspondence mentions some ordered with silver stars and thumb pieces as decoration.

The three illustrated specimens shown here are by C. Gumpf, J. Dickert and H. DeHuff—all of Lancaster, Pennsylvania. They have remarkably similar configuration, furthering the contention that most, if not all, followed similar styling. Other known makers were J. Henry, H. Guest and P. Brong, H. Pickel, J. Welschans, A. Angstadt, J. Nicholson, P. Gonter, J. Groff and A. Morrow—all Pennsylvania gunsmiths and all well known Kentucky rifle makers.

The 1792 "Contract" style rifles as indicated by these specimens and as is apparent from correspondence were all made on the classic Pennsylvania-Kentucky rifle pattern. Specimens observed have a rather distinctive patchbox as shown here; they vary slightly in contours and dimensions. Although barrel lengths believed established at 44-1/2 inches; specimens recorded have varied usually 42 inches to 44 inches. Observed specimens were part octagon/part round with the octagon section smoothly tapering and blending into the round section rather than a clearly defined sharp line where the octagon becomes round; this also corresponds to the Tench Coxe letter calling for the barrels to be "pressed round." Although 1792 Contract specified caliber 50 for these rifles, specimens vary from 45 to 50 (and larger calibers likely). Contract of **1792** rifles were not believed to bear government markings. **1794** Contract markings denoting government ownership presumed began after Feb. or March, 1794. Maker markings, when present, usually appear in large script. Various barrel markings have been observed including large, deep stamped U.S. at top of breech, deep sunken oval cartouche with small eaglehead in center; deep sunken oval proof with eaglehead over P; or deep sunken oval proof with P in center. The DeHuff specimen had three of the above described proofs while the Gumpf was unmarked except for maker.

Locks varied in contour styling, being the early Germanic type, typical Kentucky style lock. They were unmarked except for the Gumpf which bore large deep U.S. markings at its rear. The Coxe correspondence mentions that the U.S. government was furnishing locks and that they were to be "… carefully and minutely inspected and the maker's name to be marked on each rifle."

Stocks also showed a conformity to a general style. All observed were quite sturdily made, with small cheekrest, and not having the grace or delicacy of the more classic Kentucky. This also follows Coxe's description "… they are to be common, plain rifles substantially made." All used curly maple wood, but not the select, pronounced tiger stripe grain of the finer crafted "civilian" pieces. There is certainly every possibility that plain maple and even walnut were used for stocks and that they may be encountered.

The vagaries surrounding these rifles are again mentioned. Except for the facts that these types may be considered among the most rare of early American military longarms, and that they have been identified as representative of the style believed supplied c. 1792 to 1809, they can as yet, not be pinpointed to exact years of manufacture. Whether they are representative of the pre-1807 intermittent purchases or post-1808 contract purchases—or for that matter, whether there is any distinction between the two remains to be discovered. In all likelihood there was no difference, the contract purchases merely being a different means of acquiring the rifles.

Significant additional information about these rifles will be found in "*American Military Shoulder Arms,*" Vol. II (Moller, *q.v.*); *Man at Arms* No. 3, 1999; and *The Kentucky Rifle Association Bulletin*, Winter 1998.

9B-001   Values—Good **$10,000**   Fine **$27,500**
As above; converted to percussion:
9B-002   Values—Good **$4,500**   Fine **$11,500**

Bridgewater Flintlock Muskets

9B-003
Style A

9B-005
Style B

Bridgewater Flintlock Muskets with pin-fastened stocks, a.k.a. Model 1807 Indian Musket (a collector's term of convenience which may be a misnomer). Believed made by Rufus Perkins of Bridgewater, Massachusetts, c. 1808-1820. Quantity unknown.

Two distinct types illustrated and described below, but other variations are known with closely similar configurations. Features common to all are the full walnut stocks pin-fastened (in place of barrel bands); all 69 caliber; all with brass furniture fashioned very closely after the style of the British Brown Bess; three brass ramrod pipes; iron ramrod with button head tip; brass tip on forend of stock.

Little definitive information available on these arms. Strongly believed that many were made under contract for the U.S. Office of Indian Trade to give as treaty payment as well as to arm Indian allies in the 1812, Creek and Seminole Wars. Perkins was a maker of contract muskets (*see listing under 1808 contracts*) and is also known to have received a contract as early as 1808 from the Indian Office for "…smooth bored guns brass mounted…full stocked." In 1813 the U.S. government released Perkins from his 1808 contract for flintlock muskets. He was known to have had a large stock of parts on hand which he apparently either sold to another maker or used himself to fabricate muskets for privateer and other military and quasi-military purposes.

Although the two styles shown here differ considerably, the die stamps used to mark the locks of each style were identical.

Style A; 39" barrel (but 42" barrels are encountered and were the length specified in 1808 Indian Office contract); small "civilian" type 5-1/2" lockplate with two deep vertical flutings and projecting teat at rear; gooseneck hammer; integral forged rounded iron flashpan. Lock marked ahead of hammer with eagle over small oval panel with US in center; marked at rear BRIDGWATER in arch curving inward and date 1815. Others dated to 1819 have been observed in this identical type. Barrel marked at top near breech UNITED STATES and two deep sunken oval cartouches with proofs V and P respectively:

9B-003   Values—Good **$1,650**   Fine **$3,250**

As above; converted to percussion:
9B-004   Values—Good **$750**   Fine **$1,150**

Style B; 41" barrel; lock is classic military pattern identical to that used by Perkins on his U.S. 1808 contract musket and obviously surplus from that contract. Stock patterned very closely after the British military musket, displaying classic "Brown Bess" features such as the notch at the forward edge of the comb and the broad relief plateau carving around barrel tang. Barrel unmarked. Lock with markings identical Type I above; dated 1818; other dates known:

9B-005   Values—Good **$1,750**   Fine **$3,250**

As above; converted to percussion:
9B-006   Values—Good **$750**   Fine **$1,000**

Deringer Flintlock Military Rifle

9B-007

Deringer Flintlock Military Rifle. Made by Henry Deringer, Philadelphia, Pennsylvania, c. 1810-1820. Quantities unknown.

56 caliber, single shot; muzzleloader. 33" part octagon/part round barrel. Full walnut stock wedge fastened; lug for socket type bayonet on underside near muzzle.

Lock marked H. DERINGER/PHIL^A. Barrel markings indicating ownership and contract by the Commonwealth of Pennsylvania and appear at breech CP over a serial number and oval cartouche with P proof at breech. Stock also bears CP stamping near lock screw with matching serial number to barrel.

Brass furniture with trigger guard having tapered, pointed finials each end and rudimentary finger ridges just below the trigger bow; brass sideplate; three ramrod pipes; brass forend

tip. The gun is quickly distinguished by its unique large patchbox with the finial in the outline/silhouette shape of the upper part of an eagle with its head turned to the left.

Very little recorded information about these arms and it is possible to encounter them with variations of lock and barrel markings. The patchbox seems to be unique to Henry Deringer. These arms were evidently made for private sale as well as for state contracts. Prices shown here are for martially marked specimens; those with no martial markings or apparent military usage or intention should be priced approximately twenty percent less:

9B-007 Values—Good **$4,000** Fine **$7,500**
Same as above; converted to percussion:
9B-008 Values—Good **$1,500** Fine **$3,750**

Ellis-Jennings Repeating Flintlock Rifle

9B-009

9B-010

9B-010

Ellis-Jennings Sliding Lock Repeating Flintlock Rifle. Made by R. & J.D. Johnson, Middletown, Conn. 1829. Total quantity 520.

Unique, self priming, sliding lock with two distinct types adapted for either four shots or ten shots. The barrels accepting superposed loads. The individual touchholes for each load have swivel covers which also act to position and align the lock for the prior charge.

One of the great American military rarities and oddities. Reuben Ellis of Albany, New York, acting as agent and contractor, received a *Federal* contract for 520 of these unique arms patented by Isiah Jennings of New York City in 1821. The arms were specifically authorized for and delivered to the state of New York after Federal inspection.

About identical to the Model 1817 "Common Rifle" and utilizing many parts of that model. Many distinctive features on

the rifle, including its lack of provision for a side-plate have proven this unique piece *not* to be an alteration of Model 1817.

36" barrel; 54 caliber rifled bore. Barrel and stock with U.S. proof and inspector initials. Unmarked lock closely similar to that used on Model 1826 pistol.

This identical, unique, Ellis-Jennings Sliding Lock Repeating Flintlock System is also known in an all brass (stock and barrel) breech-loading flintlock, 12-shot sporting rifle. (See Chapter 12-009.5 Jennings Rifle.)

Four Shot Model as delivered under contract:
9B-009 Values—Good **$12,000** Fine **$27,500**
Ten Shot Model; extremely rare; likely experimental only:
9B-010 Values—Good **$25,000** Fine **$50,000**

Flintlock Militia Musketoon

9B-011

Flintlock Militia Musketoon. With lock of M.1826 Navy pistol, c. 1831; total produced unknown.

69 caliber smoothbore. Single shot muzzleloader. 24-5/8" round barrel, two barrel bands.

Brass mountings. Metal parts finished bright. Steel ramrod with button shaped end. Walnut stock of full length.

Lock markings: W.L.EVANS/V. FORGE, forward of the hammer; behind hammer, stamped vertically: 1831/USN with no markings on barrel or inspectors markings on stock.

Distinguishing features are the round trigger guard contour, the sweeping curve of the bottom contour of the buttstock and the saddle ring merely attached to a small eye-bolt screwed into the underside of the butt.

An enigma for collectors, no documentary, or other, evidence shows U.S. purchase. Most specimens seen have commercial, sporting type locks with various maker/dealer names. General low quality of workmanship (especially the flimsy eye bolt saddle ring) casts doubt on its purported mounted use. Likely intended for militia sale, collector is cautioned that there is little likelihood of U.S. Navy use or association:

9B-011   Values—Good **$425**   Fine **$750**

Jenks Flintlock Rifle

9B-012

Jenks Flintlock Rifle. Made for William Jenks by the Chicopee Falls Company, Chicopee Falls, Massachusetts; c. 1838-39; total quantity estimated less than 100.

54 caliber. Single shot muzzleloader. 35-1/4" round barrel, semi-octagonal breech section; three barrel bands.

Iron mountings. All metal parts bright finished. Steel ramrod with trumpet shaped head.

Walnut stock.

Lockplate marking, behind hammer: CHICOPEE FALLS CO./MS (or CHICOPEE ARMS MFG. CO./MS.) Barrel marking at breech inspector's initials NWP or JH; beneath initials proofmark P, within circle. Inspector initials on left side of stock (opposite lock) and on comb near buttplate tang.

This extremely rare rifle is believed to have preceded the Jenks Flintlock Breech-Loading Carbine. It appears likely that production was in an attempt to interest the U.S. Ordnance

9B-012

Department. Among the important features are the back action type lock, the lack of bayonet lug, and the detachable brass pan having quite high fence. An unusual detail is the reverse positioning of the frizzen spring:

9B-012   Values—Good **$4,500**   Fine **$12,500**

New England Flintlock Militia Musket

New England Flintlock Militia Musket c. 1800-1830s. Quantities unknown.

These arms constitute a distinct American military type and are often encountered, evidencing that they were produced in reasonably large quantities. They are directly identified with New England manufacture and usage. The name most often applied to them and in common collector usage is **NEW ENGLAND MILITIA MUSKET.** The majority were likely made for and issued in the State of Massachusetts and possibly even paid for by local towns or counties. They do conform to a general pattern and style as illustrated, although numerous variations are seen.

The most generally observed style is quickly distinguished by its full pin fastened black walnut stock, rather than the use of barrel bands; approximately 39" round barrel (which varies in length) 69 caliber with front sight doubling as stud for socket type bayonet. Furniture is invariably brass and most often of sporting type with tear shaped escutcheons for lock screws and three ramrod pipes or thimbles. Locks are usually sporting types with gooseneck hammers; iron or wooden ramrods.

A great variety of barrel markings have been observed—the most often being proof or inspection letters P and M at breech of barrel quite often accompanied by a date (with most from 1810 through the 1830s). Locks either unmarked or with a variety of American and English makers or agents names (KETLAND often seen) and occasionally followed by WARRANTED. Names almost invariably will indicate lock maker or supplier only. The well known Boston firm of LANE and READ is a marking quite often seen.

9B-013

There is every likelihood that these arms, due to their lightweight and semi-sporting style, were intended for dual purposes—to be used as a citizen-soldier militia arm and for private game shooting at home. The statement is speculative, but the evidence of their appearance throughout New England and general background of ownership would seem to point in that direction. For a greater understanding of these arms and their usage, the collector will find *Massachusetts Military Shoulder Arms 1784-1877* by George Moller (*q.v.*) an important source.

Values indicated are for pieces generally following above described types. Minor variations generally tend to bring the same values—however, premiums may be added for such other often encountered features as cherry wood stock (which is worth slight premium), curly maple stock (will bring 20 percent to 50 percent premium depending on quality of wood and tiger stripe grain), the use of military style furniture with brass barrel bands of scaled down size U.S. musket type, or the presence of important markings such as known contractors of U.S. arms on locks (makers like A. Waters have been observed with a military type small lock):

9B-013   Values—Good **$850**   Fine **$1,750**

As above; converted to percussion:
9B-014   Values—Good **$450**   Fine **$850**

South Carolina Contract Flintlock Military Rifle

South Carolina Contract Flintlock Military Rifle. Various makers c. 1820-1830. Quantities unknown.

Caliber 56, single shot, muzzleloader; rifled bore. 38" octagon barrel with 3" at muzzle turned round to accept a socket type, angular bayonet.

Full black walnut stock, wedge fastened. Brass furniture with large plain shaped patchbox; iron sling swivels.

This weapon has been observed with various makers markings on lock. Specimen shown here J. J. HENRY/BOULTON. On all specimens observed markings SOUTH CAROLINA appeared in large letters at top of barrel near breech.

No information has yet been published on these. They were obviously made under state contract and probably to arm a company of riflemen for the state. Variations and dimensions will undoubtedly occur. Value reflected here is for South Carolina marked military specimen. If encountered without such marking or barrel not adapted for socket bayonet, value should be lessened approximately 40 percent or more:

9B-015   Values—Good **$6,000**   Fine **$11,500**

Same as above; converted to percussion:
9B-016   Values—Good **$3,000**   Fine **$6,000**

9B-015

Virginia Manufactory Flintlock Rifle

9B-017
First Model

9B-019
Second Model

Virginia Manufactory Flintlock Rifle. Made at Richmond, Virginia, c. 1803-1821.

Flintlock military rifles were first produced at the Virginia Manufactory in 1803 and 1804. No known specimens of the 72 believed made can be identified from that era. Considerable variance appears in early production, but generally they all conform in basic configuration and major features.

1st Model 1805-1808: Approximate quantity made 200 to 240. Quickly recognized by its distinctive iron patchbox with finial in shape of a large coiled rattlesnake. 46" part octagon/part round barrel; 45 caliber; iron furniture (one extremely rare 1805 dated specimen known in brass). Full stock pin fastened. Flat lock with projecting teat or point at rear marked identically to the musket

VIRGINIA (in block letters) over MANUFACTORY (in script) ahead of hammer; marked vertically at rear RICHMOND in curved arch over date of manufacture. Gooseneck hammer. Surviving specimens very rare:

9B-017   Values—Good **$14,000**   Fine **$40,000**
As above; converted to percussion:
9B-018   Values—Good **$6,000**   Fine **$15,000**
2nd Model c. 1812-1821: Approximate quantity made 1,700. 39" octagon barrel. 50 caliber. Full stock wedge fastened; usually walnut, but maple occasionally used. Plain design large brass patchbox and mountings. Considerable quantities of finished and marked 1st Model lockplates were on hand at the armory when production of this 2nd Model commenced. Hence, it is not unusual to encounter this model with earlier dates prior to 1811, which, in such cases do not indicate actual year of production of the rifle. Such locks were evidently used up to 1817 when the

manufacture of locks resumed. Markings from mid-1817 to 1821 bore year of manufacture stamped at rear and omitted the word MANUFACTORY:

9B-019   Values—Good **$6,000**   Fine **$10,000**
As above; converted to percussion:
9B-020   Values—Good **$3,000**   Fine **$5,500**

Virginia Flintlock Rifle Contracts 1808-15 & 1819

9B-021

Virginia Flintlock Rifle Contracts 1808-1815, and 1819: Total quantity 2,145 divided between 20 contractors. Definitive data not available. Generally conform to full stock Kentucky style rifles with varying brass patchboxes; the illustrated specimen displaying a style more often encountered. Key identification features are the county and regimental markings appearing in large letters along top of barrels, as required by contract. Further data will be found in the Cromwell book *Virginia Manufactory Of Arms*. Specimens quite rare; values only approximate:

9B-021   Values—Good **$6,000**   Fine **$15,000**
As above; converted to percussion:
9B-022   Values—Good **$3,000**   Fine **$5,500**

PERCUSSION   *See "U.S. Purchased Sporting Rifles During Civil War" 12-014.5*
See "Turner Rifles" 12-018.5

Blunt-Enfield Rifle Musket

9B-023

Blunt-Enfield Rifle Musket. (Not illus.) Made for Orison Blunt, New York City, c. 1861-62; total quantity of several hundred.

58 caliber muzzleloader. Single shot. 40" round barrel, with three barrel bands. In appearance almost identical to the standard British Enfield 577 rifle musket.

Iron mountings, with Enfield type brass buttplate and brass forend cap. All metal parts finished bright, except for blued barrel bands and ramrod. The latter of knurled, slotted head type.

Walnut stock, of American wood and American manufacture.

The only marking a proof stamp, CP/B, contained within an oval on breech of the barrel. Double engraved lines encircling the lock plate, and engraving also on hammer.

This quite scarce piece is considered a product of attempts by prominent New York arms dealer and gunmaker Orison Blunt to fill a U.S. government contract for 20,000 Enfield pattern rifle muskets. Only 500+ are known to have been completed for the contract, and all were rejected. Various structural details suggest that some parts, e.g., the locks and barrels, were made in England. Assembly is believed, however, to have been in the U.S.

9B-023   Values—Good **$950**   Fine **$2,000**

J. Henry & Son Percussion Rifle

9B-024

J. Henry & Son Percussion Rifle. Made in Philadelphia, Pennsylvania; c. 1861-62; total quantity about 600.

58 caliber. Single shot muzzleloader. 35" round barrel, fastened by barrel bands.

Brass mountings. All metal parts bright, excepting browned barrel, and casehardened (sometimes blued) lock. Ramrod of knurled, slotted type.

Walnut stock; with Sharps style patchbox on right side of butt.

Serial number stamped on muzzle forward of bayonet lug. Lockplate marking J. HENRY/& SON at rear section. Barrel marked at breech: J. HENRY/& SON.

Production of these arms is believed to have been on contract for the State of Pennsylvania. J. Henry & Son were descended from the well known Philadelphia arms manufacturer, J. J.

Henry. Note some similarity between the Henry rifles and contract arms by Justice (*q.v.*). Variations noted in placement of markings and other minor features and configuration.

Type with reverse curve style trigger guard; (of Justice type); flat lockplate fitted flush with stock; hammer more vertical than model noted below. Stock overall length of 45-3/4", with 10-1/2" comb. Bayonet lug on side of barrel, to accept saber type bayonet:

9B-024	Values Good **$950**	Fine **$2,500**

Type with conventional trigger guard; lockplate with beveled edges; hammer angling somewhat forward. Stock overall length of 47-1/2", with 8-1/2" comb. Bayonet lug on top of barrel, to accept socket (angular) bayonet:

9B-025	Values—Good **$850**	Fine **$2,000**

P. S. Justice Percussion Rifle

9B-026

P. S. Justice Percussion Rifle. Made by P. S. Justice, Philadelphia, Pennsylvania; c. 1861; total quantity made estimated at about 2,500.

58 caliber. Single shot muzzleloader. 35" round barrel, fastened by two barrel bands. Lug on side of muzzle for attaching saber type bayonet. Variance in types and shapes of nipple bolsters.

Brass mountings standard, although iron also known. All metal parts finished bright, excepting browned barrel.

Walnut full stock includes Sharps style patchbox at butt. Stocks usually observed with warpage and shrinking.

Some specimens serial numbered (marked on trigger guard plate behind bow). Lockplates used were from earlier U.S. models, and have the original markings removed (vestiges may often be seen) and the following marking added: P.S. JUSTICE/PHILAD[A]. Eagle motif retained from original stamping. P.S. JUSTICE/PHILAD[A] also stamped at breech of barrel.

The Justice Rifles are in the same category as the Justice Rifle-Muskets (*q.v.*) and are considered to represent a patriot's attempt to make quick deliveries for the Civil War effort. The result, though often a product not up to usual Ordnance standards, was one of the earliest deliveries by any supplier of martial longarms for the war. Specimens were issued mainly to Pennsylvania volunteer units. Usual types listed below with variations encountered not altering values.

Brass mounted specimens; featuring unusual reverse curve trigger guard profile, and the rear sling swivel on integral stud:

9B-026	Values—Good **$950**	Fine **$2,000**

Iron mounted specimens; having conventional type trigger guard, and the rear sling swivel of conventional type:

9B-027	Values—Good **$900**	Fine **$1,750**

P. S. Justice Rifled Musket

P. S. Justice Rifled Musket. (Not illus.) Made by P. S. Justice, Philadelphia, c. 1861; total quantity 2,174.

69 caliber muzzleloaders. Single shot. 39" barrel length, round; most having semi-octagonal breech section. The three basic variations are described below, under values.

Walnut stocks.

Not serial numbered, except as noted below. Usual lockplate marking P. S. JUSTICE/PHILAD[A]. Considerable variation noted in locks.

Although not of the quality associated with most Rifled Musket production of the Civil War era, the Justice arms represent a sincere attempt to answer the Union's severe demands for military arms. Justice's deliveries were among the fastest from any American manufacturer during the War years. Usual types listed below, with variations encountered not altering values.

First Type Justice; made up from parts, e.g., Model 1816 musket lock/trigger assemblies, Model 1816 stock pattern (though lacking comb), and three Model 1840 or Model 1842 barrel bands and band springs. Bolster type conversion of barrel breech; the barrel rifled. Iron mountings; made without patchbox. Long range type rear sight. Model 1863 type tulip head ramrod. Muzzle area sometimes marked with a number; P. S. JUSTICE/PHILADA. on barrel at breech:

9B-028	Values—Good **$800**	Fine **$1,650**

Second Type Justice; easily distinguished by the lack of barrel bands. Rifling of three shallow grooves. Barrel breech marked: P. S. JUSTICE/PHILADA. Rear sights of V-notch type or long range type. Brass mountings; distinctive double curve profile to trigger guard and patchbox. Lacks sling swivels. Browned finish on barrel. Tulip type ramrod head; the steel rod passing through two ferrules:

9B-029	Values—Good **$800**	Fine **$1,650**

Third Type Justice; variation most often observed by collectors (identical to Justice rifle illustrated above). Does not use parts of earlier U.S. arms. Rifled barrel; finished brown; front sight of brass; barrel marked at breech; P. S. JUSTICE/PHILADA. Brass mountings with three barrel bands. Double curve profile of the trigger guard; patchbox; sling swivels present:

9B-030	Values—Good **$850**	Fine **$1,750**

J. H. Krider Militia Rifle and Rifled Musket

9B-031

J. H. Krider Militia Rifle and Rifled Musket. Made by John H. Krider, Philadelphia, Pennsylvania; c. 1861; total quantity estimated but a few hundred.

58 caliber. Single shot percussion muzzleloader. 33" and 36" round barrels fastened by two barrel bands (rifle) and 39" barrel fastened by three bands (musket). Front sight doubles as lug for angular type bayonet. Enfield style lock.

Brass mountings (or combination of brass and iron). All metal parts finished bright, excepting browned barrel and casehardened lock. Steel ramrod with unusual constructed tulip shape head.

Walnut stock; brass Sharps style patchbox at butt.

Serial numbers sometimes present, on barrel breech. Lock marking simply: KRIDER, toward forward end. Barrel marked at breech PHILADA.

Also observed with flush-fitted lock similar in profile to U.S. Model 1842; marked only KRIDER.

Production of these arms is believed to have been on contract to the State of Pennsylvania, in an effort to provide arms early in the Civil War. Krider was a maker of quality firearms, and these rifles reflect that fact admirably:

9B-031   Values—Good **$2,500**   Fine **$4,500**

H. E. Leman Militia Rifle

9B-032

H. E. Leman Militia Rifle. Made by H. E. Leman, Lancaster, Pennsylvania; c. early 1860s; total quantity estimated at about 500.

58 caliber. Single shot percussion muzzleloader. 33" round barrel, fastened by two barrel bands.

Walnut stock.

Brass or iron mountings. Metal parts finished bright, excepting browned barrel and casehardened lock. Steel ramrod with tulip shaped head.

Lockplate marking: H. E. LEMAN/LANCASTER, P^A, forward of hammer and at breech of barrel.

Leman is best known as a maker of Indian trade arms and of Kentucky type rifles. It is believed that these Militia Rifles were to fill contract(s) from the State of Pennsylvania, probably for Civil War use. In the upper range of condition, iron mounted specimens worth premium of 20 percent.

9B-032   Values—Good **$2,500**   Fine **$4,500**

Lins Rifled Musket

9B-033

Lins Rifled Musket. Made by A. Frederick Lins, Philadelphia, Pennsylvania; c. 1861-62; total quantity limited, probably considerably less than a few hundred.

58 caliber. Single shot percussion muzzleloader. 39" round barrel, fastened by three barrel bands. Long range type rear sight.

Iron mountings; forend cap of brass. All metal parts finished bright. Steel ramrod with modified trumpet end (believed machined down from Model 1842 rod). Front sight doubles for bayonet lug.

Walnut stock.

Lockplate altered from surplus U.S. Model 1816 musket with original markings removed; marked with eagle/U.S. *and* A. FRED^KLINS/PHILADA, forward of hammer and beneath nipple bolster respectively.

Production believed for militia requirements early in Civil War. Less than handful of known specimens:

9B-033   Values—Good **$2,500**   Fine **$4,500**

Moore-Enfield Rifle-Musket

9B-034

Moore-Enfield Rifle-Musket. Made by J. P. Moore's Sons, New York City; c. 1861-63; total quantity estimated at a few thousand.

58 caliber. Single shot muzzleloader. 39" round barrel; three barrel bands; front sight doubles as lug for angular bayonet.

Iron mountings, excepting brass trigger guard, buttplate, forend cap and side screw ferrules. All metal parts finished bright. Steel ramrod of knurled, slotted head type.

Walnut stock.

Lock marking of date (1862, 1863, or 1864) forward of the hammer. At rear of lock an eagle motif atop a shield, central to the upper section of which is M (for Moore). Hammer and lockplate hand engraved with double line borders. Variety of barrel markings noted, including British proofmarks, script initials, and/or batch numbers. Variations of the eagle/shield/M lock mark indicate that it was apparently hand engraved.

J. P. Moore's Sons were one of the Colt Fire Arms Company's jobbers, and it appears likely that Colt's was the source for some of the parts on these scarce Rifle-Muskets. E.g., barrels had been purchased in Europe, but Colt decided against using certain of these, and they were either refused, or resold in the arms trade. A number of parts used on the Moore muskets were imported. Although some references have belabored the theory, to the point of tedium, that this musket is Confederate, proof positive exists in the form of correspondence by J.P. Moore on their letterhead, Jan. 13, 1862, that the musket was theirs:

9B-034   Values—Good **$1,000**   Fine **$2,000**

New Hampshire Marked Rifled Musket

New Hampshire Marked Percussion Rifled Musket. (Not illus.) Made 1858 by E. Whitney, New Haven, Conn. using combination of surplus Model 1842 Springfield barrels and production over-run locks from Whitney's earlier M.1841 rifle contracts.

Conforming in general appearance to the Model 1842 with noted variance of lock (unmarked); three barrel bands, the upper one of equal width to the lower two instead of the wide double strap M.1842 band; wide iron forend cap; brass trigger bow with iron strap. Some barrels still retain Springfield proofs and tang dates 1852 or 1853. Typical Whitney seven-groove rifling; 69 caliber. Numerous other features identify this as a Whitney "good and serviceable" arm (q.v.).

Barrel marked at breech NH or NEW HAMPSHIRE. Quantity made possibly 2,000 (1,270 recorded as delivered). Thrifty New Hampshire was by 1858 getting around to replacing flintlocks still in the hands of local militias "...for new percussion muskets of modern style...equal if not superior to the arms delivered...from the Ordnance Dept.":

9B-035   Values—Good **$1,100**   Fine **$2,750**

Schalk Rifle-Musket

9B-036

Schalk Rifle-Musket. Made by G. S. Schalk, Pottsville, Pennsylvania; c. 1861; total quantity estimated less than 100.

58 caliber. Single shot muzzleloader. 40-3/16" round barrel; three barrel bands. Lockplate a surplus U.S. Model 1817 with markings removed.

Iron mountings. All metal parts finished bright. Steel ramrod with brass tip, mounted on left side of the stock, and entering through thimble on the forward barrel band. Lug for unique styled angular bayonet mounted under muzzle.

Walnut stock.

Barrel marked near breech: G. SCHALK POTTSVILLE 1861.

Believed made by Schalk to prove his abilities and in seeking a substantial contract for Rifle-Muskets. Sale of these very likely to State of Pennsylvania for militia or Volunteer Regiment issuance:

9B-036   Values—Good **$3,000**   Fine **$6,500**

"Windsor" British Enfield Type Rifle-Muskct

"Windsor" British Enfield Type Rifle-Musket. (Not illus.) Made by Robbins & Lawrence, Windsor, Vermont and Hartford, Connecticut; c. 1855-58; total quantity about 16,000.

577 caliber. Single shot muzzleloader. 39" round barrel; three barrel bands.

Brass mountings. All metal parts finished bright. Steel ramrod of knurled, slotted type and having swelled shank (as on Model 1855 and Model 1861 Rifle-Muskets). Front sight doubles as lug for angular bayonet.

Walnut stock.

Lock marking: (date)/WINDSOR forward of hammer; crown motif stamped on rear section of lockplate. Double line border on lockplate and hammer, which also bears slight decorative engraving. British proof marks at breech of barrel.

These so-called American Enfield arms were the result of an earlier favorable impression made by Robbins & Lawrence on the British Small Arms Commission, causing the Commission to seek out Robbins & Lawrence for arms needs at the outbreak of the Crimean War. 25,000 muskets of the British Enfield type were ordered in 1855. In expectation of substantial further orders, Robbins & Lawrence made a considerable investment in tooling and expansion. The quick ending of the Crimean War left the company without the further orders they expected, resulting in bankruptcy and preventing their completion of the 25,000 musket contract. A number of the 16,000 pieces completed never reached England; selling instead in America, as surplus. Many probably also returned to America at the outbreak of the Civil War. This is the only Enfield pattern arm made entirely in America. As a collector's item this is quite a scarce piece, and even though made in large quantity, specimens are seldom observed:

9B-037   Values—Good **$1,500**   Fine **$3,500**

Breech-Loading

Experimental and Trial Breech-Loading Rifles and Carbines For U.S. Service

In the final years of the Civil War and the decade following, the U.S. Government held competition trials for the examination and ultimate adoption of improved breech-loading weapons for issuance to U.S. Military services…all of which are illustrated, described and valued in the following pages of this chapter. However, there was a wide variety of other carbines (and some rifles) made as prototypes or very abbreviated production runs. Quite a few of those experimental or trial carbines (and an occasional rifle) have reached the collectors' market. Many of them are seen valued in the low to mid-four-figures, occasionally substantially higher. Among

factors to consider in arriving at a value are: the inventor's name and notoriety; the manufacturer; the uniqueness or oddity of the breech system and its exterior appearance (it should look like a military saddle-ring carbine!); its markings; date of manufacture and the government trial in which it may have been entered in competition; background and historical information that might be available. Two studies especially helpful in identifying such trial guns are *"The Breech-Loader in Service 1816-1917"* (Fuller) and *"Digest of Patent Relating to Breech-Loading and Magazine Small Arms in the U.S. 1836-1873"* (Stockbridge; See Biblio).

Breech-loading Carbines U.S. Trials 1865

ROBERTSON & SIMPSON
GOULDING
GWYN
GREY
BEAL
PERCY
ROOT
HAMMOND
ALLEN
FIELDS
JOHNSTON
REMINGTON
STRAW · 2
GWYN · 2
WRIGHT

Illustrated here are 15 typical examples of such experimental / prototype / trial carbines which were among a larger group of similar types entered by various American makers and inventors for the U.S. trials in 1865. The illustrations were taken from the 1925 edition of the Francis Bannerman, New York Military Goods catalog (with similar illustrations appearing in later years as well). Those catalogs are also a fine source for identification of trial and other types.

Carbine Slings for Mounted Soldiers to Carry (and not lose) Their Long Arms While on the March or in the Heat of Battle!

As elementary as it may appear (and often taken for granted by collectors familiar with American military longarms) it is surprising how many collectors (and non-collectors, too) unfamiliar with cavalry longarms have no idea what that loose-fitting, iron ring affixed to the left side of most 19th century carbines was utilized for! Nor do many of those who know what its purpose was, have any notion of what the accessory that affixed to it resembled, either! Illustrated here (attached to a Spencer Cavalry Carbine) is the standard U.S. issue, large, wide leather carbine sling (folded in center) that was worn over the left shoulder with its buckle facing to the back. The sling was normally 56" long and 2-1/2" wide and fitted with a brass tip. Its length was adjusted by use of the large, frame type brass buckle. A solidly built iron slide is fitted with a short iron chain and a massive, hook-type iron, spring clip that very simply snaps onto the standard swivel ring, usually affixed to the left side of almost every cavalry carbine. Earlier belts were made of black buff leather. By 1861 black harness leather was used, dressed on the outside only. It has been stated that cavalrymen wore the sling while both mounted or dismounted. (The slings are collector's items and quite scarce.)

Ball Repeating Carbine

9B-038

Ball Repeating Carbine. Made by Lamson & Co., Windsor, Vermont. Total quantity 1,002.

50 rimfire; 7-shot repeater; operated by lever which also acts as trigger guard. Walnut stock. Sling ring on receiver. 20-1/2" round barrel. Two-piece walnut stock with three-quarter length forend fastened by single barrel band.

Marked on left side of receiver: E. G. LAMSON & CO/WINDSOR, VT./U.S./BALL'S PATENT/JUNE 23, 1863/MAR 15, 1864. Inspector markings on left side of buttstock, top of wrist near receiver.

Records indicate that the government contracted for these arms in 1864 and delivery was made in May, 1865, following the cessation of hostilities. The arm is generally considered by collectors as a Civil War weapon even though it does not appear to have seen actual service:

9B-038   Values—Very Good **$2,000**   Exc. **$3,500**

Ballard Carbines and Rifles   *See Marlin, Chapter V-D.*

Blake Bolt Action Repeating Rifle

9B-039

Blake Bolt Action Repeating Rifle. Made by J. H. Blake, New York, c. 1890s to 1910, approximately. Quantity unknown; limited.

Caliber 30-40 Krag most often encountered, but others known. Unique seven-shot rotary magazine inserted from underside. 30" barrel usual with full walnut stock having checkered pistol grip and fastened by three barrel bands; wood cover over breech of barrel.

Very little accurate or significant information about this maker. (see 13-000.5.) Although the company issued an impressive catalog with many models in many grades and calibers, all with the rotary magazine, it is believed it was greatly overstated. Previously mentioned that this military model was reported on favorably in the U.S. trials of 1893, losing out to the Krag, it seems that just the opposite was the case. The U.S. Ordnance report for those trials actually states "(Blake) system entirely unsuited to the military service." Further research may find the same as to its recommendation after the 1896 N.Y. trials:

9B-039   Values—Very Good **$950**   Exc. **$2,250**

Brand Breech-Loading Single Shot Carbine

9B-040

Brand Breech-Loading Single Shot Carbine. Made by E. Robinson, New York, c. 1863-1865. Quantities unknown; very limited.

50 rimfire. 22" round barrel fastened by single barrel band. Swivel bar and ring on left frame. Markings BRAND'S PATENT JULY 29, 1862/E. ROBINSON MANFR/NEW YORK.

Although very little is known about these carbines, they were made in limited production quantities and used in field trials during the Civil War. They were evidently privately sold to officers or militia units as well. Promotional literature by the manufacturer lists quite a few actual testimonials as to their field and campaign usage.

Christopher C. Brand of Norwich, Connecticut, was more well known for his percussion whaling bomb-lance gun of the 1850s *(see 18-001* and also *8A-030.8 Brand Pistol).* These breech-loading carbines are rare:

9B-040   Values—Good **$2,750**   Fine **$5,500**

Brown Bolt Action Rifle

9B-041

Brown Bolt Action Rifle. Made by Brown Manufacturing Company, Newburyport, Massachusetts, c. 1869-1873. Quantity unknown; believed limited.

58 caliber rimfire. Single shot. Short bolt handle at extreme breech lifts upward; when pulled back exposes top loading chamber and simultaneously cocks the small centrally hung hammer immediately behind it. Bolt locking latch on right of receiver. 34" barrel fastened by three Enfield style iron barrel bands.

The full Enfield style stock shows distinct signs on all specimens observed of alteration from earlier side lock usage. The lock aperture and the left sideplates (lock screw escutcheon area) have both been very neatly filled with matching walnut wood. Brass Enfield style furniture. Iron cleaning rod.

Markings on bolt BROWN MFG. CO. NEWBURYPORT, MASS./PATENTED OCT. 17, 1871.

Brown Mfg. Co. was successor to the Merrimack Arms Co. and better known for manufacture of Southerner deringers and Ballard rifles (q.v.). Substantial information of the history of this relatively obscure rifle appeared in an article in the 2003 edition of *Gun Digest.* The rifle was made under the George Merrill patent of October, 1871. Submitted for a test in caliber 50-70 to the U.S. Ordnance Department in 1872, it was not recommended for adoption, further testing or issuance. That same 2003 article offers evidence that the rifle may have seen service in the ill-fated Fenian troubles at the Canadian-U.S. border in Vermont in 1870. A Newburyport, Mass. newspaper in March, 1872 reported that Brown had received and completed a contract to convert 2,000 Enfield rifles to breech-loaders:

9B-041   Values—Good **$600**   Fine **$900**

Burnside Carbines

Burnside Carbines. Made by Bristol Firearms Co., and its successor the Burnside Rifle Co., as noted under models below. Total quantities listed under variations. Manufactured c. 1857-1865.

54 caliber; percussion breechloader. The Burnside arms are of special collector interest due to the identity of their designer, Ambrose E. Burnside, Treasurer of Bristol Firearms Co. (financial difficulties caused him to sell his interest June, 1859) and famous Union general during the Civil War. The cartridge is also unusual, having either a copper casing, or of tapered foil.

First Model. Made in Bristol, R.I., by Bristol Firearms Co. c. 1857-58; total quantity under 300. Tape primer device within frame. Breech opened by lever adjacent to hammer, also actuating the primer device. 22" round barrel. Iron mountings; finish blue and casehardened. Walnut stock *without* forend. Serial numbered

9B-042
First Model

9B-043
Second Model

9B-045
Fourth and Fifth Model

from 1 on up. Top of frame marked: BURNSIDE'S/PATENT./ MARCH 25TH/1856. Left side of stock usually bearing inspector cartouche: RHKW. The U.S. purchased at least 200 of these, with most being issued to the 1st U.S. Cavalry at Ft. Leavenworth, Kansas, about Jan. 1858 and carried on various expeditions. A few experimental types and possibly as many as 50 sporting types were also made:

9B-042   Values—Good **$5,000**   Fine **$15,000**

Factory Altered/Transition (First/Second Model). (Not illus.) Believed made for trials, incorporating improvements suggested from Army field use of the First Model and other design improvements. A standard first model (serial number under 300) with side lever removed and the round aperture on the side of frame (where lever was fitted) plugged. An inside (Foster Patent) spring latch fitted to the breech lever. The round plug and a small area on the frame around it are neatly engraved in a simple scroll design, conjectured as an attempt to disguise the plug's unsightliness. U.S. markings on both sides of the frame. Estimated less than 50 so altered:

9B-042.5   Values—Good **$3,000**   Fine **$5,500**

Second Model. Made by Bristol Firearms Co. and by the Burnside Rifle Co., the latter in Providence, R.I. Manufactured in a total quantity of about 2,000; c. 1860-62. The breech mechanism opened by the inside latch device on the trigger guard. 21" round barrel. Iron mountings. Although finish often mentioned as case-hardened frame, it is noted that blued frames are mostly encountered. Walnut stock *without* forend. Serial numbered from about 250 on up, continuing the range begun by the First Model. Lockplate marked either BRISTOL FIREARM CO. *or* BURNSIDE RIFLE C°./PROVIDENCE=R.I. Barrel marked: CAST STEEL 1861. Top of frame: BURNSIDE'S PATENT/MARCH 25TH, 1856. Some breechblock latches marked: G.P.FOSTER PAT/APRIL 10TH 1860. The left side of the stock usually will bear inspector marking cartouche. It is known that this model was issued to the First Rhode Island Infantry who were in the opening attack at First Bull Run, July 21, 1861. Issues in smaller quantities were made to many cavalry units, including the 1st Maine, 1st New Jersey, 1st Pennsylvania, 1st and 2nd Indiana, 1st and 2nd Rhode Island, and 1st U.S.:

9B-043   Values—Good **$1,850**   Fine **$4,500**

Third Model. (Not illus.) Made by Burnside Rifle Co., Providence, R.I. Total quantity estimated 1,500; all made in 1862. 21" round barrel. This model differs from the Second type in having a forestock, and a somewhat modified hammer. Mountings, sling ring, stock, and finishes basically as on Second Model, except for the addition of a forend and barrel band. On outward appearance this 3rd Model very closely resembles the more often encountered 4th and 5th Models. Its most apparent difference is that it retains the solid, unhinged or pivoted breechblock found on the Second Model. Serial numbered from about 1500 on up, continuing the range from the Second Model. Lockplate marked BURNSIDE RIFLE C°/PROVIDENCE=R.I. Barrel

marked CAST STEEL, and sometimes 1862. Top of frame: BURNSIDE'S PATENT/MARCH 25TH, 1856. Some breechblock latches marked: G.P.FOSTER PAT/APRIL 10TH 1860:

9B-044   Values—Good **$1,250**   Fine **$3,250**

4th and 5th Models. Made by Burnside Rifle Co. Quantities as below. 1862-1865.

Identifying these "models" or variations presents no difficulty; understanding terminology is confusing, at best. In attempting to sort this out, the author hopes he does not further muddy the waters!

Most writers on the subject, including this one, have classified Burnsides into four "models" or "types;" all, collector terms of convenience. A fifth model has been either unmentioned, or specifically stated as not existing. The author of *Burnside Breech Loading Carbines*, Edward Hull (*q.v.*) makes the best case for the 5th model and beginning with the 6th Edition of this "Guide" it is so included.

Curiously enough, the U.S. Ordnance Dept. officially used "Model 1863" to cover both types, while the 5th type is actually marked MODEL OF 1864. Yet, neither official term has ever been adopted by a cataloger or arms writer.

Serial numbers: Models 1 through 4 seem to follow in sequence; Model 5 was apparently numbered in its own series.

Many cavalry regiments are known to have been armed with these models during the Civil War; among them: 1st Michigan, 3rd Indiana, 5th, 6th, 7th Ohio, 1st New Jersey, 3rd West Virginia, 3rd, 14th, 18th Pennsylvania, 2nd, 12th, 14th, 16th Illinois.

4th Model. Formerly No. 9B-046 "Transition type" in first five editions of this Guide and generally unmentioned elsewhere. Made 1863-1864. Quantity approximately 7,000. Breech mechanism differs significantly from preceding models, featuring a hinged center section of breech block, allowing for easier insertion of the unique Burnside cartridge. Mountings, saddle ring, stock basically same as 3rd model. Lockplate and barrel marks as on 3rd model with varying barrel dates. Frame marks same as 3rd model. Inspector's marks in cartouches on left side of buttstock. Barrel blued; frame blued or casehardened. Note: frame has no provision for the centrally located guide screw on the left side:

9B-045   Values—Good **$950** Fine **$2,500** Exc. **$3,750**

5th Model. Formerly No. 9B-045 the "Standard Model" or "4th Model" in the first five editions of this Guide; also termed "4th Model" by most other references. This is the model made, sold to government and issued in largest quantities; approximately 43,000 c.1863-1865. About identical to 4th model but with very noticeable guide screw in the center of the right frame that allows smoother operation of the breech as it rides in the corresponding curved groove in the breech block. Although first deliveries were made in 1863 the marking at top frame BURNSIDE'S PATENT/MODEL OF 1864 (an anomaly yet to be explained). Finish: blued barrel and casehardened frame:

9B-046   Values—Good **$950** Fine **$2,250** Exc. **$3,250**

Colt Military Longarms   *See Colt, Chapter V-B.*

Cosmopolitan Carbine

9B-047
Early Variant

9B-047.5
"Contract Type"

Cosmopolitan Carbine. Made by Cosmopolitan Arms Co., Hamilton, Ohio (owned by E. Gwyn and A.C. Campbell (*q.v.*). Manufactured in a total of about 1200 c. 1859-1862.

52 caliber, percussion, breechloader. Single shot falling block action. 19" round barrel with octagonal section at breech.

Iron mountings; finish in blue. Walnut buttstock. Sling ring mount on left side of frame.

Serial numbered from 1 on up, usually in company with an assembly number. Oddly sloped downward angled lockplate marking: COSMOPOLITAN ARMS CO./HAMILTON O. US./GROSS' PATENT/1859. On frame: UNION/RIFLE.

This carbine is a predecessor of the Gwyn & Campbell (*q.v.*), a very similar appearing arm made later, and by the same factory. The unusual hammer is a distinctive identifying feature for both types. The single contract for 1,140 of these was by the State of Illinois, ordered through the U.S. Ordnance Dept., Dec. 1861. Delivered by July, 1862.

The large majority issued to the 6th Illinois Cavalry and carried by them on the famous "Grierson's Raid" April-May, 1863 through Mississippi to divert Confederate attention from Grant's Vicksburg campaign. Considered among most daring foray of the Civil War, covering 600 miles in 16 days. The 5th Illinois Cavalry, which saw much service in raids and expeditions throughout Arkansas and Mississippi were issued over 400 of that contract.

There are quite a few variants, preproduction and transitional types known (all very scarce), especially of the early "Double loop, enclosed lever" style. All merit premium values. They are best identified through the Rentschler book *"Cosmopolitan and Gwyn & Campbell Carbines"* (2000; *q.v.*)

Earliest Type with "Double Loop, Enclosed Lever:" Locking latch for breech inside loop. Quantity approx. 50 with variations:
9B-047   Values—Good **$2,750**   Fine **$4,750**
Contract Type. Large rounded hammer and serpentine lever. Total 1,140 contract to Illinois. Transitional types known:
9B-047.5   Values—Good **$2,500**   Fine **$4,500**

Cosmopolitan Breech-Loading Rifle

9B-048

Cosmopolitan Breech-Loading Rifle. Made by Cosmopolitan Arms Company, Hamilton, Ohio; c. 1859-62; total quantity under 100; possibly under 50.

52 caliber. Single shot percussion. 31" round barrel, made with or without barrel band. Breechblock pivots downward when trigger guard/lever is opened downward.

Iron mountings. Blued barrel. Walnut buttstock with unusual feature of varnished finish; note lack of forend.

Serial numbered. Frame marking, on the separate lockplate: COSMOPOLITAN ARMS CO. (in arc)/HAMILTON O. US./GROSS' PATENT, to rear of the distinctive and unusually large hammer.

One of the rarest of Civil War period breech-loading longarms, comparison should also be made with the Cosmopolitan Carbine (*q.v.*). A number of variations have been observed in the Rifle, despite the quite limited total number produced. Bayonet lug on right side of muzzle for use with a large knife style bayonet. Sling swivels are sometimes present, mounted on the single barrel band, and on bottom of the buttstock:
9B-048   Values—Good **$3,250**   Fine **$6,500**

Evans Repeating Carbine   *See Chapter XIII, Repeating Rifles.*

Fogerty Repeating Rifle and Carbine

9B-049
"Carbine"

9B-050
"Rifle"

Fogerty Breech-Loading Repeating Rifle and Carbine. Made by American Repeating Rifle Company of Boston, c. 1867 to 1869. Quantities unknown; very limited.

50 rimfire. Repeating lever action mechanism; varying carbine and rifle barrel lengths. Carbine has short forend fastened by single barrel band; rifle full forend fastened by three barrel bands. Magazine and buttstock. Finish: Blued barrel with casehardened action.

Very little known about these arms and specimens are rare. They were evidently manufactured in short production quantities and they are for collector purposes often classified with "experimentals." A number of variations have been observed in them including specimens made for single shot use only (without loading devices in stock) but otherwise identical in appearance (values apparently the same as for repeating types). Very likely developed and submitted for military trials and contracts by the inventor. Valentine Fogerty commenced business in Boston c. 1866 as the Fogerty Repeating Rifle Company, subsequently becoming the American Repeating Rifle Company which was purchased in its entirety by Winchester Repeating Arms Company in 1869. Winchester turned an almost immediate profit on the deal by reselling the Fogerty machinery and made no attempt to utilize the Fogerty patents. It is surmised that Winchester's sole interest was to lessen any possible competition:

Carbine:

9B-049 Values—Very Good **$4,000** Exc. **$6,500**

Rifle:

9B-050 Values—Very Good **$4,000** Exc. **$6,500**

Gallager Carbine

Gallager Carbine. Made by Richardson & Overman, Philadelphia. Total quantity of about 17,728+ (5,000 chambered for 56-52 Spencer cartridge).

50 caliber, percussion, breechloader. Single shot, the barrel sliding forward to load. 22-1/4" round barrel.

Iron mountings; blued barrel with casehardened frame. Walnut buttstock with long iron patchbox (usually casehardened). Sling ring bar on left side opposite lock.

Serial numbered from 1 on up. Lockplate marking of two major types; see below. Inspector markings on left side of the stock at breech area.

Schuyler, Hartley & Graham, N.Y., are known to have converted 200 Gallagers to 44 cal. and a few to 50 cal. in the 1870s for commercial sale. Others are encountered with smooth, shotgun bores. Although conceivable factory made, all were most likely late, post-war conversions. Bannerman's, N.Y., in their 1889 catalog listed surplus Gallagers and offered to alter them to shotgun for an extra charge of $2.00.

The Gallager saw extensive service during the Civil War. Among the many cavalry regiments armed with it were the 2nd, 3rd, 4th and 6th Ohio, the 13th Tennessee and the 3rd West Virginia. Ironically, the inventor, Mahlon J. Gallager was from South Carolina. A number of minor variations are observed in trigger shape, sights, breech details, etc. Basic variants are:

Early Production Carbine; the lockplate marked: GALLAGER/ PATENTED JULY 17TH 1860/(serial number):

9B-051 Values—Good **$1,250** Fine **$3,000**

Standard Model; the lockplate marked: MANUFACT^D BY/RICHARDSON & OVERMAN/PHILADA/(serial number), and GALLAGER'S PATENT/JULY 17TH 1860

9B-052 Values—Good **$1,100** Fine **$2,500**

Final Model; as above, chambered for the Spencer 56-52 cartridge; about 5,000 produced; has cartridge extractor and a firing pin device (instead of percussion nipple). Often observed with blued frame apparently original contracted March 1865; delivered May 1865. At least 2500 of them sold 1870 as surplus eventually bought by France for Franco-Prussian War.

9B-053 Values—Good **$950** Fine **$2,250**

9B-051
Gallagher Carbine

9B-052

Gibbs Carbine

Gibbs Carbine. Made by William F. Brooks, New York City. Total quantity about 1,052.

52 caliber, percussion, breechloader. Single shot, the barrel sliding forward to load. 22" round barrel.

Iron mountings; blued, with casehardened breech, lockplate, and trigger guard/lever. Walnut stock. Sling ring mount on left side of the breech.

Standard marking on the lock of an American eagle, and W F. BROOKS/MANF^ED NEW YORK/1863. At breech: L.H. GIBBS/PAT'D/JANY 8, 1856. (Note: Earlier production specimens marked on lock only: W F. BROOKS/MANF^ED NEW YORK- and will bring higher values.) Inspector markings on left side of stock near butt, US on tang of buttplate, and B at breech end of the barrel.

The production of the Gibbs was cut off when the Phenix Armory (owned by Brooks and W. W. Marston) was destroyed by fire during the New York Draft Riots of 1863. The government had contracted for a total of 10,000 specimens, but only 1,052 were completed. About 500 Gibbs were issued to the 10th Missouri Cavalry with lesser quantities to the 13th and 16th New York Cavalry:

9B-054   Values—Good **$2,500**   Fine **$5,000**

**9B-054
Gibbs Carbine**

9B-054

Greene Breech-Loading Rifle

9B-055

Greene Breech-Loading Rifle. Made by A. H. Waters Armory, Milbury, Massachusetts; c. 1859 to early 1860s; total quantity about 1,500 U.S. plus 3,000 Russian contract.

53 caliber. Single shot percussion; underhammer bolt action mechanism of rather complex type, in which the bolt must go through two motions, and priming is done by placing percussion cap on nipple located forward of the trigger guard. 35" round barrel; three barrel bands.

Iron mountings. Blued finish, with casehardened hammer. Bright finished ramrod of trumpet head type. Front sight doubles as lug for angular type bayonet. Walnut stock.

Serial numbered. Upper tang of breech marked: GREENE'S PATENT/NOV. 17, 1857. Serial number marked on bottom of bolt.

This unusual arm was patented by Lt. Col. J. Durrell Greene, of the U.S. Army, and is historically significant as the first bolt action firearm adopted by U.S. Ordnance. Besides the curious nature of the mechanism, the weapon features an oval bore, cleaning brush aperture in the buttplate, and is somewhat European in styling. Although appearing to be smooth, the bore is the type of rifling invented by London gunmaker Charles Lancaster. 900 Greene Rifles were bought by U.S. Ordnance and delivered March, 1863. Very small quantities appear to have been sold to state militia units through the well known Boston firm of William Read & Sons which will likely account for the occasional specimen without inspector markings. 3000 were made and delivered circa 1859-1860 to fill a Russian government contract, none of which are known, nor are details of their markings or physical characteristics:

9B-055   Values—Very Good **$1,600**   Exc. **$2,750**

Greene Carbine

Greene Carbine. Made by Massachusetts Arms Co., Chicopee Falls, Mass. Total quantity of about 300; c. 1855-1857.

54 caliber, percussion, breechloader, with Maynard tape primer. Single shot, the barrel pivoting down and to the right for loading. 22" round barrel.

Finish: barrel browned, receiver blued with casehardened

lock and breech tang. Buttplate and patchbox are brass. Walnut stock. Sling ring mounted on rear of trigger guard.

Marked in the breech area: MAYNARD'S PATENT/SEP. 22, 1845, and MASS. ARMS CO/CHICOPEE FALLS, and GREENE'S PATENT./JUNE 27, 1854.

200 were delivered March, 1856 to fill a U.S. contract. 170 of

9B-056

them were sent west and issued to the 1st Cavalry for field test and carried on the Cheyenne Expedition May, 1857. Most of the others appear to have been sent to Florida for field trials. A small quantity in U.S. arsenals at the outbreak of the Civil War are known issued to the 6th Ohio Cavalry. Specimens are known with tinned finish, longer barrels and smaller calibers; all quite rare. Martially marked examples are worth premium:

9B-056   Values—Good **$4,750**   Fine **$15,000**

Greene (British Type) Carbine

9B-057

9B-057
Greene Carbine
British Type

Greene (British Type) Carbine. Made by Massachusetts Arms Co., Chicopee Falls, Massachusetts. Total quantity of about 2,000; made c. 1855-1857.

Very similar to the U.S. Type, with the following exceptions: Large crown over the cypher of Queen Victoria VR on the lockplate; British proof marks on barrel and on stock behind trigger plate; lock markings: MASS. ARMS CO/CHICOPEE FALLS/U.S.A.; shorter 18" blued barrel; 16-sided hand grasp section in center of the barrel; sling ring affixed to lower trigger plate; blued iron patchbox and buttplate.

2,000 of these arms were made under contract to the British government in 1855, for use in the Crimean War, but evidently they saw little actual service. Indications are that many of the carbines were destroyed and stripped for parts (which accounts for the large lot of mint condition locks that were on the market in the 1970s) before the British Government sold these as surplus. It is the author's opinion that more than the reported 200 survived. Legend has it that a number of the British Type Greenes were repurchased by the U.S. during the Civil War, but there is no substantive evidence of this. However, over the years collectors have very much tended to include this arm in a U.S. Carbine group, and on the American collecting market it is a desirable item. Scarce:

9B-057   Values—Very Good **$2,250**   Exc. **$4,000**

Gwyn & Campbell Carbine

Gwyn & Campbell Carbine, a.k.a. "Union Carbine" and "Grapevine Carbine." Made by Edward Gwyn and Abner C. Campbell, Hamilton, Ohio. Manufactured in a total quantity of about 8,200. c. 1863-1864.

52 caliber, percussion, breechloader. Single shot falling block action. 20" round barrel with octagonal section at breech.

Iron mountings; blued barrel, casehardened frame, lock and hammer. Walnut buttstock, with inspector markings on left side near frame. Sling ring mount on left side of frame.

Serial numbered from 1 on up. Lockplate marking: GWYN & CAMPBELL/PATENT/1862/HAMILTON. O. On frame: UNION/RIFLE.

The Gwyn & Campbell was successor to the Cosmopolitan (q.v.), and manufactured in the same factory. U.S. Ordnance issued a total of 13 contracts for the Gwyn & Campbell, totaling 8,202 carbines. Commercial sales were limited. Quite a few Union cavalry outfits were armed with these, including the 7th Tennessee, 5th & 8th Ohio, 4th & 8th Missouri, 3rd Wisconsin,

9B-058
Type I

9B-059
Type II

2nd & 3rd Iowa, 2nd & 3rd Arkansas, 5th, 6th, 16th Illinois, 2nd, 6th, 14th Kansas, 10th, 12th, 14th Kentucky.

Type I Carbine; a.k.a. the "Grapevine." Quantity 4,200. Both the hammer and lever are long serpentine shaped and rounded; long base rear sight and rear lockplate screw entering from the right side. Lever latch a long trigger-like spur inside bottom loop of lever. Two variations recognized: (1) Long base sight; adjustable leaf to 900 yards. Quantity made 4200. (2) Short base rear sight (Illus.); leaf adjustable to 600 yards. Quantity 700; serial range 4300 to 5150. Although scarcer, market values reflect only modest premium, at best:

9B-058   Values—Good **$1,250**   Fine **$2,750**

Type II Carbine; quantity 4,000 the most often encountered; the hammer flat with beveled edge; lever shorter, not as serpentine and only slightly rounded; short base rear sight; lockplate screw enters from the left. Small, claw-like, vertical mounted latch above tip of lever. Three variations recognized: (1) Curvature and projection on heel of butt plate more pronounced than illustrated. Quantity 1,380. (2) With butt plate as illus. Quantity 1,370. (3) With more efficient, horizontal, pivot-type lever latch mounted below tip of lever. Quantity 500. Scarce, but current market reflects only modest premium:

9B-059   Values—Good **$1,200**   Fine **$2,500**

Henry Lever Action Repeating Rifle   *See Winchester Firearms, Chapter V-K.*

Jenks Breech-Loading Flintlock Musketoon

Jenks Breech-Loading Flintlock Musketoon. Made by William Jenks, Chicopee Falls, Massachusetts; c. 1839-40; total known quantity manufactured 100 with possible total of 350.

64 caliber smoothbore. Single shot. Breech operated by pulling upward and rearward on a lever mounted in the upper tang area, exposing the chamber for loading. 25-9/16" round barrel, semi-octagonal breech section; two barrel bands.

Iron mountings (one known with brass mounts). Metal parts finished bright. Steel ramrods with button tip. Walnut stock of full length.

Serial numbered. Lock marking: CHICOPEE FALLS CO./MS.On the barrel breech: US/1839/WM JENKS/P/EB (later initials may be NWP). Left side of stock (opposite lock) bear inspector initials: NWP. Heel of butt marked with sub-inspector initials MPL.

Recommendations were made to shorten the barrel for use by mounted troops; specimens known with 19-1/2" barrel.

Distinctive features besides the unusual breech-loading mechanism are the back action type lock, the reversed positioning of the frizzen spring, and the use of serial numbers.

U.S. Ordnance Dept. ordered 100 November 1839; delivered February 1840. 25 sent to 2nd U.S. Dragoons in Florida for field test and 25 to 1st U.S. Dragoons at Carlisle, Pennsylvania for

9B-060

trials. By 1842 65 were on hand at Springfield Armory and ordered to be altered by purchasing new percussion locks from Jenks. Apparently the conversions were not performed and it is likely that the surviving examples were still in flintlock state when sold as obsolete arms in the 1850s along with the loose percussion locks.

It is known that 250 Jenks were ordered by the Republic of Texas and that they reached New Orleans by August, 1840. 100 of them described as "rifles" in the hands of Texas General A.S. Johnson by 1842 and 37 described as "carbines" were recorded transferred to the Galveston Hussars. To date no positively identified Texas-Jenks is known. It is quite possible that it was identical to the U.S. purchased musketoon:

9B-060   Values—Good **$9,500**   Fine **$25,000**

Jenks Carbine

9B-061

Jenks Carbine, a.k.a. "Mule Ear." Made by N. P. Ames, Springfield, Massachusetts. Total quantity of about 4,250; made c. 1843-46.

54 caliber, percussion, sidehammer breechloader. Single shot, loaded by pulling up and back on the hooked lever located on the breechblock. 24-1/4" round barrel, with two barrel bands.

Brass mountings, finished bright; the barrel browned, the lockplate and breech lever casehardened. Walnut full stock; not fitted for ramrod. Sling ring mounted on the rear section of the trigger plate.

Marked on lockplate: N. P. AMES/SPRINGFIELD/MASS, and W JENKS. On the barrel breech: W JENKS/USN/(inspector initials— either RC, RP, JCB, or JL)/P/(date). Inspector initials within cartouche on left side of stock in breech area. Earlier production were 54 caliber smoothbore and are worth a

9B-061
"Round Loading Aperture"

30 percent premium over values shown. Loading was through the round aperture at the breech (with ball and loose powder). Majority were later altered for use with a paper cartridge (circa 1861) having the loading aperture enlarged to oval shape and the bores rifled.

Production was on contract for the Navy and the Bureau of Ordnance and Hydrography. The Jenks percussion carbines and rifles are recognized as the only mule-ear type arms officially accepted by U.S. armed forces. An advantage of this type was the limited number of moving parts.

Ten Jenks carbines were given U.S. Army trials, 1842. Markings and particulars unknown. 40 were subsequently ordered (half of them smoothbore) and delivered Jan., 1844. All were issued for field testing to Co. "D" and "E" of U.S. 1st Dragoons. Markings unknown. Authenticated specimens very rare; worth premium.

Three specimens of this model known with the usual lock (i.e. not made with Maynard primer as on 9B-063) marked only REMINGTON'S/HERKIMER, N.Y. Presumably fabricated in c. 1846-47 in the interim during transfer of the Navy contract and the equipment from Ames to Remington. Very rare.

9B-061
"Oval
Loading Aperture"

Standard model; U.S.N. marked specimens:
9B-061   Values—Good **$1,250**   Fine **$3,500**
Scarce variation; marked U.S.R. and date, inspector initials, at barrel breech, indicating purchase and issuance by the U.S. Revenue Cutter Service; encountered with round loading aperture and without the sling ring. Rare:
9B-062   Values—Good **$3,250**   Fine **$7,500**

Jenks Carbine With Tape Primer

Jenks Carbine With Tape Primer. Made by E. Remington & Son, Herkimer, New York. Made 1847-48. Total quantity of about 1,000.

9B-063

54 caliber, percussion, breechloader with sidehammer, a.k.a. "Mule-Ear" type. Identical action as the Ames-made Jenks carbine. 24-1/4" round barrel, with two barrel bands. Long, oval loading aperture.

Brass mountings, finishes, stocks, and sling ring as on above Jenks-Ames carbine.

Marked on lockplate REMINGTON'S/HERKIMER/N.Y. On breech of barrel: W. JENKS/USN/RC/P/CAST STEEL/(date).

A distinguishing feature of the Jenks-Remington is the Maynard tape primer mechanism. E. Remington & Son bought from the Ames Manufacturing Company a contract which had been awarded for 1,000 Jenks carbines fitted with Maynard tape primers. The result was a noticeably modified arm, made on the original Jenks machinery, which was also purchased from Ames:
9B-063   Values—Good **$1,450**   Fine **$4,000**

Jenks Navy Rifle

9B-064

Jenks Navy Rifle. Made by N. P. Ames, Springfield, Massachusetts; c. 1841-42; total quantity 1,000.

54 caliber, rifled, percussion, breechloader with side hammer, a.k.a. "Mule-Ear"; also known in 52 caliber smoothbore. 35" round barrel fastened by three barrel bands. Lug on bottom of muzzle for attaching angular type bayonet.

Brass mountings. All metal parts finished bright, excepting browned barrel and casehardened lock.

Walnut full stock; not fitted for ramrod.

Lockplate marking: N. P. AMES/SPRINGFIELD/MASS, to rear of hammer. Rear section of lock marked: W JENKS. Breech of barrel marked W JENKS/USN/(inspector initials)/P/(date). Inspector initials on left side of stock, opposite lock.

The 1,000 specimens of the Jenks rifles were made on a contract of 1841 from the U.S. Navy; all delivered by 1844.
9B-064   Values—Good **$1,850**   Fine **$4,250**

Jenks-Merrill Carbine

Jenks-Merrill Carbine. Altered by James H. Merrill, Baltimore, Maryland; c. 1858-60. Total quantity of about 300.

54 caliber, percussion, breechloader. Single shot, loaded by pulling up and back on the breech lever device, which is secured

by an oval latch engaging the rear sight. 24-1/4" round barrel, with two barrel bands.

Mountings, finishes, stocks, and sling rings as on Jenks Carbine described above.

9B-065

Marked on breech lever J. H. MERRILL BALTO./PAT. JULY 1858 *or* JAS. H. MERRILL/BALTO. PATENTED/JULY 1858. On breech of the barrel: W JENKS/USN/RC/P/(date).

The breech action is identical in style and operation to the Merrill carbines (*q.v.*). Conventional Jenks carbines were sent to Merrill in Baltimore for alteration to his system to test the practicality and ease of using the Merrill type combustible cartridge rather than the more cumbersome loose powder and ball as required by the Jenks system.

Major distinguishing features are the breech mechanism and lever, the altered lock shape at forward end and the use of a conventional shaped hammer:

9B-065   Values—Good **$3,000**   Fine **$7,000**

Joslyn Model 1855 Carbine

9B-066

Joslyn Model 1855 Carbine, a.k.a. "Monkey Tail." Made by A. H. Waters, Milbury, Massachusetts. Made c. 1855-56. Total quantity unknown. Estimated quantity under 1,500 with 1,200 known sold to U.S.

54 caliber, percussion, breechloader. Single shot, loaded by pulling up and forward the breech lever device which is fitted and recessed along the upper wrist of the buttstock. 22-1/2" round barrel, with one barrel band.

Brass mountings, finished bright; the iron parts blued, except for the casehardened lock, breech, and breech lever. Walnut stock. Sling ring mounted on the left side of the stock.

Serial numbered on breech lever. Lockplate marked: A. H. WATERS & CO./MILBURY MASS. Breech lever marked: PAT^D BY/B.F. JOSLYN./AUG. 23, 1855. Inspector initials on left side of the stock, opposite lock.

The earliest of breech-loading carbines made under patents of B. F. Joslyn, the Model 1855 has added historic interest as the last firearms made by the A. H. Waters firm. Early in the Civil War the 2nd, 3rd and 4th Ohio Cavalry were known to have been issued 100 each of these Joslyns and 250 of them to the 6th Ohio:

9B-066   Values—Good **$2,500**   Fine **$5,000**

Joslyn Model 1855 Rifle

Joslyn Model 1855 Rifle. (Not illus.) Made by A. H. Waters & Company, Milbury, Massachusetts; c. 1860; total produced believed a few hundred or less.

58 caliber, percussion, breechloader. 30" round barrel; one barrel band. Lug on side of muzzle for attaching saber type bayonet.

Identical to the Joslyn carbine described above in configuration, mountings and markings with major distinguishing feature the long 30" barrel, bayonet lug, larger caliber and lack of sling ring. Serial numbered in sequence with the carbine.

The U.S. Navy Department ordered 500 Model 1855 Joslyn Rifles; it is believed less than 200 were delivered—the order likely to have been changed to carbines:

9B-067   Values—Good **$3,500**   Fine **$8,000**

Joslyn Model 1862 and 1864 Carbines

Joslyn Model 1862 and 1864 Carbines. Made by the Joslyn Fire Arms Co., Stonington, Ct. Total quantity of about 16,500.

52 rimfire caliber. Single shot, loaded by pivoting the breechblock up and to the left. 22" round barrel, with one barrel band.

Finishes and mountings described below. Walnut stock. Sling ring mounted on the left side of the stock, opposite the lock.

Serial numbered from 1 on up. Markings as indicated below; both models have inspector stampings on left side of the stock, opposite the lockplate.

The Joslyn proved to be one of the more widely used of Civil War carbines. Deliveries began early in the War, and continued through early 1865. A number of variations are known in both models and values will increase according to established

9B-068
Model 1862

9B-069
Model 1864

9B-068
Percussion Action,
Early Model 1862

Union cavalry regiments issued the Joslyn were the 4th and 8th Indiana; 19th New York; 13th Tennessee; 9th Pennsylvania; 3rd West Virginia; 2nd Wisconsin; 1st Nebraska; 1st Nevada and 11th Ohio:

Model 1862; mountings of brass, finished bright; barrel blued, lockplate casehardened. Lock marking: JOSLYN FIRE ARMS C°/STONINGTON/CONN. Top of breechblock marked: B.F. JOSLYN'S PATENT/OCTOBER 8TH 1861/JUNE 24TH 1862/(serial number). Trigger guard plate measures about 8" in length. 4-1/2" long breech tang. Hook type friction latch for the breechblock, and exposed firing pin extension. U.S. Government purchase 2,200; private purchase approx. 1,300. Transitional model with M1864 type breech/pull-out knob latch, etc. is found in approx. 2400-3600 serial range. Very scarce; worth premium:

9B-068   Values—Good **$1,250**   Fine **$3,000**

Model 1864; mountings of iron, casehardened, as is the lockplate. Lock marking: JOSLYN FIRE ARMS C°/STONINGTON CONN./1864. Breechblock marked as above. Trigger guard plate measure 7". 2" long breech tang. Knob type pull-out latch for breechblock, and protected or hooded type firing pin. Bulk of production was this model. U.S. Government purchase 8,000; private purchase 4,500:

9B-069   Values—Good **$1,100**   Fine **$2,750**

authenticity and desirability of such variants. The more interesting variations are those that appear on the earliest Model 1862s which are encountered with percussion ignition system and considered quite rare; on late production Model 1864s odd calibers (such as 44 rimfire) are known as are varied barrel lengths. Joslyns occasionally found without inspector markings; such specimens most likely those privately sold (see quantities below) through major military outfitters such as the noted Schuyler, Hartley & Graham of New York, where they may be found advertised in their famous 1864 catalog. Among the many

Lee Single Shot Carbine

Lee Single Shot Carbine. Made by Lee Firearms Company, Milwaukee, Wisconsin, c. 1864-1865. Quantities very limited. (*See also illus. No. 14-016, Chapter XIV.*)

44 rimfire. Centrally hung hammer. 21-1/2" round barrel swivels sideways to right to load; manual extraction by lug at right side of barrel breech. Sling ring and bar on left side of receiver. Walnut buttstock; made without forend.

Barrel marked LEE'S FIREARMS CO. MILWAUKEE, WISC., PAT'D JULY 22, 1862. Serial numbered.

One of the very few arms made in the West during the Civil War. Very little recorded about the arm, but it is known that in late 1866 Lee had completed 255 carbines (of which 102 were already sold) and that approximately 200 more were in various stages of near completion with a few more hundred in partial states. His sales were very likely privately made to officers or militia units; surviving specimens are very scarce. An identical sporting style rifle is encountered with longer, varied length, octagon barrels. Values of sporters about 30 percent less than the carbine.

9B-070

A source of confusion about the Lee is the fact that the U.S. War Department placed an order for 1,000 carbines on April 18, 1865. Lee subcontracted barrels to Remington at Ilion, New York. Due to a misunderstanding the barrels were bored to an incorrect caliber and the entire lot was rejected by government inspection. There is no record of further assembly of the arms of that contract and it is assumed they were never completed:

9B-070   Values—Good **$2,500**   Fine **$5,000**

Lee Bolt Action Magazine Rifle   *See Chapter V-E; Remington Arms, Remington-Lee Magazine Rifle.*

Lindner Carbine

Lindner Carbine. Made by Edward Lindner, Manchester, New Hampshire, probably at Amoskeag Mfg. Co. Total quantity of about 6,500.

58 caliber, percussion, breechloader. Single shot loaded by turning a rotating collar locking device on the barrel 180 degrees to the left; the breechblock then pushed upward by a spring. 20" round barrel, without barrel band.

Iron mountings, polished bright. Walnut stock. Sling ring mounted on left side of the stock, opposite the lock.

Breechblock marking: EDWARD LINDNER'S/PATENT/MARCH 29, 1859.

9B-071
First Type

**9B-072
Second Type**

A collecting anomaly due to lack of information was fact that the Second Type formerly was valued higher than the First Type. That situation has changed.

First Type. Two contracts total 892. (Nov. 1861, 391 to 1st Michigan Cavalry; late 1863, 501 to 8th West Va. Mounted Infantry.) Markings on breech only; lock unmarked. Overall length of stock 27-1/2"; square profile of buttplate. Rear sight behind breechblock. Sling ring left side opposite lock:

9B-071 Values—Good **$2,500** Fine **$5,000**

Second Type. Recent research indicated changes were made at request of Ordnance Dept. and Amoskeag given an order for 6,000

April, 1863. Amoskeag requested U.S. inspection of completed contract April, 1864, but for reasons yet unknown such never took place and delivery was refused. Amoskeag lost a lengthy law suit, the carbines believed ultimately sold c. 1870 to one of the European countries engaged in Franco-Prussian wars.

The carbine has many features of the Special Model 1861 Rifle-Musket (*q.v.*) Amoskeag then making under contract, the stock appearing as an altered musket type and an identical lock with same markings "U. (eagle) S. / AMOSKEAG M^{fg} C$^{o.}$ / MANCHESTER, N.H." with date at rear. Trigger guard apparently a musket type with sling ring attached to the reversed bow:

9B-072 Values—Good **$2,250** Fine **$3,000**

Maynard Carbine and Rifle

Maynard Carbine and Rifle. Manufactured by the Massachusetts Arms Co., Chicopee Falls, Massachusetts. (*See history of this noted maker with 7A-054 and 14-017.*)

35 and 50 caliber, percussion, breechloader. Single shot; barrel tips downward to load by lowering the trigger guard and pushing it forward. 20" round barrel with octagonal section at breech.

Iron mountings; blue finished with casehardened frame. Walnut stock; made without forend.

Serial numbered from 1 on up. Markings noted below.

Designed by Dr. Edward Maynard, inventor of the mechanical system for priming firearms (utilized in other U.S. arms) both models will also be found in various sporting configurations, calibers and barrel lengths. Percussion sporters tend to bring less than these military types. (*See also Chapter XIV.*)

First Model Carbine; made c. 1858-1859. Quantity estimated all types 5000. Fitted with the Maynard tape primer mechanism on right frame. Thick iron buttplate with iron patchbox door marked: MAYNARD PATENTEE/MAY 27, 1851/JUNE 17, 1856 (earliest have added date SEPT 22, 1845). Right frame: MAYNARD ARMS CO./WASHINGTON. Left frame: MANUFACTURED BY/MASS. ARMS CO., CHICOPEE FALLS. 20" barrel. Earlier types made with simple open barrel sights, most of which were replaced by maker with the long folding tang sight found on most specimens. Sling swivel on later production on lower trigger plate. Patchbox for spare rolls of Maynard tapes.

Known U.S. purchases, all in 50 caliber: 400 U.S. Army, delivered by March, 1859. Sent to St. Louis Arsenal of which 60 known issued from Ft. Union, New Mexico Territory to the

Regiment of Mounted Rifles; approximately 100 each to Co. I (1859) and Co. H (1860) 1st Cavalry which saw service on Indian campaigns. By the outbreak of the Civil War Co. I, 1st Cavalry, the 9th Pennsylvania and 1st Wisconsin were partially armed with it. U.S. Revenue Service acquired 200, all delivered by December 1860. The U.S. Navy purchased 60 in February 1860 and some were known issued to Marines aboard the U.S.S. Saratoga.

Southern State Purchases. There were sufficient purchases of this First Model by Southern states in the immediate months preceding the Civil War to actually include the gun in 35 and 50 caliber in their later issued Confederate ordnance manuals as an official weapon. The Mass. Arms Co., taking advantage of the crisis, made great efforts to dispose of their large inventory and were able to sell and deliver sizable quantities. Known purchases: to state of Mississippi 325 carbines in 50 cal. and 300 in 35 cal. To the state of Florida 1000 carbines in 35 cal. To the state of Georgia 650 in 50 cal. Approximately 800 (calibers unknown; likely mixed) were sold to various militia outfits in South Carolina and Louisiana while small quantity purchases are known to most other southern states in those hectic months.

As late as 1864 this 1st model was offered for commercial sale in the catalog of the noted New York City outfitter Schuyler, Hartley & Graham. U.S. inspector markings have not been observed by author; if specimens are found with authentic government markings, values would increase at least 50 percent over those shown below. No known authentic Southern or Confederate markings are recorded and collector is cautioned to

**9B-073
First Model**

**9B-074
Second Model**

**9B-073
Maynard Carbine**

be extremely wary of any. Such marks, if authentic would increase values substantially:

9B-073   Values—Good **$2,250**   Fine **$5,500**

First Model Rifle; Southern State Purchase identical to above; made without sling swivel; longer 26" barrel. (Not illus.) State of Mississippi purchased under contract 175 in 50 cal. Dec., 1860; likely small quantities sold to militia outfits. Georgia contracted for 250 of them but were never delivered:

9B-073.5   Values—Good **$1,500**   Fine **$3,750**

Second Model; a.k.a. in company literature as "Model 1863." Made c. 1863-65; total about 20,202. 50 caliber. Stock lacks patchbox and has thin, somewhat squared profile buttplate. Frame right side marked MANUFACTURED BY/MASS. ARMS CO./CHICOPEE FALLS. The left side: EDWARD MAYNARD/PATENTEE/MAY 27, 1851/DEC. 6, 1859. Made without the tape primer and tang sight. Sling ring on left side of frame; government inspector markings on left side of stock. Among the Union cavalry regiments armed with it were 9th and 11th Indiana and the 11th Tennessee. (Quite often seen in better states of condition):

9B-074   Values—Good **$1,000** Fine **$1,800** Exc. **$3,000**

Merrill Carbines

Merrill Carbines. Made by H. Merrill, Baltimore. Total quantity about 14,495.

54 caliber, percussion, breechloader. Single shot, loaded by lifting up and pulling back of the breech lever. 22-1/8" round barrel, with one barrel band.

Brass mountings; finished bright. Iron parts blued, or may be finished bright; excepting the casehardened lock, breech, and breech lever. Walnut stock. Sling ring mounted on left side of the stock, opposite the lock.

Serial numbered from 1 on up. Breech lever marked: J. H. MERRILL BALTO./PAT. JULY 1858. Other markings noted below. Stock stamped with inspector initials on left side, opposite the lock.

Government purchases of the Merrill Carbine were rather substantial, and an unusual feature of the Second Type production was the copper-faced breech plunger, serving to secure the percussion cartridge (combustible type) into the breech and form a gas seal. A number of highly interesting variants appear in Merrill carbines which can and do affect value upwards considerably. The very earliest have completely flat, flush fitted lockplates with staple type (open-pierced U-shaped) front sights; others have iron furniture and marking variations. These earlier pieces command considerable premiums and are seldom encountered. Those listed below are standard issue types. Merrills were known issued to the following Union cavalry regiments: N.Y. 1st, 5th, 18th; Penna. 11th, 17th, 18th; N.J. 1st; Indiana 7th; Wisc. 1st, 3rd; Ky. 27th; Del. 1st.

First Type; marked on lockplate forward of hammer: J. H. MERRILL BALTO./PAT. JULY 1858/APL. 9 MAY 21-28-61, and (rear

of hammer) the serial number. Stock fitted with brass patchbox, and the forend tip has sharply tapered contour. Breech lever is secured by latch of flat, knurled type:

9B-075   Values—Good **$1,250**   Fine **$3,600**

Second Type: lockplate marked as above, with addition of an American eagle design in center; behind hammer the serial replaced by the year of manufacture. Stock made without patchbox, and the forend tip has a rounder and thicker shape. Breech lever is secured by a rounded, button type latch:

9B-076   Values—Good **$1,400**   Fine **$4,000**

**9B-075 / 9B-076
Merrill Carbine**

**9B-075
First Type**

**9B-076
Second Type**

Merrill Rifle

Merrill Rifle. Made by James H. Merrill, Baltimore, Maryland; c. 1862-65; total quantity estimated at about 800+.

54 caliber, percussion, breechloader with action identical to Carbine. 33" round barrel; full walnut stock with two barrel bands. Lug on right side of barrel at muzzle end for attaching saber type bayonet.

Brass mountings and patchbox. Metal parts finished bright, excepting casehardened lock and browned barrel (some finished blue). Steel ramrod with button shape head.

Serial numbered, sharing range with Merrill Breech-Loading Carbine. Rifle numbers between about 5000-14000. Standard lockplate and lever marking identical to Carbine: J. H. MERRILL BALTO./PAT. JULY 1858/APL. 9 MAY 21-28-61, forward of hammer.

Inspector initials on left side of stock, opposite lock. Batch numbers also noted on various parts, e.g., inside patchbox cover.

A total of 770 Merrill Rifles were bought by the U.S. government during the Civil War period. They are ranked among the more rare and sought-after of percussion breech-loading rifles. Variations are also known and quite rare on this model; specimens with iron mountings have been encountered and will bring a premium. The only regiment known to have been almost entirely armed with them was the 21st Indiana. Small quantity issues were made to individual sharpshooters in the 7th, 10th Mich.; 4th Ark.; 1st Mass. A few rifles known issued to cavalry outfits also.

Standard model; as above:
9B-077   Values—Good **$2,000**   Fine **$5,000**

Late production specimens, with button latch release for the breechblock lever; rare, and found above serial range 14000. Lock marking of name/address/patent dates moved to forward section of plate, a small eagle motif marked to right of hammer, and the date of manufacture added at rear section (replacing the serial number):
9B-078   Values—Good **$2,250**   Fine **$5,000**

9B-077

Merrill, Latrobe & Thomas Carbine

Merrill, Latrobe & Thomas Carbine. Made by S. Remington, Ilion, New York. Made c. 1855. Total quantity about 170.

58 caliber, percussion, breechloader. Single shot, loaded by lifting up and pulling forward the breech lever. 21" round barrel, with one barrel band.

Brass mountings; finished bright. Iron parts blued. Walnut stock. Sling ring mounted on left side, opposite the lock.

Serial number marked on bottom of the breech lever. Lockplate marked: S. REMINGTON/ILION, N.Y. On top of breech: MERRILL, LATROBE & THOMAS/BALTIMORE, MD./PATENT APPLIED FOR. Left side of stock, opposite the lock: RHKW and ADK inspector stampings.

A rare and eagerly sought after Civil War carbine, only 170 are known to have been bought by the U.S. Ordnance Department, for trial use. The fact that Samuel Remington was the manufacturer adds to the collector importance of this extreme rarity. Among the important mechanical features of this model was the rammer mounted in the rear section of the breech (within the stock wrist) used to push the combustible cartridge into the barrel. Another distinct detail is the use of a Maynard primer:
9B-079   Values—Good **$12,500**   Fine **$35,000**

9B-079

Mont Storm Carbine

Mont Storm Breechloading Percussion Carbine. Invented by William Mont Storm (see also 9A-349). Although not finding favor with the U.S. Ordnance Dept., 2000 were ordered through that facility April, 1862 at request of the governor of Indiana

9B-079.5

through the Secretary of War with the endorsement of Col. Ripley of Ordnance (who had previously given it an adverse report). The order was placed with the well-known N.Y. military outfitters/arms dealers Schuyler, Hartley & Graham, acting as agents for the manufacturer (as yet unidentified, although Alsop of Conn. most likely; British maker possible). Records indicate 500 carbines completed by Dec., 1862 but delivery refused by the Ordnance Dept. as the contract had expired. No others likely made; the disposition of the 500 unknown.

58 caliber. 19-1/2" blued barrel (21-1/2" overall with the casehardened receiver); "trap door" type action; breech lifts upward. Marked on receiver "W. MONT STORM / PATENT JULY 1856." Enfield style, unmarked lock.

With the war in full swing and a desperate need for arms there were obviously political and other machinations affecting

9B-079.5

acquisition of this enigma. Less than handful of known specimens. The gun has a very English look to it and is closely similar to an English counterpart (variance in receiver size, etc.). Best and only reference about it by E.A. Hull in July, 1981 issue *"Man At Arms."* Undoubtedly there is more to the story:

9B-079.5   Values—Good **$4,500**   Fine **$12,500**

Palmer Bolt Action Carbine

9B-080

Palmer Bolt Action Carbine. Made by E. G. Lamson and Company, Windsor, Vermont; c. 1865. Quantity estimated 1,001.

50 caliber rimfire; single shot. The first bolt action metallic cartridge arm accepted for U.S. issuance. A quarter-turn of the short handle at rear of breech operates the bolt and exposes chamber for loading. Full side lock; hammer directly strikes cartridge rim for firing.

20" round barrel fastened by single barrel band. Barrel and furniture blued with casehardened lock. Walnut stock.

Receiver marked on top: W PALMER/PATENT/DEC. 22, 1863

Lockplate marked forward of hammer: U.S./E. G. LAMSON & CO./WINDSOR, VT. and 1865 at rear.

The Palmer was contracted for late in the Civil War with delivery not being made until June, 1865, after the cessation of hostilities; thus received too late for issuance. It is not accurately known how many were manufactured, but as all specimens encountered have borne government inspector markings, it is assumed that the 1,001 pieces known to have been purchased and delivered to the U.S. government are about the complete quantity made. A non-inspected piece, although rare, would not bring a premium. These arms when encountered, are quite often in excellent condition:

9B-080   Values—Very Good **$2,000**   Exc. **$3,500**

Peabody Carbines and Rifles

Peabody Carbines and Rifles. Made by the Providence Tool Company, Providence, Rhode Island; c. 1866-71. Total quantity all models 112,000.

Calibers 433 and 43 Spanish, 45 Peabody rimfire, 45-70, 50 rimfire and 50-70, and some European calibers. Breechloading, single shot. Trigger guard acts as breech lever, lowering the breechblock for top loading. Back action style lock and side hammer. Markings on receiver PEABODY'S PATENT JULY 22, 1862/MAN'F'D BY PROVIDENCE TOOL CO. PROV. R.I.

Iron mountings; blued finish with casehardened receiver. Walnut stock.

Development began in the early Civil War years; a few were entered in the trials of 1864 with favorable reports. Six were made at Springfield Armory for trials. The cessation of hostilities terminated all further U.S. interest. The great majority of Peabody's production was for foreign contracts, all of which are detailed in the authoritative "Providence Tool Co. Military Arms" (*see Bibliography*).

The end of the Franco-Prussian War, January, 1871, left Peabody with a large inventory of 50 rimfire carbines and the so-called "Spanish Model" rifle of which 10,000 were made for Spain, 8,500 for Mexico and 33,000 for France; all in caliber 43 Spanish (same as American designation caliber 433) with 33" barrel, full stock, etc. In order to dispose of those arms the company reduced prices sufficiently to win in competitive

bidding three state contracts; these were the only American military orders acquired:

Connecticut: c. 1871-72. Contract for 2,000 Spanish Model; caliber 433. By 1877, after rough treatment by state regiments, Connecticut negotiated a contract with Peabody to refurbish the rifles and replace the barrels in 45-70 cal. (barrels similar to Martini type). Rifles then continued in use until 1896 when sold to military and surplus dealers Francis Bannerman of New York. They are found advertised in their 1903 catalog; their later 1907 catalog shows them as having been "...altered to cadet size" with 30" barrels. The only identifying state marking is CONN. with serial stamped on the sling swivel plate on lower butt.

Massachusetts: c. 1872. Contract for 2,941 rifles. Identical as above Spanish Model, caliber 433. Marking MASS. with serial on swivel plate on butt. All declared surplus and sold 1883. A few Peabody's were purchased in 45-70 cal. in 1875 for competitive target shooting.

South Carolina: c. 1877. Purchased 350 carbines (part of original French contract) caliber 50 rimfire. Not until 1881 did the state have a die stamp S.C. made and mark those still in service on the heel of the buttplate.

Stock Inspector Mark: WC inside an oval cartouche (similar to the type marks used by U.S. inspectors) is found on all

9B-081

foreign contract Peabody arms except the Canadian contract. These initials were of a company, not government, inspector.

Canadian Contract: c. 1866. Strained relations between Canada and U.S. were partially causes of Canada's re-arming it's militia. Although 5000 rifles ordered and made, it seems that only 3000 were delivered and paid for. They were issued mostly to volunteer forces stationed along the border. Caliber 50-60 rimfire. Full stock fastened by three barrel bands to 36" barrel. Inspector mark DWB in oval on left wrist. Approx. 2,500 of these sold by Canada as surplus, 1898 to N.Y. dealers Hartley & Graham.

It is apparent that quite a few Peabodys in various military and sporting configurations were sold to the general public as evidenced by company catalogs 1865 to 1878 (*see also Chapter*

XIV). **Values** are mostly dependent on condition and caliber; 45-70 being among the more desirable and worth a 10 to 20 percent premium. Those with foreign proofmarks have been found less in demand with values usually 10 to 20 percent less than those below. Martially marked American and Canadian specimens as described above usually bring a 10 to 25 percent premium over values for the most often observed types described below:

Carbine: 20" barrel; forend fastened by single barrel band; sling ring on left side:

9B-081   Values—Very Good **$850**   Exc. **$1,650**

Rifle: 33" barrel; full stock, forend fastened by two barrel bands; front sight doubles as lug for angular bayonet:

9B-082   Values—Very Good **$700**   Exc. **$950**

Peabody-Martini Military Rifle and Carbine

Made by Providence Tool Co. c. 1873-1882. Never adopted or purchased for any U.S. military issuance, over 600,000 were sold under 3 contracts to the Turkish government; used during Russo-Turkish War. Delayed payment and default by Turkey caused bankruptcy of company, 1882. Advertised and sold on civilian market in very limited quantity in many calibers from 45-70 to 50-70 (worth premiums). Markings "PEABODY & MARTINI PATENTS / MAN'FD BY / PROV. TOOL" (etc.) with profuse Arabic marks on Turkish contracts which found their way to U.S. collectors' market in large quantity post WW II. 7000

known sold to Japanese Navy, 1882, bear both Turkish and Japanese marks. (Not illus; action identical to sporting rifle; *q.v.*) Values for Turkish contract; cal .45 Turkish:

Rifle: 32-1/2" barrel; 2 band fastened full forend (in 1911 some shortened to 29" and bore sleeved to 7.65mm):

9B-082.4   Values—Good **$450**   Fine **$750**

Carbine: 21-1/2" barrel. Single band fastened short forend; saddle ring:

9B-082.6   Values—Good **$575**   Fine **$900**

Perry Carbine

9B-083

Perry Carbine. Made by the Perry Patent Arms Co., Newark, New Jersey. Total quantity of the Navy type "long frame" (as shown) carbine estimated 250 with some sold on the commercial market. Made c. 1857.

54 caliber, percussion, breechloader. Single shot, loaded by pulling downward on the trigger assembly, which pivots the breechblock upward. 20-3/4" round barrel, with one band. A removable tubular magazine in the buttstock holds 50 percussion caps which are automatically spring fed to the nipple, and are actuated by the use of the breechblock. Specimens are known without this feature.

Iron mountings; standard finish blued, with casehardened breech. Walnut stocks. Most of production made without sling ring mount.

Serial numbering inconsistent. Many observed with all mismatched numbers and are presumed assembled accordingly. Several marking variations have been observed on the Perry, e.g.: PERRY PATENT ARMS CO, or PERRY PATENT ARM, or PERRY PATENT ARMS CO./NEWARK, N.J., or A. D. PERRY/NEWARK, N.J., etc.

9B-083

U.S. Navy ordered 150 in 1856; only 50 were accepted after twice rejecting them; made without saddle ring; iron mounted. U.S. Army ordered 200 of so-called short frame model, with saddle ring, c. 1855. Although an estimated 25 produced, recent research maintains none believed ever made for the order; no recorded deliveries against the order. Reason unknown.

A total of 1500 Perry breechloaders is estimated, which includes their many and varied configuration sporting arms which comprise a large majority of their production. Values below are for the Navy type carbine. If authentic U.S. martial marks are present, values should be increased at least 50 percent:

9B-083   Values—Good **$3,000**   Fine **$7,000**

Remington   *See Remington Firearms, Chapter V-E.*

Schroeder Needle Fire Carbine

Schroeder Needle Fire Carbine. Made by Hermann Schroeder, William Schmidt and Louis Salewski, Bloomington, Illinois, U.S. contract 1857 for 10 carbines.

9B-084

53 needle fire caliber. Single shot; action operated by rotating large side lever downward/rearward which moves barrel forward for loading and cocking the hammer; double set triggers. 26-3/4" octagonal barrel; cleaning rod beneath barrel.

Brass mountings finished bright; elaborate scroll type trigger guard. Barrel browned. Walnut stock with small cheekpiece.

Inspector marking RHKW on right side of the stock (inverted). Tang of breech has brass disc affixed on top marked in relief U.S. and American eagle motif.

This very rare and unusual arm has the distinction of being the only needle fire weapon purchased on contract by the U.S. government. The order for ten is believed all that were purchased. Given government trials 1860 and found unsuitable for military service.

9B-084   Values—Very Good **$25,000**   Exc. **$65,000**

Sharps, Various Models   *See Sharps Firearms, Chapter V-F.*

Sharps & Hankins Models   *See Sharps Firearms, Chapter V-F.*

Smith Carbine

9B-085

Smith Carbine. Made by American Machine Works, Springfield, Massachusetts, Massachusetts Arms Co. and American Arms Co., both of Chicopee Falls, Massachusetts, c. 1861-65. Total quantity estimated over 30,000.

50 caliber, percussion, breechloader. Single shot, loaded by depressing the latch ahead of the trigger which releases barrel allowing it to pivot downward giving the appearance of folding in half. 21-5/8" round barrel, octagonal to rear of barrel band.

Iron mountings; standard finish blued, with casehardened breech. Walnut stocks. Sling ring mounted on left side of the breech; early carbines by Mass. Arms Co. (only) under serial range 11000 (August, 1863) with sling swivels on barrel band and lower butt; worth small premium. It is recorded that the agents Poultney & Trimble handled the adaptation of some for the saddle ring and bar.

Serial numbered from 1 on up. On left side of the breech: ADDRESS/POULTNEY & TRIMBLE/BALTIMORE, U.S.A.and SMITH'S PATENT/JUNE 23 1857, and also the 3-line markings

of the contractors; either: MANUFACTURED BY/AM'N M'CH'N WKS/SPRINGFIELD MASS or MANUFACTURED BY/MASS ARMS CO/CHICOPEE FALLS. Values shown are for these two types. A third manufacturer marking in two lines, AMERICAN ARMS CO/CHICOPEE FALLS, is scarcer and will bring a slightly higher value.

Made in a significant quantity, the Smith was patented by Gilbert Smith, Buttermilk Falls, New York, and agents were Thomas Poultney and D. B. Trimble, Baltimore. Almost the entire production was purchased by the government with some sold commercially. The famous Civil War military outfitters Schuyler, Hartley & Graham of N.Y. prominently advertised the Smith and its special ammunition in their 1864 catalog, which will likely account for the occasional very fine condition specimen lacking inspector markings.

Among the Union cavalry regiments issued the Smith were the 3rd W.Va., 7th, 11th Ill., 1st Conn., 7th, 17th Penna., 6th, 9th Ohio, and 1st Mass.:

9B-085   Values—Very Good **$1,450**   Exc. **$3,000**

Spencer Repeating Rifles and Carbines

**9B-086
Carbine–Civil War**

Spencer Repeating Rifles and Carbines. Made by Spencer Repeating Rifle Company, Boston, Massachusetts, with some production subcontracted by Burnside Rifle Company, Providence, Rhode Island. Total carbines and rifles approximately 144,500 of which 107,372 rifles and carbines sold to the United States government.

Rimfire calibers as listed below. Seven-shot repeater; loaded by magazine tube fitted through center of buttstock. Operated by lowering and raising the combination trigger guard-lever. Various barrel lengths as noted below.

Iron mountings; standard finish casehardened receiver, buttplate and barrel bands; blued barrel. Walnut stocks.

Usual markings on top of frame SPENCER REPEATING/RIFLE CO. BOSTON, MASS./PAT'D MARCH 6, 1860 with other markings as noted below.

One of the most colorful, widely used and popular Civil War firearms, the Spencer received the unique advantage and distinction, after a trial firing demonstration, of gaining the personal endorsement of President Lincoln. Toward the end of the Civil War, the Spencer established itself firmly as the main arm for cavalry use and was widely issued during the Indian Wars eras also. It was a dazed, somewhat incredulous Confederate soldier, after capture by Custer's 5th Michigan Cavalry at Gettyburg (only outfit armed with the Spencer that day) who is credited with the oft-repeated remark that "(Spencers) load in the morning and fire all day!" Although seldom mentioned, it was the Spencer "Army Model" **RIFLE** (9B-093) with 30-inch barrel and full stock that the Fifth Cavalry was armed with; carbines were yet to be issued, the rifle being the first group purchased and issued by the government (see 9B-093 for serial range).

A major source of confusion arising in the nomenclature, and oftentimes description and identification, are the caliber designations originally assigned to various models and not in common usage by present day collectors.

The rimfire metallic cartridge used in the Civil War issue Spencer Rifle and Carbine was known as the "No. 56" or 56-56, these latter numbers referring to the measurements at the top and bottom of the copper case, indicating it was straight. In actuality, the bore measurement of the arms in which this case was used is 52 caliber, and in present day collector terms such arms are described usually as 52 caliber.

The cartridges used in the post-Civil War models were officially termed the 56-52 and 56-50, each being very slightly tapered and both used interchangeably in all models of the post-Civil War era. Present day collector terms usually describe such arms as 50 caliber, referring to bore diameters. Hence, for ease of identification, the most often encountered bore sizes of 52 and 50 are used herewith to describe the various models. From studies made of these arms it is noted that Spencer always used six groove rifling while those made by Burnside or converted at the armory have three groove rifling.

A few rare variations of Spencers are known in lesser calibers and smaller, lighter weight frame sizes. They are considered as early trial developmental types and are quite rare. Their values are considerably in excess of those for the usual production types. Sporting models are occasionally encountered. Many variations, sporting model and foreign copies are identified in *"Spencer Repeating Firearms"* by R. Marcot (see Biblio.).

CARBINES: Sling ring bar with ring on left side; short forend fastened by single barrel band; sling swivel on underside of butt.

Civil War Model: Made c. 1863-1865. 52 caliber rimfire (56-56). 22" barrel with six groove rifling; sling swivel at butt. Approximately 50,000 manufactured. Serial number range 11000 to 61000:

9B-086 Values—Good **$1,850** Fine **$4,000**

Post-War Alteration of Above: Altered by Springfield Armory c. 1867-1874. 50 caliber rimfire (56-52 and 56-50 interchangeable). 22" barrel sleeved for smaller caliber; three groove rifling. Small swivel device known as the "Stabler cut-off" added forward of the trigger to allow for use as a single shot (keeps breech from opening completely.) These arms very often arsenal refinished and restocked; markings will often appear weak or thin. They are desirable and the amount of reblue and recasehardening is important to evaluating. Over 11,000 altered. Stock bears ESA inspector markings in oval cartouche on left side:

9B-087 Values—Good **$1,600** Fine **$3,000**

Model 1865: Made c. 1865-1866. 50 caliber. 20" barrel; six groove rifling. Approximately 50 percent are fitted with the Stabler cut-off. Serial numbered approximately 1 to 23000. Additional marking at breech of barrel M 1865:

9B-088 Values—Good **$1,600** Fine **$2,750**

Canadian Marked Model 1865 Carbine. Although Canadian records are vague, it is known that Spencer contracted with the Canadian government in 1866 (and probably earlier) for both carbines and rifles. Quantities unknown, but estimated a few thousand delivered. Both types (along with other varied arms) were issued to the Royal Canadian Mounted Police as well as Canadian volunteers and citizens along U.S.-Canada Frontiers to aid in repelling and suppressing raids by the Irish Fenian Society in their attempt to procure independence from Great Britain. Whether those particular Spencers were marked or not by the Canadian government is unknown. However, specimens with official Canadian markings are noted bearing stampings on the extreme breech of barrel of a small flaming bomb motif over a rectangular panel with large "W.D." (War Department) and a date. A close-up illustration of one of these marks with the date "1864" clearly indicates that *some* of these Spencers were earlier models as well. Spencer's so-marked are extremely scarce and likely to bring premium values of 25 to 50 percent.

9B-088.2

Contract Model 1865: By Burnside Rifle Company c. 1865. Identical to above, but with three groove rifling. Approximately 34,000 made of which U.S. government purchased 30,502. It can only be surmised as to where the balance of 3,500 went. Possibly destroyed as government rejects or privately sold; the latter being the most likely. Markings on top of receiver SPENCER REPEATING RIFLE/PAT'D MARCH 6, 1860/MANUF'D AT PROV. R.I./BY BURNSIDE RIFLE CO./MODEL 1865. Serial numbered in their own range 1 to 34000. Approximately 19,000 of these are fitted with the

9B-092
Military Rifle

9B-097
Springfield Armory Alteration of Carbine to Infantry Rifle

Stabler cut-off, hence specimens without it tend to bring a slight premium:

9B-089   Values—Good **$1,600**   Fine **$2,750**

Mexican Military Marked Spencer "Contract Model 1865" Carbine as above. Quantities unknown; purchased as U.S. surplus arms and deeply marked on the top and right side of the receiver with small oval panel having liberty cap-like motif in center surrounded with a sunburst design over the large letter R.M. (Republic of Mexico). Values approximately the same as 9B-089 although premium of 10 to 20 percent justified.

9B-089.2

Model 1867: Made c. 1867. 50 caliber. 20" barrel; six groove rifling; additional marking at breech of barrel M 1867. A distinguishing feature of many of these (but not all) is the Spencer patent magazine cut-off; an extra wide device in place of the usual very narrow cartridge ejector guide at the top of the breechblock; pivoting the top prevents the breechblock from traveling rearward sufficiently to accept the next cartridge in the magazine. Estimated production 3,000. Serial numbered in the range of 91000 to over 101000 along with the Model 1867 rifles:

9B-090   Values—Good **$1,600**   Fine **$2,750**

"New Model": Manufactured c. 1868. Identical to above, but with marking N.M. at breech of barrel. Has Spencer patent cut-off. Estimated production 2,500. Numbered with the New Model rifle series in range of about 101000 to over 108000:

9B-091   Values—Good **$1,600**   Fine **$2,750**

MILITARY RIFLE OR MUSKET: 30" barrel; full stock forend with iron tip; fastened by three barrel bands; sling swivels.

Navy Model: Civil War production; made c. 1862-1864. 52 caliber. Six groove rifling; large lug underside of muzzle for saber type bayonet. Total purchase by U.S. Navy of 1,009 pieces of which 709 are of this pattern; the balance of the contract believed filled with Army style as below. Serial numbers fall in the range of 1 to 750. This represents the first Spencer of any type purchased by the U.S.:

9B-092   Values—Good **$2,250**   Fine **$5,000**

Army Model: Civil War production; made c. 1863-1864. 52 caliber. Six groove rifling; front sight doubles as lug for socket type bayonet. 11,470 delivered. Serial range from approximately 700 to 11000 with another small group in the 28000 range. It was this "Army Model" **rifle** with which Custer's Fifth Michigan Cavalry was armed at Gettysburg. Those rifles are presumed to fall within serial ranges 100 to 1550. With their historical significance to the Spencer story and American military history (and further substantiation of serial ranges) specimens are likely to fetch a premium yet to be determined.

9B-093   Values—Good **$2,000**   Fine **$3,750**

Post-war alterations of Army Model rifle by Springfield Armory c. 1867-74. Caliber 50 rimfire, fitted with "Stabler Cut-Off" device. Total 1,215 altered:

9B-093.5 Values—Good **$1,400**   Fine **$2,500**

Model 1865: 50 caliber, six groove rifling. Barrel also marked at breech M 1865. Front sight doubles as lug for socket bayonet. Estimated production approximately 1,000. Serial numbers in Carbine range approximately from 1 to 23000. No recorded U.S. Government purchase:

9B-094   Values—Good **$1,400**   Fine **$2,750**

Model 1867: Identical to above, but with markings M 1867 at breech of barrel; some encountered with the Spencer patent cut-off. Estimated production 7,000; serial numbered in range 91000 to over 101000:

9B-095   Values—Good **$1,400**   Fine **$2,000**

"New Model": Identical to above with markings N.M. at breech of barrel. Observed with either lug for saber type bayonet under muzzle or with front sight doubling as lug for socket bayonet; made in about equal quantities and value the same. Estimated production 5,000; serial range approximately 101000 to over 108000:

9B-096   Values—Good **$1,400**   Fine **$2,000**

ALTERATION OF CAVALRY CARBINE TO INFANTRY RIFLE: Performed at Springfield Armory c. 1871. The arms used were the Burnside marked Model 1865 carbines with receivers refinished at the Armory. The Armory added a new 32-1/2" round 50 caliber barrel with three groove rifling, Stabler cut-off, full forend fastened by two barrel bands and an iron ramrod with ribbed head. 1,108 arms so altered. Serial number marked at breech of barrel to correspond to original receiver number. Stock bears ESA inspector markings in oval cartouche on left side of butt:

9B-097   Values—Very Good **$1,750**   Exc. **$3,000**

Starr Percussion Carbine

Starr Percussion Carbine. Made by Starr Arms Co., Yonkers, New York, c. 1862-65. Total quantity 20,601.

54 caliber, breechloader. Single shot, loaded by pulling down on the combination trigger guard/lever, which allows the breechblock to lower and tip backwards. 21" round barrel, fastened by single band.

Brass barrel band and buttplate; iron parts blued, with casehardened lock and frame. Walnut stocks. Sling ring on left side of the breech.

Serial numbered. Lock marked: STARR ARMS Cº/YONKERS, N.Y. On barrel: STARR ARMS Cº YONKERS, N.Y. On breech: STARR'S PATENT/SEPT. 14th 1858. Inspector initials on left side of buttstock.

9B-098

The inventor, Ebenezer T. Starr, was a son of gunmaker Nathan Starr, Jr., and in government tests the carbine was rated as better than the Sharps. A number of the Starrs were issued for service in the West, primarily to the following Union cavalry regiments: 1st Ark., 5th Kansas, 11th Missouri and 24th N.Y. The 1st Arkansas is the only one known to have officially identified their carbines. Authentic, but awkwardly and unevenly stamped (with single letter dies) three line markings 1/ARK/(co. Letter) at the top of the frame over breech. (Exercise caution to verify originality of markings as they are the type subject to abuse.) Worth premium of 50 percent and greater:

9B-098   Values—Good **$1,250**   Fine **$3,000**

Starr Cartridge Carbine

9B-099

Starr Cartridge Carbine. Made by Starr Arms Co., Yonkers, New York. Total quantity 5,002. The first 1000 of these were delivered by March 9, 1865 and were those that were issued to the Winchester (Va.) Ordnance Depot at the end of the month. By April 10th 2,000 more were received; the balance of the order completed by May 25, 1865.

52 caliber rimfire. Single shot, falling block breech mechanism. 21" round barrel.

Iron barrel band, buttplate and barrel blued, with casehardened lock and frame. Walnut stocks. Sling ring mounted on left side of the breech.

Identical in most respects to its percussion predecessor, this model has a smaller, straight hammer. Major markings are the same as for the percussion model, and serial numbering continued from those arms. The Starr company went out of business in 1867:

9B-099   Values—Good **$1,100**   Fine **$2,750**

Symmes Carbine

9B-100

Symmes Carbine. Designed by Lt. John C. Symmes, U.S. Army. Made c. 1857. Made by Bruce & Davis, Worcester, Massachusetts. Total quantity about 20.

54 caliber, percussion, breechloader. Single shot, loaded by pulling down and forward on the combination trigger guard/lever, which pivots up the breechblock backward exposing chamber. 21-7/8" round barrel with pentagonal rifling.

Brass mountings; iron parts blued. Walnut stocks with three-quarter length forend fastened by two bands. Sling ring on left side of breech.

Tang of breech marked: LT. SYMMES PATENT. Inspector cartouche with initials RHKW on left side of buttstock.

Lt. Symmes' unique carbine received a government contract order for 200 specimens, but only 20 were delivered. In tests, problems of gas leakage at the breech and excessive fouling caused the gun to be rejected as not up to service requirements. The result for collectors is one of the ultimate rarities in U.S. Military Carbines:

9B-100   Values—Good **$25,000**   Fine **$50,000**

Triplett & Scott Repeating Carbine

Triplett & Scott Repeating Carbine. Made by the Meriden Manufacturing Company, Meriden, Connecticut, c. 1864-1865. Total quantity estimated 5,000.

50 caliber rimfire. Seven-shot magazine tube in butt. Unusual loading action: depressing latch in frame behind hammer allows barrel to twist in circular motion to come in line with magazine protruding through butt. Made in two barrel lengths: 30" round barrel (3,000 estimated) and most often observed; also 22" round barrel (2,000 estimated) quite scarce and will bring approximately 20 percent premium value over that listed below.

Iron mountings with single barrel band for forend. Sling swivels on the underside as well as heel of butt. Barrel, sights, and tubular socket blued with receiver and other parts casehardened.

Markings: On tang TRIPLETT & SCOTT/PATENT DEC. 6, 1864 on left side of receiver MERIDEN MAN'FG. CO./MERIDEN, CONN. with serial number on right side. Marked KENTUCKY left side of breech.

A contract for 5,000 Triplett & Scott carbines was executed January 2, 1865, with the state of Kentucky to arm 5,000 Home

9B-101

9B-101
Triplett & Scott Carbine

Guard troops mustered into service to protect the supply lines of the Union Army under General W. T. Sherman, then engaged in the Atlanta Campaign. They were received too late for service in the Civil War. Markings believed to be inspector's noted on most N/W.B. in small block letters on left side of stock near buttplate.

These carbines are often seen in fine condition and with line cracks in buttstock, which were weakened by the method with which the magazine tube is embedded in it.

This carbine has dual historical association. It represents the second venture into arms making by Charles Parker, co-founder of the Meriden Manufacturing Co. and soon to become (1866-67) co-founder of what became the most famous of all American shotgun manufacturing firms. See full story Chap. XVII and also Parker's manufacture of a Civil War military musket (9A-324):

9B-101   Values—Very Good **$1,500**   Exc. **$2,750**

Warner Carbine

9B-102
Made by Warner

9B-103
Made by Greene

Warner Carbine. Made for James Warner of Springfield, Mass. by the Massachusetts Arms Co. Made c. 1864. Total quantity 1,501.

50 Warner rimfire (many changed to 56-50 Spencer). Single shot; breechblock hinged on right side; loaded by lifting upward. Extraction by a manual slide at rear underside of forestock. 20" round barrel, fastened by single iron band.

Brass frame, breech, trigger guard assembly, buttplate, finished bright. Barrels usually blued. Walnut stocks. Sling ring mounted on eye bolt on left side of breech.

Serial numbered. Markings on left side of frame: JAMES WARNER, SPRINGFIELD, MASS./WARNER'S/PATENT(earliest production, believed first 200, without frame markings, are thought to be those made for Warner before the patent was officially issued). Release for breechblock is a thumb lever in recoil shield to left of the hammer. Buttstock with CSL inspector marking on left side near breech. Specimens known with iron frames very rare and will bring values considerably higher than brass frame styles:

9B-102   Values—Good **$2,250**   Fine **$4,750**
Variant by Greene Rifle Works: Made for James Warner for his 2nd contract for 2500. Delivered between Feb. and March, 1865. Chambered for the 56-50 Spencer cartridge. Identical action, all brass frame and breech with significant manufacturing differences such as a friction locked breech merely kept closed by the hammer; a sling ring bar on left side of frame in place of the eye-bolt and a larger and heavier manual extractor under forend. Marked: GREENE RIFLE WORKS/WORCESTER, MASS.PAT. FEB. 1864

Warners were known issued to the 3rd Mass. and 1st Wisc. Cavalry Regiments. By 1870 almost 2500 of them (possibly both types) were sold as surplus to a noted N.Y. dealer who immediately resold them to France for use in the Franco-Prussian War:

9B-103   Values—Good **$2,000**   Fine **$4,500**

Wesson Carbine   *See Frank Wesson Arms, Chapter V-I.*

Chapter X

Confederate Firearms

One of the most difficult and challenging areas of collecting is that of Confederate arms. Broad in scope, the field encompasses just about every American firearm made up to 1861, as well as a great many European pieces. In their desperate struggle to arm themselves and engage in full-fledged war, the Southern states used almost every conceivable weapon on hand while sending agents abroad to purchase whatever was currently available from European markets.

This chapter is limited to those weapons actually made in the Confederate states (with the one notable exception of the LeMat) during the period 1861 to 1865 and touches upon other Confederate associated and used firearms.

A few salient features should be noted: (1) All surviving specimens are scarce and a great majority are rare. There are no common Confederate arms on the collectors' market. (2) Almost all Confederate made firearms display workmanship and quality not commensurate with those manufactured in the North or in Europe. Many specimens may be accurately termed crude or primitive; it is quite often this feature, and at times an awkward appearance, that holds the greatest attraction and desirability for the collector. (3) Almost all Confederate made guns saw service—and extensive service at that; hence, surviving examples in any condition are desirable. Guns in fine or mint condition may be considered extreme rarities. A few of the more widely manufactured types, such as the Richmond muskets or Fayetteville rifles, may be found in better grades of condition (and considered rare) while for many other makes the collector would consider himself quite fortunate to find a complete piece (or often even parts thereof) in any grade of condition.

Herein listed are almost all known Confederate manufactured handguns and longarms. It must be stated that some of these rarely, if ever, become available. The author has seldom encountered specimens of some of these makers in more than half a century of collecting and dealing. It will become quite apparent when reviewing this section which pieces those are. Due to the great rarity of such arms and the lack of accurate information on reported sales, the value ranges shown for them are very broad based estimates. Although the effort was made to list all known Confederate arms about which information is available, the reader should be aware that there are other Confederate makes that might be encountered but for which information is too sparse or examples either unknown or unavailable for study. Arms of the Montgomery (Ala.) Arsenal, Florence (N.C.) Armory, Holly Springs (Miss.), Memphis (Tenn.) Arsenal and L.G. Sturdivant & Co. (Ala.) are a few such reported types.

A few handguns occasionally found listed in other treatises on Confederate arms have been purposely omitted from this work. They were either one-of-a-kind or were questionable as to their origin of manufacture; the likelihood of either type being encountered is decidedly remote. The author felt that without further substantiation of such arms, he might be perpetuating a myth by their inclusion.

SIGNIFICANT NEW INFORMATION ABOUT C.S. ARMS

This field owes much to the tireless efforts of the late William A. Albaugh III, who almost single handedly was the pillar of knowledge in the study of Confederate weapons. His highly respected, prolific writings have been a major source of reference. In very recent years a few excellent studies have been published which add substantially to Confederate arms lore. The most recent, *"Confederate Rifles and Muskets"* by Murphy & Madaus (*q.v.*) offers a new approach for collecting both Confederate and pre-Civil War American firearms. Its very broad coverage of southern arms makers is the most thorough yet undertaken, affording a comprehensive insight to Confederate contract and manufacturing procedures. It is also the first extensive examination and identification of southern private contractors that altered flintlock arms to the newer percussion system. Invariably, they did not mark or otherwise identify their work. The altered arms, however, possess a number of distinctive features, especially in the area of bolsters, that allow for both tentative, and in some instances positive, identification. There is little doubt but that this opens a new vista for collecting both U.S. and C.S. arms.

Immediately apparent are the vast numbers of small firms engaged in the Confederate arms business and the extremely limited quantities of weapons many, if not most, actually delivered. It is equally apparent that the trial and error manufacturing processes and unavailability of materials led to a great many variations in their finished arms. Thus, most Confederate weapons are not as easily or neatly classified as those made in the Union; all of which leads to possible abuses today by the unscrupulous. The mere fact that various conversions are illustrated in this important work is not in itself always proof that specific types are Confederate, nor positive identifications of various arsenals, beyond shadow-of-doubt.

The authors specifically state in some instances that their identifications are tentative. The reader is urged to read the accompanying text. This caveat is issued as this author has observed that too often collectors tend to jump to conclusions without reading the "fine print!"

Virtually unstudied and unexploited, this new mine of information opens another avenue for collectors. It's yet too early to survey what effect it may have on the marketability and value of many newly identified and tentatively identified conversions, but it should prove interesting to see how the collectors' market reacts to them. What this new study clearly shows is how much yet remains to be known about Confederate arms and arms manufacture.

ALL THAT GLITTERS, ETC.

Present data are reasonably accurate and reliable for the more well-known Confederate arms. On the many supra-rare makes, so little reliable information and so few specimens have survived, that the collector should have some experience under his belt and be well armed with all factual information currently available.

In collecting Confederate arms it is not quite possible simply to use the available reference sources for complete verification and comparison of all types as variances are so often encountered. Thus, the accumulation and study of them is a rather inexact science. The neophyte, especially, is often apt to find himself travelling in somewhat muddy waters.

In some instances makers are known whose products have yet to be identified. Occasionally unmarked, poorly made (if not crude) unidentified firearms appear on the market labeled "Confederate"—and priced accordingly! Of course, it is possible that some are just that. It has been the author's experience that with a lack of verification (and that is invariably the case) such arms may just as easily be of Mexican, Spanish, Turkish or Indian origin (often copies of American-made pieces of the same era) or even frontier American-made arms of the pre-Civil War era. Some types more often encountered are copies of the Colt Dragoons. There is little doubt that such pieces are good collectors' items. However, as they are generally unidentified and most certainly are not substantiated as of genuine Confederate manufacture, they must be categorized as "unknown origins," with prices judged accordingly.

WORTH BEARING IN MIND

A classic case of misidentified arms often classified as "Confederate" is the array of percussion military muskets made by Eli Whitney of Connecticut during the period 1857 to 1864, and actually termed by him as "good and serviceable arms." These consisted of composites assembled from surplus government weapons as well as his own production, sold on the open market to states and militia units. The reader is referred to Chapter V-J, Whitney Arms, where a review quite poignantly illustrates the ease with which these weapons could be misidentified. The Eli Whitney story is merely one positively known instance of composite arms which were sold to the private and government market of the Civil War era. Other dealers, agents or even makers in the gun trade were engaged in the same activities; their products, too, when encountered could just as easily fall into the "Confederate" category today and thus the collector is urged to exercise caution and good judgment when contemplating the purchase of otherwise unidentified but seemingly "Confederate" arms.

SPURIOUS AND PSEUDO-SOUTHERN

Regrettably, Confederate weapons have been the subject of many abuses over the years. Very likely they are the easiest to pass off as "genuine" to the unsuspecting due to the dearth of definitive detail about many of them. The term "Confederate made" tends to be a great catch-all for almost any unidentified, crudely made weapon that falls within the Civil War era of manufacture and has a military-like appearance. Some such arms are actually what they are purported to be, but, before the reader jumps to conclusions, it's very important to separate fiction from fact and he should explore every avenue available to verify the originality and authenticity of any questionable pieces if buying them as "Confederate." Bear in mind that some

references, especially those of an earlier day, may contain misinformation.

The field has long been a very popular one for collectors. As genuine specimens have consistently brought good prices on the market, the speciality has not lacked for its share of scoundrels; hence, spurious specimens are reasonably abundant. Most often these are of the various makes which are directly copied after the Colt Navy and Dragoon model revolvers; not a few heavily worn Colts have been reworked and marked to resemble their Confederate counterparts. As earlier stated, Confederate arms usually show considerable wear; combined with their often poor quality manufacture, they are often found in mutilated or badly broken condition. Due to value and rarity, specimens are worthy of restoration and thus the buyer is urged to exercise extreme caution when acquiring a specimen. These matters are discussed in Chapter III and the observations are especially applicable to these arms. Extra scrutiny should be given to patina, aging, pitting and markings.

Among the more flagrant abuses found on spurious Confederate longarms is the insertion of original Confederate made locks on U.S. made or British percussion rifle-muskets. Rather large quantities of original RICHMOND ARMORY LOCKPLATES were found and sold after the Civil War and during the ensuing years to the present day. The subject is treated in detail with the description of Richmond-made muskets in the following section. Other Confederate locks have turned up in small quantities from time to time and occasionally these too have been fitted on incorrect guns. One of the more common examples is the Confederate COOK & BROTHER—ATHENS, GEORGIA marked lock which has been encountered with some frequency on standard British Enfield percussion muskets.

CAVEATS

When the war began in 1861, the individual states and the Confederate government issued a call for weapons of all types to hastily arm their rapidly mobilized forces. Just about every conceivable style of firearm was sent to a great many contractors and gunsmiths commissioned to convert such pieces for military use. These ran the gamut from Kentucky rifles to double barrel shotguns and handguns of every type. To the best of the author's knowledge, none was officially marked after alteration and issuance. Undoubtedly a great many cut-down, bored out and otherwise altered civilian and U.S. issue pre-Civil War American military firearms are those items officially altered for Confederate military use. Regrettably, in present day most of these must be classified "unidentified" and sold (and justly so) for prices much less than if in their original condition. Had they been officially marked by either the Confederate contractor or government, their value and historical importance would be considerably enhanced. Such was not the case. It is in this gray area that the forger or gun trader with larceny in his heart has operated prolifically. Not a few altered civilian or U.S. military arms with otherwise minimal value have been marked C.S. or variants thereof indicating Confederate ownership and use to enhance their demand and value. There is the possibility that some such markings are authentic. However, it has been the author's experience both as a collector and dealer in Confederate arms that the instance of originality of such surcharged marks is extremely rare and the buyer should examine such items with a jaundiced eye, relying on expert opinion or documentary evidence for originality.

Secondary Confederate weapons are a class unto themselves. Many of these will be found listed elsewhere in this work. Any firearm manufactured in the South or intended for Southern usage (and so marked) prior to the Civil War is classified and considered as "Secondary Confederate." These will include the well known products of the Palmetto Armory at Columbia,

South Carolina, and the various flintlock pistols and muskets (and their percussion conversions) made at the Virginia Manufactory at Richmond. Such arms are cross-indexed throughout this Confederate chapter.

Some U.S. military flintlocks, most notably the Models 1816 North pistol and 1836 Johnson and Waters pistols, are found bearing SOUTH CAROLINA or NORTH CAROLINA markings, indicating ownership and issuance by those states. Such pieces as well as any others with authentic markings indicating Southern state ownership are also placed in the category of "Secondary Confederate" weapons. Their values are usually enhanced considerably by these Southern markings, as indicated where listed in this book.

A complete cross-section of American firearms from deringer-type pocket pistols to sporting rifles and shotguns which bear Southern makers' or agents' names of pre-Civil War vintage are generally considered as Secondary Confederate types also. As a rule-of-thumb, any American arm of pre-Civil War Southern manufacture or association has an immediate built-in demand factor and a subsequent price increase due to its valid or imagined Confederate relationship. Thus, a host of Philadelphia-type deringers encountered with agent's markings on their barrels will fetch slightly higher prices for Southern agent markings as compared to Northern.

At the outbreak of hostilities the Southern governments seized all U.S. Federal armories throughout their states; these combined with the capture during combat of other U.S. made arms accounted for a large percentage of Union weapons in common usage by Confederate units. If such weapons can be positively established as Confederate used, the values are enhanced considerably. Colt, Remington and other Northern-made handguns were highly popular with Confederate forces; instances of known inscribed pieces with Confederate associations are quite rare. Such arms when fully authenticated have values substantially in excess of similar guns with Northern-associated histories or inscriptions.

Foreign arms of all types were widely purchased and imported by both the North and South at the outbreak of hostilities. The British Enfield 577 percussion rifle-musket was the most popular imported arm and was purchased in large quantities by both sides. It is considered both a Secondary Union piece as well as Confederate. Specimens bearing markings actually attesting to their usage by either side are quite rare and when encountered should be carefully scrutinized.

The most often observed handguns that are considered Secondary Confederate are the various types of English Adams, Tranter and Kerr patent percussion revolvers that were either known to have been purchased under Confederate military contract or privately imported by well known military goods dealers. Not a few double action Tranters will be found fully inscribed along the topstrap and barrel with the British maker's name accompanied by that of the Southern importer. Most notable are those bearing the names Hyde and Goodrich and A. B. Griswold & Company, both of New Orleans. Exact period of manufacture and import is not known, but probably would coincide with the very beginnings of the war if not immediately preceding it.

Such pieces when verified original will normally bring at least double the value of the same specimen with only their English makers' marks and oftentimes, depending on the Southern agent's name, the price may be triple or more.

A rather interesting, incidental fact to collecting Confederate arms, is the observation that a great majority of specimens (often in the finest condition) have been found and unearthed in homes in the North! With the cessation of hostilities, the majority of Confederate weapons were either captured or destroyed and the proportion of such items actually carried home by Southern soldiers was evidently very small, at least judging by the percentage of specimens found over the years still in Southern hands. It is evident that a great many Southern weapons were taken or sent home as souvenirs by Northern forces during and immediately following the war—as is the case with victorious armies of all eras—thus accounting for this seeming anomaly.

BIBLIOGRAPHY

(Note: Information about Confederate arms may be found in several other books covering a broad field of American firearms. These volumes appear in complete bibliographic listings elsewhere in this work, notably Chapters IV and IX. They are: *The Collecting Of Guns*, edited by Serven: *Civil War Guns* by Edwards; and *Small Arms And Ammunition In The United States Service* by Lewis.)

*Adams, Doug. *The Confederate LeMat Revolver*. Woonsocket, R.I. Mowbray Publishing, 2005. Fine coverage of the invention, manufacture and variations of this famous handguns; its purchase and issuance by the Confederate Government and even those sold privately and the individuals involved in the commercial sales.

*Albaugh III, William A. *The Confederate Brass-Framed Colt And Whitney*. Falls Church, Virginia: Privately published by author, 1955. The first important detailed study of the Griswold and Gunnison and Spiller and Burr revolvers. Reprint 1993 by Broadfoot Pub. Co., Wilmington N.C.

*Albaugh III, William A. *Tyler, Texas, C.S.A.* Harrisburg, Pennsylvania: Stackpole Company, 1958. Detailed account with exact entries from the day-book of the Confederate Ordnance Works at Tyler, Texas. Reprint 1993 by Broadfoot Pub. Co., Wilmington N.C.

Albaugh, William A. and Simmons, Edward N. *Confederate Arms*. Harrisburg, Pennsylvania: Stackpole Company, 1957. Most important and classic guide to collecting Confederate longarms, handguns, edged weapons, accessories. Important *Directory* of all known Confederate makers with brief histories of each. Reprint 1993 by Broadfoot Pub. Co., Wilmington N.C.

*Albaugh III, William A., Benet, Hugh, Jr., Simmons, Edward N. *Confederate Handguns*. Philadelphia: Riling & Lentz, 1963. Highly definitive, classic guide to the subject. Widely respected and used. Reprint 1993 by Broadfoot Pub. Co., Wilmington N.C.

*Albaugh III, William A. and Steuart, Richard D. *The Original Confederate Colt: The Story of the Leach & Rigdon and Rigdon-Ansley Revolvers*. New York: Greenberg Publisher, 1953. Detailed account of both well known Confederate makers and their arms. Reprint 1993 by Broadfoot Pub. Co., Wilmington N.C.

Cromwell, Giles. *The Virginia Manufactory Of Arms*. Charlottesville, Virginia: University Press of Virginia, 1975. Detailed history of this famed Southern armory and the numerous weapons produced including considerable illustrations of converted specimens very likely seeing Confederate service.

*Davies, Paul J. *C. S. Armory Richmond*. Carlisle, Pennsylvania: Published by author, 2000. Reconstructs month-by-month the history of that Confederate armory, its monthly production and details of the firearms produced. Important reference.

Forgett, Valmore J. & Serpette, A.F. & M-A. *LeMat; The Man, the Gun*. Privately printed, 1996. Ridgefield, N.J. Well detailed and illus.; all models. Considerably expanded from the 1995 French work.

Fuller, Claud E. and Steuart, Richard D. *Firearms Of The Confederacy*. Huntington, West Virginia: Standard

Publications, Inc., 1944. (Reprint c.1978, publisher unknown.) The first important guide to the field. Some material has since been superseded or changed, but contains wealth of important data still of significant importance to the collector and student.

Gary, W. A. *Confederate Revolvers*. Dallas, Texas: Taylor Publishing Company, 1987. Detailed, well illustrated study shedding new light on some models.

*Hartzler, D. D. *Confederate Presentation & Inscribed Swords & Revolvers*. Gaithersburg, Maryland: Olde Soldier Books, Inc., 1988.

Hill, R. T. & Anthony, W. E. *Confederate Longarms and Pistols: A Pictorial Study*. Charlotte, North Carolina: Privately published by the authors 1978. Very broad coverage with excellent photographs; however, includes a number of pieces of questionable attribution and text lacks depth. Conjecture is often stated as fact.

Hughes, Jr., James B. *Confederate Gun Makers, Armories And Arsenals*. Publisher unknown, 1961. Alphabetical listing with short historical accounts of each entry.

*Kusrow, Bruce (compiler) *"William A. Albaugh, III 1908-1983; His Life & Writings."* Wilmington, N.C. Broadfoot Publishing, 1993. Important compilation of his many articles; significant information not found elsewhere.

Meredith, Edward J. *Variations of the Leech & Rigdon Revolver* from Bulletin No. 32 American Society of Arms Collectors, 1995.

Meyer, J. A. *William Glaze & the Palmetto Armory*. Columbia, S.C.: South Carolina State Museum 1982. Glaze was one of few makers who provided weapons to South prior to and during Civil War. Informative data with exceptional illustrations of markings on guns and edged weapons. 2nd Edition 1994. S.C. State Museum. Columbia, S.C. Revised and enlarged.

*Murphy, John M. *Confederate Carbine & Musketoons*. Dallas, Texas: Privately published by author, 1986. Important new material accompanied by detailed photographs. Expanded /

revised second edition of 2002. Santa Ana, Calif: Graphic Publishers. Significant reference.

*Murphy, John M. and Madaus, Howard M. *Confederate Rifles & Muskets; Infantry Small arms Manufactured in the Southern Confederacy 1861-1865*. Newport Beach, Calif. Privately published by author, 1996. Major reference to this field.

Murphy, John M. *The Story Of Confederate Carbines*, from Bulletin No. 32 American Society of Arms Collectors. Dallas, Texas, 1975.

*Norman, Matthew W. *Colonel Burton's Spiller & Burr Revolver; An Untimely Venture in C.S. Small Arms Mfg*. Macon, Ga., Mercer Univ. Press, 1996. New data on serials; private production at Atlanta v.s. C.S. contract as Macon.

Serpette, Alain F. Colonel Francois Alexandre LeMat. Concremiers, France; privately published by author circa 1999. Small pocket size booklet with individual full page illustrations of each model and variations as well as experimental types, along with copies of patent drawings. Intended as an "easy-to-consult guide" for collectors. English text.

Serpette, M-A & A.F. (collaboration with Forgett, V.) *Col. Francois LeMat 1821-1895*. Privately published. France, 1995. French text.

*Sword, Wiley. *Firepower From Abroad; The Confederate Enfield and the LeMat Revolver*. Lincoln, R.I.: Andrew Mowbray, Inc., 1986. Much new data on a variety of Confederate small arms.

*Whisker, J.B.; Hartzler D.D.; Yantz, L.W. *Arming The Glorious Cause: Weapons of The Second War for Independence. A Photographic Study of Confederate Weapons*. Bedford, Penn.: Old Bedford Village Press, 1998.

Wiggins, Gary. *Dance & Brothers, Texas Gunmakers of the Confederacy*. Orange, Virginia: Moss Publications, 1986. New information on the gun and its maker.

*---- *Arms & Equipment of the Confederacy*. N.Y., *Time-Life* Books. 1991. Fine color illus.; general survey.

(*) Preceding a title indicates the book is currently in print.

HANDGUNS

Augusta Machine Works Revolver

10-001
Six-notch Style

10-001
Twelve-notch Style

Augusta Machine Works, Augusta, Georgia. Revolver of Colt Model 1851 Navy type. Made *c*. 1861-1864; total quantity very limited, estimated at approximately 100.

36 caliber. 6-shot round cylinder, with 6 or 12 stop slots. Octagonal barrel of about 7-11/16" (lengths vary slightly).

One piece wooden grips. Browned finish; the brass gripstraps left bright. Both very rare. 12 "notch" type least encountered.

Serial numbers noted have been letters, e.g., K, and numbers, e.g., 48; profusely marked. No other markings.

These well-made arms are distinct rarities, and only a few specimens are known. Research into original records has revealed but a smattering of background information. Added features to note for identification are the faint six groove rifling, twisting slightly to the right, the 1-11/16" long cylinder, and the 3-3/16" long frame. An important model believed made under C. S. government auspices at facilities erected for the purpose of small arms manufacture:

10-001 Values—Fair **$20,000** Very Good **$45,000**

Clark, Sherrard & Co. *See also Tucker, Sherrard, 10-022*

T. W. Cofer Revolver

Thomas W. Cofer, Portsmouth, Virginia. Navy Type Revolver modeled partially after the Whitney Navy. Made c. 1861-1862. Total quantity estimated between 86 and 140 with less than ten known specimens.

36 caliber. 6-shot round cylinder. 7-1/2" octagonal barrel.

Two-piece walnut grips. Blued finish; the frame of brass, left bright. Spur or sheath type trigger.

Serial numbers or assembly markings present, but have yet to be fully interpreted. Standard marking on topstrap (individually stamped letter by letter): T. W. COFER'S/PATENT Marked on top of barrel with individual die stamps PORTSMOUTH, VA. Letter or number markings on screw heads and major parts.

T. W. Cofer, a gunsmith and arms dealer, had the distinction of holding one of the first patents issued by the Confederate States of America. The specifications covered his invention of a system whereby a revolver could utilize both the conventional loading system or a special auxiliary chamber—metallic cartridge with nipple in a uniquely designed split cylinder. The Cofer revolvers known are particularly intriguing to the collector, but relatively little data is available on them. Recent research reveals that Cofer received and completed a C.S.

10-002

Government order for 82 revolvers by May, 1862; all delivered to the 5th Virginia Cavalry. One of the greatest, most sought after C.S. rarities, with few recorded sales:

Patent Cylinder Model; a.k.a. First Type. Made with split cylinder; blind screws:

10-002 Values—Fair **$75,000** Very Good **$150,000**

Transition Model; a.k.a. Second Type. Similar above, but fitted with percussion cylinder only; barrel threads visible:

10-003 Values—Fair **$45,000** Very Good **$125,000**

Production Model; a.k.a. Third Type. Has shoulder present at point where cylinder meets breech of barrel and thus barrel threads are not visible:

10-004 Values—Fair **$45,000** Very Good **$125,000**

Columbus Fire Arms Mfg. Co. Revolver

10-005

The Columbus Fire Arms Manufacturing Company (L. Haiman and Brother), Columbus, Georgia. Revolver of the Colt Model 1851 Navy Type. Made c. 1863-64; total quantity about 100.

36 caliber. 6-shot round cylinder, with 6 stop slots. 7-1/2" part round/part octagon barrel (full octagon very rare).

One piece wooden grips. Browned finish; the brass gripstraps left bright.

Serial numbers (in small size stampings) from 1 on up. Barrel marking in two lines: COLUMBUS FIRE ARMS MANUF. CO/COLUMBUS, GA. On cylinder: COLUMBUS FIRE ARMS/MANUF. CO/COLUMBUS, GA. (Note: Variations of markings known, as listed in Albaugh, Benet and Simmons, *Confederate Handguns*.)

Awarded a contract by the Confederate government for manufacture of 10,000 Navy revolvers of Colt type (August 26, 1862), the Columbus Fire Arms firm had high hopes that never materialized. In the spring of 1864 the Haimans sold out to the Confederate States government, which intended to establish a major facility, the Columbus Arsenal and Armory, for the manufacture of various military small arms and armaments. Union forces destroyed the works in 1865, and it is doubtful that any revolvers were completed by the C. S. A. after their acquisition of the Haiman plant, other than one sample specimen:

10-005 Values—Fair **$75,000** Very Good **$150,000**

J. H. Dance & Brothers Revolvers

J. H. Dance & Brothers, Columbia, Texas. Dragoon Type Percussion Revolvers in calibers 36 and 44. Estimated total quantities manufactured approximately 325 to a maximum of 500, of which 275 to 350 were in the larger 44 caliber size.

The Dance is easily distinguishable by the complete absence of the recoil shield protrusions, giving it a very flat appearing frame.

All models bear numerous matched serial number markings on various parts, but no maker markings. Both sizes are 6-shot with part octagon, part round barrels. One piece walnut grips. Blued finish; brass gripstraps left bright.

The J. H. Dance & Brothers firm commenced the manufacture of firearms in 1862, the need for small arms being so great that the Governor of Texas granted exemption for the company's work force from military service. The Union's knowledge of Dance's operation was apparent in 1863 by the subsequent removal of the

10-006

factory from Columbia to a new site a few miles away to prevent possible shelling by Union gunboats. Following that move the manufacture of revolvers was apparently not resumed.

44 Caliber Model; 8" barrel. (Note: A very few in the higher serial number range have full octagon barrels and will command a premium value):

10-006 Values—Fair **$25,000** Very Good **$60,000**

36 Caliber Model; (Not illus.) scaled down version of above, lighter weight and size and having 7-3/8" barrel. (Note: Buyers must be especially wary when acquiring this model as a great many spurious specimens exist, being simply fashioned by milling off the recoil shield, and otherwise altering worn Colt 1851 Navies):

10-007 Values—Fair **$40,000** Very Good **$85,000**

Deane & Adams Revolvers   *See Introductory note to this chapter.*

Fayetteville Model 1855 Type Pistol-Carbine

Fayetteville Model 1855 Type Pistol Carbine. (Not illus.) Almost identical in appearance to U.S. Model made at Springfield Armory (*see 6A-051/052*) except the "high hump" lockplate never milled for the Maynard primer unit.

Allegedly made by the Confederate Arsenal at Fayetteville, N.C. from parts made at the captured Harpers Ferry Arsenal, the collector is advised to use extreme caution before acquiring this model. The author has never viewed an authentic specimen, nor has he found reliable authorities to verify the existence of such specimens:

10-007.5

J. and F. Garrett Single Shot Pistol

J. and F. Garrett and Company, Greensboro, North Carolina. Single Shot (Blunt & Syms type) Pistol. Made c. 1862-63; total quantity about 500.

54 caliber. 8-1/2" round barrel, with swivel type ramrod having tulip shaped tip.

Two piece walnut grips. Barrels finished bright, as were the case brass frames.

10-008

Serial numbered from 1 on up, marked on side of the gripstrap and inside the sideplate. Initials, e.g., G.W. or S.R. on breech end of the barrel, beneath which is the letter P. Maker's name stamping not known to be present on any specimens.

Best known to collectors as makers of the brass framed J. H. Tarpley breech-loading carbine, the J. and F. Garrett firm has been attributed by Albaugh, Benet, and Simmons as the source of this so-called "Blunt & Syms" type pistol. The barrels and ramrods on these arms are considered to have been from Model 1842 U.S. Pistol production, and thus the main production requirement was in the frame castings and internal parts.

Considerable controversy surrounds this piece and a number of students are of the opinion that this gun has no Southern association but is rather a Northern, pre-Civil War, Secondary Martial. Because of its long accepted place in Confederate collecting and the lack of definitive information to term it otherwise it is included herein:

10-008 Values—Good **$1,500** Fine **$3,500**

Griswold and Gunnison Revolver

Griswold and Gunnison, Griswoldville, Georgia. Revolver of the Colt Model 1851 Navy type. Made c. 1862-64; total quantity about 3,700.

36 caliber. 6-shot round cylinder, with 6 stop slots. Dragoon type barrel of about 7-1/2". Wedge made without spring.

One piece walnut grips. Blued finish; the brass frame and gripstraps, left bright.

Serial numbers from 1 on up, standard on the frame, barrel lug, and cylinder. Secondary serials were marked on most parts but no maker identification legend was used. The secondary number is one or two digits from the actual serial. Roman numeral benchmarks (e.g., XXV) on gripstraps and frame. A cryptic inspector stamping (generally like a capital letter backward) on major parts was also employed.

Details of construction helpful for identifying this model include the upward angle of the butt profile, the twist lines on the cylinder (running from left to right), 1-3/4" cylinder length, and the 6 groove rifling with right gain twist. Safety pins were standard on the back of the cylinder, positioned between each nipple. And grips often appear too small, having shrunk slightly.

Samuel Griswold, whose factory made these revolvers, was a transplanted Yankee from Connecticut. His first munitions production for the Confederacy was an infantryman's pike, in

10-009

10-010

1862. The success of that venture soon led to revolver production, and no Confederate maker outdid Griswold in quantity; few equaled him in quality. The C.S.A. contracted with Griswold for revolvers, an important point to collectors. The factory was thoroughly destroyed by Union forces in November of 1864. Early collectors identified these arms as the

Griswold and Grier, and sometimes that terminology is encountered today.
Standard model, as above with octagonal barrel lug:

10-009	Values—Fair **$12,000**	Very Good **$25,000**

As above, but with rounded barrel lug contour:

10-010	Values—Fair **$14,000**	Very Good **$30,000**

Leech and Rigdon Revolver

10-011

Leech and Rigdon, Columbus, Mississippi, and Greensboro, Georgia (bulk of production at the latter). **Revolver of the Colt Model 1851 Navy type.** Note: About the last 500 specimens completed at Rigdon & Ansley plant, Augusta, Georgia (*q.v.*). Made c. 1863-64; total quantity about 1,500.

36 caliber. 6-shot round cylinder, with 6 stop slots. Dragoon type part round-part octagon barrel of about 7-1/2". Wedge includes spring. Pin and ball or Colt type loading lever latch. Face of recoil shield not channeled. Roller bearing on hammer. Casting flaws often seen although there is no visible twist pattern in barrels.

One piece walnut grips. Blued barrel and cylinder; casehardened frame; brass guard and backstrap left bright.

Serial numbered from 1 on up on various parts; all should match. Standard barrel marking: LEECH & RIGDON CSAon top flat with few variations known which, if authentic, will increase value. Inspection or assembly mark on side of the trigger guard; generally a cross made of four square dots, or (less common) a capital letter (e.g., J or N). High serial number specimens may bear C.S.A. inspector stamping W.H. within a diamond, or script *W.H.* within a parallelogram. Very rare markings known such as LEECH & RIGDON NOVELTY WORKS, CSAin low serial range; worth considerable premium.

Thomas Leech and Charles H. Rigdon appear to have first become acquainted in Memphis, Tennessee, where the former is believed to have financed the Memphis Novelty Works. The Novelty Works concentrated on sword manufacture, early in the Civil War effort, and when moved to Columbus May, 1862, replaced sword-making with revolvers. In 1864 the company was dissolved, and Rigdon moved to Augusta, Georgia, soon forming the firm Rigdon, Ansley & Co. Approximately the last 500 Leech and Rigdon revolvers were completed by the new company, but still bearing the standard LEECH & RIGDON CSAbarrel marking. It is important to note that the 1,500 gun total by Leech & Rigdon had been made on a C.S.A. government contract:

10-011	Values—Fair **$12,500**	Very Good **$30,000**

LeMat Two-Barrel Revolver

10-012
First Model

10-013
Second Model

LeMat Two-Barrel 10-Shot Percussion Revolver by Dr. Jean Alexandre Francois LeMat, of New Orleans; production at Liege, Belgium, Paris, France, and Birmingham, England. Army and Navy Model Revolvers; a.k.a. "Grape Shot Revolver." Made c. 1856-65; total quantity less than 2,900.

The inclusion of this arm here is purely arbitrary as it is strictly of foreign manufacture—made for commercial sale abroad. It is known that a substantial number were purchased under direct C.S.A. contract. The known use by a few Confederate high ranking officers as a favorite personal handgun, its own unusual design and mechanical features and the fact that it was invented by an American (and a Southerner at that) has firmly placed it over the years as worthy of an equal listing and placement in a C.S.A. handgun collection.

42 caliber, 9-shot round cylinder (with 6-1/2" barrel) revolving on a center axis which was also a smoothbore 5" barrel of 63 caliber (for firing buckshot). The hammer fitted with a pivoting striker, to accommodate the set of cylinder nipples and the single nipple at top of frame for the shot barrel.

Checkered walnut grips. Blued finish; casehardened hammer and loading lever.

Serial number ranges and markings noted under variations below.

Dr. LeMat's extremely novel revolver was first patented in America, in 1856, and was later patented in several European countries. Initially he was aided in developing manufacture and sales by P. G. T. Beauregard, later one of the Confederacy's outstanding generals. John Krider of Philadelphia made what were believed to have been prototype percussion LeMat revolvers in 1859. Estimated that 25 were produced, of which five are known. Markings MADE BY JOHN KRIDER, PHILA. LeMAT'S GRAPESHOT REVOLVER PATENT.Extremely rare; premium value. The first production specimens were made in

Liege, under the supervision of Dr. Charles F. Girard, who soon became major owner of the enterprise. Confederate government contracts were awarded with deliveries of about 900 for the Army, and approximately 600 for the Navy. (*See also Confederate Longarms.*)

First Model revolver; made in Liege, Belgium, 1862, serial numbers 1-450; *L* and *M* script letters within circle marking (LeMat trademark), spurred trigger guard, part round/part octagonal barrel, loading lever mounted on right side, and swivel lanyard ring in butt. Barrel marking: COL. LeMAT'S PATENT and E/LG in oval proof:

10-012	Values—Good **$20,000**	Fine **$50,000**

Second Model revolver; made in Paris, France, 1864-65, round trigger guard, full octagonal barrel, loading lever on left side, fixed lanyard ring in butt; L and M block letters beneath

5-pointed star (trademark). On the earliest of these a transitional feature of spur on trigger guard will be found (worth premium).

Considerable variation occurs in markings and other manufacturing details, for which the reader is referred to Albaugh, Simmons and Benet *Confederate Handguns*. Serial number range 451 - 2500. Most often encountered are the markings: (1) COL. LeMAT BTE. s.g.d.g. PARIS; (2) SYST. LeMAT BTE. s.g.d.g. PARIS; (3) SYSTme LEMAT Bte S.G.D.G. PARIS. London proofs markings and M inspector stamp of C.S.A. Lt. Murdaugh (of the Confederate Navy) or other bona fide C.S.A. markings will increase values according to their importance:

10-013   Values—Good **$15,000**   Fine **$25,000**

LE MAT & GIRARD'S PATENT LONDON marked on barrel. Manufactured in England 1865 and bearing Birmingham proofmarks, crown over V and crown over P proof stampings. Serial ranges 1 - 128, 5200, 8000, and 9000:

10-014   Values—Good **$17,500**   Fine **$30,000**

Baby LeMat; 32 caliber, 9-shot round cylinder (with 4-1/4" octagon barrel) revolving on a center axis doubling as a 2-3/4" smoothbore barrel of 41 caliber (for firing buckshot). The Baby Model is a scaled down version of the Army and Navy LeMats; it is based on the so-called Second Model production features.

10-015
"Baby LeMat"

Checkered walnut grips. Blued finish; casehardened hammer and loading lever. Serial numbered in individual range from 1 on up. Barrel marking: ***Systeme Le Mat Bte s.g.d.g. Paris***. Bearing Birmingham proofmarks (crown over V and crown over P) and the M stamping of Lt. Murdaugh of the C.S. Navy.

The Baby Model is one of the scarcest of LeMat production, and its known history of order by C.S.A. contract adds to its desirability. The original government order called for a total of 2,000 revolvers, of which about 100 are believed to have been delivered:

10-015   Values—Good **$17,500**   Fine **$40,000**

London Armoury Company, Kerr Patent   *See Introductory note to this chapter.*

Palmetto Armory Single Shot Pistol   *See Chapter VI, U. S. Military Single Shot Pistols, Model 1842 Percussion Pistol for technical details. A scarce and desirable Confederate-associated (secondary Confederate) arm.*

Rigdon, Ansley Revolver

Rigdon, Ansley, & Co., Augusta, Georgia. Revolver of the Colt Model 1851 Navy type. Made c. 1864-1865. Total quantity about 1,000.

36 caliber. 6-shot round cylinder. The most quickly distinguishing features are the 12 stop slots on cylinder. Part octagon/part round dragoon type barrel of about 7-1/2". Colt type loading lever latch. Face of recoil shield channeled; roller bearing on hammer.

One-piece walnut grips. Blued finish; the brass gripstraps left bright.

Serial numbered from about 1501 to approximately 2500, continuing the range begun by the Leech and Rigdon revolvers. Standard barrel markings as noted below, but other variants known. Inspector and assembler markings same as noted for the Leech and Rigdon revolvers (*q.v.*).

After dissolution of his former association, Rigdon formed the Rigdon, Ansley & Co. in Augusta, Georgia. The new firm completed the few hundred revolvers of the Leech and Rigdon C.S.A. contract (*q.v.*) and began production of an improved

10-016

revolver. Sherman's march to the sea and occupation of Georgia forced a halt to all manufacturing operations by January of 1865.

Early Production; barrel marking AUGUSTA, GA. C.S.A. Serial range about 1501 to 1700; although these markings with added line "C.H. RIGDON" are known in higher serial range: very rare:

10-016   Values—Fair **$25,000**   Very Good **$60,000**

Standard Model; barrel marking C.S.A. Serial range about 1700 to end of production:

10-017   Values—Fair **$17,500**   Very Good **$45,000**

Schneider and Glassick Revolver

Schneider and Glassick, Memphis, Tennessee. Navy Revolver of Colt Model 1851 type. Made c. 1861-1862. Total quantity estimated at about 50, or less.

36 caliber. 6-shot round cylinder. 7-1/2" octagonal barrel. One-piece walnut grip. Blued or browned finish; the frame and gripstraps of unfinished brass.

Serial numbered from 1 on up. Top of barrel marked: SCHNEIDER & GLASSICK, MEMPHIS, TENNESSEE.

There is a single known specimen bearing the same markings as noted above (but applied letter by letter), which has part octagon/part round barrel and an iron frame. Established authentic specimens should be worth a premium over the style valued here.

First listed in Memphis city directories in 1860, the firm was

10-018

formed by two gunsmiths, and their Colt Navy type revolver was the subject of an interesting article in the Memphis *Daily Appeal* early in December, 1861. Surviving specimens are of extreme rarity, and relatively little is known of the firm or its products. Great caution is suggested on the acquisition of this model, especially specimens that bear markings applied with individual die stamps:

10-018 Values—Fair **$65,000** Very Good **$125,000**

Spiller and Burr Revolver

Spiller and Burr, Atlanta, Georgia, c. 1862-1864 with later production at the Macon Armory, Macon, Georgia c. 1864-1865. Revolver of the Whitney Navy type. Total quantity estimated about 1,450.

36 caliber. 6-shot round cylinder with six stop slots and twist design visible on surface of cylinder. Safety slots between nipples on rear of cylinder. Octagonal barrel 6" or 6-1/2" length.

Two-piece walnut grips. Blued finish; brass frame.

Serial numbered from 1 on up. Barrels may or may not be marked: SPILLER & BURR Government markings C.S. usually present on left or right side of frame.

The history of Spiller & Burr revolvers began with an optimistic government contract calling for a total of 15,000 pieces! The company first set up shop in Richmond, Virginia, and moved in 1862 to Atlanta, Georgia, where 762 revolvers have been estimated manufactured. After purchase of the firm by the C.S. government in January, 1864, production commenced again at the Macon Armory where an estimated 689 revolvers were made. Differences between the two types are minor, with the main detail being the apparent greater angle between the frame and the grip:

10-019 Values—Fair **$17,500** Very Good **$40,000**

10-019

Earliest Production Spiller & Burr Revolvers (a.k.a. 1st Model or "Open Frame Type"). Show distinct design differences, following closely the appearance of the Whitney Navy Model. Approximately 50 are estimated to have been manufactured and to have been numbered in their own serial range beginning with No. 1. The most apparent distinguishing feature is the forward section of the brass frame (the section into which the barrel is screwed). Only 5/8" thick (versus the conventional model which is 7/8" thick) thus leaving 1/4" of the barrel threads exposed, just as on the Whitney revolver. Thinner topstrap also noticeable. Only a few specimens are known to date. Very rare and worth premium over values shown above:

10-020

George Todd Revolver

George Todd, Austin, Texas. Navy Model Revolver of Colt 1851 type. Made c. 1857-61; total quantity unknown, but thus far less than a handful of known specimens.

36 caliber. 6-shot round cylinder. 7-1/2" barrels both full octagon as well as part round-part octagon. Iron frame, having thick recoil shields.

One piece walnut grips. Blued or browned finish; gripstraps of unfinished brass.

Serial numbered from 1 on up. GEORGE TODD, AUSTIN marked on frame; and GEORGE TODD on top of the barrel.

Although production is considered to have taken place prior to the War, the Todd Navy revolvers are considered Confederate arms due to their likely C.S.A. use. During the war years Todd is

10-021

believed to have worked for a government armory, since he was a highly skilled gunsmith. With no known sales, value is an approximation only:

10-021 Values—Fair **$35,000** Very Good **$75,000**

Tranter Revolvers   *See Introductory note to this chapter.*

Tucker, Sherrard and Company Revolvers

Tucker, Sherrard and Company (Clark, Sherrard & Co.), Lancaster, Texas. Dragoon and Navy Model Revolvers of Colt

10-022

type. Made c. 1862-67; parts made during the Civil War, but production not completed until following the end of hostilities. Total quantity about 400 and believed to all be the 44 caliber type.

The company rather ambitiously entered into a contract with the State of Texas to manufacture 1,500 36 caliber and 1,500 44 caliber revolvers, all of the Colt type. Due largely to the conscription of workmen by the Confederate Army only a handful (perhaps only one sample) were completed before the end of the War. It is believed that c. 1867 the sets of parts were finally finished, assembled and sold. A distinctive feature of the Tucker, Sherrard and Company product is the lack of a loading aperture on the right side of the barrel lug; it otherwise resembles the Colt Second and Third Model Dragoon in both

large size and shape; having both square back and round trigger guards. Barrel marking: CLARK, SHERRARD & CO., LANCASTER, TEXAS. Acid etched design on cylinder of two decorative panels, one containing a coat-of-arms and crossed cannon, the other a large five pointed star and the words TEXAS ARMS.
Dragoon Model:

10-022   Values—Fair **$25,000**   Very Good **$100,000**
(Note: There is but one known specimen of the 36 caliber model which bears the acid etched legend L.E. Tucker Sons on its 7-3/4" dragoon type barrel. Rarity of other specimens should they appear would be obvious, and extreme caution should be exercised should the collector acquire one.)

Virginia Manufactory   *See U.S. Military Single Shot Pistols, Chapter VI.*

LONGARMS

Arkadelphia Ordnance Works Rifles

Arkadelphia Ordnance Works, Arkadelphia, Arkansas. Percussion Rifle; a.k.a. "Hindman Rifle" after Confederate Major-General Thomas C. Hindman, commanding the Trans-Mississippi District and whose units were believed to have been issued some of these rifles. Quantity produced unknown; believed extremely limited. Specimens extremely rare. Circa 1863.

Only in recent years has one specimen been authenticated and a second specimen, similar but altered with a replaced barrel, been tentatively accepted as genuine. Although records clearly indicated that Arkansas Ordnance Works produced rifles, they were reasonably believed to have been reworked/made-over sporting rifles. A consensus by knowledgeable students has generally agreed that the specimen examined is representative of what that ordnance facility turned out in limited quantity, and that such arms were definitely produced.

The crudely made rifle bears a resemblance to the U.S. Model 1841 "Mississippi Rifle" and the British Enfield with noticeable variances. Although the dimensions and features mentioned here are likely to vary on other examples from that same production, they are believed to reasonably represent what other Arkadelphia rifles may feature. 47-3/4" overall; fitted with a 32-1/2" round barrel (octagon-shaped at 6 inches of its breech end with a gradual transition to round). Caliber 58, rifled with three lands and three grooves. (the barrel possibly reworked

from other earlier manufacture.). "V"-notched open rear sight with a simple shaped folding blade. Lock oddly shaped, resembling a cross between a Model 1841 and an Enfield style; possibly a re-shaped lockplate from another military arm (measurement unknown). Markings, which are regarded authentic, in center of lock in two lines ARKADELPHIA / ARK, and at rear behind hammer perpendicular to lock CS / 1863.

Full walnut stock fastened by a single, rather crudely made, iron Enfield type barrel band in mid-forend and roughly fashioned sheet iron forend tip. Buttstock noticeably formed without a comb (whether intended originally or the comb was lowered at later date yet to be determined). Matching serial or assembly numbers (single digit) on many parts. All mountings are iron with exception of crudely-fashioned brass thimble/lower pipe for the ramrod. No provision made for sling, although the trigger guard (generally shaped as a Model 1841 rifle type) has a small hole at the front of the overly large trigger bow, possibly intended for a swivel.

To the date of this 9th edition, the only article describing and illustrating the rifle appeared in the Spring 2003 edition of The Texas Gun Collector periodical. Collectors should exercise extreme caution and seek expert opinion on the acquisition of other examples of this extremely rare Confederate longarm. Values would certainly be logical in five figures.
10-022.5

Asheville Armory Model 1841 / 1855 Style Rifle

Asheville Armory, Asheville, North Carolina. Percussion muzzle-loading rifle with features of both Model 1841 & 1855 U.S. Rifles. (Not illus.) Made 1862-1863. Total quantity estimated 875.

58 caliber. 33" barrel and lock are M1841 style. Walnut stock fastened by two split type (screw tightened) bands. Brass mountings. Early manufacture with flat buttplate; later with the curved M1855 buttplate. Iron ramrod. Lug for saber-type bayonet.

Lock plate marking ASHEVILLE, N.C. (with or without added letters "C.S.") or only "ASHEVILLE". Lockplates on early production may have been from captured U.S. parts as remains of burnished markings "HARPERS FERRY" still visible on a few.

The Asheville Armory's first contract (1861-2) was "for repairing and fitting up double barrel shotguns for service." The description of the M1841/1855 type rifle update corrects the "Enfield Type" rifle reported in earlier editions:
10-023   Values—Fair **$17,500**   Very Good **$37,500**

M.A. Baker Conversion of U.S. Rifles & Muskets & Baker C.S. Rifle

10-024
Rifled Musket

M.A. Baker, Fayetteville, North Carolina. Altered flintlock U.S. Model 1816 muskets and Model 1817 rifles for the C.S. government 1862-3. Many of both types will have "N. CAROLINA" barrel markings. No known musket with BAKER markings has yet been recorded. Rifles are known with lockplates marked "M.A. BAKER / FAYETTEVILLE, N.C." *Values shown here* are for the BAKER marked specimens. On either the rifle or the musket with the conversion attributed to Baker, but not so-marked, values considerably less.

A single recorded example of a completely C.S.-made percussion rifle (as illus.) bears Baker markings as above. M1841 style; brass mounted; 2 barrel bands. 35" barrel 50 caliber. It is unknown if Baker made the entire rifle or merely the lock. It is known that he had a contract Sept. 1862 for 500 "rifle locks." Other specimens have yet to surface. In late 1861 Baker known to have sold N.C. 100 double barrel shotguns a contract for "...cutting off and swiveling 100 double barrel shotguns." These obviously intended for cavalry issuance:

10-024   Values—Fair **$17,500**   Very Good **$30,000**

J.B. Barrett (Read & Watson) Rifles and Carbines

10-025
Carbine without Ramrod Lug

10-025
Carbine with Ramrod Lug

10-025
Rifle

J. B. Barrett (Read & Watson) Rifles and Carbines. Formerly believed to have been the work of J. B. Barrett of Wytheville, Virginia (whose foundry did fill C.S. contract for converting and altering civilian and military arms for government service), these arms are recently identified as the product of **N. T. Read and John T. Watson of Danville, Virginia,** c. 1862-1863. Research by M. T. Madaus of the Milwaukee Public Museum as reported in the J. M. Murphy book, *Confederate Carbines and Musketoons* (q.v.) presents this more credible attribution. Estimated total quantity of rifles and carbines is 900. Made c. 1862-1863.

Made for the state of Virginia and their forces from standard issue Hall Model 1819 rifles and various Hall carbines already in Virginia Militia inventories ... and *not* from parts captured at Harper's Ferry, as previously believed.

The only known instance of military arms originally designed for breech-loading converted to muzzle-loading!

A new bronze breech unit (two distinct types are known) with the nipple in line with barrel at its extreme rear, surrounded by a flash shield, was installed. Although the stocks are of Hall pattern, they are apparently not altered and have obviously been made and fitted for this distinct Confederate version as evidenced by the fit and contour around the breech area. Numerous variations are noted in furniture, fittings and stock contours (i.e., a carbine utilizing Hall M 1819 rifle parts has distinctly different contours and furniture from one utilizing Hall M 1833 carbine components, etc.).

Carbines most often seen generally follow the style of the Model 1833 Hall Carbine; found with or without the ramrod lugs intact under muzzle of the 26" barrel. Carbines utilizing M 1819 rifle parts reported in 22" barrel lengths (other lengths likely).

Rifles usually with 32-1/2" barrel; 54 caliber and full stock and three-band fastened; the upper band of double strap type as on the Model 1819 Hall rifle. On some specimens observed of the rifle, stock was made in two pieces with the seam appearing under the center band. Values for rifles; carbines worth 20 to 25 percent premium:

10-025   Values—Fair **$12,500**   Very Good **$20,000**

Bilharz, Hall & Co.   *See Hodgkins & Sons, and also "Rising Breech Carbine."*

C. Chapman Rifle and Carbine/Musketoon

10-026
Rifle

10-026
"Carbine / Musketoon"

C. Chapman Rifle and Carbine/Musketoon. Recent evidence indicates manufacture may have been at the Nashville Arsenal or Sumner Armory in Tennessee. Quantity manufactured unknown; only a handful of recorded specimens, all with low serial numbers. Quantity estimated under 100.

54 caliber percussion muzzleloader. Fashioned directly after the U. S. Model 1841. Brass mountings; made without patchbox; both types with two barrel bands, the upper being double strapped as on the Model 1841. Both iron and brass triggers reported. Walnut stock. Only markings: C. CHAPMAN on lockplate; numerals (serial numbers) stamped on various parts. Rifle has 33" barrel; carbine/musketoon has 24" barrel. Workmanship quite crude as usually encountered on Confederate arms. (Note: Exercise extreme caution as a number of loose locks are known, some of which have been fitted to similar appearing guns.)

Values for rifles; carbines worth approx. 50 percent premium:

10-026   Values—Fair **$20,000**   Very Good **$40,000**

Clapp, Gates & Company Percussion Rifles

10-026.3

Clapp, Gates & Company, Cedar Hill Foundry, Alamance Creek, North Carolina. Made c. 1862-1864. Total of 1031 recorded delivered of which only 661 are shown as being accepted.

Although 4 distinct types identified (CONFEDERATE RIFLES & MUSKETS, *q.v.*) there is no known marked specimen. All have been identified from artifacts recovered at site of the original foundry which had been destroyed by occupying Union troops, by distinctive features common to all four (such as the odd shaped lug for saber bayonet) and, in the case of the first style, specific mention in state records of rifles with "hammer inside locks."

Earliest production, likely under 50, with very unusual box-lock with hammer inside lockplate. Approx. 36" barrel. 50 caliber. Brass mounted. Two barrel bands, spring-retained with top band serving also as the forend tip.

10-026.3

Other types with odd, awkward shaped Enfield-type lock. Caliber 50 and 577. Barrel lengths reported from 32" to 36". Two spring-retained barrel bands. Brass and/or iron mounted. Forend tip. Two crudely fashioned Enfield-type lock screw escutcheons:

10-026.3   Values—Fair **$10,000**   Very Good **$30,000**

M. Cody & Son Model 1841 Type Rifle

Michael Cody & Son Model 1841 type percussion rifle. Most likely Tennessee, exact location unknown. (Not illus.) Procured through the C.S. Arsenal at Nashville 1861-1862. Quantity estimated under 100.

Although no known marked specimen, tentative identification made through a number of distinctive features on all recorded specimens.

Very closely fashioned after the U.S. M1841 even retaining the large brass patchbox. Civilian type, plain, flat, flush fitted side lock retained by just single lock screw. Pin fastened brass barrel bands. Large, hand engraved serial number on the barrel tang. 33" barrel. 54 caliber:

10-026.5   Values—Fair **$7,500**   Very Good **$25,000**

Columbus Armory Carbine

Columbus Armory, Columbus, Georgia. John D. Gray (reported to be brother of William C. Gray, Columbus, Georgia, maker of J. P. Murray Artillery carbine…see 10-047) c. 1861-63.

An elusive gun, evidence of its existence first reported in the 7th edition of this "GUIDE." One authenticated, marked specimen now known as well as a matching, marked excavated lock. Closely similar to the J. P. Murray Artillery Carbine (*q.v.*) with same dimensions and the wide, double strap top barrel band. Lock marked in bold block letters "COLUMBUS ARMORY."

23-2/3" barrel marked PRO/FCH. Lower sling swivel on front of trigger bow.

There is a strong likelihood of a direct association between the Columbus Armory and J. P. Murray; hence the possibility that unmarked Murrays may indeed be the product of the Columbus Armory! Thus far records indicate 183 were delivered against a 1000 piece contract. An extreme rarity:

10-026.7   Values—Fair **$40,000**   Very Good **$75,000**

Cook & Brother Musketoon, Carbine, Rifle

10-027
Musketoon

10-028
Carbine

10-029
Rifle

Cook and Brother, New Orleans, and (later) Athens, Georgia. Musketoon, Carbine and Rifle. Made c. 1861-1862 at New Orleans, and c. 1863-1864 at Athens. Total quantity estimated at a few thousand; serial numbered.

58 caliber percussion muzzleloaders; barrels display a twist grain, characteristic of these arms. Two barrel bands on all models.

Finished in the white. Brass mountings including the sling swivels; these latter are attached to forward barrel band and lower trigger guard tang. Iron ramrod. Stocks of walnut or maple, with some believed of pecan wood. Markings as indicated below.

Ferdinand W. C. and Francis Cook were Englishmen: the longarms they produced were of British Enfield pattern. They were forced to leave New Orleans with the approach of Northern troops, and eventually settled on Athens, Georgia, as a safe locale for resuming their manufacturing operations.

Artillery Carbine or Musketoon; 24" barrel. Lockplate marking: COOK & BROTHER ATHENS GA/1864 Marked behind hammer with a Confederate flag design. Wide, flat button type ramrod head (that shown in illustration is incorrect). The earlier, New Orleans made musketoon features a shorter and smaller lockplate, unmarked, with the barrel often found marked COOK & BROTHER NO 1862 Stock on this latter type is not as well

designed as the Athens product and has a larger overall configuration in the butt area. New Orleans specimens are considered very rare and will bring considerable premium over the Athens type valued here:

10-027   Values—Fair **$10,000**   Very Good **$25,000**
Cavalry Carbine; 21" barrel. Earlier production has iron ramrod with swivels and a sling ring bar with ring on left side opposite lock. Both these features were discontinued on later production with sling swivels added; hence, they resembled the musketoon except for the shorter length. Lock markings identical as those described for artillery musketoon with Athens, Georgia address. A few specimens reported of New Orleans manufacture marked as on New Orleans musketoon described above, considered very rare and will bring a premium:

10-028   Values—Fair **$12,500**   Very Good **$30,000**
Infantry Rifle; Production in both New Orleans and Athens, Georgia. 33" barrel. Found with or without a lug for saber type bayonet near muzzle. Lock markings identical to musketoon above. Barrel marked PROVED at breech. Surviving specimens with the earlier New Orleans marks are scarcer and will bring a 10 to 20 percent premium over values shown below. A few of the New Orleans-made rifles are seen with a large, oval, brass patchbox:

10-029   Values—Fair **$15,000**   Very Good **$35,000**

Davis & Bozeman Percussion Rifle & Carbine

Henry J. Davis and David W. Bozeman, Equality, Elmore County, Alabama. Muzzle-Loading Rifle. (Not illus.) Total quantity made estimated approximately 900 rifles and 90 carbines.

58 caliber, muzzleloader. 33" barrel, secured by two barrel bands.

Finished in the white. Mountings of brass. Iron ramrod. Made to accept saber type bayonet. Stocks usually of walnut.

Lockplate marking forward of hammer: D. & B. and ALA., with the date; serial number may be found at rear. On barrel at

breech: ALA. and date.

Fashioned after the U. S. Model 1841 rifle with notable differences being lack of a patchbox and fastened with two narrow barrel bands, the forend having brass cap at its tip. Rare. Records indicate 89 carbines made by D. & B. for Alabama. Known specimens have 24" barrels; some made from rejected rifle barrels, while others special as carbine. Extremely rare. Values shown for the rifle:

10-030   Values—Fair **$15,000**   Very Good **$40,000**

Dickson, Nelson Carbine and Rifle

Dickson, Nelson Carbine and Rifle. Made by Dickson, Nelson & Co. Total quantity estimated 3600 at Adairsville, Georgia (1862-3), Macon (1863-4) and Dawson, Georgia February, 1864 to

April, 1865. The firm was founded by William Dickson and Owen O. Nelson, and was known as the Shakanoosa Arms Company.

**10-031
Carbine**

**10-032
Rifle**

Approximately 58 caliber, muzzleloaders. Lockplates styled after U. S. Model 1841 pattern.

Finish unknown. Mountings generally of brass. Stock of walnut or cherry.

Lockplate marking: DICKSON/NELSON & CO./C.S., forward of hammer. At rear of lock, marked vertically: ALA./(date). Barrel may also be marked: ALA (date), at breech. Stocks may bear stamping: F. ZUNDT.

Surviving specimens are rare. Most bear lock date "1865". Very seldom seen date "1864" and only two recorded "1863" date on an unattached lockplate, the other on a two-band rifle. **Carbine;** 24" barrel fastened by single band. Full stock with brass cap at tip of forend. Iron ramrod with swivels:
10-031   Values—Fair **$12,500**   Very Good **$35,000**
Rifle; 33" barrel fastened by two bands of equal size; brass cap at tip of forend. Made without patchbox:
10-032   Values—Fair **$12,500**   Very Good **$37,500**

Fayetteville Armory Rifles

**10-033
Early Production**

**10-034
Standard Production**

Fayetteville Armory, Fayetteville, North Carolina. Altered many captured flintlock U.S. pistols and longarms. Many identifiable by a distinctively shaped hammer (*Confederate Rifles & Muskets; q.v.*) and made Model 1855-type rifle from parts captured at the U.S. Arsenals at Harpers Ferry and Fayetteville. Estimated 8000 to 9000 made c. 1862-65 (majority seem to be of Type IV; estimated 5000).

58 caliber, muzzleloader. 33" barrel, secured by two barrel bands.

Finished in the white or browned. Mountings of brass; patchbox sometimes present on early specimens using Harpers Ferry stocks. Lug for saber bayonet usually on barrel. Iron ramrod. Stocks of walnut.

Lockplate marking of FAYETTEVILLE at forward section; just forward of hammer, an eagle motif above C.S.A.; to rear of hammer, the date. Tang of buttplate marked C.S.A. On barrel breech: V.P. and eaglehead motif and the date.
Type I; Early production; c. 1861-1862 made from captured Harpers Ferry parts. The lockplate with the high humpback shape (from Maynard primer profile, although primer not

present). Lock marking: C.S.A./FAYETTEVILLE, N.C. No eagle or date stamp present. Seen with or without small brass patchbox. Markings "C.S.A." usually not present on buttplate:
10-033   Values—Fair **$10,000**   Very Good **$30,000**
Type II; With low lumpback, and marked: (eagle motif)/C.S.A. and FAYETTEVILLE, forward of hammer. Date 1862 to rear of hammer. Made from Harpers Ferry parts. Markings "C.S.A." on some brass buttplates:
10-034   Values—Fair **$10,000**   Very Good **$35,000**
Type III; Lockplate without humpback profile and on the general contour of the U. S. Model 1861 musket; standard markings as above with "1863" date; a few transitional specimens dated "1862." Hammer of distinctive S contour. Lug for saber bayonet added to right side near muzzle:
10-035   Values—Fair **$8,500**   Very Good **$25,000**
Type IV; About identical with slight variance in the eagle die stamp. Accepts socket-type bayonet with front sight acting also as bayonet lug. Lock markings as above with 1864 or 1865 dates:
10-035.5   Values—Fair **$8,000**   Very Good **$22,500**

Georgia Armory Percussion Rifle

Georgia Armory, Milledgeville, Georgia (at state penitentiary building) contract percussion rifle. Estimated approximately 400 made c. 1862-63. (Not illus.)

Patterned closely after the U.S. Model 1855.
58 caliber muzzleloader. 33" to 38" barrel. Brass mountings. Stock fastened by two flat, narrow bands; brass forend tip; brass

patchbox of M1855 type but slightly smaller. Two small Enfield type escutcheons for lockplate screws. Unusual feature is the trigger bow which is cast integral as one piece with the tang.

Lockplate is in M1841 profile, but flat and flush fitted.

Marked vertically at rear "GA. ARMORY" over date "1862" or "1863." Extreme caution should be exercised. On acquisition; loose lockplates are known:

10-035.7   Values—Fair **$20,000**   Very Good **$60,000**

Greenwood & Gray Carbines & Rifles   *See J.P. Murray.*

Gillam & Miller Contract Rifle

L.M. Gillam & James Miller, High Point, North Carolina percussion rifle. Total 739 delivered to N.C. 1863 before contract cancelled. (212 of those rejected.) Patterned closely after U.S. Model 1841 but without patchbox. (Not illus.)

58 caliber. 33" barrel with "P" proof, brass mountings. Stock fastened by 2 split type (screw tightened) narrow, oval brass bands; brass forend tip. M1841 style lock unmarked. Few specimens observed with "GILLAM & / MILLER" deeply stamped

in the wood on comb of buttstock (collectors should be extremely wary of spurious markings). Serial numbers stamped inside lockplate and elsewhere (if markings present values double those shown).

The company had a C.S. government contract also, but it is not known if they delivered any rifles towards it. They are also known to have supplied stocks to other contractors:

10-035.9   Values—Fair **$7,500**   Very Good **$12,500**

Hindman Rifle   *See Arkadelphia Rifle 10-022.5*

D.C. Hodgkins & Sons Percussion Carbine

10-036

D. C. Hodgkins & Sons Percussion Carbine. Originally attributed to D. C. Hodgkins & Sons, Macon, Georgia, and traditionally so-listed. More recent research by H. M. Madaus, and reported by J. M. Murphy in *Confederate Carbines and Musketoons* (q.v.), convincingly indicates the carbine was made by **Bilharz, Hall and Co. of Pittsylvania Courthouse, Virginia,** in late 1863 to early 1864. Quantity manufactured for the C.S. Government estimated between 400 and 700.

58 caliber muzzleloader, copied closely after the Springfield Model 1855 carbine. 22" barrel.

Iron mountings with brass or pewter (scarce) forend cap.

Ramrod attached to barrel by means of iron swivels. Sling ring mounted on rear of trigger guard bow. Walnut stock.

Assembly numbers present on various parts. Breech of barrel marked: CSA over P. If unmarked or markings not visible values tend to be about 20 percent less.

These apparently handmade arms, as to be expected, show small variations in shapes and contours. As an example, rear sections of locks may be rounded, or somewhat pointed. Letter and number stampings will be observed on some parts, both external and internal:

10-036   Values—Fair **$10,000**   Very Good **$25,000**

Kean, Walker & Co. Carbine   *See Maynard-Perry.*

H.C. Lamb & Co. Contract Rifle

10-037

Henry C. Lamb & Co., Jamestown, North Carolina. State Contract for percussion rifles. Quantities unknown. Total recorded delivered 1862-3 was 532 of which about 15 percent rejected.

Patterned generally after the U.S. Model 1841, the few surviving examples have evidenced three varying types, all with

many common features such as brass mountings; two split type (screw tightened) flat, barrel bands and 33" (approx.) round barrels with about 7" at breech being octagon.

Earliest type 58 caliber with lockplate almost Enfield shaped and just two very small, round escutcheons under lock screws (v.s. the M1841 style sideplates on all other types). Later production encountered in 50 and 58 caliber and distinctive M1841 style unmarked lockplates. Barrel marking usually "P" proof and seen with and without "N.C." A few rifles are known stamped in the wood near the sideplate with serial number and "H. C. LAMB & CO. / N.C." (worth 25 percent premium, often much greater on upper condition; be wary of spurious markings):

10-037   Values—Fair **$8,500**   Very Good **$17,500**

LeMat Two-Barrel Revolving Carbine

10-038

LeMat Two-Barrel Ten-Shot Percussion Revolving Carbine. (*See Confederate Handguns section for full details about this maker and his arms, also see bibliography.*)

The inclusion of this carbine is arbitrary, as it is of French manufacture. Very little is known about the quantity made or their purchase or use by Confederate forces. It is most often seen in either pinfire or centerfire models, but only the percussion model listed here (very rare) has been traditionally considered by collectors as a secondary Confederate weapon. In action it is identical to the pistol (*q.v.*).

42 caliber. Nine-shot cylinder with 20" part octagon/part round barrel revolving on a center axis which is also a smoothbore 63 caliber 20" barrel firing a single load of buckshot. Overall length approximately 38". Variations noted.

Three different barrel markings observed as on the pistol (*q.v.*):

10-038   Values—Fair **$22,500**   Very Good **$60,000**

Maynard (by Mass. Arms Co.) First Model Carbine with primer.   *See 9B-073.*

Maynard or Perry Brass Frame Carbine

10-039

10-039

Maynard or Perry (so-called) Brass Frame Tilting Breech Carbine. Evidence strongly indicates they were made by **Keen, Walker & Co. of Danville, Virginia,** between May and September, 1862, for the C.S. Government. Total quantity made believed 280.

Originally reported to be the design of N. T. Read, later evidence indicates that it is not the Read patent. Externally somewhat similar to the U.S. Maynard Carbine with the breechblock similar to the Perry action.

54 caliber, breechloader; the breechblock tilting upwards as the trigger guard/lever is lowered 22-1/2" barrel.

Blued or browned barrel; balance of iron parts believed casehardened. Brass or bronze frame. Walnut stock. Sling ring and bar on left side of frame.

P stamping may be on breech of barrel. Roman numeral stamps of large size cut on various parts, e.g., upper and lower tang, inside stock, and on barrel. A distinctive arm, with positive Confederate origins:

10-039   Values—Fair **$15,000**   Very Good **$30,000**

Mendenhall, Jones & Gardner Contract Rifle

10-040

Cyrus P. Mendenhall, Ezekial Jones & Grafton Gardner. Percussion, muzzle-loading rifles styled after the U.S. Model 1841 (without patchbox) made under contract for state of North Carolina 1862-64.

Although 2239 recorded as accepted by the state, survival rate minimal; rare.

The small number of existing specimens studied are categorized in four types. There are common features on all. 33" barrel fastened by two spring retained, flat, brass barrel bands; brass forend cap. Brass mountings (except on earliest which has iron buttplate). 58 caliber on almost all except earliest type (50 caliber with under 100 recorded delivered in 1862). Two small Enfield type brass escutcheons under lock screws on most; earlier examples with brass M1841 style side plate (worth premium).

Barrels marked "N.C." over "P." Lockplates "M.J.& G. / N.C." in center (the county marking "GUILFORD" also appears as an added line on some early examples) and marked vertically at rear "C.S." over the date. "1863" and "1864" most often seen; "1862" very rare:

10-040   Values—Fair **$12,500**   Very Good **$30',000**

Morse Carbine

10-041

Morse Carbine, made by the State Military Works, Greenville, South Carolina. This unusual breechloader invented by George W. Morse was made on machinery which had been captured by the Confederates from the Harpers Ferry Armory. Total quantity made estimated at approximately 1,000.

50 caliber, chambering a forerunner of the centerfire metallic cartridge. The breechblock tilts upward for loading. 20" round barrel.

Brass frame and mountings. Butternut stock; brass buttplate has small friction fitted accessory in center which removes and screws onto end of ramrod. Only a few of the very last types were marked other than with serial numbers (see below).

Serial numbered (from 1 on up) and visible on bottom of frame.

Production of the Morse carbines was mainly for the state militia of South Carolina. Specimens were also used to some extent by other C.S.A. forces.

Prototype Morse; most notable distinguishing feature is the wooden forend which has a very long tail extension reaching back to the trigger guard. All later production has a brass plate covering that same area. Sights differ with rear sight

approximately 2" further forward than all Greenville types; latch configuration also differs. Larger 54 caliber. Very rare:

10-041   Values—Fair **$12,000**   Very Good **$37,500**

Greenville Production Types:

First Type; distinguished by use of the firing pin to lock the action. Very low serial numbers, under 200. Barrels are often part octagon shaped at breech while others are all round. The sides of the breech lever (observable when lever is lifted upward) have three deep cut-out indentations each side:

10-042   Values—Fair **$10,000**   Very Good **$30,000**

Second Type; the action locked by a latch which engaged a bolt head on the breechblock:

10-043   Values—Fair **$9,000**   Very Good **$27,500**

Third Type; action locked by latch which engaged breechblock's rounded iron top section:

10-044   Values—Fair **$8,000**   Very Good **$22,500**

Marked specimens; on very late production with high serial numbers the markings MORSE may be seen on the right frame plate. Rare:

10-045   Values—Fair **$12,500**   Very Good **$35,000**

Morse Inside Lock Musket

10-046

Morse Inside Lock (so-called) Musket by George W. Morse, Greenville, South Carolina. Total quantity recorded as 80 muskets and 60 rifles, April-June, 1864. Only one rifle in 54 caliber known; unmarked.

71 caliber, smoothbore, muzzleloader. 42" barrel, secured by three barrel bands.

Mountings of brass. Iron ramrod. Walnut stock closely resembles those used on Palmetto Armory muskets.

Serial numbered. Markings are stamped on the lower brass trigger tang "MORSE'S LOCK / STATE WORKS / GREENVILLE, S.C." with serial number at the extreme tip. The date "1863" stamped on the brass finial ahead of trigger bow. (The anomaly of that date and the April-June 1864 reported delivery date is unresolved.)

One of the most unusual designs in C.S.A. small arms, distinguished by the economy of mechanism, reduced to the very barest essentials:

10-046   Values—Fair **$25,000**   Very Good **$65,000**

J. P. Murray (Greenwood & Gray) Rifles & Carbines

Eldridge S. Greenwood and William C. Gray (and possibly John D. Gray), none of whom were gunmakers, purchased facilities to manufacture firearms in Columbus, Georgia in 1862 and

employed John P. Murray, a skilled gunmaker as their master armorer. Quantities unknown but likely limited 1862-64. It is known that in 1864 they made and delivered under Alabama

10-047
Artillery Musketoon Variant

10-047
Artillery Musketoon Variant

10-049
Rifle

state contract 262 rifles and 73 carbines (which bear barrel markings "ALA 1864"). SEE ALSO "COLUMBUS ARMORY" (John D. Gray).

58 caliber, muzzleloaders. Barrel lengths as noted below.

Finish believed to have been bright. Mountings generally of brass with high copper tint; iron sling swivels and ramrod. Walnut stock.

Marked with serial or assembly numbers. Lockplate of U.S. Model 1841 style usually marked forward of hammer: J. P. MURRAY/COLUMBUS GA. Inspector initials usually marked at breech of barrel such as PRO, F.C.H., or ALA. A windmill or cross-like mark may be found on underside of barrels.

Artillery carbine or musketoon; made in two basic variations about equal in value. Barrel lengths 23-1/2" and 24". Variations of brass or iron triggers; rounded or flat bolt heads. Those with unmarked locks marked at breech of barrel ALA and date with

inspector markings. Although all have full stocks, two-band fastened, they may be found and are correct with either the narrow upper band and a brass cap on forend tip, or a wide double strap band at top of forend which precludes the use of a forend cap:

10-047   Values—Fair **$10,000**   Very Good **$27,500**

Cavalry carbine; 23" barrel; swivel type iron ramrod with flat head. Lock markings as above; various letter and number stampings on barrel and breech. Flat bolt heads. Large sling swivel on rear of trigger guard:

10-048   Values—Fair **$10,000**   Very Good **$30,000**

Rifle; 33" barrel; fastened by two narrow, flat, spring retained bands; brass forend cap. Many specimens found with the wide, brass adapter ring and stud for a saber type bayonet; bears markings "B.G.& M / Richmond / Va. / Sept. 2, 1861." (Note: Spurious copies of the adapter ring are known):

10-049   Values—Fair **$10,000**   Very Good **$30,000**

Palmetto Armory—William Glaze & Company, Columbia, South Carolina   *See U. S. Military Longarms, Chapter IX (Model 1841 Rifle and Model 1842 Musket).*

Pulaski Armory Rifle

Pulaski Armory, Pulaski, Tennessee. Percussion, muzzle-loading rifle patterned after the U.S. Model 1841 but without patchbox. (Not illus.) Made c. 1861. Quantity unknown; very limited. Very rare.

54 caliber. 33" barrel fastened by two barrel bands (top band double strap M1841 type). Brass mountings. Most distinguishing feature is the use of sporting type side locks of varying dimensions attached by just a single screw with small diamond shaped escutcheon. A distinctive shaped bolster with nipple is

common to all specimens.

Locks, commandeered from various civilian sources throughout the state, bear many and varied markings (LEMAN / LANCASTER ; GOULCHER ; TRUITT WARRANTED etc.). Barrels on most viewed specimens are marked with small, deep, block letters on left side near breech "PULASKI, T. CSA 61." (Genuine marking variations are known, however, caution advised to authenticate):

10-049.5   Values—Fair **$9,500**   Very Good **$25,000**

Read & Watson Carbines and Rifles   *See J. B. Barrett.*

Richmond Armory Carbines, Musketoons, Rifle-Muskets

Richmond Armory, Richmond, Virginia. Carbines, Musketoons, Rifle-Muskets. Made c. 1861-1865. Total quantities unknown, but in larger numbers than all other Confederate longarms manufactured during the Civil War.

58 caliber percussion muzzleloaders conforming to general configuration of U.S. Models 1855 and 1861 rifled-muskets. Iron

mountings with brass buttplate and forend cap (iron occasionally encountered, but buyer should be cautious). Iron ramrod with tulip head. Walnut stock. Barrel markings usually V P and eaglehead; seen both with or without date at top of breech. Finished bright with casehardened lock.

These arms were made with machinery and parts captured at

10-050

10-051

10-052

Harpers Ferry Armory in April, 1861, and moved to Confederate ordnance facilities in Richmond. They are quite distinctive by their use of the so-called "humpback" lockplate. Early locks were made from forgings and dies taken from Harpers Ferry and originally intended for use with the Maynard tape primer on the U. S. Model 1855 rifled musket. Having no use for the Maynard device, the Richmond Armory merely utilized the old dies as the most expedient means of production. In 1862 new dies were evidently made shortening the "hump" by approximately 3/8" making it noticeably lower. This style was used for the balance of production and is the most often seen. There are variations noted especially in the earliest manufactured arms. Three major types of Richmond locks and markings are:

Type I: Earliest manufacture with full humpback lockplate marked forward of hammer RICHMOND, VA. and vertically at rear 1861. Produced under the auspices of the State of Virginia before the armory was turned over to the Confederate government. These will bring a premium value over the prices indicated below.

Type II: Similar to above. Identical markings, but with the addition of the letters CS above RICHMOND, VA. and dated 1862 at rear. Made immediately after the Confederate government takeover of the armory. These also will bring a premium value over the more often seen styles.

Type III: Easily distinguished by the lower humpback lock as described above. Markings same as Type II with two die variations of "RICHMOND" noted and date "1862" to "1864" usual ("1865" very rare).

Caution and good judgment should be exercised in the acquisition of these arms. It is worth noting that quite a few Richmond humpback lockplates were on hand at the close of the Civil War—eventually finding their way to the souvenir and ultimately collectors' market. For years they were merely curiosities sold at very minimal sums. In the decades following World War II, prices rose steadily in direct proportion to their value to unscrupulous traders for use on U.S. Model 1855 and 1861 muskets to create a more profitable Confederate gun. The humpback Richmond locks neatly fit the U.S. counterparts; hence, a very careful inspection is in order, especially on the musket size. The lock aperture on all Richmonds should be carefully inspected; an original does not have the groove or channel required for the Maynard primer device. This is merely the most cursory check and not in itself conclusive. The rear sight must be removed for a second important area to inspect. On the U.S. M1855 barrel and the Richmond-made barrel the

wide mortise on the barrel has a small "T" shaped, perpendicular cut-out at the front (to allow for a small bead on the underside of the sight to fit, preventing side-to-side shifting (date will also allow for distinguishing origin). The U.S. Model 1861 musket barrel, which will fit the M1855/Richmond, does not have that small "T" slot; thus unless it is proven that there was a battlefield emergency repair from a captured Yankee musket, there is every likelihood that the Richmond is a composite assembled in a more recent era.

Carbine; 25" barrel. Full stock fastened by two barrel bands. Sling swivels on upper band and front of trigger guard with a third swivel screwed directly into underside of buttstock and a distinct feature of the carbine. The iron front sight is also a key feature of identification, having a wide base tapering inward on each side to form a tall blade:
10-050   Values—Fair **$5,500**   Very Good **$20,000**

Musketoon; 30" barrel. Full stock fastened by two barrel bands. Front sight doubles as lug for socket type bayonet. Sling swivels on upper band and front of trigger guard. All recorded specimens have iron mounts with few only having brass forend tip. Termed a "Navy Musketoon" in some earlier works, but undoubtedly for artillery use also. Often found bored smooth to 60 or 62 caliber and believed issued that way. Rare variant of this musketoon is known with an original 33" barrel, also two-band fastened. Not fitted for bayonet; also distinguished by its distinctive front sight. Authentic specimens valued in low to almost mid-five figures. Caution urged on all musketoons especially 30-inch barrels as many observed with post-war alterations (believed by Bannerman's); some with stocks from M1873 Springfield rifles:
10-051   Values—Fair **$5,000**   Very Good **$17,500**

Rifled musket; 40" barrel; three barrel bands; sling swivels; front sight acts as lug for socket type bayonet. Most recent study (*C.S. Rifles & Muskets, q.v.*) recognizes three distinct types, classified basically by lock types (see above). The earliest production April to August, 1861 had considerably intermixed, captured parts and Richmond-made parts as supplies were exhausted. By mid-1862 all stocks were produced in Georgia and shipped back to Richmond for assembly. Although muskets are valued less than the above models in "fair" as they are more often encountered, they command higher values in better grades as most saw hard service and survival rate of finer specimens is less. It also has been found that C.S. infantry arms have a greater "demand." "1861" and "1864" dates bring premium:
10-052   Values—Fair **$7,000**   Very Good **$25,000**

Rising Breech Carbine

10-053

10-053

Rising Breech Carbine. Recent research attributes manufacture of this unique breechloading percussion carbine to **Bilharz, Hall and Company, of Pittsylvania Courthouse, Virginia**. Attribution is based on the similarity of the barrel markings and the rifling of the bore to the Bilharz, Hall and Company carbine (formerly called the "D. C. Hodgkins" carbine (*q.v.*). Quantity estimated at 100.

54 caliber, firing a paper cartridge; the breechblock rising vertically when the trigger guard/lever is lowered. 21" barrel, secured by a single barrel band.

Barrels believed to have been browned, and breechblock and frame casehardened. Iron mountings, including barrel band and buttplate. Walnut stock. Sling ring on left side of frame. Two variations of lever latches.

Serial numbered. Marked on breech of barrel and on breechblock with proof or inspection mark P over C.S.

These well made (hand constructed and fitted) arms remain an enigma to the collector and researcher. A rare and very desirable Confederate arm:

10-053   Values—Fair **$25,000**   Very Good **$65,000**

S.C. Robinson, Sharps Type Carbines

10-054

Sharps Type Carbines. Made at Richmond, Virginia, c. 1862-1864. Total quantity of two distinct styles approximately 5,000.

52 caliber, percussion, breechloader. 21" barrel. Fashioned directly after the Hartford-made Model 1859 Sharps with a few noticeable differences: simple V-notch rear sight and tapered iron front sight; lockplate has lower profile as it is made without provision for the pellet primers; sling ring bar is affixed to long narrow iron plate which is inletted in left side of stock and edge of receiver; sling swivel on underside of buttstock; no provision for patchbox; mountings are brass. Workmanship throughout does not have the refinements viewed on the Hartford products with often crude, if not primitive, features observed in the stock work. Finish uncertain, but probably blued.

First Type; Made by S. C. Robinson, c. 1862-1863. Estimated production 1,900. Serial numbered from 1 on up. Lockplate marked S. C. ROBINSON./ARMS MANUFACTORY./RICHMOND, VA./1862 with serial number at extreme rear of lock. Top of

barrel usually marked (ahead of rear sight) S. C. ROBINSON/ARMS MANUFACTORY; and marked behind rear sight RICHMOND, VA./1862:

10-054   Values—Fair **$7,000**   Very Good **$25,000**

Second Type; Made under the auspices of the Confederate government after their purchase of Robinson's factory in March 1863. Production continued approximately one year with estimated quantity of 3,000 carbines made. Serial number ranges continued from the end of the Robinson production (approximately 1900) to slightly over 5000. Identical to the Robinson made First Type carbine (above) with only markings RICHMOND, VA. at the top of breech of barrel and the serial number marked at extreme rear of lock. Because of its manufacture under the auspices of the C.S. Gov't., its value, once slightly less than the 1st Type, has been found to be the same:

10-055   Values—Fair **$6,500**   Very Good **$22,500**

Brass Frame Sharps Carbine

Brass Frame Sharps Carbine. a.k.a. "Getty Brass Frame Sharps," a conjectural name applied by the first study to

recognize this rare arm ("Confederate Carbines & Musketoons" *q.v.*). Maker and quantity produced unknown. Questionable

10-055.5

origin was Huntersville, Va. (later W. Va.) based on correspondence by officer at C.S. carbine factory, Richmond Feb. 26, 1863, to Brig. General Gorgas, Chief of C.S. Ordnance. Mention was made that a report was enclosed (contents unknown) of the "...Master Armorer on the altered Sharps carbine presented by Capt. Getty" (G.T. Getty, then commanding C.S. Ordnance Depot at Lynchburg, Va.). Future studies may reveal more about the guns.

Six specimens are thus far known and recorded. None bear maker markings; all have crudely marked Roman numerals on

various metal and wood parts. Key feature is the Sharps-style brass frame and breechblock. Overall length 41"; barrel 25-3/4". Caliber 52; the lands and grooves of the rifled bores may vary. One specimen known 58 cal. smoothbore. Iron fittings may be those of Hall carbine; centrally mounted hammer also may be Hall carbine. No provision made for lever latch. Rifle-type sling swivel screw mounted to left frame; some specimens with upper swivel mounted on pin fastened barrel band. Walnut (or possible other, yet to be determined) stock and long, tapered forend:

10-055.5   Values—Fair **$35,000**   Very Good **$75,000**

Tallassee Enfield Pattern Carbine

10-056

Tallassee Enfield Pattern Carbine, a.k.a. "New Model Carbine." Made by the Confederate Armory at Tallassee, Alabama, c. 1864. Total quantity estimated about 500.

58 caliber percussion muzzleloader, patterned closely after the British Enfield carbine. 25" barrel fastened by two barrel bands.

All brass mountings with iron ramrod and swivels; iron sling swivels on forward band and bottom of stock near butt. Full walnut stock.

Lockplate marked forward of hammer: C.S./TALLASSEE/ALA. Dated at rear of lock 1864.

Apparently the only officially adopted Confederate cavalry weapon. Made with machinery moved (for safety against threatened capture) from the former Robinson/Confederate government factory producing Sharps type carbines at Richmond. Production commenced late in the war and it is believed that completion of approximately 500 pieces in the spring of 1865 was too late for issuance. Very rare; extreme caution advised:

10-056   Values—Fair **$44,000**   Very Good **$100,000**

Tarpley Breech-Loading Carbine

10-057

Tarpley Breech-Loading Carbine. Invented by Jere H. Tarpley, Greensboro, North Carolina, and granted C.S.A. patent in February, 1863. Made by the J. and F. Garrett Company, Greensboro; c. 1863-1864; total quantity estimated a few hundred.

52 caliber, breechloader; firing paper cartridge. 22" round barrel.

Blued barrel; the frame of unfinished brass, having a copper

coloration; casehardened hammer. No ramrod or forend. Front sight of brass; two-leaf iron rear sight. Iron buttplate, trigger guard, sling ring and ring bar. Buttstock of walnut.

Serial numbered. Upper tang of frame stamped: J H TARPLEY'S./PAT FEB 14./1863. Stock may also bear marking of MANUFACTURED BY/J. & F. GARRETT & CO/GREENSBORO N.C. CSA.

Production of this rarity was primarily for the State of North Carolina. 200 recorded delivered 1863. This weapon is also distinguished as the only Confederate firearm known to have also been available on a commercial basis:

10-057   Values—Fair **$50,000**   Very Good **$90,000**

George H. Todd Rifled Musket

George H. Todd, Montgomery, Alabama. Rifled Musket. (Not illus.) Quantity unknown.

Although reported in earlier Confederate references, this musket is conspicuously absent from well-respected works published in the last two decades. Hence, collectors should exercise extreme caution if contemplating acquisition of this arm. *"Confederate Arms"* (Albaugh, 1957) specifically mentions known fakes of the musket...but the reader should also be aware that this author and Confederate specialists have yet to view a

specimen judged to be authentic.

The musket was reported to be fashioned directly after the U.S. Model 1861 cal 58 rifled-musket, but with brass mountings, including the lockplate and hammer; markings of TODD. MONTGOMERY / ALA., etc., on lock. Should such a specimen come to light and be adjudged authentic it would command a value commensurate with other great C.S. rarities. For reasons above, there is no value assigned here:

10-058

Tyler Texas Rifle, et al.

Tyler Ordnance Works, Tyler, Texas. Various styles of infantry rifles, known through documents, records and markings as the Long and Short Patterns of the **Hill Rifle** and the **Texas Rifle** with others the **Enfield, Austrian** and **Tyler** models.

Surviving specimens of complete arms are extremely rare with but a handful known. A number of locks only are known from which much of the marking information has been recorded. One lot of 29 locks was brought to light in 1931 and a

10-059

few others have been found intermittently since.

Total quantities made are unknown; believed in excess of several hundreds; c. 1863-1865. There was evidently a very wide range of dimensions and not enough specimens are known to give particulars. It is apparent that barrels of all types were utilized in their assembly, from discarded civilian rifles with octagon barrels to many styles of military barrels running the gamut from Hall carbines to British Enfields.

The one feature which apparently is common to all varieties is the Enfield style lockplate which is fastened by a single screw to the gun. A great many lock marking variations have been observed. The following (all marked ahead of hammer) are some of those recorded: TEXAS RIFLE/TYLER with or without a third line marked CAL. 57; or ENFIELD RIFLE/TYLER/TEX/CAL .57; or HILL RIFLE/TYLER/TEXAS; or AUSTRIAN RIFLE/TYLER TEXAS/CAL .54.

Locks may be found marked vertically at rear C.S. with date or serial numbers.

Of two distinct styles observed and from markings it is surmised that the arms are generally 54 and 57 caliber. Barrels are of various lengths and shapes, 28" to 38" with and without lugs for saber type bayonet. Walnut full stocks were most probably fastened by two barrel bands.

Of two known types, a specimen marked AUSTRIAN RIFLE had a 37-1/2" barrel, 54 caliber, all iron mountings and two barrel bands with top band similar in appearance to a European Austrian rifle. The second specimen marked TEXAS RIFLE had a 33" barrel, 57 caliber, all brass mountings and was styled more closely after the Enfield artillery rifle, also having two barrel bands of equal width and a brass forend cap.

Extreme care should be exercised in the acquisition of these very rare guns:

10-059   Values—Fair **$20,000**   Very Good **$50,000**

Virginia Mfty. Conversion of Second Model Flintlock Musket

Virginia Manufactory, Richmond, Virginia, Second Model Flintlock Musket (Model 1812 U.S. type) made circa 1812-1821 and converted to percussion during the Civil War years (1861-1865) under direct contract of the Confederate Government. Four known contractors, all of Richmond, identified as S. C. Robinson (see 10-055); Francis Persignon, a Richmond gunsmith; the (ambiguously named) Union Mfg. Company of Richmond; and Thomas J. Adams, also a Richmond gunsmith. All utilized the bolster-type alteration. A significant article, "The Alteration of Virginia Manufactory Weapons 1813-1863" by Giles Cromwell in the *Journal of the American*

Society of Arms Collectors, Issue No. 52 (Spring, 1985), identifies, describes and illustrates those Confederate alterations as well as many other conversions of Virginia Manufactory muskets by various gunsmiths. (Also refer to works by Murphy in Biblio.)

Usually percussion conversions of flintlock arms tend to lower values considerably. However, with these identified Confederate Contract conversions present, they are likely to be valued equal to original flintlock muskets, possibly greater. (See flintlock listings for these arms, items 9A-179; 9A-181; 9A-183.)

10-060

Wytheville Rifle or Carbine   *See J. B. Barrett.*

British "Brunswick" percussion rifle purchased and issued by the Confederate government and its stock carved by the soldier that carried it. Vast numbers of British and other European arms were purchased by the South during the Civil War. This Brunswick rifle is a rare example of a known type issued. Its exceptional feature is the large, fine quality incised carving that fills the right butt: "JOHN C. GILLESPIE... CO.K... 18TH ARK. INF. VOL...C.S.A."

Close-up view of the manner by which common sporting weapons were adapted for military issuance by the Confederacy during the Civil War. Although massive quantities of civilian shotguns and squirrel rifles were acquired by the Southern armies (many brought their own weapons from home) and supposedly huge numbers were so altered to accept a bayonet, but a handful are known which actually have that alteration. The large brass fixture attached to an otherwise undistinguished percussion half stock low quality English shotgun is an example of the alteration and is accompanied by its original matching brass hilt bayonet specially fitted to it. The two pieces were brought home as souvenirs by a Union soldier of a Massachusetts regiment during the Civil War and have always been kept together. (*N. Flayderman & Co., c.1963*)

Chapter XI

Kentucky Rifles and Pistols

The very nature of this subject and the fact it is often likened to an American art form, makes any discussion a highly subjective one. The individuality of each rifle makes for an obvious lack of objectivity. Although the rifles of various makers have notable similarities and "earmarks" there are no two exactly alike. Since the subject is broad in scope with many complexities and subtleties, the author, governed by the nature of this particular work must limit himself to broad generalities and overall personal observations as to what constitutes the field of collecting "Kentuckies" and their market values. He hopes to acquaint the reader with the various types and styles and arm him with the facts necessary to interpret their relative importance and, consequently value. To truly understand the field requires careful study and research.

In its most esoteric sense a discussion of Kentucky rifles invokes the use of highly aesthetic terminology. This usually begins with comparisons to Roman and Greek sculpture, progressing through time to the American Federal and Victorian eras with parallels to contemporary furniture, carving, mouldings and even gaudiness. All of these discussions are liberally spiced with architectural terms (such as "… smooth, uncluttered lines …") and their intended functions; proportions of the various elements of the rifle; and the intricacies—and often perplexities—of straight, convex or concave stock profiles along their drop and castoff!!

To be truly involved in collecting "Kentuckies" one must have, or acquire, the same feeling for these rifles as does the collector of any art form—be it paintings or sculpture or otherwise. There is a great similarity in the proper appreciation of them all. As attested to by the bibliography accompanying this section, the subject has been widely covered with many published works containing much excellent information. However, as with most original art forms, this one still offers virtually unlimited possibilities for the researcher, student and author; with almost bottomless depths to plumb.

Keeping within the main guidelines established for this book, i.e., identification and evaluation, the author will not attempt to encapsulate or oversimplify the subject, but rather make a few general observations that he has noted in his years of collecting and dealing in these distinguished American arms. He will but lightly touch upon the aesthetic principles involved for true understanding and appreciation, but again emphasizes their importance and the undeniable fact that a knowledge of same is essential to the formation of a representative Kentucky collection. The reader need not be overawed or dissuaded from pursuing this field by what might be taken as the need for overly great intellectual capacities or involvement which all the foregoing might seem to require. The field is one that is easily mastered and

it is strictly a matter of personal choice and preference as to how far the collector wishes to progress upward on the ladder to the ultimate in quality and beauty. It is very much akin to having a fine example of the work of a noted artist, which for most collectors would be sufficient and satisfying. There are, however, those ultimate perfectionists who would seek only the most choice example of that same artist's work; Kentucky rifles—at the risk of oversimplification— can be thusly compared.

There is likely more lore and romance surrounding the Kentucky rifle than any other American gun—or for that matter any style of firearm in the world. The generic name "Kentucky Rifle" is widely recognized by most Americans (non-gun collectors included!) who have but a smattering of knowledge of their own history; the name is almost equally well-known and recognized by the arms collecting fraternity of Europe. These rifles have never lacked for devotees; even during the "dark ages" of American gun collecting (i.e., the turn of the century through the 1920s) they held a place of esteem in the hierarchy of weapons.

Quite a few qualities give Kentucky rifles their unique appeal. First, distinctive American flavor—they are truly one of the few indigenous American weapons. Secondly, sheer beauty—they are all attractive and pleasing to the eye. Aesthetically, Kentuckies represent the most handsome of all early American weapons, ranking with the finest products of Europe. Lastly, their unparalleled role in the development of American history—from use prior to and during the American Revolution and the War of 1812 to their integral part in forging and expanding the western frontiers. These classic arms have acquired an aura of importance quite justly due them.

THE ORIGIN OF THE NAME

As every neophyte entering the gun collecting field knows, the use of "Kentucky Rifle" is a misnomer. The name has, however, become deeply rooted in gun lore and terminology as well as that of the casual (often scholarly) writer of American history; so much so that it has been generally accepted as a common generic term for a peculiarly American rifle. A knowledge of how the Kentucky acquired its name is of vital interest to the collector and student and will do much to place the entire subject in a clearer perspective by pointing out that the name is just that—a generic term—embracing a relatively broad cross section of American made rifles all of which follow a general form and style. It follows suit that many collectors (purists if you will) specialize in varied forms of the Kentucky rifle and will thus modify or expand the use of the generic term to properly identify the gun's variations.

The most popular and credible theory of origin traces the name to a popular ballad of the decade following the War of 1812 (i.e., the early 1820s). American rifles until that time were widely known and acclaimed but were merely known as "rifles." The government when ordering rifled longarms in the late 18th and early 19th centuries from various Pennsylvania makers called them "rifles," sometimes modifying the name to be "plain" or "common" rifle. During the War of 1812 a somewhat ragtag army of 5,000 Americans under General Andrew Jackson (including about 800 regulars of the U.S. Army) succeeded in performing a veritable military miracle in defeating the British at the strategically important Battle of New Orleans (1815). Among the Americans were approximately 2,000 frontiersmen from the area of the Ohio River Valley including a great many from Tennessee with lesser numbers from Kentucky and other states and territories. The frontiersmen played an instrumental role in the important victory and are generally credited as causing the turning point of the battle to favor the American forces. Those riflemen were memorialized within a decade after the battle in a ballad that immediately caught the public imagination and became popular throughout the United States; the title was "The Hunters of Kentucky, or the Battle of New Orleans." The lyrics of the ballad (circulated in broadside form) overly romanticized and recounted the role played by the riflemen in that New Orleans victory. With typical literary license the unnamed writer credited all the riflemen as being from Kentucky to the complete exclusion of other areas. Included in the recounting of the prowess of those fearless Kentuckians is the following verse that has obviously had far reaching consequences for the American arms collector:

But Jackson he was wide awake,
and wasn't scar'd at trifles,

for well he knew what aim we take
with our Kentucky Rifles.

With the wide circulation of the broadsheet and the popular acceptance of the tune (which remained popular for years), it is evident that combined with a gradual evolutionary process and the passage of time that all long barreled full stock American rifles came to be termed "Kentuckies." Some writers like to use the dialect of the frontier, "Kaintuck" which is a much later, romanticized term that had no contemporary use.

It seems that impetus was added to the use of "Kentucky Rifle" by some Pennsylvania gunmakers of the mid-19th century. There is record of a Pittsburgh gunsmith in 1848 actually stating that he was the maker of the "… celebrated Kentucky Rifle." The pioneer book on the subject *The Kentucky Rifle* by Captain John Dillin (first published in 1924 and since reprinted numerous times), has permanently embedded the term in collecting lore. It should be noted however that Dillin was not the first popular gun writer to use the terminology. Another, milestone work in American gun collecting literature, *Firearms In American History* by Charles Winthrop Sawyer (1910) made liberal use of the name "Kentucky Rifle," and W. W. Greener did likewise in his classic *The Gun And Its Development*, published in the late 19th century.

The incongruity of all this is the fact that the "Kentucky" was widely made in a number of other states to the almost complete exclusion of known examples from Kentucky itself!

ORIGIN OF THE KENTUCKY RIFLE

Lancaster, Pennsylvania has been generally credited as the birthplace of the American rifle (the so-called Kentucky). By far the greatest number of makers and extant specimens are credited and attributed to Pennsylvania. Many present day writers and collectors often prefer to term these arms as "the Pennsylvania Rifle," certainly a more accurate attribution. By the same token however, a great many of this same general type of rifle (each

with its own stylistic features) were quite widely made in Maryland, Virginia, the Carolinas, Tennessee, Ohio, Indiana, New York and even New England (*see Chapter XII for this latter type*). Thus, what one wishes to call them may be very much a matter of personal preference. For our purposes and those of the general gun collecting world the term "Kentucky Rifle" suffices quite nicely and has been found widely acceptable.

CLASSIFICATION OF THE KENTUCKY

For study purposes most modern day writers have established three major classifications for Kentucky rifles. It should be clearly understood that these are broad categories and considerable overlapping exists as well as many "sub-species." The subject is still in its infancy, regardless of the number of available published works, and a single qualified student, researcher and author approaching the field in a different light could completely rearrange thinking as well as classifications. Thus, the reader should be aware that the three major divisions are merely terms of convenience which have been relatively recently established and have yet to be embedded in collecting lore.

The "transition period," as the earliest era is known, commenced circa the 1720s (some writers place it as early as 1710) with the arrival of German and Swiss gunsmiths who settled in the Lancaster, Pennsylvania area and produced rifles closely similar to those they had brought from central Europe. Those same gunsmiths slowly introduced features making the rifle more adaptable to the needs of the environment: providing meat for the table and defense of the homestead. That general evolutionary era extended to about the period of the American Revolution, circa, the 1770s. The *jaeger* rifle of Germany—the direct ancestor of the Kentucky—was short, octagonal barreled (about 30" to 36") with a rifled bore (approximately 60 to 75 caliber). In its American development during this transition era the barrels were generally lengthened to 40" or more (a few were considerably longer) for greater accuracy, with the calibers averaging about 60". Native American woods were used for stocks with maple predominating. Earliest specimens normally had sliding wood patchboxes on the right side of the buttstock to hold cloth patches, tools, flints and other accessories; a style directly fashioned after the European mode. At approximately the mid-18th century iron or brass became the basic material for the patchbox and it was permanently affixed to the buttstock with its cover (or door) hinged for both practicality and accessibility. These early "transition era" arms are relatively plain, although some simple embellishments such as relief or incised carving are seen on many. They are very rare, very much in demand and highly sought in any state of condition.

Terminology for the second era or classification of Kentucky rifles is ambiguous at best. In its entirety (i.e., covering the era of the end of the Revolution to the beginning of the percussion ignition system) the period has yet to be named and thus the nomenclature "post Revolutionary flintlock era," although a mouthful, will nicely suffice until more apt phraseology is coined. The late Joe Kindig, Jr., of York, Pennsylvania, undoubtedly the most erudite and knowledgeable collector of Kentucky rifles and the author of a classic work on the subject (*see Bibliography*) coined the term "Golden Age." However, that served to describe only a major segment of this second era of the Kentucky Rifle, covering those rather elegant examples made from the close of the Revolution to approximately 1810 or 1815. It should definitely be understood that the "Golden Age" does not embrace all flintlock Kentucky rifles but merely an important segment of a specific style and quality.

Through Mr. Kindig's interpretation it has become generally accepted among collectors that examples of the Kentucky rifle of the "Golden Age" reflect the highest developments of elegance in the rococo design of the patchboxes (one of the major and outstanding elements of the rifle and an indigenous American innovation) as well as the rococo style of sophisticated relief carving (largely exemplified by the "C" and "S" scroll motifs intertwined with foliated designs). Both of these features are major elements contributing to the elegance and importance of the Kentucky in its so-called "Golden Age." It is an understanding and appreciation of these features and their many ramifications and variances that form the essence of Kentucky collecting and of course evaluation. Although the "Golden Age" was the period when the Kentucky achieved its apex in form, design and decoration, it should be clearly understood that the same riflesmiths who turned out the elegant "Golden Age" specimens also made some plain ones. Other lesser makers turned out rifles for the trade that were rather simply formed and embellished. All of the above are equally representative of the era but not all would be classified under the umbrella term of "Golden Age." It is the author's opinion—as well as that of many collectors—that all Kentuckies are beautiful and that all have great desirability and demand on the collectors' market. It is further maintained that all have equally important American significance as collectors' items and that it is merely a matter of distinguishing the quality of workmanship possessed by each that will indicate their individual increase in demand and consequently value.

The post-Revolutionary and "Golden Age" eras saw a number of refinements to the Kentucky. Barrels were lengthened (42" to 46" average); bores reduced (to approximately 50 caliber average), finer grains of maple (the highly desirable curly or "tiger stripe") generally replaced plainer grades of wood, and carving (both incised and relief) was often found embellishing the left side of the buttstock. It is this carving which is often a major distinguishing feature of finest quality specimens (and affects values significantly). Not a few writers have compared the workmanship of carving and other stock features to that of fine American furniture of the same period. That singular feature places them out of the confining category of antique guns and into the high plane of American art. The second era saw patchbox design flourish to elaborate heights, becoming highly embellished and ornamented with side pieces added and often taking elegant, if not exquisite, forms. The styles of carving as well as patchboxes and sideplates often serve to identify the makers of otherwise unsigned specimens.

The final phase of Kentucky manufacture began with the introduction of the percussion ignition system (circa the mid-1820s) and extended through the late 1850s. The innovation and subsequent popularity of the metallic cartridge breechloader generally signaled the Kentucky's demise. Barrels in the percussion phase were shortened (34" to 36" average) and bores were also generally reduced (40 caliber being a mean average although many smaller ones are known). Other simplifications were made, depending on the market to which they were geared, including the use of plain maple, while some were artificially striped to resemble the handsome tiger stripe grain. The use of fine grains of maple continued however, and many specimens of the percussion era are of fine quality craftsmanship, displaying artistic elegance representative of their later period.

As barrel and bore sizes were reduced, stocks proportionately followed suit, as did furniture and mountings. Even patchboxes, still a key feature of ornamentation, are seen on later specimens reduced to simpler round or elliptical shapes, centered on the butt. Relief carving is rare in the later era although incised carving is occasionally encountered. Inlay work is especially notable on these later pieces and reached its height of elegance and profuseness on percussion Kentuckies. The author has always been amused to read critical reviews

(theater or art; with guns included in the latter) in which omnipotent judgments (often accompanied with snide remarks) seem to be *de rigueur*. In the case of these third phase Kentucky percussion rifles, all too often, self-styled arbiters of collecting taste take apparent relish in such glib observations that these rifles are "degenerate forms" of the Kentucky, hence implying, regardless of their quality or elegance, that they are not worthy of the writer's or collector's attentions. These self-appointed pundits merely reflect the limited scope of their own personal interests and tastes; the latter more often emulated than personally arrived at! Most certainly, a great disparity exists among Kentucky rifles and many are singled out as exemplary specimens. It is however completely unfair and unjust to do so at the expense of the more usually encountered (and hence available) types which are equally representative of an important and significant indigenous American firearm—and a handsome one at that!

Varied schools of thought debate what constitutes either "true" or "fine" Kentuckies. Each group is quite adamant in their beliefs. The author wishes to neither adjudicate nor mediate the dispute, but rather presents existing viewpoints. Primary in the thinking of the "purist" is the opinion that only those great artistic "Golden Age" Kentuckies are important, valuable and collectible. Such rifles reflect the general attributes of relief carving and architectural perfection and are representative of the "better" schools of Pennsylvania makers. Such schools were developed in various towns and counties of Pennsylvania, each having stylistic differences and changes unique to those particular areas. The opposing view regards the entire evolutionary development of the Kentucky rifle, placing each era in its proper perspective and finding pleasure in examples representative of the best workman of each period.

KENTUCKY VALUES

Establishing price ranges and standards for evaluating Kentucky rifles may be likened to the same task for oil paintings or other forms of art. It is accomplished reasonably well with the lesser important, more often encountered styles and grades (in Kentuckies primarily those under $10,000) whereas with the masterpieces, or specimens representative of the highest development of the art, evaluation guidelines become very difficult and certainly vague, if not practically impossible.

With paintings, the lesser artist, whose work is often seen but is not in great demand, will reflect values that quite readily fall into a reasonably established price range. Artists of great reputation, whose paintings are highly valued and equally sought after, become quite difficult to place within those same guidelines; prices will fluctuate tremendously. To further complicate the situation, and offer proof that a name or signature alone is not sufficient to establish values, note that even the very best of artists (and riflemakers) had their off days, and that some of their handiwork just doesn't stand up to their normal standards! Thus the mere fact that a rifle—or a painting—is the work of a noted artisan is insufficient to evaluate it with all other specimens of the same maker unless the item possesses the same standards of quality for which that artist—or gunsmith—was known. In the case of Kentucky rifles the collector should be aware that many specimens are of composite assembly (as such they are still prized collectors' items, assuming assembly was contemporary to their use). Almost all these rifles saw heavy use; when worn out or badly broken all usable parts were salvaged, reused and in many cases modified (particularly so with barrels and locks). Hence, it is quite possible to find a barrel bearing the name of a famous maker that has been restocked by another gunsmith of a somewhat later era.

Thus, there is no easy, simple formula for categorizing or pricing Kentuckies. This does require some experience and the personal handling and viewing of a number of specimens in order to get the hang of it.

Decided eccentricities exist in establishing values for Kentucky rifles as well as distinguishing and weighing the importance of the varied features that set apart (in demand and value) one Kentucky from another.

The nature of the subject does not lend itself to the neat categorization of those antique firearms which were mass produced. As each rifle is an entity in itself, only the broadest guidelines may be given for evaluation. Thus it is very much up to the reader to go out into the field and actually see the rifles firsthand (at museums, gun shows or private collections) and to review the several published works on the subject in order to grasp the wide range of Kentuckies that were made and are consequently available on the collector's market.

RELIC KENTUCKIES

The "Golden Age" Kentuckies (i.e., those that are relief carved and otherwise bear characteristics of the famed makers of that era) and all of the pre-Revolutionary "Transition Era" Kentuckies are in great demand and eagerly sought after in any condition. Even "relics" and badly mutilated specimens maintain a high demand and usually fetch prices proportionately far greater than similar condition specimens of common grades and those of the later eras. Of course, those prices are not comparable to what that same specimen would bring in complete, and higher grades, of condition, but to the unfamiliar and the unpracticed eye there is little doubt that "relic" values are far greater than would normally be expected. The astute collector may often become ecstatic over a specimen of a famed early maker regardless of its condition as long as there is enough to identify the gun and a potential is evident for restoration. Such instances would be the ultimate example of the "rarity" factor taking precedence. The reader should note however, that although such mutilated or "relic" types may often fetch high values, there exists but a small group of devotees willing to actually pay cash for such rifles and that they are not easily sold on the open market for what those same devotees generally feel they are worth! The market for such types is highly irregular and inconsistent; spasmodic is a more accurate classification. The situation is very much akin to acquiring an extremely rare painting in badly mutilated— though possibly restorable—condition. Both market and demand are strong for such an item. Conversely a painting in similarly poor condition by a lesser known and lesser sought after artist would be practically worthless. Hence, in the broadest of generalities it may be said for the "average" Kentucky most often seen and available on the collectors' market, and not considered either pre-Revolutionary or of fine quality "Golden Age," that condition takes precedence in pricing and very much plays a dominant role in demand. On such rifles, the replacement of sections of stock (very often forestocks were shortened and it is necessary to reconstruct the wood in order to place them in presentable appearance), shortened barrels, missing inlays, repairs to bad breaks in the stock (most notably in the wrist area where Kentuckies were very susceptible to damage) and, of course, reconversions or restorations to flintlock all play important roles in evaluation.

At the risk of redundancy it is again noted that demand is still strong for Kentucky rifles of all types and of all conditions as long as they are priced consistently—and logically—with their quality and condition.

RESTORATION vs. VALUE

There have been evolutionary changes in the factors determining values on Kentucky rifles over the past decade. Foremost is the matter of acceptability of restoration as well as the desirability of rifles restored to flintlock. This subject has been covered in broad terms in Chapter III, to which the reader is referred. Note further, as particularly applicable to the Kentucky, and as regards the "demand" factor, reconversion is very much of secondary importance. This holds true for Kentuckies of all eras in which quality is the primary factor on which to base value. The matter of original flintlock vs. conversion to percussion (or reconversion) has importance in establishing value, but to a lesser degree than quality and condition, and plays a decidedly less important role with Kentuckies than it does on martial firearms. In order that the reader is not misled by this statement, the author modifies it by calling the reader's attention to the fact that an original flintlock Kentucky is certainly far more valuable than one converted to percussion or restored to flintlock. This element plays a far more important role in values with the more commonly encountered, plainer grades of Kentuckies than with those of the "Golden Age" or the pre-Revolutionary specimens. It has been the author's experience that original, unaltered flintlock Kentuckies of all types and enjoy a very strong demand. To repeat, most of these arms saw hard usage, especially the earlier ones. Many enjoyed long lives with a great proportion of the flintlock types simply converted to the newer percussion system in the 1830s, continuing in service until either phased out by breechloaders or simply worn out. It is also important to bear in mind that whereas the fine quality and fine art European arms were only occasionally used and then well stored in private armories or castles by caretakers, that most Kentuckies were used day in and day out as an integral part of a man's life and were passed down from generation to generation for that same usage.

There is a decided divergence of opinion in collecting circles on the matter of original flintlock vs. conversion/reconversion. The author takes to task a well-known writer in the field of Kentuckies as well as some collectors who have tended to downgrade the importance of the original flintlock in making claim that the locks were relatively unimportant to the overall aesthetics of the rifle as they were for the most part not made by the riflesmith who made the gun (the lock most likely purchased separately). As the essence of the Kentucky is its aesthetic and artistic qualities this school of thought would have it that the matter of locks is of relative unimportance. This position does have aesthetic validity and more so with the earlier pieces, but it certainly does not hold water when it comes to evaluation or for that matter "demand" and/or "desirability." When functioning in the sphere of collecting the word "originality" still predominates, and particularly carries weight in regard to values. Kentucky rifles in original flintlock condition are definitely established as rare (estimates indicate that over 80 percent were converted, thus further attesting to rarity). With that factor confirmed, it follows suit that such rifles are worth considerably more price-wise than the same rifles when converted or restored. In handling a great many Kentuckies over the years and having appraised some of the largest collections ever formed, the author is firm in his opinion that these arms in original flintlock condition (i.e., unrestored and untouched) are great rarities. Additionally, the factor of "total originality," although not the prime consideration for either demand or value in this field, will still play a strong role in price.

In the evolutionary process of collecting, and with the general acceptability of restored flintlocks (*see Chapter III, under "Reconversions"*) the Kentucky rifle is very much in the forefront of discussion. The subject is considerably less debatable currently than ever before; as a matter of fact it is deemed by many to be aesthetically desirable to restore Kentuckies to flintlock if that was their original ignition system. The matter is indeed one of personal preference these days. If it is to be done, the reconversion should be accurately and well performed or not at all.

KENTUCKY STOCKS

A major consideration affecting value is the type of wood used for the stock. The classic Kentucky of the post-Revolutionary era is stocked in native American curly maple (quite often called "tiger stripe" maple) having contrasting dark and light graining which possesses great eye appeal and adds immensely to the overall artistic value of the gun itself. These "tiger stripe" grains vary immensely in appearance from broad deep colors very widely spaced to very narrow stripes extremely closely aligned. To the discerning eye there are innumerable subtleties in judging appearance and relative beauty. The word "patina" (*see Chapter III*) is one that is closely associated with the character of the wood and has much to do with grading its appeal and value also. The curly maple stocks vary considerably with the areas in which the guns were made; those from Tennessee and Virginia are quite noticeably different than the same "tiger stripe" maples from the Pennsylvania area. New England made "Kentuckies" are normally encountered with cherry or walnut stocks. Plain grades of maple or walnut, or even birch, are most often seen on Revolutionary and colonial era rifles. Late flintlock and percussion era specimens quite often used plain maple or walnut also; in many instances artificial "tiger stripe" graining (through staining or burning by tarred rope) will be observed. Although curly maple is the most desirable wood to be found on a Kentucky, the statement is merely rule-of-thumb and must be strongly tempered as contradictions will occur. The mere fact that curly maple is used for the stock is not sufficient to categorize the piece.

Stocks are evaluated also on the basis of their patina or "color," a major aesthetic factor of the rifle. The quality, color and condition of the patina will often play a very strong role in demand as well as value. Many a fine Kentucky has been badly damaged by improper cleaning and refinishing of the stock, thereby removing the genuine age patina.

KENTUCKY BORES

Bores are decidedly a factor of lesser importance in evaluating Kentuckies. Although they do have some influence on value, it is to a much lesser degree than with other collectors' arms (i.e., sporting rifles, target rifles, etc.). Generally speaking, bores are the last feature to be taken into consideration when evaluating a Kentucky. A Kentucky will bring the same value with or without a good bore—and even, in most instances with a complete lack of rifling remaining. Quite likely with the disappearance of larger game many were purposely bored smooth during their era of use (for buckshot). The "demand" factor might change somewhat for these smooth bored rifles, depending mostly on the era of their manufacture and only the very late percussion types have been apparently affected to any measurable degree in current day collector values. Such smooth bored rifles might be slightly more difficult to sell to a few "sticklers" who wish to have the rifling intact (or even a good bore) whereas most collectors are interested in outward characteristics, which for apparent reasons are of the essence! The author has never known of bore conditions to have played any role in evaluation of the "Transition Era" or fine "Golden Age" Kentuckies. On the more common, plainer grade Kentuckies (and later ones) good bores have been found to change values slightly. Generally, the later the piece in era the more the bore condition might play a role in affecting values.

PATCHBOXES AND INLAYS

Patchboxes are a distinctive feature of Kentucky rifles and quite often are important in identifying the maker or the school of makers of an otherwise unsigned rifle. They are also influential in affecting values, especially on the more commonly encountered, decorative examples of the post-1800 through percussion eras. As the name implies, patchboxes were originally devised to hold greased cloth patches with which to insert the bullet more easily in the rifled bore and hold it tight. They were, however, multi-purpose and undoubtedly held many other small articles and accessories (spare flints, or caps, touch-hole picks and even small tools). Earlier specimens of the "Transition Era" were equipped with sliding wood patchboxes, a direct carryover from their European ancestry. However, the mere presence of a sliding wood patchbox is not sufficient to positively identify and date a Kentucky rifle as pre-Revolutionary. A few schools (notably around the Allentown, Pennsylvania, area) had makers that used such sliding wood patchboxes into the early 19th century, although admittedly very infrequently. Possibly one of the first major changes in the evolutionary pattern of the Kentucky was that from the European style sliding wood patchbox to a distinctively American one of metal, permanently affixed to the gun and its rectangular door hinged. Although most were made of brass, a few iron specimens are known. The earliest forms are very simple and functional to the complete absence of any elaborate designs associated with the "Golden Age" and later.

Patchboxes underwent a gradual evolutionary change with side pieces added, and enlarged finials and embellishments of all manner from delicate, lacy piercings to profuse engraving. On "Golden Age" specimens the patchbox is a major segment of the rifle and is considered equally with other factors such as carving, maker's name, general style and school of workmanship. On later made rifles or those of lesser quality (which are the most often encountered types on the collectors' market) the patchbox, along with the type of wood, are often the determining factors for both demand and price. It is on these later types—by far the ones most often seen and sold—that the patchbox most quickly identifies a gun as a "Kentucky" and makes it aesthetically desirable. Thus, the patchbox is the center of attraction and attention for many Kentucky rifles. It has been considered of such importance that a detailed book has been written on the subject, illustrating 800 examples. For the more commonly observed styles, if one were to rate patchboxes for desirability, those that are the largest and fill most of the butt area and have the largest number of piercings (i.e., open work designs) would be rated among the most desirable and would show proportionately larger value increases. Engraving on patchboxes may also tend to increase values depending on both the quality and profuseness of the designs. Progressing further down the patchbox scale, those that might be considered not as valuable (but still in very strong demand) are those of the mid-19th Century representative of the last period of Kentucky manufacture, having circular or long oval patchboxes inset in the center of the buttstock with varying degrees and qualities of finials and decoration. These also vary greatly in style with some achieving ornateness both in shape and engraved motifs.

Inlays, their number and quality, are determinants in Kentucky rifle values. The mere presence—or absence—of them does not necessarily indicate the quality of a rifle or its value, however. Profuse and lavishly inlaid Kentuckies are usually of the later eras. Inlays are judged on their quality of workmanship as well as quantity. Inlay materials were normally brass, German silver or silver with the latter often worth a premium. The least valuable styles are those in very simple geometric shapes (i.e., circles, squares, rectangles, diamonds, etc.) progressing upward in beauty (and consequently value) to complex and delicate designs of animals, fish, and human motifs, and even including lacy-like open work motifs. Engraving when present lends the inlays further importance.

MAKERS' SIGNATURES

Signatures on Kentucky rifles (i.e., the maker's name or initials on the barrel or elsewhere) are quite often significant determinants of value; very much the same as a signature on a painting. The absence of a name, however, does not detract or lessen the importance of the rifle, for by far the great majority of Kentuckies are unsigned. Advanced students are often able to identify the maker of unsigned rifles merely by their general appearance or special details and features. Many have distinctive characteristics of style peculiar to individual makers, the same way as with paintings or furniture. Most of the better—and more prolific—makers have peculiarities of workmanship (i.e., distinctive sideplates or patchboxes or carving details, etc.) which the practiced eye is able to easily identify. In some instances where individual makers are not identifiable, the schools of workmanship are readily distinguishable and the gun may be quickly placed as an example of a specific area (i.e., state, county or even town).

KENTUCKY LOCKS

The locks on a great majority of Kentucky rifles especially of the post Revolutionary period through the percussion eras, were not made by the riflemaker, but were purchased in their entirety as ready-made units, (the Bedford, Pennsylvania, style Kentucky rifles seem to be an exception to this rule). It is important to note that the name appearing on the lock is rarely that of the riflemaker but may very well be that of the European lockmaker, an American hardware merchant who imported and sold the lock, or other name associated with the lock making process and having nothing to do with the rifle on which it appears.

STYLES, TYPES AND ERAS

The values reflected for the Kentucky rifles listed here are generally for Pennsylvania made pieces, or those that are otherwise unmarked and not definitely attributed to other geographic areas. Premiums may often be added to values for Kentuckies that are definitely established as the handiwork of gunsmiths in areas such as Virginia, Maryland, North Carolina, Tennessee, Ohio, or Indiana, etc. (New England made "Kentucky" types are specifically treated in Chapter XII). The mere fact of their manufacture in areas other than Pennsylvania is not sufficient to place premium values on them, nor are such values, when justifiable, always easy to acquire. Such collectors' markets are often very local in nature. This subject is also discussed in great length in Chapter XII.

All of the foregoing are merely rules-of-thumb and very broad generalities which are certainly not applicable to all specimens. No single feature on all rifles tends to increase or decrease value or importance, but rather the entire Kentucky and its period of manufacture must be considered with quality of workmanship a significant factor.

In the diverse schools of thought among Kentucky collectors there are those who confine themselves to the "Golden Age," preferring the simpler types in which form is the overall determinant, quite often accompanied by elegant touches of relief carving and delicate mouldings and one or a very few engraved silver inlays on the butt. Others search for ornateness,

with profusion and delicateness of inlay work a chief factor in determining their interest, confining themselves to later dates and eras of manufacture. All this is purely a matter of personal preference and taste as each style of Kentucky is representative of a completely different era of riflemaking and each is an excellent representative example of Americana of that respective period. The author looks askance at those who would attempt to deem it otherwise and remind them of a number of analogies in gun collecting wherein certain items or types were thought desirable to the complete exclusion of others (or at best, were thought second rate) but which over the years have proven themselves to be of equal importance. These same comparisons may be readily made in other fields of collecting; examples are myriad. The author admonishes certain of those writers who establish themselves as arbiters of quality and taste in the field of American firearms, and cautions the reader to let his own judgment and taste as well as common sense be his best guides!

THE KENTUCKY AS FINE ART

If any American weapon deserves the appellation "fine art" it is certainly the Kentucky rifle—or at least many outstanding examples of the type. They may justifiably take their place among the finest of early Americana with many specimens ranking with the best handiwork of American artisans in other fields of the 18th and 19th Centuries. It has always been the author's feeling that of all early American arms—or for that matter antique arms of all types—the Kentucky represents one of the highest achievements in the art of gunmaking, and that it holds the greatest potential for the future. Although always in the forefront of arms collecting, and among the most eagerly sought after of firearms, they are still in their infancy in relation to the worldwide collecting field. During the past decade the finest examples of European gunsmiths of the 16th through 18th centuries have risen, value-wise, to undreamed of heights, setting record prices for the finest specimens. Although American arms have risen considerably in proportion to the world firearms market, they have yet to realize their ultimate potential. The Kentucky rifle—the American counterpart of the European "fine art" weapon—is only newly emerging in that role. At the risk of appearing to create a greater demand for an already popular firearm, the author cannot help but hazard the opinion that the Kentucky rifle will one day be among the greatest "sleepers" in the collecting field, and asks the reader's indulgence in allowing him this speculative conclusion.

The author has departed from the usual method used throughout this book of illustrating a specimen and describing it in its many variations, accompanied by individual pricings. More preferable here was to illustrate general types of Kentuckies with broad explanatory text accompanying each and a discussion of the salient features, which might be found on that particular type, along with general price ranges. The reader should bear in mind that on this subject a great many inconsistencies exist that are not simply explained and there are neither hard, nor fast, nor easy methods of setting forth exact values. Many of the influencing factors have been discussed herein; the reader will find in his own research that other nuances exist and may often play special roles.

KENTUCKY RIFLES

Transition Era

The earliest or first style Kentuckies, from the early 18th century through the Revolutionary period; all as discussed in the preceding text. Some key features to assist in identification (but none of which is the sole determinant) as follows:

(a) Relatively straight, heavy or thick stock, lacking the characteristic drop to the butt as observed on the later and "classic" Kentuckies.

(b) Thick, heavy butts *vs.* the thinner, narrower butt types of the post Revolutionary era (*see illustration*). Earliest types readily distinguishable by the thickness at the heel, a feature common to all early specimens. A decided slendering of the butt is noticeable with the increase in era of manufacture. The three illustrated are of (top) pre-Revolutionary (middle) "Golden Age" late 18th- early 19th century, and (bottom) very late flintlock and the percussion era.

(c) The butt (when viewed from the side) is relatively flat without the noticeable crescent shape of post-Revolutionary and later pieces.

(d) The mountings (or furniture) of brass (and occasionally iron) are very similar to that of the German *jaeger* rifles on the earliest forms of Transition Era Kentuckies and gradually conform to the more classic style with later forms. The trigger guard on almost all Transition Era specimens is quite low arched, heavy in weight, and wide.

(e) Trigger of early form quite often exhibits the characteristic 18th century curl or scroll at its bottom; double set triggers rarely seen.

(f) Relatively plain lockplate usually of Germanic style. Most often flat with beveled edges. Usually pointed or teat-like projection present at rear of lock, also often accompanied by two deep vertical flutes.

(g) Relatively narrow and short metal forend cap of brass or iron.

(h) Quite often a sliding wood patchbox (*see illustration*) or, on the mid-era specimens a very simple hinged iron or brass patchbox quite primitive in appearance.

(i) An important feature noted on almost all Transition Era specimens is the decided flare at the muzzle of the barrel (will often be found in arms literature described as a "swamped" barrel). The flaring or widening shape at the muzzle is a direct carryover from the earlier German *jaeger* and will vary considerably from rifle to rifle. On some it is quite pronounced and noticeable while on others the "swamping" or flare is but slight and not readily seen on first glance. However, when shouldering the gun and sighting along the top of the barrel the flare can be easily seen.

(j) Carving, when present, may be either incised or relief and usually takes but very simple scroll form, appearing at the tang or cheek piece. Such carving will normally increase values. Some writers have claimed that carving is quite common to these early pieces while others maintain it is relatively rare. The author's experience is that the latter has been more often the case. These early pieces are also characterized by the almost complete lack of other decorations.

Transition Era Rifles; plain; unembellished; no maker's marks, dates or other identifying features; plain maple, walnut, birch or other American wood. Original flintlock condition:

11-001   Values—Poor **$2,750-6,000**   Fair **$5,500-14,500**
             Very Good **$14,000-45,000** and over

Identical to above; converted to percussion:

11-002   Values—Poor **$2,250-4,500**   Fair **$4,500-7,000**
             Very Good **$7,500-25,000** and over

Transition Era Kentucky as described above but of better quality with simple relief scroll carving; curly maple stock (but rarely of the fine type tiger stripe grains seen on later era pieces) and overall possessing workmanship and refinement placing it in a better grade than above. Original flintlock condition:

11-003   Values—Poor **$4,500-10,000**   Fair **$10,000-25,000**
             Very Good **$25,000-60,000** and over

Identical to above; converted to percussion:

11-004   Values—Poor **$3,500-6,500**   Fair **$6,500-14,000**
             Very Good **$12,500-45,000** and over

"Golden Age" Kentuckies

This significant type has been described in general terms in the preceding introductory text and its importance established. Only the very broadest guidelines and value ranges are shown here. The reader is reminded that vast differences exist among this type with several influencing value factors. Representative specimens illustrated and valued here have full curly maple stocks with average amounts of relief rococo carving (mostly on left side of butt with small amounts elsewhere) and feature large, handsome and well-made patchboxes; barrels either unmarked or bearing signatures of well-known (but not the most famous) makers. In original flintlock condition:

11-005   Values—Poor **$5,000-10,000**   Fair **$10,000-25,000**
             Very Good **$25,000-85,000** and over

As above; converted to percussion:
11-006   Values—Poor **$2,500-6,500**   Fair **$6,500-12,500**
       Very Good **$12,500-50,000** and over
"Golden Age" Kentucky; as described above but without relief carving. Otherwise shows distinctive "Golden Age" features; may have some incised decorative carving (but not of the most ornate or elaborate nature). Original flintlock condition:

11-007   Values—Poor **$2,250-4,000**   Fair **$4,000-7,000**
       Very Good **$7,000-22,500** and over
Identical to above; converted to percussion:
11-008   Values—Poor **$1,000-2,500**   Fair **$2,250-3,750**
       Very Good **$3,500-11,000** and over

Flintlock Kentucky Rifles c. 1790s-1830

This style of Kentucky is the more often encountered on the collectors' market. Specimens here are representative of the plainer types. Full stocked in curly maple; large patchboxes but not of the most ornate nature; inlays, if any, are few; carving if present of the incised type only and quite simple. Barrels either unmarked or with signatures of known and recorded makers but not of the famed schools. Earlier specimens (late 18th century) tend to bring higher values. Those shown here generally of the period 1800 to 1830s. Original flintlock condition:

11-009   Values—Fair **$1,750-3,250**   Good **$3,250-6,000**
       Very Good **$4,000-11,000**

11-009
Flintlock Kentucky Rifles

11-011
Flintlock Kentucky Rifles

Identical to above; converted to percussion:
11-010   Values—Fair **$850-1,400**   Good **$1,250-2,500**
       Very Good **$2,000-5,000**
Flintlock Kentucky Rifles. Generally identical to above but finer quality workmanship, fancier patchboxes; some inlays (usually a large engraved one oftentimes with an eagle motif on cheekrest), incised carving may be present on buttstocks. Original flintlock condition:
11-011   Values—Fair **$2,000-4,000**   Good **$3,500-7,500**
       Very Good **$6,000-15,000** and over
Identical to above; converted to percussion:
11-012   Values—Fair **$1,100-2,500**   Good **$2,000-5,000**
       Very Good **$3,500-7,500** and over

Heavy Barreled Kentucky Match Rifles

11-013
(without patchbox)

11-015

11-015

Made solely for rifle match competition these very heavy barreled rifles generally conform stylistically to the plainer grades of Kentucky rifles but with greater overall proportions. They are almost invariably encountered in flintlock (or conversions to percussion) and rarely seen as original percussion. (Such a piece however would not be worth more.) Some show lesser qualities of workmanship on the exterior finishing than on the usual Kentucky and on many form is somewhat graceless causing their demand—and consequently values—to drop off somewhat. Specimen illustrated and valued here has the classic Kentucky style stock but much heavier throughout with typical Kentucky style brass furniture and made without patchbox (quite often seen on this type). Bores frequently play a role in evaluations and better bores do seem to sell more quickly and fetch premiums. Original flintlock condition:
11-013   Values—Fair **$500-800**   Good **$850-1,100**
       Very Good **$1,100-2,250**

Identical to above; converted to percussion:

11-014 Values—Fair **$400-600** Good **$600-850**
Very Good **$850-1,400**

Heavy barreled flintlock match rifle; very similar to above but better quality workmanship throughout. Typical of Kentucky styling with classic brass furniture, large well-made patchbox

and possibly a few inlays:

11-015 Values—Fair **$1,000-1,500** Good **$1,500-2,500**
Very Good **$2,000-4,500**

Identical to above; converted to percussion:

11-016 Values—Fair **$850-1,250** Good **$1,100-2,000**
Very Good **$2,000-3,000**

Original Percussion Full Stock Rifles

11-017
Original Percussion Full Stock Rifles Plain Type

11-018
Original Percussion Full Stock Rifles

Plain type. Curly maple stock; brass patchbox with a long rectangular door and finial (possibly with piercing) simply shaped side pieces; no inlays:

11-017 Values—Fair **$850-1,400** Good **$1,250-2,000**
Very Good **$1,400-2,500**

Original percussion Kentucky similar to above but fancier grade in quality; large patchbox of finer and fancier quality work

as often accompanied with a few piercings; some inlays or simple incised carved designs on left side of butt:

11-018 Values—Fair **$950-1,750** Good **$1,500-2,500**
Very Good **$2,250-4,000**

Original percussion Kentucky rifle similar to above but fancier; very fine quality patchbox with numerous piercings; some fancy inlays (approximately 6 to 12) mostly along left side of buttstock with few along forend and underside:

11-019 Values—Fair **$1,250-2,250** Good **$2,000-3,000**
Very Good **$2,750-6,000**

11-019
Original Percussion Full Stock Rifles

**11-020
Original Percussion
Full Stock Rifles**

11-021

11-023

11-023

Original percussion Kentucky rifle; plain grade with small circular or oval patchbox with slight finial at top; curly maple stock, one or two inlays:
11-021 Values—Fair **$550-900** Good **$800-1,150**
Very Good **$1,000-2,000**

Identical to above; also with circular or oval patchbox, but fancier, larger shape; few inlays and possibly some incised carving:
11-022 Values—Fair **$600-1,100** Good **$1,100-1,750**
Very Good **$1,500-3,500**

Original percussion Kentucky as above. Very fancy grade with 20 to 30 inlays (quality of same greatly influences value); large fancy pierced patchbox; fine grained curly maple stock:
11-020 Values—Fair **$1,600-3,250** Good **$3,000-8,000**
Very Good **$6,000-22,500** or more

"Plain" Kentucky Rifles

An often abused, misused and certainly misunderstood term in gun collecting is "plain rifle" *vs.* "plains rifle." The subject is discussed in greater depth with the differentiation between the two clearly made in Chapter XII, to which the reader is referred. Illustrated and evaluated here is the plainest form of Kentucky rifle. Manufactured to sell for the lowest price, this is usually a piece that has seen considerably hard wear and use. Values fluctuate with both barrel and lock markings; the majority

apparently were unsigned. Stocks are normally plain maple without the fancy tiger stripe grains and usually lack embellishments, patchboxes or inlays although they do have the classic style brass Kentucky furniture. Original flintlock full stock specimen:
11-023 Values—Fair **$850-1,250** Good **$1,100-1,750**
Very Good **$1,400-3,000**

Identical to above; converted to percussion or original percussion:
11-024 Values—Fair **$400-600** Good **$600-1,100**
Very Good **$1,000-1,750**

Double Barrel Kentucky Rifles

The most commonly seen double barrel Kentucky rifles are these "swivel breech" types; i.e., those with over-and-under

barrels which are manually revolved and fired by a single lock. Side-by-side Kentuckies are quite rare, especially in flintlock.

11-025
Side-by-Side Full Stock Rile

11-027
Swivel Breech

11-031
Original Percussion Swivel Breech

11-031
Original Percussion Swivel Breech

11-032
Original Percussion Swivel Breech Better Quality

11-033
Original Percussion Late Type

11-034
Double Bbl. Over-and-Under Solid Breech

The first double Kentuckies were undoubtedly side-by-side style with but a handful of known specimens predating 1790. The majority of side by side doubles are of the percussion era.

The swivel breech seems to have made its first appearance in the early 19th century. Specimens in original flintlock are considered rare.

Side-by-side full stock Kentucky rifle; original percussion; simple classic Kentucky style furniture; oval or round patchbox with finial; full curly maple stock:

11-025   Values—Fair **$850-1,400**   Good **$1,400-2,500**
          Very Good **$2,500-5,000**

Double barrel side-by-side Kentucky; as above with fancy large full patchbox, few inlays and possibly some incised carving:

11-026   Values—Fair **$950-1,750**   Good **$2,000-3,500**
          Very Good **$3,000-6,500**

Swivel breech flintlock Kentucky rifle. Large patchbox; few inlays; both barrels rifled or one rifled and one smooth bore (prices apparently are not affected by this feature) good quality:

11-027   Values—Fair **$1,400-3,500**   Good **$3,250-7,000**
          Very Good **$6,500-22,500**

Identical to above; converted to percussion:

11-028   Values—Fair **$950-1,750**   Good **$1,750-4,500**
          Very Good **$3,250-7,500**

Swivel breech original flintlock Kentucky rifle as above but finer quality, fancier patchbox, few inlays; maker's name and some incised carving or decoration:

11-029   Values—Fair **$2,250-4,000**   Good **$4,000-7,500**
          Very Good **$7,000-30,000**

Identical to above; converted to percussion:

11-030   Values—Fair **$1,100-2,250**   Good **$2,000-5,000**
          Very Good **$4,000-11,000**

Original percussion swivel breech Kentucky rifle. Plain grade; large patchbox, few inlays if any; plain or very slight incised carving:

11-031   Values—Fair **$950-1,500**   Good **$1,500-3,000**
          Very Good **$1,750-4,500**

Swivel breech Kentucky identical to above but finer quality; original percussion; fancier patchbox with some piercing; few inlays and possibly more profuse incised carving:

11-032   Values—Fair **$1,100-1,750**   Good **$1,600-3,000**
          Very Good **$2,750-5,500**

Swivel breech original percussion Kentucky as above. Late type; round or oval patchbox in butt; plain with possibly few inlays:

11-033   Values—Fair **$700-1,000**   Good **$850-1,600**
          Very Good **$1,500-2,750**

Double barrel over-and-under solid breech (barrels do not swivel) original percussion Kentucky rifle. Dual locks mounted on left and right side (or possibly right lock only with an underhammer to fire bottom barrel); barrels are either both rifled or one rifled and one smooth (apparently does not affect value). Plain grade; circular or oval patchbox with fancy finial:

11-034   Values—Fair **$450-700**   Good **$650-1,250**
          Very Good **$1,000-2,500**

Side Lock Kentucky Rifles

11-035

11-035

A distinctive and unique form of lock mechanism often seen on Kentucky rifles is the side lock, also known as the "mule ear" lock. The analogy is to the shape of the cocking spur of the hammer which often resembles a mule's ear. This style of mechanism is seen with considerably less frequency than a normal side lock. The mere fact of the decided difference is not sufficient to place side lock rifles in a higher value category, although slight premiums are often added. In general side lock arms are priced similarly to other percussion Kentuckies based on their quality, elaborateness and, of course, condition:
11-035

Half-Stock Kentucky Rifles

11-036
Original Half-Stock

11-036
Original Half-Stock

11-037
Original Half-Stock–Finer Quality

This is somewhat of a "gray" area, for many of these types are just as easily classified as half-stock sporting or target rifles (and are discussed in Chapter XII). Generically, just about anything having a patchbox is often called on today's collector market a "Kentucky." By the strongest stretch of the term (and one's imagination), there is a reasonable accuracy for so doing! For our purposes here, it may be assumed that the half-stock Kentucky is identical in appearance to the full-stock type, generally including curly wood with classic Kentucky style furniture and, most importantly, the classic Kentucky large patchbox; the only basic difference being that the stock is half length rather than full to the muzzle. Not a few exceptionally elegant, lavishly embellished specimens are known in this type, with their demand and consequently values commensurate with the finest of full stocks.

In an earlier era of collecting there was an unexplained stigma attached to the half-stock rifle *vs.* the full stock, as if a gun was bought by its weight and the total amount of wood it carried! The fact that a gun had been half-stocked (usually merely indicating its later period of manufacture) immediately placed it as a second-class citizen in gun collecting. This was especially noticeable on two specimens possessing similar qualities made by the same maker; the half stock fetching less than its full stock counterpart. Although the stigma is fast disappearing and demand for these half stocks is just as great as full stocks, there is no doubt that in the plainer grades they do tend to fetch lesser values.

Original half-stock percussion Kentucky rifles; curly maple stock with large patchbox; classic Kentucky style furniture; inlays (if present) very slight:

11-036 Values—Fair **$650-1,000**   Good **$900-1,600**
           Very Good **$1,250-2,250**

Identical to above; finer quality workmanship; fancier patchbox with some piercings; few inlays:

11-037 Values—Fair **$750-1,250**   Good **$1,100-2,000**
           Very Good **$1,750-3,500** or more

KENTUCKY PISTOLS

Just what constitutes a "Kentucky" pistol is indeed a nebulous area. Although not defying description, it will be found that naming clear-cut characteristics common to all is impossible. In its most all-inclusive definition, the Kentucky pistol is one made by the same makers of Kentucky rifles and/or a handgun that displays the same characteristics as are shown by a Kentucky rifle. It then becomes a matter of semantics and personal preference as to whether a pistol may be accurately or aptly classified as a "Kentucky" or merely an American "holster" or "belt" type. It is, however, neither the classification nor the nomenclature that affects its value but rather the pistol's quality, general period of manufacture and condition.

Although the Kentucky pistol started life considerably later than the rifle (the earliest specimens are believed to date from the late 1760s) their development from that point was simultaneous with the rifle and in the same general geographical areas; most notably Pennsylvania. From the frequency with which they appear it is obvious that considerably fewer pistols were made than rifles. Reasonable estimates as to relative rarity have placed the ratio at approximately one pistol made for every 250 rifles.

Such figures are of course subject to modification. Whereas the rifle was made for the dual purpose of putting meat on the table and for protection of life, the pistol was invariably made as a protective weapon only. It is this fact that undoubtedly accounts for the observation that pistols are generally found in much better average condition than rifles, having seen less hard use. It is a further observation that pistols are more often found in their original flintlock condition than rifles with a lesser proportion of them having been altered to percussion.

Undoubtedly major characteristics that qualify a pistol to be termed a "Kentucky" are in the stock, furniture and other mountings and decoration. Kentucky pistols were stocked in all types of wood as were the rifles. Although curly maple was the most prominent wood, cherry and walnut followed very closely.

A study of Kentucky pistols and the collecting of them is quite subjective. Features differentiating an early American holster pistol from a "Kentucky" pistol are often very moot points. For example, the mere fact that curly maple may have been used for the stock is not sufficient to call an early flintlock American handgun a "Kentucky" pistol (however great a rarity it may be).

It is generally considered by present day collectors that there were three major eras of manufacture of the Kentucky pistol:

(a) Circa 1760 to the Revolution. Specimens of that era were invariably directly copied from British (or occasionally French) styles prevalent during the era, and are often identical to them. Barrels are either all round or part round/part octagon (with no full octagon barrels observed) and are of iron or brass. Cherry or walnut were the predominant stock woods. The furniture (brass or silver) was quite often identical to European style with the lionhead design buttcap quite popular. It seems that a majority of these handguns were unmarked and hence are quite often difficult to positively identify. It is in this area that the generic use of the term "Kentucky pistol" becomes very hazy. If for instance a pure English style pistol was made by a Pennsylvania gunsmith (who also made Kentucky rifles) then that particular pistol is quite legitimately termed a "Kentucky pistol." If however a New England maker made the identical appearing English style pistol (and so marked it with his name) that gun, although equally rare and valuable, is merely called a "colonial American" handgun!

(b) Circa 1780 to 1812. It is in this era that the true American form of flintlock pistols usually referred to as the "Kentucky" made its emergence. Stocks were in curly maple, cherry or walnut with either brass or silver mountings and with many having full octagon (either rifled or smooth) barrels. In this era maker's names are also much more in evidence. These handguns took on the characteristics of the rifles with furniture and sideplates having close similarities to the rifle parts made by these same Pennsylvania gunsmiths. Earliest specimens have a decided Germanic appearance, although in general the pistols tend to evolve to look less European. The majority of such pistols are believed to have been made either during the Revolutionary era or the War of 1812 (the latter predominating) to the general exclusion of interim eras. Their need was quite obviously predicated by the urgency of military requirements of such pistols as sidearms for American officers and, to a lesser degree, for cavalry troops.

(c) Circa 1814 to 1825. The American military flintlock pistol was standardized during this era and reasonably large contracts were given for its manufacture. The requirements of the earlier war years for private contracts diminished considerably, while the beginning of limited mass production lessened demand for the handcrafted Kentuckies and undoubtedly accounts for the relatively few privately made American flintlock handguns in the post-1814 period. The so-called "Kentuckies" made during those later years are either of very plain, simple workmanship or at the opposite end of the spectrum displaying exceptionally high quality workmanship, obviously made for sale to a wealthy individual.

In its present day, most commonly used application the terminology "Kentucky pistol" applies to those particular arms generally falling in the three above categories but will also cover just about any American percussion handmade pistol that has a curly maple stock and an octagon barrel! Thus, the boundaries are defined quite loosely.

The terminology in itself really has nothing to do with either the desirability, the demand, or the values of the guns themselves. They all will stand on their own merits. The subject has been discussed in only the broadest of terms to make the reader aware that in some collecting fields there are problems of semantics which are not always easily resolved. In other words—a rose by any other name smells just as sweet!

Most likely a majority of Kentucky pistols were made originally as matched pairs. When seen and found to be truly matching in workmanship and condition, premiums may be added to value. A reasonable figure would be 20 percent. However, this is subject to increase considerably depending on the exact type, period and quality of the pair itself.

Illustrated herein is a reasonable sampling of American Kentucky pistols of the late 18th to early 19th centuries which should give a general idea of their wide variance in appearance and style. Small features such as the shape of sideplates, furniture and inlays do much to affect value as does relief carving (only occasionally encountered). Just the broadest of price ranges are indicated below for these types. It is important that the reader or collector survey the market himself in order to get a better understanding of the importance of any specific specimen.

11-038

11-038

Original flintlock Kentucky pistol; full stock curly maple; barrels full octagon, full round or octagon/round. Large holster size with 8" to 12" barrels; brass furniture; no inlays. Generally attributed to Revolutionary and late 18th Century eras:

11-038   Values—Good **$3,500-6,000**
                      Fine **$5,000-10,000** or more

Identical to above; converted to percussion:

11-039   Values—Good **$2,500-4,500**
                      Fine **$3,750-7,500** or more

Original flintlock Kentucky style pistol; same as above. Circa War of 1812 era. Classic "Kentucky" styling and appearance; carvings or inlays not present:

11-040   Values—Good **$2,500-5,000**
                      Fine **$5,000-10,000** or more

Identical to above; converted to percussion:

11-041   Values—Good **$2,000-4,000**
                      Fine **$3,250-6,500** or more

Kentucky flintlock pistol identical to above but fancier workmanship and quality with some silver or brass inlays;

All Guns 11-042

All Guns 11-040

graceful proportions to stock (curly maple usually brings premium over walnut or cherry):

11-042   Values—Good **$3,250-5,500**
        Fine **$6,000-12,000** or more

Identical to above; converted to percussion:

11-043   Values—Good **$2,500-4,500**
        Fine **$4,000-7,500** or more

Kentucky flintlock pistol similar to above but fancier quality and workmanship; some silver or brass inlays and/or some relief carving. Stock gracefully proportioned. Large holster size; curly maple usually (but not always) brings a premium value:

11-044   Values—Good **$4,500-10,000**
        Fine **$10,000-25,000** or more

Both Guns 11-044

Identical to above; converted to percussion:

11-045   Values—Good **$3,500-7,000**
        Fine **$6,000-15,000** or more

Kentucky pistol similar to above not showing the general quality nor styling nor graceful proportions of the above illustrated types but yet classically "Kentucky" in appearance. May have plain maple or walnut stock or simulated striped grain (seen on some of the later Kentucky rifles). Most likely 1820s to 1830s:

11-046   Values—Good **$1,000-2,250**   Fine **$2,000-4,250**

Identical to above; converted to percussion:

11-047   Values—Good **$800-1,400**   Fine **$1,150-2,750**

Belt sized Kentucky pistols. Identical in contour to their larger counterparts; approximately 5" to 7" barrels; distinctive "Kentucky" characteristics and quite often curly maple stocks. Original flintlock:

11-048   Values—Good **$950-2,250**   Fine **$1,750-4,000**

11-046

11-048

11-050

11-051

Identical to above; converted to percussion:
11-049   Values—Good **$700-1,750**   Fine **$1,250-3,000**

Original percussion Kentucky style pistols c. 1830 to 1850. Large holster type; 8" to 12" barrel most often with octagonal, rifled barrels. Shows excellent quality of workmanship and very well proportioned. Classic Kentucky style furniture:
11-050   Values—Good **$1,000-2,000**   Fine **$1,500-4,500**

Original percussion Kentucky style pistols as above having a number of classic features such as barrels or stocks identifying them as "Kentucky" types but of considerably lesser quality and in some cases appearing crude if not almost primitive; not marked by maker:
11-051   Values—Good **$650-1,000**   Fine **$1,000-2,250**
Identical to above; but in small belt sizes:
11-052   Values—Good **$350-600**   Fine **$450-1,000**

BIBLIOGRAPHY

(Note: A great deal of information about Kentucky rifles may be found in numerous books in Chapter IV "The Arms Library", especially those dealing with maker listings, and in several other works listed in bibliographies elsewhere in this book. They are: *Arms And Armour In Colonial America* by Harold Peterson; *The History Of Weapons Of The American Revolution* by George Neumann; *The Muzzle- Loading Cap Lock Rifle* by Ned H. Roberts; *The Plains Rifle* by Charles E. Hansen, Jr.; *The Collecting Of Guns* edited by James E. Serven.)

Alexander, Peter A. *The Gunsmith of Greenville County: Building the American Longrifle*. Texarkana, TX: Scurlock Publishing Co., 2002. Excellent guide for making/repairing Kentucky longrifles; historical background on antique longrifles. Illus. with drawings and photographs. Ring bound for easy use on work benches.

Bivins, John, Jr. *Longrifles of North Carolina*. York, Pa.: George Shumway, Publisher, 1968. A definitive study accompanied by photographic illustrations of "Kentucky" type rifles of that state.

Bowers, William S. *Gunsmiths of Pen-Mar-Va 1790-1840*. Mercersburg, Pennsylvania: Irwinton Publishers, 1979. Considerable important biographical data on many makers of Pennsylvania, Maryland and Virginia.

*Butler, J. T. Jr. & Whisker, J. B. *Long Rifles of Virginia*. Bedford, Pennsylvania: Old Bedford Village Press, 1996.

Chandler, Roy F. *Kentucky Rifle Patchboxes and Barrel Marks*. Duncannon, Pennsylvania: David E. Little Press, 1971. Photographic catalog of 800 Kentucky patchboxes and identification of their makers. Volume II; Chandler and J. B. Whisker; Old Bedford Press, 1992.

Chandler, R. F. and Whisker, J. B. *Pennsylvania Gunmakers—A Collection*. Bedford, Pennsylvania: Privately published, 1984.

Chandler, R.F. & Whisker, J.B. *The Kentucky Pistol*. Bedford, Pa: Old Bedford Village Press, 1994. Fine photos with almost complete absence of text.

Chandler, R.F. & Whisker, J.B. *Behold The Longrifle*. Bedford, Pa: Old Bedford Village Press, 1993. *Behold The Longrifle Again* by J. B Whisker; Old Bedford Press, 1997.

Cooper, Edith G. *The Kentucky Rifle and Me*. Port Royal, Pennsylvania: Privately published by author, 1977. Part catalog of personal collection assembled over fifty years, part reference and part reminiscences.

Dillin, Captain John G. W. *The Kentucky Rifle*. Washington, D.C.: The National Rifle Association, 1924. Numerous subsequent additions and reprintings. The pioneer work on the subject with considerable information of value not duplicated by present day works. Later editions contain extra chapters on the Kentucky pistol and Bedford County rifle.

Dyke, S. E. *Thoughts on the American Flintlock Pistol*. York, Pennsylvania: George Shumway, Publisher, 1959 and 1974. Entirely devoted to the "Kentucky" pistol with wide range of photographic illustrations.

Gabel, R. G. *The Lehigh County Long Rifle*. Allentown, Pennsylvania: Privately published by author (not dated, c. 1980s).

Hartzler, D.D. & Whisker, J.B. *Maryland Longrifles*. Bedford, Pa: Old Bedford Village Press, 1991. Detailed listing of makers and their rifles.

*Hetrick, Calvin. *The Bedford County Rifle and its Makers*. York, Pennsylvania: George Shumway, Publisher, 1973. Detailed monograph of this specific and unique styled Kentucky.

Huddleston, J. *Colonial Riflemen in the American Revolution*. York, Pennsylvania: George Shumway, Publisher, 1978. Discusses controversy of actual effect of longrifle on outcome of Revolution; includes material on rifles of the era with details of ownership and history.

Hutslar, Donald A. *Gunsmiths of Ohio - 18th and 19th Centuries - Volume I, Biographical Data*. York, Pennsylvania: George Shumway, Publisher, 1973. Wealth of detail on makers of "Kentucky" type rifles of that state with some illustrations. Valuable reference.

Kauffman, Henry J. *The Pennsylvania-Kentucky Rifle*. Harrisburg, Pennsylvania: The Stackpole Company, 1960, with subsequent reprintings. Definitive treatise; widely used and referred to.

Kentucky Rifle Association. *The Kentucky Rifle. A True American Heritage in Picture*. Washington, D.C.: Kentucky Rifle Association, 1967. Reprinted, Alexandria, Virginia: The Forte Group, 1985. Detailed photographic survey of a selection of exceptionally fine specimens.

*Kentucky Rifle Association. *Kentucky Rifles And Pistols 1750-1850*. Delaware, Ohio: Golden Age Arms Company and James R. Johnston, 1976. Detailed photographic survey of a broad selection of exemplary specimens that are not shown in the above listed work.

*Kindig, Joe, Jr. *Thoughts on the Kentucky Rifle in its Golden Age*. Wilmington, Delaware: George N. Hyatt, Publisher, 1960; Numerous subsequent reprintings by George Shumway, York, Pennsylvania. The classic work on the "Golden Age" Kentuckies. One of the most often cited and referred works on the subject.

Kindig, J. *Artistic Ingredients of the Long Rifle*. York, Pennsylvania: 1989.

*Klay, Frank. *Samuel E. Dyke Collection of Kentucky Pistols.* Highland Park, New Jersey: The Gun Room Press, 1964. Monograph illustrating thirteen fine Kentucky pistols with background history of makers and description.

Lagemann, R. & Manucy, A. *The Longrifle.* New York: Publishing Center for Cultural Resources 1980. Overview of history of the longrifle, its military uses, gunsmiths.

*Lambert, F. & Whisker, J. B. *Gunsmiths of West Virginia.* Bedford, Pennsylvania: Old Bedford Village Press, 1995.

Lindsay, Merrill. *The Kentucky Rifle.* New York: Arma Press for the York County, Pennsylvania Historical Society, 1972. General survey of the development of the Kentucky Rifle as told through a fine selection of a special exhibition at the York County Historical Society.

Rosenberger, R.F. & Kaufmann, C. *The Longrifles of Western Pennsylvania: Allegheny & Westmoreland Counties.* Pittsburgh, Pa: Univ. of Pittsburgh, 1993. Fine coverage; biographies of makers; details and illustrations of their rifles.

*Shumway, George. *Longrifles of Note, Pennsylvania.* York, Pennsylvania: George Shumway Publisher, 1968. Representative photographic and textual coverage of the various schools of Pennsylvania makers.

*Shumway, Geo. *Rifles of Colonial America. Vols. I & II.* York, Pennsylvania: George Shumway, Publisher, 1980. Highly important, extensive coverage nearly all of rifles that have survived from pre-Revolutionary era. Profuse photo illustrations in exacting detail.

Shumway, George. *George Schreyer Senior & Junior, Gunmakers Of Hanover, York County, Penna.* York, Pa: G. Shumway Publisher, 1990. Excellent study of these very noted makers.

*Whisker, Vaughn Sr. & Whisker, J.B. *Gunsmiths of Bedford, Somerset And Fulton Counties.* Bedford, Pa: Old Bedford Village Press, 1991.

*Whisker, James B. *Gunsmiths of York County, PA.* Bedford, Pennsylvania: Old Bedford Village Press, 1995.

Whisker, J. B. *Gunsmiths of Lancaster County, PA.* Bedford, Pennsylvania: Old Bedford Village Press, 1995.

*Whisker, J. B. *Arms Makers of Western PA.* Bedford, Pennsylvania: Old Bedford Village Press, 1994.

Whisker, J. B. *The Gunsmiths and Gunmakers of Eastern Pennsylvania.* Bedford, Pennsylvania: Old Bedford Village Press, 1982. Listing of 18th and 19th century makers. Pamphlet.

Whisker, J. B. *Ohio Long Rifles* Vol. I. Bedford, Pennsylvania: 1988.

*Whisker, J. B. *Gunsmiths of Adams, Franklin & Cumberland Counties.* Bedford, Pennsylvania: 1989.

Whisker, James & Vaughn. *Gun Makers & Gunsmiths of Western Penna.* Bedford, Pennsylvania: Old Bedford Village, 1981. Listing of 18th & 19th Century makers of that region.

Whisker, J. B. & V. E. *Bedford County Gunsmiths & Gunmakers.* Bedford, Pennsylvania: Published by the authors; 1981. An extension of the Hetrick work (*q.v.*), *The Bedford County Rifle & its Makers.*

*Whisker, J.B. *Gunsmiths Of Virginia.* Bedford, Pa: Old Bedford Village Press, 1992.

-- *Selected articles from the Kentucky Rifle Association Bulletin, Vol. 1-30.* Roswell, Georgia: Kentucky Rifle Foundation, 2005. Reprints 157 articles from 30 years of their "Bulletins." Articles grouped by subject matter, i.e. origin of the Kentucky; architecture and ornamentation of the rifles; variations; gunsmiths, etc... Illustrated.

(*) Preceding a title indicates the book is currently in print.

Chapter XII

Percussion Sporting and Target Rifles, Plains Rifles, Flintlock New England Rifles & Pistols

Although rarely are two percussion muzzle-loading rifles alike, and all are individually handcrafted, it is possible to categorize them for identification and evaluation purposes. The subject is broad in scope with a great variety of available specimens on the collectors' market, yet, no wealth of relevant substantive data is available in print. The field offers a rich potential to both the collector in accumulating specimens and the student gathering information. Values for both the buyer and seller are very much a "what the market will bear" arrangement; those with a practiced eye for aesthetics and quality and also armed with some historical insight will be ahead of the game. It would be presumptuous for the author to claim any detailed coverage of the subject in the short space allotted here, and the reader is forewarned that an understanding of the many facets necessary to comprehend the field is only acquired by research on individual specimens. By so doing one can appreciate the importance and significance of a specific rifle or maker which may alter value. Reducing the subject to its basic fundamentals the key factors influencing values are "quality," closely followed by "condition."

All of the rifles discussed in this chapter are classified in the general category of "sporting guns." In their broadest definition this includes all rifles designed for hunting and target shooting. Obviously, many were originally intended solely for utilitarian purposes, i.e., to put meat in the pot for the farmer, the frontiersman, pioneer or settler, and thus could hardly be called "sporting" if narrowly defined. Such rifles however are usually considered under this same grouping and hence are included in the present discussion. The reader is quite free to define the term as narrowly as he wishes.

Just where the dividing line comes between what the collector calls a "Kentucky Rifle" and a "sporting rifle" is sometimes a fine one indeed! Both terms as commonly used are quite broad in scope, with "Kentucky" quite loosely and liberally applied. A discussion of its origin and a more accurate definition appear in the preceding chapter. Undoubtedly there is considerable misapplication—if not corruption—of the term and it is quite casually applied to almost any kind of American rifle, especially one that has a patchbox of any size and shape! In the interest of accuracy, and not wishing to depreciate the importance of other American sporting rifles it should be noted that they are decidedly a distinct category. Only a handful of them are borderline cases which may be aptly termed "Kentucky" or "Kentucky-style." Let a spade be called a spade!

With the introduction of the percussion ignition system in the 1830s there rapidly grew a flourishing arms trade throughout the United States in the manufacture of muzzle-loading sporting rifles of all types. The trade generally prospered through the early 1870s and some hangers-on remained active to almost the turn of the century in certain types. A general demise was signaled by the introduction of breech-loading metallic cartridge rifles. Muzzleloaders were, for the most part, handcrafted by a great many individual gunsmiths throughout the country. Some of the more accomplished gunsmiths produced specimens in many varying degrees of quality (either at their own whim or on custom order of clients) while others seemed to have turned out more-or-less "average" rifles with but slight variance in either quality or ornateness. It is evident also that some makers were highly prolific in output, a few even achieving a proximity of limited mass production for general sale via arms shops and hardware dealers throughout the country with many of the lesser quality, plainer specimens destined for the Western emigrant and Indian trade markets. It is often quite difficult to positively identify these latter arms, especially when unsigned.

Percussion sporting rifles reflect a spectrum of quality from awkward, crudely made specimens apparently turned out by country blacksmiths to highly ornate, elaborately embellished, superbly crafted masterpieces embodying the highest talents of accomplished gunsmiths and artisans. These latter types are often representative of the highest form of arms design and decoration of their era. Many bear maker's signatures, but it is surprising to note that numerous examples of such high quality rifles are seen lacking maker's names. The author has always been puzzled why a gunsmith would lavish such great effort and yet neglect to sign his work. The same is true in other forms of art and paintings. Modesty, perhaps?

MAKERS' NAMES

The name (and consequent fame), origin and geographic location of the maker often play significant roles in evaluating a percussion rifle. On the very finest quality arms the absence of a name will not normally affect value, while on very plain, unembellished rifles a signature may often add considerably to value.

Quite a few very well known Eastern makers are in more demand than others and their works command value premiums. The premium, of course, varies greatly depending on the name and type of rifle under consideration. Generally, classification may be divided into three major categories: (a) Northern (or Eastern). (b) Southern, and (c) Western. A general rule-of-thumb for evaluation places premium values on rifles in the latter two categories, with Western associated specimens decidedly having the edge. Hence, a common style half-stock rifle normally of modest value bearing a Northern (or Eastern) maker's name may very well be worth double that value, or more, if found bearing a Western maker's name. The foregoing example will be tempered greatly by the actual maker's name and the quality of the gun itself. Note also that the maker's name and geographic location, although affecting value upward, may do so only in that very area where the gun was actually made. Thus, a rifle of a specific county or town in Indiana or Ohio may be worth more only in those same general areas where a handful of collectors are looking for specimens of local guns. On the general collectors' market those same markings and identification may be completely overlooked by the casual buyer, hence, in order to obtain the best, or ultimate, value for specific rifles the seller may have to advertise the piece and hope to virtually pull a "needle out of the haystack" to locate a buyer from that locale to attain its top price. By the same token, the collector with a practiced eye still has the opportunity to purchase many bargains in those same rifles that are offered at attractive prices in areas out of the region where they were made.

REMINGTON (or P&S REMINGTON) is the one name often seen marked on barrels of percussion sporting rifles; frequently on the underside. In all instances thus far recorded the markings merely indicate Remington's manufacture of the barrel blank only. They were among the largest suppliers of such barrels to the gunsmith trade throughout the U.S. Their markings are occasionally seen on locks also, again indicating Remington's sale of that prefabricated part to the trade. REMINGTON markings alone, with no other names present, rarely add significantly, if at all, to the rifle's value. (*See Chapter V-E "Remington Firearms" [Longarms section] for detailed discussion of the subject.*)

BORES

Bore conditions decidedly affect values of percussion rifles, and in varying degrees will affect demand. On the plainer, more common grades a fine bore, allowing for use by black powder shooters will increase values 10 percent to 30 percent; a poor bore may decrease values by these same percentages. The same plain grade rifle, if bored out smooth, is decreased in value by at least 25 percent or more. Bore condition is of decreasing importance, and is a minor determinant of value for the more ornate and lavishly embellished rifles. Such specimens of high quality if bored smooth would have their values lessened somewhat, however the quality and general beauty of the rifle are still the major determinants for such pieces.

Bore condition for high grade match rifles, designed solely for target shooting, is a major factor. A poor bore will decrease values 50 percent and more and diminish the "demand" accordingly. Value figures for heavy, bench rest match rifles (fitted with false muzzles) are very much determined by bore condition. Thus, generally speaking, the more a rifle is designed strictly for fine target shooting the greater the role played by bore condition in determining value. The reader is referred to Chapter II (Other Factors Affecting Value, Section 8) for further discussion of the subject.

FALSE MUZZLES

A false muzzle is a device specifically made for, and only found with, rifles designed solely for accurate target shooting. Although generally associated with muzzle-loading percussion rifles, this attachment was occasionally made for breech-loading single shot metallic cartridge target rifles (Harry Pope was one of the more notable gunsmiths who utilized this feature). The false muzzle was designed to facilitate loading of a target rifle and to lessen any possible wear at the critical point of the barrel where the bullet left the bore and to prevent damage to its muzzle while loading. It was invented by Alvan Clark of Boston, 1840, who assigned sole rights to its use to Edwin Wesson, Worcester, Mass., maker of fine target rifles. Wesson licensed others to make false muzzles, 1848.

False muzzles were an integral part of the barrel during its original manufacturing process. The barrel was made several inches longer than intended for shooting; after completion a segment (approximately 2-1/2" to 3-1/2") at the muzzle was removed, that piece then becoming the false muzzle. The segment underwent a few other processes (such as facing-off for a perfect fit) and a series of four hardened steel pins were fitted. Corresponding holes were bored in the front of the barrel into which the false muzzle was then friction fitted for quick removal, then barrel and muzzle rifled together. (Alternative method, not preferable by fine makers, was to rifle barrel first then cut off false muzzle which did not allow for as perfect alignment.) Key to all this was the fact that both the false muzzle and the full barrel were rifled as one unit with the rifling of each perfectly coinciding. Other accessories were used as well (such as a bullet starter) but these were not integral parts of the false muzzle or barrel and if lost could be replaced. The false muzzle, however, (which was removed before firing) took the majority of the wear in the loading and cleaning processes and lengthened the life of the rifle itself, preserving its accuracy.

False muzzles play highly important roles in evaluating percussion rifles fitted for that accessory. These are quite often found on off-hand, half-stock target rifles and their mere presence usually indicates rifles of accuracy and of fine quality workmanship. When present on an off-hand size rifle, value can be increased by 20 percent to 25 percent. When the false muzzle is missing, the value is diminished by at least 20 percent if not more. If the gun happens to be of very fine quality and fancy grade, it still remains highly desirable and in strong demand. However, if the gun is plain and unembellished, the lack of the false muzzle will seriously affect demand as well as value.

The false muzzle was a major, integral part of many heavy bench rest match rifles and when missing will detract from value 20 percent to 50 percent and lessen demand even further. Such heavy match rifles are usually purchased only for their great accuracy and completeness. When the false muzzle is missing it is akin to finding a fine percussion Colt revolver missing its barrel and cylinder!

False muzzles cannot be replaced for they were an integral part of the barrel making and bore drilling processes. Weak attempts are often made to fit missing muzzles (usually for window-dressing purposes) but there is no way that rifling can be perfectly lined up to match the original bore on such replacements.

BIBLIOGRAPHY

(Note: Considerable information about sporting rifles may be found in many of the books listed in the Bibliography of Chapter XI "Kentucky Rifles and Pistols." Further information about New England rifles is found in *The New England Gun - The First Two Hundred Years* by Merrill Lindsay [*see Chapter XVI Bibliography*].)

Baird, John D. *Hawken Rifles - The Mountain Man's Choice.* Pence, Indiana: Privately published by the author, 1968 with subsequent editions. Definitive guide to the subject, highly detailed and well illustrated.

*Baird, John D. *Fifteen Years in the Hawken Lode.* Big Timber, Montana: The Buckskin Press, 1971. Reprinted 1972, 1976. Companion volume to the author's *Hawken Rifles.* A collection of thoughts and observations about Hawkens illustrated with drawings and photographs.

*Demeritt, Dwight B., Jr. *Maine Made Guns And Their Makers.* Hallowell, Maine: Maine State Museum, 1973. A vast amount of information on sporting rifles from that state.

*Hamilton, John and Rowe, Tom. *The American Percussion Schuetzen Rifle.* Rochester, N.Y.: Rowe Publications, 2005. Arranged by region of U.S. where rifles made rather than alphabetical by maker to underscore stylistic differences. Only work devoted to the subject; profusely illustrated.

*Hanson, Charles E., Jr. *The Hawken Rifle: Its Place In History:.* Chadron, Nebraska: The Fur Press, 1979.

*Hanson, Charles E., Jr. *The Plains Rifle.* Harrisburg, Pennsylvania: The Stackpole Company, 1960 and subsequent reprintings by Gunroom Press. The basic reference in its field. Highly respected and often referred to.

Liu, Allan J. (after the editor) *The American Sporting Collector's Handbook.* New York City: Winchester Press, 1976. Contains chapter by Norm Flayderman, *Sporting Firearms,* encompassing material pertinent to this section.

*Rentschler, Thomas B. *Rifles and Blades of the German-American Militia and the Civil War.* Hamilton, OH: Blue Hills Press, 2003. Comprehensive history of that unique American militia group, The "Turners" and their arms (see 12-018.5 this chapter)

Roberts, Ned H. *The Muzzle-Loading Cap Lock Rifle.* Harrisburg, Pennsylvania: The Stackpole Company, 1940, 1944, 1947 and subsequent reprintings. The all-time classic on the subject. The basic work on percussion American sporting and target rifles; often referred to and cited.

Russell, Carl P. *Firearms, Traps, & Tools Of The Mountain Men.* New York: Alfred Knopf Publishers, 1967. An important work on the subject with cursory information on firearms.

Serven, James E. *Conquering The Frontiers - Stories Of American Pioneers And The Guns Which Helped Them Establish A New Life.* La Habra, California: Foundation Press Publications, 1974. Fine work by a noted arms authority with considerable information on muzzle-loading percussion sporting and plains rifles.

(*) Preceding a title indicates the book is currently in print.

Half Stock Percussion Sporting Rifles

12-001
Plain Grade with Patchbox

12-002
Plain Grade with Patchbox

12-003
Fancier Grade

12-003
Fancier Grade

The following are a representative sampling of American half stock percussion sporting rifles and their values in varying degrees of ornateness or quality. The reader is again cautioned that such values are very much subject to variation by the many factors discussed in the preceding text. It should be further assumed that bore conditions for the condition grades given below are at least commensurate, if not one degree higher than the general exterior.

Plain grade, brass or iron mountings: average quality; made without patchbox or inlays:

12-001 Values—Good **$400-650**   Very Good **$500-900**
Exc. **$750-1,250**

Plain grade as above with patchbox; slightly fancier features including possibly checkering at wrist and forend; few simple inlays:

12-002 Values—Good **$450-750**   Very Good **$650-1,000**
Exc. **$850-1,750**

Fancier grade and quality; usually brass furniture; larger fancier patchbox; displays other features such as few good quality inlays and possibly stock checkering and finer grades of wood and grains for stock:

12-003 Values—Good **$600-1,000** Very Good **$800-1,600**
Exc. **$1,250-3,000**

Fancy grade; displaying highest quality workmanship and corresponding grades of wood for stock; fancy furniture, inlays and (when present) patchboxes:

12-004
Highest Quality (both guns)

12-004 Values—Good **$850-1,750** Very Good **$2,000-4,500**
Exc. **$4,000-9,000 or more**

A.H. Babcock, Charlestown, Mass. *See Chapter XVII "Shotguns" 17-001.3*

Wm. Briggs, Norristown, PA. *See Chapter XVII "Shotguns" 17-011.5*

Full Stock Sporting Rifles

Full stock sporting rifles (other than those distinctly classified as "Kentuckies") are seen with much less frequency than half stocks. Although they may be considered as "very scarce" or even "rare" in comparison to half stocks this feature in itself is not sufficient to add significantly to value. They were generally by the same makers who produced the above described half stock rifles, and most likely on custom order. General appearance and degree of quality will follow almost identical classifications as outlined above for half stocks. Values are about the same also with premiums of 10 percent to 20 percent an average mean figure for those of better quality.

12-005

Pre-1800 New England-Made Rifles

One of the few known signed and dated 18th century New England-made rifles. Longarms made in New England pre-800 are invariably smoothbore fowling pieces or muskets. Rifles did not achieve any modicum of popularity until a decade or more after the turn of the century. This well-made, sturdy example bears the signature of a famous maker "J. HILLS" on its lock and "VERMONT" on the octagon barrel. Engraved in large letters on the heel of the buttplate: "BY J. HILLS, CHARLOTTE" - a distinctive feature found on most guns made by him. The stock also bears an inlay dated "1794" and the name of the man for whom the rifle was made on the brass sideplate. (*N. Flayderman & Co. Catalog No. 106 of October 1982*)

Pre-1800 New England-Made Rifles. The manufacture of rifles in New England was very slow in starting. Specimens dating back to the Revolutionary War or earlier are extremely rare with but a handful known. It was generally not until the latter part of the 18th century and the beginning of the 19th when the fabrication of sporting, target and other flintlock rifles first commenced in New England. Although quite a few of those turn-of-the-century specimens will be found to have been manufactured in the Worcester, Massachusetts vicinity, a few rare examples are known from other New England areas. Illustrated here is one of the few known signed and dated examples of that 18th century, New England rifle. Signed on its lock in a decorative panel J. HILLS (a noted early gunmaker) and also engraved in large letters "VERMONT" on the 44-inch octagon barrel; 56-caliber rifled bore. An engraved oval inlay at its wrist is dated "1794" while the long tang at the heel of the butt plate is also engraved in bold letters "BY J. HILLS, CHARLOTTE," (name of

his Vermont town). The side plate bears a similar style inscription with the name of a man for whom the rifle was made. The full, curly maple stock is fitted with a simple almost primitive appearing patchbox (a rare feature for this early type of rifle). As each example of these rarities differs, establishing a range of values is a broad generalization, at best, with many features necessary to consider such as: signature of maker; place of origin; date of fabrication, quality of workmanship and condition… among others. The two broadest, generalized ranges that follow offer a reasonable estimate of their relative values.

12-005.5 plain, full-stock; unsigned, yet credibly identified as New England made 18th century original flintlock rifle. Values range from high four to mid-five figures.

12-005.6 Signed and fully identified as to maker, original flintlock, full stock, New England rifle displaying professional, competent craftsmanship. Values estimated in low to mid/high five figures.

Flintlock New England "Kentucky" Rifles

12-006
Original Flintlock

"Typical New England Rifle Patchboxes and trigger guard"

It was not until the early 19th century that the more commonplace, popular manufacture of sporting, target and other rifles began in New England, centered mostly in the Worcester, Massachusetts, area. Although a wide variety of rifle types were made in New England, the most commonly seen and recognized is that illustrated here which may be compared quite closely to the "Kentucky" or "Pennsylvania" rifle of the era. The jargon that has generally crept into the gun collector's vocabulary for this specific type is the "New England Kentucky." All are usually quite well made and gracefully proportioned with not a few achieving superlative status in the lavish use of inlays, engraving and silver wire work. On a relative rarity basis specimens are considerably scarcer than a Pennsylvania made Kentucky and have in recent years become much more widely recognized, sought after and studied.

It is quite interesting to note that a great majority of the so-called New England "Kentucky" rifles made during the first quarter of the 19th Century invariably followed the same general patterns in mountings and patchboxes and are readily identifiable by such features. It has been the author's experience that 75 percent or more of the New England rifles that he has seen and handled retain the same identical features: (a) Long rectangular patchbox door without side pieces and distinctive circular top piece or hinge with a tall pointed finial (so-called ball & spike). Although variations of engraving and shape of finials are seen the patchboxes are identical to this form. (b) Distinctive pointed teat like projection on the front of the trigger guard (*see illustration*). This feature invariably accompanies the above described patchbox.

Quite often the New England rifle is fitted with a small oval silver thumbpiece/escutcheon plate at the wrist, surrounded with

silver wire work often was used around the area of the barrel tang and the cheekrest. Illustrated here are the most often seen New England style "Kentuckies" although rarely are two identical, the amount of silver inlay work, fancy engraving, maker's name and any major variances in style and shape of patchboxes do much to affect value. On the latter it should be noted that a few exceptional horsehead and eagle finials are known. Prices reflected here are merely for average illustrated specimens.

These very same rifles are often seen in original half stock configuration with a few exceptionally fine specimens known. Most often the New England rifle is stocked in cherry or walnut with plain maple and curly (or "tiger stripe") maple in lesser frequencies. The latter will normally command a premium merely because of its handsome appearance.

Original flintlock full stock New England "Kentucky" type rifle; cherry, walnut or plain maple stock; brass mountings and patchbox as shown:

12-006 Values—Good **$1,750-3,000** Fine **$3,250-6,500**

Identical to above; converted to percussion:

12-007 Values—Good **$1,250-2,000** Fine **$2,000-3,500**

12-007
Percussion Conversion
(both guns)

12-008
Original Percussion

Original percussion New England half stock rifle:
12-008 Values—Good **$750-1,400**   Very Good **$1,000-2,250**
Exc. **$1,250-3,500**

New England Flintlock Pistols

12-008.5

Very loosely applied and defined terminology to a broad range of handguns (i.e., any made in the northeast section of the U.S.). Among arms collectors its use is limited to a general style of large holster pistol circa 1800-1830s, most often made by the same gunsmiths that created these New England "Kentucky" rifles. The majority are full stocked in cherry or walnut and quite often display the same features found on the rifles of those same makers, such as delicate silver wire inlay designs surrounding the (mostly brass) mountings. A variety of barrel styles are seen, with a rifled bore in a full octagon brass or iron barrel especially desirable and worthy of a premium value. Quality and general appearance significantly affect value:

12-008.5 Values—Good **$1,750-$2,500**
Fine **$2,500-$6,500 or more**
Identical to above; Converted to percussion:
12-008.6 Values—Good **$950-$1,750**
Fine **$1,500-$3,500 or more**

18th Century New England Flintlock Pistols

A few early New England made handguns have distinguishing characteristics that deserve to place them in a separate category. Most collectors would not consider it appropriate to merely classify them as "Secondary Martial." Similar to the above post-1800 New England pistols, these c. 1775-1800 handguns display features often viewed on the fowling pieces (rifles rarely made) of the same makers (see Chapter 16). Specimens that can be positively identified, especially signed by maker, are very rare. The example illustrated displays many of the most desirable qualities sought in the type: Large holster size, stocked in "tiger stripe" curly maple, with bold markings "J(ohn) HILLS/CHARLOTTE/VERMONT" as well as the individual for whom made. This noted maker worked in Vermont c. 1775-1810. He was earlier associated with his brother, Medad Hills in Goshen, Connecticut.

Values are subjective, at best. Much like Kentucky pistols (Chapter 11) each pistol must be judged on its individual merits which take into account quality, markings, type of stock and mountings, and any special features. All of them are rare. If *positive* identification can be established...and that is the key

12-008.8

word...the very lowliest specimen should be in the value range $1,000 to $2,000. From that starting point, it is within the realm of possibility that exceptional specimens might fetch values in substantial five figures:

12-008.8

Hall's Patent Breech-Loading Flintlock Sporting Rifle

12-009

12-009.2

Hall's Patent Breech-Loading Flintlock Sporting Rifle Made by John H. Hall, Portland, Maine, c. 1811-1818. Quantity unknown; estimated under 150.

Although no two of these highly desirable rifles are identical, they do retain close similarities in many features. The specimen illustrated is typical of the type most often encountered. The breechblock pivots upward for loading and is released by a lever device protruding through the bottom of the stock. Calibers vary from approximately 32 to 52. Octagon barrels have been recorded from 29" to 35". The slender, full stocks are usually encountered of curly maple wood; brass patchboxes, which are found on most specimens, are of an identical pattern (as shown).

Most (but not all) specimens recorded are marked on the top of the breechblock JOHN H./HALL/PATENT. Numbers (believed serials) are found on most specimens on the breechblock as are various initials believed those of factory workmen.

Earlier types than that shown, with unique or evolutionary features, are worth premium values (*See also Chapter IX-A, Model 1819 U.S. Breech-Loading Rifle*):

12-009 Values—Good **$6,500**   Fine **$17,500**

Variant Hall's Patent Breech-Loading Sporting Rifles. Other unusual variations of early Hall sporting rifles are possible to encounter (see also Hall pistol 6B-029). A unique double-barrel, half-stock specimen is described and illustrated by C.W. Sawyer in his pioneering work *Our Rifles*, 1920 (q.v.) with side-by-side octagon barrels and double side-by-side breech-blocks. Variants of Hall sporting rifles are known with brass barrels and/or brass breech-blocks. All display differences and are extremely rare. Hall even advertised his breech-loading sporter as a "fowling piece" (smooth-bore Hall Patent shotguns as yet unknown). Illustrated is a Hall's Patent breech-loading, half-stock original percussion sporting rifle; marked in bold, fancy script "H. KEITH PHILADELPHIA" on its octagon barrel. The well-proportioned stock fitted with a fancy brass patchbox, elegantly engraved with an American eagle, shield and ribbon, with motto, filling its lid. A unique feature is the maker's original printed label yet intact within the patchbox: "**Manufactured and sold by H. Keith and B. Butterfield**" with street address, Philadelphia. Other examples by Keith known in flintlock. Values of variant Hall Patent sporting breech-loaders, made by Hall in Portland, Maine or other listed American makers, and of commensurate quality, are estimated to be values in the high four to low five-figure range.

12-009.2

Jennings All Metal Breech-Loading Flintlock Rifle

Jennings All Metal Breech-Loading Flintlock Rifle. Invented by Isaiah Jennings, New York City, 1818 and likely made by him also. Quantity limited. (See also 9B-009 Repeating flintlock.)

Specimens viewed and recorded, although varying in dimensions and quality, do have common features of removable barrel that takes-down by quarter twist to load at breech as well as to shorten overall length for portability; integal made skeleton type stock. Varying barrel lengths, calibers (some smooth bore).

Markings vary: JENNINGS on lock and INVENTED BY ISAIAH JENNINGS APR 11, 1818 viewed on some examples. Rare:

12-009.5   Values—Good **$4,500** Fine **$8,000**

12-009.5

Jennings All-Metal, Muzzleloading Multi-Shot Flintlock Rifle

12-009.6

Isaiah Jennings All-Metal Muzzleloading Flintlock Repeating Rifle. Invented and patented by Isaiah Jennings of New York City, 1821. Quantity unknown; extremely rare. Illustrated here is a twelve-shot specimen; a three-shot variant similar in appearance is illustrated and described in C.W. Sawyer's *Our Rifles, 1800-1920.* All brass construction, skeleton-type shoulder stock (identical to above) that is easily removable; the 21-inch octagon barrel is also quickly removable by merely loosening the thumbscrew at the breech and twisting. Lock marked I.JENNINGS. The multi-shot rifle illustrated takes twelve individual, superposed loads of powder and ball, one on top of the other, and is fitted with twelve individual touchholes, each with a swivel cover which also act to position and align the lock as it slides from its forward position towards the rear to align the shots in reverse order. 21-inch octagon brass barrel; rifled 44 caliber bore. (See also Ellis-Jennings Repeating Flintlock Military Rifles 9B-009/010 purchased under contract by U.S. Government, 1829.) Value for these rarities indeterminate; estimates in mid- to high five-figure range would not be inordinate. **12-009.6**

Underhammer Rifles

12-010
Plain Grade Underhammer Rifle

12-011
Fancier Grade
(all 3 guns)

Quite a variety of underhammer percussion rifles are seen on the collectors' market. They represent an interesting cross-section of arms by American makers. By far the great majority of underhammers were made in New England, although certainly all Eastern states are well represented as is California; these latter worth a premium. Underhammers are found in a wider range of sizes than almost any other American rifle. Quite a few are seen in lightweight "boys" or "buggy" sizes with correspondingly smaller proportions and dimensions while others increase to massive 20-pound and 25-pound bench rest match target rifles made by some of the era's most noted riflesmiths, e.g., Billinghurst and Brockway. Specimens illustrated here are the most typical of those encountered. Underhammers run the gamut in quality from primitive, awkward, unmarked specimens to those displaying the very highest quality of workmanship and possessing pleasing, artistic qualities.

As the underhammer mechanism was more simply fashioned than the full side lock type, their manufacture was obviously attempted by not a few unskilled craftsmen and gunsmiths—or more likely, blacksmiths! Thus, quite a few primitive appearing specimens are to be seen. If identifiable markings as to maker and localities are present, values may be increased proportionally.

A factor to be considered for evaluation is the type of wood used for the stock; curly maple being quite desirable and worth a premium and is in equally stronger demand.

Undoubtedly one of the most prolific makers was Nicanor Kendall of Windsor, Vermont. Judging by the specimens seen over the years, he turned out a notable number of underhammers in varying degrees of quality circa 1830s to 1840s. Another well-known maker of this type was David H. Hilliard of Cornish, New Hampshire. The reader is referred to Chapter VII, American Percussion Pistols (Section E) for further information about the principle and use of the underhammer, and to the classic work on the subject, *Underhammer Guns*, by Herschel C. Logan.

The specimens illustrated here are all of the off-hand size and weight. Heavy bench rest match type underhammer rifles are classed and evaluated in the "Bench Rest Rifles" section of this chapter.

Plain grade underhammer rifle usually brass mounted; made without patchbox, plain walnut or maple stock (curly maple worth 10 percent to 20 percent premium on this type):
12-010 Values—Good $300-600   Fine $500-900

Fancier grade underhammer. With large circular or oval patchbox; possibly few small inlays; usually brass mounted.

Curly maple stocks worth 10 percent to 20 percent premium:
12-011 Values—Good **$500-1,000**   Fine **$850-1,750**

"Mule Ear" Side-Hammer Rifles

12-011.5

A distinct and separate category of percussion rifles, almost all of which are sporting types, an exception is the U.S. Navy Jenks carbine, 9B-061. Readily identified by the distinctive percussion lock on which the hammer is brought to full cock by drawing it back sideways. The "**Mule Ear**" designation refers to the configuration of the cocking spur on the hammer which has a fancied, if sometimes vague, resemblance to a mule's ear. Regardless of reports to the contrary, research indicates the nickname was coined in the early 20th century by antique arms collectors; it ultimately became the most often heard or read way to describe this style of lock mechanism and firearm. An earlier work on collecting noted this style of lock as a "Side Striker,"

that terminology has not always remained in common usage.

A broad range of styles and qualities of American percussion sporting rifles are to be encountered with "mule ear" locks. The majority observed have been in either plain or less fancy grades, occasionally fitted with patchboxes or a few inlays. They invariably were crafted by competent, professional gunsmiths. The style achieved its greatest popularity in New England and parts of New York. Specimens displaying backwoods, primitive worksmanship are seldom encountered and would not be worth a premium. Almost all are single-shot with but a few being multi-barreled. Value-wise they may be classified identically to single-shot percussion sporting rifles or underhammer rifles. Although the style is scarcer that usual, they have not been observed to attract premium values.
12-011.5

Pill Lock Rifles

The "**Pill Lock**" (a.k.a. "Punch Lock") was a short-lived transitional gun lock ignition system and mechanism between the flintlock and percussion methods. The primer charge was a small pellet of fulminate (the "pill") often coated with a metallic foil to make it water-resistant. It was placed directly on a semi-enclosed touchhole at the breech of the barrel and held in place with a smear of tallow, beeswax or similar viscous substance.

12-011.6

Upon firing, the pill was struck by a projection on the end of the hammer (most often a laterally-operating hammer, occasionally a side "mule ear" hammer as illustrated here) causing a detonation of the "pill" and subsequently the main powder charge. The system had many obvious drawbacks and was short-lived, but was important for the ultimate development of the more practical percussion cap.

The pill lock illustrated here was fitted on a well-made, half-stock sporting rifle by Ephraim Gilbert working in Rochester, New York 1822-1837. It appears there was a patent issued in 1829 for the lock (patent number not known). The engraved lock marked E. GILBERT / PATENT / ROCHESTER.

Pill-lock firearms are rare and are seldom encountered on American-made arms. A premium for their value is justified. However, unless the firearm on which that pill lock mechanism is used has other unique or outstanding features, that premium in value over a similarly styled and quality percussion rifle is usually modest.
12-011.6

Plains Rifle vs. Plain Rifle

Two of the most often misused and misunderstood terms in gun collecting are "plains rifles" and "plain rifle." The latter pertains solely to the so-called "Kentucky" type rifle and was the actual terminology used by various makers and merchants to describe their (Kentucky) rifles that were simple and unembellished (quite often without patchboxes) and usually of the late flintlock and percussion eras.

"Plains rifle" is a generic term coined by collectors and authorities of the 20th century to denote those rifles made and intended for use on the expanding Western frontiers, i.e., the Western plains. They were manufactured from the early 19th century through the 1870s, and were more often referred to in their day as "mountain rifles" or even "buffalo rifles." A more accurate definition would be those rifles made mostly in and around St. Louis, Missouri—adaptations from the long

Kentucky rifle first carried to that part of the West by emigrants opening and settling the frontier. These were modifications of the Eastern Pennsylvania-Kentucky style rifle by Western (St. Louis) gunsmiths seeking to provide shorter rifles for big game and for use on horseback. Modifications were achieved by shortening barrels and enlarging bores. Earliest development and distinctive designs are directly traced to the famed Hawken brothers (Jacob and Samuel) of St. Louis, circa 1820s, gunsmiths originally emigrating from Maryland.

Although the Pennsylvania makers did devote some of their production to the "plains" rifle, notably Leman of Lancaster, and James Henry of Philadelphia and Boulton, the majority of production was instead sold to Indian traders and smaller merchants.

It is often a moot point as to what is merely a "plain"

12-012
Hawken St. Louis, Percussion

12-012
Gemmer, St. Louis, Percussion

12-014
O'Dell, Natchez, Mississippi

Kentucky as opposed to a true "plains rifle"; the author leaves it to the dilettante and semanticist to resolve the problem. An excellent work, entirely devoted to the subject *The Plains Rifle* by Charles Hanson (*see Bibliography*), is highly recommended for definitive details.

Without doubt the markings of the Hawken brothers and their St. Louis address are magic on any plains rifle. Not only were they the originators of the type but their rifle was so widely accepted, used and respected that in some instances the Hawken name, like that of Henry Deringer, became a generic term for the entire style of rifle. "Hawken" was occasionally used synonymously to indicate a "mountain" or "buffalo" rifle of the era (or "plains rifle" of current day). Examples of their work are now quite rare and any genuine specimen brings far in excess of what other plains rifles of contemporary makers fetch.

For the most part plains rifles have all seen considerable use. They are sought on the basis of great historical association and although condition certainly plays an instrumental role in values, the demand is great for all of them in all conditions.

As with all guns of this nature that were handcrafted, varying from piece to piece, a great many factors affect values. The reader is cautioned to spend time researching the subject in the referenced works in order to better understand their significance.

Although some examples were made in full stock, the usual plains rifle follows the half-stock pattern (with simple furniture and patchbox) most often made by the Hawkens. Quite often double wedges and escutcheons fastening the barrel to the forend were used. Patchboxes when present are normally quite simple and circular or oval in shape; special order full rectangular patchboxes were occasionally made. Note that these rifles were made for rough, hard usage and delicacy was not a design detail. They are proportionately larger and heavier than the usual percussion half-stock sporting rifle; trigger guards were very often rounded and scrolled type with no projecting spurs or fancy work to catch on clothing or saddle. Average barrel lengths were usually 36" to 38" with bores averaging 50 to 60. Overall weights averaged 9 pounds to 14 pounds; stocks

though well proportioned were ruggedly made of plain maple or walnut.

Specimens shown here are the average, more easily recognized plains type. Also to consider, and very pertinent to the collecting of these types, are such factors as possible Indian usage. The presence of brass tacks or rawhide wrappings play a role in evaluation. As with other collectors' weapons in which usage or historical associations are aspects of value, these latter features (subject to abuses in present day) are ones to which the collector should exercise caution and common sense.

Hawken, St. Louis marked Plains Rifles. Earliest specimens were made by Jacob Hawken c. 1815 and are mostly flintlock (many full stock) and worth premiums over values shown here. Samuel Hawken joined his brother in St. Louis circa 1822 and dual markings J & S HAWKEN are in evidence circa 1822 - 1849, followed by the markings S. HAWKEN, ST. LOUIS to circa 1861. After Samuel's retirement the business was sold to one of his employees J. P. Gemmer, who continued making the same style of rifle. Gemmer was known to have used the original S. HAWKEN stamp on his earlier products changing soon afterward to J. P. GEMMER ST. LOUIS. Later Hawken rifles show a progression to smaller calibers as the muzzleloader was relegated to more target shooting roles. A majority of Hawken rifles saw heavy usage and the survival rate was small:

12-012 Values—Fair **$12,500**   Good **$17,500-25,000**
     Very Good **$30,000-60,000+**

St. Louis made Percussion Plains Rifles bearing markings and signatures of established makers of the same general era, and stylistically similar to the Hawkens. The presence of a patchbox does not affect value. Research is necessary to more accurately determine value as many maker's names are worth premiums:

12-013 Values—Fair **$1,500-3,000**   Good **$3,000-5,000**
     Very Good **$4,000-7,500+**

Plains Rifles by other makers. Illustrated here is a fine quality specimen by the noted gunsmith, S. O'Dell of Natchez, Mississippi. This type is generally priced by the quality of workmanship, the maker's name and location. Eastern (mostly Pennsylvania) marked specimens tend to bring lesser values. Those west of the Mississippi (as valued here) normally are in the higher price ranges and in greater demand:

12-014 Values—Good **$2,500-5,500** Fine **$4,500-9,500**

U.S. Purchased Sporting Rifles During Civil War

Records clearly reveal the government purchased 2,707 "COMMON SPORTSMAN RIFLES" 1861-62; likely more. Well known St. Louis maker Horace Dimick received a contract from

General J.C. Fremont for 1,000 percussion sporting rifles to arm the 14th Missouri ("Birge's Sharpshooters", later the 66th Ill. Inf'y). All likely delivered; 472 recorded in May, 1862. To fill contract Dimick acquired some from other makers/dealers. Existing photographs reveal guns as half stock rifles varying in features (double and single wedge forends; back action and bar locks; with and without patchbox, etc.) Early correspondence mentioned saber type bayonets, but likely only a few so-fitted. Known to have been serial numbered (likely on face of muzzle)

and issued with bullet mold (likely numbered to match. (See Chapter II...*An Underutilized Research Tool.* Calibers 48 to 55). Values shown for authenticated, documented specimens (Note: Colorado Territory also purchased "sporting rifles" to arm their 1st Reg't of Volunteers, Sept. 1861):

12-014.5   Values—Good **$1,750**   Fine **$5,500**

Bench Rest Rifles

12-015

12-015

Labeled Civil War Union Sharpshooter's Rifle. Heavy barreled percussion bench rifle by Worcester, Mass. gunmaker Cyrus Baldwin Holden. Affixed to the lid of its original wooden box is the rare label indicating its manufacture or purchase in 1861 and specific use by Captain Saunder's Company of Massachusetts Sharpshooters (named after Governor Andrews of Mass.). The outfit was initially attached (and later separated) to the famous Berdan's Sharpshooter Regiment.

LANGDON'S ADVICE,
TO CAPT. SAUNDERS SHARP SHOOTERS.

1st. In taking the Gun from the Box, put the left hand under the centre of the barrel, the right hand at the small part of the stock, lift it up, in all cases the breech first.

2d. If the Gun has remained some time without being used, wipe with a dry swab, and snap one or two Caps to clean the oil.

3d. In loading for war purposes use an oiled patch, to prevent the barrel from rusting near the chamber.

4th. When the Gun is fired every day, it need not be wiped out with a swab wet by the mouth, but a little oil.

5th. (And last) Trust in GOD, keep the sight straight, and POWDER DRY.

Boston, Mass. Sept. 3, 1861.

No. ....

Ungainly—and often homely—in appearance, these distinctive appearing. massive sized, muzzle-loading target rifles were made to obtain the very best accuracy (i.e., make the smallest target groups) and were shot from a rest position (often a special wooden bench). Operation was characterized by a very slow and exact loading procedure with minute measurements of charges and the hand trimming of the bullet as well as painstaking sight adjustments. A few of these types were used as sharpshooters rifles during the Civil War. Quite often a special iron or bronze attachment affixed under the muzzle, allowed the barrel to slide (without tilting) on a fixed stand.

Rifles of this type usually weigh in from 18 to 25 pounds although those tipping the scales at 30 to 40 pounds are not unusual. Generally embellishments of any type are lacking with the focus of workmanship solely around the barrel and its bore; that latter feature is the essence for evaluation. Invariably these rifles are equipped with false muzzles (*see discussion of same in preceding text*) and this feature too, plays a key role in evaluation. Maker's names are also important and thus it is the collector's task to research signatures if they appear. Some names like Norman Brockway of Bellows Falls, Vermont, Nelson Lewis of Troy, New York, and Morgan James of Utica, New York, are

highly important and will add considerably to value for their renowned craftsmanship and accuracy. Exteriors of these heavy pieces do not usually show the quality that the normal off-hand rifle displays; embellishments and fittings are usually plain and simple, though well made. The maker's efforts were lavished upon the bore and thus bore condition is a key to pricing. For a rifle to be in demand and bring a price commensurate with its importance, the bore should be excellent and better—if not perfect! Anything less will considerably diminish both demand and value. Just a "good" or "fair" bore will lessen value 50 percent or more. The rifle has a value for a modern-day shooter and for re-rifling, but as far as collectibility is concerned its glamour has been lost! As most were fitted with false muzzles, it is also of extreme importance that the original false muzzle be intact with the gun; if missing, value will diminish at least 25 percent and probably more.

Often these heavy match rifles are found in their original boxes which were usually heavy pine wood, with simple wooden compartments and usually containing a number of spare accessories, most important of which is the brass bullet starter and mold. These all add proportionately to values if intact. Heavy bench rest rifles are occasionally found in their original, sturdily-built wooden box accompanied with numerous accessories (as illustrated), and worthy of premium values. Such boxed outfits might also include a maker's label (rare) or (as illustrated) a label directly linking the gun to military usage as a "sharpshooter's rifle" during the Civil War. Whether the rifleman brought his own bench rifle with him (it is known that a cash bounty was offered such enlistees by some sharpshooter outfits) or the rifle was purchased by the state or federal government is uncertain. The inclusion of a marking or label validating the use of a bench rifle for military sharpshooter service in the Civil War enhances its value considerably; Premiums of 100 percent and greater. Authentic specimens are rare and highly prized.

Bench rest match rifle (side lock or underhammer) with original false muzzle. Known and recorded makers with premiums added for the most famous. The presence or absence of patchbox does not affect value:

12-015 Values—Very good exterior with fine to excellent bore: **$2,250-5,000**

12-016 Values—Excellent condition with almost (if not) perfect bore: **$3,250-7,500**

Schuetzen Rifles

12-017 Plain Grade

12-018 Fancier Grade

The Schuetzen rifle was a highly specialized percussion target rifle developed to the point where it was almost a precision instrument. As discussed here and as used in America, the Schuetzen was only a target arm and completely impractical for any other sporting purposes. The word is a variant form of the German *schütze* or *schützen*, a marksman, sharpshooter, rifleman—or even "member of a rifle club." In its broadest, most accurate sense the word simply means: Any off-hand (standing and without artificial support) shooting. As applied to American percussion target rifles, it indicates one intended solely for off-hand shooting and of a weight generally too heavy, and a contour and configuration too clumsy for hunting or normal sporting purposes. The rifle type and even the shooting match for which it was designed originated in Germany. Popularity in America in the Germanic form commenced c. 1860s and lasted until the turn of the century. Judging from the many surviving specimens, a large proportion were made by German gunsmiths who emigrated to the United States. Evidently, many such craftsmen devoted their entire work only to the German Schuetzen style rifle. A great many shooting clubs, all with Germanic/Teutonic names formed throughout America during the second half of the 19th Century for the sole purpose of target shooting, with national matches and national organizations following suit. The matches themselves, or meetings, were known by the German name *Schützenfest*. The percussion Schuetzen rifle was in its heaviest use from the 1860s through the early 1880s but survived to the very end of the era (c. 1900) and was used simultaneously with the breech-loading Schuetzen style rifles, e.g., the Marlin-Ballards, Winchester High Walls and Stevens Ideals.

Invariably, the muzzle-loading variety is fitted with a false muzzle. The presence of that appurtenance is extremely important in evaluation.

Note that many of the maker's names are Germanic while another noticeable feature is that markings are often seen with Midwest and far West addresses as well as many from the New York and New Jersey areas.

As far as can be determined, any style of rifle was acceptable in the Schuetzen matches, in any form or weight and in any sized charge. Calibers range from the 30s to approximately 45 with rifle weights averaging 11 to 12 pounds, although 14 to 16 pounds are not uncommon. Just as the shooting matches were characterized by their individuality of equipment, so are the guns! An extremely wide range of elaborateness of embellishments are to be seen. Likely the single common denominator for all is quality of workmanship. Even plainer grades show fine craftsmanship. Specimens illustrated are of plainer, medium grades that might be encountered; however, some rifles may bear extremely fine relief carvings varying from simple leaf and floral designs to elaborate detailed hunting and patriotic motifs. The quality and profuseness of such carving will do much to affect increase in values.

Bore conditions are important on this type and should be at least as good as the exterior condition if not better. On a fine, elaborate specimen the bore condition would be secondary; such rifles would be basically valued for their artistic qualities and eye appeal. On plainer grades the bore plays a more influential role in values. Rear peep sights of these percussion Schuetzens were usually quite elaborate and precision made, each handcrafted for the specific rifle to which it was fitted. They are extremely difficult to replace and when missing will lessen both value and demand.

Plain grade (but fine quality) Schuetzen percussion half stock rifle; signed by maker; complete with sights and false muzzle:
12-017 Values—Good **$900-1,500**   Very Good **$1,250-2,500**   Exc. **$2,250-4,500**

Schuetzen rifle of fancier (but not most elaborate) grade; fancy buttplate and trigger guard; complete with false muzzle, sights; signed by maker; finer grade of wood for stock:
12-018 Values—Good **$1,000-1,500**   Very Good **$1,500-3,000**   Exc. **$2,750-5,500**

Turner Rifles

12-018.5
Typical "Turner Rifle"...shown with the distinctive pattern, large, Brass Hilt Bayonet unique to this style rifle.

"**Turner Rifles**" so-called American percussion rifles made almost exclusively in Ohio (a few in Kentucky near border) for the "TURNVEREIN" (athletic/gymnast clubs) the fraternal, social, paramilitary societies of German immigrants and German-Americans formed to preserve their heritage, traditions and habits, c. 1848; very active throughout the 1850s. Cincinnati, with its large German population was the central focus of activities and rifle makers. Known for their strong feelings of patriotism and on social issues, anti-slavery, labor movements etc. Occasionally had to defend those views by force of arms. Their rifles, although not identical, follow a distinct style: Generally fullstock with barrel fastened by two wedges. Average weight 9 pounds; approx. 31" rifled octagon barrel; back action lock and double set trigger. Invariably present are sling swivels and a massive stud at muzzle for a large, distinct

style, brass hilt saber-bayonet. Caliber 40 to 45. Rifles very plain; most bear Ohio maker names but Philadelphia and New York German-American makers known. Variances often due to personal preferences and income and owner's finances. At outbreak of Civil War Turners enlisted in great numbers, but liklihood of taking their rifles with them believed minimal. Possibly carried in the "Turner Rifles" (militia) formed to protect Cincinnati against threat of invasion (value does not include bayonet). A comprehensive, well-illustrated history of the various forms of these rifles and their many accessories is told by T.P. Rentschler in *Rifles and Blades of the German-American Militia and the Civil War*, 2003 (q.v.):

12-018.5   Values—Good **$1,000-1,750**   Exc. **$2,000-4,000**

Multi-Barrel Percussion Rifles

12-019
Common Type Double Barreled

12-019
Common Type
Over-Under Rifle

12-020
Over-Under Rifle-Shotgun
(finer quality)

12-019
Three Barreled
Rifle-Shotgun

12-021
Four Barreled Rifle

12-021
Four Barreled
Rifle-Shotgun

There are numerous types of variations and combinations of multi-barreled percussion sporting rifles. The most commonly encountered are double barreled over-and-under styles (usually combinations of rifle over smooth bore shotgun) followed in frequency by double barreled side-by-side types. Three barreled variations (usually double barreled shotgun over single rifle barrel) would be considered scarce although they are seen with a reasonable frequency. Four barreled styles (they normally swivel) would be classified as rare, while combinations of five barrels or more would be classed as very rare.

For the more common double barreled types quality of workmanship, maker's name, and condition are key factors for evaluation. In broad general terms either side-by-side or over-under styles will bring prices comparable to the same quality single barreled specimens, although a 10 percent to 20 percent premium for better condition pieces would not be unreasonable. **The three barrel styles** usually have double sidelocks for the upper two barrels with an underhammer for the rifled barrel. Plain specimen is similar to that illustrated:

12-019 Values—Good **$750-1,400** Fine **$1,000-2,500**
Similar to above; finer quality often with patchbox, few inlays; select grain wood; better overall workmanship:
12-020 Values—Good **$900-1,850**
Fine **$1,500-4,000**

Four barreled rifles (or rifles over shotgun barrels or combinations thereof) are very difficult to categorize price-wise as they do not conform to common styles or patterns as do the double and triple barrel types and reflect much greater individuality of workmanship. For the most part they all display fine quality (primitive specimens are occasionally seen which fetch values commensurate with the quality of their workmanship). Only the broadest price ranges are shown here as general guidelines for good and fine quality professionally made four barrel types:

12-021 Values—Good **$1,000-2,250**
Fine **$2,500-5,000**

Breech-Loading Percussion Sporting Rifles

It is apparent from the frequency with which they appear that breech-loading percussion sporting rifles, except for the Sharps and to some extent the Maynard, did not achieve great popularity (*see Chapter V-F and Chapter XIV for information on these latter two*). There were but few "patented" types manufactured in any quantity; the Allen & Wheelock so-called "faucet" or "tap" breech is among the better known of that style (*see Chapter V-A*) with the Marston and Perry breechloaders following respectively (*see below*). The collector will occasionally encounter oddball, one-of-a-kind types; evaluated on the basis of their quality and uniqueness of mechanical action; in that order.

Sporting variations of military percussion breechloaders infrequently occur also. Thus, it's possible to encounter such

well-known military breechloaders as the Burnside, Gallager, Joslyn, Merrill and even the Smith in pure sporting variations (not merely conversions of former military models). *See Chapter IX-B for illustrations and details of those breech actions.* Although such sporting types are rare, it will be found that the "demand" factor is not strong for them and usually they are worth but small premium values over their military counterparts. Of course, beautifully decorated, superb conditioned specimens would be in a class by themselves and evaluated on an individual basis for their elaborateness. These same types may possibly be encountered as smooth bore/shotgun variations, also. See also Chapter V-K *WInchester* for details of the Smith and the Smith-Jennings breech loading percussion rifles (5K-002 et al).

Marston Breech-Loading Percussion Rifle

W. W. Marston, New York City. Breech-loading single-shot lever action rifle. Made circa mid-1850s. Total quantity limited; estimated at less than 300 (including shotguns).

Calibers and barrel length vary; specimens observed in 31, 36 and 54 caliber. Barrel lengths vary; standard approximately 28"; observed mostly round with some barrels part octagon, part round. Made without provision for a forend; cleaning rod mounted below barrel. Double set triggers on some specimens. Finished brown or blued with other parts case-hardened. Stock usually walnut; occasionally bird's eye maple. Serial numbered underside of frame. Usual markings on frame: W. W. MARSTON, PATENTED 1850. NEW YORK. Broad, scroll engraving on frame standard. Sprague & Marston markings also known.

Best known to collectors for his various percussion pepperboxes, single and multibarreled percussion and cartridge handguns (*q.v.*). Marston also produced this unique breech-

12-022

loading action in handgun form (*see Chapter VII-C*). Although the shotgun is probably scarcer than the rifle, it does not usually fetch as much because of a slightly lessened demand factor. One specimen has been recorded in military musket style; a great rarity and worth a considerable premium. Variations are known in frame sizes, barrel types, contours.

Rifle: Various calibers and barrel lengths:
12-022 Values—Good **$950** Fine **$3,000**
Shotgun: Approximately 70 caliber. Various barrel lengths:
12-023 Values—Good **$800** Fine **$2,000**

Perry Breech-Loading Percussion Sporting Rifle

12-024

Alonzo Perry, Newark, NJ. Breech-Loading Rifle. Made circa late 1850s-1860. Quantity unknown; limited. Same style action as

found on his military carbine and single shot percussion pistol (*q.v.*).

Various calibers, barrel lengths and barrel weights reported. Apparently most, if not all, specimens were on a custom order basis using the same patented action. Barrels usually are full octagonal.

Finish browned; walnut stocks with wedge-fastened matching forend. Markings identical to military carbine (*see Chapter IX-B*). Broad scroll engraving on frame standard (some specimens with very fancy profuse engraving noted; worth premium). Specimens are known with round or part-octagon, part-round shotgun/smoothbore barrels in large caliber; although scarcer than rifles do not usually fetch as much; worth approximately 25 percent less:

12-024 Values—Good **$950**   Fine **$2,750**

J.B Revol Breech-Loading Hammerless Percussion Rifle

12-025

Jean Baptiste Revol, New Orleans, Breech-Loading, Hammerless Percussion Sporting Rifle. Made circa 1850's. Quantity unknown; limited.

36 caliber; 21-inch octagon barrel, lengths and calibers will vary, with open-type rear sight and mounting post affixed to rear of barrel tang allowing for a removable peep sight. Long, narrow iron frame with circular handle ahead of trigger guard to open the pivoting breech block with nipple for percussion cap affixed. Large forward trigger cocks hammer; smaller single set rear trigger for firing. Browned barrel finish; case-hardened frame. Walnut stock; not provided or fitted with forend; iron mountings. J. B. REVOL/N.ORLEANS marked on left frame. Revol in business circa 1850-1880s; known to have made fine target rifles, shotguns and a few breech-loading rifles such as this. Scarce.

12-025 Values—Good **$1,250**   Fine **$3,250**

Chapter XIII

Lever Action and Other Repeating Rifles

Magazine repeating arms were developed as early as the 17th century. Several variations are known, almost all of fine quality, with most of European manufacture and in flintlock ignition. As all were basically impractical and many quite hazardous to use they were produced in extremely limited quantities and hence all are considered great collector's prizes. The introduction of fixed ammunition (i.e., self-contained metallic cartridge incorporating the bullet, powder and primer in one unit) presaged the possibility for a practical magazine repeating arm. This significant advancement has been generally credited to Walter Hunt of New York, with the patent and manufacture of his "Volition Repeater." Hunt's rifle is also regarded as the direct ancestor of the Winchester lever action. A complicated arrangement of two levers and a series of small and delicate parts, the novel weapon was destined to failure in terms of manufacturing feasibility and success. The rifle was adapted for the inventor's "Rocket Ball" patented loaded bullet, equally unfeasible commercially. Although there were a number of other preceding and simultaneous developments along both lines, the Hunt inventions are generally credited with a role of great significance in American arms history and are widely accepted in the collecting field as ancestors of the lever action repeater and the self-contained cartridge. The Hunt rifle and its direct line of descendants is best viewed in the section dealing with Winchester arms (Chapter V) in which progress and subsequent change is traced from the Hunt Repeater to the Jennings, the Smith & Wesson "Volcanics," the varied brass frame Volcanics, the Henry Rifle, and finally the host of famed Winchesters.

The 1850s through the 1870s spawned tremendous developments and experimentation in America and Europe with the devices and systems for mechanically (automatically) and manually breech-loading firearms of all types. While many never went beyond the drawing or prototype stage a number of patents were filed both here and abroad. A few books, notably the *Digest Of Patents Relating To Breech-Loading And Magazine Smallarms* (by V. D. Stockbridge, 1874) readily verify this fact.

In broad terms, the breech actions as they pertain to the repeating rifle take three basic forms: (a) lever actions, (b) bolt actions, and (c) revolving cylinders. Recoil operated semi-automatic operation and pump (or slide) actions followed later, descending from these three earlier forms.

The pump repeating mechanism (a.k.a. "trombone" or "slide" action), was developed as early as the mid 1850s in England, but not practically adapted or manufactured. A few subsequent pump repeaters were developed in the interim, none of them reaching beyond the experimental stage. The Christopher Spencer and Sylvester Roper patents of 1882 and 1885 are generally recognized as the first American application of pump actions. The John Browning patents of 1888 and 1890 were responsible for Winchester's first pump rifles and shotguns while the 1883 patents of W. H. Elliott (noted also for his association with Remington in the development of various deringers) and subsequent patents by Carl J. Ebbets were responsible for the development of Colt's popular line of pump action "Lightning" type rifles commencing in 1884.

The lever action rifle, defined in its simplest and most easily observed terms, identifies a firearm in which the lever (usually acting in the dual capacity of trigger guard) is manually activated to expose, close and lock the breech. In its normal application the lever is hinged at its forward end on the underside of the receiver and when opened and dropped downward, simultaneously exposes the breech; the lever when returned closes and locks the breech. As will be seen by an overall survey of patents and experimental types, the lever has taken many forms other than the above, but mainly performed the same functions. With the development of self-contained cartridges and the introduction of repeating mechanisms, the downward and then upward motions of the lever/trigger guard simultaneously ejected the spent cartridge in the chamber, cocked the hammer, loaded a full cartridge in its place, and locked the breech behind it. It is just these functions in their great many variations running from minute differences in manufacturing to often bizarre systems that make the study and collection of lever action and other repeating rifles intriguing.

The complete story of lever actions, pump actions and other repeaters has yet to be told in either its entire history from the 17th century to modern times, or solely in its American form. Either way it would be a fascinating one and worth the diligent efforts of an arms historian. Not a few collections are devoted entirely to lever action rifles, with the products of Winchester and Marlin predominating on a simple numerical basis. The field is one that offers considerable challenge for the collector and has sufficient historical—as well as eye—appeal to make it interesting for merely the casual viewer.

This section alphabetically lists most American made repeating arms of the 19th century, describing and detailing those considered to be quantity or mass produced. There are, of course, borderline cases, most notably the Robinson. Heavy use of cross-indexing appears throughout this section since many of the makers have been treated in their own individual sections in Chapter V. Also noted are exceptions such as those repeating arms considered "secondary martial longarms" (*see Chapter IX*) which were almost exclusively made in military styles and for which an occasional sporting model might have been made in an attempt to seek a commercial market which never materialized. The latter arms (most notable examples are Spencers) would certainly be considered scarce, and in many instances very rare. Although certainly worth in excess of their military counterparts, they have not always enjoyed the greatest market demand. Sporting values are normally higher than the military types, but when priced disproportionately they tend to suffer in salability and demand. Experimentals, prototypes and other one-of-a-kind lever actions and repeaters are infrequently encountered on the collectors' market and must be priced on their individual merit based on their quality, maker's name, unique principles, historical significance (if any) and, condition. The subject has been discussed throughout this work in general terms and at greater length in Chapter II.

The popularity of the lever action repeater has never waned; it continues to this very day to be one of the most widely used and popularly accepted mechanisms on the American arms market. A few 19th century arms are still currently manufactured in their almost identical original configurations and mechanisms (such as the Marlin Model 1893, the Winchester 1894, and the Savage 1899) attesting to both the reliability of the arms and the justifiable pride of their respective manufacturers. Other makers have entered the field in the 20th century and certainly these and other later developments have their significance and relative importance to the evolution of the type and are worthy of collectibility. But for our general purposes they are considered in the "modern" category and hence not within the scope of coverage of this work.

Ornate embellishments, select and fancy grained stocks, checkering and pistol grips and many variations of sights are also seen on most of the rifles listed in this section and premiums may be added to the values depending on the significance of the extra features and of course the overall condition of the arm itself. To avoid redundancy, the author refers the reader to those other sections throughout this work dealing with single shot and lever action rifles (notably Chapters V and XIV as well as Chapter II where the subject of values as assessed for extra features is discussed at length).

Condition plays an important determining role in demand and consequently values for most of the arms in this section. For the more commonly seen makes such as Bullard, Evans, Burgess and Savage in their most frequently observed models (i.e., sporting rifles) condition is an even greater determinant than with the very scarce, less frequently encountered makes (as the Robinson) or less frequently seen models (e.g., military muskets and carbines). With these latter types collectors often sacrifice condition to acquire a specimen and demand is quite strong for even the lower condition grades, being in direct proportion to rarity.

BIBLIOGRAPHY

With the exception of the volume listed below the subject lacks an overall definitive guide. The reader is referred to those sections in Chapter V pertaining to the individual makers, e.g., Winchester, Marlin, and Whitney. Other general material on the subject may be found in works listed elsewhere throughout this book, notably *Colt Burgess Magazine Rifle* by S. L. Maxwell, *Maine Made Guns* by D. Demeritt (major source for Evans rifles), *Spencer Repeating Firearms* by Roy Marcot, *The Rifle In America* by Philip B. Sharpe, *Identifying Old U.S. Muskets And Carbines* by Col. A. Gluckman, some slight references in *Single Shot Rifles* and *More Single Shot Rifles* by James Grant, general surveys of antique arms such as *Guns And Rifles Of The World* by Howard Blackmore, *One Hundred Great Guns* by Merrill Lindsay, *A History Of Firearms* by Major H. B. C. Pollard, *Bullard Arms* by G. S. Jamieson, "*Savage and Stevens Arms & History,*" by B. West and many original (or reprint) catalogues of American gun dealers and manufacturers of the late 19th century.

*Kimmel, Jay. *Savage and Stevens Arms Collector's History*. Portland, Oregon: Corey-Stevens Pub. Co., 1990. Reprints of important articles and original catalogs plus textual material by the author; much valuable information.

Maxwell, S. L. Sr., *Lever Action Magazine Rifles* Bellevue, Washington: Privately published by the author, 1976. Covers only those lever action rifles derived from the patents of Andrew Burgess including the 1872-75 Burgess, 1878 Burgess, Kennedy, 1881 Marlin, Colt-Burgess and 1886 Whitney. Pioneer work with a wealth of definitive detail.

(Author unknown.) *Savage Arms Company 1895-1945*. (monograph) Canton, Conn.: Arms Co. Press, c. 1995.

(*) Preceding a title indicates the book is currently in print.

Adirondack Firearms Company   *See O. M. Robinson.*

Blake Bolt Action Repeating Sporting Rifle

Blake Bolt Action Repeating Sporting Rifle. Made by J. H. Blake, New York, c. mid-1890s to 1910 approximately. Quantity unknown; limited. (Not illus.—see Number 9B-039 for military version; this model about identical with sporting type half stock.)

Blake catalog stated calibers made to order for each gun from wide choice offered. Unique seven-shot rotary magazine inserted from underneath.

First marketed in grades A (their best), B,C,D. After turn of century, grades changed to a very wide variety under such names as "Antelope Grade/Caribou Grade/Elk Grade ..." and "Deer, Moose, Grizzly, Tiger, Elephant Grades ..." and more! Judging by the few specimens to appear on the market and the little known about the company, their guns were individually custom-made only after receipt of an order. Their catalogs were error-filled and highly exaggerated:

13-000.5   Values—Very Good **$850**   Exc. **$2,000**

Bullard Lever Action Sporting Rifles

Bullard Repeating Arms Company, Springfield, Massachusetts, Lever Action Sporting Rifles. Made c. 1886 to 1890. Quantity estimated at 10,000 to 12,000.

Overall blued finish or casehardened frame with blued barrel. Walnut stocks.

Marked on left side of receiver: BULLARD REPEATING ARMS COMPANY/SPRINGFIELD, MASS. U.S.A. PAT. AUG. 16, 1881. Top of receiver marked with caliber.

James H. Bullard, a former employee of Smith & Wesson and one of their top mechanics, developed a lever action mechanism

13-002
"Large Frame"

13-003
*Military Musket
and close-up of action*

considered of exceptional quality and design, allowing for loading the magazine from the bottom and equally permitting loading for single shot firing while the magazine was full. The company was unable to survive stiff competition from Winchester and Marlin.

Deluxe models are occasionally seen in varying grades and will bring premium values.

Small Frame Model. Calibers 32-40 and 38-45. 26" octagon barrel. Full or half magazine; rifle or shotgun buttplate. Open sights standard (variety of options available):

13-001   Values—Very Good **$1,250**   Exc. **$3,500**

Large Frame Model. Calibers 40-75, 40-60, 45-70, and 45-85. Also available on special order in Express calibers 50-95 and 50-115 and will bring premiums. 28" octagon barrel; full or half magazine. Numerous options available in barrel shapes, sights:

13-002   Values—Very Good **$1,750**   Exc. **$5,500**

Military Musket. Caliber 45-70 only. 30" round barrel. Full stock. Provided with sliding cover device on right side of receiver serving as magazine cut-off. Encountered either with or without maker's markings but does have serial number and caliber markings. Rare:

13-003   Values—Very Good **$3,500**   Exc. **$6,000**

Carbine. 22" round barrel. Full magazine. Caliber 45-70 only. Similar sliding cover device on left side of receiver. Rare:

13-004   Values—Very Good **$3,750**   Exc. **$7,000**

Burgess Slide Action Rifles and Shotguns

13-005
12 Gauge Shotgun

13-006
Folding Gun

Burgess "Folding Gun."

-1897-

ESPECIALLY ADAPTED FOR
**POLICE SERVICE,
EXPRESS MESSENGERS,
U. S. MARSHALS,
PRISONS, BANKS, &c.**

LIST PRICE.

FOR SALE BY

Burgess Gun Company, Buffalo, New York, Slide Action Repeating Rifles and Shotguns. Made c. 1892 to 1899. Total quantity unknown; estimated at few thousand.

Unique action designed by the famed American inventor Andrew Burgess. Also notable for his lever action rifles made by Whitney and Colt (*q.v.*). Established himself in business 1892 for the manufacture of this unusual repeating longarm distinguished by its iron sleeve fitted over the wrist of the stock which activates the bolt and breech mechanism when slid rearward.

Blued finish. Marked on top of breech: BURGESS GUN CO./BUFFALO N.Y. U.S.A. Underside of frame with various patent dates. Damascus or steel barrels.

Although the firm made fine quality arms, it was short lived. Purchased in its entirety in 1899 by Winchester, who withdrew the line from the market and evidently made no further use of the Burgess patent. Manufacture was almost exclusively confined to 12 gauge shotguns with rifles quite rare. Values shown for plain, standard grades; deluxe fancy specimens will bring premiums.

12 Gauge Shotgun. 28" and 30" barrels. Tubular magazine:

13-005   Values—Very Good **$550**   Exc. **$1,400**

"Folding Gun." 12 gauge shotgun. 19-1/2" barrel. Hinged on underside of receiver with lift lever to open on top. Folds in half for concealment. Advertised in company literature as "...especially adapted for police service, express messengers, U.S. marshals, prison and bank guards." Company sold a unique "quick draw" waist holster to go with it:

13-006   Values—Very Good **$1,750**   Exc. **$4,500**

Rifles. Reported in calibers 30/30 and 45/70. Round barrels. The longer forend conceals the full length of the magazine tube. Very scarce:

13-007   Values—Very Good **$2,000**   Exc. **$4,500**

Burgess Lever Action Rifle   *See Chapter V: Whitney Firearms (V-J) or Colt Firearms (V-B).*

Colt Lever and Pump Action Rifles   *See Colt Firearms, Chapter V-B.*

Evans Lever Action Rifles

13-008
Old Model

13-013
Transition Model Carbine

13-016
New Model Military Musket

Evans Repeating Rifle Company, Mechanic Falls, Maine, Lever Action Repeating Rifles. Made c. 1873 to 1879. Total quantity estimated at approximately 12,200.

Caliber 44 Evans centerfire all models (1" shell on "Old Model" and "Transition Model" with longer 1-1/2" shell on "New Model").

Blued finish on barrel and frame standard. Walnut stocks. Nickeled buttplates and cocking levers occasionally seen and correct, but not worth premium.

Markings as noted below. "Old Model" and "Transition Model" serial numbered from 1 to approximately 2185. New Models are not serial numbered (the numbers that appear on them are assembly numbers and not serials).

The Evans was one of the more novel repeating rifles of the 19th century. It enjoys the distinction of being the only mass produced firearm ever attempted in the state of Maine and also holds the greatest capacity of any repeating rifle ever mass produced and marketed in the United States. The magazine was of a revolving type with the full complement of cartridges loaded through the butt. In place of the usual top hammer on most lever action rifles, the Evans hammer was mounted on the underside of the frame, just ahead of the breech lever and could also be manually cocked. Earliest specimens (extreme rarities with no examples known) held 38 rounds while the standard manufactured types had capacities of 34 and 28 rounds respectively.

As with other arms companies of their era, Evans made a practice of presenting for promotional purposes, special elaborately embellished models of their rifles to notables of the time. They included famous shooters, personalities and governmental officials instrumental in passing judgment on the acceptability of weapons for possible quantity contracts. Such

arms are rare and eagerly sought after; some are exemplary for their ornateness and superb quality reflecting the highest degrees of the engraver's art. Such rifles are one-of-a-kind and are evaluated similarly to those of other makes on the basis of their quality, elaborateness of workmanship, historical significance and, of course, condition. They have been recorded in all models of Evans with known examples presented to famous Westerners, Presidents of various Central and South American Republics and a number of Russian officers whom Evans was actively courting, seeking military contracts.

The best reference for information about Evans may be found in *Maine Made Guns And Their Makers* by Dwight B. Demeritt, Jr. (Maine State Museum, Hallowell, Maine, 1973).

Old Model. Made c. 1874 to 1876. Quantity estimated at approximately 500. Serial numbered 1 to approximately 500. 34-shot capacity. Fitted with upper buttstock only with the iron magazine entirely exposed on underside; buttplate has an inverted appearance with the heel on the underside. Flat top of frame; wooden forend fits into cut-out sides of forward section of frame. Earliest production made without the small lever retaining stud; later production (approximately serial numbers 100 to 500) with small locking stud. Exposed loading aperture on right frame without cover. Barrel marked EVANS REPEATING RIFLE/PAT.DEC 8, 1868 & SEPT 16, 1871.

Sporting Rifle. Estimated quantity made 300. 26", 28", and 30" octagon barrels:

13-008   Values—Very Good **$850**   Exc. **$2,250**

Military Musket. Estimated quantity less than 50. 30" barrel fitted for either socket type or saber bayonet. Full forend fastened by two barrel bands:

13-009   Values—Very Good **$2,500**   Exc. **$4,000**

Carbine. Estimated quantity made 150. 22" barrel. Short carbine forend with single barrel band and sling swivel:

13-010   Values—Very Good **$1,450**   Exc. **$2,750**

13-017
New Model Carbine

13-018
Evans Sporting Rifle

Transition Model. Made c. 1876 to 1877. Estimated quantity 1,650. 34-shot capacity. Serial numbers approximately 500 to 2185. Same frame shape and exposed loading port as above, but has addition of a lower butt piece with the magazine exposed in center. Thinner buttplate with no heel piece as above. Barrel marked: EVANS REPEATING RIFLE MECHANIC FALLS ME/PAT DEC 8, 1868 & Sep 16, 1871.

Sporting Rifle. Estimated quantity made 1,050. 26", 28", and 30" octagon barrels:
13-011   Values—Very Good **$850**   Exc. **$1,500**

Military Musket. Estimated quantity made 150. 30" round barrel; full forend fastened by two or three barrel bands:
13-012   Values—Very Good **$2,250**   Exc. **$3,500**

Carbine. Estimated quantity made 450. 22" barrel; short carbine forend fastened by single barrel band and sling swivel:
13-013   Values—Very Good **$1,000**   Exc. **$2,250**

"Montreal" Marked Carbine. A few specimens have been observed marked only EVANS REPEATING RIFLE - PAT JULY 24, 1873 - MONTREAL. These are believed made for and sold by Evans' Canadian representative Ralph H. Kilby. Estimated quantity 50 to 100:
13-014   Values—Very Good **$1,500**   Exc. **$3,250**

New Model. Made c. 1877 to 1879. Estimated quantity 10,000. 28-shot magazine capacity. Easily distinguished by its new frame shape; rounded at top and no cut-outs on side; the forend fits square to the front of the receiver; dust cover over the redesigned loading aperture on receiver. The hammer and cocking mechanism were redesigned and shaped; late production has slightly redesigned shape of lever with reverse curve at tip. Markings identical to the above Transition Model but are in one line with the addition at end of U.S.A.

Sporting Rifle. Estimated quantity 3,000. 26", 28", and 30" octagon barrels:
13-015   Values—Very Good **$775**   Exc. **$1,250**

Military Musket. Estimated quantity 3,000 plus (many converted to sporting rifles). 30" round barrel. Full forend fastened by two barrel bands:
13-016   Values—Very Good **$1,750**   Exc. **$3,000**

Carbine. Estimated quantity made 4,000 plus. 22" barrel; short carbine forend fastened by single barrel band with sling swivel. A few specimens found with stud for saber type bayonet at muzzle and are worth premium:
13-017   Values—Very Good **$850**   Exc. **$1,600**

"EVANS SPORTING RIFLE" marked specimens (in place of the usual Evans barrel markings). Believed assembled from parts on hand after the company entered bankruptcy. These markings are seen on 30" round barrel Evans military muskets with a short screw fastened sporting type forend in place of the usual full two-band fastened forend. The shape of the sporting forend is quite different than the usual Evans. These are believed assembled by E. G. Ridout & Company of New York or G. W. Turner & Ross of Boston, the firms that purchased the remaining stock of the Evans Company:
13-018   Values—Very Good **$700**   Exc. **$1,000**

Henry Lever Action Rifle   *See Winchester Firearms, Chapter V-K.*

Hunt Repeating Rifle   *See Winchester Firearms, Chapter V-K.*

Jennings Rifles   *See Winchester Firearms, Chapter V-K, and Chapter XII.*

Kennedy Lever Action Rifles   *See Whitney Firearms, Chapter V-J.*

Marlin Lever and Pump Action Rifles   *See Marlin Firearms Company, Chapter V-D.*

Morse Lever Action Rifle   *See Whitney Firearms, Chapter V-J.*

Remington Bolt Action Repeating Rifles   *See Remington Firearms, Chapter V-E.*

O.M. Robinson Tube Loading Rifles

Orvil M. Robinson Patent, Tube Loading Repeating Rifles. Manufactured by Adirondack Arms Company and A. S. Babbitt, both of Plattsburgh, New York. Made c. 1870 to 1874. Less than 600 estimated manufactured.

38 and 44 rimfire calibers. Varying length octagon barrels; 26" and 28" average; few also known with part octagon/part round barrels. Three-quarter length magazine tube on most; few with full magazine. Brass frames standard with iron frames occasionally seen and considered scarcer and worth premium. Blued barrels.

Two distinct types have been noted, but variances on all of them are quite evident, seemingly indicating their individual hand manufacture. Markings vary on most, but all apparently bear: O. M. ROBINSON PATENT and accompanied by markings of

13-019
Type I

13-020
Type II (frame variations)

either A. S. BABBITT PLATTSBURGH N.Y. or ADIRONDACK FIREARMS COMPANY PLATTSBURGH, N.Y.

Very little is known about the inventor or the manufacturers of this arm which has been variously described as a "Modified Bolt Action." It is believed that Babbitt was the manufacturer of all of them and that his name will appear on the earlier specimens made c. 1870 to 1872. It is also theorized that the later production (1872 to 1874) bears the Adirondack Firearms Company markings and that the company was a financial entity only, formed to market them. This latter firm was purchased in its entirety by Winchester in 1874 who apparently never utilized the patents nor marketed the guns.

Type I, a.k.a. Model 1870. Wing-like grippers for fingers at each side of the hammer for activating mechanism and cocking:
13-019   Values—Very Good **$2,500**   Exc. **$5,500**

Type II, a.k.a. Model 1872. Mechanism actuated by two small round button-like knobs at the top center of receiver which pull back bolt and cock. Various loading ports and apertures noted on receiver:
13-020   Values—Very Good **$2,500**   Exc. **$5,500**

Savage Model 1895 Lever Action Rifle

Savage Repeating Arms Company, Utica, New York, Model 1895 Lever Action Sporting Rifle. (Not illus.) Made c. 1895 to 1899. Total quantity estimated at 5,000. Manufactured by the Marlin Firearms Company of New Haven. Similar to Model 1899 (*q.v.*) but with distinctive fluted/scalloped sides of frame.

Caliber 303 Savage. 26" round or octagon barrel. Six-shot rotary magazine. Open sporting type sights. Hammerless type action; side ejection.

Blued finish. Walnut stocks. Serial numbered.

Barrel marking: SAVAGE REPEATING ARMS CO. UTICA, N.Y. U.S.A./PATENTED FEB. 7. 1893, JULY 25. 1893. Caliber markings also present.

The forerunner of the Model 1899, the inventor, A. W. Savage, initially attempted to produce this in a military version (in its prototype form) with subsequent production in sporting types for commercial sale. Specimens with part round/part octagonal barrels are worth premium. Major distinguishing feature from the Model 1899 is the presence of a 1/4" hole through the top of the bolt (approximately 3/4" from the front) through which the firing pin may be seen. When the bolt is cocked, the letter "C" appears on the firing pin when viewed through the hole; when fired, the letter "S" appears:
13-021   Values—Very Good **$800**   Exc. **$2,250**

Savage Model 1899 Lever Action Rifle

Savage Repeating Arms Company, Utica, New York, Model 1899 Lever Action Sporting Rifle. Made c. 1899 to date. Total quantity in the hundreds of thousands.

Made in a great many calibers, variations and styles. The Model 1899 was an improved version of the Model 1895, and was of such superior design and construction that it remains to this day a key part of the Savage line. A great many variations

Model 1899 Sporting Rifle, Early Model. 26" octagonal or part round/part octagonal barrels. Open type sights. Blued finish:
13-022   Values—Very Good **$600**   Exc. **$1,100**
Model 1899 Carbine. 20" round barrel with short forend fastened by single barrel band; carbine style buttplate and sights; saddle ring on left side of frame:
13-023   Values—Very Good **$850**   Exc. **$2,250**

13-024
Military Rifle

exist in this model. Generally they are considered as "modern" collectors' items and hence, are not covered in detail herein. The following few types are those that often are considered in the "antique" collectors' category:

Model 1899 Military Rifle. Calibers 303 and 30-30. 30" barrel with full forend fastened by two barrel bands. Bayonet lug on muzzle for angular or sword bayonet:
13-024   Values—Very Good **$2,250**   Exc. **$4,500**

Spencer Repeating Arms Company, Boston, Massachusetts, Lever Action Repeating Sporting Rifles
See Spencer Rifles and Carbines, Chapter IX-B American Military Longarms (Secondary).

Standard Arms Co. Gas & Slide Action Rifles

13-025

Standard Arms Co. (1909-1911) & Standard Arms. Mfg. Co. (1912-1914) Wilmington, Delaware gas operated and slide action, hammerless rifles. Quantity estimated as high as 12,000; likely less.

An intriguing appearing rifle with eye-appeal and little published information. Handsome, high relief decorated, wide brass grip covers the front slide, with matching brass buttplate. Achieved little commercial success. Two basic models as shown, offered in various qualities and custom features. Calibers 25-35; 30-30; 35 Rem. Barrels 22" (25" on earlier G/H models). After 1912, "CAMP MODEL" advertised for 50 cal. buckshot or round ball; rare; worth premium.

"MODEL G" gas operated **"AUTOMATIC RIFLE."** Early attempt to employ gas to operate a piston driven gun mechanism. Gas tube under barrel almost full length to muzzle has switch at gas port to allow for semiauto use or conventional, manual slide action (The "G" believed replacing, near identical, short-lived "Model H"):

13-025   Values—Very Good **$550**   Exc. **$875**

"MODEL M" (Not illus.) manual slide action. About identical; magazine tube ends midway:

13-026   Values—Very Good **$475**   Exc. **$750**

Stevens Lever and Pump Action Rifles
See Stevens Arms, Chapter V-H.

Volcanic Repeating Rifle & Carbines
See Winchester Firearms, Chapter V-K.

Whitney Lever Action Rifles
See Whitney Firearms, Chapter V-J.

Winchester Lever and Pump Action Rifles
See Winchester Firearms, Chapter V-K.

Chapter XIV

Single Shot Breech-Loading Cartridge Rifles

Single Shot collectors are a breed apart! The field is one of many nuances, several of which are irrelevant in other areas of antique gun collecting. Often the collector has a deep interest in cartridges and ballistics and may be extremely skilled as a shooter. Where the collector of specific makes, e.g., Colts, Winchesters, Sharps, Remingtons, etc., may seek specimens of different models and types (including single shots) and often sacrifices minor features to acquire a specimen, generally the Single Shot enthusiast is more demanding in his quest for exactness, completeness and frequently condition.

The terminology "Single Shot" as commonly used and accepted throughout the gun collecting world denotes a breech-loading one-shot rifle taking a metallic cartridge. Of course, in its very truest sense, the term applies to any type of one-shot rifle—but to gun collectors it means only that type described above. Most Single Shots were made in the era immediately following the Civil War and their development was simultaneous with that of the metallic self-contained cartridge, the general evolution being quite noticeable as distinctive and specialized types developed. A general rise in popularity of match target shooting combined with the founding and growth of the National Rifle Association (1871) was certainly responsible for the wide public following and equally wide manufacture of this highly stylized type. Very likely no other American firearm was made in as wide a range of styles and qualities as these Single Shots, and variations are seemingly endless. By the 1890s the era of the Single Shot waned. The Stevens Arms Company was apparently the only firm manufacturing examples in any quantity after that period and the rifle's final demise was signaled by the outbreak of hostilities in World War I.

The subject is sufficiently broad to be treated by several specialized works and even series of volumes (*see Bibliography*). Listings and descriptions herein are a cursory survey of the field setting forth basic models, styles and types of the popular, well known makers considered to have "mass produced" their rifles, although for some quantities were limited at best. Listings are alphabetically by manufacturer and considerable cross-indexing has been used. Descriptions are for the rifles in their basic styles, either as most often seen and available on the collectors' market, or exactly as listed in original manufacturers' catalogs or other literature. The values shown are for those basic types and styles. For most makes a great many options (i.e., extra features) were available, such details making for the infinite varieties possible. Each such optional feature must be assessed on individual merits and importance with values altered or premiums assigned proportionately. In many instances factory catalogs and other literature has itemized such options and are certainly the best collector's guide to follow (many of them have been reprinted in present day) lending the very best insight into what might be encountered on the collectors' market. Such features include a wide range of calibers, barrel lengths, weights, finishes, qualities of stocks, buttplates, sights, set triggers, telescopes and much more.

Numerous makers of lesser notoriety (and success) produced but a handful of rifles for which either insufficient information is available, or specimens are so infrequent as to be considered almost "experimental." Each of these rifles when encountered by the collector must be individually researched with values assigned on the basis of their relative importance, quality, condition and, of course, caliber. Although many such rifles and their makers would be considered rare, the guns themselves do not necessarily bring values commensurate with their rarity factor.

In broadest general terms, Single Shots consist of large, full size rifles chambered for a wide range of calibers from 22 rimfire to 50 caliber centerfire and are intended for both general sporting and target purposes. The latter styles were usually made in the premium grades of quality and consequently are found today in the premium ranges of values. Just where the fine point of "Single Shot" rifles leaves off and that of the "Boys' Rifles" begins is often a moot point. Size and weight are the determinants rather than caliber. Quite a few "border-line cases" are included in this section, such as the Wurffleins, Hopkins and Allen and small spur trigger Holdens, which are just as often found included in works about (and collections of) the so-called "Boys' Rifles." The author has chosen to list them herein as they have been seen to possess sufficiently collectible qualities, especially in the finer/higher grades, as to be often seen in a well rounded Single Shot collection.

An entire line of single shot rifles not covered in this work, but one which has increasing popularity with collectors in more recent years is that of "Boys' Rifles." Such arms are all of small bore, small size and weight, and for the most part, made to sell at inexpensive cost to the youth market of the latter 19th and early 20th Centuries. Of these too, variations are virtually endless. Such rifles have but recently come into their own, so to speak, and although a few are found within this section and other chapters (i.e., Stevens, Winchester, Remington), quite a few other makes such as Hamilton and Quackenbush have shown increasing demand in recent years. A whole host of names of makers and models are quite often seen and readily available; these are quite well discussed and described in the James Grant book, *Boys' Single Shot Rifles.* In broadest generalities, it would be an accurate observation that most of them in excellent condition but less than "factory new" are found on the collectors' market in the $200 to $500 price range. Those in "factory new" condition have a strong demand and desirability and values have risen for the most part to the $300 to $650 range, unless some exceptional features are found to place them in higher and premium grades. In the lesser grades of condition (N.R.A. "Fine" or below), prices and demand fall off drastically, averaging $75 to $150.

Another major segment of the Single Shot field that should not be overlooked and in which specimens will often be seen on the collectors' market is that of "customized" rifles. This category covers specimens having standard actions (e.g., Winchester high walls, Ballards and Stevens) which have been rerifled and/or rebarreled by private gunsmiths and often restocked as well. They may be generally grouped in two distinct categories: (a) Those made during the height of the popular shooting eras of the late 19th or early 20th centuries, and (b) modern made customized rifles utilizing antique actions. The latter is completely beyond the realm of this book, and specimens are considered as modern shooters' rifles possessing little, if any, value to the "antique" collector. Quite another matter, however are those earlier rifles customized during the height of the popular single shot era. Many are classified and considered on a par with factory made pieces and occasionally may even fetch higher prices. The best rule-of-thumb to judge by is the signature of the gunsmith who performed the alteration and, of course, the condition of the gun itself. In a few cases such as special work performed by Frank W. Freund (of Denver, Colorado and later Cheyenne, Wyoming Territory) on Sharps New Model 1874 rifles (*see Chapter V-F*) and by Harry W. Pope on Stevens, Ballard and other rifles, specimens so marked will often bring considerably in excess of the standard factory made piece. Many other noted makers and craftsmen, e.g., August and William Zischang, Axel W. Peterson, Carlos Gove, George Schoyen and various members of the Berg family of Iowa, are prominent in customized Single Shots; their products are quite actively sought and highly regarded.

Note, however, that the market for such rifles is still one created equally by shooters and collectors; hence, the major determinant is not merely the name of the gunsmith (except in cases like Freund or Pope), but rather condition, with the emphasis on bores. As the very reason for rerifling or rebarreling and hence, customizing, the rifle originally was not for cosmetic purposes, but rather to improve shooting qualities, it is essential that those qualities are still intact and in a fine state of preservation. Thus in order for the gun to have any demand on the collectors'/shooters' market bores, in particular, must be fine. These rifles must be priced on an individual basis, since the workmanship varies on each. It does take a familiarity with the market, the fine distinctions thereof in order to make proper evaluations. For the most part, it has been the author's experience that in order to sell such rifles for values commensurate with their individual importance, one must often go out of the normal antique collecting channels to find the highly esoteric collector/shooter group which quite often is a field apart and not always allied to pure collecting avenues.

As discussed in the "Introduction," there was a noticeable change since the mid-1980's of acceptable condition standards for collecting Single Shot Rifles. This field numbers among the first to be highly condition conscious. Where previously demand and value fell drastically for guns anything less than mint or near mint condition, recent years have quite reversed the trend.

Although those gem quality rifles are still eagerly sought after, almost all lesser quality and condition examples now find ready buyers and strong demand as long as they are priced accordingly. For the very top condition single shots, slight fluctuations in the amount of original blue finish can affect value considerably in the higher grades. Although percentages of blue (and casehardening) are the usual guidelines for evaluations, the actual condition of those finishes is a further point to be considered, i.e.: Is the remaining blue still bright and where missing has it merely flaked from storage or age, or has it become dulled and flat from use? Thus, pure percentage figures often tend to mislead and, to be truly accurate, a description must modify percentages. The subject is sufficiently complex that a further study of the guns themselves, at first hand, is highly recommended.

As noted briefly above, bore condition plays a highly important role in demand and values. Very much *de rigueur* is to closely examine the bore on all Single Shots before properly assessing values. Although chances are slim that any will ever be shot again, the collector rightfully feels that the value of the gun and its importance during its original era of manufacture and use was the very quality and shootability of that bore. He is equally desirous of retaining those same qualities in as close to their original condition as possible. For pure academic or nostalgic purposes he might choose (after purchase!) to fire a few rounds to test these qualities. The more a rifle was designed for use as an accurate competition sporting arm, the greater the feature of bore and condition is to value. On a fine conditioned piece or one of very high quality, a mediocre (or poor) bore, or one in lesser condition than the exterior of the gun, would decidedly detract from demand and hence, value. This is true on all types listed herein and is a general rule-of-thumb with most antique Single Shots. Exceptions may be made on those very rare or one-of-a-kind types in which often a specimen in any condition is considered a rarity.

Among some of the more important features affecting demand and values are calibers, barrel lengths, qualities of stocks, sights, etc. It is neither possible nor practical to list and evaluate each caliber of each model herein, and hence, average values are given for each style in all calibers. It should be recognized that where guns were made in numerous calibers (32-40 was probably the most popular and widely made) the more well-liked, shootable or currently available calibers will often bring premiums and are consequently in stronger collector demand. A simplified example of this is a rifle listed in four calibers, three of which are obscure while the fourth is 45-70, a caliber that has always been highly desirable among collectors of antique arms. Another example where premium values may be added is for a rifle commonly listed in multiple barrel lengths of 28", 30", and 32". In almost all cases it will be found that the longest, 32" length, is most desirable. When such features as long lengths or popular calibers are standard and the only ones listed, then of course the values shown herein reflect those specific features and premiums are not in order. The absence of a Vernier tang sight on a mid-range or long-range Creedmoor rifle, where it was standard equipment and so listed, is very much a detriment to value and demand.

Engraved or otherwise lavishly decorated Single Shots are highly sought after and are quite scarce in all makes (unless otherwise listed as standard). Designs and motifs are seen from the most simple scroll and floral decoration to extremely fancy, profusely engraved panels depicting sporting, animal or even target shooting scenes, with some approaching almost banknote quality in delicacy and minuteness of detail. Much of such ornamentation was executed by famous engravers of the era. Prices for such elaborate arms must be individually arrived at and assessed on the unique merits of the designs and quality of engraving (and, of course, their originality to the period of manufacture) as well as the rifle and its condition.

A few words or terms that the reader will often encounter in this field might be unfamiliar and have been deemed worthy of defining in order that the subject might be less perplexing. Very likely "Schuetzen" is that most commonly noted. A derivative from the German *schützen* meaning marksman, sharpshooter, rifleman (or even "member of a rifle club"), in its broadest and most accurate sense it merely means: Any off-hand (standing and without artificial support) shooting; as applied to American single shot target rifles, the name usually indicated a rifle intended solely for off-hand target shooting and of a weight generally too heavy, and a contour and configuration too clumsy, for hunting or normal sporting purposes. The so-called Single Shot Schuetzen rifle weights will average around 12 pounds with up to 16 pounds not unknown. Schuetzen stocks were often specially fitted to the shooter by whom they were ordered and they are also occasionally found provided with folding palm rests under the forends. Thus, the so-called Schuetzen grades by the various American makers were usually their most elaborate styles, with high combed stocks having large cheek rests, massive pronged Swiss type buttplates and (quite often) folding palm rests. The term Schuetzen Rifle as used on earlier percussion and European rifles generally has different connotations. In modern day terminology, the Schuetzen or off-hand rifle is called the "Free" or "International" rifle.

"Creedmoor" is another common term applicable to single shot rifles and quite often used synonymously for long-range target rifles. These very long barreled arms (usually 32" or 34") were designed to be shot prone and thus have a noticeably straight mounted stock with little drop and with flat or shotgun style buttplates. They were actually developed to conform to the rules of the National Rifle Association of the 1870s and were generally chambered for 40, 44, or 45 caliber with the latter two predominant, and are invariably found with two-position Vernier tang sights and spirit level, windgauge front sights. The terminology "Creedmoor" was in honor of their use as (and many actually designed for) the famed rifle matches held on the Creedmoor Range owned by the National Rifle Association on Long Island, New York (originally Creed's Farm). Specific rules were in force governing Creedmoor types, such as a complete prohibition of telescope sights, set triggers and prong type buttplates.

A third group of Single Shot rifles, rarely encountered in the breechloader, are those with extremely heavy barrels designed solely for bench rest shooting. As mentioned throughout the text in this chapter, and in other sections pertaining to Single Shots, those with very heavy barrels usually bring premium prices. Their use and popularity was much less wide spread than either the off-hand or long-range styles with the great majority of such heavy barreled American specimens being made in both percussion and flintlock types.

BIBLIOGRAPHY

(Note: Material on Single Shot rifles may be found in many other books covering American firearms appearing in complete bibliographic listings elsewhere in this book, notably in Chapter IV and Chapter V [the arms of specific makers such as Stevens, Winchester, Remington, Marlin, etc.]) plus *The Rifle 1885-1888* and *Shooting & Fishing 1886-1906. Ballard, the Great American Single Shot Rifle* by J.T. Dutcher; *10 Old Gun Catalogs* [and] *14 Old Gun Catalogs*, both compiled by L.D. Satterlee.

Carder, Charles E. *Falling Blocks And Other Single Shots From Hopkins & Allen*. Delphos, Ohio: Avril Publishing Co., 1995

*deHaas, Frank. *Single Shot Rifles and Actions* (John T. Amber, Editor). Ridgeway, Missouri: Mark deHaas, 1969. General broad coverage, with numerous exploded view illustrations.

deHaas, Frank. *Mr. Single Shot's Gunsmithing Idea Book*. Summit, Pennsylvania: Blue Ridge Books, 1983.

deHaas, F. & M. *Single Shot Actions…Their Design and Construction*. Orange City, Iowa: Frank deHaas; 1986.

Grant, James J. *Single Shot Rifles*. New York: William Morrow and Company, 1947. Reprinted by Gun Room Press, Highland Park, New Jersey, 1982.

Grant, James J. *More Single Shot Rifles*. New York: William Morrow and Company, 1959.

*Grant, James J. *Still More Single Shot Rifles*. Union City, Tennessee: Pioneer Press 1979. Companion to author's other volumes on same subject.

Grant, James J. *Single Shot Rifles Finale*. Prescott, Arizona: Wolfe Publishing Co., 1992.

Grant, James J. *Boys' Single Shot Rifles*. New York: William Morrow and Company, 1967. Not really an accurate title, for although it contains very detailed information on single shot rifles made for young boys, it also has a wealth of other data about the large caliber and full size single shots also.

James, Edsall. *The Golden Age Of Single Shot Rifles*. Nashville, Tennessee: Curley Printing Company, 1974. Small monograph; general and very cursory survey of the field.

Jamieson, G. S. *Bullard Arms*. Erin, Ontario: Boston Mills Press, 1988. Definitive, well illustrated and researched study of these fine lever action, single shot and repeating rifles.

*Kelver, Gerald O. *Schuetzen Rifles—History and Loadings*. Boulder, Colorado: Paddock Publishing Company, 1972.

*Kelver, Gerald O. *Major Ned H. Roberts and the Schuetzen Rifle*. Osceola, Indiana: Published by author, 1951.

*Kelver, Gerald O. *Reloading Tools, Sights & Telescopes for Single Shot Rifles*. Ft. Collins, Colorado: Robinson Press, 1982.

Kelver, Gerald O. *100 Years Of Shooters And Gun Makers Of Single Shot Rifles*. Fort Collins, Colorado: Robinson Press, Inc., 1975.

Kelver, Gerald O. (compiler) *Respectfully Yours—H.M. Pope. The Pope Story As Told From His Correspondence*. 1978.

*Layman, George J. *A Guide To The Maynard Breech-Loader*. Ayer, Mass: Neshoba Publications, 1993. Revised, enlarged 1998, Pioneer Press, Tenn.

*Leech, Arthur B. *Irish Riflemen In America*. London, England & New York: Van Nostrand, 1875. Wealth of important information on early Creedmoor matches, rifles used, trophies.

Perkins, Jim *American Boys Rifles 1890-1945*. Pittsburgh, Pennsylvania: RTP Publishers, 1976. Definitive work on the wide variety of these rifles. Opens a fertile and little exploited category for collectors.

Roberts, Ned and Waters, Ken. *The Breech Loading Single Shot Match Rifle*. New Jersey: Van Nostrand Company, Inc., 1967. Wealth of valuable data on the rifles and shooting them.

Satterlee, L. D. *A Catalog Of Firearms For The Collector*. Detroit, Michigan: privately printed for the author, 1927 and 1934. Alphabetical listing of makers with some data on their arms.

*Smith, Ray M. *The Story Of Pope's Barrels*. Harrisburg, Pennsylvania: The Stackpole Company, 1960. Definitive work on one of the most famed of American riflesmiths.

Sharpe, Philip B. *The Rifle In America*. New York: Funk & Wagnalls Company, 1947. Great deal of data on most American makes. Considerable amounts that have since been revised and updated by other works.

(*) Preceding a title indicates the book is currently in print.

NOTE: Sights are key features in valuing Single Shot rifles. Although always an important feature, by the 1990s even greater emphasis and value have been placed on tang, Vernier, Beach, spirit level types when specified as original accessories. (Prices for detached sights have risen considerably.) If missing, values of rifles should be lessened 20 to 30 percent and more, depending on the model.

Ballard Rifles   *See Marlin/Marlin-Ballard, Chapter V-D.*

Bay State Arms Co.   *See Hopkins & Allen Rifle.*

Brown Mfg. Co.   *See Marlin Ballard, Chapter V-D. Also see 9B-041 Brown Bolt Action Rifle.*

H.A. Buck Single Shot Rifle

14-000

H.A. Buck of West Stafford, Connecticut and Chicopee, Massachusetts, Single Shot Rifle. Made c. 1880s. Quantity unknown; very limited.

Mostly large caliber centerfire rifles (45-70 caliber known and desirable) with smaller action for 22 rimfire reported. Round or octagon barrels; lengths vary.

Lever actuated, rolling block type action. Frame markings H.A. BUCK/CHICOPEE, MASS.USA/PAT'D APR. 8,1879 or H.A. BUCK & CO/WEST STAFFORD, CT.USA, PAT'D APR 8, 1879
14-000   Values—Good **$1,100**   Fine **$2,250**

Bullard Single Shot Rifles

14-002

Bullard Repeating Arms Company, Springfield, Massachusetts, Single Shot Rifles. Made c. 1883 to 1890. Quantity unknown, but believe rather limited.

Standard finish: Casehardened or blued receivers with blued barrels. Top of receiver faceted (a few rounded receivers are known and considered very rare) and marked: BULLARD REPEATING ARMS COMPANY/SPRINGFIELD, MASS. USA PAT. JULY 6, 1886.

James H. Bullard had earlier distinguished himself as master mechanic for Smith & Wesson, and is best known for his lever action repeating rifles (*q.v.*). Bullard single shots are noted for the speed and smoothness of their operation. They are easily distinguished by their very thin receivers and several parts of their mechanism are interchangeable with the lever action rifles. They are also quite noted for excellent quality and workmanship.

Target Rifle. Basic calibers 32, 38, 45, and 50 (worth premium) centerfire with others known. Approximately 24" to 28" full octagon or part octagon/part round barrels. Vernier tang sight

and windgauge front sight standard. Select grain, checkered pistol grip stock and forend. Swiss type or rifle buttplate:
14-001   Values—Very Good **$2,000**   Exc. **$4,500**
Schuetzen Rifle. Available in a variety of calibers. 30" part round/part octagon barrel. Vernier tang peep sight and a variety of optional target type front sights. Select grain checkered walnut pistol grip stock with cheek piece; nickel plated Swiss buttplate; double set triggers:
14-002   Values—Very Good **$2,250**   Exc. **$5,000**
Target Gallery and Hunting Rifle. Lightweight model. Available in a variety of calibers and barrel lengths up to 28". Open sights. Pistol grip stock; rifle type buttplate:
14-003   Values—Very Good **$1,100**   Exc. **$3,500**
Identical to above, in 22 caliber rimfire; 26" barrel:
14-004   Values—Very Good **$1,000**   Exc. **$3,000**
Interchangeable Barrel Model. 32 and 38 caliber centerfire (will bring 10 to 20 percent premium) and 22 caliber rimfire. If accompanied by extra matching number barrel and forend, add approximately 50 percent premium:
14-005   Values—Very Good **$1,250**   Exc. **$3,500**
Military Rifle. 45-70 caliber. 32" barrel, full forend. Muzzle accepts a triangular bayonet; locking system differs from sporting and target models:
14-006   Values—Very Good **$3,000**   Exc. **$5,000**

Farrow Arms Co. Falling Block Rifle

Farrow Arms Company, Holyoke, Massachusetts and later Mason, Tennessee, Single Shot Falling Block Rifle. (Not illus.) Made c. 1885 to early 1900s. Total quantity unknown, but believe

very limited. A very distinctive short, falling block action with center hammer. Made in a variety of calibers. 28" to 36" octagon barrels (longest types will bring premiums). Either full octagon, full round or part octagon/part round. Tang peep sight; varied barrel sights.

Finish either full blued or nickel plated receiver and blued barrel. Pistol grip walnut stock with rifle buttplate.

W. Milton Farrow (1848-1934) was a renowned target shooter of his day and had earlier been associated with the Marlin Firearms Company. He was responsible for several improvements on the Marlin Ballards, among them the Model 6-1/2 Off-Hand buttplate which was named for him in Marlin

advertising. Farrow single shots are highly prized by collectors with specimens very scarce. Two basic grades were produced, but variations are not unusual in all of them.

No. 1 Model. Their best quality; deluxe fancy grained walnut stock; finely checkered and finished; Schuetzen buttplate standard:

14-007   Values—Very Good **$4,000**   Exc. **$10,000**

No. 2 Model. American black walnut stock, plain, uncheckered:

14-008   Values—Very Good **$3,750**   Exc. **$8,500**

Forehand & Wadsworth Drop Breech Rifle

Forehand and Wadsworth, Worcester, Massachusetts, Single Shot, Drop Breech Target Rifle. (Not illus.) Made c. 1871 to 1880s. Quantity estimated at a few thousand.

About identical to the "Drop Breech Rimfire Rifle" made by Allen and Wheelock (q.v., *Chapter V*) and merely a continuation

of manufacture of it by Forehand and Wadsworth with a few minor changes, most notably in the sight. Made in a variety of calibers from 22 rimfire (will usually bring a premium) through 44 rimfire:

14-009   Values—Good **$500**   Fine **$900**

Granville Henry Single Shot Rifles

14-009.5

14-009.5 Close-up "Henry" Breech-Loading Single-Shot Rifle

Granville Henry, Boulton, Pennsylvania Single Shot Rifles. Manufactured 1872 to 1896; quantity estimated at 1,000 or less. Sales apparently were made through the American Midwest and west predominately. Calibers 22 and 32 rimfire. 24-inch octagon barrel, other lengths likely. Breech of barrel is integral with the front part of the receiver and twists to the right to expose chamber for loading. Manual ejector rod enclosed on left side of the breech. Small thumb depressed lever at top of frame releases barrel for loading. Apparently majority of production were not marked "Henry" or company name.

This seemingly unnoteworthy, small-caliber, modest rifle may appear out of place in company with notable, mostly target type single shots in this chapter. It was deemed worthy of inclusion as it, along with a breech-loading shotgun in Chapter XVII, represent the last of a long line of American firearms

produced from the mid-18th century to the turn of the 20th century by any prominent Pennsylvania gunmaker. William Henry, the first of the dynasty, was a gunmaker of Lancaster, PA in the 1750s; other members continued and expanded that business over a long span of time. Most noted was John Joseph Henry, 1786-1836, whose many government contracts for flintlock pistols and muskets, percussion rifles made for the Indian trade, and Civil War military muskets, have all been eagerly sought by American collectors. Continuing to operate from the Boulton, PA factory in the post-war years under direction of Granville Henry, the company remained in operation until production ceased in 1895, with guns assembled from parts on hand until 1907. This rifle, and the shotgun, represent the last of that distinguished line of American firearms. The story is best told in *Henry of Boulton: A Pennsylvania Gunmaking Family and its Firearms* (see biblio. Chapter IV). Values shown are for unmarked Henry rifles. Marked specimens worth premium of 50 percent or greater.

14-009.5   Values—Very Good **$150**   Exc **$275**

C.B. Holden Open Frame Rifle

14-010

C. B. Holden, Worcester, Massachusetts, Single Shot Open Frame Rifle, a.k.a. Model 1862, as that was the year in which the patent was issued. Made c. 1862 to possibly early 1870s. Total quantity very limited, estimated at less than 200.

44 caliber rimfire. 28" octagon barrel. Open sporting type sights.

Bronze frame with unique action. Entire right side of receiver exposed with the oddly shaped hammer and breechblock having large circular finger apertures for cocking and loading; trigger guard assembly acts as locking device and is lowered to open breech.

Barrel markings: C. B. HOLDEN WORCESTER, MASS.

Holden was a former employee of Frank Wesson. Details of his manufacturing career are elusive, although it is known that he held a few patents for breech-loading rifles. This open frame so-called 1862 is one of the best known of his scarce, often obscure types. Others include the tip-up in the following description and a quite rare falling block, full side lock action Creedmoor rifle:

14-010   Values—Very Good **$750**   Exc. **$1,500**

C.B. Holden Tip-Up Rifle

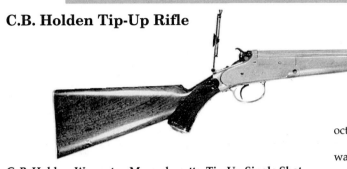

14-012

C. B. Holden, Worcester, Massachusetts, Tip-Up Single Shot Rifle. Made c. 1876 and possibly as late as 1890s. Total quantity estimated at a few hundred of small frame spur trigger type and very limited quantity of medium frame conventional trigger style.

22 caliber rimfire with larger calibers reported on medium frame style. Barrel lengths vary with 24" part round/part octagonal average. Tang peep and globe front sight.

Nickel plated frame and mountings; blued barrel. Select grain walnut stocks with checkered pistol grip; shotgun style buttplate.

Barrel marking: C. B. HOLDEN, MAKER, WORCESTER, MASS. Light decorative scroll engraving standard on frame.

Spur trigger, small frame style (most often seen). (Not illus.):
14-011   Values—Very Good **$950**   Exc. **$2,250**
Conventional trigger, medium frame style:
14-012   Values—Very Good **$950**   Exc. **$2,250**

C.B. Holden Long-Range Rifle

14-012.5

C. B. Holden, Worcester, Massachusetts, Under-Lever, Falling-Block Action Rifle (a.k.a. Holden Fifth Model Rifle). Made circa 1870s; quantity unknown; very limited; specimens rare. The identical action with varying length barrels, calibers and styles of stocks are known. This long-range model has been called a "Creedmoor Rifle" but no known use of it at those famous Long Island rifle matches. Caliber 45, 34-inch round barrel marked "C.B. HOLDEN, Mfr. WORCESTER, MASS."brass frame. Conventional type trigger guard. Checkered pistol grip and forend; long range target site affixed to heel of stock (with no provision for tang sight). Globe front sight.

Cyrus B. Holden, 1827-1906, popularly believed to have been employed by Frank Wesson in Worcester in the early 1870s. By 1877, he is listed in city directions as a "rifle manufacturer," which continued until 1904.

14-012.5   Values—Very Good **$2,000**   Exc **$3,250**

Hopkins & Allen Falling Block Rifles

14-015
"Solid Breech Rifle"

14-014
"Schuetzen Rifle"

Hopkins and Allen Manufacturing Company (1868 to 1898) and Hopkins and Allen Arms Company (1898 to early 1900s), Norwich, Connecticut, Lever Action, Falling Breechblock Single Shot Rifles. Quantity estimated at several thousands.

Usual finish: Casehardened frame; blued barrel. Walnut stock. Standard markings usually company name, address and patent dates.

Prolific makers over a long period of single shot rifles, shotguns, pistols, a great many of which do not fall within the realm of coverage of this book and many of lighter weight so-called "boys" types. A few of them are more eagerly sought after and are occasionally classified in the "single shot" collectors' categories.

Also made as shotgun. Values and demand low.

The predecessors of these falling blocks were made by the Bay State Arms Co. of Uxbridge, Massachusetts, c. mid-1880s. Their rifle was about identical to the Hopkins & Allen, but apparently of finer workmanship and quality. The company was acquired by H&A who continued to manufacture similar rifles on identical style actions. In top grades of condition Bay State Arms Co. specimens tend to bring slightly higher values. Some are found with "Merwin Hulbert & Co" markings; values about same.

Lever Action, Falling Block Rifle. Calibers 22 rimfire to 38-55. The larger calibers (worth premiums) usually encountered on heavier frames. 24", 26", and 28" octagon barrels. Made c. 1888 to 1892. Lever actuates breech. Rimfire calibers tend to bring 10 to 30 percent less. Occasionally found with extra shotgun barrel when sold as a set. *Only* if matching number to rifle worth premium of 25 percent or more.

14-013 Values—Very Good **$450** Exc. **$950**

Schuetzen Rifle. Action as above; often called a "Ladies Type" by collectors. Caliber 22 rimfire and 25-20. 26" octagon barrel. Select grain checkered walnut stocks with a "fish-belly"

appearance to the underside of butt; Swiss type buttplate; made with or without double set triggers:

14-014 Values—Very Good **$950** Exc. **$2,250**

Target and Sporting Rifles; Solid Breech Type. Calibers 22, 25 Stevens, 32 and 38 rimfire and 38 S&W centerfire. Barrel lengths from 18" (22 caliber) to 24". Largest calibers are worth small premiums to value:

14-015 Values—Very Good **$300** Exc. **$650**

Howard Single Shot Rifle   *See Whitney Arms, Chapter V-J.*

Lee Fire Arms Co. Single Shot Rifle

14-016

Lee Firearms Company, Milwaukee, Wisconsin, Breech-Loading Single Shot Rifle. Made c. 1865 to 1866. Total quantity estimated at approximately 1,000.

Calibers 38 and 44 rimfire. Full octagon barrels varying in length with 28" average; swivels sideways for loading. Sporting type open sights.

Iron frame. Overall finish blued and standard, although case-

hardened frames are reported. Walnut stock; made without forend.

Barrel marked on left side: LEE'S FIRE ARMS CO. MILWAUKEE, WIS./PAT[D] JULY 22[D] 1862. Serial numbers intermixed with the military carbines. (*See 9B-070.*)

One of the earliest patents and manufacturing enterprises of James P. Lee, a noted and highly respected American arms inventor, more well remembered for his bolt action and straight pull rifles manufactured by Remington and Winchester respectively:

14-016 Values—Good **$475** Fine **$900**

Marlin-Ballard Rifles   *See Marlin Firearms, Chapter V-D.*

Maynard Patent Single Shot Rifles

Maynard Patent Single Shot Rifles manufactured by the Massachusetts Arms Company of Chicopee Falls, Mass. Made c. 1860s to 1890. Production quantities unknown, but were apparently quite large. (**See history of Mass. Arms Co. chapter VII-A.**)

Maynard variations are virtually limitless. The wide range of original options available was myriad. For the collector, identification may be reasonably made by the basic guidelines established by the Massachusetts Arms Company in their original catalog listings of the 1870s to late 1880s and as used herein. Valuations are for basic models as shown; when found with optional accessories premiums may possibly be added, to varying degrees, depending on their importance and, of course, the overall condition of the rifle itself.

As with the two-trigger Wessons, these rifles have been relatively common on the collectors' market, attesting to their wide manufacture as well as their popular acceptance over a lengthy period. Their relative commonness (until recently) for many years on the collectors' market, the close similarity in appearance of most models, and their very simplicity (a key to their original popularity) left them relatively unappreciated.

As a generalization, their demand, and consequently values are created and established by: (a) condition; (b) model or type, with fancier grades, e.g., those with forends, checkered pistol grip stocks, etc., more eagerly sought after; (c) calibers, with 22 rimfire usually bringing a premium over values listed below and those in the more popular larger calibers, e.g., 45-70, etc., also worth premiums and in stronger demand.

Model 1865s usually seen only with casehardened frames and blued barrels, while Models 1873 and 1882 were found with

similar finishes and also overall blued or nickeled frame and blued barrels. Oil finished straight walnut stocks common to most types unless otherwise noted below. Only the Models 15 and 16 were standard with wooden forends. All other types not provided with same, however, this accessory was available as an option at a slight additional price.

Basic models were the Model 1865 (see listing below), the Model 1873 and Model 1882. These latter two styles were made and available in each of the below named rifles (e.g., the "Gallery Rifle No. 1" could be purchased in either the 1873 style or the 1882 style) with differentiating features as follows:

Model 1873: The first Maynard with standard chambering for centerfire metallic cartridges with a special accessory (Hadley's Patent device) simply added to the breech to convert for rimfire cartridges. Very similar appearance to the percussion model with a slightly offset hammer and the firing pin contained within the bolster on recoil shield (in place of a nipple). Most easily distinguished feature is the very wide gap between the breech of the barrel and the recoil shield in order to accept the very thick rimmed brass shell (most commonly known among collectors as the "thick head Maynard").

Model 1882: An improved version of the above; centrally mounted hammer with firing pin in the center of the recoil shield. Also easily distinguished by its very narrow, thin gap between the breech of barrel and recoil shield as it accepts the normal and much thinner rimmed (or head) cartridge.

Generally speaking, prices on the collectors' market have been about the same for the 1873 and the 1882 types with the latter worth a premium to highly advanced single shot or Maynard collectors in some of their more desirable or popular

14-019
Gallery and Small Game Rifle No. 2

14-031
Long-Range Creedmoor Rifle No. 14

calibers. Condition, especially in the lesser grade models, has very much played the dominant role in pricing Maynards.

A major feature of the 1873s and 1882s (especially the latter) was interchangeability of barrels (they were easily and readily available from the Massachusetts Arms Company). Quite a few specimens are found still accompanied by their extra barrels. An approximate increase in value of 25 percent to 35 percent would not be unreasonable for each matched number accompanying barrel. If numbers are mismatched, a 10 percent to 20 percent premium seems sufficient. Occasionally these barrels are offered separately on the collectors' market.

Engraved Maynards are quite rare. However, a few very fine specimens are known; valuations are based on quality of workmanship and overall condition. Not a few exceptional cased Maynard outfits are known containing numerous interchangeable spare barrels of varying calibers and accessories. Such outfits are worth substantial premiums and, of course, must be valued for their completeness, the quality of cases (some exceptional workmanship has been noted in Maynard casings) and condition.

Model 1865 Percussion Sporting Rifle. Although so mentioned in later Maynard catalogs as the "MODEL 1865," these rifles were first produced during 1863-65 simultaneous with wartime carbines. The post war manufacture (M. 1865) merely utilized incomplete or unfinished actions of military carbines, often with date "1865" marked on lower tang of buttstock. Varying barrel lengths. Calibers 35, 40, 50:
14-017   Values—Very Good **$600**   Exc. **$1,250**
(The following models all available in both 1873 and 1882 styles.)
Gallery Rifle No. 1. 22 rimfire only (the 1873 has the Hadley device attached). 20", 24", and 26" barrels; open sights:
14-018   Values—Very Good **$750**   Exc. **$1,750**
Gallery and Small Game Rifle No. 2. 22 rimfire only; 20", 24", and 26" barrels. Elevated, graduated tang peep sight; open type barrel sights:
14-019   Values—Very Good **$750**   Exc. **$1,750**
Improved Hunting and Target Rifle No. 3. 32 caliber centerfire (with Hadley attachment for rimfire on 1873 types). 24" and 26" barrels; open sights:
14-020   Values—Very Good **$750**   Exc. **$1,750**
Improved Hunting and Target Rifle No. 4. 32 caliber. 24" and 26" barrels. Elevating tang peep sight and open barrel sights:
14-021   Values—Very Good **$750**   Exc. **$1,750**
Improved Hunter's Rifle No. 5. 38 caliber. 26", 28", 30" barrels. Open sporting sights:
14-022   Values—Very Good **$650**   Exc. **$1,400**

Improved Sporting Rifle No. 6. Same as above, but with elevating tang peep sight and open barrel sights:
14-023   Values—Very Good **$750**   Exc. **$1,750**
Improved Hunter's Rifle No. 7. 35-30 Maynard caliber. 20" barrel; open hunting sights:
14-024   Values—Very Good **$650**   Exc. **$1,400**
Improved Hunter's Rifle No. 8. Identical to above, but with elevating tang peep sight and open barrel sights:
14-025   Values—Very Good **$750**   Exc. **$1,750**
Improved Hunting or Target Rifle No. 9. 35-30 or 40-40 Maynard caliber. 26" barrel. Elevating tang peep sight, open type rear barrel sight and Beach front sight:
14-026   Values—Very Good **$825**   Exc. **$1,850**
Improved Mid-Range Target and Hunting Rifle No. 10. Calibers 35-30, 45-40, 40-40, 40-60, and 40-70. 28", 30", and 32" barrels, the latter worth premium. Elevating tang peep sight, open rear barrel sight and Beach type front sight. Checkered or fancy wood stocks and sight options factory recommended (and worth premium):
14-027   Values—Very Good **$1,100**   Exc. **$3,250**
Improved Hunter's Rifle No. 11. Advertised as "… for large and dangerous game." Calibers 44-60, 44-70, 44-100, 45-70 (premium), 50-70, and 50-100. 26", 28", 30", and 32" barrels (the latter worth a premium). Elevating tang peep sight, open rear and Beach front sights:
14-028   Values—Very Good **$1,100**   Exc. **$3,500**
Improved Mid-Range Target Rifle No. 12. Calibers 40-60 and 40-70. 28", 30", and 32" barrels (the latter worth a premium). Elevating tang peep sight with open sporting and Beach front sights. Checkered straight stock standard:
14-029   Values—Very Good **$1,000**   Exc. **$3,250**
Improved Mid-Range Target Rifle No. 13. Similar to above, but with Vernier tang peep sight and spirit level windgauge front sight:
14-030   Values—Very Good **$1,600**   Exc. **$4,500**
Long-Range Creedmoor Rifle No. 14. Caliber 44-100; 32" barrel. Two position (tang and heel) Vernier tang peep sight and windgauge, spirit level front sight. Checkered pistol grip stock and deluxe wood standard:
14-031   Values—Very Good **$4,250**   Exc. **$9,500**
Improved Target Rifle No. 15. Calibers 22, 38-50, 40-60, and 40-70. 26", 28", 30", and 32" barrels (the latter worth a premium). Elevating tang peep sight and windgauge spirit level front sight; folding or open rear barrel sight. Checkered select grain straight walnut stock; nickel plated Swiss type (or rifle) buttplate. A plain or checkered forearm was available as a recommended option and worth a premium:
14-032   Values—Very Good **$1,500**   Exc. **$3,250**
Improved Target Rifle No. 16. Calibers 22 rimfire, 38-50, 40-60, 40-70. 26", 28", 30", and 32" barrels (the latter worth a premium).

14-032
Improved Target Rifle No. 15

14-033
Improved Target Rifle No. 16

Vernier tang peep sight; windgauge spirit level front sight, open rear barrel sight. Extra fancy grained checkered pistol grip stock and matching checkered forend. Swiss type buttplate

interchangeable with hunting style buttplate:
14-033   Values—Very Good **$2,250**   Exc. **$4,500**
Improved Breech-Loading Shotguns. Available 1873 or 1882 types. "No. 1" 55 caliber with 26" barrel; "No. 2" 64 caliber with 26" barrel; "No. 3 Sportsman's Favorite" 64 cal, 20 gauge (worth premium); 28", 30", 32" barrels:
14-034   Values—Very Good **$400**   Exc. **$750**

Merrimac Arms Co. Rifles   *See Marlin Ballard, Chapter V-D.*

Merwin Hulbert & Co.   *See Hopkins & Allen Rifles.*

Peabody and Peabody-Martini Rifles

Peabody and Peabody-Martini Rifles. Made by the Providence Tool Company, Providence, Rhode Island, c. 1860s to 1880s. Quantities unknown, but estimated at few thousand total all types sporting models.

Standard finish: Blued barrels with casehardened frames. Walnut stocks in varying grades as noted below.

Designed by Henry O. Peabody, Boston, Massachusetts, the rifle is seen in two basic types: (a) Outside hammer model, hinged breechblock; and (b) hammerless design (European in appearance), an improved design of the earlier side hammer developed by the Swiss inventor Friedrich von Martini.

Outside Hammer Peabody Sporting Rifles. Made c. 1866 to 1875 approximately. Calibers 44 rimfire, 45-70, 40-70 centerfire and others. 26" and 28" round barrels average, although known in heavier weights (and worth premiums). Varnished walnut straight type sporting stocks; forend affixed by screw on underside. Select wood grains and checkered stocks occasionally seen and worth premiums. Adjustable sporting type sights. Marked on frame: PEABODY'S PATENT, JULY 22, 1862/MAN'F'D BY PROVIDENCE TOOL CO., PROV. R.I.(*See also "Secondary U.S. Military Longarms" Chapter IX-B*):
14-035   Values—Very Good **$1,850**   Exc. **$4,500**

Peabody-Martini Sporting and Target Rifles. Made c. 1875 to 1880s. Various models; easily identified as model names are hand engraved in large, Gothic style letters almost entirely filling left side of frame. Hand inscribed in a similar Gothic style right side of frame: PEABODY & MARTINI PATENTS. Both sides of frame are also edged in a simple hand engraved scroll border. Barrels all bear markings in single line: MANUFACTURED BY THE PROVIDENCE TOOL CO. PROVIDENCE R.I. U.S.A.

Data accumulated from a study of serial numbers indicates that less than 1,000 Peabody-Martini sporters were made.

The name "What Cheer" quite often associated with Peabody-Martini rifles and ammunition was used to honor a famous rifle and target range of that same name located a few miles from Providence, Rhode Island.

The Peabody-Martini military rifle was also sold on the civilian market. See full details with No. 9B-082.4.

CREEDMOOR (inscribed on left frame in Gothic letters) long-range Creedmoor rifle. Caliber 44-100 (40-90 also made; scarce; worth premium). 32" part round/part octagon barrel. Two-position (tang and heel of butt) Vernier rear peep sight; interchangeable globe and bead front sight with windgauge

14-035
Outside Hammer Sporting Rifle

14-036
Peabody Creedmoor

14-039
What Cheer Mid-Range

and spirit level. Checkered pistol grip deluxe walnut wood stock; shotgun buttplate:
14-036   Values—Very Good **$4,250**   Exc. **$8,500**

WHAT CHEER (inscribed on left frame) long-range Creedmoor rifle. Identical to above, but with checkered straight grip stock:
14-037   Values—Very Good **$4,000**   Exc. **$7,500**

CREEDMOOR MID RANGE (inscribed on left frame) mid-range Creedmoor rifle. Calibers 40-70 and 40-90. 28" part round/part octagon barrel. Vernier tang peep sight; windgauge front sight. Checkered pistol grip stock; rifle type buttplate:
14-038   Values—Very Good **$4,000**   Exc. **$7,500**

WHAT CHEER MID-RANGE (inscribed on left frame) mid-range Creedmoor rifle. Identical to above, but with checkered straight grip stock:
14-039   Values—Very Good **$3,250**   Exc. **$6,500**

KILL DEER (inscribed on left frame) sporting rifle caliber 45-70. 28" or 30" part round/part octagon barrel. Interchangeable globe and peep sights. Plain, straight grip stock with shotgun buttplate:
14-040   Values—Very Good **$5,000**   Exc. **$9,000**

ROUGH AND READY (inscribed on left frame) sporting rifle caliber 45-70. 30" round barrel. The most elusive of all Peabody-Martinis. Specimens have been reported only, but not viewed. The gun itself was advertised in a few 1880 period gun catalogs and is believed to have been merely a plainer grade "Kill Deer" as above. No known sales on the collectors' market and to an advanced Peabody collector, it would be worth at least the value of the long-range Creedmoor, if not more:
14-041

Phoenix Rifles   *See Whitney Arms, Chapter V-J.*

Remington Single Shot Rifles   *See Remington Arms, Chapter V-E.*

Sharps Single Shot Rifles   *See Sharps Firearms, Chapter V-F.*

Stevens Single Shot Rifles   *See Stevens Arms, Chapter V-H.*

Frank Wesson Single Shot Rifles   *See Wesson Arms, Chapter V-I.*

Whitney Single Shot Rifles   *See Whitney Arms, Chapter V-J.*

Winchester Single Shot Rifles   *See Winchester Firearms, Chapter V-K.*

Wm. Wurfflein Tip-Up Rifles

William Wurfflein, Philadelphia, Pennsylvania, Single Shot Rifles with Tip-Up Action (various models). Made c. 1880s to 1890s. Quantities made unknown, estimated at a few thousand.

On highest grade "Mid-Range" models, Nos. 20, 22, and 25, standard finish was blued barrels and frames, with nickel plated buttplates. All lesser grades have nickel plated finish on frames and buttplates with blued barrels. Walnut stocks with straight or pistol grip as noted, in varying grades, depending on model.

Markings at breech of barrel: WM. WURFFLEIN/PHILADELPHIA/PAT. JUNE 24, 1884.

A famous family name in Philadelphia gun making, William Wurfflein, the son of Andrew Wurfflein, was known for his percussion deringers, double barrel shotguns and other muzzle-loading arms, was active c. 1874 to 1910 as the W. Wurfflein Gun Company. This single shot rifle has a very simple mechanism, with a small thumb lever located on the tang behind the hammer acting as breech latch. Although advertised in the Wurfflein catalogs in many models and grades, with numerous options available (including double set triggers, engraved and silver finishes), they were not believed too popular in their day

14-045

---

and specimens are reasonably scarce, especially in the finer, larger sizes. (The same tip-up action was used for a single shot target pistol; see 8A-194.) Examples are sought primarily on the basis of their condition with minor differentiating points not playing key roles in either collecting or evaluating them. They are listed in broad categories below by general type:

Sporting and Gallery Types. Various models. 22 and 32 rimfire and 32, 38, and 44 centerfire *(rimfire brings 10 to 20 percent less)*. Sporting type sights with Vernier tang sights worth premium. 24" and 28" octagon or octagon/round barrels.

Models Not Fitted For Forend Centerfire Calibers:
14-042   Values—Very Good **$500**   Exc. **$1,100**

Models With Straight Stock and Forend:
14-043   Values—Very Good **$550**   Exc. **$1,250**

Models With Checkered Pistol Grip Stock and Checkered Forend:
14-044   Values—Very Good **$950**   Exc. **$2,000**

Mid-Range Types: Calibers 22-15, 32-35, 32-40, 38-55, and 40-70 (the latter will bring slight premium). 28" and 30" part octagon/part round barrels.

Models With Checkered Pistol Grip Stock and Forend, Tang Peep Sight and Open Type Barrel Sights, Rifle or Shotgun Style Butt. (Swiss buttplate worth premium):
14-045   Values—Very Good **$1,250**   Exc. **$3,500**

Special Mid-Range Model No. 25. The top of the Wurfflein single shot line. Vernier rear peep sight; select grain pistol grip stock and forend with horn pistol grip cap and forend tip, otherwise same as above:
14-046   Values—Very Good **$1,750**   Exc. **$4,000**

Shotgun. 12, 16 and 20 gauge. Pistol grip stock. Very plain:
14-047   Values—Very Good **$300**   Fine **$500**

Advertisements from an 1886 sporting periodical for single-shot rifles.

Chapter XV

Revolving Rifles

One of the more fascinating fields of American arms collecting is that of revolving rifles. The attraction of this specialized group is mainly in the very wide variety of arms made as well as their often intriguing appearances and unusual configurations. Revolving rifles hold a special appeal for the collector and non-collector alike.

Offering a broad potential to the arms student and literally begging for a definitive guide, the field is rich in lore with a number of often over-romanticized legends surrounding some types, not a few of which have little basis in fact. Some of these "old wives' tales" have been set straight here. A great deal remains to be known about these guns and it is often this very feature that offers the greatest challenge to the collector and stands as one of the strongest reasons for choosing this specialty.

Revolving rifles have played an interesting and at times significant role in the development of firearms. The search for multi-shot weapons began early in arms history; revolving specimens date to the matchlock era of the 16th century. The first nearly practical American revolving arm was that invented and patented by Artemus Wheeler of Boston in 1818, but it is quite conceivable that other American revolving arms were individually handmade or experimented with prior to that date.

Enlightenment about the background of revolving shoulder arms, the reasons for their development, and their practicality offer an insight to the field. The facts, though sometimes quite obvious, have often been overlooked by collectors and thus certain basic features of their significance have been missed.

In the constant innovative quest for improved firepower, which led to the development and evolution of multi-shot weapons, the revolving arms (i.e., those adapted with a multi-shot cylinder for a revolving breech) were a marked improvement over the multi-barreled types in one significant and salient area—weight. This feature had greater importance when applied to longarms than handguns, where the necessity for lighter weight was not as important. The earlier development and longer, more widespread use of the pepperbox or many-barreled revolving handguns bear witness to that fact. A review of the history of revolving arms, including those only (or most often) seen in handgun form will evidence that the original designs and patents were often for revolving shoulder arms. A prime example is the Colt revolver, for which the initial patent issued to Samuel Colt featured a revolving rifle. It is also significant that Colt's first production (as well as his last) at his Paterson, New Jersey plant was of revolving shoulder arms.

There are two major schools of thought regarding the relative scarcity of revolving arms and/or their impact (or lack of it) in the general development of firearms in the early and mid-19th century, especially in America. The position most often heard may have as its only strength the fact that it has appeared in print on several occasions and has become implanted, by virtue of repetition, as traditional "gospel." This view acknowledges that the principle of the revolving breech/cylinder had greater importance and direct application in rifle form spawning numerous attempts and innovations over three centuries, but that its practicality was doomed to failure as applied to rifles, whereas the same principle survived and prospered on the handgun. It attributes the revolving rifle's demise to the major defect of gas escape when the gun was fired (a result of the gap or spacing between the cylinder and the barrel). Although the gas escape occurred with both shoulder arms and handguns, on the former it was held highly objectionable and oftentimes dangerous, whereas on the handgun it was assumed to be of little or no significance.

It is a further contention of the established school of thought that upon discharge of a firearm (especially the black powder muzzle-loading types), there is a considerable flash of fire between chamber and barrel breech, and that on the larger shoulder arms of heavier calibers taking proportionately greater powder loads, the flash and pressure caused by the discharge (increased by the longer barrel lengths also) often caused a severe flash in proximity to the shooter's face. Continuing this train of thought such was not the case with a smaller load handgun, which was fired at a longer distance from the head. Another feature deemed detrimental, and certainly a greater liability on the shoulder arm, was the unfortunate occurrence that could be caused by an extenuated flash which occasionally set off a chain reaction, igniting the other chambers of the cylinder and resulting in an almost simultaneous discharge. This danger was more obvious—and certainly more disconcerting—on the rifle than the handgun, as one of the shooter's hands was supporting the forearm just forward of the cylinder. Note that Samuel Colt in his published instructions for the correct manner of using his revolving rifle urged the shooter to support the piece with the hand ahead of the trigger guard and behind the cylinder in the event that any of the chambers fired accidentally.

Although the foregoing theories are logical and certainly credible, it would appear that considerable gray areas are left unexplained. Examination and dissection of the subject clearly indicates there is a lot more to note than has been commonly accepted and presented by arms literature for the past half-century and more. If the truth of the matter is not entirely as outlined in the following, it at least lies somewhere in between and should subject to question (if not fully dispelling) the over-simplified explanation presented above.

The more clearly thought out approach to this subject (presented here for the first time) has every reason to refute the foregoing as based on erroneous assumptions that have been parroted for the last 50 years or more, apparently based on earlier statements from firearms auction catalogs in the era of 1910 to the 1930s, the major source of antique arms sales in that period. Very little of credible or reliable arms literature was available in those years and catalogers of the era quite often embellished their descriptions (just as is done today!) to increase the desirability of their merchandise. It seems that revolving rifles fell prey to just such statements which in an evolutionary manner have become part and parcel of American gun literature.

The more plausible and certainly well grounded theories hold that American revolving rifles were successful in relation to the period in which they were introduced and made; that their demise was caused neither by their gas escape problem nor their greater danger in event of multiple explosion, but solely by the introduction and popularity of the lever action repeating rifle which rendered them obsolescent. The major obstacles that befronted revolving rifles and will account for their smaller quantities of manufacture were likely the nature of the times during which they were introduced, their higher production costs and consequently prices for public consumption, and the general lethargy and stubbornness of the military in accepting and adopting innovations.

It is quite significant to remember that even Samuel Colt failed in attempting to manufacture revolving arms at his first try at Paterson, New Jersey. His handguns suffered the same lack of acceptability and sales as did his longarms; and as earlier mentioned, he had even devoted greater energies to the longarms, both commencing and ending his venture with their manufacture. The 1839 model carbine was the only successful Colt Paterson and even after the factory's closing, John Ehlers of New York completed and sold the parts of every available carbine.

As far as gas escape was concerned, there were a number of practical methods which solved the problem reasonably well, such as those used by Wheeler, Daniels, and Nichols & Childs in their tight seal of the chamber by forward motion of the cylinder and chamfering at the joint. Even Colt's use of an affixed loading lever which tightly sealed the bullet into the chamber has been attributed as resulting in commercial success of his shoulder arm in the 1850s. One of the chief features of the 1855 model Colt solid frame Hartford revolving rifle was the adjustment of the rear bearing of the receiver that permitted tightening of the cylinder against the barrel breech to cut down leakage after considerable wear and corrosion. It would thus seem that the attendant hazards of the revolving rifle have been very much over-emphasized.

Another significant factor quite often overlooked is the general era of development of most revolving rifles *vs.* handguns. A majority of these appeared in the great era of revolving arms innovations of the 1830s through the early 1850s simultaneous with the same experimentation (and same very low production figures) of revolving handguns. The patents held by Colt made all revolver production (handguns or rifles) highly restrictive. It would quite clearly seem that the major difficulty was in arranging financing to manufacture any of the more well-designed types as well as the general public's acceptability of them due to their higher prices—and not their danger in use. The fact that the Colt factory turned out approximately 20,000 revolving longarms in the 1850s is reasonable verification of this.

Another factor to be considered is the short length of time between the expiration of Colt's patent protection and the introduction of lever action repeating rifles with which revolving percussion arms had to compete on the open market; very short indeed—considerably less than ten years. Worth investigating further is the fact that one of his two major competitors in the 1849 era was Warner of Springfield,

Massachusetts, whose total revolving rifle production, though small by comparison to Colt, must have been well received judging by the heavy use which almost all known specimens seem to have experienced (*q.v.*).

The Ordnance Department of the U.S. Army in that pre-Civil War era was notorious for its stubborn resistance toward adopting more modern—and proven superior—firearms. It is an often-told story and one that held far reaching consequences in those as well as later years. The single shot muzzle-loading musket was then secure in its dominant position, with the possibility of supplanting it virtually impossible.

Thus, the arms student should look with considerably greater kindness and reverence on the importance of revolving longarms and realize that their relative rarity was due more to their innovation and high cost rather than any attendant dangers—and they were far more successful for their era of manufacture than has been commonly believed.

The revolving rifles and shotguns (and their major variations) illustrated, described and evaluated in this chapter are those which are generally considered to have achieved some degree of "mass production." They represent examples by known makers who produced specimens resembling one another quite closely and which may be encountered on the collectors' market. Although quantities are extremely limited of many types, these arms on the whole will conform stylistically to those illustrated and described. The reader should bear in mind that a great many other variations may possibly be seen and that contradictions in data will occur. Such variances should be considered on their own merits, using good common sense and clear judgment when assessing values and rarity factors. This field of collecting is one in which many unusual, unique and even bizarre arms, most of them one-of-a-kind, may be seen. Rarity-wise such guns may be rated in the highest category; value-wise, though, it may be a horse of a different color. The subject has been covered in general terms in Chapter II as well as in the prefatory text of several other chapters throughout this book. The best rule-of-thumb is to assess unique pieces on the basis of their quality of workmanship, condition, markings, period of manufacture, uniqueness of mechanical operation and any historical significance (in that general order) after first establishing their genuineness.

Many prominent, qualified and highly skilled gunsmiths as well as back-woods country gun makers (or even blacksmiths) tried their hand at making revolving rifles. They seemed to do so at a far greater degree than with handguns, which adds further credence to our discussion earlier in this text as to the significance of the revolving principle on rifles *vs.* handguns. A tremendous variety of interesting, and often ingenious, revolving methods were adopted to shoulder arms. There is an entire category often termed "Kentucky-type" because of the propensity of the makers to use tiger striped/curly maple wood for the stocks. In actuality the term "Kentucky" is not aptly applied, for the guns were more likely of New England manufacture (where curly maple was a commonly used wood also) than of Pennsylvania "Kentucky" manufacture.

A few other features such as elaborate embellishments (i.e., engraving or stock inlays) may occasionally be seen on revolving rifles. If determined to be original, values should be increased proportionate to the quality of ornateness or elaborateness of the work and, of course, any historical significance that might be attached to it. Such features are quite rare, but do not necessarily increase values in direct proportion to their rarity. As with all collectors' arms, variations (from calibers and barrel lengths to mechanical innovations) will affect values and advanced collectors ardently seek them. Bizarre lengths or remarkable calibers (either for extremely small size or over-sizes) decidedly affect values, especially if the overall proportions and configurations of the guns on which they appear are correspondingly altered.

The field of revolving rifle collecting is noticeably less condition-conscious than most other American arms specialties. The usually low production figures of various makers and their relative scarcity on the collectors' market, combined with a certain erudition on the part of collectors who fancy these types, has placed emphasis (and consequently values) on their rarity factor with condition decidedly taking a back seat. Many of these types may be considered in great demand and eagerly sought after in almost any degree of condition. The foregoing, however, should certainly be modified and tempered by the fact that condition still plays a role in determining value.

BIBLIOGRAPHY

(Note: There is a decided lack of published definitive information about American revolving rifles. Some material about them may be found in several books having general coverage of American firearms and appearing in complete bibliographic listings elsewhere in this book. Most notable and valuable for the collector is *American Percussion Revolvers* by Frank Sellers and Samuel Smith. Others are *The Collecting Of Guns* edited by James E. Serven, *Spencer Repeating Firearms* by R. Marcot (best details on Ropers) and the numerous works covering Colt Firearms [the revolving rifles of this maker only have been adequately and completely covered].)

James, Edsall. *The Revolver Rifles*. Nashville, Tenn. Pioneer Press, 1974. Short monograph well illustrated on general history of revolving rifles.

(Author unknown.) *The J. C. Lowe Collection Of Cylinder Guns.* Issue No. 35 (February, 1951) *The Gun Collector* Magazine, Published Whitewater, Wisconsin. For many years a major source of reference on revolving longarms of all types. The entire issue devoted to a study of those in the collection of J. Churchill Lowe of St. Louis.

(*) Preceding a title indicates the book is currently in print.

Allen & Wheelock Revolving Lip Fire and Percussion Rifles and Carbines
See E. Allen Arms, Chapter V-A.

Bennett & Haviland Many Chambered Revolving Rifle

15-000

15-000

Epenetus A. Bennett and Frederick P. Haviland, Waterville, Maine, Many Chambered Revolving Rifle. Made c. 1838-40. U.S. Patent No. 603, Feb. 15, 1838. Quantity unknown; likely less than ten.

Twelve-shot. 40 caliber. 29" octagon barrel (dimensions, caliber likely will vary on all specimens).

Rectangular brass chambers horizontally mounted in linked belt fashion. Manually revolved by rotating disc at rear of chambers. Locking latch for chambers on topstrap. Marking of well-known gunsmith N. KENDALL, WINDSOR, VT. observed on barrel of one specimen with BENNETT'S PATENT on frame. Markings likely will vary on each. Very rare. Unique system:

15-000   Values—Good **$9,500**   Fine **$20,000**

Billinghurst Revolving Pill Lock Rifles   *See J. & J. Miller*

Cochran Underhammer Revolving Turret Rifle

John W. Cochran, New York City, Underhammer Revolving Turret Rifle. Made by C. B. Allen, Springfield, Massachusetts c. mid-late 1830s. Total quantity estimated at slightly over 200.

36 and 40 caliber horizontally mounted turret or radial cylinder. First and Second Types nine-shot; Third Type seven-shot. Manually revolved. Single action; underhammer. Octagon barrels of varying length; 31" to 32" average.

Finish: Frames and turrets casehardened; barrels blued or browned. Walnut stock.

Topstrap over turret marked on forward section: COCHRAN'S/MANY/CHAMBERD/ & /NON RECOIL/RIFLE Marked on rear of topstrap: C. B. ALLEN/SPRINGFIELD/MASS, and often, but not always, accompanied by an eagle motif.

Serial numbered from 1 to slightly over 200. Key to understanding variations of these arms as well as spotting occasional skullduggery with serial numbers, is the sequence in which patents were granted. The initial patent claim filed by Cochran was followed closely by a claim for an improvement. Surprisingly, the improvement patent (which was the hinged top plate) was granted first (Patent No. 183) on April 29, 1837, while the original patent claim followed after as Patent No. 188, and granted on the same date. The Second Type bearing very low serial numbers would therefore be quite inconsistent.

(a) First Type: Topstrap completely circular in center with short vertical projection of narrow width at either end and bolted securely down over the turret by two screws; turret is not easily removable for loading. The underhammer is gracefully curved and entirely encircles the trigger acting in a dual capacity as trigger guard. Estimated quantity made approximately 30; serial numbers in the range of 1 to 30:
15-001   Values—Good **$5,000**   Fine **$12,500**

15-001
First Type

15-002
Second Type

15-003
Third Type

its open trigger without encircling trigger guard. The lower profile arched hammer is mounted ahead of the trigger as on the Cochran pistol (*q.v.*). Quantity estimated made approximately 50. Serial number range approximately 155 to slightly over 200:

15-003   Values—Good **$4,500**   Fine **$10,000**

(d) Carbine: Action identical to Third Type described above, but with 27" full round barrel. Markings on top strap over turret identical to those described for the rifle but with the last line changed to read NON RECOIL/CARBINE:

15-004   Values—Good **$5,000**   Fine **$11,000**

Revolving turret rifles utilizing this same invention and marked on the barrel COCHRANS PATENT have been encountered. Usually such specimens have eight-shot turrets and a long monkey-tail lever extending from the topstrap (used to lift it up) along the back of the stock almost to the comb. Maker unknown, believed from Poughkeepsie, New York, same general era c. 1830s. Although undoubtedly more rare than the C. B. Allen made specimen, quality not as fine and they tend to be valued in the same price range.

(b) Second Type: Similar in appearance to above, but the topstrap is long and rectangular in shape and of even width for entire length and hinged on forward section; the rear retaining latch also acts as open type rear sight. Turret easily removed for loading. Quantity estimated made approx. 125. Serial numbers generally in the range of 30 to 155:

15-002   Values—Good **$4,500**   Fine **$10,000**

(c) Third Type: Generally similar to above with hinged top plate; smaller seven-shot turret and quickly distinguished by

Collier Revolving Flintlocks

15-005

Elisha H. Collier, Boston, Massachusetts and London, England, Revolving Flintlock Shoulder Arms. Made c. 1818 to early 1820s in London, England. Estimated quantity approximately 150.

A great many variations have been noted in these rare and highly desirable arms that were made in carbine, rifle and shotgun sizes. Although they generally conform in overall appearance and configuration, dimensions will vary from piece to piece. The most often encountered type (as illustrated) has a five-shot fluted cylinder (earliest types apparently had straight cylinders) and tops of frame, topstrap and locks as well as hammers display fine quality profuse engraved scroll, floral, military trophy motifs. The more standardized form has a round barrel with a relief fluted rib extending along lower section of barrel and acting also as topstrap over the manually revolved cylinder; automatically primed flashpan with very large, thick frizzen acting as reservoir for the priming powder.

Although the original English patent filed by Collier illustrated and described a spring mechanism for automatic rotation of the cylinder when the hammer was cocked, such features were evidently abandoned very early, for all known specimens are manually revolved. A key feature of the Collier is the very tight gas seal between the cylinder and the breech of the barrel. The cylinder is held tight over a protruding lip at the barrel breech by a piston wedge that forces the cylinder forward and must be manually withdrawn prior to revolving. The Collier

patent for the self priming pan did not follow the system of Wheeler, but rather follows that developed by Wilson of the Minories, London c. 1811.

Usual finish: Barrel and cylinder browned, lock and topstrap casehardened; furniture blued.

Usual markings (many variances noted): E. H. COLLIER LONDON on rib; E. H. COLLIER/(serial number) PATENT on lock; E. H. COLLIER/PATENT on side of frizzen.

Five-shot cylinder standard, although other sizes (seven-shot notably) known and recorded.

The inclusion of the Collier in this chapter is arbitrary. The arm is strictly foreign made, displaying fine quality workmanship typical of British makers of the era. However, the gun has a distinct and direct American association that gives it an optional choice for inclusion in an American collection. Although exact circumstances are not known (and the story that Collier could not get American financial backing for his invention and had to go abroad to manufacture the arm does not bear up under critical scrutiny), it has been thoroughly established that Collier worked with or for Artemus Wheeler (*q.v.*) in helping to manufacture or perfect the latter's revolving flintlock in Boston. Using the Wheeler principle, Collier went abroad, patented it in England, while Wheeler apparently gave up interest in manufacturing and marketing the gun in America. Collier's gun achieved considerable success (it was also made in pistol and pistol-carbine sizes) and may also lay claim to being the first revolving rifle produced and sold in substantial quantities.

Specimens are also known in both percussion conversions (and worth proportionately less) and in original percussion. The latter, although far more rare than original flintlock, normally do not bring as much. The entire Collier story is yet to be told. Important data about them may be found in *English Guns And Rifles* by J. N. George (Small-Arms Technical Publishing Company, Plantersville, South Carolina, 1947 and more recent reprint editions):

15-005   Values—Good **$12,500**   Fine **$35,000**

Colt Revolving Percussion Rifles and Shotguns   *See Colt Firearms, Chapter V-B.*

Daniels Underhammer Percussion Turret Rifle

15-006

Henry and Charles Daniels of Chester, Connecticut, Underhammer Percussion Turret Rifle. Made by C. B. Allen, Springfield, Massachusetts c. late 1830s. Patent No. 610, February 15, 1838 and Patent No. 677, April 3, 1838. Quantity made unknown, estimated at less than 50. Rare.

Calibers and dimensions vary; average approximately 40 caliber with 34" octagon barrel. Eight-shot horizontal turret or radial cylinder of octagon shape. Manually revolved. Turret removed for loading by raising the hinged topstrap (as on the Second and Third Type Cochran) with the latch also acting as rear sight. Unique protruding lip at each chamber which locks into breech of barrel to form a tight gas seal; actuated by lever mounted beneath breech on left side of frame that moves turret forward to effect gas seal.

Finish: Frame and turret casehardened; barrels blued or browned.

Marked on forward section of topstrap: H & C DANIELS/ PATENT/CHESTER, CONN. Marked at rear of topstrap: C. B. ALLEN/SPRINGFIELD/MASS. accompanied with an eagle motif.

Walnut stock and forend; German silver furniture.

It is quite apparent that C. B. Allen made this shortly after his manufacture of the Third Type Cochran (*q.v.*). Note the similarities in design with the hammer mounted ahead of trigger:

15-006   Values—Good **$7,000**   Fine **$12,500**

Hall 15-Shot Percussion Revolving Rifle

15-007

Alexander Hall of New York City, New York, 15-Shot Percussion Revolving Rifle. Made c. mid-1850s. Quantity unknown. Very rare.

Calibers and dimensions will undoubtedly vary; specimen viewed was 38 caliber.

Bronze frame; concealed hammer; large cocking lever/spur located inside the very wide trigger guard just ahead of trigger.

Massive 15-chambered cylinder suspended from frame by a hinge.

Marked in script on cylinder *HALL'S/REPEATING RIFLE/PATENTED JUNE 10/1856.*

Value estimated only with no known recorded recent sales:

15-007   Values—Good **$9,500**   Fine **$20,000**

Jaquith Revolving Underhammer Rifle

15-008

Elijah Jaquith of Brattleboro, Vermont, Revolving Percussion Underhammer Rifle. Made c. late 1830s; manufacturer unknown, but believed same as for Nichols and Childs (*q.v.*). Patent No. 832 of July 12, 1838. Quantity made unknown; extremely limited, estimated at approximately 25.

Calibers and dimensions vary; approximately 36 to 40. Barrels 30" to 34" part round/part octagon. Seven- and eight-shot.

The unique feature of these distinctive appearing arms is the hollow cylinder with sighting through the axis or the center of the cylinder. The cylinder itself is mounted above the barrel discharging from its bottom chambers. The deep star shaped revolving and locking cuts on the rear of the cylinder were utilized in the Jaquith pistol made by Springfield Arms Company to avoid infringement on the Colt's Patent at later date.

Finish: Frame and cylinder casehardened; barrel browned.

Barrel markings: E. JAQUITH BRATTLEBORO. V^T. (with small design of hand and pointing finger) and PATENT.

Loading lever for cylinder is mounted on the right side of barrel identical to the type found on some Nichols and Childs' revolvers. No provision made for trigger guard.

Walnut stock with distinctive Gothic style brass patchbox identical in contour and size to that used on the Nichols and Childs' revolving rifles (*q.v.*):

15-008   Values—Good **$7,500**   Fine **$17,500**

LeMat Percussion Revolving Carbine   *See Chapter X, Confederate Firearms.*

J. & J. Miller Revolving Pill Lock Rifles

15-009
Billinghurst Type

15-009
Billinghurst Type

15-010
Double Barreled
Rifle-Shotgun

J.&J. Miller of Rochester, New York, Revolving Rifles. Most commonly called Billinghurst rifles as he was the most prolific and well known maker of them. Made c. 1835 to 1850. Total quantity made unknown; total of all makers estimated at a few hundred. Quite a few gunsmiths made revolving rifles under the Miller Patent. Known at this writing are:

Benjamin Bigelow of Marysville, California. Estimated as the second most often encountered maker. He worked for Billinghurst in New York and later moved to California where he produced revolving arms. His revolving rifles bring a premium due to their association with early California and the gold mining era.

William Billinghurst of Rochester, New York. The most often encountered.

George A. Brown of Dansville, New York.

C. E. Bunge of Geneva, New York.

T. P. Cherington, Jr. of Catawissa, Pennsylvania.

Antrobres Edwards of Rochester, New York.

E. S. Ormsby. Address unknown.

H. V. Perry of Fredonia, New York.

A. S. Sizer. Address unknown.

Patrick Smith of Buffalo, New York.

W. H. Smith of Rochester, New York, and New York City. He worked for Billinghurst for many years and his name often appears on the underside of barrels of Billinghurst marked guns and later made some of these for himself. Workmanship usually fine quality.

Elijah Snell of Auburn, New York.

A. W. Spies of New York City.

H. Volpious of Cincinnati, Ohio.

There is considerable variety in the work of these various makers, but they all generally follow the pattern set forth by the Miller and Billinghurst arms, and all apparently have at least one feature in common—the distinctive front latch on the cylinder. They may be found in varying calibers and barrel lengths as well as all styles of barrels, i.e., octagon, round or part octagon/part round. Seven-shot cylinder usual with specimens recorded from four shots to nine shots.

All are of pill lock ignition; the very tiny pills containing the fulminate are retained in small receptacles in the cylinder by use of beeswax. Patchboxes when present on some specimens were intended for holding a supply of beeswax (and often it will be found still present). Although these arms are often found with percussion nipples on the cylinder, it is believed that all were converted at later dates due to the lack of pills or as use of percussion caps became more common.

Stocks are usually walnut. Finish either blued or browned with casehardened frame or a combination of finishes.

Information on the brothers James and John Miller is incomplete. James was granted a patent in June, 1829, (prior to issuance of patent numbers) for "… An improvement in rifles, muskets and fowling pieces, etc., … the magazine (cylinder) to contain a number of charges." Thought lost in Patent Office fire of 1829, the only surviving copy of the Miller Patent has only recently come to light. Patent protection was granted for their system of revolving the cylinder and the cylinder stop-lock below the barrel breech into the periphery of the cylinder.

This was one of the earliest revolving arms patented in the United States, but lacked the important feature of automatic cocking and locking of the cylinder which was later claimed by Colt in his first U.S. revolver patent of 1836. Quality is the key factor for pricing these Miller Patent style revolving arms—and not just rarity of maker. Specimens are known marked J. & J. MILLER/ROCHESTER on barrel as well as lockplate, and are scarcer and normally bring premium values over the most often encountered style marked W. BILLINGHURST, ROCHESTER, NEW YORK on top of barrel. Lesser quality pieces will bring proportionately less than those values indicated here and, of course, finer quality or fancier specimens will bring premiums:

15-009 Values—Good **$3,250** Fine **$6,500**

Other variants are known such as double barreled (over/under) rifle- shotgun (*see illustration*) and considered quite rare. Probably less than 25 were made of such types. The upper barrel is rifled and used with the revolving cylinder. The lower barrel is smoothbore/shotgun and just single shot; fired by the underhammer:

15-010 Values—Good **$6,000** Fine **$17,500**

Morris & Brown Conical Repeating Rifle

15-011

W. H. Morris and C. L. Brown, Conical Repeating Rifle. Believed made New York City, c. early 1860s. Patent No. 26,919 of January 24, 1860. Quantity made unknown, estimated at approximately 50 or slightly more.

Although not a revolving rifle, it has usually been classed in that category by collectors and also considered a distinct firearms oddity.

44 caliber rimfire. 23-1/2" round tapered barrel. Six-shot with all six chambers in the breech funneled into the single barrel. Concealed revolving firing pin in frame is rotated and cocked by the ring lever behind trigger; no provision made for trigger guard. Heavy all bronze frame.

Marked in Old English style letters on right side of frame: MORRIS & BROWN'S/PATENT.and in script *JANUARY 24th 1860.* Marked on left side of frame: CONICAL REPEATER

Maple (often bird's eye maple) stock; brass buttplate:

15-011 Values—Good **$7,500** Fine **$17,500**

Nichols & Childs Percussion Revolving Rifle

15-012
Gothic Patchbox

15-012
Lacy Patchbox with Loading Lever and Internal Mechanism

Rufus Nichols and Edward Childs of Conway, Massachusetts, Inventors of Six-Shot Percussion Revolving Rifle. Made c. late 1830s. Manufacturer unknown. Total quantity estimated at approx. 100 to 150. U.S. Patent No. 707 of April 24, 1838. Rare.

Calibers and dimensions vary; 36 to 40 caliber approximately average on specimens viewed. Average barrel lengths 26" to 30"; either part octagon/part round or all round barrels. Also seen in so-called carbine lengths of 22". Six-shot cylinder most often recorded, but also made in 5-, 7-, and 9-shot.

Finish: Frame and cylinder casehardened; barrel browned.

Cylinder automatically rotated by outside ratchet mechanism when hammer is cocked; later models known with internal mechanisms; considered very rare and worth premium.

A lever affixed to left side of frame locks cylinder and must be released prior to cocking. Variations have been noted in contours of barrel and other parts. A few specimens (usually those with the internal rotating mechanism) are found with hinged loading lever mounted below barrel (a rare feature and worth premium in value).

No provision for use of a forestock is made on this arm; the barrel must be removed to disassemble the cylinder from the frame (a major weakness), therefore dispensing with the forestock.

Two styles of patchboxes were used: (a) Fancy lacy edged pierced brass patchbox and (b) German silver patchbox of a Gothic style and identical to that used on the Jaquith Revolving Rifle (*q.v.*). The use of this distinctive, latter described patchbox on both arms plus other features strongly suggests that one maker, yet unknown, produced both arms:

15-012 Values—Good **$6,000** Fine **$15,000**

North & Skinner Revolving Rifle

H. S. North and C. D. Skinner of Middletown, Connecticut, Percussion Revolving Rifle. Made by H. S. North and Edward

Savage of Middletown, c. 1856 to 1859. Total quantity estimated at about 600. Patent No. 8,982 of June 1, 1852 by North & Skinner.

15-013

Barrel marked: NORTH & SAVAGE/MIDDLETOWN CONN along top; PATENTED JUNE 1 1852 and CAST STEEL along sides. Additional markings also encountered THE WORLD'S REVOLVER

Also made in shotgun size of approximately 60 caliber with average 27" part octagonal/part round barrel, slightly longer frame and a full shield in front of cylinder. In place of the loading lever of the rifle there is a shotgun tamping rod/loading tool mounted below the barrel. Although fewer made, values either the same as rifle or slightly less as demand is not quite as strong:

Average caliber 44, but could vary. Six-shot cylinder revolved, locked into position and hammer cocked by a downward motion of combination trigger guard and cocking lever. Round or part round/part octagonal barrels varying lengths; 23-1/2" average. Finish blued. Walnut stock.

15-013   Values—Good **$3,500**   Fine **$7,500**

P.W. Porter Revolving Turret Rifles

15-014
Early Model with Cannister Magazine

15-015
First Model

Parry W. Porter of Memphis, Tennessee and New York City, Revolving Turret Rifles. Made c. 1850s. All (except for earliest model with cannister magazine) made by G. P. Foster of Taunton, Massachusetts. Total quantity estimated about 1,250. U.S. Patent No. 8,210 of July 18, 1851.

Calibers and dimensions as below. The vertically mounted radial cylinder or turret is rotated and locked by movement of the under-lever which simultaneously cocks hammer.

Markings on the barrels of all New York era types: ADDRESS/ P. W. PORTER/NEW YORKand P. W. PORTER'S/PATENT 1851

An intriguing, though fictitious, legend has grown around Porter and his turret rifles stating that the inventor was killed while giving a demonstration of his arm to Colonel Samuel Colt, implying that but a few were made. Research has proven this story untrue and it seems likely that it was fabricated in the pre-World War II era to give color to an arms auction catalog! The wonderment is that so many specimens were produced since the arm had the same basic failing as the Cochran—at least one chamber aiming in the direction of the shooter at all times. **Early Porter With Cannister Magazine.** Believed made in Tennessee prior to Porter's move to New York to seek financial assistance for mass production. Quantity unknown; estimated at approximately 25. Very rare. It is a matter of record that this type was given government trials at the Washington, D. C. arsenal in February of 1853.

Automatic loading and priming; with a distinctive large round German silver cannister magazine mounted above the turret holding balls (on ramp around outer periphery), black powder (in mid section of cannister) and fulminate (in the tube mounted over center). 30 shots are held in the magazine; that

combined with the 8 loaded chambers gave the shooter a total of 38 shots providing all worked according to principle. Caliber average approximately 40; octagon barrels of varying lengths. All known specimens quite fancy with engraved symbolistic designs on the frame as well as the magazines and plaques inlaid in stocks (motifs such as clasped hands, sheaves of wheat, Masonic eye, town views and even an engraving of the capitol building at Washington, D.C.).

Most of those known specimens are without the magazine intact. Thus, prices reflected are for specimens without the cannister magazine. A premium of approximately 50 percent may be added to the price if complete with original magazine:

15-014   Values—Good **$9,500**   Fine **$27,500**

New York Types (Made by Foster in Massachusetts). Total quantity made estimated about 1,225 for all three models.

In debunking another arms collecting myth, it should be specifically noted that the First and Second Model Porters *are not pill lock ignition as invariably described,* but rather, are all percussion ignition, accepting the standard type percussion caps of the era and not pills. Caps are spring forced into alignment with the hammer as the gun is used. When the hammer struck, the cap was smashed flat against the outer wall of the turret (over the tiny flash hole which is often confused as a receptacle for pills) and the residue of the exploded cap fell clear through the slot provided underneath the magazine.

In the First and Second Models occasionally nipples may be found screwed into the frame (with magazines often removed or partly missing). Such alterations are usually performed by parties unfamiliar with the Porter system; thereby making it

15-016
Second Model

15-017
Third Model

necessary to manually cap for each shot. Such alterations will detract from value and desirability.

First Model. Nine-shot turret. Approximately 44 caliber. Octagon barrels average length 26" to 28". Approximately 300 estimated manufactured. Serial numbered 1 through approximately 300. Finish: Blued barrel with casehardened frame and turret. Straight shaped, mule-ear side hammer. Offset front and rear sights. Serpentine shaped loading lever mounted on top of barrel at breech. Quickly recognized by its square shaped magazine cover with rounded front edge; swivels downward for loading with long locking latch underneath.

Originally provided with a "U" shaped iron cover which fitted over the top of the turret, but invariably missing. Prices reflect those without cover. A premium of approximately 10 percent to 15 percent may be added if the removable turret cover intact.

Considerable evidence exists to suggest that when originally sold, the rifle was accompanied by an extra matching numbered cylinder and if same is still intact, a premium of approximately 15 percent to 20 percent may be added.

This model was also made in carbine size with a 22" to 24" round barrel. Original specimens will bring approximately 25 percent premium:

15-015   Values—Good **$5,000**   Fine **$12,500**

Second Model. Very similar to above. Easily distinguished by its circular magazine with screw-off cover; the hammer must be cocked in order to remove the cover.

Nine-shot; straight mule-ear side hammer; serpentine loading lever at breech of barrel. Finish as above. Quantity made estimated at about 350 to 400. Serial numbers from approximately 300 to 679 or more.

This model was also supplied with the turret cover, but is usually found missing and prices reflect those without cover. A premium of approximately 10 percent to 15 percent may be added if the removable turret cover intact.

Also made in carbine length with round barrel of 22" to 24". Original specimens worth a premium of approximately 25 percent. Sights also are offset to the left:

15-016   Values—Good **$5,000**   Fine **$12,500**

Third Model. Quickly distinguished by the absence of a magazine and percussion nipples visibly mounted on the exterior of the turret. Eight-shot, manually capped and loaded. No provision made for loading lever or for turret cover. The side hammer is offset or bent/angular type. Finish and markings as above. Offset sights.

Quantity made estimated at approximately 550. Serial numbered approximately 680 to 1225:

15-017   Values—Good **$4,500**   Fine **$11,000**

Remington Percussion Revolving Rifle   *See Remington Firearms, Chapter V-E.*

Roper Revolving Rifles and Shotguns

15-018
Shotgun

Sylvester H. Roper of Amherst, Massachusetts, Revolving Rifles and Shotguns. Basic Patent No. 53881 of April 10, 1866. First production at Amherst, Massachusetts 1867 to 1868 by the Roper Repeating Rifle Company with later production at Hartford, Connecticut 1869 to 1876 by the Roper Sporting Arms Company. Serial number ranges separate for each location, each starting with No. 1.

Basic principle of these arms was the use of a reloadable steel cartridge (or auxiliary chamber) which formed a tight gas seal. Insertion and removal was performed from either a cylinder or a web carrier depending on the model. Insertion was either complete or partial depending on the model. Two types of steel reloadable cartridges were used. The earliest was primed with a percussion cap over a nipple at the rear being supplanted by one with a recessed cavity at its rear in which a primer was pressed. Shotguns featured a variable choke threaded on the muzzle of the barrel.

Markings on the hinged door/loading gate at top of the cylinder housing: ROPER REPEATING RIFLE CO/AMHERST, MASS./PATENTED APRIL 10. 1866 or ROPER SPORTING ARMS CO./HARTFORD, CONN./PAT. APR. 10, 1866. JULY 14, 1866

Considerable variations have been noted on the Ropers. Until a definitive treatise is written and data on estimated quantities of variants are known, prices will not be seen to fluctuate greatly for variations other than those noted.

Shotguns. All have four-shot carriers (consisting of a series of fins) enclosed within a large rounded housing with hinged

15-019
Rifle

15-020
Baby Model

15-021
Cloverleaf Cylinder

loading gate at top. Encountered with both Amherst and Hartford markings; values are about the same for either. 12 and 16 gauge, the latter believed made in smaller quantities and might bring a small premium. Barrels vary approximately 24" to 28" with the variable choke threaded at muzzle. Barrels blued; housing and frame casehardened; pewter forend tip. Walnut stock with shotgun butt. Made without rear sight; top of frame grooved for sighting:

15-018   Values—Very Good **$2,250**   Exc. **$4,500**
Rifles. Six-shot carriers also enclosed within large rounded housing as on shotguns above. 41 caliber. Round or octagon barrels varying in length; 26" to 28" average. Finish as above. Found with both styles of markings; values about the same for either.

Walnut stocks with either crescent style (rifle) or shotgun style buttplates; the latter presumed originally made and sold with interchangeable shotgun and rifle barrels as a combination outfit. If both barrels present and matching numbers, premiums may be added. Rifles have standard rear barrel sight as well as the sighting groove along top of frame:

15-019   Values—Very Good **$5,000**   Exc. **$9,500**
32 Caliber "Baby Model" (so-called) Rifle. Six-shot. 21-1/2" round barrel. Rear sight mortised on frame. Massive hammer spur with large circular piercing. Miniaturized version of the

rifle and shotgun, but in diminutive size. Estimated quantity made 10. All specimens known unmarked. Believed made only at Amherst, Massachusetts:

15-020   Values—Good **$7,500**   Fine **$15,000**
Cloverleaf Cylinder Shotgun. Four-shot exposed cylinder made without the enclosed housing. Quantity made estimated at less than 25. Round barrels average 26" to 30". Most specimens unmarked and unnumbered (one known marked specimen bears Amherst address).

Manufactured in two distinct types: (a) Solid frame; cylinder manually removed for loading by sliding center-pin forward, and (b) hinged frame; lifting topstrap allows barrel to tip downward for removal of cylinder.

The rear cocking trigger pulls back and withdraws the spent cartridge from its tight gas seal at the breech while simultaneously revolving the cylinder. Upon firing, the hammer drives the steel cartridge chamber into a recessed ring (approximately 1/4" deep) at the breech of the barrel to form tight gas seal. Cartridge does not enter full length as in previous models.

Note the high comb stock which is also seen on some late production Amherst marked standard shotguns.

Some of these were made as a combination rifle/shotgun and were quickly altered by merely inserting a specially designed rifle barrel inside the shotgun barrel and locking it at the muzzle with the variable choke threads. Such barrels were also accompanied by matching interchangeable cylinders. When such accessories are intact, a premium of at least 25 percent may be added to value:

15-021   Values—Good **$6,000**   Fine **$12,500**

Smith & Wesson Revolving Rifle Caliber 320 Centerfire   *See Smith & Wesson Firearms, Chapter V-G.*

Springfield Arms Company Revolving Percussion Rifle   *See James Warner.*

Stanton Percussion Turret Rifle

15-022

S. F. Stanton, New York City, Revolving Percussion Turret Rifle with Suspended Hinged Chambers. Made c. late 1850s. Patent No. 14780 of April 29, 1856. Estimated quantity less than 50.

Six-shot. Caliber 50. 23-1/2" octagon barrel. Unmarked. Finish casehardened frame and chambers; browned barrel.

Unique lever action cams chambers into firing position. Each chamber has nipple at rear. For loading the entire turret with chambers is removed. Opening the lever cams the chamber into line with cylinder; when lever closed, it slides a gas seal around the face of the chamber. The mechanical functioning of this uniquely designed arm is exceptionally speedy.

Walnut stock with iron furniture:

15-022   Values—Good **$10,000**   Fine **$20,000**

Storm Revolving "Fire Gun"

15-022.5

William Mont Storm Revolving Percussion Fire Extinguisher Gun. Invented by Storm; maker unknown; c. 1855. Extremely rare; quantity unknown.

A unique firearm intended to fire a special cartridge in form of a paper wrapped cake of nitrate of soda, sulfur and charcoal into a fire, the combustible mix igniting, thereby generating a gas to extinguish fire!

Overall 37". Massive 17-1/2" brass barrel widely flared at the muzzle. 3" bore. Brass frame and lever; 8-chambered cylinder.

Very large, fancy engraved barrel markings BALLISTA FIRE GUN/WM. MT. STORM PATENTEE/OCT. 9, 1855

Walnut stock; all brass mountings. Large rectangular patchbox and smaller circular patchbox for caps:

15-022.5   Values—Good **$7,000**   Fine **$11,000**

Warner Open Frame Revolving Carbines

15-023
Retractable Cylinder Type

15-024
Grooved Cylinder Type

15-025
Automatic Revolving Type

James Warner, Springfield, Massachusetts, Open Frame Percussion Revolving Carbines. Made c. 1849 to early 1850s. Warner built these arms in expectation of the expiration of Colt's Patent. Colt, however, received a patent extension and Warner had to modify these arms in order to avoid suit for patent infringement. The deep grooves cut on the rear of the outside wall of the cylinder (between the nipple recesses) were one of the means chosen by Warner; another system abandoned the Warner method entirely, substituting manual rotation.

The earliest of this open frame style were most likely made by James Warner at Springfield while latter adaptations of it (as below) were manufactured by the Springfield Arms Company.

Numerous variations have been observed on this open frame style. Those described below show major distinguishing features as well as illustrate their general chronological sequence.

Average calibers all models approximately 40. Octagon barrels vary in length from 20" to 24". All are six-shot.

An observation of interest to collectors in evaluating these specimens is the fact that invariably all Warner carbines as well as their solid frame rifle (*q.v.*) are found in very heavily used and quite worn condition. Whether this feature indicates that this particular group of arms saw heavier service than most other makes is open to debate and must await a future treatise on the subject. The values reflected here are for specimens in generally lower ranges of condition ("fair" and "very good") than used for most other revolving arms in this chapter.

Retractable Cylinder Type. Usually likened to the Collier system with chamfers at the mouth of each chamber which fit over the breech of barrel to form a tight gas seal. Cylinder held in forward or locking position by a spring around the cylinder pin; cylinder must be manually retracted in order to manually rotate to next chamber position. The cylinder release latch operated by a small button ahead of trigger. No locking notches are visible at rear of cylinder.

Marked on right side of frame: JAMES WARNER/SPRINGFIELD MASS accompanied by an eagle motif over U.S. (not indicating martial usage). Marked on left frame: PATENT APPLIED FOR

Cylinder bears etched floral and scroll designs. Made without provision for loading lever. Walnut stock with brass patchbox.

Quantity made estimated at less than 30; c. 1849:

15-023   Values—Fair **$2,750**   Very Good **$6,000**

Grooved Cylinder, Manually Revolved Type. Most obvious external feature, the long hook type cylinder release latch located ahead of trigger and passing through the front of the trigger guard (appearing as a second trigger). Cylinder is non-retracting (does not have the chamfers for gas seal). Has etched scroll designs and locking notches at rear outside wall which are easily seen without disassembly. Made without provision for loading lever. Markings on right frame: JAMES WARNER/SPRINGFIELD MASS. Walnut stock with brass patchbox. Quantity made estimated between 50 and 100; c. 1849:

15-024　　Values—Fair **$2,500**　　Very Good **$4,500**

Springfield Arms Company Manufacture Automatic Revolving Warner. Has almost identical cylinder as found on the Wesson & Leavitt dragoon percussion revolver and revolving carbine (*q.v.*) with the nipples and nipple wells recessed at 45 degree angle and the identical floral/scroll cylinder etched design. The rear of the cylinder, however, does not have the Wesson & Leavitt gear and is revolved on the Warner system by use of a lever in a deep star cut groove at rear of cylinder wall (externally cylinder identical to Wesson & Leavitt, but on disassembly there is a vast difference on the rear wall which causes rotation).

Loading lever of Warner type with plunger mounted at angle. Walnut stock with small cheek piece. Iron furniture; no provision for patchbox.

Markings on right frame: WARNER'S PATENT/JAN. 1851. Markings on topstrap: SPRINGFIELD ARMS CO.

Quantity made estimated between 100 and 200:

15-025　　Values—Fair **$2,500**　　Very Good **$4,500**

Brass Frame Type. Believed to have preceded the above described Springfield-Warner, and about identical to above except the barrel lug and topstrap only (one piece integral) are of brass, balance of frame iron. Identical Wesson & Leavitt type cylinder as above. Walnut stock with small cheek piece; iron furniture; no provision for patchbox.

Marked only on right frame: WARNER'S PATENT/JAN. 1851.

Quantity unknown; estimated at less than 25:

15-026　　Values—Fair **$3,000**　　Very Good **$6,000**

Warner Solid Frame Revolving Rifle

15-027

James Warner, Springfield, Massachusetts, Solid Frame Percussion Revolving Rifle. Made c. 1850s. Total quantity estimated at approximately 300 to 350.

40 caliber apparently standard, but may vary. Six-shot. 26" to 30" octagon barrels. Walnut stock without patchbox.

Markings on topstrap (or occasionally cylinder): JAMES WARNER/SPRINGFIELD, MASS.

Manually revolved cylinder with locking notches at rear of cylinder wall visible on exterior. The cylinder latch is a short hook shaped lever just ahead of trigger.

Variations are noted in this model also. Approximately the first 100 were made with a safety shield ahead of cylinder and no provision for loading lever and worth premium. Later production (most often encountered) eliminated the safety shield and was provided with loading lever. The removable wood ramrods fitted into the tip of the loading lever more or less locking it into its closed position. A small receptacle in the bottom of the buttplate held the short screw-on extension for the ramrod. Variants have also been noted in both round and spurred trigger guards. Brass frame types have also been reported and would be considered rare and worth a considerable premium.

Some cylinders are equipped for variant type priming systems that might appear as pill lock. Some accept a percussion pellet and are readily recognizable by their square nipples with recessed cavity at the top opening, into which the tiny pellet is fitted (retained by beeswax). When found with these variant ignition systems in complete and intact condition, premium of approximately 25 percent may be added to value:

15-027　　Values—Fair **$2,500**　　Very Good **$4,750**

Wesson & Leavitt Revolving Rifle

15-028

Edwin Wesson and Daniel Leavitt Patent, Percussion Revolving Rifle. Made under Wesson's Patent No. 6669 of August 28, 1849, and Leavitt's Patent No. 182 of April 29, 1837. Made by the Massachusetts Arms Company of Chicopee Falls, Massachusetts. Quantity made estimated at less than 50 and very probably less than 20.

Made on the frame of the 40 caliber "Army" size Wesson & Leavitt/Mass Arms Co. percussion revolver (*q.v.*). Round, two-step barrels varying from 16" to 24". 40 caliber. Etched cylinder designs and markings same as Army revolver and numbered in same series with them.

Although detachable shoulder stocks reported, on specimens viewed the stock and handle, although appearing as a detachable type, were actually made as one piece with no provision for removing:

15-028　　Values—Good **$3,750**　　Fine **$7,500**

Artemus Wheeler Revolving Cylinder Flintlocks

Artemus Wheeler of Boston, Massachusetts, Revolving Cylinder Flintlock Carbines and Muskets. Believed made by William Bishop of Boston, Massachusetts, c. 1820.

Of the most often reported and occasionally encountered

styles, both are seven-shot and approximately 52 caliber with manually revolved cylinders: (a) musket with 32" barrel; cylinder released by manual catch inside trigger guard; (b) carbine with pepperbox-like cluster of 12-1/2" barrels with positive locking on each turn by spring resting in ratchet at rear of cylinder. This type is also reported in rifle size with similar spring latch. Most specimens are believed unmarked.

The first revolving firearm patented in the United States (June 10, 1818), this arm also holds the distinction of being the first rotating cylinder repeating arm to be officially purchased by the United States government. Four of them (two pepperboxes and two muskets) were purchased for testing by the U.S. Navy in 1821. Wheeler has been credited with introducing the first practical revolving arm and his invention was the basis for the more famed Collier flintlock revolving rifle (q.v.). Both very rare. Values shown (approximate only) for carbine; premium of 40 to 50 percent for musket:

15-029
Both guns

15-029   Values—Fair **$25,000**   Good **$50,000**

Whittier Percussion Revolving Rifle

15-030

O. W. Whittier, Enfield, New Hampshire, Percussion Revolving Rifle. Made under Patent No. 216 of May 30, 1837. Made c. late 1830s. Total quantity estimated at approximately 100.

44 caliber probably average, but will vary. Reported in six-, nine-, and ten-shot variations. A distinguishing feature is the very deep zig-zag grooves cut on outside surface of the cylinder to facilitate revolving. Actuating the rear trigger cocked the hammer and rotated cylinder simultaneously. Octagonal barrels approximately 31" to 32" average.

Walnut or maple stock with patchbox on right side. Finish browned.

Barrel marked: WHITTIER'S/PATENT with additional marking PATENT occasionally found on upper tang.

A specimen of this unusual design was in the personal arms collection of Samuel Colt. The zig-zag cylinder system was later modified and improved upon by Colt engineer, E. K. Root, and patented.

This arm was also made as a revolving shotgun of approximately 70 caliber. Part round/part octagonal barrel of approximately 36". Value approximately the same for all types. Variations in all will be noted due to hand workmanship:

15-030   Values—Good **$8,000**   Fine **$17,500**

Wurfflein & Psotta Percussion Revolving Rifle

15-031

John Wurfflein and Frederick Psotta, Philadelphia, Percussion Revolving Rifle. Made c. 1840s. Total quantity unknown; likely less than 20.

44 caliber. Eight-shot. 27" octagon barrel retained by two horizontal keys fitting through center pin. The fully hooded cylinder gives this rifle its ungainly appearance. Internal striker/hammer with centrally hung cocking piece. Barrel must be detached and cylinder removed to load. Very complex, delicate, almost clockwork mechanism for automatic cylinder rotation.

Barrel and both sideplates marked J. WURFFLEIN & PSOTTA, PHILAD'A:

15-031   Values—Good **$5,750**   Fine **$14,000**

Chapter XVI

American Colonial and Revolutionary War Firearms

T he collecting of these earliest of American arms is a highly challenging, and exciting field. Until circa 1960s it attracted a small but extremely enthusiastic nucleus of connoisseurs who have been mostly centered in the East and Northeast. The appreciation of good Colonial American arms has always held a place of respect in the collecting fraternity, but its following until recently has been limited. This has been due to: (a) a lack of awareness of the importance of many of the weapons: (b) a lack of sufficient definitive publications on the subject; (c) the longer period of experience necessary to acquire knowledge in the field; and (d) insufficient understanding or appreciation of our own American heritage and beginnings—very much a case of not seeing the forest for the trees!

Surprisingly enough, sufficient examples of Revolutionary and Colonial American arms have been available on the market over the years to form a number of fine collections. Further surprising is the fact that many of the best and most extensive of such arms groups have been formed by, and still remain in, private hands rather than museums. This well illustrates the fact that Americans are only recently coming to realize the importance of their own heritage and poignantly exemplifies the fact that we are really a new nation in relation to the "Old World." This same phenomenon has been true in other fields of antiques, e.g., American primitive art and various handicrafts, that for years lay fallow (beneath one's nose so to speak) and have been "discovered" in relatively recent times.

It does require a certain appreciation, knowledge and insight to understand (and, of course, evaluate) Revolutionary and earlier American arms. Their study is a continuing and ongoing one. The publication within recent years of several reference books has made available to the collector a wealth of important information that assists greatly in the pursuit of this field. Interest has been widely disseminated and is now nationwide in scope rather than limited to the cadre of Eastern collectors of former days. This latter phenomenon has been erroneously attributed to the celebrations associated with the American Bicentennial in 1976; however, the author is of the opinion that this is merely a coincidence. The field has shown over a long period of time a steady, strong, progressive rise in interest and it is merely coincidental that the highest values realized were during the Bicentennial period—the awakening was by no means sudden. The author also feels that these same arms will continue to increase in popularity both in the private and public sectors (i.e., museums) as awareness of their historical significance becomes more widespread. Many of these weapons played a direct part in the very forging of the independence which this country enjoys today—a role that can be hardly understated.

The preponderance of weapons used in America up to the end of the Revolution were of European manufacture; hence a study of these is essential to prepare the student for an understanding of arms having Colonial associations. Only rarely will one find European made pieces with known, documented or otherwise fully substantiated American associations. When available they will command values far in excess of their normal price as an antique gun, depending on the amount of verification accompanying them. European weapons that have been established as types used in Colonial America have acquired dual interest both as antique European arms and as American-associated arms. In many instances premium values may be placed on them as general types suitable for inclusion in Colonial American collections. Almost all British service arms of the 17th and 18th centuries are in this category; the most notable is the famed British "Brown Bess." Such European weapons have taken on a far greater significance in recent decades; in some instances their values are greater today in America because of the Colonial association than in their European homelands.

Essential to understanding the significance and usage of various types of firearms in early America is a reasonable working knowledge of colonial history, the various evolutionary stages of expansion and a cognizance of the countries that settled and explored the American continent. An indispensable reference for the student and collector and considered a classic on the subject is *Arms And Armour In Colonial America 1526-1783* (*see Bibliography*). A number of monographs published over the years pertaining to excavations at historical sites shed considerable light on the earliest eras of American colonial weapons while the later Revolutionary era is quite adequately covered by published works found in the Bibliography.

The first Europeans to settle what is today the continental United States were Spaniards, establishing forts in the early 16th century in North Carolina, southern Virginia and Florida with explorations along the Gulf Coast and in the Southwest. Following them in 1562 were the French, who established a settlement in Port Royal, South Carolina, and Fort Carolina in Florida in 1564; all their subsequent colonization turned northward to what is now Canada. The English, Dutch and Swedes followed in the late 16th century with the English multiplying rapidly beginning with the early 17th century.

These European settlers, explorers, adventurers and military men brought along the usual, or standard, arms and equipment then in use in their respective countries. The first era of exploration and colonization through to the 17th century was characterized by a change in the usual European situation (i.e., white man fighting white man) to meet the environment of the New World, typified by a struggle for existence against the wilderness and often against hostile and uncivilized peoples. The crossbow and matchlock of those early eras were found slow and clumsy against the Indians who did not fight in the conventional European manner. American conditions certainly did much to create a demand for better arms from Europe, such as the wheel-lock and ultimately the flintlock.

It is well recorded that both the crossbow and matchlock were the first style of arms in general usage during the Colonial eras with the former generally superseded in the mid-16th century; a few uses are recorded as late as the 1570s but by then the crossbow was of secondary importance.

It is often difficult to discern in early references exactly what type of arm was used at a specific period, the matchlock as well as subsequent weapons were often called (for many years) by generic terms which were apparently interchangeable; e.g., arquebus, caliver, musket, fusil, fuzee and firelock.

The Matchlock (often referred to as arquebus) was brought to America with the first expedition and excavated examples show considerable evolutionary changes over their period of development in the 16th century. The wheel-lock was developed as early as 1520 with the snaphaunce following by 1570 and primitive forms of flintlock as early as 1600.

The earliest shoulder arms were characterized by rather heavy weights, reduced about mid-17th century to an average of 16 pounds for a musket with approximately a 10 gauge bore. By early 18th century the general characteristics of the musket averaged weights of 8 to 12 pounds with 40" to 46" for barrel lengths and smooth bores approximating 65 through 80. Invariably the muskets were fitted with front sights only. Not until the turn of the 18th century did a small stud acting as a guide for the socket type bayonet serve the dual function of front sight also.

Much less is known about the role of **The Wheel-Lock** than any other type of firearm ignition form. As mentioned, early references were quite often not specific as to the exact ignition type and generic terms tend to be confusing. Although specific mentions are limited, there have been a small amount of wheel-lock fragments excavated from historic sites. Competent authorities believe wheel-locks were more widely used than has been generally supposed (see *Arms And Armour In Colonial America* by Harold Peterson). Of much greater reliability than the matchlock, the wheel-lock's requirements of closer manufacturing tolerances and considerably greater expense did much to limit its widespread military issuance and usage. Hence, the great majority of wheel-locks were made for sporting purposes and were obviously owned by men of wealth and means.

The introduction of the **flintlock ignition system** in mid-16th century and its gradual development in various evolutionary stages precipitated its widespread manufacture and use throughout all European countries and its gradual introduction to the American continent. This firearms system saw greater and longer usage than any other type, and was utilized on all basic weapons of all countries beginning with the late 16th century. The system was in general use in America and Europe through to the 1840s, a reign of some 300 years!

The evolutionary development of the flintlock was governed primarily by regional and geographic differences, and is generally broken down into six distinct types:

(1) The Snaphaunce: Developed in the Scandinavian and Low countries in mid-16th century; the very first form of flintlock ignition, which very quickly spread to all countries of Europe and England. There is considerable misunderstanding and misconception about the use of the snaphaunce in Colonial America. This situation has presumably been created by the generic terminology of the era used to describe it (from the Dutch word *schnapphahns* meaning "snapping cock or rooster") a term misapplied to all subsequent flintlock forms also, not merely indicating the true first form described here. It is apparent from the handful of lock relics excavated at historic sites that the actual snaphaunce system was used less here than any other flintlock form.

(2) The English Lock: This quickly superseded the snaphaunce in England, and subsequently America. Named after country of origin it was developed about c. 1610-20 and ushered in a major innovation, combining the battery (or frizzen) and separate flashpan cover of the snaphaunce into a single piece, pivoting on the outside of the lockplate and held in a rigid position over the flashpan by an outside mounted spring (the frizzen spring). The battery (or frizzen) when struck by the flint (held between the teeth of the hammer or "cock") simultaneously caused a sparking action and knocked the battery (frizzen) out of the way uncovering the pan and thus making the lock considerably faster in operation than the earlier snaphaunce. The new "English lock" also provided for a "safety" or "half cock" position, by utilizing a notch internally on the tumbler which was engaged by the sear.

(3) The Dog Lock: An evolutionary development of the English lock (with its own variations and history of evolution) in which the "half cock" or "safety" position was achieved by means of a swivel, hooked type latch mounted externally behind the hammer. The small hook (known as a "dog") engaged a notch in the hammer itself.

Both above types of English locks underwent long periods of changes and a great many variations are seen. The lock shape also changed form as did several of the major parts. The dog-lock remained in use until the turn of the century (circa 1700) and quite a few of this style saw service in Colonial America. The type is eagerly sought after.

(4) The Miquelet Lock: Developed in Spain and quickly becoming popular and spreading throughout the Mediterranean area and east to Italy in the mid-16th century. Its basic differentiating feature is the mounting of the mainspring externally on the lock with the tension of the spring acting directly upon an external notch in the hammer itself (rather than internally on the tumbler). The general lock part shapes are quite distinctive and easily recognized from other flintlocks. Only the slightest evidence points to use of the miquelet system in the Eastern United States, with but a handful of relic locks excavated (at Jamestown, Virginia, and in Massachusetts). However, the system was quite widespread throughout other Spanish settlements and explored areas in Florida and the Southwest. Types of weapons on which they were used are well illustrated and described in the classic work *Spanish Military Weapons In Colonial America 1700-1821* (*see Bibliography*).

(5) The Scandinavian Lock or "Snap" Lock: Similar to the miquelet, with a mainspring on the outside acting directly on a notch on the hammer. The mainspring acted in a dual capacity supplying tension to the battery (frizzen) also. Quite distinctive in appearance with a flashpan having its own cover; in some forms, resembles the snaphaunce. Made in many variations, the major ones are of Swedish and Norwegian types. The introduction of this system was approximately mid-16th century and it has but the slightest association with Colonial America, apparently being used only in the short-lived Swedish settlements along the Delaware River c. 1638-55, and even there the matchlock undoubtedly took precedence.

(6) The French or "true" Flintlock: The ultimate development of the flintlock ignition system that continued in use for over two centuries. Perfected about 1610 in France and quickly spreading throughout western Europe, reaching America in large quantities by the 1660s. By the third quarter of the 17th century it had entirely supplanted the English dog lock. This simplified system had two major characteristics distinguishing it from all other earlier flintlock actions: (a) Internally the sear moved vertically to engage the tumbler notches, and (b) the tumbler was provided with two notches for half cock (safety) and full cock positions.

From existing evidence it is quite apparent that the principal weapon of the English colonies in the East was the matchlock musket through to the 1630s when the general transition to flintlock (dog lock, etc.) began. By the 1640s both flintlock and matchlock were on an equal footing in importance and use, but by the late 1640s all matchlocks although still in use were very much considered secondary weapons for private ownership only. Whereas public arms (of Plymouth Colony) only allowed the flintlock or wheel-lock, specific orders in the early 1670s indicate the purchase of flintlocks only for Colonial use and by the end of King Philip's war in 1677 matchlocks as a military weapon were outlawed.

Connecticut allowed both matchlocks and flintlocks in the colony's early formative years in the 1640s, but by 1649 only the latter were allowed for public use, and a system was devised to convert matchlocks to the flintlock system. In the mid 1670s Connecticut recognized only flintlocks as acceptable militia weapons.

The Dutch in New York (New Netherlands) also favored the matchlock in their early settlements in the 1620s, although records extant show the use of both flintlock and wheel-lock in that era with the former gaining much private favor while the public sector clung stubbornly to the matchlock as an official weapon. The colony requested aid in 1655 for a few thousand soldiers to assist in their struggle against hostile Indians, specifically requesting that the men be armed about equally with wheel-locks and flintlocks. It is reasoned though, that regardless of this Dutch colonist's request for supporting military forces to be armed with wheel-locks that likely but few were brought with the relief forces. In the private sector, however, the governing body of the colony by official resolution allowed that future immigrants were to be armed personally only with matchlocks. It is not known however if this resolution was enforced and of course there is every likelihood that the newer flintlocks were substituted surreptitiously.

With the withdrawal of the Dutch in 1664 and the occupation of New York (New Amsterdam) by English forces, firearms in general use throughout the colony followed similar customs of those throughout the Eastern settlements, with the flintlock the dominant style.

The study and collecting of Colonial American made arms is one requiring insight, common sense, the viewing of known documented specimens and a discerning eye. Although at times fraught with pitfalls, it can be exceptionally rewarding if pursued with patience and diligence.

Values are very much "seat of the pants" or "what the market will bear" for true 17th century specimens. No simplified or codified method exists for the layman as a guide, other than to advise study and research on such specimens that may fall within this category. Both quality of workmanship and historic association play dominant roles. It is quite accurate and safe to say that all American made specimens (i.e., those that are primitive as well as finely made, or even those that are composite) are in great demand in almost any state of condition or completeness. Prices however run the gamut from the low three figures to five figures with the latter including extremely historical, documented arms or those possessing maker's names or other exemplary qualities.

Very little of substance has been written of the gun making from the earliest periods. The reader is referred to those works in the Bibliography, most of which touch upon the subject but are by no means complete nor definitive. Note that American gunsmiths from the earliest periods not only made entire guns but did a considerable amount of repairing of those brought in from abroad; one notes a decided lack of uniformity throughout. Further, those arms considered unfit for additional use or service were not discarded, but rather cannibalized for every usable part to be remounted, restocked or assembled as a composite weapon. The bulk of Colonial and American made arms existing today reflect just such usage, and these features are by no means detrimental to their collectibility nor their value; as a matter of fact just the opposite is true. Quite conceivably the same parts were used in many forms over a lengthy period of time and in a number of guns until the parts themselves were literally worn beyond any further use.

A majority of arms made and used by the Colonists followed British designs and patterns. A few distinctive types (as described below) are the most often seen on the collectors' market and are quite easily recognizable by specific characteristics. They do fall into general value categories.

"Committee of Safety" weapons (discussed later in this chapter) form a much abused subject in gun collecting. Very likely a number of those so-called muskets considered of Revolutionary period American manufacture are in actuality much earlier in date, probably of assembly and use in the era of the French-Indian Wars, and possibly even earlier campaigns. Proving earlier backgrounds, however, becomes quite difficult if not impossible in many instances, and, as the Revolution has the most glamour of the 18th century, such weapons are usually attributed to this latter date which seems to add to their general popularity and acceptability by collectors.

Some of the most easily identified features of American made or assembled arms of the Colonial era are the types of wood used for the stocks and their general British characteristics (i.e., barrels pin fastened to the forestock rather than the use of barrel bands; British style furniture, with iron often substituted for brass). The use of American maple and cherry quite easily distinguish the arms as American manufacture to even the novice collector. Often the characteristics and configuration of the stock and general workmanship are also major identifying features. Markings or signatures are rare during the early periods and such specimens are seldom available or offered. However, due to the rarity (and consequent substantial values) of such markings and the usually simple manner in which they were applied, the collector should proceed with extreme caution in instances where markings indicating colonial manufacture, ownership or usage appear. A notable number of spuriously marked (but otherwise authentic) specimens were altered as far back as the pre-World War II era, and such nefarious practices have continued to the present day. The field is rife with such marked, fraudulent examples, some of which have attained an air of respectability by their inclusion in earlier arms literature. Not a few have been traceable to the handiwork of specific individuals in the 1930s through 1950s whose *modus operandi* followed stylistically similar patterns on most of their output. Recent years have brought on rashes of lesser gifted craftsmen and there is always a new crop coming up! Thus, markings should be the subject of very close scrutiny, and if possible, backgrounds and pedigrees are worth investigating. These latter are oftentimes helpful, but should by no means be the sole deciding factor, for the old conundrum "…it must be good because of where it came from" doesn't always hold water!

Most early American made arms had to serve the dual purposes of providing food and protection. In the latter instance the gun was often used by the colonist during his militia service and thus it is difficult at times to specifically classify the purpose or type of arm and easily categorize it. Many of these early muskets lack sling swivels and do not have provision for bayonet studs, as the owner was allowed the option of bringing either a sword or a bayonet. This situation apparently was in effect until the era of the Revolution and thus pre-Revolutionary arms of military significance will take a great many shapes and forms. Although most follow the British pattern with many conforming quite closely, others will vary vastly. Thus the too-hastily used and improper generic application of the term "Committee of Safety" for many of these muskets is somewhat unfair. Many deserve better treatment as they possess even

16-001
Flintlock Colonial Military Dual Purpose Muskets

greater significance for their earlier manufacture and usage. The "Committee of Safety" terminology is merely a matter of oversimplification and over-identification with one era of American history at the complete expense of others of equal, if not greater, importance.

Firearms of Colonial American manufacture and/or assembly, and of distinct military or combination military-sporting design are generally valued for their: (a) Aesthetic appearance and appeal; (b) type of stock wood; (c) originality of ignition system (i.e., flintlock *vs.* percussion conversion); (d) amount of repairs or replacement; and (e) condition—in that general order. Without doubt those having curly maple wood for their stocks are the most readily identified, and sometimes (depending on the condition of that wood, the tiger-striping and grain as well as the patina) fetch somewhat better values merely for the eye appeal. It should be noted thought that those with plain maple, cherry or other fruitwoods, or American black walnut are equally desirable and equally in demand. Several other American characteristics are often identifiable to the discerning eye, e.g., varying degrees of awkwardness and primitiveness, readily distinguishing these arms from their European counterparts. However, such qualities are not in themselves sufficient to identify an arm as American for there are awkward, crude European pieces also! Such primitive features on American pieces often lend to their attractiveness; although certainly an oversimplification and a broad generalization, it is often said that for some specimens in their awkwardness and their primitiveness is in fact their beauty! The statement will certainly not hold true for all specimens; some are just so badly made and so homely in appearance that these features can be detrimental. The subject is indeed an esoteric one and only the discerning and experienced eye can make the choice for both collecting and evaluation purposes. A relative range of values for such military or semi-military pre-Revolutionary and Colonial arms is indicated below. The reader should be very much aware that these are the broadest guideposts only and that it is probable that superlative specimens, or unique pieces, or those possessing historical significance will fall in ranges far beyond those shown:
Original Flintlock Colonial American Military or Dual Purpose Musket; full stock; approximately 42" to 46" or longer barrel (exceptional lengths will bring premiums based on length

alone); no maker's name appearing but decidedly of American manufacture and/or assembly:

16-001   Values—Fair **$950-1,750**   Good **$1,500-3,000**
    Very Good **$2,500-5,000**

Identical to above; converted to percussion:

16-002   Values—Fair **$650-1,400**   Good **$900-2,000**
    Very Good **$1,400-3,000**

New England Flintlock Fowling Pieces; 18th century; also known as "Queen Anne" stock type. Generally made in New England and environs. Most often stocked in cherry or plain maple (only rarely seen in curly maple and worth premium), full stock; slender, gracefully made; fashioned directly after the British full stock fowling guns of the era; utilizing English, Dutch or French barrels, furniture and locks; not bearing American maker's markings (although European markings may appear on barrels and locks); stock plain, uncarved (relief carving worth premiums depending on quality and profuseness with such carving usually found around the tang, lower ramrod pipe and occasionally around the lock); varying barrel lengths averaging 45" to 55" (longer lengths with accompanying full stocks worth premium):

16-003   Values—Fair **$850-1,400**   Good **$1,000-2,000**
    Very Good **$1,600-3,500**

Identical to above; converted to percussion:

16-004   Values—Fair **$500-900**   Good **$650-1,500**
    Very Good **$1,100-2,500**

Club Butt Musket/Fowling Pieces. A distinct category of typically New England made arms with a uniquely shaped stock. Considering the number of specimens extant of this distinctive style, surprisingly little has been written about them. Very well known to collectors of Colonial weapons, this is a specific type that is always found in an early American collection. The style seems to have been generally made around Massachusetts with quite a few specimens traced to the South Shore area. Stylistically, the massive club butt was in general use from the third quarter of the 17th century to about the period of the American Revolution, with a few specimens even dating to the turn of the century and an occasional "straggler" having these general club butt features known in original percussion! Butts are invariably massive in size with a unique "fish belly," heavily curved underside. Barrel lengths vary from 40" to specimens almost 6 if not longer in length (worth premium values). Average specimens illustrated and valued here are

16-003
New England Flintlock Fowling Pieces

**16-005 / 16-006
Club Butt
Musket / Fowling Pieces**

normally with British proofed barrels and either British military or French style locks; stocks usually of plain maple or walnut (curly maple worth a premium). Values dependent on aesthetic qualities with premiums added for relief carving (usually appearing in the shape of a shell or fan around the barrel tang or cheek piece) or fancy moldings along forend and other quality features such as unusually deep or fancy flutings alongside a high comb (just behind the wrist area) which lend pleasing qualities and eye appeal to the type. Furniture most often brass and composites of British or French military styles. Values indicated here for average specimens, without American maker's markings; barrels approximately 40" to 50" in length and full stocks:

16-005   Values—Fair **$1,400-3,000**   Good **$2,500-5,000**
                    Very Good **$3,500-7,000**

Identical to above; converted to percussion:

16-006   Values—Fair **$1,000-1,600**   Good **$1,400-3,250**
                    Very Good **$2,500-5,000**

Hudson Valley Fowling Pieces. A highly desirable, very distinctive appearing American type of the pre-Revolutionary era. Generally similar distinguishing characteristics common to the type are very long overall lengths and massive stocks with high combs. Specimens usually date from the late 17th to mid-18th century. They are found in quite long lengths usually 5-1/2" to 7-1/2" overall (longest lengths usually bring premiums for size). Those valued here average 5-1/2" to 6" overall with curly maple stocks, just slight carving around the tang area. Premiums are added for greater amounts of carving (often found with extremely fine quality relief work); mountings are usually of brass and Dutch style, simply yet well made, although on finest quality types sideplates and mountings are often elaborate; barrels are quite often of English manufacture and proofed although Dutch and other European barrels are seen; locks normally rounded with broad scroll and floral designs and similar matching work on the hammer. No two specimens alike; values indicated here are just broad ranges and guideposts for

plainer specimens similar to those illustrated. Exemplary specimens often fetch values far in excess of those indicated:

16-007   Values—Fair **$2,500-4,000**   Good **$3,500-7,000**
                    Very Good **$5,000-12,500+**

Identical to above; converted to percussion:

16-008   Values—Fair **$1,500-2,500**   Good **$2,500-4,500**
                    Very Good **$3,500-7,500+**

The 18th century in America was characterized by a return to European military fighting tactics; conflict was no longer against the wilderness and hostile Indians but rather between Europeans on American soil. The era ushered in by the "Glorious Revolution" in England in 1688 and generally commencing in the American colonies in the early 18th century saw a gradual standardization of military firearms. The hodge-podge of weapons of the various countries which settled America was outmoded and, for the first time, specific models (i.e., one closely fashioned similar to the other) were introduced. The French were first with their model of 1717, the English following suit about the mid-1720s.

By far, the majority of weapons used by various European military organizations had been purchased from private contractors, each of which generally designed and chose details of manufacture most suited to their own purposes. The gradual standardization by governments (notably the French and English) brought about patterns and standard dimensions which were followed with a reasonable resemblance and proximity to each other allowing for variations of hand workmanship.

As has been stated, English models were the most popular and widely used throughout the colonies, followed during the Revolutionary era by French weapons. By the end of the Revolutionary War the French musket became the most common and popular as well as the one preferred by American forces; it became the basis for official U.S. muskets in the years following the war.

Almost any European made weapon of the American Revolutionary (or immediately pre-Revolutionary) era might conceivably have an American association; such arms were purchased abroad in all types and imported for American military service. These covered a wide range of styles, types and manufacture. While many specific styles have known histories of

**16-007
Hudson Valley Fowling Pieces**

usage, others are merely thought to have been a general style purchased, imported and issued. The subject is well covered in several of the works listed in the Bibliography, to which the reader is referred. Certainly, many such arms are only peripheral in their possible American association and values normally reflect this. Others, however, are known to have played major roles during the War (i.e., the French Model 1763 and the British "Brown Bess") and are of such importance that they must be considered integral to any American Revolutionary or Colonial collection. The subject is certainly a vast one, with many facets as yet unexplored. However some very excellent works have been written about those foreign made weapons, especially those of British manufacture (*see Bibliography*). The foreign made nature of the arms precludes an in-depth discussion and detailed descriptions in this particular work, but it would be a major oversight not to mention them, at least in brief. Those British muskets bearing regimental markings which may be ascribed to units known to have served and participated on the American continent during the War are worth considerable premiums and value. Although all French models of the various 1763 and subsequent styles known to have been used in America are considered of direct American importance, there is a group of them actually bearing surcharged markings, indicating American ownership and issuance, quite decidedly placing them in a unique category (to be discussed later).

With the outbreak of hostilities of 1775, signaling the American Revolution, there was a very urgent need for firearms. The Americans employed every means of acquisition including confiscation, European and Colonial purchases, and actual contracts to Colonial gunsmiths. A large number of soldiers went off to war carrying a very great variety of their personal weapons.

COMMITTEE OF SAFETY MUSKETS

An often misused, misunderstood, and certainly abused term associated with Revolutionary American firearms is "Committee of Safety." Used loosely by the great majority of those buying, trading and collecting weapons of that era it has come to denote almost any American musket manufactured during the Revolutionary War years. The Committees of Safety were colonial societies originally organized clandestinely in 1775 with the authority to mobilize a militia, seize military stores and otherwise exercise the functions of state governments for keeping order and furnishing men and supplies to the Army. They did not issue actual arms-making contracts until mid-1775. Thus guns delivered under those contracts could not have been used at the Battles of Lexington or Concord or Bunker Hill. Most of the Committees of Safety were short-lived (until 1777 or 1778) and hence the arms delivered under their contracts are believed to have been small in relative quantities. Thus, a great many American arms made during the Revolutionary War are not by true definitions of the term "Committee of Safety" models (which, in all accuracy, had to be made on specific contracts) but are nevertheless equally historic, important and rare.

Study of the actual Committee of Safety contracts affords the collector, historian and student the opportunity to obtain reasonably detailed specifications of the muskets, as well as the general types of arms manufactured during the entire era. Thus, it is important for the collector, and even the casual gun trader, to perform research on his own to better understand, and hence identify, American made arms of the period. Quickly apparent are considerable differences in dimensions; some colonies and the Continental Congress each established specifications and wide variances exist among them. For instance, the Continental Congress in 1775 specified a 44" musket barrel, while the colony of Massachusetts Bay in 1775 specified one of 45" in length, and Connecticut, in that same year, specified a 46" length. The Pennsylvania specifications called for 44" barrels while

Maryland only required those of 42". The New York Committee of Safety merely supplied contractors with a standard pattern British "Brown Bess" musket and the request that contractors follow it in design. Interestingly, some Committees purchased imported barrels and locks, giving them to contractors for fitting of stocks and furniture/mountings. Not only were there wide variances in the specifications themselves, but it is reasonably assumed that contractors were both granted and took on their own, a wide latitude in the actual manufacture of the weapons. What inspection was made was undoubtedly very loose and liberal, created by the pressing needs of the times.

The general consensus among students holds that there are a few common elements and close similarities with all the so-called "Committee of Safety" and other American Revolutionary manufactured muskets: (a) Calibers average about 75, and (b) barrel lengths vary from 42" to 46" and are pin fastened in the British manner (i.e., without the use of barrel bands) and most generally resemble the British "Brown Bess."

The vast majority of American made arms which qualify as Revolutionary War era in manufacture are unsigned by the makers. With the absence of such markings it becomes difficult, if not impossible, to classify or differentiate them as a true "Committee of Safety" or an American Revolutionary made weapon. The difference is, of course, slight as far as historical significance is concerned. Both are of equal importance to the collector. Thus the very loose terminology in common collector usage of "Committee of Safety" has become a generic term for all Revolutionary American made muskets.

Although the original Committee of Safety specifications called for maker's signatures or initials on their contract arms, such signed pieces are rarely seen (very likely another area where the makers deviated from the specifications). The collector is urged to exercise extreme caution on the acquisition of signed or otherwise marked specimens as the area is one which has been (and continues to be) subject to many abuses. Values of genuine marked pieces, especially when the makers are both known and identifiable, will be at least double or triple (if not more) those for unmarked pieces as generally illustrated and evaluated herein.

Arms of all types and makes were purchased in Europe by the Continental Congress as well as by individual states and colonies. French weapons were in preponderance, with original purchases made in devious manners through false trading companies and private means until 1778 when the French openly declared war against Great Britain. The French government thereafter directly supplied the colonies with arms. As in all wars, profiteering was rife, and hence a great many low quality, as well as obsolete, arms found their way to America from various ports of Europe.

SURCHARGED U.S. MARKINGS

Early in 1777 the Continental Congress passed a resolution requiring, and authorizing, the marking of all arms and accoutrements owned by the United States, requiring these to be marked "U.S." or "United States." The exact wording stated that such marks be placed on"… such parts as will receive the impression." Markings were either applied by stamps (on iron parts) or heated brands on the stock. Quite a few variations are known. The author personally encountered five different styles of markings on one relic French Model 1763 some years back. The most often seen markings on the locks and barrels are U S while the brands generally viewed on stocks are U. STATES and UNITED STATES. The practice of marking applied only to government owned pieces and not those of either personal or state ownership. The presence of such markings on weapons of any type of the American Revolution adds immeasurably to their value. Because of the many abuses to which such marks lend themselves and the numbers of suspect and otherwise proven spurious markings (on otherwise genuine antique guns), the collector should proceed *cautiously* when acquiring and paying premiums for such features. Genuine markings proving U.S. ownership, and hence assumed usage during the Revolution, will normally increase the value of a firearm 25 to 50 percent, and sometimes considerably more. Many factors should be taken into account when evaluating them, such as known backgrounds and pedigrees, historical association, the model on which they appear, overall completeness, condition, and quality. Such markings are possible to encounter on American made guns as well as imported pieces. The most usual arm of the latter type is the French Model 1763 Charleville (or Maubeuge) musket and variations of same.

The mere presence of a "U.S." marking does not always indicate Revolutionary War usage. This same mark was often applied to American made, as well as American owned, arms in government warehouses and arsenals as late as the turn of the century. For the most part these later type marks are much smaller in size than those of the War period; however, this last statement is a very broad generality and the collector and

student is urged to read further on the subject. The William Guthman work *U.S. Army Weapons 1784-1791* (*see Bibliography*) discusses the subject quite well. That book is especially valuable in its coverage of arms of the immediate post-Revolutionary years and lends considerable insight to American made muskets for the entire era of the Revolution to 1800.

So-called "Committee of Safety" Muskets. The type most often encountered on the collectors' market. Patterned after the British "Brown Bess." Average barrels measuring from 42" to 46" (although shorter lengths may be seen and are known to be original). Walnut, pin fastened full stocks (curly maple will usually bring premium values of 20 percent to 40 percent depending on the overall quality of the gun), utilizing a mixture of unmarked locks (either American made or possibly imported European) or salvaged locks and barrels from British and French muskets. Value premiums may also be added (depending on the quality of the gun itself) for the furniture/mountings if determined of American manufacture. Specimens marked by American makers are very rare and their values are two to five times those listed here. The presence of "U.S." surcharged markings on locks, barrels or stocks on otherwise unmarked specimens is worth a premium of 25 percent to 50 percent and possibly more; caution should be exercised when encountering such markings:

16-009   Values—Fair **$1,250-2,000**   Good **$1,750-3,250**   Very Good **$3,000-6,000**

     As above; converted to percussion:

16-010   Values—Fair **$800-1,150**   Good **$1,000-1,600**   Very Good **$1,250-3,000**

British "Brown Bess" Flintlock Muskets. The three basic types are listed here. There are a great many variations, sub-types, and transitional types; all of great interest to the American collector. Definitive data is to be found in many of the books listed in the Bibliography:

    First Model Brown Bess. 46" barrel. In general manufacture circa 1710 to 1760:

16-011   Values—Fair **$3,750-5,000**   Good **$5,000-7,500**   Very Good **$7,500-12,500**

16-009
"Committee of Safety" Muskets

16-011
British "Brown Bess"

16-017
French Model 1763 Flintlock

Identical to above; converted to percussion:
16-012   Values—Fair **$1,500-2,250**   Good **$2,750-4,000**
          Very Good **$4,000-6,000**

Second Model Brown Bess. 42" barrel manufactured circa 1760 through mid 1770s:
16-013   Values—Good **$2,750-3,750**   Fine **$4,250-7,500**

Identical to above; converted to percussion:
16-014   Values—Good **$1,500-2,000**   Fine **$2,250-4,000**

Third Model Brown Bess. (a.k.a. "India" pattern). Although not formally adopted by the British Army until the 1790s, the earliest manufacture of this pattern began mid-1770s with a great many made for the British East India Company and bearing their markings and datings in the 1770s. Those types as well as the earliest forms of third pattern (e.g., those with goose-neck hammers and earlier features such as the thickening or swell around the lower thimble) have come to be generally accepted as a model worthy of inclusion in American Revolutionary collections. Recent evidence from excavated relics at a Revolutionary American battle site proving the use of this model has added further credibility to their inclusion in an Revolutionary collection:
16-015   Values—Good **$1,500-2,000**   Fine **$2,500-3,250**

Identical to above; converted to percussion:
16-016   Values—Good **$650-950**   Fine **$1,000-1,250**

French Model 1763 Flintlock Musket: Locks bearing markings of either CHARLEVILLE or MAUBEUGE, the French National Armories. This musket was used in later years as the pattern for the first U.S. Armory produced weapon, the Model 1795 (*see Chapter IX*). The nomenclature "Model 1763," although both a specific model and official French designation, has been used by the collecting world to embrace quite a few variations and modifications, each of which has been classified by advanced students (with some having official French model year markings) until superseded by the distinctively different Model 1777. For the most part the variations are slight, not affecting the general contours and characteristics of the musket. Values indicated are general ranges for the Model 1763 and later modifications. The Model 1763 is the most often encountered type with U S surcharges on barrels, locks or stocks (or combination of same). Such markings denoting American ownership and issuance are worth at least a 50 percent or greater premium depending on the condition of the gun:
16-017   Values—Good **$2,000-2,500**   Fine **$3,250-5,000**

Identical to above; converted to percussion:
16-018   Values—Good **$850-1,250**   Fine **$1,250-2,000**

THE RAPPAHANNOCK FORGE AND THE FREDRICKSBURG MANUFACTORY

Due to their apparent total quantities made and the numbers of surviving specimens of handguns, the output of the Rappahannock Forge is treated separately. The handguns manufactured there are generally considered by many arms writers and collectors as the first or earliest American military handgun. These were actually made under contract for the state of Virginia during the Revolution and qualify as the best marked of early martial pistols made for American usage. There can be no slighting the significance of these historic arms.

Virginia had established its own state manufacturing facilities at the commencement of the Revolution, known as the Fredericksburg Manufactory. In 1775 that facility concentrated on repairs of weapons already owned by the Colony with actual manufacture of muskets beginning about mid-1776. These latter pieces very closely followed the Brown Bess in configuration.

The State of Virginia also contracted with private firms and gunsmiths for weapons. From surviving specimens it appears that the leading contractor was James Hunter, owner of the Hunter Iron Works, also known as the Rappahannock Forge, since it was located along the Rappahannock River at Falmouth, Virginia, near Fredericksburg. The Hunter Works was right across the river from the Fredericksburg Manufactory.

The Rappahannock Forge was in production prior to May of 1776 through to the end of the War, suspending operations in 1780 when it was necessary to move equipment to prevent falling into British hands; the Forge was re-established in 1781.

Rappahannock Forge Pistol. Modeled directly after the British Light Dragoon pistol of the era. Approximately a dozen authentic specimens are recorded to date. Dimensions differ slightly on all and other slight features show variations from specimen to specimen. Average overall length 15" and average barrel length 9"; Calibers approximately 66 to 69. Most barrels bear hand engraved markings along top near breech I. HUNTER. Flat lockplate with vertical flute and pointed teat at rear. Marked vertically at rear in two lines RAP^A/FORGE. Gooseneck shaped hammer. Stocks are noted both with and without relief carved section around the barrel tang. Mountings are brass. Sideplates on some specimens observed with Virginia regimental markings. Collectors are urged to exercise extreme caution on the acquisition of this handgun as not a few spurious specimens are known, the majority merely alterations from the standard British made pistol with fraudulent markings. Another distinctive version of the Rappahannock Forge pistol with a bulbous hexagonal shaped butt has been described in many earlier published works. Such pistols have been proven to be 20th century work and are completely spurious:
16-019   Values—Fair **$15,000**   Good **$30,000**
          Very Good **$35,000-50,000+**

16-019

16-021
Rappahannock Forge Musket and Pistol

Identical to above; converted to percussion:
16-020   Values—Fair **$12,500**   Good **$22,500**
                Very Good **$25,000-35,000+**
Rappahannock Forge Musket. Fashioned closely after the first model Brown Bess but shorter in length. On the two known and recorded specimens (both 80 caliber) overall lengths were 57-3/4" with 41-1/2" barrel and 60-1/8" with a 44" barrel respectively. Flat lockplate similar in shape to that of the pistol but larger with a vertical flute and pointed teat at rear. Markings identical to that of the pistol described above. The I. HUNTER markings also hand engraved on top of barrel near breech:
16-021   Values—Fair **$15,000**   Good **$30,000**
                Very Good **$35,000+-50,000+**
Identical to above; converted to percussion:
16-022   Values—Fair **$12,500**   Good **$22,500**
                Very Good **$22,500-30,000+**

Fredericksburg Manufactory Musket. Patterned after the British Brown Bess musket, but somewhat lighter in construction. Barrel lengths recorded from 39" to 45"; considerable variation in details on all known specimens; no provision for ramrod; lock plates similar profile to Rappahannock above, flat with rear tapering to a point; large gooseneck hammer is flat with beveled edges. Two-line engraved markings, vertically at rear of lock FRED^G and date. (The years **1776**, **1777** and **1778** recorded on the few known specimens.) Other markings observed on inside, rear of lock plate W. G. indicating William Grady the master armorer at the Manufactory. Some specimens noted with iron mountings in place of brass.
16-022.5   Values—Fair **$17,500**   Good **$35,000**
                  Very Good **$40,000 to $60,000+**
Identical to above; converted to percussion:
16-022.6   Values—Fair **$15,000**   Good **$25,000**
                  Very Good **$30,000 to $40,000+**

PISTOLS

Flintlock pistols were carried by officers of all branches, by cavalry troopers and by men of the Navy. The British pistol had a major influencing role in American design and use. In its military version, it was standardized somewhat later than the musket and is found in several models in many variations. The role of French handguns is secondary; their pistol was not standardized until 1763.

Few pistols were made in Colonial America and those that were followed closely British designs and styles. Those Americans able to afford handguns quite obviously purchased imported British made fine quality arms. It is only during the Revolution that there was an apparent expansion of manufacturing of handguns. Two general styles have been

noted: (a) Those closely patterned after the British holster pistols of the period; often distinguishable by the type of materials used, such as the different wood and very often the lesser quality of workmanship, and (b) The so-called "Kentucky" type (*see Chapter XI*). Although distinctly American in appearance the earliest specimens retained very Germanic characteristics. The Kentucky type usually have rather sharp angles to the handle with a closely fitted (or the complete absence of) buttcaps. See the aforementioned chapter for discussion of the type.

As with muskets, the majority of handguns used during the American Revolution were purchased from abroad or came from captured British stocks. Thus, almost all British flintlock pistols of the era and that immediately preceding it are suitable for inclusion in an American collection. French pistols of the era (notably the Model 1763 and to a lesser degree the Model 1777) were supplied by the French and are also considered by many collectors an integral part of a Revolutionary collection.

American Light Dragoon Flintlock Pistol; fashioned directly after British cavalry pistols of the Revolutionary War era. A number of this identical style flintlock handgun, all with closely similar markings, are recognized as American military handguns of that historic era…and from which many similarly patterned pistols were made in the late 18th and very early 19th century in America, comparable to those illustrated in Chapter 6-B *Secondary Military Single Shot Pistols*. The key feature that distinguishes these (aside from their similar lock shapes and

Pair American made c. 1760-1770 flintlock belt size pistols by Perkin, New York, closely fashioned after the popular British style of the era. Silver mounted.

16-022.8

mountings,) are the markings, a large "US" or "U. States" on the lock and/or barrel with similar marks burned deeply into the wood stock itself. Four of these identical types are to be seen in detail in the Smith & Bitter work *Historic Pistols: The American Martial Flintlock 1760-1845 (qv)*. The typical example illustrated here is 67 caliber with a 9" round barrel engraved with large letters "LD" (Light Dragoons) and deeply die-stamped "US" at

top of breech. Lockplate engraved "US"; large deep burnt "U. STATES" underside of the pin-fastened walnut stock; brass mountings. Minor variations on all specimens viewed.

16-022.8   Values—Fair **$8,500+**
           Good **$15,000-20,000**
           Very Good **$20,000-$40,000+**

BIBLIOGRAPHY

(Note: Information concerning Colonial and Revolutionary era firearms may be found listed in bibliographies elsewhere in this book. They are: *A Pictorial History Of U.S. Single Shot Martial Pistols* by James Kalman and C. M. Patterson; *U.S. Martial And Semi-Martial Single-Shot Pistols* by C. E. Chapel; *Identifying U.S. Muskets, Rifles And Carbines* by Col. A. Gluckman; *Thoughts On The Kentucky Rifle In Its Golden Age* by Joe Kindig, Jr.; *American Military Shoulder Arms: Colonial and Revolutionary War Arms.* Vol. 1. by G. Moller.)

*Ahearn, Bill. *Muskets of the Revolution and the French & Indian Wars.* Woonsocket, Rhode Island: Mowbray Publishers, 2005. Broad coverage of the smoothbore longarm in early America, including British, French, Dutch, German, Spanish and American weapons. Lots of details and close-up illustrations of the guns and locks. Fine identification guide.

Bailey, D. W. *British Military Longarms 1715-1815.* Harrisburg, Pennsylvania: Stackpole Books, 1971. A wealth of detailed information with excellent coverage of variations not discussed elsewhere.

Blackmore, Howard L. *British Military Firearms 1650-1850.* London, England: Herbert Jenkins, Publisher, 1961 with subsequent American reprintings. A basic and highly important guide. Widely cited and referred to.

Boehret, Paul C. *The Committee-of-Safety Musket.* Sellersville, Penna.: published by author, 1956. Paper covered pamphlet; early study with important information and listing of makers

Brinckerhoff, Sidney B. and Chamberlain, Pierce A. *Spanish Military Weapons In Colonial America 1700-1821.* Harrisburg, Pennsylvania: The Stackpole Company, 1972. A major guide to the subject. Very well illustrated.

Brown, M. L. *Firearms in Colonial America.* Washington, D. C.: Smithsonian Institution Press 1980. Traces firearms and their development from earliest days in Europe through evolution and use in America to 1792. Wealth of information not available elsewhere.

*Darling, Anthony D. *Red Coat And Brown Bess.* Ottawa, Ontario, Canada: Museum Restoration Service, 1970. Monograph containing definitive data on basic models and many variance.

Gill, Harold B. Jr. *The Gunsmith in Colonial Virginia.* Williamsburg, Virginia: The Colonial Williamsburg Foundation, 1974. Listing all known makers 1608 to 1800. Details of tools and actual gunsmith's accounts, information on Committee of Safety muskets and rifles.

*Grinslade, Tom. *Flintlock Fowlers: The First Guns Made in America.* Texarkana, Texas: Scurlock Publishing Co., 2005. Long overlooked, these longarms were the most commonplace of all antique American firearms and yet, until now, were neglected. Very important coverage of this widely varied type with profuse and detailed photographic illustrations; coverage from 1700 to 1820.

Guthman, William H. *U.S. Army Weapons 1784-1791.* St. Louis, Missouri: The American Society of Arms Collectors, 1975. The

only work covering arms of this era with highly significant information.

Hicks, Major James E. *French Military Weapons 1717-1938.* New Milford, Connecticut: N. Flayderman & Co., 1964. Originally published 1938 as *Notes On French Ordnance.* The only work specifically devoted to the subject in English.

Lindsay, Merrill. *The New England Gun - The First 200 Years.* New Haven, Connecticut and New York, New York: New Haven Colony Historical Society and David McKay Company, 1975. Catalog of a major museum exhibit with outstanding examples of Colonial and Revolutionary guns.

Mayer, Joseph R. *Flintlocks Of The Iroquois 1620-1687.* Rochester, New York: Rochester Museum of Arts & Sciences, 1943. Important and well illustrated monograph on firearms relics from historic sites.

Moore, Warren. *Weapons Of The American Revolution And Accoutrements.* New York, New York: Funk & Wagnalls, 1967. Very well illustrated guide; includes weapons of America and Europe.

Neumann, George C. *The History Of Weapons Of The American Revolution.* New York, New York: Harper & Row, Publishers, 1967. Basic guide with arms of all countries of Europe and America; heavily illustrated.

*Neumann, George C. *Battle Weapons Of The American Revolution.* Texarkana, Texas: Scurlock Pub. Co., 1998. Similar to the above work with expanded coverage.

*Neumann, George C. *Collector's Illustrated Encyclopedia Of The American Revolution.* Harrisburg, Pennsylvania: Stackpole Books, 1975. A vast amount of material on artifacts and equipment with sections on firearms. Reprinted, 1992, Texarkana, Texas: Rebel Publishing Co.

Peterson, Harold L. *Arms And Armour In Colonial America 1526-1783.* Harrisburg, Pennsylvania: The Stackpole Company, 1956. The classic in its field, the basic and most important guide to the subject.

Peterson, Harold L. *The Book Of The Continental Soldier.* Harrisburg, Pennsylvania: The Stackpole Company, 1968. Complete coverage with chapters devoted to firearms.

Peterson, Harold L. *Arms and Armor of the Pilgrims.* Plymouth, Mass: Plimouth [sic] Plantation, Inc. & Pilgrim Society, 1954. Monograph; author a noted arms researcher.

Rogers, Col. H. C. B. *Weapons Of The British Soldier.* London, England: Seeley Service & Co., 1960. General survey of edged weapons and firearms with cursory information on early flintlocks.

Sawyer, Charles Winthrop. *Firearms In American History 1600-1800.* Boston, Massachusetts: Privately printed for the author, 1910. A long-time classic on the subject; considerable of its material has been updated and improved upon by more recently published works.

Swayze, Nathan L. *The Rappahannock Forge.* St. Louis, Missouri: The American Society of Arms Collectors, 1976. Well illustrated monograph of lecture given before the society. Definitive data obtained from most recorded specimens.

(*) Preceding a title indicates the book is currently in print.

Chapter XVII

American Shotguns and Fowling Pieces

It's an interesting observation, a fact worthy of noting, that shotguns and fowling pieces were likely the most commonly owned and used of all antique American arms; the type of gun that just about every household had at one time or another; America before 1900 being essentially rural. Some estimates have it that almost 90 percent of the population owned a gun. Certainly, if a home was to have one firearm of any type it most likely would have been a shotgun/fowling piece. Yet, conversely, these antique (or pre-1900) American shotguns have, until recently, been of but slight interest to the antique arms collector. Of course, there have been exceptions to this generality; notably in the outstanding handcrafted work of individual makers and of other famous manufacturers (e.g. Colt, Parker, Remington, Winchester, etc.) which have always possessed a reasonable *demand* on the collectors' market. Even such finer quality, popular named pieces suffered somewhat by being on the lower end of the price scale in each of their respective fields. By far, the great majority of so-called "Damascus barrel, black powder" types, of which vast quantities were made and sold, have stirred very little interest until the last few years. Terming the field unexploited until now would be more apt than calling it "undiscovered." Those fine quality, famous name makes have evidenced considerable increases in price and demand in recent years. The vast numbers of medium and lower grade makes by relatively unknown or unrecognized manufacturers have shown similar, though not as dramatic, price and demand increases. Some of these latter types have very little to offer in the way of collector interest, surrounded with similar obscurities to the "Suicide Specials" revolvers (*see Chapter VIII-A*), and are obviously merely riding the coattails of the general antique collecting market, akin to the "Suicide Specials" by being "… unique in that they have almost no historical significance!" With few relatively inexpensive firearms remaining for the collector with a minimal budget, this field offers many opportunities to assemble an interesting collection. Many fascinating variations are encountered.

COVERAGE

As with many other areas of "antique" gun collecting, there is a very fine line (if any at all!) that divides what is "antique" from "modern" or even "semi-modern" and thus, suitable for inclusion in this work. As discussed earlier, the word "antique" as applicable to collecting quite often defies an exacting description. Coverage includes Muzzle-Loading Flintlock and Percussion Shotguns as well as **Black Powder Damascus Barrel, Breech-Loading Double Barrel Shotguns (hammer and hammerless types)**, a category that has been generally accepted as "antique" by a majority of the collecting world. It was necessary due to the limitations of space and the nature of this generalized coverage to make exceptions … both inclusions and exclusions. In the following listing will be found a few shotguns of special historical interest (e.g. the Spencer pump action shotgun) or of unique design (e.g. the Young two-shot repeating shotgun and the Hollenbeck three-barrel gun) that are occasionally available on the collectors' market and of sufficient interest to warrant bringing to the reader's attention.

No attempt has been made to list every known or recorded name found on the Damascus, black powder doubles. The greatest obstacle to ever having a complete compilation is the fact that a vast amount of such shotguns were not actually made by the parties whose names appear on them. Large quantities of shotguns were manufactured in Europe and America by makers (in many instances unknown) who marked on the guns only the names of the importers, large wholesale hardware dealers, sporting goods firms or various distributors who sold them in the United States. Others were marked merely with brand names … a similar occurrence to the markings often found on "Suicide Special" revolvers (Chapter VIII-A). Quite often identical make and model shotguns are encountered with differing company or brand markings. Similar conditions prevailed for muzzle-loading percussion shotguns also but not quite to the extent as observed on the Damascus breechloaders.

FOREIGN MADE—IMPORTED PARTS

A feature unique to shotguns and fowling pieces, and one the collector should prominently bear in mind, is the fact that a great majority of *American-made* muzzle-loading and breech-loading shotguns have utilized foreign imported parts, mostly *barrels*. Although certainly many shotguns were entirely of American manufacture, it should be noted that this is one area of American arms collecting in which there is a preponderance of imported parts. Knowledge of this fact and realization that rarely did American barrel-making approach the quality and price of the European product, especially English barrels, may upset some misconceptions and notions previously held by American gun collectors. In the years of the rise in popularity of arms collecting, unknowing collectors have attached an unjustified stigma to many American-made guns on which some foreign parts may have been used. No valid reasons are apparent other than some vague sense or implication of being "un-American!"

Obviously, in instances where an entire gun was of European manufacture and then marked with an American dealer's or agent's name, it will command a lesser value than an identical gun of entirely American manufacture. A notable example of such price differentials is seen in American dueling pistols. Such reasoning should definitely not be the case, though, with fine shotguns or fowling pieces. Many of the finest muzzleloaders and breechloaders utilize imported barrels; generally of British manufacture. The very essence of shotgun collecting is an understanding of the development of the gun and the markets to which it was directed.

The American shotgun market was oriented towards "meat" hunters. Although American makers produced many shotguns in the first half of the 19th century, they were usually sturdy, rough, big-bore affairs made for hard work and not sporting purposes. American makers devoted their finest efforts to rifle making for sporting purposes, turning out but a few shotguns and often on special order basis only. Those Americans that took up the sporting or "gentlemanly art" of wing shooting invariably bought a fine, English-made shotgun … be it muzzleloading or breech-loading. The English shotgun dominated the American market until well into the 1870s; by then American gun-makers began "getting into the act." Not only was the British product costly, but most often it had many features about it (i.e. fancy engraving and stock work) that were completely unnecessary for the American market. The sharply defined structure of British society and their social system most often allowed only the upper classes to engage in the sport, and the British gunsmith tailored his product accordingly. Conversely, the American market encompassed all strata of society and, hence, a much broader spectrum of gun buyers. American makers, recognizing this market, incorporated the most functional of the British gun features and gave a much wider range to their product by offering them in varying states of ruggedness and a wide range of ornamentation; commencing with the very plainest grades at minimal cost.

MAJOR FACTORS AFFECTING VALUE

Quality and condition generally are the most important features that determine value of American shotguns and fowling pieces. Intriguing or unique mechanisms are highly important factors with breechloaders. Makers' names are significant, especially on the more famous lines (e.g. Parker, Colt, etc.) while for those of lesser name and fame it may be generalized that the more well-known and respected the maker, the greater the demand and likely the value of the gun. As no specific "pecking order" has been established in this field, it is strictly a "seat-of-the-pants" instinctive reasoning process that is involved to establish price! Reasonableness should be the watchword.

Maker's name and geographic location often play a significant role in establishing shotgun prices, very similar to the methods applied to American percussion sporting and target rifles (*see Chapter XII*). Premium values may often be placed on shotguns and fowling pieces depending on the maker's, agent's, or dealer's name found marked on them. A very loose rule of thumb for percussion muzzleloaders gives greater weight and premium prices to Western and Southern markings (the latter for their possible Confederate association) with Midwestern and Eastern markings respectively less. It is interesting to note that on the Damascus double shotguns, Long Island and Chesapeake Bay area makers and names are apparently among the most sought after and worth premiums. Often collectors seeking guns made in their own locality offer premium prices for such pieces;

for the collector or dealer looking to sell such "local" shotguns it's much like finding the proverbial needle-in-the-haystack.

Mechanical condition quite often alters both demand and price of shotguns. On the earlier muzzle-loading varieties and the better grade breechloaders, mechanical condition may often be secondary, and the cost of repairs merely factored into the value of the gun. With many of the lesser quality, low valued shotguns, mechanical condition does play a major role in both demand and value. As with "Suicide Specials," it is often found that cost of repairs may be more than the entire gun is worth. Hence, lacking completeness and proper mechanical functioning and with the absence of any other redeeming feature, such shotguns should be bought only at "distress" prices. Values fall off drastically on lower grade pieces as condition diminishes. Many are relatively unattractive due to their lower quality workmanship, offering but slight incentive other than "decorative value" for the collector. Such shotguns normally create but slight demand, and consequently minimal values, unless in pristine almost new condition. Values are often on a "… what-the-market-will-bear" basis. Those collectors with a practiced eye for aesthetics will be very much ahead of the game.

The most common gauges or bore sizes encountered are 10 gauge and 12 gauge. Prices shown here generally reflect those bore sizes. A general rule-of-thumb for both breech-loading and muzzle-loading varieties has it that the larger bores (i.e., 8 gauge, 6 gauge and even 4 gauge) will increase in both demand and value in direct proportion to their increasing enormity. Smaller bores (i.e., 16 gauge, 20 gauge or smaller) also increase in both demand and value in direct proportion to their decreasing diminutiveness … but not nearly as much or worth the premiums priced on the large gauges. Big bores seem to be in much greater demand and predominate in interest and price.

HAMMER vs. HAMMERLESS BREECHLOADING SHOTGUNS

Although the hammer type doubles are earlier and for many years seemed to be in greater demand and to fetch slightly higher values than comparable hammerless types, it is readily apparent that such conditions no longer exist. As a matter of fact in many instances the highest grade hammerless types might surpass all others in demand and value. Many of the finest quality very high grade hammerless Damascus doubles were rebarreled over the years by their original owners, by later shooters who acquired them or by dealers and/or modern gun collectors upgrading what was then considered an obsolete, yet still fine quality, shotgun to make it more valuable and desirable on the modern gun market. Rebarreling was performed in many instances by the same maker that originally produced the gun. Parker Brothers for instance is well known to have supplied on custom order fluid steel barrels for customers who wished to "modernize" or upgrade their earlier Damascus barrel Parker guns; some other makers updated their own products similarly. Such guns of course are of dual interest both as collector's items and as "modern" firearms.

In instances where rebarreling was performed outside the factory, by private gunsmiths, the "antique" collector value and desirability has been diminished. Such shotguns are usually revalued upward strictly as "modern" sporting firearms and are outside the coverage of this treatise.

From the foregoing it becomes readily apparent that many of the high grade American hammerless types may in actuality be among the scarcest of Damascus shotguns as it's quite possible that less have survived in their original unaltered condition. The Damascus double market being more or less in its infancy has yet to have statistical surveys or in-depth scrutiny to verify that fact. It certainly offers considerable potential for the diligent researcher and, of course, the discriminating collector.

BORES

Condition of bores in muzzle-loading shotguns/fowling pieces seems to play a very minor role in determining value. The author can recall less than a handful of instances where a collector has made even an inquiry about a shotgun bore in a muzzleloader. Catalog descriptions of them rarely, if ever, mention the feature. Bores do play a role of considerable importance with the breech-loading Damascus doubles; more or less in direct relationship to the outside condition of the gun as well as its increasingly higher degree of quality or grade.

Although chances are slight that the gun will ever be shot again (*see section below cautioning against shooting*), it is perfectly proper for the collector to feel that part of the value of the Damascus double should be reasonably weighed by its bore condition, as the very quality and shootability of that bore was important during its era of original use. Although likely a minor determinant for value with the lowest grade doubles, it is of ever-increasing importance for the top quality guns.

A factor often overlooked, but one the prospective buyer should bear in mind, is reboring. Although occurring to a lesser degree on Damascus barrels than on the modern steel barreled doubles, it may affect desirability and will very likely alter value; especially so on the better grades. Reboring (i.e., the drilling and reaming out of the inside of a barrel) on the antique doubles was most likely done for pure cosmetic purposes; to clean up a ruined, poor conditioned bore and to make it look new. Aside from changing the shooting quality of the gun, this practice rendered the already thin walls of the barrel even thinner, making the black powder Damascus shotgun even more hazardous should one attempt to shoot it! If such reboring is readily apparent, it will alter value in varying degrees depending on the quality of the shotgun; if not readily apparent yet the buyer is suspect and the gun is of sufficient importance, he would do well to perform micrometer and bore gauge verifications as is commonly practiced with modern shotguns.

STOCKS

Almost all makers of Damascus doubles (at least the very well known ones) offered their arms in varying qualities of stocks; commencing with the plainest grain American walnut and proceeding through various levels to the fanciest figured, imported English walnut or fancy grained French Circassian walnut. Even the most unpracticed eye can quickly distinguish those fancy grain stocks from the plainer types. Values are judged proportionally. The quality of checkering and, occasionally, carving also varies considerably from the plainest, most coarse, to highly detailed and delicate; prices and values are set accordingly.

There is no systematic means to establish or recognize each degree of quality; even the makers themselves use the most ambiguous and dubious, if not downright questionable terminology. Distinguishing quality is not a difficult skill to master; merely being observant of the many specimens that are available on the collectors' market should make these differences readily apparent.

ENGRAVING

Profuseness and quality of engraving (or its complete lack of it) are determinants of shotgun values; to a greater degree with the more noted makes. Recognizing engraving quality is also a skill that can be readily mastered by the keen observer of the wide range of specimens available and which may usually be seen by the collector at almost any large gun show. The reader is referred to Chapter II where a discussion of engraved guns and their importance may be found in greater depth.

Most makers of quality shotguns as well as all the larger makers offered their doubles in varying degrees of ornateness. Some of the most elaborate specimens included delicate gold inlay work depicting wildfowl and other game scenes. The amount of such engraving designs (i.e., the total area of the gun that it might cover from locks to breech of barrels to all the mountings) and its overall delicateness and detail or, its uniqueness of design, are factors the discriminating collector recognizes as important when determining desirability and consequently values. Gun decoration and embellishments are quite significant in the shotgun collecting field. The originality of such engraving should be carefully gauged and studied; in not a few instances, very fine shotguns have been "upgraded" by the addition, in modern times, of extra engraving and designs (including gold inlay work) to immeasurably add to their value! Thus, the buyer of highly embellished shotguns should be reasonably knowledgeable on the subject of firearms decoration and engraving.

DAMASCUS, TWIST AND LAMINATED BARRELS

These most commonly used terms ... **Damascus, Twist, Laminated** ... each indicated a different method of barrel type in their day, but for the gun collector of today, have become, for all practical purposes, one and the same. They are all generally referred to in the generic sense as *Damascus barrels*. In its most common usage the terminology *Damascus shotguns* or, *Damascus doubles*, is applied to the entire group of double barrel, breech-loading, hammer and hammerless type *shotguns* with nonfluid steel barrels, most of which are made to accept black powder loaded shells only, and on which the barrels may be seen to have twist or spiral-like design in their manufacture and finish.

Should the reader wish to be thoroughly confused and delve into the subject at greater length, he might find it interesting, if not amusing, to wade through the many dissertations on the subject (some at odds with one another) to arrive at a simple definition, and distinction, of each of those three terms denoting types of barrels made and used on black powder breech-loading shotguns of the 1870 through early 1900s era! Although not defying plain definition (and there are some beauts!) it presents a challenge rendering them to their most simplistic terms.

During the actual time those terms (and barrel manufacturing processes) were employed, they were often used synonymously by dealers, agents and manufacturers. Over the past decades, in their general usage by sportsmen and authors, they tended to become very much one and the same. For instance, in *Small Arms Lexicon* (Muller and Olson; Shooter's Bible; New Jersey) there is the following definition: "*Damascus Barrel, also known as 'Laminated' or 'twist' barrel.*" In *English Sporting Guns & Accessories* (Hastings; Ward Lock & Co., London), the author says of Damascus barrels: "... Rigby of Dublin made the first Damascus Barrel ... prior to that barrels were twisted out of horseshoe nail stubs. Damascus barrels ... were worked into their beautifully herringbone patterns by the mingling of iron and steel." Other well-known authors such as Harold Peterson in the *Encyclopedia of Firearms* (Dutton & Co.; New York) and George Nonte in the *Firearms Encyclopedia* (Outdoor Life/Harper & Row; New York) both discuss "Damascus barrel" with very accurate descriptions but neglect to mention completely "laminated" or "twist" barrels, or even list or mention them elsewhere in their books. Yet, both other forms decidedly existed, were widely made and were heavily advertised.

It's not quite anyone's guess as to the distinction between these three terms; there apparently was one. The best witness to that fact is seen in any 19th century catalog of a gun dealer or maker. It's quickly apparent that "twist" barrels were commonly used on their most inexpensive grades and are seen at the very bottom of their advertised lines, while the top of almost every line (Winchester shotguns seem to be the exception) was almost universally reserved for "Damascus" barrels only, this latter type being offered in many varying grades too. "Laminated" barrels are usually found in the middle of most makers'/dealers' shotgun lines but quite often they'll be found to overlap into the lower "twist" as well as the upper "Damascus" grades, thus leading today's collector to believe that the catalog descriptions may very well have been more a play on words than an actual description of a manufacturing process.

The noted New York dealer Homer Fisher's 1880 catalog usage of various barrel terminology makes intriguing reading. For instance, Fisher described his muzzle-loading percussion single barrel shotguns with "Belgian Sham Twist Barrels" and "English … genuine twist barrels" while also offering "American guns made from muskets." On the same catalog page are found listed muzzle-loading percussion Belgian doubles with "… imitation twist barrels" and "…real twist barrels," while English percussion doubles are offered with "… English twist barrels … laminated steel barrels … and fine laminated steel barrels!"

Among the numerous well-known makers whose lines Fisher offered were Parker Brothers of Meriden, Connecticut, seen listed with "… plain twist barrels … fine English twist barrels … fine Damascus steel barrels … extra fine steel barrels … finest Damascus steel barrels." The lowest quality Remington Damascus doubles were offered in "… decarbonized steel barrels" progressing to "twist barrels" and ultimately to their best grade "Damascus barrels." Lowest grade Daly shotguns were those mounted with "… fine laminated steel barrels" progressing through various stages to Daly's top-of-the-line with "… extra quality Turkish or superb Damascus barrels." Colt shotguns were shown in two grades only—"twist" or "laminated" barrels. Numerous other makes were offered in that same catalog, each with varying barrel types and names furthering the contention that the terminology of the era was loosely applied and that actual manufacturing processes had become obscured even then. Such was certainly the case with the very cheapest, most inexpensive grade shotguns of the era which are found actually marked on their barrels or locks "best Damascus steel" or "… Fine London Laminated" and a host of similar markings, none of which likely designate any specific manufacturing process used in their production but, rather, was puffery, if not outright falsity, used to sell them!

"*DAMASCUS*" as applied to gun barrels is strictly a generic term indicating what had originally been a specific manufacturing, laminating and welding technique to give special strength and decorative structure to *sword blades*. It was developed in and around the famous, ancient Mid-East city of

Coil Wound Around Mandrel

Damascus (now in Syria). The date of application of this technique to the manufacture of barrels and the first usage of the word "Damascus" is obscure and certainly, a highly esoteric subject outside the scope of this treatise. In broadest, and simplest, terms the types of barrels to which this generic name is applied are those made by a process, which varied from country to country, in which alternating strips or rods of iron and steel were twisted and welded into larger rods and were then combined and twisted or coiled around a mandrel or core, with the abutting edges of the rods or bars then welded. The more strands of steel and iron that are twisted and braided before winding on the mandrel, the stronger and lighter the barrels could be made; the finer the twist, the less chance of a carbon inclusion from welding, further adding to the barrel's lightness, strength and safety. When the mandrel was removed, the welded tube, or rough barrel, that remained was filed, bored and finished. There were a great many qualities and grades involved (as witnessed by descriptions from the Fisher catalog). Often the alternating strips/rods were in themselves separately forged into wire and twisted about each other. Those strips when set side-by-side were heated and forged into a solid bar. After finishing and boring, the barrel was acid etched on the exterior to bring out the design formed by those varied strips of twisted metal.

The "Damascus" process achieved a number of important results, most important of which was the manufacture of much lighter weight barrels than were possible at the time with the conventional barrel manufacturing techniques then in use. The process combined the desirable properties of wrought iron with steel and made possible the manufacture of shotguns (especially double barrel types) with thin walled barrels, in many cases making them less expensive.

An eye-appealing aesthetic feature, important for today's collector when assessing values, was the almost limitless artistic opportunities available to the barrel maker when creating the complex pattern this "Damascus" process created. When the barrels had been filed and polished to a mirror-like finish and treated with various acids and browning processes, there emerged on the outside of the barrel highly recognizable, intricate patterns of close, tight-wound tiny coils alternating with various stripings and coils of brown colors, some of them approximating herringbone and swirled patterns … all of them in varying degrees of delicateness and in an overall twisted design corresponding to the artistic abilities of the maker and pocketbook of the purchaser.

There were endless variations of designs; larger makers even offered a broad selection of patterns to their customers. The Colt Firearms Company (who, incidentally, imported all of their twist and Damascus barrels from Belgium for their Model 1878 and 1883 shotguns) advertised in their catalogs that barrels could be ordered with four varying types of patterns "… twist … fine twist … laminated … Damascus"; prices rising respectively. Quite a few interesting variations have been noted, a customer occasionally ordering the left and right barrels in different grades to give contrasting patterns! While the Liége, Belgium, makers were noted for their delicateness of patterns, the British makers favored larger designs. That feature was of such importance in selling shotguns, and their quality often judged by them, that not a few nefarious makers engaged in a brisk

Gun Barrel Iron, Tristed & Formed into a Thin, Flexible Metal Brand

Section of Gun Barrel Coil

business of simulating the Damascus patterns on cheap grade twist barrels to fleece the unwary. Today's collector should be aware that such counterfeit and spurious "Damascus" barrels were made in considerable quantity. Many surviving specimens of these less expensive grade shotguns with poor quality barrels on which "Damascus" patterns have been merely acid etched are to be seen on the current collector's market. At the time they were actually sold and used, both the quality and strength of such barrels had been proportionately lessened to the point where the shooter might have been risking life and limb!

Discussions of the subject, to be found in a great many gun books over the past century, often tend to be overly complicated and confusing. The early Parker Brothers catalogs contain a reasonably accurate and clear description of the process as does one of the most classic gun books of all times *The Gun & Its Development* by W.W. Greener (published in nine editions 1881 to 1910 with modern day reprints). This latter book also tends to be a superb source for detailed information on American and European Damascus breech-loading doubles of all types. The author tends to favor the description, worth repeating here in abbreviated form, from *Farrow's Military Encyclopedia* (Military-Naval Publishing Company, New York, 1895; 2nd Edition):

> The iron for all good barrels contains a portion of steel, or undergoes some kind of steeling process. Horseshoe-nails or stubs, after much violent usage, yield a tough kind of iron when reheated; English gun-makers have been accustomed to buy such refuse on the Continent. The best barrels are now made of *laminated, twisted and Damascus* steel. To prepare "*laminated*" steel, Mr. Greener, a celebrated Birmingham gunsmith, collects scraps of saws, files, springs and steel tools from various workshops, cuts them into small pieces, cleans and polishes them then fuses them into a semi-fluid state; gathers them into a "bloom" or mass and forges this bloom, hardens and solidifies it (then) rolls it into rods which are cut into pieces six inches long and welded together, repeating the rolling, cutting, welding several times finally bringing the metal into a very hard,

Two-Iron Damascus Barrel

Skelp Gun Barrel

Three-Iron Stub Damascus Barrel

Single-Iron Damascus Barrel

tough, fibrous and uniform state. "*Twisted steel*" for barrels is made by taking thin plates of iron and steel, laying them alternating on one on another in a pile, welding them by heat and hammering and twisting them by a very powerful, mechanical agency until there are twelve or fourteen complete turns to an inch; the length becomes reduced one-half and the thickness doubled by this twisting. "*Damascus steel*" barrels are made of steel which has undergone a still further series of welding and twisting operations. "*Stub Damascus*" barrels are made of a mixture of old files with old horseshoe nails; the files are heated, cooled in water, broken with hammers and pounded with mortar into small fragments, then mixed with stub and the mixture is fused, forged, rolled and twisted. An inferior Damascus twist is made by interlaying scraps of sheet iron with charcoal and producing an appearance of twist but without the proper qualities. Three penny-skelp and two penny-skelp are inferior kinds of barrel iron; the worst of all is "Sham-dam skelp" of which gun barrels are made for hawking at a cheap price at country fairs and for barter with natives in Africa and backwoods and prairies of America.

Thus, the watchword was "caveat emptor" for the shotgun buyer … then … and now! The very cheapest or "twist" barrels were formed by merely welding a strip of flat metal that had been "twisted" or wound around a mandrel or core; not much of a safety factor.

Although a few aficionados may wish to quibble about these often ambiguous terms, the collector will be quite proper in merely calling them *DAMASCUS DOUBLES*. It seems worthy, however, to recall their less obscure beginnings.

CAUTION AGAINST SHOOTING DAMASCUS DOUBLES

The collector should be aware that all of these "twist" or "Damascus" barreled shotguns were made primarily for use with **Black Powder Loaded Shells** only. Many are dangerous even with those shells in their chambers! All are unreliable … if not extremely hazardous … if used with modern, smokeless powder loaded shotshells. The majority of all modern, smokeless or nitro powder shotshells produced through the first half of the 20th century retain the printed warning on their labels "… caution … do not use these shells in guns having Damascus or other twist steel barrels" or words to that effect.

Black powder loaded shotshells for use in Damascus doubles were offered by some of the largest manufacturers as late as the 1930s; Remington listed them in a 1935 price list, while the 1933 Winchester catalog still had them available.

Not a few weaknesses have been noted in Damascus barrels; notably their inability to stand up under excessive pressures. If original manufacture was faulty (i.e., welding), they were susceptible to "unwinding." Barrels were also subject to bursting if small areas were allowed to rust thin or become heavily pitted. The author has often heard jeering comments about such warnings; the scoffers claiming that finer grade Damascus doubles are perfectly safe to fire and that they have done so with no ill-effect. Conversely … many are the stories heard and known of injuries received from blown barrels when those same cautions were not heeded. Just about every writer on the subject of Damascus shotguns has cautioned against firing them; the author joins that chorus of disapprovers and, at the risk of triteness, can only advise that if one plays with fire long enough, he gets burned! It's true that some of the makers specifically stated that their Damascus barrels would hold "nitro or smokeless powder" loads. Parker stated that fact in their 1899 catalog. The collector or prospective shooter is doubly cautioned to discount these statements in the light of experience of many that have preceded him and further realize that such guarantees and warranties hold no validity today.

FOWLING PIECE vs. SHOTGUN

Terminologies, and their definitions, play an important role in gun collecting. *"FOWLING PIECE"* and *"SHOTGUN,"* are terms that are defined identically and which may be used interchangeably. In common usage, however, in the collecting world, breechloaders are invariably known only as "shotguns" whereas muzzleloaders utilize both terms. Single barrel muzzleloaders are most often known as "fowling pieces" while double barreled flintlock and percussion types are called by both names, depending on the author's or collector's preference and collecting experience.

A "fowling piece" or "shotgun" is a smooth bore longarm specifically designed to fire a quantity of pellets simultaneously on one discharge. It was intended for use in hunting small game, especially birds … hence, the incorporation of the word "fowl" in its nomenclature. Early literature often termed it a "birding" piece while in modern times it has become universally known as a "shotgun." The evolutionary use of larger shot and the massive single slug widened the possible uses of the gun for hunting big game, for target firing and as an offensive and defensive weapon as is witnessed by those pieces carried as guard guns (i.e., Wells Fargo shotguns) to repeating riot shotguns and U.S. military trench shotguns … and even the sawed-off shotguns of the gangster era of the 1920s!

Earliest muzzle-loading shotguns were single shot, long barreled pieces; some exceeding 6" in overall length, the theory being that it could achieve longer range and flatter trajectory with longer barrels that held greater charges of powder. Such arms were intended to be used primarily near feeding areas and fired from blinds at waterfowl. All American Colonial fowling pieces were long and heavy; all shooting in that early era was from blinds. Shooting in flight was strictly a matter of chance! Their fowling pieces were designed strictly for killing; the shooting of birds on the wing … or even running, played no notable role. With the Americans it was strictly "for the pot" whereas the British developed such bird shooting as a gentleman's sport. The very first fowling pieces in Colonial America were brought from England with the settlers. A prominent member of the Pilgrim Colony in 1621 wrote home to England to others planning to join them to "… let your piece be long in barrel and fear not the weight of it for most of our shooting is from stands." It was not until the invention of the percussion cap that the fowling piece/shotgun assumed greater importance and became practical for use with moving game and also for sport and target.

The evolutionary changes in ignition systems (i.e., flintlock to percussion to self-contained cartridge) primarily at the end of the 18th and early 19th centuries and a great many improvements in firearms design led to lighter weight and balance in fowling pieces. Barrels were successively shortened, leading to lighter weight arms, thus allowing the double barrel side-by-side fowling piece/shotgun to be acceptable, if not practical. Their earlier use had never been popular due to their size and weight which made them clumsy and cumbersome. Popularity increased with the invention (by Joseph Manton of England in 1806) of the elevated sighting rib which facilitated aiming and increased accuracy considerably. It was the British who not only initiated and developed shooting "on the wing" but refined it to a very gentlemanly art. Their shotguns were tailored for their patrician pocketbooks by the well-established, high quality British gunmaking trade. Americans who were interested in such shooting almost exclusively purchased the British-made product with but a few American gunsmiths devoting their efforts to producing shotguns.

Although there were many changes and improvements in shotguns, especially the double barreled types, in the 19th century, American public acceptance of such changes was slow. Breechloaders appeared as early as 1812. By the 1860s improved versions were utilizing centerfire, self-contained cartridges. Hammerless models were introduced in the late 1870s. The flintlock double shotgun was relatively scarce (and American versions a rarity) having been made during a short time span only. The percussion double lasted well into the breech-loading era, overlapping usage and manufacture of the hammer type double shotgun, which in turn overlapped the era of its successor, the hammerless double. The same was true with the first repeating and automatic shotguns which appeared in the 1880s.

The 1870s was the decade that American sportsmen and hunters … and consequently manufacturers … entered the shotgun market en masse. Many features about the British-made shotguns, notably their exceptional quality and fancy embellishments, made them prohibitively priced for the average American buyer. Many of those quality features were just not necessary for the general American market. Both American ingenuity and mass production techniques combined to turn out a wide range of shotguns in less expensive, affordable price ranges. Of course, as this market grew in popularity and demand on the vast American market, so too did the British, Belgian, and other European makers alter some of their manufacturing techniques to compete with the American product. The American hunter and sportsman by the 1880s had a tremendous range of shotguns to choose from in both homegrown and foreign varieties.

Multi-shot and various types of repeating shotguns had been made and marketed over various eras, none with any resounding commercial success. It was not until the mid-1880s that the Spencer pump action shotgun achieved a modicum of success due to both its practicality as well as its additional fire power for the hunter, making general inroads to the double barrel gun market. Other makers, notably Winchester with their lever action repeating shotgun and Burgess with their slide action shotgun entered the repeating market in the late '80s and early '90s with some success. It was not until the late 1890s that Winchester successfully marketed a repeating slide action shotgun. Made under the patent of the famous American inventors the Browning Brothers it was superior to anything then on the market. Its immediate public acceptance and success in the field overtook and surpassed in popularity the dominant position that had been held by the double barrel shotgun.

IDENTIFICATION AND CLASSIFICATION

Muzzleloaders

The basic distinguishing feature on *percussion, muzzle-loading fowling pieces and double shotguns* is lock style. This major component is normally mentioned in any description and immediately allows the collector a general mental picture of the appearance and style of the gun itself. Although there are numerous variations of locks, the following two types were in most common usage and hence, most often encountered today:

Bar or Front Action Lock

Bar Action or Front Action Locks: A full removable lock plate with the outside hammer mounted towards the *rear* of the plate; the lock plate itself extending forward alongside the percussion bolster and under the barrel breech. The mainspring is located inside the lock *in front of the hammer* exerting its force downward against the tumbler. Many variations in lock plate shapes and styles are seen. Quite commonly known as a "side lock" which has come into common usage in collecting jargon. It should be noted that the term has quite different connotations when applied to breech-loading guns.

*Hammer Type Damascus Double with
Bar/Front Action Locks and Top Lever*

Back Action Lock

Back Action Lock: The hammer located on the very front end of the lock plate while the mainspring inside is located behind the hammer; its force exerted upward against the tumbler in reverse of the bar lock. When fitted to a gun it was mortised/inletted into the wrist of the stock allowing the forestock to be lightened; a feature which proved quite important in the design and manufacture of shotguns and improved a gun's balance. The back action lock first appeared in the 1830s becoming in common usage by 1850; older bar action locks continued in use simultaneously. Some percussion shotguns were still manufactured as late as the 1880s with the back action lock. A major objection to the back action lock was the possible weakening of the stock at the wrist where it was necessary to inlet more of the wood to accommodate it.

Disparaging remarks are occasionally overheard about back action locks; another example of the eccentricities of gun collecting. Although diminishing in frequency, one can still hear off-handed caustic utterances when eavesdropping on a gun-trade: A particular shotgun (or rifle) should not be worth as much … or not as desirable … merely because it has a back action lock! There is very little rhyme or reason for the stigma. Although it's likely correct that back action locks were less expensive to make and it's certainly true that they are quite often found on lower grade, less expensive guns, both muzzle-loading and breech-loading, it should be recognized that they were developed not for their cost advantages but

rather to allow for the lightening and better balance of the firearms to which they were applied. Therefore, there are numerous top quality, even exceptional, firearms displaying the very height of the gunmaker's art that are fitted with back action locks. It certainly isn't logical to tar them all with the same brush. The disparity is apparently vanishing with the fast-growing popularity of this group of arms.

Breechloaders

The most readily apparent difference in the breech-loading "Damascus doubles" and the two major categories into which they are separated are:

Hammer Guns on which the hammers are mounted on the outside and are manually cocked.

Hammerless Guns on which the lock mechanism for firing is placed within the gun and is not visible on the exterior.

Of course, on both above types numerous variants and transitional forms (e.g., the semi-hammerless action) are encountered; many of them intriguing for appearance and mechanical innovation. Although the majority of hammerless types are self-cocking, quite a few of the earlier evolutionary styles are fitted with various forms of outside cocking levers and devices.

Another major distinguishing feature categorizing Damascus doubles is lock style.

Outside Hammer Guns have the same two basic styles found on muzzleloaders; i.e. the *Bar/Front Action Lock* and the *Back Action Lock*. Here, too, variant forms are found such as the modified or semi-box lock Whitney and the distinctive Ithaca semi-box lock.

Hammerless Doubles are most often encountered in two basic styles:

Box Lock: A style in which the entire mechanism is enclosed within the action. Often the stock must be removed in order to get to the mechanism. This type of lock or action is almost exclusive to "hammerless" breechloaders although occasionally variances are encountered with outside hammers fitted. Many variations of the box lock exist with some of the later, top-grade types having detachable box locks or "drop locks" which are removed from the underside of the frame. Box lock actions are usually self-cocking.

*Semi-Hammerless Double
and Box Lock Type
Action with Manual
(Side) Cocking Lever*

*Ithaca Hammer Type Double
with Semi-Box Lock Action*

Hammerless Double Box Lock Action

Double with Side Lever

Hammerless Damascus Double with Side Locks

Side Lock: Basically a modernized, refined variant of the traditional bar lock with the hammer mounted *inside* the lock plate. The entire lock plate is removable from the action (or frame). They are generally thought to be more efficient but considerably more expensive to produce. The two major variants within this style are the:

Bar Action Side Lock in which the mainspring projects forward of the tumbler necessitating a section of the lock plate to project forward to hold it; the type most widely used. Typical examples are seen on L. C. Smiths.

Back Action Side Lock on which the mainspring is fitted behind the tumbler usually allowing for a shorter lock plate that fits flush to the frame. Early Baker shotguns are excellent examples of this type.

Once again the collector should be aware that there are many variant forms of the above styles (for example: the false side lock, which is merely a box lock action made to resemble the more expensive side lock action with dummy side plates). The seeking out and acquisition of those variants make for a fascinating collection.

BREECH LEVERS AND LATCHES

The third important feature for categorizing Damascus doubles is the method by which barrels are opened. These, too, are many and varied in style and shape with numerous intriguing innovations and improvements.

The most often used and commonly seen early locking arrangements are those that open with an *underlever*; usually found on shotguns circa 1860s through 1870s; manufactured simultaneously with the *side lever*. Both types were superseded by the *top lever* which is a vertically pivoted narrow bar or lever at the

Double with Underlever

upper rear of the receiver which actuates various mechanisms used to lock the barrels to the breech/action. This system, in use to the present time, offers the most advantages: making it possible to carry the gun in any position without catching the lever; allowing the shooter to quickly detect if the action was securely locked; offering the capability of working the lever without the necessity for loosening the grip on the stock; and ease of operation. The multitude of various locking levers combined with an equally great variety of "hold-down bolts" or "grip-bolts" make for almost limitless possibilities in locking systems.

The ejection system is a feature that holds fascination for many advanced collectors; one which they often take into consideration when arriving at value. Here, too, many interesting innovations are to be encountered showing the evolutionary process and development of a suitable system to automatically eject spent shot shells from the chamber of the barrel when the gun was opened.

WELLS FARGO EXPRESS COMPANY, CONFEDERATE AND OTHER HISTORICAL MARKINGS

Quite often the most insignificant appearing, worn, beat-up shotgun (muzzleloader or breechloader) is seen with die-stamped or engraved markings indicating usage by the famous Wells Fargo Company or other well known American/Western Express or Stagecoach companies … or, on percussion shotguns, "C.S.A." markings indicating ownership by the Confederate States of America. Prospective buyers should immediately be suspect of such guns. Unless the buyer has experience with such markings (it is possible to have a feel for them) or there is documentary evidence or other substantiating data that proves beyond doubt that the piece is legitimate and has a provenance, then the watchword should be *BEWARE*!

When such markings are proven authentic, they add considerably to both interest and value of the guns on which they appear, placing them in the realm of historical firearms. Values are arrived at based on the wealth of substantiating data and the importance of the historical association of the gun.

Likely the most often encountered … and certainly the most widely applied … mark is that of the WELLS FARGO & COMPANY EXPRESS on many double barrel breech-loading Damascus shotguns. Wells Fargo bought large quantities of them in the last quarter of the 19th century and early 20th century to arm their company guards. Other express companies undoubtedly ordered large quantities also, but only the Wells Fargo examples seem to have survived in quantity and were apparently those best preserved and documented. During the late 1950s and early 1960s quite a few were released for public sale by their successor, the Railway Express Co.; all of them with accompanying supporting documents verifying their historical background. By the 1970s all those shotguns were disbursed and scattered throughout the collecting world. They are now considered quite rare and highly desirable. The majority were Ithaca hammer-type Damascus doubles; most with short, heavy weight barrels, having been made for rugged, rough duty and wear. Almost all had markings on their frames or barrels (sometimes both) and occasionally the stock, indicating Wells Fargo & Co. ownership. Fortunately there was a wealth of documentary material from the Railway Express Co. indicating their ownership and sale of the shotguns (each was listed with serial numbers) and it was easy to verify their original manufacture for Wells Fargo by merely writing to the Ithaca Gun Company who, at that time supplied full verification from their factory records. The Railway Express Agency also released a few other "Wells Fargo" marked shotguns which included Winchester lever actions, Hopkins & Allen, L.C. Smith, and a few low-grade English doubles … all of which were ruggedly made and which had evidently been originally purchased singly or in small groups by Wells Fargo from various dealers rather than direct from the factory. The Railway Express Company gave supporting documents for each of those types too. Armed with this knowledge various nefarious individuals over the ensuing years have spuriously marked not a few worn, beat-up, ruggedly made Damascus doubles "Wells Fargo." Such shotguns are usually sold "tongue-in-cheek" with the sellers answering queries as to originality with such bland replies as "… I don't know … that's the way I got it" … or … "I'm positive its original because of where I got it!" … or … "The fellow I got it from had the papers but couldn't find them and is going to send them to me." Undoubtedly there are many legitimate Wells Fargo and other similarly marked shotguns (some handguns, too) which are completely authentic and for which no substantiating paperwork is available. It's very much a matter of experience for the collector who buys such items. Markings do have their own "character" as to style and appearance of originality. At that point, only one's experience can be a guide, taken along with the reliability of the party selling it. Armed with the knowledge that there are a great many outright fakes on the market, the buyer should certainly proceed with caution.

Gilding The Lily

In 1998 collectors were treated to news of a scam on a par with the old Spanish Prisoner Swindle. Not merely one, but three double shotguns, each reported bearing spurious "Wells Fargo & Co." markings on their stocks and accompanied with a bogus letter of authenticity from the Colt factory were sold for $58,000. to an unsuspecting collector. That's just half the story. The trio of guns were also inscribed, respectively, with the names of the legendary brothers of the Old West: *Wyatt, Virgil and Morgan Earp*! The same buyer also was said to have paid $20,000. for a fourth Wells Fargo marked gun bearing yet another falsified inscription. The seller was charged with theft by deception and simulating objects of antiquity. As hackneyed as it may be, the prospective buyer, confronted with similar situations, should take heed of the oft-quoted adage...*if it's too good to be true, it probably is*.

CONFEDERATE MARKINGS

C.S. or C.S.A. are markings that may be encountered on well worn, if not beat-up, percussion double shotguns … many of them with their barrels shortened. Such markings suggest their usage by the Southern or "Confederate States of America" military forces during the Civil War. The same comments noted for the "Wells Fargo" shotguns are equally applicable here. It should be further noted that in the author's personal experience he has never seen an authentic C.S. marking on any shotgun and that on every example thus far examined the marking has proven spurious. Although certainly not outside the realm of possibility to have such a marking indicating ownership and issuance by the Confederate forces, it's highly unlikely.

The possibilities of markings establishing an historical association for an antique shotgun are limitless; bounded only by the imagination of the faker. They are encountered bearing ownership and/or issuance markings of police departments, famous penitentiaries, railroads, mining companies … ad infinitum. Given the tremendous quantity of such doubles on the market over the past years, with many of them having minimal value at best if they were heavily worn and abused, it is not difficult to understand the strong temptation for those few with larceny in their soul to transform a practically worthless relic into a highly desirable collector's item by adding an imposing or distinguished name merely by striking it with a few marking dies. It's highly likely that such worn doubles will continue to be the treasure trove for such inspirations! The author does not wish to imply that there is an epidemic of such spurious markings; such is definitely not the case. They are in sufficient evidence, though; just enough to keep the collector on his toes!

Values for Muzzle-Loading Fowling Pieces and Shotguns

It's highly necessary, though redundant, to again bring to the reader's attention the fact that fowling pieces and shotguns in both muzzle-loading and breech-loading eras very often utilize imported parts … especially barrels. On most of the finer grade muzzleloaders they were usually English barrels; on the breechloaders they were English and Belgian mostly with some German imports, too.

The collector will seldom see a *fine quality* percussion or flintlock single or double shotgun which is entirely of American manufacture. Having foreign-proofed barrels is not … and should not be … a deterrent in demand, desirability or price; a feature that is occasionally factored into other types of antique firearms. The mere fact that there is no proof on a barrel is not sufficient to say that the barrel was not imported! Such proof markings are easily found and most often appear, on the underside of the barrels near the breech. Usually it is necessary to disassemble the barrels in order to view them. The finer quality, better grade shotguns will quite often bear British proof marks (usually Birmingham) while many of the lower grade types may be observed with the familiar LEG marking inside an oval panel indicating manufacture at Liége, Belgium. This latter proof, however, does not necessarily indicate a poor quality or lower grade barrel, for that country turned out numerous superlative products also. Of course, other barrel proofs from continental European countries are also in evidence. The astute collector learns to recognize spurious proofmarks, originally applied to dupe the indiscriminate buyer to believe he was getting a better product than it actually was. That such practices are in wider evidence and more prevalent with shotguns than any other field of firearms manufacture in itself strengthens the premise, made in the opening paragraph of this chapter, that shotguns and fowling pieces were likely the most commonly owned and used of all antique American guns. The mere fact that there was such a tremendous market for them in all strata of society that made for a huge and competitive shotgun manufacturing industry obviously led to some abuses and evil practices.

Single Barrel Full and Half Stock Flintlocks

An important guide to this subject is *Flintlock Fowlers: The First Guns Made in America*, by T. Grinslade, (Biblio. Chap. 16). Extensive treatment and profuse illustrations, especially in detail of locks, side plates, markings, etc, of the "fowlers" from 1700-1820. Much information is of direct relevance to similar fowlers of the later eras discussed in this chapter.

The normally encountered types are mediocre quality, full stock, single barrel fowling pieces of the 1790 to 1830 period, very similar in appearance to the classic "New England Flintlock Militia Musket" (*see Chapter IX-B, Item 9B-013*) but made without provision for a socket or other type bayonet. Such fowling pieces are seldom marked with maker's name; usually fitted with a Warranted (marked) or other imported type lock which may possibly bear an agent's or lockmaker's name. The large majority are walnut stocked with plain brass or iron mountings, often simply engraved. A small premium value (if any) may be added if wood is cherry; a 25 percent to 50 percent increase in value is quite proper if the wood used is a well striped and grained curly maple. Condition and general quality of workmanship are, of course, important factors in arriving at value. As no two are alike, values shown here are approximate only, for an "average" specimen stocked in walnut:

Full Stock Original Flintlock:
17-001 Values—Good **$600 to $750** Fine **$1,250 to $2,000**
Converted to percussion:
17-002 Values—Good **$300 to $500** Fine **$500 to $850**

Half Stock Flintlock Fowling Pieces of American manufacture; generally following description of above types; of medium quality:

Original flintlock:
17-003 Values—Good **$500 to $700** Fine **$850 to $1,500**

Converted to percussion:
17-004 Values—Good **$200 to $350** Fine **$350 to $550**

Half Stock Flintlock Fowling Pieces of European manufacture (usually English); fine quality with American lock and/or barrel markings:

Original flintlock:
17-005 Values—Good **$500 to $850** Fine **$850 to $2,000**

Converted to percussion:
17-006 Values—Good **$275 to $475** Fine **$350 to $850**

American Colonial and Revolutionary Era Flintlock Fowling Pieces   *See Chapter XVI.*

Double Barrel Flintlocks

Double barrel flintlock shotguns of American manufacture or assembly are rare. The author has seen but a handful of them over the years and every one bore either American maker or dealer name and utilized imported European (mostly English) parts. All are half stock and modeled identically after fine British flintlock doubles of the same era. No two are identical. The most important factors to determine value are quality of workmanship and condition; in that order. The mere fact that a double flintlock might be encountered of entirely American manufacture, but having rather crude proportions and coarse

workmanship, although a rarity, would not necessarily make its value commensurate. Quality is still a major determinant.
Values: For a good quality, well-made, well-proportioned double barrel flintlock with walnut or cherry half stock, brass or iron mountings of good quality (usually well-engraved) with well-made imported locks:

In original flintlock:
17-007 Values—Good **$950 to $2,000**
            Fine **$2,000 to $3,750**

Converted to percussion:
17-008 Values—Good **$450**   Fine **$1,250**

Percussion Single Barrel Fowling Pieces/Shotguns

These are priced similarly to "Percussion Sporting and Target Rifles, etc." discussed in the introduction to Chapter XII. Rarely are two muzzle-loading fowling pieces identical as most were individually handcrafted. The same factors discussed in the opening paragraphs of Chapter XII are equally applicable here. Shotguns, however, normally fetch lesser values than similarly decorated or embellished, or marked rifles. They are encountered in a very wide range of quality with varying amounts of fancy embellishments. However, they rarely, if ever, approach the ornateness of the fancier grade rifles. An important … or rare … maker's name may often be worth a premium to the value. Full stock percussion fowlers are encountered with considerably less frequency than the half stock types; this feature adds moderately to value; for average specimens a 20 percent to 30 percent increase is a reasonable guide.

The general appearance (i.e. the overall lines and proportions as well as the type wood used) of the stock plays a significant role in determining value. Aesthetics are very much a factor that

must be considered. On simplest, least embellished, plain grades, cherry wood would likely fetch a small premium over walnut, while a handsomely tiger-stripe grained curly maple would easily bring from 50 percent to 100 percent more. The very same curly maple would fetch a proportionately smaller percentage increase as the quality of the fowling piece increased. (See also *Chapters V-A "Ethan Allen", V-E "Remington" and V-J, "Whitney".*)

Percussion half stock fowling piece of plain grade, without patchbox, with average quality brass or iron mountings:
17-009 Values—Good **$225**   Fine **$375**

Plain grade as above with patchbox, including possibly checkering at wrist and forend and a few simple inlays:
17-010 Values—Good **$275**   Fine **$550**

Fancy grade, as above, with or without patchbox; fine grade of wood (fancy-figured grains) fine quality, fancy mountings; possibly a few inlays of fine quality:
17-011 Values—Good **$350 to $550** Fine **$550 to $1,250**

Babcock Open-Frame Percussion Shotgun

Moses Babcock, Charlestown, Massachusetts Open-Frame Percussion Muzzle-Loading Shotgun, circa 1850s. Quantity unknown; very limited; scarce.

*17-011.3
"Babcock"*

Unique and distinctive construction and appearance. The trigger guard also serves as the mainspring. The trigger, which projects upwards through the frame, also serves as the sear. Centrally mounted hammer. Caliber 44; other calibers likely. 20, 24 and 26-inch barrels recorded; other lengths also likely; iron forend with walnut buttstock. Bead type front sight; no provision for rear sight. Marked on barrel M. BABCOCK / CHARLESTOWN / MASS.

This identical odd-looking action also made by Babcock in rifle form with varying lengths octagon barrels. A specimen is illustrated in the 1920 edition of the notable work *"Our Rifles"* by C. W. Sawyer (*see Chapter IV*).

17-011.3   Values—Good **$550**   Fine **$1,250**

Briggs Underhammer Percussion Shotgun

11-011.5

William Briggs, Norristown, Pennsylvania, Patent 1860 Underhammer Muzzle-Loading Shotgun. C. 1860. Quantity unknown; estimated less than 50. The identical gun is also known to have been made as a percussion muzzle-loading rifle. Quantities unknown; likely less than 50.

The distinctive construction and appearance of this unique shotgun classifies it as an American arms oddity. The entire buttstock is hollow iron with circular patchbox on right side. The lock, trigger and trigger guard consist of but two pieces for which the inventor claimed "… it is not subject to get out of order … having less pieces … than any other gun ever patented … and will last anyone a lifetime." The flat bar type hammer and trigger bow are fashioned integral with the outside mounted mainspring, all as one piece.

Marked on barrel WILLIAM BRIGGS, NORRISTOWN.PA./PATENTED AUG,13,1860

17-011.5   Values—Good **$550**   Fine **$1,250**

Breech-Loading Percussion Shotguns

There are but few breech-loading percussion shotguns; almost all merely variants of sporting or military rifles using identical breech actions. They include those shotguns made by Sharps (Chapter V-F) and Maynard (Chapter XIV) and the lesser known, occasionally encountered models by Marston and Perry. The reader is referred to Chapter XII "Percussion Sporting and Target Rifles" ("Breech-Loading Percussion Sporting Rifles") for details equally applicable to shotguns.

Revolving Percussion Shotguns   *See Chapter V-B "Colt" and Chapter XV "Revolving Rifles" for shotgun variants.*

Double Barrel (Side-by-Side) Percussion Shotguns

These are valued on a similar basis to the half-stock fowling pieces as discussed above. Gracefulness, proportion and balance are also taken into account; the presence or absence of a patchbox is of much lesser consequence to value except on the very lowest, most inexpensive grades. The author again emphasizes that the best grades invariably will be found with European (mostly British) barrels. Bore sizes are of greater consequence when pricing doubles; 10 gauge through 14 gauge are the most commonly encountered size. A generalization has it that the larger the bore size the more eagerly sought after the double may be, and the larger the premium may be placed on it. Smaller bores, too, are worth premiums; the smaller the gauge, the larger the premium … but they do not command the large percentages that big bores do. Quality is very much the key word when assessing values.

Double Barrel Percussion Shotguns of plainest grade; brass or iron mountings of simple form without embellishments or inlays:
17-012   Values—Good **$200**   Fine **$600**
Plain grade double as above; slightly fancier features, including slight engraving on locks, good quality checkering at wrist and forend; better grade of wood; few simple inlays:
17-013   Values—Good **$250**   Fine **$750**
Fancier grade and quality; select grain wood stock; few good quality inlays; finely-made and usually well-engraved locks; iron or brass mountings; displays quality workmanship throughout with excellent proportions and balance:
17-014   Values—Good **$300 to $550**   Fine **$650 to $1,500**

Market Hunting and Punt Guns

Until 1918 when "Market Hunting" was prohibited by Federal legislation, not a few made their full-time livelihood as professional "market hunters"; many others supplemented their incomes similarly by supplying the American commercial wildfowl market from the plentiful supply of game in season. Such commercial markets with their corresponding number of professional hunters reached their apex in the 1880s. Those hunters most often turned to very large bore and correspondingly longer barreled firearms. Thus, many of the 8 gauge, 6 gauge, and larger bore shotguns of American manufacture that are occasionally encountered on the collector's market had every likelihood of being made and used by (but not exclusively) such market hunters. Often, exceptionally huge, cannon-size "punt" and swivel type guns are also seen. Such tremendous shotguns were made and used mostly in East Coast areas of America; utilized most often (but not exclusively) by commercial market hunters, mounted on the bow of a small "punt" or flat-bottomed boat having broad, square ends and most often propelled by a long pole. Hiding in a blind, hunters with punt guns literally decimated flocks of waterfowl as they settled on the surface nearby. Such huge bore pieces of gigantic proportions could be fired from the shoulder, but, as they increased in massive proportions (some approached 50 pounds and even more in weight) they were most often mounted rigidly to the bow and aimed by pointing the boat towards the target; the boat taking the recoil and often moving backwards on firing. Batteries of barrels were even assembled, usually crude homemade affairs. As many as ten in a row were utilized in the same manner, all firing simultaneously at a resting flock. Those death-dealing batteries were known to have taken over 500 ducks in a day, cutting wide swaths, if not completely obliterating, a resting flock. In America, "punts" of one form or another were mostly used, although canoes, and even light rowboats were employed.

The huge punt guns were apparently outlawed in most states by the late 1860s. Thus, American specimens that are seen are invariably percussion muzzleloaders, normally quite crude in appearance and design, though sturdily made. They appear in very great variety; some being merely oversized versions of a typical single barrel percussion fowler while others take on the appearance of a crudely-made wall or "rampart" gun of very awkward dimensions and form. The huge breech-loaded punt guns occasionally encountered are invariably of English or European manufacture and thus beyond the coverage of this book.

The market hunter along both East and West coasts of America and the inland lakes specialized in the slaughter of American waterfowl while the commercial market hunter of the Midwest devoted his attentions to the "prairie chicken" (the pinnated grouse) supplying huge quantities to local markets and even to some of the well-known, large meat-packing firms. "Market hunting" at first decimated the tremendous American bird population for its food value. By the 1880s with the bird population considerably thinned, the death knell was sounded by the dictates of ladies' fashion. The "feather hunter" entered the scene, supplying the craze for bird feathers for use on ladies'

hats that reached a fevered peak. Just as the beaver (and later, to some extent the buffalo) nearly passed from the scene because of the demands of fashion, so too did America lose tremendous quantities of birds of all types that were taken to fill the demands for fancy-plumed headwear. Public outcries at the urging of the Audubon Society, led to Congressional action in 1899. The Lacey Act which prohibited the shipping of wild game, feathers, and skins in interstate commerce effectively stopped the selling and wearing of such hats. This put an end to the wanton slaughter and eventually led to the elimination of the market hunter. Various states, and then the Federal government, passed a series of laws over the following years restricting bird hunters, eventually prohibiting, in 1918, the sale of waterfowl; the actual enforcement of the act, not commencing until 1920.

Punt guns and those huge half stock percussion fowling pieces of massive proportions enjoy a reasonably strong demand on the collectors' market, mostly for their curiosity value. Although no two are alike and they run the gamut in appearance, size, weight, form and quality of workmanship, they do fall into general price categories which seem to be arrived at by their overall eye appeal. Except for the very crudest-made, homeliest-appearing, poorest-quality specimens, they may be divided into two categories:

Punt guns or market guns that resemble half stock single barrel or double barrel percussion fowling pieces. Generally, the more tremendous in size and heavier in weight, the larger the price:

17-015   Values—Good **$600 to $2,000**
               Fine **$950 to $3,500**

Punt guns generally resembling a small cannon or wall or "rampart" gun; intended to be mounted rigidly on the bow of a flat-bottomed "punt" or boat:

17-016   Values—Good **$650 to $2,250**
               Fine **$950 to $3,500**

"Damascus" Double Barrel Breech-Loading Shotguns

Quality is to be considered as the major determinant of value for Damascus doubles. Condition and mechanical variation are slightly less important and of about equal weight. As earlier noted, the use of imported parts, especially barrels, was the rule rather than the exception. Any lessening of interest, or demand, or value because of the appearance of a foreign proof-mark on an American-made gun would not be consistent with collecting this type of firearm.

As the entire field of collecting Damascus doubles is more or less in its infancy and one that has only recently started to "hum," it is a reasonable assumption that these shotguns will generally fall into a few broad-priced categories. As yet, only a handful of the finest quality doubles and those with markings of the most well-known makers such as Winchester, Colt, Parker, L. C. Smith, etc., enjoy a strong demand in almost any condition, as well as marketability and values commensurate with their varying degrees of condition from "poor" through "mint/factory new." Lesser quality, lesser name shotguns enjoy the status of strong "demand" with yet moderate price levels achieved *only* in the very upper grades of condition (external and mechanical). Unless there is something unusual or unique about the gun, such as agent's or maker's name or other marking, lending it a historical association, only the very top condition specimens fetch any appreciable price; both demand and price fall off radically as condition diminishes.

A point of interest for collectors…and possibly arms historians…concerns the last manufacture of Damascus barrels. The introduction of smokeless powder and fluid steel barrels did not immediately halt the demand or production and sales of

Damascus types. Their demise was yet quite a few years away. Damascus barrels continued to be made and offered during the first two decades of the 20th century. World War I generally signaled their end. The noted L.C. Smith did not drop them from their catalogue line until approximately 1919 with Parker Brothers offering them as late as 1919 or 1920. It is, of course, possible that those Damascus barrels being offered in the last years were actually "shelf" items that had been made prior to World War I; certainly demand for them waned. Nevertheless, they still had a following and were made concurrently with fluid steel barrels for quite a few years.

TRADE AND BRAND NAMES

No complete list is yet compiled of all known names to be found on Damascus, American-made or American-imported doubles. The largest yet assembled, and that most often referred to is found in *The Golden Age of Shotgunning* (*see Bibliography*). Trade name markings are often those of hardware stores (e.g. CAROLINA ARMS COMPANY, the Smith-Wadsworth Hardware Store in Charlotte, N.C. or PIEDMONT, The Piedmont Hardware Co. of Danville, PA.) or merely brand names (e.g. ARISTOCRAT, CHAMPION, CONTINENTAL, ECLIPSE or PREMIER) some of which were used exclusively by various distributors or sporting goods dealers.

The firm of **H. & D. Folsom Arms Company** of New York must be singled out as unique in this area of collecting. It literally dominated the field at the turn-of-century era. As major distributors and dealers, their purchase of Crescent Firearms Co. Norwich, CT, large manufacturers of shotguns, allowed Folsom to offer an even wider selection. Thus, Folsom was not only importing English and Continental shotguns, but also manufacturing American (Crescent) shotguns simultaneously, offering both types (in low and medium price ranges) to the public directly under their own "house" and "brand" names, as well as making other "house/brand" names under direct contract to hardware stores, mail order houses, and distributors; using any names specifically requested by the purchaser. Over 100 of those known brand names used by Folsom have been listed in *The Golden Age of Shotgunning*; alphabetically commencing with the AMERICAN GUN COMPANY (Folsom's principal house brand name sold directly to stores or firms not wishing to have their own special names marked) to WORTHINGTON ARMS COMPANY (a Crescent-made shotgun made for the Worthington Hardware Company of Cleveland). Another 22 brand names are listed that are believed to be Folsom products by virtue of certain distinguishing features; such names ranging from CHICAGO LONG RANGE WONDER (made for Sears Roebuck) to the WHIPPET (a brand name for a well-known Chicago hardware firm).

Undoubtedly, many other, as yet unknown, names will be found and recorded. The author is not certain if all of those listed names refer only to "Damascus" doubles or to some turn-of-century shotguns made with steel barrels also. The foregoing discussion, however, allows the collector to realize that there are broad vistas to set his sights on in this area of collecting.

Some of the finest sources for information and research in this field are to be found in the original manufacturers', dealers', and distributors' catalogs. Quite a few have survived with many of the more famous issues reproduced in recent years. Considerable intriguing and factual information is to be gleaned from them. Immediately apparent to the collector when reading them is the tremendous variety of "house" and imported types with a plethora of names readily available to the sportsman of the latter 19th century. These catalogs do much to rectify erroneous facts that have been perpetuated by not a few modern-day authors on the subject.

Damascus Doubles Values

17-025

The following is a representative sampling of Damascus double barrel breech-loading shotguns and their collector values for varying degrees of quality and condition. As with other types of antique firearms (notably Kentucky rifles, percussion sporting and target rifles, etc.) there is no simple formula to neatly categorize shotguns. The many nuances involved in the collecting of them, the numerous models and variations offered by the makers in their catalogs, and the fact that customers most often did not order "standard" pieces, but rather had them customized when built requires some background knowledge and experience in handling and viewing a cross-section of types. The reader is therefore cautioned that the values reflected below are very much subject to variation by the numerous influencing factors discussed in the preceding text. Bore conditions should at least be commensurate with the general exterior condition ... or better.

The field is one deserving of a definitive guide book; one which will refine the broad categories listed here and hopefully better define the classifications to alleviate the highly subjective nature of evaluation and ease the collector's burden. The broad price ranges shown below are approximate only; extremely fine quality specimens, of which there are many, could certainly fall outside those ranges and be worth in excess of values shown.

The collector should take cognizance of one further, salient point. During their period of use, many of these Damascus doubles were altered (restocked) or modernized (barrels replaced with fluid steel for use with smokeless powder) or otherwise changed to adapt them to the uses and desires of their later owners/shooters. Such modifications usually detract from their desirability, hence both their *demand* and *value* factors as far as the collector is concerned. Those same guns, however, might very well retain excellent *demand* and *value* on the modern shooter's market (depending on the modifications) which is outside the scope of this work.

Most common, plain grades marked with well-known names; simple engraving (where standard); very plain grain wood; rough checkering; mechanically complete and functioning. 10 or 12 gauge:

17-025 Values—Fine **$225 to $450**
Exc. to Factory New **$550 to $900**

Identical to above with select wood grain stock of medium grade; better quality checkering and finer, fancier Damascus finish to barrels:

17-026 Values—Fine **$350 to $650**
Exc. to Factory New **$750 to $1,500**

Identical to above with very fancy select grain wood stock; delicate detailed checkering; fancy, delicate detailed Damascus designs on barrels; identifiable known names of makers or well-known dealers (not merely a brand name):

17-027 Values—Fine **$550 to $950**
Exc. to Factory New **$850 to $2,500**

AMERICAN (AND ASSOCIATED) MAKERS OF DAMASCUS DOUBLES

The following list is by no means complete. Many of these makers are to be found listed with short biographical sketches in other well-known American bibliographies such as *Small Arms Makers* (Gardner), *American Gun Makers* (Gluckman), *Gunsmiths of Ohio* (Hutslar), and *The Golden Age of Shotgunning* (Hinman). **This compilation represents a near complete listing of the larger, well-known American manufacturers whose shotguns the collector is most likely to encounter** along with a reasonably broad, cross section of lesser-known (in some cases obscure) American makers of shotguns. Many offered a wide selection of shotguns in varying grades over reasonably long periods of

time. Prices for most of the makers listed here will generally fall within the categories defined above. The output of a few makers, notably **PARKER BROTHERS**, is of such importance to the Damascus double collecting field that the author has given expanded coverage and data about them. There are also a few interesting, unusual and even unique types of Damascus shotguns that are occasionally available and have always been considered good collectors' items that are included and evaluated (e.g., Baker and Hollenbeck Three-Barrel Guns, Spencer Pump Action Repeating Shotgun and the Young Two-Shot Repeater, etc.).

E. ALLEN & CO., Worcester, Massachusetts. (*See Chapter V-A.*)

AMERICAN ARMS CO., Boston, Massachusetts. Circa 1860s to 1900. Well-known for their G.H. Fox Patent swing-out, hammer shotgun (not to be confused with the A.H. Fox Gun Co. of Philadelphia). Ultimately acquired 1901 by Marlin Fire Arms Co. of Connecticut. **17-100**

17-113

17-101

BAKER GUN CO., Batavia, New York. Circa 1880s to 1933. Well-known makers offering a wide range of models and grades. L.C. Smith, an early partner of this firm. Their "Three-Barrel Gun" (a double shotgun over single rifle similar to a German "Drilling") has always had good collector interest. This outside hammer type with an intriguing barrel locking arrangement was invented by Frank Hollenbeck (originally a principal of the Baker Gun Co.), later owner of the "Three-Barrel Gun Co." and "Hollenbeck Gun Co." of Wheeling, West Virginia (*q.v.*) making a similar combination rifle-shotgun:

Three-Barrel Gun:
17-101   Values—Very Good **$650**   Exc. **$2,000**

BALDWIN AND COMPANY, New Orleans, Louisiana. Double barrel shotguns with octagonal barrels. **17-102**

BALTIMORE ARMS CO., Baltimore, Maryland. Circa 1895-1902. **17-103**

BANNERMAN, New York. Slide action repeating shotgun. (*See Spencer Arms Co.*) **17-104**

BECK, SAMUEL. Indianapolis, Indiana. Circa 1860s-1885. **17-105**

BLICKENSDOEFER & SCHILLING. St. Louis, Missouri. Circa 1870s. **17-106**

BOYD BREECH-LOADING ARMS CO., Boston, Massachusetts. Circa 1870s **17-107**

BROOKS, C. (and BROOKS ARMS CO.) East Wilton, Cape Elizabeth & Portland, Maine. Circa 1890s. Double shotguns. Also known for patent and manufacture of a unique three barrel gun with under-lever release (single barrel rifle over double barrel shotgun). No recent sales known by author. Approximate price range only:

Three Barrel combination:
17-108   Values—Very Good **$850**   Exc. **$2,000**

BROWN, R.H. & CO. Westville and New Haven, Connecticut. Circa 1883-1904. **17-109**

BURGESS GUN CO., Buffalo, New York. (*See Chapter XIII.*)

COLT FIREARMS CO. (*See Chapter V-B.*)

COLTON FIREARMS CO. Toledo, Ohio. Circa 1890s. Bicycle manufacturer and sporting goods dealer; might have made shotguns but more likely importer and distributor. **17-110**

COLVIN, M.S. Syracuse, East Randolph, Salamanca, New York. Circa 1872-1880s. **17-111**

CRESCENT FIREARMS CO. Meriden and Norwich, Connecticut. Circa 1890s-1930s. Acquired by H.D. Folsom Arms Company (*q.v.*). Circa 1893. Eventually absorbed by J. Stevens Arms & Tool Company, Massachusetts. Circa 1932. Manufacturers of large quantities of low and medium priced shotguns under their own house and various trade names. **17-112**

DALY, CHARLES. European-made, imported, fine quality shotguns using "Daly" as a house brand name of Schoverling, Daly, and Gales, large New York Sporting Goods dealers and distributors; successors (1888) to the well-known New York firm of John P. Moore (originally established 1823). DALY marked shotguns were made by various German firms (including J.P. Sauer) under contract for this New York firm. Various grades and gauges offered. Early specimens (under serial number 2600) were built in Prussia by Charles Lindner are most eagerly sought after and worth premium.

Among the more interesting Dalys is a three barrel outside hammer combination double shotgun (10 or 12 gauge) over a single barrel rifle which was offered in quite a few calibers from 32 to 45-70. This latter caliber usually brings a 25 percent premium value. Average prices for the 3-barrel Daly only:

17-113   Values—Very Good **$600**   Exc. **$1,75**0

DANE, JOSEPH. LaCrosse, Wisconsin. Circa 1870s. **17-114**

DAVENPORT FIREARMS COMPANY. Providence, Rhode Island and Norwich, Connecticut. Circa 1880-1900. The founder, William H. Davenport, held a great many patents on breech-loading firearms. The company apparently devoted its energies almost exclusively to single barrel shotguns of very inexpensive grades, making them under both house and brand names. **17-115**

DAVIS, N.R. & CO. Circa 1880s—early 1900s. Eventually absorbed by Crescent-Davis Arms Company (including Crescent Firearms Co., *q.v.*). Ultimately taken over by the Stevens Arms & Tool Co. of Massachusetts circa 1930s. **17-116**

DODDS, JAMES. Xenia (1863-1868) and Dayton (1868-1908) Ohio. **17-117**

ENTERPRISE GUN WORKS. Pittsburgh, Pennsylvania. Circa 1848-1880s. Originally established by Bown & Tetley (1848); James Bown, sole owner 1862. Succeeded 1870s by Bown & Hirth. Large makers, importers, and distributors of American and foreign Damascus doubles; usually of low and medium grades. **17-118**

FOGERTY, GEORGE. Cambridge, Massachusetts. Circa 1890s. **17-119**

FOLK'S GUN WORKS. Brian, Ohio. Circa 1865-1890s. **17-120**

FOLSOM, H&D ARMS COMPANY. New York, New York. *See details described earlier in this chapter.* **17-121**

FOREHAND & WADSWORTH, 1871-1890; **FOREHAND ARMS CO.,** 1890-1898. Worcester, Mass. Successors to E. Allen & Co. (q.v.) Made wide range of hammer & hammerless single and double shotguns of low and medium prices under their own and various brand names. **17-122**

FOX, ANSLEY H. GUN CO. Philadelphia, Pennsylvania. Boxlock, hammerless type doubles only. Medium and high grade types. Very well-known name and make. Circa 1880s-1930s. Eventually taken over by Savage Repeating Arms Company of Massachusetts. **17-123**

GARDNER GUN COMPANY. Cleveland, Ohio. Circa 1887-1895. **17-124**

GODFREY, CHARLES. New York, New York. Circa 1880s-1890s. Importers and dealers only. **17-125**

GREAT WESTERN GUN WORKS. Pittsburgh, Pennsylvania. Circa 1860s-1916. Makers, distributors, and importers of inexpensive lines of shotguns all types. Their company motto aptly describes their products ... "cheap guns for the people." **17-126**

HARRINGTON & RICHARDSON. Worcester, Massachusetts. Circa 1880s to present. (*See Chapter V-I, Item 5I-070.*)

HARTLEY & GRAHAM. (*See Schuyler, Hartley & Graham.*)

HIBBARD, SPENCER, BARTLETT & CO. Chicago, Illinois. Circa 1880s-early 1900s. Importers and distributors of many different American and European shotguns of various brand names. See also "Spencer Gun Co." **17-127**

HOLLENBECK GUN COMPANY. Wheeling, West Virginia. Known mostly for their three barrel combination hammerless type double shotgun over single rifle; usually 12 gauge over 32-40; other combinations known. Made and marked with three various trade names: HOLLENBECK GUN COMPANY ... THREE BARREL GUN COMPANY (1905) ...ROYAL ARMS COMPANY. Circa 1901-1910. Frank Hollenbeck originally a principal of the Baker Arms Company and Syracuse Arms Company of New York:

17-128   Values—Very Good **$800**   Excellent **$2,250**

HOOD FIREARMS CO. Norwich, Connecticut. (*See Chapter VIII-A.*) Makers or distributors of inexpensive grade doubles under various brand names. Circa 1870s-1880s. **17-129**

HOPKINS & ALLEN Norwich, Connecticut. Circa 1868-1917. Makers of extensive line of handguns and also a wide selection of double barrel hammer and hammerless-type double shotguns as well as single barrel models. (See also "Merwin, Hulbert and CO.) **17-130**

HUNTER ARMS CO. (*See L.C. Smith Co.*)

17-131

ITHACA GUN CO. Ithaca, New York. 1873 to present. Manufacturers of sturdy, well-made Damascus doubles of medium price range, both hammer and hammerless types (the latter introduced circa 1893) both with boxlock type actions. Expanded their selection to numerous grades after the turn of the century. Ithaca eventually absorbed the Union Firearms Co., Syracuse Arms Co., Wilkes-Barre Gun Co. and Lefever Arms Co. **17-131**

IVER JOHNSON ARMS & CYCLE WORKS. Fitchburg, Massachusetts. 1871 to present. Manufacturers of inexpensive grades single and double shotguns; many made under various trade names. (*See Chapter VIII-A.*) **17-132**

    CUTAWAY SALESMAN SAMPLE/DEMONSTRATOR I.J. "NEW MODEL CHAMPION MODEL 36". single 12 Ga. shotgun. c. 1910. Special lot of 199 produced; serial No. 1 to 199. Numerous apertures of varying size and shape on receiver, barrel and stock in order to view interior. It is subject to the provisions and restrictions of the N.F.A. After complying with same it would be valued at:
17-132.5 Values—Good **$250**   Fine **$550**

JORDAN, LOUIS. Chicago, Illinois. Circa 1891-1894.   **17-133**

17-134

KENNEDY, MARTIN, F. (1867); M. F. KENNEDY & BRO. (1875); & BROS. (1877); KENNEDY BROS. ARMS CO. (1905-1960). St. Paul, Minn. Double shotguns assembled and stocked from imported English actions and barrels. **17-134**

KIRKWOOD, DANIEL. Boston, Massachusetts. Circa 1875-1890s. Originally "Mortimer & Kirkwood" 1875-1880; "David Kirkwood" 1882-1888 and "Kirkwood Brothers" to early 1900s. **17-135**

KITTREDGE & CO. Cincinnati, Ohio. 1845-1900. Well-known dealers, agents and distributors for many major manufacturers. Importers of European firearms including many shotguns of Belgian make. **17-136**

LEFEVER, DANIEL M. & LEFEVER ARMS CO. Syracuse, New York. Circa 1850s-1915 when purchased by Ithaca Gun Co. During years 1876-1878 in partnership with John A. Nichols as Nichols & Lefever for the manufacture of fine grade Damascus barrel shotguns. 1879-1902 as Lefever Arms Co. manufacturing excellent quality Damascus doubles including one of the first American hammerless shotguns with side-cocking lever. After 1902 operating as "D.M. Lefever Sons & Co." Wide range of medium and high quality Damascus hammer and hammerless doubles. **17-137**

LOVELL, J.P. & SONS AND LOVELL ARMS CO. Boston, Massachusetts. Circa 1840s-1900. Primarily dealers and importers; uncertain of their actual manufacture of shotguns which were marketed under their name. **17-138**

MARLIN FIREARMS CO. New Haven, Connecticut. (*See Chapter V-D.*)

MEACHAM ARMS CO. St. Louis, Missouri. Circa 1880s-1890s. Believed dealers only. Hammerless shotguns observed with their markings have been imported types. **17-139**

MERIDEN FIREARMS CO. Meriden, Connecticut. 1900-1915. Not to be confused with the Meriden Manufacturing Company, makers of the Triplett and Scott carbine that is associated with Parker Brothers shotguns. Meriden's shotguns believed made exclusively for large mail order firms; also importers of European doubles sold under their name. **17-140**

MERWIN HULBERT & CO. New York. 1871-1896 Sole agents and part owners of Hopkins & Allen. Their name marked on many of H&A shotguns. **17-140.5**

MOORE, JOHN P. New York City, New York. Circa 1830s-1880s. Large dealers and importers. Purchased by Schoverling, Daly, & Gales (*q.v.*) 1888. **17-141**

MORTIMER & KIRKWOOD. Boston, Massachusetts. (*See D. Kirkwood.*)

NICHOLS, JOHN A. Syracuse and Geddes, New York. Circa 1870s-1880s. (*See also "Lefever".*) **17-142**

PARK & McLEISH. Columbus, Ohio. Circa early 1880s. **17-143**

PARK & GARBER. Columbus, Ohio. Successors circa late-1880s to Park & McLeish. **17-144**

PARKER BROTHERS. Meriden, Connecticut. Circa 1860s-1942.

Rated with the best of American-made shotguns, the Parker is considered by many to have been the finest American shotgun ever produced. The very titles of the two books devoted to the subject are adequate testimonials to that fact: *The Parker Gun ... An Immortal American Classic* (Baer) and *Parker ... America's Finest Shotgun* (Johnson).

Parker shotguns ... notably their Damascus doubles ... offer much to the collector; representing a wide line of high quality shotguns by one of the largest makers over a long period of time. The Parker, along with a few other American Damascus doubles (such as Colts, Winchesters, etc.) has always been in the forefront of the shotgun collecting field and has always enjoyed a strong demand on the collectors' market. Hence, in this new era of Damascus double collecting, with all of these types acquiring higher status as collectible "antiques," the Parkers are elevated to even higher plateaus.

As Parkers play a major role in the American shotgun field and as their price levels are quite often in higher value ranges, the author has chosen to devote more attention to them. It is neither practical nor within the scope of this book to cover the entire line in depth. This discussion will be limited to those generally considered "antiques," i.e., those with Damascus barrels or those generally considered "black powder" models. Although there are two published works devoted solely to the Parker shotgun, both are sadly lacking in clarity and completeness. The collector with a flair for research will find it a fertile field and ready market for a comprehensive, definitive guide; one very much in need of such a work. It's worth noting that just about all Parkers are quite desirable and eagerly sought after, being highly collectible and possessing strong demand.

No attempt has been made to list all the variants of Damascus barreled Parkers; even the early catalogs are vague on those points, merely establishing nuances, in highly subjective terms, for differing grades of shotguns. Hopefully this general survey will be sufficient to impart the importance of these fine firearms and shed further light on their background, making the collector aware of their "regal" status in American shotguns.

The very earliest history of the firm, as related in other works, and the year of manufacture of their first shotgun is somewhat cloudy. The author hopes he is not muddying the waters with this encapsulated history pieced together from available material and assumed to be reasonably accurate:

The firm was founded circa 1830s by Charles Parker (1809-1902) a manufacturer of hardware items in Meriden, Connecticut. He was especially noted for his coffee mills (grinders) which bear his firm name, many of which are still in evidence and considered interesting Parker collector's items. His first gun-making venture was during the Civil War in partnership with Gamaliel F. Snow and Brooks (first name unknown) when they subcontracted for gun parts (locks and trigger guards, etc.) for the Model 1861 Springfield 58 caliber percussion rifled-musket, then being built in vast quantities by numerous government contractors. In 1863, they received a contract for 15,000 complete muskets which they subsequently made and delivered in late 1864 (*see Chapter IX-A, Item 9A-324*). That musket may actually be termed the first Parker gun. Charles Parker in partnership with William and George Miller under the firm name of "Meriden Manufacturing Co." next manufactured the Triplett and Scott Patent repeating carbine (*see Chapter IX-B, Item 9B-101*) of which approximately 5,000 were made, almost the entire production being sold to the state of Kentucky but delivered too late in 1865 for actual service in the Civil War. During the years 1865 to 1867 (approximate) Meriden Mfg. Co. altered a group of Civil War Model 1861 muzzle-loading muskets (quantity unknown) to breech-loading utilizing the Miller Patent of May 23, 1865 (*see Chapter IX-A, Item 9A-346*).

With that gun-making experience under his belt, Charles Parker, in partnership with his sons Wilbur and Dexter, circa 1866-1867 formed the newly-named firm Parker Brothers in Meriden to make sporting shotguns. Their first side-by-side shotgun has yet to be positively identified; it has been variously reported by most researchers as being "14 gauge" however this seems unlikely as their earliest catalogs do not mention that gauge at all; the 14 gauge not introduced until the 1880s. One prominent researcher has stated that the first shotgun was an "under-lever release" while another mentions it as being the well-known Parker "lifter" action; yet a third advises it was a "lifter bolting action ... keywedge fastened forend." As a matter of fact, even the date of manufacture of the first shotgun is somewhat cloudy, being reported anywhere from 1865 to 1868. Very recent evidence appears to indicate that latter date. The firm stayed in continuous operation to January 1934, when it was acquired by the Remington Arms Co. who continued to make the Parker shotgun in Meriden until 1938 when production was moved to Ilion, New York. Shotguns were marketed under the Parker name until approximately 1942 after which the name and line was discontinued.

The subleties of Parker collecting are multifold. Barrel lengths, chokes, style and length of stock and certain other features apparently have much more importance in determining values in the later steel barrel "modern" types than they do with Damascus values. Basic features such as engraving styles, unusually long barrel lengths, or odd gauges are major determinants with the Damascus line.

On medium and lower grades, the singularly, most important factor that apparently still determines value and consequently demand is **condition**, while on the *finest (top)* grades the **rarity** factor plays the dominant role, taking precedence over condition.

A great many variations are to be seen in Parker firing pins, shapes and design of recoil shields (frame shoulders), lever placement, locking systems, and even markings. Profuseness and elaborateness of engraving will also be seen to vary greatly, another important factor in arriving at value. Even the noted American engraver Gustave Young has been reported to have decorated a few Parkers.

Studying early Parker catalogs offers much basic information for the collector. Just a quick glance will attest to the many variations a customer could order ... and hence, a collector may encounter. The 1869 catalog, believed their first, and their 1899 catalog both said, "... We are prepared to make any style of gun desired, but any deviation from our regular weights or measurements compels us to make an additional charge"; a statement that remained in effect over 30 years. An in-depth study of Parkers will certainly attest to its veracity.

It was not until the 1880s that Parker Brothers first assigned and/or stamped their guns with an alphabet letter designation to indicate the level of quality or grade of their various models; a marking system that certainly simplified it for collectors of later eras. Prior to that time, no specific marking differentiates each level of quality; it's strictly the practiced eye that can spot the variances.

Their first (1869) catalog offered guns only in 10, 11, and 12 gauges with standard barrel lengths of 24" to 32". The following listing taken from that catalog (shown here in reverse order from their lowest to their best quality) is a useful guide for the modern-day collector:

(Lowest grade) **"Best gun iron barrels, plain finish, 12 gauge" (lock style not mentioned)**

(Next better grade) **"Decarbonized steel barrels, solid breech,** *back action locks.* **12 gauge"**

"Laminated or Damascus steel barrels, solid breech, *back action locks.* **11 or 12 gauge"**

"Laminated or Damascus steel barrels, solid breech, *back action locks*. 10 gauge"

"Laminated or Damascus steel barrels, solid breech, *front action locks*. 11 or 12 gauge"

(Next to best quality) "Laminated or Damascus steel barrels, solid breech, *front action lock*, 10 gauge"

(Their very best grade) "Laminated or Damascus steel barrels, solid breech, *front action locks*, 10, 11 or 12 gauge, superior finish"

Thus, using Parker's own terminology, the collector is afforded an exact and simple categorized listing of their earliest line of shotguns. **All of them have the lifter type action.** It's significant to note that the four lowest grades had *back action locks*, which, judging from the frequency with which they appear on the collectors' market, were likely dropped from the Parker line in their early years and may be considered quite scarce and worth premium values of at least 30 to 50 percent.

It is not known exactly which year the back action lock was dropped from the line. In their 1874 catalog, expanded somewhat and offering but one model in 11 gauge, there is no specific mention made to "back action lock" but they list both their lowest grades with "rebounding locks" while all others are shown with "front action" locks specifically; hence, one might reasonably assume that those two lowest grades were back action locks. By 1877 no mention of locks is made and one may assume that back actions were gone from the line.

By 1877 Parker's line had expanded considerably, but there was yet to be introduced any grading system or marking that could assist today's collector! By then, their least expensive quality was simply shown as:

"Plain twist barrels, no engraving or checkering, *straight grip*, 12 gauge"

This same gun with a "pistol grip" was one step higher and just slightly more expensive.

In edited form, their line for that year (and likely for the few following years) was listed thusly in ascending order of qualities:

(Next to their bottom grade) "Fine *English*, twist barrels, fine American stock, no checkering or engraving, with pistol grip, 10 or 12 gauge"

"Fine Damascus steel barrels, fine American stock, checkered and engraved; pistol grip, 10 or 12 gauge"

"Fine Damascus steel barrels, finest American stock, silver mounted, fine checkering and engraving, straight or pistol grip, 10 or 12 gauge"

"Fine Damascus steel barrels, fine English walnut stock, silver mounted, fine checkering and engraving, straight or pistol grip, 10 or 12 gauge"

(Their next to top grade) "Extra fine Damascus steel barrels, extra fine English stock, gold mounted, extra fine checkering and engraving, straight or pistol grip, 10 or 12 gauge"

(Their very top grade) "Finest Damascus steel barrels, finest English walnut stock, gold mounted, finest checkering and engraving, combined with finest workmanship and finished throughout. Straight or pistol grip, 10 or 12 gauge"

Catalogs of the 1890s are significant as they contain detailed listings of every quality/grade of Parker then made, utilizing the alphabetical system that all subsequent Parkers bore. It is significant that this grading system was used for both their *lifter* action as well as their *top lever* action even as late as 1899, when both types were still made and offered simultaneously. This alphabetical grading system was equally applied to their "hammerless" shotgun by merely adding the letter "H" after each "quality." Thus, grade "G" in the hammer-type guns will be found listed as "GH" for the hammerless type; that latter type was not offered in as wide a range as the hammer gun.

It is equally significant to note that when this grading system was adopted the guns were actually marked with the alphabet letter designating quality on the underside of the barrels and the frame.

In edited, simplified form, from their lowest quality to their best, Parker in 1899 described their line as follows:

"U" Quality: Twist barrels, American stock, engraved and checkered, straight grip, hard rubber buttplate. Gauges 12, 14, 16 and 20.

"T" Quality: Identical to above but with pistol grip.

"S" Quality: Identical to above but in 10 gauge only; straight grip.

"R" Quality: Identical to above; 10 gauge only; pistol grip.

"I" Quality: Fine laminated steel barrels, fine figured American stock, checkered and engraved, pistol grip, hard rubber buttplate. 10 gauge only.

"H" Quality: Fine Damascus steel barrel, fine figured American or imported stock, checkered and engraved, straight grip, hard rubber buttplate. 12, 14, 16 or 20 gauge.

"G" Quality: Identical to above but with pistol grip.

"F" Quality: Fine Damascus steel barrel, fine figured American or imported stock, checkered and engraved, straight grip, hard rubber buttplate, 10 gauge only.

"E" Quality: Identical to above, 10 gauge only with pistol grip.

"D" Quality: Fine Damascus steel barrels, fine imported stock, silver shield, fine checkering and engraving, skeleton buttplate, straight or pistol grip. 10, 12, 14, 16 and 20 gauge.

"C" Quality: Fine Bernard steel barrel, fine imported walnut stock, silver shield, fine checkering and engraving, skeleton buttplate, straight or pistol grip. 10, 12, 14, 16 or 20 gauge.

"B" Quality: Extra fine Damascus steel barrel, Extra fine imported stock, gold shield, extra fine checkering and engraving, skeleton buttplate, straight or pistol grip. 10, 12, 14, 16, or 20 gauge.

"A" Quality: Finest Damascus steel barrels, finest imported walnut stock, gold shield, finest checkering and engraving combined with finest workmanship and finished throughout. Skeleton buttplate. Straight or pistol grip. 10, 12, 14, 16, and 20 gauge.

"AA PIGEON GUN" Quality: Whitworth fluid pressed steel barrels, finest imported Circassian walnut stock, gold shield, finest checkering and engraving combined with finest workmanship and finish throughout. Skeleton buttplate. Straight or pistol grip. 12 gauge only.

The Parker Top Lever Shotgun

The Parker Hammerless Shotgun

The *hammerless* line was offered in their "AA PIGEON GUN" and qualities "A" through "E" and "G" identical to the hammer guns with the addition of two other qualities:

> **"NH" Quality: Fine English twist barrels, fine American stock, checkered and engraved, straight or pistol grip. Hard rubber buttplate. 10 gauge only.**
>
> **"PH" Quality: Identical to above but in gauges 12, 14, 16 and 20.**

In addition to the foregoing "Quality" levels, there were a few others, dropped prior to 1899: grades K, L, M, O, Q, and R. All were in lower quality ranges, fitted with "twist" and/or "laminated" type barrels; none believed approaching the fine Damascus grades. However, they might prove to be relatively scarce.

Parkers are most often observed in 10 gauge through 14 gauge sizes. 16 gauge is apparently quite scarce and worth a premium while the very largest (8 gauge) and smallest (20 gauge) are both quite rare and worth at least a 50 percent premium—and often, more.

Barrel lengths vary considerably. Usually anything over 34 inches in length is considered rare and worth a considerable premium—50 percent to 100 percent, if not more; barrels of original length of 26" or under are also very rare and worth premiums. It should be noted that odd barrel lengths in 1/2-inch graduations are occasionally encountered, but not necessarily worth premium value.

Parker Hammer Gun with Lifter Action

The first breech locking system on Parkers was a push-bar type called the "LIFTER ACTION." The latch, or bar, was located on the underside of the frame, just ahead of the trigger guard; three variations have been noted. The TOP LEVER style generally supplanted it in later years (variations of that type also), but the lifter action was made and offered simultaneous with it right to the turn of the century, and possibly later. Considerable variations have also been noted in hammer shape and contours of the recoil shield (shoulders).

Twist designs on Damascus barrels were offered in a wide range of choices, depending on the purchaser's pocketbook—from an inexpensive two-strand style to an exquisite eight-strand design. The common fallacy that Parker made fluid steel barrels with a Damascus pattern for clients desiring that special finish has been generally disproved by advanced Parker students.

Although reported in recent published works that hammerless Parker double shotguns were introduced in 1875, a study of catalogs seems to indicate they were introduced considerably later, probably 1891. Parker's statement (in their 1899 catalog) that they had "eight years of pronounced success with (the hammerless)" would seem to be verification of that fact. This is generally corroborated by another author on the subject whose chronology of major Parker events lists 1889 as being their year of adoption of the hammerless type, being "… the most radical change up to that time"; assuming that a period of 2 years after that would have been necessary for the actual manufacture and marketing of it.

The total Parker production of all models in all grades approximated a quarter of a million before their demise in 1942.

Slightly less than 100,000 were manufactured prior to 1900. One author has noted the inconsistency in serial number sequences used by the factory. A study of numbers with known manufacturing and shipping dates, has shown that occasionally a span of a few years existed between serials in close proximity to one another, seemingly indicating that frames were manufactured, numbered, and then shelved or stored, being held in reserve for custom orders. The hammer shotgun was believed to have been in production as late as 1920 and possibly offered even after that date on special order only. It has been generally assumed but not substantiated, that Parker shotguns under serial number 89,350 were made prior to December 31, 1898.

Parker Shotgun Manufacturing Records. The Parker Gun Collectors Association in 1998 was allowed to make copies of original Parker factory records, owned by Remington, allowing them to research those records for specific information for a fee for both members and collectors at large. By checking **www.parkergun.org**, it is possible to find out if information is available about a specific serial number as well as directions for acquiring that information. Typical information includes barrel length and chokes; stock configuration, date the gun was ordered and shipped, as well as other information about the gun. Replies are sent by mail on "factory" letterhead.

VALUING PARKERS:

In establishing broad categories for valuation guides the author has used descriptions from the 1869, 1877, and 1899 catalogs as listed in this section.

Higher values and stronger demand for *Damascus* Parkers are evidenced in the later (c. 1890s and after) Parkers; those that are actually *marked* (on undersides of barrels and frames) with the factory established *grades/qualities* and follow catalog configurations. The earlier types are more difficult to categorize because of the highly subjective catalog descriptions and the lack of a factory quality/grade marking; they are also more susceptible to spurious "up-grading" in recent eras.

It should be noted by the collector that values shown here are extremely variable due to the broad range of decoration, engraving and custom features that may be encountered on almost all models. Automatic ejectors (on hammerless types) are especially illustrative of price variables: on higher grade types they could add as much as one-third to the price while the same feature on lower grade models would add only approximately 15 percent to the price.

Very earliest markings, observed on both back action and bar lock types on center rib: CHARLES PARKER MAKER, MERIDEN, CONN. Less than 50 estimated; very rare; worth substantial premium.

Parker Values

Early models with back action locks and lifter type actions (first four descriptions listed in 1869 catalog):
17-150   Values—Very Good **$800** Fine **$1,000** Exc. **$2,500**

All other models; hammer guns with lifter or top lever and hammerless guns:

> **Lowest grades** (first three listed descriptions 1877 catalog and first nine listed descriptions 1899 catalog):
> 17-155   Values—Very Good **$500 to $700**
>   Fine **$700 to $1,200**
>   Exc. **$1,250 to $2,250**

> **Medium grades** (Fifth and sixth listed in 1869 catalog; fourth and fifth listed in 1877 catalog; Qualities B, C, D in 1899 catalog). Values are based on "D" grades:
> 17-160   Values—Very Good **$900 to $1,500**
>   *Fine **$1,200 to $2,000**
>   Exc. **$3,000 to $5,000**

*(This very broad price-range created by the tremendous amount of variables and possible configurations encountered in this category.)

Highest grades (Last listed in 1869 catalog; last two listed in 1877 catalog; "A" quality of 1899 catalog with premium for their "AA PIGEON GUN"):

17-165   Good **Values—Very Good $2,500 to $6,000**
   Fine **$3,750 to $9,500**
   Exc. **$8,000 to $15,000**

REMINGTON. (*See Chapter V-E.*)

ROYAL ARMS CO. (*See "Hollenbeck Gun Co.".*) reorganized from 3 Bbl Gun Co. 1908-1910.

SCHUYLER, HARTLEY & GRAHAM. New York, New York. Circa 1860-1876. Well-known sporting and military goods dealers. Agents, distributors, importers for many well-known shotguns. Succeeded by Hartley & Graham circa 1876 to turn of century (acquired the Union Metallic Cartridge Co. [1867] and in 1888 secured control of Remington Arms Co. ... merging both firms in 1912).   **17-170**

SMITH, LYMAN C. Syracuse, New York. Circa 1877 to 1971. Famous name in American shotguns. The commercial history of the firm is a bit complex, undergoing four distinct name changes while Lyman Smith was also involved with other gun-making ventures in New York state.

Smith's entry into gun manufacturing was in partnership with his brother Leroy and W.H. Baker who, in 1877, formed the W.H. Baker & Co. and commenced with the manufacture of Baker's three-barrel shotgun-rifle and a double shotgun of similar Baker design. By 1880 the partnership dissolved, Baker and Leroy Smith going their separate ways leaving Lyman Smith in business still manufacturing the Baker shotguns and shotgun-rifle under his name as "L.C. Smith, Maker of the Baker Gun." In 1884, the Baker gun was superseded by a new hammer shotgun designed and patented by an employee Alexander T. Brown; the hammerless model, also by Brown, was introduced in 1886. It was both of those models that have ever since been known as the "L.C. Smith shotgun." During those early formative years, his guns were marketed merely under the name "L.C. SMITH, Maker" and, not as occasionally, erroneously mentioned "L.C. SMITH & CO." or "L.C. SMITH CO."

In 1888, L.C. Smith sold his business to John Hunter of Fulton, New York. Smith left the gun business and went into the manufacture of typewriters (the later well-known Smith-Corona). By 1890, the Hunter Arms Co. was in full production of the "L.C. Smith Shotgun" at their newly-built factory in Fulton, New York, where they offered both the hammer and hammerless type L.C. Smith doubles. Made in a great many grades, the side-lock Smiths, as manufactured by Hunter, were medium and top quality American shotguns, highly regarded by the hunter and sportsman of their day. Those well-made, often elegant embellished, Damascus doubles enjoy a strong demand on the collectors' market of today.

Hunter Arms Co. underwent bankruptcy proceedings in 1917 due to their inability to keep up with manufacturing innovations of the era. The company went into receivership and continued under limited operation until 1920 when purchased by investors who had only passing interest in the manufacture of firearms. They continued to limp along until filing bankruptcy in 1945, at which time their entire assets were purchased by the Marlin Fire Arms Co. of New Haven, Conn. Marlin revitalized the firm, renaming it the "L.C. Smith Gun Co." for the production of double shotguns. After a disastrous collapse of the building in 1949, production ceased with remaining on-hand parts and tooling sent to Marlin's New Haven plant for storage. In 1967, Marlin resurrected the L.C. Smith side-lock shotguns and discontinued them in 1971. L.C. Smith manufacturing

L.C. Smith

records are at the Cody Firearms Museum which offers a service for collectors to identify those shotguns for which records are still on file, for a modest fee of $55 per gun, or $30 to members of the Historical Center. Address letters to:

Cody Firearms Museum
c/o Buffalo Bill Historical Center
720 Sheridan Ave.
Cody, WY 82414

(Records mostly contain only gauge and barrel lengths. Only a small number of shotguns have information available.)

L.C. Smith Values

BAKER THREE-BARREL SHOTGUN-RIFLE. L.C. Smith's first gun-making venture. Side-lock double shotgun over rifle. Made 1880 to 1884. Two distinct types (exacting details to be found in *L.C. Smith Shotguns* (*see Bibliography*). Offered in five grades from plain "English twist barrels" to "... Finest Damascus barrels, finest English walnut stock, elegantly engraved." Offered in 10 or 12 gauge over 44 caliber centerfire:

Plainer grades:
17-171   Values—Very Good **$750**   Exc. **$2,250**
Fancier grades:
17-172   Values—Very Good **$900 to $2,750**
   Exc. **$2,250 to $3,500**

17-173

BAKER PATENT DOUBLE SHOTGUNS MADE by L.C. SMITH, Syracuse, New York, Circa 1880 to 1884. Offered in six grades:
Plainest grades: (approximate only):
17-173   Values—Very Good **$275 to $550** Exc. **$650 to $900**
Fancier grades:
17-174   Values—Very Good **$500 to $900**
   Exc. **$850 to $1,750**

L.C. SMITH HAMMER SHOTGUNS. This model was made in almost identical form from its first manufacture and introduction by L.C. Smith in 1884 and continued manufacture by the Hunter Arms Co. Smith made it available in seven varying grades while it is assumed the Hunter Arms Co. offered those identical grades, then altered them from time to time over the long span of its manufacture. Best details about them are to be found in *L.C. Smith Shotguns* (*see Bibliography*). Values for these Damascus doubles will generally fall in the same groupings shown preceding this section under "Damascus Doubles Values."   **17-175**

L.C. SMITH HAMMERLESS SHOTGUNS. Introduced 1886 and in production (with varying interruptions as discussed above) to present day; underwent modifications and changes throughout.

17-177

17-187

The Damascus doubles were offered in approximately seven grades. They included not a few superb quality shotguns which are in high collector's "demand" fetching values commensurate with their various degrees of quality. Seldom encountered, their very finest doubles display superb quality workmanship and fetch values in excess of those shown for the general range of Damascus shotguns. As the *demand* factor is less than evidenced for Parkers, they generally fetch one-third to one-half of the values of commensurate highest grade Parkers.　**17-176**

SMITH & WESSON (*See Chapter V-G, Item 5G-065.*)

SPENCER ARMS CO., Windsor, Connecticut. Circa 1882-1889. First successful American slide or "pump" action repeating shotgun. An interesting and important collector's item from the historical viewpoint. It achieved a modicum of popularity in the mid-1880s and may be said to be the first widely sold and publicly accepted repeater, eventually leading to the end of the supremacy of the double barrel shotgun. Invented by Christopher M. Spencer, who was noted for his famed Civil War and Indian War era Spencer military carbines and rifles (*see Chapter IX-B*). The shotgun was offered in both solid and take-down models (the latter worth about 10 to 20 percent premiums) and in varying quality grades. 12 gauge most often encountered; 10 gauge scarce and worth premium.

Encountering financial difficulties, Spencer Patents were bought by the famed military equipment dealers (and America's first antique gun dealers) Francis Bannerman Sons of New York City about 1890 who continued to manufacture them until approximately 1907. These later Bannerman models worth approximately 20 percent less than the SPENCER ARMS CO. marked specimens whose values are shown as follows:
Plainer grades:

17-177　Values—Very Good **$450 to $650**
　　　　　Exc. **$800 to $1,250**

U.S. ARMY PURCHASE SPENCERS. The U.S. Army Ordnance Dept. purchased 354 of these Spencer pump action 12-gauge shotguns under four contracts between April, 1886 and January, 1893 (largest contract for 240 in 1886); all were delivered between May, 1886 and February 1893. On identified specimens the martial markings appeared with inspector initials in a stamped cartouche on the left side of the wrist of the buttstock FH (initials of Springfield Armory inspector Frank Heath) and on the right wrist D.F.C. (inspector David F. Clark). Other markings possible as additional specimens are identified. Among recorded numbers of those accepted were ten in the 1800 serial range. Authenticated examples rare. With no established history of sales, it is estimated that values would easily bring at least double those estimated above for "plainer grades," possibly higher.　**17-177.2**

SPENCER GUN COMPANY. Trade name found on a variety of Crescent, Stevens and Hopkins & Allen shotguns made for Chicago distributors Hibbard, Bartlett & Spencer Co. 1883-1929. 17-177.5

SQUIRES, HENRY C. New York City, New York. Circa 1870-1900. Well-known dealers, agents and importers.　**17-178**

STEVENS ARMS & TOOL COMPANY. (*See Chapter V-H.*) Manufacturers of inexpensive doubles and single shotguns.　**17-179**

SUTHERLAND, S. Richmond, Virginia. Circa 1850s-1870s. Maker and importer.　**17-180**

SYRACUSE ARMS CO. Syracuse, New York. Circa 1893-1910. Manufacturers of a wide range of inexpensive and medium quality doubles, many for large mail-order firms under brand names formed by Hollenbeck who left in 1895.　**17-181**

SYRACUSE FORGING & GUN COMPANY. Syracuse and Batavia, N.Y. Circa 1887 to 1890 (when it became Baker Gun Co.).

THREE-BARREL GUN COMPANY (*Reorganized 1905 from Hollenbeck (q.v.) until 1908 changed to ROYAL GUN CO.*)

TONKS, JOSEPH. Boston, Massachusetts. Circa 1850s-1880s.　**17-182**

TORKELSON ARMS CO. Worcester, Massachusetts. Circa 1880s-1908.　**17-183**

UNION ARMS COMPANY. Toledo, Ohio. Circa 1903-1913.　**17-184**

WHITNEY FIREARMS CO. New Haven, Connecticut (*See Chapter V-J*).

WHITNEY SAFETY FIREARMS CO. Florence, Massachusetts. Circa 1890s.　**17-185**

WILKES-BARRE GUN COMPANY. Wilkes-Barre, Pennsylvania. Circa 1890s. Shotguns made under their own and various brand names.　**17-186**

WINCHESTER REPEATING ARMS COMPANY (*See Chapter V-K*).

YOUNG REPEATING ARMS CO. Columbus, Ohio. 1902-1904. Manufactured a unique single barrel two-shot repeating shotgun designed by Charles "Sparrow" Young, a ranking trapshooter of the era:

17-187　Values—Very Good **$500**　　Exc. **$1,100**

Single Barrel Shotguns; Hammer and Hammerless Types

These single Damascus barrel types are usually singularly uninteresting! Very little interest or demand for them has been evidenced on the collectors' market. They all generally seem to fall in the same price ranges and categories. Of course, a uniquely designed specimen with some unusual breech feature or a truly remarkable single barrel (if such exists!) with exquisite engraving or gold inlays ... or possibly a special exhibition piece made by the manufacturer ... or occasionally a plain specimen in gem condition bearing the name of a famous maker, might possibly stir a latent interest deep within the breast of a kindly collector and thereby fetch a value worth noting.

The most humble of firearms, often called "farm guns", it seems their very commonness caused them to be disregarded. Little has been done to study their many diverse types. Single barrel Damascus shotguns were normally the most inexpensive grade, most modestly priced fowler of their day, made for those who could not afford even the least expensive double; made

17-188

17-189
"Zulu" Shotgun

strictly to put meat in the pot or maybe ward off an itinerant vagrant. They have a redeeming and historical feature though—as what was likely the most common, often-seen firearm in what was essentially a rural United States at the turn of the 20th century! They rarely possess quality workmanship or features that enamour them to any but the most unsuspecting novice or pure-bargain hunter! Their "demand" factor is minimal at best and normally, they're salable only when offered in an attractive, very low price range. The few that are found in brand-spanking new "mint" condition do have a following; there are collectors who buy "mint" guns of any type merely because they are in that pristine state.

Values:

Damascus Single of "garden variety" type in gauges 10, 12 or 16 and "Factory New" condition. Values fall off substantially for those same above "garden variety" shotguns when in less than "Factory New" condition; often 50 percent (possibly even greater if condition less than Fine.

17-188   Values—**$100 to $300**

Damascus Single of "garden variety" type of 20 gauge or smaller. The 20 ga. size in "Factory New" worth premium of approx. 20 percent more than 12 ga. variety (17-188) above.
Smaller gauges as follow:
28 gauge Damascus Single Shotgun
17-188.2   Values—**$250 to $750**
Same as above in 410 bore
17-188.3   Values—**$150 to $400**
Same as above in 8 ga. or larger size
      Values—**$550 to $1750**

"ZULU" SHOTGUNS. Among the most commonly encountered antique shotgun; of very little demand on the collectors' market; likely all of European manufacture c.1850s-1860s with alterations c.1880s. Included here to head off inquiries and unnecessary correspondence!

Utilizing a French version of the British Snider breech-loading action (invented by an American), the breechblock is hinged on right side and lifts upwards to expose chamber for loading. One of the most inexpensive shotguns of its day, produced in large quantities and apparently sold mostly through American mail order houses (including Sears, Roebuck) for very modest prices ($3.40 to $4.50) in the 1880s and early 1890s. Most are 10 and 12 gauge; varying barrel lengths.

Described in earlier editions of this work as "of no historical interest," the author stands corrected by the intriguing research article of J.B. Hughes (*Man At Arms*, Oct., 1993) which proves that even the most ordinary and unassuming of objects may posses a fascinating background if thoroughly studied.

French breech-loading Zulus started life as French military System 1857 muzzle-loading percussion rifled muskets. In the late 1860s they were converted to breechloaders using the Snider type action, many seeing service in the Franco-Prussian War, 1870. Sold as obsolete and surplus to Belgian arms dealers circa 1874, they were quickly altered into inexpensive shotguns to make them saleable to a civilian market. Apparently it was those Belgian dealers who coined the "ZULU" name, likely to give some punch to their marketing of these rather homely shotguns, just as is done today with everything from automobiles to wrist watches. The Zulu was among the most widely advertised shotgun (occasionally named "THE HUNTER") in American sporting goods mail order catalogs of the 1880s. It seems that it was so widely sold that there were even knock-offs, copies, of it using other surplus military parts.

One particular ZULU has an intriguing background. Those with brass breech blocks were produced during the Franco-Prussian War under siege conditions. The brass was obtained from French church bells donated to meet the dire emergency. For the history buff these would certainly be worth a premium.
17-189   Values—Good **$100**   Fine **$250**

BIBLIOGRAPHY

(Note: Both W.W. Greener books *The Gun and Its Development* and *Modern Breechloaders: Sporting and Military* [*see listing Chapter IV*] are among the most significant works for the collector in the study of breech-loading Damascus shotguns. Further biographical information about American shotgun makers will be found in the numerous works about American gun makers found listed in Chapter IV and elsewhere. See also *Spencer Repeating Firearms* by R. Marcot and "*Flintlock Fowlers; The First Guns Made in America*" by T. Grinslade.)

Akehurst, Richard. *Sporting Guns*. New York: G. P. Putnam's Sons, 1968. General survey from flintlock to breechloader with good background information on fowling pieces and double shotguns.

Arnold, R. *Automatic and Repeating Shotguns*. New York: A. S. Barnes & Company, 1962.

Askins, C. *The Shotgunner's Book*. Harrisburg, Pennsylvania: The Stackpole Company, 1958.

*Baer, Larry. *The Parker Gun … An Immortal American Classic*. Los Angeles, California: Beinfeld Publications. Vol. I. 1974; Vol. II. 1976, Highland Park, New Jersey: The Gun Room Press, 1980. Compilation of uncorrelated and often unsubstantiated information without given sources; more or less a scrapbook of the author's collecting experiences and gripes. Liberally illustrated but much of the uncaptioned material difficult to identify. Information on Damascus doubles meager.

*Brophy, Lt. Col. William S. *L. C. Smith Shotguns*. North Hollywood, California: Beinfeld Publishing Company, 1977 and Highland Park, New Jersey: The Gun Room Press, 1983. Definitive treatise; well documented; heavily illustrated. Basic reference source.

Brophy, Lt. Col. William S. *Plans and Specifications of the L. C. Smith Shotguns*. Montezuma, Iowa: F. Brownell and Son, 1981.

*Butler, D. F. *The American Shotgun*. New York: The Winchester Press, 1973.

*Canfield, Bruce. *U.S. Combat Shotguns*. Lincoln, R.I.: Andrew Mowbray, Inc., 1992. Earliest types to present.

Carder, C. E. *The Side-By-Side; History & Digest of Double Barrel Breechloading Shotguns.*1989. Wealth of details; 800 trade names; profuse illustrations; many Damascus doubles included.

Carder, C.E. *Tip Up Shotguns From Hopkins & Allen*. Delphos, Ohio: Avil Onze Publishing, c. 1995. Monograph

Carder, C.E. *Side By Sides Of The World*. Delphos, Ohio: Avil Onze Publishing, c.1998. Double shotguns early 1800's to present. 1295 names list.

Crudgington, I. M. & Baker, D. J. *The British Shotgun 1850-1870*. Volume 1. London, England: Barrie and Jenkins, 1979. Detailed; definitive; well-illustrated. Of importance to American shotgun collectors.

*Elliot, R. W. & Cobb, J. *LeFever: Guns of Lasting Fame*. Lindale, Texas: 1986. Well illustrated, includes production estimates.

*Elliot, Robert W. *Uncle Dan Lefever: Master Gunmaker*. Lindale, Texas: Privately printed by author, 2002.

*Grozdik, Richard S. *Game Guns*. Iola, Wisconsin: Krause Publications, 2002 (Second Edition). The leading shotguns of yesterday and today for hunting game and birds.

*Gunther, R. W., Mullins, W. L. and Parker, L. C. III. *The Parker Story*. East Jordan, Michigan: The Double Gun Journal, 2000. A two-volume set and major work on subject, superbly illustrated.

Hastings, MacDonald. *English Sporting Guns and Accessories* London, England: Ward Lock & Company, 1969. General coverage flintlock to breech-loading Damascus types. Of interest to American shotgun collectors.

Hinman, Bob. *The Golden Age of Shotgunning*. New York: Winchester Press, 1971; Reprint Prescott Arizona: Wolfe Publishing Company, 1982. Basic reference. Best overall coverage for background on the rise and demise of the Damascus double in America; the punt gun; market hunting; target shooting. Includes lengthiest compiled list of known makers and trade names. Often referred to.

Johnson, Peter H. *Parker—America's Finest Shotgun*. Harrisburg, Pennsylvania: The Stackpole Company, 1961 and 1985. Basic information but lacking definitive detail for the collector; some unsubstantiated facts.

Keith, Elmer. *Shotguns By Keith*. Harrisburg, Pennsylvania: The Stackpole Company, 1950.

*McIntosh, Michael. *A.H. Fox - The Finest Gun in the World*. Traverse City, Mich: Privately published, 1992. All models of their shotguns...and automobiles.

*Muderlak, E. *Parker Guns, The Old Reliable*. California: 1997.

*Snyder, W.C. *The Ithaca Company From the Beginning*. Marceline, Missouri: Privately published, 1991. Complete coverage of guns and company.

Vorisek, J.T. *Shotgun Markings 1865 to 1940*. Canton, Conn.: Armsco Press, 1998.

*Walsh, H. M. *The Outlaw Gunner*. Centreville, Maryland: Tidewater Publishers, 1971. Detailed coverage and illustrations of market hunting and huge punt guns.

Zutz, Don. *The Double Shotgun*. New York: The Winchester Press, 1978.

(*) Preceding a title indicates the book is currently in print.

The biggest Winchester of them all! Twenty foot overall length; weighing about 450 pounds. Antique hand-carved wooden trade sign in perfect scale of the Model 1873 Winchester rifle. Made circa 1880-1890, mounted for over half-century over the store of a Winchester dealer in New York City. (*N. Flayderman & Co. Catalog No. 101, 1977*)

Paul Bunyan model double shotgun! Trade sign - in exact scale - carved of wood, 14 feet overall length, weighing over 100 pounds. Made around the 1890s; was mounted outdoors for nearly half a century over the front of the famous IVER JOHNSON GUN AND SPORTING GOODS store at the corner of Washington Street and Cornhill, Boston. Original gold-painted finish. (*N. Flayderman & Co. Catalog No. 101, 1977*)

CHAPTER XVIII

Miscellanea

Whaling Guns, Indian Guns, Alarm Guns, Blunderbusses, Spring and Air Guns, Harmonica Guns, Needle Fire Guns and Salute Cannon

Most firearms discussed in this chapter are rarely mentioned in general guides to collecting antique American guns. Many have seemingly been relegated to obscurity. The author always felt they were deserving of better treatment; they just did not fit into the neatly defined categories of the preceding seventeen chapters. In some areas the collector following has been somewhat limited, as is the case of whaling guns, while specialties such as air guns have been considered on the periphery of antique gun collecting.

Regrettably, much of the published literature on most of these subjects is obscure or long out of print and not easily available. By no means is the information presented here intended to be definitive in any single category. However, it is the first time to be made available to collectors at large, having been given but short shrift until now. Possibly this chapter will broaden horizons for some American collectors while allowing these very collectible antique guns to be more fully recognized, understood and appreciated.

WHALING GUNS

To the unfamiliar, these large, cumbersome, unwieldy appearing firearms are looked upon as merely "curiosa". True, some are quite homely, even awkward, were they to be judged on their aesthetic qualities (although brass types often have a wider audience for their eye appeal when burnished bright!). And, true, they don't lend themselves easily to mounting on a wall with a pair of gun hooks. However, they possess dual

interest for American collectors as a distinct category of firearms and as historic artifacts that played an important role in the American whaling industry. Regardless of how whaling may be viewed today by environmentalists for its association with an endangered species, it was, during much of the 19th century, a major industry dominated by American ships and by Yankee seamen. To lend further appreciation for these arms, let the reader visualize that Yankee seaman proving his mettle, balancing precariously in the bow of the pitching, frail whaleboat, shouldering one of these 20 pound (or heavier) guns. After shooting a forty ton monster he still had to fasten to it, do further battle, then "reel" it in.

Whaleboat with Greener's Gun Mounted

Greener Swivel Gun

Whaling guns are recognized as a distinct category, specimens often appearing on the market. Yet, surprisingly little has been written about them. Frequently mentioned in whaling literature, specific details about them are seldom offered. As for antique arms literature, there is a deafening silence! For the student and researcher but one book treats the subject at any depth, "HARPOONS AND OTHER WHALECRAFT" by Thomas G. Lytle (Whaling Museum; The Old Dartmouth Historical Society, New Bedford, Mass., 1984). These interesting antique firearms are deserving of further research.

As a generalization, all whaling guns are quite scarce and enjoy a reasonably strong demand on the collectors' market. That market, however, is not usually among antique arms collectors, where often these guns are seen and can be acquired at reasonable values … although rarely as sleepers! Their strongest demand, and consequently highest values, have always been among nautical, notably whaling, collectors. Those two diverse collector markets may possibly level out with added knowledge of their history and usage and appreciation of the role they played in an historic American Industry.

The whaling guns illustrated and discussed here are among the most well known, often encountered models. As with many other collectible obsolete firearms there are manufacturing variances. Such differences in dimensions, bore sizes, weight, etc. have seldom been found to make any appreciable differences in values … yet.

NON-WHALING HARPOON GUNS: A type of "harpoon gun" much too small for use in whaling is occasionally seen. Often built on popular gun actions (such as the Remington rolling block, etc.) and fitted with very light weight harpoons, they are intriguing oddities and may be considered "firearms curiosa"; most often anyone's guess as to their intended use. Likely the best clue to all of them is found on a specimen made by the famous London gunmaker, W.W. Greener marked on the barrel "HARPOON GUN". Printed on the label of the case which holds the gun is an advertisement of the period: "SMALL

Mid 18th Century Flintlock Whale Harpoon Swivel Gun

MAMMAL HARPOON GUN … For Taking Small Mammals and Larger Game Fish". Greener's description would appear to put the entire category in clear perspective. Judging by the frequency with which such pieces are encountered they did not achieve great popularity (*see also Ingersoll Life Line Gun, Chapter V-E; No. 5E-104.5*).

Flintlock Harpoon Guns to the Development of the Bomb Lance: The use of various apparatus to fire large, iron whale harpoons with lines attached is traced to the mid-18th century. Such firearms never achieved any measure of popularity; surviving examples are rarities. The unreliability of the flintlock ignition system, combined with damp, if not soaking wet, conditions of an open whaleboat was but one detriment. Innovations in the flintlock mechanism, such as double

Bomb Lances

hammers and protective covering, did little to solve the problem. Those massive guns, swivel mounted on the bow of a pitching and rolling whaleboat were severely limited to use in calm seas only. The increased dependability of the percussion cap allowed for the more practical, improved harpoon gun developed, made and marketed c. 1837 by the noted British gunmaker, William Greener, famous for his shotguns and rifles. Greener swivel types, weighing 55 pounds, 4-1/2 feet long, firing an iron harpoon about 40 yards, were first advertised in the U.S. circa 1850s. The gun had little competition, enjoying wide American use. The exploding bomb lance, designed for percussion, much lighter weight shoulder fired guns, was developed by Christopher C. Brand and Charles Tracy, both of Norwich, Conn. and quickly gained wide popularity and use in the whaling industry. Many various inventions, innovations and types of bomb lances were developed and perfected through to the 1880s, most to fit bores from 7/8" to 1-1/4". The bomb lance, a pointed steel projectile about 20" long and 1" in diameter (average), filled with black powder, with fins or other device to help guide it in flight was designed to explode on impact and penetration. If the aim was true it rendered the whale senseless or dead. They did not revolutionize the whaling

industry, but were of great aid, making the taking of those behemoths somewhat less hazardous. The threat of sudden death was always present. Although bomb lances were the projectiles of choice, the shoulder-fired gun was adaptable for use with harpoons, albeit limited. The lighter weight harpoon it could handle was not practical, while the attached line often caused it to be deflected, limiting accuracy. The very heavy powder charge needed to propel the harpoon and line any great distance often knocked the whaleman off his feet (the charge for the bomb lance, occasionally did the same), a most disconcerting turn of events.

Most common bomb lances were designed for three bore diameters: 7/8", 1-1/8", 1-1/4". Overall length of the gun varied approx. 32"-38" while weights usually were between 15-25 lbs. Many guns, if not most, when sold were cased in a plain, thick, serviceable pine wood box which would stand the rigors of being tossed around in a pitching, rolling whaleboat. Accessories included were normally a powder container and loading tools in their respective wood compartments. It is assumed that most cases had a large printed label "Directions For Use", etc. on the inner lid. When found complete with label intact values are enhanced by approx. $1,000 to $2,000.

SHOULDER-FIRED WHALING GUNS

C. C. Brand, Norwich Connecticut

18-001

18-002

The most popular, widely used and longest in service bomb lance muzzle loading percussion shoulder gun was by Christopher C. Brand of Norwich, Conn. (after 1876 by Junius A. Brand). First used circa 1850, some were still in service after the turn of the 20th century. Made in the three bore sizes mentioned above, and a few manufacturing variations. Only one specimen of these Brands has been recorded (in C.W. Sawyer's 1920 edition *"Our Rifles"*) with markings BRAND ARMS COMPANY; all other known and observed whaling guns by C.C. Brand are unmarked. General configurations make them readily identifiable. Weighing between 19 and 25 lbs., average length 22", the part octagon, part round barrel is usually fitted with ramrod pipes underneath for a removable wooden loading rod. Most specimens also have the skeleton type pistol grip. The open iron loop just below trigger bow is for attaching a lanyard in event gun falls overboard. Earliest type as shown is fitted with walnut butt stock and iron butt plate. The author suspects early wood stock type may have been made for C.C. Brand by ALLEN THURBER & CO. of Worcester, Mass. (See their whale gun # 5A-097.5 for specifics). Brand may not have commenced his own manufacturing operation until the 1860s, which further strengthens the opinion. An early Brand has been mentioned

with a hollow brass stock in place of the walnut stock; it would be considered extremely rare and worth a considerable premium. Barrels either blued or browned, but rarely seen with finish remaining.

18-001   Values—Good **$2,250**   Fine **$3,750**

Most often seen is the all iron C.C. Brand with the heavy skeleton type iron stock cast integral with the frame; also unmarked. There is a variation with much thinner but similar integral skeleton type iron stock, quite scarce, but there has not been a noticeable difference in values.

18-002   Values—Good **$2,000**   Fine **$3,250**

**18-003
Grudchos & Eggers**

JULIUS GRUDCHOS & SELMAR EGGERS, NEW BEDFORD, MASSACHUSETTS circa 1857, muzzle loading percussion whaling gun. Considerably scarcer than the Brand.

A ponderous piece, specimens are most often found with a rifled bore to take a Grudchos & Egger patented bomb lance. Among the lightest of bomb lance guns; 18 lbs., 40" overall; 24" octagon/round barrel, Walnut half stock of massive proportions with oversize back action lock. Maker markings "GRUDCHOS & EGGERS/NEW BEDFORD, MASS." on barrel and lock.

18-003   Values—Good **$3,500**   Fine **$6,000**

**18-004
Brown**

ROBERT BROWN, NEW LONDON, CONNECTICUT, all brass, percussion muzzle loading harpoon/bomb lance gun circa 1850s.

Specifically intended to utilize harpoons and bomb lances designed by Brown, it had a bore much larger than all others and was likely the heaviest of the shoulder-fired guns at about 30 lbs. All brass frame cast integral with hollow brass stock; 34 lbs.; 31"

brass barrel with cannon-turned muzzle. Bore approx. 1-1/2". Although contemporary accounts of its use and advertisements are known, the gun likely did not gain much favor as the huge charge it took to propel the harpoon and lance created tremendous recoil. Seldom encountered. Variations noted in shape of hammer; a double width type used to strike 2 nipples to insure ignition.

Markings: ROBERT BROWN / NEW LONDON, CT. Also known marked "ALBERTSON, DOUGLAS & CO." of New London; (who also patented a shoulder-fired harpoon gun hinged at center in order to be folded for ease of transport; no specimen yet recorded).

18-004   Values—Good **$4,500**   Fine **$7,500**

**18-005
William Lewis (Chapman Patent)**

BREECH-LOADING ALL BRASS WHALING GUN BY WILLIAM LEWIS OF NEW BEDFORD, MASS. UNDER THE IMPROVED 1877 PATENT OF H. W. CHAPMAN OF NEWARK, NJ.

Thirty six inches overall; weight about 20 lbs.; 7/8" bore, 18" round barrel. Narrow breech block swivels upward to expose chamber and load. Entire frame, stock and trigger bow cast integral as one piece; matching brass barrel believed superior to iron as it would not become brittle or easily break in the cold of the arctic when whaling in those climes. Manufactured by William Lewis of New Bedford. Maker markings not present.

18-005   Values—Good **$4,000**   Fine **$6,500**

**18-006
Iron Cunningham & Cogan**

Breech loading all iron whaling gun by Patrick Cunningham & Bernard Cogan, on the H. W. Chapman patent of 1877 (This preceded item 18-005 above in date of manufacture.) Heavy iron frame, skeleton stock, trigger bow all cast integral as one piece. Breech action same as above. Dimensions about same as above. No maker markings.

18-006   Values—Good **$3,000**   Fine **$5,000**

**18-007
Pierce & Eggers**

Breech-loading whaling gun circa 1878 by Ebenezer Pierce & Selmar Eggers, New Bedford, Massachusetts.

Massive lever opens breech; all brass with frame and skeleton stock cast integral. Weight 25 lbs. Specimens both marked and unmarked S. EGGERS / N. BEDFORD MASS / PAT. FEB. 12. 1878. Variations noted in shape of lever; long, thick rifle-like style most often.

18-007   Values—Good **$4,500**   Fine **$7,500**

**18-008
Pierce**

Breech-loading whaling gun by Ebenezer Pierce, New Bedford, Mass. Circa 1882. Made by Frank E. Brown, New Bedford, Massachusetts (nephew of E. Pierce).

All brass with skeleton type stock (two styles noted) cast integral with frame. Barrel tips downward to load. 39" overall; weight approx. 24 lbs. No maker markings.

18-008   Values—Good **$4,000**   Fine **$7,000**

DARTING GUNS

**18-009
Pierce Patent 1865**

**18-009
Luscomb Patent 1894**

**18-009
Cunningham Patent 1875**

Although widely used from 1860s through early 20th century and made in both muzzle-loading percussion and breech-loading metallic cartridge, specimens are quite scarce. A dual purpose whaling implement used to fire a bomb lance (as in shoulder fired guns) while simultaneously fastening to the whale with a toggle type harpoon, or "darting iron". The oddly shaped, unusual appearing device is usually brass, about 20" overall. Although the gun and barrel mechanism are quickly apparent, its intended use is obscure to those not familiar. The device was triggered by a slender round iron rod protruding approximately 30" on side of the barrel; mounting rings were integral to hold the darting iron. The entire apparatus, with harpoon, was mounted on a six foot sturdy wooden shaft and used in the time-honored method by a whaleman balancing at the bow of a small whaleboat. When in range of his prey, he sunk the harpoon into the whale, fastening to it while at the same time triggering the firearms device, shooting the bomb lance into the whale. Originally invented by Ebenezer Pierce circa 1865, the darting gun was modified by him and made in various configurations and shapes by other makers until the end of the century; the last patent for one was issued in 1894. Percussion specimens are scarcer and are worth a premium of 25 percent at least. If the original six foot wood shaft still affixed worth 20 percent premium.

18-009   Values—Good **$2,750**   Fine **$4,000**

INDIAN TRADE GUNS AND INDIAN OWNED GUNS

Firearms made specifically for the Indian trade and firearms owned and used by American Indians have received increasing recognition by the collecting world. They embrace and overlap three distinct fields of specialty: antique firearms … American Indian artifacts … and are equally prized for their role in the history and lore of the American frontier and the West. Seldom following traditional collecting patterns these arms, most often plain in features, possessing minimal embellishments and decorations and often well-used, if not abused, are invariably relegated to a vague status in most collecting guides and arms literature. That they are routinely disregarded may be attributable to the unique, one-of-a-kind characteristic of many Indian firearms, making generalizations difficult. A second contributing factor may also be the English or Belgian manufacture of many, causing them to be overlooked as non-American. That they were designed, manufactured and sold only to the North American Indian trade merits their inclusion here.

Commencing with the latter decades of the 19th century, there has been increasing fascination and collectibility for guns identified with Indian usage in their various heated combat encounters with the U.S. military and settlers heading to the Western frontiers. The more famous (or notorious) of such encounters, the more desirable (hence valuable) are relics of those engagements. Typical of that early interest is the entry seen in the 1889 catalog of noted militaria dealers Francis Bannerman of New York advertising a "Lot of 50 Assorted Rifles, Muskets and Carbines, part of the lot surrendered by the Indian Chief Sitting Bull, to the U.S. Government after the Custer Massacre; some of the rifles are the Leman Indian Sporting Rifle with heavy barrels and fine sights; stocks and woodwork are worn thin; some stocks are repaired with buckskin; some are still loaded. [Those loads] will be withdrawn before shipment. …Carbines $3; muskets $4; sporting rifles $5; some Henry Repeating Rifles in the lot $7." The famous 1899 catalog of the A.E. Brooks collection of Hartford, (See Chap. I) also described and illustrated numerous longarms found at Indian battle sites.

Although space limitations allow but cursory coverage, the intent is to arm the collector with sufficient facts to recognize many of the trade types and equip him with basic information about other guns that may have been Indian-owned and used, along with a caveat or two for buying or trading. The field does not lack for carpetbaggers.

Trade guns have a fascinating background of usage in America. From the earliest European settlement there were extensive dealings in firearms with Indians by trade, sale and outright gift. Seventeenth and early eighteenth century predecessors of the "true" trade gun were inexpensive small

bore European (mostly English) fowling pieces. By the mid-18th century those English fowlers tended to conform to a loosely uniform pattern specifically made to use in the American Indian trade. By the mid-1770s that pattern, having found favor with Indians, became quite standardized: A gun that was inexpensive, dependable and large enough to take big game yet could be carried for lengthy periods. Mostly intended for trading in the prime fur trapping areas of the Great Lakes, Illinois and Hudson's Bay, then known as the "NORTHWEST TERRITORY"

Common English Flintlock Fowling Piece of 1720-1770 with Dragon Sideplate

Classic Examples of Dragon Sideplate "Standarized" Trade Musket (note also the usual oversize trigger bow)

Examples of "Standardized" Trade Guns. Lower specimen c. 1800. Note lack of carving, pointed tail of lock, gooseneck hammer; rounded nain fastened buttplate. Upper gun (dated "1861" converted to percussion (although likely left factory in this configuration), screw fastened squared butt-plate; carving at lock and tang; rounded tail of lock.

the guns were actually mentioned in correspondence as early as 1777 as the "Northwest gun" (pre-dating the formation of the famous Northwest Company by seven years). Richard Wilson and William Grice appeared to have been among the more prolific makers of the earlier "fire locks" for the American Indian trade. The flintlock trade gun as it was standardized, had more wide spread use for a longer period of time (circa 1775-1875 approx.) than any other firearm in American history except the Colt single action. The gun was bartered and sold by all major fur trading companies, at every frontier post and by independent traders to all tribes from Canada to the border of Mexico; from Western Pennsylvania to the Rockies. Many thousands were given as treaty payments by the U.S. Government, which is known to have purchased, under contract, English-made guns as well as those of American manufacture. Flintlocks remained popular well into the late 19th century as the cost of using them was minimal. Although percussion firearms were advantageous, they required copper primer caps not always readily available and for some, expensive. For those same reasons muzzle-loading firearms, both flintlock and percussion, may still be found in use with primitive societies throughout the world where metallic cartridges are either too expensive or rigidly controlled by the respective governments which may prefer to keep their natives from getting restless. During earlier periods of use the trade gun was often termed "The Hudson Bay Gun" or "Mackinaw Gun" or the "Northwest Gun". The term most often in use by collectors today is merely "Indian trade gun".

A number of features are common to almost all American and European manufactured types; those made for and sold by various British trading companies in North America as well as the famous American Fur Company of John Jacob Astor and other American firms. The most prolific maker was John Barnett of London whose name is most often seen. There is little doubt that the market was dominated by British makers and the Hudson's Bay Company in earlier years. By 1840 the American Fur Company and American makers had become pronounced factors. Much is yet to be known about these firearms; various makers produced specific types for some of the larger companies with markings that may identify them. The most important study of them remains "THE NORTHWEST GUN" by Charles E. Hanson, Jr. (Nebraska State Historical Society, 1955). Other valuable references for Indian trade and Indian owned guns are: "*Arms Of The American West*" (Vol. I & II; Garavaglia and Worman); "*Custer Battle Guns*" (DuMont and Hutchins); "*Indian Trade Guns*" (Hamilton, compiler); "*Guns Of The Western Indian War*" (Dorsey); "*Guns Of The Early Frontiers*" (Russell)' "*American Military Shoulder Arms*" (Moller). "*Firearms in the Custer Battle*" by Parsons & DuMont; "*Guns at the Little Bighorn: Weapons of Custer's Last Stand*" Mowbray Publishers. "*Trade Guns of the Hudson's Bay Company 1670-1970*" by S. J. Gooding. All are listed in Chapter IV "The Arms Library." The highly regarded, well-known **MUSEUM OF THE FUR TRADE**, as its name implies has long devoted itself to the history and artifacts associated with that broad subject. Its collections and its important *"Quarterly"* publication (now in its 41st year) have included numerous important articles on trade guns and other firearms associated with Indian usage. The collector interested in this subject would do well to seek membership. Further information may be obtained by writing to 6321 Hwy 20, Chadron, Nebraska 69337 (www.furtrade.org).

The most prominent, easily distinguished feature on almost all trade types is a large brass sideplate (with many variations) cast in the well defined, relief design of a sea serpent or coiled dragon. For reasons now obscure, that motif gained great favor with the Indians. It has been suggested that the serpent design was merely a common English and Dutch decoration on many of the early fowling pieces in the late 16th/early 17th century, one fancied by the Indian, eventually becoming tantamount to a seal of approval, if not a good omen, The serpent sideplate was usually fastened to the lock with three large screws. About 1820 the use of two lock screws became common with one small wood screw fastening the rear of the serpent to the stock.

All Indian trade guns are full stock, usually walnut, pin fastened. Varying overall length, approximately 46"-64". Locks follow general sporting patterns; earlier markings usually engraved in script and pointed tail while later ones are die stamped in block letters and became successively more rounded. Goose neck hammers were used until about 1840 overlapping with the thick double necked hammer, used until the 1870's. Very earliest types had no relief carving. By the 1830's a long, relief carved tear drop design is seen around the barrel tang and each side of the wrist-, towards later production the long wrist carvings are very shortened. Most are fitted with two brass, closely ribbed ramrod ferrules, lacking the third lower thimble/ramrod ferrule. Although barrels vary in length they almost invariably are part octagon, part round with circular turnings near their center; original finishes were blue or brown; caliber approx. 60 (24 gauge). Barrel tangs were fastened with a screw from the underside near the trigger, changing placement to the tang around 1830's. Two other very distinctive features common to almost every trade gun are the very large iron trigger guard with massive oversize trigger bow having simply shaped finials (thin iron on earlier types) and the flat brass buttplate with very short tang of heel. Buttplates were fastened by square iron nails as late as the 1820's; replaced with five screws, eventually two.

Earliest formalized markings were the design of a seated fox within a circular panel stamped on the lock and barrel along with "LONDON", circa 1780. Generally in use through to 1810-1820 at which time the so called "TOMBSTONE FOX" came to general use. Invariably struck on the barrel, occasionally the lock also, in many sizes, shapes and variations, the mark appears as a small, deeply struck, sunken marking in the shape of a tombstone with a seated fox motif in its center. Variations of the markings and overlapping of dates in use are quite common, however all are unique to Indian trade guns. British government markings are often seen on locks indicating their purchase and use of the guns as gifts or to arm Indian allies, mostly War of 1812 era. Locks are quite often dated after 1805 through to the mid-1870's.

Many thousands of trade guns were produced by a host of makers, yet <u>survival rate</u> was minimal. Owing to their hard wear and rough usage with very little thought given to maintenance, it is assumed they were carried until they possessed no further function and discarded. Many borderline salvageable specimens were likely unrecognized or discarded in the 20th century before gun collecting became popular. There is considerable leeway and disparity in demand and values of trade guns depending on which collecting market they are sold (i.e. gun collecting, Indian artifacts or Western history). Values reflected here are those most often used for the gun collector's market. Frequently the firearms are found shortened or otherwise altered for saddle use. Depending on the collector's taste and appearance of the gun, values may be the same as for an unaltered specimen. The use of brass tack decoration and rawhide repairs often adds considerably to value (see following discussion).

ENGLISH-MADE FLINTLOCK INDIAN TRADE GUN of "standardized" pattern as described above (earlier specimens prior to circa 1800 worth premium values):

18-030	Values—Fair **$2,250**	Very Good **$5,000**

As above; converted to percussion:

18-031	Values—Fair **$1,750**	Very Good **$3,000**

Leman (all three)

Tryon

Deringer

A sampling of the type of markings used by three famous makers: Henry Leman of Lancaster, PA, Henry Deringer and Edward and George Tryon of Philadelphia and applied to their respective flintlock trade muskets, and typical of other American-made trade guns. Note especially the spurious / imitation proof marks intended to resemble British proof marks and also that odd "tombstone fox" motif to which the Indians had become accustomed to accept on these style arms. Often the very names of the makers are stamped in a more crude manner than viewed on their better quality weapons for the home market.

AMERICAN-MADE "standardized style" flintlock Northwest Trade gun identical to above with markings of many varied Pennsylvania makers known to have produced these such as H.E. Leman of Lancaster, Penna., Henry Deringer and J. Henry & Sons, Boulton, Penna. among others. Their guns were properly marked by the respective maker, also stamped with the "tombstone fox" along with spurious British proofs, markings which the Indian had become accustomed to.

18-032   Values—Fair **$3,500**   Very Good **$6,500**

Identical above converted to percussion:

18-033   Values—Fair **$2,500**   Very Good **$5,000**

BELGIAN MADE "standardized style" flintlock Northwest Trade gun about identical above. An interesting variant, quite genuine and of "the period", are various Belgian trade guns bearing spurious, well known British maker markings; "LONDON" often on barrel; crude imitation of British proof marks along with standard Liege ("LEG" in oval) Belgian proof values usually the same as for the regular English made types although some collectors may pay premium.

18-034   Values—Fair **$2,250**   Very Good **$5,000**

Identical converted to percussion:

18-035   Values—Fair **$1,750**   Very Good **$3,000**

ORIGINAL PERCUSSION English-made Northwest Trade gun. Stylistically about identical to the so-called "standardized" type showing its later manufacture with a military style Enfield lock and hammer. Otherwise about identical.

18-036   Values—Fair **$1,750**   Very Good **$3,750**

CHIEF'S GRADE FLINTLOCK TRADE GUNS: Commonly accepted as being made for presentation to friendly Indian chiefs, possibly as diplomatic or treaty gifts out of the usual trade channels. These better quality flintlock fowling pieces, popularly termed "Chief's Grade" are a distinctive type with easily recognizable features: pin fastened full stock; British proofed part octagon/round barrel often (not always) with the seated fox-in-circle marking. Invariably seen with an engraved boar's head within a round, curled hunting horn design at rear of lock; same motif occasionally on heel of butt plate with large

18-037

engraved arrow (or merely the arrow only); bow and arrow engraved motifs on the trigger bow and the large, flat side plate (not the usual dragon type); finial of trigger guard most often seen in cloverlike pattern. Singularly most obvious feature is oval silver inlay at wrist with large, relief, detailed profile

Indian wearing feathered headdress and carrying bow and arrows.

18-037   Values—Fair **$3,750**   Very Good **$7,500**
Identical; converted to percussion:
18-038   Values—Fair **$2,250**   Very Good **$4,750**

INDIAN TRADE RIFLES

18-040

Considerable documentation exists concerning the manufacture of flintlock and percussion rifles for both trade and treaty gifts to American Indians (see "THE NORTHWEST GUN" by Hanson and "AMERICAN MILITARY SHOULDER ARMS" by Moller). Pennsylvania-Kentucky rifle makers dominated the field. Conversely, the rifles themselves are about impossible to positively identify as Indian trade guns. They rarely bear special markings and are indistinguishable from the plainer grade of brass-mounted Kentucky rifles. Significant quantities of those less expensive, simply decorated rifles by various makers (Henry Deringer especially noted) were sold on the commercial market over a lengthy period of time. Documents and correspondents mention two specific types ordered: the "LANCASTER" style and far less popular "ENGLISH PATTERN"; both of American make. Such rifles were made under contract to the U.S. Government through the "Office of Indian Trade" and the "Bureau of Indian Affairs" from the 1790s through the 1840s. Quite a few contracts mentioned quantities of

one thousand with as many as two thousand seven hundred and fifty in the 1837 contract to Henry Deringer. Although not fancy, there is evidence they were well-constructed according to rigid specifications and subject to government inspection. As distinguishing marks are yet to be known, collectors are cautioned to be wary when offered specimens.
18-039

The author is familiar with but one "U.S." marked U.S. Government purchased percussion rifle believed intended as treaty gifts to friendly Indians. The type is seen with reasonable frequency on the collectors market. Approximately 70 percent of those encountered bear authentic "U.S." markings stamped on the underside of the buttstock, just below the trigger guard. Made in varying barrel lengths and calibers, all follow an identical pattern: walnut half stock with small brass forend tip, Enfield style lockplate; iron trigger guard and crescent buttplate. Marked on both the octagon barrel and lock "J. HENRY & SONS". Specimens without "U.S." markings valued at approximately 20-30 percent less (NOTE: extreme caution should exercised should similar markings appear on the stock of other firearms attributed as Indian treaty or trade guns).
18-040   Values—Fair **$1,500**   Very Good **$3,750**

BRASS TACK DECORATIONS AND RAWHIDE REPAIRS
INDIAN OWNED AND INDIAN USED FIREARMS

Just about any firearm made in America from colonial times to the end of the Indian Wars, circa 1890s, as well as European types from those same eras, could be and was used by the American Indian. Many became adept in their use for hunting and war, acquiring them by gift, trade, purchase or capture in battle. To the collector, the only indication of Indian usage (other than substantiated, documented pedigrees; rare indeed) is the presence of typical Indian decoration, most often in the form of brass tacks hammered into the stock in symmetrical patterns, beadwork, carved Indian symbol designs, motifs applied with a hot file and repairs to the stock in the form of wide pieces of rawhide, sinew sewn with an occasional piece of red trade cloth. Such decoration, if authentic, adds considerably to the value of the weapon, regardless of its condition. Of course the type of firearm, the ornateness and profusion of the decoration and condition are considered. A broad generalization of value for such weapons ranges from a minimum of $500 dollars; with four figures not uncommon. A substantiated historical background will add immeasurably.

The mere mention of the importance of such decorations should immediately set off an alarm in the collector's mind as such ornamentation is rife for nefarious activities. The easy availability of brass tacks and rawhide has proven tempting for a few rascals dealing with Indian artifacts. Their handiwork is

often seen at arms shows. Guns in very poor condition are primary candidates for "upgrading" by the bogus application of brass tacks, rawhide repairs, trade cloth, bead work and other Indian-associated materials. Often used are weapons of the 1850-1870s including Winchesters, Springfield "trap door" rifles and carbines, many makes of half-stock and fullstock rifles; especially eligible are cut-down percussion conversion military muskets. **WIDE RAWHIDE** repairs to the wrist or forearm of a longarm was not an uncommon practice by frontier people when no gunsmith was handy; applied when wet it made a very tight repair as it shrunk. With an Indian association, adding considerable "character", it becomes another category.

BRASS TACK DECORATIONS have instant recognition as Indian owned firearms and is the area subject to most abuses. The large domed head tacks are available to this day. During the 19th century such tacks were available to Indians at most frontier trading posts who purchased and sold them in large quantities. Even the U.S. Government purchased them for Indian trade. They were also used by manufacturers of the era to decorate large leather trunks and other household objects, finding reuse in the 19th century by Indians to decorate firearms and in the 20th century by the more clever of the scam artists to do likewise.

A definitive history of the manufacture of dome headed brass tacks has yet to be written. Inquiries to knowledgeable parties

18-041

indicate that most tacks prior to circa 1875 were solid brass, cast integral as one piece with a square brass shank. American made types were likely very rough finished, often ragged around the edge, while the typical British tack was well finished with a heavier, longer square brass shank. The introduction of two piece tacks with brass head and steel shank apparently was the late 1860s; by the 1870s such two piece tacks were commonly manufactured, having round steel shanks, although the earliest patent for such a type does not seem to occur until around 1900.

Most modern made "Brass Tacks" are not brass at all but iron, with a thin brass plating or flashing. Revealing them with the use of a common magnet would make suspect the originality of an "Indian gun".

There is no easy, simplified method for determining authenticity of such Indian guns. If collecting such pieces, it's best to have some experience under one's belt. A practiced eye for aging and patina is important. Telltale clues to originality are aging as it appears around the tacks and on the rawhide, coloration, patina and wear. If possible, and allowable by the owner, the removal of a tack without damaging the wood is often significant as the wood underneath might also tell a story; it should show aging pattern (i.e. discoloration or patina) quite different than that of other parts of the stock.
18-041

SEE ALSO U.S. SPRINGFIELD MODEL 1807 INDIAN CARBINE 9A-116 AND BRIDGEWATER FLINTLOCK MUSKET 9B-003/004/005/006.

AMERICAN BLUNDERBUSSES

The blunderbuss never gained great favor in the American colonies or early United States. Except for U.S. Naval service even the mention of them is slight. American made blunderbusses are very scarce; those bearing maker markings are great rarities with very few known specimens. Their often liberal mention in early literature has been the cause for some confusion. The word was frequently used interchangeably with "musketoon" and "carbine." In some instances the word was correctly used to describe a "true" blunderbuss (as described below) while for other usages it cannot be determined if the firearm intended was merely a short barreled gun, i.e. musketoon/carbine with a straight, unflared barrel. It appears that such literature has occasionally been interpreted by later arms writers to mean what <u>they</u> wanted it to indicate rather than leaving the definition questionable.

The 1711 edition of "MILITARY AND SEA DICTIONARY" has a fine definition of Blunderbuss as "...a short firearm with a very large bore to carry a number of musket or pistol bullets proper to do execution in a crowd or to make good a narrow passage." It is primarily a scatter gun, invariably a short barreled flintlock with an expanding bore and usually a flared or belled muzzle; the 18th century riot gun, designed to scatter many lead bullets at short range. The dictionary says it is "...a short musket of wide bore with expanded muzzle to scatter shot, bullet or slugs at close range". It seems to have escaped an exacting definition, acceptable by all and has been interpreted quite differently by many arms authors, though most give the reader a reasonably coherent depiction of its appearance. A recent paper defined it as a "short shoulder arm or pistol with bell or flared muzzle," while another called it the "... 18th century version of sawed off shotgun; a short barrel shotgun carried by stagecoach guards, prison guards and ship boarders." Yet, another describes it as "... a weapon designed to do great

execution against a tight group in confined spaces". The origin of "blunderbuss" also is elusive, most acceptable theories derive it from the German "dunder" (thunder) and "buchse" (gun) or the Dutch "donderbus".

BLUNDERBUSS MYTHS. No. 1: It was intended to fire many round lead balls or buck shot and also loaded with stones, glass, nails, etc. Not so. The latter objects would have ruined the bore; by a long stretch of the imagination, possibly used only in a greatest emergency.

Myth No. 2 The size and shape of the flare or bell at the muzzle determined the pattern or spread of the bullets. Not so. Wide spread of bullets or shot is determined by both large caliber and a **gradual** expanding of the bore. In many cases short barreled, large bore shotguns will get that same wide spread. That principle was known from the mid-18th century but not always followed.

Most blunderbusses were made only during the flint lock period, but a few exist in both earlier and later ignition systems. By 1840 popularity of the blunderbuss waned. Most were made in Europe, especially in England; extremely few in America. Those imported in the late 18th, early 19th century found little popular favor.

The author of *"THE BLUNDERBUSS 1500-1900"* (James D. Forman, 1994) theorized the almost complete absence of them from the American scene versus the extremely wide manufacturing and usage in England was the fact that American firearms of the 18th century and early 19th centuries were limited to hunting and militia types with relatively small amount of "road traffic or urban unrest … consequently little crime". Quite the opposite was the case in England; as many as 1,500 stagecoaches left for various destinations from London daily, the roads literally crawling with footpads, highwaymen and brigands. Although many books on American firearms

18-050

touch upon the blunderbuss, few discuss them in any depth. *"BOARDERS AWAY; FIREARMS OF THE AGE OF FIGHTING SAIL"* Volume II (W. Gilkerson, 1993) and *"U.S. MARTIAL FLINTLOCKS"* (R.N. Reilly, 1986) treat the subject well.

The notable feature of colonial and early American blunderbusses is their dissimilarity; rarely are two alike, or even closely similar. Almost all are unmarked, although some may have imported barrels or locks. The major feature of their American identification is appearance, workmanship and, most important, the wood used for stocks and, quite often, style of the furniture/mountings. In general, values, would be about identical to Colonial military muskets (see 16-001), New England flintlock fowling pieces (see 16-003) and Hudson Valley fowling pieces (16-007). A maker marking of proven American origin is a great rarity and would be worth a considerable premium.

18-050

By far, the majority of blunderbusses made in America were for the U.S. Navy, especially in the War of 1812 era. Their use by the naval service is well known; regulations actually specify their issuance, yet extremely few have ever turned up. It is further believed that a quantity were privately purchased by privateers, i.e. owners and vessels given official government "letters of marque" license to prey upon enemy shipping for commercial gain. One American naval manual of the era specifies the issuance of one blunderbuss for every gun aboard ship, while an American naval gunner's inventory c.1830's specifies six blunderbusses for issuance to a frigate and twelve to a ship carrying 74 guns. Definite records of their issuance and use exist. In 1793 arsenal inventories showed 2,262 "blunderbusses" on hand. Many other mentions are found in the archives and naval correspondence, yet there are no known specifications for their pattern or size. Inexplicably less than a handful have been tentatively identified as U.S. Naval issue, mostly due to the standard U.S. contract 1808 flint locks they are fitted with. Values, if proven authentic and not later era composite "married" weapons, would be commensurate with swivel guns discussed below.

18-051

A mere handful of the large naval swivel blunderbuss or "Espingoles" are known. Their only common features are

their massive size and weight. Too heavy to be shoulder fired, they are fitted with a large oarlock-like swivel affixed to the midsection of the stock, allowing it to be mounted onto a ship's rail. Primarily a scatter gun used most often on a man-of-war's "fighting top", the highest of a vessel's battle stations; a solidly built platform surrounded with rails built high on the mast. Sailors and marines were stationed there to rain a hail of fire onto an enemy's unexposed decks. Depending on a vessel's size, such platforms could accommodate up to 20 men. As with the shoulder fired type, there are no known patterns or models. Identified specimens reveal a very wide range of size, weight and appearance. Overall length approx. 38" to 45"; weights from 14 lbs. to 35 lbs.; maple or walnut stocks; brass or iron barrels; ring-turned or plain muzzles.

LARGE FLINTLOCK SWIVEL BLUNDERBUSS. c.1800-1815. Lock marked by American maker (most often seen is U.S. musket lock by 1808 contract makers and brass or iron barrel also with American maker or U.S. military proofs possibly with date (a few specimens known.) Oval or round flared muzzle, Typical specimen illustrated is 42" overall; 24" barrel; weight 15 pounds. (Often considerable variance of size and weight.)

18-052	Values—Good **$9,500**	Fine **$20,000+**
Converted to percussion:		
18-053	Values—Good **$7,500**	Fine **$15,000+**

LARGE FLINTLOCK SWIVEL BLUNDERBUSS; similar to above; Lock or barrel marked by American maker (usually 1808 U.S. contract type). Size and weight varies.

18-054	Values—Good **$8,000**	Fine **$17,500+**
Converted to percussion:		
18-055	Values—Good **$5,500**	Fine **$12,500+**

LARGE FLINTLOCK SWIVEL BLUNDERBUSS; Private manufacture type with American maker markings; very often massive in size; workmanship not of the quality of professional gunmaker. Great variance in weight, dimensions and profile. Specimen illustrated is 39" overall; weight 35 pounds. Value shown for brass barrel type; iron barrel about 20 percent less.

18-056	Values—Good **$8,000**	Fine **$17,500+**
Converted to percussion:		
18-057	Values—Good **$5,500**	Fine **$12,500+**

Similar above (not illus.) lacking maker markings. Identified by workmanship, quality, wood or other features as American manufacture:

18-058	Values—**$4,000**	Fine **$9,500**
Converted to percussion:		
18-059	Values—**$3,000**	Fine **$6,000**

18-052
Contract Type

18-056
Private Manufacture Type

RAMPART, WALL AND SWIVEL GUNS

Designed to deliver very heavy loads of lead at moderately close range, these massive pieces (some weighing over 50 pounds and up to 60 inches in overall length) are a unique category of "military curiosa" occasionally encountered by the collector. All are considered rarities. It is known and recorded that Harpers Ferry Arsenal produced one of these in 1807 (likely as a pattern gun) and that six more were manufactured in 1808 at that arsenal. Another is known manufactured at the U.S. Allegheny Arsenal at Pittsburgh; correspondence on record indicates the Arsenal shipped at least 16 of those wall guns prior to 1821 to western U.S. territories. It's quite likely no two are identical, but the main determining feature for them would be use of U.S. military locks of musket size and pattern. Other wall guns are known completely unmarked, but from the style and quality of their manufacture there is no doubt as to their American origins. Their usually massive size and corresponding weight obviously precluded their ease in transportation and portability; they were primarily intended for the defense of fortresses. Almost all known specimens are found fitted with a large iron swivel at their approximate mid-point to facilitate mounting on the wall (or rampart) of a fort. All are collector rarities with values established based on markings, quality, period of mfr....and of course, condition.

Belonging in this same category of massive swivel guns is the unique **U.S. NAVY BOAT SWIVEL GUN** illustrated here (in the collection of the U.S. Marine Corps Museum at Quantico, Virginia). Fitted with the standard U.S. Model 1842 Musket percussion lock marked HARPERS FERRY 1858. All brass construction (including the large swivel); overall length 33-1/2";

**18-060
U.S. Navy Boat
Swivel Gun**

bore 1-1/2"; weight 58 pounds; barrel marked near breech BOAT SWIVEL / 1858 / N.Y. WASHINGTON along with the inspector initials J. B. S. and serial "No. 1." Markings indicate manufacture at the "Navy Yard," Washington, D.C., an important naval facility known to have made other trial and pattern guns. (See 9A-312.5).

Establishing values for any of these massive wall and rampart guns...or others similar to boat swivel guns must be determined on an individual basis. Specimens with official U.S. government or other military markings while also displaying workmanship indicative of government facilities are extremely rare; values are broadly estimated in the mid-five figures...possibly higher. Other examples, considered equally rare, would be evaluated based on appearance, condition, the quality of manufacture and markings (if any). They are more apt to fall in the range of the large flintlock swivel blunderbusses (18-056).

18-060

ALARM GUNS

Distinctly classified as "firearms curiosa", this category does indeed fit that label. The dictionary defines "curiosa" as "unusual things", while a few synonyms from a thesaurus are "curio, rarity, freak" ... all of which may be applicable. Curiously the single book treating the field, if not naming it, *"Firearms Curiosa"*, by Lewis Winant (1955) never defines the subject until the very last chapter, where the author says "... a gun to be classed as curiosa must have some bizarre feature that tends to astonish the student ... but just what is a bizarre feature? We may say ... an oddity will always provoke a sympathetic smile or derisive laugh, etc." At that point even the definition became curious!! These alarm guns certainly fit the bill.

Until recently most of these devices were relatively unnoticed in the collecting world, reflecting extremely modest prices and very slight demand. A few of the large, earlier types (especially those in combination with animal trap guns) and those having some aesthetic quality interested a few collectors of oddities. Later, and simple-appearing, types went unnoticed. In recent years a few impressive collections of them have been formed and the market now shows a decided interest.

In broadest, most generalized terms, the alarm gun explodes a powder charge sufficient to sound an alert against unwanted, unannounced intrusion to a building or structure (and on occasion to furniture such as a desk or trunk). Some were made in combination with an animal (or burglar) trap gun to simultaneously sound an alarm while felling the animal or perpetrator (see 7C-033; 7C-035; 7C-035.4; 7C-040; 7B-012). The major differentiation for collectors is the size of the device and the presence of barrels large enough to hold a full charge to impel a bullet of sufficient weight for its intended purpose. Other forms of alarm guns such as sundial guns (intended to ignite a charge to announce hour of the day) and those with clock

mechanisms firing shells at regular intervals to scare birds in fields, etc. are not included here as all are apparently of European manufacture.

The invention of the percussion system and easy availability of the copper primer cap was the stimulus for the invention and marketing of a wide variety of small, inexpensive devices intended for fastening to doors or windows that, when opened, exploded a powder charge announcing unwanted intrusion, possibly scaring off the intruder. A rising petty crime rate in America likely played a role. Approx. 300 patents have been issued for such devices, many likely never getting beyond the prototype stage. Surviving alarm guns exhibit a wide range of clever, imaginative and innovative design; some bordering on the incredible.

Collectors are cautioned to verify the legal status of certain model breech-loading <u>cartridge</u> model alarm guns before acquisition. It is the author's understanding (but not an ATF legal determination) that such models that fire blanks only likely will not fall under GCA or NFA restrictions. Determinations normally handled by ATF on a case-by-case basis. In general pre-1898 manufacture considered "Antique". However, model alarms designed to chamber a cartridge with bullet, or suitable to be modified to do so, likely fall under such restrictions; their legal status should be verified.

COMBINATION ANIMAL TRAP AND ALARM GUNS: As the primary purpose of those oddities is apparently for trapping of game and/or the itinerant miscreant, only antique percussion models are included and are found in Chapter VII-C. Most, if not all, cartridge models may likely fall under NFA restrictions and their legal status should be verified.

PERCUSSION ALARM GUNS

Bigelow's Patent Percussion Burglar Alarm Made by J. M. Marlin & Co. New Haven, Connecticut circa mid-1860's. *See Chapter V-D Marlin Firearms item No. 5D-006.7.*

D. Coon Patent Burglar Alarm Gun

David Coon, Ithaca, New York, Percussion Burglar Alarm Gun. Quantity limited.

28 caliber; 4-3/4" overall. Marked on barrel CHESEBROUGH & CO. ITHACA PATENTED MAY 26, 1857. Coon specified on patent that it was intended for use on a door, so that when "...burglarious (sic) entrance feared … the door when forced a little way open shall discharge the pistol endangering the burglar and alarming the occupants." The folding unit fastens to door jamb; barrel, with nipple, movable:

18-070

18-070 Values—Good **$225** Fine **$400**

S. Coon Patent Burglar Alarm Gun

Simon Coon, Ithaca, New York, Percussion Burglar Alarm Gun. C. 1857. Quantity unknown; likely limited.

25 caliber. 2-1/2" overall. Marked on side S. COON/PATENT/SEP. 22,1857. Also seen mkd. Maf'd for R.M. Patchin/Springfield, Ill.

18-071

The folding, tapered screw device allows gun to be affixed to door jamb, window or other movable object and fire a blank charge when disturbed, mainspring also acts as hammer:

18-071 Values—Good **$200** Fine **$375**

J. G. Clark Patent Percussion Burglar Alarm Gun

John G. Clark, August, Georgia, 1859. Quantity unknown; limited.

28 caliber. 4-3/4" overall. Two piece gravity device with 3 nipples for caps on large section. Attached to door or window by chain (or other means); when opened, causes device to drop to floor or sill and strike the dome-shaped "hammer" underneath, firing all 3 caps. Marked CLARKS PAT/JUNE 7, 59:

18-072

18-072 Values—Good **$225** Fine **$350**

Dewey Percussion Burglar Alarm Gun

Dewey Percussion Burglar Alarm Gun; made by Henry and William Holding, New York, N.Y. 1895.

Small, rectangular shape, 3-1/2" tall, just 1/2" thick. Double hammer fulcrumed in center with cocking spurs each end; percussion caps inserted through "C" shape slits on sides. Adaptable for doors, windows and elsewhere. Marked both sides DEWEY BURGLAR ALARM/PAT. OCT. 1, '95

18-073

18-073 Values—Good **$225** Fine **$350**

Haldeman Percussion Burglar Alarm Gun

Daniel Haldeman, Morgantown, (West) Virginia. Percussion Burglar Alarm Gun. Patent No. 12,351 of Feb. 6, 1855. Maker and quantity unknown. Limited.

25 caliber. All brass construction with drilled bore along bottom of the frame. Flat hammer with cocking spur. Complex design; its exact method of use puzzling. Serial numbered and marked D. HALDEMAN PATENTED FEB. 6, 1855.

18-073.5

18-073.5 Values—Good **$475** Fine **$700**

A. F. Hammond Patent Burglar Alarm Gun

18-074

A. F. Hammond, Houston, Ohio Percussion Burglar Alarm Gun. Manufactured by Gross Arms Co., Tiffin, Ohio c. 1866. Quantity unknown; limited.

Brass 2-3/4" octagon barrel cast integral with brass frame. 3-1/2" overall. 25 caliber. Attached to door or window or could be clamped to mantle, etc. Tripped by cord or wire. Small hole on left side of barrel to hold thin rod or wire fixture that could hold a common wooden match over muzzle; when device fired, the blast lit the match thus exposing the intruder and his location (while simultaneously igniting the homestead, the burglar having knocked over the device in his haste to exit!!).

Marked on barrel A. F. HAMMOND/PATENTED 1866/GROSS ARMS CO./TIFFIN, OHIO:

18-074   Values—Good **$400**   Fine **$700**

A. F. Hammond Burglar Alarm Gun

18-074.1

A. F. Hammond, Houston, Ohio Percussion Burglar Alarm Gun. Patent No. 54,531 of May 8, 1866. Maker and quantity unknown; limited.

Another match-lighting, curious alarm device fraught with hazard. All brass construction; 3-1/2" overall. Flat bar type hammer upon striking nipple fires blank charge in the 2" barrel bored along top of the block. Caliber 30. The fired charge lit a common wooden kitchen match affixed to a wire type arm over the muzzle. Unmarked. Integral swivel clamp fastens to window sill, mantle or door frame.

18-074.1   Values—Good **$375**   Fine **$600**

D. E. McDougall Percussion Alarm Gun

D. E. McDougall, Springfield, Mass. Percussion Burglar Alarm Gun. Patent No. 11,131 of June 20, 1854 based on his earlier patent No. 9,753 of May 31, 1853 for a "Door Securer" device. Maker and quantity unknown; limited.

Combining the two patents, McDougall added a 2" round 38 cal. iron barrel (with a cannon turned muzzle) and a percussion hammer, nipple and lock mechanism to the all brass, unique

18-074.5

door locking device. Overall 3-1/2" by 5-1/2". Markings D. E. MCDOUGALL/PATENTED/MAY 31, 1853.

18-074.5   Values—Good **$550**   Fine **$875**

R.M. Patchin   *See "S. Coon" Alarm Gun*

Pratt Alarm & Trap Gun   *See 7C-033 (Chapter 7C).*

George Smith Alarm & Trap Gun   *See 7C-035.4 (Chapter 7C).*

Smith, Torrey & Co. Percussion Alarm Gun

Smith, Torrey & Company, New York, Percussion Alarm. Made c. 1850s. Muzzle-loading; all brass construction with iron hammer. 2-3/4" overall with short 3/4" octagon barrel. Not intended to take a projectile.

Intended to affix to door jamb or window and fire blank charge when disturbed.

Profusely marked. On the right side: SMITH, TORREY & CO/50 MAIDEN LANE, N.Y. On left side LOFT'S DETECTOR/1851 PATENT Pg:

18-075

18-075   Values—Good **$400**   Fine **$700**

Wilson Percussion Alarm

J. P. Wilson, Ilion, New York, joint inventor with J. F. Thomas (the inventor of the Remington cane gun), Percussion Alarm. Manufacturer unknown. Circa 1850s.

22 caliber muzzleloading. 7/8" by 1-5/8" rectangular brass block with small bored chamber to accept black powder charge. Not intended to take a projectile. Spring retained iron swivel

arm at top acts as hammer. When device is disturbed (usually by opening or closing a door or window), the arm/hammer snaps closed, striking the nipple mounted inside causing the charge to explode.

Usually mounted with a gimlet screw and base which fits into the mortised slot at bottom. The alternative method (shown here) has a wide, curved brass plate which fits the mortise, allowing the device to be used in numerous positions on doors and windows. Surprisingly, the original patent states it can be loaded with a projectile for "extra protection."

18-076

Markings: J.P. WILSON/PATENTED FEB.8.1859/ILION.N.Y.:

18-076   Values—Good **$450**   Fine **$750**

Two variations are known, both same configuration, but in place of the removable base plate they are fitted with a large, well designed swivel screw mounted on side opposite the hammer-arm.

Smaller type; exact size and markings as above:

18-076.1   Values—Good **$450**   Fine **$750**

Larger type; 1" x 2" marked "Wilson Mfg. Co./New York/Pat'd Feb. 8. 1859."

18-076.2   Values—Good **$350**   Fine **$675**

BREECH LOADING METALLIC CARTRIDGE ALARM GUNS

"The American Portable Burglar Alarm" Gun

"The American Portable Burglar Alarm" Gun. circa 1895. Maker and quantity unknown.

Caliber 22 rimfire blank. Although breech loading, it is very close in design to the J.P. Wilson percussion alarm gun (*q.v.*) and may be an improvement on that earlier patent.

All brass construction. 1-3/4" overall. Large folding arms set against door or window. When disturbed snaps shut, striking cartridge. Illustrated with original labelled box; worth 100 percent premium if intact.

18-076.4   Values—Very Good **$185**   Exc. **$300**

18-076.4

"Automatic Alarm Defender" Burglar Alarm Gun

18-076.5

Automatic Alarm Company, Detroit Michigan Burglar alarm gun. circa 1920's. Quantity unknown.

Caliber 22 rimfire blank. Stamped sheet metal of very simplest design and construction. Spring loaded bolt fires blank cartridge when long rod type lever is disturbed by motion of door or window opening...or, chicken coop is raided, as pointed out by the instruction sheet that accompanied it. Illustrated with the original labelled box; worth 100 percent or greater premium if intact.

18-076.5   Values—Very Good **$175**   Exc. **$275**

S. R. Brooks Burglar Alarm Gun

Invented by S. R. Brooks, Salamanca, New York, c. 1880. Quantity unknown.

22RF blank. 5" overall. Cast iron with high relief, ornate scroll decoration. After device fires, the hammer arm prevents door from opening further. Hammer adjustable to use on doors that open left or right. Nickel finish. High relief markings BURGLAR ALARM LOCK & BOLT/S. R. BROOKS LOCK EXPERT/PATSAPPL'D FOR. SALAMANCA, N.Y.:

18-077   Values—Very Good **$275**   Exc. **$500**

18-077

T. Carr Burglar Alarm Gun

Tom Carr, Chicago, Illinois. Alarm gun circa 1920. Maker and quantity unknown.

32 caliber centerfire blank. Lightweight cast metal with metallic bronze painted finish. 5" overall. Two mounting holes

on base to affix to door or window frame. Spring loaded bolt fires blank cartridge chambered in the short, stubby three-stepped receptacle. Triggered by lever-arm on side or by trip wire. Relief markings on top of housing TOM CARR BURGLAR ALARM CO./PAT. CHICAGO, ILL./MADE IN U.S.A.

18-077.1   Values—Very Good **$150**   Exc. **$250**

18-077.1

E. N. Case Steamer Trunk Alarm Lock

Invented by Dr. E. N. Case, Chicago, Illinois. Patented 1898. Maker and quantity unknown. Very limited.

32 CF blank (38 blank also reported). Large two piece brass 7-1/2" x 3" identically resembling common steamer trunk lock; complicated mechanism on reverse of the keyed section. Any attempt to pry open (or even pick lock) triggers and fires device. Very rare.

Dr. Case also patented unique padlock alarm guns for 32CF blanks, 1897 and 1898 and alarm gun device for desk drawer (no known specimen):

18-078

18-078   Values—Very Good **$1,850**   Exc. **$3,000**

Chaffee Burglar Alarm Gun

Chaffee Alarm Gun. Invented by Noah Chaffee of Athens, Pennsylvania. patented July 1895. Manufacturer unknown; quantity very limited.

22 Rimfire blank. All brass construction. 2-1/4" round "barrel", 3-3/4" overall. Steel swivel breech and hammer; large mainspring on top. The long tapered mounting screw on underside allows it to be used in various positions on window and door jambs. Intended to explode a charge only and not fire a projectile.

Markings on side of the "barrel" PAT.JULY 9,95:

18-079

18-079   Values—Very Good **$225**   Exc. **$325**

G. S. Clements Burglar Alarm Gun

G. S. Clements, New Lexington, Ohio Burglar Alarm Gun. Patent No. 197,334, Nov. 20, 1877. Maker and quantity unknown; limited.

22 rimfire blank. Iron frame; painted finish. Approx. 3-1/2" overall. Small sliding bolt below hammer is set against the closed door or window. Pressure on opening causes bolt to push inward and trigger device. The blank cartridge is fitted into head/top of the long nickel plated hammer; fires up and outward when it strikes fixed projection cast on front of base. Only markings Pat'd/Nov. 20, 1877.

18-079.2   Values—Very Good **$225**   Exc. **$325**

18-079.3
Conklin & Hauser

18-079.2
Clements

Conklin & Hauser Burglar Alarm Gun

Manufactured by Conklin & Hauser of Chicago, Illinois. Late 19th, early 20th century. Quantity unknown.

Caliber 22 blank. 4 inches overall. Markings THE MODEL BURGLAR ALARM / TS. / CONKLIN & HAUSER MFRS. / CHICAGO / PAT. PENDING. Factory box with direction label: "Can be attached to any door as quickly as one can open and close the door" with printed details how to attach. (Values without box):

18-079.3   Values—Very Good **$115**   Exc. **$175**

Cyclone Door Locking Burglar Alarm Gun

Cyclone Door Locking Burglar Alarm Gun, Indianapolis, Indiana. Patent No. 528,206 on Oct. 30, 1894 by H.J. Mitchell of Chicago, Ill. Manufactured Indianapolis; quantity unknown.

Caliber 38 centerfire blank. Two piece. 7-1/2" overall. Iron with nickel finish. Serrated teeth on base plate partially used to affix to door or window frame. Short 3/4" receptacle in center holds cartridge with integral cast smoke/flame shield slightly ahead of it. Spring loaded bolt fires device. Only markings Pat Oct. 30, 94. Originally sold with labelled box having instructions for use and "Mfd. only by CYCLONE ALARM CO. INDIANAPOLIS."

18-079.4   Values—Very Good **$225**   Exc. **$325**

18-079.4

Ferris Burglar Alarm Gun

Invented by Hudson Ferris, Chicago, Illinois. Patented 1883 and 1886. Maker and quantity unknown.

22RF blank. Made in few variations; 3-1/2" to 4-1/2" overall. Iron; wedge shaped; screws to floor. After firing prevents door from opening further. Some unmarked; most FERRIS/PAT.OCT 16,83 (illus. here). Later PAT. DEC.28,86 unusual variant (worth premium) has protruding lip front of base to hold bent iron tube for a common wood match and serrations on head of hammer. When device triggered it simultaneously fires blank cartridges and lights match to expose intruder hopefully not igniting the entire structure in the process!

18-080   Values—Very Good **$275**   Exc. **$375**

18-080

Kunz Burglar Alarm Gun

C. T. Kunz, New York City Burglar Alarm Gun. Patent No. 617,931 of Jan. 17, 1899 by Kunz and assigned by him same year to Francis Schnugg of N.Y.C. Maker and quantity unknown.

Caliber 22 rimfire blank. Cast iron casing; nickel plated finish. 6" overall. Trigger-like cocking lever on side. Prevents door or window opening by wedging between frame; slight pressure on either trip the alarm. Small prongs on end prevent device from slipping on rug, floor or other surface. Unmarked.

18-080.5   Values—Very Good **$225**   Exc. **$325**

18-080.5

Lauffer Burglar Alarm Gun

Invented by Simon D. Lauffer, Irwin Station, Penna. Patented 1878. Maker and quantity unknown.

Door alarm: made in left and right hand models marked respectively "L" and "R". When door opened, hammer fires device and prevents door from opening further. 4-1/2" overall. High relief fancy scroll designs marked PATENTED FEB. 5, 1878.

Window alarm: 3-1/2" overall, plain design; separate mounting plate. Both types cast steel with brass hammers. 22RF blank. Marked PAT'd FEB 5'78. Values same for all 3 types.

18-081   Values—Very Good **$250**   Exc. **$375**

18-081

Lauffer, Bilhimer & Williams Alarm Gun

Invented by S. D. Lauffer, C. F. Bilhimer & W. Williams. Patented November 30, 1886. Maker and quantity unknown.

Door alarm; caliber 22 rimfire blank. The patent and the device itself are improvements to the earlier Lauffer alarm gun patent of Feb. 5, 1878 (see 18-081 above) in order that travelers might use these devices to secure their rooms against intruders. Many were made in two models, the first of which (shown here) has a swiveling arm with teeth to attach to the door frame. Second model has a removable plate with teeth for attaching to the door frame. Either will work with left- or right-hand opening doors. The arm that holds the blank cartridge, when turned by the opening of a door drops into a notch that locks the door. All brass

18-081.2

with nickel finish. Earlier model 3-1/8" overall; later model 4" overall. Although improvement manufactured and patented in 1886, it retained the earlier markings "PATd FEB 5, 78."

18-081.2   Values—Very Good **$185**   Exc. **$285**

Liberty Alarm Co. Cash Box Alarm Gun

18-082

18-082

Liberty Alarm and Accessories Company, New York City Alarm Box Bell and Gun. *Patent No. 1,301,783 by J.M. Butcher on April 22, 1919.* Manufactured by Liberty Alarm Co.; quantity unknown.

Caliber 22 rimfire blank. Selective dual alarm: 3-1/2" diameter, nickel plated, key wound bell and alarm gun. Although sold with a well made, sturdy, locking type cash box, complete with printed label and instructions, the patented device was suitable for a valise or other container. Triggering mechanism is a round steel ball fitted in housing that protrudes through a lower corner of the cash box; attached internally to a delicately suspended pendulum. Moving, lifting or otherwise disturbing box (or other continuator) trips alarm causing bell to ring (until it winds down) and fires gun simultaneously. Bell, firearm and trip mechanism mounted on a 4 " x 5" sheet steel plate marked in corner PAT APLD FOR/PATENTED APRIL 22, 1919. Values for complete unit in cash box with label. If mechanism only value about 50 percent less.

18-082   Values—Very Good **$450**   Exc. **$800**

Mintern Burglar Alarm Gun

J. A. Mintern, Indianapolis, Indiana Burglar Alarm Gun. Patent No. 752,174 of Feb. 16, 1904. Maker and quantity unknown.

Caliber 22 rimfire blank. Small device stamped from sheet steel. Rounded hook-like top of plate has receptacle for cartridge. Attaches to door or window with two screws. Hammer/firing rod is merely a long, round wire spring. To set alarm, the rod is depressed and locked in position by small projecting spur on base plate. Releases by opening motion of door or window. Unmarked. Originally sold wholesale for $1.00 per dozen (Winant, *"Firearms Curiosa"*).

18-083   Values—Very Good **$100**   Exc. **$175**

18-083

Night Hawk Burglar Alarm Gun

Night Hawk Alarm Company, Danville, Illinois Burglar Alarm Gun circa 1915-1920's. Quantity unknown.

Caliber 38 centerfire blank. Cast white metal device 6" wide with top of the curved bar hammer hooked to a long coil spring; simple lever trigger which can be attached by cords/trip wires to two or more doors or windows simultaneously. The metal unit is screw mounted on original factory 6" square plywood board with large attached paper label illustrating the device and various uses; made by BLACK HAWK ALARM CO./DANVILLE, ILLINOIS/PRICE $2.50. Value based on completeness with full label. If lacking or poor condition 50 percent less.

18-084   Values—Very Good **$375**   Exc. **$600**

18-084

Patchin Burglar Alarm Gun

R. N. Patchin, Waylin, New York circa 1881 and later. Manufacturer and quantity unknown.

Caliber 22 rimfire; patented March 15, 1881. Designed for dual use as a door bolt and alarm gun. Patchin also claimed that when device was removed from door a separately fitted grip could be attached for use as a pistol! Iron barrel with a brass adjustable sliding device for attaching to door. 4-1/2" overall. Only markings PAT'D US 238,805. Very few known; rare.

18-084.2   Values—Very Good **$250**   Exc. **$375**

18-084.2

Reichard Burglar Alarm Gun

Edwin D. Reichard, Reading, Pennsylvania Patent Burglar Alarm Gun circa 1870s-80s. Quantity unknown.

Caliber 32 rimfire blank. Rectangular iron plate 3 inches overall; made for mounting in place on a doorjamb or window. Examples observed with original gold wash finish for improved appearance. Only markings large PAT. DEC 11 '77 (under patent no. 198,044 issued to Reichard that date).

18-084.5   Values—Very Good **$300**   Fine **$425**

18-084.5

Reiff Burglar Alarm Gun

W. H. Reiff, Philadelphia, Penn. Burglar Alarm Gun. Patent No. 150,712 of May 12, 1874. Maker and quantity unknown.

Caliber 22 rimfire blank. Small brass frame about 2-1/2" overall; nickel plated. Wood screw for fastening to door or window is made integral. Flat swivel arm acts as a hammer. drilled bore at end holds cartridge. Marked "W. H. Reiff/Pat. May 12, 74/ Chicago, Ill." This is the earliest of Reiff's total thirteen patents for such devices.

18-085   Values—Very Good **$175**   Exc. **$275**

18-085

Similar and Larger model made under later Reiff patent No. 179,060 of June 20, 1876 by the U.S. Burglar Alarm Co. (possibly of Philadelphia). Quantity unknown. Very similar in appearance to 18-085.

Caliber 22 rimfire blank. Rectangular iron block 2-1/4" overall. Has integral wood screw. Drilled bore 5/8" full width of end. Large "V" type mainspring affixed at top. Although not supplied with device, patent drawing indicates that a curved wooden handle could be attached to the wood screw to make a very awkward appearing handgun. Marked U.S.B.A. CO./PAT JUNE 20, 76/PHILA. PA."

18-085.2   Values—Very Good **$200**   Exc. **$300**

18-085.4

W. H. Reiff, Philadelphia, Penn. Burglar Alarm Gun Patent No. 284,980 of Sept. 11, 1883. Maker and quantity unknown.

Caliber 22 rimfire blank. A two-piece, gravity-actuated device; attached to a door or window by a bent wire. Constructed of nickel-plated brass tubing. The 1-1/4" brass "barrel" held in place by a machine screw. Device consists of a telescopic-barrel; gravity-actuated anvil in the lower section; blank cartridge in upper. Overall, 5 inches empty and not set; approx. 6 inches overall when cocked and set. Note: illustration depicts device horizontally. In usage it is suspended vertically from an iron loop at top.

18-085.4   Values—Very Good **$165**   Exc. **$250**

Reiff & McDowell Burglar Alarm Gun

W. H. Reiff and H. F. McDowell Burglar Alarm Gun. Patent No. 499,365 to W. H. Reiff on June 13, 1893. Maker and quantity unknown.

Caliber 22 rimfire blank. Similar to earlier Reiff models, with improvements. Nickel finished brass frame; 2" overall; large detachable wood screw. Long, inletted swivel arm acts as hammer. Cartridge fits in drilled 5/8" long drilled bore at end of device. Rounded swivel cover on side is receptacle for nine spare cartridges. Marked REIFF & MCDOWELL/PAT JUNE 13, 1893.

18-086   Values—Very Good **$225**   Exc. **$350**

18-086

St. Louis Burglar Alarm Gun

St. Louis Burglar Protection Company, St. Louis, Missouri Burglar Alarm Gun. Circa 1900. Quantity unknown.

    Caliber 22 rimfire blank. Small iron frame construction; just 3-3/8" overall. Short bolt on firing mechanism pulls rearward to engage notch on the swivel arm of the triggering lever. Any movement of door or window trips device when set in place. Marked ST. LOUIS BURGLAR PROTECTION CO., ST. LOUIS MO. PRICE $1.00 PAT. APD. FOR.

18-086.2

18-086.2   Values—Very Good **$250**   Exc. **$375**

"Super Automatic Wireless" Burglar Alarm Gun

18-087

Caliber 38 centerfire blank. Cartridge is fastened into 3/4" long receptacle by a knurled set screw. Sheet metal construction; zinc plated. 4-1/2" overall. Spring loaded firing pin. Markings on housing PAT. APPLD. FOR. Supplied with 2 small metal WARNING plates to ward off miscreants; both bore name of gun as well as "D & H/Chicago, etc." (if still with the device add premium to value.)

18-087

"Super Automatic Wireless" Burglar Alarm Gun. Maker and quantity unknown. Circa 1900 to 1920s. Sales brochure with device stated "Copyrighted and sold by D & H Sales Co., Chicago, Ill."

18-087   Values—Very Good **$200**   Exc. **$265**

Sur-Shot Burglar Alarm Gun

Sur-Shot Alarm Company, Long Beach, Cal. Burglar Alarm Gun. Circa 1900-1920s. Quantity unknown.

    Caliber 22 rimfire blank. Very inexpensively made of sheet metal; nickel plated; integral, long wood screw fixture. Cartridge fits into small 1/4" wide ring cast in upper corner. Hammer is hooked shaped squared rod. Marked Patents Pending/Sur-Shot Alarm Co./Long Beach, Calif.

18-088

18-088   Values—Very Good **$135**   Exc. **$200**

Swallow Burglar Alarm Gun

Invented by Freeman M. Swallow, Springfield, Mass., July, 1877. Maker and quantity unknown.

    22RF blank. Iron. 3-3/8" by 2-1/2" high. Attaches to door or window. Small steel pin locks hammer to frame in cocked position. Chain, wire, string fixed to door or window; when either opened, pulls out the locking pin firing the device. Markings PATENTED JULY 31, 1877.

18-089

18-089   Values—Very Good **$250**   Exc. **$400**

Tierny "Thief Signal" Burglar Alarm Gun

W. Tierny, Seattle, Wash. "Thief Signal" Burglar Alarm gun. Patent No. 1,306, 789 of June 17, 1919. Maker and quantity unknown.

    Caliber 32 centerfire blank. Cast brass base with nickel finish. 4-1/4" overall. Intended to be fastened in an upright/vertical position with two woodscrews to door or window frame. Short 1/2" wide receptacle at top holds cartridge. Fired by long spring loaded bolt which can be tripped by movement of long, narrow lever/arm resting against door, or by cord/trip wire. Marked on center of base Tierny's/Automatic/Thief Signal/Pat. June 17-19.

18-089.1

18-089.1   Values—Very Good **$165**   Exc. **$300**

U.S.B.A. Co. *See "REIFF" Alarm Gun.*

AIR AND SPRING GUNS

The principle of compressing air to use as a propellant force was known as early as ancient Egyptian times and first used with a catapult. The earliest known air gun dates to the 16th century; various innovations, experiments and improvements were made in following eras. The most usual methods of storing compressed air were in the hollow iron buttstock of a shoulder arm or in a large round copper ball-like device screwed to the underside of the breech of the barrel; both were filled by use of a hand pump. Although most were considered merely novelties, one type was adopted by the Austrian army for military use in the late 18th century. Rarely considered anything other than target weapons, their noiseless feature gave rise to occasional alarm for fear of their suitability of use by assassins and poachers; ownership or use at various times was forbidden by law.

Pre-1850 American manufacture and use of air guns was extremely limited and specimens are rare. It is well-recorded that one was carried on the historic Lewis & Clark exploring expedition 1804-06 and demonstrated many times before Indians.

In recent decades, most modern accounts of that air gun carried on the famous western trek had presumed it to be a muzzle-loading, single-shot air gun of the butt reservoir type, generally attributed to Isaiah Lukens of Philadelphia. That assumption has since been disproved by substantiated, exhaustive research. Those findings, first disclosed in *"The Gun Report"* (January, 2003) in an article by Michael Carrick, received wide acceptance by historians as well as arms scholars. It is now acknowledged that Meriwether Lewis most likely carried with him on that 1804-1806 expedition a breech-loading, multi-shot (22 balls; 464 caliber) repeating air gun of the butt reservoir type (filled by use of a pump) of the style designed by Italian gunmaker of Vienna, Austria, Bartolomeo Girandoni (1744-1799). He made approximately 1500 of those air rifles (circa 1780s-1790s) for the Austrian army. They may represent the very first example of interchangeable parts on military guns! Recent research discloses that when issued to units of the Austrian army each gun was fully loaded and accompanied by a pack containing two additional pressurized butt reservoirs plus four additional tubes, each containing 20 balls. Thus, 100 shots were quickly available for each soldier. The exhausted air reservoirs were exchanged at a central mobile station which contained a large air pump for re-filling. Several hundred of those Austrian air guns were lost in various battles, commencing 1787. It is now surmised (but yet to be conclusively determined) that Lewis acquired that Girandoni air rifle from French immigrants with whom he socialized at meetings in Pittsburgh while awaiting the completion of his keelboat.

Further research to dispel the Isaiah Lukens (Philadelphia) long-held relevance to the air gun saga on that famous expedition asserts that he was too young to have made the gun in 1803 for Lewis. At that time Lukens was apprenticed to his father in Horsham, Penn. (twenty miles outside of Phila.) and is unlikely to have ever met Lewis. He was primarily a clockmaker and a machinist. He is known to have enjoyed shooting air guns. The single Girandoni rifle known to have been owned by Lukens (and recorded in his estate, 1847) is presumed to have been acquired through the Peale museum in Phila., where it is presumed that rifle had been deposited after Lewis's death in that same city. That Girandoni had a provenance of original ownership and use by Lewis on the historic exploring expedition.

Ball reservoir type American air rifles are very rare. Most examples are styled as "Kentucky" rifles with typical brass mountings and large brass patchbox; worth premium values. Values shown are for American **maker marked** specimens. Quality and appearance are important factors and vary considerably … as do values!:

18-090   Values—Good **$5,000**   Fine **$20,000**

It was not until the mid-19th century and the introduction of *"Gallery Guns"* that the air guns achieved a modicum of popularity in America. The earliest types were introduced shortly before the Civil War, remaining in vogue not much over a decade following the war. They were used almost exclusively for indoor gallery target shooting. Almost all were developed from European breech loading types with American innovations. A large majority of makers were of German origins. All utilized spring power pistons with leather bushings; almost all were intended to fire only darts.

The only work to seriously study early American types (*"Air Guns"*, Wolff. q.v.), completed in 1955, classified them into five general categories based on their method of operations (i.e. crank lifting upward to cock; trigger guard pulling downward, etc.), and the geographic region where each type was believed (at the time of the Wolff study) to have been made. More recent

Isaiah Lukens, Philadelphia

Peter Kunz, Philadelphia

B. Girandoni, Vienna, Austria

Butt Reservoir American Air Rifles circa 1800. Hollow iron butts are removable, air filled by use of small pump then replaced. Flint hammers merely a cocking device. Both by Philadelphia makers, upper by Isaiah Lukens; lower by Peter Kunz. Butt reservoir air rifle made circa 1780s-1790s by B. Girandoni of Vienna, Austria which recent research credibly assumes to have been the gun carried on the historic Lewis and Clark Exploring Expedition (see accompanying text above).

18-091
Primary N.Y. City Type

18-091
Primary N.Y. City Type

18-092
Secondary N.Y. City Type

18-093
Upstate N.Y. Type

18-094
St. Louis Type

18-095
Fancy Grade New England Type

18-095
New England Type

information seems to indicate that there are many exceptions and cross-overs of styles vs regions and that the 1955 treatise is too narrowly circumscribed. It has also been found by this author in his own research that there are two schools of thought to the study and collecting of these guns. One views it casually based on the five categories established by Wolff as, admittedly, there is no other published guide. The other catalogs them by their method of operation. Thus, the so-called "Primary N.Y. City Type" may be made by a St. Louis maker, in which case that address would be lesser valued commensurate with guns of that region. New England maker marks usually are worth small premiums. It would be presumptuous to arbitrarily reclassify the entire field without the benefit of a more current analysis. Hence, with hesitation, the early, pioneering nomenclature of the Wolff study is retained. Air guns are another example of the relative newness of American antique arms research; they offer the historian and collector a fine opportunity to add to the lore of this hobby. See also *Air Rifles* by Hiller (Chapt. IV Arms Library).

Much like "Whaling Guns" (q.v.) there are dual collector markets for air guns. The anomalies were quickly made apparent during the author's research of the field. For instance, among air gun specialists, whose marketplace often differs from that of general antique arms collecting, St. Louis types are the most common and maker marks of that city and region are given but of slight importance, while the broader market prized those markings and values them commensurately. The reverse seems to happen with the very rare early Luken and Kunz type rifles,

considered among the rarest of all American types and accorded high values on the air gun market, but not fully understood or appreciated by the general market and considerably undervalued. Only a competent guide to the subject will level the disparity.

The gallery guns illustrated and valued here are not all known types or models. Numerous variations are encountered and there are many differences in quality and profusion of decoration (worth premium). Values are for plain grade specimens in working order (up to 50 percent less if incomplete/not in working order) and with maker markings (20 to 30 percent less unmarked).

New York City Type: Large detachable crank fits into right frame; barrel twists for loading; center section of rifle has appearance of being a wide iron cylinder. Separate wooden forearm. Most makers all New City c. mid 1850s to 1880 approx. (25 percent less approx. if lacking crank).

18-091 Values—Good **$400** Fine **$1,000**

Secondary New York City Type: General appearance of above. Not fitted for crank; trigger guard pulls downward for cocking (similar to St. Louis style, below). Makers from various area: N.Y. City, Baltimore, Cincinnati, etc. Circa 1850s-1870s.

18-092 Values—Good **$300** Fine **$800**

Upstate New York Revolving Type: Rigid affixed or removable cocking lever; manually revolved cylinder. Two upstate N.Y. makers-Bunge (Geneva) and Werner (Rochester) identified, each with 12 shot cylinders. Makers also believed from other regions. Circa 1860-70s:

18-093 Values—Good **$1,500** Fine **$3,500**

St. Louis Type: Trigger guard pulls down and back to cock; barrel tips downward to load; forend most often is brass. Although most makers are of St. Louis, a few are noted from Ohio, Penna., New Jersey. Circa 1860s-1880. (Values for St. Louis are markings):

18-094   Values—Good **$400**   Fine **$925**

New England Type: Most noticeable is the one-piece walnut stock. Permanent affixed cocking lever right side pulls upward to cock; cylinder which houses mechanism narrower width and diameter than above types. Very scarce; Massachusetts makers identified; c. 1850s-1870:

18-095   Values—Good **$500**   Fine **$1,500**

QUACKENBUSH, HERKIMER, NEW YORK

18-096 / Model No. 1

18-097 / Model No. 2

18-100 / Model No. 5

More than any other inventor or manufacturer, Henry Marcus Quackenbush was responsible for the earliest development of mass produced, serious air guns for short range target and small game shooting. The pioneer in the field started in 1871 and by 1874 his products were popular. First employed in 1861 at age 14 by Remington Arms Company, he rose quickly to expert tool maker and gunsmith. In 1871, the same year he left Remington, he patented his first air pistol, successfully advertising and selling it himself. Known as the EUREKA, cocked by pushing the barrel, creating compression, he soon sold the patent to the Pope Brothers of Boston who continued its manufacture. The gun was found an effective substitute for more expensive hand-made gallery guns of preceding years, receiving glowing testimonials, including one from U.S. Army General Sherman in 1875. With fewer parts and lighter weight it was highly successful competing against earlier styles. Its production techniques and design simplified manufacture, allowing for mass production at a reduced cost. The 1870s and 1880s saw the shooting gallery trade grow extremely large. Quackenbush undersold almost all competition, quickly becoming leader in the field. The basic action for Quackenbush guns was the patent purchased from Haviland and Gunn of Ilion, New York. Of the eight models and variations Quackenbush manufactured, seven were variations of his MODEL 1 Haviland and Gunn patent, with barrel pushing in to cock. Various models were chambered to take 21 caliber feathered, steel, long pointed darts (advertised to penetrate through 3/8" pine at 35 feet) 21 caliber shot pointed slugs, 22 caliber round shot and 22 rim fire cartridges in various combinations. Quackenbush's attempt to substitute a rubber band for the wound spiral spring (patented 1884) was used in their short-lived LIGHTNING model rifle, discontinued after but a few hundred were made; very rare. Quackenbush air guns were serial numbered; their 22RF rifles were not.

Other inventors and manufacturers produced excellent quality air guns during the same era, most unsuccessful. By the early 1900s the manufacturers of BB Guns reversed the tables for Quackenbush, whose desire not to sacrifice quality eventually doomed his production. Uncertain if production had actually ceased or deliveries were made from existing stock, by 1921

factory records indicate less than 500 per year of all models were shipped and by 1930 less than 100 per year. After approximately 50,000 air guns were manufactured production and/or shipping concluded in 1943 with but 74 air guns. BB Guns, the so-called "tin-plate" rifles, a radically new process using folding metal, assumed command of the market … but that is another story.

The publication of *Quackenbush Guns*, by John Groenwold in 2000 has added measurably to the study of these air guns. The collector may also find the pamphlet *"Henry Marcus Quackenbush: Investor and Manufacturer,"* by Margaret Thompson Quackenbush, a worthy read. As available production figures and dates on introduction of various models are in conflict, the most reasonable estimates are shown here. Arriving at accurate evaluations presented a challenge. Not only was there considerable disparity in opinions of dealer/collectors involved in the general antique arms market versus air gun specialists, but that same disparity existed within that latter field itself. Values reflected here are felt to be the most reasonable average from all and are subject to change depending on the market on which the guns are traded.

Values shown are for standard nickel finish; blue finish worth 25 to 50 percent premium. If mechanically inoperative values approx. 50 percent less.

Model No. 1 Improved Air Gun: Quantity made approx. 185,00. Introduced 1877, weight 4 pounds. Made to fire 21 caliber darts or slugs:

18-096   Values—Fine **$150**   Exc. **$300**

Model No. 2 New Model Air Gun: Quantity made approx. 7,000. 21 caliber darts or slugs; heavier barrel and construction; 37" overall; 4-1/2 pounds. Held to frame by large spring guard. Company advertising, 1889, said this "… adopted on practice ships of the U.S. Navy:"

18-097   Values—Fine **$160**   Exc. **$325**

Model No. 3 Shot Model: (Not illus. same as above.) Quantity approx. 2,700. Common F shot (22 caliber round shot):

18-098   Values—Fine **$175**   Exc. **$350**

Model No. 4 Magazine Shot: (Not illus.). About identical above with magazine at breech to hold 20 "F" shot so as to be "… ready at any instant for shooting rats or small game." Shot only. Quantity made approx. 850:

18-099   Values—Fine **$300**   Exc. **$600**

**18-104
Safety Cartridge Rifle**

**18-105
Junior Safety Cartridge Rifle**

**18-103
Champion**

**18-103
Eureka**

**18-106
Bicycle Rifle**

Model No. 5 Combination: 21-1/2 darts or slugs, TT shot (smooth bore barrel) or 22 rimfire (rifled barrel) with the use of an auxiliary chamber provided and stored in butt. Original patent of Benjamin Haviland and George Gunn, Herkimer, N.Y. 1871 (specimens known with their markings; very scarce; worth premium); purchased by Quackenbush 1887. Total 3,185 made up to 1907. Brown or nickel finish:

18-100   Values—Fine **$300**   Exc. **$600**

Models No. 6 & 7: (Not illus.). Least expensive of the line. One-piece slab type stock without buttplate fastened by large knurled screw on underside. Cal. 175 dart or BB shot. Location of loading port at top of breech (on No. 7) only difference. Barrel pushes in to cock. Model 6 approx. quantity 2,400; worth premium. Model 7 approx. quantity 15,000:

18-101   Values—Fine **$125**   Exc. **$250**

Models No. 9 & 10: (Not illus.). About identical to Models No. 2 & 3. Lighter weight. Caliber 175 for darts or BB shot. Bore of No. 9 at upper edge (not center) of barrel; loading port oval. No. 10 barrel has bore in center; loading port round. Both barrels of tubing:

18-102   Values—Fine **$200**   Exc. **$650**

Quackenbush Air Pistols: Two models CHAMPION and EUREKA as shown. All metal construction. 21 caliber for darts or slugs. Standard finish black, japanned handle; nickeled barrel or full nickel. Both available with detachable skeleton type shoulder stock. Values same:

18-103   Values—Fine **$150**   Exc. **$375**

Safety Cartridge Rifle: Introduced 1886 to approx. 1922. Calibers 22 RF (S, L, LR or BB Cap). 18" & 22" barrels (about same amount of each). Quantity about 50,000. Nickel finish; casehardened breech swivels sideways to load. Various wood forends and sights offered.

18-104   Values—Fine **$175**   Exc. **$400**

Junior Safety Cartridge Rifle: Quantity approx. 7,000. Introduced about 1893 to 1920. Same action as above. Caliber 22 RF. Nickel finish; 18" barrel. Skeleton/wire type detachable stock made as one-piece with trigger bow. (Current legal status should be verified before acquiring):

18-105   Values—Fine **$300**   Exc. **$475**

Bicycle Rifle: Quantity approx. 4,000. Introduced about 1899 to 1919. Same action as above; 22RF. 12" barrel. Offered with a special bicycle holster (worth premium). Skeleton/wire type pistol handle and skeleton stock affixed by bracket to frame allows it to adjust to various lengths or close for carrying. (Current legal status should be verified before acquiring):

18-106   Values—Fine **$350**   Exc. **$600**

NOTE: Item 18-105 (if made after 1898) and 18-106 are subject to GCA only and also qualify as "Curios & Relics."

HARMONICA GUNS

**18-110
Chamberlain Patent by C.B. Allen**

**18-110
Browning "Slide Repeater"**

18-110
Browning "Slide Repeater"

The group of unusual appearing, multi-shot repeating antique arms known as "harmonica guns" are so-termed by collectors from likening the appearance of the arrangement of bullet chambers to the harmonica or "mouth organ"; the small, inexpensive, common wind instruments.

This odd attempt to make a repeating firearm with varying numbers of chambers never gained popularity. The system was used in the percussion and metallic cartridge eras on rifles and hand guns; the latter were almost entirely made in France. Few harmonica rifles were successful in America; as such they represent rarities, all made in extremely small quantities. Specimens vary greatly in decoration, length, caliber and number of chambers/shots. On almost all American types there are a varying number of chambers in a rectangular bar which slides horizontally through the breech of the gun barrel, much

like a harmonica. A variant type has chambers in a triangular bar which swivels horizontally, retained by a vertical pin at its rear, center. All are rare. Specimens are known with two interchangeable sets of chambers i.e. three shot and six shot etc. A spare set would increase value 25 to 40 percent. Values shown are for marked specimens. Names that might be encountered include C.B.ALLEN/SPRING-FIELD, MASS./CHAMBERLAIN PATENT; OSGOOD AND TOWN-SEND/PAINTED POST, N.Y.; NICANOR KENDALL/WINDSOR, VT; HENRY GROSS/TIFFIN, OHIO; CURTIS PARKHURST/LAWRENCE-VILLE, PENNA. For unmarked specimens value as a "rule of thumb" would be 20-30 percent less, although quality of the rifle should be taken into account and may alter those percentages considerably. A few known examples exist of a five shot percussion harmonica rifle made by Mormon gunsmith Jonathan Browning (father of famed American inventor, John Moses Browning) in Utah Territory circa 1850s; actually advertised as his "Slide Repeater." It is possible, as with other great rarities, of historical importance, that these rarely seen or traded on the open marketplace specimens would be worth a premium of 50-100 percent of values shown. When actually exposed to the buying public, they tend to shatter expectations. In 2007, a Browning "Slide Repeater" sold at auction in the mid to high five-figures.

Marked Percussion Harmonica Rifle:
18-110   Values—Good **$5,000** to **10,000**
         Fine **$12,500** to **25,000 (and more)**

See also F. Schopp Harmonica Pistol 8A-165.5

NEEDLE-FIRE RIFLES

KLEIN'S PATENT NEEDLE-FIRE, BOLT ACTION RIFLES. Made by George P. Foster of Taunton, Massachusetts, and Bristol, Rhode Island. Circa 1850's. Quantity unknown; limited.

The needle-fire system played a highly important role in the development of the self-contained cartridge and the breech-loading system as they evolved to present day. Its influence in both areas was considerable. Achieving commercial success in Europe, it received but little attention in America in its day and even less by the collector and arms historian of present. It is due better recognition.

The Massachusetts-made Klein patented rifle is the sole example of this fascinating, historically significant ignition system to reach even a modicum of popularity here. Of the few other attempts made, only the Schroeder military carbine (see 9B-084) is ever given mention. Its production seems limited to but ten guns, made in 1857, given U.S. trials in 1860 and found "...unfitted for the military service."

The needle-fire system is credited to Johann Nikolaus Von Dreyse of Prussia, and patented by him in 1827. He was earlier

employed in Paris (1804-1814) as a lockmaker for Samuel Pauly, noted French inventor, credited with the first firearm to use fixed ammunition. Returning to Prussia, Dreyse's experiments with self-contained/"self-igniting" needle-fire ammunition was not only a major advance in cartridge systems, one adopted for wide use, but also led to his invention of the first successful military breech-loading, bolt action rifle made to chamber self-contained ammunition. Both developments had great impact on the world's weapons; the rifle being the fore-runner of all bolt action rifles. The Prussian army adopted Dreyse's needle-fire system in 1840 with an initial contract for 60,000 of them. The gun was used with deadly effect in the war with Denmark, 1864 and later with Austria, 1866. The French army adopted a needle-fire type rifle, the Chassepot, in 1866; various sporting type needle-fire rifles and hand guns were made in England and the continent during those years. Occasionally the term **NEEDLE GUN** was used in contemporary Western literature applied to early "trap-door" Springfield breech-loading rifles Models 1865 to 1870. Very much a misnomer, it merely described the firing pin of those rifles and not the ignition form.

The needle-fire cartridge, historically important as an ignition system and a great rarity in American forms, consists of a combustible paper wrapped or molded paper case (papier mache) with various shaped lead bullets (conical apparently most often seen) seated on a pressed paper sabot which contained the primer fulminate in a form of percussion cap imbedded in it. The sabot and bullet is seated on top of the powder charge. The system acquired its name form the firing pin/striker on the bolt of the action which resembles a long, tapered, slender, pointed needle. When fired the needle passes first through the general large powder charge then strikes the primer fitted just below the lead bullet.

The U.S. needle-fire patent was issued November, 1849 to Charles Hartung, New York City (also listed from Prussia) who

18-120 / 121

18-120

18-121
(early mfr.)

likely reassigned it under that same date to John B. Klein of New York. Manufacture was by the well-known gun maker, George P. Foster of Taunton, Mass. also known as maker of the Porter Revolving Turret Rifle (q.v.) and, in partnership with Ambrose E. Burnside, formed the Bristol Firearms Company that made the early models of the well-known carbine bearing the general's name.

American needle-fire rifles are very scarce. Like other sporting arms they vary in caliber and dimensions. Specimens viewed were mostly calibers 40 to 46 with varying length octagon barrels of light and medium weights. Barrels are marked G.P. FOSTER/TAUNTON/MASS. Receivers marked KLEIN'S PATENT/NOV. 1849/NEW-YORK, often with a few simple, decorative leaf and scroll engraved designs which may also be seen on some of the iron mountings. Walnut, sporting type halfstocks.

18-120   Values—Good **$1,250**   Fine **$3,500**

Early Manufacture: Entire bolt and bolt handle of brass. Lighter weight, shorter, part round/octagon barrel; caliber noted up to 60. Large double leaf brass rear sight. Walnut stock fastened to forend by brass band; brass patchbox and mount. Unmarked.

18-121   Values—Good **$2,500**   Fine **$5,500**

YACHT & OTHER SALUTE CANNON

Cannon and artillery pieces of all sizes and types, from miniatures and those designed to fire blank salutes to large field pieces have always been an integral part of antique arms collecting. A wide variety of **small muzzle-loading cannon**, all too puny to be employed as weapons, were made throughout the 19th century. Their only intended use was to fire salutes and as noise makers at parades, political rallies and important holiday celebrations; July 4th was of special significance. Rarely are two identical. Such types are valued for their aesthetic appeal, quality of workmanship (many are crude) and type of carriage on which they may be mounted. Values, usually what the market will bear. NOTE TO THE UNWARY: these mostly unimposing pieces, handsome though some may be, are occasionally offered as weapons that were intended for a combat situation. It is true that there are small "bow cannon" and "rail guns," etc., and only a fine line might separate the two. Unless there is substantial evidence that the barrel was designed as a weapon, it should be valued considerably less...as a salute gun.

BREECH-LOADING YACHT CANNON (their correct terminology) of the late 19th century are another sub-category. Specifically designed to fire black powder blanks only, they were intended solely as noisemakers, to signal the start or finish of yacht, or other, races and salutes for various celebrations. In an era of rising affluence, it apparently was as popular as it was fashionable for yachtsmen and growing number of pleasure boat owners to be so-equipped. A few manufacturers entered the market, most offering brass barrel, 8 or 10 gauge models on naval type carriages. Early 20th century catalogs of Francis Bannerman, N.Y. offered a few "pre-owned" examples of a least three types. Their descriptions sometimes even mentioned the name of the yacht from where acquired. Most were made in limited quantity. Although styles, breech variations and makers may be rare, all are valued principally for eye-appeal, quality, size and type of carriage. A Hartley & Graham, N.Y., catalog circa 1890 offers fine insight to the subject. Among the wide range of models by various makers were many more humble models geared to the plebian boating crowd. Although all bear the grandiloquent title "Yacht Cannon," it does require some stretch of the imagination to envision them in that lofty context. One steel barrel, breech-loading model, available only in caliber 44 C.F. (or R.F) Blank (10-1/2" overall) on a two wheel "mahogany finish mount" at just $6.50 was said to be "...noisy but will meet the demand for a low priced Breech Loading Yacht Gun, suitable for club houses and small yachts." The same model on the same mount (less wheels) was offered as a "Muzzle Loading Yacht Cannon" in three sizes from 8-1/2" to 10-1/2" overall at just $1.50 to $4.00. And it didn't end there. Row boat and bathtub sizes (if the reader will allow) were also available. For a mere 50 or 75 cents the less endowed boatsman was offered iron-mounted models in 22 cal. blank (7" long) and 32 cal. RF blank (8-1/2" long) respectively. The general collecting market has not evidenced much interest in these lesser sized, steel barrel types. It merely takes a survey of the field and a printed guide to stir interest. As with the "Alarm Guns" discussed here, the collector is cautioned to verify the legal status of certain cartridge models before acquiring. It is suspected that the same guidelines may apply.

18-122

Just one firm, the **Strong Firearms Company,** dominated the market. Their own words on an advertisement places the entire salute cannon genre in clear perspective: "The distressing accidents which so frequently result in the killing and maiming of our enthusiastic and patriotic citizens by the use of antiquated and unsafe Cannon (sic), either by bursting or accidental discharge, cease to occur when by happy foresight one of our beautiful Bronze Breech Loaders is substituted for the played-out dangerous old Muzzle Loader."

Strong Firearms Company, New Haven, Conn. 1878-1890. Makers of yacht cannon, sub-caliber tubes, rifles and ammunition (the latter product bought out by Winchester in 1884). Quantity of cannon unknown.

Basic model as illustrated, offered in a remarkable diversity of sizes, all with the same general contours. Hinged breech (opens upwards), thick-walled, tapered, brass barrels; mounted on proportional sized, mahogany, naval type, two wheel (wood) carriages (4 wheels available at extra charge most sizes); all brass fittings and elevation wheel under breech.

Company literature (subtly pretentious and a tribute to the Madison Ave. of its day!) advertised ten distinct models. They ranged from 13" barrel (10 Ga. "Suitable for 12 ft. to 30 ft. yacht"); 15" barrel (8 Ga. "suitable for 20 ft. to 40 ft. yacht"); 20" barrel (4 Ga. "suitable for a 35 ft. to 60 ft. yacht") up to a 36" barrel taking a 1" dia. Hotchkiss brass casing holding half a pound of black powder ("suitable for a 150 ft. yacht") and their king size 54"

barrel taking a 7" long Hotchkiss case holding one pound of black powder "suitable for a yacht 200 ft. or longer."

Among the great prizes of the Strong cannon are those 54" barrel models mounted on large field type artillery carriages with tall, wooden spoke wheels (offered in 3 ft., 4 ft. and larger diameters). They were available complete with matching limbers and various accessories. Specifically offered for "Military Schools, G.A.R. Posts, Boys' Brigades, Private Batteries, Patriotic and other organizations." Only a handful have ever shown up on the market; their value would easily command low five figures. One other Strong carriage was offered, but is unlikely to have enjoyed commercial success. It, too, was a large, field type mount, but of heavy cast iron and rather shapeless, if not unattractive, in appearance. Supported by two large, cast iron spoke wheels, its size indicated it was designed only for the largest of the company's barrels. They advertised it as "...designed for club houses or lawns and not for parading...may be exposed to weather without injury." It does not pass notice that immediately following that description, the company added "Muzzle loaders converted to breech loaders at reasonable prices or taken in exchange."

Judging from specimens observed, the two or three smallest sizes were most popular, and valued here. All are scarce. Rarity increases in ascending order to size. Those with 25" and large barrels, rare; the 42" and 54" very rare.

18-122   Values—Very Good **$1,250** to **$3,000**
                       Exc. **$1,750** to **$4,000**

The Lyle Lifesaving Gun

Often misidentified as salute cannons or signal guns, these ungainly-appearing, muzzle-loading cannon are occasionally encountered in the gun collectors' marketplace. Much like the various whaling guns (described earlier this chapter) their strongest demand (and consequently highest values) is decidedly not with the arms collecting world, but rather, is to be found among nautical collectors in general or specialists for material associated with the United States Life Saving Service (USLSS). Purpose here is to correctly identify these devices, pay them the respect due and offer a general idea of values for collectors.

The idea of using a firearm to throw a line to help in the rescue of people threatened with death in a sinking ship or other perilous situations (usually nautical in nature) has origins that revert to the 18th century or earlier. David A. Lyle is specifically noted for creating a design in the 1870s that was officially adopted by the United States for issuance as standard equipment. The model he designed was made in numerous various styles (and copied by many others in similar design) continued in use through World War II. Its history and numerous variations is best read in *"The Lifesaving Guns of David Lyle"* by J. P. Barnett, 1976 (*see Chapter IV*). Although the rather homely, but sturdy carriage is usually all iron, it appears from various advertisements that the barrels were made of both brass and iron (although iron is the most commonly encountered). Specimens all conform to the same general configuration similar to illustration; most notable differences are in profile of carriages. Bores standard at 2-1/2"; barrels are all muzzle-loading and vary; 24 inches about average; weights reported from 85 to 150 pounds. The original advertising from a noted Boston dealer's catalog of the 1890s best describes its usage and general appeal to the then-existing market: "For use of Steamships, Barges, Towboats and Yachts for throwing a line from one vessel to another or communicating with the shore in case of shipwreck...the law now enforced compels all ocean steam vessels carrying passengers to be provided with a line-carrying projectile and means of propelling such as may have

18-123

received the formal approval of the Board of Supervising Inspectors. [This Lyle gun] is the regular government pattern and size as today in use by over 200 Government Life Saving Stations...and can be used as a signal gun as well as a line thrower." All Lyle Guns used blackpowder (or in later 20th century years, a form of blackpowder especially made by some of the largest powder works) and were fired by friction primers (of the type used to fire Civil War muzzle-loading cannon) with later innovations and devices made to simplify ignition. The mounts (or "carriage") on which they are fitted is termed the "sled type" and is invariably not fitted for or provided with wheels of any type. Earliest mounts on Lyle guns were a heavy oak wood, iron edged (will bring a premium in value). They were replaced rather quickly with cast iron mounts (similar to that illustrated here, varying in profiles. This style, too, was replaced with an almost triangular looking iron mount). When originally acquired, cannons came equipped with accessories of a projectile, a patent reel type device for dispensing the line and a box containing other accessories. When such implements accompany the line guns they add premiums to both value and desirability.

Lyle guns bearing authentic "U.S.L.S.S." markings, often seen on the trunnions (i.e. the two cylindrical projections from sides of the cannon near the mid-point for mounting barrel on the carriage)…or occasionally on the rim of the muzzle, will add substantially to values (often double or more than shown below). The familiar caveat is applicable: markings should be fully authenticated before acquisition. Other markings are quite likely indicating the foundry, the mfr. or the company that originally sold the cannon.

Lyle Guns with early, iron edged, oak wood mounts and brass barrels
18-123   Values—Good **$1,250**   Fine **$2,500**

Lyle Guns as above with iron barrels
18-124   Values—Good **$750**   Fine **$1,000**

Lyle Guns on heavy iron mounts (various shapes and sizes) with brass barrels
18-125   Values—Good **$850**   Fine **$2,000**

Lyle Guns on iron mounts with iron barrels
18-126   Values—Good **$500**   Fine **$750**

A spectacular array of Henry brass-frame rifles. Of the 120 catalogs of N. Flayderman & Co. issued over the past half-century, the cover of No. 95, the edition of June 1974, received the most comment. Occasionally someone still remarks about the illustration (which was very carefully composed with no harm to any rifle!) and the selection of those great rarities. They included two engraved Henrys, a martially marked one, a presentation example with dual inscriptions and Serial No. 46 – among the lowest recorded.

Acknowledgments

The hardest task the author has ever undertaken was the preparation of the manuscript for this book. The project turned out to be much more complex than even the most meticulous planning envisioned.

The most satisfying aspect of compiling the broad range of data and seeing it through to the completed text was the unfailing and gratifying support of fellow collectors and dealers who were asked for help. Even with the most casual glance it is obvious that assembling a work of this size and scope would have been impossible without the cooperation of many individuals and organizations. In no instance was that support denied—whether from an individual's specialized knowledge, access to unpublished notes and manuscripts, or from information gleaned from years of research in various fields. That unfailing assistance has left a lasting impression of the kindness and generosity of those who people the world of collecting. Often characterized as the "gun fraternity," the author can testify that the term is indeed apt. This project has poignantly illustrated those qualities of kinship and brotherhood our fraternity represents.

The author gratefully acknowledges and tenders his sincere thanks and deep appreciation for the unselfish assistance of his fellow collectors. Though some are singled out for special contributions, let him note that the significance of all assistance was equally appreciated and of distinct importance to the satisfactory completion of this work.

Many of these same individuals were consulted for this revised edition. In all instances their support and cooperation was generous. The author also wishes to recognize, thank and acknowledge those collectors who thoughtfully brought to his attention data that had been previously overlooked or otherwise assisted in making this revision more accurate, up-to-date and complete.

The valued editorial assistance of R.L. Wilson of Connecticut and his encouragement at the inception of this project were deeply appreciated. A noted author and arms historian, his formidable efforts during the preparation and completion of the initial first edition of this work are particularly noteworthy.

Other important contributors were:

Mark Aziz of Rutgers Book Center, specialist in books about firearms, weapons and collecting, at 127 Raritan Avenue, Highland Park, New Jersey, for his patience in reviewing the various bibliographies for up-to-date information on new titles and others currently in print.

Robert B. Berryman of Mountain Home, Texas, and T. M. Hutcheson, for their generosity in allowing unlimited access to their photographic files of the late William M. Locke's famed collection of American firearms.

L. P. Bassinger of Pasadena, Texas, for long days of arduous labor reflected in the Allen firearms chapter, and help in placing Allen Pepperboxes in perspective for the first time.

William S. Brophy, Lt. Col., USA (Ret.) of Marlin Firearms Co. for his devoted efforts toward making the Marlin chapter the most up-to-date and comprehensive yet to see print.

Michael F. Carrick of Turner, Oregon, for pointing the author in the right direction for researching obscure subjects and for revamping the history of an historic air rifle.

Kenneth L. Cope of Milwaukee, Wisconsin, for his guidance, assistance, and the use of illustrations that helped complete the Stevens chapter and certain other sections.

Dwight B. Demeritt, Jr., of Brooklyn, New York, for verifying and placing in perspective the various Evans repeating rifles and Maine-made guns and supplying up-to-date information on them.

L.D. Eberhart of Alpharetta, Georgia, for sharing his wealth of knowledge... and many photographs...of percussion and cartridge deringers.

Melvin W. Flanagan of Denver, Colorado, for loan of photographs, research and guidance in assembling the new section about Alarm Guns.

Jim Gordon of Sante Fe, New Mexico, for allowing access to his private museum (and supplying photographs) from his remarkable collection of Western Armerican-made, early firearms and associated historic artifacts.

William H. Guthman of Westport, Connecticut, for his highly valued assistance and guidance on those chapters dealing with Kentucky Rifles, American Colonial Arms and early U.S. Flintlock Longarms, and for his willingness to lend an ever-ready ear on technical and esoteric points.

Thomas E. Hall, Curator of the famed Winchester Gun Museum for his kindness and patience in supplying data, and allowing unlimited use for photographic purposes.

Herbert S. Hoffman of Boston, Massachusetts, for his sage advice and wise counsel over a great many years. His observations, comments and suggestions always highly valued.

Herbert G. Houze of Cody, Wyoming, eminent arms authority and author for his generous assistance with the research for the story of the first famous American antique gun collection.

Jay Huber, Jr. of Fort Lauderdale, Florida, indefatigable researcher of Remington lore and arms, who takes no greater delight than sharing that information with fellow collectors.

Edward A. Hull, Cypress, California, for his contributions to the lore of American arms and patience in answering the author's inquiries.

Roy G. Jinks, Historian, Smith & Wesson Inc., (Springfield, Mass.) and author of two classic books on the subject, for his untiring efforts and continued counsel on the products of that venerable firm.

Burton Kellerstedt of New Britain, Connecticut, who played a major role in the presentation of Springfield Armory firearms from all eras. Burt lent unstintingly of his time and many years of accumulated notes—a treasure house of data— to place this important segment of American military firearms in proper perspective for the first time. Numerous illustrations are from his extensive collection.

George Layman of Wallingford, Connecticut, for bringing to light the importance of a formerly obscure firearm and assisting the author to interpret that firearm and its many variations for this *Guide*...and for the many photographs of same.

Tom Lewis of Evergreen, Colorado, for his expertise on Spencer repeating arms and for his help in sorting out that specialty and providing several key details.

Richard Littlefield of Jaffrey, New Hampshire, for access to his data and unpublished manuscript on the history of Frank Wesson, Wesson & Harrington, and Harrington & Richardson firearms, and his efforts in helping place them in perspective for the first time. His counsel and advice as a professional dealer in American arms was of great assistance.

Andrew F. Lustyik of Middletown, New York, respected authority on American military carbines, for access to his voluminous notes on the subject and assistance in reviewing considerable material about them for presentation here.

Howard Michael Madaus, Curator of the Cody Firearms Museum, Cody, Wyoming and widely repected arms historian, for sharing his unpublished manuscript on Ballards and guidance on use of his published material.

Karl F. Moldenhauer of Cedarburg, Wisconsin, for his many hours of pouring over Remington notes and his enduring patience in answering the author's endless questions about the finer points.

Arthur F. Nehrbass of Pittsburgh, Pennsylvania, and Robert D. Schofield of Hyde Park, New York, for access to their unpublished notes and manuscripts on early American flintlock longarms. The lengthy correspondence and many days of meetings that ensued resulted in a major reappraisal of the collector's view of such arms.

William R. Orbelo of San Antonio, Texas, for generous assistance and appreciated comments about the author's conclusions on American dueling and dueling pistols.

Robert D. Palmer of Brevard, No. Carolina, for his continuing assistance with information on arms curiosa, deringers and loan of photographs.

Robert M. Reilly of Baton Rouge, Louisiana, author of major works on American military weapons, for aiding me in the presentation of U.S. martial arms, and for his cooperation in supplying data and frank opinion.

Larry Riling of Ray Riling Books, dealers in a wide range of works about firearms and collecting at 6844 Gorsten St., Philadelphia, for his generous assistance in reviewing and updating the many bibliographies throughout this 9th Edition.

Frank M. Sellers of Alstead, New Hampshire, for letting me tap his encyclopedic knowledge of American arms. His kindness in sharing personal notes on Sharps firearms was responsible for placing all models of that famed make in clear focus for the first time. Frank's generous assistance with many of the book's sections, including those on American cartridge and percussion handguns, was a highly regarded, valuable asset. His observations and opinions as a professional dealer were equally appreciated.

James B. Shaffer II of Irwin, Pennsylvania for providing facts and figures on cartridge deringers as well as considerable archival data on other cartridge handguns.

Anita Sylvia, secretary to T. E. Hall at the Winchester Gun Museum, for her kind help in supplying data from the original factory records and assistance during photographic sessions.

Samuel E. Smith of Markesan, Wisconsin, for an always-available ear to questions about single shot martial pistols, and for adding significant material and data about many of them.

Henry M. Stewart, Jr. of Wynnewood, Pennsylvania, for his many years of devoted efforts to collecting and the collector, and his constant quest for information, and for willingness to share his findings freely. His untiring assistance on revolving rifles has resulted in the first and most comprehensive presentation of that specialized field in print.

Charles W. Thrower of Wellesley, Massachusetts, for allowing access to the wealth of data gleaned over many years in preparing his own as yet unpublished manuscript about Whitney firearms.

Peter Tillou of Litchfield, Connecticut, collector and connoisseur of American art, for confirming the author's thoughts (during a long night flight to Iceland!) on the importance and potential of the Kentucky rifle.

Richard R. Wagner, Jr. of Marlborough, Massachusetts, for sharing his notes and photographs of small caliber metallic cartridge revolvers and allowing access to his hard earned data on Prescott revolvers.

Tom Wallace, Curator of the Springfield Armory Museum (Springfield, Mass.) for his assistance with information pertaining to the Armory, and access to photographic files.

Extensive assistance and invaluable advice was rendered by the following professionals in the field of collector's firearms. All were frequently consulted, and all gave freely of their time in reviewing substantial data submitted to, or asked of, them. Their opinions were highly valued and respected. To each goes my deepest appreciation and thanks:

Douglas R. Carlson, DesMoines, Iowa
David Carroll, Birmingham, Alabama
David Carter, Boulder, Colorado
Mike Clark of Collectors Arms, Houston, Texas
Richard Ellis, Rock Island, Illinois
Fred Fiet, Thomson, Illinois
Neil and Julia Gutterman, Pearl River, New York
Larry Hannusch, Houston, Texas
William "Pete" Harvey, Falmouth, Massachusetts
David Kleiner, Bloomingburg, New York
Martin Lane, New York, New York
John J. Malloy, Wye Mills, Maryland
Greg Martin, San Francisco, California
LeRoy Merz, Fergus Falls, Minnesota
Steven S. Miller, Portland, Oregon
Damon Mills, Montgomery, Alabama
Ron Peterson, Albuquerque, New Mexico
John Rinaldi, Kennebunkport, Maine
Bob Ruben, Oyster Bay, New York
Ray Saign, Minneapolis, Minnesota
John Sexton, Grayson, Georgia
James Supica, Lenexa, Kansas
Eric Vaule, Bridgewater, Connecticut
Norman Vegely, St. Louis, Missouri

Four auction houses, particularly well-known for specializing in the sale of firearms, were most generous in their cooperation for supplying information and photographs of material from their widely circulated catalogs:

James D. Julia, Inc. Auctions, Fairfield, Maine
Little John's Auction Service, Orange, California
Greg Martin Auctions, San Francisco, California
Rock Island Auction Co., Moline, Illinois

Among the many others who gave of their time and knowledge, allowed the use of photographs from their collections, and to whom the author offers his sincere appreciation are:

Donald S. Ball, Clearwater, Florida
John Battaglia, Tulsa, Oklahoma
Robert J. Berger, Monroe, Connecticut
Taylor G. Bowen, Sedona, Arizona
Thomas Brady, Kent, Connecticut
Kurt F. Brandenburg, Director, Museum of the Confederacy, Richmond, Virginia
Bernard Braverman, Monroeville, Pennsylvania
Graham Burnside, Dundee, Illinois
James Cameron, East Meadow, New York
Charles E. Carder, Delphos, Ohio
Robert E. P. Cherry, Geneseo, Illinois
Stephen R. Cole, Fort Myers, Florida
W. R. Cole, Brookline, Massachusetts
Giles Cromwell, Richmond, Virginia
Mark Cross, Au Sable Forks, New York
Pete Dickey, Washington, D.C.
Ken Domina, Ritzville, Washington
Arni Dunathan, Escanaba, Michigan
John Dutcher, Aurora, Colorado
Vern Eklund, Rockford, Illinois
Marc Fagan, Neal Auction Co., New Orleans, Louisiana

Firearms Technology Branch, BATF, Washington, D.C.
David H. Fink, Atlanta, Georgia
Robert Fisch, West Point Museum, New York
James D. Forman, Port Washington, New York
William Francis, New Milford, Connecticut
Stuart M. Frank, Director, The Kendall Whaling Museum, Sharon, Massachusetts
E. F. Furler, Jr., Bellaire, Texas
Ronald T. Gabel, Slatington, Pennsylvania
Louis A. Garavaglia, Melbourne, Florida
Roderick S. George, Virginia
William Gilkerson, Nova Scotia, Canada
Craddock R. Goins, Jr., Curator, Division of Military History, Smithsonian Institution, Washington, D.C.
Edwin C. Hall, Santa Ana, California
Charles E. Hanson, Jr. & James A. Hanson, Directors, Museum of the Fur Trade, Chadron, Nebraska
C. Vance Haynes, Jr., Tuscon, Arizona
Doug Heiser, Altamonte Springs, Florida
Gary Herman, Ridgefield, Connecticut
Bob Hinman, Peoria, Illinois
Col. J. C. Hitz, Abingdon, Virginia
Peter Hlinka, New York, New York
James L. Hudson, Jr., Vista, California
Harry Hunter, National Museum of American History, Smithsonian Institution, Washington, D.C.
Robert D. Jeska, Plainwell, Michigan
Edwin Kennedy, Santa Fe, New Mexico
Michael D. Kramer, Morristown, New Jersey
Carl Bruce Kusrow, Herndon, Virginia
Eric Larson, Takoma Park, Maryland
George F. LeBlanc, Fitchburg, Massachusetts
Aaron J. Littlefield, Jaffrey, New Hampshire
Jim Lovell, Albuquerque, New Mexico
Dennis E. Lowe, Hamburg, Pennsylvania
John B. Lundstrom, Assistant Curator and the Milwaukee Public Museum, Milwaukee, Wisconsin
Albert C. Mayer, Jr., Bethany, Connecticut
E. S. McCauley, Remington Arms Co., Bridgeport, Conn.
George S. McCluney, Berger, Missouri
R. Bruce McDowell, Metuchen, New Jersey
O. H. McKagen, Falls Church, Virginia
Don McMahon, Meridan, Connecticut
Roy Marcot, San Ramon, California
Harold R. Mouillesseaux, South Orleans, Massachusetts
Stuart Mowbray, Woonsocket, Rhode Island
Roger Muckerheide, Plano, Texas
Bluford Muir, Chevy Chase, Maryland
John M. Murphy, M.D., La Jolla, California
R. E. Neville, Mobile, Alabama
David Nigh, San Jose, California
Col. Brooke Nihart, USMC (Ret.) Director Marine Corps Museums, Washington, D.C.
Hayes Otoupalik, Missoula, Montana
Dr. Harry J. Parker, Dallas, Texas
Raymond Petry, Newton Square, Pennsylvania
Thomas Pirone, Brookfield, Connecticut
Neil Poppensiek, Ithaca, New York
Richard Rattenbury, Oklahoma City, Oklahoma
Kit Ravenshear, Benton, Pennsylvania
Glode Requa, Monsey, New York
Thomas B. Rentschler, Hamilton, Ohio
Edward J. Rogalski, Norwich, Connecticut
Joseph Schroeder, Glenview, Illinois
Edward D. Seeber, Bloomington, Illinois
Tom Seymour, Fort Worth, Texas
George Shumway, York, Pennsylvania
Donald M. Simmons, Patagonia, Arizona
Paul Sorrell, Beaumont, Texas
David C. Squire, Wilton, Connecticut
William Stelma, Trumbull, Connecticut
Holman J. Swinney, Syracuse, New York
Jerald T. Teesdale, Madison, Wisconsin
H. H. Thomas, Lexington, Kentucky
Lowell J. Wagner, St. Louis Park, Minnesota
James M. Wertenberger, Huntington, Indiana
Robert F. Wheeler, Baltimore, Maryland
James B. Whisker, Ph. D., Bedford, Pennsylvania
Peregrine White, East Rindge, New Hampshire
George Whiting, Lexington, Virginia
Bleeker Williams, Madison, Connecticut
Vonnie S. Zullo, Fairfax, Virginia

My sincere thanks also to the following organizations for allowing the use of photographs and other materials:

The University Press of Virginia, Charlottesville, Va., the Maine State Museum at Augusta, Maine, the National Rifle Association, Washington, D.C., the National Museum of American History at the Smithsonian Institution, the U.S. Marine Corps Museum at Quantico, Virginia and the New Bedford Whaling Museum, New Bedford, Massachusetts.

The author hopes he has included all of those who helped so generously in the preparation of this book. If any names have been omitted he asks their forgiveness and indulgence for the oversight. Please bring any such omissions to his attention for use in future editions.

A great debt of gratitude is due those who, closely associated with the author, have in many ways lent valuable assistance, and have been invariably forbearing and patient with him during some quite difficult and trying times. His deepest appreciation and thanks to Linda Kuhne, Linda Clarke, Bonnie Shepherd,

Johanna Welter, George Lassen and Claudyne Terrell for their perseverance and generous assistance on the previous editions. And to Carrie DeRosa for her long tedious hours in suffering through the preparation of the corrections for this 9th Edition.

Steve Augutis' steadfast editorial support was indispensable; his demonstrated photographic competence responsible for many of the images in this 9th Edition.

Lastly ... to Ruthie Flayderman ... a champion and All-American in her world of Trapshooting ... and a superstar in shepherding the author through the myriad of paper and correspondence necessary to get this revised edition to print!

Norm Flayderman
P.O. Box 2446
Fort Lauderdale,
Florida   33303

CONDITION STANDARDS FOR ANTIQUE FIREARMS

FACTORY NEW—all original parts; 100 percent original finish; in perfect condition in every respect, inside and out.

EXCELLENT—all original parts; over 80 percent original finish; sharp lettering, numerals and design on metal and wood; unmarred wood, fine bore.

FINE—all original parts; over 30 percentoriginal finish; sharp lettering, numerals and design on metal and wood; minor marks in wood; good bore.

VERY GOOD—all original parts; none to 30 percent original finish; original metal surfaces smooth with all edges sharp; clear lettering, numerals and design on metal; wood slightly scratched or bruised; fore disregarded for collectors firearms.

*GOOD—some minor replacement parts; metal smoothly rusted or lightly pitted in places, cleaned or reblued, principal lettering, numerals and design on metal legible; wood refinished, scratched, bruised or minor cracks repaired; in good working order.

FAIR—some major parts replaced; minor replacement parts may be required; metal rusted, may be lightly pitted all over, vigorously cleaned or reblued; rounded edges of metal and wood; principal lettering, numerals and design on metal partly obliterated; wood scratched, bruised, cracked or repaired where broken; in fair working order or can be easily repaired and placed in working order.

POOR—major and minor parts replaced; major replacement parts required and extensive restoration needed; metal deeply pitted; principal lettering, numerals and design obliterated, wood badly scratched, bruised, cracked or broken; mechanically inoperative; generally undesirable as a collectors firearm.

These various condition grades have been established as "Standards" by NRA collecting committees specifically for antique firearms. They were used as guidelines in determining the values shown in this new edition. The reader is urged to regularly review these "Standards" as they are essential to accurately assess values. **Chapter II "VALUES & CONDITION"** discusses the subject at length, offering insight to other factors that may enhance values considerably.

FOR FIREARMS ON WHICH BLUE (or nickel) FINISH IS A MAJOR DETERMINANT OF VALUE: the wide latitude given to "original finish" in the NRA "Standards" has been refined for this GUIDE:

> **"VERY GOOD"** indicates a crisp piece with but traces of finish

> **"FINE"** is a specimen with 30 percent finish

> **"EXCELLENT"** indicates 80 percent finish

BLUE vs. NICKEL: On mass-produced guns, invariably cartridge models, that list "blue" or "nickel" as standard, it is observed that blue frequently tends to bring a premium. That occurs more often on guns in the upper grades of condition and (on handguns) in the larger caliber models. Premiums are modest for **FINE**, rising substantially for **EXC.** and **FACTORY NEW/MINT.** This axiom is a very broad generalization and not applicable across the board.

A DUAL RANGE OF CONDITIONS (AND THEIR ACCOMPANYING VALUES) HAVE BEEN USED THROUGHOUT THIS GUIDE. Condition ranges shown for each piece are those in which it is most likely to be encountered.

"GOOD": universally used, abused and misunderstood terminology. Be sure to read discussion relevant to it in "Introduction" of this new 9th Edition.

Major Manufacturers Index

ETHAN ALLEN
(Allen & Thurber, Allen & Wheelock, E. Allen & Co.)

COLT FIREARMS

MANHATTAN FIREARMS COMPANY

MARLIN
(Marlin-Ballard, Ballard)

REMINGTON FIREARMS

Remington Firearms (cont.)

SHARPS FIREARMS

SMITH & WESSON

STEVENS ARMS COMPANY

FRANK WESSON
(Wesson & Harrington and Harrington and Richardson)

WHITNEY ARMS COMPANY

WINCHESTER FIREARMS
(and their Predecessor Arms)

Alphabetical Index

A

Adams Revolving Arms Co., New York *See Massachusetts Arms Co.*, 352
Adirondack Firearms Company *See O. M. Robinson*, 692
Aetna Arms Co. Pocket Revolver, 462
Afferbach, W., Pocket Pistol, 410
Air and Spring Guns (History and Values of), 775
Alarm Guns (History of), 766
Allen & Thurber *See Chapter V, Ethan Allen*, 352
Allen & Wheelock *See Chapter V, Ethan Allen*, 352
Allen, Amasa, Grant, Samuel, and Bernard, Joseph, U.S. 1798 Contract Flintlock Muskets, 541
Allen, C. B., *See Elgin Cutlass Pistols*, 388
Allen, Ethan Allen, Allen & Thurber, Allen & Wheelock, E. Allen and Ethan Allen & Co. *See Ethan Allen; Major Manufacturers Index*, 711
Allen, S., Independent Maker of 1808 Contract Flintlock Musket, 549
Alling *See Aetna*, 462
All Metal Revolver *See Reid, James, Model No. 3 Deringer*, 510
"All Metal Waters." *See Waters "All Metal" Single Shot Percussion Pistol*, 333
All Right Firearms Co. Palm Pistol, 462
Alsop, C. R., Navy Model Revolver, 352
Alsop, C. R., Pocket Model Revolver, 353
American Arms. Co. Fox Patent Double Shotgun, 746
American Arms Co. Double Barrel Deringers, 463
American Arms Co. Top-Break Revolver, 463
American Arms Co. Top-Break Revolvers, 463
American Blunderbusses (History of), 764
"American Bulldog" Marked Revolver *See Iver Johnson 8A-068.9*, 464
American Colonial and Revolutionary Era Flintlock Fowling Pieces *See Chapter XVI*, 742
American Colonial and Revolutionary War Firearms (History of), 722
American Light Dragoon Flintlock Pistol, 731
American-Made Flintlock Northwest Trade Gun, 762
American Military Longarms (History of), 530
"American Portable Burglar Alarm, The" Gun, 769
American Shotguns and Fowling Pieces (History of), 733
American Standard Tool Company *See Chapter V-C, Manhattan Firearms (5C-022/023)*, 464
American Standard Tool Company *See Manhattan Firearms, Chapter V*, 388
Anderson (so-called) Unmarked Underhammer Pistol, 423
Andrews, Ferry & Co. Underhammer Pistol, 423
Andrus & Osborn Underhammer Pistol, 423
Angstadt Contract Flintlock Pistol, 339
Arkadelphia Ordnance Works Rifles, 646
Asheville Armory Model 1841 / 1855 Style Rifle, 646
Ashton, P. or W., Underhammer Pistol, 424
Auer, B., Pocket Pistol, 410
Augusta Machine Works Revolver, 640
"Automatic Alarm Defender" Burglar Alarm Gun, 769

B

Babcock, A.H., Charlestown, Mass. *See Chapter XVII "Shotguns" 17-001.3*, 679
Babcock Marked Single Shot Pistol *See T. J. Stafford*, 464
Babcock Open-Frame Percussion Shotgun, 742
Babcock Underhammer Cane Gun, 424
Baby Hammerless & New Baby Pocket Revolvers, 464
Bacon & Co. All Metal Ring Trigger Pistol, 388

Bacon & Co. Single Shot, Single Action Pistol, 388
Bacon & Co. Single Shot Bar Hammer Pistol, 388
Bacon & Co. Single Shot Ring Trigger Pistol, 388
Bacon & Co. Underhammer Pistol, 424
Bacon, Thomas K., Firearms Manufacturer (History of), 465
Bacon Arms Co. Pepperbox Revolver, 468
Bacon Arms Co. Pocket Model Revolver, 353
Bacon Arms Co. Pocket Revolver, 467
Bacon Arms Co. Pocket Revolver, 468
Bacon Mfg. Co. Navy Model Revolvers, 466
Bacon Mfg. Co. Pocket Model Revolvers, 353
Bacon Mfg. Co. Pocket Revolver, 467
Bacon Mfg. Co. Removable Trigger Guard Pocket Revolver, 467
Bacon Mfg. Co. Single Shot Pistols, 468
Bacon Mfg. Co. Swing-Out Cylinder Revolver, 466
Bacon, Thomas K., Single Action Underhammer Pepperbox, 379
Baggett, Elijah, U.S. 1798 Contract Flintlock Muskets, 541
Bailey, T., Pocket Pistols, 410
Baker, J., Private Contractor of Model 1816 Flintlock Musket, 553
Baker, M. A., Conversion of U.S. Rifles & Muskets & Baker C.S. Rifle, 646
Baker, Melchior, Commonwealth of Pennsylvania Flintlock Musket (1797), 543
Baker Gun Co. Three-Barrel Shotgun/Rifle, 746
Baldwin & Company Shotgun, 746
Ballard, C. H., Single Shot Deringer, 469
Ballard Carbines & Rifles *See Marlin; Major Manufacturers Index*, 701
Ballard Carbines and Rifles *See Marlin; Major Manufacturers Index*, 616
Ball Repeating Carbine, 616
Baltimore Arms Co. Shotgun, 746
Bannerman Slide Action Shotgun, 746
Barns, T., Underhammer Pistol, 424
Barrett, J. B., (Read & Watson) Rifles and Carbines, 647
Barstow, Joshua and Charles, 1808 Contract Flintlock Muskets, 547
Bartlett, Asher and Pliny, 1808 Contract Flintlock Muskets, 547
Bay State Arms Co. *See Hopkins & Allen Rifle*, 701
Beck, Samuel, Shotgun, 746
Beerstecher, F., Superposed Load Pocket Pistol, 411
Belgian-Made Flintlock Northwest Trade Gun, 762
Bench Rest Rifles (History and Values of), 686
Bennett & Haviland Many Chambered Revolving Rifle, 711
Bennett & Haviland Many Chambered Revolving Rifle, 711
Bicknell, Thomas, U.S. 1798 Contract Flintlock Muskets, 541
Bidwell, Oliver, 1808 Contract Flintlock Muskets, 548
Bigelow, Benjamin, Maker of Miller Revolving Rifle. *See Miller, J. & J.*, 714
Bigelow's Patent Percussion Burglar Alarm *See Marlin Firearms; Major Manufacturers Index*, 767
Bilharz, Hall & Co. *See Hodgkins & Sons, and also "Rising Breech Carbine,"* 647
Billinghurst, W., Underhammer Pistol, 424
Billinghurst, William, Maker of Miller Revolving Rifle. *See Miller, J. & J.*, 714
Billinghurst Revolving Pill Lock Rifles *See Miller, J. & J.*, 711
Billings Combination Bowie Knife-Pistol, 469
Billings Vest Pocket Single Shot Deringer, 469
Bird, C. & Co. Flintlock Pistols, 339
Bismarck Pocket Revolver, 469
Bitterlich, Frank J., Pocket Pistols, 411
Blake, P. & E. W., Private Contractor of Model 1816 Flintlock Musket, 553
Blake Bolt Action Repeating Rifle, 616
Blake Bolt Action Repeating Sporting Rifle, 692

Blickensdoefer & Schilling Shotgun, 746
Bliss & Goodyear Pocket Model Revolver, 354
Bliss, F. D., Pocket Revolver, 470
Blunt & Syms Dbl. Bbl. Underhammer Pistol, 390
Blunt & Syms Deringer *See Percussion Deringers, Chapter VII-D*, 390
Blunt & Syms Double Barreled Underhammer Percussion Pistol *See Blunt & Syms*, 425
Blunt & Syms Double Barrel Pistol, 390
Blunt & Syms Pocket Pistol, 411
Blunt & Syms Ring Trigger Pistol, 390
Blunt & Syms Single Shot Bar Hammer Pistol, 389
Blunt & Syms Single Shot Pistol, 389
Blunt & Syms Single Shot Side Hammer Pistol, 389
Blunt & Syms Single Shot Side Hammer Pocket Pistol, 389
Blunt & Syms Target or Dueling Pistol, 390
Blunt & Syms Underhammer Pepperbox, 379
Blunt-Enfield Rifle Musket, 611
Bolen, J. G., New York, an agent for Allen Pepperboxes *See Allen Firearms, Chapter V*, 379
Bonnie Blue 22 Blank Deringer, 470
Boom Pocket Revolver, 470
Booth, William, Flintlock Pistol, 339
Boss Single Shot Blank Deringer, 470
Bosworth, B. M., Underhammer Pistol, 425
Boyd Breech-Loading Arms Co. Shotgun, 746
Brand, C. C., 757
Brand Breech-Loading Single Shot Carbine, 617
Brass Frame Sharps Carbine, 656
Brass Tack Decorations and Rawhide Repairs Indian Owned and Indian Used Firearms (History of), 763
Breech-Loading Percussion Shotguns, 743
Breech-Loading Percussion Sporting Rifles (History and Values of), 689
Brettell & Frisbie Pocket Revolver, 354
Bridgewater Flintlock Light Dragoon Pistol, 340
Bridgewater Flintlock Muskets, 607
Briggs, H. A., Single Shot Deringer, 471
Briggs, Wm., Norristown, PA. *See Chapter XVII "Shotguns" 17-011.5*, 679
Briggs Underhammer Percussion Shotgun, 743
British "Brown Bess" Flintlock Muskets, 729
"BRITISH BULL DOG" Marked Revolver *See Iver Johnson 8A-068.8*, 471
"British Bull-Dogs" (History of), 481
Broad, I., Independent Maker of 1808 Contract Flintlock Musket, 549
Brong (or Brang), Peter, Commonwealth of Pennsylvania Flintlock Musket (1797), 543
Brooke, John, James and Nathan, 1808 Contract Flintlock Muskets, 548
Brooklyn Firearms Co. Pocket Revolver, 471
Brooks, C., & Brooks Arms. Co. Shotgun, 746
Brooks, S. R., Burglar Alarm Gun, 769
Brown, D., Underhammer Pistol, 425
Brown, Elisha, U.S. 1798 Contract Flintlock Muskets, 541
Brown, George A., Maker of Miller Revolving Rifle. *See Miller, J. & J.*, 714
Brown, R.H. & Co., 746
Brown, Robert, Percussion Muzzle Loading Harpoon/Bomb Lance Gun, 758
Brown, W.H., Pocket Rifle, 472
Brown Bolt Action Rifle, 617
Brown Mfg. (& Merrimack Arms Co.) Southerner Deringer, 472
Brown Mfg. Co. *See Marlin Ballard, Chapter V-D. Also see 9B-041 Brown Bolt Action Rifle*, 701
Bruce & Davis Double Barrel Pistol, 390
Bruff, R. P., Pocket Pistol, 412
Bryce, Wm. & Co. markings on percussion revolver. *See Sharps, Chapter V-F (5F-072)*, 354
Buck, H. A., Single Shot Rifle, 701
Buell, E., Independent Manufacturer of the Charleville-Model 1795 Springfield Style Flintlock Muskets, 545
Buell, E., Private Contractor of Model 1816 Flintlock Musket, 553
Buell, Elisha, Independent Maker of 1812 Musket, 552

792 ✳ FLAYDERMAN'S GUIDE

Nichols and Childs Belt Model Revolver, 365
Nichols, John, Shotgun, 747
Nichols, Jonathan Jr., U.S. 1798 Contract Flint-
lock Muskets, 542
Night Hawk Burglar Alarm Gun, 772
Nippes, D., Private Contractor of Model 1816
Flintlock Musket, 554
Nippes, D., Private Contractor of U.S. Model
1840 Flintlock Musket, 559
Norfolk, Private Contractor of U.S. Model 1861
Percussion Rifle-Musket, 571
Norris, S. and Clement, W. T., Private Contrac-
tor of U.S. Model 1861 Percussion Rifle-
Musket, 571
North & Couch Hand Held and Animal Trap
Pepperbox, 382
North & Savage *See Savage*, 366
North & Skinner Revolving Rifle, 715
North, Simeon, Private Contractor of U.S. Mod-
el 1817 Flintlock Rifle, 555
Norwich, Private Contractor of U.S. Model 1861
Percussion Rifle-Musket, 571

O

O.K. Single Shot Deringer, 499
O'Dell, Stephen, Pocket Pistols, 417
"Officer's Sporting Rifle" Modification of Mod-
el 1873 Rifle, 583
"Officer's Sporting Rifle" of Model 1866 Allin,
578
"Officer's Sporting Rifles" of Models 1868 and
1870, 579
Onion & Wheelock *See Chapter V-A, Ethan Allen*,
383
Original Flintlock Colonial American Military
or Dual Purpose Musket, 726
Original Percussion English-Made Northwest
Trade Gun, 762
Ormsby, E. S., Maker of Miller Revolving Rifle.
See Miller, J. & J., 714
Osborn, S., Underhammer Pistol, 429
Osborne, H., Independent Maker of 1808 Con-
tract Flintlock Musket, 549
Osborne, H., Private Contractor of Model 1816
Flintlock Musket, 554
Osborne, Independent Maker of 1812 Musket,
552
Osgood Gun Works Duplex Revolver, 500

P

Palmer Bolt Action Carbine, 630
Palmetto Armory Single Shot Pistol *See Chapter
VI, U. S. Military Single Shot Pistols, Model
1842 Percussion Pistol*, 644
Palmetto Armory, Private Contractor of U.S.
Model 1841 Percussion Model, 564
Palmetto Armory, Private Contractor of U.S.
Model 1842 Percussion Model, 565
Palmetto Armory—William Glaze & Company,
Columbia, South Carolina *See U. S. Military
Longarms, Chapter IX (Model 1841 Rifle and
Model 1842 Musket)*, 654
Paragon Marked Spur Trigger Revolvers
(32/38/41 Rimfire) *See Prescott Pistol Com-
pany Revolvers*, 500
Park & Garber Shotgun, 747
Park & McLeish Shotgun, 747
Parker, Albert, Pocket Model Revolvers, 366
Parker Brothers (Values of), 750
Parker Brothers Shotguns (History of), 748
Parker Four-Shot Pistol, 398
Parkers' Snow & Co., Private Contractor of U.S.
Model 1861 Percussion Rifle-Musket, 571
Parkhurst Clip Loading Attachment, 594
Patchin, R.M., *See "S. Coon" Alarm Gun*, 768
Patchin Burglar Alarm Gun, 773
Peabody and Peabody-Martini Rifles, 706
Peabody Carbines and Rifles, 630
Peabody-Martini Military Rifle and Carbine,
631
Peavey, A. J., Clasp Knife-Pistol, 500
Pecare & Smith Four-Shot Pepperbox, 383
Pecare & Smith Ten-Shot Pepperbox, 383

Peck, Abijah, U.S. 1798 Contract Flintlock Mus-
kets, 542
Peck, J., Pocket Model Revolver, 366
Percival & Smith Repeating Magazine Pistol,
398
PERCUSSION *See "U.S. Purchased Sporting Ri-
fles During Civil War" 12-014.5 See "Turner
Rifles" 12-018.5*, 611
Percussion Single Barrel Fowling Pieces/Shot-
guns (Values of), 742
Percussion Sporting and Target Rifles, Plains
Rifles, Flintlock New England Rifles (Histo-
ry of), 676
Perkins, Rufus, 1808 Contract Flintlock Mus-
kets, 548
Perpetual Revolver *See Perry and Goddard Single
Barrel 2-Shot Deringer*, 500
Perry, H. V., Maker of Miller Revolving Rifle.
See Miller, J. & J., 714
Perry and Goddard Single Barrel 2-Shot De-
ringer, 500
Perry Breech-Loading Percussion Sporting Ri-
fle, 689
Perry Breech-Loading Single Shot Pistol, 399
Perry Carbine, 631
Pettengill, C. S., Army Model Revolver, 367
Pettengill, C. S., Navy or Belt Model Revolver,
367
Pettengill, C.S., Pocket Model Revolver, 366
Phenix Armory *See W. W. Marston*, 384
Phenix, The, *See Reid, James, Pocket Revolver
Model 2*, 501
Phoenix Pocket Automatic, 526
Phoenix Rifles *See Whitney Arms, Chapter V-J*,
707
Pickell, Independent Manufacturer of the Char-
leville-Model 1795 Springfield Style Flint-
lock Muskets, 545
Pierce, Ebenezer, 759
Plains Rifle (History and Values of), 684
Plains Rifle vs. Plain Rifle, 684
Plant's Mfg. Co., Belt Model Revolver *See Chap-
ter VIII*, 367
Plant's Mfg. Co., Pocket Model Revolver *See
Chapter VIII*, 367
Plant's Mfg. Co. Front-Loading "Army" Re-
volvers, 501
Plant's Mfg. Co. Front Loading Pocket Revolv-
er, 502
Pocket Model *See Mass. Arms Co. Wesson &
Leavitt Belt Revolver*, 362
"Pocket Rifle" marked underhammer Pistol *See
Anderson*, 429
"Pocket Rifle" marked underhammer Pistol *See
Anderson*, 429
Pointer Single Shot Deringer, 502
Polhemus "Little Pal" Knife-Pistol, 502
Pomeroy, Independent Maker of 1808 Contract
Flintlock Musket, 549
Pomeroy, L., Private Contractor of Model 1816
Flintlock Musket, 554
Pomeroy, L., Private Contractor of U.S. Model
1840 Flintlock Musket, 559
Pond, Lucius W., Front Loading Separate
Chambers Revolvers, 503
Pond, Lucius W., Single Action "Army" Re-
volver, 502
Pond, Lucius W., Single Action Pocket or Belt
Revolver, 503
Porter, P. W., Revolving Turret Rifles, 716
Porter, P. W., Turret Revolver, 367
Post, J., Double Action Pepperbox, 384
Pratt, A., Independent Maker of 1808 Contract
Flintlock Musket, 549
Pratt, A., Independent Manufacturer of the
Charleville-Model 1795 Springfield Style
Flintlock Muskets, 545
Pratt, H., Underhammer Pistol, 429
Pratt Alarm & Trap Gun *See 7C-033 (Chapter
7C)*, 768
Pratt Burglar Alarm and Animal Trap Gun, 399
Pre-1800 New England-Made Rifles, 679
Prescott, E. A., Pocket Model Revolver, 367
Prescott, E.A., Pocket Model Revolvers, 504

Prescott, E.A., S&W Style Pocket and Belt Re-
volvers, 503
Prescott, E.A., Single Action "Army" Revolver,
504
Prescott, E.A., Single Action "Navy" Revolver,
503
Prescott Pistol Co. Single Action 44 Revolver,
506
Prescott Pistol Company Magazine Deringer,
505
Prescott Pistol Company Revolvers, 505
"Protector" *See Reid, James, New Model Knuckle-
Duster*, 510
Protection Pocket Model Revolver, 368
Protector Pocket Revolver *See Rupertus, Jacob*,
506
Providence, Private Contractor of U.S. Model
1861 Percussion Rifle-Musket, 571
Providence Tool Company, Private Contractor
of U.S. Model 1861 Percussion Rifle-Mus-
ket, 571
Pulaski Armory Rifle, 654

Q

Quackenbush, Herkimer, New York Air Guns,
777
Quackenbush Air Pistols, 778
Quackenbush Bicycle Rifle, 778
Quackenbush Junior Safety Cartridge Rifle, 778
Quackenbush Model No. 1 Improved Air Gun,
777
Quackenbush Model No. 2 New Model Air
Gun, 777
Quackenbush Model No. 3 Shot Model, 777
Quackenbush Model No. 4 Magazine Shot, 777
Quackenbush Model No. 5 Combination, 778
Quackenbush Models No. 6 & 7, 778
Quackenbush Models No. 9 & 10, 778
Quackenbush Safety Cartridge Rifle, 778
Queen Single Shot Deringer, 506
Quinabaug Rifle Mfg. Co. Underhammer Pis-
tol, 429

R

"Ramrod-Bayonet Model" *See U.S. Model 1888
"Trapdoor" Rifle*, 587
Ramsdell, C. V., Underhammer Pistol, 429
Rappahannock Forge (History of), 730
Rappahannock Forge Musket, 731
Rappahannock Forge Pistol, 730
Read & Watson Carbines and Rifles *See Barrett,
J. B.*, 654
Reichard Burglar Alarm Gun, 773
Reid, James, 1-3/4" Barrel Knuckle-Duster *See
Reid, James, Model No. 2 Knuckle-Duster*, 510
Reid, James, 22 Caliber Knuckle-Duster Revolv-
er, 509
Reid, James, 3" Barrel Knuckle-Duster *See Reid,
James, Model No. 1 Knuckle-Duster*, 509
Reid, James, 32 Caliber Knuckle-Duster Revolv-
er, 509
Reid, James, 41 Caliber Knuckle-Duster Revolv-
er, 509
Reid, James, Model No. 1 Knuckle-Duster, 509
Reid, James, Model No. 2 Knuckle-Duster, 510
Reid, James, Model No. 3 Deringer, 510
Reid, James, Model No. 4 Deringer, 510
Reid, James, New Model Knuckle-Duster, 510
Reid, James, New Model Revolver, 510
Reid, James, New York City (History of), 507
Reid, James, Pocket Model Revolver *See Chapter
VIII*, 368
Reid, James, Pocket Revolver Model 1, 507
Reid, James, Pocket Revolver Model 2, 508
Reid, James, Pocket Revolver Models 3 and 3A,
508
Reid, James, Pocket Revolver Models 4 and 4A,
508
Reid, Wm., Breechloading Percussion Pistol *See
Rollin White*, 399
Reid's Extractor *See Reid, James, Model No. 4 De-
ringer*, 510
Reiff & McDowell Burglar Alarm Gun, 773
Reiff Burglar Alarm Gun, 773